Y0-CDB-715

Chicago Public Library

REFERENCE

JAN . . - 2006   Form 178 rev. 11-00

Chicago Public Library
Clearing Branch
6423 West 63rd Place
Chicago, Illinois 60638-5005

Joseph B. Heroux
2035 West 79th Place
Chicago, Illinois 60652

Editorial Board

EDITOR IN CHIEF

John J. McCusker

Halsell Distinguished Professor of American History, professor of
economics at Trinity University, San Antonio, Texas, and adjunct
professor in the department of history at the University of Texas,
Austin.

ASSOCIATE EDITORS

Louis P. Cain

Professor of economics at Loyola University Chicago and adjunct
professor of economics at Northwestern University.

Stanley L. Engerman

John H. Munro Professor of Economics and professor of history at
the University of Rochester.

David Hancock

Associate professor of British, American, and Atlantic history at
the University of Michigan in Ann Arbor.

Kenneth Pomeranz

Chancellor's Professor of History and professor of East Asian
languages and literatures at the University of California, Irvine,
and director of the University of California Multi-Campus
Research Group in world history.

HISTORY of WORLD TRADE since 1450

John J. McCusker
EDITOR IN CHIEF

VOLUME

1
A-K

MACMILLAN REFERENCE USA
An imprint of Thomson Gale, a part of The Thomson Corporation

Detroit • New York • San Francisco • San Diego • New Haven, Conn. • Waterville, Maine • London • Munich

History of World Trade since 1450
John J. McCusker, Editor in Chief

© 2006 Thomson Gale, a part of The Thomson Corporation.

Thomson, Star Logo and Macmillan Reference USA are trademarks and Gale is a registered trademark used herein under license.

For more information, contact
Macmillan Reference USA
An imprint of Thomson Gale
27500 Drake Rd.
Farmington, Hills, MI 48331-3535
Or you can visit our Internet site at
http://www.gale.com

ALL RIGHTS RESERVED
No part of this work covered by the copyright hereon may be reproduced or used in any form or by any means—graphic, electronic, or mechanical, including photocopying, recording, taping, Web distribution, or information storage retrieval systems—without the written permission of the publisher.

For permission to use material from this product, submit your request via Web at http://www.gale-edit.com/permissions, or you may download our Permissions Request form and submit your request by fax or mail to:

Permissions
Thomson Gale
27500 Drake Rd.
Farmington Hills, MI 48331-3535
Permissions Hotline:
248-699-8006 or 800-877-4253 ext. 8006
Fax: 248-699-8074 or 800-762-4058

Since this page cannot legibly accommodate all copyright notices, the acknowledgments constitute an extension of the copyright notice.

While every effort has been made to ensure the reliability of the information presented in this publication, Thomson Gale does not guarantee the accuracy of the data contained herein. Thomson Gale accepts no payment for listing; and inclusion in the publication of any organization, agency, institution, publication, service, or individual does not imply endorsement of the editors or publisher. Errors brought to the attention of the publisher and verified to the satisfaction of the publisher will be corrected in future editions.

LIBRARY OF CONGRESS CATALOGING-IN-PUBLICATION DATA

History of world trade since 1450 / John J. McCusker, editor in chief.
    p. cm.
        Includes bibliographical references and index.
        ISBN 0-02-865840-X (set hardcover : alk. paper) —
        ISBN 0-02-865841-8 (volume 1) —
        ISBN 0-02-865842-6 (volume 2)
        1. International trade—History. 2. Commerce—History.
        I. McCusker, John J.
HF1379.H574 2005
382′.09—dc22

2005018624

This title is also available as an e-book.
ISBN 0-02-866070-6
Contact your Thomson Gale representative for ordering information.

Printed in the United States of America
10 9 8 7 6 5 4 3 2 1

R03126 13511

Editorial and Production Staff

EXECUTIVE VICE PRESIDENT AND PUBLISHER
Frank Menchaca

DIRECTOR, NEW PRODUCT DEVELOPMENT
Hélène Potter

PROJECT EDITORS
Ray Abruzzi
Mark Drouillard

CONTRIBUTING EDITORS
Jennifer Albers
Shawn Corridor
Kate Milson
Jenai Mynatt
Nicole Watkins

EDITORIAL TECHNICAL SUPPORT
Mark Springer

MANUSCRIPT EDITORS
Marc Borbely
Anne Davidson
Matthew May

ADDITIONAL EDITORIAL SUPPORT
David J. Clarke
Justin Crawford
Ryan Peacock

PROOFREADERS
Dorothy Bauhoff
Eleanor Stanford

TRANSLATOR
Paul Ellis

INDEXER
Wendy Allex

PRODUCT DESIGN
Michelle Dimercurio
Kate Scheible

IMAGING
Dean Dauphinais
Lezlie Light
Christine O'Bryan
Denay Wilding

GRAPHIC ART
GGS Information Services
XNR Productions

RIGHTS ACQUISITION AND MANAGEMENT
Margaret Chamberlain-Gaston
Susan Rudolph

COMPOSITION
Evi Seoud
Mary Beth Trimper

MANUFACTURING
Rhonda Williams

Contents

Preface

The *History of World Trade since 1450* offers help in understanding the complex interactions between peoples over time as they sought to exchange goods and services to their own benefit. Economics activity has been described as "getting" and "spending." All people have done this since humankind began. Individually, people cannot do as well for themselves as they can collectively, either in getting or in spending. Trade broadens the return from such activities, widening the audience for what people have to offer as they try to get as much as they can to spend, and widening their range of choices as they seek the most when they spend. Geographical constraints limit what individuals are able to accomplish in selling the fruits of their labor and in maximizing their gains.

Over time some individuals began to occupy the middle ground between buyer and seller, offering to help individuals earn more and buy more, quantitatively and qualitatively. Traders charged fees to function as business brokers and bring together buyers and sellers, but diminished the competitive disadvantage suffered by anyone who initiated a transaction. With their help, trade grew from neighborly to local, to regional, to national, to international. With the growth of trade, peoples' worlds grew and—ideally—the returns from their efforts and their standards of living grew, too.

The 500 years since the middle of the fifteenth century witnessed a spectacular expansion of world trade. These volumes are designed to offer the reader information about the changes in the world that caused and were caused by this expansion. Precipitated largely by European voyages of exploration and discovery that had as their primary purpose a search for better markets in which to sell and to buy, the growth of world trade has had numerous consequences, including the ending of the very empires that started and initially prospered from that expansion. It is a tale with many players, a story with many parts, all told here.

The *History of World Trade since 1450* is intended for general readers with a high-school or college-level education, but the editors and authors expect that many others also will find much here of use and interest. There are more than 400 entries in the encyclopedia, arranged in alphabetical order for easy reference. The entries vary in length from 200 to 3,000 words and concern everything that has to do with the subject in the period from 1450, the beginning of European expansion, to the present day. The entries explore all regions of the world. Thus they deal with persons and places, and developments and ideas that are global in their reach and global in their implications. The stories told are not always wonderful; the consequences of world trade have not always been good. The expansion of world trade across the Atlantic Ocean included the expansion of African slavery to the Western Hemisphere, for instance. But all is fodder for this discussion.

The entries have been written by experts, authorities in their respective fields; each contributor is identified by name. Like the topics they address, the authors are international. As much as possible, the authors and editors have used language that should be easily accessible to the public at large. The result is a set of entries reflecting immense and solid scholarship. A glossary of terms with which the reader might be unfamiliar appears at the end of volume 2, and each entry concludes with a short list of articles and books to guide readers to further sources of information. Cross-references at the end of each entry refer to related topics. In addition, an outline of contents at the beginning of volume 1 groups the entries thematically.

The *History of World Trade since 1450* contains historical images and contemporary photographs to illustrate the entries. Particularly for this topic, it is often difficult to visualize the subjects discussed. The editors have chosen the images carefully to provide further information and representation of the things included. There are sidebars that expand on an interesting aspect of a subject. At the end of the second volume, further material is included to assist the reader. In addition to the glossary, the concluding matter includes primary source documents and a comprehensive subject index. The primary documents may be of particular interest to those undertaking research in this field (for instance, extracts from United States Secretary of the Treasury Alexander Hamilton's 1791 "Report on Manufactures"; and key passages from the famed "Navigation Acts" issued by the British Parliament during the reign of King Charles II). The editorial board and contributors have all benefited from the editorial assistance given by individuals at Macmillan Reference USA, in particular Hélène Potter and Mark Drouillard. Their dedication to the project and infinite capacity for work inspired everyone. We express our thanks to them and to the others who contributed by suggesting authors, entries, and materials for the set.

John J. McCusker

Introduction

Globalization is a word on many people's lips at the dawn of this new millennium, not always with positive connotations. Yet, like it or not, the world in which we live has changed mightily over the past five centuries. We have gone from thinking very small indeed to thinking large: we have been globalized. Before the middle of the fifteenth century, however expansive one's perspective, his or her worldview was startlingly limited compared to today's. In the ancient world, both the emperor of Han dynasty China and the emperor of Rome thought of himself as the ruler of all of the world that mattered, yet even at their grandest they held sway over only a very small portion of the globe. They were barely even aware of each other. Neither had any notion of the Western Hemisphere.

If anything, people's worldview shrank between 500 and 1500. It certainly did not broaden. Europeans' focus had become local and limited after Rome withdrew its imperial presence. One risked ridicule, and possibly even death, just for thinking beyond the bounds during the "Dark Ages" in Europe. For the Chinese the Middle Kingdom was all that counted; its limits were known, and everything outside it was barbarian. Trade within Europe and trade across Asia flourished and declined with periods of peace and periods of war. The trade that existed between distant parts of the world, which was never very great anyhow, was kept alive along precarious silk roads linking East and West. The century before 1450 was an especially hard time in Europe and in Asia, punctuated by the plague— the "Black Death"—which, ironically for our story, was spread and intensified by an earlier boom time in long-distance trade. Europe and Asia now knew more of each other, and suffered for it, but still neither had any notion of the Western Hemisphere. Nor were the mighty empires of the Americas aware of much beyond their own borders. Some sailed ships long distances, hugging the coasts, or across some well-charted seas, but very few dared the open oceans. The high seas set limits.

To citizens of the twenty-first century, the world before 1500 seems almost as strange as the future. Yet one aspect of our future is sure: people are steadily becoming less foreign, at a steadily increasing rate. We are becoming more and more globalized citizens of the world, and the agency most responsible for this is expanded international trade, a process that had its start 500 years ago. It is a tale often told and, in its outlines, already well known. The purpose of the *History of World Trade since 1450* is to color in that outline and to enhance the picture to include much seen only dimly before, if at all. As a consequence of that expanded trade, the peoples of Asia, Africa, Europe, and the Americas have discovered each other in ways that ultimately have enriched us all. The world begins at oceans' edge. The high seas have become shipping lanes.

After 1450, Europe was the first to take advantage of these changes. Once recovery from the plague was underway, networks of trade in both the East and the West were revived and extended, but for a long period it was Western Europeans who gained the most from global interaction. Europe, for a thousand years a backwater, became the center of the first truly global economic and political order through its dominance of world trade. The agencies of European imperial expansion ultimately pushed into every corner of the globe, finding new goods to trade and new markets for the things they had to offer. Exploiting every opportunity, subjugating many who challenged them and enslaving some, doing deals with those they encountered who were locally as strong or stronger than they, and turning regional rivalries to their own good purposes, European nations created empires which from the start were at war with each other. Over the eighteenth century, having triumphed over the other contestants, the two nations with the strongest European empires, France and Great Britain, fought increasingly intense wars that culminated in worldwide wars. Britain's ultimate victory in its Second Hundred Years' War with France ushered in a hundred years of relative peace across the nineteenth century, when London reigned as the center of world trade and finance. Such great power only provoked newer rivals and a final war for empire in two parts—World War I and II—that resulted in the destruction of all those empires. Five centuries of European expansion came to a stunning end in a global firestorm that threatened to destroy the very planet itself.

The twentieth century, which had begun with a world tightly enthralled by empire, ended with a world bound loosely by a legacy of empire. World trade, which had been a function of the empires of Europe and the means of their sustenance, outlasted their demise. The peoples of the world, who had conducted business as best they could within the constraints of European imperialism, found new opportunities—and room to make their own mistakes—once freed from European domination. Slowly during the second half of the twentieth century newer, smaller counties and larger, older countries sought each other out as trading partners under a new world order, each as usual trying to advance its own best interest, but also working out anew the patterns of interaction. Symptomatically, already at the start of the century, as a direct consequence of World War I, the center of world trade and finance had migrated across the Atlantic Ocean, leaving London and Europe behind, to settle in New York. Where and when it will move next, who knows, but the trajectory is clear. From the Italian city-states of Genoa and Venice at the time of the Renaissance, to London at the end of the seventeenth century, to New York at the beginning of the twentieth century, the line of march was clear: ever westward. On to Singapore or Hong Kong or, perhaps, Shanghai! Or, perhaps, given the Internet and the World Wide Web, dispersed everywhere. Thus the globalization of the world. Thus the history of world trade since 1450.

THE EDITORS

The composition of the board of editors reflects the obvious necessity of a broad-based, interdisciplinary approach to the complex subjects addressed the *History of World Trade since 1450.*

John J. McCusker is the Halsell Distinguished Professor of American History and a professor of economics at Trinity University, San Antonio, Texas. He also serves as adjunct professor in the Department of History of the University of Texas, Austin. He has held major fellowships and grants from, among others: the Fulbright Senior Scholar Program, the Smithsonian Institution, Harvard University, Katholieke Universiteit Leuven (Belgium), the National Endowment for the Humanities, the American Council of Learned Societies, the American Enterprise Institute, the Leverhulme Trust (Great Britain), the Institute of Early American History and Culture, the John Simon Guggenheim Memorial Foundation, the University of Oxford, and the University of Cambridge. His teaching and his research have focused on the Atlantic World during the seventeenth and eighteenth centuries. His major publications include: *Money and Exchange in Europe and America, 1600–1775* (1978; revised edition, 1992); with Russell R. Menard, *The Economy of British America, 1607–1789* (1985; revised edition, 1991); with Cora Gravesteijn, *The Beginnings of Commercial and Financial Journalism: The Commodity Price Currents, Exchange Rate Currents, and Money Currents of Early Modern Europe* (1991); *Essays in the Economic History of the Atlantic World* (1997); *How Much Is That in Real Money? A Historical Price Index for Use as a Deflator of Money Values in the Economy of the United States* (1992; revised edition, 2001); and, edited with Kenneth Morgan, *The Early Modern Atlantic Economy* (2001). His most recent article is "The Demise of Distance: The Business Press and the Origins of the Information Revolution in the Early Modern Atlantic World" (*American Historical Review,* April 2005). His next book is tentatively titled *The Price of Sugar and the Economic Integration of the Early Modern Atlantic World.* He and his wife, Ann Van Pelt, have five children and eight grandchildren.

Louis P. Cain is professor of economics at Loyola University Chicago and adjunct professor of economics at Northwestern University. He is currently serving as visiting codirector of research in the Center for Population Economics and visiting professor at the Graduate School of Business of the University of Chicago. With the late Jonathan R. T. Hughes, he is author of *American Economic History* (sixth edition, 2003). Cain has served as an area editor for the *Oxford Encyclopedia of Economic History* (2003), a chapter editor for the *Historical Statistics of the United States, Millennial Edition* (2005), and a consulting editor to the *Encyclopedia of Chicago* (2004). He also has served as chairman of the Board of Trustees of the Cliometric Society and as a trustee of the Business History Conference and the Economic History Association. He is currently researching entrepreneurship in the United States before 1865. He and his wife are empty nesters who share a house in Glenview, Illinois, with the family dog.

Stanley L. Engerman is John H. Munro Professor of Economics and professor of history at the University of Rochester, where he has taught since 1963. He received a B.S. cum laude from New York University in 1956 and an M.B.A. there in 1958. After two years of working as an accountant, he went to The Johns Hopkins University and received a Ph.D. in economics in 1962. His major areas of research and writing have been American and British economic history and the history of slavery in the United States, the Caribbean, and elsewhere. Among his publications are: edited with Robert W. Fogel, *The Reinterpretation of American Economic History* (1971; winner of the American Historical Association's Bancroft Prize in American History); with Robert W. Fogel, *Time on the Cross: The Economics of American Negro Slavery* (1974; reissued 1995); edited with Robert Gallman, *Long-Term Factors in American Economic Growth* (1986); edited with Seymour Drescher, *A Historical Guide to World Slavery* (1998); and, edited with Robert Gallman, the three-volume *Cambridge Economic History of the United States* (1996–2000). He is currently coediting, with David Eltis, the four-volume *Cambridge World History of Slavery.* He is a fellow of the American Academy of Arts and Sciences and has been a fellow of the Center for Advanced Study in the Behavioral Sciences. He is a past president of the Economic History Association and the Social Science History Association, and was Pitt Professor of American History and Institutions at the University of Cambridge. He has three married sons and a total of five grandchildren.

David Hancock is associate professor of British, American, and Atlantic history at the University of Michigan in Ann Arbor. A specialist on the eighteenth century, he is the author of *Citizens of the World: London Merchants and the Integration of the British Atlantic Community, 1735–1785* (1995), and the editor of *The Letters of William Freeman, London Merchant 1678–1685* (2002) and of *Guerre et Économie dans le Monde Atlantique du XVIe au XXe Siecle: Stratégies en Échec, Logiques d'Adaptation* (2005). He has just completed a study, titled *Oceans of Wine, Empires of Commerce,* of the emergence and self-organization of the Atlantic economy between 1640 and 1815 as viewed through the lens of Madeira wine production, distribution, and consumption. Professor Hancock was born in New York and received his A. B. degree in history and music from the College of William and Mary, an A. M. degree in music from Yale University in 1983, and a Ph.D. degree in History from Harvard University in 1990. He has also taught history at Harvard University (1990–1997) and the *École des Hautes Études en Sciences Sociales* in Paris (2003).

Kenneth Pomeranz is Chancellor's Professor of History and professor of East Asian languages and literatures at the University of California, Irvine, and director of the University of California Multi-Campus Research Group in world history. He received his Ph.D. from Yale University in 1988, and has been at UC Irvine ever since. His publications include: *The Great Divergence: China, Europe, and the Making of the Modern World Economy* (2000); with Steven Topik, *The World that Trade Created: Society, Culture, and the World Economy, 1400 to the Present* (1999; second edition, 2005); and *The Making of a Hinterland: State, Society, and Economy in Inland North China, 1853–1937* (1993). *The Making of a Hinterland* won the John King Fairbank Prize of the American Historical Association for the best book on East Asian history in 1994; *The Great Divergence* won the Fairbank Prize for 2000, shared the World History Association Book Prize for 2000, and been the subject of more than a dozen symposia and panel discussions at sites around the world. Pomeranz has held fellowships from the Guggenheim Foundation, the American Council of Learned Societies, the Social Science Research Council, and the American Philosophical Society, among others. Although the bulk of his work has revolved around Chinese and comparative economic development, rural social change, environmental change, and state formation, he has also written on the history of popular religion, and on the history of family organization and gender roles. He lives in Irvine, California, with his wife and two children.

Louis P. Cain
Stanley L. Engerman
David Hancock
John J. McCusker
Kenneth Pomeranz

List of Articles

Thematic Outline

This systematic outline provides a general overview of the conceptual scheme of the *History of World Trade since 1450,* listing the titles of each entry and subentry. The outline is divided into sixteen parts.

1. Business Families
2. Cities
3. Commodities
4. Concepts and Ideas (Economic)
5. Concepts and Ideas (General)
6. Corporations and Businesses
7. Countries and Regions
8. Economic Agents
9. Empires
10. Industries
11. Infrastructure
12. Labor
13. Organizations and Institutions
14. People
15. Phenomena
16. Shipping

1. BUSINESS FAMILIES
Agnelli Family
Astor Family
Brown Family
Cabot Family
Dole Family
Duke Family
du Pont de Nemours Family
Fugger Family
Guggenheim Family
Hope Family
Mitsubishi

Mitsui
Nanyang Brothers Tobacco
Philips
Rockefeller Family
Rothschild Family
Saʿud Family
Schlumberger Family
Siemens
Sumitomo
Tagore Family
Tata Family Enterprises
Wallenberg Family
Zheng Family

2. CITIES
Amsterdam
Antwerp
Bahia
Baltimore
Barcelona
Bordeaux
Boston
Bristol
Cádiz
Calcutta
Cartagena
Chambers of Commerce
Charleston
Entrepôt System
Factories
Free Ports
Gdansk
Genoa
Glasgow
Guangzhou
Guilds
Hamburg
Hanseatic League (Hansa or Hanse)
Havana

Hong Kong
La Rochelle
Lisbon
Liverpool
London
Los Angeles–Long Beach
Madras
Marseilles
Melaka
Mumbai
Nagasaki
Nantes
New Orleans
Newport
New York
Paris
Philadelphia
Porto
Potosí
Rio de Janeiro
Rotterdam
Salem
San Francisco–Oakland
Seville
Shanghai
Singapore
Sydney
Venice
Veracruz
Yokohama

3. COMMODITIES
Coal
Coffee
Cotton
Counterfeit Goods
Cowries
Drugs, Illicit
Furs

Contributors

Pascal Acot
Professor, Department of the History of Science, Centre National de la Recherche Scientifique, France
CLIMATE
FAMINE

Olutayo Charles Adesina
Senior Lecturer and Ag. Head of Department, Department of History, University of Ibadan, Oyo State, Nigeria
KENYA

Peter Alonzi
Associate Professor of Economics and Finance, School of Business, Dominican University
CHICAGO BOARD OF TRADE

Morris Altman
Professor and Head of the Department of Economics, University of Saskatchewan, Canada
PROTECTION COSTS
STAPLES AND STAPLE THEORY

Ignacio Amate-Fortes
Associate Professor, Department of Economics, Faculty of Economics and Business Studies, University of Almeria, Spain
MERCOSUR

Frederick F. Anscombe
Lecturer in Contemporary History, School of History, Classics and Archaeology, Birbeck College, University of London
ARAMCO

Ian W. Archer
Fellow and Tutor in Modern History, Faculty of History, University of Oxford
GRESHAM, SIR THOMAS

John Armstrong
Professor, School of Business, Thames Valley University, London
SHIPPING, COASTAL

Peter E. Austin
Professor, Department of History, St. Edward's University
ANGLO AMERICAN CORPORATION
ANGOLA
ASTOR FAMILY
BANGLADESH
BARING, ALEXANDER
BOSTON
ETHNIC GROUPS, ARMENIANS
GDANSK
HUSKISSON, WILLIAM
MARCONI, GUGLIELMO
OPEC
RAFFLES, SIR THOMAS STAMFORD
SMITH, ADAM

Amiya Kumar Bagchi
Professor, Director, Institute of Development Studies Kolkata, Calcutta University Alipore Campus
HOME CHARGES (INDIA)

Vinay Bahl
Associate Professor, Department of Sociology, Pennsylvania College of Technology (Penn State)
TATA FAMILY ENTERPRISES

Peter Bakewell
Professor, Department of History, Southern Methodist University
POTOSÍ

Daniel Barbezat
Professor, Department of Economics, Amherst College
MONNET, JEAN
SUBSIDIES

David Baronov
Associate Professor, Department of Sociology, St. John Fisher College
BAHIA

Fred Bateman
Professor, Department of Economics, University of Georgia
NEW ORLEANS

Alun Buumler
Assistant Professor of History, Department of History, Indiana University of Pennsylvania
DRUGS, ILLICIT

Edward Beatty
Associate Professor, Department of History and the Kellogg Institute for International Studies, University of Notre Dame
MINING

Stéphane Beaulac (Cantab)
Associate Professor, Faculty of Law, University of Montreal
BODIN, JEAN

Contributors

Sven Beckert
Professor, Department of History, Harvard University
COTTON

Marco Beretta
Professor, Department of Philosophy, Universitá di Bologna
GLASSWARE

Antonio-Miguel Bernal
Professor, Departamento de Historia e Instituciones Económicas, Facultad de Economía, Universidad de Sevilla, Spain
NATIONALISM
SEVILLE

Leslie Bessant
Professor, Department of History, Ripon College
AFRICA, LABOR TAXES (HEAD TAXES)
SOUTH AFRICA

Leonard Blussé
Professor, Departments of History and Southeast Asian Studies, Leiden University
EAST INDIA COMPANY, DUTCH FACTORIES

Federico Boffa
Assistant Professor and Doctoral Candidate, Department of Economics, Northwestern University; Free University of Bolzano/Bozen
BONAPARTE, NAPOLEON
GETTY, JEAN PAUL
GILBERT, HUMPHREY
PHILIPS
SCHLUMBERGER FAMILY

Hubert Bonin
Professor, Montesquieu Center for Economic History, Institut d'études politicques de Bordeaux
ARTISTIC REPRESENTATIONS OF TRADE
EMPIRE, FRENCH: 1815–PRESENT
FINANCE, CREDIT AND MONEY LENDING
GHANA
RUSSIA
SENEGAMBIA

J. F. Bosher
Professor, Department of History, York University Toronto
BRUNEL, ISAMBARD KINGDOM
EMPIRE, BRITISH: 1783–PRESENT
ETHNIC GROUPS, HUGUENOTS
LA ROCHELLE
PEEL, SIR ROBERT
SHIPPING, AIDS TO
TREATIES

Maristella Botticini
Associate Professor, Department of Economics, Boston University and Università di Torino
ETHNIC GROUPS, JEWS

James M. Boughton
Historian, International Monetary Fund
INTERNATIONAL MONETARY FUND (IMF)

Gordon Boyce
Professor, Faculty of Business, Queensland University of Technology
SHIPBUILDING

George R. Boyer
Professor, Department of Labor Economics, School of Industrial and Labor Relations, Cornell University
CORN LAWS

Fabio Braggion
Doctoral Candidate, Department of Economics, Northwestern University
GUGGENHEIM FAMILY

Loren Brandt
Professor, Department of Economics, University of Toronto
CHINA

Elizabeth Brayer
Independent Historian, Author of
George Eastman: A Biography (1995)
EASTMAN, GEORGE

Timothy Brook
Professor, Department of History, University of Toronto
ZHANG HAN

Jonathan C. Brown
Professor, Department of History, University of Texas at Austin
ARGENTINA
PEMEX

Marcelo Bucheli
Assistant Professor of Business Administration and History, Business Administration and History, University of Illinois, Urbana-Champaign
UNITED FRUIT COMPANY

José Céspedes-Lorente
Professor of Management, Department of Mangement, Faculty of Economics and Business Studies, University of Almeria, Spain
eBAY

Ann M. Carlos
Professor, Department of Economics, University of Colorado
FURS

Leonard A. Carlson
Associate Professor, Department of Economics, Emory University
ETHNIC GROUPS, NATIVE AMERICANS

Selwyn H. H. Carrington
Professor, Department of History, Howard University
SUGAR, MOLASSES, AND RUM

Sarah Anne Carter
Doctoral Candidate, History of American Civilization, Harvard University
TOYS

Christopher J. Castaneda
Professor and Chair, Department of History, California State University, Sacramento
CAPITALISM

Edward J. Chambers
Research Professor, School of Business, University of Alberta
NAFTA

Cheuk-Wah Sunny Chan
Associate Professor, Public Administration Program, Macao Polytechnic Institute
HONG KONG

Ming Chan
Research Fellow and Coordinator of the Hong Kong Documentary Archives, Hoover Institution, Stanford University
TUNG CHEE-HWA

Alfred D. Chandler Jr.
Professor of Business History, Emeritus, Harvard Business School, Harvard University
DU PONT DE NEMOURS FAMILY

Maria Christina Chatziioannou
Director of Research, Institute for Neohellenic Research, National Hellenic Research Foundation
GREECE

Sushil Chaudhury
Professor, Department of History, Calcutta University
TAGORE FAMILY

Yong Chen
Associate Professor, Department of History, University of California, Irvine
ETHNIC GROUPS, CANTONESE
GUANGZHOU

Martin Chick
Senior Lecturer, Department of
Economic History, University of
Edinburgh
NATIONALIZATION

David J. Clarke
Doctoral Candidate, Department of
History, University of Newfoundland
DEBEERS
EMPIRE, BRITISH: 1450–1783
SHIPPING, TECHNOLOGICAL
CHANGE
SHIP TYPES
WARS

Karen Clay
Assistant Professor of Economics,
Heinz School of Public Policy and
Management, Carnegie Mellon
University
GOLD RUSHES

Peter A. Coclanis
Professor, Department of History,
University of North Carolina at
Chapel Hill
RICE

Alfredo Manuel Coelho
Research Assistant, Department of
Economics, Business and Social
Sciences, Umr Moisa Agro, France
FRANCHISING, INTERNATIONAL
PHARMACEUTICALS

Jeremy Cohen
Adjunct Assistant Professor,
Department of History, University of
Florida
SMUGGLING

Andrea Colli
Professor, Economic History
Institute, Bocconi University, Milan,
Italy
AGNELLI FAMILY

Catherine Coquery-Vidrovitch
Professor Emeritus, Laboratoire
SEDET/CNRS, Université Paris
DAHOMEY

Howard Cox
Professor, Worchester Business
School, University College Worcester
BRITISH-AMERICAN TOBACCO

Gerald Crompton
Reader in Economics and Business
History, Kent Business School,
University of Kent
SHIPPING, INLAND WATERWAYS,
NORTH AMERICA

Mario J. Crucini
Associate Professor, Department of
Economics, Vanderbilt University
PROTECTIONISM AND TARIFF
WARS

Javier Cuenca-Esteban
Professor, Department of Economics,
University of Waterloo, Canada
CARGOES, FREIGHT

L. M. Cullen
Professor Emeritus of modern Irish
history, Modern history, Trinity
College, Dublin
ETHNIC GROUPS, IRISH

Guillaume Daudin
Économiste, Department of the
Economics of Globalization,
Observatoire Français des
Conjonctures Économiques, Sciences
Po
FRANCE

Karel Davids
Professor, Department of History,
Vrije Universiteit Amsterdam
AMSTERDAM

Peter N. Davies
Professor Emeritus, The Centre for
Port and Maritime History, The
School of History, University of
Liverpool
CUNARD, SAMUEL
LIVERPOOL

Lance E. Davis
Professor of Social Science, Division
of Humanities and Social Sciences,
California Institute of Technology
BLOCKADES IN PEACE

Alexander H. De Groot
Reader in Islamic Institutions,
Department of the Languages and
Cultures of the Islamic Middle East,
Leiden University
LEVANT COMPANY

Greta Devos
Professor, Centrum for
Bedrijfsgeschiedenis, University of
Antwerp
ANTWERP

Sheila C. Dow
Professor, Department of Economics,
University of Stirling
HUME, DAVID

Paul Duguid
Professor, Centre for Business
Management, Queen Mary,
University of London
PORTO

Robert F. Durden
Professor Emeritus of History,
Department of History, Duke
University
DUKE FAMILY

Jonathan Eacott
Doctoral Candidate, Department of
History, University of Michigan
MAGELLAN, FERDINAND
ROTHSCHILD FAMILY

John Richard Edwards
Professor, Cardiff Business School,
Cardiff University
ACCOUNTING AND ACCOUNTING
PRACTICES

Anene Ejikeme
Assistant Professor, Department of
History, Trinity University
JAJA, KING OF OPOBO

Peter P. Ekeh
Professor, Department of African
American Studies, State University of
New York at Buffalo
ROYAL NIGER COMPANY

Walter Eltis
Emeritis Fellow, Exeter College,
Oxford University
PHYSIOCRATS

Pieter Emmer
Professor, Department of History,
University of Leiden
WEST INDIA COMPANY, DUTCH

Stanley L. Engerman
Professor, Department of Economics,
University of Rochester
INTERNATIONAL TRADE AGREE-
MENTS

Victor Enthoven
Associate Professor, International
Security Studies, Royal Netherlands
Naval College
COEN, JAN PIETERSZOON
HOPE FAMILY
JOINT-STOCK COMPANY
WAR, GOVERNMENT CONTRACT-
ING

Chris Evans
Principal Lecturer, School of
Humanities, Law and Social Sciences,
University of Glamorgan
HARDWARE

Tommaso Fanfani
Professor, Department of Economics,
Università di Pisa
ITALY

Contributors

Peter Fearon
Professor, School of Historical Studies, University of Leicester
GREAT DEPRESSION OF THE 1930S

Harvey M. Feinberg
Professor, Department of History, Southern Connecticut State University
AFRICA, NATIVES LAND ACT
GOLD COAST
SARBAH, JOHN

Bruce Fetter
Professor, Department of History, University of Wisconsin-Milwaukee
DISEASE AND PESTILENCE

Richard J. Finlay
Professor, Chair of Scottish History, Department of History, University of Strathclyde, Glasgow
ETHNIC GROUPS, SCOTS SINCE 1800

Price V. Fishback
Professor, Department of Economics, University of Arizona
ROOSEVELT, FRANKLIN DELANO

David Flath
Professor, Department of Economics, North Carolina State University
JAPANESE MINISTRY OF INTERNATIONAL TRADE AND INDUSTRY (METI)

Dennis O. Flynn
Professor, Department of Economics, University of the Pacific
GOLD AND SILVER

Laurence Fontaine
Professor, Department of History, CNRS-EHESS-Paris
PEDDLERS

Lionel Frost
Associate Professor, Department of Economics and Institute for Regional Studies, Monash University, Australia
SYDNEY

Marcia J. Frost
Assistant Professor of Economics, Department of Economics, Wittenberg University
GUJARAT

Maria Fusaro
Assistant Professor, Department of History, University of Chicago
MEDITERRANEAN

Donato Gómez-Díaz
Professor of Economic History, Department of Economics, Faculty of Economics and Business Studies, University of Almeria, Spain
EBAY
MERCOSUR

Robert Gardella
Professor, Department of Humanitites, U.S. Merchant Marine Academy
COMPRADORS
TEA

H. A. Gemery
Professor Emeritus, Department of Economics, Colby College
COMMODITY MONEY

Thomas M. Geraghty
Assistant Professor, Department of Economics, University of North Carolina at Chapel Hill
INDUSTRIALIZATION

Ruthy Gertwagen
School of History, Byzantine and Post Byzantine Studies, Haifa University
VENICE

Árturo Giraldez
Professor of Modern Language and and Literature (Spanish), Department of Modern Language and Literature, University of the Pacific
GOLD AND SILVER

Paul Gootenberg
Professor of History, Department of History, Stony Brook University
PERU

David M. Gordon
Assistant Professor, Department of History, Bowdoin College
KONGO

Regina Grafe
Prize Fellow, Nuffield College, Oxford University
FAIRS

Robert G. Greenhill
Economics, Finance and International Banking, London Metropolitan University
CAPITAL FLOWS
FLOWS OF FACTORS OF PRODUCTION

Farley Grubb
Professor, Department of Economics, University of Delaware
LABORERS, CONTRACT

Jorge Guzman-Gutierrez
Scott Polar Research Institute, University of Cambridge
LAW, INTERNATIONAL (LAW OF NATIONS AND LAW OF THE SEA)

Sheryllynne Haggerty
Fellow, School of History, University of Liverpool
PHILADELPHIA

Michael R. Haines
Professor of Economics, Department of Economics, Colgate University
POPULATION—EMIGRATION AND IMMIGRATION

John R. Hanson II
Professor, Department of Economics, Texas A and M University
COPPER

C. Knick Harley
University Lecturer in Economic History, Department of Economics, University of Oxford
INDUSTRIAL REVOLUTION

Robert Harms
Professor, Department of History, Yale University
LEOPOLD II

Ellen Hartigan-O'Connor
Professor, Department of History, San Jose State University
NEWPORT
SEX AND GENDER

Philippe Haudrère
Professor, Department of History, University of Angers, France
EAST INDIA COMPANY, OTHER

Marc D. Hayford
Associate Professor, Department of Economics, School of Business Administration, Loyola Unviersity Chicago
MONEY AND MONETARY POLICY

Ingo Heidbrink
German Maritime Museum
SHIPPING, INLAND WATERWAYS, EUROPE
UNILEVER

Charles R. Hickson
Senior Lecturer, School of Management and Economics, Queen's University, Belfast
CORPORATION, OR LIMITED LIABILITY COMPANY
GUILDS
PARTNERSHIP

B. W. Higman
Professor, History Program, Research
School of Social Sciences, Australian
National University
JAMAICA

Diana Davids Hinton
Professor, Department of History,
The University of Texas of the
Permian Basin
PETROLEUM

Philip T. Hoffman
Professor, Division of Humanities
and Social Sciences, California
Institute of Technology
PARIS

Jan Hogendorn
Professor Emeritus, Department of
Economics, Colby College
COWRIES

Christopher Howe
Research Professor, Department of
Finance and Management Studies,
School of Oriental and African
Studies, University of London
EMPIRE, JAPANESE

Gary Clyde Hufbauer
Senior Fellow, Institute for
International Economics
BLOCKADES IN WAR

W. G. Huff
Reader in Economics, Department of
Economics, University of Glasgow
LEE KUAN YEW

William K. Hutchinson
Visiting Professor, Department of
Economics, Vanderbilt University
AGRICULTURE
CANALS
INSTITUTIONAL ASPECTS OF
WORLD TRADE
MONOPOLY AND OLIGOPOLY

Joseph E. Inikori
Professor, Department of History,
University of Rochester
NIGERIA

Kris Inwood
Professor, Department of Economics,
University of Guelph
CANADA

Christopher Isett
Associate Professor, Department of
History, University of Minnesota,
Twin Cities
MANCHURIA

Gordon Jackson
Honorary Research Fellow Economic
History, Department of History,
University of Strathclyde, Glasgow
HARBORS

Evelyn Powell Jennings
Chair of Latin American History,
Department of History, Saint
Lawrence University
HAVANA

Hans Chr. Johansen
Professor, Department of History,
University of Southern Denmark
DENMARK

Louis D. Johnston
Associate Professor of Economics,
Department of Economics, College of
Saint Benedict
BALANCE OF PAYMENTS

Charles Jones
Director of the Centre of Latin
American Studies, Centre of
International Studies, University of
Cambridge
IMPERIALISM

Evan Jones
Lecturer in Economic and Social
History, Department of Historical
Studies, University of Bristol
BRISTOL

Anu Mai Kōll
Professor of Baltic History,
Department of History, Stockholm
University
BALTIC STATES

Elisabeth Köll
Associate Professor, Department of
History, Case Western Reserve
University
JARDINE MATHESON
NANYANG BROTHERS TOBACCO

Alan L. Karras
Professor, International and Area
Studies Teaching Program, University
of California, Berkeley
ETHNIC GROUPS, SCOTS BEFORE
1800

Yrjö Kaukiainen
Professor, Department of History,
University of Helsinki
FINLAND
SHIPPING LANES

Harry Kelsey
Research Scholar, Huntington Library
HAWKINS, JOHN

B. Zorina Khan
Associate Professor, Department of
Economics, Bowdoin College and
UBER
GATES, BILL
PATENT LAWS AND INTELLECTUAL
PROPERTY RIGHTS

John E. Kicza
Professor, Department of History,
Washington State University
EMPIRE, SPANISH

Daniel Kilbride
Associate Professor, Department of
History, John Carroll University
TRAVELERS AND TRAVEL

John M. Kleeberg
D.Phil. in Modern History from
Oxford; former curator of modern
coins and currency at the American
Numismatic Society
BLACK SEA
COUNTERFEIT GOODS

Wim Klooster
Assistant Professor, Department of
History, Clark University
EMPIRE, DUTCH

Sandra Kuntz Ficker
Professor, Centro de Estudios
Históricos, El colegio de México
MEXICO

Sumner J. La Croix
Professor, Department of Economics,
University of Hawaii and East-West
Center
DOLE FAMILY

Miguel-Ángel Ladero Quesada
Real Academia de la Historia,
Madrid, Spain
BOARD OF TRADE, SPANISH

Chi-Kong Lai
Reader in Modern Chinese History,
Department of History, School of
HPRC, University of Queensland
ALCOCK, RUTHERFORD
HONG KONG AND SHANGHAI
BANK

Pedro Lains
Associate Research Fellow, Instituto
de Ciências Sociais, University of
Lisbon
PORTUGAL

Sergio Lamarão
Associate Researcher at Research and
Documentation Center in Brazilian
Contemporary History, Getulio
Vargas Foundation, Rio de Janeiro,
Brazil
RIO DE JANEIRO

Kris Lane
Associate Professor, Department of
History, College of William & Mary
PIRACY

A. J. H. Latham
Department of History, University of
Wales, Swansea (retired)
MARKET INTEGRATION

Adebayo A. Lawal
Professor, Department of History
and Strategic Studies, University of
Lagos, Nigeria
VOLCANIC ERUPTIONS

Christian Leitz
Corporate Historian, UBS AG
KRUPP

Graham Lemke
Assistant Professor, Department of
Business, Northwestern College, Iowa
RELIGION

Carol Scott Leonard
University Lecturer in Regional
Studies of the Post-Communist
States, Russian and East European
Graduate Studies, Oxford University
SOCIALISM AND COMMUNISM

David W. Lesch
Professor of Middle East History,
Department of History, Trinity
University
SA'UD FAMILY

Barry Levy
Associate Professor, Department of
History, University of Massachusetts,
Amherst
SALEM

David M. Levy
Director and Professor, Department
of Economics, Baldwin-Wallace
College
ECONOMICS, NEOCLASSICAL

Wayne Lewchuk
Professor, Department of Labour
Studies & Economics, McMaster
University
AUTOMOBILE
FORD, HENRY

James B. Lewis
University Lecturer in Korean,
Department of Oriental Studies,
University of Oxford
KOREA

Michael Limberger
Associate Professor, Department of
History, Catholic University of
Brussels (KUBrussel), Belgium
ANTWERP

Nancy S. Lind
Professor, Department of Politics and
Government, Illinois State University
MOST-FAVORED-NATION PROVI-
SIONS

Hanchao Lu
Professor, Department of History,
Technology, and Society, Georgia
Institute of Technology
SHANGHAI

Shu Shin Luh
Freelance Journalist, Author of
Business the Sony Way (2003)
SONY

Jan Luiten van Zanden
Professor, International Institute for
Social History
INDONESIA

Mats Lundahl
Professor of Development
Economics, Department of
Economics, Stockholm School of
Economics
HAITI

Sari Mäenpää
Research Associate, School of
History, University of Liverpool,
England
SEAMEN WAGES

Leos Müller
Associate Professor of History,
Department of History, Uppsala
University, Sweden
NETWORKS, SUPPLY, DISTRIBU-
TION, AND CUSTOMER
SWEDEN

Debin Ma
Associate Professor, National
Graduate Institute for Policy Studies,
Tokyo, Japan
SILK

Lars Magnusson
Professor, Vice Chancellor of Uppsala
University, Department of Economic
History, University of Uppsala,
Sweden
MERCANTILISM

John Majewski
Associate Professor, Department of
History, University of California at
Santa Barbara
AMERICAN SYSTEM

John Major
Department of History, University of
Hull, United Kingdom (retired)
PANAMA CANAL

Jay R. Mandle
Professor, Department of Economics,
Colgate University
GLOBALIZATION, PRO AND CON

Andrea Maneschi
Professor, Department of Economics,
Vanderbilt University
THEORIES OF INTERNATIONAL
TRADE BEFORE 1900
THEORIES OF INTERNATIONAL
TRADE SINCE 1900

Edward Marcus
Professor Emeritus and Former Chair
of the Department of Economics,
Department of Economics, City
University of New York; Brooklyn
College
WORLD BANK

Daan Marks
International Institute for Social
History
INDONESIA

José-Ignacio Martínez Ruiz
Faculty of Economics and Business
Administration, University of Seville,
Spain
FREE PORTS
NITRATES

Silvia Marzagalli
Professor, Department of History,
Université of Nice, France
BALTIMORE
BORDEAUX
EMPIRE, FRENCH: 1450–1815
FINANCE, CREDIT AND MONEY
LENDING

Rudi Matthee
Professor, Department of History,
University of Delaware
IRAN

Alistair McCleery
Professor, Scottish Centre for the
Book, Napier University
BOOKS

Marvin McInnis
Professor Emeritus, Department of
Economics, Queen's University,
Kingston, Ontario
TIMBER

Peter McNamara
Associate Professor, Department of
Political Science, Utah State
University
HAMILTON, ALEXANDER

Kenneth McPherson
Professor, South Asia Institute,
University of Heidelberg, Germany
CONTAINERIZATION

Christopher M. Meissner
Lecturer, Faculty of Economics, University of Cambridge and King's College, Cambridge
PRICES AND INFLATION

Ronald Michener
Associate Professor, Department of Economics, University of Virginia
QUANTITY THEORY OF MONEY

Graeme J. Milne
Postdoctoral Researcher, Department of History, University of Liverpool
INFORMATION AND COMMUNICATIONS

Thomas J. Misa
Associate Professor of History, Department of Humanities, Illinois Institute of Technology
BESSEMER, HENRY

David Mitch
Associate Professor, Department of Economics, University of Maryland, Baltimore County
EDUCATION, OVERVIEW

Douglas Moggach
Professor, School of Political Studies and Department of Philosophy, University of Ottawa
MARX, KARL

Michael Monteón
Professor, Department of History, University of California, San Diego
CHILE

Carl Mosk
Professor, Department of Economics, University of Victoria
IMPERIAL PREFERENCE
INTERNATIONAL LABOUR ORGANIZATION
IRON AND STEEL

Larry Neal
Professor, Department of Economics, University of Illinois
COMMON MARKET AND THE EUROPEAN UNION
MARKETS, STOCK

J. Peter Neary
Professor, Department of Economics, University College Dublin
PURCHASING POWER PARITY
STOLPER-SAMUELSON THEOREM

Chin-keong Ng
Adjunct Professor, Department of History, National University of Singapore
ETHNIC GROUPS, FUJIANESE

August H. Nimtz Jr.
Professor, Department of Political Science, University of Minnesota
ENGELS, FRIEDRICH

Omar Noman
Human Development Report Office, United Nations
PAKISTAN

Michael North
Professor, Department of History, University of Greifswald, Germany
FUGGER FAMILY
GERMANY

John V. C. Nye
Associate Professor of Economics and History, Department of Economics, Washington University, St. Louis
FREE TRADE, THEORY AND PRACTICE
TRANSACTIONS COSTS

Kevin H. O'Rourke
Professor, Department of Economics, Trinity College, Dublin
HECKSCHER-OHLIN

Kerry A. Odell
Professor, Department of Economics, Scripps College, Claremont
SAN FRANCISCO–OAKLAND

Barbara Oegg
Institute for International Economics
BLOCKADES IN WAR

Lawrence H. Officer
Professor, Department of Economics, University of Illinois, Chicago
CHURCHILL, WINSTON
RATES OF EXCHANGE

Roger M. Olien
Professor, J. Conrad Dunagan Chair in Regional and Business History, The University of Texas of the Permian Basin (retired)
ROCKEFELLER FAMILY

Michael J. Oliver
Associate Professor, Department of Economics, Bates College
BRETTON WOODS

Ayodeji Olukoju
Professor, Department of History and Strategic Studies, University of Lagos, Nigeria
BOYCOTT
CARGOES, PASSENGER

Kenkichi Omi
Associate Professor, Faculty of Law and Economics, Mie Chukyo University
NAVIGATION ACTS

John Orbell
Former head of Corporate Information Services, ING Bank NV, London
BANKING

Norman G. Owen
Visiting Scholar, Department of History, Duke University; University of North Carolina-Chapel Hill
LONEY, NICHOLAS
PHILIPPINES

Olivier Pétré-Grenouilleau
Professor, Department of History, University of Bretagne Sud, Lorient, France
NANTES

Sarah Palmer
Professor, Greenwich Maritime Institute, University of Greenwich
LONDON

Jan Parmentier
Coordinator European research Eurindia, Department of Early Modern History, Ghent University
OSTEND EAST INDIA COMPANY

Benjamin Passty
Doctoral Candidate, Department of Economics, Northwestern University
HEARST, WILLIAM RANDOLPH
KEYNES, JOHN MAYNARD
ONASSIS, ARISTOTLE
SIEMENS

Donald G. Paterson
Professor, Department of Economics, University of British Columbia
UNITED KINGDOM

Michael N. Pearson
Professor, Humanities and Social Sciences, University of Technology, Sydney
ETHNIC GROUPS, GUJARATI
GAMA, VASCO DA
INDIAN OCEAN
PERSIAN GULF

Robin Pearson
Senior Lecturer in Economic History, Department of History, University of Hull, UK
FINANCE, INSURANCE
LLOYD'S OF LONDON

Contributors

Sandra J. Peart
Professor, Department of Economics, Baldwin-Wallace College
ECONOMICS, NEOCLASSICAL

Jorge M. Pedreira
Professor, Institute of Historical Sociology, Universidade Nova de Lisboa
EMPIRE, PORTUGUESE

Edwin J. Perkins
Professor Emeritus, Department of History, University of Southern California
BROWN FAMILY

Christine Philliou
Teaching Fellow, Yale Center for International and Area Studies, Yale University
MILLETS AND CAPITULATIONS

William D. Phillips Jr.
Professor, Department of History, University of Minnesota
COLUMBUS, CHRISTOPHER

Peter Pierson
Professor Emeritus, Department of History, Santa Clara University
PHILIP II

Kenneth Pomeranz
Chancellor's Professor, Department of History, University of California, Irvine
CARAVAN TRADE
DENG XIAOPING
HART, ROBERT
LIN ZEXU
PERRY, MATTHEW
SPECIAL ECONOMIC ZONES (SEZs)
TRIBUTE SYSTEM

Peter E. Pope
Professor, Archaeology Unit, Memorial University of Newfoundland
CABOT FAMILY

Om Prakash
Professor, Department of Economics, Delhi School of Economics, University of Delhi
BENGAL
EAST INDIA COMPANY, BRITISH
EMPIRE, MUGHAL

Jacob M. Price
Professor Emeritus, Department of History, University of Michigan
BOARD OF TRADE, BRITISH
CORRESPONDENTS, FACTORS, AND BROKERS
TOBACCO

John Ravenhill
Professor, Department of International Relations, Australian National University
REGIONAL TRADE AGREEMENTS

Himanshu Prabha Ray
Associate Professor, Centre for Historical Studies, School of Social Sciences, Jawaharlal Nehru University
CALCUTTA

Vera Blinn Reber
Professor, Department of History, Shippensburg University
BUNGE AND BORN

Anthony Reid
Professor, Asia Research Institute, National University of Singapore
MELAKA
WOMEN TRADERS OF SOUTHEAST ASIA

Erik Reinart
Professor, Department of Humanities and Social Science, Tallinn University of Technology, Estonia
DEVELOPMENTAL STATE, CONCEPT OF THE

Paul Rhode
Professor, Department of Economics, University of North Carolina, Chapel Hill
LOS ANGELES–LONG BEACH

David Richardson
Professor, Department of History and Wilberforce Institute for Study of Slavery and Emancipation, University of Hull, United Kingdom
SLAVERY AND THE AFRICAN SLAVE TRADE

Nigel Rigby
Head of Research, National Maritime Museum, Greenwich, UK
COOK, JAMES

Hugh Rockoff
Professor, Department of Economics, Rutgers University and NBER
BULLION (SPECIE)

Richard Rosecrance
Distinguished Research Professor, UCLA and Senior Fellow, Belfer Center, Kennedy School of Government, Harvard University
POLITICAL SYSTEMS

Robert I. Rotberg
Professor, Kennedy School of Government, Harvard University
ZIMBABWE

Dietmar Rothermund
Professor Emeritus, Department of History, South Asia Institute of Heidelberg University
MADRAS
MUMBAI

Tirthankar Roy
Professor, Gokhale Institute of Politics and Economics, India
IMPORT SUBSTITUTION
INDIA

John C. Rule
Professor Emeritus, Department of History, Ohio State University
COLBERT, JEAN-BAPTISTE

Brett Rushforth
Assistant Professor, Department of History, Brigham Young University
LABORERS, NATIVE AMERICAN, EASTERN WOODLAND, AND FAR WESTERN

Frank Safford
Professor, Department of History, Northwestern University
CARTAGENA
COLOMBIA

Mohammed Bashir Salau
Doctoral Candidate, Department of History, York University, Canada
ETHNIC GROUPS, AFRICANS

Lars G. Sandberg
Professor Emeritus, Department of Economics, Ohio State University
TEXTILES SINCE 1800
WALLENBERG FAMILY

Michelle Sanson
Lecturer and Director of Undergraduate Programs, Faculty of Law, University of Technology, Sydney, Australia
GATT, WTO
TRADE FORMS, ORGANIZATIONAL, AND LEGAL INSTITUTIONS

Joseph Santos
Associate Professor, Department of Economics, South Dakota State University
WHEAT AND OTHER CEREAL GRAINS

Jörg Schendel
Assistant Professor, Department of History, University of Toronto
BURMA

Daniel Schroeter
Professor, Department of History, University of California, Irvine
MOROCCO

Ralph Shlomowitz
Reader in Economic History, School
of Business Economics, Flinders
University, Adelaide, Australia
LABORERS, COERCED
LABOR, TYPES OF

John Singleton
Reader in Economic History, School
of Economics and Finance, Victoria
University of Wellington
ARMS, ARMAMENTS

Edward W. Sloan
Professor Emeritus, Department of
History, Trinity College, Hartford
PACKET BOATS

John Smail
Professor, Department of History,
University of North Carolina at
Charlotte
TEXTILES BEFORE 1800

Gene Smiley
Professor Emeritus, Department of
Economics, Marquette University
HOOVER, HERBERT

Gene A. Smith
Professor, Department of History,
Texas Christian University
MONROE, JAMES

Byung Khun Song
Associate Professor, School of
Economics, Sungkyunkwan
University, Seoul
HYUNDAI

George Bryan Souza
Adjunct Associate Professor,
Department of History, University of
Texas, San Antonio
ALBUQUERQUE, AFONSO DE
SPICES AND THE SPICE TRADE

David J. Starkey
Lecturer in Maritime History,
Department of History, University of
Hull, United Kingdom
ELIZABETH I
PRIVATEERING
SHIPPING, MERCHANT

Randall W. Stone
Associate Professor, Department of
Political Science, University of
Rochester
COMECON

Martin Stopford
Managing Director, Clarkson
Research Studies, Finance Institute,
Cass Business School, London
BALTIC EXCHANGE

Kaoru Sugihara
Professor, Graduate School of
Economics, Osaka University
JAPAN

S. Sugiyama
Professor, Department of Economics,
Keio University
SINGAPORE

Carl E. Swanson
Associate Professor, Department of
History, East Carolina University
CHARLESTON

Stefan Szymanski
Professor, Tanaka Business School,
Imperial College, London
SPORTS

Li Tana
Fellow, Division of Pacific and Asian
History, Research
School of Pacific and Asian Studies,
The Australian National University
VIETNAM

Mariko Tatsuki
Professor, Department of Economics,
Aoyama Gakuin University
YOKOHAMA

Stig Tenold
Associate Professor, Economic
History Section, Department of
Economics, Norwegian School of
Economics and Business
Administration
NORWAY

Robert Tignor
Professor of Modern and
Contemporary History, Department
of History, Princeton University
ALI, MUHAMMAD
EGYPT
PASHA, ISMA'IL
SUEZ CANAL

Miguel Tinker Salas
Professor, Chicano Studies, History,
Latin American Studies, Pomona
College
VENEZUELA

Alexander Tokarev
Assistant Professor, Department of
Economics, St. John's University
RELIGION

Maria Elisabetta Tonizzi
Department for European Research,
University of Genoa
GENOA

Steven Topik
Professor, Department of History,
University of California, Irvine
BRAZIL
COFFEE
DÍAZ, PORFIRIO

Thomas M. Truxes
Visiting Lecturer, Department of
History, Trinity College, Hartford,
Connecticut
SERVICES

Ernest Tucker
Associate Professor, Department of
History, United States Naval Academy
EMPIRE, OTTOMAN

Richard P. Tucker
Adjuct Professor, School of Natural
Resources and Environment,
University of Michigan
RUBBER

Malcolm Tull
Associate Professor, Department of
Economics, Murdoch Business
School, Murdoch University
AUSTRALIA AND NEW ZEALAND
PORT CITIES

John D. Turner
Senior Lecturer, School of
Management and Economics,
Queen's University, Belfast
CORPORATION, OR LIMITED LIA-
BILITY COMPANY
GUILDS
PARTNERSHIP

Richard W. Unger
Professor, Department of History,
University of British Columbia
SHIPS AND SHIPPING

Tim Unwin
Professor, Department of Geography,
Royal Holloway, University of
London, United Kingdom
WINE

Jesús M. Valdaliso
Professor of Economic History,
University of the Basque Country,
Spain
SPAIN

James E. Valle
Professor, Department of History
and Political Science, Delaware State
University
MORGAN, J. P.

Paul van de Laar
Professor, Faculty of History and
Arts, Erasmus University, Rotterdam
ROTTERDAM

Contributors

Guy Vanthemsche
Professor, Department of History,
Free University Brussels
EMPIRE, BELGIAN

Carmel Vassallo
Coordinator of the Mediterranean
Maritime History Network,
Mediterranean Institute, University
of Malta
CHAMBERS OF COMMERCE

Patrick Verley
Professor, Department of Economic
History, University of Geneva
DEPRESSIONS AND RECOVERIES

Simon Ville
Professor, School of Economics and
Information Systems, University of
Wollongong
COAL
WOOL

Timothy D. Walker
Assistant Professor, Department of
History, University of Massachusetts,
Dartmouth; Universidade Aberta de
Lisboa
LISBON
POMBAL, MARQUÊS DE

Claire Walsh
Associate Lecturer, Faculty of Arts,
Open University
RETAILING

John Walsh
Assistant Professor, School of
Management, Shinawatra University
THAILAND

Jason L. Ward
Assistant Professor, Department of
History and Political Science, Lee
University
CONQUISTADORS
ENCOMIENDA AND REPARTIMIEN-
TO
LABORERS, AZTEC AND INCA
NEW SPAIN

James L. A. Webb Jr.
Professor, Department of History,
Colby College
COMMODITY MONEY
SRI LANKA

Simone A. Wegge
Associate Professor of Economics,
Department of Economics, City
University of New York
HAMBURG
NEW YORK

Robert Whaples
Professor, Department of Economics,
Wake Forest University
UNITED STATES

Christopher A. Whatley
Professor of Scottish History,
Department of History, University of
Dundee
GLASGOW

Charles Wheeler
Assistant Professor, Department of
History, University of California,
Irvine
DE RHODES, ALEXANDRE
SOUTH CHINA SEA

Lawrence H. White
Professor, Department of Economics,
University of Missouri-St. Louis
GOLD STANDARD

James Q. Whitman
Professor of Comparative and
Foreign Law, School of Law, Yale
University
LAW, COMMON AND CIVIL

John E. Wills Jr.
Professor Emeritus, Department of
History, University of Southern
California
CANTON SYSTEM
EMPIRE, MING
EMPIRE, QING
ENTREPÔT SYSTEM
ZHENG FAMILY

John Y. Wong
Reader in History, Department of
History, University of Sydney
IMPERIAL MARITIME CUSTOMS,
CHINA

R. Bin Wong
Professor of History and Director of
UCLA Asia Institute, Department of
History, University of California, Los
Angeles
ZHANG HAN

Jeffrey Wood
Graduate Student, Department of
Economics, Northwestern University
GULBENKIAN, CALOUSTE
HAKLUYT, RICHARD, THE
YOUNGER
RHODES, CECIL
STALIN, JOSEPH
WATSON, THOMAS, SR., AND
THOMAS, JR.

Ralph Lee Woodward Jr.
Professor of History Emeritus,
Department of History, Tulane
University
BARCELONA
CÁDIZ
CONDORCET, MARIE-JEAN-
ANTOINE-NICOLAS DE CARITAT,
MARQUIS DE
CUBA
HANSEATIC LEAGUE (HANSA OR
HANSE)
MARSEILLES
MILL, JOHN STUART
VERACRUZ

William Wray
Associate Professor, Department of
History, University of British
Columbia
MITSUBISHI
MITSUI
NAGASAKI
SUMITOMO

Tsong-Min Wu
Professor, Department of Economics,
National Taiwan University
TAIWAN

Selected Metric Conversions

WHEN YOU KNOW	MULTIPLY BY	TO FIND
Temperature		
Celsius (˚C)	1.8 (˚C) +32	Fahrenheit (˚F)
Celsius (˚C)	˚C +273.15	Kelvin (K)
degree change (Celsius)	1.8	degree change (Fahrenheit)
Fahrenheit (˚F)	[(˚F) −32] / 1.8	Celsius (˚C)
Fahrenheit (˚F)	[(˚F −32) / 1.8] +273.15	Kelvin (K)
Kelvin (K)	K −273.15	Celsius (˚C)
Kelvin (K)	1.8(K −273.15) +32	Fahrenheit (˚F)

WHEN YOU KNOW	MULTIPLY BY	TO FIND
Distance/Length		
centimeters	0.3937	inches
kilometers	0.6214	miles
meters	3.281	feet
meters	39.37	inches
meters	0.0006214	miles
microns	0.000001	meters
millimeters	0.03937	inches

WHEN YOU KNOW	MULTIPLY BY	TO FIND
Capacity/Volume		
cubic kilometers	0.2399	cubic miles
cubic meters	35.31	cubic feet
cubic meters	1.308	cubic yards
cubic meters	8.107×10^{-4}	acre-feet
liters	0.2642	gallons
liters	33.81	fluid ounces

WHEN YOU KNOW	MULTIPLY BY	TO FIND
Area		
hectares (10,000 square meters)	2.471	acres
hectares (10,000 square meters)	107,600	square feet
square meters	10.76	square feet
square kilometers	247.1	acres
square kilometers	0.3861	square miles

WHEN YOU KNOW	MULTIPLY BY	TO FIND
Weight/Mass		
kilograms	2.205	pounds
metric tons	2205	pounds
micrograms (μg)	10^{-6}	grams
milligrams (mg)	10^{-3}	grams
nanograms (ng)	10^{-9}	grams

WHEN YOU KNOW	MULTIPLY BY	TO FIND
Speed		
kilometers per hour	0.6214	miles per hour
knots	1.151	miles per hour

ACCOUNTING AND ACCOUNTING PRACTICES

The system of record keeping in widespread use throughout the world today, double-entry bookkeeping (DEB), is thought to have been initially developed by banking and trading partnerships operating in the Italian city-states of Genoa, Florence, and Venice during the thirteenth and fourteenth centuries.

The impetus for the adoption of the "Italian system," as it was initially often described, has been the subject of study, and scholars have identified as relevant factors the level of business activity, the size and complexity of organizational structures, the ready availability of relevant literature, the socialization of capital, and the technique's disciplinary potential. Globalization of the "Italian system" occurred as firms set up business in new countries, and it first arrived in England when used by the London branch of an Italian firm of merchants—the Gallerani company of Siena—between 1305 and 1308. Among Eastern countries, it has been argued that DEB was introduced to Japan in the early seventeenth century by the Dutch East India Company (Camfferman and Cooke 2001). Sometimes, adoption followed conquest. China was forced to open its borders to Western powers following its defeat in the Opium War of 1840 and, with capital flowing into that country, administration systems, including DEB, were brought in by Western businessmen. New systems do not always gain immediate footholds, and it seems clear that DEB only began to achieve widespread adoption in Japan when the country was reopened to Western influence in the second half of the nineteenth century.

Dissemination of the new technique was also achieved through the publication of manuals that first appeared in Italy in 1494 (the first book on DEB authored by Luca Pacioli) and in Britain in 1543 (by Hugh Oldcastle). In the centuries that followed, in countries all over the world, hundreds of texts made both fair and extravagant claims for the system's contribution to the efficient conduct of business and domestic affairs. The actual advantages of double-entry compared with single-entry record keeping are that the records are more comprehensive and orderly, the duality of entries provides a convenient check on the accuracy or completeness of the ledger, and, perhaps most important, the underlying records can be designed to facilitate the preparation of two fundamental financial statements—the profit and loss account and the balance sheet (Yamey 1956).

ACCOUNTING FOR MANAGEMENT

For many centuries, it was the usual practice for owners and managers to consult directly the contents of accounting records, such as the ledger, to monitor the financial progress and condition of their enterprises. During the nineteenth century, it became increasingly common for managers of larger companies to arrange for the preparation of accounting statements for the purposes of planning, decision making, and control. The profit and loss account and balance sheet play an important part in these processes because of the degree of detail that they contain (e.g., departmental figures). Many other financial statements have been developed to meet management's information requirements, and these may be constructed on the basis of information generated both within and outside the formal system of record keeping. Some fairly advanced applications of cost accounting for manufacturing activity have been revealed in the fifteenth- and sixteenth-century cloth-manufacturing records of the Medici family and the printing records of the Flemish printer Christopher Plantin.

Britain was the first industrialized nation but, in the estimation of the noted British economic historian, Sidney Pollard, the "practice of using accounts as direct aids to management was not one of the achievements of the British industrial revolution; in a sense, it does not even belong to the later nineteenth century, but to the twentieth" (Pollard 1968, p. 248). More recent research (e.g., Boyns and Edwards, 1997; Jones, 1985) has shown that at least some eighteenth- and nineteenth-century companies constructed costing systems that contained fundamental features that persist to the present day. The post-1850 period saw the development and adoption of cost and management accounting systems by companies throughout the world. The practices of leading companies and leading industries were widely disseminated, and new procedures were developed for subsequent emulation. In the last years of the nineteenth century, scientific management procedures were developed in the United States, which are associated within the accounting domain with the formulation of the techniques of standard costing and budgetary control. The twentieth century saw the dissemination of numerous other aids to management such as the discounted cash-flow technique of capital project appraisal, target costing, zero-based budgeting, and activity-based costing. Methods that proved suitable in certain communities sometimes failed to gain acceptance in different environments. Where certain Western cost-accounting practices were adopted, as in Japan, modification was required to meet local cultural conditions.

The initial development of cost accounting occurred in countries such as Britain with little support from the published literature. Indeed, practice preceded theory to the end of the nineteenth century, although the position may since have reversed. In France, in contrast, numerous books containing in-depth discussions of industrial accounting issues such as overhead apportionment, transfer pricing, depreciation, fixed and variable costs, and break-even analysis were published before 1880. Whereas the British were content with "learning by doing," there was a much greater interest on the other side of the English Channel in developing a theoretical understanding of cost-accounting practice.

MEASURING BUSINESS ACTIVITY

The profit and loss account and balance sheet require decisions about how incomes, expenditures, assets, and liabilities are to be measured. For much of accounting's history, these items have been computed and reported on the same basis that they were recorded—the value at the date of the transaction, commonly described as "historical cost." Accounting theorists (Edwards 1994) have argued plausibly that whereas it is entirely appropriate to use the original transaction value to record rights and obligations (e.g., how much a customer owes you and how much you owe the bank), historical cost is not necessarily relevant for financial reporting and decision-making purposes. Criticism of the use of historical cost usually rises with the general rate of inflation. Alternative proposals include adjustment of historical data for changes in the purchasing power of money and the restatement of recorded figures for assets and liabilities at replacement cost, market price, or present value.

PUBLISHED ACCOUNTS

What we describe today as "the published accounts" developed from the need to raise capital from the general public and the consequent separation of ownership from management. The balance sheet (initially termed *ballance account*) was "by far the most important financial statement" (Chatfield 1977, p. 69). Interest in the balance sheet stemmed from the fact that it was useful in answering traditional stewardship questions such as managements' honesty and ability to account for resources entrusted to them.

The colossal publicly funded chartered companies that carried British trade and government to many parts of the globe date from the sixteenth century; the most famous early example is the East India Company, established in 1600. Its officers were required to "deliver up a perfect Ballance of all the said accompts unto the Company [shareholders], by the last day of June yearely" (Baladouni 1986, p. 20). The first surviving "Ballance of the Estate" (balance sheet) was published in 1641. The more widespread development of published financial reports was the British contribution to accounting, largely due to the British capital market being the first to develop a significant trade in corporate stock, beginning with the railways in the 1830s.

The joint-stock company has proved immensely successful in providing a vehicle for the expansion of national and world trade since 1450. The history of the joint-stock company, from the South Sea Bubble (1719) to Enron (2001), has also been marked by instances of fraud, mismanagement, and growing regulation. Demands for more transparent accountability have expanded the size and content of the published data set enormously, and this trend has been reinforced by recognition of the need to provide information to a widening array of corporate stakeholders. The desire for more effective regulation has also led to the development of the external audit and to ever-increasing disclosure requirements. Many countries introduced their own national financial-reporting requirements—in the United States, for example, the Financial Accounting Standards Board was created in 1973 to prepare and issue its series of Financial Accounting Standards. Internationally, strenuous efforts have been made to gain global acceptance for International Accounting Standards that are intended to achieve, among other things, harmonization and therefore worldwide comparability of corporate financial-reporting practices.

SEE ALSO CAPITALISM; CORPORATION, OR LIMITED LIABILITY COMPANY; INFORMATION AND COMMUNICATIONS; ITALY.

BIBLIOGRAPHY

Baladouni, Vahe. "Financial Reporting in the Early Years of the East India Company." *Accounting Historians Journal* 13 (Spring 1986): 63–80.

Boyns, Trevor, and Edwards, John Richard. "The Construction of Cost Accounting Systems in Britain to 1900: The Case of the Coal, Iron, and Steel Industries." *Business History* 39 (July 1997): 1–29.

Camfferman, Kees, and Cooke, Terry E. "Dutch Accounting in Japan 1609–1850: Isolation or Observation?" *Accounting, Business and Financial History* 11 (2001): 369–382.

Chatfield, Michael. *A History of Accounting Thought.* New York: Krieger Publishing, 1977.

Edwards, John Richard, ed. *Twentieth-Century Accounting Thinkers.* London: Routledge, 1994.

Jones, Haydn. *Accounting, Costing and Cost Estimation.* Cardiff: University of Wales Press, 1985.

Pollard, Sidney. *The Genesis of Modern Management.* London: Penguin, 1968.

Yamey, Basil S. "Introduction." In *Studies in the History of Accounting,* eds. A. C. Littleton and B. S. Yamey. London: Sweet and Maxwell, 1956.

John Richard Edwards

AFRICA, LABOR TAXES (HEAD TAXES)

In all African colonies, taxes and labor policies were designed to force Africans to work for the benefit of white colonizers. These taxes and labor policies took three basic forms: head taxes, labor rents, and forced labor.

Colonial governments used head taxes (or poll taxes) and hut taxes to force Africans into the colonial economy. To get the cash for taxes, Africans had to work for colonial employers at low wages or sell crops at low prices. Employers claimed that the low wages were justified because workers only had to pay their own expenses;

EDUCATIONAL EXERCISE

The slave trade did not end the world's hunt for cheap labor. To satisfy that hunger, colonial governments devised various strategies to compel native Africans to work. These included oppressive taxes and laws restricting the independence of indigenous peoples. In some cases, such measures were accompanied by missions intended to "civilize" native Africans. The continued economic exploitation of native peoples could therefore be justified by colonial administrators as an educational exercise.

Justin Crawford

workers' families were expected to support themselves through farming. Tax defaulters were arrested and sent to work on plantations and mines as contract laborers. The contract work was dangerous and the pay was extremely low.

Labor rents forced Africans to work for white settlers and private companies. Families who refused to work were beaten, arrested, or evicted. Settlers ordered African tenants to work in the settlers' fields. The amount of rent ranged from working a few days a week to working every day during planting and harvest. Private companies forced tenants to produce cash crops. Company agents dictated the amount to be harvested and the price to be paid for the crop. Families had to tend the cash crops before they could work in their own fields. Food shortages frequently resulted, forcing families to buy food from company-owned stores on credit. The families' debt made them more vulnerable to the companies' demands.

Colonial officials also forced Africans to work on roads, railways, and other public projects. In the early 1900s police officers surrounded villages, kidnapped men, and took them for forced labor. By the 1930s violence had given way to threat, and colonial officials simply ordered chiefs to provide workers. Men worked between 60 and 120 days per year building roads and laying railway tracks; they were also forced to work for settlers and private companies. Women and children were forced to clear ditches, repair local roads, and work on soil conservation measures. Men were paid very low wages; women and children received no pay.

In the early 1900s Africans openly rebelled against colonial taxes and labor policies. When colonial govern-

Native workers tend tobacco plants on a Southwest African plantation in 1918. *Large plantations across the continent often coerced locals into harsh working conditions through head or poll taxes. Tax defaulters were sent to plantations and mines to work as contract laborers.* © BETTMANN/CORBIS. REPRODUCED BY PERMISSION.

ments responded by hanging rebel leaders and burning villages, Africans turned to more subtle forms of resistance. Men ran away from home to avoid being taken for forced labor or sent to the mines for defaulting on their taxes. Tenant families sabotaged cash crops in the hope that company agents would leave them alone after the crop failed. Some families managed to earn the money they needed for taxes by selling cash crops such as coffee, cocoa, and peanuts for export, or food crops for local consumption. These families escaped from having to work for colonial employers, but colonial governments forced them to sell their crops at low prices.

Colonial governments combined taxes and labor policies in various ways. In the Congo, company agents relied on terror tactics to make Africans deliver set quotas of raw rubber. If a family failed to deliver their quota, the agent mutilated their children. Horrified families produced over 5,000 metric tons of rubber per year between 1900 and 1908. When the rubber tree population declined, company plantations turned to palm oil and cot-

ton. Tenants on palm plantations had to harvest 128 kilograms of palm kernels to pay their tax and rent. Palm oil exports rose from 1,500 tons in 1900 to 36,000 tons in 1930. Tax defaulters were arrested and sent to the copper mines in Katanga (now Shaba) in Zaire. The steady flow of forced labor allowed the copper mines to increase production to 162,000 tons in 1941. In addition to paying taxes and labor rents, men were also forced to work for sixty days on public projects.

Forced labor played a crucial role in French West Africa. By law, the colonial *prestation* (the official French term for "forced labor") required men to work on public projects for only twelve days every year. In practice, however, officials conscripted men and forced them to work for private companies for much longer periods. The number of conscripts and their families on cotton plantations alone reached 28,000 in 1944. Despite the abundance of cheap labor, the plantations failed; production ranged from 550 metric tons of ginned cotton in 1923, to 950 tons in 1929, to 100 tons in 1932.

Many Africans in Southern Rhodesia (now Zimbabwe) were able to earn money for taxes by selling food crops rather than working for white settlers and mine owners. Colonial employers responded by raising taxes in the British colonies to the north—Northern Rhodesia (now Zambia) and Nyasaland (now Malawi)—forcing men to take work on mines and farms in Southern Rhodesia. The supply of cheap migrant labor made Southern Rhodesian mining profitable, and gold exports rose from 5,000,000 pounds British sterling in 1924 to 13,000,000 pounds in 1940. White settlers also benefited: tobacco production increased from 200 tons in 1917 to 23,500 tons in 1944.

In Mozambique the Portuguese government allowed private companies to impose exorbitant labor rents. Most companies forced their tenants to grow and sell a set amount of cotton to company agents. When the demand for cheap cotton grew in the 1930s, agents used violence to increase the number of cotton producers from 80,000 in 1937 to 800,000 in 1944. The amount of cotton produced rose to 90,000 tons in 1951, but the increase came at the cost of extreme food shortages and hardship.

Colonial officials used racist stereotypes to justify their tax and labor policies. They claimed that Africans were lazy and that whites had to teach Africans the "dignity of hard labor." Officials argued that taxes and forced labor were simply tools for turning Africans into good workers. The fact was that colonial employers needed cheap labor to survive. Settlers, mine owners, and company plantations lacked the capital and expertise they needed to compete on the world market. African wages were the only expense they could control, and they used every available method to force Africans to work more for less pay. Critics denounced forced labor policies, but their protests had little effect. In the early 1900s the Congo Reform Campaign raised a public outcry over the violent measures used to force Africans to collect rubber. The Belgian government promised to abolish forced labor in the colony, but company plantations continued to impose labor rents on tenants. The International Labour Organization's Forced Labour Convention of 1930 called on governments to outlaw all forms of forced labor. However, the document permitted the use of forced labor on public projects. This loophole allowed colonial labor practices to continue essentially unchanged until the 1950s.

SEE ALSO AFRICA, NATIVE LANDS ACTS; AGRICULTURE; ANGOLA; DAHOMEY; EMPIRE, BELGIAN; EMPIRE, BRITISH; EMPIRE, DUTCH; EMPIRE, FRENCH; EMPIRE, PORTUGUESE; ENCOMIENDA AND REPARTIMIENTO; FREE TRADE, THEORY AND PRACTICE; GHANA; INTERNATIONAL LABOUR ORGANIZATION; IMPERIALISM; INDIA; KENYA; LABORERS, COERCED; LABORERS, CONTRACT; NIGERIA; ROYAL NIGER COMPANY; RUBBER; SLAVERY AND THE AFRICAN SLAVE TRADE; SOUTH AFRICA; ZIMBABWE.

BIBLIOGRAPHY

Conklin, Alice L. "Colonialism and Human Rights, A Contradiction in Terms? The Case of France and West Africa, 1895–1914." *American Historical Review* 103 (1998): 419–442.

Cooper, Frederick. *Decolonization and African Society: The Labor Question in French and British Africa.* Cambridge, U.K.: Cambridge University Press, 1996.

Fieldhouse, David K. "The Economic Exploitation of Africa: Some British and French Comparisons." In *France and Britain in Africa: Imperial Rivalry and Colonial Rule,* ed. P. Gifford and W. R. Louis. New Haven, CT: Yale University Press, 1971.

Freund, Bill. *The Making of Contemporary Africa: The Development of African Society since 1800,* 2nd edition. Boulder, CO: Lynne Rienner Publishers, 1998.

Isaacman, Allen. *Cotton is the Mother of Poverty: Peasants, Work, and Rural Struggle in Colonial Mozambique, 1938–1961.* Portsmouth, NH: Heinemann, 1996.

Jewsiewicki, Bogumil. "Rural Society and the Belgian Colonial Economy." In *History of Central Africa,* vol. 2, ed. D. Birmingham and P. M. Martin. London and New York: Longman, 1983.

Manning, Patrick. *Francophone Sub-Saharan Africa, 1880–1985.* Cambridge, U.K.: Cambridge University Press, 1988.

Miracle, Marvin. *Agriculture in the Congo Basin: Tradition and Change in African Rural Economies.* Madison, WI: University of Wisconsin Press, 1967.

Nzula, A. T.; Potekhin, I. I.; and Zusmanovich, A. Z. *Forced Labour in Colonial Africa,* ed. R. Cohen, trans. H. Jenkins. London: Zed Books, 1979.

Perrings, Charles. *Black Mineworkers in Central Africa: Industrial Strategies and the Evolution of an African Proletariat in the Copperbelt, 1911–1941.* London: Heinemann, 1979.

Roberts, Richard L. *Two Worlds of Cotton: Colonialism and the Regional Economy in the French Soudan, 1800–1946.* Stanford, CA: Stanford University Press, 1996.

Rubert, Steven C. *A Most Promising Weed: A History of Tobacco Farming and Labor in Colonial Zimbabwe, 1890–1945.* Athens: Ohio University Press, 1998.

Van Onselen, Charles. *Chibaro: African Mine Labour in Southern Rhodesia, 1900–1933.* London: Pluto Press, 1976.

Vellut, Jean-Luc. "Mining in the Belgian Congo." In *History of Central Africa,* vol. 2, ed. D. Birmingham and P. M. Martin. London and New York: Longman, 1983.

Leslie Bessant

AFRICA, NATIVES LAND ACT

The Union of South Africa, formed in 1910, included the Cape, Natal, Transvaal, and Orange Free State provinces.

Whites (about 1.25 million), divided between Afrikaans- and English-speakers, controlled political and economic power. The Africans (about 4 million) had been subordinated to European control during the nineteenth century, and most African societies lost substantial amounts of land. Most Africans lived in rural South Africa, many on reserves (similar to American Indian reservations); only a few Africans owned any land in freehold outside the reserves. As of 1910, however, Africans living in the Cape, Natal, and Transvaal provinces could buy land; this was not allowed in the Free State.

HISTORY OF THE ACT

Parliament passed the Natives Land Act in 1913 to promote a vague plan of territorial segregation within the Union and to stop Africans from buying more land. The act, which was a political maneuver to retain the support of the Free State members of Parliament, was one of the most important segregation laws in South African history, and included three major provisions:

(1) Africans were prohibited from buying land outside so-called "scheduled areas," which included the reserves and most farms owned by Africans at that time, and whites were prohibited from buying land in the scheduled zones. The act identified the scheduled areas, approximately 21 million acres, equaling only about 7 percent of the area of South Africa. Equally important, the act included an exception clause, allowing the government to approve African requests to buy or lease land outside the "schedules areas."

(2) The act included antisquatting provisions intended to restrict severely the opportunity for African sharecroppers to remain on white-owned farms, especially in the Free State. As a result, many Africans were evicted from land where they had lived for generations, or left rather than give up the privileges they were enjoying.

(3) The act established a Land Commission to recommend additional land for the use of Africans. The Natives Land Commission in 1916 recommended adding about 17 million acres, which would allow the Africans (almost 70% of the population) only about 12.5 percent of the area of South Africa. Even that miserly recommendation did not pass Parliament, however. Between 1918 and 1936 Parliament failed to pass any new land legislation.

The government in 1913 knew that many of the reserves were overcrowded, and officials also understood the land hunger of many Africans. Consequently, after Parliament failed to increase the amount of land for Africans, the government used its discretion under the excep-

---

AN EXCERPT FROM THE NATIVES LAND ACT OF 1913

INTRODUCTION The Natives Land Act of 1913 reserved just 7 percent of South Africa's land for native South Africans. It promoted a plan of territorial segregation within the Union and stopped Africans from buying more land. It is often described as one of the most important segregation laws in South African history. ∎

THE NATIVES' LAND ACT OF 1913
Be it enacted by the King's Most Excellent Majesty, the Senate and the House of Assembly of the Union of South Africa, as follows:—

1. (1) From and after the commencement of this Act, land outside the scheduled native areas shall, until Parliament, acting upon the report of the commission appointed under this Act, shall have made other provision, be subjected to the following provisions, that is to say:—

Except with the approval of the Governor-General—

1. A native shall not enter into any agreement or transaction for the purchase, hire, or other acquisition from a person other than a native, of any such land or of any right thereto, interest therein, or servitude thereover; and

2. A person other than a native shall not enter into any agreement or transaction for the purchase, hire, or other acquisition from a native of any such land or of any right thereto, interest therein, or servitude thereover.

Justin Crawford

---

tion clause in the act to approve requests from Africans to buy land. Between 1918 and 1936 the government approved, in increasing numbers, hundreds of applications to buy farms. Finally, in 1936 Parliament passed the Native Trust and Land Act, which enlarged the reserves, but only by 14.5 million acres purchased over many years. The aim of the new trust was for the government to buy land and allot the use of this "trust" land to Africans; private sales of land to Africans was a low priority.

The Natives Land Act affected the African population in several ways. The limited amount of land available for Africans meant that the reserves became very crowded with both people and cattle, leading to serious soil erosion and declining fertility. The overcrowding forced some men and women to migrate to the cities. A portion of the men went to work in the mines, particularly the gold mines, for gold was an export critical for South Africa. Many black leaders blamed specifically the Land Act and its antisquatting provisions for this migration and the resulting decline in morality among black city dwellers. The effects of the act produced an abiding bitterness in prominent black leaders: consistently between 1913 and 1936, African leaders singled out the Land Act as a catastrophe and condemned the failure of the government to make more land available. Thousands of Africans formed partnerships to buy farms after 1913, but these owners were only a small proportion of the African population. The Natives Land Act remained in force after apartheid became the policy of the government in 1948. One important policy of the apartheid system was to create segregated "homelands" exclusively for different African societies; the reserves created in 1913 formed the core of the new homelands.

The Natives Land Act was repealed only in 1991 as South Africa eliminated apartheid, but land continued to be a significant political issue after Nelson Mandela (b. 1918) was elected president in 1994. One law Parliament passed allowed Africans who had lost their land as a result of discrimination to lodge restitution claims. The date for the beginning of the legally defined discriminatory period was 1913.

LAND POLICIES IN OTHER PARTS OF AFRICA

In comparing South Africa's colonial land history to those of other African nations, it is more or less similar, depending on whether those nations were white-settler colonies or colonies without settlers, especially those under British and French rule. In other white-settler colonies, especially Kenya and Southern Rhodesia (today's Zimbabwe), the settlers took over vast amounts of land, but the methods used and the amounts Europeans controlled varied between the colonies, and the percentage of land left for the African population also differed. The two colonial governments also required official approval to buy land and created reserves for the Africans, similar to those in South Africa, where the Africans had exclusive rights. The Southern Rhodesia government limited the black majority to about 40 percent of the land, often in remote areas with poor soils. Also, in Southern Rhodesia, the Land Apportionment Act of 1931 prohibited Africans from acquiring permanent rights in European areas (Wills 1973). In Kenya the Europeans, who made up a very small percentage of the population, controlled 20 to 25 percent of the best habitable land, and it was very diffi-

cult for Africans to buy land outside the reserves. White control of the best agricultural land allowed the Rhodesians to produce tobacco for export, and the Kenyans, sisal and coffee.

In most of the other tropical African colonies, where there were few or no white settlers, the colonial governments often took control of lands that officials deemed to be unused or empty (even though they almost always were claimed by African societies). However, most of the land remained in the hands of the African population. In British West Africa governments prohibited whites from buying land, but in French West Africa authorities alienated 352,968 acres to European planters (Crowder 1968, p. 317). Alternatively, in many colonies, Africans accepted the European system of purchase with title deeds. Whatever evolved, Africans' loss of land never engendered the anger and bitterness in most other parts of tropical Africa that it did in South Africa, Kenya, and Southern Rhodesia.

SEE ALSO AFRICA, LABOR TAXES (HEAD TAXES); CORN LAWS; EMPIRE, BRITISH; EMPIRE, FRENCH; GOLD AND SILVER; IMPERIALISM; KENYA; LABORERS, COERCED; LABORERS, CONTRACT; MINING; SOUTH AFRICA; TOBACCO; ZIMBABWE.

BIBLIOGRAPHY

Brett, E. A. *Colonialism and Underdevelopment in East Africa.* London: Heinemann, 1973.

Crowder, Michael. *West Africa under Colonial Rule.* Evanston, IL: Northwestern University Press, 1968.

Feinberg, Harvey. "The Natives Land Act of 1913 in South Africa: Politics, Race, and Segregation in the Early 20th Century." *International Journal of African Historical Studies* 26, no. 1 (1993): 65–109.

Gann, Lewis H. *A History of Southern Rhodesia.* London: Chatto and Windus, 1965.

Mungeam, Gordon H., ed. *Kenya: Select Historical Documents, 1884–1923.* Nairobi, Kenya: East African Publishing House, 1978.

Palmer, Robin H. *Aspects of Rhodesian Land Policy, 1890–1936.* Salisbury, Southern Rhodesia: Central African Historical Association, 1968.

Tignor, Robert L. *The Colonial Transformation of Kenya.* Princeton, NJ: Princeton University Press, 1976.

Wills, Alfred J. *An Introduction to the History of Central Africa.* 3rd edition. London: Oxford University Press, 1973.

Harvey M. Feinberg

AGNELLI FAMILY

Giovanni Agnelli was born in 1866 in the Piedmontese Val Pellice. In July 1899 he founded, along with many other landowners and aristocrats, the Fabbrica Italiana Automobili Torino (Fiat), of which he was appointed chief executive officer (CEO) in 1902. By the end of World War I, Fiat was among the largest concerns in Italy, with more than 40,000 employees. The profits financed the modern production plant in Lingotto (1923) as well as the integration in steel production. Agnelli transformed Fiat's organizational structure as well, hiring new managers including Vittorio Valletta, who was appointed general manager in 1928.

Fond of mass-production methods, Agnelli drove Fiat toward the production of small, cheap cars; in 1936 the manufacturing of an economy car (the famous "Topolino") began. After Agnelli's death in 1945, Valletta was appointed president and CEO and oversaw the realization of Agnelli's dream with the mass production of two models, the 600 and the 500. In 1963 Giovanni Agnelli's grandson Gianni became CEO, and the Agnelli family was back at the firm's helm. Gianni and his brother Umberto oversaw a difficult reform of the monochromic organizational structure built by Valletta, and further expansion in the 1960s and 1970s.

Around the mid-1970s Cesare Romiti proved to be a key leader for Fiat. He succeeded in improving the company's performance, and in 1991 Agnelli acceded Fiat's managing and strategic responsibilities to him. The representatives of the Agnelli family maintained control over key strategic decisions, for example in 1985, when a merger with Ford Europe, a project that could undermine Fiat's autonomy, was rejected, or in 2000, when a deal with General Motors, which foresaw an industrial cooperation without threatening Fiat's autonomy, was accepted.

In 1986 Fiat bought Alfa Romeo, which was privatized and became a pure monopolist on the Italian market. However, this had no positive influence upon Fiat's competitiveness, which steadily declined. During the 1990s the family was not able to regain influence over Fiat, particularly because in 1997 Umberto's son, Giovanni Alberto, died, and in 2000 Gianni's son, Edoardo, committed suicide.

Gianni died on January 24, 2003, and one month later Umberto became Fiat's president, but he died suddenly the following year, on May 27. Fiat's presidency has since been taken over by Luca Cordero di Montezemolo, who represents the interests of the Agnelli family.

SEE ALSO Automobile; Italy.

BIBLIOGRAPHY

Annibaldi, Cesare, and Berta, Giuseppe, eds. *Grande impresa e sviluppo italiano: Studi per i cento anni della Fiat* (Big Business and Italian Development: Studies for the centennial anniversary of Fiat). Bologna: Il Mulino, 1999.

Berta, Giuseppe, *Mirafior (Mirafiori)*. Bologna: Il Mulino, 1998.

Castronovo, Valerio. *Fiat, 1899–1999: Un secolo di storia italiana* (Fiat 1899–1999: A century of Italian history). Milan: Rizzoli, 1999.

Scotti, Gino. *Fiat, auto e non solo: I dilemmi strategici degli Agnelli dalle origini alla crisi di oggi* (Fiat, not only cars: The strategic dilemmas of the Angelli family to today's crisis). Rome: Donzelli, 2003.

Andrea Colli

AGRICULTURE

During several centuries people evolved from hunting and gathering to growing produce in a single location; this was the beginning of the agricultural age. Agriculture spread from the fertile crescent area westward into Europe and North Africa. Intensive food production allowed for greater population density and, as food surpluses were produced, the opportunity arose for trade among the settlements in which different types of agricultural surpluses were produced. As agricultural settlements expanded in number and size, trade in agricultural goods expanded as well.

AGRICULTURAL TRADE THROUGH THE NINETEENTH CENTURY

Early trade followed water routes because it was easier to float people and goods on water than it was to haul them over land, where few if any roads existed. Shipments of grain, fruits, and vegetables were among the first items in recorded trade among countries. The Egyptians traded grain and vegetables with the Romans and others in the Mediterranean region, and trade flourished in the Indian Ocean and China Sea area as well. Germans, French, English, and, to a lesser extent, Italians built canals in the fifteenth and sixteenth centuries to complement existing rivers in the formation of water routes to connect interior agricultural areas with cities and seaports. Once the technology of sailing progressed to where it allowed explorers to venture forth in search of new land to settle, agricultural goods were exchanged between the explorers and those they encountered.

Beginning in the seventeenth century, trade between Western European countries and the New World began to prosper. Spanish explorers searched for and found silver in Central and South America. They also found a thriving agricultural system that produced products such as maize, tobacco, and sugar. The Portuguese established a colony in Brazil that produced and exported agricultural goods. Unlike the Spanish, the English and Dutch explorers developed settlements and colonized North America and the Caribbean islands. These colonies pro-

JETHRO TULL

In 1701 Jethro Tull (1674–1741) created the first modern seed drill.

Prior to Tull's invention, English farmers had scattered seed by hand on the surface of the soil. Many seeds were thus lost to devouring birds, and the germination rate was low. Tull's device incorporated mechanisms for furrowing the soil and evenly distributing the seeds in orderly rows. Modern sowing machines still use the rotating cylinder design that Tull pioneered.

Born in Basildon, England, Tull strove to be a politician until poor health compelled him to abandon that aspiration. He became a farmer-inventor instead, and his innovations improved agriculture's efficiency and yield.

Tull went on to advocate a method of farming without manure that depended on aeration of the soil. He published a controversial book about the method, *New Horse-Houghing Husbandry* (1731), which he revised and expanded in subsequent years.

Justin Crawford

duced agricultural goods that were shipped to Europe in exchange for manufactured goods. The British colonies in North America became major producers of wheat and corn as well as rice, tobacco, and cotton. Sugar was produced in the Caribbean colonies. Tobacco was the major export product for the colonies (and later the United States) until the early nineteenth century, when exports of cotton exceeded exports of any other single product. Eli Whitney's cotton gin (1793) made it feasible to profitably grow cotton in a much larger geographic region of the United States, and technological improvements in British textile mills created a strong demand for this cotton.

The Napoleonic Wars made international trade very risky, as both the British and French navies seized ships and cargo thought to be destined for "enemy" ports. The Jeffersonian Embargo in 1807, which was a reaction to foreign harassment of United States ships, was a major disruption to trans-Atlantic trade, and this disruption was continued by the War of 1812 and the British blockade of the United States. The war ended in 1815, and

trade resumed. However, United States trade volume did not return to pre-1808 levels until the 1830s.

Britain imported large quantities of grain from Australia and Canada and, during the last half of the nineteenth century, Argentina began exporting grain and meat products to Europe. The opening of the Suez Canal in 1869 shortened the voyage from India and Australia to Britain and allowed producers there to compete more directly with farmers in the United States and Canada for the European markets.

Between 1870 and 1910, four of the top five exports from the United States were agricultural goods (the top five U.S. exports to Britain were all agricultural goods). By the 1890s refrigeration aboard oceangoing ships allowed for the export of chilled beef to Europe, especially Britain, which was also a large market for pork and live cattle exports from the United States during the last half of the nineteenth century. Wheat, wheat flour, and corn were among the top five United States exports to Europe. Europeans also purchased large quantities of oil-seed cake and vegetable oil, both of which were derivatives from processing cotton, along with lard and tallow from the United States. Agricultural exports from the United States to East Asia were also growing during the last half of the nineteenth century. Central and Eastern Europe produced large quantities of various grains and pulses, but little of this was traded across national borders due to their remoteness and the lack of an exportable surplus. It was not until the turn of the century that United States exports of agricultural goods were less than exports of manufactured goods, but even then agricultural exports continued to expand in the twentieth century.

WORLD AGRICULTURE SINCE THE TWENTIETH CENTURY

Opening of the Panama Canal in 1914 reduced costs for Midwestern U.S. farmers to ship to Pacific and East Asian countries. It also allowed Australia to ship raw wool directly to the United States, instead of through London. U.S. West Coast producers of wheat and other agricultural goods could compete more effectively in the European market.

The mechanization of agriculture, along with a persistent search for better and more disease-resistant seeds, accounted for the productivity advantage enjoyed by farmers in the United States and Canada relative to most other countries before World War I. Horse-drawn harvesters and combines were common before the Civil War, but they increased in size, efficiency, and availability in the post–Civil War period. Wheat seeds imported from Europe, including winter wheat and hard red wheat, were resistant to disease and the harsh climate of the upper Midwest. Farmers saved seed from those plants

A tractor moves across a field to prepare the soil for planting season. *Farming machinery advances revolutionized agricultural production, allowing farmers to produce a wider volume of crops across a greater area of land.* © LESTER LEFKOWITZ/CORBIS. REPRODUCED BY PERMISSION.

that did well, and in the process created seed lines that were resistant to many diseases. There was also selective breeding in cattle as well as swine and sheep during the post–Civil War era, resulting in increased productivity in dairy, meat, and wool production. World War I interrupted the flow of world trade in all types of goods. The interwar years were marked by slow growth in international trade in all products as countries became increasingly protectionist.

In the aftermath of World War II, both the political and the economic structure of the world was radically different. Five-year plans announced by the Soviet Union (first announced in 1928) advertised large increases in agricultural productivity and reduced dependence on imports. China began announcing five-year plans in 1953; besides having a heavy-industry component, these aimed to reduce China's reliance on trade for agriculture goods. The United States realized even greater mechanization of agriculture with the adoption of tractors and tractor-drawn machinery, which replaced horse-drawn machinery and increased the optimal size for the average farm. New developments of hybrid seeds and selective

breeding further increased the productivity advantage of United States agriculture. Rubber-tired tractors were adopted in the 1930s and 1940s and became commonplace in the 1950s as tractors replaced horses on most farms. Horse-drawn combines were replaced by tractor-drawn versions, then self-propelled combines. Moreover, disease-resistant hybrid corn that grew to uniform height became common after World War II, making it possible to further mechanize corn harvesting. Hybrid corn also improved the yield per acre and increased the surplus available for export.

Exports of agricultural goods from the United States threatened the agricultural sectors in many other countries, which responded by erecting protective barriers against imports. During the first two decades after World War II, Japan, South Korea, members of the European Common Market, and most Latin American countries created tariff or nontariff barriers to protect their domestic agriculture sector. The consequent decline in the world price of agricultural goods forced the United States and other countries to subsidize their domestic agricultural sectors to prevent them from shrinking. Price-

A farmer in Melk, Austria, steers a horse-drawn plow. *Farmers in many industrialized nations replaced their draft horses with tractors and other machines after World War II, a transition that contributed to booming agricultural productivity in those countries.* © ADAM WOOLFITT/CORBIS. REPRODUCED BY PERMISSION.

support schemes produced substantial surpluses or stockpiles of agricultural goods in the United States and Europe which often were donated to less-developed countries as aid, and this destroyed the domestic agricultural sectors in many of those countries. South Korean and Japanese agricultural sectors have such a high rate of protection that the effective rate of protection on manufactured food products is negative—that is, it is as if the manufactured food companies in these two countries are paying a tax in the form of higher prices for unprocessed agricultural goods, which are the inputs to their production process. As a result of all of this protection for domestic agriculture by various countries, the volume of international trade in agricultural goods is considerably lower than it would otherwise be.

The effect of the Common Agricultural Policy (CAP) of the European Union, which was meant to protect European agriculture, has been production of surpluses that require export subsidies to create trade. For example, people jokingly refer to Europe's "mountains of butter" when discussing the outcome of European agricultural policies that protect dairy farmers. In Asia, Japan and Korea both protect domestic agriculture to an even great-

er extent than the European Union does. The United States also protects its agriculture sector, but not the degree that these other countries do so.

Various rounds of multilateral trade negotiations under the General Agreement on Tariffs and Trade (GATT) generally excluded agriculture from the negotiations. Finally, in the Uruguay Round of negotiations that ended in 1995, all of the countries agreed to discuss the issue of agricultural protection and to act upon it at the next round. The World Trade Organization (WTO) was created as a result of the Uruguay Round, and its dispute-settlement board has ruled that subsidies provided by the United States for cotton farmers are in violation of the WTO rules. If this ruling stands, it could mark the beginning of the dismantling of protection for agriculture, because many other countries use similar types of methods to protect domestic agriculture.

What would removal of all of this protection for agriculture mean for world trade in agricultural goods? The volume of trade in agricultural goods would increase rather significantly as agricultural output in some countries decreased and in others expanded. The optimal scale for most types of agriculture is quite large, especially when growing grains, pulses, and beef cattle. Even dairy farming, which is protected in Europe and the United States, would be forced to remove price supports that allow high-cost producers to remain in operation. Thus, many smaller, higher-cost producers would cease to produce due to the low profits, but consumers would pay far less for agricultural products than they currently do. The result would be a readjustment of resources within the countries where protective barriers have sustained unprofitable agricultural producers.

Trade liberalization has already expanded the rice trade considerably as new exports have entered markets. Japan imports rice from the United States for industrial uses, as domestic Japanese rice is preferred for human consumption. Vietnam has also benefited from trade liberalization in rice, as the well-being of its rice growers has improved significantly. China has reduced its efforts to be agriculturally self-sufficient, and imports increasing amounts of agricultural goods. Chile, in moving toward freer trade with the United States, has exploited the reversed seasons of the Southern Hemisphere and expanded its exports of fruits and vegetables to the United States and other markets. And as a result of the North American Free Trade Agreement, Mexico exports fruits and vegetables to the United States and Canada and imports grains.

As is the case with all products, there are particular countries that possess comparative advantages in producing agricultural goods. Multilateral reductions in trade barriers will allow people worldwide to realize the benefits of less expensive agricultural products, not only in lower food costs, but lower costs for many manufactured goods that are produced from agricultural goods.

SEE ALSO DISEASE AND PESTILENCE; FAMINE; FURS; LABOR, COERCED; LABOR, CONTRACT; LABOR, TYPES OF; RICE; SILK; SLAVERY AND THE AFRICAN SLAVE TRADE; SUGAR, MOLASSES, AND RUM; TIMBER; TOBACCO; WHEAT AND OTHER CEREAL GRAINS; WINE.

BIBLIOGRAPHY

Atack, Jeremy, and Passell, Peter. *A New Economic View of American History,* 2nd edition. New York: W. W. Norton, 1994.

Curtin, Philip D. *Cross-Cultural Trade in World History.* Cambridge, U.K.: Cambridge University Press, 1984.

Diamond, Jared. *Guns, Germs, and Steel.* New York: W. W. Norton, 1999.

Rosegrant, Mark W., and Hazell, Peter B. R. *Transforming the Rural Asian Economy: The Unfinished Revolution.* Oxford, U.K.: Oxford University Press, 2000.

United States Treasury. *Commerce and Navigation Reports.* Washington, DC: Government Printing Office, 1870–1910.

William K. Hutchinson

AFONSO DE ALBUQUERQUE
1453–1515

Afonso de Albuquerque, a Portuguese naval-military commander and imperial administrator, was responsible for designing and executing the strategy that established the first European maritime empire in Asia in the early modern period. Based on the occupation of a series of strategically located and fortifiable port cities that dominated the principal maritime trading lanes, the strategy was designed to control the spice trade (primarily pepper, cloves, nutmeg, and mace) and redirect it from Muslim-controlled Persian Gulf and Red Sea routes to the Cape of Good Hope route around Africa to Europe.

In less than twelve years of furious activity, from 1503 to 1515, Albuquerque sought to establish this ambitious strategy. Initially, he supported indigenous Portuguese allies on the western coast of India at Cochin and established a trading post at Quilon to access larger deliveries of pepper. He shifted his focus toward the disruption of trade through the Red Sea with the establishment of a fortress at Socotra and through the Persian Gulf by temporarily taking Hormuz. Faced with continued resistance to their efforts on the western coast of India, his forces took Goa in 1510 to establish an independent base and seat of government for the Portuguese trading-post empire in Asia. The capture of Melaka, on the Malay Peninsula, in 1511 secured immediate and eventual access to the Spice Islands, China, and Japan. Albuquerque did suffer a few operational failures and reversals, such as the abandonment of building a fortress at Hormuz in 1507, and thwarted attempts to seize Cochin in 1510 and Aden in 1512.

The Portuguese successes were possible, in part, through their introduction of Mediterranean practices of armed trade to the Indian Ocean and new technology in naval and military designs. Innovative ships were constructed to provide stable platforms for the operation of large-caliber cannons that radically changed the level of violence at sea and permitted the projection of seapower over great distances. New fortresses were designed to withstand siege and await relief from the sea. Albuquerque was brutal, ruthless, and pragmatic in implementing imperial strategy. According to contemporary reports and surviving records, Albuquerque also was a charismatic leader, well-educated, and, extraordinary for the time, an avid writer of letters and reports.

SEE ALSO EAST INDIA COMPANY, DUTCH; EMPIRE, DUTCH; EMPIRE, PORTUGUESE; GAMA, VASCO DA; INDIA; INDIAN OCEAN; INDONESIA; LISBON; MELAKA; PORTUGAL; PROTECTION COSTS; SPICES AND THE SPICE TRADE.

BIBLIOGRAPHY

Albuquerque, Afonso de. *The Commentaries of the Great Afonso Dalboquerque, Second Viceroy of India*. Trans. Walter de Gray Birch. London: Printed for the Hakluyt Society, 1875–1884; Reprinted 1970.

Albuquerque, Afonso de. *Albuquerque Caesar of the East: Selected Texts by Afonso de Albuquerque and His Son.* Trans. and ed. T. F. Earle and John Villiers. Oxford: Aires and Phillips, 1991.

George Bryan Souza

RUTHERFORD ALCOCK
1809–1897

Sir Rutherford Alcock, a British diplomat in East Asia, was a wholehearted advocate of commercial imperialism. Alcock entered the consular service at Fuzhou in 1844; he was moved to Shanghai in 1846 and to Canton briefly in 1855. In 1854 he invented the "foreign-inspectorate system" of taxing foreign trade at Shanghai, leading to the founding of the Imperial Maritime Customs. In 1858 Alcock was appointed the first consul-general to the newly opened empire of Japan. He advocated gunboat diplomacy to open Japan further. In 1864 he was transferred to Beijing as British minister to China until 1871. He advised the Chinese government regarding the adoption of various Western innovations. Alcock was responsible for the opening of Taiwan and negotiated the revision of the Treaty of Tianjin in 1869—the first equal treaty between China and a Western maritime nation—but the Alcock Convention was never ratified. He estimated that China spent about 10 million taels on opium annually while selling only 2 million taels worth of tea; China's new export was people. He tried to force the Chinese government to enter into a treaty to allow their subjects to take opium and pushed for the legalization of the opium and coolie trade. He was for some years president of the Royal Geographical Society, and was author of several books.

SEE ALSO CANTON SYSTEM; CHINA; DRUGS, ILLICIT; EMPIRE, BRITISH; EMPIRE, QING; FACTORIES; GUANGZHOU; HART, ROBERT; HONG KONG; IMPERIALISM; IMPERIAL MARITIME CUSTOMS, CHINA; JAPAN; JARDINE MATHESON; LIN ZEXU; SHANGHAI; TEA; TREATIES.

BIBLIOGRAPHY

Michie, Alexander. *An Englishman in China during the Victorian Era: As Illustrated in the Career of Sir Rutherford Alcock, Many Years Consul and Minister in China and Japan.* Taipei: Zhengwen, 1966.

Smith, Richard J.; Fairbank, John K.; and Bruner, Katherine F.; eds. *Robert Hart and China's Early Modernization: His Journals, 1863–1866.* Cambridge, MA: Council on East Asian Studies, Harvard University, 1991.

Chi-Kong Lai

MUHAMMAD ALI
1760?–1849

Muhammad Ali is without question the most significant historical figure in modern Egyptian history (since 1800), at least until Gamal Abdel Nasser (1918–1970) came to power in the military coup d'état of 1952. The son of an Ottoman-Albanian military figure, in 1801 Muhammad Ali led Ottoman forces drawn from the Albanian region of the Ottoman Empire to help in the ultimately successful campaign to repel the invading French forces from Egypt, which was a province of the Ottoman Empire at the time. Refusing, however, to subordinate himself or his soldiers to Ottoman authority, the pasha, or *wali* (as Muhammad Ali was often referred to) emerged as the most powerful political figure in Egypt in 1805. By 1811 he had defeated all pockets of military resistance to his power.

Enjoying virtually unchecked political authority, he proceeded to carry out a far-reaching reform program to introduce modern European military, economic, and educational institutions into Egypt. He sent educational missions to Europe, brought European technicians and teachers to Egypt, had European works of science translated into Arabic, expanded the Egyptian army and reorganized it along European lines, introduced long-staple cotton into the agricultural economy and made it Egypt's primary export, and set up local textile- and food-processing factories. His successes were considerable, and by the 1830s Egypt had become the most powerful state in the eastern Mediterranean. But the pasha's successes worried the major European powers, notably Britain, which feared the presence of a strong state astride one of its key trade routes to India. In 1840 to 1841 a concert of European powers led by the British forced the Egyptian ruler to give up territorial conquests outside of Egypt, restricted the size of the Egyptian army to 18,000 men, and opened the country to European merchants. The reforming zeal went out of the sails of the Egyptian leadership, whose zest for modernizing the state and the economy did not revive until Khedive Isma'il came to power in 1863.

SEE ALSO COTTON; DEVELOPMENTAL STATE, CONCEPT OF THE; EGYPT; EMPIRE, BRITISH; EMPIRE, OTTOMAN; INDUSTRIALIZATION; MEDITERRANEAN; NATIONALISM; PASHA, ISMAIL; SUEZ CANAL; TEXTILES.

BIBLIOGRAPHY

Daly, Martin W., ed. *Modern Egypt from 1517 to the End of the Twentieth Century.* Cambridge, U.K.: Cambridge University Press, 1998.

Marsot, Afaf Lutfi al-Sayyid. *Egypt in the Reign of Muhammad Ali.* Cambridge, U.K.: Cambridge University Press, 1984.

Toledano, Ehud. R. "Muhammad Ali Pasha." *Encyclopedia of Islam,* vol. 7, ed. E. J. van Donzel. Leiden, Netherlands: Brill, 1993.

Robert L. Tignor

AMERICAN SYSTEM

The American System was a protectionist policy first put forward by the Kentucky politician Henry Clay (1777–1852) in 1824. Clay argued that protecting U.S. industry from foreign manufacturers would create large internal markets for cotton, foodstuffs, and other U.S. agricultural products. By 1832 Clay had added two other major elements to the American System: a government-financed system of transportation improvements and a national bank. Although the American System met a decidedly mixed political fate in the antebellum period, it nevertheless became a focal point in debates over national planning and global trade. Almost all of the elements of the American System became national policy after the Civil War.

Clay himself embodied many of the values and interests that the American System sought to promote. Born and raised in Virginia, Clay moved to the Bluegrass region of Kentucky, where he became a prosperous lawyer and slaveholding planter. Ever ambitious, Clay quickly made his way into politics as a devoted nationalist, and he became a leader of the War Hawk faction that supported war with Great Britain in 1812. Clay, like many planters in the Bluegrass region, grew hemp that was manufactured into rope and cotton bagging. The region's strong manufacturing connections gave Clay a direct financial and political interest in protectionism. On a more general level, the Bluegrass region's mix of prosperous farmers, vibrant manufacturing, and growing cities represented the diversified economy that Clay hoped to create across the nation.

Clay first supported a protectionist agenda in 1816. Thomas Jefferson's embargo of 1807 and the War of 1812 had limited British competition in U.S. markets for nearly a decade, but observers noted with alarm that a flood of inexpensive British textiles and other goods threatened to undermine the United States' fledgling manufacturing sector. Clay's attempts to pass a protective tariff met with only mixed success—import duties on cotton and woolen textiles, for example, were fixed at only 25 percent of

Henry Clay (1777–1852). Clay, who proposed the protectionist American System policy, was nicknamed the "Great Pacificator." He brokered several compromises, including the Missouri Compromise, which prevented civil war—at least until after his death. LIBRARY OF CONGRESS.

the product's value. Repeated attempts to raise the tariff in the aftermath of the Depression of 1819, which struck manufacturing particularly hard, narrowly failed. Protectionists, however, made more headway in tariff bills passed in 1824 and in 1828, which significantly raised duties on woolen goods, iron, cotton bagging, and other important goods.

In these legislative debates, Clay and other advocates of the American System argued that high tariffs would benefit all sectors of the economy. Manufacturers would flourish, safely protected from cheap foreign goods. Farmers and planters would also prosper as a safe, dependable home market replaced uncertain foreign markets as the major outlet for U.S. agricultural products. Merchants who coordinated the exchanges between cities and countryside would see their business grow as well. The American System thus rested on the harmony of interests among manufacturing, commerce, and agriculture. All would benefit from a growing home market. Clay frequently emphasized the importance of home markets as a way of appealing to those who most opposed the American System. He argued that even the farmers and planters who initially paid higher prices for consumer goods would benefit in the long run from protectionist policies as the markets for their own produce expanded, prices for what they sold rose, and their return of trade consequently improved. Would not cotton planters of the South, Clay rhetorically asked in 1824, benefit from the development of more dependable American buyers for their crop?

A strong sense of nationalism pervaded the appeals on behalf of the American System. Protectionists repeatedly stressed the importance of industry to national defense, reminding listeners of shortages of arms, munitions, uniforms, and other supplies that had hampered U.S. forces during the War of 1812. Clay and other supporters of protectionism portrayed free trade as a form of colonial dependency that subjected Americans to the whims of European states and consumers. A large internal market, in contrast, would link the various regions of the country together with the bonds of mutual dependency. Dependence on international markets, in other words, created weakness; but dependence upon domestic markets cultivated patriotism. Defenders of the American System also stressed that domestic markets created homogeneity—consumers throughout the nation would buy the same goods and read the same news, thus reducing regional loyalties and creating a more unified nation.

Because of their deep belief in the importance of the home market, Clay and other proponents of the American System also supported government-financed internal improvements and a national bank. Federal funding of roads, canals, and railroads would connect all U.S. localities to the domestic market. Clay and his allies also vigorously defended the Second Bank of the United States, which they believed would regulate state banks, insure a stable currency, and supply businesses across the nation with much-needed capital. A national system of internal improvements and a national bank would also strengthen commercial ties and provide a shared set of common economic interests that would transcend regional loyalties. In this sense the American System resembled Alexander Hamilton's economic nationalism of 1790s, which sought to unify the new nation through large national debt, a powerful national bank, and moderately higher tariffs. It should be noted, however, that Clay's American System went far beyond many of Hamilton's relatively moderate proposals. Whereas Hamilton's famous *Report on Manufactures* called for a tariff of 10 percent, Clay and other proponents of the American System regularly pushed for duties that exceeded 50 percent.

The economic and nationalistic appeals of the American System became an important part of Clay's platform during his presidential bids in 1824, 1832, and 1844. The nationalistic wing of the Jeffersonian party—known as the National Republicans—embraced the American System in the 1820s. The Whig Party, formed in the early 1830s, endorsed the American System as the centerpiece of its economic agenda. Influential editors and writers, such as Hezekiah Niles (1777–1839) and Henry Carey (1793–1879), strongly supported the American System. Politically, the American System found strong support in larger, more industrial, northeastern states such as New York and Pennsylvania.

Despite some success in the 1820s, the political fortunes of the American System waned in the 1830s. High tariffs were especially unpopular in the South, where planters opposed paying higher prices that, they charged, benefited only northeastern manufacturers. Some southerners also feared that the centralization of power inherent in the American System presented a long-term threat to slavery. If the federal government had the power to protect industry, build canals, and regulate banking, they reasoned, then why would it not have the power to abolish slavery as well? During the winter of 1832 to 1833, South Carolina took the dramatic step of nullifying the Tariff of 1828, which was known in the state as the "Tariff of Abominations." South Carolina's response to the tariff, although extreme, nevertheless highlighted a central political problem of protectionism and other elements of the American System. Opponents successfully portrayed the American System as a zero-sum game in which some interests (northern manufacturers) won and other interests (farmers and planters) lost.

Nullification won South Carolina few allies even within the South, but the state's radical stand forced Clay to back a compromise tariff in 1832 that gradually lowered rates. Major tariff bills in 1844 and 1857 adopted the concept of a revenue tariff, in which rates were set to meet the financial needs of the government rather than to help protect industry. Although tariff revenues provided some incidental protection, their generally lower rates were a far cry from the protectionism promised in the American System. Other policies associated with the American System also fared poorly. In 1830 Andrew Jackson, a long-time political rival of Clay's, vetoed the Maysville Road Bill, which would have provided federal funding to an important project in Clay's own state of Kentucky. Even more importantly, Jackson vetoed in 1832 a bill to recharter the Second Bank of the United States. Jackson soundly defeated Clay in the election of 1832, effectively dooming the American System. Most Americans apparently shared Jackson's fears that the American System, in mixing economic power with political centralization, would invite political corruption.

The American System never became a reality in the antebellum period, but many of its important elements were passed during the Civil War. Abraham Lincoln and many other Republicans were long-time admirers of Clay and his ideas. When the South left the Union, Republicans eagerly subsidized railroads with generous land grants, passed a highly protective tariff, and enacted national banking regulation. The American System was alive and well even after the death of Henry Clay and the Second Party System.

SEE ALSO HAMILTON, ALEXANDER.

BIBLIOGRAPHY

Baxter, Maurice G. *Henry Clay and the American System.* Lexington: University of Kentucky Press, 1995.

Howe, Daniel Walker. *The Political Culture of the American Whigs.* Chicago: University of Chicago Press, 1979.

Watson, Harry L. *Liberty and Power: The Politics of Jacksonian America.* New York: Noonday Press, 1990.

Watson, Harry L. *Andrew Jackson vs. Henry Clay: Democracy and Development in Antebellum America.* Boston: Bedford/ St. Martin's Press, 1998.

John Majewski

AMSTERDAM

Amsterdam arose as a village of fishermen and craftsmen at the mouth of the river Amstel, near the Zuider Zee, in Holland in the early thirteenth century. Having received a city charter about 1300, this settlement slowly developed into a sizable port, reaching a population of around 10,000 in 1500. Throughout most of the sixteenth century, Amsterdam still ranked second to Antwerp in the hierarchy of port towns in the Low Countries. Although customs records by 1580 showed already a quite large variety of import and export products (numbering roughly 300 of the latter and half that many of the former), Amsterdam's share in the seaborne and inland trade of the Habsburg Netherlands as a whole was at that time much lower than that of Antwerp, and its commerce and shipping exhibited a more pronounced penchant for particular products and regions. Grain imports and the exportation of textiles and beverages formed the bulk of its trade, and northwest Germany and the Baltic were the main areas of origin and destination.

The revolt against Habsburg rule and the subsequent political and economic breakup of the Low Countries at the end of the sixteenth century prepared the way for Amsterdam's rise to the status of a port of global importance. Thanks to the massive inflow of financially strong, well-connected merchants from Antwerp following the reconquest of that city by the Spanish army in 1585, and the rapid ascent of the newly founded Dutch Republic as a major political and military power, Amsterdam succeeded between 1590 and 1630 to grow into the hub of a far-flung maritime and commercial network that ranged from India, the Indonesian archipelago, and Japan to the Caribbean and North America, and from Archangel and the Baltic to West Africa, Spain, Italy, and the Levant. The volume of shipping and trade vastly expanded, and an increasing part of the imports consisted of products such as spices, sugar, silk, copper, cotton, timber, tar, tobacco, and furs. In the eighteenth century Amsterdam developed into a dominant center of international finance as well. During its swift expansion about 1600, Amsterdam moreover saw the foundation of a number of institutions that strengthened its leading role in shipping, commerce, and finance by facilitating money flows, easing the exchange of information, guarding the proper conduct of transactions, and improving protection for ships and trade routes: a stock exchange, an exchange bank, a chamber of insurance and average, an admiralty, boards of directors for the Baltic and Levant trades, and joint-stock companies that monopolized the trade with the East and West Indies. The growth of trade and shipping in turn led to the rise of various new industries such as sugar refining, calico printing, tobacco spinning; and diamond cutting generated a large influx of skilled and unskilled labor, including many seamen from Germany and Scandinavia. The population of the city exploded from about 30,000 in the 1570s to 105,000 c. 1620, and to about 240,000 in the early eighteenth century.

Due to the changing structure of world trade, the loss of its lead as a center of information, and the progressive decline of the international power of the Dutch state, Amsterdam from the late eighteenth century onwards fell back to the position of a second-rank economic center whose prosperity for a long time rested mainly on its financial service sector, its trade and shipping links with the East Indies, and a restricted array of processing industries. As a port and trading town, it received a new lease on life beginning at the end of the nineteenth century with the industrialization of the Netherlands and the German hinterland and the construction of new, direct waterways to the North Sea and the Rhine (and later, the construction of a large international airport). Although it was outdistanced by Rotterdam, Antwerp, and Hamburg as far as the scale of its shipping activities was concerned, the city of Amsterdam, which in the twentieth century expanded into a metropolitan area with over one million people, nevertheless managed to maintain the status of one of the major commercial and financial centers in northwest Europe.

SEE ALSO AGRICULTURE; BANKING; CANALS; CARGOES, FREIGHT; CARGOES, PASSENGER; CHAMBERS OF COMMERCE; COEN, JAN PIETERSZOON;

Containerization; East India Company, Dutch; Empire, Dutch; Ethnic Groups, Armenians; Free Ports; Harbors; Indonesia; Port Cities; Shipping, Merchant; South Africa; Spices and the Spice Trade; Tea; West India Company, Dutch.

BIBLIOGRAPHY

Israel, Jonathan I. *Dutch Primacy in World Trade, 1585–1740.* Oxford, U.K.: Clarendon Press, 1989.

Jonker, Joost. *Merchants, Bankers, Middlemen: The Amsterdam Money Market during the First Half of the 19th Century.* Amsterdam: Nederlands Economisch Historisch Archief, 1996.

Lesger, Clé. "Intraregional Trade and the Port System in Holland, 1400–1700." In *The Dutch Economy in the Golden Age,* ed. Karel Davids and Leo Noordegraaf. Amsterdam: Nederlands Economisch Historisch Archief, 1993.

Postma, Johannes, and Enthoven, Victor, eds. *The Atlantic World, Vol. 1: Riches from Atlantic Commerce: Dutch Trans-Atlantic Trade and Shipping, 1585–1817.* Leiden, Netherlands: E. J. Brill, 2003.

Riley, James C. *International Government Finance and the Amsterdam Capital Market, 1740–1815.* Cambridge, U.K.: Cambridge University Press, 1980.

Van Tielhof, Milja. *The "Mother of All Trades": The Baltic Grain Trade in Amsterdam from the Late 16th to the Early 19th Century.* Leiden, Netherlands: E. J. Brill, 2002.

Karel Davids

ANGLO AMERICAN CORPORATION

Anglo American is South Africa's largest company and the world's leading mining enterprise, with interests in gold, coal, ferrous and base metals, platinum, and diamonds. It also has more than 100 subsidiaries throughout the world in banking and insurance, paper and packaging, timber, publishing, and steel.

Today, Anglo and its subsidiaries own 45 percent of DeBeers Consolidated Mines; in turn, DeBeers owns nearly 40 percent of Anglo American. DeBeers is the world's largest diamond group, controlling between 60 and 90 percent of the rough-diamond market through its management of the so-called Central Selling Organization (CSO), an international diamond cartel. While not a monopoly in DeBeers in diamonds, Anglo remains the West's largest producer of gold, and has mined 11,000 tons since the middle of the twentieth century, or one-tenth of the world total.

The story of Anglo American is closely tied to the emergence of South Africa as a nation in the twentieth century. The company's fortunes were, and continue to be, intertwined with South African politics, social structure, and overall economic development. Company operations also have drawn workers from Angola, Lesotho, Zimbabwe, and other neighboring states and kingdoms, thereby affecting the African subcontinent as a whole.

Ernest Oppenheimer (1880–1957) created Anglo American Corporation in September 1917, seven years after the Union of South Africa came into being in the wake of the second Boer War (1899–1902). The German-born Oppenheimers came to South Africa in 1905 and bought a major interest in the Premier Transvaal Diamond Company, together with some of the region's richest gold-producing lands. Until then, southern Africa's foreign investors had been British and European, but Oppenheimer's success attracted the first U.S. venture capital—including some from J. P. Morgan (1837–1913)—ever invested south of the Limpopo River. Formed during World War I, Anglo American's name was chosen to disguise its German background and because the original suggestion, African-American, was unacceptable to U.S. investors.

DIAMONDS

Diamonds are the hardest natural mineral on earth, which makes them ideal for many applications that require extremely durable, precise, or sharp tools. Because only the finest diamonds are suitable for gemstones, many small or imperfect diamonds are used to grind, polish, or cut other hard materials.

One example of this use is the diamond-impregnated drill bit, which can be small enough to fit in a dental patient's mouth, or large enough to drill an oil well. Diamond drill bits are expensive, but they cut rapidly.

In addition to their hardness, diamonds have unique optical properties that make them especially suitable for certain laser tools. Diamonds are transparent to beams of light well beyond the visible range, and they are durable even in intense heat and radiation, which means that high-powered infrared lasers can pass through them with minimal diffusion. By using a special chemical process, diamonds can be shaped into a window or lens through which an infrared beam can exit a laser device.

Justin Crawford

Loading copper at Anglo American's mine in Phalaborwa, South Africa, 1997. The Oppenheimers, the founders of the Anglo American Corporation, first came to South Africa in 1905. AP/WIDE WORLD PHOTOS. REPRODUCED BY PERMISSION.

Anglo American represented the consolidation of a fragmented industry. More than 500 "wildcat" companies had mined diamonds discovered near the upper Vaal River in central South Africa in 1871, and the vast gold deposits on a ridge called the Witwatersrand ("Rand") in 1886 in the northeast. By century's end, however, less than ten companies remained, steered by a remarkable group of mostly English finance-mining entrepreneurs, including Cecil John Rhodes (1853–1902).

Shortly after its formation, Anglo added diamond fields in German Southwest Africa (now Namibia) to its facilities in Angola and Congo, and broke the DeBeers monopoly in diamond production. The diamond monopoly was reestablished in 1926 when Anglo took control of DeBeers, which, since its establishment by Rhodes in 1888, had controlled the South African diamond industry. By this time DeBeers had diversified into cattle ranching, agriculture, wine production, explosives, railroads, and coal. In 1928 Anglo spearheaded the development of the Zambian Cooperbelt, a mining region in

south central Africa and one of the richest sources of copper, cobalt, and selenium in the world.

In the depressed 1930s, Great Britain, the United States, and others, including South Africa, abandoned the gold standard for their currencies. This destabilized Anglo for several years, but DeBeers experienced rising demand as diamonds began to have industrial applications, replacing steel blades formerly used to cut precision tools. The industrial challenges of the 1940s created massive demand for minerals, diamond dust, and resins. South Africa supported the Allies during World War II, and the United States was by far Anglo's largest customer.

After World War II, Anglo American became the world's foremost mining company, able to prospect for and extract minerals at unprecedented depths. Anglo expanded its grip on the South African gold industry, becoming the largest producer by 1958 with a 40 percent share; DeBeers did likewise with diamonds, gaining nearly 80 percent of the world market by 1958. In the 1950s

Anglo American also made major uranium strikes. As the raw material of atomic weaponry, uranium complicated the relations of all major powers with South Africa during the Cold War, particularly as issues of racial segregation and equity gained worldwide attention.

The booming mineral industry spawned a huge growth of supporting infrastructure within South Africa—including roads, railways, harbors, and manufacturing—and created such cities as Johannesburg and Kimberley. Mining also led to an almost insatiable hunger for labor that, from the start, had a hierarchy of tasks based on race. Dirt diggers were black; sorters of small gold nuggets and small diamonds were mixed race (African, Chinese, Indian); processors of the large nuggets and diamonds were white. There were huge disparities between black and white wages. In 1920 some 21,000 white workers on the gold mines earned twice as much as the total earnings of 180,000 black workers, or roughly seventeen times as much per capita; the same average ratio held in 1961.

In the 1930s South Africa began calling the institutional separation of races *apartheid*. From 1948 to 1989 nationalist regimes made apartheid the official policy of South African society. Labor unrest, strikes, and government pressure to conform to strict apartheid standards put Anglo in an awkward position. Not only at home, but also as an enterprise doing business abroad, Anglo American was sensitive to being associated with a government becoming an international pariah.

The Oppenheimer family was loyal to South Africa, and Ernest always had maintained Anglo's national character and outlook. In the decades following World War II, the family supported moderate opposition politicians and black labor unions, and provided funding for worker housing, education, and training. In the late 1960s and early 1970s, however, domestic difficulties connected to apartheid obliged the company to look outside South Africa, and Anglo invested in mines in the United States, Australia, Portugal, Canada, and Malaysia, as well as in newly independent Zambia and Tanzania. To manage its overseas interests, Anglo created a Luxembourg-based holding company—first called Charter Consolidated, then the Mineral and Resources Corporation (Minorco).

In 1993 Minorco paid U.S.$1.4 billion for Anglo American's and DeBeers's European, Australian, and South American operations as part of a swap that put all of Anglo's non-African assets, except diamonds, into Minorco's hands, and out of reach of possible nationalization by the black-controlled South African governments. Five years later, Anglo and Minorco combined to form Anglo American plc to provide "a better base for international expansion and to access capital markets"(Annual Report 2004). Since 1998, the company also has unraveled many of its former crossholdings.

Though its origins are South African, Anglo is today more British than African. The company lists its shares primarily on the London Stock Exchange, is majority-owned by U.K. institutions, and maintains its headquarters in London. Two-thirds of its sales come from outside South Africa. The Oppenheimer family retains management control of DeBeers and a seat on Anglo's Non-Executive Board. Revenues for the first half of 2004 were nearly U.S.$12 billion.

SEE ALSO AFRICA, LABOR TAXES (HEAD TAXES); ANGOLA; COAL; DEBEERS; EMPIRE, BRITISH; GOLD AND SILVER; GOLD RUSHES; LABORERS, CONTRACT; LABOR, TYPES OF; MINING; RHODES, CECIL; SOUTH AFRICA; TIMBER; UNITED KINGDOM; UNITED STATES; ZIMBABWE.

BIBLIOGRAPHY

Kanfer, Stefan. *The Last Empire.* New York: Farrar, Straus and Giroux, 1993.

Sanderson, G. L., et al. *Cambridge History of Africa,* vols. 6–8. Cambridge, U.K.: Cambridge University Press, 1975.

Wheatcroft, Geoffrey. *The Randlords.* New York: Weidenfeld and Nicholson, 1986.

Peter E. Austin

ANGOLA

Angola, formerly known as Portuguese West Africa, is an independent state in southwest Africa that was administered by Portugal from 1483 to 1975. It is important in the regional economy of southern Africa as well as in the Atlantic trading economy, particularly regarding Brazil.

The first inhabitants of present-day Angola are thought to have been members of the hunter-gatherer Khoisan group. Bantu-speaking peoples from West Africa arrived in the region in the thirteenth century, partially displacing the Khoisan and establishing a number of powerful kingdoms, most notably the Kongo in the north. The Portuguese first explored coastal Angola in the late fifteenth century, and except for a short occupation (1641–1648) by the Dutch, the country was under Portuguese control until they left late in the twentieth century. Although Portugal's presence in Angola lasted for nearly five centuries, for most of this time it was restricted to port cities such as Benguela and the country's present capital, Luanda. Despite its apparent shallowness, European colonization had a profound influence on Angolan society and on its internal and external trade patterns.

Portuguese explorations of the west coast of Africa in the 1480s sought silver, spices, ivory, and gold. Those

ELEPHANTS AND IVORY

Elephant tusks are the primary source of natural ivory, which is a toothlike material prized for its beauty. Humans have used ivory for decorative carvings since prehistoric times, and ivory still embellishes modern goods such as furniture and jewelry.

To satisfy global demand for ivory in the late twentieth century, poachers in Africa killed hundreds of thousands of elephants. Between 1979 and 1989 the price of ivory climbed to $140 a pound, and the number of elephants in Africa decreased by nearly half (to an estimated 700,000 animals).

In 1989 the United States led a handful of nations in banning the importation of ivory. Fearing the imminent extinction of the species, 150 nations agreed that same year to completely halt the ivory trade. The price of ivory fell to less than $5 per pound.

The ban is a subject of ongoing debate among African nations. Some, such as Kenya, want to see elephants recover from their near extinction. Others, such as Zimbabwe, consider the ban to be an economic hardship imposed on them by outside interests.

In the meantime, the export of tusks continues. In 2004, 1,000 tusks (from 500 animals) left Zimbabwe as hunting trophies, according to the web site of the Convention on International Trade in Endangered Species.

Justin Crawford

first European contacts with the Kongo were beneficial to both parties, who exchanged ideas and supplies, though Portugal had an advantage in weaponry. Slavery was part of this relationship from the start. The Kongo supplied coastal traders with slaves from the interior, who were sent either to sugar plantations on the islands of São Tomé and Principe in the Gulf of Guinea or, after 1550, across the Atlantic to the slave-receiving stations of Rio de Janeiro, Salvador, and Recife in the developing Portuguese colony of Brazil. Angola was the primary slave supplier to Brazil, and indeed, may have supplied as many as one-third of all the slaves taken from western Africa over 300 years.

In addition to supplying slaves, until the nineteenth century Angola was a dumping ground for criminals and undesirables of the Portuguese Crown. Its status changed profoundly, however, with Brazil's independence in 1822, with the formal abolition of slave transport on the open seas in 1836, and after the Berlin Conference of European colonial powers recognized Portuguese rights, possession, and most boundaries of Angola and Mozambique in 1885. Vigorous exploration of the Angolan interior then began. To offset economic losses of the decline of slavery, Portugal developed a series of mono-crop economies designed for export from its colony. The first of these was the development of the ivory trade, which continued until elephant extinctions in about 1900 forced a change to wild rubber, Angola's main export in most years from 1900 to 1916. Due to strong competition in the rubber trade from Southeast Asia, coffee became the new main export cash earner in the 1920s, then diamonds in the 1930s, and finally oil in the late 1960s following discoveries by Belgian and U.S. oil companies in the northern area of Cabinda. Throughout this changing economic landscape, sugarcane was a constant and significant export crop for Angola from the 1830s to the 1930s.

Virtually every region of Angola found a substitute for the export of human beings, but severe demographic damage continued due to Portuguese policies. In the late nineteenth century Portugal had imposed a "hut tax" payable in currency or tradable goods. Labor for very low wages—utterly unregulated, unrestricted, and enforced by military force—was made compulsory for Angolans in the cultivation of cash-export products, but also in the construction of roads and railway links to the copperbelt of Katanga, Zaire, and to the newly discovered gold fields of the South African Rand. Compulsory labor service had a high death rate, and thousands of Angolans migrated to neighboring countries to avoid it. Additionally, between 1885 and 1903 Portuguese officials in Angola sent more 56,000 Angolan laborers to São Tomé and Principe for the cultivation of cocoa to keep the islands in surplus. Portuguese officials also received fees from South African companies for the many workers they sent to labor in the gold mines.

As Portugal sought export production, it also sought increased administrative control over Angola's interior, which it accomplished by military force in 1917. The Angolan countryside was reorganized into villages and townships to which thousands were forced to move. The reorganization for export production continued the churning of the Angolan population and destabilized still further the already splintered systems of authority and culture caused by years of slave seizures from the Angolan interior.

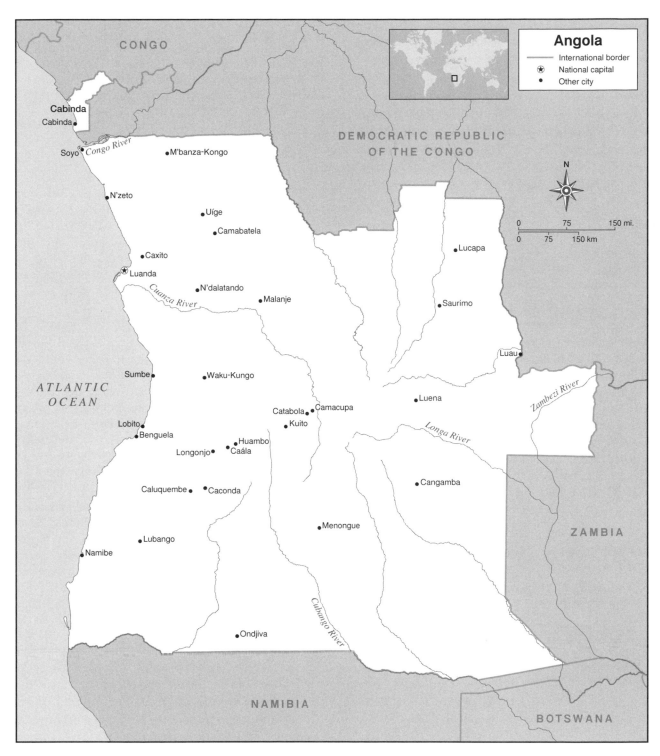

MAP BY XNR PRODUCTIONS. THE GALE GROUP.

With increased organization and growth in the colony came Portuguese settlers, whose numbers swelled from 10,000 in 1900, to 40,000 in 1940, and to 340,000 in 1974. Every arrival of Europeans contributed to a reduction in the status of the indigenous population, and Angolan society became increasingly stratified. Particularly in the central highlands around the Bie Plateau and Kwanza River Valley, land expropriations and expulsions of Africans to make way for colonial farms became increasingly common, and the villages and the townships were governed by regulations separating the races. Angola was one of the most profitable colonies on the African subcontinent, but its population was one of the most displaced and damaged.

Politics in Portugal had great bearing on what policies came to pass in its colonies. Perhaps the greatest example of this was the Colonial Act of 1930, which, for the first time, made the writ of Lisbon count for something in its colonies. Suddenly, the stated goal was to bind Angola closely to Portugal in order to create prosperity to benefit Portugal. Tariff laws and laws to discourage foreign investment were passed, and considerable new financial commitments were made to develop Angolan infrastructure. The aim was to develop Angola from a collection of separate customs zones, railroad corridors, and administrative districts to a modern unified state.

Despite its intentions, Portugal began modern development of Angola only after World War II. In 1951 Portugal designated its colonies as overseas provinces and initiated plans to develop industries, infrastructure, and hydroelectric power. Although the Portuguese professed the aim of a multiracial society of equals in Angola, most Africans still suffered repression and labor dislocation. Inspired by nationalist movements elsewhere, native Angolans rose in revolt in 1961. When the Portuguese army quelled the uprising, many fled to Congo (Kinshasa) and other neighboring countries. Portugal granted Angola independence in 1975, together with the other Portuguese African colonies, Mozambique, São Tomé, and Principe.

Following independence, Angola retreated from the world of trade and slid into twenty-seven years of civil war from which it has yet to recover fully. In 2004 the economy was booming due to peace and high oil prices. Inflation was down from quadruple digits in the mid-1990s, and GDP was expected to grow by 13 percent in 2005. Still, the country relies on outside donors to feed itself, poverty is widespread, most of its population is under twenty-four years old, and foreign direct investment from private sources remains cautious. Oil, cotton, and diamonds are Angola's main exports, and Portugal remains its main trading partner, followed by South Africa.

SEE ALSO AFRICA, LABOR TAXES (HEAD TAXES); ARMS, ARMAMENTS; BRAZIL; EMPIRE, DUTCH; EMPIRE, PORTUGUESE; ETHNIC GROUPS, AFRICANS; FACTORIES; IMPERIALISM; INTERNATIONAL MONETARY FUND (IMF); KONGO; LABORERS, CONTRACT; LABOR, TYPES OF; SLAVERY AND THE AFRICAN SLAVE TRADE; SOUTH AFRICA; SUGAR, MOLASSES, AND RUM; TEXTILES.

BIBLIOGRAPHY
Parry, J. H. *The Age of Reconnaissance.* Berkeley: University of California Press, 1963.
Sanderson, G. N., et al. *Cambridge History of Africa,* vols. 6–8. Cambridge, U.K.: Cambridge University Press, 1975.
Tvedten, Inge. *Angola: Struggle for Peace and Reconstruction.* Boulder, CO: Westview Press, 1997.

Peter E. Austin

ANTWERP

After being a port of some importance and a fair town in the thirteenth and fourteenth centuries, Antwerp, a port town in modern-day Belgium, with access to the North Sea via the River Schedlt, grew into a major commercial center at the end of the fifteenth century. The exchange of English cloth, Central European precious metals, and Portuguese spices made it one of the leading trading places of the Atlantic coast.

The period between about 1490 and 1585 can be considered the Golden Age of Antwerp. It was then seen by contemporaries as the "metropolis of the West," the major meeting place of international trade and finance, a center of art production and luxury industries. The city reached about 100,000 inhabitants around 1565, which made it one of the largest cities of Europe at that time. The presence of wealthy Southern German and Italian merchant-bankers at Antwerp contributed to the rise of one of the major financial markets of Europe, both for commercial credit and for government loans.

After an initial period, lasting until the 1530s, when Antwerp's significance lay mainly in international transit trade, the role of the regional economy of the Low Countries, both in export and consumption, increased. On an international level, Italian silk and luxury products and American silver replaced Portuguese spices and Central European metals as the leading products in the second half of the century. Antwerp lost much of its appeal as a result of the popular unrest and political instability that resulted from the religious troubles after about 1565. The blockade of the river Scheldt by the Dutch in 1585 resulted in the end of Antwerp's commercial dominance and the beginning of Amsterdam's.

During the first half of the seventeenth century, the town remained an important commercial and financial center, and it still had very good contacts with major European trading places. During this period Antwerp was also a major center of art production, with such masters as Peter Paul Rubens and Sir Anthony Van Dyck. After the Treaty of Munster (1648), which recognized the United Provinces as well as the closure of the river Scheldt, Antwerp's economic importance decreased.

Only after the reopening of the Scheldt for direct international navigation, in 1796, could the town recover its position as a major international port. As before, the port offered structural advantages: its favorable location deep inland and the proximity of an extensive hinterland with exceptional rail connections. Port infrastructure and expansion increased, especially from the 1860s. In these years the old Spanish town ramparts from the sixteenth century were demolished. Population boomed: Figures show a population of 50,000 in 1796, 302,000 in 1910, and 450,000 (for the whole metropolitan area) in 2004.

Since the 1950s, increasing port traffic (thanks to the creation of the European Common Market) went hand in hand with industrialization in the port, chiefly by multinationals (especially new branches such as automotive, chemical, and petrochemical industries). By the early twenty-first century the Antwerp port ranked third in trade volume on the continent (after Rotterdam and Hamburg), fourth for international general cargo, and tenth in the world for container traffic. It had become the second petrochemical cluster in the world, after Houston.

SEE ALSO AGRICULTURE; BANKING; BLOCKADES IN PEACE; BLOCKADES IN WAR; CARGOES, FREIGHT; CARGOES, PASSENGER; CHAMBERS OF COMMERCE; CONTAINERIZATION; EMPIRE, BELGIAN; FREE PORTS; HARBORS; LEOPOLD II; PORT CITIES; POTOSÍ; SHIPPING, INLAND WATERWAYS, EUROPE; SHIPPING, MERCHANT; SPICES AND THE SPICE TRADE; WOOL.

BIBLIOGRAPHY

Blomme, Jan; Devos, Greta; Nauwelaerts, Mandy, et al. *Momentum: Antwerp's Port between 1880 and the Present Day.* Antwerp: Pandora, 2002.

Suykens, Fernand, et al. *Antwerp: A Port for All Seasons.* Antwerp: MIM, 1986.

Van der Wee, Herman. *The Growth of the Antwerp Market and the European Economy (Fourteenth to Sixteenth Centuries).* 3 vols. The Hague: Nijhoff, 1963.

Greta Devos
Michael Limberger

INCREASES IN OIL USE

Prior to 1900, crude oil found on the surface of the earth had been used for hundreds of years by Middle Easterners and Europeans in a variety of applications, including caulking ships and waterproofing cloth. But a series of discoveries—the production of distillations such as kerosene, for example, and the techniques of petroleum exploration and extraction—made possible a rapid global transition from coal to oil energy during the twentieth century.

For World War I, the British Royal Navy outfitted a new fleet with oil-only engines. These new ships could travel farther and faster than coal boats, and they were much easier to refuel.

At the same time, engineers and industrial innovators were making automobiles, powered by internal-combustion gasoline engines, more powerful and affordable. More than 8 million Americans owned internal-combustion automobiles by 1920, and by the end of the century there was approximately one such vehicle for every licensed driver in the country.

Industrialized nations around the world, such as Japan in the 1960s, experienced similar explosive growth in automobile ownership. As new economic powers and consumer markets emerged, they put increasing pressure on global oil supplies. At the start of the twenty-first century, China's government released a plan to begin producing 1 million cars per year.

Justin Crawford

ARAMCO

The Arabian American Oil Company (ARAMCO) was the engine that pulled the Kingdom of Saudi Arabia into full participation in the world economy. The company's forerunner, the California-Arabian Standard Oil Company (CASOC), discovered oil in the kingdom's Eastern Province in 1938, and after World War II, ARAMCO developed what proved to be the world's largest reservoir of petroleum. In the first years of the twenty-first century Saudi Arabia remains the global leader in production and exportation of oil, making ARAMCO arguably the most influential company in the petroleum industry.

Before World War II, Saudi Arabia had few trade ties reaching beyond the Red Sea, Persian Gulf, and India; its main source of income was from pilgrims visiting Islam's holiest cities, Mecca and Medina. State revenues in 1938 (at the time, essentially the money accruing to the first Saudi king, Abd al-Aziz Ibn Sa'ud [1902–1953], and now to his descendants) were estimated to be $4 million. Limited oil exports in the 1940s raised revenues to $13.5 million in 1946 and $113 million in 1950, the first year of large-scale exports. Saudi oil-export revenue peaked at almost $103 billion in 1980.

The first Arabian American Oil Company (ARAMCO) well in Saudi Arabia, c. 1955. Since the discovery of Saudi oil in 1938, ARAMCO has developed the nation's reservoir, the largest in the world. HULTON ARCHIVE/GETTY IMAGES. REPRODUCED BY PERMISSION.

The rapidity of the rise of the Saʿud family's wealth was boosted by a series of generally amicable renegotiations of revenue sharing. CASOC, a U.S. consortium of Standard Oil of California (Chevron) and Texas Oil (Texaco), initially paid Ibn Saʿud a modest fee on each ton of oil produced. ARAMCO (which saw Standard Oil of New Jersey [Exxon] and Standard Oil of New York [Mobil] added to the CASOC partnership) agreed to a fifty-fifty revenue split with the king in 1950. In 1973 the Saudis took one-quarter ownership of ARAMCO, then 60 percent in 1974, and finally full ownership in 1980. These agreements were often copied later by other oil companies and producer states, although nationalization elsewhere was not always accomplished so amicably.

Long before Saudi ownership of ARAMCO, the company was the leading agent in using the oil income to transform the country's physical infrastructure and develop its human resources. At Ibn Saʿud's request it built Arabia's first railway since 1908, when the Ottomans completed the Hijaz Railway linking Medina to Damascus, constructed the road and pipeline networks crisscrossing the peninsula, and dug water wells to support population growth in the largely desert land. ARAMCO also invested in schools and offered employment to thousands under a policy of gradual "Saudization." Although much of the physical infrastructure was needed for company operations, other development projects were undertaken as a defensive measure against pressures to better the lot of the population and workers, especially in the Eastern Province. ARAMCO imported to its work camps some of the discriminatory practices common in the United States before the 1960s Civil Rights era, including segregation not only at the level of living quarters but down to the marking of some water fountains in the American Camp as "For Saudis Only." Those practices led to riots and strikes by Saudi workers in the 1950s. The unrest, coupled with rising tensions over the politics of Palestine/Israel, helped to push ARAMCO into adopting more proactive, accommodationist policies. The training offered through the policy of Saudization fostered the rise of a skilled technical and administrative middle class, which has been heavily involved in the kingdom's economic and political life. The ultimate success of Saudization was marked by the appointment in 1989 of the first Saudi to head ARAMCO.

With its control over ARAMCO deepening in the 1970s, Saudi Arabia was able to establish its leading role in the Organization of Petroleum Exporting Countries (OPEC). OPEC was founded in 1960 but first seized the world's attention in the early 1970s by forcing up the price of oil by controlling exports. When Arab members organized a boycott of exports to states supporting Israel following the 1973 Arab-Israeli War, the "oil shock" rocked the economies of industrialized countries. Prices rose from $2 per barrel in 1970 to $40 per barrel in 1980. Saudi Arabia began to rethink its policies supporting OPEC's restrictive export quota system, however, in part because of reduced world dependence on OPEC (and Saudi) oil with the rise of fuel efficiency and alternative energy sources in the industrialized economies. Moreover, as Saudi income soared it realized that it, too, was harmed by economic turmoil, because it had invested much of its wealth in those countries hit hardest by high oil prices. ARAMCO boosted production in the mid-1980s, causing a sharp fall in world petroleum prices. After 1986 Saudi Arabia generally acted as "swing producer," raising or lowering production to keep world oil markets relatively steady.

The supply and price stabilization policies followed by ARAMCO helped to bolster Saudi Arabia's good relations with its most important trade and security partner, the United States. Recognizing the mutual importance of their relationship, both states have been careful to avoid direct confrontation with each other. King Ibn Saud turned to U.S. oil companies in the 1930s in order to get a better deal than was offered by the region's dominant British/European oil companies. U.S. interest in oil led to Saudi Arabia being offered Lend-Lease aid, the American program for selling the Allies war supplies (including food, weapons, and machinery) under flexible terms of payment in 1943, and then to a meeting between Ibn Saud and President Franklin Roosevelt in 1945, during which the king and the U.S. president established the basis of a military relationship that grew steadily through the remainder of the century. Saudi Arabia, a huge land with indistinct borders and a relatively small population, came to rely upon U.S. security assistance against possible threats from states tempted to seize its tremendous oil wealth. U.S. military support rested on the sheer size of Arabian oil deposits and Riyadh's willingness to act as the main petroleum market stabilizer, but it also grew out of Washington's appreciation of strong Saudi distrust of communism. In the 1980s the Saudis were able to buy very advanced U.S. weaponry, including fighter jets and AWACS planes, and for more than a decade after the 1990 Iraqi invasion of Kuwait, U.S. troops were stationed in the kingdom to guard against any further threat from Iraq. Although U.S. troops were withdrawn in 2004, the ties between the two countries are likely to remain strong for as long as the primary architect of the relationship, CASOC/ARAMCO, continues to play such an important role in the world oil trade.

SEE ALSO Nationalization; OPEC; Petroleum; Roosevelt, Franklin Delano; Saʿud Family.

BIBLIOGRAPHY

Al-Naqeeb, Khaldoun. *Society and State in the Gulf and Arab Peninsula*, trans. L. M. Kenny. New York: Routledge, 1990.

Al-Rasheed, Madawi. *A History of Saudi Arabia.* New York: Cambridge University Press, 2002.

Anderson, Irvine. *Aramco, the United States, and Saudi Arabia: A Study of the Dynamics of Foreign Oil Policy.* Princeton, NJ: Princeton University Press, 1981.

Bahgat, Gawdat. *American Oil Diplomacy in the Persian Gulf and the Caspian Sea.* Gainesville: University Press of Florida, 2003.

Yergin, Daniel. *The Prize: The Epic Quest for Oil, Money, and Power.* New York: Free Press, 1993.

Frederick F. Anscombe

ARGENTINA

In its historic trade relations, Argentina has been an exporter of raw materials and an importer of manufactured goods and industrial inputs. Buenos Aires became the region's chief port soon after its founding in 1580, connecting the hinterlands of southern South America to the Atlantic world. Its first cargoes consisted of silver bullion from the mines of Potosí in present-day Bolivia. This commerce was illegal, as Spanish mercantilism dictated that all silver was to be exported through Lima and Panama, thence to Spain. Colonial authorities tried unsuccessfully to restrict exchange at Buenos Aires, which was

BUENOS AIRES

From its resettlement in 1580, Buenos Aires was subject to mercantilist regulation by Spain, which outlawed overseas trade into the port. However, despite Spains best attempts to control Buenos Aires, merchant ships from other European nations were able to smuggle slaves into the port and to take away hides, silver, and tea.

Trade in the colony continued illegally for the next two centuries. Regional governors appointed by Spain were more concerned with their own economic well-being than with enforcing colonial regulations. One such governor, Diego de G ngora, was found guilty after his death of dealing illegally in slaves. His estate was fined 23,000 ducats as punishment.

A decree signed on February 2, 1778, finally lifted trade restrictions on Buenos Aires and the surrounding region. Slave ships poured into the port, and the slaves they brought contributed to the economic productivity of the city. Cattle exports brought wealth to the city, ensuring its economic and cultural vitality through the fight for independence that soon followed.

Justin Crawford

accomplished mostly on the ships of Spain's enemies, the Portuguese, Dutch, and British. In 1776 the Spanish Crown recognized the commercial importance of Argentina, making Buenos Aires the capital of the viceroyalty of the Río de la Plata, which included the mines of Bolivia.

The regional wars that eventually won Argentina's political independence, which was proclaimed in 1816, led to the collapse of Bolivia's mining industry but did not destroy Argentina's trade with Northern Europe. Expansion of cattle *estancias* (ranches) on the fertile pampas made Argentina the leading source of leather hides for the North Atlantic economies; by 1860 wool exports dominated Argentine commerce. The arrival of the railroad contributed to trade diversification beginning in the 1870s, as *estancieros* added wheat and meat to their exports. Capital, technology, and a variety of consumer goods flowed into Argentina, as did European immigrants to produce exports and build the economic infrastructure. Great Britain emerged as the most important

market—and source of capital—and Italy and Spain contributed emigrants. As the hub of internal and external trade as well as the nation's capital, Buenos Aires grew to become South America's largest city in 1936, with 2.5 million residents.

The Great Depression discredited Argentina's liberal trade relations with Europe and stimulated economic policies favoring import substitution industrialization (ISI). The Roca-Runciman Treaty of 1934, which guaranteed access of Argentine products to British markets, failed to reestablish the formidable Anglo-Argentine trade relationship of the previous age. Under the influence of Argentine economist Raúl Prebisch (1901–1985), policy makers utilized protective tariffs and subsidies to promote industrialization, which was equated with economic independence, modernity, and national power. State takeover of foreign-owned utilities also became a hallmark of industrial policies, as typified in 1947 by the nationalization of the British-owned railways by President Juan D. Perón (1895–1974). The state petroleum company controlled oil prices for the benefit of consumers even though the country did not produce enough to satisfy industrial demand. Besides oil, many other inputs for industrialization also had to be imported—technology, capital, chemicals, and steel—and foreign multinationals gained footholds in the newest industries such as business machines (IBM) and automobiles (Ford and Renault).

In the meanwhile, agricultural exports lost competitiveness on world markets, as monetary exchange controls taxed the rural sector and as the state forced down food prices to satisfy urban workers. ISI reached its limits in the 1960s. Inflation rates and the international debt increased as the aging economic infrastructure began to break down. By 1989 two decades of political turmoil and economic havoc came to an end with a return to freer trade relations. President Carlos Menem (b. 1930) spearheaded these economic reforms by pegging the value of the Argentine peso to the U.S. dollar, by selling off state industries to private capital, by dropping tariff rates, and by permitting unrestricted foreign investment in the economy. In 1991 he helped to inaugurate the common market known as MERCOSUR (*El Mercado Común del Cono Sur*, or Common Market of the Southern Cone) between Argentina, Uruguay, Paraguay, and Brazil. Thereafter, Argentina's regional trade grew faster than its European and U.S. trade, and rural producers flourished by exporting to Brazil. However, many domestic manufacturers lost market share to Brazilian industrialists. In curing inflation, the rigid peso-dollar exchange rate made imports relatively cheap, further undermining domestic industry. Then, the Argentina peso collapsed in 2001. A period of painful economic adjustments, including high unemployment and spreading poverty, ushered in a resurgence of agricultural exports in 2003.

SEE ALSO AGRICULTURE; BALANCE OF PAYMENTS; BRITISH-AMERICAN TOBACCO; BUNGE AND BORN; CARGOES, FREIGHT; CARGOES, PASSENGER; CONTAINERIZATION; EMPIRE, SPANISH; ENCOMIENDA AND REPARTIMIENTO; FREE PORTS; FREE TRADE, THEORY AND PRACTICE; GATT, WTO; GREAT DEPRESSION OF THE 1930S; HARBORS; IMPORT SUBSTITUTION; INDUSTRIALIZATION; INTERNATIONAL TRADE AGREEMENTS; MINING; MONROE, JAMES; PERU; PORT CITIES; POTOSÍ; SHIPPING LANES; SHIPPING, MERCHANT; STAPLES AND STAPLE THEORY; WHEAT AND OTHER CEREAL GRAINS.

BIBLIOGRAPHY

Brown, Jonathan C. *A Brief History of Argentina.* New York: Facts on File, 2002.

Lewis, Paul. *The Crisis of Argentine Capitalism.* Chapel Hill: University of North Carolina Press, 1990.

Jonathan C. Brown

ARMS, ARMAMENTS

Trade in arms, like trade in drugs and slaves, is often regarded as morally different from other types of commerce. The arms trade is unusual in that every sale potentially expands unmet demand, as the rival of whichever state made the purchase suddenly feels the need for offsetting purchases. In the early twentieth century, arms traders were called "merchants of death" and accused of provoking wars in order to sell more weapons, although actually wars are started by those who buy weapons. The arms trade remained controversial at the close of the twentieth century, given the risks of nuclear, biological, and chemical proliferation, the excessive weapons expenditures of poor nations, and the political embarrassments of arms sales to notorious regimes.

Bribery of customers (politicians, civil servants, and military and naval officers) has always been commonplace in the arms trade. Both Britain and Germany used corrupt methods to win contracts in Chile before 1914. The arms trade is also bound up with politics. At times, arms exporters could call upon diplomatic support for their sales drives. In the 1920s the French government awarded medals to Latvian officials who had been helpful in allocating naval contracts to French firms. More recently, arms sales have been a source of political embarrassment. During the Iran-Iraq War in the 1980s, Saddam Hussein (b. 1937) received arms shipments from thirty countries. The Soviet Union was his main supplier, but France was next in importance, and both the United

A 1901 Smith & Wesson poster boasts of sales to the Japanese navy. The American gun manufacturer expanded its international trade early in the century by selling firearms overseas to foreign countries and their military forces.
© BETTMANN/CORBIS. REPRODUCED BY PERMISSION.

States and Britain were also involved. After Saddam's invasion of Kuwait in 1990, the United States, Britain, and France regretted that their firms had supplied him in the first place.

ARMS TRADE BEFORE THE WORLD WARS

Rulers, states, and empires have always required arms for defense, aggression, and the suppression of dissent. The term *arms* calls to mind guns, swords, aircraft carriers, and other hardware, but it can also include anything useful in fighting, including animals and mercenaries. War elephants were trained in sixteenth-century Ceylon (Sri Lanka) and exported to India. There was a thriving trade in warhorses from Persia and Arabia to India, and from Central Asia to the Middle East, China, and Mediterranean. Central Asian warhorses were also exported to China for centuries (usually in exchange for tea) until the mid-eighteenth century, when the Qing were able to

A ballistic missile launch at White Sands Missile Range in New Mexico. The destructive capabilities of such missiles, which can threaten distant places with nuclear payloads, prompted nearly 100 nations in 2002 to sign an international code of conduct intended to limit ballistic-missile proliferation. © CORBIS. REPRODUCED BY PERMISSION.

breed their own successfully. Within Europe, there was a large military trade in horses until World War I, when the British began shipping horses from the Americas for military use in France and Belgium.

Traffic in mercenaries also counts as trade in services. Until the early nineteenth century Swiss mercenaries were incorporated into the French army. Some countries still hire mercenaries: France has the Foreign Legion, and Britain the Gurkhas from Nepal.

For centuries, the manufacture of swords, armor, and firearms was the province of skilled artisans scattered across Europe, the Middle East, and Asia. Gun manufacturing built on traditions of metalworking. It was advantageous for cannons to be made close to iron ore and fuel supplies. (Charcoal was the main fuel until the adoption of coke.) Sweden, with its plentiful iron ore deposits, forests, and metallurgical prowess, dominated the trade in cannons until the late eighteenth century. In small-arms production, proximity to raw materials was less important. Certain districts began to specialize in arms production and exporting. One such district was Liège, a formerly neutral territory in what is now Belgium, which for 250 years accepted orders for arms from all sides in the campaigns in the Low Countries. Liège benefited from its proximity to large and discerning markets, and from the local agglomeration of skills. Small arms from the area around Birmingham in England were prominent among the goods exported from Europe to Africa during the eighteenth century. Proceeds from this trade were used to purchase slaves for the Americas.

INDUSTRIALIZATION TO THE PRESENT

Industrialization in Western Europe and the United States led to major changes in the scale and structure of the arms industry. Whereas the arms industry had previously consisted of a few state-owned arsenals and dockyards supplemented by networks of artisans and small firms, in the new industrial climate large-scale business corporations took a leading role. These corporations were outgrowths of the iron and steel and shipbuilding industries, and had access to superior technology and organizational methods. Industrial advance was most rapid in regions with plenty of coal (of which coke was a derivative) such as northern England, Scotland, and the Ruhr Valley in Germany.

Changes in technology and organizational methods ensured that the armies and navies of 1914 (during World War I) were many times more powerful than those of 1815 (during the Napoleonic Wars). Each soldier had the capacity to fire more often and with greater accuracy than his predecessors. The battleship represented the apogee of Victorian technology—it was the most sophisticated machine in the world.

Only the most advanced nations established self-sufficient armaments sectors before 1914. Krupp of Essen in the Ruhr Valley became the world's largest arms maker, offering a full range of naval and military products, from small arms to steel battleships. The British firms Vickers and Armstrong-Whitworth operated on a comparable scale. Schneider was the leading French firm. The United States became self-sufficient in weapons systems and developed a successful export trade in small arms. Other countries, including Brazil, Chile, China, Greece, Turkey, Japan, Russia, and Italy, relied on British, German, and French companies for arms supplies. Western European firms had no qualms about selling arms to deadly rivals, including China and Japan, and Greece and Turkey. Japan, Russia, and Italy eventually graduated to the manufacture of modern armaments, often through joint ventures with firms such as Armstrong-Whitworth and Vickers. The most notorious arms merchant was

Basil Zaharoff (1849–1936), an entrepreneur from Constantinople who became a highly successful salesman in the Mediterranean and Eastern Europe. Zaharoff was made a director of Vickers and was knighted by the king of England, although he was a French citizen.

The two world wars brought increased opportunities for some arms exporters, especially those based in the United States. U.S. firms supplied vast quantities of munitions to the Allies during both conflicts. During wartime, the arms industry extended far beyond the firms that made weapons in peacetime. General engineering, shipbuilding, and automobile producers were induced into the arms trade. Under the 1941 Lend Lease scheme, the U.S. government financed wartime arms shipments to the British Empire and the Soviet Union. Thus, arms exports were not always balanced by payments from the country of destination.

Between 1918 and the early 1930s there was a slump in the arms trade. Under the Treaty of Versailles (1919) draconian controls were imposed over Germany's armed forces and arms industry. Britain, the United States, and Japan agreed to restrict naval armaments under the Treaty of Washington (1922). Arms factories and naval shipyards languished until Japan and Germany, followed by Britain and France, began to rearm in the 1930s.

Between the 1930s and the 1950s a decisive shift occurred in the center of gravity of the world arms industry. The United States developed a technical lead in most branches of arms production, particularly the aircraft and electronics industries, which were becoming central to modern warfare. Silicon Valley in California was prominent in the development of defense-electronics products. After 1945 military research and development had some important civilian spin-offs, especially in the fields of aviation and information technology.

In view of the United States' emerging rivalry with the Soviet Union, U.S. arms procurement remained at a high level after 1945. U.S. arms producers were able to achieve long runs of production and to reap scale economies. Given the limited size of home markets in Europe, British and French firms could not reduce their costs to U.S. levels. U.S. arms exports became highly competitive in price and quality. In an effort to extend their home markets, Western European firms began to cooperate in multinational consortia, particularly in the aircraft industry. Export orders were vital to the survival of Western European producers, but hard to come by.

After 1945 the Soviet Union became a major arms exporter, especially to Eastern Europe, the Third World, and, until a split in the early 1960s, China. The arms trade became even more politicized. The United States and its allies competed with the Soviets to supply weapons to countries in the Third World—often on credit—as part of wider geopolitical strategies. Soviet weapons exports, for instance, strengthened Fidel Castro's regime in Cuba and gave the Russians a presence in the Western Hemisphere. Many arms-export contracts were heavily subsidized, both for political reasons and to preserve jobs. The dismantling of the European empires led to political fragmentation and the emergence of new regional rivalries in Asia, including conflicts between Israel and the Arab states and between India and Pakistan. A substantial new market was created.

The commercial ambitions of arms producers were not allowed to negate political considerations. Although the leading international powers were all, at various times, involved in the production of nuclear, chemical, and biological weapons, they had no interest in the proliferation of these technologies. Presumably, both the United States and the U.S.S.R. could have offset some of the costs of developing nuclear weapons by selling missiles and warheads to the highest bidder, but they refrained from such action. Embargos were imposed on sales of conventional weapons to rogue states, including South Africa.

After the collapse of the Soviet Union and its former empire in the early 1990s, the arms trade languished. Cold War rivalry had been a major driver of arms exports and imports, but now arms budgets were slashed. With the scaling down of the Soviet and East European armed forces, a big secondhand trade developed, and competition for those markets intensified. Out of the five largest arms producers in the world in 1997, four were from the United States (Lockheed Martin, Boeing, General Motors, and Northrop Grumman) and the other was British Aerospace. The 1990s also saw a new emphasis on multilateral arms control under the auspices of the United Nations and other international bodies. In 1997, for instance, 121 countries signed the Ottawa Convention prohibiting land mines. It is too early to say whether such measures will be effective.

The arms trade was worth at least U.S.$25 billion per annum in the late 1990s. Economics textbooks argue that trade enhances welfare. The arms trade clearly benefits the managers, shareholders, and workers of firms making weapons, and it also benefits the armed forces and politicians of importing countries. However, the arms trade imposes a heavy burden on taxpayers in exporting and importing countries, and absorbs resources that could be put to other uses.

SEE ALSO Ali, Muhammad; Blockades in War; Bonaparte, Napoleon; Boycott; Brazil; China; Drugs, Illicit; Du Pont de Nemours Family; East India Company, British; East India Company, Dutch; East India Company, Other; Empire, British; Empire, Dutch; Empire, French; Empire, Japanese; Empire Ming; Empire, Mughal; Empire, Ottoman; Empire, Portuguese; Fairs; Ford, Henry; France; Genoa; Germany; Imperialism; Import Substitution; Iron and Steel; Italy; Japan; Krupp; Mercantilism; Mitsubishi; Nationalism; Nationalization; Pakistan; Pasha, Isma'il; Piracy; Privateering; Roosevelt, Franklin Delano; Siemens; Slavery and the African Slave Trade; Socialism and Communism; South Africa; Stalin, Joseph; Subsidies; Sumitomo; Sweden; United Kingdom; United States; Venice; War, Government Contracting; Zheng Family.

BIBLIOGRAPHY

Hartley, Keith, and Hooper, Nick, eds. *The Economics of Defence, Disarmament, and Peace: An Annotated Bibliography.* Aldershot, U.K.: Edward Elgar, 1990.

Hartley, Keith, and Sandler, Todd, eds. *Handbook of Defense Economics.* Amsterdam: Elsevier, 1995.

Heinrich, Thomas. "Cold War Armory: Military Contracting in Silicon Valley." *Enterprise and Society* 3, no. 2 (June 2002): 285–317.

Koistinen, Paul A. C. *The Military-Industrial Complex: A Historical Perspective.* New York: Praeger, 1980.

Manchester, William. *The Arms of Krupp, 1587–1968.* London: Michael Joseph, 1968.

McNeill, William H. *The Pursuit of Power: Technology, Armed Force, and Society Since AD 1000.* Oxford, U.K.: Blackwell, 1983.

Stockholm International Peace Research Institute. *SIPRI Yearbook 2003: Armaments, Disarmament, and International Security.* Oxford, U.K.: Oxford University Press, 2003.

O'Connell, Robert L. *Of Arms and Men: A History of War, Weapons, and Aggression.* New York: Oxford University Press, 1989.

Scott, J. D. *Vickers: A History.* London: Weidenfeld and Nicolson, 1962.

Stoker, Donald J., Jr., and Grant, Jonathan A., eds. *Girding for Battle: The Arms Trade in a Global Perspective, 1815–1940.* Westport, CT: Praeger, 2003.

John Singleton

ARTISTIC REPRESENTATIONS OF TRADE

In antiquity, artistic representations of trade had the purpose of warding off business failure by invoking the gods of trade. From the Middle Ages and the Renaissance, merchants aimed to gain legitimacy usually granted only to practitioners of "noble" military or religious administrative professions and productive activities, such as agriculture. Their representation in works of art was a way of marking their social status and economic utility.

The Usurers *by Marinus van Reymerswaele (1490–1567) depicts a scene of bankers and lenders. The artist's intention was not to satirize the occupation, but to highlight the sins of greed, vanity, and materialism. According to a Flemish proverb, the four evangelists of the devil are a banker, a usurer, a tax collector, and a miller.* © DAVID LEES/CORBIS. REPRODUCED BY PERMISSION.

A CRITICAL VIEW

In the cultural milieu of Europe in the Middle Ages and Renaissance, financial profit had to be "purified" by charitable works and submission to the religious principles of sharing. The notion of purgatory allowed for the washing away of part of the sins of merchants, whose souls were endangered by their greed. The bad reputation of money dealers and public resentment of commercial brokers and financiers can be seen in the popular rejection of excessive ostentation, hence the arrest of the French merchant bankers Jacques Coeur in 1453 (there is a miniature of his sentencing in the Bibliothèque nationale, Paris) and Jean Fouquet in 1661, who were suspected of enriching themselves via excessive charges. The acquisition of wealth by the *nouveaux riches* shocked France's rural society, which was used to slow growth. Molière's 1670 play *Bourgeois gentilhomme* is a case in point: it criticized ambitious merchants who wanted to become part of the upper class—merchants and bankers were too fond of the whole game of deals and speculation. The

power of the big businessman fascinated the artist Quinten Metsijs, but in his painting *The Lender and His Wife* (1514, Paris, Louvre) the vanity mirror and the woman's devotion reveal mistrust of the money dealer's trade. (Another work by the same artist, *The Usurers,* deals with a similar theme.) Paintings of the time criticized the dealers on the Bourse (stock exchange), worship of the golden calf (e.g., Nicolas Poussin's *Dance around the Golden Calf,* mid-seventeenth century), and materialism as opposed to religious values and social morals (e.g., *Battle of the Chests and Moneyboxes,* engraving in the style of Pieter Bruegel, and several copies of *Wealth Breeds Thieves*), with players surrounding a rich future victim, and often attributed dreadful fates to big businessmen in depictions of the Apocalypse. William Shakespeare's character Shylock (*The Merchant of Venice*) is another example of a cunning and dishonest merchant.

IN SEARCH OF IDENTITY

The formation of a bourgeois class and its insistence on an identity explains the wish to be recognized by society at large. Between the thirteenth and sixteenth centuries, merchants were "in the background" in religiously themed scenes in churches or paintings, appearing in group scenes of the adoration of the Magi or processions connected to some religious festival. The decoration of chapels by professional guilds in Italy or Flanders provided the opportunity for this discreet development. Merchant dealings appeared with details of everyday trades in stained-glass windows in chapels (e.g., *The Drapers,* stained glass of Saint James the Greater; and *The Winesellers,* stained glass of Saint Lubin, Chartres Cathedral, thirteenth century). Undoubtedly, these works were paid for by guilds. During the sixteenth to eighteenth centuries merchant activities were represented in the corners of numerous paintings depicting scenes from antiquity— merchants and their staff can be seen working on the port docks. Next, seascapes depicted (trading) ships in port or at sea. Flemish and Dutch painters such as Saloman van Ruysdael, Frans Hals, Jan van Goyen, and Willem Van de Velde specialized in such scenes, but there were similar works by some French artists (see Claude Lorrain's *Harbor with Medici Villa,* 1677, Uffizi, Florence) and British ones (for example, the paintings housed at the National Maritime Museum in Greenwich, London). Scenes of fairs and markets attracted (often Flemish) painters because, like battles, they suited large-scale works, which were typically picturesque representations of merchant professions. Drawings on Chinese porcelain plates depicting ships (*The Vrijburg,* 1756, Musée Guimet, Paris) marked the opening of the Orient to European trade.

As the economic basis of the merchant sphere expanded and their influence in society grew, the bourgeoisie constructed their own representation in the world. The architecture and particularly the decoration of houses was ostentatious, with towers as symbols of power, such as at San Gimignano. In market towns such as Bruges, Tuscany, Lyons, Antwerp, Bavaria, and Frankfurt the buildings of the merchant community—guild and national edifices, stock exchanges (e.g., Gerrit Berckheyde's *Interior of the Old Market at Amsterdam,* 1668, Rijksmuseum), and bonded warehouses—demonstrated their power. The painters Canaletto and Francesco Guardi provided numerous illustrations of Venice in the eighteenth century.

Some paintings combined religious subjects with illustrations of the artists' patrons. For example, the *Portinari Triptych* by Hugo van der Goes (1440–1482) depicts the merchant Tommaso Portinari and his two sons protected by Saint Anthony. Later, portraits—hitherto restricted to depictions of aristocrats or famous religious figures—were dedicated to the success of the head of a trading house (e.g., the portrait *Oswolt Krel,* of a rich Swabian merchant, by Albrecht Dürer, 1499; and Hans Holbein's portrait *Georg Gisze,* depicting a Hanseatic merchant in London, 1532) or bank (e.g., Jan van Eyck's *Portrait of Giovanni Arnolfini and His Wife,* 1434; and Hans Memling's *Tommaso Portinari,* c. 1470). The Medici celebrated their glory in a number of works in which they are present at historical scenes (Benozzo Gozzoli's *Procession of the Magi,* 1459). A mid-sixteenth-century engraving by Jost Amman, *German Trade and Bank,* celebrates traders with an allegorical representation of the central qualities of a merchant (integrity, discretion, knowledge of languages). This anticipates the eighteenth-century works praising the profession, including trade manuals (such as Jacques Savary des Bruslons's *Dictionnaire universel du commerce,* Paris, 1723), theatrical works, and the writings of Voltaire.

THE MERCHANT WORLD

During the French Revolution, the Terror (1793–1794) allowed open hatred of *accapareurs* (monopolizers), and in a number of cities (e.g., Paris, Lyons, Bordeaux, Nantes) the guillotine punished members of the upper bourgeoisie. This was an indication that the old and new social orders were in confrontation, with the entrepreneurial merchants kicking against the old order and provoking a hostile reaction. The novels of Honoré de Balzac describe the machinations of greedy, swaggering bankers and businessmen. In Stendhal's novel *Lucien Leuwen* the hero's father is a banker, businessman, and prime minister. Honoré Daumier, whose many satires appeared in the press at the end of the century (as in *L'Assiette au Beurre*), caricatured *hommes d'affaires* in *Robert Macaire* (1836–1838). Novels and theatrical works stressed the fragile nature of the business world: Stendhal's Leuwen senior dies as soon as he gains power; a number of businessmen in novels by Balzac and Émile Zola are ruined, falling victim to speculation or fraud. In the Thomas Mann novel *Buddenbrooks* (1901) the fate of a Hanseatic family is uncertain due to the business failure of a son and other risks of business.

UPPER-MIDDLE-CLASS LEGITIMACY

In all parts of the world today, the business world has become part of high society, with its flashy character and social networks. Commissioned artists provide paintings of members of the mercantile dynasties and their family members. In the nineteenth century it was mostly lesser painters who offered this service—examples include François Gérard's 1805 work *Juliette Récamier* (the wife of a merchant banker) and Wilhelm Schlesinger's *Salomon von Rothschild* (1838). Conversely, merchants collect the works of the great masters, either for their private collections or to bequeath to museums, gaining prestige as patrons among the art elite. Hence, the merchant is both a collector of painting and its subject.

The business profession itself shines through in art objects. The values of hard work and saving are depicted in sculptures and allegorical paintings that are intended to be instructive (murals on the walls of bank buildings, for example, are usually devoted to moral enlightenment). Allegorical sculptures decorate the walls of private (particularly institutional) buildings and even monuments. Enormous paintings recalling trade in the ports and colonies hang in international or colonial exhibition buildings (e.g., the Musée des colonies, Paris), in museums, or in company buildings. Trade is advanced as a means of spreading economic prosperity, world progress, and "civilization." The East India Company set up its own museum of Asian artifacts in London in 1801, which was bequeathed to the South Kensington Museum in 1880. Painters portrayed everyday business activities, for commissions or to represent modern locations (e.g., *Cotton Market, New Orleans,* by Edgar Degas, 1873; Fitz Hugh Lane, *Boston Harbor at Sunset,* early twentieth century). And, at the start of the twentieth century, advertisers used attractive posters to promote brands, often depicting exotic scenes to reinvent the atmosphere in which the product is sold.

SEE ALSO FRANCE; GUILDS; ITALY.

BIBLIOGRAPHY

Chaline, Jean-Pierre. *Les bourgeois de Rouen: Une élite urbaine au XIXe siècle (The Bourgeois of Rouen: An Urban Elite).* Paris: Presses de la Fondation nationale des sciences politiques, 1982.

Favier, Jean. *De l'or et des épices. Naissance de l'homme d'affaires au Moyen Age (Gold and Spices. The Businessmen of the Middle Ages)*. Paris: Fayard, 1987.

Green, Edwin. *Banking: An Illustrated History*. Oxford, U.K.: Phaidon, 1993.

Hubert Bonin

ASTOR FAMILY

The Astors are a notable Anglo-American family, originally from Walldorf, Germany, who amassed great wealth from the fur-trading business of John Jacob Astor (1763–1848), who emigrated to the United States in 1783. Astor's American Fur Company initially did business in Europe and the eastern United States. His employees were among the first settlers of the Great Lakes region. After the Louisiana Purchase in 1803, he set up a chain of western trading posts with a main base at Astoria on the coast of present-day Oregon, and dominated the North American consignment trade with China in goods such as tea, silks, furs, ginseng, cochineal, and guns. By the 1820s Astor controlled an international trading house with several hundred employees and more than 200 ships. He died the richest man in the United States, with an estimated net worth of $20 million based on considerable Manhattan real estate holdings.

For the most part, the four generations of Astors since John Jacob have not entered business or trade, but rather politics, architecture, publishing, military intelligence, and diplomacy. In 1890 William Waldorf Astor moved to England, and to this day the Astors remain a truly transatlantic family. They have collected two English peerages and provided over $250 million of philanthropic support to American and British colleges, museums, urban renewal projects, and scientific research.

SEE ALSO CARGOES, FREIGHT; FURS; UNITED STATES.

BIBLIOGRAPHY

Astor, Brooke. *Footprints, An Autobiography*. New York: Doubleday, 1980.

Irving, Washington. *Astoria*. Philadelphia: Lippincott, 1961.

Wilson, Derek. *The Astors, 1763–1992*. New York: St. Martin Press, 1993.

Peter E. Austin

AUSTRALIA AND NEW ZEALAND

Although both Australia and New Zealand are island nations, there are major differences in land area and in the scale of their economies. Australia covers an area of 7.7 million square kilometers and New Zealand 0.3 million square kilometers. In 1998 Australia's population was al-

most 19 million, or about five times larger than New Zealand's; Australia's real gross domestic product (GDP) per capita was U.S.$20,400 (1990 prices), or about 1.3 times larger than New Zealand's; and exports were U.S.$69,300 million (1990 prices), or about 4.5 times larger than New Zealand's (Maddison 2003). The relative dominance of Australia has led to proposals—mainly by Australians— that New Zealand become the seventh state of Australia.

COLONIAL EXPANSION

White settlement of Australia dates from 1829, when a British penal colony was established at Port Jackson (Sydney). After struggling in its early years, the colony started to prosper during the 1830s with the arrival of larger numbers of free migrants and an increase in exports, especially of wool. The 1769 visit to New Zealand by Captain James Cook (1728–1779) was the trigger for the arrival of other Europeans, but it was not until the 1840s that British settlers began to arrive in large numbers, attracted by the country's rich agricultural potential. Both nations' economies were transformed by gold rushes, in the 1850s in Australia and in the 1860s in New Zealand. The exploitation of their natural resources and expanding world markets for their exports propelled per capita income to high levels. Australia acquired the reputation of being a "workingman's paradise." The success of exports was due to Australia and New Zealand's comparative advantage in the supply of food products, minerals, and energy needed by industrialized nations such as Great Britain. Technological changes, such as the development of refrigerated shipping in the latter part of the nineteenth century, played a key role in opening up these isolated economies to world markets.

GROWTH SINCE THE TWENTIETH CENTURY

During the twentieth century Australia and New Zealand grew more slowly than most other Organisation for Economic Cooperation and Development (OECD) countries, especially during the long boom after World War II. Between 1960 and 1997 real GDP per capita (1990 prices) grew by 139 percent in other OECD countries, by 122 percent in Australia, and by 60 percent in New Zealand. Over the same period the real value of exports (1990 prices) from all OECD countries grew by 819 percent, by 932 percent for Australia, and by 403 percent for New Zealand (New Zealand Institute of Economic Research 2001, p. 1). This relatively poor economic performance (except for Australian exports) led to concerns about future growth in both countries. In Australia Prime Minister Paul Keating (1944–) talked of the dangers of becoming "a banana republic," and in New Zealand there were fears of "slip-sliding away" (New Zealand Institute of Economic Research 2001, p. 1). It is generally

An overhead view of Sydney Harbor in Australia. *The harbor is a major trading port, a waterway for ferries, and a recreational playground filled with sailboats. It stretches twelve miles inland from the Parramatta River and is dotted with famous landmarks such as the Sydney Opera House.* © DAVID BALL/CORBIS. REPRODUCED BY PERMISSION.

agreed that while there are many factors that explain the relatively poor growth performance of both countries, the following were important: first, the focus on primary exports and not manufactures meant that both countries were in the "slow lane" of world economic growth; second, high tariffs and inward-looking growth strategies led to the development of inefficient and noncompetitive manufacturing sectors; and third, both countries were attached to traditional markets and slow to see the potential of Asia.

The end of the long boom in the early 1970s forced both countries to begin restructuring in order to keep pace with the rapidly growing economies of the Asian region. In the 1980s economic policy in both countries underwent a sea change as markets were deregulated, tariffs reduced, and public enterprises corporatized or privatized. In Australia these reforms contributed to a surge in productivity and GDP growth. In the 1990s per capita GDP grew at 3 percent per annum, one of the highest growth rates among the developed economies (Nieuwen-

huysen et.al 2001). Successful efforts were made to increase the downstream processing of minerals, promote exports of elaborately transformed manufactures, and increase exports of services such as banking, tourism, and education. In the early 1900s Australia famously "rode on the sheep's back," but by the late 1990s farm products accounted for only 20 percent of total exports, and the combined share of manufactures and services approached 66 percent of total exports. Trade intensity (the ratio of imports plus exports to GDP) increased from 31 percent in 1974 to 1975—a low ratio by comparison to other countries with comparable population and living standards—to 45 percent in 2001 to 2002. The increased trade intensity is evidence of Australia's successful integration into the competitive world economy.

By contrast, New Zealand's growth rate is still below average for an OECD country. Although New Zealand has experienced growth in service exports, especially tourism and education, the small size of its manufacturing sector has limited export diversfication. According to

Sheep flock in South Island, Otago Peninsula, New Zealand. *Although both Australia and New Zealand "rode on the sheep's back" to economic prosperity, exports of manufactures and services are supplanting farm products.* WILFRIED KRECICHWOST/GETTY IMAGES. REPRODUCED BY PERMISSION.

one assessment, "it appears that the economic reformers underestimated the difficulties in changing the economic structure, and the trading patterns, of the New Zealand economy" (New Zealand Institute of Economic Research 2001, p. 13). Currently, policy focuses on the development of "knowledge-based" industries (Briggs 2003). As small trading nations, both Australia and New Zealand have to work hard to compete in an increasingly globalized economy.

At the beginning of the twentieth century the United Kingdom was the major trading partner of both Australia and New Zealand. In the case of Australia, total trade with the United Kingdom was more than five times greater than the total trade with its second-largest trading partner, the United States; the other major trading partners were either European countries or members of the British Empire (Australian Government 2001).

Manufactured goods dominated the imports of both countries, a feature that persists to this day. Between 1900 and 1935 the United Kingdom's share of Australia's imports dropped from over 60 percent to about 40 percent, and Australian governments became concerned about the United Kingdom's declining share of its import trade. The Ottawa Conference of 1932 had already put forward the idea of Imperial Preference to strengthen the British Empire. U.K. manufacturers were facing increasing competition from the United States for motor-vehicle parts and from Japan for textiles. In 1936 the Australian government introduced the infamous trade-diversion policy, which used penal tariffs to divert trade away from the United States and Japan toward Britain (Meredith and Dyster 1999). Before it was quickly abandoned it already had seriously damaged Australia's relations with these two countries, but protectionist squabbles were soon overshadowed by the outbreak of World War II.

After the war, initially the United Kingdom remained both Australia and New Zealand's major trading partner, in the case of Australia accounting for about 37 percent of exports and 50 percent of imports. In the mid-1950s Australia and New Zealand received about 10 percent and 5 percent, respectively, of the United Kingdom's total exports, and Australia was the United Kingdom's major export market (Singleton 2001). But, as far as both Britain and Australia were concerned, the relative importance of the relationship rapidly declined in the 1960s. In 1960 the Australian government lifted the export embargo on iron ore, which it had introduced in 1938, and this led to rapid development of the known reserves, especially in the Pilbara region of northwestern Australia. By 1970 minerals (mainly iron ore, bauxite, and coal) and fuels accounted for about 17 percent of Australia's total exports.

Due to the high complementarity of the Australian and Japanese economies (which measures the extent to which the commodity composition of a country's trade matches that of its trading partner), Japan became the main customer for Australia's mineral exports, and from the mid-1960s it replaced the United Kingdom as Australia's major trading partner. The prospect of British entry into the European Economic Community (now the European Union) had increased Australian interest in trading with Asia, but, for a variety of reasons, until the 1970s Australia had only limited success in gaining access to Asian markets other than Japan (Tweedie 1994). When the United Kingdom finally succeeded in gaining entry to the European Union in 1973, it effectively meant the loss of a traditional market. By 1970 the United Kingdom accounted for only 12 percent, the United States 15 percent, and Japan 25 percent of Australia's total exports.

By contrast, New Zealand lacked Australia's abundant mineral resources and continued to rely heavily on exports of farm products such as lamb and butter. New Zealand negotiated some special concessions with the European Union, but was forced to diversify export markets, especially towards the Pacific Rim countries (Hawke and Lattimore 1999; Singleton and Robertson 2002). In 1970 the United Kingdom accounted for 36 percent, the United States 15 percent, and Japan 10 percent of New Zealand's total exports. Export composition, however, has changed only slowly, and is still dominated by dairy, meat, and forestry products.

By the 1970s the progress of industrialization was creating a prosperous middle class and expanding markets in raw materials and food products for both Australia and New Zealand in Hong Kong, Singapore, South Korea, and Taiwan. In the 1990s Australia especially was also gaining from growing complementarity with China. With GDP growth of about 10 percent per annum during the last two decades of the twentieth century and a population approaching 1.3 billion, China has emerged as a major market for minerals and energy. By the early 1990s about 55 percent of Australia's exports were going to East and Southeast Asia, and 37 percent of imports were coming from this region (Tweedie 1994).

Since the nineteenth century Australia and New Zealand have been important trading partners for each other. Trade was facilitated by the New Zealand Australia Free Trade Agreement of 1965 and the much more effective Australia Closer Economic Relations Trade Agreement (CER) of 1983. New Zealand has probably gained more than Australia from the free-trade agreements, as it has gained access to the much larger Australian market (Pinkstone 1992). Both countries have been involved in international trade negotiations such as the Uruguay Round (1986–1994) of GATT (now the World Trade Organization) and, from 1989, the Asia-Pacific Economic Cooperation Community. As trading nations with substantial primary exports, many economists believe that in the long run the two countries have more to gain from multilateral agreements brokered by the World Trade Organization than from regional or bilateral trade agreements. However, New Zealand signed a free-trade agreement with Singapore in 2000. Australia has completed free-trade agreements with Singapore (2003), Thailand (2004), and the United States (2004).

SEE ALSO Agriculture; Balance of Payments; Cargoes, Freight; Cargoes, Passenger; Containerization; Cook, James; Free Trade, Theory and Practice; GATT, WTO; Gold Rushes; Great Depression of the 1930s; Imperial Preference; Import Substitution; Indian Ocean; Industrialization; International Trade Agreements; Laborers, Contract; Law, Common and Civil; Mining; Staples and Staple Theory; Sydney; Wheat and Other Cereal Grains; Wine; Wool.

BIBLIOGRAPHY

Altman, Morris. "Staple Theory and Export-Led Growth: Constructing Differential Growth." *Australian Economic History Review* 43, no. 3 (November 2003): 230–255.

Australian Government. *Year Book.* Canberra: Australian Government Publishing Service, 2001.

Briggs, Phil. *Looking at the Numbers: A View of New Zealand's Economic History.* Wellington: New Zealand Institute of Economic Research, 2003.

Caves, Richard E., and Krause, Lawrence B., eds. *The Australian Economy: A View from the North.* Sydney: Allen and Unwin, 1984.

Economic Analytical Unit. *Globalisation: Keeping the Gains.* Canberra: Department of Foreign Affairs and Trade, 2003.

Hawke, Gary, and Lattimore, Ralph. *Visionaries, Farmers, and Markets: An Economic History of New Zealand Agriculture.* Working Paper No.1. Wellington: New Zealand Trade Consortium and New Zealand Institute of Economic Research, 1999.

Meredith, David, and Dyster, Barrie. *Australia In the Global Economy: Continuity and Change.* Cambridge, U.K.: Cambridge University Press, 1999.

New Zealand Institute of Economic Research. *New Zealand's Economic Growth: Why Has It Been Low?* Wellington: Author, 2001.

Nieuwenhuysen, John; Lloyd, Peter; and Mead, Margaret.; eds. *Reshaping Australia's Economy: Growth with Equity and Sustainability.* Cambridge, U.K.: Cambridge University Press, 2001.

Pinkstone, Brian. *Global Connections: A History of Exports and the Australian Economy.* Canberra: Australian Government Publishing Service, 1992.

Singleton, John. "Introduction." *Australian Economic History Review* (special issue: *Australia and New Zealand in a Changing World: Commercial Policies in the 1960s*) 41, no. 3 (November 2001): 233–240.

Singleton, John, and Robertson, Paul L. *Economic Relations Between Britain and Australasia, 1945–1970.* Basingstoke, U.K.: Palgrave, 2002.

Tweedie, Sandra. *Trading Partners: Australia and Asia, 1790–1993.* Sydney: University of New South Wales Press, 1994.

Malcolm Tull

AUTOMOBILE

The automobile industry played a central role in shaping twentieth-century societies and economic institutions. It gave rise to a number of major multinational companies, including General Motors, Ford, Daimler-Chrysler, Toyota, Honda, and Volkswagen, which to this day are im-

The Ford Model A. *The world's first mass-produced car on the assembly line at the Rouge Plant in Dearborn, Michigan, in 1932.* AP/WIDE WORLD PHOTOS. REPRODUCED BY PERMISSION.

portant players in the global economy. The production of large volumes of low-cost vehicles created the need for new systems of production and new institutions for regulating the relationship between managers and employees. Finally, the ease of travel that cars made possible changed the physical and social landscape of the communities we inhabit.

ORIGINS OF THE INDUSTRY

The first automobiles appeared in Europe around 1890. Although German, French, and British firms were the pioneers in vehicle design and manufacture, by the first decade of the twentieth century American firms dominated the industry. The first European vehicles were expensive luxury products produced in small batches of a few dozen or perhaps a few hundred by skilled craft workers. Ease of entrance led hundreds of firms to try their hand at making cars, many producing only a handful of vehicles

and lasting only a few years. However, by World War I consolidation was underway, driven by a number of American manufacturers who began producing tens of thousands of vehicles per year.

This process was accelerated by Henry Ford, who revolutionized the industry with the introduction of the Model T in 1908. Ford's idea was a simple one: design a basic car; use interchangeable components; produce in large volumes. This allowed Ford to reduce dramatically the price of his vehicles and open up mass markets. On the eve of the introduction of the Model T, Ford was producing about five thousand vehicles, employing approximately five hundred workers and reporting total assets of less than $2 million. Within five years of the introduction of the Model T, Ford was producing nearly 200,000 vehicles, employing nearly fifteen thousand workers and reporting over $35 million in assets.

Lincoln Mercury division president Darryl Hazel (left) and group vice president Phil Martens drive a new model off the assembly line in Dearborn, Michigan, 2005. The automobile industry is evolving rapidly, and many of the world's most successful firms have become globalized. AP/WIDE WORLD PHOTOS. REPRODUCED BY PERMISSION.

Volume production led to the introduction of the first moving assembly line at Ford in 1913 and to the famous Five Dollar Day employee compensation policy in 1914. Ford's dominance of the early industry was almost total. By World War I he was producing more cars in the United States than the next ten U.S. producers combined and over forty times more than the next largest non-American producer.

THE EMERGENCE OF THE BIG THREE

To this day, Ford remains an important producer, but in the 1930s he was forced to share the sector with a number of other innovative firms. In 1908, William Crapo Durant formed General Motors (GM) by merging a number of firms, including Oldsmobile, Cadillac, Pontiac, Buick, and Chevrolet. He created a multidivisional structure, with each division operating in a different price bracket. This allowed GM to offer vehicles to suit different income levels and gave consumers the option of purchasing

more expensive vehicles as their earnings rose without having to turn to another manufacturer.

Alfred P. Sloan, who replaced Durant as the head of GM, introduced the idea of the annual model change during the 1920s, giving consumers further incentive to change vehicles and purchase a more expensive model. This strategy contrasted with Ford, who through most of the 1920s was producing a single model, the Model T, and for many years offering it in only one color, black. While Ford was interested in serving a basic need for cheap transport, Sloan turned the industry into one where style and image were as important as cost and functionality.

The other important innovator in the American industry was Walter Chrysler. Relying on state of the art engineering, the latest techniques in mass production, and a move from owner management to a more bureaucratic management model, Chrysler surpassed Ford in the early 1930s, becoming the number-two producer of vehicles behind GM. A number of other firms, including Packard, Hudson, Studebaker, and Nash, made significant numbers of vehicles in the United States, but by the early 1960s they had either failed or been bought out by one of the "Big Three"—GM, Ford, and Chrysler. The success of the American firms was based on their willingness to produce less expensive models for a mass market, innovative forms of work organization, and the expanding purchasing power of the growing American middle class.

THE EUROPEAN PRODUCERS

Despite the fact that European firms, such as Daimler, pioneered the technical design of motor vehicles, they quickly became less significant players outside of the high-end luxury segment of the market, which they continued to dominate. In 1913 the largest British-owned manufacturer of cars, Wolseley, was making 3,000 cars per year, compared to the 200,000 produced by Ford. Even mid-size American producers such as Willys-Overland and Studebaker were making ten times more vehicles than Wolseley.

These differences in production volumes also masked important differences in production techniques. Many American producers had adopted the techniques of standardization, interchangeability of parts, and mass production, while in Europe many early vehicle manufacturers continued to rely on hand-crafted components. Ford's near dominance of European markets after World War I led to some gradual changes in strategy at firms like Austin and Morris in Britain and Renault and Peugeot in France, which became important European producers. These firms were able to thrive in their local markets but did not rival the American dominance of the global industry.

THE END OF AMERICAN DOMINANCE

The decades following World War II are often referred to as the Golden Age, two decades of unprecedented economic growth. The automobile industry was at the heart of this growth. Prior to the war, total global vehicle ownership was around 50 million, and annual global production was around 5 million. By 1980 there were over 400 million cars worldwide, and annual production exceeded 50 million.

During this same period there was a change in the global pattern of vehicle production. At the beginning of the period, the United States was the dominant producer, manufacturing over 80 percent of the world's cars in 1950. By 1975 U.S. manufacturers were producing less than 25 percent of the world's cars, as Japan and West Germany became major producers. Since 1975 this shift has continued, as vehicle manufacture has expanded in Mexico, Brazil, South Korea, and Eastern Europe. The first decade of the twentieth century witnessed a dramatic expansion of Chinese manufacturing capacity.

PATTERNS OF INTERNATIONAL TRADE

Unlike many other products, the majority of motor vehicles tended to be produced relatively near where they were consumed. Until the 1970s, the United States imported and exported very few cars. Instead, the major American producers set up branch plants in key markets. For a brief period, Ford used his Canadian plant in Windsor as a base for exports to Britain and Australia, taking advantage of the preferential tariffs between Canada and Britain. But by 1911 he decided that the British market warranted its own manufacturing facility, and a plant was built in Manchester. GM followed Ford to Britain and Europe, after World War I.

It was not until the 1970s that this pattern of production shifted to an export pattern, driven by the rapid expansion of Japanese and later Korean production. During the 1970s and 1980s, a significant share of the U.S. demand for vehicles was satisfied by the importation of cars from Japan and to a lesser extent from Europe. However, political pressure to produce and provide jobs in the areas where cars were being sold led the Japanese to change their strategy during the 1980s: They began building new production facilities in North America and Europe. By the end of the century they were producing almost as many cars in these markets as they were selling.

SOCIAL AND ECONOMIC EFFECTS

The expansion of motor vehicle production in North American and Europe had a dramatic effect on the nature of society. The ability to produce trucks and military equipment in large volumes revolutionized the practice of warfare, drove radical changes in urban architecture, gave rise to the suburbs, and paved the way for new models of collective bargaining between ever-expanding workforces and their employers. In the United States, the United Automobile Workers (UAW) emerged as a key social player under its flamboyant leader Walter Reuther.

The UAW began organizing U.S. workers in the mid-1930s. Reuther challenged the unilateral rights of employers to hire and fire at will and to set working conditions unilaterally. The UAW was one of the earliest unions to bring collective bargaining to the ranks of the less skilled worker.

Following World War II, Reuther and management at GM hammered out a deal that would set the pattern in American industry for the next half century. The UAW agreed to concede to management control over how and which vehicles were made. In return, GM agreed to recognize the union as the bargaining agent for labor and to share productivity increases through an annual cost of living adjustment and an annual improvement factor. Known as the Treaty of Detroit, this deal created stability in the industry and made automobile workers among the best-paid industrial workers in North America. Automobile workers outside of North America also enjoyed significant improvements in their standard of living, although few could rival the gains made by the UAW.

SOCIAL COSTS

The growth in the industry has not come without costs. Cars and trucks consume large quantities of oil and have a negative impact on the environment. Though roads crisscross the landscape of most developed countries, congestion is a major problem. And finally, accidents continue to be a concern, with cars involved in tens of thousands of fatalities each year.

SEE ALSO AGNELLI FAMILY; FORD, HENRY.

BIBLIOGRAPHY

Alshuler, Alan, et al. *The Future of the Automobile: The Report of MIT's International Automobile Program.* Cambridge, MA: MIT Press, 1984.

Bardou, Jean-Pierre, et al. *The Automobile Revolution: The Impact of an Industry.* Chapel Hill: University of North Carolina Press, 1982.

Cusumano, Michael. *The Japanese Automobile Industry: Technology and Management at Nissan and Toyota.* Cambridge, MA: Council on East Asian Studies, 1985.

Davis, Donald Finlay. *Conspicuous Production: Automobiles and Elites in Detroit, 1899–1933.* Philadelphia: Temple University Press, 1988.

Foreman-Peck, James; Bowden, Sue; and McKinlay, Alan. *The British Motor Industry.* Manchester, U.K.: Manchester University Press, 1985.

Gartman, David. *Auto Opium: A Social History of American Automobile Design.* London: Routledge, 1994.

Lewchuk, Wayne. *American Technology and the British Vehicle Industry.* Cambridge, U.K.: Cambridge University Press, 1987.

Meyer, Stephen, III. *The Five Dollar Day: Labor Management and Social Control in the Ford Motor Company, 1908–1921.* Albany: State University of New York Press: 1981.

Nevins, Allan. *Ford.* New York: Scribners, 1954.

Rae, John B. *The American Automobile: A Brief History.* Chicago: University of Chicago Press, 1965.

Wilkins, Mira, and Hill, Frank Ernest. *American Business Abroad: Ford on Six Continents.* Detroit: Wayne State University Press, 1964.

Wayne Lewchuk

Bahia

From the time that the Portuguese Crown granted Francisco Pereira Coutinho (1498–1549) the captaincy of Bahia in 1535, this state in the northeast region of Brazil has had a prominent role within the world economy. Indeed, Bahian planters were instrumental in shaping the development of large-scale plantation economies across the colonial world and spurring the Atlantic slave trade—as well as slave resistance. Bahia also played a central role in financing the British Empire, and today it feeds the global petrochemical industry.

From its inception, Bahia was characterized by a monocultural, plantation economy for export—an economic institution that became a staple feature across the globe throughout the colonial era. The Portuguese initially established plantations in Bahia for the purpose of exporting sugar to European markets, and during the seventeenth and eighteenth centuries Bahia was singularly identified with large-scale sugar plantations. As a result of the success of Bahia's sugar industry, Salvador, the state's capitol, became a thriving international port city.

The development of the plantation economy in Bahia borrowed techniques from an earlier generation of Portuguese colonizers in the Azores Islands. Bahian plantation owners created large-scale, labor-intensive plantations that relied on great numbers of African slaves. Salvador became one of the most prosperous slave-trade centers in the world. As slave labor grew in Bahia, however, so did slave rebellion. Following several slave revolts in the early nineteenth century, Bahia developed an international reputation for formidable slave resistance.

Importantly, the Bahian plantation model was exported to other regions of the capitalist world economy. The Dutch occupied Bahia for a brief period in the seventeenth century, and, before their defeat, they studied the Bahian plantation and were able to replicate its basic features in their own colonial holdings in the Americas and Southeast Asia.

One of Bahia's most pivotal roles in the world economy concerned its financing of the British Empire. This resulted from a unique relationship between the Portuguese and the British. A series of seventeenth-century treaties, along with the Methuen Treaty of 1703, effectively reduced Portugal to the status of a protectorate of Britain for several centuries. By virtue of this arrangement, the British Empire reaped a major share of the profits from Bahian exports.

Though of secondary importance to sugar in the first few centuries, tobacco was also an export crop of significance in Bahia. Tobacco's role in the world economy was first tied to trade with Africa. Later, the Dutch popularized its use in Europe. The quality of the Bahian leaf gained an international reputation and tobacco remained a major export crop of Bahia throughout its history.

With the decline of Brazil's sugar plantations in the late eighteenth century, Bahia's role in the world economy waned. This persisted into the twentieth century, when rich deposits of gold, rock salt, chromite, magnesite, copper concentrate, barite, and manganese were found throughout Bahia. Global investors, attracted to Bahia for its vast mineral resources, established the Polo Petroquimico de Camaçari (the Petrochemical Center of Camaçari) in the Bahian region of Camaçari in the 1970s.

As a result, Salvador today remains a major port city within the capitalist world economy, linking the prosperous petrochemical and metallurgy industries of Bahia to global industrial centers.

SEE ALSO AGRICULTURE; BRAZIL; CARGOES, FREIGHT; CHAMBERS OF COMMERCE; COFFEE; CONTAINERIZATION; EMPIRE, PORTUGUESE; FREE PORTS; HARBORS; PORT CITIES; PORTUGAL; SLAVERY AND THE AFRICAN SLAVE TRADE.

BIBLIOGRAPHY

Barickman, B. *A Bahian Counterpoint: Sugar, Tobacco, Cassava, and Slavery in the Recôncavo, 1780–1860.* Stanford, CA: Stanford University Press, 1998.

Furtado, Celso. *The Economic Growth of Brazil: A Survey from Colonial to Modern Times.* Berkeley: University of California Press, 1963.

Manchester, Alan. *British Pre-eminence in Brazil, Its Rise and Decline: A Study in European Expansion.* New York: Octagon Books, 1972.

Reis, João José. *Slave Rebellion in Brazil: The Muslim Uprising of 1835 in Bahia.* Baltimore, MD: Johns Hopkins University Press, 1993.

David Baronov

U.S. ACCOUNT DEFICIT

The Bureau of Economic Analysis, a branch of the U.S. Department of Commerce, regularly publishes data about the balance of payments on its web site (http://www.bea.gov).

In 2004 the U.S. current account deficit increased to $666 billion, up from $546 billion the year before. As a share of the U.S. gross domestic product, those numbers equal 5.7 percent and 4.8 percent, respectively. The largest contributors to the deficit were imported goods such as petroleum, industrial supplies, and consumer products.

Both U.S. investment abroad and foreign investment in the United States increased in 2004. Foreign investment in the United States was larger than U.S. investment abroad, by some $600 billion.

Justin Crawford

BALANCE OF PAYMENTS

A country's balance of payments is the record of all market transactions between that nation and the rest of the world. The term *balance* comes from the fact that each international transaction creates both a debit and a credit in the country's international account. These items should therefore balance; that is, the sum of all debit transactions should equal the sum of all credit transactions over the course of a given time period. The term *payments* refers to the fact that the transactions are recorded as market values in the currency of the country in question. The balance of payments is typically measured annually, but data for shorter periods are frequently reported.

BALANCE-OF-PAYMENTS ACCOUNTS

The balance of payments consists of three accounts: the current account, the capital account, and the official reserves balance.

The *current account* is the sum of net exports plus unilateral transfers. *Net exports* are the difference between the market value of a country's exports of goods and services minus the market value of all that country's imports of goods and services. This is where a researcher can find information regarding, for example, trade in spices, oil, or automobiles. Further, this account also includes insurance fees, interest payments, and dividends on foreign bonds and stocks. Thus, if one wants to study maritime insurance, or returns on foreign investment, the current account is the place to look first.

Unilateral transfers consist of the net amount of gift transactions between the country in question and foreign counties. Examples include foreign aid donated from one country to another, and remittances sent by immigrants back to their home countries.

The *capital account* reports the difference between the market value of capital imports and the market value of capital exports. These flows of capital fall into two broad types: portfolio investment and direct investment. Portfolio investment includes purchases and sales of securities along with deposits and withdrawals from banks. Direct investment involves control and ownership of productive facilities outside the home country. This category thus includes purchases and sales of factories, mines, and plantations in other countries, for example, whereas portfolio investment involves buying stocks and/or bonds in manufacturing firms, mining companies, and agricultural enterprises.

The *official reserves balance* measures the net change in a country's foreign-reserve holdings. These assets currently include gold, foreign-exchange holdings, and Special Drawing Rights issued by the International Monetary Fund. Historically, gold was the most important reserve holding, with foreign-exchange holdings (especially of British pounds sterling and U.S. dollars) becoming dominant from the late nineteenth century onward.

The "balance" in the balance of payments can now be seen more clearly. Suppose, for example, that the United States exports $100,000 of goods to Canada. This creates a $100,000 credit in the current account (from the sale of the goods) and a $100,000 debit in the capital account (with the creation of a claim on foreign assets). This debit could take the form of a deposit in a Canadian bank, the purchase of bond denominated in Canadian dollars, the purchase of stock in a Canadian company, or some combination of all three transactions.

CAPITAL FLOWS OVER TIME

Balance-of-payments data are especially useful in studying capital flows. The sizes and directions of international capital movements have varied greatly over time and place. Before 1800 capital-account flows were small relative to gross domestic product (GDP). This changed with European industrialization. According to Angus Maddison, foreign-owned capital as a percentage of GDP in developing countries rose to 8.6 percent by 1870 and reached 32.4 percent by 1914 (Maddison 2001, 128). These figures fell to 4.4 percent in 1950 and then rose again during the next fifty years, to 10.9 percent in 1973 and 21.7 percent in 1998.

Different regions of the world were at various times net importers or net exporters of capital. Europe generally has been a capital exporter to the rest of the world. North America (especially the United States and Canada) imported capital until World War I and then exported capital until the 1980s, when it again began importing capital on a net basis. Asia historically has imported large amounts of capital; however, since the 1970s Japanese capital exports pushed the region toward balance, and in many years to net capital-export status. South America suffered through regular periods of large inflows, debt default, capital outflows, and then a resumption of capital inflows from the 1840s to the present. Africa imported capital until the 1980s. Beginning in the early 1980s, exports and imports balanced out until, in the 1990s, repayments of debt actually outstripped new capital flows and made the continent a (small) net capital exporter.

BALANCE-OF-PAYMENTS ADJUSTMENT

History is replete with "balance-of-payments crises." Although the overall balance of payments must balance, the individual accounts need not balance. For example, during the 1960s the United States experienced a balance-of-payments crisis when it began running large current-account deficits in order to finance the Vietnam War. The deficit in the current account was financed initially by flows of reserves, but eventually the United States had to begin importing capital.

The importance of these types of events has led economists to develop two basic theories of how the balance of payments maintains equilibrium: the expenditure method and the monetary approach. Both theories are based on the price-specie-flow mechanism first described by the Scottish historian David Hume (1711–1776).

It is easiest to understand the price-specie-flow mechanism through an example. Suppose the world is composed of two countries: one has a current-account surplus, the other has a current-account deficit. The deficit country sends gold to the surplus country to pay for its imports, and the surplus country absorbs gold in return for its exports. The increase in the surplus country's gold stock then causes an increase in its money supply. Assuming that the country is at full employment, the increase in the money supply causes inflation and thus a rise in the surplus country's export prices relative to prices of similar goods in the deficit country. At the same time, the gold outflow from the deficit country causes deflation and reinforces the relative decline in the prices of domestic goods. Taken together, the export surplus in the surplus country shrinks, the deficit in the deficit country shrinks, and the two countries move toward current-account balance.

Notice that, in this version of the story, causation runs from spending to gold flows to changes in money stocks to changes in prices to changes in spending patterns. This is the essence of the expenditure approach to the balance of payments. Changes in spending patterns of households and businesses cause changes in exports and imports, thus affecting the current account. The changes in the money stock (via gold flows) are caused by the changes in expenditures.

The expenditure approach builds on the price-specie-flow mechanism in an important way. In this model, countries can pay for their current-account deficits by borrowing funds from abroad rather than (or in addition to) exporting gold. Thus, changes in the current account affect the capital account generally, not just gold flows.

Further, the capital account itself reflects changes in spending because it includes portfolio and direct investment. For example, in the nineteenth century Canadian and U.S. railways issued bonds in European capital markets (primarily London) in order to construct intercontinental rail networks. European investors loaned their resources because they were told that the railroads would open up new tracts of fertile farmland and allow North American manufacturers to grow and prosper. The railways would then be profitable and yield a stream of revenue adequate to service the debt payments. Balance-of-payments crises erupted when the railways and other capital-intensive investments failed and the revenues available for debt service disappeared. Similarly, many governments issued bonds and then used the proceeds not for investment but for consumption purposes. Thus, no productive assets were purchased, and a debt crisis was inevitable.

There is another way to view the price-specie-flow mechanism. Again suppose that there are two countries, each with a zero balance in the current account. Then if there is a change in money demand or money supply in one of the countries, interest rates will adjust, causing either an outflow or inflow of gold or foreign exchange. The country that begins absorbing gold will experience a rise in its relative prices, making imports cheaper and exports more expensive and thus producing current-account deficit, whereas the country that exports gold will see its relative prices fall and find itself with a current-account surplus.

This is the foundation for the monetary approach to the balance of payments. In this theory, current account and capital-account movements are driven by changes in the worldwide demands for and supplies of money. Changes in spending patterns are then caused by the changes in relative prices that result from capital and reserve flows.

SEE ALSO CAPITAL FLOWS; HUME, DAVID; RATES OF EXCHANGE.

BIBLIOGRAPHY

Eichengreen, Barry, and Flandreau, Marc, eds. *The Gold Standard in Theory and History.* 2nd edition. London: Routledge, 1997.

International Monetary Fund. *International Financial Statistics.* Washington, DC: Author, various years.

Lindert, Peter H. *Key Currencies and Gold, 1900–1913.* Princeton, NJ: Princeton University Press, 1969.

McCusker, John J. *Rum and the American Revolution: The Rum Trade and the Balance of Payments of the Thirteen Continental Colonies.* New York: Garland Publishers, 1989.

Maddison, Angus. *The World Economy: A Millennial Perspective.* Paris: Organisation for Economic Cooperation and Development, 2001.

Mitchell, B. R. *International Historical Statistics.* 2nd rev. edition. New York: Stockton Press, 1995.

Newman, Peter; Milgate, Murray; and Eatwell, John. *The New Palgrave Dictionary of Money and Finance.* New York: Stockton Press, 1992.

Louis D. Johnston

BALTIC EXCHANGE

The Baltic Exchange started life as the Virginia Wine House, which opened at 61 Threadneedle Street in 1603, just across the road from London's busy Royal Exchange (Braudel 1984, p. 355). By this time the Royal Exchange, London's marketplace for overseas trade, was prospering and had become "a kind of emporium for the whole of the earth" (Ackroyd 2001, p. 306). Its trading floor was arranged in "walks" where merchants trading with different parts of the world could meet from 12 to 2 P.M. each day. There were about twenty-five of these "walks"; the Virginia Walk was located by the southern entrance. When merchants had finished their business they would retire to a convenient tavern to meet others in the same trade; the Virginia Wine House was the meeting place for merchants from the Virginia Walk.

When coffee became fashionable the Wine House was renamed the Virginia Coffee House, then in 1743 the Virginia and Maryland Coffee House. By that time it was used by merchants and traders supplying the Navy Board with stores from the plantations of Virginia and Maryland. However, the Baltic was also an important source of these goods, and in May 1744 the house's name was changed again, to the Virginia and Baltick Coffee House. It was advertising that the late Virginia and Maryland Coffee-House in Threadneedle Street took in foreign and domestic news, letters and parcels directed to merchants or captains in the Virginia or Baltic trade. The new hostelry got an unexpected bonus when a fire in 1748 burned down many of the other coffeehouses around the Royal Exchange, leaving the Virginia and Baltic untouched.

After the American Revolution ended in 1789 the Baltic trade became dominant, with 4,113 ships cleared through English ports in the Baltic trades in 1792, compared with 1,047 from North America (Fayle 1931, p. 223). In 1810 the Virginia and Baltick Coffee House closed and reopened at 58 Threadneedle Street as the Baltic Coffee House. By this time tallow, the primary material used for candles, had become one of the major commodities traded by the coffeehouse's clientele. It was imported from St. Petersburg, Riga, and Archangel and traded on the Baltic Walk of the Royal Exchange. In 1823 there was such a wave of speculation in the tallow market that the Baltic Coffee House became an establishment of note from the large speculations which at different periods had been carried among subscribers. To rectify this, a committee was set up to improve standards, and a members-only subscription room was opened on May 1, 1823, where subscribers could meet and consult a large number of newspapers, directories, and other market intelligence. The refurbished Baltic Coffee House consisted of the subscription room for subscribers, a dining room, a sale room upstairs where tallow and oil were auctioned,

Traders from the London Baltic Mercantile Exchange weigh commodities in 1920. The exchange was formed in 1900 and became one of the key centers for shipping of industrial bulk commodities across the Baltic Sea and to several other international destinations. © HULTON-DEUTSCH COLLECTION/ CORBIS. REPRODUCED BY PERMISSION.

and a coffee room. There were 300 subscribers, and membership was strictly regulated. Six references were required to become a member, and members whose conduct was judged unsatisfactory could be expelled.

In the 1840s the Baltic Coffee House's transformation into a commodity exchange was helped first by a fire that closed the Royal Exchange from 1838 until 1847, and then by the 1848 repeal of the Corn Laws, which opened up new grain trades. By 1854 membership had increased from 300 to 325 and new premises were purchased at South Sea House, an imposing building further down Threadneedle Street with "the finest Banking Room in the Metropolis"—this became the new subscription room. Grain by then had replaced tallow as the main commodity traded, and "the Baltic," as it was now known, was also becoming a tramp freight market. Over the next thirty years its role as a physical exchange was boosted enormously by the overseas cable network, which developed between 1866 and 1890. This transformed shipping because for the first time cargoes could

be fixed in anticipation of a ship's arrival at port and backhaul cargoes arranged.

The Baltic benefited because London was at the heart of the new communications network, and a trading floor was the most economic way to exploit the opportunities offered by instant communications. The problem was that cables were prohibitively expensive. The first Atlantic cable in 1866 cost $1.25 per word (about 5 British shillings), and although by 1894 rates across the Atlantic had fallen, outlying areas such as southeastern Africa still cost over $1.25 per word. (In 2005 that equates to about $300 per word.) Given these prohibitive costs, agents and brokers would arrange transport on the exchange floor and then cable the briefest details to their principals. Trading sessions ("changes") were held twice a day, and Leon Benham, a shipbroker with H. Clarkson, "was in constant attendance at the Baltic Exchange. Several times a day he would return to the office to dispatch telegrams, invariably drafted on the stiff cuffs of his shirt" (Clarkson 1853, p. 20).

By 1880 Baltic membership had quadrupled to 1,337 members, and the facilities at South Sea House were inadequate. When the Baltic Exchange Company Limited failed to deal with this problem, in 1893 a breakaway group formed the London Shipping Exchange, and its superior premises in Billitier Street were an instant success, attracting 1,500 members and causing a decline in Baltic membership. After six years of competition the two organizations merged in 1899 and a new organization, the Baltic Mercantile and Shipping Exchange, was set up to build a new exchange that would reflect the interests of both merchants and shippers.

The new cathedral-like Baltic Exchange, opened in St. Mary Axe in 1903, continued to trade commodities, particularly grain and soybeans, as well as freight. But by the 1920s freight was becoming more important as the amalgamation of grain interests (the Miller's Union) undermined the grain trade, and by the end of the 1930s the membership was composed of 50 percent shipping, 37 percent grain, and 13 percent oilseed trade. By the 1950s the Baltic was almost exclusively a shipping exchange, chartering tramp vessels for the deep-sea and short-sea trades. Trading sessions still took place twice a day, and in the course of a few brief conversations on the floor of the Baltic, a chartering clerk could obtain a firm offer of a vessel and a firm bid for carriage of cargo far more easily and swiftly than was possible by telephone, telegram, or letter. All of this depended on the ability of members to rely on deals struck in a few words on the exchange floor—hence the Baltic's maxim, "our word is our bond."

Over the next fifty years the advantage of the physical exchange was eroded by communications technology.

Broadcast telex, automatic switchboards, fax, and e-mail progressively reduced the need for a physical trading floor as brokers, shippers, and ship owners networked from their offices. By the 1980s trading sessions were reduced to Monday lunchtimes only, and the Baltic Exchange launched itself in the futures market. In 1985 it started to compile the Baltic Freight Index, published every day at 1 P.M. This was the settlement Index for Contract Trading through the London futures market. During the 1990s contract trading gradually gave way to negotiated agreements, and the range of routes was widely extended. In 2004 the Baltic published more than forty routes on its web site, in addition to providing dining facilities, a bar, and, of course, a coffee room.

SEE ALSO CARGOES, FREIGHT; CHAMBERS OF COMMERCE; CONTAINERIZATION; LLOYD'S OF LONDON; UNITED KINGDOM.

BIBLIOGRAPHY

Ackroyd, Peter. *London: The Biography*. London: Vintage, 2001.

Barty-King, Hugh. *The Baltic Exchange: Baltick Coffee House to Baltic Exchange, 1744–1994*. London: Quiller Press, 1994.

Blake, George. *Lloyd's Register of Shipping, 1760–1960*. London: Lloyd's Register, 1960.

Braudel, Fernand. *Civilization and Capitalism, Fifteenth to Eighteenth Century: The Perspective of the World*. New York: Harper and Row, 1984.

Clarkson. *The Clarkson Chronicle, 1852–1952*. London: Harley, 1953.

Cochran, Ian. *The Baltic Exchange: 250th Anniversary*. London: Lloyd's List, 1994.

Fayle, C. Ernest. *A Short History of the World's Shipping Industry*. London: Allen and Unwin, 1931.

Martin Stopford

BALTIC STATES

The Baltic states Estonia, Latvia, and Lithuania are situated between the Baltic Sea and Russia. Their trade patterns have often been determined by the neighborhood and by the interests of both Russia and its trading partners to access and control the Russian market. Accordingly, transit trade in Baltic ports has been important, from the age of the Vikings until the present.

In 1450 the Hanseatic League, an organization of important German traders, was still the major power holder of the Baltic Sea, although it was challenged by the new trading power the Netherlands. Several of the Baltic towns of the time, Riga, Reval, Dorpat, and others, belonged to the Hanseatic League. German traders and German culture dominated the Baltic towns. Furs, bees-wax, tar, hemp, grain, and timber were exported from the Baltic towns. The strategic importance of these items deserves some attention. In this period, the Netherlands and England were building fleets to rule the seas, and lesser powers such as Sweden and Denmark tried to emulate their success at controlling trade. The Baltic exports were important since they contained all of the necessary naval stores. They were producers of timber and tar for the building of ships, flax and hemp for the making of sails, and hemp again for the innumerable cables, ropes, and cords needed to make ships sail. Riga was the center of the international hemp trade, and the Baltic area was an important if not exclusive producer of strategic goods.

In the seventeenth century, the focus of timber trade moved northward in the Baltic Sea area, from Danzig and Königsberg to Riga and, for tar, to Finland. At the same time, the significance of Baltic grain was growing. The most important import items were salt, fish, cloth, and wine. The trade was dominated by the Netherlands during the sixteenth and seventeenth century, but in the eighteenth century English and Scottish traders in the Baltic ports replaced Dutch traders.

By the mid-sixteenth century, Sweden's interest in the Baltic area increased. The expanding Russian empire lacked ports in the Baltic Sea, and controlling the Baltic provinces was a way of controlling Russian expansion and trade. Sweden acquired the Baltic provinces Estonia and Livonia through wars and agreements. In Sweden, the variety of mercantilism called cameralism and its policies promoted trade in the interest of the central Swedish area, and exchanges were basically in its favor. Grain was becoming the most important contribution of the Baltic provinces to the motherland. Formally, the grain was not delivered in the course of trade but as delivery of various taxes and contributions. Livonia became an important granary for Swedish garrisons throughout the Swedish territory and helped Swedish war efforts, particularly in preparations for the Great Northern War in 1700–1721.

The grand duchy of Lithuania also developed grain trade in this period. Riverboats carried grain to Königsberg, Riga, Klaipeda, and Gdansk. Already in the first half of the sixteenth century, landlords gained the right to trade with foreign countries without any customs and taxes, which negatively influenced the domestic market. Lithuania also held an important place in oriental trade, through its intensive contacts with the Crimean Khan. Courland under the suzerainty of the king of Poland-Lithuania went through a period of growth in the mid-seventeenth century, with exports of grain and flax. The Couronian duke built a considerable fleet and even founded overseas colonies, which, however, soon were lost to England.

At the end of the Great Northern War in 1721, the Baltic provinces were incorporated into czarist Russia. Riga became the transit port for trade between Russia and Western Europe. Five hundred to eight hundred ships per year visited Riga in the eighteenth century. When the harvest was poor in Russia, exports of Baltic grain were prohibited. Flax from Livonia and Courland was sold in Riga and was important for the emancipation of the peasantry there. By selling flax, peasants were able to buy relatively substantial farms. An owner-occupier peasantry, crucial for subsequent political development and economic growth, started to form in the nineteenth century.

The state-led industrialization of Russia in the late nineteenth century was rapid in the western areas, among them the Baltic provinces. Railways, built in the second half of the century, contributed to integration of the Russian market and to transit trade over Riga and Liepaja. Factories built in Riga, Narva, and other places were typically large-scale, often foreign-owned, and oriented to the needs of the state. Imports became more varied, with an eye to the needs of the industries, mostly metallurgy, textile, and food.

After the Russian revolution, the Baltic States gained their independence in 1919. They were totally cut off from the Russian market. The large-scale industries catering to the Russian army and home market failed, and the young republics were forced to reorient the economy. New, small-scale industries had difficulties reaching foreign markets in the bleak economic opportunities of the interwar years, but agricultural cooperatives found new markets for butter and bacon in the British and German markets. Timber and oil shale were other important export items. In the depression of the 1930s, agrarian exports were in severe crisis, but they recovered with German war preparations. Subsequent growth was closely related to German imports through bilateral trade.

In World War II, the Baltic countries were devastated and once again were incorporated in the large Soviet internal market. Exports were few to the outside world, but large-scale industries were rebuilt in the Baltic republics. The region grew more quickly than the rest of the Soviet Union. At the demise of the Soviet Union, the industries again collapsed, and the Baltic states had to start reconstruction again in the 1990s. After independence, agriculture was in crisis. Foreign-owned companies, many based in Finland, Sweden, and Germany, bought existing production plants, and trade became reoriented toward Western Europe. Simultaneously, formerly important trade links with Russia were severed in Estonia and Latvia, and to a lesser extent in Lithuania. The Baltic states are dependent on foreign trade and have to struggle to keep the balance of trade even. The lack of vital re-sources of raw materials, in particular energy, is a continuous challenge to their trade policies.

SEE ALSO AGRICULTURE; CARGOES, FREIGHT; FINLAND; GATT, WTO; GERMANY; GREAT DEPRESSION OF THE 1930S; HANSEATIC LEAGUE (HANSA OR HANSE); RUSSIA; TIMBER.

BIBLIOGRAPHY

Attman, Artur. *Swedish Aspirations and the Russian Market during the 17th Century.* Göteborg, Sweden: Vetenskaps-och Vitterhets-Samhället, 1985.

Johansson, Anders; Kangeris, Karlis; Loit, Aleksander; and Nordlund, Sven, eds. *Emancipation and Interdependence: The Baltic States as New Entities in the International Economy 1918–1940.* Studia Baltica Stockholmiensia series, no. 13. Stockholm: Almqvist & Wiksell, 1994.

Kahk, Juhan, and Tarvel, Enn. *An Economic History of the Baltic Countries.* Studia Baltica Stockholmiensia series, no. 20. Stockholm: Almqvist & Wiksell, 1997.

Van Arkadie, Brian, and Karlsson, Mats. *Economic Survey of the Baltic States.* New York: New York University Press, 1992.

Anu Mai Kõll

BALTIMORE

The tobacco economy of colonial Maryland fostered broad settlement patterns and discouraged the growth of major staple ports. The city of Baltimore was established as a town in 1729 on the Patapsco River, a tributary of the Chesapeake River, but had only twenty-five houses in 1752 according to a contemporary observer. The increasing demand for cereals in the West Indies in the second half of the eighteenth century, as well as European food shortages in the late 1780s and early 1790s, greatly benefited Baltimore. Its population grew from 3,000 inhabitants in 1760 to 13,500 in 1790 and 54,000 in 1810. Warfare made local shipowners and merchants switch to privateering, in which the city excelled during the American Revolution, as well as during the War of 1812.

The location of Baltimore took advantage of the relative depth of the port, the mildness of the Chesapeake Bay, which allowed shipping all year round, and a fertile hinterland with rapid-moving streams ideal to mill sites. By the late 1780s, the city competed in most markets with Philadelphia, which was at that time the main U.S. port. French and European wars boosted Baltimore's worldwide trade, adding re-export trade to the more traditional import-export activities and allowing entrepreneurial merchants such as Robert Oliver to become millionaires. Baltimore's technological advances in shipbuilding (e.g., the Baltimore clipper) at Fells Point made the city a leader in the industry from 1790 to 1815.

After 1815 Baltimore resumed a vigorous foreign trade in flour, and by 1825 the city was the second-largest

THE STAR SPANGLED BANNER

Francis Scott Key (1779–1843), an American soldier and patriot during the War of 1812, was detained by the British during their bombardment of Fort McHenry in Baltimore when he approached their ships to secure the release of a friend and fellow soldier. He was successful, but the British kept him while they launched an assault on the fort.

During a fierce twenty-four hours, the British flotilla fired more than 1,800 shells at the fort, finally stopping just before dawn on September 14, 1814. Key was uncertain about the fate of his fellow Americans on shore until, at sunrise, he saw the U.S. flag still flying above the fort.

Deeply moved, he described the sight in a poem he called "The Defense of Fort McHenry." The poem was later put to music. In 1815 it was renamed "The Star Spangled Banner."

In 1931 it became the United States' national anthem.

Justin Crawford

municipality in the United States. But after sixty years of extraordinary growth and prosperity, Baltimore experienced a decline relative to other U.S. ports. Whereas the Erie Canal (1825) enhanced New York trade to the advancing U.S. frontier, Baltimore's Chesapeake and Ohio Canal project (1828) to link the Potomac and Ohio River Valleys met with major construction difficulties and unexpected costs. It was not until 1850 that the canal, which operated until 1924, reached Cumberland (184 miles). By 1836 the port developed the first railcar ferry in the United States, and the Baltimore and Ohio Railroad allowed a buoyant grain trade from the Midwest in the decades after the Civil War. In the second half of the nineteenth century Baltimore was still an important port city, combining trade (in cereals), passenger transport (of European immigrants), and industry (shipbuilding, canning of oysters). Despite a destructive fire in 1904, the city progressed well into the 1920s, but then suffered severely from the Great Depression and World War II.

The postwar recovery made Baltimore the seventh port of the United States in terms of the value of its imports (U.S.$20 billion in 2003). Exports are less relevant

by far (one-fourth of imports, both in terms of value and of volume). Baltimore ranks as the tenth U.S. port in the number of vessels calling, but is first in roll-on-roll-off transport. Particular efforts have been made to modernize facilities on the 2,000 acres of the marine terminals of the Port of Baltimore, which is one of the major economic engines of its region. The port employs about 16,000 people directly, and at least that many indirectly.

SEE ALSO AGRICULTURE; BOSTON; CARGOES, FREIGHT; CARGOES, PASSENGER; CHAMBERS OF COMMERCE; CHARLESTON; CONTAINERIZATION; EMPIRE, BRITISH; FREE PORTS; HARBORS; LOS ANGELES–LONG BEACH; NEW ORLEANS; NEWPORT; NEW YORK; PHILADELPHIA; PORT CITIES; SALEM; SAN FRANCISCO–OAKLAND; UNITED STATES.

BIBLIOGRAPHY

Bruchey, Stuart Weems. *Robert Oliver, Merchant of Baltimore, 1783–1819.* Baltimore, MD: Johns Hopkins University Press, 1956.

Gould, Clarence P. "The Economic Causes of the Rise of Baltimore." In *Essays in Colonial History Presented to Charles McLean Andrews by His Students.* New Haven, CT: Yale University Press, 1931.

Livingood, James Weston. *The Philadelphia-Baltimore Trade Rivalry, 1780–1860.* New York: Arno Press, 1970.

Silvia Marzagalli

BANGLADESH

Bangladesh (2004 pop. 141,349,476), is historically part of Bengal, a former province of British India that encompassed West Bengal (now in India) and East Bengal (now Bangladesh). From the mid-eighteenth century to the mid-twentieth century, the area of present-day Bangladesh was part of the Bengal province of British India. In 1905, Bengal was divided roughly along religious lines into Hindu West Bengal (now India) and Muslim East Bengal (now Bangladesh). East Bengal became East Pakistan in 1947, and Bangladesh in 1971. Bangladesh is one of the world's poorest and most densely populated countries.

During the prosperous years of the Mughal Empire in the sixteenth and seventeenth centuries, northeast India attracted new and increasingly powerful European interests, including French, Dutch, and British trading companies, and the Bangladeshi cities of Chittagong and the present capital, Dhaka (Dacca), became centers of the textile trade. By 1765, however, the British had become *de facto* rulers of Bengal, and had made Calcutta in West Bengal their commercial and administrative center in South Asia. For the most part, the development of Muslim East Bengal was thereafter limited to agriculture, as the colonial infrastructure of the eighteenth and nineteenth centuries reinforced the area's function as a supplier of materials—chiefly jute and rice—to processors and traders in urban economy around Calcutta.

Before the British period, East Bengal was already part of an international trading system. Europe took Indian and Chinese products that it could not produce itself, such as spices, exotic woods, tea, and silk and cotton textiles. Asia—particularly China—took mostly South American silver in return. East Bengal was known specifically in aristocratic circles of Asia and Europe, and later North America, for its dyes, yarn, and fine handwoven muslin and silk fabrics that it produced far more cheaply than could Europe.

At the turn of the nineteenth century the British decision to develop West Bengal, government imposition of disadvantageous work rules on weavers, and the production of machine-made textiles by English factories spelled great difficulties for the Bengali traditional handloom process and trade. Cotton cultivation in the United States largely replaced Bengali cotton growing, and the textile industry became dependent on imported yarn. With the industrialization of Europe, trade balances generally tipped against India in the nineteenth century.

The opening of the Suez Canal contributed to a sevenfold increase in India's general trade volume between 1869 and 1929, but these increases did not benefit East Bengal because of its subsidiary status to Calcutta. Rapid population growth—made possible in part by favorable natural conditions for agriculture—constrained per capita growth in the region, traditional agricultural methods inhibited farming modernization, and riverine geography limited maintenance of a modern transportation system.

The partition of India in 1947 and Bangladesh's subsequent war for independence from West Pakistan caused great loss of life and vast damage to national infrastructure. The main shipping port at Chittagong was unusable for years. The connection that former British East Bengal had maintained to the reliable urban economy around Calcutta for jute and rice ended.

Bangladesh has had a negative trade balance since independence in 1971. Raw jute and textiles continue to dominate the economy, accounting for almost 90 percent of merchandise exports. Rice cultivation occupies over 70 percent of fertile land, and nearly 80 percent of the population is engaged in agriculture. Additional exports include tea, seafood, and wood products, as well as modest amounts of petroleum and natural gas. As of the late 1990s imports were more than triple exports, and the country relies on development aid, with India its largest donor. In recent decades Bangladesh has exported workers to wealthy, often Islamic, countries; remittances from these workers have become a major source of foreign exchange.

SEE ALSO Bengal; Cotton; Famine; Import Substitution; India; International Trade Agreements; Pakistan; Textiles.

BIBLIOGRAPHY

Bayley, Christopher, ed. *Atlas of the British Empire.* New York: Facts on File, 1989.

Brown, Judith. *Modern India: Origins of an Asian Democracy.* Oxford, England: Oxford University Press, 1994.

Lawson, Philip. *The East India Company: A History.* London: Longman, 1993.

O'Donnell, Charles Peter. *Bangladesh: Biography of a Muslim Nation.* Boulder, CO: Westview, 1984.

Peter E. Austin

BANKING

The international trade of merchants played a pivotal role in the early development of banking. Along with state and city governments, merchants trading internationally were the most important customers by far for bankers. Generally speaking, they operated on a larger scale and in a more sophisticated way than other business sectors and, as a matter of routine, needed to exchange currencies and to finance goods in long transit between places of purchase and sale. As important users of banking services, their involvement in the promotion and ownership of banks was inevitable, and many managed banking alongside merchanting activities. By the second half of the nineteenth century, however, their dominance had greatly reduced as more complex requirements of other business sectors emerged.

EARLY DEVELOPMENTS IN SOUTHERN EUROPE

Banking originated in ancient Greece in the fifth and fourth centuries B.C.E. when the Athenian economy began to shift from subsistence to coin-based transactions. Our knowledge of their banking processes remains sketchy and their significance is debated, but they included distinctive elements of banking such as the receipt of deposits for safekeeping (but without payment of interest) and the provision of advances. Bankers also authenticated and exchanged currencies in the form of coin, which was essential for the conduct of long-distance trade. By the second century B.C.E., bankers in Egypt were acting on written instructions from depositors for fund transfer, another essential feature of banking.

Banking structures reappeared in the twelfth and thirteenth centuries, although on a very limited scale

Banking in the Depression era. *In the wake of the great economic collapse following the 1929 stock-market crash, the United States government legislated banking reforms, such as deposit insurance, intended to restore consumer confidence in the country's financial infrastructure.* THE LIBRARY OF CONGRESS.

given the continuing feudalism, which placed emphasis on subsistence, barter, and payment in kind, and not on money, loans, and capital. International trade was growing fast in the eastern Mediterranean, where leading merchants in cities such as Genoa, Venice, Florence, and Siena began to provide recognizable banking services. These embraced currency exchange, deposit taking, provision of loans, and arrangement of transfers for merchants and city-states. The trading and banking activities of the most powerful of these merchant bankers were focused on great commercial fairs such as those of Champagne, to which they traveled to exchange currencies, settle debts, and provide credit.

By the fifteenth century, banking was adopting a more specialized and institutionalized form. It remained concentrated in southern Europe, in particular in the city-states of Italy and Spain, and embraced the earliest elements of public banking, although private ownership of banks by a single family or small number of partners remained the dominant ownership form. These public institutions accepted the savings of citizens and financed city-state governments. Another category, *monte di pietá*, developed as quasi-charitable institutions which received

funds from wealthy citizens and made loans secured on pawns to borrowers of modest means. But of much greater importance for international trade and finance was the emergence of a small number of great private merchant-banking houses, of which the Florentine bank of Medici, formed in 1397, was the most powerful and sophisticated. Its network of branches and agents, stretching across Europe, cooperated in gathering and sharing commercial intelligence, spreading risk, and effecting international payments in support of its merchant and sovereign clients in a highly efficient way. The later German house of Fugger is another example from this period of a successful private banking house, albeit one with wider economic interests.

EARLY BANKING IN NORTHERN EUROPE

The seventeenth century witnessed a shift in economic growth and innovation in banking to northern Europe. Publicly owned banks based in north European cities led the way into an era of greater stability and continuity. In the greatest financial and trading center of all, Amsterdam, the city and merchant community promoted the Wisselbank (Exchange Bank), which opened in 1609 and

Jacob Fugger, also known as "Jacob the Rich," and his bookkeeper. Fugger came from a family of German financiers. He expanded the family's wealth and power and established a virtual monopoly over Central Europe's precious metals industry. ERIC SCHAAL/TIME LIFE PICTURES/GETTY IMAGES. REPRODUCED BY PERMISSION.

acted as a prototype for similar city banks established elsewhere in northern Europe. It dominated banking in Amsterdam, receiving deposits, making transfers between customer accounts, advancing funds to merchants and public authorities, and, not least, taking responsibility for coinage and exchange.

The creation of state banks—as opposed to city banks—more closely linked public banking with the management of government finance in northern Europe. The Bank of Sweden, formed in 1668 and closely modeled on the Wisselbank, was the first such institution, but more notable was the Bank of England, formed in 1694.

As with so many similar formations, merchants took the lead in establishing this public bank that replaced private goldsmith bankers in lending funds to the British government and also provided the government with debt management and other banking services. Alongside this, important commercial banking was undertaken, largely for merchant customers, and banknotes were issued, first by the Bank of Stockholm in 1661. Other early state-bank developments occurred in France in 1716, Prussia in 1765, and the United States in 1791.

State and city banks apart, the commercial banking scene in northern Europe in the eighteenth century was dominated by small private banks owned and managed by partnerships, family members, or sole traders. In this period, on the back of an unprecedented rise in economic prosperity, the banking system in England was as advanced as in any country. In the seventeenth century banking had been largely restricted to London, and was in the hands of goldsmiths who, inter alia, provided safe custody for valuable property, accepted deposits, discounted bills of exchange and advanced funds, especially to the government. By the late century the goldsmith-related activities of these bankers were being discontinued as their commercial banking services were broadened. In the eighteenth century numbers expanded rapidly as private commercial banks became well established outside London; by 1800 every town had at least one bank, and often several. As a distinct exception to this pattern, a more permissive legal system in Scotland encouraged the formation of public commercial banks operating on joint-stock principles with multishareholders. Three were established after 1695 and several more immediately after 1800, although private banks also existed in Scotland and thrived.

MERCHANT BANKING AND BILLS OF EXCHANGE

In the eighteenth century a specialized form of banking emerged in northwest Europe—by now the center of world trade—for the finance of international merchants. Known as merchant banking, it was intricately linked to the bill of exchange, and was conducted by small private banks based in cities such as Amsterdam, Hamburg, and, particularly in the nineteenth century, London. These banks had invariably been formed as merchant firms trading internationally in commodities on their own account and also providing agency services such as arranging warehousing and insurance, buying and selling commodities, and making and collecting payments for merchants in other centers of international trade. It was a small step to include banking in their portfolio of services, simply by providing advances when a payment needed to be made ahead of a collection or holding deposits when a collection was received before a payment

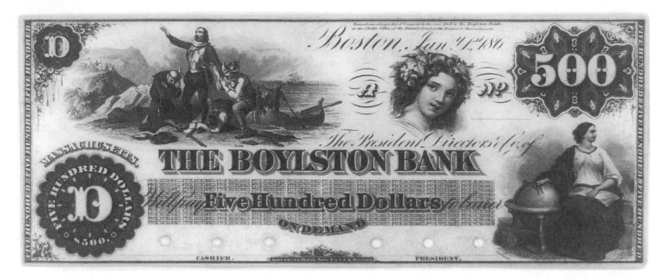

An 1862 banknote from Boylston Bank in Boston. *The American Bank Note Company produced this banknote for Boylston Bank in Boston. Notes were one of several lending instruments that became prominent in the U.S. banking industry during the industrial development of the nineteenth century.* THE LIBRARY OF CONGRESS.

needed to be made. However, although these merchant banks did provide merchants with advances, much more frequently their facilities were based on their acceptance—or guarantee—of the bills of exchange of their customers.

Bills are one of the most durable banking instruments, originating as "letters of exchange" issued by Genoese bankers from the late twelve century and used widely by fourteenth-century Italian bankers for, inter alia, finance of trade emanating from the Champagne fairs. A bill represents a promise to make a payment in the future (often three months or more) for goods received in the present. If guaranteed—or "accepted"—by a well-known bank of high standing, bills could be sold on—or "discounted"—by the holder. Thus, merchant banks of high standing accepted the bills of their merchant customers in return for a commission and guaranteed to pay the bill when it fell due for settlement. Accepted bills thereby became easily transferable and were included in the short-term asset portfolios of commercial banks. But as well as being an important means of raising short-term finance, they were also a highly effective means of making payment internationally. In the nineteenth century the international bill market became centered on London, where merchant banks were of prime importance in the finance of international trade until 1914.

In the eighteenth century Hope and Company of Amsterdam was the most important merchant bank; in the next century London houses, led by Barings and Rothschilds and including firms such as Hambros, Schroders, George Peabody and Company, and Morgan Stanley and Company were preeminent. From the mid-

nineteenth century these houses were also at the heart of the emergent London international capital market, now the world leader in making bond issues and providing other security-management services for sovereign, municipal, and corporate clients in all parts of the world. This was the beginning of modern investment banking, and in due course the London banks were joined by similar private banks in the other major international capital markets which developed before 1914, namely Paris, Berlin, and New York.

DEVELOPMENT OF MODERN COMMERCIAL BANKING

The massive growth in economic activity in the nineteenth century took place in an environment of burgeoning population growth and increasing personal wealth, larger and more sophisticated producers of goods and services, more extensive government activity and expenditure, and, not least, the international movement of goods, people, and capital on an unprecedented scale. All had profound effects on banking, which transformed itself from an industry characterized by small, privately owned entities to one dominated by giant public corporations.

Among state banks, the Bank of England remained the most powerful, but significant developments occurred in France, Prussia, Belgium, Italy, the Netherlands, the United States, Russia, Japan, and elsewhere. Although the objectives, activities, and ownership of no two state banks were hardly ever the same, common themes included raising and managing government debt and influence over the wider economy through activity in the money markets and control of banknote issue. In this period many state banks were given a monopoly of note issue and, given their national strategic importance, were sometimes subject to state controls or ownership.

But the most important change of all was the virtual disappearance of private banks and their replacement by joint-stock banking, which had its origins in the city-state banks of fifteenth-century Italy and, later, in state banks such as the Wisselbank and the Bank of England. The essence of joint-stock banking is public ownership by a large body of shareholders who provided a major proportion of the bank's assets in the form of share capital. Shareholders elected a board to direct the business and appoint professional bankers as managers, and they often benefited from limited liability. Their large shareholder base meant that they could command far greater resources than private banks, which were reliant on the restricted resources of a handful of partners and their families. They offered greater stability to depositors and larger and more sophisticated facilities to increasing numbers of big-business customers.

U.S. bankers were early and enthusiastic proponents of joint-stock banks, launching their first, the Bank of New York and the Bank of Boston, in 1784; by 1850 over 1,000 promotions had been handled. Rapid progress was also made in England following the passing of enabling legislation in the 1820s. Within ten years 100 joint-stock banks had been promoted, and their impact was extended through the acquisition of small private banks and their establishment of branches; by 1850 some 1,700 bank branches existed in the United Kingdom.

Adoption was much slower and restricted and more specialized in the rest of Europe. Between the 1820s and 1860s it was invariably associated with industrial development and company formation, and included names such as Société Genérale de Belgique and the French Crédit Mobilier. It was not until the second half of the century that joint-stock deposit banks with branch networks took hold.

The joint-stock model was exported to the European empires and to nonaligned areas such as Latin America to provide local banking services to which quasi-state banking functions were sometimes attached. British formations, promoted from 1817, invariably headquartered in London and using capital provided by U.K.-based shareholders, were by far the most numerous, followed by those of France and Germany. Some sixty-eight British formations were launched between 1853 and 1913 and comprised an important element of economic imperialism. They were the earliest banks in Australia, Canada, India, Africa, and South America; hardly a territory existed to which their branch networks did not extend.

In the second half of the nineteenth century concentration of joint-stock banking into fewer and fewer units became characteristic of banking development. Banks grew in size through acquisition or merger and developed into regionally and then nationally spread entities with management focused in the great financial centers of London, Paris, New York, and Berlin. Such concentration was explained in terms of the need for increased capacity when serving the largest customers, the need to demonstrate the stability that comes with size and geographical spread, and the need to respond to fierce competition. But the accumulation of such power in fewer and fewer hands became a source of concern from the early twentieth century, and checks—both formal and informal—were introduced to curtail it.

CRISES IN BANKING

The history of banking is punctuated by bank failure and loss of deposits and capital by customers and owners, either through the collapse of a single institution due to its mismanagement or the widespread failure of banks due to a general financial crisis leading to panic and withdrawal of deposits by customers. Numerous examples are to be found from the outset of banking in Italy in the Middle Ages, most notably the collapse of the leading Florentine houses as a result of default between 1339 and 1343 on huge loans they had made to King Edward III of England (1312–1377).

The nineteenth century provides good examples of all types of bank failure—the wholesale collapse of British private deposit banks in the 1820s as a result of the bursting of a stock market boom, especially in Latin American securities; the devastation of merchant banking in the United States and Europe in the 1830s and 1840s as a result of financial crises that crossed the Atlantic; the widespread failure of Australian banking in the 1890s following the collapse of a boom in land prices; and the 1866 failure of Overend Gurney, a discount house at the heart of the London money market, due to mismanagement.

However, in the nineteenth century important forces were at work to ensure greater stability, at least in deposit banking. The move to larger units operating regionally or nationally meant that being spread over a wider and more diverse area of economic activity mitigated a bank's risk. Improved education and professional standards in banking and more rigorous reporting by banks to shareholders (and customers) were also important.

The banking panic arising out of the 1866 collapse of Overend Gurney underlined the need for the banking community to support banks in difficulty and thereby stave off crisis. Therefore, in 1890, when Barings, the leading London merchant bank, suffered a liquidity crisis, its collapse was prevented through a rescue operation launched by the Bank of England. It was the first such operation conducted by a state—or central—bank, and it marked an important future role for them. The 1929 Wall Street Crash, which caused the failure of some 5,000 U.S. banks and created the greatest crisis in modern banking, resulted in the first comprehensive legislation to regulate banking. At its heart was the separation of commercial banking and deposit taking from investment banking and direct exposure to the security markets.

EARLY INTERNATIONAL COOPERATION IN BANKING

World War I—the first period of total war—and its aftermath provided a huge shock and challenge for banking. Certain lines of business (e.g., the trade-finance activities of merchant banks) were severely damaged and the administration of banks was disrupted. At war's end Russian banking was in ruins, German banking was severely damaged, and in the United States banking was in the ascendancy. The importance of the dollar and of the New York international capital market had increased steadily before the war; after the war the United States was the most important creditor nation and the role of U.S. banks in international finance had been hugely enhanced.

The economic damage brought by war was especially exposed in the interwar years. Whereas U.S. banks extended their international activities, those of European banks were increasingly confined to domestic markets. The functioning of the international economy was hindered by the legacy of huge wartime loans between the Allies and by unrealistic reparation payments imposed on Germany. The 1929 Young Plan dealt with the reparations legacy and paved the way for the establishment of the Bank for International Settlements in Basel in 1930. It was a vehicle for communication and cooperation between central banks in the management of international financial affairs and was the first supranational bank.

In the new era that followed World War II more durable solutions were sought in creating stability in the international economy. Of huge importance was the 1944 Bretton Woods Conference of the Allies, which led to the formation of two more supranational institutions, the International Monetary Fund (IMF) and the International Bank for Reconstruction and Development (the World Bank). The former aimed to promote world trade through economic good order, in particular via the stability of exchange rates and the financing of trade deficits, whereas the latter, at least initially, funded the rehabilitation of infrastructure in those countries most damaged by war.

SEE ALSO ACCOUNTING AND ACCOUNTING PRACTICES; CAPITAL FLOWS; CAPITALISM; GREAT DEPRESSION OF THE 1930S; HOPE FAMILY; INTERNATIONAL MONETARY FUND (IMF); MONEY AND MONETARY POLICY; MORGAN, J. P.; WORLD BANK.

BIBLIOGRAPHY

Born, Karl Erich. *International Banking in the Nineteenth and Twentieth Centuries.* Leamington Spa, U.K.: Berg Publishers, 1983.

Capie, Forest, ed. *History of Banking.* 10 vols. London: Pickering and Chatto, 1993.

Carosso, V. P. *Investment Banking in America: A History.* Cambridge, MA: Harvard University Press, 1970.

Chapman, S. D. *The Rise of Merchant Banking.* London: Allen and Unwin, 1984.

Chapman, S. D. *Merchant Enterprise in Britain from the Industrial Revolution to World War I.* Cambridge, U.K.: Cambridge University Press, 1992.

Green, Edwin. *Banking: An Illustrated History.* New York: Rizzoli International, 1989.

Jones, Geoffrey, ed. *Banks as Multinationals.* London: Routledge, 1990.

Kirshner, Julius, ed. *Business, Banking, and Economic Thought in Late Medieval and Early Modern Europe: Selected Studies of Raymond de Roover.* Chicago: University of Chicago Press, 1974.

Klebaner, Benjamin J. *American Commercial Banking: A History.* Boston: Twayne, 1990.

Kynaston, David. *The City of London.* 4 vols. London: Chatto and Windus, 1994–2001.

Mokyr, Joel, ed. *The Oxford Encyclopedia of Economic History.* New York: Oxford University Press, 2003.

Pressnell, L. S. *Country Banking in the Industrial Revolution.* Oxford, U.K.: Clarendon, 1956.

Teichova, A.; Kurgan-Van Hentenrijk, G.; and Ziegler, D., eds. *Banking, Trade and Industry: Europe, America, and Asia from the Thirteenth to the Twentieth Century.* Cambridge, U.K.: Cambridge University Press, 1997.

John Orbell

BARCELONA

Barcelona emerged in the late Middle Ages as the principal port of the western Mediterranean, closely associated with the rise of Catalonian commerce and the Kingdom of Aragon. The Black Death of the fourteenth century arrested this growth, but its fleet had extended Aragonese power over the Balearic Islands, Italy, Sicily, and beyond to the Levant. Barcelona's merchants and navigators, represented by a powerful guild, the *Consulat de Mer,* traded throughout the Mediterranean and brought prosperity to the city. Construction begun in 1477 protected and progressively expanded its harbor.

Turkish power in the Mediterranean, Castilian hegemony following the unification of Spain, and the discovery and conquest of America all tended to diminish Barcelona's importance after 1450, especially with Seville's designation as the exclusive port for trade with America in 1503. French and Italian ports also seriously challenged Barcelona's role in Mediterranean trade from the fifteenth through the seventeenth centuries.

Barcelona suffered new damage in the War of the Spanish Succession (1701–1714) when it sought to secede from Spain and supported the Habsburg claim to the Spanish throne. Spain treated Catalonia as a conquered province and continued to subordinate its interests to those of Castile. Nevertheless, military expenditures stimulated Barcelona's economic recovery, and Bourbon reforms later in the eighteenth century triggered an industrial revolution, especially in cotton textile manufacture. After 1778 Barcelona's merchants began to participate in the American trade, and by the end of the century its commerce had grown greatly as the city expanded beyond its medieval walls.

After 1792 the French Revolution and Napoleonic Wars damaged Barcelona again. The city shared much of the turmoil and social upheaval that characterized the rest of Spain in the struggle between republicanism and monarchy during the following century. Yet it enjoyed substantial growth in commerce and industry as its population grew from 115,000 in 1800 to more than 500,000 in 1900, and more than 1 million by 1930. Rising trade-union activity and immigration accompanied Barcelona's industrial prosperity and accounted for the city's leftist politics, but the establishment of the republic at Barcelona in 1931 brought more turmoil and damage during the Spanish Civil War (1936–1939), followed by political repression and economic stagnation under the fascist rule of General Francisco Franco (1892–1975).

Since Franco's death, as the capital of the Autonomous Catalonian Community, Barcelona led Spain's democratization. Its production of about 20 percent of Spain's industrial goods—notably chemicals, pharmaceuticals, automobiles, household appliances, and electronics—increased its exports, and its free economic zone (*zona franca*) encouraged a substantial re-export trade. Its imports of natural gas supply a large region of Spain and France. With its stock exchange, World Trade Center, a modern transportation system, and ferries connecting the port with the Balearics and Genoa, Barcelona is an international commercial and financial center. The city has a population of more than 4 million in its metropolitan area, and as one of Europe's most important ports it has looked outward to the world. Its hosting of the 1992 Olympics reinforced that trend and gave an important boost to Barcelona's economy.

SEE ALSO AGRICULTURE; CÁDIZ; CARGOES, FREIGHT; CARGOES, PASSENGER; CHAMBERS OF COMMERCE; CONTAINERIZATION; EMPIRE, SPANISH; FREE PORTS; HARBORS; MEDITERRANEAN; NEW SPAIN; PERU; PORT CITIES; POTOSÍ; SEVILLE; SPAIN.

BIBLIOGRAPHY

Chaytor, Henry John. *A History of Aragon and Catalonia.* New York: AMS Press, 1969.

Fernández-Armesto, Felipe. *Barcelona: A Thousand Years of the City's Past.* Oxford and New York: Oxford University Press, 1992.

Hughes, Robert. *Barcelona.* New York: Vintage, 1993.

Ralph Lee Woodward Jr.

ALEXANDER BARING
1774–1848

Alexander Baring, the first Baron Ashburton, was a British banker and statesman. He assumed the helm in 1810 of the merchant bank Baring Brothers and Company, which his father, Sir Francis Baring, had built into a major banking force, and created a global institution with operations in Asia, Canada, Latin America, and Europe, with interests in shipping, debt finance, and commodities such as cotton, indigo, tea, timber, and wool. Baring made his reputation from the management of reconstruction loans to rebuild Europe after the Napoleonic Wars. He expanded operations in the emerging United States after 1815, including the agency of the Bank of the United States and American government accounts. He married into the Philadelphia establishment (1798) and helped to negotiate and finance the Louisiana Purchase (1803). As a member of Parliament (1806–1835), Baring opposed the Reform Bill (1832) and advocated repeal of the English Corn Laws and the trade monopoly of the East India Company (1833). He served as president of the Board of Trade (1834–1835) and received peerage in 1835. He negotiated the boundary between the eastern United States and Canada (Webster-Ashburton Treaty, 1842). The partnership he assembled is considered the greatest in Baring Brothers' history, which successfully navigated the world economic downturns of 1820s and 1830s, and assisted the Bank of England in preserving the vitality of the transatlantic economy. Baring was eulogized by Benjamin Disraeli as "the greatest merchant England ever had."

SEE ALSO CANADA; TREATIES; UNITED KINGDOM; UNITED STATES.

BIBLIOGRAPHY

Austin, Peter E. *Baring Brothers and the Panic of 1837.* Austin: University of Texas Press, 1999.

Jenks, L. H. *The Migration of British Capital to 1875.* London, 1927.

Ziegler, P. *The Sixth Great Power.* New York: Knopf, 1988.

Peter E. Austin

FAMINE

Bengal has suffered through a number of devastating famines, particularly during the period of British rule, commonly called the Raj. A particularly severe famine hit the region in 1770, with as many as 5 million people—one-third of the population—perishing. Bengal suffered famine again in the nineteenth century, and in 1943 to 1944 endured the "Great Famine," in which upwards of 3 million died, mostly due to their lowered resistance to disease. Scholar Amartya Sen believes that price increases, possibly linked to the war with Japan, and an influx of urban construction workers increased demand for available foodstuffs. This drove up food prices to the point where rural Bengalis could not afford basic staples such as rice. The tragic result was severe famine.

David J. Clarke

BENGAL

Bengal traditionally has been a major trading region of the Indian subcontinent. Features particular to the region have included (a) a great abundance of rice and other provisions, such as sugar and oil, which were exported in large quantities both to other parts of the subcontinent as well as to neighboring areas such as Ceylon and the Maldives islands; (b) manufacturing of textiles—cotton, silk, and of mixed yarns—of exquisite quality and unparalleled fineness; and (c) an excess of commodity exports over commodity imports, involving an inflow of a certain amount of precious metals on a regular basis. Bengal rice was sent up the Ganges to Agra via Patna, to Coromandel, and around the Cape Comorin to Kerala and various port towns on India's west coast. The Gujarat silk industry was almost entirely dependent on the import of raw silk from Bengal, and Gujarat in turn provided large quantities of cotton for the Bengal textile industry. Large consignments of Bengal silk also went to Agra, whence 20,000 to 30,000 bales were sent yearly to Persia and Turkey. As far as the import of precious metals—mainly silver—was concerned, by far the most important region was the Middle East, both the Persian Gulf and the Red Sea.

India had always played a central role in the Indian Ocean trade. The subcontinent's capacity to put on the market a wide range of tradable goods at highly competitive prices was a key element in this. Bengal figured prominently in Indian trading networks, mainly as a provider of high-quality textiles manufactured from cotton and silk. The principal items imported into the province were spices and nonprecious metals such as tin from Southeast Asia and wines and precious metals from the Middle East. Although Bengali merchants certainly constituted an important part of the trading community of the region, the significant role played by immigrant merchants from other parts of the subcontinent (particularly the Gujarati Shahs) as well as from other Asian countries (e.g., Persia) must be emphasized. Another distinguishing feature of the mercantile community of Bengal engaged in coastal and high-seas trade was the considerable participation in trade by state officials at all levels. In the seventeenth century the highest-ranking among these included Subahdars Mir Jumla and Shaista Khan. Misuse of provisions aimed at facilitating the procurement of goods for use by the government at highly concessional prices for procuring goods for their private trade contributed to a significant enhancement in the profit made by these officials.

With the arrival of the Europeans in the Indian Ocean at the beginning of the sixteenth century, Bengal became important for European corporate enterprises and private traders. The Portuguese concession holders, for example, engaged trade from Bengal, but it was only in the seventeenth century, when both the Dutch and the British East India Companies established trading stations in the region, that Bengal became a hub in the Europeans' trade. The single most important distinguishing feature of the Dutch East India Company was an extensive participation in intra-Asian trade, and from about 1640 onward, Bengal was at the heart of the Dutch intra-Asian trading network. It supplied almost half of the total cargo for the crucial bullion-providing Japan trade. At the same time, Bengal opium accounted for a very substantial proportion of the total cargo imported by the company into the Malay-Indonesian archipelago. From the last quarter of the seventeenth century, the fashion revolution in Europe brought Indian textiles and raw silk to the top rung of the export cargo from Asia. Because Bengal was by far the largest Asian supplier of these two items, at the turn of the eighteenth century it accounted for around 40 percent of the total Asian cargo imported by the Dutch East India Company into Europe. The figure for the British East India Company was similar. This trade led to a substantive expansion in the income, output, and employment in the textile-manufacturing sector in the province. The average annual rate of growth of demand for Bengal textiles and raw silk regularly exceeded the average annual rate of growth of supply of these items, and the market increasingly turned into a sellers' market, further reinforcing the positive effects of the European trade in the region.

This scenario changed dramatically in the second half of the eighteenth century when, following the Treaty of Allahabad in 1765, the British East India Company managed to acquire revenue collection rights in the province. The availability of substantive political leverage made it possible for the company to impose arbitrary and unilaterally determined terms on the producers and the intermediary merchants it dealt with to procure the export cargo. For the most part, this brought to an end the positive implications of the European trade for the region. By siphoning off a part of the province's revenues for the procurement of the export goods, the British Company was increasingly able to manage without importing much bullion from home.

At the time of the renewal of its charter in 1813 the company's monopoly of the India trade was withdrawn. In 1833 the company altogether ceased to be a trading body. India was now fully exposed to the consequences of the Industrial Revolution in Britain, which was turning Bengal and other regions of the subcontinent into absorbers of finished manufactured goods—mainly cotton textiles produced in Manchester and Lancashire—and providers of raw materials and food. The loss of the foreign market and increasing British intrusion into the domestic market for textiles manufactured in India created a growing crisis in the textile-manufacturing sector in Bengal and other regions of the subcontinent.

SEE ALSO BANGLADESH; CALCUTTA; CARAVAN TRADE; COTTON; EAST INDIA COMPANY, BRITISH; EMPIRE, BRITISH; EMPIRE, MUGHAL; FAMINE; INDIA; INDIAN OCEAN; SILK; TAGORE FAMILY; TEXTILES.

BIBLIOGRAPHY

Chaudhuri, K.N. *The Trading World of Asia and the English East India Company, 1660–1760.* Cambridge, U.K.: Cambridge University Press, 1978.

Prakash, Om. *The Dutch East India Company and the Economy of Bengal, 1630–1720.* Princeton, NJ: Princeton University Press, 1985.

Prakash, Om. *European Commercial Enterprise in Pre-Colonial India.* Cambridge, U.K.: Cambridge University Press, 1998.

Om Prakash

BENIN

SEE DAHOMEY

HENRY BESSEMER
1813–1898

Henry Bessemer was a talented and successful British inventor and steel manufacturer who introduced the first process that made large amounts of steel at low cost. Low-cost steel was a key input to the emerging industrial economy of the nineteenth century and an important commodity in world trade. Bessemer made steel simply by blowing large volumes of air through molten pig iron. Oxygen in the air combined with carbon and other impurities in the iron to generate great heat while refining the iron into steel. From 1855 to 1857 Bessemer patented the key concepts and mechanical apparatus for his steel-making process and also several applications for railway building, shipbuilding, and gun making. Bessemer steel, along with a close variant known as Thomas steel, was widely used for building railroads, bridges, ships, factories, and many other key elements in the economy.

Bessemer's steel-making process influenced world trade in several ways. First, a problem posed by the French military had inspired Bessemer to invent a better metal for cannons. French shipbuilders were early users of the material. Second, all the major steel-making countries adopted the Bessemer process, which remained a leading source of steel for decades. By 1899 world production of Bessemer steel stood at 10 million tons. In the twentieth century, however, steel makers increasingly turned to the open-hearth process and electric steel making. Yet, curiously, the basic oxygen furnace used worldwide to produce steel today strikingly resembles a classic pear-shaped Bessemer converter, except that it uses pure oxygen.

SEE ALSO INDUSTRIALIZATION; IRON AND STEEL.

BIBLIOGRAPHY

Misa, Thomas J. *A Nation of Steel: The Making of Modern America, 1865–1925.* Baltimore: Johns Hopkins University Press, 1995.

Wengenroth, Ulrich. *Enterprise and Technology: The German and British Steel Industries, 1865–1895.* Cambridge, U.K.: Cambridge University Press, 1994.

Thomas J. Misa

BLACK SEA

Six countries border the Black Sea: Bulgaria, Romania, the Ukraine, Russia, Georgia, and Turkey. Five major rivers flow into the Black Sea: the Kuban, the Don, the Dniepr, the Dniestr, and the Danube. Below 200 meters, the sea's anoxic waters do not support life. When the Bosporus was formed, the saltwater killed the organic de-

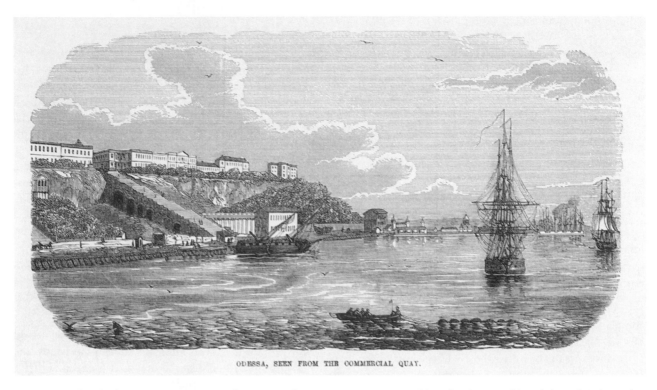

ODESSA, SEEN FROM THE COMMERCIAL QUAY.

Odessa, on the Black Sea, c. 1854. *During the nineteenth century enormous quantities of grain were shipped through Odessa, the first commercial port in Russia (1794).* © CORBIS. REPRODUCED BY PERMISSION.

posits from the rivers. Bacteria then produced deadly hydrogen sulfide. "Turnover" of these layers would result in an environmental catastrophe on the level of the Ice Age; fortunately, this threat is remote.

The continental shelf of the northwest part of the Black Sea is above the 200-meter level, allowing the growth of benthic red algae, the basis of a food chain that supported the Black Sea's abundant anchovies, sturgeon, bonitos, and dolphins. Eutrophication through fertilizer runoff (the result of massive fertilizer pollution) has led to repeated phytoplankton blooms that killed off the red algae and the life-forms it supported. The comb jellyfish (mnemiompsis), which had been introduced into the Black Sea from the U.S. East Coast in the water ballast tanks of freighters, drove out many of the other life forms. In 1990 the catch of comb jellyfish weighed 1 billion tons wet. Since 1990 this environmental crisis has moderated, partly because economic crises in the formerly Communist countries has reduced the use of fertilizer.

A surface current flows out of the Black Sea via the Bosporus, and a deeper, more saline current flows into the Black Sea; thus its level remains stable. The inward current divides into two, with a western branch flowing north to Odessa and an eastern branch flowing to the Crimea, and then moving clockwise around the shores of the Black Sea. It surfaces at the Caucasus, and is partly responsible for the mild and fruitful climate of Georgia.

These currents need to be taken into account when navigating the Black Sea.

Ottoman conquests made the Black Sea into a Turkish lake. Constantinople fell in 1453, Trebizond in 1461, the Genoese colony of Caffa in 1475. The Golden Horde (Mongols) disintegrated in the mid-fifteenth century; the Crimean Tatars established their own khanate in 1443, which came under Ottoman suzerainty in 1478. The Ottoman Empire reserved the Black Sea trade for itself, to supply the huge city of Istanbul with foodstuffs—grain, fish, and meat—and with slaves. Extensive raiding by the Crimean Tatars provided more than 10,000 slaves a year for the Ottoman Empire.

During the reign of Catherine II (1762–1796), Russia permanently conquered the northern shores of the Black Sea. In 1794 Catherine founded Odessa. Odessa's exports included grain, merino wool, tallow, linseed, and wine, but grain, especially wheat, crowded out the other exports so that the area became a wheat monoculture. The wheat was of two types: soft wheat, sold to northern Europe to make bread, and hard wheat, sold to the Mediterranean to make pasta. The growth of the grain trade was explosive because the abolition of the Corn Laws in Britain had opened new export markets. The grain trade received only a check during the Crimean War (1853–1855) when Russia pressured the Western powers with a grain embargo and northern European countries bought grain from the United States instead. The Black Sea lost out because the quality of its wheat was poor, with much contaminating dirt, and because the transportation links to the ports, in particular the rail links and the dock facilities, were inadequate. Grain was left to rot in the open because there were not enough railroad cars to transport it. The United States standardized its grain and flour types and produced five to six types of grain and three bleached flours; Russia, by contrast, produced fifty to sixty types of grain and fourteen types of flour, all unbleached.

The leading export houses of Odessa in the first half of the nineteenth century were owned by Greeks; in the second half, Jews owned the leading houses. The British, who dominated the trade because they had a convenient return freight in British coals, set the contract terms; the introduction of high Russian tariffs on coal in 1883 shifted much grain trade from Britain to Germany. By the early twentieth century the most important import for Odessa was cotton from India and Egypt, which was destined for the spinning works of Łodz. Another major import was tea; Russia sent out soldiers and stores to Vladivostok, and brought tea back to Odessa.

By 1945 every country on the Black Sea, with the sole exception of Turkey, was under Communist control. As the warmest regions in the region, the Crimea and the Bulgarian coast were popular tourist destinations. The Ukrainian Black Sea coast, in particular the port of Mykolaiv, became a major center of shipbuilding. The construction of pipelines to link with Caspian oil reserves made Rostov on the Don a petroleum port.

Hopes for a boom in trade across the Black Sea since the end of Communism have not been realized because of repeated economic crises in both the former Soviet Union and in Turkey, and because of bitter civil wars in the Caucasus. The Black Sea is, however, one of the shortest routes to the pipelines from the Caspian Sea, which has the greatest oil reserves outside the Persian Gulf. The oil trade in the twenty-first century in the Black Sea may dwarf the grain trade of the nineteenth century.

SEE ALSO Blockades in War; Caravan Trade; Climate; Empire, Ottoman; Ethnic Groups, Armenians; Ethnic Groups, Gujarati; Ethnic Groups, Jews; Genoa; Gold and Silver; Greece; Imperialism; Iran; Mercantilism; Millets and Capitulations; Petroleum; Piracy; Privateering; Protection Costs; Russia; Ship Types; Smuggling; Spices and the Spice Trade; Textiles; Venice; Wheat and Other Cereal Grains.

BIBLIOGRAPHY

Ascherson, Neal. *Black Sea*. New York: Hill and Wang, 1995.

Aybak, Tunç, ed. *Politics of the Black Sea: Dynamics of Cooperation and Conflict*. London: I. B. Tauris, 2001.

Friebel, Otto. *Der Handelshafen Odessa* (*The Commercial Port Odessa*). Leipzig and Berlin: B. G. Teubner, 1921.

Helihy, Patricia. *Odessa: A History, 1794–1914*. Cambridge, MA: Harvard University Press, 1986.

Inalcik, Halil, and Quataert, Donald, eds. *An Economic and Social History of the Ottoman Empire, 1300–1914*. Cambridge, U.K.: Cambridge University Press, 1994.

John M. Kleeberg

BLOCKADES IN PEACE

The laws of international relations deal with three broad categories of actions in response to disagreements among nations—four, if one option is to do nothing. The three are (1) amicable measures short of war, (2) non-amicable measures short of war, and (3) war. The first of these are formal understandings among nations, designed to avoid warfare. They are usually based on some mutual agreement—the product of negotiations that include mediation or arbitration. The second represents an attempt to avoid warfare through the adoption of policies that impose a sufficiently high cost on the targeted nation, so that the target submits to certain terms to avoid military action. These policies—often termed "sanctions"—include measures of an economic, political, or diplomatic nature that are imposed unilaterally by one nation or a coalition of nations. Among economic sanctions are pacific blockades and various other forms of restrictions on trade, financial flows, and the movement of people. What types of sanctions to impose, and what their appropriate breadth and magnitude should be, are questions that must be answered by any potential targeting nation (or nations); the answers to those questions indicate the wide range of possible actions.

There is no generally accepted legal definition of what constitutes a sanction representing a measure short of war. It is recognized that sanctions are a prerogative of a government or of governments, taking coercive measures to discourage behavior. Sanctions are often considered to be the government-inspired withdrawal, or threat of withdrawal, of customary trade or financial relations. Customary does not mean contractual; it simply means the levels of trade and financial activity that would probably have occurred in the absence of sanctions. In the words of M. S. Daoudi and M. S. Dajani (1983), sanctions are the "penalty attached to transgression and breach of international law." They are unilateral or "collective action against a state considered to be violating international law taken to compel that state to conform."

In the past, sanctions have involved diplomatic, economic, and military actions. As such, sanctions represent

American-made 1950s-model cars for rent to tourists in Havana, Cuba, 2003. *The United States has maintained a trade embargo on Cuba since 1961.* JORGE REY/GETTY IMAGES. REPRODUCED BY PERMISSION.

compromise between "a slap on the wrist" and "more extreme measures," such as covert action or "military measures" (Hufbauer, Schott, and Elliot 1990). Most studies of the efficiency of sanctions have focused on the degree to which the target relies on the sender for its imports and exports and on the economic and political stability of the target. Because sender countries are more likely to enjoy a dominant market position in the export rather than the import market, historically, when weapons against trade have been deployed, the sender is more likely to have used export rather than import controls. The greater the reliance on trade and the weaker the target, the more likely it is that the sanction will succeed. Furthermore, it appears probable that the longer the sanctions remain in force, the higher the costs incurred by the target; this empirical relationship probably helps explain the apparent positive correlation between the duration of the sanction and the level of success.

It appears that the sanctions that are most likely to induce the desired political and policy changes in the target country are those that concentrate income losses not on the country at large, but on groups that benefit "from the target government's policies, those which signal political support to opposition interest groups, or those which threaten increased pain in the future and therefore create an incentive for individual supporters of the target to free ride on the political activities of their group as a whole" (Kaempfer and Lowenberg 1988). In operational terms, because of the sender's political structure, a sanction might be imposed or renewed only occasionally but enforced continuously; and legislation can be enacted that would require the executive or judiciary to lift the sanctions as soon as the target met the sender's conditions. Finally, to prevent the target from adopting and adjusting, the imposition of a sanction should be swift; and the sender should not devote too many resources to securing multilateral cooperation, since that is far from necessary for a successful sanction (Drezner 1999).

Economists, political scientists, and lawyers, as well as interested laymen, have explored the underlying reasons for the imposition of sanctions; although there is a rough consensus, there is still a lack of precise agreement. For example, Jonathan Eaton and Maxim Engers (1992) argue that there are "two types of actions that the sender might wish to affect. One is the target's ongoing choice of some action, such as its debt-service payment, trade policies, pollution, or degree of protection of intellectual property. Another is the target's once-and-for-all choice of an irreversible action, such as ceding territory, releasing a hostage, extraditing an accused criminal, or relinquishing power to a new government." Again, Hufbauer, Schott, and Elliot (1990) identify five major foreign policy goals that sanctions have been used to achieve: (1) change the target's policies "in a relatively modest way"; (2) "destabilize the target government"; (3) "disrupt a minor military adventure"; (4) "impair the military potential of the target country"; and (5) "change the target country policies in a major way."

The type of sanction must also be considered. The most common are restrictions imposed on exports and imports; but those that affect the target's finances—for example, by freezing assets or by cutting off the access of the ruling elites to foreign assets and currency—have proven to be even more important and effective.

If the international political situation is relatively stable, the imposition of tough sanctions by a sender country that is relatively equal in size to the potential target is not likely to touch off a war. Thus the primary constraint on the sender's behavior is the economic impact of the loss of that country's business with the target. Given the potential costs, the options of the sender are

(1) to do nothing and accept the status quo, (2) to impose sanctions that are stringent enough to have an economic impact on the target but also result in a high cost for the source, or (3) to impose

sanctions that are relatively limited in scope because of the unwillingness of the source states to bear the economic costs of forgoing lost business with the target. (Lenway 1988)

Although sanctions have most frequently been a response to an action or a policy of the target, in some cases the domestic political goals of the sender have been the force behind their imposition. Such a measure may, by inflaming public opinion or by quenching the public's demand for action, strengthen the political position of the government in power.

SEE ALSO BLOCKADES IN WAR; BOYCOTT; SMUGGLING.

BIBLIOGRAPHY

Daoudi, M. S., and Dajani, M. S. *Economic Sanctions: Ideals and Experience*. London: Routledge, 1983.

Drezner, Daniel W. *The Sanctioning Paradox: Statecraft and International Relations*. Cambridge, U.K.: Cambridge University Press, 1999.

Eaton, Jonathan, and Engers, Maxim. "Sanctions." *Journal of Political Economy* 100 (October 1992): 899–928.

Hufbauer, Gary Clyde; Schott, Jeffrey J.; and Elliot, Kimberly Ann. *Economic Sanctions Reconsidered: History and Current Policy,* 2nd edition. Washington, DC: Institute for International Economics, 1990.

Kaempfer, William, and Lowenberg, Anton D. "The Theory of International Sanctions: A Public Choice Approach." *American Economic Review* 78 (September 1988): 786–793.

Lenway, Stefanie Ann. "Between Law and Commerce: Economic Sanctions as a Tool of Statecraft." *International Organization* 42 (Spring 1988): 397–426.

Lance E. Davis

BLOCKADES IN WAR

Economic statecraft was part of the diplomatic armory long before modern times. One of the first documented uses dates back to 423 B.C.E., when the Athenian trade embargo on Megara played a role in triggering the Peloponnesian War. In fact, from ancient Greece through the nineteenth century, economic sanctions almost always foreshadowed or accompanied warfare. Combatants frequently employed economic tools, such as naval blockades, to directly or indirectly reduce the enemy's economic strength and thus its capacity to launch or sustain a war.

BLOCKADES DURING WARTIME

There are two main ways by which a government tries to inflict costs on its foreign target: (1) with trade restrictions that limit the target's exports or reduce its imports, and (2) with financial measures that impede its access to

DECLARATION CONCERNING LAWS OF NAVAL WAR

Rules on wartime blockades have normally been unwritten conventions. The 1856 Paris Declaration had attempted to set out a formal groundwork for imposing blockades, but it was not systematic—contraband was not defined, for instance. In 1908 to 1909 the major European naval powers, plus the United States and Japan, made a new attempt at formally codifying the laws of blockade, and tried to establish an international court with real authority. The "Declaration Concerning the Laws of Naval War," drafted in London, contained seventy-one articles defining matters such as the geographical limits of a place under blockade, and the consequences to vessels found guilty of breeching a blockade. The interests of neutral nations were well represented, and the document also addressed the issues of contraband and prizes.

Although it was ratified by the U.S. senate, Britain's House of Lords rejected the 1909 declaration, and it never officially came into force. Many nations nonetheless agreed to abide by the declaration, as Germany initially did in World War I. As the world's greatest naval power, Britain had the most to lose by restrictions on its freedom to blockade, and it refused U.S. entreaties to abide by the 1909 code.

David J. Clarke

foreign exchange. Export bans are intended to reduce a target's foreign sales and thus deprive it of both markets and foreign currency, whereas import restrictions are meant to deny critical goods to the target country. Financial sanctions, such as asset freezes and the interruption of commercial finance, are intended to deprive the target country of resources to pay for imports and limit the target's access to affordable credit. In addition, a key goal of an assets freeze is to deny an invading country the full fruits of its aggression. Such measures were used against Japan for that purpose just before and during World War II. And in the 1990 Iraq crisis, the U.S. government and its allies froze Kuwait's assets to stop Saddam Hussein's plunder.

During the Napoleonic Wars (1803–1815) both France and Britain employed economic tools to gain the

A British illustration depicting the American use of torpedoes and other explosive devices against a British blockade of New York during the summer of 1813. The naval blockade was an attempt to cut off crucial shipping and transportation routes as part of the War of 1812. THE LIBRARY OF CONGRESS.

strategic upper hand. Great Britain imposed a naval blockade in an effort to contain French expansion and eventually defeat Napoleon. In retaliation France introduced the Continental System. The comprehensive trade embargo closed the continental European market to British exports and denied Britain access to strategic goods from the Baltics. By isolating Great Britain, Napoleon hoped to bring its economy to the brink of collapse. Neither Britain nor France was able to effectively enforce its embargo. Enemy trade with neutral countries and widespread smuggling undermined the effectiveness of the blockades. The desire to eliminate third-party trade compelled Napoleon to seize large parts of Europe, and his push into Russia was in part triggered by Russia's refusal to comply with the Continental System. In fact, neutral nations frequently found themselves drawn into conflicts as a result of the adverse effects of blockades on their economies. The United States, for example, imposed a trade embargo on Britain in retaliation for Britain's violation of its neutral rights and interference with its trade with France. The conflict over trade further strained bilateral relations and ultimately led to the War of 1812.

Even if the economic costs are high, naval blockades and trade embargoes have not always forced belligerents to yield. This point is illustrated by the Union's naval blockade of the Confederate States during the U.S. Civil War (1861–1865). The South depended heavily on the export of cotton to finance its imports of manufactured goods, arms, and ammunition. The Union's naval blockade drastically diminished the South's foreign imports and caused severe inflation. However, despite the devastating effect, the Confederate States managed to obtain sufficient amounts of military matériel, and in the end it "was the shortages of manpower, not of strategic goods, that led to the collapse of the Confederate war effort" (Naylor 2001, p. 16).

These experiences inspired attempts to establish an international legal framework for the imposition of naval blockades, the rights of neutral states, and differentiation between civilian and military goods. These efforts culminated in the London Declaration of 1909 stipulating that blockades had to be formally declared and limited to enemy or enemy-occupied ports. Commodity trade was divided into three categories: goods of purely military use (*absolute contraband*), which could be seized immediately; items that could be used both for civilian and for military purposes (*conditional contraband*), which could be seized only if intended for military use by the enemy; and purely civilian goods (*noncontraband*), which could not be seized at all. The declaration was never ratified, and was soon overtaken by the events of World War I. The concerns raised, however, are still relevant for the contemporary debate about economic sanctions. Questions about the legality of comprehensive embargoes, economic costs experienced by third states, and the need for humanitarian exceptions to limit the impact on the civilian population were at the center of the debate about the comprehensive United Nations (UN) embargo against Iraq (1990–2003).

The principles of the London Declaration were abandoned during World War I (1914–1918). The comprehensive British blockade and the navicert (a certificate issued to a neutral ship by a belligerent certifying that the inspected ship is free of contraband) system established to administer it were rather successful in strangling the German economy. Belligerents imposed tight capital controls and froze foreign interest payments and assets of enemy citizens. As the cost of the war and blockade mounted and food supplies decreased, Germany resorted to unrestricted submarine warfare, eventually drawing the United States into the war.

ECONOMIC SANCTIONS AS ALTERNATIVE TO USE OF FORCE

The horrors of World War I led U.S. President Woodrow Wilson to advocate economic sanctions as an alternative to armed conflict. Economic sanctions were subsequently incorporated as a tool of enforcement in each of the two collective security systems established in the twentieth century—the League of Nations and United Nations. However, hopes that economic sanctions would be an effective deterrent against aggression faded when the league's embargo against Italy failed to deter Benito Mussolini's conquest of Ethiopia in 1935 and 1936. When hostilities broke out again in Europe in 1939, economic warfare, trade embargoes, asset freezes, and preemptive buying once again played a major role in the struggle to defeat Germany and Japan.

Following World War II, economic sanctions were imposed for an increasingly broad range of foreign-policy purposes. Economic sanctions have been utilized to combat weapons proliferation, to support nuclear disarmament, to stop drug trafficking, to fight terrorism, to end civil wars, and to promote democracy and human rights. Some sanctions have been drastic and comprehensive, such as the UN sanctions against Iraq and the U.S. unilateral sanctions imposed on North Korea, but most were far less severe.

Motives behind the use of sanctions have also changed. Economic sanctions during wartime were focused primarily on reducing a target's capabilities. In modern times, the core motives shifted to changing a target state's behavior, deterring others, demonstrating resolve to allies and domestic constituencies, or simply sending a message of disapproval in response to objectionable behavior. When military action would be too expensive and diplomatic protest too mild, world leaders increasingly resorted to sanctions.

Since the 1920s the use of economic sanctions for foreign-policy purposes has increased decade by decade. Although the majority of economic sanctions imposed were unilateral adventures, the end of the cold war allowed for greater cooperation between the major powers. This is reflected in the fact that the U.N. Security Council imposed mandatory sanctions thirteen times in the 1990s compared to just twice—against South Africa and Rhodesia—in previous decades. But the increasingly frequent deployment of sanctions in the late 1980s and the 1990s generated intense debate among policy makers and scholars about their effectiveness in shaping a target country's policies. Advocates of economic sanctions regard them as an important middle-of-the-road policy between diplomatic protest and military force. Opponents, on the other hand, stress that economic sanctions are generally ineffective in achieving policy changes abroad, and that the costs to the sender country's economy, third states, and civilians in the target country are seldom worth the benefits derived.

Lessons learned from the frequent use of economic sanctions as a tool of international policy in the 1990s have led to their reevaluation. Reform efforts focus on "fine tuning" sanctions to become a more useful tool while inflicting less economic cost on civilian populations, third states, and the sender countries. Targeted sanctions are meant to focus their impact on leaders and political elites responsible for objectionable behavior. UN Security Council actions in Angola, for example, focused on one particular internal actor—the rebel group UNITA. Targeted sanctions operate at a level of intervention in internal affairs of states that was unknown in previous decades. They also constitute a departure from the traditional sanctions philosophy that civilian pain leads to political change. Because they focus on certain groups and individuals within the targeted country, they assume that the leaders do not represent the population and can actually be separated from it.

SEE ALSO BLOCKADES IN PEACE; WARS.

BIBLIOGRAPHY

Baldwin, David A. *Economic Statecraft*. Princeton, NJ: Princeton University Press, 1985.

Hufbauer, Gary C.; Schott, Jeffrey J.; and Elliott, Kimberly A. *Economic Sanctions Reconsidered,* 2nd edition. Washington, DC: Institute for International Economics, 1990.

Jack, Daniel Thompson. *Studies in Economic Warfare.* New York: Chemical, 1941.

Knorr, Klaus. *The Power of Nations: The Political Economy of International Relations.* New York: Basic Books, 1975.

Naylor, R. T. *Economic Warfare: Sanctions, Embargo Busting, and Their Human Cost.* Boston: Northeastern University Press, 2001.

Renwick, Robin. *Economic Sanctions.* Harvard Studies in International Affairs, no. 45. Cambridge, MA: Harvard University, 1981.

Wu, Yuan-Li. *Economic Warfare.* New York: Prentice-Hall, 1952.

Gary Clyde Hufbauer
Barbara Oegg

BOARD OF TRADE, BRITISH

As English foreign trade and colonial activity expanded in the seventeenth century, the king's government was increasingly faced with the problem of finding effective modes of supervision. Formally, the secretary of state for the southern department was the person who transmitted royal commands to the colonies, but he had many other responsibilities. The treasury and its subordinate bodies were also involved insofar as trade and colonies created opportunities for taxation. Policy was left to the king's senior advisors sitting as the full privy council. Gradually there were calls for some sort of supervisory body that could advise on trade and the colonies, taking part of this responsibility away from the privy council. There was, however, no clear consensus about the personnel or authority envisioned for such a body. Should it be a single entity, or should there be separate boards for the colonies and trade? If a single body, was it to be a free-standing entity or a subcommittee of the privy council? Throughout most of the seventeenth century there were relatively short-lived experiments with different solutions to these questions, until a more lasting answer was reached in 1696.

SEVENTEENTH-CENTURY EXPERIMENTS

The earliest experimental commissions were focused on trade and had little to do with the colonies. These included the board established by James I (1566–1625) in 1622 and its successor, authorized by Charles I (1600–1649) in 1625. More carefully planned was the Committee of Privy Council, which was authorized in 1630 and still focused primarily on trade. Its members included the two secretaries of state and the lord treasurer, and its meetings were sometimes attended by the king, giving it exec-

utive as well as advisory functions. It drafted regulations and issued orders on its own authority, but sometimes appointed subcommittees to investigate specific questions. Despite its considerable authority, this committee could not answer all the needs of the state. In 1638 and 1639 separate boards of commissioners were appointed to look into the problems of the cloth industry.

As these various trade bodies did not concern themselves with colonial questions, from time to time between 1623–1624 and the early 1630s separate short-lived, ad hoc committees were appointed by the privy council to look into specific colonial problems, particularly those involving Virginia and the New England colonies. A more regular standing committee for the colonies, appointed by the king in April 1634, lasted until 1641. On paper, this body had the most sweeping powers. It could make laws and orders for the colonies; impose penalties and imprisonment for ecclesiastical offenses; remove governors and require reports from them; establish courts both civil and ecclesiastical and appoint judges and magistrates to them; hear judicial appeals and administrative complaints from the colonies; and investigate all patents and charters relating to a colony and revoke any that were irregularly obtained. This commission has been the focus of much attention from historians, yet in retrospect it achieved very little. More was accomplished by the various aforementioned short-lived ad hoc subcommittees of the Privy Council.

In 1643, during the English Civil War, Parliament assumed the functions of the king in council, and in November it appointed a commission of eighteen members of Parliament to supervise colonial affairs. An act of Parliament in 1650 also created a commission, or Council of Trade. The responsibilities entrusted to this commission were exceptionally broad, including regulation of domestic and foreign trade, trading companies, manufactures, free ports, customs, excise, coinage, exchange, fisheries, and plantations. Specifically, it was instructed to investigate ways in which the colonies could be encouraged to produce the raw materials needed by English industry. It received instructions and information from the Council of State, to which it reported. It was an exceptionally energetic body, devoting particular attention to the wool and cloth trades. In addition to this Council of Trade, the Council of State of the revolutionary government itself acted as a board supervising the colonies, and it had the power to appoint subcommittees of its members to consider particular questions relating to trade and plantations.

In all this, a spirit of improvisation continued. The 1650 Council of Trade was replaced in December 1651 by a standing committee of the Council of State on trade, plantations, and foreign affairs. Its scope may have been too wide. New committees of trade and plantations were established in 1653 and 1655 (twice). The body established in November 1655 was called the Committee and Standing Council for the Advancing and Regulating the Trade and Navigation of the Commonwealth. It had more than seventy members, including ten London merchants and port representatives from Newcastle, Yarmouth, Dover, Bristol, Lyme, Southampton, and Exeter. In addition, any member of the Council of State could attend its meetings and vote. With its cumbersome size and procedures, this institution accomplished relatively little, and ceased operation after 1657.

At the restoration of the monarchy in 1660, an effort was apparent to move away from the disorderly improvisation of the trade bodies under both Charles I and the revolutionary government. Even so, a willingness to innovate persisted. Charles II (1630–1685) in 1660 appointed two distinct bodies. One was a Council of Trade of sixty-two unsalaried members; the other was a Council of Foreign Plantations of forty-nine unsalaried members. The majority of members of each were privy councillors and other members of the House of Lords and House of Commons. The former included fifteen merchants; the latter only three. In the Council of Trade reappointed in 1669, the number of merchants was reduced to five. The Council of Foreign Plantations was replaced in 1670 with a new body of the same name and which consisted partly of *ex officio* commissioners (the lord chancellor, the lord treasurer, the chancellor of the exchequer, and the two secretaries of state), and partly of nominated and salaried commissioners, but no recognizable merchants.

These two separate councils were replaced in 1672 by a combined Council of Trade and Plantations. Its membership consisted of three groups: the same *ex officio* members; nine unpaid councilors or commissioners; and paid commissioners. John Locke (1632–1704) was briefly the secretary of the board. This Council of Trade and Plantations, an independent body, was replaced in 1675 by a committee of the privy council for Trade and Plantations. Because it was a committee of the privy council, its membership was overwhelmingly drawn from the House of Lords.

TOWARD GREATER STABILITY, 1696–1782

After the Revolution of 1688 and the start in 1689 of the war against France, the dissatisfaction of the merchant community—caused in part by heavy shipping losses to privateers—provoked discussion in the House of Commons about the desirability of returning to the separate boards of 1660 to 1672, with a substantial merchant representation on at least one of them. The king and his ministers interpreted the agitation for parliamentary action as a challenge to the Crown. To check the campaign

for separate boards, in 1696 William III (1650–1702) created a new combined Council of Trade and Plantations, which lasted until 1782. It continued the trend toward a smaller but well-remunerated body. The unsalaried *ex officio* members again included the lord chancellor, the lord president of the council, the lord privy seal, the lord treasurer, the lord admiral, the secretaries of state, and the chancellor of the exchequer (the minister of finance in the House of Commons). To these were added, in 1702, the bishop of London (with authority over the colonial church), and in 1721, the surveyor and auditor general of the plantations (who happened to be the brother of the prime minister at that time). In addition there were seven or eight salaried commissioners, the most senior of whom was usually known as the first lord. The salaried commissioners were paid £1,000 per annum with individual first lords allowed between £500 to £1,500 extra. The only member who had any mercantile experience was John Pollexfen (1696–1707), a London merchant trading to Portugal and the West Indies.

The formal structure of the boards influenced their personnel and sensitivity to economic interests. When there were separate boards for trade and the colonies (as from 1660 to 1672), it was easier to get a fair number of merchants onto the trade board; when the boards were united, political pressures left little room for merchants. Similarly, when the united board was outside the privy council, there was a chance that it would include men with relevant experience. This was unlikely when the board was a subcommittee of the privy council. The personnel and activity of the board of 1696 to 1782 thus ultimately reflected the balance of influence in the political nation. And just as there was hardly any place for merchants on that board, so was there little room for men with direct colonial experience. Of the seventy-five men who served on the board between 1696 and 1775, only five had any conspicuous connection with the Americas.

Because there was very little experience of either commerce or colonies on the Georgian board, its operation and sense of continuity leaned heavily on the services of its subordinate staff. At the top was the secretary to the board. One of these, William Blathwayt (1675–1696), was an important politician who subsequently became a member of Parliament and regular member of the board (1696–1707), among other offices. He was succeeded as secretary by William Popple I (1696–1707), who was succeeded by his own son, William Popple Jr. (1707–1722), and his grandson, Alured Popple (1722–1737); another grandson, William Popple III, became solicitor to the board. In addition to the long-established position of solicitor, a more senior legal position—counsel to the board—was established in 1718. All four men who held this position between 1718 and 1782 were also members of Parliament and king's counsels (the highest rank of barristers). Their legal opinions would have greatly influenced the allowance or disallowance of colonial legislation.

The Board of Trade has a reputation of having been particularly inactive during the long administration of Sir Robert Walpole (1721–1742), who was not inclined to antagonize the colonies. Even so, it did make some significant decisions. The Virginians in the 1720s were particularly upset by a decline in the price of tobacco (the most valuable export of the continental colonies), which they ascribed to overproduction and attempted to check by imposing a heavy duty on the importation of slaves. When merchants trading to Africa complained against this measure, on the recommendation of the Board of Trade, the Virginia act was disallowed by the Crown. This step greatly offended the Virginians; Thomas Jefferson remembered it half a century later and wanted to include it as an example of Britain's promotion of slavery in his preliminary draft of the Declaration of Independence. The board was particularly active only from 1748 to 1760, when the earl of Halifax was the first lord and a member of the cabinet. In an age in which control of patronage was one of the most sensitive political questions, Halifax's most significant accomplishment, in 1752, was regaining for the board the control of colonial patronage that it had lost in 1704.

NINETEENTH-CENTURY ACHIEVEMENT

Reflecting the anti-imperial, anti-establishment mood associated with British failures in the American Revolution, the Board of Trade was abolished in 1782. Most responsibility for colonial matters was transferred to one of the secretaries of state, but trade required special attention. In 1784 William Pitt (1759–1806), the prime minister, made a temporary arrangement by establishing a Committee of the Privy Council for Trade and Plantations. As this committee consisted only of privy councillors, it proved not entirely satisfactory, and was replaced in 1786 by a committee of the privy council with the same name but a different composition. Its membership thereafter consisted of ten or more *ex officio* members and an indefinite number of nominated members, headed by the president and vice president of the board. Both the nominal and effective membership shrank in the nineteenth century, with some meetings attended only by the president. At the same time, however, the expansion of overseas trade and the progress of the Industrial Revolution, with its railroads and steamships, swelled the amount of business allotted to the board. Although the board itself dwindled in members, its staff increased from twelve to fifteen in the eighteenth century to ninety-seven in 1867 and about 7,500 in 1914. In this expansion it evolved

from the advisory body of the seventeenth and eighteenth century into an administrative agency comparable to most of the government ministries of the late nineteenth century. Organizationally it came to be divided into several departments, the most important of which were headed by assistant secretaries. Some of these departments became so important that they were spun off and became independent ministries (e.g., transportation, labor). In retrospect, the nineteenth-century Board of Trade was very much the godfather of the interventionist state.

SEE ALSO BOARD OF TRADE, SPANISH; EMPIRE, BRITISH.

BIBLIOGRAPHY

Andrews, Charles McLean. *British Committees, Commissions, and Councils of Trade and Plantations, 1622–1675.* Baltimore, MD: Johns Hopkins University Press, 1908.

Andrews, Charles McLean. *The Colonial Period of American History.* 4 vols. New Haven, CT: Yale University Press, 1934–1938.

Basye, Arthur Herbert. *The Lords Commissioners of Trade and Plantations Commonly Known as the Board of Trade, 1748–1782.* New Haven, CT: Yale University Press, 1925.

Bieber, Ralph Paul. "The Lords of Trade and Plantations, 1675–1696." Ph.D. diss., University of Pennsylvania, Allentown, 1919.

Prouty, Roger. *The Transformation of the Board of Trade, 1830–1855.* London: Heinemann, 1957.

Sainty, J. C. *Officials of the Boards of Trade, 1660–1870.* London: Athlone, 1974.

Smith, Sir Hubert Llewellyn. *The Board of Trade.* London: G. P. Putnam, 1928

Steele, I. K. *The Politics of Colonial Policy: The Board of Trade in Colonial Administration, 1696–1720.* Oxford, U.K.: Oxford University Press, 1958.

Jacob M. Price

BOARD OF TRADE, SPANISH

The Catholic kings founded the Spanish Board of Trade (*Casa de la Contratación de las Indias,* hereafter referred to as *Casa*) in January 1503 as the institution responsible for the regulation of trade and movement of goods with the Indies. The Crown did not hold a monopoly, as was the case with the Portuguese *Casa da Guiné e Mina* and the *Casa da India,* but rather allowed individual merchants to take the initiative. The *Casa* was established in Seville because this was the main Spanish center for Atlantic trade, a principal location of merchants and capital, with a port, customs facilities, a population of 40,000, and an extremely productive rural hinterland. Its first *factor* and controller was Francisco Pinelo (d. 1509), a Genoese who had settled in Seville.

The duties of the *Casa* consisted of: (1) organizing the monopoly of the traffic of goods during the prepara-

A Spanish galleon on the high seas, c. 1550. The primary function of the Casa de Contratación was to organize the trade fleets that sailed between Spain and the Indies. HULTON ARCHIVE/GETTY IMAGES. REPRODUCED BY PERMISSION.

tions for expeditions to the Indies; (2) licensing and registering the ships involved and their cargo; (3) nominating those in charge and accepting bonds; (4) controlling passengers; (5) repatriating the belongings of those who had died; and (6) holding the money from this trade that was the property of the king (the so-called *quinto real,* or "royal fifth," on precious metals and other imported goods, other taxes, etc.). From 1511 it held civil and criminal jurisdiction over everything relating to trade and shipping for the Indies, and its three main officials were known as *jueces oficiales* (official judges). The *Consejo de Indias* (Council of the Indies), founded in 1524, was the court of appeal for criminal cases and civil suits involving amounts of more than 40,000 maravedis, and the *Consulado,* or *Universidad de cargadores a Indias* in Seville, established in 1543, was responsible for lesser cases. In 1579 the role of president of the *Casa* was created, and in 1583 the *Casa* was divided into two distinct courts, administrative and judicial.

The main duty of the *Casa* was to organize the fleets that went on the *Carrera de Indias.* Although it was already common for ships to sail as a group in the early years, for safety reasons this practice became the norm because ships were so often captured by pirates (189 between 1536 and 1568). Philip II (1527–1598) made it compulsory to travel in a fleet from 1561 onward. The fleets sailed from Seville-Sanlúcar de Barrameda in April and August and, after a stopover in the Canaries, reached the Caribbean. From either La Dominica or Guadaloupe, where one fleet sailed on to New Spain (Veracruz) and the other to Tierra Firme (Cartagena de Indias/Nombre de Dios or Porto Bello). The return trip went via Havana, where the two fleets and the royal armada, which had spent the winter there, were reunited before August to avoid the hurricanes. The journey home, which had a stopover in the Azores, lasted two months. The number of ships in each fleet varied, although it was normally between ten and thirty. The frequency of voyages eventually was reduced from twice a year to once and, by the seventeenth century, to a fleet every two or three years. This pattern was maintained in the eighteenth century. The establishment of registered shipping from 1754 and the regulations on *Comercio Libre* (free trade) of 1765 and 1778 meant the end of the fleets, which remained, although in a much reduced form, for Venezuela and Mexico until 1783.

The *Casa* came to be the first genuine naval academy in Europe (Pérez-Mallaína 1992). In 1508 the king established the post of *piloto mayor* (master pilot), which carried the duty of drawing up the *padrón real* (royal register) showing the results of geographical discoveries. From this register, sailing charts were copied for use by pilots onboard ships. The master pilot also had the task of testing those who hoped to be pilots on the route to the Indies. The first master pilot was Amerigo Vespucci (d. 1512). In December 1552 a chair in Cosmography and Navigation was established in the *Casa*, the first of its kind, because of the need to train an increasingly large number of pilots to undertake the Indies voyages.

The controlling duties exercised by the *Casa* meant that it became an ideological filter of the books and people that traveled to the Indies, with the explicit intention of avoiding any "spiritual risk" to the natives or the colonists, as well as preventing spying. The following were thus forbidden: foreigners, Jews, Muslims, converts who had been disciplined or reconciled by the Inquisition, along with their children and grandchildren, gypsies (from 1570), clergy without royal permission, and unmarried women and slaves, unless either of these latter groups were in service. As far as books were concerned, carrying nonreligious works such as romantic, "chivalrous" novels was banned. The export of prayer books was encouraged, and Philip II granted a monopoly to the monastery of San Lorenzo de El Escorial for their sale in the Indies.

The fleets generally sailed from the bay of Cadiz in the last third of the seventeenth century to avoid the dangers and high accident rates of sailing the Guadalquivir. The change was also the result of the growing influence of merchants from Cadiz. The *Casa* officially moved to Cadiz in 1717. The administrative arm (*Sala de Gobierno*) disappeared, for its functions were transferred to the *Intendencia General de Marina*; only the judicial part remained (the *Sala de Justicia*), continuing to regulate the licensing of sailing and travel to the Indies, administering the possessions of those who died in the Indies, and resolving civil suits of the stevedores and sailors. However, trading conditions had already changed a great deal, and the *Comercio Libre* decrees of Charles III (1765, 1778) put an end to the remaining duties of the *Casa*. In 1783 the teaching and examination of pilots was transferred to the Colegio de San Telmo in Seville. Finally, in June 1790, a port court was created in Cadiz, and the *Casa* disappeared for good.

SEE ALSO EDUCATION; EMPIRE, SPANISH; MERCANTILISM; NEW SPAIN; SHIPPING, AIDS TO; SHIPS AND SHIPPING.

BIBLIOGRAPHY

Bernal, A. M. *La financiación de la Carrera de Indias (1492–1824)*. Madrid: Tabapress-El Monte, 1993.

Caballero Juárez, J. A. *El régimen jurídico de las armadas de la Carrera de Indias*. Mexico: 1997.

Cervera Pery, J. *La Casa de Contratación y el Consejo de Indias (Las razones de un superministerio)*. Madrid: Ministerio de Defensa, 1997.

España y América: Un océano de negocios. Quinto centenario de la Casa de la Contratación, 1503–2003. Madrid: Sociedad Estatal de Conmemoraciones Culturales, 2003.

García-Baquero, A. *Cádiz y el Atlántico, 1717–1778. El comercio coloniall español bajo el monopolio gaditano*. Seville: Escuela de Estudios Hispanoamericanos, 1976.

García-Baquero, A. *La Carrera de Indias: Suma de la contratación y océano de negocios*. Seville: Algaida, 1992.

Ladero Quesada, Miguel-Ángel. *El primer oro de América: Los comienzos de la Casa de la Contratación de las Yndias (1503–1511)*. Madrid: Real Academia de la Historia, 2002.

Martín-Merás, M. L. *La cartografía marítima hispana: La imagen de América*. Madrid: Instituto de Historia Naval, 1993.

Pérez-Mallaína Bueno, P. E. *Los hombres del océano: Vida cotidiana de los tripulares de las flotas de Indias, Siglo XVI*. Seville: University of Seville, 1992.

Pulido Ortega, I., dir. *Obras españolas de náutica relacionadas con la Casa de la Contratación de Sevilla*. Madrid: Escuela de Estudios Hispanoamericanos, 1992.

Schäfer, E. *El Consejo Real y Supremo de las Indias: Su historia, organización y labor administrativa hasta la terminación de la Casa de Austria*. 2 vols. Seville: University of Seville, 1935–1947; reprinted 1975, 2003.

Miguel-Ángel Ladero Quesada

JEAN BODIN
1530–1596

Jean Bodin is considered to be the father of *sovereignty* because, with *Les six livres de la République* (1576), he provided the first theoretical definition and application of this extraordinary, powerful idea that shaped approaches to politics and economics in the world. "Sovereignty is the most high, absolute, and perpetual power over the citizens and subjects in a Commonwealth," (1606, p. 84) wrote Bodin, albeit "subject to the laws of God and of nature, and even to certain human laws common to all nations" (1606, p. 90). The sovereign is thus placed at the apex of a pyramid of authority where he or she enjoys the supreme power in the hierarchical organizational structure of society. Bodin's *sovereignty* has had a creative and transforming social effect on the shared consciousness of humanity, standing for the proposition that there is indeed one single entity that holds the greatest and final authority on earth. This self-empowerment idea was used not only as a justification for the international nation-state system since the seventeenth century, but also later as a basis for antislavery thought in the nineteenth century and, along with self-determination, as a force behind decolonization in the second half of the twentieth century.

Bodin's numerous other works deal with a method of study for universal history, a system of universal law, the economics of inflation, witchcraft and demonology, principles of natural science, the nature of religion.

SEE ALSO EMPIRE, FRENCH; MERCANTILISM; SLAVERY AND THE SLAVE TRADE.

BIBLIOGRAPHY

Beaulac, Stéphane. *The Power of Language in the Making of International Law: The Word Sovereignty in Bodin and Vattel and the Myth of Westphalia.* Leiden, Netherlands, and Boston: Martinus Nijhoff, 2004.

Bodin, Jean. *The Six Bookes of a Commonweale,* trans. by Richard Knolles. London, Bishop, 1606.

Franklin, Julian H. *Jean Bodin and the Rise of Absolutist Theory.* Cambridge, U.K.: Cambridge University Press, 1973.

Stéphane Beaulac

BOMBAY
SEE MUMBAI

NAPOLEON BONAPARTE
1769-1821

Napoleon Bonaparte, soldier and politician, was born in 1769 in Ajaccio, on the Mediterranean island of Corsica. He died in St. Helen, a remote island in the South Atlantic Ocean, on May 5, 1821, after having reshaped and ruled continental Europe and France's colonies abroad (e.g., Haiti and Louisiana). He promulgated the "Code Napoleon," a modern system of civil laws, and reorganized the French bureaucracy and school system. His military campaigns began early in his career; he conquered Italy in 1796 and Ottoman-ruled Egypt in 1798. Back in France, he was named consul after a coup d'état in 1799, consul for life (1802), and emperor (1804). After defeating Austria (Austerlitz, 1805) and Prussia (Jena, 1806), Spain, and Portugal, Napoleon modernized the social and economic structures of the countries he conquered. He then allied with Russia and, in order to weaken Britain, imposed the Continental System, a blockade

of all English goods. This was one of Napoleon's biggest errors as it limited trade, thus causing the discontent of the bourgeois, previously his most supportive social block. Napoleon's success ended with the disastrous attempt to invade Russia, and his army's retreat (1812), followed by his exile to the island of Elba. He escaped in 1815, shortly ruled France again, but was defeated in Waterloo (1815) and exiled to St. Helen.

SEE ALSO BLOCKADES IN WAR; EGYPT; EMPIRE, FRENCH; FRANCE; HAITI; LEVANT COMPANY; MEDITERRANEAN; NEW ORLEANS; UNITED KINGDOM; UNITED STATES.

BIBLIOGRAPHY

Broers, Michael. *Europe under Napoleon: 1799–1815.* Oxford, U.K.: Oxford University Press, 1996.

Schom, Alan. *Napoleon Bonaparte: A Life.* London: HarperCollins, 1997.

Federico Boffa

BOOKS

The trade in books predated the invention of printing. The great European *scriptoria* of the Middle Ages such as that in the Abbey of Cluny in France produced manuscript books for cloistered monastic libraries. As literacy rates increased and the demand from universities for books grew, so too did commercial manuscript production, which by that time was also serving a market of luxury book collectors. Limited trade networks that the later printing industry exploited and expanded serviced this manuscript production. After Johannes Gutenberg (c. 1390–1468) first used the process of printing with movable metal type around 1455, his innovation spread rapidly throughout Europe. The more rapid, more inexpensive production of multiple copies transformed books into a widespread commodity that required, like any other commodity, a system of production, sales, and distribution. Where books were different was in their dual nature as physical objects and containers for knowledge and ideas.

THE SPREAD OF IDEAS

In Germany printing presses had been established in six towns by 1470, and by the end of the century presses existed in more than fifty German towns. Print became the vehicle for the scholarship of learned reformers, and the ideas of the Protestant Reformation spread rapidly in permanent form. The first Italian books were printed in the monastery of Subiaco near Rome in 1465. Presses in Rome, Florence, and Milan followed, but it was Venice's position as a commercial and cultural crossroads that

A 16th-century printing shop. *Mechanization of the printing press made books—and thus ideas—much easier to copy and preserve, which had profound impacts on nearly every aspect of Western culture, from politics to law to commerce.*
© HILTON-DEUTSCH COLLECTION/CORBIS. REPRODUCED BY PERMISSION.

helped to quickly establish it as the printing capital of Italy, and indeed of Europe. Its publications were the treatises and manuals for the expanding class of educated laity to which Renaissance learning was addressed. Printers found a market and humanists found a means of broadcasting their message. The Italian humanist movement was able to develop into a European-wide "republic of letters" partly because the printing press allowed transmission of the new learning beyond the Alps.

TRADE STRUCTURE

Within fifty years of its invention, printing had spread throughout Europe. Most enduring printing firms tended to be in commercial and trading centers rather than the intellectual centers around universities and monasteries. Early printers combined the roles of printer, publisher, and bookseller, but could not do so for long, even when serving a small, local market. The large capital required up front to run a print shop soon forced both a separation of responsibilities and the pursuit of wider markets. Master printers began to concentrate on the chief publishing tasks of securing financial backing and establishing sales networks in order to ensure survival in the trade and a sufficient return on investments.

DISTRIBUTION NETWORKS

Traditionally, tutors had sold books to pupils or peddlers had touted them at markets, but much higher sales figures were needed than these channels could provide. Successful publishers began printing stock lists, setting up branch offices in large towns and cities, attending international book fairs, and acting as agents for other publishers. The major book fairs in Europe were those at Antwerp, Lyons, Leipzig, and Frankfurt. Frankfurt, traditionally a center for the sale of manuscripts, soon became the biggest fair for printed works too. It retains this preeminence even into the twenty-first century.

Agents who originally did the rounds of fairs as middlemen for big publishers developed into wholesale dealers concentrating on the major events such as the Lyons and Frankfurt fairs, and on supplying the booksellers in big cities such as Paris. Itinerant peddlers carrying small quantities of books continued into the eighteenth century, but they could only reach a limited market.

Major publishers established warehouses at Frankfurt to keep stock between one fair and the next; branch offices in Europe's main cities also served as distribution points. In France, Paris and Lyons could take advantage of major rivers to aid distribution, and the Rhine and the Elbe carried stock through Germany. Venice was able to become the preeminent publishing city in Europe, partly because its established commercial network provided for such an effective distribution of stock.

INTO THE NEW WORLDS

As the European powers began to establish colonies overseas, books accompanied the flag and the cross. In turn, they were rapidly followed by the printing press. Often authors and publishers sought the freedom overseas to produce material that was banned in their mother countries. Rather than simply spreading the established culture to the new colonies, books became the vehicles for fresh ideas about religion and politics that were reexported to the countries of origin. Laws that had been established to protect the intellectual property rights of authors and publishers from the beginning of the eighteenth century were ignored in this international trafficking of texts. In particular, publishers in the United States during the nineteenth century seized on the lack of international protection to reproduce foreign works without payment. Eventually, international copyright protection was established through treaties such as the Berne Convention of 1886 and the Universal Copyright Convention of 1952. English-language publishers in the United States and the United Kingdom made agreements to parcel out "traditional" trading territories. These agreements lasted until the second half of the twentieth century, when they fell foul of U.S. antitrust legislation and British entry into what is now the European Union.

INDUSTRIAL PROCESS

The nineteenth century saw a revolution in publishing. Industrialization of most of the book production process meant lowered costs and increased output. Inventions such as the steam-powered press, mechanical typecasting and setting, stereotyping, and innovations in the reproduction of illustration ensured that book production was more efficient and much, much faster. Enhanced channels of communication and distribution helped the book trade: improved roads, telephones, and railways. The increased populations of Europe and the United States of America (during the nineteenth century Europe's population doubled, the United States's increased fifteen-fold)

provided an eager audience for books and magazines. Books were required for reading on train journeys, in the new public schools, and in libraries, and for information in new trades brought about by industrialization. The paperback was an extension of the democratization of the book, as was the diversity of outlets, from supermarkets to drugstores, through which it was sold.

TRADING IN RIGHTS

The distribution of the physical book has today given way to the increased sale of publishing rights and the decentralization of production. Over the past few decades the global publishing industry has undergone a process of consolidation and concentration. During this period the profile and structure of the publishing industry has experienced significant change with merger and acquisition deals that have resulted in a number of "global transmedia conglomerates" that include significant book publishing operations within their portfolios.

In addition, there are a number of other factors that indicate that the global publishing business is likely to continue to undergo further structural changes in the next decades. These include developments in delivery systems such as electronic publishing, the growth of "on-demand publishing," and potential improvements in the format of the "electronic book." Digital content and e-learning, for example, are already changing the face of the academic, educational, and scientific, technical, and medical sectors, but not as yet the general or leisure sectors.

At the other end of the scale, the global book industry comprises a large number of small, independent indigenous publishing companies, where the domestic market represents their primary focus and source of titles and revenue. The nature of the book, as a creative and cultural product, is generally less susceptible to standardization than products in other industries, and it is likely that these smaller publishing houses will continue to thrive.

SEE ALSO GERMANY; INFORMATION AND COMMUNICATIONS; TRIBUTE SYSTEM.

BIBLIOGRAPHY

Eisenstein, Elizabeth. *The Printing Press as an Agent of Change.* Cambridge, U.K.: Cambridge University Press, 1983.

Febvre, Lucien, and Martin, Henri-Jean. *The Coming of the Book: The Impact of Printing, 1450–1800,* English trans. David Gerard. London: Verso, 1976.

Finkelstein, David, and McCleery, Alistair, eds. *The Book History Reader.* London and New York: Routledge, 2001.

Jordan, John O., and Patten, Robert L., eds. *Literature in the Marketplace: Nineteenth-Century British Publishing and Reading Practices.* Cambridge, U.K.: Cambridge University Press, 1995.

Rose, Mark. *Authors and Owners: The Invention of Copyright.* Cambridge, MA: Harvard University Press, 1993.

Schiffrin, André. *The Business of Books.* London: Verso, 2000.

Alistair McCleery

BORDEAUX

Bordeaux, the French city located on the left bank of the Garonne, around 50 miles from its mouth, has been a center for maritime trade since the Middle Ages because of its rich wine-growing hinterland. Its international trade history has involved several phases of growth and change. The end of English rule over Aquitaine (1152–1453) modified its trading position, which had previously consisted mainly of exporting wine to England. In the fifteenth century, the sale of Toulouse pastel produced a great deal of prosperity among the merchants of Bordeaux, who started shipping to the New World in the sixteenth century.

In the final quarter of the seventeenth century, the inhabitants of Bordeaux formed relations with the West Indies; the Indian Ocean was off limits until the dissolution of the Compagnie des Indes Orientales in 1769. Beginning in the years between 1730 and 1740, Bordeaux was the main French port used in shipping to the West Indies. The wealth of Bordeaux merchants in the eighteenth century, regarded as a golden age for their maritime trade, was economically connected with the Atlantic. It relied upon selling to the West Indies manufactured goods from northern France and agricultural produce from its rich hinterland, which had been able to adapt its flour and wine to the requirements of the colonies. Imports from the West Indies included sugar, coffee, and indigo. Bordeaux merchants re-exported 80 percent of colonial produce to northern Europe (Amsterdam, Hamburg, and ports in the Baltic). Slave-trading expeditions took place on a regular basis beginning in the 1730s and grew more frequent between 1783 and 1792 (there were 205 slavers during this decade). Although the slave-trade and colonial expeditions (there were 267 shipments in 1785) were restricted to French shipowners via the Exclusif system, foreign agents were essential for the re-export of colonial goods and for the export of Bordeaux wines, which had improved greatly since the end of the seventeenth century. In 1785, 724 foreign vessels came to Bordeaux for these goods. Bordeaux thus had significant communities of merchants (Sephardic Jews from the Iberian peninsula, Germans, Dutch, and Irish), while half of French shipowners were Protestant. The colonial trade made Bordeaux, via its Chamber of Commerce, a staunch defender of the Exclusif system, opposed to the abolition of the slave trade and slavery.

The loss of Saint-Domingue, which became Haiti in 1804, necessitated a number of changes to the trade of Bordeaux; before the French Revolution this island had provided three-quarters of the colonial goods imported to Bordeaux. While trade in wine and colonial goods remained most significant, Bordeaux increased its trade with Africa, which France had colonized from the 1830s onwards, and in the second half of the nineteenth century, Bordeaux also specialized in trade on routes that were little used by steamships (Chile, Argentina, Oceania).

While the overall volume of maritime trade has increased (from 0.7 to 4.2 million tons between 1860 and 1913; 14.4 million tons in 1972, a figure unequaled since), Bordeaux declined compared to Le Havre and Marseille. In those ports, trade has outstripped that in Bordeaux since the 1820s. At the beginning of the twenty-first century, Bordeaux was France's seventh most important port. The makeup of trade changed fundamentally during the course of the nineteenth century and even more so during the twentieth. From being a major international trading post, Bordeaux became a city providing imports supplying the needs of industry, with coal in the nineteenth century and oil in the twentieth century being the main imports. Most wine is transported by rail, road, and even by air; only corn is still moved by ship in large volume, like the wood of the Landes region in the past for the mines of northern Europe.

This transition from an international emporium to a regional port has been accompanied by a decline in the decision-making role of Bordeaux businesses, which have generally been absorbed by larger French or foreign companies. The port of Bordeaux, once at the heart of the town, has gradually been moved outside the city in successive stages, between the mouth of the estuary and Bassens. The city's image is no longer tied up with its port and sea trade. But it retains its reputation for wine: 650 million bottles were sold per year during the 1990s; 40 percent of its production is exported; 1.27 billion euros of wine was sold abroad in 1998. Japan and the United States are its first- and fifth-best customers respectively, amounting to a quarter of the value of wine exports, while the traditional markets of northern Europe account for half of exports.

SEE ALSO AGRICULTURE; CARGOES, FREIGHT; CARGOES, PASSENGER; CHAMBERS OF COMMERCE; CONTAINERIZATION; EMPIRE, FRENCH; FRANCE; FREE PORTS; HAITI; HARBORS; LA ROCHELLE; MARSEILLES; NANTES; PARIS; PORT CITIES.

BIBLIOGRAPHY

Butel, Paul. *Les négociants bordelais, l'Europe et les Iles au XVIIIe siècle.* Reprinted in 1996. Paris, Aubier-Montaigne, 1974.

Figeac, Michel, and Guillaume, Pierre, eds. *Histoire des Bordelais.* 2 vols. Bordeaux: Mollat, 2002.

Saugera, Eric. *Bordeaux, port négrier: Chronologie, économie, idéologie, XVIIe-XIXe siècles.* Paris: Karthala, 1995.

Higounet, Charles, ed. *Histoire de Bordeaux.* Vols. 4–7. Bordeaux: Fédération Historique du Sud-Ouest, 1968.

Silvia Marzagalli

BOSTON

Boston, New England's largest city and the capital of Massachusetts, is a seaport trading center, rail hub, and the oldest continually active major port in the Western Hemisphere. The city's early commercial fortunes were determined by its proximity to the sea. Early settlers of the Boston area became enterprising maritime traders engaged in a vigorous overseas trade. Boston-owned whalers; "slavers" trading with Guinea; ships returning with molasses from the West Indies (for which Massachusetts built distilleries), mahogany from Honduras, and lumber from Maine; and ships carrying salted fish to foreign markets all contributed to a sophisticated maritime economy. Until the ascendancy of New York and Philadelphia in the 1750s, Boston was the primary trading hub of the American colonies, situated on the peninsula closest to Europe of any major colonial city, and endowed with a magnificent natural harbor.

Boston enjoyed robust growth after the Revolutionary War. Though devastated by the British occupation, the city built a new fleet of fast deepwater trading ships, and U.S. vessels were seen around the world from Tripoli to Canton. The merchant and fishing fleets of Massachusetts increased by ten times from 1790 to 1810, but due to foreign trade disruptions associated with the War of 1812, the Boston economy diversified into inland manufacturing. This coincided with the start of the United States' Industrial Revolution, which was centered in areas adjacent to Boston proper. Based on technology and abundant water power for factories, early-nineteenth-century Boston took the lead in the manufacture of textiles, paper, and printing, and became the center of the U.S. shoe and leather industries and the wholesale wool trade.

In the nineteenth century coastwise and domestic traffic surpassed international trade in importance to the U.S. economy. The port of Boston became a center for a vital coastwise trade bringing southern raw cotton and wool, cane sugar, and turpentine northward, and returning finished goods either south or west, or exporting them to Europe. At mid-century Boston's shipyards reached their zenith with the development of clipper ships, the fastest commercial sailing ships ever built.

After the Civil War, Boston's national importance was tempered by other cities. New York, for example, took a commanding lead in the United States' international trade, as well as financial control of many of Boston's local shipping lines. Boston failed to adapt to assembly-line techniques of iron and steam-powered ship construction, and the port went through a period of relative dormancy as production facilities moved closer to raw materials: the textile mills moved south and the leather manufactures west. The decline of traditional shipbuilding in the 1880s marked a change in the character of the waterfront. Railroad companies built huge coal and grain terminals on expanding landfill of South Bay and East Boston. The United States government developed large shipbuilding facilities in the Boston area, backed by enormous railyards, vital to the world wars. In the 1950s Boston lost traditional manufacturing jobs to other states but began to transform itself into a leader in cutting-edge industries. Drawing on the intellectual capital from its fifty colleges and universities, Boston developed such value-added sectors such as electronics, lasers, computer hardware and software, medical devices, imaging, and genomic research. These industries have spawned a revival of the Boston area, and have maintained the city's status as the financial, educational, and economic hub of New England.

The Port of Boston was at the forefront in the use of shipping containers in the transatlantic trade, and by the 1970s containers had become the most common method of transportation in the shipping world. In 2004 the port handled about 13 million metric cargo tons worth nearly U.S.$10 billion. Major transported products include petroleum, liquefied natural gas, automobiles, salt, and scrap metals. Additionally, Boston welcomes over 200,000 cruise-ship passengers every year.

SEE ALSO BALTIMORE; CARGOES, FREIGHT; CARGOES, PASSENGER; CHAMBERS OF COMMERCE; CHARLESTON; CONTAINERIZATION; EMPIRE, BRITISH; FREE PORTS; HARBORS; LOS ANGELES–LONG BEACH; NEW ORLEANS; NEW YORK; PORT CITIES; SAN FRANCISCO–OAKLAND; UNITED STATES.

BIBLIOGRAPHY

Allison, Robert J. *A Short History of Boston.* Boston: Commonwealth Editions, 2004.

Whitehill, Walter, and Kennedy, Lawrence. *Boston: A Topographical History.* Cambridge, U.K.: Belknap Press, 2000.

Peter E. Austin

BOYCOTT

The practice of organized boycotts of specific commodities, firms, and countries was named after Captain

A 1978 poster encourages a consumer boycott of lettuce and grapes. Cesar Chavez, a prominent labor rights figure, led the boycott to draw attention to migrant worker conditions. THE LIBRARY OF CONGRESS

Charles C. Boycott (1832–1897), an English land agent in Ireland who was so ruthless that his employees ostracized him and his family. His employees' action could be described as a *primary* boycott, in which aggrieved employees (and their sympathizers) refuse to buy the products of their employer. A *secondary* boycott targets a third party that has dealings with or is presumed to be sympathetic to the original target of the boycott. A *tertiary* boycott extends the action to other firms that deal with the target(s) of the secondary boycott. Boycotts could be organized by sovereign states or a union of states, and by subnational and nonstate actors to attain particular ends in war and peacetime. Those organized by states could be backed by legislation, while powerful interests, such as multinational firms, could get state actors to initiate or support a boycott. Boycotts usually ended when the goal was accomplished, or when failure was too glaring or continuation too costly. Boycotts are inherently discriminatory and punitive, the aim being to ensure a predetermined outcome.

AMERICAN COLONISTS' BOYCOTT OF BRITISH GOODS

American colonists reacted to the Townshend Act of 1767, which taxed American imports from Britain, by agreeing not to import British goods, especially luxury products. Consequently, British imports dropped by half within a year, and the Townshend Act was repealed, thereby removing all taxes and duties on goods, except for tea. The Tea Act of 1773 provoked the colonists' resentment by giving the British East India Company a monopoly, and it revived the clamor against taxation without representation. Hence, the colonists reacted by boycotting tea, and local patriots attacked three ships in Boston Harbor. On the evening of December 16, 1773, 150 "Sons of Liberty" boarded the ships and dumped forty-five tons of tea into the harbor. The "Boston tea party" was emulated at other seaports, though the British government later imposed stiff sanctions on Massachusetts via the so-called Coercive Acts. But the boycott effectively disrupted British tea exports to America.

INDIAN BOYCOTT OF BRITISH TEXTILES

Since its formal colonization by the British in the mid-eighteenth century, India had provided a huge market for British exports, especially Lancashire textiles. However, apart from the Sepoy Mutiny of 1857, Indians had opposed British rule in various forms up to the onset of middle-class nationalism in the late nineteenth century. The partition of Bengal in 1905 radicalized the nationalist movement and necessitated recourse to a boycott of British textiles as a means of reversing the unpopular measure. Boycott was coupled with *swadeshi* (the promotion of homemade goods), and both had a devastating effect on British textile exports to India. Even after Bengal was departitioned in 1911, Indian nationalists, led by Mahatma Gandhi (1869–1948) after 1920, continued to employ the boycott weapon—coupled with *swadeshi, hartals* (business strikes), and acts of civil disobedience or noncooperation—and this had a long-term effect on the British textile industry, which had lost its major market in India by 1925. In particular, there were job losses and an irreversible decline of what had been a major industry in Britain.

U.S. AND BRITISH BOYCOTT OF MEXICAN OIL EXPORTS

At the beginning of the twentieth century the Mexican government of Porfirio Díaz (1830–1915) had granted foreign oil companies favorable terms for their operations, including rights of ownership of oil deposits and tax concessions. The aim was to attract foreign investment in the oil industry and to develop the economy. But by the 1920s Mexico had come under revolutionary governments that ventilated popular opposition to the unfavorable terms under which U.S. and British oil companies operated in the country. The government sought to earn revenue from taxation on Mexican oil exports, but the foreign companies stoutly resisted such measures, and even intimidated successive governments into acquiescence. By the mid-1920s Mexican oil production declined and the country became a marginal exporter. However, the discovery of the Poza Rica oil fields in 1930 increased the stakes, and the government of Lázaro Cárdenas (1895–1970), armed with the Expropriation Law of 1936, sought to claim its rights of ownership to the oil fields. In 1935 it successfully negotiated a settlement with the British oil company, El Aguila, by which the company agreed to pay taxes ranging between 15 and 35 percent of production. But U.S. oil companies were unyielding.

Eventually, on March 18, 1938, Cárdenas announced the nationalization of the Mexican oil industry. Diplomatic relations between Mexico and Britain were severed, and U.S. and British firms spearheaded a boycott of Mexican oil and an embargo of exports to the country. The Mexican oil industry and the country's oil company, PEMEX, faced hard times, although internal demand and exports to the Axis powers mitigated the impact of the boycott. Moreover, as oil became scarce during World War II, the United States and Britain abandoned the boycott of Mexican oil exports. Meanwhile, Mexico had embarked upon import-substitution industrialization to deal with the embargo of imports of industrial goods. Eventually, in 1942, Mexico reached an agreement with the foreign oil companies at a cost of $130 million. The boycott had robbed Mexico of foreign investment, access to markets, loans, and oil technology, and slowed down the pace of the reform program of the Cárdenas government. But Mexico succeeded in securing control of its oil industry.

ANTI-ISRAEL ARAB BOYCOTT

With the impending creation of the State of Israel, a boycott was formally declared against it by the Arab League Council on December 2, 1945. Arab countries were enjoined to "refuse to deal in, distribute, or consume Zionist products or manufactured goods." After 1948 the boycott consisted of a primary boycott of direct trade between Israel and the Arab nations; a secondary boycott of companies that traded with Israel; and a tertiary boycott of firms which traded with other companies that did business with Israel. The boycott was meant to isolate Israel from its Arab neighbors and the wider world in order to undermine its military and economic strength.

It largely succeeded in isolating Israel, especially from its nearest markets, but it did not undermine Israel's economic and military strength to any great extent,

largely because the U.S. Congress in 1977 prohibited U.S. companies from joining the Arab boycott on the grounds of the defense of free trade. In any case, there were divisions among the Arabs themselves, and the Taba Declaration of February 8, 1995, signed by Egyptian, U.S., Jordanian, and Palestinian trade leaders, endorsed "all efforts to end the boycott of Israel." Israel's peace agreements with the Palestine Liberation Organization and Jordan further weakened the boycott. The primary boycott has been breached by Qatar, Oman, and Morocco, but Saudi Arabia, for example, continues to comply.

ANTI-PEPSI BOYCOTT IN BURMA

Since gaining independence from Britain in 1950, Burma (now Myanmar) has been mainly under authoritarian rule. Hopes that civil rule would be entrenched were dashed with the annulment of the 1990 election won by Aung San Suu Kyi (b. 1945), and the tightening of military dictatorship by the State Law and Order Restoration Council (SLORC). Hence, a boycott of foreign firms still doing business with the regime was organized to stop foreign investment in the country until civil rule was restored. The soft drinks giant PepsiCo was a target of a major boycott organized by the All Burma Students' Democratic Front (ABSDF), which was founded by refugees who had fled SLORC's student massacres in 1988.

Local and international groups combined to pressure the company, especially with the use of the internet, cartoons, analyses and news in the media, flyers, and stickers to carry the campaign to the shareholders and university communities in North America and Europe. U.S. states and cities consequently passed selective purchasing laws that excluded companies with ties to Burma from contracts and other business opportunities. At Harvard University the students succeeded on April 8, 1996, in denying PepsiCo a $1 million contract. Eventually, on May 31, 1997, PepsiCo formally announced that it had cut all ties to Burma. Although it did not result in the restoration of democratic rule, the ouster of a major multinational company was a major accomplishment of the democracy movement in Burma.

SEE ALSO ANGLO AMERICAN CORPORATION; ARMS, ARMAMENTS; BURMA; CUBA; DEBEERS; EMPIRE, BELGIAN; EMPIRE, BRITISH; GATT, WTO; GERMANY; INDIA; IRAN; JAPAN; LEOPOLD II; MEXICO; NATIONALISM; OPEC; PEMEX; ROOSEVELT, FRANKLIN DELANO; SLAVERY AND THE AFRICAN SLAVE TRADE; SMUGGLING; TEA; TOBACCO; UNITED KINGDOM; UNITED STATES.

BIBLIOGRAPHY

Brown, Jonathan C., and Knight, Allan, eds. *The Mexican Petroleum Industry in the Twentieth Century.* Austin: University of Texas Press, 1992.

Chatterji, Basudev. *Trade, Tariffs, and Empire: Lancashire and British Policy in India, 1919–1939.* Delhi: Oxford University Press, 1992.

Chill, Dan. *The Arab Boycott of Israel.* New York: Praeger, 1976.

Jayne, Catherine. *Oil, War, and Anglo-American Relations: American and British Reactions to Mexico's Expropriation of Foreign Properties, 1937–1941.* Westport, CT: Greenwood Press, 2000.

Lintner, Bertil. *Outrage: Burma's Struggle for Democracy.* Edinburgh: Kiscadale, 1995.

Prittie, Terence, and Nelson, Walter. *The Economic War against the Jews.* London: Corgi Books, 1977.

Puth, Robert C. *American Economic History,* 2nd edition. Chicago: Dryden Books, 1988.

Victor, Barbara. *The Lady: Aung San Kyi, The Nobel Laureate and Burma's Prisoner.* Boston and London: Faber and Faber, 1998.

Ayodeji Olukoju

BRAZIL

Brazil is one of the world's only countries to be named for a trade good, which is appropriate because few other countries have been so much created by the world economy. Brazilwood, used for dye, first attracted European interest in the region, but its boom was brief and its harvest difficult. The first boom and bust that was already declining by 1600 led Brazilians to perceive foreign trade as a brittle foundation upon which to build the national economy, and indeed some Brazilians became leading theoreticians of "dependency theory," which warned of the dangers of opening to the world economy. But a closer and longer-term inspection of Brazil's participation in the world economy reveals a complex, dynamic relationship.

EARLY FOREIGN TRADE

Foreign trade arrived only with the Portuguese after 1500. The indigenous subsistence producers who occasionally engaged in barter exchanges did not attract the first Portuguese to Brazil: in 1500 Pedro Alvares Cabral (1467–1520) spent ten days exploring the area, then set about his mission to Asia, never to return to Brazil. The king of Portugal awarded the new land as a commercial monopoly to a New Christian (former Jews who converted to Christianity) company that wanted to exploit its dyewood through coastal trading posts. For the first thirty years of the sixteenth century the only export was brazilwood, which was collected in private coastal trading posts. Native Tupi traded logs for European wares. However, when the French vied for the dyewood trade and control of Brazil, it became clear to the Portuguese that they needed settlements and another trade good to secure

Brazil and, in turn, the South Atlantic and the Cape of Good Hope route to Asia. They transferred sugar production to Brazil from their African colonies such as São Tomé, and by the end of the 1500s Brazil was the world leader in sugar growing. Although still an expensive luxury because of high transport costs, the market for sugar widened beyond the elite in the 1600s. Sugar's primary destination was Europe via Portugal, but a large trade with Africa also developed. Brazilian sugar, rum, and tobacco, carried sometimes in Brazilian-built ships, bought slaves. Eventually Brazil would import some 40 percent of all the Africans brought across the Atlantic, approximately 3.6 million by 1852, when the Atlantic trade was outlawed. So profitable did the sugar and slave trades become that the Dutch seized major sugar-growing areas in Brazil's northeast between 1623 and 1654. After leaving Brazil, the Dutch transferred sugar technology and the slave trade to the Caribbean, which began to out produce and undercut Brazil, further reducing the price of sugar and stimulating consumption.

The decline of sugar was compensated for by the discoveries of gold and then diamonds in the interior of Brazil after 1695. There followed the world's first great gold rush in the first half of the eighteenth century. Over 300,000 Portuguese immigrants stimulated the internal and external markets. Brazil provided more than half the world's supply of gold in the seventeenth century. Even as gold began to run out toward the end of the century, sugar, cotton, and cacao gave Brazil a substantial trade surplus with Portugal, which still officially had a monopoly on Brazilian trade (despite rife contraband). Indeed, by some measures the colony was richer per capita than the mother country. Researchers have discovered that prosperity was due not only to exports—there was also a dynamic internal economy.

RISE OF COFFEE

Brazil's ports were thrown open in 1808 when prince regent Dom João VI (1767–1826) was forced to flee from Portugal to Brazil ahead of Napoleon Bonaparte's troops. After Brazil gained independence in 1822, high imports continued while exports faltered, causing trade deficits. Then a new crop came to the rescue—coffee. Although it had been growing in Brazil already for 100 years, coffee only became an important export in the nineteenth century after a slave rebellion in Haiti nearly halted what had been the world's leading coffee-exporting producer. By 1832 Brazilian coffee exports surpassed sugar; five years later coffee accounted for one-half of all exports, and by the end of the century, two-thirds. Total Brazilian coffee exports jumped seventy-five-fold between 1822 and 1899, which helped world consumption grow more than fifteen-fold in the nineteenth century. By 1850 Brazil was

Teatro Amazonas, a grand opera house in Manaus, Brazil. *Work on the opera house was completed in 1896, when Manaus was a bustling trade center for goods harvested from the rainforest, especially rubber.*PHOTOGRAPH BY SUSAN D. ROCK. REPRODUCED BY PERMISSION.

producing over half the world's coffee. Indeed, about 80 percent of the expansion of world coffee production in the nineteenth century occurred in Brazil alone. As Brazil had previously done with sugar and gold, it stimulated worldwide demand for coffee, transforming it from a drink for the elite to a beverage for the masses. By 1900 coffee was the world's third-most-valuable internationally traded good, and Brazil produced most of it. In 1906 it produced almost five times as much as the rest of the world combined. Brazil's dramatic surge in production of Amazonic rubber between the 1870s and 1912 also revolutionized world rubber usage, particularly by making bicycle and then automobile tires widely available. Coffee and rubber, combined with cotton exports especially in the period 1863 to 1872 and cacao after 1898, gave Brazil trade surpluses from 1861 to 1955. The real value of total trade grew sixfold between 1822 and 1900, while the population quadrupled in that same period. Despite these impressive numbers, it is likely that the domestic economy grew even faster than the external sector as railroads, telegraph, electricity, and factories began to

tie together the growing urban population. The abolition of slavery in 1888 further intensified market relations.

Brazil's trade partners and the composition of international goods also changed. From Portugal in the colonial period, Brazil turned to Britain in the first half of the nineteenth century. Imports, which were mostly finished goods and machinery, continued to come mostly from the United Kingdom, with important French, German, and Belgian contributions. Exports, primarily coffee and later, rubber, began to flow to the United States by the 1840s. Beginning during World War I, Brazil also turned primarily to the United States for imports. The export boom, development of transportation and communications, and the almost sevenfold growth in population between independence and World War I, stimulated import-substitution industrialization.

Although Brazil's domination in almost all of the boom products did eventually go bust, coffee was a notable exception, in good part because of state intervention. Officially, Brazilian government officials subscribed to free trade after independence, but demands of the treasury forced import and export taxes. Duties on imports grew so that by the early twentieth century they were some of the highest in the world. Public involvement in the international market was particularly striking in the coffee trade, where first the state of São Paulo (1906) and then the federal government engaged in price-support schemes, warehousing, and financing of the trade. Government involvement in commerce continued after 1930 when the export oligarchy's grip on the state weakened as import-substitution policies erected import barriers and exchange controls to privilege the industrial sector. Coffee continued to dominate exports into the 1960s when the International Coffee Organization (ICO) was created as an outgrowth of the earlier Inter-American Coffee Agreement. Brazil's leadership position was sustained by this international price-support system. Since the ICO's demise in 1989, Brazil has continued to be the world leader, though its share of world production has fallen to around 25 percent.

This apparent continuity masks the fact that Brazil's external sector has been radically transformed. Exports as a percentage of GNP fell steadily because of the rapid growth of the domestic economy, financed in good part by foreign borrowing; today exports account for only about 7 percent of total production of goods and services. Coffee is responsible for only 5 percent of total exports because of diversification. Brazil is still a major player in world trade as a leader in soy and orange exports through giant agro-industrial corporations. Brazil also exports semifinished goods such as steel, as well as sophisticated industrial products such as automobile parts, airplanes, and audio equipment. Where manufactured exports accounted for only 2 percent of Brazil's total in 1960, they had risen to 37 percent by 1980 and 41 percent in 2000. The surge of capital-intensive exports has allowed Brazil to expand its capacity to import fifteenfold since 1900, and sixfold in just the thirty years since 1970. It also diversified its trade partners, turning more to Western Europe, Latin America, and Japan while conducting less than a quarter of its trade with the United States.

A prosperous export sector, heavily assisted by the state, has helped make Brazil the world's eighth-largest economy. But despite the government's neoliberal policies since the 1980s directed at increased opening to the world economy, Brazil was in 2000 the second-least trade-dependent country in the world (*Economist* 2001, p. 30). This is certainly not an outcome dependency theorists would have predicted. Yet they were not completely wrong: along with its giant cities and factories, Brazil has the world's largest foreign debt incurred from state-led attempts at industrialization, and one of its most unequal distributions of wealth, two consequences of which are its giant urban slums and the extreme violence in them.

SEE ALSO Bahia; Coffee; Conquistadors; Cotton; Empire, British; Empire, Dutch; Empire, Portuguese; Gold and Silver; Gold Rushes; Lisbon; MERCOSUR; Pharmaceuticals; Portugal; Rio de Janeiro; Rubber; Slavery and the African Slave Trade; Sugar, Molasses, and Rum; Textiles; Tobacco; United Kingdom; United States; West India Company, Dutch.

BIBLIOGRAPHY

Baer, Werner. *The Brazilian Economy: Growth and Development*. Westport, CT: Praeger, 2001.

Dean, Warren. *Brazil and the Struggle for Rubber*. New York: Cambridge University Press, 1987.

The Economist. "Pocket World in Figures, 2001." London: Profile Books, 2001.

Schwartz, Stuart. *Sugar Plantations in the Formation of Brazilian Society, Bahia 1550–1835*. New York: Cambridge University Press, 1985.

Topik, Steven. *The Political Economy of the Brazilian State, 1889–1930*. Austin: University of Texas Press, 1987.

Steven Topik

BRETTON WOODS

Following the introduction of a new system of exchange-parity values in December 1971 (the Smithsonian Agreement), U.S. President Richard M. Nixon (1913–1994) hailed the outcome as the "most significant monetary agreement in the history of the world." In reality, this was the final attempt by the international community to shore up the fixed but adjustable par-value system, which had served the world since its inception at Bretton Woods, New Hampshire, in July 1944. Within fifteen months of the Smithsonian Agreement, most countries had moved to floating exchange rates and with this, one of the central tenets of the 1944 international monetary settlement had been lost. Of course, the Bretton Woods Conference encompassed more than an agreement on fixing exchange rates. Two institutions that were established at the conference, the International Monetary Fund and the World Bank, live on to this day. However, even with the passing of the fixed-exchange rate era and despite calls for the reform of the Bretton Woods institutions, sixty years of hindsight suggests that the outcome of the three-week conference held at Bretton Woods was both more important for the world and had greater longevity than any other international monetary conference before or since.

The ideas behind Bretton Woods were conceived in the interwar years when inflation, depression, mass unemployment, trade wars, and political instability had produced economic devastation across the globe. Few

Plenary session of the United Nations Monetary Conference in Bretton Woods, New Hampshire, July 4, 1944. *Delegates from forty-four countries turn their attention to Senator Charles W. Tobey, R-NH, the speaker in center background.* PHOTOGRAPH BY ABE FOX. AP/WIDE WORLD PHOTOS. REPRODUCED BY PERMISSION.

had realized that the economic landscape would change so dramatically after World War I and that the cornerstone of international economic policy, the gold standard, would be the prime culprit of the chaos. The sharp inflation that accompanied the postwar boom in 1918 led to a scramble to return to gold, as it was believed that this would restore prewar order and stability. It was not to be. There was only limited economic cooperation among the major powers, and in particular there was now sharp rivalry between the key financial centers of London, Paris, and New York. Moreover, increasing restrictions on trade, payments, and resource flows, together with less flexibility in domestic price systems, made it more difficult for adjustments to take place. Most importantly, cost and price relationships between countries had been so distorted by the war and the subsequent violent inflation in Europe that it was extremely difficult to determine equilibrium exchange rates in such volatile conditions.

The disintegration of the gold standard in the 1930s was followed by managed exchange-rate systems and autarkic regimes.

World War II galvanized policy makers in the United States and the United Kingdom to consider how to strengthen the international economy in general and the international monetary system in particular when the hostilities ceased. One of the most undesirable consequences of the gold standard was that some countries accumulated surpluses on their balance of payments and others accumulated deficits. When a country had a balance-of-payments deficit, it was required to reduce its domestic money base. The British economist John Maynard Keynes (1883–1946) in particular wished to avoid the deflation associated with this adjustment mechanism, which would produce a decline in national income and a rise in unemployment. In his original plan for an international clearing union, those countries with a balance-of-payments surplus would provide credits to the deficit countries through the clearing union. This was deemed unacceptable to the United States (the country with the largest surplus). Instead, the U.S. economist Harry Dexter White (1892–1948) proposed the establishment of an International Stabilization Fund and an International Bank for Reconstruction and Development (IBRD). The former would maintain stable exchange rates and provide finance for deficit countries and thereby prevent members from having to deflate their economy and the international economy. The latter would provide credits for postwar reconstruction and long-term loans for development; it became known as the World Bank.

The discussions in the early 1940s were not confined to the United States and the United Kingdom; they also involved the Soviet Union, China, the free French, and a number of British Commonwealth countries. In April 1944 it was agreed that an International Monetary Fund (IMF) should be established. It was agreed at a pre-conference in Atlantic City, New Jersey, in mid-June that the United Nations Monetary and Financial Conference to be held at Bretton Woods in July would legally establish the IMF and the World Bank. At Bretton Woods, White presided over a commission on the setting up of the IMF, and Keynes took responsibility for the World Bank.

The outcome of the Bretton Woods Agreement was for the most part in favor of the United States, although the Americans did make some concessions to the British. However, Keynes's ideas for a clearing union were dropped or partitioned off to separate institutions such as the World Bank and an International Trade Organization (which came to nothing). Broadly speaking, the Articles of Agreement, which came out of the conference, contained three main features.

First, every member of the IMF had to establish a par value for its currency and to maintain it within a 1 percent margin on either side of the declared par value. Although currencies were treated equally in the articles, Article IV defined the linchpin of the system as either gold or the U.S. dollar (the fixed price of gold was $35 per ounce). As the United States was the only country that pegged its currency in terms of gold, all other countries would fix their parities in terms of dollars and would intervene to monitor their exchange rates within 1 percent of parity with the dollar. In the event of a "fundamental disequilibrium" with the balance of payments, the parity could be changed only if the fund member had consulted with other members (Article IV, Section 5). The phrase "fundamental disequilibrium" was never defined, and it later proved to be a source of contention among some members. The escape clause differed from that of the

gold standard because countries were not expected at a later date to return their currencies to the original parity. Secondly, under Article VIII, members were expected to make their currencies convertible for current account transactions, but were allowed a three-year transitional period to achieve this (Article XIV). Capital controls were allowed (Article VI, Section 3), and members had to avoid discriminatory currency and multiple-currency arrangements. Thirdly, the IMF could help finance members with short- or medium-term payment difficulties and issue sanctions against countries with large surpluses. The rights of members to draw on the fund, along with their contributions and voting powers, were based on members' quotas. The world share the member country had according to national income, international trade, and international reserves decided each quota. The quota would be paid by gold or U.S. dollars (25%) and the member's own currency (75%). Although members could draw on their quotas at will, stringent conditions were attached to further borrowing beyond the existing allotments. At the outset, the total fund was set at $8.8 billion and could be raised every five years by a majority vote. For those countries that ran a large surplus, the IMF was able to invoke the scarce-currency clause (Article VII). Members would then have to adopt exchange controls on imports and other current-account purchases from the surplus country.

The required number of countries ratified the treaties, creating the two organizations at the end of 1945, and by the summer of 1946 they had begun operation. Although it would be wrong to attribute the success of post-1945 international economic relations solely to the Bretton Woods institutions, they undoubtedly played their part in facilitating trade liberalization and the expansion of economic growth. The IMF's central function of maintaining fixed-nominal exchange rates persisted until 1973, but it has continued to act as crisis manager and international lender of last resort. Although the growth of private capital flows since 1946 has marginalized the original remit of the World Bank, it has continued to evolve, and it is currently separated into five agencies.

SEE ALSO Churchill, Winston; International Monetary Fund (IMF); Keynes, John Maynard; World Bank.

BIBLIOGRAPHY

Aldcroft, Derek H., and Oliver, Michael J. *Exchange Rate Regimes in the Twentieth Century.* Northampton, MA: Edward Elgar, 1998.

Bordo, Michael D., and Eichengreen, Barry, eds. *A Retrospective on the Bretton Woods System: Lessons for International Monetary Reform.* Chicago, IL: University of Chicago Press, 1993.

Horsefield, John K. *The International Monetary Find, 1945–1965: Twenty Years of International Monetary Cooperation,* Volume 1: *Chronicle.* Washington, D.C.: International Monetary Fund, 1969.

James, Harold. *International Monetary Cooperation since Bretton Woods.* Oxford, U.K.: Oxford University Press, 1996.

Scammell, William M. *International Monetary Policy: Bretton Woods and After.* London: Macmillan, 1975.

Michael J. Oliver

BRISTOL

Until the end of the Hundred Years' War (1453), most of Bristol's trade had been to Gascony, then an English possession. At Bordeaux, English woolen cloth was exchanged for wine, salt, and woad (a plant used to make a blue dye). After the loss of Gascony, Bristol merchants diversified their interests, increasing their trade to Spain and Portugal over the next century. In an attempt to expand their markets, Bristol merchants also financed voyages of exploration during this period—the most famous being John Cabot's 1497 voyage to North America.

In the seventeenth and eighteenth centuries Bristol was a major center for the emerging Atlantic economy. This included a "triangular trade" that connected Europe, West Africa, and the Americas. This trade involved the export of manufactured goods, such as cloth and firearms, to West Africa. These were used to buy African slaves for shipment to plantations in the Americas. The sugar and tobacco produced on these plantations was then taken back to England for processing and consumption.

During the eighteenth century Bristol's shipping industry became a byword for efficiency, while its merchants were renowned for their solid business practices. Nevertheless, by the early nineteenth century the port was in decline. Despite the construction of a great "floating harbor," the river Avon proved unable to accommodate the largest ships of the day. In the late nineteenth century the city responded to this problem by building docks on the Bristol Channel itself, which were linked to the city by railway. Nevertheless, the high costs of both operating these docks and dredging the Bristol Channel made it difficult for the city to compete with lower-cost ports. As a result, Bristol gradually lost out to other ports, such as Glasgow, Liverpool, and Southampton.

Although the city center docks finally ceased to be used for commercial purposes in the mid-twentieth century, the processing of some old colonial products, such as tobacco, continued in Bristol. New growth was provided by high-technology industries, including aerospace, film media, computing, financial services, and tertiary education. The development of these sectors has meant that, at the start of the twenty-first century, Bristol has again become one of Britain's most prosperous cities.

SEE ALSO CANADA; CARGOES, FREIGHT; CARGOES, PASSENGER; CHAMBERS OF COMMERCE; CONTAINERIZATION; EMPIRE, BRITISH; FREE PORTS; GLASGOW; HARBORS; LIVERPOOL; LONDON; PORT CITIES; SLAVERY AND THE SLAVE TRADE; UNITED KINGDOM.

BIBLIOGRAPHY

Dresser, Madge, and Ollerenshaw, Philip, eds. *The Making of Modern Bristol.* Tiverton, U.K.: Redcliffe Press, 1996.

Morgan, Kenneth. *Bristol and the Atlantic Trade in the 18th Century.* Cambridge, U.K.: Cambridge University Press, 1993.

Sacks, David H. *The Widening Gate: Bristol and the Atlantic Economy, 1450–1700.* Berkeley: University of California Press, 1991.

Evan Jones

BRITISH-AMERICAN TOBACCO

The foundation of the British-American Tobacco Company in 1902 marked an important shift in the history of the international tobacco industry. Trade in tobacco leaf, either in raw or semiprocessed state, began with the colonization of America by Europeans in the sixteenth century, and tobacco became a staple product of international trade in the early modern period. Relatively little long-distance trade occurred in the final product as purchased by consumers. The onset of industrial production in the nineteenth century, however, created urban lifestyles and working patterns that encouraged new, more convenient forms of consumption. In the tobacco industry, this new demand was ultimately satisfied by the development of cigarettes. To begin with, these products were handmade, luxury goods, but with the development of more advanced forms of mechanization, cigarettes emerged during the last two decades of the nineteenth century as articles of mass production. From this base was built the tobacco multinationals of the modern era.

The first firm to successfully exploit the potential of the mass-produced cigarette was the American Tobacco Company, formed through a process of amalgamation in 1890 by the self-made business tycoon James Buchanan Duke (1856–1925). Recognizing the potentially global market for this type of tobacco product, Duke hired salesmen to promote his cigarette brands extensively throughout North and Central America, Europe, Asia, Australasia, and southern Africa. Between 1891 and 1901 the proportion of the company's cigarette sales accounted for by exports rose from 11.1 percent to 36.7 percent. This success often bred resentment among local manufacturers of tobacco products, which characterized the Americans as foreign invaders and lobbied their national governments to introduce protective tariffs. Duke's company responded to such moves by setting up production facilities directly in the markets concerned, often through the acquisition of one of the leading local tobacco firms. Thus the tobacco industry provides one of the earliest examples in which manufacturing firms used foreign direct investment as a strategic response to overcome government controls on their export trade.

In Great Britain, American Tobacco's success in promoting its products through an import agency led the leading cigarette manufacturer, W. D. & H. O. Wills, to draw up plans to form a rival British-based business enterprise incorporating the combined forces of a group of leading national firms. When Duke responded to a rise in the tariff on cigarette imports by buying control of the Liverpool-based firm of Ogden's in 1901, the management of Wills carried out its plan and drew together thirteen of Britain's leading tobacco manufacturers under the banner of the Imperial Tobacco Company (of Great Britain and Ireland). After a year of commercial conflict, Imperial and American Tobacco called a truce and drew up an agreement to stabilize the market. In essence, the two companies agreed to limit their own spheres of operation to their national markets, and jointly formed the British-American Tobacco Company to handle their business in the rest of the world. Because it surrendered brand rights to British-American in worldwide markets, this agreement created numerous complexities regarding international brand ownership when the American Tobacco Company was forced to divest its shareholding in British-American by the U.S. antitrust authorities in 1911.

Although the British-American Tobacco Company began its life as an enterprise wholly owned by American Tobacco (67%) and Imperial (33%), it nevertheless was granted a great deal of operational autonomy, controlling its own export factories in Britain and the United States and managing foreign subsidiaries in countries such as Canada, Australia, South Africa, Germany, and Japan. When the company was forcibly ejected from Japan in 1904, its export trade was focused on developing the huge potential for cheap machine-made cigarettes that existed in China. By 1913 over 10 billion cigarettes were being exported to China annually from Britain and the United States combined, and these sales were supplemented by local production facilities within the Chinese Treaty Ports and hinterland. Between 1921 and 1941 around 40 percent of all cigarettes produced by British-American were sold in China.

The international growth of British-American's production system had implications for the trade in leaf, too. Locating factories abroad meant that shipments of flue-cured Virginia leaf from the United States were now required to support foreign production, and British-American set up the Export Leaf Tobacco Company to handle this business. Increasingly, however, in large markets such as China, Brazil, and India, the company helped to facilitate local cultivators to produce the leaf that their factories required. The Indian Leaf Tobacco Development Company was a subsidiary concern that British-American initially used to develop leaf production for its own needs, but it eventually began to export leaf tobacco on its own account, helping the Indian economy to become a significant exporter of flue-cured leaf tobacco from the mid-1920s.

Britain's exports of cigarettes grew rapidly during the 1920s as British-American sought to expand the number of markets in which it operated, particularly in Latin America. Exports were used to build up the business in different countries until a market was sufficiently established to support local manufacturing. Following the Great Crash of 1929, however, this export trade fell off markedly, although it recovered well after the World War II. For British-American as a whole, the 1930s and 1940s were a difficult period during which growth in volumes was sustained mainly by reducing profit margins. During these years the company became more focused on its individual operations in the less industrialized regions of the world, although important developments were put in place in Germany and the United States, where it had purchased the Brown & Williamson Tobacco Corporation in 1927.

The importance of cigarettes and tobacco goods as a source of tax revenue meant that British-American tended to cultivate close links with governments in many of the countries in which it operated. Although this served their interests well in the short run, in the longer term it often meant that the company was aligned with regimes that fell out of favor in the postcolonial climate of the 1950s and 1960s. The China market was lost following the Communist Revolution, and significant problems were experienced in countries such as Egypt, India, and Indonesia. Moreover, a number of tobacco firms who had previously refrained from extensive international activity began in the 1950s to expand into British-American's markets. In Latin America, for example, R. J. Reynolds, American Tobacco, and Liggett & Myers began to set up licensing agreements to produce their international brands. The growth of a global marketing media in the 1960s helped to promote this type of pan-national product, exploited particularly adeptly by Philip Morris with Marlboro and Rothmans International with

Dunhill. Having built up its reputation with brands that tended to be country-specific, British-American found it difficult to compete effectively with this new type of product strategy.

As with all the leading cigarette-manufacturing companies, faced with adverse publicity following the disclosure of evidence linking tobacco consumption with lung cancer, in the 1960s British-American began to engage in a strategy of diversification. The company became active in other consumer products, paper manufacturing, retailing, and, later, financial services. The strategy helped to reduce the company's orientation towards less-developed economies, but it ultimately fell victim to the late 1980s trend away from conglomerates as financially credible forms of business. During the 1990s the company refocused itself as a dedicated tobacco company, taking advantage of the collapse of Communism to expand its activities in Eastern Europe and China. In 1998 the company divested its financial-services arm and, shortly after, merged with Rothmans International to place itself within touching distance of Philip Morris as the world's leading cigarette manufacturer.

BIBLIOGRAPHY

Cochran, Sherman. *Big Business in China: Sino-Foreign Rivalry in the Cigarette Industry, 1890–1930.* Cambridge, MA: Harvard University Press, 1980.

Corina, Maurice. *Trust in Tobacco: The Anglo-American Struggle for Power.* London: Michael Joseph, 1975.

Cox, Howard. *The Global Cigarette: Origins and Evolution of British American Tobacco, 1880–1945.* Oxford, U.K.: Oxford University Press, 2000.

Kluger, Richard. *Ashes to Ashes: America's Hundred-Year Cigarette War, the Public Health, and the Unabashed Triumph of Philip Morris.* New York: Alfred A. Knopf, 1996.

Howard Cox

BROWN FAMILY

Based in Providence, Rhode Island, a succession of Brown family members headed mercantile firms that were active in international trade for over a century, beginning with James in the 1720s and ending in the 1830s. In the colonial era their ships conducted trade mainly with Caribbean islands and along the northern coast of South America. Exports consisted mainly of tobacco, horses, spermaceti candles, flour, and salted meats. The return cargoes were primarily sugar and molasses, supplemented by coffee and cocoa. To process traded goods, the Browns established in their home port a slaughterhouse, a candle-making shop, and a distillery. An iron plantation outside Providence—where ore, timber, and water were readily available—produced bars for the near-

by coastal trade and for shipment to Great Britain. Return cargoes from the mother country were mostly fancy goods. A few vessels carried slaves from Africa to the Western Hemisphere, but after Moses Brown became an outspoken critic of the institution of slavery, the family's involvement in the African trade ceased.

After American independence, the firm expanded its horizons by participating in the tea trade to China. Their vessels sailed eastward to Canton and stopped along the way at ports in the Atlantic Ocean, India, and the Dutch East Indies. In the early nineteenth century, the firm became more active in the transatlantic trade to Europe, with port destinations from the Baltic to the Mediterranean. Meanwhile, voyages to Surinam (Dutch) and other countries in Latin America continued.

The Browns were early investors in the U.S. cotton textile industry. In the 1790s, in a cooperative venture with Samuel Slater, a recent immigrant from England with knowledge of the new technology, the firm built a water-powered spinning mill in Rhode Island. In the 1840s the family withdrew from their overseas mercantile activities and concentrated its efforts on textile manufacturing. In the realm of philanthropy, the Browns spearheaded the creation of a local, prominent university that bears the family name.

SEE ALSO NEWPORT; SHIPS AND SHIPPING; UNITED STATES.

BIBLIOGRAPHY

Hedges, James. *The Browns of Providence Plantation: The Nineteenth Century.* Providence, RI: Brown University Press, 1968.

Perkins, Edwin J. *The Economy of Colonial America.* New York: Columbia University Press, 1988.

Edwin J. Perkins

ISAMBARD KINGDOM BRUNEL
1806–1859

Born at Portsmouth, England, a year before Robert Fulton launched his steamboat on the Hudson River, Isambard Kingdom Brunel was the inspired engineer who founded transatlantic travel by iron steamship. His three amazing steamships—each bigger, better, and more original than the last—were the *Great Western*, launched in 1837 to be an extension of his Great Western Railway from London to Bristol; the *Great Britain*, built in 1843 of riveted iron plates and fitted with the first propeller so used, as well as paddle-wheels; and the *Great Eastern*, launched at Bristol in 1858.

Bigger than the average liner a century later, the *Great Eastern* was too far ahead of her time, and a commercial failure. Brunel died of nervous strain before her maiden voyage to New York in June 1860.

The *Great Eastern* was built large to carry the coal needed in a world without coaling stations and, unlike most ships, could hold all the cable, fuel, food supplies, and technical staff required for laying a transatlantic cable. The Telegraph Construction and Maintenance Company bought her after Cyrus Field, the American promoter of the transatlantic cable venture, met Brunel by chance on a train. After several failures, the *Great Eastern* laid the first cable across the Atlantic in September 1866.

A great engineer of the Victorian age, Brunel applied the British development of rolling mills, steam hammers, coke furnaces, and the iron-puddling process in constructing iron steamships with screw propellers.

SEE ALSO SHIPPING LANES; SHIPPING, TECHNOLOGICAL CHANGE.

BIBLIOGRAPHY

Bowen, Frank C. *A Century of Atlantic Travel, 1830–1930.* Boston: Little, Brown; London: Sampson Low, Marston, 1930.

Dugan, James. *The Great Iron Ship.* New York: Harper and Brothers, 1953.

Fishlock, Trevor. *Conquerors of Time: Exploration and Invention in the Age of Daring.* London: John Murray, 2004.

Gordon, John Steele. *A Thread Across the Ocean: The Heroic Story of the Transatlantic Cable.* New York: Perennial, 2003.

Pudney, John. *Brunel and His World.* London: Thames and Hudson, 1975.

Vaughan, Adrian. *Isambard Kingdom Brunel, Engineering Knight-Errant.* London: John Murray, 1997.

J. F. Bosher

BULLION (SPECIE)

Gold and silver have played an important role in international trade since ancient times as raw materials for works of art and coins. Ultimately, the roles played by gold and silver in international trade were derived from their physical properties. Gold, the most malleable of all metals, can be worked into exquisite jewelry using simple tools. It may well have been the first metal worked by man. Gold is also chemically inactive, so objects made of it are likely to survive for long periods of time, justifying intense working, and also making it a good choice for cooking and eating utensils. Silver is similar to gold: it is malleable, chemically inactive, and beautiful. These physical properties also made gold and silver natural choices for coins. The high value of gold and silver in the decorative arts, moreover, meant that coins made of these metals would have some credibility in international trade, even when the private firms or governments that issued them lacked authority. Coins could be melted down and sold as the raw material for works of art, and gold and silver plate could be melted down and minted into new coins. Indeed, prior to the nineteenth century people may have thought of their total monetary assets as the value of the sum of their plate and coins, rather than as the value of their coins alone. Gold and silver were, in short, ideal choices for means of payment in international transactions. The earliest known coins are said to have been made at Lydia in Greece in the seventh century B.C.E. of electrum, a naturally occurring alloy of gold and silver. Many other commodities have been used as money—tea, cowrie shells, tobacco, and so on, but none were as widely used as gold and silver.

By the end of the Middle Ages merchants had perfected the bill of exchange to conserve the use of precious metals in international transactions. Nevertheless, until the twentieth century gold and silver played a unique role in settling accounts. Wars confirmed and enlarged the special role of the precious metals. Traditional trading relationships were strained, and military expenditures including the hire or mercenaries often had to be paid for with precious metals.

The development of gold or silver coins (together known as specie) with outstanding reputations facilitated international trade. Florence first issued its famous gold florin in the thirteenth century, and it soon won an international reputation for reliability of weight and fineness. Venice's gold ducat of the same weight was first issued at about the same time. The ducat circulated widely in Europe and the Middle East, and was widely imitated. Shakespeare made reference to the ducat in plays with foreign settings, reflecting the coin's international use and renown. Hamlet, for example, says when he kills Polonius: "How now? A Rat? Dead, for a ducat, dead!" (Hamlet III, iv, 23). In fact, Denmark minted a fine gold coin called the ducat.

Silver coins also circulated internationally. The term *dollar* derives from a German silver coin, the *joachimstaler,* first struck in the sixteenth century and known colloquially as the *thaler.* In the United States during the colonial period silver pesos, usually Mexican, circulated throughout the colonies and were known as dollars. The U.S. dollar that was introduced after the American Revolution was modeled on the peso. Silver pesos were popular in many other parts of the world, for example in China. In the nineteenth century the United States minted a so-called "trade dollar." This coin contained a bit more silver than the standard U.S. dollar, and was in-

Gold bars. *Coins and bars made from precious metals were the base unit of trade in much of the Western world until the 20th century; now, some investors consider bullion to be a hedge against fluctuations in national currencies.* © CHARLES O'REAR/CORBIS. REPRODUCED BY PERMISSION.

tended to challenge the peso, particularly in the China trade.

BIMETALLIC SYSTEMS

Although the first coins were made of an alloy of gold and silver, the two metals generally have been kept separate and have had an uneasy relationship. Many monetary systems have utilized both gold and silver coins in what is called a bimetallic system. There are two advantages to such a system. First, in a bimetallic system coins can cover a wider range of values. Gold can be used for high-valued coins; silver for low-valued coins. A second, and more important advantage of a bimetallic system is that it provides a better chance of avoiding deflation. If the supply of one metal fails to provide sufficient growth in the money supply to maintain a stable price level, the other metal may be able to do the job.

The "bimetallic ratio," the ratio of silver to gold in the basic monetary unit, was a crucial variable in a bimetallic system. In the system established in the United States after the American Revolution, for example, the silver dollar was defined as 371.25 grains of silver and the gold dollar was defined as 24.75 grains of gold, creating a bimetallic ratio of 15:1. If the market ratio in another part of the world differed, it may have paid to export one metal and import the other, according to Gresham's Law. In our example, if the ratio of silver to gold in Europe was 16:1, it might pay to export gold from the United States and import silver. The 24.75 grains of gold in the gold dollar, when exported to Europe, could be converted into 396 grains of silver (16 x 24.75), which would be worth $1.07 in the United States when converted into silver coins. The process of exporting gold and importing silver would be costly, but if the foreign ratio was high enough, arbitrage would pay. It was often hard in practice, because of these flows, to maintain both gold and silver in circulation simultaneously. Although this was not a fundamental weakness, it did undermine confidence in bimetallism and create shortages of certain denominations of coins. There was a tendency, moreover, once the bimetallic system had tipped toward gold (the more valuable and therefore more prestigious metal) to prevent it from tipping back toward silver by closing the mint to silver.

ECONOMICS OF MONETARY SYSTEMS

The discovery of new mines sometimes had a profound effect on monetary systems, price levels, and the countries in which the mines were found. The gold and silver that poured into Spain after the discovery of the New World provided revenues for the expansion of the Spanish Empire and set in motion a long period of rising prices in Europe known to historians as the Price Revolution. The discovery of gold in California in 1848 and the subsequent discoveries in Australia launched a long period of rising prices and a long economic boom. And at the end of the nineteenth century the development of gold fields in South Africa and other parts of the world produced a long period of rising prices in those countries that adhered to the gold standard. Even the largest discoveries of gold and silver, however, did not produce inflations of the scope that have occurred from time to time under paper-money regimes.

Until the end of the eighteenth century it was difficult for governments to maintain the value in circulation of token coins—that is, coins with face values greater than the market value of the metals they contained. One of the main problems was that coins could be easily counterfeited, and would be if their legal value exceeded the value of silver, copper, or other metal they contained. Toward the end of the eighteenth century, however, machinery was developed that produced coins that were hard to counterfeit. It was then possible to have a currency that consisted of gold coins for large denominations and international transactions and token coins for smaller transactions. England adopted this system in 1816. The availability of token coins for smaller transactions and the prestige of Britain led to the spread of the gold standard throughout much of the developed world during the second half of the nineteenth century. The heyday of the gold standard was the period from 1879, when the United States adopted the gold standard after the Civil War era of paper money, and 1914, when many countries left the gold standard as a result of the outbreak of World War I. An attempt to reinstitute the gold standard was made in the 1920s, and a modest role for gold was created under the Bretton Woods system. It was not until the final abandonment of the link between the dollar and gold in 1973 that there was finally a world monetary system in which neither gold nor silver played a significant role. The time since then is unique in human history.

SEE ALSO GOLD AND SILVER; GOLD STANDARD; MINING; MONEY AND MONETARY POLICY.

BIBLIOGRAPHY

Craig, Sir John H. M. *The Mint: A History of the London Mint from AD 287 to 1948.* Cambridge, U.K.: Cambridge University Press, 1953.

McCusker, John J. *Money and Exchange in Europe and America, 1600–1775: A Handbook,* 2nd revised edition. Chapel Hill: University of North Carolina Press, 1992.

Redish, Angela. "The Evolution of the Gold Standard in England." *The Journal of Economic History* 50, no. 4. (December 1990): 789–805.

Rockoff, Hugh. "Some Evidence on the Real Price of Gold, Its Cost of Production and Commodity Prices" and "Reply to Barro." In *A Retrospective on the Classical Gold Standard, 1821–1931,* ed. Michael D. Bordo and Anna J. Schwartz. Chicago: University of Chicago Press, 1984.

Sargent, Thomas J., and Velde, Francois R. *The Big Problem of Small Change.* Princeton, NJ: Princeton University Press, 2002.

Watson, Andrew M. "Back to Gold—and Silver." *The Economic History Review,* new series 20, no. 1 (April 1967): 1–34.

Hugh Rockoff

BUNGE AND BORN

Bunge and Born is a multinational agribusiness, linked by financial, commercial, and industrial operations to more than eighty countries on all continents. The total wealth and influence of the company is difficult to evaluate because it operates under various names, including Bunge and Born, Bunge and Company, and Bunge Limited, and includes dozens of affiliates, often privately owned and secretly linked to the parent company. It markets 10 percent of the world's grains, is one of the largest food processing companies in South America, and supplies one-third of the world's edible oils. Bunge Limited, the U.S. company, had revenues of U.S.$14 billion in 2003.

La Sociédad Bunge y Cía originated in 1818 in Amsterdam, and in 1851 moved to Antwerp. Bunge transported and stored Russian, U.S., Canadian, and Argentine grain. In 1876 Ernesto Bunge settled in Buenos Aires, leaving his younger brother, Eduardo (1851–1927), to direct the Antwerp company. Profitable investments in the trade of colonial profits underwrote the South American venture. In Argentina, Ernesto Bunge purchased productive agricultural and pasture lands. In 1880 he founded Banco de Tarapaca y Argentina, which in 1925, under the name Anglo-South American Bank, was the largest foreign bank in Buenos Aires. In 1884 Ernesto Bunge associated with his brother-in-law, Jorge Born, to establish Bunge and Born. In 1897 two German merchants, Alfredo Hirsch and Jorge Oster, brought additional capital and expertise to the company's expanding grain business. By 1900 Bunge and Born, together with three other companies, controlled the Argentine grain trade.

In the twentieth century Bunge and Born invested in manufacturing, first in Argentina and then in Brazil.

BUNGE LIMITED

Bunge Limited became a public company listed on the New York Stock Exchange in 2001; it is one of the oldest companies listed on the exchange. It employs more than 25,000 people in 32 countries. It is:

• The world's largest oilseed processor
• The world's largest seller of bottled vegetable oil
• The world's largest corn dry miller
• The largest manufacturer and seller of fertilizer
• The largest exporter of soy products in Asia
• A leading biodiesel producer

Source: www.bunge.com

Bunge and Born survived the stigma of their German affiliations during World War I and expanded rapidly in the 1920s in the international trade of cotton fibers and seeds, the production of cotton and sunflower oils for animal feed and human consumption, and the manufacture of flour, vegetable oils, and textiles.

Bunge and Born (Argentina), Bunge and Company (London), Bunge Corporation (United States), and Bunge (Antwerp), continued to expand during the 1930s. Despite depressed grain prices, the organization purchased more U.S. storage facilities and ships and expanded Argentine textile production. Argentina's high import tariffs favored Bunge and Born's vertical diversification in vegetable oils, paints, enamels, and dyes, with parallel expansion into Brazil, Peru, and Uruguay. Grain exports remained the core business, and in the 1930s Bunge and Born exported more than 30 percent of Argentine grains.

World War II favored industrialism in South America, but postwar political developments and market conditions within Latin America determined the direction of Bunge and Born investments. The adverse policies of Juan Perón (1895–1974) in 1946 in Argentina led to a shift of resources to Brazil, where, after 1945, Getúlio Vargas encouraged foreign investment in food processing, textiles, chemicals, pesticides, fertilizers, and soybeans. Liberal economic policies in Peru between 1948 and 1968 attracted Bunge and Born investments. With the exile of Perón in 1955, Bunge and Born expanded investments in Argentine chemical and textile factories. Military control in Brazil from 1964 to 1986 assured Bunge and Born's position as a major exporter of soybeans and related products. The 1976 Argentine military coup provided Bunge and Born opportunities in the petrochemical industry. By 1979 Bunge and Born companies in Argentina controlled 42 percent of the domestic food sector, 36 percent of the chemical industry, 11 percent of textiles, 8 percent of packing, and 8.1 percent of cereal exports.

In the 1970s Bunge Limited was a grain merchant handling from 10 to 15 percent of the U.S. grain exports, but by the 1980s it was one of the three largest U.S. producers of soybean oil. It has continued its diversification in the food industry. In August 2001 it sold 20 percent of its shares on the New York Stock Exchange. The European operations of Antwerp and London remain important financial centers for Bunge and Born, and they trade with former British, Belgian, and French colonies.

From 1884 until the 1930s Bunge and Born, Buenos Aires, and Bunge y Cía, Antwerp, were legally independent. The death of Eduardo Bunge in 1927 in Antwerp shifted power to Argentina. Financial decisions and global strategy resided in families: Ernesto Bunge in Antwerp and Bunge, Born, Oster, and Hirsch in Argentina. By the 1940s there were four geographical centers of operations: Bunge and Born S.A. (Argentina, Brazil, Paraguay, Panama, Peru, and Uruguay), Bunge Sociédad (Belgium, France, Germany, Spain, and Switzerland), Bunge and Company of London (Australia, South Africa, and Japan), and Bunge Limited (United States, Canada, and Venezuela). Family members of diverse nationalities sat on the boards of directors of both private and public companies to promote a global strategy while allowing company autonomy.

On September 19, 1974, the Montoneros, an Argentine leftist guerrilla movement, kidnapped Juan and Jorge Born. To obtain release of the two brothers, Bunge and Born paid a ransom of U.S.$60 million and distributed $1.2 million in food and clothing to the Argentine poor. This shocking event led the Bunge, Born, and Hirsch families to transfer headquarters to São Paulo, Brazil.

In 1989 Bunge and Born provided the Argentine government of Carlos Menem (b. 1930) with its first two economic ministers. Involvement in politics and lackluster company performance led to dissatisfaction among the family members. They hired a professional manager, who sold money-losing businesses in Argentina and Brazil, and refocused on agribusiness in grains and oilseeds. In 1994 the members of the principal families—Bunge, Born, Hirsch, Engels, and De la Tour—replaced the previous ownership system, which consisted of individual shareholders holding investments in the various Bunge companies, with the Bermuda-registered Bunge International, in which family members currently hold shares.

In 1999 Bunge and Born transferred its company headquarters from São Paulo to White Plains, New York.

SEE ALSO AGRICULTURE; ARGENTINA; BANKING; BRAZIL; CHICAGO BOARD OF TRADE; FINANCE, INSURANCE; IMPORT SUBSTITUTION; POPULATION— EMIGRATION AND IMMIGRATION; RUSSIA; TEXTILES; UNITED KINGDOM; WHEAT AND OTHER CEREAL GRAINS.

BIBLIOGRAPHY

Bryne, Harlan. "Global Agribusiness Goliath Bunge Ltd. Feeds the World and Nourishes Stockholders." *Barron's* 82, no. 42 (October 21, 2002): 20–21.

Green, Raúl, and Laurent, Catherine. *El Poder de Bunge & Born (Power of Bunge and Born)*. Buenos Aires, Argentina: Legasa, 1988.

Kandell, Jonathan. "Argentine Ransom Is Put at $60 Million." *New York Times*, June 21, 1975.

Kilman, Scott. "Bunge Increases Grain Position with Bid of $830 Million for Cereol." *Wall Street Journal*, July 22, 2002, Eastern edition.

Schvarzer, Jorge. *Bunge & Born: Crecimiento y diversificación de un grupo económico (Bunge and Born: Growth and Diversification of a Company)*. Buenos Aires, Argentina: CISEA: Grupo Editor Latinoamerico, 1989.

Smith, Tony. "Grain Trader Restores Its Argentine Homestead." *New York Times*, 25 December 2003, Late Edition: W.1.

Vera Blinn Reber

BURMA

Situated on the sea lanes of the Bay of Bengal and wedged between India and China, Burma offers rich opportunities for both overland and maritime trade. Over the last six centuries the country has realized this potential within varying degrees. The volume and direction of Burma's foreign trade have shifted several times, as has the relationship of foreign trade with the domestic economy.

In the fifteenth and sixteenth centuries' relative peace, population growth and the expansion and diversification of agriculture boosted trade. Burma shipped increasing amounts of rice, ceramics, gems, and forest items to the Malayan ports, and became an important site for shipbuilding and repairs, using locally abundant teak. With India, Burma exchanged local products and imports from the east in return for cotton cloth and yarn.

The state played a strong role in early modern trade, levying fees and customs duties, administering royal trade, and farming monopolies of lucrative items. Foreigners, including Indians, Armenians, Persians, other Muslims, and Chinese, controlled external trade after 1600, if not before. A dip in maritime trade in the seven-

Rice exports from Burma, 1855–1998

Thousand metric tons, five-year averages

Year		Year	
1855–1859	225	1925–1929	2,902
1860–1864	337	1930–1934	3,052
1865–1869	361	1935–1940	2,901
1870–1874	636	1950–1954	1,229
1875–1879	770	1955–1959	1,672
1880–1884	921	1960–1964	1,636
1885–1889	947	1965–1969	779
1890–1894	1,245	1970–1974	463
1895–1899	1,209	1975–1979	505
1900–1904	2,042	1980–1984	721
1905–1909	2,234	1985–1989	332
1910–1914	2,379	1990–1994	374
1915–1919	2,136	1995–1998	146
1920–1924	2,365		

SOURCE: Compiled from Schendel (2003); Cheng (1968); Saito and Kiong (1999); Khin Win, *A Century of Rice Improvement in Burma*. Manila: International Rice Research Institute, 1991; B. R. Mitchell, *International Historical Statistics: Africa, Asia & Oceania, 1750–1988*, 2nd ed. New York: Stockton, 1995; J. W. Grant, *The Rice Crop in Burma: Its History, Cultivation, Marketing and Improvement*. Rangoon: Superintendent Government Printing and Stationery, Burma, 1932; David I. Steinberg, *Burma: The State of Myanmar*. Washington, D. C.: Georgetown University Press, 2001.

THE GALE GROUP.

teenth century was later replaced by moderate, steady growth. More rice from the south was diverted to central Burma, and other bulk items such as teak and cutch came to dominate exports.

Raw cotton became precolonial Burma's main item of overland export to Yunnan (in southwest China), supplemented by rubies, amber, jade, and, at times, imported textiles. Burma imported firearms, copper, iron, and silver, and, from the eighteenth century onward, raw silk. Around 1800 overland trade almost matched Burma's maritime trade. Total foreign trade made up only a small share of Burma's precolonial economy, but provided important incentives for commercialization and monetization.

After the establishment of British rule (1826–1886) Burma's economy was geared toward maritime trade. Burma became the world's leading rice exporter (1934–1935: 3.4 million metric tons), sending more than half of its harvest abroad (1930–1935: 63%) and running large trade surpluses. Exports made up between 30 (1901–1902) and 50 percent (1936–1937) of NDP. Great Britain was the largest rice customer (1870–1875: 72%) until higher demand redirected the trade to India (1935–1940: 53%) and other parts of Asia (1935–1940: 31%). The overriding importance of rice for the export trade (1890–1895: 73% of export value) declined over time (1935–

1940: 44%). Teak (1935–1940: 8%) and petroleum (1930–1935: 33%) diversified exports. Largely, Burmese cultivators, Indian Chettiar capital, Burmese, Indian, and Chinese traders, and European exporters controlled trade. These foreigners expatriated profits from trade and investments. Manufactures dominated imports. Reliance on trade was felt severely during the Great Depression, when plummeting rice prices plunged Burmese cultivators into crisis.

World War II and the Japanese occupation interrupted Burma's trade links. Sustained fighting and scorched-earth tactics inflicted considerable damage. The new Burmese government (1948) nationalized the rice trade and the timber industry and converted the Burma Oil Company into a joint venture. Exports fell to 20 percent of GDP by 1958/1959 and continued to be mostly primary products. Imports were tightly regulated, but attempts at import substitution failed to stimulate new industries.

From 1962 to 1988 a military government pursued nationalist and socialist economic policies, making foreign trade into a state monopoly. Official trade was halved between 1961/1962 and 1968/1969. It climbed in the early 1980s but fell back below 1961/1962 levels by 1988/1989. The trade deficit widened to 40 percent of imports that year, and exports made up less than 4 percent of GDP. Rice exports declined to about 500,000 tons (1990/1991), and other primary items (forestry, minerals, marine products) gained a larger export share. Import controls marginalized consumer goods and fostered smuggling. Asian countries remained Burma's main trading partners.

A new (1988) military regime proclaimed an interest in free-market economics and foreign trade and investment. However, many export items, such as rice, teak, petroleum, gas, and precious stones, remained state monopolies. Exports more than quadrupled between 1987/1988 and 1994/1995. Subsequently, export growth continued, but more slowly. Imports rose roughly eightfold from 1987/1988 to 1999/2000. As the trade deficit reached 59 percent of imports in 1997/1998, the state restricted imports, which, in turn, slowed export growth. Official exports account for less than 1 percent of GDP. Agricultural exports gained in importance until 1995, after which rice exports declined and textile exports increased. In 1999/2000 primary goods, including marine products, still made up almost 60 percent of exports. Consumer goods accounted for 40 percent of official imports. The structure of trade had changed little, reflecting Burma's failure to develop its economy. Much trade in imported consumer items and Burmese timber and narcotics is conducted illegally and not registered.

SEE ALSO Bangladesh; Bengal; Drugs, Illicit; East India Company, British; Empire, British; Entrepôt System; Import Substitution; India; Indian Ocean; Rice; Socialism and Communism; Women Traders of Southeast Asia.

BIBLIOGRAPHY

Adas, Michael. *The Burma Delta: Economic Development and Social Change on an Asian Rice Frontier, 1852–1941.* Madison: University of Wisconsin Press, 1974.

Aye Hlaing. "Trends of Economic Growth and Income Distribution in Burma, 1870–1940." *Journal of the Burma Research Society* 47, no. 1 (June 1964): 89–148.

Booth, Anne. "The Burma Development Disaster in Comparative Historical Perspective." *South East Asia Research* 11, no. 2 (July 2003): 141–171.

Cheng Siok-Hwa. *The Rice Industry of Burma.* Kuala Lumpur: University of Malaysia Press, 1968.

Lieberman, Victor B. "One Basin, Two Poles: The Western Mainland and the Formation of Burma." In *Strange Parallels: Southeast Asia in Global Context, c. 800–1830,* Vol. 1: *Integration on the Mainland.* Studies in Comparative World History. Cambridge, U.K.: Cambridge University Press, 2003.

Longmuir, Marilyn Violet. *Oil in Burma: The Extraction of "Earth-Oil" to 1914.* Bangkok, Thailand: White Lotus, 2001.

Myat Thein. *Economic Development of Myanmar.* Singapore: Institute of Southeast Asian Studies, 2004.

Nishizawa, Nobuyoshi. *Economic Development of Burma in Colonial Times.* Institute for Peace Science, Hiroshima University, Research Report Series, no. 15. Hiroshima, Japan: Hiroshima University, Institute for Peace Science, 1991.

Resnick, Stephen A. "The Decline of Rural Industry under Export Expansion: A Comparison among Burma, Philippines, and Thailand, 1870–1938." *The Journal of Economic History* 30, no. 1 (March 1970): 51–73.

Saito, Teruko, and Kiong, Lee Kin, eds. *Statistics on the Burmese Economy: The 19th and 20th Centuries.* Data Paper Series, Sources for the Economic History of Southeast Asia, no. 7. Singapore: Institute of Southeast Asian Studies, 1999.

Schendel, Jörg. "The Mandalay Economy: Upper Burma's External Trade, c. 1850–90." Ph.D. diss., University of Heidelberg, 2003.

Shein. *Burma's Transport and Foreign Trade, 1885–1914.* Rangoon, Myanmar: University of Rangoon, Department of Economics, 1964.

Walinsky, Louis J. *Economic Development in Burma, 1951–1960.* New York: Twentieth Century Fund, 1962.

Jörg Schendel

BUSINESSMEN AND WOMEN
SEE SEX AND GENDER

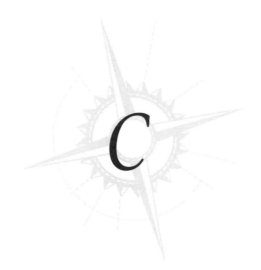

CABOT FAMILY

John Cabot (c. 1450–1499) was a Venetian pilot and merchant active in the Black Sea and Spain. About 1495 he moved to Bristol, England. Like Columbus, Cabot believed that only the Atlantic separated Europe and Asia, which he hoped to reach by sailing to the north. Backed by English merchants and Henry VII's promise of a trading monopoly, he set out in May 1497 on the fifty-ton *Matthew*. Probably following the old Norse route to Greenland, he and his eighteen men reached North America, likely Newfoundland, on June 24, exploring as far as southern Labrador. On their return to Bristol, his crew told of immense stocks of codfish. Cabot's geographic vision and trade estimates convinced Henry to invest in several ships for another voyage, which set sail in 1498, only to disappear. John's son Sebastian (c. 1480–1557) probably made the 1497 voyage with his father and certainly made later voyages to the Americas between 1504 and 1526. After a career as pilot major of Spain, he returned to England in 1548 to act as an advisor to the Muscovy Company. The southern skills in celestial navigation that he brought with him were a key intellectual asset for the new company, which was opening a trade to Russia through the White Sea.

SEE ALSO CANADA; EMPIRE, BRITISH.

BIBLIOGRAPHY

Pope, Peter E. *The Many Landfalls of John Cabot.* Toronto: University of Toronto Press, 1997.

Williamson, James A., ed. *The Cabot Voyages and Bristol Discovery Under Henry VII.* 2nd series, vol. 120. London: Hakluyt Society, 1962.

Peter E. Pope

CÁDIZ

Located on Spain's southern Atlantic coast, Cádiz dates from about 1100 B.C.E., when Phoenician merchants established the port of Gadir on the island of León, forming the southwest side of the Bay of Cádiz. Its residents are still called *gaditanos*. Following Christopher Columbus's 1492 discovery of America, Cádiz's vulnerability to attack led Isabella I (1451–1504) to grant the inland port of Seville a favored position in trade with the New World. Yet Columbus launched subsequent voyages to America from Cádiz, and a piloting school opened there in 1500. In 1509 the Crown authorized fleets for America to leave from Cádiz as an alternative to Seville. The Board of Trade (*Casa de la Contratación*) in Seville established a permanent office (*Juzgado de Indias*) at Cádiz in 1535. The annual fleets carried passengers, supplies, and merchandise to Spain's American kingdoms and returned with gold, silver, cacao, sugar, tobacco, indigo, and other plantation crops. In 1587 Francis Drake (1540?–1596) destroyed many ships at Cádiz. After his defeat of the Spanish Armada in the following year, Cádiz was even more vulnerable, and in 1596 an English-Dutch expedition burned the city. The 100-foot high signal tower (*Torre de Vigía*) is a reminder of the greater fortifications built during the seventeenth century.

Most of the colonial trade used Cádiz by 1680, when the government finally designated it as the principal port for that commerce. Not until 1717, however, did the Board of Trade and Chamber of Commerce (*Consulado*) formally move from Seville to Cádiz. Exports of Spanish wine, olive oil, flour, textiles, and other manufactures were always important to this trade, but by the eighteenth

A painting from 1847 depicts the seafront of the city of Cádiz in southern Spain. *Cádiz, located on a peninsula along the Atlantic Ocean, was a major trading port during the eighteenth century involved with commodities from the Indies and exporting industrial goods across Europe.* © HULTON-DEUTSCH COLLECTION/CORBIS. REPRODUCED BY PERMISSION.

century Cádiz had become the emporium for all of Europe, and its exports included large volumes of textiles and other industrial goods from Italy, France, Britain, Flanders, and Holland. Despite Spain's official policy of excluding foreigners from its colonial trade, foreign merchants in Cádiz engaged (operating through Spanish merchants) in large-scale legal and illegal trade with Spanish America. With the wealth of the Indies flowing through its port, Cádiz in the eighteenth century was a wealthy and prosperous financial center.

Commercial reforms in the eighteenth century, aimed at developing Spain's lagging economy, eventually ended Cádiz's domination of the colonial trade. The Crown chartered colonial trading companies in other Spanish ports, ended the fleet system, encouraged other ports to participate, and replaced Cádiz with La Coruña as the terminus of a new overseas postal service established in 1764. The 1778 Free Trade Act ended altogether Cádiz's monopoly on colonial trade. For a time, the strength of its financial resources, shipyards, and experience in the colonial trade gave Cádiz a competitive advantage, but with the outbreak of war in 1793 its trade plummeted. The British blockaded the port in 1797 to 1798 and bombarded it in 1800.

Cádiz became the seat of Spanish resistance to Napoleon Bonaparte's invading armies in 1810, resulting in the Constitution of 1812, but Spain's colonies abandoned old trade routes in favor of free trade and then won independence. By 1820 Spanish-American privateers were sinking Spanish ships within view of Cádiz and the British were rapidly taking over most of Latin America's commerce. Cádiz became a "free port" in the 1820s, but without the colonial trade its merchant community withered. Cádiz remained a naval center, but the loss of the fleet in the 1898 war with the United States was a further blow to the port. In 1947 an explosion at its naval arsenal caused great damage. Since then, improvement in its port facilities, regional agricultural production, some industrial growth, and passenger cruise calls have contributed to economic growth.

SEE ALSO AGRICULTURE; BARCELONA; CARGOES, FREIGHT; CARGOES, PASSENGER; CHAMBERS OF COMMERCE; CONTAINERIZATION; EMPIRE, SPANISH; FREE PORTS; HARBORS; MEDITERRANEAN; PERU; PORT CITIES; POTOSÍ; SEVILLE; SPAIN.

BIBLIOGRAPHY

Bustos Rodríguez, Manuel, ed. *Historia de Cádiz*, 4 vols. Madrid: Silex, 1991–1993.

García-Baquero González, Antonio, ed. *Comercio y burguesía mercantil en el Cádiz de la Carrera de Indias*. Cádiz: Diputación Provincial de Cádiz, 1991.

Girard, Albert. *La rivalité commerciale et maritime entre Séville et Cadix jusqu'à la fin du XVIIIe siècle*. Paris: E. de Boccard, 1932.

Haring, Clarence H. *Trade and Navigation between Spain and the Indies in the Time of the Habsburgs*. Cambridge, MA: Harvard University Press, 1918. Reprint, Gloucester, MA: P. Smith, 1964.

Stein, Stanley J., and Stein, Barbara. *Silver, Trade, and War: Spain and America in the Making of Early Modern Europe*. Baltimore, MD: Johns Hopkins University Press, 2000.

Walker, Geoffrey. *Spanish Politics and Imperial Trade, 1700–1789*. Bloomington: Indiana University Press, 1979.

Ralph Lee Woodward Jr.

CALCUTTA

The city of Calcutta, or Kolkata as it has been known since the 1990s, is about 100 miles from the sea. Until a High Court judgment in 2003, it was accepted that on August 24, 1690, Job Charnock, an agent of the East India Company, established a British trade settlement on the river Ganga at the site of three villages, Gobindapur, Sutanuti, and Kalikata. The 2003 judgment rules that the city had grown over a period of time and that no fixed date can be established for its birth.

A major outlet in eastern India under the Mughals was at Hooghly, on the opposite bank of the Ganga, where a fleet comprising 400- to 600-ton ships of the Mughal nobility was stationed. In the sixteenth century, Hooghly formed a part of the Indian Ocean trading network, with an effective linking of the land routes and sea lanes as a result of the rise of continental monarchies, such as the Mughal Empire in India, the Safavid Empire in Persia, and the Ottoman Empire in Iraq, Syria, and Egypt (Das Gupta 2001).

In the eighteenth century the picture changed again, with the collapse of the Indian political order and with the growth of European private trade. In 1717 the Mughal emperor granted the East India Company duty-free trade in return for a yearly payment of 3,000 rupees. Though this privilege was meant for the Company's trade to Europe, it was used for the benefit of English trade in general and as a result the Company could undercut its competitors and sell Bengal goods cheaply in the Indian Ocean.

The Calcutta fleet made rapid strides between 1715 and 1740, with both the English and the Dutch increas-ingly employing military force to protect their trade in Bengal and along the Ganga (Das Gupta 2001). In 1772 Calcutta became the capital of British India. It retained this status until 1912, when the capital was moved to Delhi.

The eighteenth century also saw the entry of American ships in the Indian Ocean. These brought mainly Spanish dollars, but also wine, provisions, and naval stores for the European settlements; they took away textiles, pepper, sugar, and jute. Calcutta was an important destination for these vessels, but so was Canton in China. The nature of trade changed, and the agency house in Calcutta became crucial for trade, with profits from trade increasingly depending on successful politics.

After Indian independence in 1947, Calcutta became the capital of the state of West Bengal and changed its role from being primarily a port to being a capital city with a port attached. Dramatic changes in shipping had taken place since World War II with the containerization of trade and the development of intermodal ports, which linked road, rail, and ship in one operation. The Haldia dock complex was commissioned, and facilities at Calcutta port were expanded; these now include oil jetties, a coal-handling plant, and container parking yards. The city is thus poised to participate in the changing trading system.

SEE ALSO AGRICULTURE; CARGOES, FREIGHT; CARGOES, PASSENGER; CHAMBERS OF COMMERCE; CONTAINERIZATION; DRUGS, ILLICIT; EAST INDIA COMPANY, BRITISH; EMPIRE, BRITISH; EMPIRE, MUGHAL; EMPIRE, OTTOMAN; ENTREPÔT SYSTEM; ETHNIC GROUPS, GUJARATI; FACTORIES; FREE PORTS; HARBORS; INDIA; INDIAN OCEAN; MADRAS; PORT CITIES; RICE; SPICES AND THE SPICE TRADE; TAGORE FAMILY; WOMEN TRADERS OF SOUTHEAST ASIA.

BIBLIOGRAPHY

Das Gupta, Ashin. *The World of the Indian Ocean Merchant 1500–1800*. New Delhi: Oxford University Press, 2001.

Pearson, Michael. *The Indian Ocean*. London: Routledge, 2003.

Ray, Rajat Kanta. "Calcutta or Alinagar: Contending Conceptions in the Mughal-English Confrontation of 1756–1757." In *Ports and Their Hinterlands in India, 1700–1950*, ed. I. Banga. New Delhi: Manohar, 1992.

Himanshu Prabha Ray

CANADA

The history of Canada, a large and sparsely populated country, is inextricably linked to its import and export trades. The first exports from what is now Canada were

An idealized illustration of Quebec, Canada's largest province. *Quebec has the third largest freshwater supply in the world, which fuels a healthy and rich supply of natural resources and agricultural production.* THE LIBRARY OF CONGRESS.

cargoes of fish caught by West European mariners during the fifteenth century. The provisioning and the drying of fish for transport to Europe spawned seasonal settlements on shore, and then the first permanent communities on Canada's Atlantic coast. Fishing for export continued to be important for the Atlantic Canadian economy, society, and politics into twentieth century, although the dwindling of fish populations in recent decades has diminished this once-great trade.

The collection and export of animal furs defined the leading edge of European invasion inland during the seventeenth and eighteenth centuries. The Hudson's Bay Company, founded by Royal Charter in 1670 and now the world's oldest chartered trading company, established a network of fur-trading posts along Hudson's Bay and James Bay in the Canadian sub arctic. These posts collected furs in competition with French and mixed-blood traders who traveled by canoe from Montreal to acquire furs from aboriginal communities in the interior of the continent. The buying and export of furs continued to be a principal European interest in the west and north of Canada through much of the nineteenth century. At the heart of this trade were the aboriginal communities, who exchanged furs for goods manufactured in Europe. The Hudson's Bay Company sale of much of its western land in 1870 was a critically important step in the development of Canada.

The export of timber followed close upon the fur trade in forested areas of eastern Canada. Exports of white pine and other forest products for shipbuilding were particularly important to the Royal Navy during the wars with France that followed the loss of Britain's American colonies. Indeed, large numbers of ships built in Atlantic ports were exported. Wood was the first commodity exported in large volumes to the United States, as well as to Britain.

The last export boom to be driven almost exclusively by European demand was that of agricultural products. Ontario farmers shipped considerable quantities of wheat to Europe during the middle decades of the nineteenth century. When lower-cost western grains eroded Ontario's competitive edge in field grains during the final third of the century, farmers took advantage of improvements in transportation and refrigeration technology to launch a successful trade in live beef, cheese, and other livestock products. Eventually, during the early twentieth century, the settling of the prairie provinces contributed to a second surge in wheat export, this time from the west. Many scholars believe that the rapid expansion of western population and economy during the celebrated "wheat boom" of the early twentieth century precipitated a dramatic transformation of Canadian economy and society.

Subsequent export booms increasingly focused on the American rather than the transatlantic market. The fast growth of the U.S. economy and its sizable balance-of-payments surplus from the 1920s to the 1960s contributed to a reorientation of Canadian trade along north-south lines. U.S. companies became the least-cost supplier of a wide range of imports to Canada. At the same time, U.S. investment in Canadian industry and raw-material supply facilitated the growing exports of nickel, pulpwood, petroleum, automobiles, and other new commodities.

The succession of exports may have shaped the character of economy and society more fundamentally in Canada than in other many other countries, but the importance of international trade should not be overstated. In all periods most Canadians worked to provide goods and services for consumption in local and national markets. Indeed, the early appearance of manufacturing to meet local needs contributed to a powerful and relentless pattern of Canadian industrialization.

During the early nineteenth century Canadians imported all but the most rudimentary consumer goods, home furnishings, machinery, metals, and even food from Britain and the United States. Local manufacturers gradually developed an ability to compete with these imports. The earliest success was achieved in the processing of raw materials such as basic foodstuffs, leather, and forest products. The wood-based manufacturing industries employed especially large numbers of artisans and workers.

Politicians and the educated elite monitored and encouraged the gradual evolution of a larger and more diversified manufacturing sector during the second half of the nineteenth century. A steady decline in the transportation cost of importing to Canada and the close proximity to Canadian consumers of the U.S. industrial heartland undoubtedly slowed the expansion and diversification of Canadian industry. In part to offset the effect of transportation change and technological improvements elsewhere, Canadian politicians created subsidies and tariffs to encourage local manufacturing.

Tariffs, or taxes on imports, are of particular interest because they provided the single largest source of revenue for the nascent Canadian state. British North America and the United States agreed to a free exchange of raw materials during the years 1854 to 1866. Abandonment of this "reciprocity treaty" on the eve of the Canadian political union of 1867 set the stage for successive rounds of tariff increases. The raising of protective tariffs in Canada followed, and to some extent was inspired by, the rise of protectionism in the United States. The most important rounds of tariff expansion came in 1879 and in 1887 (in which year protection was extended to primary iron manufacture). A change of ruling party in the 1896 national election led the following year to a discriminatory policy that favored trade within the British Empire.

This system of "imperial preference" for a time facilitated the export of agricultural implements and other goods to Empire markets. Nevertheless, the failure to pay large dividends and the undeniable advantages of trading with a large, prosperous, and close-at-hand neighbor led to abandonment of this policy during the trade depression of the 1930s. Joint planning of production by Canada and the United States during World War II reinforced the trend toward continental integration.

Canada participated in the international movement to reduce trade barriers after World War II. The result was an acceleration of trade and national economic growth not unlike that of many other countries during the 1950s and 1960s. Canada benefited particularly from a movement to continental free trade that began in 1964 with the Canada–United States Auto Pact. The 1988 Free Trade Agreement between Canada and the United States, which committed the two countries to a further lowering of trade barriers, was extended in 1994 to include Mexico. Since that date the Canadian government has continued to establish trade agreements with more and more countries. Increasingly, these agreements govern investment and the trade in services as well as commodity trade.

Not surprisingly, Canada's participation in international trade has continued to increase. By 2000 the value of Canadian imports was roughly 40 percent of gross domestic product (GDP), while exports accounted for more 45 percent of Canadian GDP. In the same year the United States accepted nearly 90 percent of Canadian exports and provided slightly less than two-thirds of imports. Today, more than ever before, the Canadian economic and its continued prosperity relies on international trade and on trade with the United States.

SEE ALSO AGRICULTURE; BALANCE OF PAYMENTS; BARING, ALEXANDER; CABOT FAMILY; CANALS; CARGOES, FREIGHT; CARGOES, PASSENGER; COAL; COLBERT, JEAN-BAPTISTE; CORN LAWS; DEPRESSIONS AND RECOVERIES; EMPIRE, BRITISH; EMPIRE, FRENCH; ETHNIC GROUPS, CANTONESE; ETHNIC GROUPS, FUJIANESE; ETHNIC GROUPS, HUGENOTS; ETHNIC GROUPS, JEWS; ETHNIC GROUPS, SCOTS; FRANCE; FREE TRADE, THEORY AND PRACTICE; FURS; GATT, WTO; GILBERT, HUMPHREY; GOLD RUSHES; GREAT

DEPRESSION OF THE 1930S; INTERNATIONAL MONETARY FUND (IMF); IMPERIAL PREFERENCE; IMPORT SUBSTITUTION; INDUSTRIALIZATION; INTERNATIONAL TRADE AGREEMENTS; IRON AND STEEL; LA ROCHELLE; LABORERS, NATIVE AMERICAN; LAW, COMMON AND CIVIL; MERCANTILISM; MINING; NAFTA; NAVIGATION ACTS; OPEC; PETROLEUM; PROTECTIONISM AND TARIFF WARS; REGIONAL TRADE AGREEMENTS; SHIPBUILDING; STAPLES AND STAPLE THEORY; TIMBER; TREATIES; UNITED STATES; WHEAT AND OTHER CEREAL GRAINS.

BIBLIOGRAPHY

Bothwell, Robert; Drummond, Ian; and English, John. *Canada, 1900–1945.* Toronto: University of Toronto Press, 1987.

Carlos, Ann, and Lewis, Frank. "Marketing in the Land of Hudson Bay: Indian Consumers and the Hudson's Bay Company, 1670–1770." *Enterprise and Society* 3, no. 2 (June 2002): 285–317.

Forster, Ben. *A Conjunction of Interests: Business, Politics, and Tariffs, 1825–1879.* Toronto: University of Toronto Press, 1986.

Forster, Ben, and Inwood, Kris. "Markets and the Industrial Revolution in Ontario Furniture Manufacture." *Enterprise and Society* 4, no. 2 June 2003): 326–371.

Green, A. G., and Urquhart, M. C. "Estimates of Output Growth in Canada: Measurement and Interpretation." In *Perspectives on Canadian Economic History,* 2nd edition, ed. D. McCalla and M. Huberman. Toronto: Copp Clark, 1993.

Hart, Michael. *A Trading Nation: Canadian Trade Policy from Colonialism to Globalization.* Vancouver: University of British Columbia Press, 2002.

Innis, Harold. *The Cod Fisheries: The History of an International Economy.* Toronto: University of Toronto Press, 1940.

Lower, Arthur. *The North American Assault on the Canadian Forest.* Toronto: Ryerson Press, 1938.

McCalla, Douglas. "Forest Products and Upper Canadian Development, 1815–46." *Canadian Historical Review* 68, no. 2 (June 1987): 159–198.

McCallum, John. *Unequal Beginnings: Agriculture and Economic Development in Quebec and Ontario until 1870.* Toronto: University of Toronto Press, 1980.

Norrie, Kenneth; Owram, Doug; and Emery, J. C. Herbert. *A History of the Canadian Economy,* 3rd edition. Toronto: Nelson, 2002.

Ray, Arthur, and Freeman, Donald. *"Give Us Good Measure": An Economic Analysis of Relations between the Indians and the Hudson's Bay Company before 1963.* Toronto: University of Toronto Press, 1978.

Kris Inwood

CANALS

Perhaps as early as 7000 B.C.E. Egyptians, Chaldeans, and probably the Chinese used canals first for irrigation and subsequently for transport of goods. Riparian canalization, that is, canals that took advantage of existing rivers, constituted the first type of canal construction. People dug out rivers to allow for easier movement of "barges," which were initially little more than rafts. Connecting natural waterways was the next natural step in promoting commerce between villages or cities. The primary difficulty these first canal builders encountered was variation in elevation between natural waterways. Rivers naturally flow from higher to lower elevations, but connecting two rivers that were several meters apart in elevation without redirecting one of the rivers was a daunting task. Accomplishing this feat required the invention of a system to lift or lower vessels loaded with cargo as one progressed from one elevation to another. At first this was accomplished by what are referred to as "flash" locks, which amounted to dams used to retain water for raising vessels to higher elevations and to release water to float vessels to lower elevations. Using flash locks was very time consuming, often taking several weeks to move less than 100 kilometers (60 miles).

China's Grand Canal, completed during the thirteenth century, took nearly 600 years to complete the connection between Beijing and Hangzhou. By the twelfth century, 200 years ahead of the Europeans, China had developed the pound lock that is in use today. The Dutch, around 1400, and the Italians, around 1480, developed the pound lock in Europe. The pound lock is a closed container built into the canal, in which a vessel could be floated to a higher or lower elevation by adding water or removing water, respectively. With the gate at the other end shut, a vessel would enter the lock from one end and a gate would shut behind it. Water would be added if the vessel was going to a higher elevation or water would be let out if the vessel was going to lower elevation. One of Leonardo da Vinci's many inventions was the "mitre gate" in 1497. The pressure of the water was employed to force together mitred edges of double gates so that water would not leak out of the lock. Managing an adequate water supply for the canal and lock system was a major problem in the early stages of canal building.

Early canals were built to connect one city to another or to a particular larger body of water such as an ocean. Milan's rise to power as a trading center in the thirteenth century depended on riparian canalization of the surrounding watershed, and pound locks in the fifteenth century gave Milan access to the Po River. The Canal de Briare in 1642, the first modern summit level canal in Europe, was followed by the Canal d'Orleans and Canal du Loing, which created an interlinked transport system connecting the provinces with Paris. Louis XIV's success with the Briare, which employed forty locks to cross a

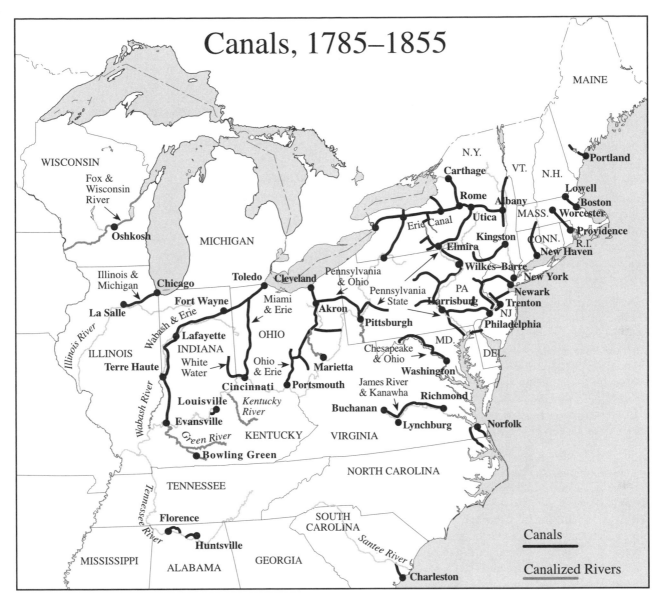

Canals, 1785–1855

MAP BY DONALD S. FRAZIER. THE GALE GROUP.

summit of 281 meters, prompted him to support construction of the Midi Canal from Sète on the Mediterranean to Bordeaux on the Atlantic. This was to provide an alternate route from the Mediterranean to the Atlantic that the British could not control as easily as they did the Strait of Gibraltar. Using 101 locks over 240 kilometers, the Midi was a true ship canal that used lock staircases of up to eight rises, and the first canal tunnel in Europe. It first opened for traffic in 1681 and was completed in 1692.

Both the United States and Britain experienced canal periods before their railroad eras. By 1790 Britain's four major estuaries were linked by canals, and the Forth and Clyde Canal in Scotland provided an alternate route to

avoid the dangerous route around northern Scotland. Manchester, England, became a seaport as a result of a canal built in 1894, the Manchester Ship Canal. The Becquey Program (1820–1850) of canal building provided France with the first waterway network in the Western world. Completion of this program made France the third major country to experience a "canal age" prior to the "railroad age."

In the United States merchants looked inward due to the loss of British markets in the early nineteenth century. The British controlled the Saint Lawrence River, and New Orleans, at the mouth of the Mississippi, was controlled first by the Spanish and then by the French until 1803, when the United States purchased the Louisiana Territory. Finished in 1825 and financed by New York State, the Erie Canal was the most logical route for inland trade: it would connect the Hudson and Mohawk Rivers to Lake Erie. Entering the Great Lakes system south of Niagara Falls gave merchants access to the Midwest and opened up a vast feasible market area for grain production. Eventually, the Detroit River Canal connected Lake Huron with Lake Michigan and the Sault Sainte Marie Canal connected Lake Huron with Lake Superior, providing a shipping route from northern Minnesota to New York City, with off loading from ships to barges required only at the Lake Erie end of the Erie Canal. The Cincinnati and Erie Canal connected the Great Lakes with the Ohio River and, thus, the Mississippi River and New Orleans. These canals opened the heartland of the United States to world trade and enhanced the internal flow of goods.

The Dutch built canals in 1826 and 1876 to expand the port of Amsterdam, and in the latter part of the nineteenth century connected Amsterdam and Rotterdam with the lower Rhine River. In what was to become Germany a set of canals were built by 1750 that formed a cross with Berlin as the center. The Kiel Canal, finished in 1895, connected the Baltic to the North Sea while avoiding the dangerous route around Denmark. During World War I it provided protection for the German fleet as well.

Following up their successes in canal building during the middle of the nineteenth century, the French decided to build the Suez Canal to connect the Mediterranean Sea with the Indian Ocean. Although a predecessor to the Suez Canal had been constructed around 500 B.C.E. connecting the Nile to the Red Sea, it had been destroyed in 767 C.E. Ferdinand de Lesseps (1805–1894), a French engineer, directed the building of the 100-mile, sea-level ship canal, which was finished in 1889. The Suez Canal reduced the time it took to go from Europe to India or any other South Asian port because ships no longer had to travel all the way around the Cape of Good Hope at the southern tip of Africa. De Lesseps soon considered building a canal across the Isthmus of Panama to reduce the shipping time between Atlantic and Pacific ports. Unprepared for the unique engineering challenges and the worker casualties, de Lesseps's company went bankrupt in 1888. After facilitating the independence of Panama from Colombia in 1903, the United States agreed to pay Panama an annual fee for use of the canal and paid France for the right to take over the construction of the Panama Canal, which opened for business in 1914. Not only was the Panama Canal of strategic political value to the United States, but it also increased world trade.

Many canals remain in use today, but alternative forms of transport have replaced canals as a major mode of shipping, especially for higher-value and perishable goods.

SEE ALSO AGRICULTURE; AMSTERDAM; CANADA; CARGOES, FREIGHT; CARGOES, PASSENGER; FRANCE; GERMANY; PANAMA CANAL; SHIPPING, COASTAL; SHIPPING, INLAND WATERWAYS, EUROPE; SHIPPING, INLAND WATERWAYS, NORTH AMERICA; SUEZ CANAL; UNITED KINGDOM; UNITED STATES; VENICE.

BIBLIOGRAPHY

Doolittle, William E. *Canal Irrigation in Prehistoric Mexico.* Austin: University of Texas Press, 1914.

Geiger, Reed G. *Planning the French Canals: Bureaucracy, Politics, and Enterprise under the Restoration.* Newark: University of Delaware Press, 1994.

Hadfield, Charles. *World Canals: Inland Navigation Past and Present.* New York: Facts on File, 1986.

Helpburn, A. Barton. *Artificial Waterways of the World.* New York: Macmillan, 1914.

Hugill, Peter J. *World Trade since 1431: Geography, Technology, and Capitalism.* Baltimore, MD: Johns Hopkins University Press, 1993.

Vance, James E., Jr. *Capturing the Horizon: The Historical Geography of Transportation since the Transportation Revolution for the Sixteenth Century.* Baltimore, MD: Johns Hopkins University Press, 1990.

William K. Hutchinson

CANTON
SEE GUANGZHOU

CANTON SYSTEM

The Canton system was a complex of institutions and practices by which the Qing dynasty (1644–1911) rulers of China controlled, taxed, and facilitated the trade of foreigners at the southern port of Guangzhou, capital of Guangdong province, which the foreigners called *Canton*. The Canton system sometimes is referred to as *cohong* (Mandarin *gonghang),* meaning public or unified firm, but this properly refers only to the phase of the system from 1760 to 1771, when the state forced an amalgamation of all the licensed Chinese merchants into a single trading entity.

Canton and a few other ports were reopened to foreign trade, and to overseas trade in Chinese shipping, in 1684. Modest tariffs on imports and exports and "measurement" charges per ship were adapted from late Ming precedents. Direct official contact with foreigners was minimal. Maritime trade seemed too politically sensitive and potentially lucrative to turn over to already powerful high provincial officials, so special supervisors of mari-

A painting of foreign factories and trading stations located along Canton Harbor in China during the early 1800s. The city of Canton, capital of Guangdong province, is located on a river delta near the South China Sea. After the Opium War (1840–1842), the Treaty of Nanjing opened the port to foreign trade and ended the Canton system. © BETTMANN/CORBIS. REPRODUCED BY PERMISSION.

time customs were dispatched from Beijing. Several of the early inspectors were from the Board of Revenue (*Hubu*), and Europeans came to call this official the *hoppo*. From the 1730s on, all were officials of the Imperial Household Department (*Neiwufu*). Statutory revenue quotas were kept low; by 1800 the surplus, which went straight to the Neiwufu, often was twenty times the quota, equaling the regular tax revenue of an entire province.

Having the government license a limited number of substantial merchants to manage an important and sensitive line of trade was common in China, and could facilitate trade and minimize disputes. For the government, this practice had the additional benefit of making formally powerless merchants responsible for keeping order in the marketplace and for collecting taxes. In 1720 the Canton officials sought to organize a *hong*, or combine of the principal firms to manage the rapidly growing

trade, but backed down when the foreigners protested. European records for the 1730s and 1740s show as many as thirty firms trading with the foreigners in these years, with no clear hierarchy or organization among them. Each foreign ship had assigned to it a "security merchant" responsible for the foreigners' good behavior and the payment of tolls on their trade. This practice received formal imperial approval in 1745.

The steady expansion of foreign trade at Canton from the early 1700s to 1820 or later did much to help integrate the early modern maritime world. It was driven above all by the newly found thirst for tea of peoples around the North Atlantic. All the tea consumed in the eighteenth-century West was Chinese. European buyers at Canton relied on their Chinese counterparts to deliver the quantities, qualities, and varieties ordered; if a batch was found deficient it could be returned for prompt repayment. The Chinese managed these deliveries through a series of market transactions, from cultivator to up-country processor to wholesale merchant to licensed exporter in Canton. Until 1760 or later, 90 percent of the payment for tea and other exports was in silver. Silver imports plateaued thereafter, and continued growth of exports was covered by growing imports of Indian cotton, English woolens (transshipped to the northern and western reaches of the Qing Empire), and opium. Silk, so important in earlier Chinese exports, was less attractive to Europeans as new sources of supply emerged in Bengal, Persia, and eventually in Europe. China exported approximately 30,000 piculs (the Asian trade "hundredweight" of about 60 kilograms) of tea in 1720, 60,000 in 1740, 120,000 in 1765, and 240,000 in 1795.

Some imports and exports were less important economically but very significant in cultural history; for example, elaborate European clocks were much sought after by officials. Europeans at Canton bought large quantities of lacquer, furniture, and other decorative goods, and above all porcelain. Porcelain could be ordered in custom sets, including shapes never seen or used in China, from the great manufacturing center at Jingdezhen. In lively commercial streets near the foreign companies' "factories" (warehouses and living quarters) in Canton, items could be custom-ordered, including family arms or Christian scenes on porcelain. The supplying and victualling of foreign ships and their movements up and down the river channels were very efficiently organized.

From the 1750s on, these remarkable arrangements ran into greater conflict, though trade continued growing. The English had increasing difficulty obtaining security merchants, who were the leading importers of clocks and other treasures for the court, which led court agents to take an unwelcome direct interest in their affairs. From 1755 to 1760 the English attempted to circumvent restrictions and private interest at Canton by trading at Ningbo in Zhejiang, slightly south of the mouth of the Yangtze River. The court and bureaucracy reacted decisively, stifling the Ningbo attempt and issuing regulations making Canton the only port for foreign trade, making licensed merchants there the landlords of the foreigners' "factories" and responsible for every aspect of their conduct, forbidding foreigners to stay in China beyond the trading season, and forbidding Chinese to borrow from foreigners. Finally, all the licensed firms were to negotiate and trade as one unit, a *gonghang* (public firm," Cantonese *cohong*). These changes gave the Chinese vastly increased negotiating leverage, and were hated by the foreigners. In 1771 some massive payments by the English and the efforts of one major Chinese merchant broke the *cohong*; Chinese merchants dealt with the foreigners as individuals thereafter. One collective practice that remained was the regular contributions by the merchants to a fund that aided merchants who got into debt.

Chinese merchants borrowed from the foreigners nonetheless. Their capital was largely locked up in the tea trade, with its long chains of credit to up-country suppliers. Some firms prospered, but several went bankrupt. Officials made conscientious efforts to arrange bankrupts to repay gradually, with the help of contributions by other merchants. For the foreigners, and especially for impatient Englishmen of the age of Adam Smith and a growing empire, the frustrations of the Canton system were emblematic of a corrupt, despotic China whose doors would have to be kicked down. The Canton system was abolished in 1842 by the Treaty of Nanjing ending the Opium War.

SEE ALSO ALCOCK, RUTHERFORD; BALANCE OF PAYMENTS; CHINA; COTTON; DRUGS, ILLICIT; EAST INDIA COMPANY, BRITISH; EAST INDIA COMPANY, DUTCH; EAST INDIA COMPANY, OTHER; EMPIRE, BRITISH; EMPIRE, FRENCH; EMPIRE, MING; EMPIRE, PORTUGUESE; EMPIRE, QING; FACTORIES; FAIRS; FREE TRADE, THEORY AND PRACTICE; GOLD AND SILVER; GUANGZHOU; HONG KONG; IMPERIALISM; JARDINE MATHESON; LIN ZEXU; MERCANTILISM; MONOPOLY AND OLIGOPOLY; NAGASAKI; RICE; SILK; SMUGGLING; TEA; TRIBUTE SYSTEM.

BIBLIOGRAPHY

Dermigny, Louis. *La Chine et l'Occident: Le Commerce à Canton au XVIIIe Siècle (China and the Occident; Commerce at Canton in the Eighteenth Century)*. 3 vols and album. Paris: S.E.V.P.E.N., 1964.

Gardella, Robert. *Harvesting the Mountains: Fujian and the China Tea Trade, 1757–1937*. Berkeley, Los Angeles, and London: University of California Press, 1994.

Morse, H. B. *Chronicles of the East India Company Trading to China*. 5 vols. Oxford, U.K.: Clarendon Press, 1926–1929. Reprint, Taipei: Ch'eng-wen, 1966.

Van Dyke, Paul A. "Port Canton and the Pearl River Delta, 1690–1845." Ph. D. diss., University of Southern California, 2002.

John E. Wills Jr.

CAPITAL FLOWS

The term *capital flows* normally refers to foreign investment—the movement of funds between countries. Capital flows take various forms such as short- and long-term, which refer as much to the nature of the investment as they do to how long the investment is held. There is no precise time period by which short-term capital movements can be measured, but the term usually refers to so-called "liquid funds" that can be easily withdrawn or repatriated to their provider within, for example, twelve months. They may take the form of overseas bank deposits or the purchase of short-dated government or treasury stock offered by a foreign state. Short-term capital flows are sometimes described as "hot" money, which moves around the global economy seeking to maximize income opportunities offered by changing interest rates. Or short-term funds might effectively be trade-related working capital used to finance a commercial transaction or economic activity abroad. By contrast, long-term capital flows—typically to an economic activity with a lifespan of five years or more—is usually represented by investment in securities or physical assets which are likely to have a long gestation period before they become remunerative. In the late nineteenth century, a classic period for investment overseas, infrastructure projects such as railway construction and public utilities were the result of long-term capital flows. Of course, short-term capital flows can effectively become long-term simply by a succession of roll-over loans.

Debtor or borrowing countries welcome flows of finance to close the gap between their domestic investment needs and their own supplies of locally owned funds, especially for capital intensive projects such as railways. Such funds can then be used to finance imports, or for development purposes, or both. Borrowing countries need to import capital because their needs are large but their savings are small, given the poverty of many of their citizens, or because their capital holders are unwilling to invest at home in such projects. Lending countries are able to supply short- and long-term capital from their balance-of-payments surpluses. Individual or corporate savings from economic transactions abroad can be recycled around the international economy and across national borders through financial intermediaries such as banks. Merchant houses operating abroad do not always repatriate their overseas profits, investing instead in the local economy. Equally, official agencies and governments, especially in the twentieth century, provided funding.

An important feature of long-term capital flows is the distinction between portfolio and direct investment. The term *portfolio* normally refers to investment, which the supplier of funds does not control, and the most obvious example is the purchase of government bonds overseas. Borrowing governments are sovereign, and may use the capital raised by selling bonds in any way they like. The bond holder is simply there to take the interest from the bond. Direct investment refers to flows of capital overseas, which the supplier does control and manage. The clearest instance of this is direct foreign investment (DFI) by companies abroad, especially multinational enterprises. In the nineteenth century many of the early flows of long-term capital were deemed portfolio in the form of debt or bonds as the borrowers were sovereign governments, which were regarded (not always accurately) as inherently less risky. Subsequently, direct investment became more important, and now modern analysis accepts that direct investment outweighed portfolio investment before 1913. Mira Wilkins has drawn attention to a particular form of direct investor, the free-standing company. This typically British corporate structure raised equity through the London Stock Exchange for investment in a single project in one overseas country— perhaps a railway in Argentina, for example. A gray area across the divide of direct and portfolio capital is ordinary capital, which carries voting rights, but small, individual shareholders are generally unable to exercise much corporate influence.

SHIFT FROM SHORT- TO LONG-TERM LENDING

Over time the balance between short- and long-term lending has changed. Before the nineteenth century capital flows were likely to be short-term. Merchants and others were unwilling to lock up capital for long periods of time, although they needed working capital abroad to finance trade and to pay for business services such as shipping and insurance. But, given the poor quality of communications with business partners abroad, the slowness of shipping, and the lack of information, few would risk lending large sums over a long term. Indeed, there were few obvious projects which would require such funding.

The nineteenth century, especially after 1850, marked an enormous growth in long-term capital flows. The onset of the steamship, the development of the submarine cable and the telegraph system, and the information revolution of the period, vastly improved communication. Furthermore, the generally favorable growth factors in the world economy opened up many more opportunities for long-term investment in different parts of the world, especially the newly settled areas in the Americas and Australasia. Many of these projects were capital intensive and dependent upon technology transfer, which made overseas financing more necessary. Unlike in the twentieth century, there were few, if any, restrictions on the export of capital in the form of exchange controls or fluctuating currency rates, an aspect of each country's adherence to the gold standard before 1913. By the outbreak of World War I some £10 billion had been invested overseas in the form of long-term capital projects, most notably by the United Kingdom (40%), France, Germany, and, to a lesser extent, the United States. This capital, almost all of it supplied from private-sector sources, reached every continent, although its distribution throughout the world was uneven. The United

A classic British steam locomotive hauls freight wagons across Argentina. The Argentinian people successfully fended off invasions by British forces in 1806 and 1807. Ironically, British investment later helped Argentina develop modern industries through the construction of production facilities, water and electricity systems, and railroads. © COLIN GARRATT; MILEPOST 92 1/2/CORBIS. REPRODUCED BY PERMISSION.

States received by far the largest amount, and in South America it was Argentina that was the major recipient. But the nineteenth century was not without its problems with regard to capital flows. There were the familiar problems of debt crisis and repayment, for example in Latin America in 1825. There were notorious defaulters, especially in South America, and financial intermediaries in the lending countries also were drawn into difficulty. One of the best known is the Baring Crisis of 1890, when that lending house found itself saddled with Argentine loans it could not sell.

After 1913 the flow of long-term capital slowed. World War I, especially her overseas position, had weakened the United Kingdom's economy and this reduced her capacity to supply loans. German and French funds for investment abroad dried up for similar reasons. The French had been burned by the failure of the newly installed Bolshevik government in Russia to honor the tsarist debts raised in Paris. Only the United States was able to lend long on a sizable scale, and even this collapsed after the Wall Street crash in 1929. During the decade of

the 1930s, worldwide economic depression led to exchange controls, balance-of-payments difficulties, and competitive devaluations. These combined to reduce long-term capital flows to a trickle. In turn, borrowing countries found great difficulty in repaying or even servicing loans that they had previously taken on during the 1920s or earlier.

POSTWAR LENDING

After World War II long-term capital flows resumed on a much greater scale. Most of the private funding took the form of direct rather than portfolio investment as multinational enterprises supplied capital overseas. But the second half of the twentieth century marked the great growth of long-term capital from the public sector and from international agencies. Governments of the usual lending countries in Western Europe and North America added to capital investment through aid and other flows to less-developed countries abroad, often former colonies in Africa and Asia, but also to capital-shortage countries in South and Central America. Government capital flows of this sort are often "tied," which means that the borrower has to spend the receipts of the loan or aid in the donor country. International agencies such as the International Monetary Fund (IMF) and the International Bank for Reconstruction and Development (IBRD—the World Bank), both set up at the Bretton Woods Conference in 1944, also supplied capital to the world economy. The IMF provided what might be termed short-term funds to countries with balance-of-payments problems. The World Bank was established with the remit of providing longer-term, project finance. Designed originally to help reconstruct Europe after World War II, it turned more to capital-shortage countries outside Europe when the continent's economic recovery was quicker than expected. In part, this recovery was due to further institutional agency funding of capital flows through the European Recovery Programme, or Marshall Plan, which supplied much-needed dollars for international reconstruction. Again, the postwar period was not entirely clear sailing for overseas investors. Many countries, including the United Kingdom, retained strict exchange controls and a strategy of nonconvertibility, which made the export of capital and the repatriation of profits to foreign investors difficult.

In the last quarter of the twentieth century the relative freedom of international capital flows created something of a paradox. On the one hand, large-scale foreign investment has not always had its anticipated beneficial effects on borrowers because funds have been wasted, leading to sovereign debt crisis among many countries in the less-developed world during the 1970s and 1980s—which, in turn, exposed banks in the Western world to the economic blizzard of debt repudiation. However, such debt burdens were in effect modest compared to those during the nineteenth century. On the other hand, today's capital flows, unencumbered by exchange controls and convertibility problems, contribute to the return to an open and integrated world economy and to twenty-first-century globalization. Firms invest abroad in manufacturing plants to outflank tariff barriers such as those of the European Union. Thus, multinational enterprises, many of them U.S. and Japanese, undertake cross-border movements of capital as a matter of course; moreover, traditional capital suppliers such as the United Kingdom now find themselves the recipients of DFI in the form of foreign-owned plants in, for example, automobile and electronic goods manufacture.

SEE ALSO BALANCE OF PAYMENTS; DEPRESSIONS AND RECOVERIES; FLOWS OF FACTORS OF PRODUCTION.

BIBLIOGRAPHY

Aldcroft, Derek. "The Twentieth-Century International Debt Problem in Historical Perspective." *Journal of European Economic History* 31 (Spring 2001): 173–202.

Cottrell, P. L. *British Overseas Investment in the Nineteenth Century.* London: Macmillan, 1975.

Gould, J. D. *Economic Growth in History: Survey and Analysis.* London: Methuen, 1972.

Kenwood, A. G., and Lougheed, A. L. *The Growth of the International Economy, 1820–2000: An Introductory Text,* 4th edition. London: Routledge, 1999.

Pollard, Sidney. "Capital Exports, 1870–1914: Harmful or Beneficial?" *Economic History Review* 38 no. 4 (November 1985): 489–514.

Stone, I. "British Long-Term Investment in Latin America, 1865–1913." *Business History Review* 42, no. 3 (Fall, 1968): 311–339.

Wilkins, Mira. "Conduits for Long-Term Foreign Investment in the Gold Standard Era." In *International Financial History in the Twentieth Century: System and Anarchy,* ed. Marc Flandreau, Carl-Ludwig Holtfrerich, and Harold James. Cambridge, U.K.: Cambridge University Press, 2003.

Robert G. Greenhill

CAPITALISM

Capitalism is an economic system characterized historically by the private ownership of wealth, market-oriented commercial activity, and a basic socioeconomic class structure. There is no precise definition for capitalism because economists, historians, political scientists, and anthropologists, among others, examine it from varying perspectives. There is general agreement that capitalism refers specifically to the production, distribution, and acquisition of wealth in a market-oriented economy. Capitalism is often defined as a system diametrically opposed to socialism. In the former, wealth is privately owned and markets are relatively free of governmental interference, whereas in socialism the state owns the means of production and directs the national economy.

The emergence of capitalism in Western society can be divided into four eras: feudalism, mercantilism, industrialization, and globalization. In historical perspective, there is an evolutionary progression of capitalism from feudalism through globalization. Full-fledged capitalism is most evident in industrialization and least operative in feudalism. Globalization, unlike mercantilism, is characterized by the increasing transparency of political borders in economic transactions.

PRECAPITALISM

Feudalism and mercantilism are systems historically linked to capitalism but better described by the term *precapitalism.* The feudal system dominated Western society from the fall of the Roman Empire (c. 500 C.E.) until the fifteenth century. In feudalism, a figurehead king oversaw lords or barons who in turn ruled vassals, including

A portrait of Adam Smith (1723–1790), the economist who examined the development of modern financial and economic systems in Europe. Smith is the author of The Wealth of Nations, *a major influence on the growth of capitalism and establishment of economics as an academic discipline. His ideas opposed a system of mercantilism in favor of the capitalistic notions of free markets and private ownership.* © BETTMANN/CORBIS. REPRODUCED BY PERMISSION.

knights, peasants, and serfs. Agriculture was the principal productive activity, but some commerce occurred, such as bartering and trade. Traveling merchants sold their wares in towns or at trade fairs. Merchants offered a variety of goods such as furs from Scandinavia, German beer, and northern European wool for Oriental spices.

The feudal system began to break down as trade increased. Italian merchants, in particular, were geographically well positioned to benefit from commerce between the Near East and Europe. With more business to transact, they developed new financial practices. These included bills of exchange and double-entry accounting. Bills of exchange were signed agreements between the buyer and seller that typically stipulated the price and amount of product per transaction. Double-entry accounting

provided a means for merchants to record their assets and liabilities, or income and expenses.

In Italy these new financial tools coincided with the rise of city-states and the Renaissance. Merchants found it increasingly profitable to become sedentary, and some established counting houses where they conducted business, including banking. Early prominent bankers such as Cosimo de' Medici (1389–1464) also served the Catholic Church and supported it through charity, and they patronized artists such as Michelangelo (1475–1564) and Raphael (1483–1520).

As political power became centralized in emerging national governments, in Italy and throughout Western Europe, merchants and political leaders understood that they shared particular economic interests: power and profit through overseas trade. Between the late fifteenth and early nineteenth centuries, mercantilist philosophy reflected commercial practice and posited that governments should seek a positive balance of trade, protect domestic manufacturing, import raw materials from colonies, and encourage exports of finished products. The beginning of the breakdown of the colonial system, represented by the American Revolution, led to the gradual dismantling of the mercantile system.

INDUSTRIALIZATION AND THE CAPITALIST SYSTEM

Industrialization, capitalism, and liberalism emerged from a similar historical context. This is most evident in the fact that Adam Smith's famous treatise *The Wealth of Nations* was published in the same year that Thomas Jefferson penned the Declaration of Independence. Smith's book postulated that business activity made efficient through the specialization of labor brought wealth to entrepreneurs, and this wealth-generating process benefited society. Consistent with European Enlightenment ideals, Smith noted that political freedom for individuals should be mirrored in freedom for business from government regulation. According to Smith, businessmen benefited from *laissez-faire* (passive) government involvement in economic activity, while allowing the market forces of supply and demand to operate freely. Market forces provided a method of self-regulation, thereby rewarding efficient firms with profit and longevity. Smith's ideas presaged an emerging Industrial Revolution in Great Britain that continued in parts of Europe and blossomed in North America.

Development of the steam engine in eighteenth-century Great Britain stimulated the Industrial Revolution. This technology led directly to the railroad, and nineteenth-century railroad firms required sophisticated engineering, accounting, and managerial practices, making them larger enterprises in scale and scope than any other industrial activity. Although textile mills were the first large businesses in both Great Britain and the United States, the railroad represented the first major capitalist enterprise in the industrial era. As this industry developed in Great Britain, Germany, and the United States, capital markets emerged in order to finance these ventures. The nineteenth-century U.S. railroad industry received substantial investment from British and European investors.

Capital for industrial ventures came from stock and bond sales as well as from bank loans. Banks, in particular, invested heavily in railroad stock, and consequently became the principal investors during much of the nineteenth century. As such, they also received representation on company boards and later developed a network of interlocking corporate directorships. German banks, especially, acquired immense financial and even political power through their financing of German industrialization.

In the early industrial era the pursuit of personal wealth became an increasingly attractive occupation for entrepreneurs and partnerships. Following the establishment of the initial railway and telegraph network, John D. Rockefeller (1839–1937) and Andrew Carnegie (1835–1919) almost single-handedly organized the petroleum and steel industries, respectively. Rockefeller's Standard Oil became the symbol of industrial monopoly as it grew from a small Cleveland refinery operation to an immense corporate structure that dominated the oil refining and transportation business in the United States. Carnegie's steel-production empire was a model of nineteenth-century industrial efficiency. In 1901 the banker J. P. Morgan (1837–1913) arranged for the purchase of Carnegie's steel operations and created U.S. Steel, the first corporation capitalized at more than $1 billion.

Entrepreneurs including Jay Gould (1836–1892), Daniel Drew (1797–1879), and Jay Cooke (1821–1905) focused on financial gain through speculation. The heyday of nineteenth-century capitalism was centered in stock-market ventures pursued by men who used industrialization and capital markets as tools to attain additional wealth. Carnegie himself succinctly articulated the magic of capitalism when he said, "Eureka, here's the goose that lays the golden eggs" upon realizing that a well-placed monetary investment might double or more in value without additional labor on the investor's part.

The coordination of industrial activity during the late nineteenth and early twentieth centuries by bankers and large stockholders marked the emergence of financial capitalism. The New York Stock Exchange in the United States, the Bourse de Paris in France, and the London Stock Exchange became the centers of capitalist activity as aggressive firms marketed and promoted their stocks

to individuals and other corporations. By the early twentieth century stockholders became corporations' primary beneficiaries, as exemplified by the United States Chamber of Commerce's Principle 13 (1924): "The primary obligation of those who direct and manage a corporation is to its stockholders . . . ." Corporate ownership became increasingly divided among numerous shareholders while salaried managers made daily business decisions that determined a firm's profitability.

Free enterprise and industrialization reigned supreme in North America and parts of Europe during the nineteenth and earlier twentieth centuries, but emerging labor organizations and critics of unrestrained economic activity did not remain silent. Karl Marx (1818–1883) was foremost among them. In *The Communist Manifesto* (1848) and *Capital* (1867) he identified social stratification and class conflict as principal evils in the capitalist system, particularly as practiced in Great Britain and Germany. For example, Andrew Carnegie's glorification of investment profit was countered by Marx's concept of surplus value and the exploitation of labor. Thus, Marx described *capitalism* as a socioeconomic system diametrically opposed to *socialism*. Although Marx's prediction of class warfare and revolution did not materialize in Western capitalist society, his trenchant insight attracted many followers and influenced governmental policy, especially in the former Union of Soviet Socialist Republics (U.S.S.R.), throughout Eastern Europe during much of the twentieth century, and in parts of Asia, including China.

The tendency for capitalists to manage their business activity efficiently led to standardization in manufacturing, mass production, and business consolidation. The limited-liability corporation became the most administratively efficient organizational structure for large businesses, and it emerged as the dominant capitalist form by the end of the nineteenth and the beginning of the twentieth century. Corporations were able to accumulate capital through stock issues and loans more efficiently and rapidly than could individual capitalists. In the United States, the New Jersey corporation law of 1889 allowed corporations chartered there to purchase and own stock in companies established in other states. This law encouraged corporations to develop holding-company structures, through which they could control a large number of subsidiaries. An era of corporate mergers ensued.

Eliminating competition through acquisition or forcing a competitor into bankruptcy also provided firms with opportunities for growth. In industries without strong competition, large firms tended to become monopolistic. In the United States, state governments responded to the increasing economic power of large busi-

Microsoft founder Bill Gates (right) talks with Warren Buffet, chairman of Berkshire Hathaway. *Microsoft, the world's largest software company, was at the forefront of technology innovations during the late twentieth century that fueled the growth of capitalism and economic development on a global level. Buffet is another key figure in modern capitalism, a major investor worth billions who focused on the business strategy of long-term growth in companies.* © JEFF CHRISTENSEN/REUTERS/CORBIS. REPRODUCED BY PERMISSION.

nesses by attempting to regulate them. Granger laws of the 1870s to 1880s in various Midwestern states first sought to regulate railroads in the "public interest." Later, Congress passed the Sherman Antitrust Act (1890) authorizing the federal government to enforce restrictions on concentrations of economic power. The federal government initially employed antitrust law against striking labor unions, but later directed it against monopolies such as Standard Oil and American Telephone and Telegraph (AT&T).

Capitalism also prompted workplace efficiency, or the rationalization of labor. "Taylorism," the system of scientific management introduced by Frederick Winslow Taylor (1856–1915) imposed rigid discipline on labor in promoting industrial efficiency, and transformed the human worker at times into a series of carefully measured movements. Henry Ford's utilization of assembly-line production with interchangeable standardized parts ("Fordism") was a prime example of scientific management.

Capitalist activity throughout the 1920s, particularly in Western nations, increased dramatically as the introduction of a wide variety of consumer goods, increasing wages, and credit availability stimulated both production and consumption. However, the international economic crises of the late 1920s, most dramatically evidenced by the Wall Street stock-market crash in October 1929, tempered popular enthusiasm for capitalism. In response to the apparent instability of free markets, the Franklin D. Roosevelt administration greatly expanded the U.S. public sector. The resulting New Deal programs of the 1930s imposed a wide array of federal controls on the economy. With an intellectual foundation established partly by British economist John Maynard Keynes (1883–1946), the United States developed a form of capitalism best described as "managed capitalism," or a "mixed economy," referring to the government's active oversight of a privately owned industrial and commercial sector. The imposition of a national social-security system further contributed to the softening of capitalism's social impact on the elderly unemployed. Government controls became even more pronounced during World War II when the War Production Board in the United States strictly regulated industrial activity in support of the Allied war effort.

During the post–World War II era the U.S. economy continued to expand. Economic strength and stability in these years was due in part to successful managed capitalism. Continuing technological innovation and new and improved consumer products also stimulated both production and consumption. But the 1973 Arab oil embargo provided clear evidence that governments controlling vital resources—Saudi Arabia and oil in this case, and the Organization of Petroleum Exporting Countries (OPEC) cartel generally—could buffet international economies in order to achieve political goals.

In the 1960s through the 1980s free-market economists including George J. Stigler (1911–1991), Alfred Kahn (b. 1917), and Milton Friedman (b. 1912) argued that federal regulations hindered economic vitality, fostered market dysfunction, and did not ultimately protect consumers. A stagnant economy, energy shortages, and inflexible government price regulation provided evidence for their claims. In the United States, Congress agreed, and an era of "deregulation" ensued. In the utility and communications industries, government prompted restructuring to foster competition, and gas pipelines and long-distance telephone lines adopted open-access rules in order to allow a variety of service providers to compete for customers. Deregulation in banking and financial services and the resulting broad assortment of income-producing investments also served as a catalyst for renewed customer competition. Internationally, Britain, France, and other countries began to privatize some state-owned enterprises so that they could compete more effectively.

CAPITALISM IN THE NEW GLOBAL ECONOMY

Globalization is defined generally by the emergence of multinational corporations, government-supported free-trade practices, and increasing opportunities for international socioeconomic contact and exchange. Some of the original multinationals were automobile firms such as Ford Motor Company. Oil companies including Royal Dutch Shell, Standard Oil of New Jersey (Exxon), Standard Oil of California (Chevron), and British Petroleum (BP), among others, developed oil production in Mexico, South America, and the Middle East and became influential in international politics. Large banks and insurance companies became increasingly international in scope. U.S. food and drink companies in many respects most fully represented the globalization movement, as McDonald's restaurants and Coca-Cola became icons of U.S. cultural imperialism and economic dominance.

By the late twentieth century, corporations had become subject to the oversight of powerful nongovernmental institutions. Institutional investors such as pension funds, arbitragers, mutual funds, and insurance companies invested tremendous amounts of capital in publicly owned corporations located worldwide and some institutional investors sought to influence the policies and practices of corporations. Principal among them was the California Public Employees' Retirement System (CalPERS), which held approximately $170 billion by the end of the twentieth century. As significant shareholders and stakeholders, institutional investors employed principles of corporate governance in order to protect their investments and sometimes to pursue particular social or economic agendas.

The invention of the World Wide Web and the resulting boom and bust in internet-company investment was an example of continuing capitalist speculation. It led to both technological innovation and financial collapse. New entrepreneurs and established firms sought to profit from the expected windfall in internet commerce, but the dramatic rise in internet investment far outpaced this new industry's ability to produce a stable return on investment or societal benefits.

Competing visions of economic organization existed at the turn of the millennium. China emerged from centuries of isolation and rapidly embraced certain market-oriented practices while remaining a "Marxist" nation, and privatization of nationalized industries continued in Europe and South America. In Europe, economic cooperation and consolidation in the form of the European Union included a pan-European stock exchange, Euronext, established in 2000 in response to globalization of capital markets. Debates over free trade and protectionism continued, but globalization represented the continuing trend toward international economic efficiency. Mercantilist practices were not entirely erased in the emerging global economy, and interdependence between producing and consuming nations was increasingly characterized by the economic power of multinational corporations.

In the era of globalization, capitalism's tendency toward efficiency and standardization remained divisive and controversial. Blamed for creating social stratification and a permanent underclass, capitalism continues to be accused of brashly spreading Western culture and ideas worldwide. It is also associated with an improving standard of living, technological innovation, and political freedoms. Although the long-term viability of pure capitalism remains unclear, capitalism in some form is likely to persist.

SEE ALSO POLITICAL SYSTEMS.

BIBLIOGRAPHY

Allen, Larry. *The ABC-CLIO World History Companion to Capitalism.* Santa Barbara, CA: ABC-CLIO, 1998.

Hartwell, R. M., and Engerman, Stanley L. "Capitalism." In *The Oxford Encyclopedia of Economic History*, Vol. 1, ed. Joel Mokyr. Oxford, U.K.: Oxford University Press, 2003.

Keynes, John Maynard. *The General Theory of Employment, Interest, and Money.* New York: Harcourt Brace, 1936.

Marx, Karl. *Capital.* 3 vols. Moscow: Foreign Languages Publishing House, 1961, 1962.

McCusker, John J. *Essays in the Economic History of the Atlantic World.* London: Routledge, 1997.

Polanyi, Karl. *The Great Transformation.* Boston: Beacon Press, 1944.

Schumpeter, Joseph A. *Capitalism, Socialism, and Democracy.* New York: Harper, 1950.

Sombart, Werner. *Luxury and Capitalism.* Munich: Duncker and Humblot, 1913, 1922.

Weber, Max. *The Protestant Ethic and the Spirit of Capitalism*, tr. Talcott Parsons. London: Allen and Unwin, 1930.

Christopher J. Castaneda

CARAVAN TRADE

The caravan trade is usually thought of as the shipment of goods across long distances on the backs of pack animals accompanied by supervising human beings. The goods could all be under the control of a single merchant, but more often the trade involved several merchants traveling together. Because the need to feed beasts of burden made overland transport relatively expensive (with a few exceptions, discussed below), the goods traded in this fashion were usually quite valuable in relation to their weight: silks, spices, gold, and so on. Caravans once accounted for a large percentage of the world's long-distance trade, but they have gradually succumbed to competition, first from relatively safe and efficient sea transport, and, after 1800, from the gradual expansion of long-distance railroads.

CARAVAN ROUTES

Most caravan trade crossed some portion of the great arid and semiarid zone that crisscrosses the Old World in a great *Z* shape, from Western China across the steppe to the Caspian and Black Seas, from northern India through mountain passes to Persia and the Middle East (reaching the Black Sea from the southeast, to form the diagonal of the *Z*) and across Arabia and North Africa to the Atlas Mountains. Because these spaces were typically sparsely populated, with large settlements located at well-watered spots often at great distances from the next one, the caravan trade resembled seaborne commerce, with its long periods of isolation punctuated by stops where new supplies could be acquired, information obtained, and some trading conducted.

SILK ROAD

Through to the Middle Ages, the Silk Road was the most important East-West trade link, forming a 7,000-mile-long conduit between China, the Near East, and Western Europe. As early as 100 B.C.E. caravans were departing from China westward through the interior of Asia, loaded with goods such as silk, gold, and spices. Western European imports included foodstuffs, woolens, and linens. Their long journey took traders through the Himalayas and the Asian deserts, where bandits were a constant threat. Through these links China and Rome maintained indirect contacts, with the Parthians long acting as middlemen. In the thirteenth century C.E. Mongol hegemony encouraged Silk Road commerce, providing the late Byzantines with most of their trade. Along with goods, ideas passed along the road; Marco Polo's account of China grew out of a family trading venture. There were more sinister exchanges as well. The Black Plague originated in Mongolia's Gobi Desert in the late 1320s; by 1345 it had reached the Black Sea along the Silk Road, where trading ships spread the pestilence to most of Europe. With the fall of Constantinople in 1453 the Silk Road became less important as European merchants turned to seaward trade routes to the East.

David J. Clarke

To some degree, crossing such sparsely populated stretches was an advantage, as it avoided the numerous customs barriers and interference from local governments or bandits common in more densely populated areas. At least equally important was the fact that much of the land traversed by caravans was grazing land: there was grass for the pack animals to eat, and because the land was not permanently settled and claimed as private property (the way farmland in more populated regions usually was) the animals could eat for free, greatly reducing the costs of the caravan. Camels, for instance, are remarkably energy-efficient animals. In some cases, such as the bullock trains of North India, it was pastoralists themselves who undertook the caravan trade. Given that they and their herds would be migrating anyway, the additional costs of carrying goods was very small, making

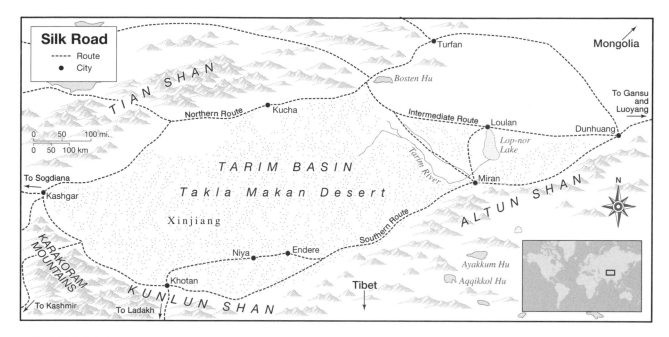

XNR PRODUCTIONS, INC. REPRODUCED BY PERMISSION OF THOMSON GALE.

them highly competitive with other possible means of transport. Traveling in large groups was in some cases simply a matter of a migratory band staying together. In other cases, when people not normally associated with each other banded together to form a caravan, there were obvious advantages. A large caravan was safer, against both robbery and natural obstacles. (Somebody crossing the desert alone whose camel gets sick is as good as dead; somebody who is part of a group can switch to another camel.) It also offered economies of scale in the supervision of the animals.

This kind of caravan trade dates back to very ancient times. The Silk Road (really, Silk *Roads*, since there were many branches) linking China with Europe and the Middle East was the most famous example, but there were others as well: for instance, gold had come north across the Sahara on caravans in exchange for salt for many centuries. The late thirteenth century, when the Mongols briefly brought northern Eurasia under one rule and provided transit passes known for hundreds of miles, was one of its golden eras. In the fourteenth century plague (which probably spread from southwest China to the Middle East and Europe along these trade routes) and the collapse of the Mongols caused a major contraction of trade. A new story began after about 1420. At that point demographic recovery and political restabilization (at least in some key areas) was well established, leading to a recovery of long-distance trade. On the other hand, the growth of maritime trade, beginning about the same time, gave the caravan trade increased competition.

OVERLAND VERSUS SEA TRADE

In many cases the caravan trade and maritime trade were complementary, with a cargo proceeding part way by sea and then finishing its journey overland. It is often claimed that the Portuguese discovery of an all-water route from Europe to India meant the beginning of the end for the caravan trade, but this is true only in the loosest sense. Portuguese mark-ups on goods transported around the Cape of Good Hope were very high, and their frequent injection of violence into the competition over intra-Asian sea routes made some maritime traders less competitive. And the Portuguese suffered considerable losses on their ocean shipments. Over the course of the 1500s, almost 20 percent of their Europe-bound ships never arrived; in the last few years of the century, as warfare with Northern European powers intensified, this number approached 50 percent. Such losses, of course, kept the mark-ups on maritime trade high, preserving a very profitable niche for caravans.

In general, the sixteenth century was one of continuing expansion for the Eurasian caravan trade. Volumes grew and profit margins were often very high, especially on luxury items. Sending a shipment of silk from Persia to Aleppo circa 1600, for instance, cost only about 3 percent of the value of the silk for transportation per se, and perhaps 10 percent more for customs and presents to officials and other security costs in stable times; the price of the silk, however, roughly doubled. A camel load from Goa to Aleppo seems to have been an even better bargain for the merchant, at least so long as the route remained secure. Although these very high rates of return must be

A heavily laden camel caravan passes en route to Timbuktu from the salt mines of Taoudenni, northern Mali, 2000. The 450-mile-long unmarked road through the Sahara Desert is a vestige of a once lucrative and vital caravan trade route. PHOTOGRAPH BY BRENNAN LINSLEY. AP/WIDE WORLD PHOTOS. REPRODUCED BY PERMISSION.

weighed against the caravans that never made it, and not all goods were as profitable as silk, in general returns were more than enough to justify the risks involved. Many different kinds of merchants were involved, but Armenians often played a prominent role, especially along the Black Sea–Caspian Sea–Mediterranean part of the route, which was linked to Europe and Russia at one end, and to India and the Silk Road to China at the other.

Serious trouble began in the seventeenth century with the arrival of the Dutch and then English East India Companies. What distinguished them from the Portuguese was not necessarily superior mercantile skill but their skill at naval warfare, which ultimately allowed them to control the protection costs of their merchants. (Because the companies themselves carried out naval warfare, they were also able to spread these costs evenly across their shipments, raise long-term capital to cover forts and other sunk costs for security, and generate sufficient trade volume to make these investments worthwhile.) Significantly, the resulting decline in protection costs for maritime shipping coincided with an increase in the cost of protection for overland travelers. The Safavid Empire (1501–1722) in Persia remained relatively

stable, and the empire's officials tended to hold office for a long time, giving them incentive to keep their charges moderate and predictable and keep the roads secure. But along the Ottoman part of the route (particularly through the Syrian desert, long one of the most dangerous sections) instability increased in the seventeenth century and protection costs rose considerably. A decline in caravan shipments meant a decline in revenue for the polities they passed through. This was one of many reasons that the eighteenth century saw very significant weakening of the Mogul, Safavid, and Ottoman Empires, making the caravan trade less and less competitive. By the end of the century the trade had shriveled and maritime shipping had become dominant.

Caravan trades existed elsewhere as well, and proved longer-lived in some of these locations. The trans-Saharan trade—particularly the exchange of gold for salt—continued into the early twentieth century in many cases, and had great cultural as well as economic significance. In many cases the trade was organized by religious figures, and was important in the spread of Islam; in others, ties and identities formed in organizing caravans became important parts of ethnic identities (as for the

Dinka). Some of these trading communities still exist today. Almost everywhere, however, the arrival of mechanized transport and of relatively secure transport routes policed by growing national states eventually supplanted anything recognizable as "caravan trade."

SEE ALSO BENGAL; BLACK SEA; BULLION (SPECIE); CHINA; CLIMATE; DAHOMEY; DRUGS, ILLICIT; EMPIRE, BRITISH; EMPIRE, MING; EMPIRE, MUGHAL; EMPIRE, OTTOMAN; EMPIRE, QING; ETHNIC GROUPS, ARMENIANS; ETHNIC GROUPS, GUJARATI; FAIRS; GHANA; GOLD COAST; GUJARAT; INDIAN OCEAN; IRAN; MEDITERRANEAN; MILLETS AND CAPITULATIONS; MOROCCO; NIGERIA; PROTECTION COSTS; ROYAL NIGER COMPANY; SILK; SMUGGLING; SPICES AND THE SPICE TRADE; TEXTILES; TRAVELERS AND TRAVEL.

BIBLIOGRAPHY

Chaudhuri, K. N. *Asia before Europe.* Cambridge, U.K.: Cambridge University Press, 1990.

Curtin, Philip. *Cross-Cultural Trade in World History.* Baltimore, MD: Johns Hopkins University Press, 1984.

Liu, Xinru. *The Silk Road.* Washington, DC: American Historical Association, 1998.

Steensgaard, Niels. *The Asian Trade Revolution of the Seventeenth Century.* Chicago: University of Chicago Press, 1973.

Kenneth Pomeranz

CARGOES, FREIGHT

By 1450 C.E. the broad lines of deep-sea transport across the known world had been shaped by the imperatives of relative costs. In the long-distance transcontinental trades, the only alternatives to the central Asian silk caravans linking Constantinople and China, and to the trans-Saharan trade in gold and slaves, were the spice routes that linked the Mediterranean with the Red Sea and with the Indian Ocean through the land crossing over Egyptian territory. On all these routes, only the goods more valuable relative to weight or bulk could easily bear the high cost of transport.

On shorter routes along the European and Asian coasts, however, lower production and shipping costs increasingly allowed for deep-sea transport of bulky cargoes of low-value commodities. The Scandinavian trades were dominated by timber, iron, and pitch and tar for the shipbuilding needs of Holland, Zeeland, England, and the Christian Mediterranean powers confronting the rising Ottoman threat. Herring caught in the Baltic Sea, and eventually along the Dutch coast, was preserved with salt from Bourgneuf (France), Setubal (Portugal), and Cádiz

ART OF CARGO STOWAGE

As historian Ralph Davis made clear, in the era of sail it was something of an art to calculate the cubic volume of a ton for shipboard stowage of commercial goods. Mixed cargoes required balancing light and heavy products to maximize the weight and the volume of goods transported. Some commodities were carried in sacks, some in wooden barrels. Other goods, including coal, were transported in bulk. Lighter goods were tricky to carry, as their low weight-to-volume ratio could make a ship unstable. Heavy items such as iron could be inserted among lighter cargoes to serve as ballast. Softwood timber was especially problematic because it was very light and difficult to stow without wasting space. Many timber vessels carried deck loads, a practice frequently blamed for capsizing these so-called "coffin ships." Bulk items had to be stored securely to prevent shifting in transit, another potential source of instability that might also cause structural damage to the vessel. Innovations such as mechanical presses increased efficiency, but the art of cargo stowage remained little changed into the steam era, revolutionized only with the advent of containerization and Ro-Ro vessels, which are ships that vehicles can drive on or off.

David J. Clarke

(Spain). The once prosperous wine trade from Bordeaux was set to recover from prolonged stagnation during the Hundred Years' War between France and England (1337–1453). The most important bulk trade in the Mediterranean—grain from Sicily, the Dalmatian coast, and Morocco—was soon to be supplemented with supplies to Portugal from Madeira and from the Azores Islands. Heavy loads of alum—a mordant that fixed natural dyes to wool fabrics—found their way from Phocaea and Smyrna to the cloth industries of Flanders and England. Trade along the coasts of Asia was still dominated by Chinese silks, Japanese silver, and Indian textiles, but it also included relatively heavy cargoes of rice and Chinese ceramics.

The Iberian voyages of discovery and the trade boom of the sixteenth century did not substantially erode the worldwide predominance of bulk cargoes. To be sure, the flows of precious metals, luxury goods, and slaves intensified as they changed direction: gold from the Caribbean, New Spain (Mexico), and eventually Japan supplemented West African supplies; massive shipments of American silver to Spain and beyond replaced the overland flows from Central Europe since the 1540s; and Portuguese spice imports from Asia through the Cape of Good Hope supplied more than half of the European market by the 1500s and 1510s. But the new transcontinental flows of high-priced commodities remained insignificant by comparison to the established and emerging bulk trades. To procure gold, ivory, slaves, and malageta pepper in West Africa, Portuguese merchants had to bring grain, livestock, raisins, shellfish, sealskins, wood, and sugar. In India the Portuguese traded German copper for pepper on very favorable terms. Imports from the Portuguese possessions in Brazil were dominated from the start by high-volume, low-priced goods such as exotic building woods and Braziletto dye. From the Spanish American "Indies" also came hides, tallow, and sugar, as well as lighter and expensive dyes; to the Indies went domestic animals, wine, and olive oil, as well as costly European textiles. By the early seventeenth century the combined plant and animal products from the Indies were said to exceed the more famous gold and silver in both value and volume.

Despite new growth in the ocean trade in Asian spices under Dutch control in the seventeenth century, the massive slave shipments from West Africa to America in the eighteenth century, and the growing presence of Indian textiles in English and Dutch holds since the 1660s, the trend toward low-value cargoes relative to weight or bulk received new impetus from the expansion of incipient seaborne trades. In Europe, wheat and rye from east of the Baltic had reached the Mediterranean by 1570 and later found increasingly dependent markets as far as Turkey and Egypt; by the eighteenth century the Baltic area was supplying hemp and flax for the cordage and linen industries, and coal shipments along the English coasts and beyond exceeded in volume those of costly manufactures. In the Far East the period 1570 to 1630 witnessed a flourishing middleman trade in Japanese copper, iron, and rice in exchange for lead ingots for ammunition, deer and shark skins, Braziletto dye, and sugar; by the mid-eighteenth century moderately priced tea was outweighing silks and porcelain in the rapidly expanding trade from Canton to Europe. The European export trade to America was enriched in the late seventeenth century with iron products, nonferrous metals, paper, wax, the cheap Spanish spirit known as *aguardiente,* and Irish provisions such as salted beef and pork. Return cargoes on the rise included tropical hardwoods, masts and timber from New Hampshire for the English navy, and pitch and tar from all the British mainland colonies. But in the eighteenth century by far the largest bulk cargoes across the Atlantic were the products of African slaves and indentured European laborers in the American plantations. Cane sugar, the most valuable import from Brazil since the seventeenth century, rose to pre-eminence in the eighteenth century with massive shipments from Saint Domingue and other West Indian islands. Other early imports from Iberian plantations—notably tobacco and cotton, but not cocoa—were eclipsed by alternative supplies from the southern United States by the end of the eighteenth century. Despite rapidly expanding shipments of Carolina rice after 1720, by mid-century more than half the volume of British imports from America was still made up of sugar and tobacco.

TRADE AND SHIPPING, 1500 TO 1800

From 1500 to 1800, for the first time in recorded history intercontinental trade appears to have grown at a faster speed than world population. On the Spanish routes to America both the number of ships and their average size doubled from the 1520s to the late sixteenth century. In the eighteenth century alone, the total carrying capacity of European fleets may have grown from 2 million to 3.5 million tons. Along with this growth in scale came a measure of technological progress—in the sense that a given load could be carried over a given distance at smaller cost of inputs. During the sixteenth century full-rigged and better-steered "long" ships gradually replaced slower and clumsier "round cogs" in the North Atlantic. In the following century, the cheaply built and fast-sailing carrier known as the flyboat (or *fluit*) brought much of the European trade in bulky and heavy commodities into Dutch hands. Further improvements in rigging and steering eventually allowed for rerouting of British vessels into the westerly winds of the North Atlantic, thus helping to reduce the average length of voyages in the tobacco trade from about nine months in the 1630s to seven months in the 1720s. But productivity gains were not limited to those arising from ship design and navigation. Recent scholarship has assigned greater importance to such broader factors as security at sea in general; piracy control, particularly beginning in the late seventeenth century; commercial organization in the Atlantic trades; and tighter packing of tobacco. In regular and large-scale trades, where prices and supplies were more readily anticipated, ships designed for particular cargoes and routes could be more fully laden, and dead times in port could be reduced. On the whole, however, the trade booms of the sixteenth and eighteenth centuries did not clearly involve a "transport revolution" in the technological sense. Skeptical historians have argued that freight rates did not generally decline over extended peacetime periods; that crew sizes per cargo ton seldom fell, and at times increased; that commodity price spreads across intercontinental ports failed to narrow; that flyboats were seldom used for commercial transport in the transatlantic routes; and that the Asian trades do not appear to have shown significant gains in shipping productivity.

Far more clear are the extent and determinants of subsequent shipping improvements. The period 1820 to 1913 witnessed an eightfold increase in the worldwide ratio of merchandise exports to gross domestic product. In the early decades of the century the largest reductions in deep-sea transport costs stemmed from the cramming of cotton bales into ship holds with screw and steam presses. From 1870 to 1913, freight rate declines were deeper and far more general despite rising seamen's wages and coal prices after the mid-1880s. One-third to one-half of the major cost reductions of this period has been attributed to a transport revolution in the technological sense. Cheaper iron and steel fostered the introduction of lighter metallic hulls and larger steam engines; improvements in steam technology brought vast gains in speed and in fuel efficiency. The result was lower prices for larger, faster, and more efficiently manned ships. Until 1860, steamers resembled today's airplanes in that they carried high-value goods such as passengers and mail. The subsequent trend toward commodities with high bulk-to-value ratios—such as American grain, Rangoon rice, and Chilean nitrates—was reinforced by the spread of railways, by the opening of the Suez Canal in 1869, and by Europe-bound shipments of Argentine frozen beef, Australian meat, and New Zealand butter in refrigerated ships beginning in the 1880s. By 1913 the transport revolution had had a dramatic impact on the worldwide division of labor, with a stark distinction between industrial and primary-producing economies.

The twentieth century saw further structural change, rising input costs, and a possibly permanent slowdown of productivity growth in deep-sea transport. Between 1913 and 1999 the share of manufactures in worldwide exports, as compared with agricultural and mineral products, rose from less than one-third to more than one-half on most routes excluding the Middle East and North and sub-Saharan Africa. Transport cost declines were far less impressive than they had been from 1870 to 1913: when compared with various aggregates of commodity prices over long peacetime periods, tramp freight rates show moderate decline during the interwar years (1919–1939) and no downward trend since 1945. An unknown proportion of this relative setback can be explained by recurrent increases in input costs—most notably in diesel oil, seamen's wages, and port charges in the 1970s. Mounting demand for shipping during World War I induced substantial improvements in shipping productivity, but recent calculations for the interwar years point to a marked slowdown in technological growth between the periods 1923 to 1925 and 1932 to 1934. Part of the explanation for this setback may lie in lagging progress in steam-engine technology since the 1900s, in the uneven adoption of diesel engines and tankers, and in persistent overcapacity in the face of rising tariffs and trade quotas during the 1920s and 1930s. Trends in productivity growth since the 1930s are yet to be ascertained; but the relative stability of tramp freight rates during this period, often in the face of soaring input costs, may have owed much to innovations such as the introduction of ship containers in the 1960s. In any event, dramatic falls in air freight rates in the 1950s, 1960s, and 1980s have led to a tenfold increase in the ratio of air-to-ocean cargoes since 1962.

SEE ALSO AGRICULTURE; CARGOES, PASSENGER; CONTAINERIZATION; COTTON; CUNARD, SAMUEL; EMPIRE, BRITISH; EMPIRE, DUTCH; EMPIRE, MING; EMPIRE, OTTOMAN; EMPIRE, PORTUGUESE; EMPIRE, QING; EMPIRE, SPANISH; ENTREPÔT SYSTEM; FREE PORTS; GATT, WTO; HANSEATIC LEAGUE (HANSA OR HANSE); HARBORS; INDUSTRIALIZATION; IRAN; IRON AND STEEL; JAPAN; LLOYD'S OF LONDON; NITRATES; PANAMA CANAL; PETROLEUM; PORT CITIES; RICE; SHIPPING, COASTAL; SHIPPING, INLAND WATERWAYS, EUROPE; SHIPPING, INLAND WATERWAYS, NORTH AMERICA; SHIPPING LANES; SHIPPING, MERCHANT; SHIPPING, TECHNOLOGICAL CHANGE; SHIP TYPES; TEA; TOBACCO; UNITED FRUIT COMPANY; WHEAT AND OTHER CEREAL GRAINS.

BIBLIOGRAPHY

Davis, Ralph. *The Rise of the English Shipping Industry in the Seventeenth and Eighteenth Centuries.* London: Macmillan, 1962.

Findlay, Ronald, and O'Rourke, Kevin H. "Commodity Market Integration, 1500–2000." In *Globalization in Historical Perspective,* eds. M. D. Bordo, A. M. Taylor, and J. G. Williamson. Chicago and London: University of Chicago Press, 2003.

Menard, R. "Transport Costs and Long-Range Trade, 1300–1800: Was There a European Transport Revolution in the Early Modern Era?" In *The Political Economy of Merchant Empires,* ed. J. D. Tracy. Cambridge, U.K.: Cambridge University Press, 1991.

O'Rourke, K. H., and Williamson, J. G. *Globalization and History: The Evolution of a Nineteenth Century Atlantic Economy.* Cambridge, MA: Massachusetts Institute of Technology Press, 1999.

Reid, Anthony. "The System of Trade and Shipping in Maritime South and Southeast Asia, and the Effects of the Development of the Cape Route to Europe." In *The European Discovery of the World and Its Economic Effects on Pre-Industrial Society, 1500–1800,* ed. Hans Pohl. Stuttgart, Germany: Steiner, 1990.

Shah Mohammed, Saif I., and Williamson, Jeffrey G. "Freight Rates and Productivity Gains in British Tramp

Shipping, 1869–1950." *Explorations in Economic History* 41 (2004): 172–203.

Steensgaard, Niels. "Commodities, Bullion, and Services in Intercontinental Transactions Before 1750." In *The European Discovery of the World and Its Economic Effects on Pre-Industrial Society, 1500–1800,* ed. Hans Pohl. Stuttgart, Germany: Steiner, 1990.

Tracy, J. D. *The Rise of Merchant Empires: Long-Distance Trade in the Early Modern World, 1350–1750.* Cambridge, U.K.: Cambridge University Press, 1990.

Williamson, Jeffrey G. "Land, Labor and Globalization in the Third World, 1870–1940." *Journal of Economic History* 62 (2002): 55–85.

Javier Cuenca-Esteban

CARGOES, PASSENGER

Historically, oceangoing passenger vessels conveyed human cargoes derived from voluntary or enforced migrations. These were vessels of various types and sizes, which covered varying distances. With a focus on deepsea passenger shipping, this article examines the nature and overall impact of the traffic.

PASSENGER SHIPPING BEFORE THE NINETEENTH CENTURY

Before the invention of steam navigation in the nineteenth century, fast sailing ships, called clippers, and other craft of various descriptions had traversed the world's sea lanes. Rowing and wind-driven sails propelled them. Human cargoes conveyed by these vessels included enslaved Africans on their way to the New World and the European colonists to the Americas and Asia. Passengers were also conveyed over shorter distances in regional waters such as the Mediterranean, the Baltic, the Indian Ocean, the Pacific, and around the Japanese archipelago. The single most significant movement was that generated by the transatlantic slave trade, by which millions of Africans were exported to plantations in the Americas. From the sixteenth to the midnineteenth century, slave ships conveyed human cargo mainly from the coast of Western Africa to the New World in long, flat sailing ships called galleys, in conditions that produced a high rate of deaths, mainly from epidemics. Voluntary seaborne migrations took English, Spanish, and Portuguese settlers to the Americas, Africa, and Asia. Sailing ships were susceptible to the vagaries of the weather, particularly storms and the direction of the monsoon winds, and passengers were vulnerable to scurvy, a disease caused by prolonged lack of fresh food at sea. To remedy this, the Dutch established a colony at the Cape of Good Hope in 1652 to victual ships of the East India Company on their way to the Orient.

PASSENGER SHIPPING LINES AND MIGRANT GROUPS IN THE AGE OF STEAM

The advent of steam navigation in the nineteenth century facilitated the ocean transportation of more humans in faster, safer vessels. By the 1830s, steamships had become dominant in the transatlantic passenger and mail transport business, as did English companies, led by the British and North American Royal Mail Steam Packet (later renamed the Cunard Line). On July 4, 1840, the Cunard ship *Britannia* began a fourteen-day transatlantic crossing from Liverpool with a cow on board to supply fresh milk to the passengers. Only four years later, pleasure cruises began as a new phase in the industry.

Cunard dominated the transatlantic passenger trade for one and a half centuries before declining in the 1950s as aircraft began to supplant ships as the bulk carriers of passengers and mail across the Atlantic. In 1998 Carnival Corporation acquired Cunard. Until 2004 its vessel the RMS *Queen Elizabeth 2* continued to make transatlantic sailings; in 2004 the RMS *Queen Mary 2* replaced it. Meanwhile, Cunard had established some sailing records: first transatlantic passenger service (*Britannia,* 1840); first passenger ship to be lit by electricity (*Servia,* 1881); first twin-screw ocean liner (*Campania,* 1893); first gymnasium and health center aboard a ship (*Franconia,* 1911); largest passenger ship (until 1996—the *Queen Elizabeth,* 1940); and largest passenger ship (*Queen Mary 2,* 2004).

Holland America, founded in 1873 as a shipping and passenger line, provided passenger shipping services between Holland and the Dutch East Indies via the Suez Canal. It was a leading carrier of immigrants (about 850,000) from Europe to the United States until the early twentieth century. In 1895 the company offered its first vacation cruise; by 1910, it had launched a leisure cruise service from New York to the Middle East. In 1971 Holland America ended its transatlantic passenger trade and shifted its focus to cruise vacations. In 1989 it too became a wholly owned subsidiary of Carnival Corporation, the largest cruise company in the world. By 2004 the line operated thirteen ships traveling to seven continents, and carried more than 600,000 cruise passengers a year.

From the 1850s ships began to specialize in carrying only passengers, no cargo or mail. Hence, luxuries such as electric lights, more deck space, and entertainment were provided aboard. Transatlantic travel, especially pleasure cruises, got a boost in the 1880s when the *British Medical Journal* certified that sea voyages served curative purposes. The period also witnessed the massive emigration of Europeans to the United States, mainly on steerage tickets. Such passengers provided their own food and slept on the floor in the cramped hold. The most significant of the population movements were the Irish to the

United States and English convicts to Australia. The ships carrying millions of famine-struck Irish émigrés were so crowded, and conditions aboard were so terrible, that they were called "coffin ships."

There are 20 million Chinese in Southeast Asia, accounting for almost 80 percent of the overseas Chinese, who had left China largely through the major ports at Fuzhou (Foochow) and Xiamen (Amoy) in Fujian province, and Shantou (Swatow) and Guangzhou (Canton) in Guangdong province. During the mid-nineteenth century large numbers of Chinese emigrated on Western ships. Some 6.3 million Chinese were estimated to have left Hong Kong alone between 1868 and 1939, and large numbers also left Xiamen (Amoy) and Shantou (Swatow). Most migrants were male indentured laborers known as coolies, but others went to seek their fortunes in alternative occupations in Australia and North America and New Zealand. The majority moved to Southeast Asian countries, which were being colonized, by the British and French. Most Chinese migrants left home intending to return home to settle down.

OCEAN LINERS AND CRUISE SHIPS

Superliners were constructed in the early twentieth century to minimize the discomfort of ocean travel by providing luxury accommodation and recreational activities. Space and passenger comfort now superseded speed in the design of passenger liners. The Cunard Line started the tradition of dressing for dinner on board, emphasizing the glamor of cruises. The White Star Line provided a swimming pool and tennis court aboard the *Olympic* and the ill-fated *Titanic*.

During World War I the building of new cruise ships was halted as many older liners were converted into troop carriers. After the war the victorious Allies took German superliners as reparations. However, transatlantic passenger shipping reached its apogee between 1920 and 1940, when luxury ships conveyed the rich and famous on cruises. The consequent patronage of ocean cruises by Americans ensured near-parity between the outflow of tourists and the declining volume of immigrants to the United States on passenger lines. The increased demand for pleasure cruises was produced by carefully placed media advertisements that glamorized life aboard the floating hotels.

World War II halted passenger cruises as cruise liners were pressed into service as troop carriers. European shipping lines, however, benefited in the postwar years by conveying refugees to North America, and tourists and businessmen to Europe. The postwar boom soon petered out, and transatlantic passenger shipping was superseded by faster air travel.

A 1912 advertisement for the White Star Line of ocean steamers. The prominent shipping company focused on vessel comfort rather than speed. This new outlook produced luxurious ships, including the company's most famous, the Titanic. © CHRISTIES IMAGES/CORBIS. REPRODUCED BY PERMISSION.

But passenger shipping persisted, as in the Israeli ZIM (Israel Navigation Company Limited) line's transport of Jews to Palestine. From 1947 it conveyed passengers and immigrants, mostly from Genoa and Marseilles. Some 1,300 passengers were carried on each voyage from several Mediterranean ports during the peak of the immigration, between December 1948 and April 1949. In 1949 alone, ZIM ships carried more than 100,000 immigrants to Israel. ZIM commenced a passenger shipping service between Haifa and New York in 1952. The *Jerusalem* made six transatlantic round-trips a year in addition to five round-trips on the Haifa–Naples–Marseilles route. When she was sold in 1959, she had carried more than 118,000 passengers and immigrants. During the winter season of 1958 to 1959, ZIM commenced its international cruise operations from the United States to the Caribbean Islands with three cruises per season. However, with the sale of ZIM's last vessel in 1969, its passenger service succumbed to the superiority of cheaper air transport.

Meanwhile, transoceanic passenger shipping had received a new lease on life in the 1960s with the emergence of the modern cruise industry. Cruise-ship companies concentrated on vacation trips in the Caribbean, advertising an exciting image exemplified by the popular U.S. television series *The Love Boat*, which aired from 1977 until 1986. From the 1980s aggressive marketing campaigns and media images, increased disposable wealth, and an aging population in the advanced economies fuelled a further resurgence. By 2000 the traffic had exceeded 10 million passengers, which could double to 22 million by 2010.

SEE ALSO Cargoes, Freight; Cunard, Samuel; Ethnic Groups, Cantonese; Ethnic Groups, Fujianese; Ethnic Groups, Irish; Ethnic Groups, Jews; Harbors; Lloyd's of London; Panama Canal; Port Cities; Shipbuilding; Ship Types; Slavery and the African Slave Trade; Suez Canal; Travelers and Travel.

BIBLIOGRAPHY

Cowley, Malcolm, and Max, Daniel P. "The Middle Passage." In *The Atlantic Slave Trade*, ed. David Northrup. Lexington, MA: D. C. Heath, 1994.

Dickinson, Bob, and Vladimir, Andy. *Selling the Sea: An Inside Look at the Cruise Industry.* New York: John Wiley and Sons, 1997.

Fayle, C. Ernest. *A Short History of the World's Shipping Industry.* London: Allen and Unwin, 1933.

Friedland, Klaus, ed. *Maritime Aspects of Migration.* Cologne, Germany: Bohlau, 1978.

Greenhill, Basil. *Travelling by Sea in the Nineteenth Century: Interior Design in Victorian Passenger Ships.* London: A and C Black, 1972.

Hall, Derek. "Ocean Cruising: Market Dynamics, Product Responses, and Offshore Impacts." In *Shipping and Ports in the Twenty-first Century: Globalisation, Technological Change, and the Environment*, eds. David Pinder and Brian Slack. London and New York: Routledge, 2004.

Ma, Laurence J. C., and Cartier, Carolyn., eds. *The Chinese Diaspora: Space, Place, Mobility, and Identity.* Lanham, MD: Rowman and Littlefield, 2003.

McDonald, John, and Shlomowitz, Ralph. "The Cost of Shipping Convicts to Australia." *International Journal of Maritime History* 2 (December 1990): 1–32.

McDonald, John, and Shlomowitz, Ralph. "Fares Charged for Transporting Indian Indentured Labour to Mauritius and the West Indies, 1850–73." *International Journal of Maritime History* 3 (June 1991): 81–99.

Ayodeji Olukoju

CARTAGENA

The economic functions of the port of Cartagena have varied considerably over time. From 1537, when the first Spanish convoyed fleet arrived in Cartagena, until the collapse of Spanish convoyed fleets after 1737, Cartagena served as a point of support and supply for Spanish trade via the Isthmus of Panama with the Pacific coast of South America. During the sixteenth century the isthmian anchorage for the South American trade was Nombre de Dios, which was troubled by a shallow bay, reefs, a miserable climate, and mortiferous disease. Spanish convoys therefore relied on Cartagena as a haven for repairs as well as for food and water. Cartagena was well suited for this purpose because of its proximity to Panama, its well-enclosed port, and the food available from the surrounding region. Convoy ships generally visited Cartagena before proceeding to the isthmus and also returned there before sailing on to Havana on the return voyage to Spain. Cartagena continued in this role after the sixteenth century when the isthmian trade moved to the better port of Portobelo. Visits of the Spanish fleet to Cartagena provided markets for cattle, pigs, and maize and other crops raised in its coastal hinterland. Cartagena also conducted active maritime commerce with Caribbean islands and along the coast of Tierra Firme.

Whereas Peruvian silver was the primary concern of Spanish convoys to the isthmus, Cartagena also was the principal port where gold produced in New Granada was exchanged for European goods. Gold moving through Cartagena attracted attacks by European privateers and naval forces from the 1540s through the 1740s. Contraband trade with the Dutch, French, and British at Riohacha and Santa Marta (northeast of Cartagena) as well as in the Cartagena region itself undermined legal trade at the port during the seventeenth and eighteenth centuries. During the seventeenth century the decline of legal shipping of consumer goods through Cartagena was compensated by the port's role as a receiver and distributor of African slaves. Cartagena's role as a distributor of slaves declined during the British *asiento* (1714–1736), as the British tended to favor Buenos Aires as a point of distribution. Nonetheless, Cartagena in the eighteenth century supplied slaves to important gold-mining sites in the Chocó and elsewhere in western Colombia.

Cartagena during the colonial period monopolized supply of the interior of New Granada with legally imported goods. It lost this role after 1830 because of the silting up of the Canal del Dique, Cartagena's link to the Magdalena River, the chief artery to the interior. From the 1830s to 1871, Santa Marta was the chief receiver of imports to Colombia, with Barranquilla taking over this role after 1871. Consequently, during half the nineteenth century Cartagena decayed and its population shrank from 17,600 in 1809 to 8,600 in 1870.

Shipments of cattle to Caribbean markets, particularly Cuba, which suffered food shortages during and after its wars against Spanish rule in 1868 to 1878 and 1895 to 1898, provided some stimulus. The reopening of the Canal del Dique in 1879 and, after the canal reclogged in 1890, the completion of a railway to the Magdalena River in 1894, aided Cartagena's recovery. But the completion of the Panama Canal encouraged the construction of railway links from the coffee zone in western Colombia to the Pacific port of Buenaventura, relegating both Barranquilla and Cartagena to secondary positions. Nonetheless, Cartagena's port activity benefited from visits of tourist cruise vessels after 1919, oil exports after 1926, and highway development after 1950, which effectively ended its dependence on the Magdalena River for connections to markets in the interior. Between 1966 and 1996 Cartagena far surpassed Buenaventura, Santa Marta, and Barranquilla in volume of freight in foreign commerce (34%, 15%, 12%, and 10% respectively). With increased port activity, tourism, and some industrial diversification, Cartagena enjoyed a rapid growth in population (from 85,000 in 1938 to more than 800,000 in 2000, and a projected 1.1 million in 2010).

SEE ALSO Agriculture; Cargoes, Freight; Cargoes, Passenger; Chambers of Commerce; Colombia; Containerization; Empire, Spanish; Encomienda and Repartimiento; Free Ports; Harbors; New Spain; Port Cities; Spain.

BIBLIOGRAPHY

Calvo Stevenson, Haroldo, and Meisel Roca, Adolfo, eds. *Cartagena de Indias en el siglo XX.* Santafé de Bogotá: Banco de la República/Universidad Jorge Tadeo Lozano, 2000.

Calvo Stevenson, Haroldo, and Meisel Roca, Adolfo, eds. *Cartagena de Indias en el siglo XIX.* Bogotá: Banco de la República/Universidad Jorge Tadeo Lozano, 2002.

Castillo Mathieu, Nicolás del. *La llave de las Indias.* Bogotá: Ediciones El Tiempo, 1981.

Chaunu, Huguette and Pierre. *Seville et l'Atlantique.* Paris: A. Colin. 8 v. in 11, 1955–1959.

Posada Carbó, Eduardo. *The Colombian Caribbean: A Regional History, 1879–1950.* New York: Oxford University Press, 1996.

Nichols, Theodore. *Tres puertos de Colombia.* Bogotá: Banco Popular, 1973.

Ybot León, Antonio. *La artería histórica del Nuevo Reino de Granada.* Bogotá: Editorial A.B.C.E.E., 1952.

Frank Safford

CEYLON
SEE Sri Lanka

CHAMBERS OF COMMERCE

Present-day chambers of commerce, sometimes encountered also as chambers of commerce and industry, are organizations of people in business dedicated to the promotion of their common interests or perceptions concerning a wide range of topics at the local, regional, state, national, and international levels. This basic definition, nevertheless, hides considerable differences in the nature of such chambers in different parts of the world, particularly between what could be called the French or Continental model and the Anglo-Saxon one.

The French or Continental chamber of commerce is typically a public institution sponsored by the state and has at times acted on the state's behalf to run public commercial institutions, commodity and stock exchanges, ports, and so on, as well as to channel the views of those in business to state authorities. Membership is often obligatory. The Anglo-Saxon chamber of commerce is a private organization independent of government, and membership is voluntary.

ORIGINS

Associations of merchants and manufacturers probably predate the earliest-known codification of laws, Hammurabi's code of 1800 B.C.E. In the Middle Ages in Europe, guilds and corporations often brought together and controlled the functioning of the few in society who lived in towns and were not involved in agricultural pursuits. Maritime tribunals eventually developed to govern the commercial dealings of emergent Italian city-states such as Venice, Genoa, Pisa, and Amalfi. Originating in the Rhodian Sea Laws, a Byzantine code, they were staffed by merchants expert in the ways of trade. These early tribunals, especially the *Curiae Maris* of Pisa, subsequently influenced the setting up of similar institutions in places such as Montpellier, Oleron, and Barcelona. Eventually called "Consulates of the Sea," they left their mark on the maritime legislation of England, France, Germany, Holland, Italy, and Spain, as well as on Spain's overseas empire.

Functioning as both tribunals and associations of merchants, the Consulates of the Sea are ordinarily considered by historians to be, at least in part, the predecessors of the later chambers of commerce, though the latter were eventually to lose their judicial function as commercial law developed.

In 1599 the King of France entrusted the city of Marseilles with the task of both organizing the trade with the

Levant and ransoming Christians enslaved by the Ottomans. In 1650 the municipal commission looking after these matters was referred to as a *chambre de commerce* for the first time and, despite some difficulties at the time of the French Revolution, became the model of chambers of commerce on the Continent and beyond, in the Modern Era.

In the Anglo-Saxon world, associations representing mercantile interests are also of long standing. By the sixteenth century, English merchants resident in communities abroad were organized to protect and promote their interests. Sixteenth-century Lisbon, for example, had a so-called British factory, here meaning an assembly of merchants and factors and not a manufacturing concern. Such British "factories" were established wherever British merchants were to be found, and they survived until the early nineteenth century in places as far afield as Buenos Aires and Singapore.

The earliest-known chambers of commerce that called themselves by that name and that were established in Britain and its dominions were in Jersey, the largest of the Channel Islands, and in the State of New York, in British North America. Both were set up in 1768.

In the nineteenth century the number of chambers of commerce, also known as boards of trade, commercial societies, importers and exporters associations, and other similar titles, grew rapidly, in line with the rapid expansion of world trade. Broadly speaking, the French model of government-controlled associations spread throughout most of mainland Europe and other non-English-speaking countries, while the English, voluntary model took hold and prospered in North America and in the British Empire. In the twentieth century many chambers widened their scope and became chambers of commerce and industry.

RECENT DEVELOPMENTS

During the latter part of the nineteenth century, officials from different chambers increasingly felt the need to meet to discuss and lobby on matters of common concern at both the national and international levels. The Association of British Chambers of Commerce was formed in 1860, but it was not until the mid-1880s that the First Congress of the Chambers of Commerce of the Empire was held. A few decades later, in 1911, the British Imperial Council of Commerce was formed, to give the periodic congresses a greater permanence. The U.S. Chamber of Commerce came into existence a year later, in 1912, when a group of seven hundred delegates from various commercial and trade organizations came together to create a unified national body of business interests. In just under a century it grew to more than three million

businesses, state and local chambers, business associations, and American chambers of commerce abroad.

The International Chamber of Commerce (ICC) was created in Paris in 1919. Its origins lay in the periodic congresses of chambers of commerce and commercial and industrial associations that had been held since 1905. At the beginning of the twenty-first century it represented thousands of member companies and associations in around 130 countries. It has the highest-level consultative status within the United Nations and its specialized agencies and makes its weight felt in intergovernmental bodies and meetings such as the G8, where decisions affecting the conduct of business are made. Apart from generally being the voice of international business and a defender of the multilateral trading system, the ICC offers a range of practical services, such as the ICC Court of Arbitration, which is the world's leading body for resolving international commercial disputes by arbitration. As the free market system gained ground in such places as Eastern Europe and the countries of the former Soviet Union, the ICC extended its operations, becoming a leading player in the fight against commercial crime.

In addition to country-based associations of chambers of commerce and the ICC, the latter half of the twentieth century also saw the emergence of regionally based associations such as Eurochambres, the association of European chambers of commerce and industry. Established in 1958, just one year after the birth of the European Community, the Brussels-based association has member organizations in forty-one countries, representing a network of over two thousand regional and local chambers with over seventeen million member companies. Other regional associations emerging subsequently included the Association of Mediterranean Chambers of Commerce (ASCAME), the Confederation of Asia-Pacific Chambers of Commerce and Industry (CACCI), and Asociación Iberoamericana de Cámaras de Comercio (AICO).

SEE ALSO FRANCE; ITALY; MARSEILLES; UNITED KINGDOM; UNITED STATES.

BIBLIOGRAPHY

Vassallo, Carmel, ed. *Consolati di Mare and Chambers of Commerce: Proceedings of a Conference Held at the Foundation for International Studies, Valletta, 1998.* Malta: Malta University Press, 2000.

INTERNET RESOURCES

International Chamber of Commerce. Available from http://www.iccwbo.org.

Eurochambres. Available from http://www.eurochambres.be.

U.S. Chamber of Commerce. Available from http://www.uschamber.com.

Carmel Vassallo

CHARLESTON

Founded in 1680, Charles Town became the fourth largest American city on the eve of independence because of its extensive Atlantic commerce (the spelling changed to Charleston after the American Revolution). Settled largely by English colonists and African slaves who moved to the mainland from Barbados, South Carolina expanded slowly in the late 1600s because it lacked a staple crop demanded in Europe. The colonists experimented with various exports including beef and timber products, which were sent to the English Caribbean, and deerskins, which were exported to England.

In the early 1700s the economic picture changed dramatically with the establishment of rice as South Carolina's staple crop. Exports to Europe soared. Charleston's fortunes improved as well, because it became the center for shipping rice. From 1700 to 1740 rice exports expanded from about 1.5 millions pounds to more than 40 million pounds annually. Accordingly, the populations of Charleston grew from about 2,000 in 1700 to 6,800 in 1742. The expansion of rice cultivation also prompted a dramatic increase in the colony's slave population, and blacks formed the majority of Charleston's, and South Carolina's, residents.

Acting primarily as commission factors for English businessmen, Charleston merchants managed rice exports. The grain was transported from low-country plantations to Charleston, where it was loaded on ships, which were primarily owned in England, for European markets. As an enumerated good under the British Navigation Acts, rice was shipped first to England and then re-exported to northern and southern Europe. Charleston merchants lobbied Parliament to allow direct exportation to the Continent. These efforts were partially successful in 1730, and vessels carried Carolina rice directly to markets in Portugal and Spain.

Imperial warfare disrupted Charleston's Atlantic commerce during the 1740s and 1750s. Stagnation in rice exports led to the development of indigo, a less bulky, higher value per unit export. Experimentation proved successful, and indigo became a second lucrative staple, with strong markets in England.

Charleston profited greatly as South Carolina's entrepôt. Merchants built substantial townhouses and imported English luxury goods. Many also purchased plantations in the low country and in Georgia and Florida and became rice planters with large numbers of slaves. Charleston merchants played active roles in the colony's political scene and were leading advocates of independence for the American colonies. They intermarried extensively with the province's planter élite and thus were part of the richest group of Americans when the American Revolution erupted.

Charleston prospered during the antebellum period. The city played an important role in southern politics while it maintained its control of rice and cotton exports, the state's leading staples. The Civil War and the abolition of slavery exerted significant economic dislocation. Rice ceased to be an important export, but as cotton rebounded, so did the port of Charleston.

Charleston depended heavily on international trade throughout the twentieth and early twenty-first centuries. In 2003 it was the busiest container port along the southeast and gulf coasts, ranking fourth nationally. Charleston ranked sixth in the value of its international shipments. Historic tourism was also a major money maker.

SEE ALSO AGRICULTURE; BALTIMORE; BOSTON; CARGOES, FREIGHT; CARGOES, PASSENGER; CHAMBERS OF COMMERCE; CONTAINERIZATION; COTTON; EMPIRE, BRITISH; FREE PORTS; HARBORS; LOS ANGELES–LONG BEACH; NEW ORLEANS; NEWPORT; NEW YORK; PHILADELPHIA; PORT CITIES; RICE; SALEM; SAN FRANCISCO–OAKLAND; SLAVERY AND THE AFRICAN SLAVE TRADE; UNITED STATES.

BIBLIOGRAPHY

McCusker, John J., and Menard, Russell R. *The Economy of British America, 1607–1789*. Chapel Hill: University of North Carolina Press, 1985.

Weir, Robert M. *Colonial South Carolina: A History*. Millwood, NY: KTO Press, 1983; reprint, Columbia: University of South Carolina Press, 1997.

Carl E. Swanson

CHICAGO BOARD OF TRADE

In 1848 the Chicago Board of Trade (CBOT) membership organization was founded to promote Chicago's commerce. It evolved into a world-leading futures exchange.

GRAIN'S ERA

In 1848 the CBOT occupied the center of an emerging U.S. grain market. Deere's plow and McCormick's reaper transformed the midwestern prairie into a global granary, and new railroads carried the burgeoning harvests to Chicago. The CBOT provided the meeting place for grain transactions. With grain flooding Chicago, automated warehouse-elevators replaced human toting with conveyors and chutes. These elevators expedited grain's flow east but required consistent grain quality. The CBOT established grain grades and a grain inspection system. Chartering the CBOT in 1859, Illinois made the CBOT's system mandatory and conferred substantial legal power on the CBOT to regulate the city's grain trade (Cronon 1991).

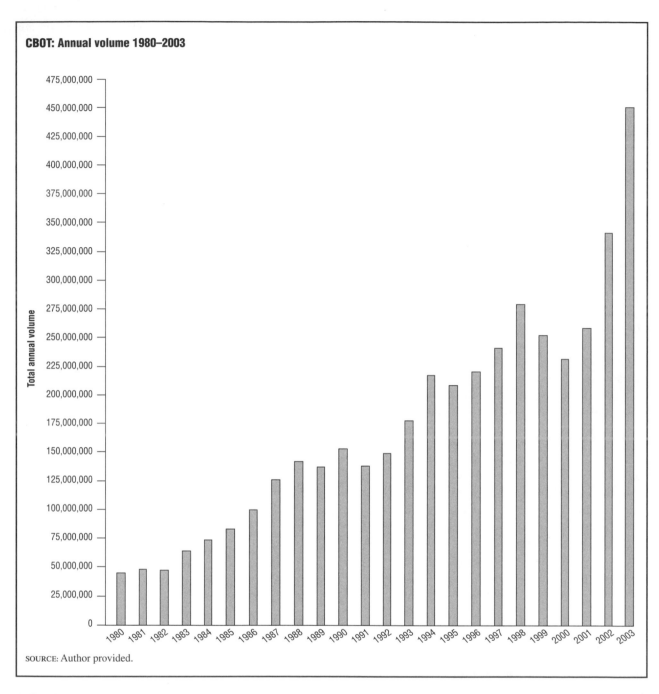

CBOT: Annual volume 1980–2003

SOURCE: Author provided.

THE GALE GROUP.

The grain market's expansion required new contracts to manage risk. Whenever grain was to change hands—farmer to elevator to exporter to food processor to consumer—owners worried, "At what price can I sell grain in the future?" Users worried about purchase price. The capacity of the two types of contracts then in use, the *forward contract* and the *to arrive* contract, was overwhelmed, spurring the evolution of CBOT futures contracts between 1860 and 1875. As with forward and to arrive contracts, futures contracts established in the present

the price at which grain would be exchanged in the future. Thus, by using futures, one could shift, or hedge, price risk. But futures added requirements: standardized terms (quality, quantity, delivery time and place) and earnest money deposits. Significantly, standardization enhanced capacity by attracting speculators to complement hedgers. Speculators bought (or sold) futures contracts sold (or bought) by hedgers. Speculators were attracted by the opportunity to make a profit without ever handling grain. Standardization allowed speculators to

Trading pits on the floor of the Chicago Board of Trade. *The trading pits are populated by brokers involved in face-to-face financial transactions throughout the day. Established in 1848, the board has become a key center for commodity futures and options trading.* © RICHARD HAMILTON SMITH/CORBIS. REPRODUCED BY PERMISSION.

offset buy (or sell) obligations by selling (or buying) a futures contract later to any willing buyer (or seller).

Increased speculation, however, raised the specter of manipulation. Buy-side speculators could corner the market and force contract value higher to squeeze earnest money out of sell-side pockets into their own. By forcing price from its appropriate commercial level, corners would make futures a less reliable hedging tool and constrict world trade.

Much CBOT activity from 1875 to 1930 tested the legitimate uses of these innovative futures contracts and resulted in the development of essential infrastructure still in use by exchanges around the world. Alleged corners conducted by Hutchinson (1888), Leiter (1898), and Patten (1909), brought about the introduction of new rules and disciplinary committees. CBOT legal disputes with bucketshops (culminating with the U.S. Supreme Court decision in 1905) established the proper use of CBOT price information by distinguishing CBOT trading from bucketshop bet-taking activity. CBOT trading produced contractual obligations to exchange grain. Bu-

cketshop activity did not. Instead, bucketshops held orders (placed them in a bucket in their offices), circumventing the CBOT contract process. Bucketshops were essentially places where anyone could bet on CBOT price changes. Bucketshops profited by keeping the losers' money and not paying winners. Winners were persuaded to bet again and again until they lost or the bucketshop went bankrupt.

The interplay between the need for default-free contracts, CBOT procedures precluding defaults, and the regulatory aims of the Department of Agriculture produced the Clearing Corporation (January 4, 1926), the heart of the guarantee system, to reduce market volatility. The Clearing Corporation protected futures contract traders from default in two steps. First it verified that a contract's buyer and seller made no error in the fury of pit trading and did, in fact, agree on price, quantity, and item traded. After a match was verified, the Clearing Corporation guaranteed performance of its members' contractual obligations by becoming a party to the contract, doing so by becoming a buyer to all clearing member sellers, and a seller to all clearing member buyers. If one of the parties were to default on a contract, the Clearing Corporation would make good on the contract.

CBOT activity evolved into pit trading. Standardized contracts had one blank to fill: price. Negotiations in the CBOT's hall readily discovered price and evolved into open-outcry trading. Surging membership created congestion, leading to the use of hand signals, larger trading halls, and trading pits.

In 1920 CBOT markets included wheat, corn, oats, and rye. When soybeans became a commercial U.S. product, the CBOT created futures for soybeans (1936), soybean oil (1950) and soybean meal (1951).

The CBOT's contribution to world grain trade was vital but hidden. It did not grow, process, or export midwestern grains, but it did provide two essential tools. First, trading at the CBOT discovered price. Illinois farmers could examine CBOT prices at spring planting time to determine whether to plant corn or soybeans, and again at harvest time to determine whether to store or sell their harvested crop. Second, trading at the CBOT shifted risk. A New York exporter's Hamburg customer wants soybeans delivered five months hence but a firm price commitment now. Committing now exposes the exporter to risk, because soybean prices could rise before the exporter has soybeans. The exporter, while negotiating with the Hamburg buyer, could shift risk by purchasing CBOT soybean futures from selling speculators (Fornari 1973).

By supplying these two tools as U.S. grain production exploded, the CBOT provided essential infrastructure and facilitated U.S. emergence as the world's leading grain exporter. Strategic location and timely innovations made the CBOT the leading U.S. futures exchange. By 1969, though still largest (43.6% of volume), the CBOT slipped from dominance (76.1% in 1962) as nongrain futures emerged and government agricultural policies slowed CBOT growth (Hieronymous 1977).

ERA OF SECURITIES

The 1960s stock and bond industry faced risks similar to those that the CBOT had managed for the grain industry since the 1860s. Applying its experience and infrastructure, the CBOT created many firsts. The CBOT opened the first stock-options exchange, Chicago Board Options Exchange (CBOE) on April 26, 1973, as a separate legal entity. CBOE quickly supplanted less efficient over-the-counter dealers and dominated all subsequent U.S. equity-option exchanges. The CBOT launched the first interest-rate futures (GNMA) on October 20, 1975. Treasury-bond futures followed on August 22, 1977. When interest-rate risk exploded in October 1979, T-bond futures volume soared to nearly 6.5 million in 1980. Notably, CBOT volume first reached 6 million in its one hundred

seventeenth year, 1965. The CBOT created five more interest-rate futures by 1990. In 1982 the CBOT fused futures and options creating eight options-on-futures contracts by 1990. These options provided 21.5 percent of CBOT volume in the 1990s. In 1984 CBOT stock index futures (Major Market Index, or MMI) began. Notably MMI was the only equity market never to close during the stock market crash of October 1987. Dow Jones Industrial Average futures began October 1997. Extending price discovery and risk shifting to world capital markets increased CBOT volume one hundred thirty-fold (4.6 million in 1968 to nearly 600 million in 2004).

INTERNATIONAL EXPLOSION

New exchanges from Asia, Europe, and South America looked to the success of the CBOT. The Commodity Trading Manual (CTM) notes twenty-nine non-U.S. futures exchanges trading in 1984 and more than fifty by 1994. Such imitation extended indirectly the CBOT's contribution to international trade. The CBOT found its relative size reduced by explosive growth in non-U.S. exchanges: in 1993 non-U.S. exchange volume surpassed U.S. exchange volume, and it accounted for nearly two-thirds of world volume in 2003. Non-U.S. exchanges sought to draw volume from CBOT contracts (notably T-bond contract in 1984 and 1985 and corn contract in 1994) by pressing time-zone advantages—that is, by trading when the CBOT was closed. The CBOT thwarted these attempts largely by opening an evening trading session. Clearly, world markets required new trading formats.

1989

In January the U.S. government revealed its undercover investigation of the CBOT and the Chicago Mercantile Exchange (CME) by subpoenaing hundreds of traders. Despite the government's claims of pervasive fraud, there were only thirteen convictions. In spring an alleged corner appeared involving the Italian conglomerate Ferruzzi. The CBOT determined that Ferruzzi's huge soybean position distorted the market, and required that Ferruzzi reduce it quickly. Without admitting guilt, Ferruzzi settled subsequent CBOT disciplinary proceedings by paying the CBOT U.S.$3 million in fines and court costs.

ELECTRONIC ERA

Computer technology improvements in the 1980s threatened the pit with obsolescence. But computerized trading had much to offer exchanges: total surveillance, global reach around the clock, and one-stop shopping. The CTM notes that eight exchanges used electronic platforms in 1990, but by 1992 twenty-one of twenty-seven exchanges with electronic platforms used them exclusively. After the venture with the CME (Globex system, 1992–1994) withered, the CBOT resurrected its Project A system. By 1995 Project A operated nearly every hour CBOT pits were closed. With Project A carrying loads exceeding its original purpose, the CBOT sought cooperative ventures (Eurex—A/C/E 2000–2003 and Euronext—LiffeConnect 2004). In 2004 61 percent of CBOT trading volume was electronic. The electronic challenge continues as evolving systems vie for dominance.

SEE ALSO AGRICULTURE; FINANCE, CREDIT AND MONEY LENDING; UNITED STATES; WHEAT AND OTHER CEREAL GRAINS.

BIBLIOGRAPHY

Alonzi, Peter, and Stebbins, Christine Depp, eds. *Commodity Trading Manual*, Patrick J. Catania, executive ed. Chicago: Board of Trade of the City of Chicago, 1994.

Cronon, William. "Pricing the Future: Grain." In *Nature's Metropolis: Chicago and the Great West*. New York: W. W. Norton, 1991.

Fallon, William D. *Market Maker: A Sesquicentennial Look at the Chicago Board of Trade*. Chicago: Board of Trade of the City of Chicago, 1998.

Fornari, Harry. *Bread Upon the Waters: A History of United States Grain Exports*. Nashville, TN: Aurora Publishers, 1973.

Hieronymus, Thomas A. *Economics of Futures Trading*, 2nd edition. New York: Commodity Research Bureau, 1977.

Lurie, Jonathan. *The Chicago Board of Trade, 1859–1905: The Dynamics of Self Regulation*. Urbana: University of Illinois Press, 1979.

Williams, Jeffrey C. "The Origin of Futures Markets." *Agricultural History* 56.1 (1982): 306–316.

INTERNET RESOURCES

Chicago Board of Trade. "Our History." Available from http://www.cbot.com/cbot/pub/page/0,3181,942.00.html.

Peter Alonzi

CHILE

Chile evolved as an outpost, first of the Spanish Empire, and then of the Atlantic World. Its economy evolved through the export of minerals. Since the establishment of European rule in 1540, Chile has produced gold, silver, nitrates, and copper, as well as quantities of iron, manganese, and iodine (a derivative of nitrate production). Trade cycles based on the technologies of production and external demand have shaped the country's overall development. Seeking to rapidly diversify its export base, in 1994 the government passed a new law (Decree Law 600) giving foreign investors the same rights as nationals under a most-favored-nation basis. The law triggered massive investment in industrial minerals, and Chile be-

came a major producer of arsenic, lead, molybdenum, selenium, borates, sulfur, potash, and potassium chloride; and, after the United States, it is the second-largest producer of lithium in the world. It has also rigorously pursued free-trade policies, concluding a major agreement with the United States in 2003.

EUROPEAN CONQUEST

The European invasion of Chile began when Diego de Almagro (1475?–1538), rich from the Peruvian conquest, went south by land in 1535 looking for gold; in three years he found only grief and ruin. Pedro de Valdivia (c. 1498–1553), in a more successful foray in 1540, established municipalities from La Serena in the north, through Santiago, Chile's capital, to Concepción in the south. The seminomadic native populations had nothing like the wealth or population of the Peruvian Incan Empire, a fact that shaped the colony's fate. Searching for commodities to send back to Peru, Valdivia and the other Europeans soon forced thousands of Indians into panning for gold. In 1553 the native Araucanians, most notably the Mapuche, rose in retaliation, burned several of the settlements to the ground, and in early 1554 killed Valdivia.

The uprising signaled the bloody economic history of the colony, which would be based on gold panning, war, and the proliferation of European livestock. Indian tribute labor produced gold under murderous conditions; indeed, a population of about one and a half million natives fell to less than half a million by 1620 as a result of war, enslavement, and tribute labor. White settlers bought cattle, sheep, and horses from Europe and set them loose, and by the 1570s were producing their own wool and rendering significant amounts of tallow. The huge increase in the number of European animals altered the Mapuche, who in a development comparable to that of the Plains Indians of North America became adept at riding horses and living off wild cattle. By 1580, with the decline in gold production, the economy became tied to war. Spain sent thousands of soldiers in the sixteenth and seventeenth centuries to create a fortified line against the natives and to fend off any rival European powers. Chile cost the Crown much more than it ever produced; its wealthiest settlers and merchants depended on feeding the troops and supplying the imperial army with leather, horses, and crude manufactures. By the eighteenth century, ships plied the South American coast between Concepción and Lima, taking wheat north and bringing European and Peruvian goods south. Trade expanded with Europe through links with Buenos Aires and through contraband shipping that came from France and England. Nonetheless, on the eve of its independence Chile was still a provincial zone of the Spanish Empire

Nitrates piled up for export from Antofagasta, a port city in northern Chile. *Along with copper, iron, petroleum, and natural gas, nitrates contribute to Chile's nearly $30 million export economy.* THREE LIONS/GETTY IMAGES. REPRODUCED BY PERMISSION.

with fewer than 750,000 inhabitants, though the underclass of peons and tenant farmers then consisted largely of *mestizos* (descendents of whites and Indians).

NINETEENTH CENTURY

Independence in the 1820s brought Chile close to Great Britain. Chilean liberals expanded trade with Britain and borrowed heavily from British merchant houses. In 1831

a conservative coalition led by Diego Portales (1793–1837) overthrew the liberals and, in 1833, established a new constitution that provided for a highly centralized government run by the president. The conservatives remained tied to Britain, and Valparaiso, the nation's major port, became little more than a British enclave. The British largely captained even the Chilean merchant marine. Chile's economy had a geographic structure with political power concentrated in Santiago, but the revenues to expand the government were tied to exports from the north (mining) and the south (wheat). For a short time in the 1850s Chile played a major role in supplying grain to the Australian and California gold fields. But the major engine of growth became copper, especially in the north around Copiapó. A new generation of liberals regained the political upper hand in the 1870s but they continued the economic policies of the Portalian regime.

Just to the north of Chile lay the Atacama Desert, then held by Bolivia (in the province of Antofagasta) and Peru (the province of Tarapacá). The desert zones boomed as European demand for commercial fertilizers led to exploitation of *salitre* (sodium nitrate). In 1879 a dispute over commercial rights in the desert led Chile to declare war on Bolivia and Peru. The War of the Pacific (1879–1883) ended with Chile seizing the nitrate zones of both nations and launching its own nitrate-based economy. British capital soon dominated the trade, and by 1890 the Chilean government under President José Manuel Balmaceda (1840–1891) was at loggerheads with the British nitrate combination led by John T. North (1842–1896). When, during a constitutional crisis, Congress rebelled against the president in 1891, the British remained formally neutral but did all they could to assist the rebellion. Congressional forces won, and in his suicide letter, Balmaceda claimed the Congress had acted on behalf of British interests.

TWENTIETH CENTURY TO THE PRESENT

The congressional victors reduced the powers of the presidency and enhanced their own, developing a complex multiparty system based on nitrate spoils. At times, a tax on nitrate exports provided the national government with 50 percent of its revenues. Import duties, which fluctuated with nitrate sales, provided the second major source of income. The British continued to manage the nitrate sector even as the Chilean work force chafed at British racism, low wages, and dangerous working conditions. Worse, Chilean politicians covered perennial deficits by printing money, causing inflation and even labor riots. During World War I the British cut off trade with Germany, then a major consumer of *salitre,* and the Germans began developing alternative, industrial sources of fertilizer. By the mid-1920s what the Chileans called "synthetic" nitrates cut deeply into the Chilean market.

U.S. capital flowed into Chile during World War I and thereafter, displacing the long century of British predominance. Led by the Guggenheims, U.S. investors sought to revive nitrate and copper exports, and U.S. banks took over lending to the government. The Guggenheims' gamble in nitrates failed during the Great Depression, leaving the Atacama Desert dotted with ghost towns. The Anaconda and Kennecott mining corporations took over investment in copper and succeeded handsomely, developing some of the world's richest ores. Chile remains the world's greatest producer of copper to this day. Just as Chileans had resented British control of the nitrate zones, they also came to resent U.S. control of the major copper mines. In 1971 the Socialist administration of President Salvador Allende (1908–1973) nationalized the mines, creating a direct confrontation with the U.S. government led by Richard Nixon (1913–1994), which ended with the United States helping the Chilean military to overthrow Allende in 1973. General Augusto Pinochet (b. 1915), with U.S. loans, consolidated a dictatorship that lasted until 1989. His advisors wrote a new constitution, approved by plebiscite, in 1981. Under Pinochet's rule the labor-union movement was permanently weakened, all political parties were banned, and the nation was thrown open to foreign investment. The economy collapsed and then began a slow recovery, led by a more diversified pattern of exports.

In 1989 another plebiscite ended Pinochet's rule and began a cycle of elected governments based on a multiparty coalition called the *Concertación.* Eventually, another socialist would be elected president, in 2000, but the economic rules after 1989 remained basically those that Pinochet had imposed. Unions remained weak and unable to mobilize as they had before 1973; the party system became representative only of capital. Chile was still trade dependent but its exports now included a mix of light manufactures, fruit, paper pulp, fish, and a large array of minerals—even though copper still made up 25 percent of the GDP. The foreign debt remained manageable but consumed up to 30 percent of foreign earnings. At the beginning of the twenty-first century Chile had a sputtering economy but compared favorably with the sad story in much of the rest of Latin America. Its economy had grown from U.S.$24 billion to over U.S.$64 billion between 1982 and 2002. About 40 percent of the population was gripped by poverty in 1990, but that figure fell to 20 percent by 2004. Adult literacy rose to over 95 percent, and per capita income was close to U.S.$4,500 a year in a population that had grown to over 15.5 million. Unemployment, nonetheless, hovered at 8 to 10 percent, and the distribution of income remained grotesque, with some 20 percent of the population taking in over 60 percent of all earnings. There was a high level of economic insecurity since no safety network existed to prevent individuals from plunging to the bottom.

SEE ALSO CONQUISTADORS; COPPER; EMPIRE, SPANISH; ENCOMIENDA AND REPARTIMIENTO; IMPORT SUBSTITUTION; LABORERS, AZTEC AND INCA; INTERNATIONAL MONETARY FUND (IMF); NATIONALIZATION; NITRATES; UNITED STATES.

BIBLIOGRAPHY

Bethell, Leslie, ed. *Chile since Independence.* Cambridge: Cambridge University Press, 1993.

Collins, Joseph and John Lear. *Chile's Free Market Miracle: A Second Look.* Oakland: Food First, 1995.

Collier, Simon and William F. Sater. *A History of Chile, 1808–2002,* 2nd edition. Cambridge: Cambridge University Press, 2004.

Loveman, Brian. *Chile: The Legacy of Hispanic Capitalism,* 3rd edition. New York and London: Oxford University Press, 2001.

Monteón, Michael. *Chile in the Nitrate Era: The Evolution of Economic Dependence, 1880–1930.* Madison: University of Wisconsin Press, 1982.

Winn, Peter, ed. *Victims of the Chilean Miracle: Workers and Neoliberalism in the Pinochet Era, 1973–2002.* Durham, NC: Duke University Press, 2004.

Michael Monteón

CHINA

Today the People's Republic of China (PRC, 1949 to present) is the third-largest trading nation in the world, behind only the United States and Japan. In 2004 imports and exports combined totaled more than U.S.$1.1 trillion, or nearly 7 percent of world trade, in an economy with a gross national product (GNP) of just over U.S.$1.5 trillion. Adjusting for differences in purchasing power parity (PPP) between China and the rest of the world, China's gross national product is U.S.$6 trillion. More than 80 percent of China's exports consists of manufactured goods, which now extend to an increasingly sophisticated array of products from apparel to machine tools to televisions. China has become the world's new manufacturing shop floor.

What is remarkable about China's current prominence in world trade is that it is almost all the product of changes occurring since the late 1970s. For the first three decades of the PRC, foreign trade was heavily planned and regulated, and largely confined to the former Soviet Union and Eastern Bloc countries. Although it served as an important source of capital goods and technology in China's immediate post-1949 industrialization efforts, and occasionally helped meet final consumer demand, in the mid-1970s China's total foreign trade was only U.S.$15 billion in current prices (Eckstein 1976).

CHINA'S ECONOMIC AND FOREIGN TRADE REFORMS

In the late 1970s China embarked on a radical economic reform path that opened its economy to the rest of the world, and gradually scrapped its Soviet-style planned economy in favor of a market-based economy with mixed ownership (Lardy 2002). Beginning in 1980 with the establishment of the four Special Economic Zones (Shenzhen, Xiamen, Zhuhai, and Shantou) and in 1984 with the setting up of Economic and Technical Development Zones in fourteen coastal cities, China encouraged foreign direct investment (FDI) as a means of developing a manufacturing export sector through the importation of much-needed capital, managerial know-how, and technology. Outside of these zones it allowed for the importation and licensing of new technologies and capital goods as part of a policy of modernizing existing domestic enterprises. China concurrently began to reduce tariff and nontariff barriers to trade, and to extend direct trading (import and export) rights to firms, culminating in its entry into the World Trade Organization (WTO) in 2001.

Domestically, China's trade reforms complemented a wide-ranging series of decentralizing economic reforms that reintroduced household farming in agriculture, expanded autonomy and increased incentives in China's state-enterprise sector, liberalized domestic markets, and allowed entry of new firms into most sectors. Aided by expanded access to overseas markets during a period of rapid globalization, China's renewed openness combined with domestic economic and institutional reform initiatives to serve as important catalysts to economic growth, which has averaged nearly 8 percent per annum in terms of GNP per capita.

Since the late 1970s FDI into China has exceeded a half a trillion U.S. dollars, much of it since the early 1990s. In 2004 alone, FDI exceeded U.S.$60 billion. Much of this investment has come from Asia—notably from firms in Hong Kong, followed by Taiwan, Japan, and Korea—who have looked to outsourcing to China as a way to reduce manufacturing costs in an increasingly competitive international environment. This has made China an integral part of global supply chains.

In the early 2000s, more than half of China's imports and exports are tied to foreign-invested enterprises (FIEs), the rest coming from domestically owned firms. Much of this FDI is from Asia, which helps explain an important regional dimension of China's trade. Nearly two-thirds of China's imports are from Asia, largely in the form of intermediate and capital goods, and, to a lesser extent, raw materials. Half of Chinese exports go to Asia. Overall, China runs a trade deficit with Asia, but a larger and rapidly expanding trade surplus with the United States. The latter has grown with the rapid increase in the outsourcing of manufacturing in Asia to China, and the decline in the trade surplus of other major Asian economies with the United States.

The historical Old Customs House and the Bank of China are shown along Shanghai's Bund roadway. Shanghai is located at the mouth of the Yangtze river and is China's largest city, serving as an important trade and financial center. The country's rise to global trading power started in the 1970s, when it expanded trading efforts beyond Communist nations and shifted to a market-based economy with mixed ownership. © MICHAEL FREEMAN/CORBIS. REPRODUCED BY PERMISSION.

TRADE WITH ASIA SINCE THE FOURTEENTH CENTURY

Intra-Asian trade has been an important feature of China's links with the international economy since at least the Ming dynasty (1368–1644), if not long before. Prior to the arrival of the Europeans in the early sixteenth century, China's trade was mostly with the Arabs, and increasingly with neighbors in Southeast Asia (Siam, Indochina, Burma, Malaya, Java. and the Philippines), as well as with Japan and Korea. Recognition of a significant China-centered trade in Asia has become central to new reinterpretations of "global" history (Franks 1999).

Some of China's trade occurred through the imperial tributary system, but probably even larger was a private trade involving its southern coastal provinces with the rest of Asia (Deng 1997). Despite frequent government bans on seaborne private trade—a ban was officially imposed between 1368 and 1567, and again under the Qing (1644–1911) between 1664 and 1684 and 1717 and 1727—private overseas trade continued, often in collaboration with local officials. Reflecting China's high com-

parative level of commercial and economic development and competitiveness in the sixteenth and seventeenth centuries, exports were made up largely of manufactured goods such as silk and cotton textiles, ceramics (porcelain), and metals (including copper coins), and imports consisted heavily of raw materials such as spices, timber, cotton, and monetary metals.

TRADE WITH EUROPEANS, SIXTEENTH CENTURY TO THE MID-1800s

The Portuguese were the first of the Europeans to develop trade with China in the early sixteenth century, through the settlement of Macao. Efforts to trade directly were resisted by Beijing. Later in the century an indirect trade with Spain also developed through Chinese merchants who traded regularly between Manila and Fujian province. In the early seventeenth century the first trade with the Dutch emerged, originally through the island of Formosa (Taiwan), but subsequently through Canton with permission from the Manchu government. The British obtained similar rights in 1637.

The British came to dominate China's direct trade with Westerners, which in 1757 was restricted to movement through the southern port of Canton. Trade with the West through Canton coexisted with the Chinese native foreign trade involving Asia, which continued to be carried on by junks at ports along the South China Coast. Institutionally, the Western trade took the form of a bilateral monopoly involving the British East India Company and the Chinese *cohong*, or trade guild system. The *cohong* was formerly established as a corporate body in 1720, with its members given exclusive rights to trade with foreigners; in 1760 they were further authorized to collect revenue on behalf of the Qing government. During the seventeenth and eighteenth centuries tea surpassed textiles and ceramics as China's largest exports, and opium became the largest import.

Several forces contributed to the demise of the *cohong* system in the early nineteenth century, the most important of which may have been Britain's persistent trade deficit with China. The British attributed this largely to the *cohong* system and limitations of trade only through Canton, and pushed for a more liberal trade regime with expanded access for Britain's manufacturers. During the early nineteenth century rapidly growing imports of opium (both legal and illegal) from India solved Britain's trade deficit, but provoked Chinese outrage. When Chinese authorities seized and burned more than 6 million silver dollars in opium, this led to the Opium Wars (1839–1842) and the Treaty of Nanjing (1842), which for the next century defined China's foreign trade regime.

Under the Treaty of Nanjing and the Treaty of Tianjin (1858), forty-eight Chinese ports were forcibly opened to foreign trade. Each of the major treaty ports had at least one foreign concession or settlement under non-Chinese rule. Rights of inland navigation were also extended to foreign vessels, with ports of call set up on both the Yangtze and Xi (West) Rivers. In 1895, following the Sino-Japanese War, foreigners were also extended full freedom to build factories in the treaty ports.

China lost all tariff autonomy with the establishment of the treaty ports. Only in 1929 under the nationalist government was it finally restored (Cheng 1956). By treaty, a low *ad valorem* tax of 5 percent was imposed on all imported goods. Moreover, all imports, after an additional 2.5 percent duty was paid, were exempt from any other additional domestic transit taxes or levies (commonly referred to as *likin*). An Inspectorate General of Customs was set up in 1854 to collect tariff duties and manage other customs matters. Robert Hart became inspector-general in 1863 and held the position until he died in 1911. A majority of the revenue collected was used to make reparation payments required by the aforementioned treaties.

Severe data limitations make it very difficult to quantify China's foreign trade up until the mid-1800s, its trends, and its effect on growth and productivity in China and elsewhere. But it is clear that prior to 1800, and in stark contrast to the late nineteenth and early twentieth centuries, China consistently exported more in merchandise than it imported. This gap was largely filled with the importation of silver, first from Japan in the fifteenth to seventeenth centuries, and later from the New World from the sixteenth through the eighteenth centuries. Imports of silver in the eighteenth century alone may have been as much as 1 billion taels (annually an amount equal to 0.5 percent of Chinese GDP) (von Glahn 2003, citing Dermigny 1964). The flow of silver into China (and occasional export of gold from China) can be linked to two key factors: (1) huge differences in the gold price of silver between China and the rest of the world, which were largely arbitraged away by the mid-eighteenth century (von Glahn 2003); and (2) an increase in demand for silver in China after the collapse of an earlier paper-money system. China's monetary system during the Ming and Qing was bimetallic, and silver and copper the two mediums of exchange. The increasing commercialization and monetization of the economy, as well as growth in its overall size—much of it related to a tripling China's population to between 350 and 400 million by the end of the eighteenth century—contributed to the growing demand for silver. But although they likely grew in absolute terms in the eighteenth century with the growth in population, at its pre-1800 peak China's annual exports probably did not exceed one or two percent of GNP. And since China consistently exported more than it imported, imports were even smaller.

TRADE SINCE 1870

The period 1870 to 1914 witnessed a rapid expansion in international trade, capital flows, and migration, which then slowed significantly during the interwar period (O'Rourke and Williamson 2002). China's foreign trade largely followed these trends. Its foreign trade quadrupled in real terms between 1868 and 1914, or at a real rate of growth between 3 and 4 percent per annum, but it then slowed to half of this rate through the late 1920s. It then declined significantly over the next two decades. Major causal factors included falling export demand for Chinese products linked to the world depression in the 1930s, the introduction of import-substitution policies with the restoration of tariff autonomy in 1929, and thirteen years of war on Chinese soil between 1936 and 1949.

As they had been prior to the Opium Wars, tea and silk—primarily raw silk as opposed to silk piece goods—were China's two largest exports through the last half of the nineteenth century. However, their share of total ex-

Pudong, Shanghai's financial, high-tech, and trading center, 2002. *Opened by Deng Xiaoping in 1992, Pudong ignited new economic development in the area.* AP/WIDE WORLD PHOTOS. REPRODUCED BY PERMISSION.

ports fell from over 90 percent to slightly less than 50 percent, as exports of tea declined with increasing competition for India and Ceylon, and exports of other agricultural goods and animal products increased. These trends continued through the early twentieth century, with the export of soya beans and bean cake from Manchuria becoming especially important. China's single-largest import up through the 1890s remained opium, followed by cotton piece goods and yarn. The share of all three declined over time, however. By agreement with the British government, opium imports largely disappeared by the end of World War I. On the other hand, imports of grain, cotton, sugar, tobacco, kerosene, metals and minerals, and machinery all increased significantly between 1900 and 1930, reflecting the growing demands of China's emerging modern manufacturing sector centered in the treaty-port cities, and its expanding urban population. Significantly, by the early 1930s Japan had become China's largest trading partner, with the United States second and Great Britain a distant third. Overall, Asia was once again China's major source of imports, and market for exports.

Changes in China's trade in cotton goods illustrate the complex impact of the treaty-port system and China's opening up of the economy during the last half of the nineteenth century and the first three decades of the twentieth century. The importation of cotton yarn led to a significant reorganization in the handicraft textile industry, as imported manufactured yarn began to replace handicraft yarn in the production of handicraft (native) cloth. The displacement occurred largely because of the sharp decline in the price of yarn relative to cotton (and therefore, the returns to labor in handicraft spinning) that occurred as China opened up. Subsequently, cotton-yarn imports were replaced with domestically manufactured yarn through a process of domestic import substitution. This can be tied to investment in the modern textile industry in China after 1895. At the outset this was a largely foreign-owned industry, dominated by British and subsequently Japanese firms. Chinese entrepreneurs followed, and by the early 1930s more than two-thirds of domestic textile output was produced by Chinese firms. In the process, China turned from being a net importer to a net exporter of yarn, with cotton yarn shipped throughout Southeast Asia. Chinese cloth manufacturing—mostly for the domestic market—also increased significantly, and helped to reduce by half net imports of cloth.

Throughout much of the period between the 1870s and 1930s, China ran a merchandise trade deficit, typically importing 20 to 25 percent more than it exported. This was largely offset by overseas Chinese remittances, much of which came from a huge Chinese population settled throughout Southeast Asia, and significant foreign direct investment from Great Britain, the United States, Germany, and Japan in the nascent modern sector in the treaty ports. China was on a silver standard up through 1935, and in most years it was a net importer of silver, but net exporter of gold. As the price of silver rose in the 1930s due to U.S. government purchases, China became a huge net exporter of silver.

Despite this half-century of growth, China's imports and exports combined never represented more than 8 to 10 percent of Chinese GDP, and was between 2 and 3 percent of world trade, or roughly its share in 1990. Yet the impact of China's opening up may have been more significant than these numbers alone indicate. On the one hand, the integration of Chinese markets for grain, cotton, and cloth with the rest of world meant that perhaps for the first time in Chinese history prices for millions of Chinese farmers and households, and thus resource allocation, were being determined internationally rather than domestically (Brandt 1989). Previously, it was likely the only differences in the price of monetary metals (gold, silver, and copper) were arbitraged through international trade. On the other hand, the introduction and early development of a modern sector in the Chinese economy, which by the 1930s was largely in Chinese hands, can be linked to the treaty ports and the early catalytic effect of foreign enterprise and investments (Rawski 1990).

SEE ALSO BOYCOTT; BRITISH–AMERICAN TOBACCO; BULLION (SPECIE); GUANGZHOU; CANTON SYSTEM; COTTON; COUNTERFEIT GOODS; DENG XIAOPING; DRUGS, ILLICIT; EAST INDIA COMPANY, BRITISH; EAST INDIA COMPANY, DUTCH; EMPIRE, BRITISH; EMPIRE, JAPANESE; EMPIRE, MING; EMPIRE, PORTUGUESE; EMPIRE, QING; ETHNIC GROUPS, CANTONESE; ETHNIC GROUPS, FUJIANESE; FURS; HART, ROBERT; HONG KONG; HONG KONG AND SHANGHAI BANK; IMPERIAL MARITIME CUSTOMS, CHINA; IRON AND STEEL; LABORERS, CONTRACT; LIN ZEXU; MANCHURIA; MOST–FAVORED–NATION PROVISIONS; NANYANG BROTHERS TOBACCO; RICE; SHANGHAI; SILK; SOUTH CHINA SEA; SPECIAL ECONOMIC ZONES (SEZs); TAIWAN; TEA; TEXTILES; TIMBER; TOBACCO; TOYS; TRIBUTE SYSTEM; TUNG CHEE–HWA; ZHANG HAN; ZHENG FAMILY.

BIBLIOGRAPHY

Brandt, Loren. *Commercialization and Agricultural Development: Central and Eastern China, 1870–1937.* New York: Cambridge University Press, 1989.

Cheng, Yu-kwei. *Foreign Trade and Industrial Development of China.* Washington, DC: University Press of Washington, DC, 1956.

Cushman, Jennifer Wayne. *Fields from the Sea: Chinese Junk Trade with Siam During the Late Eighteenth and Early Nineteenth Century.* Ithaca, NY: Cornell Southeast Asia Program, 1993.

Deng, Gang. "The Foreign Staple Trade of China in the Pre-Modern Era." *The International Economic History Review* 29, no. 2 (May 1997): 253–285.

Eckstein, Alexander. *China's Economic Revolution.* New York: Cambridge University Press, 1976.

Hsiao, Liang-lin. *China's Foreign Trade Statistics, 1864–1949.* Cambridge, MA: East Asia Research Center, Harvard University, 1974.

Fairbank, John King. *Trade and Diplomacy on the China Coast: The Opening of the Treaty Ports, 1842–1854.* Cambridge, MA: Harvard University Press, 1953.

Frank, Andre Gunder. *ReORIENT: Global Economy in the Asian Age.* Berkeley: University of California Press, 1998.

Lardy, Nicholas. *Integrating China into the Global Economy.* Washington, DC: Brookings Institution Press, 2002.

O'Rourke, Kevin, and Williamson, Jeffrey. *Globalization and World History: The Evolution of the Nineteenth-Century Atlantic Economy.* Cambridge, MA: Massachusetts Institute of Technology Press, 2000.

Rawski, Thomas. *Economic Growth in Prewar China.* Berkeley: University of California Press, 1989.

Von Glahn, Richard. "Money Use in China and Changing Patterns of Global Trade in Monetary Metals, 1500–1800." In *Global Connections and Monetary History, 1470–1800,* ed. Dennis O. Flynn, Auturo Giraldez, and Richard von Glahn. Burlington, VT: Ashgate, 2003.

Loren Brandt

WINSTON CHURCHILL
1874-1965

Winston Churchill—war correspondent, World War I army officer, historian, author (winner of the Nobel Prize for Literature in 1953), painter, First Lord of the Admiralty from 1911 to 1915 and 1939 to 1940, Chancellor of the Exchequer from 1924 to 1929, leading opponent of both Nazi Germany and postwar Stalinist Soviet Union, and Prime Minister of the United Kingdom from 1940 to 1945 and 1951 to 1955—is one of the great historical figures of the twentieth century.

Churchill's policies had two major effects on the international economy. The first was negative. Churchill was responsible for returning the United Kingdom to the gold standard in 1925 at the prewar value of the British pound. This resulted in an overvaluation of the pound of about 10 percent, meaning that British prices were 10 percent higher than those of its trading partners and competitors. The result was a depressed export sector, balance-of-payments difficulties, unemployment, and labor strife. Churchill pushed for low interest rates not to ameliorate the domestic effects of his decision, but to facilitate debt management.

The second influence was positive. In August 1941 Churchill and President Franklin D. Roosevelt of the United States issued the Atlantic Charter, which was authored in its first draft by Churchill. This document was the first statement of principles for the postwar economic order. One principle was multilateralism, via the statement that all states should have equal access to trade and raw materials. Another principle was international collaboration for improved labor standards, economic development, and social security. These principles were the genesis of the International Monetary Fund, World Bank, and General Agreement on Tariffs and Trade (which flowed from the stillborn International Trade Organization).

SEE ALSO BRETTON WOODS; GREAT DEPRESSION OF THE 1930S; UNITED KINGDOM.

BIBLIOGRAPHY

Ball, Stuart. *Winston Churchill.* New York: New York University Press, 2003.

Gardner, Richard N. *Sterling-Dollar Diplomacy,* expanded edition. New York: McGraw-Hill, 1969.

Officer, Lawrence H. *Between the Dollar-Sterling Gold Points.* Cambridge, U.K.: Cambridge University Press, 1996.

Lawrence H. Officer

CLIMATE

The use of the term *trade winds* illustrates the close relationship between climate and world trade, although the nature and scale of the influence of climatic factors on trade is a matter for debate. We know that improving climatic conditions favor the development of human societies and, accordingly, terrestrial and maritime trade, as in Europe from the tenth to the fourteenth centuries. At that time, when the earth warmed, dangerous sea routes were curved around toward higher latitudes, and the crossing of mountainous barriers was easier as passes were not as snowy.

However, this trend toward climatic determinism should be tempered. On the one hand, as regards the regional effects of general climatic changes in Northern Europe, historically, most maritime trade has been limited in winter to the non-icebound harbors. It has been the case, for example, of Bergen (in today's Norway), the harbor of which was never icebound and could belong to the Hanseatic League during the late medieval period for this very reason. Obviously, this kind of factor is ineffective in the Mediterranean, where no harbor is ever icebound. Moreover, it is clear that the technological levels of human societies that are subjected to climatic changes sometimes have been determined by climatic factors; for example, it is because of gradual climatic deterioration from the fourteenth century on that the precarious Viking settlements of southwest Greenland disappeared. The progressive cooling reduced the surface area of cultivated land, and drifting ice made sailing increasingly dangerous. Foreign incursions to North America in search of wood, and to Iceland for supplies of metal, dwindled, then ceased in about 1450. Nevertheless, the cooling that took place in the Northern Hemisphere beginning in 1550 did not prevent the regular growth of commercial relationships between Europe and America. Technological advances in horology (marine chronometers), in the making of optical instruments (sextants, octants), in shipbuilding (clippers, then steamers with metallic hulls), and in propulsion methods (twin-propelled steamers), even made possible a spectacular boom in transoceanic trade during the last cold pulsation (1800–1850) of the so-called "little ice age."

THE LITTLE ICE AGE (1550–1850)

The term *little ice age* was coined by François-Emile Matthes (1874–1948). It denotes the period between about 1550 and 1850, which was characterized in Europe by long harsh winters, rather cool and humid summers, and a general spate of glaciers. The mean temperature may have been 1–2° C (1.8–3.6° F) colder than today's. Because the cool temperatures of this period were far from the intense freeze of the great quarternary glaciations, most climatologists prefer the terms *Fernau stage* and *Fernau oscillation,* from the name of a tyrolean glacier of the time. Moreover, the consequences of the cooling period are unclear: one can observe during this period both stages of economic slump (in the course of the seventeenth century) and periods of growth (during the eighteenth century).

Climatic conditions could have played an important part in certain major historical events, including the great medieval famines in Europe up to the 1694 starvation that killed more than 2 million people in France. In another example, leading up to the French Revolution, cold years, late frosts, and rainy summers succeeded one another from 1782 to 1787. The summer of 1788 was torrid

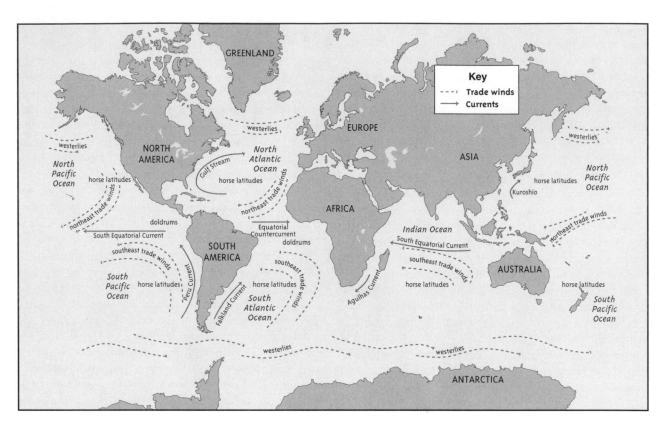

BLACKBIRCH PRESS PHOTO BANK. REPRODUCED BY PERMISSION OF THOMSON GALE.

and dry, and cereals and vineyards dried out before the crops; during the following winter, temperatures collapsed, provisions ran short, and prices rose dramatically. Wheat convoys were looted, castles were burned, and feudal taxes went unpaid. Spurred by the July 14, 1789, uprising in Paris, nearly two-thirds of the French population revolted. In this case, even the most anti-determinist historians consider that climatic conditions, in addition to political, sociological, and philosophical circumstances, played a part in launching a historical event.

Other climatic factors are sometimes put forward to explain historical events. One that occurs most frequently, and which should be very carefully assessed, is the undecennal (eleven-year) recurrence of sunspots, which denote a high solar activity caused by a perturbation of the solar magnetic field. Peaks of political agitation, cardiovascular troubles, suicides, and so on, are said to occur more frequently during periods of high solar activity. This assertion is taken seriously neither by historians nor by climatologists. However, we know that telecom networks can be disrupted during periods of high solar-flare activity, and as the mean solar luminosity paradoxically increases, solar activity has an effect on climate. But the true nature and the scale of the phenomenon are still to be determined.

THE MODERN PERIOD (1850s TO THE PRESENT)

In 1686 Edmund Halley (1656–1742) established the first world map of the trade winds known at that time, including the monsoon winds, and in 1735 the physicist and meteorologist George Hadley (1685–1768) gave an explanation of their general orientation. Climatology was thus born, but two fact conditions were still to be fulfilled at the beginning of nineteenth century before it could develop further. The first was to establish the certainty of great climatic changes in history. This evidence was obtained with the 1805 to 1812 discovery by Georges Cuvier (1769–1832) of ancient tropical fauna in the Paris area, and with the proof produced by Louis Agassiz (1807–1873) in 1840 that a huge inlandsis (a continental glacier) had covered present-day Switzerland during the last glaciation (Würm-Wisconsin). The second condition required the systematic gathering of climatologic data on a world scale. In this matter we owe Alexander von Humboldt (1769–1859) for the first world map of isotherm lines (1817).

Nevertheless, modern climatology (the science that deals with climates, i.e., weather patterns averaged over long periods, and that investigates weather phenomena and causes) began really with the discovery of the world's climate solar forcing. Between 1911 and 1957 Milutin Milankovitch (1879–1859) undertook to prove that the complex combination of different cyclical variations of the terrestrial orbit explains the alternation of warming and glaciation phases over the last 600,000 years. This theory forecasts the beginning of a new glaciation period in 70,000 years.

The discovery of the general circulation of the atmosphere was a major step for the development of modern climatology. In the 1920s Gilbert Walker (1868–1958) explained the trade-winds system in the Pacific and coined the expression *Southern oscillation* (SO) to designate the seesaw shift in surface air pressure at Darwin, Australia, and the South Pacific Island of Tahiti. Several decades later, in 1969, Jacob Bjerknes (1897–1975) linked up the Southern oscillation to El Niño events (EN), which are sporadic declines in the strength of Pacific trade winds that induce very remote and often intense atmospheric disturbances. Hence, Bjerknes coined the acronym ENSO.

Advances in the development of telecommunication networks, supercomputers, and satellite observing systems have been spectacular from the 1960s on. Meteorology (which is weather forecast, in contradistinction to *climatology,* whose aim is the understanding of long-range climatic changes) is henceforth reliable within six days and very accurate locally. These advances have promoted agriculture in developed countries and increased the security of commercial transportation.

GLOBAL WARMING

A warming trend of about 0.6° C (1° F) has been recorded on the planet Earth since 1861; melting glaciers and decreasing snow covers have been regularly observed since then. Most climatologists consider the industrial and agricultural activities of human societies to be responsible for the emissions of greenhouse gases, the main factor in global warming. However, some support the theory that water vapor is by far the main contributor to the greenhouse effect, because we can only find traces of greenhouse gases (CO_2, CO, CH_4, $NO2$, CFCs, O_3) in the chemical composition of the atmosphere.

In any case, we can expect a mean warming of as much as 6° C (10.8° F) by the end of twenty-first century—a climatic change that would be comparable to the alterations that took place during the last 20,000 years. Rainfalls and winds regime would be disrupted, and agriculture would change. The melting of glaciers as well as the thermal dilation of the oceans could lead to a gradual modification of the coastlines and even to the submersion of the lower lands. Floods, heat waves, and hurricanes would probably occur more frequently and violently. Due to the thermal inertia of oceans, the Southern Hemisphere would be less affected than the northern part of the planet. This warming would not necessarily indicate dryness, because the increasing evaporation could also increase cloud covering. Besides resultant problems in communications and transportation, climatic disturbances could also disrupt the most undermined social systems of the planet, which would not be an evolution favorable to world trade.

SEE ALSO INFORMATION AND COMMUNICATIONS; SHIPS AND SHIPPING.

BIBLIOGRAPHY

Acot, Pascal, et al. *The Concept of Biosphere.* Farmington Hills, MI: Gale, 2000.

Acot, Pascal. *Histoire du Climat,* 2nd edition. Paris: Éditions Perrin, 2003.

Burroughs, W. J. *Does the Weather Really Matter? The Social Implications of Climate Change.* Cambridge, U.K.: Cambridge University Press, 1997.

Crowley, T. G. "Causes of Climate Change over the Past 1,000 Years." *Science* 289, no. 5477 (1997): 270–277.

Hartmann, D. L. *Global Physical Climatology.* San Diego, CA: Academic Press, 1994.

Oliver J. H., and Fairbridge, R. W., eds. *Encyclopaedia of Climatology.* New York: Van Nostrand Reinhold, 1987.

McCusker, John. J. *Essays on the Economic History of the Atlantic World.* London and New York: Routledge, 1997.

Pascal Acot

COAL

The term *coal* describes an heterogeneous variety of fossilized plant materials, distinguished by different physical and chemical properties including their heating value, content of carbon and impurities, degree of moisture, solidity of structure, and melting temperature. Coal types are generally ranked according to their content of carbon, which provides most of its energy generation as measured in British thermal units per pound (BTU). In descending order, anthracite has a very high carbon content and BTU, followed by bituminous, sub-bituminous, and lignite (or brown) coal. Differences in the property of coal are reflected in their use. High- to medium-grade coals tend to be used for heating and coking, lower grades more commonly for electric power generation. Although all grades can be found in many parts of the world, Britain has mined a large supply of anthracite coal; North America, Australia, and South Africa, bituminous; and continental Europe, China, and India, brown coal. Geographical mismatches between the supply and demand for different types of coal and varying rates of mineral exploitation over time have generated an extensive national and international coal trade.

Coal mining has a long history dating back to at least the second century B.C.E. in China and evidenced in Brit-

NEWCASTLE COLLIERS

Newcastle upon Tyne was an important coastal supplier of coal to London beginning in the thirteenth century. By the 1600s true colliers (based on Dutch bulk carriers) appeared, replacing the general cargo vessels used previously. Over the course of the seventeenth century vessel size increased, with average cargoes ranging from 50 to 250 tons of coal. The small River Tyne made a flat-bottom design standard for Newcastle colliers, which could load at staiths on the river regardless of low water levels. To keep costs low it was important for colliers to handle well without ballast, so they were normally two-masted, reducing weight aloft. This allowed for small crews and easier access to cargo hatches. The colliers were often put to other uses, and three of Captain Cook's vessels—small, flat-bottomed, and able to carry large cargoes relative to crew size—were former east coast colliers. (Cook had served on colliers himself.) Little changed until the mid-1800s. In 1865 William Jevons reported that Newcastle steam colliers with a crew of twenty-one could transport more than 62,000 tons of coal to London per year, doing the work of sixteen traditional sailing colliers and 144 men.

David J. Clarke

ain by the Roman period. Before the eighteenth century coal, along with wood, was used for heating in the household and in industries such as shipbuilding, brewing, baking, glassmaking, pottery, and dye making. Wood was used for other purposes, particularly construction, such that by the eighteenth century, with population expansion and economic growth boosting demand, Britain and then many continental European nations faced a shortage of easily accessible timber located close to navigable waterways. Britain had been the dominant coal producer in the seventeenth century, accounting for more than 80 percent of world output. It was the source of most of the technological breakthroughs that increased the supply of easily mined coal and revealed important new uses for it. In 1709 Abraham Darby of Coalbrookdale (1678–1717) produced pig iron through smelting the ore with coking coal in a blast furnace. This provided labor savings compared with the use of charcoal. Concerns about the iron's quality using this method were allayed by a series of

modifications introduced by John Smeaton (1724–1792) in the 1760s. The value of blast-furnace pig iron augmented after 1784 when Henry Cort (1740–1800) found a way of converting this brittle product into wrought iron through stirring out ("puddling") the impurities and then pressing it with cylinders into a rolling mill.

A second major breakthrough was the use of coal for propulsion through the invention of the steam engine, which converted reciprocating motion into rotary motion. Thomas Newcomen (1663–1729) built the first operational steam engine in 1712 to pump water from coal mines, thereby increasing the efficiency and the depths to which mining could be undertaken. Its heavy fuel (coal) consumption limited use of the Newcomen engine mostly to coal mines. The development of a separate condenser by James Watt (1736–1819) in 1765, together with other improvements including double-acting expansion and automatic regulators, greatly reduced the steam engine's fuel consumption. Watt's engine was used in coal mining for winding and haulage. However, its greater efficiency vastly broadened the steam engine's potential application, allowing subsequent generations of engineers to adapt it for powering industrial machinery, the railways, and shipping. The greater regularity and mobility of supply of coal over water, and coal's superior thermal efficiency to wood, ensured a preference for using coal in industry and transport.

Coal was king in the nineteenth century, when its uses and efficiency continued to expand. Triple- and quadruple-expansion and turbine engines ensured the increasing efficiency of steamships and their diffusion through most international trade routes by the end of the century. Additional coal uses included the production of gas and electricity, while coal tar distillates from the coking process led to the development of a range of organic chemical compounds including dyes, fertilizers, solvents, and explosives. A widening range of construction uses for wrought iron and, by the late nineteenth century, of steel, exerted a huge increase in the derived demand for coking coal.

The expanded demand for coal in the nineteenth century was largely met by increased output without improved productivity. In Britain the exhaustion of most open-cast easily accessible underground coal seams, together with labor unrest and the slow adoption of mechanized coal cutting, meant productivity (output per man shift) was mostly constant or declining in the traditional mining areas of the northeast of England. However, a major expansion of output in South Wales occurred with the rapid growth of demand for its high quality steaming coal. Other European nations began to exploit their coal resources as major fields emerged in Westphalia (Germany), northern France, southern Netherlands, and central

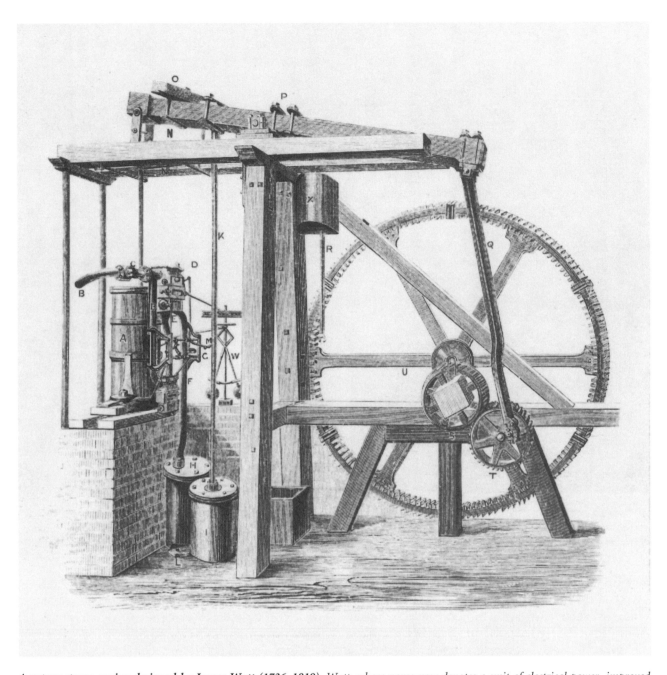

A rotary steam engine designed by James Watt (1736–1819). *Watt, whose name now denotes a unit of electrical power, improved on the designs of early steam engines by increasing their efficiency and reliability. The rotary engine that Watt patented made possible a variety of steam-powered machinery—a necessary precursor to the Industrial Revolution.* THE GRANGER COLLECTION, NEW YORK. REPRODUCED BY PERMISSION.

Belgium. Here mechanization was also limited, although the effective compression of coal into briquettes beginning in 1877 removed much of the water from brown coal and therefore improved its quality. The United States also became a major coal producer through the development of the Pennsylvania coalfields, subsequently spreading production to many other states in both the East and the West. These fields drew more heavily upon

mechanized coal cutting, and in 1899 U.S. output surpassed that of Britain.

The bulkiness of coal relative to its value made long-distance trade in the commodity uneconomic before the emergence of modern transport systems, except when producer and consumer were closely located to navigable waterways. Coal shipped coastally from the main producing area of northeast England reached the expanding

A photo from the early 1900s of a miner on a coal car in a tunnel. During the nineteenth century, higher demand for coal was met by increasing output levels instead of focusing on productivity improvement. Mining companies expanded their underground operations, creating dangerous working conditions for laborers. THE LIBRARY OF CONGRESS.

population and industries of London by way of the River Tyne and the River Thames. The expansion of Britain's system of inland waterways in the eighteenth century was motivated by the need to reduce the overland cost of coal transport. "A navigation should always have coals at the heels of it," noted the Duke of Bridgewater, whose Bridgewater Canal (1761) connected his Worsley coal mines with the expanding industrial city of Manchester. The railways, in addition to their heavy reliance on coal fuel and iron construction, counted coal companies among their major customers. Overland rail haulage of coal in the United States has been identified as a key explanation of the emergence of large-scale national manufacturing firms by the late nineteenth century.

With the new opportunities for coal use and the international expansion of industrialization, based on coal-using industries, the seaborne coal trade expanded rapidly in the second half of the nineteenth century. This was a trade principally in British coal carried in British ves-

sels. By 1913, 33 percent of British coal output was exported, which constituted 50 percent of the world coal trade and 70 percent of seaborne coal movements. Eighty percent of British coal exports went to Europe, delivering at North German ports more cheaply than overland coal could be conveyed by rail from the Ruhr fields. Welsh steam coal replenished oceanic bunkering stations throughout the world: its high calorific content, resistance to en route deterioration, and smokeless nature made it particularly appropriate. The international coal trade reduced Britain's imbalance in freight volumes, and in the process may have constrained increases in the level of freight rates. U.S. coal, though more oriented to the domestic market, included trade to other parts of the American continent.

In the twentieth century coal encountered a widening range of energy substitutes, particularly oil and its by-products, natural gas, electricity, nuclear power, and solar power. After 1918 oil began to replace coal in shipping, while the rising demand for petrol and aviation fuel stimulated the search for new oil reserves and enabled the refining industry to expand production size and thus reduce its costs. Coal's share of the United Kingdom's energy needs collapsed from 91 to 38 percent in the quarter century after 1948, a trend broadly reflected in many other nations' economies as coal's share of world energy consumption dropped below 50 percent in 1961. The main causes of the decline were the replacement of steam by diesel and electricity on the railways; the discovery of natural gas under the North Sea, and its widespread displacement of coal gas; the substitution of cleaner and more convenient electricity and oil in factories and homes; and the tentative development of nuclear power. Indeed, the only area of increased coal demand came from power stations for the manufacture of electricity, which accounted for 62 percent of world coal consumption by 1999. This market has brought little benefit to the coal industry because it involves the purchase of low-grade coals by large electricity companies with strong price-negotiating power. The profitability of coking coal has been adversely affected by new technologies including coal moisture control, dry-air compaction system, and pulverized coal injection, which made possible the introduction of lower priced "semisoft" coking coal in 1981. In addition, there has been increasing use of electric arc furnaces, which do not require coke, in steel production.

Coal, nonetheless, remains a major industry and seaborne commodity trade at the beginning of the twenty-first century, with a widening range of major producers and exporters. These include Australia (the leading exporter by 2000), South Africa, China, and Indonesia, which are the main suppliers of the expanding Asian market, particularly Japan, Korea, Taiwan, and, more generally, the Association of South-East Asian Nations (ASEAN), a body that promotes economic and political cooperation among its ten member nations. Increased consumption in these markets has helped to offset the reduced production and consumption of European countries, where natural gas is increasingly used in electricity generation. Environmental concerns together with the reduction of coal subsidies and the coal-purchase obligations of electricity producers have also affected European demand. Technological and organizational advances have been significant in increasing productivity and cutting production costs. These have included mechanical coal cutting and conveyance, computerized and remote control operations, and privatization of the industry onto a commercial basis. In the first decade of the twenty-first century, coal consumption is projected to grow at 1.9 percent per annum, 0.2 percent above world energy consumption, reflecting the continued importance of the commodity.

SEE ALSO INDUSTRIALIZATION; MINING.

BIBLIOGRAPHY

Ashworth, William. *The History of the British Coal Industry,* Volume 5: *The Nationalised Industry.* Oxford, U.K.: Clarendon Press, 1986.

Australian Bureau of Agricultural and Resource Economics (ABARE). *Global Coal Markets: Prospects to 2010.* Canberra, Australia: 2002.

Lewis, Brian. *Coal Mining in the Eighteenth and Nineteenth Centuries.* London: Longman, 1936.

Milward, Alan, and Saul, Samuel Berrick. *The Economic Development of Continental Europe, 1780–1870,* 2nd edition. London: Allen and Unwin, 1979.

Mokyr. Joel. "Technology in the Early Nineteenth Century." In *The Economic History of Britain since 1700,* eds. Roderick Floud and Donald McCloskey, 2nd edition. Cambridge, U.K.: Cambridge University Press, 1994.

Pounds, Norman John Greville. *An Historical Geography of Europe, 1800–1914.* Cambridge, U.K.: Cambridge University Press, 1985.

Palmer, Sarah. "The British Coal Export Trade, 1850–1913." In *Volumes Not Values: Canadian Sailing Ships and World Trades,* eds. David Alexander and Rosemary Ommer. Newfoundland: Memorial University of Newfoundland, 1979.

Simon Ville

JAN PIETERSZOON COEN
1587–1629

Jan Coen was born on January 8, 1587, in the Dutch town of Hoorn. He died on September 21, 1629, during a siege of Batavia. As governor-general (1618–1623 and 1627–1629) of the Dutch East India Company (Verenigde Oost-Indische Compagnie, or VOC) he forcefully established the company in Asia.

Already in 1614 Coen had outlined a strategy for the VOC: oppose European competitors; monopolize the spice trade by subduing local rulers; establish European settlements; and participate in the intra-Asiatic trade, the proceeds from which could finance the commodities for the European market.

As governor-general Coen conquered Djakarta in 1619. Renamed Batavia, the town became the administrative, commercial, and maritime center for the VOC in the Far East. Consequently Coen expelled English competitors from the Spice Islands and established for the company a monopoly in the production and trade in nutmeg and mace by "cleansing" the Banda Islands, killing three-quarters of the population. European planters and their slaves repopulated the islands. Under his direction the VOC entered the intra-Asiatic trade. By attacking Portuguese Macao and Spanish Manilla he also tried to direct the Chinese junk trade to Batavia. Although the company established itself on Taiwan, Coen's China policy failed.

SEE ALSO ALBUQUERQUE, AFONSO DE; AMSTERDAM; EAST INDIA COMPANY, DUTCH; EMPIRE, DUTCH; EMPIRE, PORTUGUESE; IMPERIALISM; INDIAN OCEAN; INDONESIA; JOINT-STOCK COMPANY; LABORERS, COERCED; MONOPOLY AND OLIGOPOLY; NAGASAKI; PRIVATEERING; PROTECTION COSTS; SOUTH AFRICA; SPICES AND THE SPICE TRADE; SUGAR, MOLASSES, AND RUM.

BIBLIOGRAPHY

Gaastra, Femme S. "The Organization of the VOC." In *De Archieven van de Verenigde Oostindische Compagnie/The Archives of the Dutch East India Company, 1602–1795,* ed. Marie A. P. Meilink-Roelofsz, Remco Raben, and Henri Spijkerman. The Hague, Netherlands: Sd Uitgevers, 1992.

Victor Enthoven

COFFEE

Coffee has been one of the world's most valuable internationally traded commodities for several centuries. One of the few commodities that was already important under early modern luxury long-distance trade, it continues today as a key trade good, with more than 10 billion pounds exported annually in the late 1990s. Coffee continues to enjoy great international importance because the nature of its appeal to consumers has shifted to conform to remarkable changes in the societies of the dominant buyers over the last four centuries. Production has also markedly shifted geographically from the Middle East to Asia, to Latin America, and now increasingly to Africa and Asia again. Control of the market moved in the sixteenth century from the producer to the exporter, in the nineteenth century to the importer, and in the twentieth century to the roaster and national and international government institutions, and finally to a few vertically integrated multinational firms.

THE BEGINNING

Although native to what is today Ethiopia and Central Africa, coffee only entered into human history once Yemenis of a Sufi Muslim order made a drink from its beans. From then on coffee was an especially export-market-oriented commodity. Initially it was almost all commercially grown from Yemen and Ethiopia. The value was important, but the amounts were tiny: only 24,000 to 30,000 pounds a year were produced in Yemen in the eighteenth century.

Prices in consuming countries varied greatly. Merchant capital was subject to the whims of peasants who brought to market small amounts they produced in their garden plots as the price or their need for money demanded. Transaction costs were very high because trans-

FIRST WAVE OF MASS CONSUMERISM

The global impact of commodities such as coffee, tea, sugar, cocoa, and tobacco that produce a "high" through ingredients such as caffeine, glucose, and nicotine has been enormous. In the eighteenth century these products became widely available and affordable, contributing to the consumer revolution. Coffee emerged as an important commodity throughout northwestern Europe, and tea became the drink of choice in England. Both were often flavored with sugar, Britain's largest single import from about 1750 to 1820. Empires such as Britain's were partly founded on a growing demand for such products. In addition, trade in coffee, sugar, and the like went hand in hand with trade in products such as Indian fabrics, transforming the way people dressed, and creating the first wave of mass consumerism, as well as major upheaval in England (from unemployment), where production costs were higher than in the colonies. Production of most of these commodities, from coffee to tobacco, was labor intensive. Europeans "solved" this problem with the massive importation into their colonies of African slaves.

David J. Clarke

portation within Yemen was rudimentary. Nonetheless, it reached a wide market: Morocco to Turkey in the Levant, west along northern Africa and the Balkans, east to India, and, beginning in the middle of the seventeenth century, north to Eastern and Western Europe. But it was a shallow market because consumption was concentrated in urban coffeehouses where it served as both a secular drug and a religious drink closely tied to Islam.

The Dutch were the first European colonial power to enjoy much success in planting coffee in their colonies when they brought it to Java in the 1690s. The Dutch indirectly controlled production but they did not change the essentially peasant nature of production: peasants were forced to grow coffee and sell the exotic crop at a set price to Dutch East Indian stores. Whereas 90 percent of Amsterdam's coffee imports in 1721 were from Mocha in Yemen, by 1726, 90 percent were from Java. A quarter century later, Amsterdam's imports of Javanese coffee were nearly matched by imports of coffee from the American colony Dutch Guyana and then the French colony of Saint-Domingue (today Haiti). By the 1780s, over 80 percent of the world's production originated in the Americas. Javanese coffee fell to only 6 percent of Europe's consumption by 1820, although later in the century Java and Ceylon would enjoy a three-decades-long renaissance. Yemen's production almost disappeared from the world market.

Coffee was different from sugar and rubber during the nineteenth century in that most of it was produced in independent countries, not in European colonies. Cheap fertile land, slave labor, and maritime transport led coffee prices to plummet after 1820 and remain low until the last quarter of the century, stimulating demand. Brazil's exports jumped seventy-five-fold between the country's independence in 1822 and 1899. World consumption grew more than fifteenfold in the nineteenth century. No colonies could either compete with Brazil in price or meet the large new demand in the colonial powers and in the United States. By 1850 Brazil was producing over half the world's coffee; in 1906 it produced almost five times as much as the rest of the world combined. Indeed, about 80 percent of the expansion of world coffee production in the nineteenth century occurred in Brazil alone. Most of the rest of the growth was in Spanish America, as African and Asian production fell from one-third of world total in the middle decades of the nineteenth century to only 5 percent on the eve of World War I. And this was no marginal market. At the dawn of the twentieth century the value of internationally traded coffee trailed only grains and sugar. Latin American production had helped to redefine the nature of consumption by dropping prices and boosting volume sufficiently to reach a mass market.

The four- to six-year gestation period necessary for coffee seedlings to become commercially viable meant that production could not be modified quickly to respond to price differences, but great price rises led to rapid expansion and geographic diversification. The Haitian Revolution in the 1790s, for example, encouraged planting in other parts of the Caribbean and Brazil's Rio state. The next rapid jump in prices, which occurred in the late 1880s and early 1890s and was caused in good part by the leaf rust in Asia, produced a fourfold jump in São Paulo's trees in fourteen years, giving it alone over half the world's production; Colombia, Mexico, and Central America also stepped up production. The protective blanket provided by the creation of the International Coffee Organization (ICO) and its quota system in the 1960s encouraged new producers, particularly in African countries such as the Ivory Coast and Ethiopia. The collapse of the ICO in 1989 and a precipitous fall in prices stimulated a stunning expansion of production in Vietnam in the 1990s and, to a lesser extent, in Indonesia (more Sumatra than Java).

MASS CONSUMPTION

During its first centuries as a Muslim drink, coffee created a narrow luxury market. It was often traded by pilgrimage caravans and went through many intermediaries. When Europeans spread production to their colonies costs fell somewhat. But mercantilist-minded colonial governments insisted on high taxes. Peasants and proletarians, if they drank a hot beverage at all, tended to drink chicory and other substitutes.

Then after the Napoleonic Wars, African slaves, semi-coerced indigenous workers and European immigrants in the Americas, and coerced migrants in the Indian Ocean made the beverage available to urban workers and even occasionally to rural residents. Coffee's heroic nineteenth century occurred not only because of Brazilian production, but also because of skyrocketing consumption in the United States and Northern Europe. Coffee became truly a mass product for the first time in the United States.

U.S. government policy also helped. The United States was the only major market to import coffee tax-free after 1832. Consequently, per capita consumption grew from one-eighteenth of a pound in 1783 to nine pounds a hundred years later. The fifteenfold explosion in the U.S. population during that century meant that total coffee imports grew 2,400 times. By the end of the nineteenth century the United States was consuming thirteen pounds per capita and importing over 40 percent of the world's coffee. (It would grow to over 60 percent after World War II.) Half of the growth in world consumption in the nineteenth century was due to increased United States purchases. The other large market was in Western Europe. It was not coincidence that the fastest-growing economies were also the biggest coffee markets. Caffeine became instrumental to the regimented time of the urban industrialized societies. U.S. and Northern European consumption continued to grow, with some fits and starts, until the 1960s.

The growing appetite for coffee fed a transformation of the global coffee market. After 1870, telegraphs carried information about prices and demand and supply between South America, New York, and London. Exporters ceased being consignment agents, becoming instead agents of importers who controlled the trade and set the prices. The creation of the New York Coffee Exchange in 1882 institutionalized access to information. (Hamburg, Le Havre, and London followed with major coffee exchanges.) After the establishment of exchanges in New York and Europe there remained difficulties in determining the quality and origins of shipments and in obtaining information about the size of annual crops. The quality problem was rectified not by planters and traders, but by a government. In 1907 the United States Pure Food and

A worker hauls a basket full of organic coffee beans harvested from the fields of a coffee plantation in Guatemala. *Since the early 2000s, certain smaller coffee producers have shifted to growing high-quality beans without using pesticides in order to compete in the international market. This type of specialty cultivation allows producers to set higher prices and sell their coffee to more affluent countries.* PHOTOGRAPH BY MOISES CASTILLO. AP/WIDE WORLD PHOTOS. REPRODUCED BY PERMISSION.

Drug Act decreed that imported coffee be marked according to its port of exit. Thus "Santos" became a specific type of coffee, as did "Java" and "Mocha." Other governments soon followed with similar acts.

By gaining the confidence of consumers and providing mass-produced roasted coffee by using advances in roasting technology, transport, and marketing, large industrial roasting firms began to control the market by integrating vertically, sometimes even buying plantations in producing countries, and certainly sending their agents into the regions' interiors to purchase directly from producers. This initially led to segmentation of the market, and specific producing countries became linked to particular markets. Government intervention worked to dampen the market's price mechanisms and brought some control back to the producing countries. Beginning in 1906 some of Brazil's states held stocks off the world market to "valorize" them. This led to a federal price-support program, the Inter-American Coffee Agreement, and finally, in 1962, the International Coffee Agreement. Since the main objective of these cartels was to stabilize prices rather than corner the market, roasters in the con-

suming countries gladly joined. Importing countries joined less for economic reasons than for political ones. Coffee became a pawn in the Cold War. It was no coincidence that the United States came on board two years after the Cuban Revolution, or that the United States abandoned the agreement in 1989, the year the Berlin Wall came down. This form of state capitalism provided conditions for rapid consolidation and vertical integration in the consuming countries. As coffee processing became increasingly industrialized, economies to scale grew and an ever-larger share of the value was added in consuming countries. The sophistication of roasting, grinding, and packaging technology grew in the twentieth century's first decades. Meanwhile, new products were created: decaffeinated coffee and, after World War II, instant coffee in which processing added increased value. Instant coffee consumption grew to the point that it provided a third of all coffee drunk in the United States in its peak year of 1978. Drinkers of instant coffee were concerned with speed and convenience, not the quality of the brew. Consequently, the small number of roasters who captured this capital-intensive market used low-priced beans, especially the robusta beans that Africa and Asia began growing. Marketing was as important as automation. The rise of chain stores in the early twentieth century such as the A & P chain, which made coffee their most profitable good, allowed wholesaling concentration. This changed in the 1950s when the supermarket was created. Selling a vastly larger number of goods, the supermarket depended upon small margins but large volume. For the first time, coffee companies competed on price rather than the quality of their blend. Giant food conglomerates such as Kraft Foods, Nestlé, Proctor and Gamble, and Sara Lee bought up smaller, successful coffee companies and had less interest in coffee as a family artisanal tradition than had earlier coffee roasters such as Chase and Sanborn, or Maxwell House. Consolidation proceeded to the extent that today, a handful of companies control 80 percent of the U.S. coffee market. Worldwide, four or five companies buy half the world's coffee beans.

CURRENT TRENDS

Despite the demise of the ICO and rise of enormous conglomerates and cheap coffee, there are countertrends. Specialty coffee such as that sold by Starbucks has grown enormously not only in the United States, but also in Western Europe and Japan. Nongovernmental organizations such as Fair Trade and Oxfam organize cooperatives to produce organic, bird-friendly coffee and capture a large share of the final price. They appeal to consumers' sense of fairness for growers and environmental concern. Although they still control only a small share of the world price-driven market, they have grown impressively since the 1980s.

The world coffee market continues to undergo great changes. U.S. per capita consumption has steadily fallen since the 1960s and accounts for less than 20 percent of world purchases, whereas European and Asian consumption imitates the United States's nineteenth-century experience, and coffee-growing countries such as Brazil dramatically escalate consumption of their own crops. For over four centuries the coffee market has ushered in the modern world and has been shaped by those transformations.

SEE ALSO BRAZIL; COLOMBIA; CUBA; EAST INDIA COMPANY, DUTCH; EMPIRE, BRITISH; EMPIRE, DUTCH; EMPIRE, FRENCH; EMPIRE, OTTOMAN; EMPIRE, SPANISH; FRANCHISING, INTERNATIONAL; GHANA; HAITI; INDONESIA; JAMAICA; KENYA; LABORERS, CONTRACT; MERCANTILISM; MEXICO; NEW ORLEANS; NEW YORK; SLAVERY AND THE AFRICAN SLAVE TRADE; UNITED STATES; VENEZUELA; VIETNAM; ZIMBABWE.

BIBLIOGRAPHY

Bates, Robert H. *Open-Economy Politics: The Political Economy of the World Coffee Trade.* Princeton, NJ: Princeton University Press, 1997.

Clarence-Smith, William, and Topik, Steven, eds. *The Global Coffee Economy in Africa, Asia, and Latin America.* New York: Cambridge University Press, 2003.

Digum, Gregordy, and Luttinger, Nina. *The Coffee Book: Anatomy of an Industry from Crop to the Last Drop.* New York: New Press, 1999.

Jacob, Heinrich. *Coffee: The Epic of a Commodity.* Short Hills, NJ: Burford Books, 1998.

Pendergrasta, Mark. *Uncommon Grounds: The History of Coffee and How It Transformed Our World.* New York: Basic Books, 1999.

Roseberry, William; Gudmundson, Lowell; and Samper Kutschbach, Mario; eds. *Coffee, Society, and Power in Latin America.* Baltimore, MD: Johns Hopkins University Press, 1995.

Topik, Steven, and Wells, Allen. *The Second Conquest of Latin America: Coffee, Henequen, and Oil during the Export Boom, 1850–1930.* Austin: University of Texas Press, 1998.

Ukers, William. *All About Coffee.* New York: Tea and Coffee Trade Journal, 1935.

Steven Topik

JEAN-BAPTISTE COLBERT
1619–1683

Jean-Baptiste Colbert was born in the French town of Reims to a family of minor French officials. Early in his career he was appointed commissioner in the French army, where he served as an agent to the secretary of state, Michel Le Tellier, and later as an agent and secretary to the prime minister, Cardinal Mazarin. With Mazarin's death in 1661, Colbert became one of Louis XIV's chief financial advisors in the midst of the Dutch wars (1672–1678). Colbert was instrumental in reforming the law codes and the Treasury. He began work on the famed palace of Versailles and was also the chief reformer of the French navy.

Patterning himself on things that the English were doing at the same time, Colbert sought to build economic strength by establishing a balanced economy. He began by creating and protecting French industries. He encouraged exports while reducing the amount France imported because he believed the country lost wealth when buying foreign luxury goods such as tapestries, lace, and porcelain. Colbert used government inspectors to standardize commercial goods. He thus encouraged internal commerce and industry and laid the groundwork for the country's expansion overseas to Canada, the West Indies, and the Far East.

Although his programs were not as successful as he wished, he did much that brought France into the modern era.

SEE ALSO EMPIRE, FRENCH; FRANCE; JOINT-STOCK COMPANY; LEVANT COMPANY.

BIBLIOGRAPHY

Ames, Glenn J. *Colbert, Mercantilism, and the French Quest for Asian Trade.* De Kalb: Northern Illinois University Press, 1996.

Cole, Charles Woolsey. *Colbert and a Century of French Mercantilism.* 2 vols. New York: Columbia University Press, 1939.

Schaeper, Thomas J. *The French Council of Commerce, 1700–1715: A Study of Mercantilism after Colbert.* Columbus: Ohio State University Press, 1983.

John C. Rule

COLOMBIA

Colombia throughout most of its history has been a relatively weak participant in foreign trade. After Spanish conquerors seized control of the interior of the country (c. 1537–1550), Iberian immigrants gravitated to the interior highlands formed by three branches of the Andes, which offered a variety of climates and an indigenous labor force less decimated by disease than on the Caribbean coast. Given the difficult transportation conditions, having most of the population in the mountainous interior for most of the country's history made it difficult for Colombia to compete in exporting agricultural products.

During the colonial period Colombia exported dyewoods, hides, and various tropical products on a small scale, but well into the republican era its only significant export was gold, which could bear easily the high cost of transportation over mountains by mule. The area now known as Colombia was the chief producer of gold in the Spanish Empire, but its value fell far short of the great wealth of silver mined in Mexico and Peru. Colonial gold mining went through two cycles. The first began about 1550, reached its zenith in 1595 to 1599, then declined rapidly to a nadir from 1640 to about 1715. Gold production, which was almost entirely in western Colombia, revived gradually between 1720 and 1760 and then accelerated, with notable growth from 1780 to the end of the colonial period in 1810.

The early peak of gold mining in the 1590s stimulated the importation of African slaves because the rapidly declining indigenous population could not supply the labor needed in the mining regions of western Colombia. In the eighteenth century the port of Cartagena was one of the chief slave emporia in Spanish America. However, the rapid increase in gold production after 1780 did not lead to large-scale slave importations because slaves and free blacks already resident apparently were reproducing an adequate labor force.

Official figures badly underestimate Colombia's total gold production figures because considerable quantities

Coffee exports from Colombia, 1870–1969	
Thousands of 60 lb. bags per year, by decade.	
1870–1879	23
1880–1889	230
1890–1899	368
1900–1909	573
1910–1919	1,041
1920–1929	2,178
1930–1939	3,561
1940–1949	4,900
1950–1959	5,430
1960–1969	6,107

SOURCE: Compiled from Ocampo (1984) and Jaramillo Uribe (1989–2001).

THE GALE GROUP.

were smuggled, particularly after the establishment of British, Dutch, and French trading entrepôts in the Caribbean during the seventeenth century. The growth of contraband trade with Jamaica and other Caribbean islands undermined legal trade with Spanish convoyed fleets and eventually brought them to an end in 1740.

From 1738 to the end of the colonial period Colombia was the site of a viceroyalty, the Nuevo Reino de Granada. After 1760 the viceroys, subordinate administrators, and Creole savants tried to develop various tropical exports, with only slight success. The Spanish Crown showed little interest: royal measures to encourage tropical exports in Venezuela and Cuba were not extended to New Granada. New Granada's exports to Spain represented only 3.2 percent of the total value from Spanish America (1782–1796), and its imports from Cádiz only 8.1 percent (1785–1796). Venezuela, with a population half as large, contributed 9.6 percent of Spanish American exports to Spain, and took 10.1 percent of Spanish American imports from Cádiz.

Independence opened ports to foreign trade, and manufactured consumer goods, chiefly British textiles, flooded in. Colombian merchants, who had carried on contraband trade with Jamaica before independence, continued to purchase goods there. But British merchants, who had commercial and credit relations in England, could bring shipments directly from British ports, and they dominated trade in the 1820s. Colombia's capacity to import was limited. Gold production had fallen as slaves deserted the mines or were recruited into armies. Exports of tropical products were inhibited by British protection of tropical commodities produced in their colonies. By the late 1820s the outflow of Colombian specie in payment for imports had contributed to an acute shortage of circulating money and economic crisis. Colombia threw up protective barriers, particularly against tropical commodities. Exports of tobacco and cinchona bark in the 1850s generated increased imports. Between 1841 to 1845 and 1865 to 1870 both exports and imports doubled. Increased volumes of trade permitted more Colombian merchants to establish direct contacts with British commission houses, and thus compete as importers.

Spurred by the tobacco model, Colombian elites tried exporting other commodities (cotton, indigo, palm hats, forest medicinals), with limited success. They found a real winner only in coffee. Coffee, first exported from Northern Santander through Venezuela, spread southward in about 1870 to mountain flanks near Bogotá, then to Antioquia, Caldas, and elsewhere in western Colombia. By 1890 coffee was the most valuable export, encouraging railway construction. An enlarged internal market (partly of small coffee growers) and partial market integration by railway supported textile and other light manufacturing.

With railway construction and incipient manufacturing, the composition of imports began to change. In the 1850s consumer goods overwhelmingly dominated imports, with textiles making up two-thirds. By 1880 to 1900 intermediate and capital goods constituted 10 to 15 percent of imports. In the 1920s raw materials and intermediate and capital goods together represented half of imports.

Nineteenth-century Colombian coffee exports went primarily to Europe. But by 1903 to 1907 the United States was taking 72 percent of Colombia's exported coffee, and had displaced Great Britain as Colombia's chief market overall. After 1914 the United States also displaced Great Britain as Colombia's principal supplier of imported goods.

Colombia's coffee exports boomed after 1905, aided by Brazil's attempts to sustain the market by withholding part of its own crop. Despite the Great Depression, Colombia's coffee exports continued to grow, though at a slowing rate after 1940 as more competitors entered the world market. In 1950 coffee still represented 72 percent of the country's exports by value. But coffee then quickly declined in relative importance; by 1990 to 1995 it represented less than 18 percent of the value of legal exports. Declining coffee income after 1980 was offset by exports of petroleum, coal, textiles, ready-made clothing, shoes, processed food, bananas, and flowers, but since 1980 the value of exported illegal drugs is believed to have been greater than that of any single legal export, including coffee. By 2005 the coffee market seemed to be reviving, despite large-scale new production in Vietnam, as coffee prices have reached unprecedented heights.

World War II, by shrinking customary supplies of imported goods, stimulated industrial development,

Harvesting coffee beans in Bolombolo, Antioquia, Colombia. Coffee, which once represented nearly 80 percent of Colombia's exports, now represents less than 20 percent.
© JEREMY HORNER/CORBIS. REPRODUCED BY PERMISSION.

North American wheat flour and finished goods from Europe. Textile imports, however, continued.

A decisive turn to external trade occurred in the 1840s. When the United Kingdom ended protection of tropical fruits produced in its colonies, Florentino González, minister of finance in 1847, urged Colombians to develop tropical products along the Magdalena River to take advantage of cheap freight costs down the river. He supported government investment in river steamboat companies and lowered import tariffs to bring more shipping to Colombian ports, thus expanding exports. Under these policies tobacco from the upper Magdalena became republican Colombia's first significant export other than gold. The tobacco "boom" of the 1850s and 1860s was relatively small, but it convinced Colombian elites that the country's economic future lay in exporting

A native Colombian uses a machete to destroy opium poppy plants growing in a rural section of the country. Before the 1980s, coffee was the main export of Colombia until the rise of the international drug trade. Indian tribes in the southwestern highlands struggle to survive with money made from producing cocaine and heroin, while facing U.S.-backed efforts to eradicate illegal drug operations. © REUTERS/CORBIS. REPRODUCED BY PERMISSION.

which was sustained, in a protected market, until the mid-1970s, with subsequent slower growth. In the early 1990s President César Gaviria (b. 1947) pursued trade liberalization, hoping to make Colombian manufacturing more competitive. Current discussions of further trade liberalization are haunted by the specter of competition from China.

SEE ALSO CARTAGENA; COFFEE; CONQUISTADORS; DRUGS, ILLICIT; EMPIRE, SPANISH; ENCOMIENDA AND REPARTIMIENTO; IMPORT SUBSTITUTION; INTERNATIONAL MONETARY FUND (IMF); LABORERS, AZTEC AND INCA; NATIONALIZATION; PANAMA CANAL; PERU; SMUGGLING; UNITED FRUIT COMPANY; UNITED STATES; VENEZUELA.

BIBLIOGRAPHY

Jaramillo Uribe, Jaime, and Tirado Mejia, Alvaro, eds. *Nueva Historia de Colombia (New History of Colombia).* 11 vols. Bogotá: Editorial Planeta, 1989–2001.

McGreevey, William Paul. *An Economic History of Colombia, 1845–1930.* Cambridge, U.K.: Cambridge University Press, 1971.

Ocampo, José Antonio. *Colombia y la economía mundial, 1830–1910 (Colombia and the World Economy).* Bogotá: Siglo Veintiuno Editores, 1984.

Palacios, Marco. *Coffee in Colombia, 1850–1970: An Economic, Social, and Political History.* Cambridge, U.K.: Cambridge University Press, 1980.

Safford, Frank, and Palacios, Marco. *Colombia: Fragmented Land, Divided Society.* New York: Oxford University Press, 2002.

Frank Safford

CHRISTOPHER COLUMBUS
1451–1506

Christopher Columbus made four transatlantic voyages in the service of Castile that established the sea routes to the Americas. His settlements in the Caribbean were the first in the Spanish American empire. He had planned to sail to Asia and enter the commercial networks there. His incorrect view of the earth's size made him believe that he had gone far enough to reach Japan when he landed in the Bahamas in 1492.

Columbus's initial plans for commercial exploitation called for him to direct salaried royal employees to trade and pan for gold. He later took animals and plants, including sugar cane, to Hispaniola to establish trading commodities. He thought he could trade in slaves, but the Spanish Crown prohibited that. His mismanagement and his enslaving of Indians caused his royal sponsors to dismiss him from many of his offices and to establish a new regime of royal officials and nonsalaried settlers that become the prototype of Spanish colonization elsewhere in the Americas. In his later voyages, Columbus explored the Central American mainland but failed to establish new colonies. He died resentful of his dismissal, even though his accomplishments had made him rich. His descendants carried on a long series of lawsuits that recovered for his son and grandson some of the offices Columbus originally held.

SEE ALSO Empire, Spain; Ships and Shipping; Spain.

BIBLIOGRAPHY

Flint, Valerie I. *The Imaginative Landscape of Christopher Columbus.* Princeton, NJ: Princeton University Press, 1992.

Henige, David P. *In Search of Columbus: The Sources for the First Voyage.* Tucson: University of Arizona Press, 1991.

Phillips, Jr., William D., and Philips, Carla Rahn. *The Worlds of Christopher Columbus.* New York: Cambridge University Press, 1992.

Zamora, Margarita. *Reading Columbus.* Berkeley: University of California Press, 1993.

William D. Phillips Jr.

COMECON

Comecon is the abbreviation for the Council of Mutual Economic Assistance (CMEA), the international economic organization of Communist countries that existed from 1949 to 1991. Comecon was established as the Cold War intensified in the late 1940s, and was conceived as the Soviet response to U.S. Marshall Plan aid to Western Europe. It gradually grew from a small secretariat to an ambitious organization that sought to coordinate the economic development strategies of the Communist countries. It was never successful in doing so, however; the Soviet satellites defended their autonomy in the economic sphere and consistently frustrated Soviet efforts to rationalize their trade and economic cooperation.

HISTORY

When Comecon was established, the Soviet Union was busily extracting resources from its new East European dependencies in the form of war reparations. The minimal cooperation that occurred took place on a bilateral basis between the Soviet central planning agency, Gosplan, and similar agencies in the Communist countries, and Comecon was simply a small office in Moscow that prepared technical reports. All of this changed as a result of the uprisings in East Germany in 1953 and in Poland and Hungary in 1956. The Soviet Union recognized the need to subsidize the new Communist states if they were to survive, and Nikita Khrushchev (1894–1971) breathed new life into Comecon. He instituted regular summit meetings of Communist premiers (the Comecon Council), an executive council (*Ispolkom*) of permanent representatives to Comecon who held the rank of deputy premiers in their respective countries, and a number of specialized agencies that brought together the chairmen of the central planning agencies and ministers of the member countries. The historian Michael Kaser argued that a speech Khrushchev gave and subsequently published in *Kommunist*, the ideology journal of the Communist Party, indicated that he was attempting to subordinate the central planning organs of the satellites to Gosplan (Kaser 1965). He never made an effort to carry this out, however, and there is some evidence that this was an ill-advised trial balloon instigated by a speechwriter. However, he articulated socialist integration as a fundamental Soviet policy goal, and it remained one until the collapse of the Communist alliance.

Comecon began to take on tangible significance with the Comprehensive Program for Socialist Economic Integration, developed in the late 1960s and launched in 1971. The Polish general secretary, Wladislaw Gomulka (1905–1982), proposed the idea for a new integration program as a means of promoting the idea of market socialism, which was currently percolating in Poland and two other relatively prosperous satellites, Czechoslovakia and Hungary. Initial discussions were wide ranging, and until the Soviet intervention to suppress the Czechoslovak reformers in 1968, it appeared to many Soviet and East European participants that the Comprehensive Program might indeed promote reform. Instead, it became a vehicle for Soviet Gosplan to engage the East Europeans in investing in Soviet mining and extraction industries under the rubric of joint planning. Two further rounds of integration programs similarly attempted to coordinate countries' development strategies through collaborative investment plans. The Long-term Target Programs of 1978 to 1979 (*Dolgosrochnye tselevye programmy sotsialisticheskogo sotrudnichestvo,* or *DTsPS*) focused on five key sectors of the economy: energy, machine building, consumer goods, agriculture, and transportation. One major project was to promote collaboration in civilian nuclear power, with the goal of building reactors in seven Comecon countries and increasing electrical generating capacity by 37 percent. The Comprehensive Program for Scientific and Technical Progress of 1985 (*Kompleksnaia programma nauchno-tekhnicheskogo progressa,* or *KPNTP*) focused on collaborative technology development in five areas of innovation: computers, robotics, new materials, nuclear energy, and biotechnology. It was not until late in the Gorbachev era that serious discussion in Comecon returned to the subject of economic reform.

As these successive programs unfolded, a plethora of Comecon committees negotiated the details of agreements that expanded economic collaboration into larger circles of activities. The agenda was always set by the Soviet Union, and it prevailed on almost every major issue. However, the debates were lively, and Soviet proposals were often significantly watered down as they were translated from general principle into concrete treaty obligations. The subsequent implementation of the agreements was very selective, and the achievements were much more modest that the formal treaties.

COMECON AND SOVIET-BLOC TRADE

The fundamental obstacle to trade among centrally planned economies was central planning. Every transaction had to be written into the plan, so trade had to be negotiated bilaterally between the countries' central planning agencies, and in effect it took the form of nonmonetary barter because none of the countries had a convertible currency. The Communist countries maintained the fiction of a common currency, the "transferable ruble," and there was a Byzantine process of determining foreign trade prices in this unit, which allowed countries to account for the balance of payments and to run trade deficits with each other. However, these prices provided no information about comparative advantage, because they were set by fiat and were not determined by scarcity. Consequently, there was no obvious way of optimizing trade flows. Finally, under central planning economic units were rewarded for meeting quantitative quotas, not for making profits, so no organization in the economy had an incentive to capture the potential gains from trade, even if they could identify them.

In principle, central planning agencies could establish a common goal, agree upon all the necessary transac-

tions, and carry them out. The problem was that the differences between the relative prices of goods within Comecon and the relative prices on world markets created incentives for the smaller countries to engage in arbitrage and optimize their import and export profiles within Comecon in terms of world prices. The prices of raw materials were set arbitrarily low in transferable rubles relative to machinery because central planning provides weak incentives to produce quality finished goods and weak mechanisms for detecting low-quality products. Consequently, East European countries faced incentives to overconsume energy and raw materials and to export shoddy manufactured goods to the Soviet Union. This formed the basis for a long-term, implicit Soviet trade subsidy that was uniformly recognized by foreign trade officials, and that expanded over time as the quality gap between East European products and world standards gradually widened. Many of the integration projects developed in Comecon were designed by the Soviet Union to reduce this one-sided flow of resources, and the satellites faced strong incentives to evade them.

PERESTROIKA AND THE COLLAPSE OF COMECON

By the late 1980s work was under way in Comecon headquarters on a Soviet plan to restructure the organization, liberalize international trade within the bloc, and promote gradual economic reforms in the Soviet satellites along the lines of Mikhail Gorbachev's *perestroika* program for reform in the Soviet Union. Many of the Soviet proposals were borrowed from proposals the East Europeans had made as early as 1968. These proposals faced a lot of criticism from the left and the right: The Poles and Hungarians were skeptical by this time about gradual reform proposals that did not go as far as their own domestic reforms had gone, and East Germany and Romania vigorously opposed any kind of reform. These objections blunted the force of each document Comecon adopted, and prevented the Soviet reform program from being adopted in its entirety. More fundamentally, however, the negotiations for the next five-year trade plan (planned to extend through 1995) demonstrated that the East Europeans did not believe in the Soviet commitment to reform. They expected the game to continue to be played by the old rules, and they frustrated efforts to implement the agreed-upon reform principles by continuing to insist on retaining features of the old regime that gave them unilateral advantages. By the end of 1989 the question of reforming Comecon was moot, as popular uprisings swept all the East European Communist regimes away. The Soviet Union was not willing to continue to subsidize the new democratic regimes, and the new leaders of most East European countries were determined to carry out rapid market transformations. Comecon was formally dissolved at the end of 1991, and the

Comecon archive was turned over to the Russian State Archive of the National Economy (TsGANKh).

SEE ALSO AGRICULTURE; COMMON MARKET AND THE EUROPEAN UNION; FREE TRADE, THEORY AND PRACTICE; GATT, WTO; GERMANY; INTERNATIONAL TRADE AGREEMENTS; REGIONAL TRADE AGREEMENTS; SOCIALISM AND COMMUNISM; RUSSIA; STALIN, JOSEPH; TRADE FORMS, ORGANIZATIONAL, AND LEGAL INSTITUTIONS.

BIBLIOGRAPHY

Harrison, Hope M. *Driving the Soviets up the Wall: Soviet–East German Relations, 1953–1961.* Princeton, NJ: Princeton University Press, 1993.

Kaser, Michael. *Comecon: Integration Problems of the Planned Economies.* London: Oxford University Press, 1965.

Kornai, Janos. *The Socialist System: The Political Economy of Socialism.* Princeton, NJ: Princeton University Press, 1992.

Marrese, Michael, and Vanous, Jan. *Soviet Subsidization of Trade with Eastern Europe: A Soviet Perspective.* Berkeley: University of California Press, 1983.

Metcalf, Lee Kendall. *The Council of Mutual Economic Assistance: The Failure of Reform.* Boulder, CO: Columbia University Press, 1998.

Stone, Randall W. *Satellites and Commissars: Strategy and Conflict in the Politics of Soviet-Bloc Trade.* Princeton, NJ: Princeton University Press, 1996.

Randall W. Stone

COMMODITY MONEY

For at least a millennium or two before 1450, merchants who engaged in international trade around the inland seas and oceanic rims of Eurasia, or along overland long-distance routes within Eurasia, tropical Africa, or the Americas, typically conducted some of their business using commodities as money. A wide array of commodities such as cattle, corn, tobacco, leather, hides and fur, cloth, olive oil, dried fish, salt, beer and liquor, slaves, copper and iron bars, gold, silver, rings, diamonds, beads, feathers, and shells served as money at various times and places.

Before the fifteenth century, in tropical Africa and the Americas the use of minted metal coin, or specie, was unknown, and monetized exchange, intermixed with barter, was facilitated by the use of commodity money. In Eurasia and North Africa, by contrast, many states minted coins, and in long-distance trade the use of commodity money often was intermixed with the use of various specie. The history of the use of these early commodity moneys is not well documented, but it is clear that some commodity currencies had lengthy historical careers.

The record of world trade since 1450 suggests two new patterns in the use of commodity money. After the

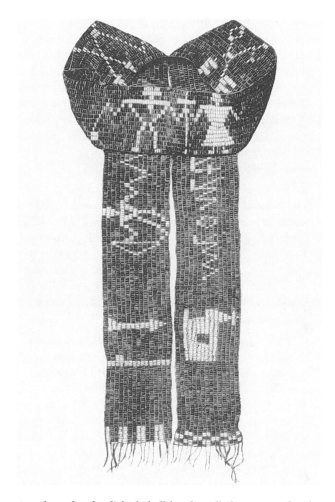

A sash made of polished shell beads, called wampum beads. Native Americans used the beads like coins, to trade for goods, while the exchange of woven articles such as this often had added ceremonial value.

discovery of the Americas (1492) and a sea route to the Indian Ocean around the southern tip of Africa (1498), the role of commodity moneys in African international trade expanded. Owing largely to the demand for labor in the New World colonies, the states of western tropical Africa came to participate in the transatlantic slave trade. During the era of the slave trade, European merchants expanded the zone of the three-quarter-inch long, creamy-white cowrie shell currency from the Indian Ocean basin, where Arab and South Asian merchants had pioneered its use, to the Atlantic coast of tropical Africa. There, cowries became one of the principal currencies of the slave trade over a period of several centuries. European traders, in response to African demand, also produced large quantities of other commodity moneys such as the open bracelets in the form of a horseshoe known as brass manillas and special-order cloth for the African markets.

A second new pattern linked the New World to the emerging nexus of truly global trade. The sixteenth-century conquest of the Incan and Aztec empires gave the Spaniards access to new sources of gold and silver. The silver ore deposits were vast. Some silver was minted in coins known as the réale and the peso, and both specie and bullion were shipped to Spain, where these imports initiated a great inflation known as the European *price revolution* of the sixteenth century.

From the late sixteenth century onward, much silver from South and Central America was shipped to China in the form of bars of bullion, where it was bartered for Chinese exports, particularly porcelain and silks. These imports of silver bullion allowed the Ming dynasty to mint more of its own silver coins and to demand that the peasantry pay taxes to the state using the new silver coins, thereby producing a more fully silverized bimetallic system with the copper currency that had replaced an earlier experiment with fiat money.

Outside of the Spanish Empire, experimentation with nonmetallic commodity currencies was ephemeral. The sugar- and coffee-exporting plantation colonies of Brazil and the Caribbean had direct economic ties to the European metropolises. They were, in effect, branches of the European economy and as such did not need to develop their own local commodity moneys, or, if so, then only very temporarily. In early British North America, by contrast, the fledgling colonies were relatively starved for specie and consequently attempted to adopt the local Native American currency or to develop new ones based on their principal agricultural products.

CHALLENGES POSED BY COMMODITY MONEY

How efficiently any of these commodities served their money role depended on a number of characteristics: ready acceptance, portability (in terms of having a high value for its weight), divisibility (so that small as well as large transactions were feasible), resistance to counterfeiting, and maintenance of value over time. Most commodities that functioned as money were deficient in one or several of these characteristics. Two notable deficiencies were a tendency toward inflation as the commodity serving as money fell in value and a susceptibility to Gresham's Law. Gresham's Law states, in its simplest form, that low-valued or "bad" money drives "good" or high-valued money out of circulation. If a choice of money forms or of money quality existed, economic agents will always place the inferior money in circulation while retaining the "good," the superior form, for consumption or saving.

The experience of the American colonists in New England and the South with wampum and tobacco, respectively, illustrates the first problem: the tendency toward inflation. Wampum, the Native American shell money in the form of beads, was adopted by the colonists and given legal tender status by the Massachusetts authorities in 1643. Tobacco, the leading staple crop of the Upper South, was an accepted medium of exchange there in the early 1600s. However, the supply of both could be readily expanded, the first by increasing the gathering of shells, and the second by increased planting. With the resulting increase in supply, the value of each as a currency unit dropped. In other words, inflation occurred. Massachusetts responded by prohibiting the use of wampum in the payment of taxes in 1648, thus ending its medium-of-exchange role.

Virginia first attempted to prevent the increase in supply by restricting the right to grow tobacco. That effort was fruitless, and the rapid expansion of tobacco cultivation doomed tobacco's career as a currency by the late 1640s. In the case of tobacco as a currency, it is certain that lower grade tobacco (bad money) would be used to settle accounts while prime tobacco leaf (good money) would be exported for consumption. In 1619, Virginia authorities attempted to forestall the operation of exactly that result of Gresham's Law by fixing the value of tobacco used in exchange at three shillings per pound for the "beste" grade but at only eighteen pence for the "seconde sort." As with most price-fixing schemes, the attempt failed, and by the 1640s, tobacco's role as a currency had failed as well.

Thus, in North America, the monetary use of any commodity other than metals in coin form declined dramatically in the seventeenth century. In tropical Africa, by contrast, commodity money remained the most important form of money until the rampant cowrie inflation of the late nineteenth century. The political efforts of European colonial administrators in the early twentieth century finally demonetized the cowrie and the manilla, the last of the African commodity moneys in wide use.

All commodity moneys had their failings. Fluctuations in the supply of precious-metal currencies could produce dramatic fluctuations in their values, and indeed the large quantity of silver bullion produced in South and Central America in the early colonial period set off a round of inflation in several regions of Eurasia. But the long Eurasian experience with a transcultural valuation of metallic moneys (gold, silver, and copper), linked with the discovery of precious metals in the New World, meant that these metals—silver in particular—would become, outside of tropical Africa, the monetary media of international trade.

An evolutionary model of money use would hold that there has been a progression from barter to commodity money, monetized metal currencies, and finally fiat money. The empirical evidence shows that this progression was not linear, and that commodity moneys continued to play a major role in international trade into the nineteenth century.

SEE ALSO COWRIES; MONEY AND MONETARY POLICY.

BIBLIOGRAPHY

Curtin, Philip D. "Africa and the Wider Monetary World, 1250–1850." In *Precious Metals in the Later Medieval and Early Modern Worlds*, ed. J. F. Richards. Durham, NC: Carolina Academic Press, 1983.

Flynn, Dennis O., and Giráldez, Arturo, eds. *Metals and Monies in an Emerging Global Economy*. Aldershot, U.K.: Variorum, 1997.

Hogendorn, Jan, and Johnson, Marion. *The Shell Money of the Slave Trade*. Cambridge, U.K.: Cambridge University Press, 1986.

Konker, Elizabeth, A. *Money in Colonial New England*. Boston: Federal Reserve Bank of Boston, 1974.

Stiansen, Endre, and Guyer, Jane I., eds. *Credit, Currencies and Culture: African Financial Institutions in Historical Perspective*. Uppsala: Nordiska Afrikainstitutet, 1999.

Von Glahn, Richard. *Fountain of Fortune: Money and Monetary Policy in China, 1000–1700*. Berkeley: University of California Press, 1996.

Webb, James L. A. Jr. "Toward the Comparative Study of Money: A Reconsideration of West African Currencies and Neo-Classical Monetary Concepts." *International Journal of African Historical Studies* 15 (1982): 455–466.

H. A. Gemery
James L. A. Webb Jr.

COMMON MARKET AND THE EUROPEAN UNION

According to the European view, the origin of the European Union was the Schuman Plan of 1950, which created the European Coal and Steel Community (ECSC). The ECSC was a supranational organization that coordinated the recovery of the coal and steel industries in France, West Germany, Italy, Belgium, the Netherlands, and Luxembourg. While acting as an internationally sanctioned cartel, the ECSC had its "own resources" and a political structure designed to be a model for further cooperative efforts in the reconstruction of Europe after World War II.

According to the U.S. view, however, the origin of the EU was the European Payments Union (EPU), also established in 1950. The EPU encouraged trade among the European participants in the Marshall Plan by allowing multilateral clearing of their trade balances with each other. To participate, however, countries had to allow trade in a given product to occur without quantitative restrictions, which encouraged them to substitute tariffs instead. The result was a rapid increase in total trade among the continental European participants, which was a marked change from the decrease in total trade and even greater decrease in intra-European trade that had occurred in the 1930s.

Belgium, West Germany, and even Italy found that their participation in both the ECSC and the EPU, combined with low tariffs and relatively stable price levels, generated export-led growth for their economies. The Netherlands, by joining in 1948 a customs union with Belgium and Luxembourg that eliminated all tariffs on manufactured goods while maintaining separate agricultural policies geared to national price-support regimes, also experienced export-led growth in the 1950s. Over the course of the 1950s, as the European Payments Union operated with increasing effectiveness, the constraints of a dollar shortage on continental European trade policy were eased considerably. This meant that members could move from a cumbersome array of bilateral trade agreements to a more efficient multilateral trade network with all the other European members of the EPU. More importantly, the governments could realize tariff proceeds cheaply by simply imposing a fixed tariff to the price of the desired good when it was imported from whatever country. The incentives then for, say, French importers, would be to import from the most efficient supplier in Europe, while the French government would garner the excess revenue in the form of customs duties.

The European Payments Union ended formally in 1958 when the countries agreed to remove all exchange controls on current-account transactions. This opened all countries to the possibility of importing goods from any other country belonging to the International Monetary Fund, especially the United States and Canada, which were long regarded as the source of the most desirable, and cheapest, manufactured goods. It is precisely this situation that a customs union is designed to prevent. For example, instead of driving German industry further away from cooperation with French industry and looking to increased trade opportunities in Scandinavia and overseas, a customs union brings German and French industry closer together, albeit at the expense of tariff revenues for each government. Inside a customs union, which erects a common external tariff around the member countries while removing all tariffs on trade among themselves, both French and German firms enjoy the same level of tariff protection from U.S. and British competition. In the French market, the German producers are given an artificial advantage over the U.S. producers by having no tariff levied against their imports, while the full tariff remains in force against the United States, Britain, Japan, or any potential competitor outside the customs union. French firms receive the same advantage on the German market.

ESTABLISHMENT OF THE COMMON MARKET

In 1958 the six members of the ECSC created an enlarged customs union, the European Economic Community (EEC), known as the Common Market. Based on the success of the Benelux customs union, and intent on extending the economic relations that had developed within the ECSC, the six countries agreed to eliminate their tariffs on all manufactured goods with respect to each other, while erecting a common external tariff (CET) against all nonmember countries. Under pressure from the rest of European members of the European Payments Union and the United States, however, the six agreed to make the CET no higher than the average of the six countries' individual tariffs. This meant reducing the much higher tariffs of France and Italy and raising the already low tariffs of the Benelux customs union and West Germany. The original intent was to eliminate the internal tariffs in stages over the next fifteen years while raising the CET to an average of 15 percent, but trade expanded very rapidly among the six, and all interior tariffs on manufactured goods were eliminated by 1968, when the average tariff had dropped to 7.4 percent. Meanwhile, successive negotiations with nonmember countries under the Dillon, Kennedy, and Tokyo Rounds of the General Agreement on Tariffs and Trade continued to reduce the level of the CET from the originally intended 15 percent to closer to 5 percent by the early 1980s.

The economic analysis of this experiment with a customs union implied that although there would be obvious gains to the countries within a customs union from the "trade creation" caused by reducing their tariffs against each other, there would also be losses through "trade diversion" away from lower-cost producers outside the customs union. These would show up mainly in lower tariff revenues. As both internal and external tariffs were reduced at the same time, the trade creation effects were much greater than foreseen. Meanwhile, the trade diversion effects were minimized as European suppliers rapidly became more efficient in response to the enlarged markets now available to them. While some economies of scale helped reduce costs for European manufacturers, modern technology was also incorporated into new capital investment, often provided by British and U.S. firms relocating their production facilities inside the customs union.

EFFECTS OF THE CUSTOMS UNION

The creation of a customs union can have a number of indirect, or dynamic, effects. The elimination of some protection can increase competition and lower transaction costs while allowing firms to benefit either from decreasing cost industries, for example, sectors with high fixed costs, or from scale economies, such as network systems. In addition, any domestic market power is eroded by the increase of competition, which increases domestic welfare by lowering deadweight losses. Thus, the reduction in market barriers can accelerate the process of technological advance. In fact, the reduction in production costs could move member states' costs closer to world prices, thus lowering any trade-diversion effect and increasing the trade-creation effect. One of the areas Europeans point to most frequently is the gains from increasing size, that is, the gains from economies of scale.

Almost all of the estimates of trade creation and trade diversion caused by the EEC show that trade creation far exceeded diversion. This is true for sectoral studies as well as for economy-wide estimates. Bela Belassa, a Hungarian-born American economist, did pioneering work on the economic effects of the European customs union. His 1975 estimates of trade creation for all goods was U.S.$11.3 billion, whereas his estimate of diversion was $0.3 billion. These figures are from a static analysis that ignores the changes through time brought on by the EEC, so they understate the actual gains from trade induced by formation of the customs union.

The essential feature of a customs union, however, is to change the pattern of trade of the member countries. The EEC has succeeded in doing this to an extent far beyond the wildest expectations of its founding fathers. From having two-thirds of their imports coming from outside the customs union when it was set up in 1958, by 1990 the original six members had over two-thirds of their imports coming from within the customs union, which had doubled its membership to twelve countries. This level of intra-EU trade compared to extra-EU trade has been maintained through 2001. Strikingly, the trade patterns of the new members after 1973 also changed to favor trade within the EEC, even in the face of the incentives to increase trade with the oil-exporting countries. The rapid economic growth of West Germany and Belgium in the 1950s was shared by the Netherlands and France in the 1960s. Meanwhile, growth rates of trade and national product in Great Britain and the United States continued at lower rates. The evident success of the customs union on the Continent led Britain and its closest European trading partners—Denmark and Ireland—to apply for membership in the 1960s, and their applications were finally accepted in 1973. The oil shocks of the 1970s disrupted trade for all nine members of the expanded Common Market, causing much slower growth and sharply rising rates of both inflation and unemployment. Nevertheless, there was no effort to retract the general tariff concessions that had been made; only specific trade goods were subjected to temporary tariffs or Voluntary Export Restrictions agreed to by lower-cost nations. The Common Market was further enlarged in 1981 with the addition of Greece; in 1986 with Spain and Portugal; and in 1995 with Austria, Finland, and Sweden. For each new member, the importance of foreign trade increased, and the direction of trade moved sharply in favor of other members of the European Union.

The trading partners that lost out in shares of trade with the EEC were not the nonmember-industrialized countries in the West, however. Rather, they were the developing countries, largely the former colonies of the European powers, which were gaining their independence but losing their access to the European markets, largely due to their own efforts to establish economic self-sufficiency along with their political independence. The significance of this change in the pattern of imports (which necessarily has been largely duplicated in the pattern of exports) is often overlooked in view of the even more dramatic increase in the total volume of foreign trade. The rapid growth of Western European foreign trade has meant that all trading partners have seen substantial increases in the volume of their exports to the European Community. Whether the growth of trade has been primarily because of technological progress or institutional changes, or because a felicitous combination of the two processes, is an open question. But there can be no doubt that the change in the geographical pattern of Western European trade has been due to the institutional changes created by the European Union.

SEE ALSO MONNET, JEAN.

BIBLIOGRAPHY

Balassa, Bela. "Trade Creation and Trade Diversion in the European Common Market: An Appraisal of the Evidence." In *European Economic Integration,* ed. Bela Balassa. Amsterdam: North-Holland, 1975.

International Monetary Fund. *Direction of Trade Statistics Yearbook.* Washington, DC: Author, annual.

Neal, Larry, and Barbezat, Daniel. *The Economics of the European Union and the Economies of Europe.* New York: Oxford University Press, 1998.

Larry Neal

COMPRADORS

The term *comprador* derives from the Portuguese language and was originally used in a South Asian context by European traders to describe native commercial middlemen. It was first applied in China with reference to those Chinese merchants involved in commercial relations with foreigners on behalf of the *cohong* (a monopolistic guild of imperially licensed Chinese merchants), during the pre-Opium War period of regulated trade under the Canton system. As a consequence of this long-term prior experience with foreign trade and foreigners themselves, Cantonese and Fujianese merchants from southeastern China were well-positioned for the even more rapid development of Sino-Western trade following the Opium War (1839–1842).

After the abolition of the *cohong* system and the opening of treaty ports in 1842, *compradors* quickly came into their own as Chinese managers for Western commercial firms in ports such as Canton, Fuzhou, Shanghai, and Hankou. Because Western merchants generally lacked language skills, local business contacts, and familiarity with China's regionally diversified commercial and social settings, *compradors* assumed central roles in Western business operations. They characteristically engaged in several business functions at once as salaried employees of foreign firms, as brokers receiving commissions from facilitating transactions, and as sales and purchasing agents for domestic and foreign goods. Among their ordinary daily duties were the recruiting and managing of Chinese staff, providing marketing intelligence, and handling native banking operations.

Compradors frequently engaged in commercial activities on their own behalf before becoming employees of foreign firms, and often expanded their personal business interests thereafter. Financial conflicts of interest became a troubling aspect of the *comprador* system. In analytical terms, principal/agent issues arose, with neither *compradors* nor their foreign employers necessarily acting in each other's best business interests. Risks thus increased for both parties. Although large firm's *compradors* rarely went bankrupt, business failures happened much more frequently at smaller, less stable firms, with *compradors* assuming heavy liabilities in both of their dual capacities as employees and private businessmen. With the rise of modern Chinese nationalism, and especially of the Chinese Communist movement in the early twentieth century, *compradors* were crudely stereotyped as traitors exploiting China's underdeveloped economy for their own gain and foreigners' illegitimate profits. Ironically, this was at a time when *compradors*' services as middlemen were quietly becoming less and less essential to foreign firms. Denounced as "running dogs" of foreign interests during the political upheavals and civil warfare of the 1920s, their positive activities were submerged by the rhetoric of Chinese anti-imperialism. Forgotten were the pioneering investments of *compradors* such as Tang Jingxing, Yu Xiaoqing, Xu Run, and Zhu Dachun in China's first modern industrial enterprises in the late Qing Dynasty and early Republic, including steamship lines, mines, milling and textile manufacturing. *Compradors*' willingness to assume novel investment risks was vital in this early phase of industrialization, which involved the use of advanced foreign technology as well as the importation of standard modern business procedures including joint-stock capitalization, insurance, and limited-liability incorporation.

SEE ALSO ACCOUNTING AND ACCOUNTING PRACTICES; BANKING; BRITISH-AMERICAN TOBACCO; CANTON SYSTEM; CHINA; DRUGS, ILLICIT; EMPIRE, BRITISH; EMPIRE, FRENCH; EMPIRE, JAPANESE; EMPIRE, QING; ETHNIC GROUPS, CANTONESE; ETHNIC GROUPS, FUJIANESE; GUANGZHOU; GUILDS; HONG KONG; IMPERIAL MARITIME CUSTOMS, CHINA; IMPERIALISM; INDUSTRIALIZATION; JARDINE MATHESON; MANCHURIA; NAGASAKI; NATIONALISM; PARTNERSHIP; POPULATION–IMMIGRATION AND EMIGRATION; SHANGHAI; SHIPPING, MERCHANT; SILK; YOKOHAMA.

BIBLIOGRAPHY

Cochran, Sherman. *Encountering Chinese Networks: Western, Japanese, and Chinese Corporations in China, 1880–1937.* Berkeley: University of California Press, 2000.

Hao, Yen-p'ing. *The Comprador in Nineteenth Century China: Bridge between East and West.* Cambridge, MA.: Harvard University Press, 1970.

Hao, Yen-p'ing. *The Commercial Revolution in Nineteenth-Century China: The Rise of Sino-Western Mercantile Capitalism.* Berkeley: University of California Press, 1986.

Robert Gardella

MARIE-JEAN-ANTOINE-NICOLAS DE CARITAT, MARQUIS DE CONDORCET
1743–1794

Born at Ribemont, Picardie, France, Condorcet was a brilliant mathematician, economic philosopher, and political activist of the French Enlightenment. Promoting the economic theories of Jacques Turgot (1727–1781), he was also associated with Voltaire (1694–1778), Jean LeRond d'Alembert (1717–1783), and Denis Diderot (1713–1784), and helped prepare the *Encyclopédie* (1751–1772), which encouraged free trade. In his *Letters on the Grain Trade* (1774) and *Reflections on the Commerce of Villages* (1776) he argued that free trade in grains would avoid famine and increase productivity. He strongly advocated natural rights, mass education, equality of nations and individuals, and economic freedom. Condorcet was an enthusiastic supporter of the French Revolution and the establishment of a republic. He was secretary of the legislative assembly in 1791 representing the more moderate Girondists, but the Jacobins forced him into hiding from 1793 to 1794, when he wrote his most cele-brated work, *Sketch for a Historical Picture of the Progress of the Human Mind* (1795). In it he traced the history of man through nine stages toward perfection. In the tenth stage ("the future progress of the human mind") he offered classical liberal views in an optimistic vision of a world in which freedom prevailed. In applying principles of natural science to the social sciences he was a precursor of the positivism of Auguste Comte (1798–1857). After his capture on March 27, 1794, Condorcet was found two days later, dead of unknown cause in his cell at Bourg-la-Reine.

SEE ALSO EDUCATION, OVERVIEW; FRANCE; FREE TRADE, THEORY AND PRACTICE; INFORMATION AND COMMUNICATIONS; THEORIES OF INTERNATIONAL TRADE.

BIBLIOGRAPHY

Goodell, Edward. *The Noble Philosopher: Condorcet and the Enlightenment.* Buffalo, NY: Prometheus Books, 1994.

Rothschild, Emma. *Economic Sentiments: Adam Smith, Condorcet, and the Enlightenment.* Cambridge, MA: Harvard University Press, 2001.

Ralph Lee Woodward Jr.

CONQUISTADORS

Conquistadors were the men who during the sixteenth century engaged in the acts of exploration and conquest in the Americas that expanded Spain's colonial empire. Although their intention was simply to better their own lives while expanding their religion to new territories, in the course of pursuing those goals conquistadors indirectly influenced the nature and scope of world trade. Not only did they serve to establish the beginnings of long-term commercial contacts between Europe, Africa, and the Americas, but their particular solutions to the problems of profiting from the conquest also laid the groundwork for later Spanish colonialism. This was especially true for conquistadors who encountered the existing complex societies of Mesoamerica and the High Andes. Undeniably, these expeditions produced great wealth and glory for individuals such as Hernán Cortés (1485–1547) and Francisco Pizarro (1471?–1541), but they also promoted important long-term changes in patterns of global production and commerce.

MOTIVATIONS OF CONQUISTADORS

Conquistadors from parts of what would later be called Spain inherited a tradition of ongoing religious warfare to claim territory for Christendom, collectively called the *reconquista,* which had persisted for seven centuries preceding Christopher Columbus's discovery of a route

The conquistador Hernán Cortés (1485–1547) among the Aztecs. *With a small force of men, Cortés marched into the Aztec capital Tenochtitlán, on the site of modern-day Mexico City. Cortés took the ruler of the Aztec Empire hostage and demanded a lavish ransom, an act that ultimately led to the empire's collapse.*

from Europe to the Americas. As a result of this background, conquistadors in the Americas adopted a number of familiar *reconquista* practices.

One of the more important of these was the combination of spiritual and material motivations for warfare itself. Conquistadors routinely engaged in practices that made little strategic or military sense, simply because they were simultaneously pursuing religious and material goals. As one member of Cortés's expedition put it, "we came to serve God, and also to get rich" (Bernal Díaz del Castillo, *Historia verdadera de la conquista de la Nueva España*, II, 394). Thus, Cortés would risk rebellion in defeated indigenous villages by insisting upon knocking down "idols" and replacing them with Catholic icons such as crosses and images of the Virgin Mary.

The conquistadors confronted difficulties resulting both from the composition of their forces and from the nature of royal support for the conquest. Very few of the armies of conquistadors were professional soldiers. Instead, they tended to be men of humble social status

whose current situations were desperate enough to warrant sailing across the Atlantic Ocean to the exotic world of the "Indies," and who therefore expected not only to serve Christendom but also to profit from their efforts. Meanwhile, the Crown was generally reluctant to invest much money in territorial conquest in the Americas, preferring to name *adelantados* (individuals licensed by the king to lead expeditions of exploration and conquest in exchange for privileges and rewards should they succeed in expanding the king's realms). Thus, the conquistadors themselves tended to be essentially private entrepreneurs. Like the spiritual aspect of the conquest, this too drew on *reconquista* precedents. Expedition members often took out loans in order to purchase equipment, expecting to risk their lives, be rewarded handsomely, and have enough profit from the journey to more than repay their creditors.

Consequently, rewards for successful conquistadors had to come from the proceeds of conquest, and they had to take material form—converting heathens would not be sufficient to cover their debts, nor to justify the risks they took. Certainly, some conquering Europeans earned considerable quantities of bullion and other wealth in the form of booty. Still, most individual soldiers led by conquistadors found themselves with too little captured gold even to repay their debts. Here, too, *reconquista* practice offered a solution. Members of conquistadors' expeditions routinely received as rewards for their efforts *encomiendas,* which were grants that conferred rights and responsibilities to the recipient. To wit, the holder of the grant of *encomienda* enjoyed the labor of a particular group of non-Christian persons, and in exchange had to arrange for their evangelization while also providing military service at the Crown's pleasure. Although this was neither gold nor land ownership, the *encomienda* shaped early Spanish colonialism in the Americas in ways that would eventually affect world trade.

CONQUISTADORS AND WORLD TRADE

The wealth, fame, and success accruing to an individual conquistador depended to great extent on the kind of indigenous society that the conqueror happened to encounter while exploring. It is no coincidence that the two best-known conquistadors, Cortés and Pizarro, were the conquerors of the two wealthiest and most powerful states in the Americas in the early sixteenth century. Hernán Cortés—unusual among conquistadors due to his minor noble family and his education—led a small expedition from Cuba in 1519 that by August 1521 had subdued the capital of the Aztec Empire. He personally earned an astonishing amount of wealth in bullion, the royal grant of a noble title, land, and *encomiendas,* but his contribution to world trade lay in subordinating to the Spanish Crown millions of Mesoamerican peoples who already lived in a complex empire and were already accustomed to paying taxes and rendering labor service. Both the *encomienda* and tribute payments became important means by which Europeans could extract surplus production from indigenous persons in the Americas.

Subsequently, several expeditions in the late 1520s and early 1530s led by Francisco Pizarro and Diego de Almagro (1475?–1538) explored the Pacific Coast of South America in search of another wealthy empire to conquer. Pizarro's men (but not Almagro's) collected thousands of pounds of gold and silver bullion in 1532 by capturing the ruler of the Incan Empire. Almagro's troops earned loot on a smaller scale when the Spanish later sacked Cuzco, the Incan capital in the Andes, to complete the conquest. Consequently, many of the conquerors of the Incas returned to Spain as rich men, rather than staying to receive *encomiendas.* However, as in Mesoamerica, the conquistadors who settled in the Incan Empire after they conquered it subordinated a complex society to Spain. As

had happened in the Aztec realms, millions of Andean peoples who had been ruled by the Incas paid taxes and rendered labor service, giving rise to substantial new trade connections.

Even those conquistadors less successful than Cortés or Pizarro contributed to the creation of a vast empire for Spain in the Americas, and this spurred world trade in several important ways. Wealth was transferred from Americans to Europeans via *encomiendas*; a second transfer of wealth took the form of tribute collected from the millions of new indigenous subjects. Another important stimulus to increased global trade was in the settlement and administration of the conquered lands and peoples, which over time in New Spain, Peru, and other American colonies promoted very complex economies that engaged in production, consumption, and exchange of commodities in an ever-larger global trading network. Although they envisioned none of this when they set out, individual conquistadors prepared the way for major shifts in world trade.

SEE ALSO EMPIRE, SPANISH; GOLD AND SILVER; MEXICO; NEW SPAIN; PERU; RELIGION.

BIBLIOGRAPHY

Cortés, Hernán. *Letters from Mexico.* Trans. and ed. Anthony Pagden. New Haven, CT: Yale University Press, 1986.

Díaz del Castillo, Bernal. *The Conquest of New Spain.* Baltimore, MD: Penguin Books, 1963.

Lockhart, James. *The Men of Cajamarca: A Social and Biographical Study of the First Conquerors of Peru.* Austin: University of Texas Press, 1972.

Lovell, W. George. *Conquest and Survival in Colonial Guatemala: A Historical Geography of the Cuchumatán Highlands, 1500–1821.* Rev. edition. Montreal: McGill-Queen's University Press, 1992 (1985).

Restall, Matthew. *Seven Myths of the Spanish Conquest.* Oxford, U.K.: Oxford University Press, 2003.

Seed, Patricia. *Ceremonies of Possession: Europe's Conquest of the New World, 1492–1640.* Cambridge, U.K.: Cambridge University Press, 1995.

Jason L. Ward

CONTAINERIZATION

In the conventional maritime technologies that served the modern world economy until the 1960s, seaborne cargoes (with the exception of oil and bulk cargoes) were packed in bags, crates, boxes, and packages that at successive stages of their voyage had to be handled, sorted, and stored individually before delivery by road, rail, river, or canal to their destination. At a time when the volume of trade was growing rapidly, this was inefficient in terms of time and cost, and such a system slowed economic globalization.

Container ships at port. *Since its introduction in the 1950s, the container ship has come to define global commercial transport. The containers it carries provide a means to transport goods across land and sea without repackaging them at the dock.* AP/WIDE WORLD PHOTOS. REPRODUCED BY PERMISSION.

Beginning in the 1950s and 1960s, the container was developed to increase the efficiency of cargo movement and handling and to create a seamless link between cargo producers and consumers—the producers being the suppliers of manufactured goods and the consumers the final customers for these goods. Until then cargoes had moved port-to-port and at either end of this process had been carried by other, separate transport systems. The standard metal container not only reduced the number of individual items of cargo in terms of packaging, but because it could be carried over sea and land by ship, truck, and train, "it broke through the fetters of shipping's isolation in the transport chain and created physical and organizational multi-modal cooperation and, later, integration where none had existed before" (Broeze 2002, pp. 10–11). In short, the container successfully established door-to-door transport between producer and consumer in place of the old port-to-port system.

But the impact of the container was even more far-reaching. It reduced the number of cargo units, simplified and accelerated stowage, slashed port time for shipping, cut the number of wharf laborers and seamen, led to a decrease in pilfering and spoilage rates, changed the face of ports around the world, reduced freight costs, and at the beginning of the twenty-first century accounted for over 90 percent by value of global nonbulk trade.

Container terminals were created at virgin sites within existing ports or at entirely new locations. Virgin sites were frequently necessary given the obsolescence of old port infrastructure and the new technology and space needed for the handling and storage of containers. Pre-existing cargo-handling facilities and warehouses were redundant with respect to container handling. Space permitting, old ports created new terminals to handle container traffic, or, if space was severely limited, new sites outside the old ports were developed as dedicated container terminals.

Not all ports were quick to make this transition, but those that did, and that possessed good "connectivity" with land and air transport systems (or were geographically situated at a meeting point of major maritime routes), rapidly emerged as major hubs whose stokes linked them to a range of destinations. This created a new hierarchy of ports dominated by great "hubs" at traditional ports such as Singapore, Hong Kong, and Rotterdam, and at entirely new ports dedicated to container traffic in various parts of the world. Many old port structures around the world decayed, although some gained new lives as tourist- and culture-oriented "maritime precincts."

The container also changed the nature of shipping itself. The container required special ships, and so its introduction sounded the death knell for the cargo-carrying ships that had dominated maritime trade since the invention of the steam engine. Also, as the container ship grew larger, and cargo movement more mechanized and seamless, crew and port labor requirements plummeted, changing the social fabric of many port communities. The fall in demand for dock labor and sailors had a sharp impact on many port communities, reducing their links with the sea. The ancient social link between ship, harbor, and city was weakened, and it continues to weaken given the ability of the container terminal to operate in relative isolation from any port-based population.

THE FIRST CONTAINER REVOLUTION, 1950 TO THE 1970S

Railway companies in Europe and North America first used containers in the 1840s. But it was not until the 1950s that Malcolm McLean, a trucking magnate in the United States, pioneered the use of containers in the U.S. coastal trade, based on the United States–Cuba Seatrain system, which had been developed by Graham Bush in the 1930s to link the U.S. and Cuban rail systems. In 1954 McLean's company, SeaLand Services, offered the first door-to-door service coordinating land and sea transport, and in the following years it pioneered the development of dedicated container terminals, beginning with Port Elizabeth in Newark, New Jersey. The Matson Line followed McLean's initiative on the West Coast–Hawaii run and also introduced the idea of land-based gantry cranes to handle containers, eliminating the old reliance upon ship-based gear. In 1960 the Grace Line opened the first foreign-going container service between the United States and Venezuela. In the same year an Australian consortium, Associated Steamships, built the first specifically designed cellular container ship, the *Kooringa*.

In the late 1960s Sea-Land began services to Northern Europe, Southeast Asia, Hong Kong, Taiwan, and Singapore. The success of Sea-Land encouraged other U.S. companies to enter the trade, and it stimulated the formation in Rotterdam of an alliance of local interests (including the Netherlands' national railway company) to construct a dedicated container terminal linked to the European rail network. At the same time, a group of European shipping companies responded to the U.S. challenge by forming a consortium, the Atlantic Container Line, to enter the North Atlantic container trade.

The consortia idea was firmly established, and through the 1960s and 1970s various combinations of shipping companies in Europe and North America (later joined by shipping interests in Australia, Japan, Korea, Taiwan, and Singapore) emerged to introduce the container to the rest of the world.

GLOBALIZATION

Between 1972 and 1980 containerization "went global" and became a worldwide cargo-movement system. In 1972 containers were introduced on the Europe–East Asia routes; in 1973, on North America–Latin America routes; and finally, in 1974, on routes linking North America with the Middle East and India. Europe was linked to the Caribbean in 1976; to South Africa and the Middle East in 1977; to India, Pakistan, and West Africa in 1978; to China in 1979; and to Latin America in 1980.

During the 1970s and 1980s consortia frequently changed in membership as individual shipping companies moved to accommodate the challenges posed by the container. Containerization required almost instantaneous change on a global scale, with entire fleets of conventional vessels condemned to obsolescence and massive investment required in alternative shipping and port facilities.

A new generation of consortia and dedicated single companies emerged, dominated by conglomerates and companies such as Maersk and Evergreen, and with increasing participation by East and Southeast Asian shipping interests as the economies of these regions began to grow rapidly. The rise of the East Asian automobile and electronics industries swung the pendulum of cargo movements away from the North Atlantic to the Asia-Pacific region, and led to greater involvement in the container trade by East Asian interests.

By the 1980s the container industry had become fully globalized and increasingly competitive and, as a result, more specialized. Attempts to cut costs and improve the quality of services led to greater sophistication in the construction, use, and tracking of containers to accommodate both dry and perishable cargoes; the construction of more efficient (in terms of both fuel and crew costs) container ships; and the development of more seamless linkages between shipping and rails services. Major operators in the industry began to take a keener interest in the development of their hub ports. Not only did they attempt to take greater control of the operation of terminals, but they also established their own dedicated feeder networks linking their hub terminals to secondary ports, thereby establishing a web of container routes enveloping the world.

In the 1990s there was a move from consortia to more integrated alliances between shipping companies to form global companies better able to deal with the demands of huge corporate customers, particularly in the fields of automobiles, electronics, chemicals, beer, and food products. This move was further encouraged by the intense competition between shipping interests and the huge capital investments needed to construct and operate dedicated shipping and shore facilities.

By the twenty-first century the importance of the container and its role in promoting both national economic interests and international trade was such that governments around the world moved to intervene in the industry to tap its perceived benefits. For example, the Singapore and Malaysian governments are active in promoting rival container depots, and globally, governments eager to attract them to their dedicated hub ports actively court the preeminent container companies and conglomerates.

The container has forever altered the hierarchy of ports. Since the 1970s there has been a shift in volume and value of activity from the North Atlantic to the Asia-Pacific, and in ranking, East and Southeast Asian hub ports are collectively far more important than the dominant hubs in Europe (Rotterdam and Hamburg), North America (Long Beach and Los Angeles), and the Middle East (Dubai).

As a means of cargo transportation the container is now preeminent. It has conquered the world and is a central part of the process of economic globalization.

SEE ALSO AGRICULTURE; CARGOES, FREIGHT; HARBORS; HONG KONG; JAPAN; PANAMA CANAL; PORT CITIES; SHIPBUILDING; SHIPPING, MERCHANT; SHIP TYPES; SUEZ CANAL.

BIBLIOGRAPHY

Beth, Hans Ludwig; Hader, Arnulf; and Kappel, Roberts. *Twenty-Five Years of World Shipping.* London: Fairplay, 1984.

Broeze, Frank. *The Globalisation of the Oceans: Containerisation from the 1950s to the Present.* Research in Maritime History, no. 23. St. John's, Newfoundland: International Maritime History Association, 2002.

Gibson, Andrew, and Donovan, Arthur. *The Abandoned Ocean: A History of United States' Maritime Policy.* Columbia: University of South Carolina Press, 2000.

Hariharan, K. V. *Containerisation Era in India.* Bombay: MVIRDC World Trade Centre, 1995.

Trinca, Helen, and Davies, Anne. *Waterfront: The Battle That Changed Australia.* Sydney: Random House, 2000.

Wijnolst, Niko, and Wergeland, Tor. *Shipping.* Delft, Netherlands: University of Delft, 1996.

Kenneth McPherson

JAMES COOK
1728–1779

James Cook led three great voyages of scientific exploration to the Pacific Ocean in the *Endeavour* (1768–1771), *Resolution* and *Adventure* (1772–1775), and *Resolution* and *Discovery* (1776–1780). He produced the first accurate charts of the Pacific that, together with his descriptions of its lands, peoples, and natural resources, quickly attracted European sealers, fur traders, whalers, and settlers. Cook had few illusions but many misgivings about what would follow him to the Pacific. He was born the son of a farm worker in Yorkshire, England, and joined the Royal Navy as an able seaman in 1755. During the Seven Years' War (1756–1763), he helped to chart the Saint Lawrence River, making possible the British attack on Quebec in 1759, and he surveyed parts of Nova Scotia and Newfoundland. Between 1763 and 1767 his reputation grew with his detailed surveys of the southern and western coasts of Newfoundland. Cook's charts of the Pacific replaced conjecture and myth with carefully observed fact, and because he rose from humble origins, was driven by the spirit of scientific inquiry, and treated native peoples with respect and consideration, he came to embody many of the values of the Enlightenment. Although he is regarded with more ambivalence today, he remains central to the history of European maritime expansion.

SEE ALSO AUSTRALIA; EMPIRE, BRITISH; SHIPPING, AIDS TO.

BIBLIOGRAPHY

Beaglehole, J. C. *The Life of Captain James Cook.* London: A and C Black, 1974.

Obeyesekere, Gananath. *The Apotheosis of Captain Cook: European Mythmaking in the Pacific.* Princeton, NJ: Princeton University Press, 1992.

Sahlins, Marshall. *How "Natives" Think: About Captain Cook For Example.* Chicago: University of Chicago Press, 1995.

Salmond, Anne. *The Trial of the Cannibal Dog: Captain Cook in the South Seas.* London: Penguin, 2003.

Smith, Bernard. *European Vision and the South Pacific.* New Haven, CT: Yale University Press, 1983.

Thomas, Nicholas. *Discoveries: The Voyages of Captain James Cook.* London: Penguin, 2003.

Nigel Rigby

COPPER

Copper mining is thought to date to prehistoric times, and during most of its known history the supply of this versatile metal has been used near mining areas. Some of the oldest mines, such as the Rio Tinto mines in southern Spain, have been worked intermittently until the present day. Both the Aztecs and the Incas in what is now known as Latin America likewise used copper and bronze tools; the inhabitants of pre-Columbian North America discovered and worked rich deposits of ore in what is now known as the Upper Peninsula of Michigan. During the Middle Ages and the early modern period, Germans led in devising new technology for mining and working copper, especially for use as an alloy in brass for cannons.

On the eve of the Industrial Revolution (c. 1800) the United Kingdom was the main consumer of copper and also producer of three-fourths of the world's output. Although it was nearly self-sufficient, it soon began to import copper ore for smelting, a process it monopolized until the mid-nineteenth century. Demand was stimulated by the booming railroad industry in those countries experiencing economic development and by growth in the shipping industry, in which copper sheaths were used to preserve the hulls of wooden ships. Britain's output remained roughly constant at 145,000 tons per year from the 1830s to the 1850s. As gradual exhaustion of the most economically extracted ore set in, lower-cost competitors entered the market. Chile profited most from British bottlenecks, increasing production from about 15,000 tons annually in the 1830s to 88,000 tons in the 1850s. Cuba was a temporary force, with production in the same years rising from about 9,500 tons to over 47,000 tons annually.

Despite an abatement of demand for copper in traditional uses and smelting, the second half of the nineteenth century and the first half of the twentieth nonetheless witnessed a further acceleration in the overall growth of demand. Copper was required for electrical transmission in the burgeoning power, lighting, and communications industries, and for copper pipe as indoor plumbing spread in developed countries. These demands could have overwhelmed traditional sources of supply and methods of production, which were based on the exploitation of concentrated lodes of ore, akin to the methods used to obtain other minerals. In 1905, however, Daniel C. Jackling (1859–1956), a now-legendary American mining engineer, discovered how to exploit low-density copper deposits (known as porphry copper) by means of open-pit methods. Although his ingenious but environmentally destructive method did not entirely replace traditional technology, the abundance of porphry copper throughout the world made the Jackling process a watershed in the history of copper.

Thus, by 1910 the United States, already the leading producer since the commercial opening of the Michigan copper lodes in the mid-nineteenth century, supplied 60 percent of the world's unrefined copper. Mass production soon was launched in South America, especially Chile, largely under the management of U.S. capital, and in Africa, especially in what is now called Zambia, under British and Belgian management. Canada also asserted itself, eventually becoming the third-ranking producer after the United States and Chile. By 1925 the United States share of world mine production was slightly more than 50 percent. This was the start of long-term erosion of the United States position; the share of non-Western countries (henceforth called "developing nations") had risen to more than 30 percent, mostly from South America.

The circle of producers continued to grow after World War II with the arrival of Peru, Yugoslavia, South Africa, and other market economies, as well as enhanced production in Communist Poland, China, and the Soviet Union. The share in world mine output of the main pre–World War II producing nations fell from over 90 percent to 55 percent by the late 1970s. Outside the Communist world much of the diversification was financed by British and U.S. investment, with the result that non-Communist copper production nonetheless remained under the control of a few large companies. In the early postwar era 60 percent of world copper output was accounted for by just four firms and 77 percent by just eight firms, of which the majority were based in the United States. Reacting against perceived imperialism and exploitation by developed countries, however, governments in some developing nations expropriated foreign mines. By 1970, 43 percent of copper-producing capacity in the non-Communist developing world had been nationalized.

Shifts in the international pattern of production were reflected in a new and more complex pattern of world exports. During the 1960s and 1970s, for example, the share of developing countries in world exports of copper ores and concentrates rose from 42 to 62 percent. The story was the same in exports of refined and unrefined copper, with developing countries gradually gaining a 65 percent share of all types of copper exported from market economies. Industrial countries—resource-poor Japan above all—remained the largest importers, especially of ores and concentrates. Overall, the demand for copper grew at over 4.5 percent per year during the first twenty-five years of the postwar era, an impressive rate.

The late twentieth century, by and large, witnessed a continuation of prior trends—production growth at about 3 percent annually, increasing shares of nontraditional producers in production and exports, and a secular downtrend in copper prices—with one dramatic exception: the implosion of the United States as a producer and exporter in the early 1980s. By 1984 U.S. mine out-

Copper miners in the Democratic Republic of Congo. *The people of this region, called Katanga, mined copper for centuries. During the colonial years, Belgium extracted copper from Katanga for shipment back to Europe, and now copper is one of the nation's most important exports.* PAUL ALMASY/CORBIS. REPRODUCED BY PERMISSION.

put represented only 13 percent of world output, and the United States and Western Europe together, only 17 percent, whereas the share of Communist countries had risen to 24 percent. Chile gained additional share, becoming the largest producer of mine copper in the world. Trends in the production of refined copper were the same. The pattern is reminiscent of the United Kingdom's demise as the top producer in the nineteenth century.

The United States collapse, which continues in the early twenty-first century, had several causes. One was the abundance of rich deposits in the newer producing areas, enabling them to undercut costs in the United States, where reduced profits or actual losses followed for inefficient U.S. firms. Another was the legal mandate to bring old or outmoded smelters into compliance with federal environmental guidelines, which led many smelters to close. The leadership of U.S. copper companies

The Morenci copper mine in Arizona, an open-pit mine. *Morenci mine is the largest copper producer in the United States. Workers there move more than 700,000 tons of rock and earth daily to get to the copper ore underneath.* AP/WIDE WORLD PHOTOS. REPRODUCED BY PERMISSION.

sometimes had been accused of managerial mediocrity as well. Thus, U.S. mines representing a joint capacity of 600,000 metric tons per year ceased production. Chile's share of world mine output, at about 30 percent, is nearly twice that of the United States, which is still the second-leading producer. Remaining production is scattered throughout the world.

The rate of growth of demand for copper returned to prewar levels in the late twentieth and early twenty-first centuries due to discoveries of new uses for the metal, especially in the computer industry, and a revival of demand in traditional uses. Yet even a continuation of this vigorous trend would not exhaust world copper supplies in the foreseeable future. Credible estimates suggest that, given extraction technologies known in 2004, about 100 years' worth of reserves exist in the world. The copper industry also has a long history of technological innovation, even during periods of declining prices. Large deposits may exist under the oceans as well. Not even pessimists expect falling production and sharp price increases, at least until late in the twenty-first century.

SEE ALSO GUGGENHEIM FAMILY; MINING.

BIBLIOGRAPHY

Hyde, Charles K. *Copper for America.* Tucson: University of Arizona Press, 1998.

Mikesell, Raymond F. *The World Copper Industry.* Washington, DC: Resources for the Future, 1979.

Prain, Ronald. *Copper.* London: Mining Journal Books Limited, 1975.

John R. Hanson II

CORN LAWS

The English Corn Laws were government regulations on the importation and exportation of grain that existed from the mid-seventeenth century to 1846 (although laws regulating the trade in grain existed as far back as the fourteenth century). The Acts of 1660 and 1663, the first true Corn Laws, permitted the export of grain when its domestic price did not exceed a certain level, and imposed a tariff on imported grain when the price was

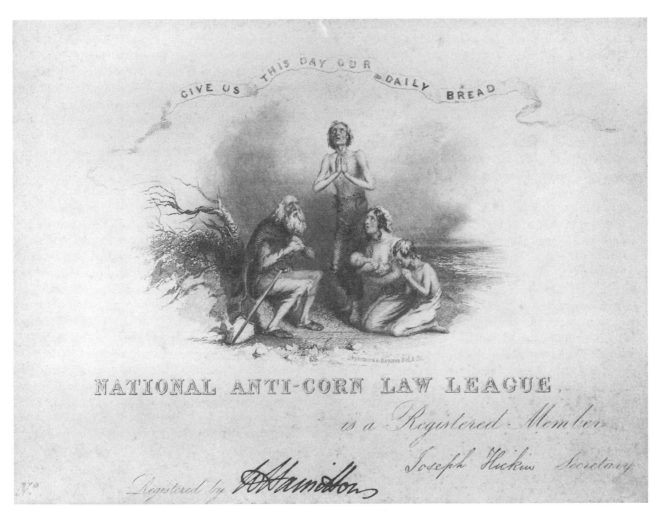

An anti–Corn Law cartoon with the title "Give Us This Day Our Daily Bread." *These laws were established by the English government in the mid-17th century to oversee imports and exports of grain. They were designed to ensure a stable economic supply while limiting reliance on other countries. A debate ensued between landowners who benefited and business owners who pushed for free trade to lower prices.* © HULTON-DEUTSCH COLLECTION/CORBIS. REPRODUCED BY PERMISSION.

below another, higher, level. The Act of 1670 established a sliding scale of import duties—the duty was high when the domestic price of wheat was relatively low, and it declined as the price of wheat increased. In 1689 Parliament established a bounty on grain exports so long as domestic prices were below a set level; the export bounty remained in effect until 1814. The sliding scale of import duties was revised several times between 1670 and 1773, and duties were suspended in years of especially high prices.

EARLY CORN LAWS

The Corn Laws of 1660 to 1747 were not nearly so contentious as those passed after 1815. The rationale for the early laws was "the further Encouragement of Tillage for the common good and welfare of this Kingdom," as the preamble to the 1670 Act stated. Import duties and export bounties were supposed to increase domestic food

production by reducing the risk associated with the grain-price fluctuations faced by farmers. When harvests were abundant, the bounties encouraged farmers to increase grain exports, which would keep domestic prices from falling too low; when harvests were meager, import duties would fall and imports would increase, which would keep prices from rising too high. The increase in stability was expected to benefit both producers and consumers of grain. Agricultural prices were relatively low during the first half of the eighteenth century, and Britain exported far more grain than it imported in all but a handful of years from 1700 to 1764.

England was not unique in its regulation of the grain trade. Denmark, Saxony, and Sweden adopted import duties on grain in the seventeenth century, and Brandenburg-Prussia did so in 1721. Several European countries prohibited the exportation of grain, in order to ensure the greatest possible food supply for their domestic populations. France, in particular, allowed the free exportation of grain during the seventeenth and eighteenth centuries.

The debate over the economic impact of the Corn Laws heated up in the last third of the eighteenth century, when rapid population growth, industrialization, and urbanization forced Britain to shift from being an exporter to an importer of grain. The Corn Law of 1773 significantly eased the tariff burden by reducing the price of grain at which only nominal import duties were charged from 80 shillings (s.) per imperial quarter of wheat (equal to eight bushels, about a quarter-ton of grain, in English measure) to 48s. per quarter. The price at which imported wheat paid only a nominal duty was increased to 54s. in 1791 and then to 66s. in 1804. The Corn Law of 1804 elicited some opposition from industrial areas in the north of Britain, but it effectively never became operational because the price of wheat remained above 66s. per quarter from 1805 through 1813. Despite the ineffectiveness of the Corn Laws during this period, Napoleon's attempted blockade of British ports during the Napoleonic Wars significantly reduced imports of grain and kept grain prices high. British farmers took advantage of the sustained high prices by increasing the acreage of arable land, as previously marginal land became profitable to cultivate.

CORN LAWS AFTER 1815

The most contentious period in the history of the Corn Laws began with the debate over the adoption of the Act of 1815 and culminated with the repeal of the Corn Laws in 1846. The price of wheat, which had averaged 107s. per quarter in 1809 to 1813, fell to 74.3s. in 1814, and again to 65.6s. in 1815. English landowners, fearing that continental grain would flood the British market upon the onset of peace, demanded increased protection. Despite antiprotection riots in London and opposition from northern manufacturers, Parliament in 1815 adopted a new law, which prohibited the importation of wheat when its domestic price was below 80s. per quarter, and allowed the free importation of wheat when the price was 80s. or above. Similarly, the importation of oats and barley was prohibited until the domestic price was 40s. and 27s. per quarter, respectively. The 1815 Corn Law clearly was intended to protect grain producers and landlords. Historian Robert Blake called it "one of the most naked pieces of class legislation in English history" (Blake 1971, p. 15), and many contemporaries and historians agree. Other countries followed England in adopting tariffs to protect domestic grain production: France in 1819, the Netherlands in 1824, and Spain in 1825. There is little doubt that the Corn Laws significantly raised the price of

grain, and the rent of agricultural land, over what it would have been if free importation had been allowed. English wheat prices were 44 percent higher than Amsterdam prices in the 1820s, and 38 percent higher than French prices. Peter Lindert (1991) estimates that during the 1820s the Corn Laws effectively raised the price of bread by 36 percent and increased the cost of living of the working class by 14 percent, while at the same time increasing the rental income of a small group of wealthy landowners.

The 1815 Act did not keep domestic wheat prices near 80s. per quarter, as landlords had hoped—and manufacturers had feared—they would. Prices fell sharply in the early 1820s, to 56.1s. per quarter in 1821 and 44.6s. in 1822. The Corn Laws were revised in 1822, when a sliding scale was reinstituted, and again in 1828. Under the 1828 Act, introduced by William Huskisson, the president of the Board of Trade, the importation of wheat was prohibited when its domestic price was below 52s. per quarter; at that price, wheat could be imported upon paying a high duty, the level of which declined as the price of wheat increased, until, when the domestic price was 73s. or above, the duty was only 1s. per quarter. The level of the duty was determined by the average price over the previous six weeks. The 1828 Corn Law was less protective than that of 1815; still, during the 1830s the price of wheat was on average 28 to 29 percent higher in England than it was in France or Amsterdam.

Criticism of the Corn Laws was relatively mild from 1828 to 1838, in part because of the low price of wheat from 1833 to 1836, but it flared up again when prices rose sharply after the bad harvest of 1838. An Anti-Corn Law Association was formed in Manchester in the fall of 1838; in the spring of 1839 this became the national Anti-Corn Law League. The League, whose leadership consisted mainly of northern manufacturers and merchants, attacked the Corn Laws on moral and humanitarian as well as on economic grounds, and called for their immediate repeal. The political power of the forces favoring repeal was strengthened by the Reform Act of 1832, which significantly increased the representation of northern industrial cities in the House of Commons.

The period from 1837 to 1842 was a time of economic crisis, especially in northern industrial cities. The economy slumped in 1837, recovered weakly in 1838 to 1839, and then slumped again, culminating in the severe depression of 1841 to 1842. The business cycle downturn coincided with a period of high grain prices from 1838 to 1841. In 1842 Prime Minister Robert Peel (1788–1850) responded to the poor economic conditions and to political pressure by modifying the Corn Laws to reduce the duties on imported corn. The revised Corn Law did not, however, satisfy the Anti-Corn Law League or other free traders, who kept up their pressure for repeal. The failure of the Irish potato crop in the fall of 1845 put pressure on Peel to at least suspend the Corn Laws. Instead, Peel called for the repeal of the Corn Laws, and, after heated debates, this was achieved on June 26, 1846. Repeal came at a serious political price; Peel's Conservative Party was split apart, and he resigned as prime minister three days later.

The short-term distributional effects of repeal were less than either its defenders or its opponents expected. From 1829 to 1846 imported wheat accounted for 7 to 8 percent of wheat consumption in England and Wales; this increased to 20 percent in 1847 to 1848 and to 27 percent in 1849 to 1859. However, the increase in imports did not lead to a sharp decline in grain prices. The average price of wheat fell from 51.7s. per quarter in 1843 to 1846 to 40.9s. in 1849 to 1852, but then increased to 57.8s. from 1853 to 1862. Domestic wheat production declined slightly as marginal land was withdrawn from production, and agricultural rent per acre remained roughly constant.

Despite the relatively small short-term effects, the repeal of the Corn Laws had major long-term, and symbolic, consequences for the British economy. Beginning in the 1880s a massive influx of North American grain caused prices to decline sharply. Domestic wheat production fell as a result, and by the first decade of the twentieth century only one-quarter of U.K. wheat consumption was domestically produced. The repeal of the Corn Laws was a major turning point in the economic history of nineteenth-century Britain because it ushered in Britain's movement to free trade, which culminated in the adoption of the Anglo-French (Cobden-Chevalier) Commercial Treaty in 1860. It also led France, Germany, Italy, and other countries to significantly lower, or abolish, their duties on grain, so that in the late 1850s and 1860s European grain prices were quite similar. The era of free trade did not last long, however. The sharp decline in prices resulting from the influx of cheap North American grain after 1870 led many European countries, but not Britain, to reinstitute tariffs on grain.

SEE ALSO HUSKISSON, WILLIAM; PEEL, SIR ROBERT.

BIBLIOGRAPHY

Abel, Wilhelm. *Agricultural Fluctuations in Europe: From the Thirteenth to the Twentieth Centuries.* 3rd edition. New York: St. Martin's Press, 1980.

Barnes, Donald G. *A History of the English Corn Laws from 1660–1846.* London: Routledge, 1930.

Blake, Robert. *The Conservative Party from Peel to Churchill.* New York: St. Martin's Press, 1971.

Edsall, Nicholas C. *Richard Cobden, Independent Radical.* Cambridge, MA: Harvard University Press, 1986.

Fairlie, Susan. "The Corn Laws and British Wheat Production, 1829–76." *Economic History Review* 22, no. 1 (April 1969): 88–116.

Fay, C. R. *The Corn Laws and Social England.* Cambridge, U.K.: Cambridge University Press, 1932.

Heckscher, Eli. *Mecantilism.* London: George Allen and Unwin, 1935.

Hilton, Boyd. *Corn, Cash, Commerce: The Economic Policies of the Tory Governments, 1815–1830.* Oxford, U.K.: Oxford University Press, 1977.

Lindert, Peter H. "Historical Patterns in Agricultural Policy." In *Agriculture and the State,* ed. C. Peter Timmer. Ithaca, NY: Cornell University Press, 1991.

McCord, Norman. *The Anti-Corn Law League, 1838–1846.* London: Allen and Unwin, 1958.

Turner, M. E.; Beckett, J. V.; and Afton, B. *Agricultural Rent in England, 1690–1914.* Cambridge, U.K.: Cambridge University Press, 1997.

Williamson, Jeffrey G. "The Impact of the Corn Laws Just Prior to Repeal." *Explorations in Economic History* 27 no. 2 (April 1990): 123–156.

George R. Boyer

CORPORATION, OR LIMITED LIABILITY COMPANY

As with a partnership, owners of a corporation pool their capital. In contrast to a partnership, a corporation has four distinctive legal characteristics: legal personality, transferability of ownership interests, a functional managerial hierarchy, and limited shareholder liability. Each one of these characteristics has added to the emerging economic dominance of the corporation.

The early corporation was a child of the state, and can be considered as an extension of its narrow mercantile interests, and, as such, it enjoyed monopoly privileges. Eventually this gave rise to state abuse of the corporation to extract wealth from its citizens. Consequently, the corporation evoked political and legal hostility that hindered its development. Once the corporation became associated with competition, companies gained freedom to incorporate.

FORMATIVE HISTORY

Forms of partnership that had unlimited and limited liability, called *societas* and *commenda* respectively, were rooted in Roman law. (Limited liability has an advantage over unlimited liability in that capital suppliers can only lose the amount of capital advanced.) However, the advent of the corporation generally is associated with the granting of a royal charter to the Russia Company in 1557, giving to it exclusive trading privileges with Russia. This charter allowed it to constitute on a joint-stock basis with a functional management. But the novel feature of the Russia Company was its joint-stock with legal personality, which through the company seal enabled it to sue and to be sued. Exclusive trading charters had been granted previously to "regulated companies" as early as the thirteenth century. The first of these was called the Merchants of the Staple, organized to govern the wool-export industry, and the last, organized in 1505, was the Merchant Adventurers. Significantly, the regulated companies governed the actions of individual merchants and had no real legal personality.

The Russia Company innovation was copied in Holland with the establishment of the Dutch East India Company. In addition, Genoa chartered a slave-trading corporation (1580) and France chartered its Africa (1561), Coral (1600), and Canadian (1602) companies.

The idea of the juristic person, or personality under the law, is attributable to Roman jurists, coming into common law, for example, by way of canon law. But through the vehicle of royal charters, the idea of legal personality enabled both ecclesiastic and lay institutions to hold and administer property in perpetuity. Royal charters conferring legal personality continued to be granted to English companies, the most significant being English East India Company (1599). When receiving a new charter in 1654, this company won the right to perpetual existence, following the precedent set by the Dutch East India Company in 1623. Free transferability of East India Company shares soon followed, setting a precedent for future corporations.

THE MERCANTILIST CORPORATION

Despite the success of the early corporation, public opinion regarding exclusive trading privileges soured under James I (1566–1625). The king was a spendthrift and had accumulated unprecedented debts. To raise additional income he regularly sold exclusive charters and renegotiated existing ones, creating a climate of investment uncertainty that undermined the long-term interests of the state. That investment uncertainty was the root cause of an economic crisis in the 1620s, intensifying political resentment against exclusive privileges. Although the attorney general, Sir Edward Coke (1552–1634), had earlier failed to restrict exclusive charters to those deemed in the public interest, Parliament was prompted to restrict royal prerogative. In 1624 it passed the Statute of Monopolies, which forbade the issuing of any further charters without its consent.

Opposition to the business corporation persisted through both the Commonwealth and Restoration eras, resulting in a decline in trading companies involved in European and the Levant trade. However, because of imperial rivalries, promotion of long-distance-trading corporations such as the East India and Hudson Bay Companies continued. Such companies were deemed essential to thwart foreign political and commercial ambitions. For example, France in 1664 chartered its own East India Company. In addition, monopoly corporations such as the East India Company were an important source of government income. For example, the need to raise additional income was an important reason behind the incorporation of the Bank of England in 1694. A notable feature of this period was the inclusion of the privilege of limited liability in company charters.

The reputation of the corporation received a further blow during the first quarter of the eighteenth century. War expenditure had led to unsustainable national debt levels, and schemes were developed to convert public debt into shares of companies, having as their primary asset the same government liabilities. The most infamous instances of these were the Mississippi Company in France (1718), and the South Sea Company in England (1720). The success of the debt conversions depended simultaneously on creditors receiving favorable terms and on government debt levels being greatly reduced. In both instances, company stock was overpromoted and stock prices soared, drawing in many thousands of investors. Eventually, rationality prevailed and investors began to doubt the promises of outlandish dividends. Consequently, stock prices fell precipitously. The Mississippi and South Sea episodes, both classic financial bubbles, further deepened suspicions regarding corporations, particularly in regard to the propensity to overpromote stocks. Given this historical context, one can understand why the physiocrats in France and Adam Smith (1723–1790) in Britain expressed disapproval toward corporations.

FREEDOM OF INCORPORATION

Negative opinion regarding corporations persisted through to the turn of the eighteenth century, although in England chartered companies made significant inroads in the insurance and transportation industries due to the need to raise large amounts of capital and to diversify risk. Moreover, quasi-corporations existed in shipping and tin mining. These sectors were under the special jurisdiction of admiralty and stannary courts. Both court systems operated under the principle of customary law, in which legal principles adapted to suit business practice instead of conforming to a set of abstract legal principles, as was characteristic of both civil and natural law.

In contrast, under the common law, many corporations had to constitute more circuitously, given the difficulty of obtaining a charter. Through the trust device, promoters hoped to establish joint-stock firms having transferable shares and the ability to sue and be sued. However, this device could not be used to attain limited

An 1858 stock certificate for Seneca Oil Company. The company hired Edwin Drake to look for oil in the United States and he set up the first oil-producing well in the country. To held help fund the company's endeavors, Seneca sold stock to shareholders, who had a stake in ownership, but limited liability related to the firm's actions. © BETTMANN/CORBIS. REPRODUCED BY PERMISSION.

liability. Beginning in the last quarter of the eighteenth century, such unincorporated companies appeared in the silk, wool, food, and beer industries, but were notably absent in the cotton and metal industries. In this period the number of companies increased fivefold, and many of them were unincorporated.

The growth in unincorporated businesses occurred despite their illegality under the Bubble Act (1720). This act had been dormant but was resurrected in a number of court rulings in the period 1808 to 1812. The legal threat to the unincorporated companies dissipated only when the act was repealed in 1825. Under a strict interpretation of the common law they were still illegal, but a business-friendly regime at both the chancery- and common-law courts had ruled that such companies were in the public interest. However, continued uncertainty prompted Parliament to enact company legislation that had as its main tenet freedom of incorporation. A chief concern focused on whether freedom to incorporate should be constrained to guard against overpromotion and stock speculation. However, lessons from incorporation experiences in the United States and France ulti-

mately resulted in the English Companies Act of 1844 granting freedom of incorporation, and leaving investors to protect themselves. However, corporations were required to accurately report half-yearly earnings to stockholders.

In the nascent United States, despite the legacy of the common law and the Bubble Act, some state legislatures had begun to freely issue charters to companies operating in many commercial sectors including banking, insurance, and manufacturing. Also, as early as 1817, Connecticut and Massachusetts had moved toward chartering corporations with limited liability. Competition among the states soon encouraged their neighbors to follow suit. Significantly, the region experienced increased economic growth.

In France hostility toward the corporation had peaked during the Revolution, when it had been outlawed it for a time, but under Napoleon, corporations were accepted as a necessary evil. Although opposition to corporations eased in successive regimes, there remained reluctance to grant charters. Paradoxically, a form of limited partnership known as a *commandite par actions* was allowed to mutate into an unofficial corporation. Firms could easily register as *commandites,* and in contrast to the chartered corporation they were free from stringent capitalization requirements. Formally, only owners not engaged in management could enjoy limited liability and the right to transfer shares. In practice, however, managers were able to circumvent such constraints. Significantly, *commandite* firms were associated with the most dynamic part of the French economy.

Freedom to incorporate with limited liability in Britain did not come until 1856. Free incorporation with limited liability soon followed in France, and by 1860 most U.S. states had adopted it. Finally, by the last quarter of the nineteenth century many continental European nations had followed suit, ushering in the modern corporate era.

SEE ALSO ANGLO AMERICAN CORPORATION; JOINT-STOCK COMPANY; LAW, COMMON AND CIVIL; PARTNERSHIP.

BIBLIOGRAPHY

Davis, Joseph S. *Essays in the Earlier History of American Corporations,* vols. 1–2. Cambridge, MA: Harvard University Press, 1917.

Ekelund, Robert B., and Tollison, Robert D. "Mercantilist Origins of the Corporation." *Bell Journal of Economics* 11, no. 1 (Spring 1980): 715–720.

Fisher, F. J. "Some Experiments in Company Organization in the Early Seventeenth Century." *Economic History Review* 4, no. 2 (April 1933): 177–194.

Freedman, Charles E. *Joint-Stock Enterprise in France 1807–1867: From Privileged Company to Modern Corporation.* Chapel Hill: University of North Carolina Press, 1979.

Handlin, Oscar, and Handlin, Mary F. "Origins of the American Business Corporation." *Journal of Economic History* 5, no. 1 (May 1945): 1–23.

Harris, Ron. *Industrialising English Law: Entrepreneurship and Business Organisation, 1720–1844.* Cambridge, UK: Cambridge University Press, 2000.

Hickson, Charles R., and Turner, John D. "The Trading of Unlimited Liability Bank Shares in Nineteenth-Century Ireland: The Bagheot Hypothesis." *Journal of Economic History* 63, no. 4 (December 2003): 931–958.

Hunt, Bishop C. *The Development of the Business Corporation in England, 1800–1867.* Cambridge, MA: Harvard University Press, 1936.

Kessler, William C. *Incorporation in New England: A Statistical Study, 1800–1875. Journal of Economic History* 8, no. 1 (May 1948): 43–62.

Livermore, Shaw. "Unlimited Liability in Early American Corporations." *Journal of Political Economy* 43, no. 5 (October 1935): 674–687.

Scott, William R. *The Constitution and Finance of English, Scottish and Irish Joint-Stock Companies to 1720,* vols. 1–3. Cambridge, U.K.: Cambridge University Press, 1912.

Charles R. Hickson
John D. Turner

CORRESPONDENTS, FACTORS, AND BROKERS

If a merchant in the seventeenth or eighteenth century had business transactions to be carried out at a distant location, he had basically two choices of instruments. He could have a merchant correspondent in the distant place who would carry out such transactions for him (buying, selling, handling bills, etc.) and charge a commission. Or, he could send an employee, or "factor," to carry out those same operations.

The correspondent option was definitely the most convenient. Two merchants corresponded; each was prepared to carry out a wide range of services for the other and charge a reasonable commission—2.0 percent in Holland, 2.5 percent in England. This was very much a mutual service. Ledgers of English merchants in these centuries show pages for commissions had both a credit and a debit side. That is, the merchant owner of the ledger credited himself with commission earned serving others, and debited himself with commissions paid to others for services performed for him.

THE NORTH EUROPEAN SCENE

Although the correspondence system was very convenient, it had its limitations. It might be relatively easy for a London merchant to find a correspondent in a major overseas center such as Amsterdam, Hamburg, or Bordeaux, but there were many lesser ports where the right sort of correspondent was not available. To get his business done in such difficult places a merchant might be forced to send an employee. Although supplied with a letter of credit from his employer, a mere clerk could not handle all the business that might be sent his way. For more complicated transactions, a more senior employee or factor was needed. Factors acted on the spot as independent commission merchants, but the firms they dealt with knew that they were representatives of English firms whose letter of credit made their activities possible. Factors, however, were not always able to operate entirely on their own, but might need support from the senior firm's correspondents. For example, a factor in the Baltic needed a lot of money to purchase the masts, deals, pitch, tar, hemp, flax, and linen cloth in demand in England, particularly for the royal and mercantile fleets. Money could not be sent to such factors directly because there was neither a market in London for bills on Baltic ports nor a market in the Baltic for bills on London. Instead, the factors in the Baltic were instructed to obtain cash by selling bills on the firm's correspondents in Hamburg or Amsterdam; the Hamburg or Amsterdam correspondents, in turn, obtained the cash to pay such bills when due by selling other bills on London. Thus the London firm's factors and correspondents supported each other in bill operations.

Because factors were usually relatively young men, they had opportunities to make local marriages, which sometimes improved their employing firm's useful connections. For example, the London merchant Samuel Holden (c. 1675–1740) brought back from Riga an intelligent Russian-born clerk whom he had naturalized in England, made a member of the Russia Company, and sent back to Riga as his factor. This factor, Mathias Shiffner (c. 1690–1756), married into the family of a Baltic German pastor whose own family was very close to Grand Duchess Anna of Courland. When Anna inherited the imperial Russian throne (1730–1740) Shiffner's in-laws had preferred access to the court at St. Petersburg and were able to obtain for him contracts and privileges from the Russian government, all to the benefit of Holden in London.

To keep their best factors, employers had to allow them some private trade. This facilitated the accumulation of capital that enabled a successful factor to return to England and set up as an independent merchant. Samuel Holden was hardly the only one who made this transition. A much more striking example is Sir Gilbert Heathcote (1652–1733), who, while still an apprentice to a major London merchant, was sent out as a clerk and then a factor in Sweden. When he accumulated enough capital he returned to London as an independent merchant, sending two of his younger brothers back as factors in Danzig and Koenigsberg. Gilbert became a member of Parliament and one of the founders of both the Bank of England and the New East India Company. At his death he was reputed to be the richest commoner in England.

THE MEDITERRANEAN SCENE

In the seventeenth and early eighteenth centuries English trade with the eastern Mediterranean (the Ottoman Empire) was limited to members of the Levant Company of London. Individual members of the company maintained factors in many ports and trading centers in that area. The most important of these were Aleppo, Istanbul, and Smyrna. In Aleppo during the first third of the eighteenth century there were thirty to forty English factor firms, including about fifty factors. To all three centers, the principal outward cargo was English woolen cloth. At Aleppo, the most important center for the English in the early part of the eighteenth century, the major return cargo was silk, obtained in bartering exchange with the local merchants, who were mostly Syrian, but also included Armenians and Jews. The typical factor firm consisted of only one or two principals. Some teenagers from families that could afford to pay a substantial premium went out as apprentices to one of these factor houses. More often, a young man in his twenties who had served an apprenticeship in England went out initially as an employee of a factor to whom his family had paid a premium roughly equivalent to that paid for an apprenticeship. If the young man demonstrated an ability to handle the business, after a year or so he was admitted as a partner. The partnership contract obliged the new partner to pay a substantial fraction of net earnings (often as much as one-half) to the senior partner for about seven years, even though the senior partner left shortly afterward to return home. The new partner expected compensation for this burden when the partnership contract terminated and he became entitled to all the profits of the factorage—and entitled also to take on a junior partner on similar terms, and ultimately return to England to enjoy his share of his successor's earnings.

The income of such a factor firm depended on the commissions and other payments it received from the London firm (or firms) for whom it worked. The standard European commission was 2 percent, although in some English trades it was commonly 2.5 percent, the extra half percent designed to cover brokerage without detailed accounting. This 2 percent charged on goods both sold and bought was, however, only the beginning of the Levant factor's earnings. Modern scholarship suggests that the factor very likely earned 3 percent on selling goods and 5 percent on purchases of return cargo—thus 8 percent on the total operation. The 2 percent on selling imports was raised to 3 percent by a "tariff" issued by the Levant Company listing the maximum rates factors could charge for a variety of expenses (customs, carriage, brokerage, weighing, etc.). In normal practice the factors paid less but charged the full amount authorized by the tariff, creating an extra 1 percent for commission. In silk exports the factors were entitled to receive compensation for the loss of weight in cleaning the silk purchased. In actuality the loss of weight was less than the margin allowed, raising the factor's earnings on silk purchases from 2 to 5 percent. Because the relevant merchants in London were commonly former factors in the Levant, both sides knew what was going on and accepted these practices as trade conventions.

The number of factors and factor firms in the Levant declined between the 1670s and 1740s, with fewer but larger firms handling the work. This was comparable to the evolution in the American sugar and tobacco trades in the same period, where progressively fewer and larger firms handled imports. In the Levant, however, this decline was influenced in part by the adverse effects of the wars starting in 1739. Despite these difficulties, the Levant Company survived until 1825.

THE EAST INDIAN SCENE

The trade of England, France, and Holland with the East Indies was to a noticeable degree controlled by money-supply problems. Although the East produced many products desired by Europeans, there was only a limited demand there for European products. Therefore, the English, French, and Dutch East India Companies had to ship coin to the East to enable their agents to make the desired purchases. Because silver was more valuable (vis-à-vis gold) in the East than in Europe, these coin shipments consisted primarily of Spanish silver dollars. However, after the British company obtained political control over Bengal and other parts of India in the mid-eighteenth century, the company had more than enough silver for its purchases and became interested in remitting money home. Like the Eastland and Levant companies, the English East India Company permitted its employees in India to venture into private trade. Because the company obtained from local rulers exemption from princely tolls for its local vessels and cargoes, by placing their cargoes on company vessels the British private traders obtained this exemption for themselves and their Indian partners. Such exemptions made the private trade quite profitable, and created a population of employee/private traders seeking ways of sending their ill-gotten gains home. The company could remit its funds by selling in Europe bills of exchange on India to the Dutch, who still had to send money outward. The company's employees sent money home by buying bills of exchange on Europe from agents of the Dutch and French companies in India.

As people in Britain became more aware of the gains being made and remitted by the company's "servants," parents in Britain became more energetic in their efforts to obtain for their sons places either as "writers" or military officers in the company's service. Throughout the seventeenth and most of the eighteenth century the normal way to get such a post was through a letter of recommendation from a director of the company duly accepted by the full board. Although this system appears to have remained in effect through the eighteenth century, in fact in the later decades some influential ministers—particularly Henry Dundas (1742–1811)—were able to influence appointments, even though the power to appoint nominally remained with the directors. Though intensely criticized, the main lines of this relaxed system remained in effect until the last days of the East India Company.

THE DIVERSITY OF AMERICAN EXPERIMENTS

The division of overseas work between correspondents and factors also appeared in the trade with the American colonies. The use of correspondents was widespread though little noted in modern accounts. A merchant in northern Ireland desiring to obtain flaxseed from the northern colonies would instruct his correspondent in New York City to buy and ship such seed for him, obtaining the necessary funds by selling bills of exchange drawn on the Irish merchant's correspondent in London. It was of course up to the Irish merchant to make sure that his London "friend" would have funds in hand when the bills came due. Similarly, a London merchant wishing to buy rice or indigo in South Carolina would instruct his correspondent in Charleston to purchase the desired quantities, using funds obtained by selling bills on London which were always in demand in the Carolinas.

In North America as in the Baltic, when suitable correspondents could not be found, factors had to be used, particularly in the Chesapeake. A very rare 1684 document survives constituting a draft service agreement between a London merchant (W. Paggen) and his Virginia factor (J. Hardman). The factor was to reside in Virginia with duties including "taking care of buyeing, selling and disposeing of such men and women servants, goods, wares and other merchandizes . . . consigned to him and in the buying, receiving in, and shipping, transporting, disposing and taking care of, preserveing and sending to England all such Tobaccoe, skinns and Furs as shall be by him bought in Virginia . . . while goods consigned to the said John Hardman . . . shall by him be laid out, bartered, sold, exchanged and disposed of for bright Tobacco, skinns or Furs and good Bills of exchange . . ." (*Perry of London,* 105–106). Although the draft leaves the compensation blank, it does specify that Hardman was not to act as factor for any other merchant and was not to trade on his own. This last provision would have been very difficult to enforce unless his employer had a supervisor on the same river in Virginia, which was unlikely in the seventeenth century. However, in the larger Scottish firms characteristic of the years after 1740, there was in fact a supervisor or chief factor in each trading area. In these Scottish firms there were two levels of factors. The lower level consisted primarily of shopkeepers who operated the stores of the firm. The upper level had supervisory duties and had the power to draw bills of exchange crucial to the operation of the firm. Such bills were sold for cash, and they enabled the Scottish stores to pay tobacco sellers partly in cash, an important element in their competitiveness.

Even the most senior factor, furnished with the most carefully drafted letters of credit, could not convey property for his principal. For anything involving buying or selling real property or foreclosing on a mortgage, the factor or other agent would need a power of attorney from the distant principal. Such powers of attorney were drafted by a recognized notary public in Britain, recorded in that notary's register, and rerecorded in the county records of the jurisdiction in America where the transaction occured.

Trading operations with America were not, however, confined to the now-familiar categories of correspondent and factor. At an early stage, the institution of factor was inverted. Instead of referring just to employees sent out from Britain, it was also made applicable to English merchants who acted on commission for planters in the West Indies and North America. That is, in the seventeenth-century West Indies, some larger planters, not satisfied with the prices and services offered them by local merchants and ship captains, opened correspondence with London and Bristol commission merchants. The latter acted as their factors, selling the sugars and other products sent to them for the usual 2.5 percent commission and returning such European and Asian goods as were ordered. Any balance on such accounts were realized by bills of exchange. The commission merchant system pioneered in the West Indies was brought into use in the Chesapeake too by the end of the seventeenth century. The bills of exchange it facilitated were in great demand in all the colonies and were particularly useful for purchasing slaves.

BROKERS

The work of a commission merchant was not as easy as it might seem. A London merchant might get an order from Germany to purchase certain grades of tobacco but might not be sufficiently conversant with the varieties and qualities involved. Another merchant might receive a consignment of tobacco for sale but might not be perfectly sure about which varieties were most suitable for which markets. Both might find it useful to consult a tobacco broker skilled in classifying and evaluating tobacco and familiar with the varieties suitable for different markets. Some of these brokers were Dutch Jews who had gained their skills in Amsterdam, where all varieties of tobacco were traded and connections maintained with all possible markets. A consignment merchant might also receive in many separate hogsheads a large variety of qualitatively variable leaf which each consigner expected him to sell separately, one hogshead at a time. However, the best sale he could arrange involved selling a large number of hogsheads at a flat price. He knew that he could not report this flat price to all consigners because they would soon learn that good leaf had not received a better price than mediocre. Therefore, the consignment merchant would ask his broker to evaluate each hogshead and recommend an adjusted price that reflected quality—an extra farthing per pound to one consigner, a farthing per pound less to another consigner. Because the costs of brokerage were included in the 2.5 percent com-

mission, the consigning planter would not find a brokerage item on his account of sales, and had difficulty learning anything about the useful brokers. But the merchants who had to sell tobacco were careful to treat brokers with the greatest respect.

Brokers of course existed in other trades and other cities. In London and presumably in other major centers, in addition to commodity brokers there were also ship brokers, exchange brokers, and bill brokers. Some eighteenth-century brokers were active in more than one sphere. The nineteenth century saw the number, size, and specialization of broker firms increase, with some of the bill-broker firms developing into major discount houses.

NON-ENGLISH EXPERIENCE

The institutions characteristic of British American trade can also be found in varying degrees in the records of French overseas trade. The French had correspondents, commission merchants (*commissionaires*), and brokers (*courtiers*). They also had one distinct institution, the *société en commandite,* that performed some of the functions of the bond between an English merchant and his overseas factor. A limited partnership could be formed in France between two or more rather junior merchants in a colony and a metropolitan sleeping partner (*commanditaire*) who provided most of the firm's capital. This gave the partners in the field the appearance of independence, yet with access to the outside capital they needed.

A specialized institution existed in the slave trade on the West African coast. There, the middlemen who linked up the captains of slave vessels (whether British, French, or Dutch) with the big slave traders of the interior were also termed brokers (*courtiers*). They settled prices with the captains, collected the trading goods, forwarded them to the interior slave traders, and brought back the slaves being traded. These were much more extensive operations than those usually undertaken by brokers in Europe.

SUBSEQUENT HISTORY

All these institutions characteristic of the seventeenth and eighteenth centuries persisted into the early nineteenth century, until overwhelmed by the arrival in the 1840s and 1850s of the steamship and oceanic telegraphic cable. These reduced the need for factors while facilitating correspondence and enabling firms to make fuller use of overseas employees.

SEE ALSO Capitalism; Law, Common and Civil.

BIBLIOGRAPHY

Davis, Ralph. *Aleppo and Devonshire Square: English Traders in the Levant in the Eighteenth Century.* London: Macmillan, 1967.

Furber, Holden. *John Company at Work: A Study of European Expansion in India in the Late Eighteenth Century.* Cambridge, U.K.: Cambridge University Press, 1951.

Pressnell, L. S. *Country Banking in the Industrial Revolution.* Oxford, U.K.: Oxford University Press, 1956.

Price, Jacob M. *Overseas Trade and Traders.* Aldershot, U.K.: Variorum, 1996.

Price, Jacob M. *Perry of London: A Family and a Firm on the Seaborne Frontier, 1615–1753.* Cambridge, MA: Harvard University Press, 1992.

Price, Jacob M. *Tobacco in Atlantic Trade: The Chesapeake, London, and Glasgow, 1675–1771.* Aldershot, U.K.: Variorum, 1995.

Solow, Barbara L., ed. *Slavery and the Rise of the Atlantic System.* Cambridge, U.K.: Cambridge University Press, 1991.

Jacob M. Price

COTTON

Throughout most of human history, cotton was processed close to where it was grown. It was only in the wake of the Industrial Revolution in the nineteenth century that vast quantities of cotton began to be shipped across continents and oceans. As cotton became one of the most valuable global commodities, networks for trading it spanned the globe with extraordinary density—from New Orleans to Bombay, from Alexandria to Liverpool.

EARLY COTTON TRADE

Before the Industrial Revolution, long-distance trade in raw cotton had loosely connected various places within Asia, the Americas, and Africa, as well as Asia with Europe. Syrian cotton was spun and woven in Egypt, Maharashtra cotton in Bengal, Henan cotton in Jiangnan, Anatolian cotton in Luzerne, Yucatecan cotton in Teotihuacan, Nubian cotton in Persia, and Macedonian cotton in Venice. This was a multipolar world of modest exchanges without significant linkages between them, not a world market.

Most of this early trade took place in Asia. Europe remained quite marginal—both because it processed relatively little cotton and because for ecological reasons it was not a significant grower of cotton. Beginning in the 1600s cotton textiles from Asia increasingly arrived in Europe, and European traders, especially those of the British East India Company, intensified sales of Indian cotton to China to pay for Chinese tea, but little cotton was worked up in Europe.

In the early seventeenth century, however, a slow but persistent increase in cotton textile production in England, France, the German lands, and the Netherlands led

EFFECTS OF BOLL WEEVIL BEETLE INFESTATION

By the 1920s all U.S. cotton-growing regions were infested with the plant's most serious pest, the boll weevil beetle. Crop destruction inflicted by boll weevils increased economic hardships suffered by U.S. cotton farmers through to the Depression. Pesticides introduced after World War II allowed cotton production to resume, but these were expensive and damaging to the environment. The global cotton industry still relies on fertilizers and insecticides, but new organic solutions are being sought to allow cotton farming while protecting the environment.

David J. Clarke

to an intensification of trade in the "white gold." Raw cotton began to arrive in greater quantities in European ports, principally from the Ottoman Empire (from Salonica and Smyrna), but small quantities also came from India, Africa, South America, and the Caribbean. Europe remained a relatively minor producer of cotton textiles, but because of its increasingly dominant position in world trade, including the trade in Indian textiles, it effectively disrupted older cotton trade networks. From a European perspective, this phase of the global cotton trade, which lasted until the late eighteenth century, was characterized by a multitude of suppliers growing cotton under various labor regimes, and by the importance of local producers and local merchants in the system of trade. There were yet no ports and merchants who specialized in the shipment of cotton to Europe, nor any parts of the world that specialized in the growing of cotton for European markets. More cotton was traded within Asia, especially within and between India and China, than into Europe.

SHIFT IN THE 1780s

This changed in the last third of the eighteenth century with the rapid expansion of cotton textile production in England and, later, on the European continent. British cotton consumption doubled from 1765 to 1774; it doubled again in the following decade. As the Ottoman Empire proved unable to meet this rapidly expanding demand, merchants and manufacturers looked elsewhere. They found responsive producers in two areas of the world that had developed a radical new way of producing agricultural commodities: the Caribbean and Brazil. Cot-

Cotton plants in bloom. *For the past 400 years, cotton's importance as a world trade good has steadily increased. The United States Department of Agriculture estimated in 2005 that world cotton consumption had surpassed 100 million bales yearly.* JLM VISUALS. REPRODUCED BY PERMISSION.

ton production there expanded rapidly, especially during the 1770s and 1780s, as they became Europe's principal providers of cotton. Britain alone imported on average about 3.7 million pounds of cotton in the late 1770s from the West Indies, and about 9.4 million pounds in the mid-1780s, about half of its total imports. Yet the West Indies's production stopped growing by the 1790s. Planters were reluctant to divert the labor and land that they had devoted to growing sugarcane, and the most important cotton island—St. Domingue—was disrupted by turmoil. Nonetheless, the expansion of Caribbean cotton production left an important legacy: from then until 1865, most cotton entering world markets was produced by slaves.

Beginning in the 1790s, the United States became the world's most important cotton exporter. Contemporary observers were surprised: indeed, a 1780s British customs official refused entry to U.S. cotton because he believed it could not possibly be from the United States. However, the United States had a climate and soil superbly suited to the growth of cotton, plus two other competitive advantages: nearly unlimited quantities of recently emptied land, as well as an ample supply of slave labor, which planters in the Upper South sold first to the Carolinas and Georgia, and later to Alabama, Mississippi, and other Southern states. Once Eli Whitney's cotton gin (1793) made separating seed and fibers of American green-seed cotton relatively easy, cotton exports from the United States exploded: in 1794 the United States exported 2 million pounds of cotton, in 1800 18 million pounds, in 1820 128 million pounds, and in 1860 1,768 million pounds. Between 1800 and 1860 an average of 68 percent of the United States's annual harvest went abroad, mostly to the United Kingdom, but increasingly also to other parts of Europe. Ever-cheaper U.S. cotton fed the explosive growth of the European textile industry, and cotton exports essentially defined the U.S. position in the world economy. Cotton remained the United States's most valuable export product from 1803 to 1936.

With U. S. cotton exports soaring, cotton growing in the West Indies and Brazil stagnated. However, by the 1920s, other regions, especially Egypt and India, became significant exporters. During the 1820s Viceroy Muhammad Ali (r. 1805–1848) tried to modernize Egypt by encouraging cotton production for export. Egypt was ecologically superbly suited for the growing of long-staple cotton—a high-quality fiber with a relatively small but lucrative market. Indian cotton was of much poorer quality and short-stapled, but pressured by Manchester manufacturers who began to fear too great a dependence on the United States, the East India Company brought small amounts of Indian cotton to Liverpool. However, until the U.S. Civil War, the major international market for Indian cotton remained China, and U.S. cotton still dominated European markets.

Between 1800 and 1860, thus, a relatively stable cotton system had emerged, with slave-grown cotton from the United States at the center, providing the raw material that fueled the British Industrial Revolution. The global center of the trade was Liverpool, entrepôt for Lancashire's booming mills. There, increasingly specialized merchants organized the global flow of cotton, prices were set, and, by the 1860s, cotton futures were first traded. Liverpool became one of the wealthiest cities in the world.

But this relatively stable trade rested on the unstable institution of slavery, which ultimately was destroyed in America by the U.S. Civil War (1861–1865). During the cotton famine, when cotton exports from the U.S. South nearly ceased, European manufacturers searched frantically for new sources of raw cotton aided by high prices and the concerted efforts of governments. Egypt, Brazil, and especially India became major suppliers to Europe, with India effectively ending its trade with China. Huge areas that had not previously produced cotton for world markets now did so, while Western merchants and capital increasingly dominated cotton trade and production not only in port cities, but also in the hinterland.

Despite widespread pessimism about the future of U.S. cotton production, the United States was again the world's most important cotton exporter by the mid-1870s, with sharecroppers and tenants, both white and black, increasing production and pushing the cotton frontier further and further west. In the United States and throughout the world, cotton was now mostly grown on small farms owned or rented by the cultivators themselves, cultivators often burdened by crushing debt and extra-economic concern. By 1900 the United States produced three times as much cotton as it had in 1860. Nonetheless, during the late nineteenth and early twentieth centuries all cotton-consuming countries in Europe made concerted efforts to secure cotton from their colonies—the United Kingdom from India; Egypt, Germany, France, Portugal, and Belgium from various places in Africa; and Russia from its new territories in Central Asia. Except for Russia, however, no European country managed to emancipate itself from its dependence on U.S.

cotton. The United States, in fact, had expanded cotton growing so rapidly that it kept up with an industry whose spinning capacity grew 3,100 percent in the century after 1800.

TWENTIETH-CENTURY RETURN TO ASIA

But by the 1920s the world of cotton that had existed since the 1780s was transformed, becoming once again multipolar and increasingly Asian. While the United Kingdom's cotton industry entered a long decline, Asian cotton-yarn and cloth production surged, above all in Japan, which became the most important consumer of cotton, most of it from India, China, and the United States. Cotton mills also grew rapidly in India and China. Thus, there was a global trend in which cotton was again worked up closer to where it was grown, including in the United States itself, which saw the rise of a large cotton industry in the South. Not geographical proximity but labor costs were the primary reason for the relocation, which slowly undermined cotton manufacturing in high-wage locations.

As industry relocated, cotton growing expanded throughout the world, finally dethroning King Cotton in the United States. China, Central Asia, and India in particular vastly expanded cotton production, not least thanks to massive investments by governments and entrepreneurs into infrastructure, water supply, and pesticides. The Soviet Union went furthest; water supplies were reallocated to cotton, resulting in grave ecological degradation throughout Central Asia. In the West, cotton became less and less important as an industry with the advent of synthetic fibers. The number of cotton farmers in the United States shrank to less than 30,000 in 2000, and their markets were now in Asia and Latin America, not Europe.

By the turn of the twenty-first century, cotton manufacturing had largely left the West. Although the United States still remained an important cotton grower (in 2000 its global market share was 19.5%), this was heavily dependent on huge government subsidies (U.S.$3.9 billion in 2001 to 2002). Countries in the global South (especially in Africa) which had expanded cotton output during the 1980s and 1990s suffered from falling prices, which dipped below the cost of production of even the lowest-cost producers, such as Mali and Benin. Today, the world's cotton industry has largely returned to where it originally sprang from, with China, India, Pakistan, and Central Asia being by far the most important growers and processors of raw cotton.

SEE ALSO AGRICULTURE; ALI, MUHAMMAD; BANGLADESH; BANKING; BENGAL; BRAZIL; BURMA; CALCUTTA; CANTON SYSTEM; CHINA; EAST INDIA

COMPANY, BRITISH; EGYPT; EMPIRE, BRITISH;
EMPIRE, FRENCH; EMPIRE, JAPANESE; EMPIRE,
MUGHAL; EMPIRE, OTTOMAN; EMPIRE, QING;
GUANGZHOU; IMPERIALISM; IMPORT SUBSTITUTION;
INDIA; INDUSTRIALIZATION; LABORERS, COERCED;
LABORERS, CONTRACT; LEVANT COMPANY; MADRAS;
MANCHURIA; MERCANTILISM; MEXICO; MUMBAI;
NEW YORK; PAKISTAN; PASHA, ISMAʿIL; PERU;
PROTECTION COSTS; SLAVERY AND THE AFRICAN
SLAVE TRADE; TEXTILES; UNITED KINGDOM; UNITED
STATES; WOOL.

BIBLIOGRAPHY

Baines, Edward. *History of the Cotton Manufacture in Great Britain.* London: H. Fisher, 1835.

Beckert, Sven. "Emancipation and Empire: Reconstructing the World Wide Web of Cotton Production in the Age of the American Civil War." *American Historical Review* (December 2004).

Chao, Kang. *The Development of Cotton Textile Production in China.* Cambridge, MA: East Asian Research Center, 1977.

Ellison, Thomas. *A Handbook of the Cotton Trade: Or, a Glance at the Past History, Present Condition, and Future Prospects of the Cotton Commerce of the World.* London: Longman, Brown, Green, Longmans, and Roberts, 1858.

Farnie, D. A. *The English Cotton Industry and the World Market, 1815–1896.* Oxford, U.K.: Clarendon Press, 1979.

Farnie, D. A., and Jeremy, David J., eds. *The Fibre That Changed the World: The Cotton Industry in International Perspective, 1600–1990s.* Oxford, U.K.: Oxford University Press, 2004.

Scherer, James Augustin. *Cotton as a World Power.* New York: Frederick A. Stokes, 1916.

Von Schulze-Gaevernitz, Gerhart. *The Cotton Trade in England and on the Continent.* London: Simpkin, Marshall, Hamilton, Kent, 1895.

Wadsworth, Alfred P., and Mann, Julia De Lacy. *The Cotton Trade and Industrial Lancashire, 1600–1780.* Manchester, U.K.: Manchester University Press, 1931.

Sven Beckert

COUNTERFEIT GOODS

Counterfeiting is the making of a fraudulent imitation with intent to deceive and to pass it off as genuine. Counterfeiting is divided into two basic types: the counterfeiting of money, and the counterfeiting of products. Art forgery defrauds collectors of art objects.

THE COUNTERFEITING OF MONEY

The counterfeiting of money was rampant in the early modern period, peaking in the late eighteenth and early nineteenth centuries. The proliferation of new coin types (ducats, thalers, eight reales) made the hard currency so

Real dollars do not bleed. *In the digital age, precise, detailed copies of currency are easy to produce using inexpensive color printers. But genuine U.S. currency incorporates numerous security features, including special optically variable inks, thread embedded in the paper, and a watermark, all designed to foil counterfeiters.* GAIL OSKIN/AP WIDE WORLD PHOTOS. REPRODUCED BY PERMISSION.

complex that counterfeiters found it easy to pass bogus money. Half of the copper halfpence in London in 1753 were counterfeit. In the 1780s ships filled with British counterfeit halfpence arrived every week in North America, where a persistent trade deficit with Britain and a lack of local mints caused a shortage of coin. Counterfeiting was led by demand. In the Middle Ages people had brewed their own beer and made their own cheese, butter, jam, and cloth, but urbanization and industrialization in the second half of the eighteenth century changed society so that people bought these products rather than making them. They needed coinage. Government mints would not produce this coin, partly because they did not understand the importance of low denomination coins; partly because they lacked a system of distributing the coin from the metropolitan mints to the rapidly industrializing provinces; and partly because they were attempting to operate a trimetallic system, with each coin worth its full weight in gold, silver, or copper, at a time of rapidly fluctuating prices for all three metals. Counterfeiters

Chinese customs agents guarding counterfeit CDs, DVDs and CD-ROMS slated for destruction in Zhuhai, 2001. U.S. accusations of product counterfeiting provoked a major trade dispute with China in the 1990s. PHOTOGRAPH BY TED ANTHONY. AP/ WIDE WORLD PHOTOS. REPRODUCED BY PERMISSION.

fulfilled the demand for circulating coin that government mints would not.

Although paper money in the American colonies bore the inscription "To counterfeit is death," this sentence was almost never carried out. In fact, counterfeiters were rarely arrested, and when arrested, they often jumped bail or escaped from jail. Juries nullified. Even if convicted, counterfeiters could plead the benefit of clergy: civil courts were not allowed to convict clergymen, so if someone could mumble a bit of Latin they were assumed to be a member of the clergy (even if a woman) and allowed to go free. Female convicts could also escape the gallows by claiming to be pregnant.

Rampant coin counterfeiting in Britain was ended by the development of better distribution methods for low-denomination coin during the Napoleonic Wars (1803–

1815) and improved production techniques, including steam machinery, at the Royal Mint.

Early U.S. coins were diverse in design, making it easy for counterfeiters to pass crude die-struck forgeries. In 1836 the United States Mint's adoption of steam machinery plus improved hubbing techniques resulted in more uniform coinage, making counterfeiting difficult.

Counterfeiters turned to attacking the paper currency. In the years 1690–1780, counterfeiters had copied the paper money issued by the American colonies and the states. This had ended when that paper money lost all value during the Revolution. Now paper money counterfeiting revived. Between 1782 and 1866, 8,000 banks and other financial institutions in the United States issued their own currency. Many were financially unsound. As merchants lost their trust in wildcat notes, their demand for notes on solid banks rose and consequently increased the market for counterfeiters' false notes of solid banks. In 1862 in New York City, 80 percent of the banknotes in circulation were counterfeit.

Counterfeiters raised notes, making $1 bills into $10s and $5s into $20s. When a bank failed, the counterfeiters bought up the junk notes and printed over them the name of a solid bank. Counterfeiters could also create notes of spurious, nonexistent banks and copy the existing notes of a legitimate bank. Crucial to the success of the counterfeiters was their nationwide distribution system that allowed them to unload their forgeries before they were exposed as bogus.

The National Bank Act of 1863 and the introduction of a "death tax" for private banknotes in 1865 eliminated the wildcat bank problem. (A "death tax" is the taxation of a product not to raise revenue, but to end its production; here, a tax upon banknotes made it unprofitable to issue them, which was the intention of the tax.) The United States Secret Service, which was established in April 1865, increased the rate at which counterfeiters were arrested and convicted. In the 1870s the Secret Service broke up the nationwide counterfeiting rings. Without the advantage of nationwide distribution, counterfeiters had difficulty unloading their bogus notes.

Counterfeiting was again widespread in Europe following World War I. The League of Nations promulgated an international convention on counterfeiting in 1929. Practical coordination was assigned to the International Criminal Police Commission (Interpol), which since 1989 has been headquartered in Lyons, France.

The most successful counterfeit of the early 1990s was a bogus New York City subway token manufactured by Alan Campbell and distributed by Kim Gibbs. Gibbs solved the distribution hurdle by circulating the tokens through his bicycle messenger service. At the peak, tens of thousands of bogus tokens were being recovered from turnstiles every day.

Color computer printers are regarded as the greatest counterfeiting threat in the early twenty-first century. Eighty-eight percent of all counterfeits passed in the United States are made on ink-jet printers. This threat led to the introduction of "NexGen" currency in the United States on October 9, 2003. NexGen currency has multiple pastel shades, security strips, and gilt ink, which the Treasury believes will be particularly difficult to counterfeit.

Both the Secret Service and Interpol claim that their rigorous enforcement of anticounterfeiting laws explains why there is so little currency counterfeiting today. Although these claims have some truth, a more likely explanation is the reduction of the number of money types that existed in the eighteenth and early nineteenth centu-

ries. With so few varieties, counterfeits stick out like sore thumbs. In addition, the numerous local branches of central banks ensure that currency is regularly submitted to and re-examined by the issuers, so counterfeits do not have a long circulating life. Counterfeits of the U.S. dollar only exist at the rate of one or two in ten thousand. Of these, the most commonly counterfeited (60–70%) is the $100 note, followed by the $20 and the $50. Most people will spend their entire lives without ever receiving a counterfeit in change.

THE COUNTERFEITING OF PRODUCTS

The U.S. economy lost $200 billion to product counterfeiting in 1995, and the European Union lost $135 billion. Product counterfeiting can be traced to the Middle Ages, when many products were counterfeited, notably bread, which was widely adulterated. Two factors aggravated the problem in the late twentieth century: the high value placed on branded items, and the development of digital technology.

In 1979 Gloria Vanderbilt lent her name to the marketing of blue jeans, allowing them to be sold for double the price of normal jeans. Counterfeiters bought their own jeans, sewed on counterfeit labels, and undercut the price of the designer jeans. Typically, counterfeit products are distributed through street peddlers and flea markets. Street peddlers in New York City in the 1980s could make $120 on a good day from selling counterfeit watches.

Digital technology created a serious counterfeiting problem at the turn of the twenty-first century by allowing the reproduction of sound and image without loss of quality: "pirated" CDs are as good as the originals. File-sharing programs on the internet, notably Napster, fostered widespread copying of music, plunging the recording industry into financial crisis. U.S. accusations of rampant product counterfeiting erupted into a major trade dispute with the People's Republic of China in 1996.

The human costs of counterfeiting have sometimes been dire. Counterfeit airplane parts and pharmaceuticals have killed people. The use of a counterfeit anti-meningitis vaccine in Niger in 1995 caused 3,000 deaths. But not all counterfeit products have bad consequences despite the intentions of those that produced them. For example, films and recordings have preserved valuable artworks that the film and recording industries had discarded.

ART FORGERY

Art forgery is the copying of an artifact meant not to deceive the original consumer, but to deceive a collector. An eighteenth-century counterfeit halfpenny was designed to deceive whoever received it in change; in contrast, a $3 gold piece, struck in gold in Lebanon in the 1960s, was designed to be sold to unsuspecting coin collectors. The former example is a contemporary (or circulating) counterfeit; the latter, a modern fake. Art forgery concerns modern fakes.

Some artists' works have been so widely forged that the forgeries outnumber the genuine pieces: 60 percent of the works attributed to Alberto Giacometti are forgeries, and there are also many more forgeries of paintings by Jean-Baptiste Camille Corot than genuine ones.

SEE ALSO GOLD AND SILVER; MONEY AND MONETARY POLICY; SMUGGLING; WINE.

BIBLIOGRAPHY
Bresler, Fenton. *Interpol.* London: Sinclair-Stevenson, 1992.
Johnson, David R. *Illegal Tender: Counterfeiting and the Secret Service in Nineteenth-Century America.* Washington, DC: Smithsonian Institution Press, 1995.
Kleeberg, John M., ed. *Circulating Counterfeits of the Americas.* New York: American Numismatic Society, 2000.
Paradise, Paul R. *Trademark Counterfeiting, Product Piracy, and the Billion Dollar Threat to the U.S. Economy.* Westport, CT: Quorum Books, 1999.
Scott, Kenneth. *Counterfeiting in Colonial America.* New York: Oxford University Press, 1958.

John M. Kleeberg

COWRIES

Cowrie shells, shipped originally from the Maldive Islands of the Indian Ocean and later in the form of a slightly different species from the East African coast near Zanzibar, played an unusual role in international trade. Cowries were historically an important part of the money supplies of two distant areas, West Africa and Bengal. They also found more limited use in China and parts of Southeast Asia. In the best-known case, cowries were the shell money of the slave trade, the major circulating medium in much of the West African region from which slaves were shipped to the New World. The shells were traded over vast distances for several hundred years until they largely disappeared from monetary use, for the most part early in the twentieth century.

The first type of cowrie shell to enter extensively into international trade was the money cowrie, *Cypraea moneta.* This milky-white shell is about three-quarters of an inch long. Its small size, physical attractiveness, low unit value, great durability, and easy identifiability made it highly suitable for money where prices levels were low. It can stand considerable wear and tear; examples found in African markets today are at least a century old and there is no simple way to determine the age of a given shell.

Undoubtedly their initial attraction was religious and magical, as impressionable minds saw in their folded underside a resemblance to female genitalia. Their transition to money use in West Africa came very early. Cheap at their source in the Maldive Islands (even though production was a royal monopoly under the control of the sultan of those isles), they could be employed as ballast in large sailing vessels, so the opportunity cost of transporting them was also low. The African case, which has been most closely studied, involved a complicated mechanism of international trade; their shipment to Bengal was much simpler and the carriage was in much smaller vessels.

The Middle Ages saw the first shipments of money cowries to West Africa by Arab traders, who moved them along the North African coast and then south by caravan across the Sahara Desert. In the sixteenth century the primary route changed as the Portuguese carried them around the Cape of Good Hope to Lisbon, where they were transshipped back to West Africa. In the seventeenth century the Portuguese predominance was ended by the English and Dutch, whose East India Companies continued as the major players until the Dutch participation was halted following the French conquest of the Netherlands in 1795. The French also carried the shells to West Africa.

The usual journey for the money cowrie involved collection in a Maldive lagoon where the mollusk clings to flotsam and jetsam, movement to burial pits where they were interred for several weeks or months to rot away the soft parts of the little creatures, collection by middlemen working with the sultan's permission, and shipment on boats to Bengal, often to the port of Balasore. The cowries that did not immediately enter the money supply of Bengal were acquired by the European trading companies. They were shipped, often as ballast in large Indiamen, to Europe, with London and Amsterdam the major destinations and sites of the most important auctions. Traders of all nationalities bound for West Africa typically found it advantageous to include cowries in the assortment of goods that they carried. The shells were used to bargain for slaves and (after the end of the slave trade) the tropical products such as palm oil that the traders carried away with them.

In an innovative development during the 1840s, German merchants sent trial shipments to West Africa of a somewhat similar shell from Tanzanian coastal islands near Zanzibar. This was the ring cowrie, *Cypraea annulus,* distinguishable by the reddish-orange ring atop the crown of every example. The experiment was a great success, as Africans proved willing to accept *annulus* in large quantities. The episode was less a reflection of Gresham's Law (because *annulus* supplemented rather

Cowrie shells. *Once used as the money of the West African slave trade, cowries largely disappeared from monetary use in the early twentieth century.* © CHRIS HELLIER/CORBIS. REPRODUCED BY PERMISSION.

than supplanted *moneta,* with the two forms treated as one) and more a verification of the quantity theory of money. So much supplementation took place as merchants flooded the market with the East African variant of the cowrie that major cowrie inflation ensued, affecting both varieties equally. (*Annulus* already had had some circulation in parts of Central Africa.)

The use of cowries in West Africa expanded well into the nineteenth century. At its greatest extent its zone of circulation included (from west to east) some parts or all of modern Mali, Burkina Faso, the Ivory Coast, Togo, Bénin, Niger, Nigeria, Cameroon, and Chad. For the most part, the shells entered Africa along the coast from Ardra and Ouidah to Lagos. They were purchased like any other import with payment in export items, mostly slaves until the nineteenth century. At the start of the twentieth century the cumulative total of cowries imported to West Africa must have been at least a hundred billion. For numbers so vast, innovative counting systems were developed to facilitate their handling.

In several ways the imported cowrie currency had unusual properties. First, the currency was inconvertible in that the Europeans who brought the shells to Africa would rarely accept them back for other goods. Once imported, they remained. Second, the cowrie was an informal rather than formal money in the sense that there was little or no government involvement with it except in the Maldives, with its sultanic monopoly over production. Local merchants and traders, often organized by lineage and as commercial diaspora, bought the shells from the Europeans and transported them inland. The payment for cowries represented the real resources that went into its production plus rents. Of course, private enterprise moneys are risky in that they can be oversupplied, leading to inflation. For hundreds of years this was prevented by the controls on production maintained at the source by the sultan of the Maldives. At the end of the cowrie's circulation, however, colonial governments did indeed intervene, usually by banning importation and prohibiting its use for tax payments. Sometimes the colonial governments employed schemes to retire the shell money altogether; French colonial authorities actually destroyed large quantities. During this period of colonial intervention prices expressed in cowries fell; that is, the value of cowries rose, with the appreciated value lasting until eventually the demand for cowries was eroded by the convenience and appeal of colonial monies, their easier acceptance in payment for imported goods, and laws requiring them to be used for tax payments. Third, in proportion to its low unit value, the cowrie was expensive to transport. There was thus a value gradient, with a given quantity of cowrie commanding more goods at locations farther away from these monies' point of importation. Fourth, the substantial investment made by Africans to acquire the shells was lost in 1900 to 1920 when the colonial authorities demonetized cowries and substituted colonial currencies. Unlike many commodity monies such as gold and silver, cloth, salt, and so forth, cowries had very little alternative market value as decoration, magical or religious significance, or when crushed for their lime content. The investment in them was almost totally lost, except in scattered locations near borders where some cowries still find local use as a means to avoid foreign-exchange transactions. In the Maldives, some cowries continue to be fished. They are exported to India not as money but for decoration and, after crushing, as a medicine.

SEE ALSO BALANCE OF PAYMENTS; BULLION (SPECIE); CARAVAN TRADE; COMMODITY MONEY; DAHOMEY; EAST INDIA COMPANY, BRITISH; EAST INDIA COMPANY, DUTCH; EAST INDIA COMPANY, OTHER; GHANA; GOLD AND SILVER; INDIA; INDIAN OCEAN; INDONESIA; KENYA; RATES OF EXCHANGE; SENEGAMBIA; SPICES AND THE SPICE TRADE.

BIBLIOGRAPHY

Cribb, Joe, ed. *Money: From Cowrie Shells to Credit Cards.* London: British Museum, 1986.

Hogendorn, Jan, and Johnson, Marion. *The Shell Money of the Slave Trade.* Cambridge, U.K.: Cambridge University Press, 1986.

Jan Hogendorn

CUBA

Following its discovery by Christopher Columbus in 1492, Cuba remained under Spanish rule until 1898. Subsistence agriculture and ranching characterized its early economic history. Havana grew in importance to service the fleets of Seville and Cádiz that monopolized Spain's trade with America. Spain prohibited trade with foreigners or even other Spanish colonies, but smuggling thrived as Cubans exchanged hides and tobacco for manufactured goods. After 1700 Spain's Bourbon monarchs began to liberalize the trading monopoly and particularly sought to promote Castilian industry by promoting trade of its manufactures for Cuban tropical commodities. Establishment of a Havana Company in 1740 moved in that direction, but was less important than reforms launched

following the British occupation of Havana in 1762, during which there was a dramatic surge in Cuba's trade, including importation of African slaves. Exports of sugar cane, coffee, tobacco, and hides grew rapidly after the Spanish Free Trade Act of 1765 and other reforms opened Cuban trade to most Spanish ports. Both legal and illegal trade with the United States grew, especially after 1776, and it soared in the 1790s, aided by the U.S. Tariff of 1789, which favored goods carried in U.S. ships, and by the neutral status of the United States during the European wars of that decade.

In 1818 Spain opened Cuba to international trade, and U.S. imports of Cuban sugar rose steadily in exchange for U.S. flour. Spanish wheat farmers pressured their government to raise tariffs against U.S. flour, and the United States responded with higher rates against Cuban coffee and other Cuban exports except sugar. This led Cuba to a dramatic shift toward slave-produced sugar. By 1850 sugar accounted for 80 percent of Cuban exports, and Cuba was the world's leading sugar producer. Despite British pressure, Cuba continued to trade in African slaves at least until 1865.

The repressiveness of Spanish governors who confronted calls for independence from Creole planters, opposition to slavery, and the discontent of workers displaced by African slaves led to the Ten Years' War (1868–1878), which devastated Cuba's sugar industry. Spain granted limited autonomy, but not independence, to Cuba, and began the gradual emancipation of the slaves, completed in 1886. The substantial modernization of cane sugar production and refining methods necessary to make Cuba again the leading sugar producer required heavy foreign investment. A commercial treaty between the United States and Spain in 1883 favored Cuba and Puerto Rico. The McKinley Tariff of 1890 provided tax-free sugar imports to the United States in exchange for a reciprocal trade agreement in 1891. The Wilson-Gorman Tariff of 1894, however, abrogated this agreement, and caused a serious economic crisis in Cuba that led to a new war for independence in 1895. Cuban trade with the United States had reached about U.S.$100 million annually, but it plummeted once the rebels began to damage sugar mills and plantations. U.S. intervention in this conflict in 1898 assured Cuban independence, but imposed a U.S. military occupation until 1902, followed by a protectorate until 1934. This period brought heavy U.S. investment and improvement to Cuba's infrastructure, but tied Cuban trade ever closer to the United States, with low tariffs for U.S. goods and a preferential position in the U.S. market for Cuban sugar. Several U.S. military interventions were followed by the establishment of a dictatorship under General Gerardo Machado (1871–1939) in 1925.

The Great Depression hit Cuba hard and resulted in a labor uprising that ousted Machado in 1933. As the head of a revolt of noncommissioned army officers in the same year, Fulgencio Batista (1901–1973) controlled the island for much of the next twenty-five years, enjoying substantial U.S. support until his overthrow by Fidel Castro (b. 1926) in 1959. Sugar continued to dominate Cuban exports, but after 1919 the tourist trade added notably to Cuban economic growth. A new reciprocal trade agreement with the U.S. in 1934 reduced Cuban tariffs on U.S. goods and established quotas for Cuban sugar and tobacco in the U.S. market. Cuban dependency on U.S. trade intensified in the decades following. Although it had one of the highest per capita incomes in Latin America by the 1950s, there was wide disparity between the wealthy and the poor and between urban and rural workers, and this contributed to the unrest that accompanied Castro's rise to power. By 1960, the Communist Party dominated Cuba under Castro's rule.

With the Cold War dominating U.S. policy considerations, the United States imposed a trade embargo on Cuba in 1960 in response to Cuban expropriation of U.S.–owned properties, then broke off diplomatic relations in January 1961. The ill-fated Bay of Pigs invasion in April 1961 and the Cuban Missile Crisis in October 1962 obviated any resumption of U.S. trade. The U.S. effort to isolate Cuba, although not entirely successful, forced Cuba into alliances with China and the Soviet Union. Cuban trade with the United States fell from more than 65 percent of its total trade to virtually nothing after 1961. Efforts to reduce Cuba's dependence on sugar exports by crop diversification were not very successful, as trade shifted to the communist-bloc countries led by the USSR and China. Cuba joined the Soviet-dominated Council for Mutual Economic Cooperation (Comecon) in 1972. Soviet aid became crucial to Cuba, with loans, oil, and military and technical assistance. Still dominated by sugar, by 1989 nearly three-quarters of Cuba's trade was with the USSR. Although the Latin American Integration Association admitted Cuba as an observer in 1986 and to full membership in 1999, Cuba was excluded from most inter-American programs, including the Free Trade of the Americas plan at the beginning of the twenty-first century. Cuban trade with Russia dropped off notably following the dissolution of the Soviet Union in 1991, when it withdrew its troops from Cuba. This forced some liberalization of Cuban economic policy, including allowing limited foreign investment, especially in the tourist industry. Some private small business development also aided the notable growth in tourism. A petroleum agreement with Venezuela also helped Cuba after 2000, but the United States remained adamantly opposed to normalizing relations. Sugar remains the principal export, followed by nickel, seafood, tobacco, and citrus fruits. Petroleum products, foods, machinery, and chemicals are the principal imports, and its main trading partners are Spain, Russia, Mexico, Holland, France, and China.

SEE ALSO BOYCOTT; CONQUISTADORS; EMPIRE, SPANISH; ENCOMIENDA AND REPARTIMIENTO; ETHNIC GROUPS, AFRICANS; POPULATION—EMIGRATION AND IMMIGRATION; IMPORT SUBSTITUTION; LABORERS, CONTRACT; LABOR, TYPES OF; NATIONALIZATION; SLAVERY AND THE AFRICAN SLAVE TRADE; SOCIALISM AND COMMUNISM; RUSSIA; SPAIN; SPORTS; SUGAR, MOLASSES, AND RUM; TOBACCO; UNITED STATES.

BIBLIOGRAPHY

Dye, Alan. *Cuban Sugar in the Age of Mass Production: Technology and the Economics of the Sugar Central, 1899–1929.* Stanford, CA: Stanford University Press, 1998.

Hudson, Rex A., ed. *Cuba: A Country Study.* Washington, DC: Federal Research Division, Library of Congress, 2002.

LeRiverand, Julio. *Economic History of Cuba,* tr. María Juana Cazabón and Homero León. Havana: Book Institute, 1967.

Morley, Morris H. *Imperial State and Revolution: The United States and Cuba, 1952–1987.* New York: Cambridge University Press, 1987.

Pérez, Louis A., Jr. *Cuba: Between Reform & Revolution,* 2nd edition. New York and Oxford, U.K.: Oxford University Press, 1995.

Pérez-López, Jorge F. *Measuring Cuban Economic Performance.* Austin: University of Texas Press, 1987.

Suchlicki, Jaime. *Historical Dictionary of Cuba,* 2nd edition. Lanham, MD: Scarecrow Press, 2001.

Zanetti, Oscar, and García, Alejandro. *Sugar and Railroads: A Cuban History, 1837–1959,* tr. Franklin Knight and Mary Todd. Chapel Hill: University of North Carolina Press, 1998.

Ralph Lee Woodward Jr.

SAMUEL CUNARD
1787–1865

Samuel Cunard, a major Canadian entrepreneur with large interests in coastal vessels, can be credited with originating the transatlantic steam shipping route—a pioneering feat that is still commemorated by the shipping line that bears his name.

Samuel, the son of a German Quaker immigrant, was born in Halifax, Nova Scotia, in 1787. After limited schooling and time with a Boston shipbroker, he joined his father's firm. Abraham Cunard and Company were mainly engaged in developing property but also handled many imported goods. After Samuel joined, it extended its activities to include the West Indian and timber trades and to shipping, and by 1840 the enterprise controlled forty sailing vessels. By then Samuel was convinced that steam was essential in shipping—he had invested in the *Royal William,* which in 1833 had been the first vessel to cross the Atlantic to Europe entirely under power—and this experience encouraged him to tender for an admiralty transatlantic contract. When this was successful he ordered three steamships from Robert Napier (1791–1876) on the River Clyde.

Napier subsequently advised that larger ships would be vital to maintain all-weather services and when Samuel was unable to raise enough capital he introduced him to George Burns and David MacIver. After making suitable financial arrangements these two Scots joined Samuel as equal partners in the British and North American Royal Mail Steam Packet Company.

Its first ship, *Britannia,* arrived in Halifax in June 1840 and the so-called "Cunard Line" then opened a regular schedule from Liverpool to Boston and New York. In spite of much competition, especially from the subsidized United States' Collins Line, Cunard continued to dominate the route with Burns and MacIver organizing the business and Samuel concentrating on his Canadian interests. These were principally his landholdings in Prince Edward Island, where he owned over 200,000 acres, and involved much work as the landlords' spokesman in settling disputes under the Land Purchase Act originally passed in 1853. Samuel died in London in April 1865, leaving at least £350,000 to his two sons and six daughters.

BIBLIOGRAPHY

"Cunard, Sir Samuel." *Dictionary of Canadian Biography,* Vol. 9 (1861–1870). Toronto and Buffalo, NY: University of Toronto Press, 1976.

Hughes, T. E. *Sea Breezes.* Vol. 39, No. 235, July 1965 pp. 503–519 and No. 236, August 1965, pp. 584–600, Journal of Commerce, Liverpool.

Hyde F. E. *Cunard and the North Atlantic.* London: Macmillan, 1975.

Peter N. Davies

DAHOMEY

The kingdom of Dahomey was a small nation-state established toward the end of the seventeenth century, following a clearly defined economic plan. The emergence of this political entity, which reached the height of its power between 1760 and 1840, and its decline in the second half of the nineteenth century, coincided with the rise and fall of the Atlantic slave trade, which itself followed the gradual expansion of sugarcane plantations from Brazil to the Caribbean.

The capital, Abomey, located in the center of the inland plateau, was established by the Agassouvi family, who came from Tado, the cultural home of the Adja and Ewe peoples. The location of the place was chosen during the reign of Houegbadja (1650–1679). His successor, Agadja (beginning of the eighteenth century), established the ruling dynasty and conquered the port of Whydah on the coast in 1727. Immediately linking himself with European (slave) traders, he recognized the three European forts that had been established during the previous century: by the French in 1671, by the Portuguese in 1680, and later by the British. The three kept each other under close watch. Thousands of captives from slave wars were transported to Abomey. The population of the town, estimated at 50,000 in the mid-nineteenth century, was double what it had been at the end of the eighteenth century.

During every dry season Dahomey's army, under the command of the king, would head out to the Ewe in the west and especially to the Mahi in the north, or towards the Yoruba in the east and northeast, to acquire slaves for supply to the trade. Their victories relied upon the slave-trade guns that had been given to the king by Europeans in exchange for slaves. During the rainy season, the soldiers would once again become peasants who devoted themselves to subsistence farming. With every generation, the slave children born in the land of Dahomey became Dahoman.

From the 1830s the English increased their efforts to make the king discontinue the slave trade. Ghezo—who launched a coup in 1818 and ruled until 1858—played the situation cleverly, retaining this basic economic resource of his kingdom while simultaneously encouraging the production of palm oil for export. Starting from 1841, and especially as a result of an 1851 agreement, he dealt with two businessmen from Marseilles, the Régis brothers, who previously had been known for their involvement in the slave trade, giving them near-monopoly rights for the export of palm oil at the expense of the British traders situated in the port of Lagos at the other end of the lagoon. Whydah, which was exporting 800 tons of oil in 1850, exported more than double that amount in 1876. The rural economy was fundamentally altered. The economic role of women, who bought palm nuts for their husbands (who gathered the nuts to ship), extracting and selling the oil, was enhanced. Large palm plantations also used slave labor.

During the reign of Ghezo the political system took on its characteristic form—a pyramid structure with the monarch and court at the top, supported by an elite body, the famous Amazon "warriors," who were specially drawn from the villages to become the king's wives. The king, who was the hereditary ruler of an inland kingdom, was not allowed to see the sea, and visited Whydah, the country's slave trading port, only in absentia, in the per-

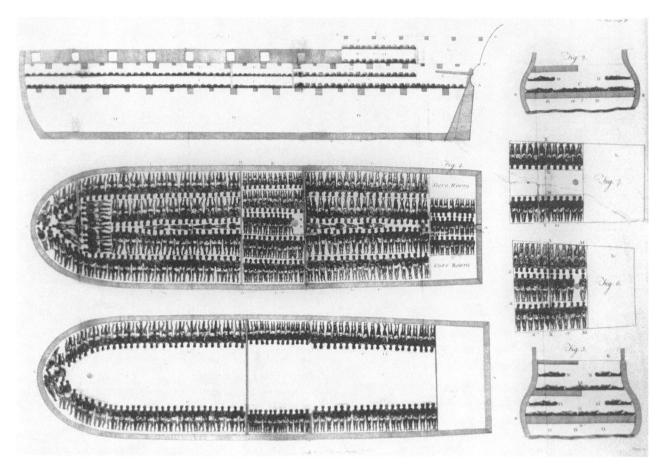

Diagram showing slaves packed tightly into a slave ship. *The African kingdom of Dahomey, in present-day Benin, owed its existence in part to the slave trade. A succession of Dahomey armies—equipped with guns from European traders—raided neighboring kingdoms for people to fill the slave ships heading west.* THE LIBRARY OF CONGRESS.

son of his important officials, the head of which was called Yovogan (chief of the whites). One of these officials was the half-Portuguese Cha Cha, also an important slave trader, who died in 1849. He left a large number of descendants and lived in enormous Western-style luxury, surrounded by hordes of dependents and slaves. Upon his death he was replaced by a new favorite, the old slave Quenum, who gave birth to a line of notables, merchants, and intellectuals in the following century. The aristocracy in the kingdom was complex, consisting of both local dignitaries and Afro-Brazilian merchants, that is, former African slaves who had returned from Brazil. They were Christians yet polygamous, businessmen and politicians.

The king ensured the country's stability, living on the taxes and tribute collected by important officials, and presided over the annual "customs" festival held in the capital. Europeans described the royal power that was demonstrated at the festival: the military power in assembling up to 10,000 soldiers, the king's economic power shown by procession of his wealth, and the religious power demonstrated by human sacrifices, which includ-

ed several dozen slaves every year, and several hundred or even more than a thousand for royal funerals.

Ghezo's son, Glele, who reigned until 1889, supported the "conservative" faction, which opposed the abolition of the slave trade. The Dahomans were defeated several times (in 1851 and again in 1864 by the Egba, who were supported by the British). Inflation was caused by large-scale cowrie shell imports by German merchants. The British, who had gained control of Lagos, imposed a series of trade embargos in 1851, 1865, and 1876. The sea outlet of Cotonou was handed over to the French by the governor of Porto-Novo (protectorates from 1863 and 1876, recognized by Glele in 1879). Glele's successor, Behanzin, resisted French conquest. National unity explains why this was the longest and hardest colonial war in the region (1890–1894).

The colony of Dahomey remained a place where forceful protest took place: alongside the small-scale French colonial administration, there existed a merchant middle class who had links with the old Brazilian or noble families. Clearly distinguishable by three characteristics—education, social status, and lifestyle—this elite continued to exercise influence over the fate of the society as a whole. The group took power upon independence, following the Gaullist referendum of September 28, 1958, and a governing body of twelve became a provisional government on December 4, 1958. The Republic of Dahomey gained full independence under the presidency of Hubert Koutoucou Maga (1916–2000) on August 1, 1960. Several coups took place before the three constituent historical regions (the North, the former kingdoms of Abomey, and Porto-Novo) shared power in a short-lived triumvirate. From 1971 Mathieu Kérékou (1933–) established a Marxist-Leninist dictatorship in 1975 that called itself the People's Republic of Benin. This lasted until 1989. After a short interlude, Kérékou was reelected, this time on the basis of liberal policies, in 1996.

SEE ALSO AFRICA, LABOR TAXES (HEAD TAXES); AGRICULTURE; ARMS, ARMAMENTS; COWRIES; EMPIRE, BRITISH; EMPIRE, DUTCH; EMPIRE, FRENCH; EMPIRE, PORTUGUESE; ETHNIC GROUPS, AFRICANS; FACTORIES; IMPERIALISM; LABORERS, COERCED; LABORERS, CONTRACT; NIGERIA; SLAVERY AND THE AFRICAN SLAVE TRADE; SUGAR, MOLASSES, AND RUM; TEXTILES, BEFORE 1800.

BIBLIOGRAPHY

Agbo, Casimir, dit Alidji. *Histoire de Ouidah du XVIᵉ au XXᵉ siècle (A History of Whydah from the Sixteenth to the Twentieth Century)* (trans.) Avignon: Les Presses Universitaires, 1959.

Akinjogbin, I. A. *Dahomey and Its Neighbours, 1708–1818.* Cambridge, U.K.: Cambridge University Press, 1967.

Argyle, William John. *The Fon of Dahomey: A History and Ethnography of the Old Kingdom.* Oxford, U.K.: Clarendon Press, 1966.

Berbain, Simone. *Le comptoir français de Juda (Ouidah) au XVIIIᵉ siècle (The French Trade Station of Whydah in the Eighteenth Century)* (trans.). Paris: Larose, 1942.

Coquery-Vidrovitch, Catherine. "Le blocus de Whydah (1876–1877) et la rivalité franco-anglaise au Dahomey" (*The Blockade of Whydah and the French-English Rivalry in Dahomey*). (trans.) *Cahiers d'Études Africaines 2 7* (1962): 373–419.

Coquery-Vidrovitch, Catherine. "La fête des coutumes au Dahomey. Historique et essai d'interprétation" (*The Festival of Customs in Dahomey: A History and an Attempt for Understanding it*). (trans.) *Annales* 19, no. 4 (1964): 696–716.

Coquery-Vidrovitch, Catherine. "De la traite des esclaves à l'exportation de l'huile de palme au Dahomey." (trans.) In *The Development of Indigenous Trade and Market in West Africa*, ed. Claude Meillassoux. Oxford, U.K.: Oxford University Press, 1971.

Glélé, Maurice Ahananzo. *Le Danxome* (trans.) Paris: Nubia, 1974.

Law, Robin. *The Social History of a West African Slaving Port, 1727–1892.* Athens: Ohio University Press, 2000.

Verger, Pierrre. *Flux et reflux de la traite des nègres entre le golfe du Bénin et Bahia de Todos os Santos du 17me au 19me siècles (Up and Down Stream of the Slave Trade Between the Bight of Benin and Bahia de Todos os Santos)* (trans.). Paris: Mouton, 1968.

Catherine Coquery-Vidrovitch

DANZIG

SEE GDANSK

DEBEERS

DeBeers is a South African and international diamond mining corporation founded in 1888 by Cecil Rhodes (1853–1902) and associates from the consolidation of smaller operators at Kimberley, South Africa. After Rhodes's death the company's primary shareholders were the Oppenheimer family, notably Sir Ernest Oppenheimer (1880–1957). For many years the company held a near monopoly on the diamond trade, operating under the principle that the quantity of diamonds on the market had to be restricted according to demand, ensuring price stability. In the recession of 1981, for example, DeBeers built up large stocks of rough gems, limiting the price drop.

Although the United States is DeBeers's largest market, from the 1940s on the company could not operate directly in the United States. The dispute originated with DeBeers's refusal to supply industrial diamonds during World War II, which might have depressed prices. In addition, officially, DeBeers was in violation of U.S. antitrust law. Sales to the United States were routed through London-based intermediaries. In the late 1990s the company rethought its traditional role in the diamond market, concentrating on selling diamonds from its own (mainly African) mines through flagship retailers. DeBeers's advertising campaigns since 1939 have expanded the world market for diamonds, and have influenced the tradition of giving diamonds for engagements.

SEE ALSO AFRICA, LABOR TAXES (HEAD TAXES); ANGLO AMERICAN CORPORATION; EMPIRE, BRITISH; GOLD AND SILVER; LABORERS, COERCED; LABORERS, CONTRACT; MINING; RHODES, CECIL; SOUTH AFRICA; ZIMBABWE.

BIBLIOGRAPHY

Heynes, Roné, ed. *South Africa 1987/1988: Official Yearbook of the Republic of South Africa.* Johannesburg: Perskor Printers, 1988.

Kanfer, Stefan. *The Last Empire. DeBeers, Diamonds, and the World.* New York: Farrar, Strous and Giroux, 1995.

David J. Clarke

DENG XIAOPING
1904–1997

Born in 1904, Deng Xiaoping spent 1920 to 1925 in France, studying and doing factory work. The experience led him to join the Chinese Communist Party, within which he advanced rapidly, holding top offices during the 1950s. He broke with Mao Zedong (1893–1976) when the Great Leap Forward (1958–1960) led to massive famines; his policies for recovery, implemented in the early 1960s, retained collective ownership but gave farmers more market incentives. Deng was purged during the Cultural Revolution (1966–1976) and fought his way back to power gradually, becoming China's *de facto* leader by 1978.

As leader, Deng made his first priority economic growth. His efforts to promote growth included opening the country to foreign trade, increasing the role of markets, and gradually eliminating both administratively set prices and various welfare guarantees, especially for urban workers, and reaching a compromise that allowed China to regain control of Hong Kong (1997). These changes produced a prolonged economic boom, both in foreign trade and in the domestic economy. The concomitant social changes were not universally welcomed, and Deng intervened on several occasions (most notably in 1992) to maintain the direction of reform. He generally resisted political liberalization, however, and backed off from rapid marketization when it appeared to threaten social stability. Deng died in 1997.

SEE ALSO CHINA; GUANGZHOU; HONG KONG; INDUSTRIALIZATION; JAPAN; MARKETS, STOCK; NATIONALISM; SHANGHAI; SOCIALISM AND COMMUNISM; SPECIAL ECONOMIC ZONES (SEZs); TUNG CHEE-HWA; UNITED STATES.

BIBLIOGRAPHY

Baum, Richard. *Burying Mao: Politics in the Age of Deng Xiaoping.* Princeton, NJ: Princeton University Press, 1996.

Lieberthal, Kenneth. *Governing China: From Revolution Through Reform.* New York: Norton, 2003.

Naughton, Barry. *Growing Out of the Plan.* New York: Cambridge University Press, 1996.

Kenneth Pomeranz

DENMARK

The composition of Danish exports and imports has, until the 1950s, been determined by the fact that the country has neither natural mineral resources nor large forests. Furthermore, industrialization came late to Denmark and, during their early existence, most factories specialized in producing for the home market. Consequently, between 1450 and the 1950s exports were largely limited to agricultural products and, until the mid-sixteenth century, herring from rich catches in the Sound, whereas imports were made up of essential raw materials, such as timber, salt, and iron, and of luxury goods for the upper class, such as wine and colonial products.

The basic agricultural product exported until late in the nineteenth century was grain. Around 1450, rye and barley were exported to northern Germany. In the first half of the sixteenth century, exports started to southern Norway of the same cereals, and in the seventeenth century the Netherlands became an important market. Annually, about 25,000 tons of grain were exported before 1700.

In the sixteenth century, oxen were another important agricultural export. The animals were fed in Danish stables and exported as live animals to towns in northern Germany and the Netherlands. In the middle of the century, about forty thousand oxen were exported every year, but the many wars in the seventeenth century were a serious impediment to this trade. Imports during the Middle Ages came from the northern German Hanseatic towns, but after 1500, Dutch merchants gradually took over most of this trade.

THE LONG EIGHTEENTH CENTURY

From the late seventeenth to the early nineteenth century, trade with Norway was of paramount importance. Both countries were united under the same king and complemented each other in a profitable way. A fleet of small coastal ships made several thousand journeys a year, bringing rye, barley, and meat to Norway and returning with timber and iron to Denmark.

These commodity flows were encouraged by privileges given as part of the monarchy's mercantilist policy. There was a Danish surplus in the trade paid by the Norwegians from their surplus in the trade with western Europe. Denmark on the other hand used its surplus and foreign currency earned from the Sound Toll—paid by ships going into and out of the Baltic—to finance imports of wine and colonial goods from France and imports of flax, hemp, potash, and oak wood from the Baltic countries. A special issue in the foreign trade resulted from acquiring overseas colonies, especially the Virgin Islands in the West Indies, and from the establishment of a chartered Asiatic Company trading in Canton and India. Especially in years with Danish neutrality in the great European wars, this trade reached impressive dimensions. The overseas commodities were taken to Denmark on board Danish ships and reexported to other European countries.

A worker in Denmark checks a butter centrifuge on a cooperative farm in 1960. *During its industrialization growth in the twentieth century, Denmark became a leader in the food processing industry, with high quality production of bacon, butter, cheeses, beers, and other items.* © PAUL ALMASY/CORBIS. REPRODUCED BY PERMISSION

THE GRAIN SALES PERIOD AND THE TRANSITION TO DAIRY FARMING

Denmark became involved in the Napoleonic wars from 1807 to 1814. The merchant navy was lost, and Norway was ceded to Sweden in 1814, resulting in the loss of privileges on that market. The following period from 1814 to about 1830 were years of crisis for Danish foreign trade, which was trying to find a new position in the world economy.

It was not until access to the British market for grain exports had become easier, after 1829, that a new outlet for the Danish grain surplus was created. Barley and wheat became the most important exported cereals; their quality had improved since the eighteenth century due to profound changes in the structure of agriculture, caused by extensive land reforms. Grain exports continued to grow until the early 1870s, reaching a peak of about 300,000 tons yearly. In these years Britain also became a more important supplier of raw materials, fuel, and manufactured goods to the Danish market.

After 1870, Danish grain exports to Britain faced increasing competition from supplies from Russia and North America, and as relative prices between vegetable and animal products developed to the advantage of the latter, Danish farmers increased their livestock, and the country became a net importer of grain from the 1880s. The animal products were processed in cooperative dairies and slaughter-houses owned by the farmers themselves, and increasing amounts of butter, bacon, and eggs were exported, mainly to Britain and to a lesser extent to Germany.

The dominance of especially butter and bacon in Danish exports continued until the late 1950s, in spite of increasing problems on the British market from the 1930s that resulted from protective measures favoring domestic and Dominion production. Export of manufactured products in large quantities was limited to a few areas in which a handful of companies had a strong position on the world market, among them shipbuilding/ diesel engines (B & W) and machinery for cement production (F. L. Smidth & Co.). Among imports, grain and raw materials were still important, but with a higher standard of living the share of finished products both for investment and consumption was increasing. Germany was the main supplier, except during World War I, during the 1930s when bilateral trade agreements made it necessary to switch some imports from Germany to Britain, and during the years of reconstruction after World War II.

JOINING THE EFTA, EEC, AND EU

The gradual liberalization of intra-European trade in the 1950s was problematic for Denmark because agricultural products were exempt from the abolition of the barriers. The Danish manufacturing industry consequently had to face increased competition, whereas agriculture met with more and more state-subsidized products on export markets. The aim of the Danish government in this situation was to become a member of the EEC to benefit from the Common Agricultural Policy, but only if Britain joined at the same time so that the British market for agricultural goods could be maintained. As this policy failed, Denmark instead became a member of the European Free Trade Area (EFTA) and obtained some privileges for bacon on the British market, but these were not sufficient to secure a future for Danish agriculture as an export trade. An industrialization process was initiated by the government and, helped by the rapid economic growth in the world economy in the 1960s, a profound change in the export structure took place. In 1958, agriculture was responsible for 58 percent of total exports; this share had declined to 27 percent in 1972, when machinery and

finished industrial goods were the main exported items. During the same period, intra-EFTA trade grew much more rapidly than trade with the rest of the world, and especially the trade with Sweden and Norway became much more important.

Denmark became a member of the European Economic Community (EEC) in 1973, at the same time as Britain. Danish agriculture came under the rules of the Common Agricultural Policy, but manufacturing continued to be the most important exporting trade. As a consequence of the removal of trade barriers within the European Union (EU), the share exported to and imported from the six original members of the EEC increased. By the early years of the twenty-first century, about three-fourths of foreign trade was with Western Europe— Germany and Sweden being the largest partners—and agricultural products, half of which was pork, represented only 11 percent of total exports.

SEE ALSO AGRICULTURE; BALANCE OF PAYMENTS; CARGOES, FREIGHT; CARGOES, PASSENGER; COMMON MARKET AND THE EUROPEAN UNION; FINLAND; FREE TRADE, THEORY AND PRACTICE; GATT, WTO; GREAT DEPRESSION OF THE 1930S; HANSEATIC LEAGUE (HANSA OR HANSE); INDUSTRIALIZATION; INTERNATIONAL TRADE AGREEMENTS; NORWAY; REGIONAL TRADE AGREEMENTS; SWEDEN.

BIBLIOGRAPHY

Enemark, Poul. *Dansk oksehandel 1450–1550, Vols. I and II.* Århus, Denmark: Århus Universitetsforlag, 2003.

Feldbæk, Ole. *Danmarks økonomiske historie, 1500–1840.* Herning, Denmark: Systime, 1993.

Hyldtoft, Ole. *Danmarks økonomiske historie, 1840–1910.* Århus, Denmark: Systime, 1999.

Johansen, Hans Chr. *The Danish Economy in the Twentieth Century.* Kent, U.K.: Croom Helm, 1987.

Johansen, Hans Chr. "The Danish Economy at the Crossroads between Scandinavia and Europe." *The Scandinavian Journal of History* 18 (1993): 37–56.

Thomsen, Birgit Nüchel, and Thomas, Brinley. *Dansk-engelsk samhandel: Et historisk rids 1661–1963.* Århus, Denmark: Århus Universitetsforlag, 1966.

Hans Chr. Johansen

DEPRESSIONS AND RECOVERIES

The existence of periodic fluctuations within the economy first became the subject of intense investigation in the second half of the nineteenth century. Clement Juglar, in 1862, was the first to articulate the idea of a cycle lasting six to eight years after studying commercial crises through troughs and peaks which consisted of a period of recovery that reached a climax, interrupted by crisis that lasted over a lapse of time to finally settle into a depression. Other scholars confounded the study of crises and the phenomenon of "business" or "trade" cycles (two terms commonly used since the end of the nineteenth century) with the aim of distinguishing them from fluctuations that had a different periodicity. These narratives are not completely analogous and overlapping. Nonetheless, crises and cycles articulate in two ways. Some think the crises are initiated by exogenous factors, which then are amplified and translated into cyclical fluctuations. Others essentially see endogenous elements resulting from disequilibrium stimulated during the growth period. Whatever the origin, business cycles are caused, amplified, and nourished by differentiated lags in the paces of economic growth. In other words, they are linked to the different inertias that exist between the decision process and investment results.

A PRECOCIOUS MULTIPLICITY OF APPROACHES

The first studies identified cycles through the statistical data then available. Juglar, for instance, pointed to the relative evolution of different elements in the balance sheet of the central bank. His aim clearly was to predict oncoming crises. This type of study was continued in the United States, where the traditions of empirical approaches through advanced statistical methods were better developed than in Europe. Responding to the crisis of 1920 and following an injunction by the commerce secretary, Herbert Hoover (1874–1964), the National Bureau of Economic Research commissioned Wesley C. Mitchell (1874–1948) to conduct a thorough investigation of the development of cycles in the leading economies. The results were published in 1927, and opened the way toward the conception of statistical material concerning business trends—that is, production, prices, employment, and various financial and monetary variables. The greater contribution of contemporary studies on business cycles remains the product of econometric approaches derived from these empirical findings.

Since the end of the nineteenth century economists have suggested numerous theoretical analyses on this subject. The repeated disequilibrium present during the 1920s, followed by the Great Depression, spurred new interest. Gottfried von Haberler provided in 1937 a new explanation when he produced a synthesis on this issue. The "purely" monetary theorists such as R. G. Hawtrey proposed a coherent analysis of the overall economic situation based on the cycle of banking loans, as seen in Great Britain, driven by the procyclical policy of the Bank of England. The nonmonetary theories of overcapitalization pointed to the primary impulses linked to the variations in the demand for consumer goods, which translate with greater intensity to the demand for capital goods as

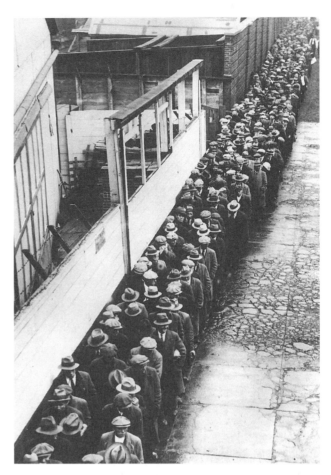

People wait in a bread line in New York City during the Great Depression. *With very little government support programs, people relied on over eighty food stations throughout the city for free meals, where they would often wait for days. The governor of New York, Franklin Delano Roosevelt, won the 1932 presidential election and enacted the New Deal— government efforts to promote economic recovery and social reform.* AP/WIDE WORLD PHOTOS. REPRODUCED BY PERMISSION.

evidenced in the accelerator model. The monetary theories of overcapitalization sought to combine the previous two approaches. Haberler finally distinguished the theories of underconsumption and the "psychological" theories based on the anticipations and their shortcomings, like those of John M. Keynes and Arthur C. Pigou.

Hence, five leading analytical approaches in the numerous studies on business cycles prevailed from the 1930s: (1) opposition between monetary and real perspectives, (2) lags in the duration and in the time lapse of responses to the different economic processes, (3) maladjustments of the supply and demand, (4) opposition in the exogenous approaches of cycles as an amplified oscillation stemming from a primitive shock, and (5) endogenous approaches.

A billboard addressing the high unemployment rate during the Great Depression. *At the height of the Great Depression (1932–1933), around 16 million people were without jobs. To understand the causes of depressions and recoveries in the economy, scholars investigate how monetary, industrial, commercial, and banking factors affect business cycles.* FRANKLIN DELANO ROOSEVELT LIBRARY.

Many economists, such as Haberler, thought that there was no single explanation for the theory of cycles, but a combination of factors. These narratives gave more or less weight to the various combinations of factors and to their hierarchy between impulses and propagation mechanism. They privileged the shocks on demand side (demand on inventories, investment, and consumption) rather than on the supply side as the initial impulse. Nevertheless, Mitchell sought an explanation by analyzing the supply-side elements, notably the variation of the costs of production during a cycle. His findings, which have since been confirmed, underlined that labor costs by unit of production evolve in a procyclical trend.

In the 1950s and 1960s the study of cycles was of secondary importance to economists who were preoccupied with conceptualizing the theory of growth. They separately studied and considered growth as dominated by supply-side elements, mostly technological, and viewed business cycles as tributary to demand factors. Thereby the cycle could initially be detected through numerous statistical indicators that became widespread, but the strength of the growth rate and anticyclical policies introduced by government measures, aimed at absorbing shocks spurred by demand, made it difficult to discern

the cycle. The instruments that have established a neoclassical consensus gave a good explanation of the dynamics in the fluctuations of demand. This has been explained by John R. Hicks in his IS/LM model (1937). In it, Hicks shows the relation, on the one hand, between the market of goods and services, which highlights the different levels of national income and its corresponding level of interest rate when investment (I) equals savings (S), and, on the other hand, the market for loanable funds, which highlights the different levels of national income and its corresponding rate of interest when the liquidity preference (L)—the demand for money—equals the supply of money (M).

THEORIES OF REAL CYCLES

The return of brutal recurrent transitions between recessions and recoveries from the 1970s, together with their concomitant shocks (oil crisis, troubles on the currency market, or financial and banking difficulties), stimulated new research on crisis and business cycles. Robert E. Lucas criticized the neoclassical synthesis and proposed a theory founded on the rational anticipations, while Milton Friedman developed a monetarist approach.

More recent analyses focus on the real cycle theory initiated by Finn E. Kydland and Edward C. Prescott. According to them, real cycles do not spring from a shock given through aggregate demand but through aggregate supply, particularly through technological shocks that induce fluctuations in average productivity of investment and consumption. These authors take up the idea of the lag of investment expenditures behind investment decision, which was first conceived by Mitchell, but they nonetheless integrate the theory of business cycle into the neoclassical theory of growth. Ironically, these authors converge towards the analyses of Karl Marx and his successors such as Tougan-Baranowski. For these two earlier writers the regular destruction of productive capital through the advent of crisis was necessary to restore the level of profit, paving the way for a new phase of accumulation.

HISTORICAL RELATIVITY OF THEORIES

From a historical vantage point, it is difficult to identify the elements of discord within the economy that stimulate cyclical fluctuations. One of the strengths of the Kydland and Prescott model was empirically validated for the U.S. economy between 1950 and 1979. For the preceding periods the lack of necessary economic data makes the econometrical models more difficult to validate.

Contrary to economists, historians think that the processes of initiation, transmission, and amplification of the fluctuations were modified and relayed over two centuries, and that the theories put forth at different periods tried to better render the realities of their times. Hawtrey, for example, insists on the role played by merchants in the transmission of the credit cycle to the real economy, because they build inventories when interest rates were low (though not indefinitely) and reduced their stock when the rates began to rise.

This analysis sheds light on the manner in which the economy functioned during the nineteenth century. One can add to this explanation that the deficiency in the spread of market knowledge as well the instability of demand for consumer goods occasioned important variations on the level of inventories. The inability to sell the goods on the market did not lead to an "economic crisis," but was rather to a "commercial crisis."

However, the acceleration of technical progress explains why technological shocks, considered by Joseph Schumpeter or Nicholas Kondratieff to be the stimulant of the long waves, come to the fore in recent theories of real cycles. Hence, a number of authors have considered, for instance, that the U.S. cycle during the 1990s depended on the *net economy*.

Historians have focused their research on crises as an integrated element of the business cycle. Crises appear to be multiform, though there is not always a consensus as to their explanations. With the growing importance of the financial sector from the 1970s, studies have turned to banking crises, currency crises, and debt crises, without, however, integrating them into the overall analysis of cycles. These new perspectives have allowed the revisiting and reevaluation of previous turbulences such as the German cycle during the 1920s. They also allow considering the 1930s more as a period stifled by a debt crisis. Likewise, the monetarist interpretation by Milton Friedman shed new light on the American crisis of 1929. If economists seek in most cases a common mechanism through space and time, historians repudiate any explanations based on a single cause, insisting instead on the differences and on various combinations between real, monetary, industrial, commercial, and banking factors. Major crises such as the one that spread in the 1930s, which had so many different aspects and spread between sectors and countries, allowed the identification of buried crises, such as the banking difficulties of 1931, when precisely an upswing in the cycle was underway in the United States. Historians believe, like the economist Mitchell, that the leading question should not be "what causes business cycles?" but rather, "how do business cycles run their course?"

MECHANISMS OF TRANSMISSION ON AN INTERNATIONAL LEVEL

Since the nineteenth century certain crises have had international repercussions. The crisis of 1857 affected at the same time the United States, Great Britain, and France, then the center of the international economic system, but scarcely spread to other countries. This coincidence does *not* mean that the various business cycles were coordinated. Between 1854 and 1938 their periodicity was on average shorter in the United States than in Europe, with twenty-one known cases in the United States and sixteen in Great Britain.

The mechanism of transmission was revealed to be more efficient during major crisis than during less severe recessions, or crisis in sectors (for example, the 1904 crisis in the German electrical industry and the 1907 crisis in the United States).

The mechanisms of relay were less efficient and slower during the other phases of the cycle, such as during the recoveries. This is the reason that the study of crises reveals a greater integration than does the study of business cycles. The growing integration of national economies into the international sphere took place over a century and a half through two different processes: First, a geographical extension of countries, and, second, a better coordination between economies.

Some mechanisms are a result of real flows that link national economies and their major economic pillars, while others pass through anticipation on the economic trend of dominant countries and are psychologically contagious.

These mechanisms are relevant at different levels of the balance of payments. The variations in volume and in prices of imported and exported goods are major factors of the transmission. Their influence is subject to the degree of openness of the economy and the importance of their trade. By the end the nineteenth century the measurable rate to which the world economy was inclined toward international trade was already high (8.7% in 1913). This level was not surpassed before the 1960s, and reached 14 percent only in the 1990s. These effects were already important before 1913, given that the commercial flows were concentrated within the dominant economic powers of the time (Great Britain, Germany, the United States, and France contributed more than half of world exports). The mechanisms of transmissions through trade are asymmetrical. First, the economic trend of the dominant power (Great Britain in the nineteenth century, the United States since 1945) influenced the economic tides of the other countries. Second, big countries such as the United States, which are less open and not dependent on foreign trade, were only slightly influenced by foreign economic fluctuations through the changes in their exports. But they transmit their commercial convulsions to their furnishers through the ebbing of their imports, which represent an important share of world trade. Prior to 1914, British merchants who bought primary products diffused their cycle into the economies of primary producers. The slowing down of U.S. imports, accentuated in 1930 by the rise in tariffs, was a vector in the propagation of the crisis for countries exporting to the United States. The smaller countries that had a high level of market openness were, for their part, influenced by the cycle of large and powerful countries through the variation of their exports to the same degree as the primary producers.

Capital flows are also a vector of transmission of cycles. Their effects are more rapid and brutal than that of merchandises, whose fall is accelerated, at the peak of a cycle, through the financing of international trade. It is also emphasized by the sudden change of anticipations. For example, in the case of the Anglo-Argentinean crisis of 1890, the difficulties faced by the London capital market, which weighed on the currency, incited the Bank of England to raise its interest rate. Of course, the consequence brought to the English market short-term capital from abroad, but it also raised the cost of credit for importers of primary products who depended on their inventories, and thereby hindered their purchasing power. The overall consequence on production was slower, but cushioned in Great Britain with the rapid revival of industrial activity. In Argentina the recovery was much slower. The London market did not undertake the refinancing of public debt; the recovery of railway constructions, which depended on the fresh capital, was slow coming; and the fall in the price of wheat depressed the value of exports over several years.

If the volume of long-term capital flows was considerable before 1914, the importance of short-term capital flows was more limited because the London money market could singularly take charge of large orders, and also because the contemporaries were convinced of the stability of the gold standard. However, during the interwar years, as well as during the last quarter of the twentieth century, these sudden and destabilizing movements became the vehicles of rapid transmission of the cycle. The psychological effect was also contagious, like the effects of regional contagion that assimilated every country of a given geographical zone (Latin America or Southeast Asia), even when they had with different economic secular trends.

The development of merchandise trade and capital flows tended to homogenize economic fluctuations between countries from the mid-nineteenth century through the twentieth century. This homogenization of economic fluctuations was nevertheless slowed down by the adoption of floating rates (in the beginning of the 1920s, during the 1930s and 1940s, and since 1971) and by the application of contracyclical policies tended to isolate national cycles. Although the degree of autonomy and the lags between the cycle set by the dominant power and the other national cycles, which were reduced little by little, they still have maintained themselves, allowing for capital flows to continue. At the end of the nineteenth century British capital arbitrated between the British and U.S. markets. Savings were exported when economic activity became stagnant in the United Kingdom and vibrant on the other side of the Atlantic and vice versa. Likewise, in the 1970s, the slowdown of growth of Western economies encouraged banks to massively lend to Latin American countries, boosting growth in some of them up to the point when disinflation precipitated them into debt crisis. These countries then went through a decade of stagnation, while in the United States the economy began a new revival.

SEE ALSO GREAT DEPRESSION OF THE 1930S.

BIBLIOGRAPHY

Bordo, Michael D. "The Impact and International Transmission of Financial Crises: Some Historical Evidence, 1870–1933." *Rivista di Storia Economica*, no. 2: 41–78. Reprinted in Bordo, Michael, ed., *Financial Crises*, vol. 2, ed. Michael Bordo. Aldershot, U.K.: Edward Elgar, 1992.

Juglar, Clément. *Des crises commerciales et de leur retour périodique en France, en Angleterre et aux États-Unis (Commercial Crises and the Periodical Recurrence in France, England and the United States).* [1862]. New York: A. M. Kelley, 1967.

Keynes, John, M. *General Theory of Employment, Interest, and Money.* London: Macmillan, 1936.

Kydland, Finn E., and Prescott, Edward C. "Time to Build and Aggregate Fluctuations." *Econometrica* 50 (Nov. 1982, no. 6): 1345–1370.

Matthews, Robert Charles Oliver. "The Trade Cycle in Britain, 1790–1850." *Oxford Economic Papers* 6 (Feb. 1954, no. 1): 1–32.

Mitchell, Wesley C. *Business Cycles: The Problem and Its Setting.* New York: National Bureau of Economic Research, 1927.

Mitchell, Wesley C. *What Happens During Business Cycles: A Progress Report.* New York: National Bureau of Economic Research, 1951.

Von Haberler, Gottfried. *Prosperity and Depression.* Geneva: League of Nations, 1938.

Zarnovitz, Victor. "Recent Work on Business Cycles in Historical Perspective: A Review of Theories and Evidence." *Journal of Economic Literature* 23, no. 2 (June 1985): 523–580.

Patrick Verley

ALEXANDRE DE RHODES
1591–1660

Born in Avignon, France on March 15, 1591, Alexandre de Rhodes entered the Jesuit novitiate in 1612 and in 1619 sailed to Asia to join the mission in Macau. In 1624 he embarked for Cochinchina, a realm in modern-day southern Vietnam, and landed in Hoi An (Faifo), a regional seaport where the missionary Francesco Buzomi had founded a church in 1615. Soon he moved north, to the realm of Cochinchina's Vietnamese rival, Tonkin. For the next two decades de Rhodes labored in both domains, to proselytize, to create indigenous societies of catechists, and to develop a strategy of vernacular translation. In contrast with the repeated failure of other European enterprises in Vietnam, the missionaries succeeded in laying the foundations for Catholicism, modern Vietnam's second-largest religion, thanks in large part to de Rhodes's accomplishments. As his greatest legacy, de Rhodes perfected a romanized alphabet for Vietnamese that French colonial rulers adopted as the standard alphabet of Vietnamese, and it remains so today. De Rhodes encountered much suspicion from both Vietnamese courts and was ultimately banished from both domains, for the last time from Cochinchina in 1646. He returned to Europe and there published numerous works about his efforts in Vietnam. He died while on a mission to Persia, in Isfahan, on November 5, 1660. During the nineteenth century French imperialists used de Rhodes's writings and legacy among Vietnamese Catholics as part of a campaign to justify French political ambitions in Vietnam.

SEE ALSO EMPIRE, FRENCH; VIETNAM.

BIBLIOGRAPHY

De Rhodes, Alexandre. *Histoire du Royaume de Tunquin* (1651). Paris: Éditions Kimé, 1999.

Hertz, Solange, trans. *Rhodes of Viet Nam: The Travels and Missions of Father Alexandre de Rhodes in China and Other Kingdoms of the Orient.* Westminster, MA: Newman Press, 1966.

Phan, Peter C. *Mission and Catechesis: Alexandre de Rhodes and Inculturation in Seventeenth-Century Vietnam.* Maryknoll, NY: Orbis Books, 1998.

Charles Wheeler

DEVELOPMENTAL STATE, CONCEPT OF THE

The idea of a developmental state is normally referred to as a post–World War II phenomenon, characterizing a transitional form of political system and type of economic policy on the path to industrialization. In spite of the novelty of the term itself—it came into general use in the 1980s—there is a high degree of continuity both in theory and in the policy tools used by nations during this transition, starting during the late 1400s lasting until the post–World War II period.

DEFINITION AND THEORY

The core idea behind the developmental state is that the productive structure of a nation may be suboptimal at the time, and may be improved with the help of active economic policy. Whether explicit or not, the concept is based on a notion that some economic activities are more conducive to growth and generalized welfare than others. In general terms the goal of the developmental state—from the policies starting in England with Henry VII in 1485 through to the policies of East Asia in the 1980s—has been to industrialize; to diversify the economy out of a dependency on agricultural and other raw materials alone. The developmental states aim at increasing national wealth by building a diversified industrial structure where economic activities with large potentials for technological upgrading, subject to increasing returns (falling unit costs), play an important role.

The developmental state bases its ideology and legitimacy on an ability to promote sustained economic development. The ability to improve the economic conditions of the inhabitants is both the goal of the ruling elite and a means to keep power. This applies as much to the so-called "enlightened despotism" of Europe in the 1700s as to the East Asian developmental states after World War II. In order to achieve its goal, the developmental state needs a strong, but not necessarily big, state and a loyal and competent bureaucracy that identifies with the national goals. The bureaucracy under Frederick the Great (King of Prussia from 1740 to 1786) and in the Japanese Ministry of Trade and Industry (MITI) in the period after World War II are suggested as ideal types of developmental bureaucrats. Elements of nation building and nationalism tend to be integral parts of the policies of developmental states.

The developmental state largely depends on private capital and ownership. Its bureaucracy is capable of stimulating, shaping, and cooperating with the private sector, identifying industrial projects where the profit-making interests of the private sector coincide with the economic goals of the nation. These interests will normally be common when the private sector invests in projects that increase the technological competence of the nation, often in industries previously dominated by companies based in wealthier countries. The prototype developmental state created by the Tudor kings—ruling England from 1485 to 1603—was based on an attempt to imitate the economic structures of the wealthy Italian city-states Venice and Florence. Under the "Tudor Plan," England—then a very poor periphery of Europe—slowly built up a textile industry, processing at home the wool which was previously all exported in bulk for manufacturing in Italy, particularly Florence, and elsewhere on the Continent. In this way England first became an industrialized nation.

POLICY TOOLS OF THE DEVELOPMENTAL STATE

The policy toolbox used by developmental states has been remarkably stable over time, although increasing in sophistication. Based on observations of the industrial structure of wealthier nations, the desired types of activities are consciously targeted and supported by different policy measures. The targeted activities are invariably more technologically advanced than those presently dominating in the nation to be developed.

Patents and tariff protection as institutions for creating and spreading new knowledge and new practices were created in the late 1400s, and used then in order to upgrade the technological skills of a nation. Entrepreneurs wishing to set up production in a backward area or country were given temporary monopolies (patents) in the area and/or temporary tariff protection. In this way new industries were forcefully spread to new areas from where they had first been set up. In Tudor England, in Prussia under Frederick the Great, and in the industrialization of

Korea, bringing in foreign skills was much more important than bringing in foreign capital. Whereas earlier, foreign skills were brought in by way of migration of skilled workers and artisans who were attracted by generous economic incentives, during Korean industrialization Japanese engineers moonlighting in Korea on weekends and on temporary assignments played a similar role.

Traditional policy tools also include tax breaks and subsidized credits for targeted activities, export bounties, and emphasis on training and education to match the needs of the targeted activities. Examples of the latter are the sophisticated apprentice system put in place in England under Elizabeth I in the late 1500s, the founding and sponsoring of scientific academies in continental Europe in the 1700s, and the emphasis on the education of a large number of engineers in the industrialization of Korea.

Praising the protectionist industry-building Navigation Acts as "the wisest of all the commercial regulations of England" in his *Wealth of Nations* (1776), Adam Smith (1723–1790) is a clear spokesman for a standard policy of the developmental state. Smith's only mention in this book of the concept of the "invisible hand" is when it works toward the goal of the developmental state, industrialization: "preferring the support of domestic to that of foreign industry" (Smith 477). Smith, however, was writing at a time when England had attained world leadership and the developmental state had outplayed its role. He therefore agrees with England's past, but not present and future, prodevelopment interventions.

In his "Report on the Subject of Manufactures" (1791) Alexander Hamilton (1755–1804)—the first U.S. secretary of the treasury—outlines a plan to industrialize the United States that is prototypical of a developmental state, employing the same theoretical arguments that were used in continental Europe at the time and that had been used in England until recently. Hamilton advocated that bounties and incentives to manufacturers be financed from the tariffs imposed on the import of manufactured goods. In the nineteenth century German economist Friedrich List (1789–1846) was the main theoretician of the developmental state. Living in the United States for several years, even becoming a U.S. citizen, List was inspired by the successful industrialization of the United States.

THE DEVELOPMENTAL STATE: TIMING, SUCCESSES, AND FAILURES

The developmental state bridges the transition from poverty to industrialization and national economic strength. Once the technological state-of-the-art—the frontier of knowledge—has been reached, the planning-based policies of the developmental state become increasingly irrelevant and inefficient. Once a nation has achieved technological leadership, there is no longer any leading nation or leading technology to aim for and to catch up with, and other, less bureaucratically oriented policy tools become more appropriate. As the manufacturing sector grows stronger, this sector also needs larger markets and will be interested in freer trade with the rest of the world. So, for more than one reason, a successful developmental state carries the seeds of its own destruction.

Both Smith and List, in different ways, emphasized the temporary nature of the policies for a developmental state. Once the desired economic structure had been achieved, free trade and openness to the world markets would be the final goal both for them both.

Whereas the East Asian developmental states have been resounding successes, similar experiments in other areas, for example Latin America and India, have been less successful. This can be accounted for partly by the different policies pursued in these areas in the post–World War II era. Whereas East Asian nations temporarily protected and targeted largely indigenously developed or indigenously improved technologies for the world markets, Latin American nations permanently protected technologies that were largely imported, for small local markets. Latin American industrialization was, consequently, much less advanced and more shallow—based on the imports of semi-manufactured goods—and much less able to compete internationally. East Asian bureaucrats also tended to place rigorous demands for technological and economic performance on the local companies they were supporting, an aspect largely absent in most of Latin America. Brazil and India represent intermediary cases, with characteristics of both these groups of nations.

In spite of the continuity both of the developmental state as a passage point to national economic welfare and of its policy toolbox, the concept itself and the related policies have been subject to recurrent debates, and there are periods when the idea has fallen completely out of favor. Examples of such periods are the 1780s (briefly), the 1840s, and the 1990s. Economic success during the early 2000s in China contains all the elements of a successful developmental state, including continuous technological upgrading and the gradual opening-up towards free trade.

SEE ALSO BANKING; CAPITALISM; FINANCE, CREDIT AND MONEY LENDING; INDUSTRIALIZATION.

BIBLIOGRAPHY

Amsden, Alice. *Asia's Next Giant: South Korea and Late Industrialization*. New York: Oxford University Press, 1989.

Evans, Peter. *Embedded Autonomy: States, Firms, and Industrial Transformation*. Princeton, NJ: Princeton University Press, 1995.

Hamilton, Alexander. "Report on the Subject of Manufactures" (1791). Reprinted in *State Papers and Speeches on the Tariff*, ed. Frank Taussig. Cambridge, MA: Harvard University Press, 1893.

Johnson, Chalmers. *MITI and the Japanese Miracle: The Growth of Industrial Policy*. Stanford, CA: Stanford University Press, 1982.

List, Friedrich. *The National System of Political Economy*. (German, 1841; English, trans. Sampson S. Lloyd.) Fairfield, NJ: Augustus M. Kelly, 1991.

Reinert, Erik. "The Role of the State in Economic Growth." *Journal of Economic Studies* 26, no. 4/5 (1999): 268–326.

Smith, Adam. *An Enquiry into the Nature and Causes of The Wealth of Nations*. Chicago: University of Chicago, 1976. Original edition, 1776.

Wade, Robert. *Governing the Market*. Princeton, NJ: Princeton University Press, 1992.

Erik Reinart

PORFIRIO DÍAZ
1830–1915

Porfirio Díaz was president (most would say dictator) of Mexico from 1876 to 1880 and 1884 to 1911, an era known as the *Porfiriato* because of Díaz's central influence. Whether Díaz's ultimate legacy was modernization of the country or the bloody Mexican Revolution (1910–1917) is disputed.

Díaz was a liberal revolutionary whose brutal hand and skillful negotiating finally led Mexico out of a half-century of foreign wars, civil wars, and revolts. The spillover effect of the rush of railroads into the U.S. West and Southwest benefited Mexico in the 1880s, expanding Mexico's rail network eighteenfold. This helped increase Mexico's exports ninefold and imports fourfold between 1880 and 1910, creating trade surpluses and securing the value of the faltering peso. The railroads carried the bulk of international trade, made possible the export of industrial metals in place of devaluing silver, Mexico's traditional export, and led Mexico to turn the bulk of its trade from Europe to the United States. Mexico was able to service its foreign debt, pay its soldiers and officials, and buy off regional warlords. By 1910 U.S., British, and French capital made Mexico one of the world's largest recipients of foreign investment.

But this export-led growth was explosive, as many indigenous villages had their lands expropriated and debt peonage was expanded. Díaz's desperation to restore Mexico's foreign credit and placate the domestic elites as well as befriend foreign investors did not prevent him from undertaking measures such as the nationalization of the country's railroads. Export-led growth led to revolution in good part because of Díaz's inability to institutionalize his charisma, creating a crisis of succession, perhaps a million casualties, and more than a decade of struggle.

SEE ALSO COPPER; COTTON; DEVELOPMENTAL STATE, CONCEPT OF THE; GERMANY; MEXICO; PETROLEUM; SUGAR, RUM, AND MOLASSES; UNITED KINGDOM; UNITED STATES.

BIBLIOGRAPHY

Knight, Alan. *The Mexican Revolution.* 2 vols. Cambridge, U.K.: Cambridge University Press, 1986.

Steven Topik

DISEASE AND PESTILENCE

Trading partners try to avoid disruptions that would threaten the profitability of their business. Diseases disturb trade only when a strong partner calculates that the loss incurred by disruption would be greater than the profits to be made on the transaction. Weak participants are often powerless to refuse exchanges, even when they bring sickness and death.

Four organic conditions curtail commerce: pandemics, which threaten whole populations; epidemics, which can kill or disable substantial numbers of people; epizootics, which threaten domestic animals; and plant diseases, which curtail agricultural output.

Generally signaled by the appearance of a previously unknown illness, pandemics, a rare phenomenon, have elicited the strongest reactions. The bubonic plague, which killed roughly one-third of the population of Europe between 1347 and 1351, immediately disrupted everyday life, trade included. Historians report the disruption of urban food supplies from the surrounding countryside, refusal to pay civil and ecclesiastical taxes, and the establishment of surveillance and management systems, which collected information about the plague and designated locations to which people thought to have the disease could be taken. Subsequently, outbreaks led to measures such as the imposition of quarantines and *cordons sanitaires,* which delayed trade by forcing merchants and their cargoes to wait outside city walls or beyond national borders for periods of up to forty days, until the danger of infection passed.

Outbreaks of diseases from which some part of the population enjoyed immunity occasioned less extreme measures. In the uncertainty of what actually caused deadly diseases, cargoes were fumigated and crews and merchants isolated. Beginning in the eighteenth century

consulates inspected ships even before they left their home ports, attesting to their safety with "clean bills of health" that certified the absence of detectable disease. These restrictions applied to reportable diseases such as smallpox, measles, cholera, and tropical diseases such as yellow fever and malaria.

Animal and plant diseases that threatened livestock or starchy staples were generally controlled by inspection. When diseased animals or plants were discovered, whole herds or food shipments were destroyed to protect domestic supplies. These restrictions applied to cattle infected with rinderpest and rye tainted with ergot, whose consumption could produce symptoms of madness.

Nineteenth-century innovations that speeded transportation and increased the size of cargoes, such as steamships and railroads, required faster response times to control disease. Sometimes news of infections arrived as quickly as the diseases themselves. One favored tactic was for national governments to pass legislation affecting vessels containing cargoes or passengers with specific reportable diseases. In the 1830s, for example, the government of the Cape Colony forbade ships known to carry measles and smallpox from landing at Cape Town. British legislation passed in 1848 barred the importation of animals with sheep pox, a prohibition extended in 1866 to animals infected with hoof-and-mouth disease.

Laissez-faire attitudes led to objections against any delay of trade at all. Opponents pointed in particular to the impotence of trade restrictions during the outbreak of cholera that devastated Western Europe and North America in the 1830s. In 1851, when the powers of individual states seemed insufficient to curb the spread of epidemics, diplomats organized the first of a series of Sanitary Conferences to discuss, among other things, how trade might be facilitated despite disease outbreaks. Once international agreements came to regulate international commerce, the list was restricted to cholera, yellow fever, and bubonic plague.

These international efforts were facilitated by changes in biomedicine. The identification in the 1870s and 1880s of the bacteria that caused rabies, tuberculosis, and the plague enabled authorities to establish more precise controls over imports. The invention of the x-ray in 1895, moreover, made it yet easier to screen passengers and crews for tuberculosis. Other microbiological tests were developed for typhoid, syphilis, and gonorrhea.

The laws protecting European and U.S. citizens from the diseases of humans and animals often did not apply to the inhabitants of tropical colonies. In 1868 the government of British India reversed a previous policy allowing colonial officials to apply *cordons sanitaires* and quarantines to prevent the spread of cholera to the Raj.

A print from the Toggenberg Bible depicts the suffering of those affected by the bubonic plague in the 15th century. The *plague, otherwise referred to as "The Black Death," had substantial economic effects, with its enormous death toll across Europe and fears that caused workers to flee affected areas.* © BETTMANN/CORBIS. REPRODUCED BY PERMISSION.

Similar policies were applied to Egypt after the invasion of 1882. In all, millions of colonial subjects unnecessarily lost their lives to diseases whose spread was successfully controlled in Europe. During this same period, previously isolated populations of the Pacific Basin suffered a devastating loss of life from diseases from which they had no immunity. In the early twentieth century many tropical environments were devastated by plant diseases associated with the monoculture of commodities such as rubber and bananas.

For most of the century, however, crops and animals were traded freely. War inhibited far more traffic than did restrictions designed to control rabies or hoof-and-mouth disease. The quantity and speed of commerce grew with the development of containerized ships and air freight. The terrorist attacks on New York City and Washington, D.C., in 2001 stimulated calls for freight inspections to prevent bioterrorism through smuggled pathogens such as Newcastle's Disease, which kills chickens, and the virulent fungus wheat rust. Nonetheless, any curtailment of trade to prevent the introduction of pathogens has been largely internal rather than international. Despite the fearful consequences of emerging diseases such as AIDS in the 1980s and SARS in 2003—the first epidemic to occasion a travel advisory by the World Health Association—few restrictions were imposed even on travelers. Health Canada reported that the main economic consequences of the SARS outbreak in Toronto were reduced tourist and business travel which, in turn, adversely affected the Canadian airline industry.

SEE ALSO AGRICULTURE.

BIBLIOGRAPHY

Carmichael, Ann G. "Epidemics and State Medicine in Fifteenth-Century Milan." In *Medicine from the Black Death to the French Disease,* ed. Roger French et al. Aldershot, U.K.: Ashgate, 1998.

Coleman, William. *Yellow Fever in the North.* Madison: University of Wisconsin Press, 1987.

Kunitz, Stephen J. *Disease and Social Diversity: The European Impact on the Health of Non-Europeans.* New York and Oxford, U.K.: Oxford University Press, 1994.

Restifo, Giuseppe, ed. *Epidemie e società nel Mediterraneo di età moderna (Epidemics and Society in the Mediterranean During the Modern Era.* Messina, Italy: Armando Siciliano Editore, 2001.

Watts, Sheldon. *Epidemics and History: Disease, Power, and Imperialism.* New Haven, CT: Yale University Press, 1997.

Woods, Abigail. "The Construction of an Animal Plague: Foot and Mouth Disease in Nineteenth-Century Britain." *Social History of Medicine* 17, no. 1 (2004): 23–40.

Bruce Fetter

DOLE FAMILY

James Drummond Dole was born in Jamaica Plain, Massachusetts, in 1877, married Belle Dickey in 1908, and died in Hawaii in 1958. Dole was instrumental in the development of Hawaii's pineapple industry and the global trade in canned and fresh pineapple. After Dole received an undergraduate degree from Harvard University in 1899, he moved to Hawaii, where his father's cousin, Sanford Dole (1844–1926), was governor of the newly annexed U.S. territory. Dole purchased 61 acres of land in central Oahu in July 1900, planted his first pineapple crop and founded the Hawaiian Pineapple Company (HAPCO) in 1901, and built a pineapple cannery near Honolulu's port in 1906. HAPCO's pineapple production expanded to 4.5 million cases in 1931, an expansion facilitated by HAPCO's development in 1913 of a machine (the Ginaca Machine) to peel, core, and slice pineapple; duty-free access to the U.S. pineapple market; and Dole's purchase of the island of Lanai in 1922. After HAPCO experienced financial problems in 1932, Castle and Cooke—one of Hawaii's "Big Five" companies—took control. It assigned Dole to the honorary position of board chairman, from which he retired in 1948.

SEE ALSO AGRICULTURE; CARGOES, FREIGHT; CORPORATION, OR LIMITED LIABILITY COMPANY; TOBACCO; UNITED STATES.

BIBLIOGRAPHY

Dole, Richard, and Porteus, Elizabeth Dole. *The Story of James Dole.* Aiea, Hawaii: Island Heritage Publishing, 1990.

Ten Bruggencate, Jan K. *Hawaii's Pineapple Century: A History of the Crowned Fruit in the Hawaiian Islands.* Honolulu: Mutual Publishing, 2004.

Sumner J. La Croix

DRUGS, ILLICIT

The trade in drugs and drug foods was crucial to the expansion of global trade. Coffee, tea, sugar, and drugs such as tobacco, rum, and opium all were high-value consumer goods that were profitable enough to attract private merchants and state interest, and most of them were at least initially regarded as morally suspect. In the cases of coffee and tobacco, this suspicion eventually died out. Other drugs such as khat and betel nut never found global markets. The opiates marijuana and cocaine, however, became as economically and politically important as coffee and sugar while gradually becoming illegal. In 1997 the illicit drug trade was estimated at U.S.$400 billion, or 8 percent of the total value of world trade. In some respects it is a fairly ordinary luxury trade: goods are produced, shipped, sold, and consumed. The trade in illicit drugs has unique economic, social, and political aspects, however. By definition, illicit drugs are substances that states want to restrict. Like drug foods, illicit drugs can be profitable and comparatively easy for states to dominate because they can be produced in limited and easily controlled areas, and their high cost-to-price ratio can finance rigorous antismuggling efforts. Sugar, opium, tobacco, and coffee have all been important to the creation of early-modern commercial empires. Low production costs, high potential prices, and high demand also make it very difficult for states to suppress the trade in these goods, as demonstrated by failures including Prohibition in the United States in the 1920s and contemporary antidrug efforts.

The modern illicit drug trade began in 1729 when the Qing dynasty outlawed sales of smoking opium in China. Despite this ban, imports of Indian opium continued to grow, as did domestic production. Some estimate that by the late nineteenth century up to 60 percent of Chinese men smoked opium at least occasionally. Indian exports of opium grew to 40,000 chests by 1854, and opium revenue was the second-largest item in the budget of British India. The Chinese government's inability to eliminate this trade sprang from the same causes that troubled later governments. Opium had legal medicinal uses, and it was difficult to distinguish illicit drugs from legal ones. Like the other illicit drugs, opium was produced in remote rural districts and uncontrollable foreign states, consumed all over, and easy to smuggle. The Chinese government also found it difficult to convince its subjects to quit smoking, growing, and selling opium. Use of the drug was popular, and its production and sale were profitable enough to attract not only common criminals but also syndicates such as the Gowned Brothers and the Green Gang. Chinese officials who had either been bribed or who saw opium taxes as a valuable source of revenue often aided the criminal drug trade. The British East India Company and the British Empire were directly involved in the trade.

In the late nineteenth century Europeans became increasingly concerned with the medical and social dangers

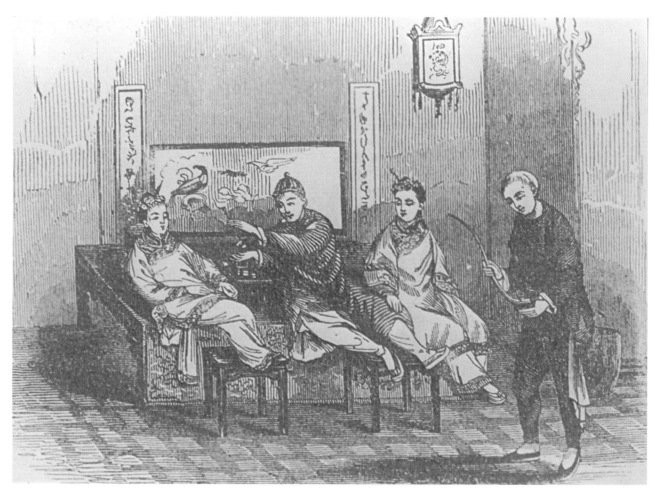

A woodcut by H. H. Kane depicts a Chinese opium den located in an American city. These dens were often found in Chinese immigrant communities and provided a location to smoke opium packed into pipes. Opium, which can be used to produce the pain killer morphine or the drug heroin, is one of the world's most valuable and illegal forms of trade. © NATIONAL LIBRARY OF MEDICINE/ SCIENCE PHOTO LIBRARY/PHOTO RESEARCHERS, INC. REPRODUCED BY PERMISSION.

of drugs. It was during this time that the modern concept of addiction was developed, and many formerly legal drugs began to be regulated. The model for later attempts to regulate the trade in drugs was the British Pharmacy Act of 1868, which established categories of medical and "luxurious" use of opiates, banning the latter and creating a licensed distribution system to supply the former. Beginning with the Hague agreements of 1912 to 1914, governments also set up a system of international treaties to govern the shipping and eventually the production of these drugs. At first this was an explicitly Eurocentric system, intended to protect only members of races assumed to be civilized. Opium continued to be sold to the subject races in colonial Asia, and the use of coca leaves by Andean laborers was encouraged as a part of the exploitation of native labor. The international treaty system initiated at The Hague was refined by later agreements, but all of the agreements focused on international cooperation to limit the production of dangerous drugs and limit their

distribution to medical and scientific channels. This has always been a very complex problem, and the history of the illicit drug trade has been one of constant change: as powerful states eliminate production and distribution channels, new ones inevitably take their place.

The illicit drug trade was made more complex by the introduction of new drugs such as morphine, heroin, and later, LSD, which began as medical drugs but could also become drugs of abuse when used outside of the medical system. Morphine and heroin were both used medically and abused from the early twentieth century. Major pharmaceutical companies produced both, and their governments (most notably Germany) fought to limit restrictions on these drugs. They also blurred the newly established distinction between medical and recreational drugs. Some doctors claimed that the best treatment for morphine addicts was a maintenance dose of morphine, a position that was opposed by the United States government not on medical grounds but because it would blur the distinction between "good" and "bad" drug use. This conflict continues today with debates about "medical marijuana."

Control of the drug trade was also made more difficult by changing patterns of consumption. In China opium was first an imported luxury used mainly by the elite, then a "backwards" habit, and finally a counterrevolutionary one. Tobacco seems to be following a related pattern today. In all cases, use of a drug is popular or unpopular as much for its social associations as for the chemical attributes of the drug. In the West use of opiates and later marijuana was first associated with outsider groups such as Chinese and Mexican laborers. Drug use was partially domesticated by its association with artistic creativity through figures ranging from the English poet Samuel Taylor Coleridge (1772–1835) to the American musician Charlie Parker (1920–1955). Marijuana use in particular became acceptable in connection with the counterculture movement in the 1960s, and it remains the most common of these illicit drugs in the developed world. Growing consumption of these drugs in some cases led to *de facto* or *de jure* relaxation of controls. Government attempts to limit demand by convincing their subjects that drugs are bad have had only limited success.

States have also had only limited success in interdicting the flow of drugs. After 1945 the colonial opium monopolies in Asia were disbanded, and officially, major states were no longer involved in the drug trade and they all cooperated in maintaining an international system of drug controls. There were many exceptions to this principle, however. Some states were openly tolerant of the drug trade. Even a handful of states remaining outside the system of international controls can have an enormous impact on the world drug trade. The United Nations estimated that between 1990 and 2002 almost all of the world's illicit opium was produced in only two countries, Afghanistan and Myanmar, with five Afghan provinces accounting for the majority. In other cases, as with the U.S. Mafia's involvement in the heroin trade or the Medellín cartel in Colombia, drug profits made it possible for nonstate groups to defy state power. In the case of the U.S. Central Intelligence Agency's complicity in the drug trade in Southeast Asia in the 1960s and 1970s, organs of the state acted in defiance of overall state policy. The official rhetoric of drug suppression is that drugs are something sold and consumed by criminals and opposed by governments and citizens. In practice, the dividing line between these categories is much less clear.

Since 1945 the illicit drug trade has been conducted in conflict with a series of national and international wars on drugs. In all cases these wars are attempts to use state power to change a whole array of political, economic,

and social relations. The only one of these wars that can be said to have ended in victory for the state was the Chinese Communists' campaign against opium after 1949. At that time almost all of China's drugs were domestically produced, so the international issues that plagued other drug efforts were not relevant. The Communists were in the process of sweeping away the old political and economic order, which had supported or tolerated the drug trade. Ultimately they were completely changing the definition of proper behavior for a citizen of China. The drug trade probably cannot be eliminated except through such a revolution, given the economic and political interests that its profits create and the popular demand for drugs that their social uses create.

SEE ALSO AGRICULTURE; BANKING; BENGAL; BURMA; CALCUTTA; CANTON SYSTEM; CHINA; COLOMBIA; EAST INDIA COMPANY, BRITISH; EAST INDIA COMPANY, DUTCH; EAST INDIA COMPANY, OTHER; EMPIRE, BRITISH; EMPIRE, DUTCH; EMPIRE, FRENCH; EMPIRE, JAPANESE; EMPIRE, MUGHAL; EMPIRE, OTTOMAN; EMPIRE, PORTUGUESE; EMPIRE, QING; GOLD AND SILVER; GUANGZHOU; HAITI; HONG KONG; IMPERIALISM; IMPORT SUBSTITUTION; INDIA; INDONESIA; JAMAICA; JARDINE MATHESON; LABORERS, COERCED; LABORERS, CONTRACT; LEVANT COMPANY; LOS ANGELES–LONG BEACH; MANCHURIA; MARSEILLES; MERCANTILISM; MITSUI; NEW YORK; PAKISTAN; PHARMACEUTICALS; PROTECTION COSTS; RAFFLES, SIR THOMAS STAMFORD; THAILAND; SINGAPORE; SMUGGLING; TEA; TOBACCO; UNITED STATES; VIETNAM.

BIBLIOGRAPHY
Bakalar, James B., and Grinspoon, Lester. *Drug Control in a Free Society.* Cambridge, U.K. and New York: Cambridge University Press, 1984.
Berridge, Virginia, and Edwards, Griffith. *Opium and the People: Opiate Use in Nineteenth-Century England.* London and New York: St. Martin's Press, 1981.
Brook, Timothy, and Tadashi Wakabayashi, Bob. *Opium Regimes: China, Britain, and Japan, 1839–1952.* Berkeley: University of California Press, 2000.
Courtwright, David T. *Forces of Habit: Drugs and the Making of the Modern World.* Cambridge, MA: Harvard University Press, 2001.
McAllister, William B. *Drug Diplomacy in the Twentieth Century: An International History.* London and New York: Routledge, 2000.
McCoy, Alfred W. *The Politics of Heroin: CIA Complicity in the Global Drug Trade: Afghanistan, Southeast Asia, Central America, Colombia.* Rev. edition. Chicago: Lawrence Hill Books, 2003.
Musto, David F. *The American Disease: Origins of Narcotic Control.* 3rd edition. New York: Oxford University Press, 1999.
Trocki, Carl A. *Opium, Empire, and the Global Political Economy: A Study of the Asian Opium Trade, 1750–1950,*

Asia's Transformations. London and New York: Routledge, 1999.

Walker, William O. *Drugs in the Western Hemisphere: An Odyssey of Cultures in Conflict.* Wilmington, DE: Scholarly Resources, 1996.

Alan Baumler

DRY GOODS

SEE COTTON; INDUSTRIALIZATION; SILK; TEXTILES; WOOL.

DUKE FAMILY

Soon after Washington Duke (1820–1905) returned as a penniless Confederate veteran in 1865 to his small farm near Durham, North Carolina, he launched his family into the home manufacture of smoking tobacco.

It was his youngest child, James Buchanan Duke (1856–1925), however, who quickly proved to be the business genius of the family. After moving into Durham and establishing W. Duke, Sons and Company in the late 1870s, the Dukes followed young "Buck" Duke's lead and gambled on the new Bonsack cigarette machine. The gamble paid off in a large way, for by the late 1880s, W. Duke, Sons and Company was the largest cigarette producer in the nation.

Realizing the immense productivity of the Bonsack machine, J. B. Duke declared in 1889, "The world is now our market." Not only did Duke play a leading role in the creation of the American Tobacco Company in 1890, he also became its first president and led the company in an aggressive program of expansion both in the United States and abroad.

Building tobacco factories in Japan, China, Germany, Australia, and other countries, J. B. Duke "invaded" Britain in 1901, bought a major tobacco firm, and engaged in a fierce competition with the Imperial Tobacco Company, a new combination of British companies. That struggle ended in 1902, when J. B. Duke and his British rivals made a deal: The American Tobacco Company would stay out of Britain, and the Imperial Tobacco Company would stay out of the United States. A new company, the British-American Tobacco Company, would engage in the tobacco trade with the rest of the world. Two-thirds of the new company was owned by the American Tobacco Company, and James B. Duke was its president, but its headquarters were in London. Tobacco globalized early.

SEE ALSO AGRICULTURE; BRITISH-AMERICAN TOBACCO; CARGOES, FREIGHT; CORPORATION, OR LIMITED LIABILITY COMPANY; EDUCATION, OVERVIEW; TOBACCO.

BIBLIOGRAPHY

Durden, Robert F. *The Dukes of Durham, 1865–1929.* Durham, NC: Duke University Press, 1975.

Durden, Robert F. *Bold Entrepreneur: A Life of James B. Duke.* Durham, NC: Carolina Academic Press, 2003.

Robert F. Durden

DU PONT DE NEMOURS FAMILY

Members of the du Pont family played a major role in the evolution of E. I. du Pont de Nemours Company. Established in 1802, it did not become involved in world trade in a major way until World War I, when it was the major provider of munitions to the Allied nations. In 1917 its senior managers, headed by Pierre S. du Pont, began to use nitrocellulose technology to produce chemicals. During the 1920s the company became and has remained the world's largest chemical enterprise.

The company's founder, Éleuthère Irénée du Pont (1771–1834), son of an eminent French physiocrat and student of Europe's leading chemist, Antoine-Laurent Lavoisier (1743–1794), was asked by U.S. president Thomas Jefferson to establish a munitions enterprise in Delaware. He and his son Henry du Pont (1812–1889) provided the gunpowder used in the nation's expansion west. During the Civil War the company became the primary supplier of the Union armies. During the nineteenth century the company's impact on world trade was only the procurement of basic raw materials—nitrates from India and Chile.

In 1902, during the era of corporate consolidation, Pierre S. du Pont (1880–1954) created the modern E. I. du Pont de Nemours Company. After meeting the demands of World War I, Pierre turned the enterprise to commercializing a broad range of chemicals, initially those based on nitroglycerin technology. After retiring as president of the family company in 1919, he became president of General Motors. There, working with Alfred P. Sloan Jr. (1875–1966), he helped to create the modern automobile industry.

At the du Pont company, Pierre's younger brothers succeeded him as president, first Irénée (1876–1963), then Lammont (1880–1954). During the 1920s E. I. du Pont de Nemours diversified broadly into chemicals based largely on German technologies commercialized before World War I. In the 1930s the company pioneered the bringing to market new products based on a new discipline, polymer chemicals. After Lammont's retirement, two of his sons-in-law became company president in succession. Since the 1960s the du Pont family's connection with the company management has decreased steadily.

SEE ALSO CARGOES, FREIGHT; CORPORATION, OR LIMITED LIABILITY COMPANY; PETROLEUM; RUBBER.

BIBLIOGRAPHY

Chandler, Alfred D., Jr., Salsbury, Steven. *Pierre S. DuPont and the Making of Modern Corporations,* New York: Harper & Row, 1971.

Dutton, William S. *Du Pont: One Hundred and Forty Years.* New York: Charles Scribner's Sons, 1949.

Alfred D. Chandler Jr.

EAST INDIA COMPANY, BRITISH

On the last day of the year 1600 Queen Elizabeth I (1533–1603) granted a charter incorporating some 219 members under the title of "The Governor and Company of Merchants of London Trading into the East Indies": this was the body that came to be known as the British or the English East India Company. Along with its rival organization in the Netherlands, the Dutch East India Company, which was chartered just over a year later, the British East India Company stood out as the most remarkable contemporary edifice of commercial capitalism. A process that we now recognize as globalization was underway, and the British East India Company played an important role in this.

As with other Europeans, the principal interest of the English in the East, initially at least, was procuring pepper and other spices for the European market. The first two voyages, of the total of twelve between 1601 and 1612 on separate and terminable account, were to Bantam in Java, where a factory was established in 1602. From 1613, Sumatra became the chief supplier of pepper to the British East India Company. The period between 1613 and 1642 witnessed the operation of three successive joint stocks. The outbreak of the English Civil War in the 1640s caused some dislocation for the company's trade, but matters improved considerably after the grant of the charter of 1657 which provided for a permanent joint stock. The company's monopoly of trade with Asia was compromised in 1813, when the new charter legalized the entry of private traders into the East Indian trade. Twenty years later, the company ceased to be a trading body and was entrusted solely with the running of the colonial ad-ministration of India, a process that had started in 1765 with the company wresting from the Mughal Emperor Shah Alam the revenue collection rights in the province of Bengal. The company was liquidated in 1858 following the assumption by the British Crown of direct responsibility for Indian affairs.

ESTABLISHMENT OF FACTORIES (TRADING STATIONS)

The crucial importance of Indian (particularly Coromandel) textiles in facilitating the spice trade had been brought home to the company quite early. A factory was established in Masulipatnam in 1611, though the first company voyage to the Coromandel coast was not organized until 1614. In the meantime, given Dutch plans to gain a monopoly on spices such as cloves, nutmeg, and mace from the Indoneisan archipelago, armed conflict with the Dutch East India Company (Vereenigde Oost-Indische Compagnie, or VOC) was becoming inevitable. The hostilities erupted in 1618, and the English emerged distinctly the worse of the two. The London agreement of 1619 provided for an English share of one-third in the trade of the Spice Islands, and of one-half in the pepper trade of Java, subject to the English contributing one-third of the cost of maintaining the Dutch garrisons in the area. But Dutch hostility and English resource shortages undermined this arrangement. The 1623 massacre at Amboyna led to a recall of the English factors from the shared centers in the archipelago to Batavia and hastened the process of English withdrawal from the Spice Islands.

Although the English had come to Coromandel in search of textiles for the Southeast Asian markets, their

BRITISH MEN AND INDIAN WOMEN

During the eighteenth century the British East India Company, mainly concerned with profit, had few thoughts of remaking the subcontinent in the British mold. Men such as Robert Clive—the so-called "nabobs"—became rich, living ostentatious lifestyles in India and at home. Many company employees were also eager to learn native ways. India's first British governor-general, Warren Hastings, was learned in several local languages, law codes, and literature. Liaisons between company men and native women were common. In one case a British official maintained a harem of thirteen women! Things changed after 1815 as an evangelical revival swept Britain. British missionaries began spreading Christian doctrines among Indians, and working to outlaw customs that clashed with their Christian sensibilities. Indians naturally resented such cultural interference. Relationships between Indian women and British men became less frequent as officials increasingly brought their wives and families with them to India. Official barriers between British families and the locals were now considered a necessity, resulting in real segregation.

David J. Clarke

attempts to penetrate the Gujarat trade were linked directly to their Euro-Asian trade. A factory was established at Surat in 1613, and regular trade started there and at Ahmedabad, Burhanpur and Agra, with a ship being sent back home directly from Surat in 1615. The president at Surat was also placed in charge of the company's trade in Persia. The Crown leased Bombay to the company in 1668, and in 1687 Bombay superseded Surat as the headquarters of the company in Western India. In the meantime, the company's trade had extended into Bengal in the early 1650s with the establishment of a factory at Hugli.

Although the company exported indigo, saltpeter, and other items from India, the most important commodity the company procured there was textiles. Initially, a part of these textiles was carried to the Indonesian archipelago to pay for the pepper and other spices bought there. The only other Asian market to which the company carried Coromandel textiles was Persia, but the quantities involved were never large. In view of the continuing

poor performance in this area, the company decided in 1661 to withdraw from participation in intra-Asian trade and concentrate its energies and resources on Euro-Asian trade.

THE ROLE OF PRECIOUS METALS

A key element in the Euro-Asian trade in the early modern period was the necessity for the Europeans to pay with precious metals for the Asian goods they procured. This was essentially due to the inability of Europe to supply goods that could be sold in Asia in reasonably large quantities at competitive terms. The growth of this trade could have been constrained by the declining, or at best stagnant, European output of silver, but fortunately, the discovery of the Cape route had coincided with the discovery of the Americas. The working of the Spanish-American silver mines had tremendously expanded the European silver stock, a part of which was available for diversion to Asia for investment in Asian goods. But the availability of silver for export to Asia was only a necessary condition: the sufficient condition was for the European corporate enterprises to be allowed to export silver to Asia. These enterprises had to contend with the prevailing mercantilist prejudice against the export of precious metals. The bullionist—particularly the vulgar bullionist—version of mercantilism equated wealth with precious metals. Considering that the stock of precious metals in the world economy at any given point in time was fixed, the export of these metals from one segment to another automatically involved impoverishment for the former and enrichment for the latter. In the context of such a worldview, the British East India Company was constantly upbraided for exporting silver. Thomas Mun, one of the directors of the company, actively participated in the pamphlet war on the issue and justified the company's policy as the most suited to promote the national interest. In any event, an overwhelming proportion of the total exports of the company continued to be in the form of precious metals.

As for the imports from Asia into Europe, the English company was way behind the Dutch until about 1670. This gap had nearly been bridged, however, by the end of the century, when the average annual English imports had reached approximately £380,000 against the Dutch figure of £420,000. By 1738 to 1740 the English had actually forged ahead of the Dutch, and by the 1770s this gap had widened enormously. Textiles and raw silk accounted for almost 70 percent of the total imports. The remainder was almost entirely accounted for by Chinese tea.

EUROPEAN TRADE AND THE INDIAN ECONOMY

The increase in the output of textiles and other export goods in the subcontinent in response to the secularly ris-

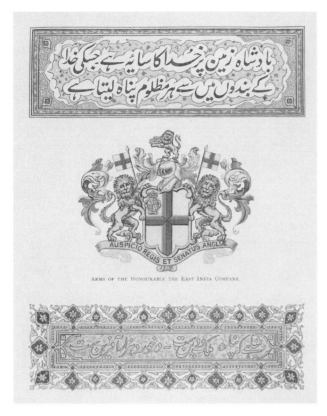

ARMS OF THE HONOURABLE THE EAST INDIA COMPANY.

A coat of arms for the British East India Company. The company was chartered by Queen Elizabeth I in 1600 to directly compete with the Dutch spice trade in the East Indies. Throughout the next two centuries, a battle was fought in the British Parliament that pitted lobbyists from the company who tried to maintain a monopoly over trade in India and private merchants who wanted to deregulate restrictions and open trading up. SURVEY OF INDIA/AKHIL BAKSHI.

ing demand for these goods by the English and the Dutch East India Companies was achieved through a reallocation of resources, a fuller utilization of existing productive capacity, and an increase over time in the capacity itself. In this scenario, the English and other European companies became a vehicle for an expansion in income, output, and employment in the subcontinent. This scenario, however, underwent a substantive modification during the second half of the eighteenth century. The starting point was the assumption of political leverage by the British East India Company in different parts of the subcontinent. The process began in southeastern India, where British victory against the French in 1761 meant that the territories of the English-backed Nawab of Arcot became a client state of the British East India Company. Much more fundamental in importance was the incorporation of Bengal as a province under actual British rule. The 1765 Treaty of Allahabad with the Mughal emperor conferred on the East India Company the *diwani* and the responsibility for the civil administration of Bengal; at

the same time the *wazir* (Mughal official in charge of the region) of Awadh accepted a British alliance and a British garrison. This settlement gave the British rule over some 20 million people in Bengal and access to revenue of about £3 million, and it took British influence nearly up to Delhi. Through an extensive misuse of its newly acquired political power, the company subjected suppliers and artisans in Bengal to complete domination, imposing upon them unilaterally determined terms and conditions which significantly cut into their margin of profit.

FINANCING OF THE IMPORTS FROM INDIA

Seemingly paradoxically, while the British East India Company exports from India were undergoing a substantial increase during the second half of the eighteenth century, the import of bullion by the company into the subcontinent was practically coming to an end. The solution to this puzzle lay in (a) the substantial quantities of rupee receipts obtained by the company locally against bills of exchange issued to English and other European private traders payable in London and other European capitals, and (b) the surplus from the Bengal provincial revenues that the company now collected. The latter represented the principal constituent element in the drain of resources from India to Britain.

MILITARY, FISCAL, AND POLITICAL DIMENSIONS

The commercial and the maritime trade dimensions of the company were thus intimately tied to the military, fiscal, and the political. From the mid-eighteenth century the company became a huge military power; thereafter, by far the largest number of British people in its service in Asia were soldiers. As Indian states passed under their control, the British began to govern provinces through the institutions of the regimes that they so derided. To support its armies and sustain an enlarged commerce, the company needed to maximize its revenues. In Bengal and in parts of South India it inherited systems of revenue extraction, which produced high yields with only limited British intervention. The company also went into partnership with Indian bankers, from whom it raised loans in anticipation of its revenue, and who enabled it to transfer money to support its armies in the field, or from one presidency to another, by their bills of exchange.

By the early nineteenth century more or less equal exchange was giving way to outright British domination. A greater degree of control was being exercised over more of the Indian economy. The so-called colonial pattern of trade involving the export to Asia of manufactured goods such as cotton textiles and the import from there of primary goods, both raw materials and food, was fast replacing the earlier pattern of trade. Colonial exploitation had become the central characteristic feature of the Indo-British encounter.

BIBLIOGRAPHY

Bowen, H. V.; Lincoln, Margarette; and Rigby, Nigel, eds. *The Worlds of the East India Company.* Woodbridge, Suffolk, U.K.: Boydell, 2000.

Chaudhuri, K. N. *The English East India Company: The Study of an Early Joint-Stock Company, 1600–1640.* London: Frank Cass and Company, 1965.

Chaudhuri, K. N. *The Trading World of Asia and the English East India Company, 1660–1760.* Cambridge, U.K.: Cambridge University Press, 1978.

Marshall, P. J. *Problems of Empire: Britain and India, 1757–1813.* London: George Allen and Unwin Ltd., 1968.

Prakash, Om. *The Dutch East India Company and the Economy of Bengal, 1630–1720.* Princeton, NJ: Princeton University Press, 1985.

Prakash, Om. *European Commercial Enterprise in Pre-Colonial India.* Cambridge, U.K.: Cambridge University Press, 1998.

Om Prakash

EAST INDIA COMPANY, DUTCH

At the beginning of the seventeenth century the establishment of two joint-stock overseas trading companies transformed European long-distance maritime commerce. Both the English East India Company (EIC), established on December 31, 1600, by a charter from the English Crown, and the Dutch United East India Company (Vereenigde Oost-Indische Compagnie, or VOC), chartered on March 20, 1602, by the States-General of the Netherlands, were granted exclusive rights to trade to all destinations east of the Cape of Good Hope. The VOC, established with a joint stock of 6 million guilders (the equivalent of about 300 million euros today), was much larger in size and quite different in organization from its English sister organization.

Comparatively speaking, the Dutch were latecomers in Asia, arriving there almost a century after the Portu-guese, although many Dutch and Flemish sailors and soldiers had already sailed to Asia on Portuguese galleons. Consequently, much information about the shipping routes was already known to the Dutch, who had secretly acquired additional rutters (guidebooks that gave sailing directions) and maps in Lisbon. The *Itinerario*, an extensive account of the Portuguese Empire in Asia written by Jan Huygen van Linschoten (1562–1611), a former secretary of the bishop of Goa, described in detail the navigational routes to and within Asia, and also made a scathing comment on the corruption that reigned in the Estado da India at the end of the sixteenth century. The manuscript accompanied the first Dutch fleet that reached West Java in 1595 and was published one year later in various languages.

ESTABLISHMENT AND PEAK YEARS

After the first fleet returned in 1596 a scramble for the Asian market broke loose. Eight different Dutch companies from different ports sent fourteen fleets with a total of sixty-five ships to the Indies, losing eleven ships en route. At the instigation of the influential *landsadvocaat* (government prosecutor) of the Province of Holland, Johan van Oldenbarnevelt (1547–1619), all these companies were combined into one. This explains the VOC's peculiar federalist organization, with six chambers spread over six ports in the provinces of Holland and Zeeland which, depending on their relative size, were represented by one or more directors in the general board of directors, the so-called Gentlemen Seventeen. (Amsterdam had eight seats.) The VOC had to have its charter renewed by the States-General every twenty-one years. Combining all the companies allowed the enormous fluctuation in the prices of Asian import goods such as pepper and spices to be controlled and a common strategy to be followed.

Whereas the EIC was first of all established as a trading organization, the VOC also had another goal: to carry the struggle for independence against the Iberian foe overseas. Thus the historian C. R. Boxer has styled the VOC as "a company of the ledger and the sword" (Boxer 1965). Because of warfare against the Portuguese in the Moluccas, no less than one-third of the original investments was spent on fortresses in those islands, which of course resulted in a much larger overhead.

One of the greatest challenges that European nations trading in Asia faced before the Industrial Revolution was how to pay for the tropical goods and luxury articles they imported. Initially, Europe had very little to offer apart from woolen cloth and bullion. Jan Pieterszoon Coen (1587–1629), who served the VOC first as director general and later as governor-general, developed a master plan to deal with this conundrum. Witnessing the success of

Engraving of a canal at Batavia, Indonesia. *Jan Pieterszoon Coen established an extensive intra-Asian trading network and set up headquarters in Batavia, present day Jakarta, Indonesia. The profits generated from trading within Asia paid for the return goods sent to Europe.* © BETTMANN/CORBIS. REPRODUCED BY PERMISSION.

his Portuguese rivals in Asia, he stressed the importance of creating an extensive intra-Asian trading network spreading from Mocha on the Arabian Peninsula to Hirado in Japan, which would enable the company to gain such high returns that the profits from intra-Asian trade could pay for the return goods sent to Europe. Textiles from Gujarat were to be traded for pepper and gold in Sumatra; pepper from Banten on West Java for silver rials and textiles from Coromandel in India; Chinese merchandise such as iron ware, silk, porcelain, and gold for sandalwood, pepper, and rials in Banten, and so on.

To improve the supervision of this trading network Coen established a new headquarters at the site of the former Javanese port principality of Jacatra (today, Jakarta) and renamed it Batavia. Batavia remained the capital of the Dutch East Indies until decolonization in 1949. According to Coen the VOC's Asian trade should rest on

at least three pillars: the highly profitable textile trade between the Coromandel Coast in India and the Indonesian archipelago, a monopoly on the spice trade in the Banda archipelago and the Moluccas in the eastern Indonesian archipelago, and trade with China and Japan. Apart from the direct trade with China, which failed to materialize, the other objectives were met, yet the goal to be relieved of the supply of precious metals from Europe was never attained. By the 1660s the VOC had dislodged and replaced the Portuguese (and Spaniards at Tidore) in the Moluccas (1603–1662), Malacca (1641) and Makassar (1667) in the Indonesian archipelago, Ceylon (1640–1657), Cochin (1663) on the Malabar coast, and Negapatnam (1659) on the Coromandel coast in India. The Dutch replaced the Portuguese on the tiny island of Deshima in Japan, but in 1662 they were driven from the island of Formosa by the Ming loyalist and warlord Zheng Chenggong (alias Coxinga).

The VOC reached its apogee in the 1690s. On average, eighty to ninety company ships were plying the Asian waters, serving twenty-two factories from Persia to Japan. In the Dutch Republic every chamber had its own warehouses and shipyards, where the workmen who built the ships who were all in the service of the local branch of the company, thus boosting the local urban economy. In addition to approximately 2,500 employees in the Netherlands, around 16,000 employees, merchants, soldiers, and sailors served the company in Asia; this number peaked at about 23,000 in 1750. The tropical climate claimed the lives of many company servants. Only one-third of the 973,000 men who traveled to Asia on 4,700 ships during the 200-year existence of the VOC eventually returned to the home country, on 3,300 ships.

Generally speaking, three fleets annually left the Dutch shores. Often warships through the English Channel as far as the Atlantic Ocean escorted the outward-bound fleets of five to ten East Indiamen. During the seventeenth century a large Dutch East Indiaman of 700 tons carried, apart from its cargo, between 250 and 300 people—that is, about 140 sailors, 120 soldiers, and a dozen passengers. The majority of sailors came from the Dutch provinces and Scandinavia, but most of the soldiers originated from the German principalities. The passengers were generally high officials with their wives and children.

Over the years the relative importance of the various trade goods changed substantially. Certain goods such as pepper and spices from the archipelago and cinnamon from Ceylon continued to form the mainstay of the trade, but from the 1680s onward the trade in sugar and textiles became increasingly important, closely followed by fashionable products such as coffee (from Java) and tea (from China), which were to revolutionize European drinking habits.

DECLINE IN THE EIGHTEENTH CENTURY

Around the middle of the eighteenth century the character of the VOC underwent a subtle change. Intra-Asian trading activities diminished while the trade between Asia and Europe intensified. At the same time, the company strengthened its grip on large territories in Ceylon and Java by intervening in local succession strife. Thus an organization, which at first had been primarily an overseas trading enterprise, increasingly developed into a large colonial empire. At the end of the eighteenth century the VOC went into a decline. In the past, corruption and lax management have been held responsible for its downfall; indeed, its acronym was even jokingly referred to as *Vergaan Onder Corruptie* ("decayed under corruption"). Increasing competition from the English East India Company, which frustrated all further Dutch activity in India after it conquered Bengal, also played a role. So did the private "country traders," who not only undercut the prices of the VOC on its trading routes but also surreptitiously evaded its monopolies. The death blow, however, was dealt by the Fourth Anglo-Dutch War (1780–1784). When the British navy seized almost all homeward-bound ships from the Indies and for a long period all ties with the colonies were cut off, the company headquarters in the Netherlands could no longer pay its large debts. Virtually bankrupt, the VOC was nationalized by the Dutch government in 1795; when the company's charter expired five years later, its debts amounted to more than 200 million guilders.

The VOC left behind extensive archives in The Hague, Jakarta, Colombo in Sri Lanka, and Chennai in India—in all, approximately 4 kilometers of manuscripts. It was a well-organized bureaucratic institution with a vast information network dedicated to maintaining the company's trading rights and its political position in Asia. With the exception of most of the bookkeeping records, the bulk of the original archives have been preserved, and part of it has even been published. These archives represent the most important source in any Western language on Monsoon Asia in the seventeenth and eighteenth centuries.

SEE ALSO AMSTERDAM; BENGAL; CHINA; COEN, JAN PIETERSZOON; COFFEE; EAST INDIA COMPANY, BRITISH; EAST INDIA COMPANY, OTHER; EMPIRE, BRITISH; EMPIRE, DUTCH; EMPIRE, FRENCH; EMPIRE, MING; EMPIRE, MUGHAL; EMPIRE, PORTUGUESE; EMPIRE, QING; EMPIRE, SPANISH; ENTREPÔT SYSTEM; ETHNIC GROUPS, CANTONESE; ETHNIC GROUPS, FUJIANESE; FACTORIES; GOLD AND SILVER; GUJARAT; IMPERIALISM; INDIA; INDIAN OCEAN; INDONESIA; JAPAN; JOINT-STOCK COMPANY; LABORERS, COERCED; MELAKA; MERCANTILISM; NAGASAKI; PRIVATEERING; PROTECTION COSTS; RAFFLES, SIR THOMAS STAMFORD; RICE; SMUGGLING; SOUTH AFRICA; SOUTH CHINA SEA; SPICES AND THE SPICE TRADE; SRI LANKA; SUGAR, MOLASSES, AND RUM; TEXTILES; TOBACCO; WOMEN TRADERS OF SOUTHEAST ASIA.

BIBLIOGRAPHY

Boxer, C. R. *The Dutch Seaborne Empire, 1600–1800.* London: Pelican, 1965.

Bruijn, J. R., et al., eds. *Dutch-Asiatic Shipping in the Seventeenth and Eighteenth Centuries.* 3 vols. The Hague, Netherlands: Rijksgeschiedkundige Publicatiën, 1979–1987.

Coolhaas, W. P. *Generale Missiven van Gouverneurs-Generaal en Raden aan Heren XVII der Verenigde Oostindische Compagnie (General Missives of the Governors-General and Councillors to the Gentlemen XVII of the United East India Company)* (trans.). 11 vols. The Hague, Netherlands: Rijksgeschiedkundige Publicatiën, 1960–2004.

Furber, Holden. *Rival Empires of the Orient, 1600–1800.*
Minneapolis: University of Minnesota Press, 1976.

Gaastra, F. S. *The Dutch East India Company: Expansion and Decline* Zutphen, Netherlands: Walburg Pers, 2002.

Raben, R., ed. *The Archives of the Dutch East India Company (1602–1795).* The Hague, Netherlands: Sdu Publishers, 1992.

The Voyage of John Huyghen van Linschoten to the East Indies. From the old English translation of 1598; 2 vols, London: Hakluyt Society 70–71 (1885).

Valentijn, F. *Oud en Nieuw Oost-Indiën* (trans.), 8 vols. [1724–1726]. Franeker, Netherlands: Van Wijnen Publishers, 2002–2004.

Leonard Blussé

EAST INDIA COMPANY, OTHER

The Danish Company (founded in 1616), the French Company (1664), and the Swedish Company (1731) had organizations similar to those of the British Company and the Dutch Company in that they were joint-stock companies holding monopolies on the maritime business between Europe and East beyond the Cape of Good Hope. However, the state retained approximately one-third of the capital in each of the former three companies, which was not the case for the British and Dutch companies. In this way the Danish, French, and Swedish Companies were closer to the Casa da India of the Portuguese, in which the Crown took care of the expenses of administration and defense of settlements as well as of the expenses of armament of vessels, in exchange for the monopoly on the transport and sale of certain spices (such as pepper) and the perception of tax of freight on the traders who wanted to load goods.

Four nations were active in the local business. The Portuguese had a good network organized in the sixteenth century, when they were the only European navigators to go in Asia. The head of this network was situated in Goa, on the western coast of India, and it extended to Timor, in the east end of the Sunda Isles, and to Macao, in southern China, with several intermediate factories. The French were established in Pondicherry on the east coast of India, in Mahé on the western coast, and in Chandernagor in Bengal. The Danes were settled in Tranquebar near Pondicherry as well as in Bengal. The Swedes traded in the ports of India, but they had no permanent settlements there because the other Europeans managed to dissuade the Moguls from accepting their installation. All could travel to Canton, a port in the south of China open to business with the Europeans, but they were forbidden to settle there. The only permanent establishment in the region was the Portuguese factory at Macao.

The French and the British competed for the market for cotton fabrics from southern India, which were very popular in Europe. The rivalry was very lively in 1749, when the sales of the French company in Europe was close to that of the sales of the English company, but it ended in 1760 with the military defeat of the French in the Seven Years' War.

An important source of profits for the French, Danes, and Swedes was tea. They obtained it in Canton from the *cohong*, the association of Chinese traders that held the monopoly on trade with the Europeans, who were not authorized to go inland. In the middle of eighteenth century the French sent three vessels to Canton each year; the Swedes, two; the Danes, one or two. The tea, which was generally of the most common variety, *bohea*, was for the most part intended for smuggling into Great Britain; the tax on tea was 106 percent in Britain. The Commutation Act of 1784, which reduced the amount of the tariff to 12.5 percent, precipitated the disappearance of the illegal trade and, consequently, a decrease in the three nations' traffic in China.

With the development of the British dominion in India in the second half of eighteenth century, these same companies found a new source of profit by offering to the employees of the East India Company services in returning their wealth to Europe. Against the delivery of capital in Asia they gave exchange letters for Paris, Stockholm, or Copenhagen. About 5 million pounds of sterling were so transferred. This arrangement suited the companies, which no longer had to bring the loads of precious metals which were previously necessary to buy return goods; it was a problem for India, which lost resources important for their currency circulation. Amidst growing British control of India, the Danes and the Swedes took advantage of their neutrality during the American and French Revolutions and the Napoleonic Wars (at least until 1807) to develop their businesses.

But the increasingly powerful presence of the British also caused problems for the companies. In Bengal the French and the Danes had to pay 25 percent more for their goods than the English, and they had to give up dealing in opium because the East India Company asserted a monopoly over production. The consequence was a drop in profits. This was amplified by the wars, during which company vessels were either detained for military operations or were condemned upon their return to Europe, following long journeys without the possibility of repair. State shareholders of the companies, who had to pay off war debts, refused to contribute to company finances, so the companies faced bankruptcy. The French Company was in this situation in 1769 after the Seven Years' War, and it was liquidated because it could not continue trafficking arms. The French then set up trade at Port Louis on the Island of France (now Mauritius), a free port where Asian goods were exchanged for European goods. The Swedish Company went bankrupt and disappeared in 1813. The same fate overtook the Danish Company in 1815, when its establishments in India were sold to the British.

SEE ALSO BENGAL; CANTON SYSTEM; CHINA; DRUGS, ILLICIT; EAST INDIA COMPANY, BRITISH; EAST INDIA COMPANY, DUTCH; EMPIRE, BRITISH; EMPIRE, DUTCH; EMPIRE, FRENCH; EMPIRE, MUGHAL; EMPIRE, PORTUGUESE; EMPIRE, QING; ENTREPÔT SYSTEM; FACTORIES; FREE PORTS; FREE TRADE, THEORY AND PRACTICE; GOLD AND SILVER; GUANGZHOU; GUJARAT; IMPERIALISM; INDIA; INDIAN OCEAN; JOINT-STOCK COMPANY; LABORERS, COERCED; MERCANTILISM; MONOPOLY AND OLIGOPOLY; PROTECTION COSTS; SMUGGLING; SPICES AND THE SPICE TRADE; SRI LANKA; TEA; TEXTILES.

BIBLIOGRAPHY

Ames, Glenn J. *Colbert, Mercantilism and the French Quest for Asian Trade.* Dekalb: Northern Illinois University Press, 1996.

Blusse, Leonard, and Gaastra, Femme, eds. *Companies and Trade: Essays on Overseas Trading Companies during the Ancient Regime.* Leiden, Netherlands: Leiden University Press, 1981.

Boxer, Charles Ralph. *The Portuguese Seaborn Empire, 1415–1825.* London: Hutchinson, 1969.

Bruijn, Jaap, and Gaastra, Femme, eds. *Ships, Sailors, and Spices: East India Companies and Their Shipping in the 16th, 17th, and 18th Centuries.* Amsterdam: Neha, 1993.

Feldboek, Ole. *India Trade under the Danish Flag, 1772–1808.* Copenhagen: Lund Studentlitteratur, 1969.

Haudrère, Philippe. *La Compagnie française des Indes au XVIIIème siècle, 1719–1795.* 2nd edition. Paris: Les Indes Savantes, 2003.

Koninckx, Christian. *The First and Second Charter Flights of the Swedish East India Company (1731–1766): A Contribution to the Maritime, Economic, and Social History of Northwestern Europe in Its Relationships with the Far East.* Courtrai, Belgium: Van Ghemmert Publishing, 1988.

Philippe Haudrère

GEORGE EASTMAN
1854–1932

George Eastman, born in Waterville, New York, took up photography as a hobby in 1877 and soon patented and marketed photographic devices in London. In 1885 he opened an English branch and in 1891 an English manufacturing company. By the time the Brownie camera was marketed worldwide in 1900, the Eastman Kodak Company was the largest photographic materials company in the world.

Eastman's success relied partly on inventions and innovations, but more on his ability to recruit skilled employees, sell his products, outmaneuver his competitors, and raise capital. His two key innovations were roll film and small, handheld Kodak cameras to replace bulky ones requiring tripods. Film found unexpected markets in the new areas of x-rays and motion pictures.

His business fundamentals included catchy trademarks and slogans ("You press the button, we do the rest"), mass production, interchangeable parts, low prices, foreign distribution, extensive advertising, selling by demonstration, the introduction of new products annually, continued improvements, and chain-store retailing.

The photographic business was highly competitive, but Eastman was able to win world dominance because he transformed photography from a cumbersome professional skill into a hobby for everyone. Beginning as a visionary entrepreneur, he became one of the great business leaders of his time.

SEE ALSO INFORMATION AND COMMUNICATIONS.

BIBLIOGRAPHY

Ackerman, Carl. *George Eastman.* Boston and New York: Houghton Mifflin, 1930.

Brayer, Elizabeth. *George Eastman: A Biography.* Baltimore and London: Johns Hopkins University Press, 1996.

Elizabeth Brayer

EBAY

Exchanges of goods between individuals and between individuals and small businesses have traditionally been carried out by means of direct sales, classified ads, secondhand markets, or intermediaries such as auctioneers. These markets are inefficient due to their regional fragmentation, which makes it both difficult and costly to exchange information and complete transactions. Additional disadvantages are the limited number of goods on offer, the high cost of transactions involving intermediaries, and the unreliability of the prices established.

To overcome some of these disadvantages, Pierre Omidyar (b. 1967), a French-born 1988 graduate of Tufts University in the United States and the son of Iranian immigrants to France, set up AuctionWeb in September 1995 using a personal web page. Soon the name was changed to eBay ("electronic Bay"), after San Francisco Bay.

The company was founded on the conviction that there was a niche to be filled in person-to-person trading over the internet. It created a virtual auction marketplace enabling at any time of night or day direct contact between buyers and vendors, who exchange information, list goods for sale, and complete transactions.

Sales, revenue, and profit, 1996–2003 (in millions of $)							
	1996	1997	1998	1999	2000	2001	2002	2003
Sales	7	95	745	2,805	5,422	9,319	14,868	23,779
Net revenues	32.1	41.4	86.1	224.7	431.4	748.8	1,214.1	2,165
Net profit	3.3	7.1	7.3	9.6	48.3	90.5	249.9	441.8

SOURCE: Compiled from eBay Annual Reports (1998–2003).

THE GALE GROUP.

In order to participate, the buyer must register in eBay through the web page before bidding in an auction. At the predetermined close time of the auction, the buyer pays the seller by bank transfer, and the seller delivers the auctioned object by post. eBay has several ways to ensure the integrity of its auctions, including a feedback forum that allows the buyer and seller in any transaction to rate the experience, and an insurance program designed to protect buyers who send their money but do not receive the goods.

Oriented at first toward collectors—for example, philatelists or numismatists—until February 1996 the service was free, and therefore attracted a large number of clients. Thereafter, a 5 percent commission was charged for goods sold for less than $25 and a 2.5 percent commission for goods over $25. The workforce of one in mid-1996 (the founder himself) had increased to 1,927 by March 2001 and to 6,000 by early 2004. The evolving company also underwent major changes in its management. In 1998 the arrival of Margaret Whitman, a former executive of Hasbro Inc., Florists Transworld Delivery, and the Walt Disney Company, injected a new dynamism into the eBay administration. That same year the company was floated on the New York Stock Exchange, and shares rose from $18 to $47 on the first day. Between September 1998 and the end of 2001 shares rose from $18 to $760 (splits), and the company's value went from $20 million in 1997 to over $16 billion in 2001, and to $40.9 billion in December 2003.

The increase in the number of products offered for sale has also been spectacular. From 300,000 listed products in 1996, the number rose to almost 26 million in 2004. There are 27,000 different listing categories, ranging from collectors' items such as stamps, coins, books, and antiques, to everyday commodities such as computers, cameras, and even cars (which accounted for sales of $4.2 billion in the third quarter of 2003 in the United States alone) and real estate.

As a company, eBay has grown by means of internal development and the acquisition of related businesses. Many of these acquisitions have been intended to com-

plement eBay's own sector with companies that can solve the problems arising from the ever-increasing scope of the business. For example, Billpoint Inc. centralized payment by credit card over the internet in 1999, and PayPal handled payments by email in thirty-eight countries in 2001. In July 2000 Half.com, a fixed-price, person-to-person trading website, was also acquired. In addition, international acquisitions have been made with a view to extending the customer base in other countries.

Table 1 shows the evolution in sales, net revenue, and net profit in the period 1996 to 2003, with a growth rate of over 75 percent in the last year. Despite the dot-com crisis that began in 2000 and competition from other e-commerce entities (including those which have utilized a similar system to eBay's), eBay has managed to maintain consistently high growth rates and increasing share prices. It is considered to be the company that has best weathered the dot-com crisis.

EBAY'S CONTRIBUTION TO INTERNATIONAL COMMERCE

The U.S. market is the driving force behind the growth of eBay's electronic commerce. This growth is based on the evolution of the company itself (sixty centers in 2002) and on the acquisition of U.S.-based companies (e.g., Jump Incorporated online auctions in 1998, and Butterfield and Butterfield jewelry and antiques in 1999), some of which are more inclined toward international trade (Kruse Inc. car auctions in 1999). eBay transactions accounted for 16 percent ($4.9 billion) of all e-commerce (not including travel, food, and drink) in the United States in 2000, and 22 percent ($13.3 billion) in the third quarter of 2003.

Since 1998 eBay has put into practice an expansion strategy in order to compete with companies such as Amazon.com, America Online, Lycos, Yahoo!, and Microsoft. Growth has been encouraged by means of establishing eBay websites in the United Kingdom, Canada, Australia, New Zealand, Austria, and Switzerland. Additionally, eBay has acquired existing e-auction companies in several countries: iBazar in France, giving access to

Meg Whitman, president and CEO of eBay, delivers a keynote address at the Comdex 2001 convention in Las Vegas. eBay revolutionized internet usage by creating the first major online marketplace that brought buyers and sellers together.
© REUTERS/CORBIS. REPRODUCED BY PERMISSION.

Italy, Spain, Belgium, Holland, and Brazil; alando.de.ag in Germany; NeoCom Technology Company Ltd. in Taiwan; and EachNet Inc. in China. In 2001 eBay invested in the Korean company Internet Auction Co. and established a strategic alliance with MercadoLibre, which has webs installed all over Latin America. All in all, eBay transactions were possible in 132 countries in 2003.

This international activity produced a rise in the number of users from 3 million in the third quarter of 2000 to 33 million in the same quarter of 2003, for an annual net revenue of $658 million. In Europe, Germany and the United Kingdom are the centers of highest activity. The data for Germany indicate a rapid rise in the number of users from 1.1 million in the third quarter of 2000 to 11.4 million in the same quarter of 2003, and a net revenue of $368 million, with 8.5 million items on sale in March 2004 (accounting for 33.3% of eBay auctions). In the United Kingdom the number of users increased from 200,000 in the third quarter of 2000 to 4.3 million in the same quarter of 2003, and a net revenue of $100 million, with 2.1 million items on sale in March

2004 (8.3% of eBay auctions). In Europe the number of users grew to 19.4 million in the third quarter of 2003, and a net revenue of $526 million, with 11.6 million items on sale in March 2004 (45% of eBay auctions).

Although the initial growth of eBay was based on trade by auction, beginning in 2000 there was a change in strategy to make the distribution system available to companies offering goods at fixed prices. Thus, certain large companies such as IBM, Palm, Sun, Disney, Kodak, and Microsoft started to sell off their goods via eBay, accounting for 5 percent of eBay trade in 2001. However, individuals and small businesses make up the bulk of eBay clients (95% in 2003). Many of them discovered that the eBay marketplace is a place to do business—to put it simply, a place to "sell things"—providing a platform that reduces the cost of managing their own websites, cutting out the middleman, and dealing directly with the customer. In January 2002 eBay Business was set up with the aim of grouping together the products that could be acquired by companies and thus make transactions easier.

Data drawn directly from the search engines show the increasing potential of the eBay Stores, whose products are separated from the usual eBay categories. In March 2004 the stores sold 10.2 million items, made up of 8 million items from the United States, 700,000 from Germany, 500,000 from the United Kingdom, and 400,000 from Canada. This clearly illustrates the growing importance of stores sales, especially in the most developed countries: 40 percent of total eBay sales in the United States, 43 percent in Canada, 19 percent in the United Kingdom, and 7.6 percent in Germany.

The 2003 United Nations report on e-commerce highlighted how society had been changed by the internet and information and communication technologies over the previous ten years. This transformation has allowed companies, governments, and the population at large to effect productive changes that enhance development. Nevertheless, an analysis of eBay's data on electronic trade shows that North America, the European Union, and Australia account for 95.9 percent of the products on sale. In contrast, Africa, Asia, and Central and South America, which are less-developed areas, account for less than 1.7 percent of the 25.5 million products on offer in the traditional eBay format in 2004 (another 10 million products were available in developed countries by means of the stores system).

SEE ALSO INFORMATION AND COMMUNICATIONS.

BIBLIOGRAPHY

Cohen, Adam. *The Perfect Store: Inside eBay.* Boston: Little, Brown, 2002.

eBay Annual Reports (1998–2003). San José, CA: Author, 2003.

United Nations. *E-commerce and Development Report 2003.* New York and Geneva: Author, 2003.

Donato Gómez-Díaz
José Céspedes-Lorente

ECONOMICS, NEOCLASSICAL

Since the publication of Adam Smith's *Wealth of Nations* in 1776, most economists have been committed to the principle that voluntary trade between equally competent agents is mutually beneficial. Those in the orthodox tradition, spanning both the classical and neoclassical periods, maintained that humans are equally competent. Smith and John Stuart Mill present the orthodox case in the earlier period, and Eli Heckscher, Jacob Viner, and Paul Samuelson make the case in the later period. From the presumption of human homogeneity, it followed that voluntary trade was mutually beneficial and restraints of trade were bad policy. For those neoclassical economists who held that competence varies—F. Y. Edgeworth, Alfred Marshall, and F. W. Taussig are discussed below—it was less clear that trade between inferior and superior agents is mutually beneficial. The key policy questions that followed were how to direct inferior decision makers, and how best to use power (national or otherwise) to restrict trade.

TRADE THEORY

Neoclassical economics is generally said to have begun in about 1870 with the near-simultaneous publication of major works by Léon Walras, William Stanley Jevons, and Carl Menger. Each of these explicated the benefits associated with voluntary exchange. Jevons attempted to distinguish his approach from "the mazy and preposterous assumptions" of the classical economists, including David Ricardo and "his equally able and wrong-headed admirer, John Stuart Mill" (Jevons 1870, pp. xliv, li). To do so, he placed utility, as opposed to cost of production, at the center of economic analysis. The key economic phenomenon requiring explanation was the act of exchange. Given prices, Jevons held that exchange between any two or more individuals, or "trading bodies," occurred as long as a preponderance of utility gain resulted (Jevons 1871, pp. 88f). As Jevons put it, "the keystone of the whole Theory of Exchange" was that exchange ceased when the ratio of exchange equaled the inverted ratio of the final degrees of utility (Jevons 1871, p. 95; Peart 2003).

In 1887 an engineer who is remembered today as the first English economist to publish supply and demand diagrams drew a picture to represent such exchanges in 1887 (Jenkin 1887, p. 150). Fleeming Jenkin's drawing shows the participants in exchange as faceless equals. In this dance-like drawing, Jenkin shows five individuals exchanging, with arrows indicating flows from one individual to another. The order is circular and nonhierarchical, each actor in the drama of markets has private goals, and these goals are revealed in the spontaneous market order. The drawing constituted Jenkin's answer to attacks on trade theory by the English art critic John Ruskin. Ruskin had argued that trade is zero-sum, and competent people gain only what incompetent people lose. By contrast, in Jenkin's society of equals no one has the power to direct others, and trade benefits all.

The key presupposition for the analysis of trade is therefore whether people are equally competent. Until about 1850, economists held that people are essentially the same. Adam Smith saw no difference between the street porter and the philosopher; the appropriate criterion for a policy advisor was the well-being of the majority. J. S. Mill argued that a sympathetic majority could be depended upon to restrain its power for predation (Peart-

Levy 2005). But post-Darwin, some economists questioned the presumption of equal capacity. Neoclassical economists, such as Edgeworth in 1881, emphasized that because humans were evolved creatures, it was unscientific to suppose that all humans possess the same capacity for work and happiness.

As a result of these supposed variations in human capacity, early neoclassical economists held that some agents are ill-equipped to make trades over time. Observing a widespread preference for present over future consumption, economists such as Jevons, Marshall, Irving Fisher, and A. C. Pigou took this as evidence that the "foresight" or "will power" of the laboring classes was defective, characterized by what Pigou called a "defective" "telescopic faculty" (Pigou 1920, p. 25). Marshall suggested that the "prudent" consumer "endeavour[s] to distribute his means between all their several uses, present and future, in such a way that they will have in each the same marginal utility" (Marshall 1890, p. 119). But, Marshall argued, the laboring classes lacked "prudence," and they consequently "discount" the future (p. 120). He pointed to the resulting "great evil" of his time: parents in the "lower ranks of society" failed to invest optimally in the education of their children, because of the "comparative weakness of their power of distinctly realizing the future" (p. 562). Fisher distinguished between "foresight" and "willpower," and argued that the lower classes were particularly susceptible to lack both attributes (Fisher 1910, p. 376).

The resulting conclusion for such early neoclassical economists was that, without direction to assist them, the laboring classes are unable to decide correctly how much to save, what investment to make in human capital, or how many children to have (Peart 2000). Neoclassical economists, who regarded the laboring classes as myopic, consequently urged policy makers to intervene and direct such choices. The issue of free versus directed choices in the context of sameness or difference also characterized the analysis of international trade.

INTERNATIONAL TRADE

In 1776 Adam Smith argued that specialization is productivity enhancing, and trade is mutually beneficial because more things can be produced. Specialization follows least-cost routes, which cross national borders. In the neoclassical period Edgeworth demonstrated that trade can be utility enhancing, even when physical output remains unchanged.

The question of equal competence becomes most important at national borders. When defined by "the immobility of industrial agents" (Edgeworth 1894, p. 35), international trade requires that we explain why costs of mobility jump discontinuously at the border. One an-

swer is immigration restrictions (Viner 1937, p. 598). Edgeworth urged that a nation is an analytical unit because our concern for others is discontinuous across national borders, and so a policy that takes from foreigners is feasible (1894, p. 49).

The key question for neoclassical trade theorists was therefore whether people in one nation differed from those in another. In 1911 Taussig argued for difference. In a restatement of Thomas Carlyle's 1849 argument (Peart-Levy 2005), Taussig claimed that the worker in warm climates "lacks endurance and spirit":

In tropical and semitropical countries the conditions of living are on the whole easier than in temperate countries. Some sorts of food are on the whole free or nearly free, and protection does not need to be provided against the cost of winter. But the climate saps energy, and checks the development of physical vigor and intellectual capacity. Hence the peoples of temperate regions, from the very obstacles they have to overcome, gain resources within themselves, which lead eventually to greater prosperity. So it is with individuals. He who has always had abundant means at his command often lacks endurance and spirit, and in the end is surpassed in happiness as well as in riches by him who had to face harder conditions at the start. (Taussig 1911, pp. 6–7)

In 1919 Heckscher made the contrary claim "that labor in different countries is of the same quality" (Heckscher 1991, p. 57). Samuelson reiterated the point in 1948 (Samuelson 1948, p. 182).

Early-twentieth-century economists who followed Taussig's reasoning urged policy makers to place restrictions on immigration from countries populated by so-called inferior workers (Peart-Levy 2005, chapter 5). The next question was whether trade restrictions on goods were also justified. Taussig addressed this in the context of the "yellow peril":

Another impression or belief, closely related to this, is that not only price and money wages, but real incomes and standards of living would be brought to one uniform level everywhere by unfettered international trade and international competition. Hence the uneasiness, even terror, about the "yellow peril"; a supposed danger that the teeming millions of the East will compete with the peoples of the West and reduce the economic conditions of all to a common low level. (Taussig 1927, p. 154)

According to Taussig, trade of this sort will not equalize incomes (Taussig 1927, p. 154).

But the line of inquiry pioneered by Hecksher (1919) and Bertil Ohlin (1924), which culminates in Samuelson (1948), showed that under traditional assumptions the costless mobility of goods obviates the movement of factors. Thus, a restriction of immigration may be insufficient to prevent the equalizing tendency of international trade.

POWER AS GOAL

Once some neoclassical economists came to embrace a hierarchy of human desert, the question emerged, how far are the people of one nation justified in exploiting the people of another? As a matter of pure theory dating from J. S. Mill, there are circumstances under which this can be done (Edgeworth 1894, Samuelson 1962). Heckscher, however, saw this as a dangerous policy road. Along with restrictive economic policy, he foresaw the use of a conjunction of policies designed to exploit helpless people in one nation in the name of national power. Mercantilism is his exemplar:

> Population policy bore the same stamp, the slave trade being in many respects only side of this policy. The innumerable letters with regard to the populating of the French colonies with young girls, who were sent thither by shiploads, usually from Houses of Correction, but sometimes also young country girls, were almost of the nature of instructions for human breeding-studs. In the same breath mention is made of shiploads of women, mares and sheep; the methods of propagating human beings and cattle being regarded as roughly on the same plane. (Heckscher 1955, 2: 300)

When a country comes to exploit those outside its boundaries, its people come to regard those others as different, perhaps even as animals. With, perhaps, eugenics policies in mind, Heckscher expressed concern at mid-twentieth century that such attitudes were returning (Heckscher 1955, p. 301). Neoclassical economists who advocated free trade, with full knowledge of the possibility of nation-specific gains from restrictions, reveal their cosmopolitan egalitarianism.

SEE ALSO KEYNES, JOHN MAYNARD; MILL, JOHN STUART; THEORIES OF INTERNATIONAL TRADE.

BIBLIOGRAPHY

Edgeworth, F. Y. *Mathematical Psychics.* London: C. Kegan Paul, 1881.

Edgeworth, F. Y. "Theory of International Values." *Economic Journal* 4 (March 1894) 35–50.

Fisher, Irving. *Elementary Principles of Economics* [1910]. New York: Macmillan, 1913.

Heckscher, Eli F. *Mercantilism,* revised edition, ed. E. F. Söderlund, tr. Mendel Shapiro. London: George Allen and Unwin, 1955.

Heckscher, Eli F., and Ohlin, Bertil. *Heckscher-Ohlin Trade Theory* [1919–1924]. Tr. and ed. Harry Flam and M. June Flanders. London: George Allen & Unwin, 1991.

Jenkin, Fleeming. *Papers, Literary, Scientific, &c.* Vol. 2. London and New York: Longmans, Green, 1887.

Jevons, William Stanley. *Theory of Political Economy* [1871]. 4th edition. London: Macmillan, 1911.

Marshall, Alfred. *Principles of Economics* [1890]. 8th edition. London: Macmillan, 1930.

Peart, Sandra J. "Irrationality and Intertemporal Choice in Early Neoclassical Thought." *Canadian Journal of Economics* 33 (February 2000): 175–188.

Peart, Sandra J. "Introduction." In *W. S. Jevons: Critical Responses,* ed. Sandra J. Peart. London: Routledge, 2003.

Peart, Sandra J., and Levy, David M. *From Equality to Hierarchy: The "Vanity of the Philosopher" in Post-Classical Economics.* Ann Arbor: University of Michigan Press, 2005.

Pigou, A. C. *The Economics of Welfare* [1920]. 3rd edition. London: Macmillan, 1929.

Samuelson, Paul A. "International Trade and the Equalization of Factor Prices." *Economic Journal* 58 (June 1948): 163–184.

Samuelson, P. A. "The Gains from International Trade Once Again." *Economic Journal* 72 (December 1962): 820–829.

Smith, Adam. *An Inquiry into the Nature and Causes of the Wealth of Nations* [1776]. Ed. W. B. Todd. Oxford, U.K.: Clarendon Press, 1976.

Taussig, F. W. *Principles of Economics* [1911]. 3rd revised edition. New York: Macmillan, 1923.

Taussig, F. W. *International Trade* [1927]. New York: Augustus M. Kelley, 1966.

Viner, Jacob. *Studies in the Theory of International Trade.* New York: Harper and Brothers, 1937.

David M. Levy
Sandra J. Peart

EDUCATION, OVERVIEW

From time immemorial, human societies have found ways to transmit cultural practices across generations, but only in the last 500 years has schooling become widespread. In 1500 there were few societies in which more than 10 percent of their populations would have attended formal schooling during childhood, or in which their adult populations had mastered the rudiments of literacy. By 1960 the majority of adults in the world did possess basic literacy skills (see Table 1). However, by then major regions of the world still varied widely in their literacy rates, and literacy rates of women were substantially below those of men (see Table 2).

By 1800 a clear majority of adults in North America, Scandinavia, and Germany possessed basic literacy skills. By 1900 the populations of not only these regions but also much of the rest of Western Europe was approaching close to universal adult literacy. Throughout the rest of the world, widespread adult literacy was still uncommon as of 1900, but there were exceptions such as Japan and

Adult literacy rates in major regions of the world c. 1960

Major region	Percent of adult population (15+) literate c. 1960
World	60
Africa	19
Northern America	97.6
Latin America	67.5
Asia	44.8
Europe	94.7
Oceania	88.5
Arab States	19

SOURCE: Adapted from Graff 1987.

THE GALE GROUP.

Male versus female literacy rates in various groups of countries c. 1970

Group of countries	Male literacy rate (age 15+)	Female literacy rate (age 15+)	Ratio of female to male literacy
World	71.5	54.8	.77
Developing countries	60.2	35.8	.59
Least developed countries	37.9	15.5	.41
Developed countries	96.9	92.0	.95

SOURCE: Adapted from the *Unesco Statistical Yearbook 1999*, II-7, II-8.

THE GALE GROUP.

possibly China. It was thus only in the twentieth century that the majority of the world's population came to possess basic literacy skills. Trends in primary school enrollment and completion rates are similar to those of literacy.

While the developing world was catching up in literacy and primary education over the course of the twentieth century, developed countries were widening the gap at the secondary and higher education level. Prior to 1900 only a small minority of adults in developed countries would have attended secondary school or universities. Between 1970 and 1997 secondary enrollment rates relative to the secondary school age population rose from 76 percent to 100 percent in developed countries, compared with from 23 percent to 52 percent for developing countries, and from 10 percent to 19.3 percent for least-developed countries. Enrollment rates in higher education relative to the university age group over the same period rose from 26 percent to 52 percent for developed countries, 3 percent to 10 percent for developing countries, and 1 percent to 3.2 percent for least-developed countries (Unesco Statistical Yearbook 1999). In 1990 the mean years of schooling completed by adults in developed countries was 10.0 years, whereas for developing countries it was only to 3.7 years (UNDP Human Development Report 1992). In accounting for both trends and disparities in education levels, factors commonly thought to be important include income per capita income, religion, and distribution of political power.

The public expenditures spent on education in the late twentieth century were substantial relative to gross national product (GNP) for both developed and developing countries. In 1970 this proportion was 5 percent for the world as a whole (Lichtenberg 1994). In the nineteenth century the share was no more than 1 percent for any group of countries (Lindert 2004).

RISING EDUCATIONAL ATTAINMENT AND THE PATTERN OF WORLD TRADE

The rise of schooling over the last half millennium can be viewed as having increased relative supplies of a distinctive factor of production—skilled labor. Because skills typically have been acquired by apprenticeship and learning on the job, it is simplistic to equate schooling with skills. Nevertheless, schooling levels do provide a convenient proxy for skill levels. The argument that skill differences in labor forces have impacted the pattern of world trade has been put forward by Adrian Wood (1994) as a characterization of trade in manufactures between industrial and developing countries. Wood's estimates show that between 1955 and 1989 the percentage of developing-country exports to developed countries that consist of manufactures rose from 5 percent to 53 percent, with a corresponding drop in the percentages of primary products, changes he attributes to falling trade barriers. Over this same period, the portion of developed-country exports to developing countries that consisted of manufactures remained roughly constant at three-quarters. Wood argues that developing countries' export manufactures during this period were intensive in unskilled labor, whereas those of developed countries became increasingly skill-intensive. In addition to other criticisms of Wood's argument, it has been noted that when more than two types of products are considered, as well as additional factors such as natural resources, capital, and skilled and unskilled labor, theoretical predictions become much less clear-cut; they depend on assumptions about interactions between the various factors of production (O' Rourke 2002; Bowen, Leamer, and Sveikauskas 1987).

Wood explicitly views his model of skill-driven trade as pertaining to the period since 1950. O'Rourke (2002) suggests that prior to 1950, a set of factors of production other than degree of labor-force skill determined international specialization patterns. Indeed, O'Rourke and Wil-

Trends in adult literacy and female to male literacy ratios 1970 to 2000

	1970	1980	1990	2000
World adult literacy rate	63	69.4	75.2	79.4
World female to male literacy ratio	.77	.80	.84	.86
Developing countries adult literacy rate	48.1	58.2	67.4	73.7
Developing countries female to male literacy ratio	.59	.68	.76	.81
Least developed countries adult literacy rate	26.8	34	42.3	50.7
Least developed countries female to male literacy ratio	.41	.49	.58	.67

SOURCE: Adapted from the *Unesco Statistical Yearbook 1999*, II-7, II-8.

THE GALE GROUP.

liamson (2002) question whether international markets were sufficiently well integrated prior to the mid-nineteenth century for models such the influential Hecksher-Ohlin model of comparative advantage to even be applicable.

Another influential line of argument emphasizes the impact of education on international technological leadership. Alfred Marshall (1919) argued that the German advantage over England in the newly emerging science-based industries could be attributed to German superiority in scientific and technical education. Nelson and Wright (1992) have attributed the rise of U.S. technological leadership over the course of the twentieth century in part to the development of its system of higher education and the research and development expertise this spawned. And Goldin (2001) has credited the rise of U.S. secondary education and the skills this cultivated in operative manufacturing workers with U.S. economic success in the twentieth century. Although these channels of influence appear plausible, their magnitude is difficult to establish.

By either line of argument, one reason for minimizing the importance of educational and skill differences to trade patterns prior to 1950, and especially prior to 1900, is simply that before then, these international differences were largely confined to the primary schooling level and basic literacy. A second consideration is the possibility that developments in technology over the past century such as the shift from steam power to electricity have increased the importance of skill and education in manufacturing (Goldin and Katz 1998).

Other possible channels of influence from rising educational attainment include increasing the divergence in growth rates across countries, resulting in income-induced variations in relative import demands in various parts of the world, and enhancing responsiveness to change as well as cultivating more cosmopolitan consumption patterns.

EDUCATION, SKILLS, AND THE DISTRIBUTION OF THE GAINS AND LOSSES FROM TRADE

By cultivating responsiveness to change, one would expect that rising educational levels would facilitate the magnitude of the general gains achieved from trade by facilitating movement of various categories of labor from declining to expanding sectors in the various countries involved.

A distinct but related issue of trade policy that has received considerable attention is what impact increasing commodity market integration has had on wages of skilled and unskilled workers, implicitly holding constant levels of educational attainment of each group. The basic expectation in Wood's influential model (1994) is that in developed countries with a comparative advantage in skill-intensive products, wages of unskilled workers will fall relative to those of skilled workers in response to the increased supply of unskilled labor-intensive imports from low-wage developing countries. Reversing the argument for developing countries, Wood's model predicts that in these countries wages of skilled workers will fall and those of unskilled workers will rise. Wood finds support for these propositions with a fall in unskilled relative to skilled wages in the United States and Europe on the one hand, and a rise in unskilled relative to skilled wages in South Korea on the other hand. However, other economists have argued that the magnitude of these trade effects in developed countries have been small; changes in technology have been more important in lowering the demand for unskilled workers relative to skilled workers, and experiences in some Central American economies have run counter to the experience of South Korea (Freeman 1995; O'Rourke 2002).

Prior to 1950 international differences in educational attainment and skill were smaller, and by some accounts the distributional impact of trade primarily has affected relative prices of other factors of production than those between various skill classes of labor (O'Rourke 2002). These considerations would lead one to expect a smaller impact of increased openness to trade on wage differences between skilled and unskilled labor before 1950.

The rise of worldwide educational attainment is one of the distinctive social developments since 1500. It is in the last half of the twentieth century that its possible links with world trade and specialization patterns became most evident.

SEE ALSO INFORMATION AND COMMUNICATIONS.

BIBLIOGRAPHY

Bowen, Harry P.; Leamer, Edward E.; and Sveikauskas, Leo. "Multicountry, Multifactor Tests of the Factor Abundance Theory." *American Economic Review* 77, no. 5 (December 1987): 791–809.

Easterlin, Richard A. "Why Isn't the Whole World Developed?" *Journal of Economic History* 41, no. 1 (March 1981): 1–17.

Freeman, Richard B. "Are Your Wages Set in Beijing?" *The Journal of Economic Perspectives* 9, no. 3 (Summer 1995): 15–32.

Goldin, Claudia. "The Human-Capital Century and American Leadership: Virtues of the Past." *Journal of Economic History* 61, no. 2 (June 2001): 263–292.

Goldin, Claudia, and Katz, Lawrence F. "The Origins of Technology-Skill Complementarity." *Quarterly Journal of Economics* 113 (June 1998): 693–732.

Graff, Harvey J. *Legacies of Literacy: Continuities and Contradictions in Western Culture and Society.* Bloomington: Indiana University Press, 1987.

Lichtenberg, Frank R. "Have International Differences in Educational Attainment Levels Narrowed?" In *Convergence and of Productivity: Cross-National Studies and Historical Evidence,* ed. William J. Baumol, Richard R. Nelson, and Edward N. Wolff. New York: Oxford University Press, 1994.

Lindert, Peter H. *Growing Public: Social Spending and Economic Growth since the Eighteenth Century.* Cambridge, U.K.: Cambridge University Press, 2004.

Mariscal, Elisa, and Sokoloff, Kenneth L. "Schooling, Suffrage, and the Persistence of Inequality in the Americas, 1800–1945." In *Political Institutions and Economic Growth in Latin America: Essays in Policy, History, and Political Economy,* ed. Stephen Haber. Stanford, CA: Hoover Institution Press, 2000.

Marshall, Alfred. *Industry and Trade: A Study of Industrial Technique and Business Organization, and of Their Influences on the Conditions of Various Classes and Nations.* London: Macmillan, 1919.

Nelson, Richard, and Wright, Gavin. "The Rise and Fall of American Technological Leadership." *Journal of Economic Literature* 30 (December 1992): 1931–1964.

O'Rourke, Kevin. "Globalization and Inequality: Historical Trends." *Aussenwirtschaft* 57, no. 1 (2002): 65–101.

O'Rourke, Kevin, and Williamson, Jeffrey G. "The Heckscher-Ohlin Model Between 1400 and 2000: When It Explained Factor Price Convergence, When It Did Not

and Why." In *Bertil Ohlin: A Centennial Celebration 1899–1999,* ed. Ronald Findlay, Lars Jonung, and Mats Lundahl. Cambridge, MA: Massachusetts Institute of Techonology Press, 2002.

United Nations Development Programme. *Human Development Report.* New York: Oxford University Press, 1992.

UNESCO. *Statistical Yearbook.* Paris: Author, 1999.

Wood, Adrian. *North-South Trade, Employment, and Inequality: Changing Fortunes in a Skill-Driven World.* Oxford, U.K.: Oxford University Press, 1994.

David Mitch

EGYPT

Throughout its long history Egypt has always been a major economic center. Whether as part of a larger empire or an independent polity, the inhabitants of the Nile River basin have had a flourishing agricultural economy and a robust commercial life. Agricultural success stemmed from annual Nile floods. These were unusually predictable and provided both crucial water supplies and rich silt from the Ethiopian highlands, which was deposited on Egyptian lands. This made the regions bordering the Nile River basin in Egypt and those in the delta north of Cairo some of the most fertile areas in the world, enabling Egypt to produce agricultural surpluses for export and to be active in long-distance trade throughout and beyond the Middle East. Throughout history, Egypt's merchant elite has been one of the world's most dynamic.

EGYPT UNDER OTTOMAN, FRENCH, AND BRITISH RULE

Egypt's more recent history begins with the Ottoman conquest in 1517. Conscious of the country's great wealth, the new rulers chose not to parcel its lands out to military men in the form of tax farms, as was the Ottoman custom elsewhere. Instead, they established a formal administration over the territory, thus securing for the central administration in Istanbul a large portion of the country's wealth in the form of tributary payments.

The Egyptian economy flourished during the first two centuries of Ottoman rule. The world economy itself was expanding, fueled in large part by silver from the Americas and reflected in increased trade across the Indian and Atlantic Oceans. Although this trade eventually would fall mostly into the hands of European merchants, for many centuries Asian and African merchants participated and grew wealthy; this included Egyptian merchants based in Cairo and Alexandria. They were instrumental in expanding the coffee and sugar trades during the sixteenth and seventeenth centuries, and for a time held a virtual monopoly over the world trade in coffee.

HIGH DAM AT ASWAN

One of President Abdel Gamal Nasser's most important goals was to modernize Egypt's economy. He proposed the huge High Dam at Aswan, just north of the Sudanese border, to provide the nation with electricity and irrigation on the Upper Nile. Initially the World Bank was to finance the dam, with support from the United States and Britain, but Nasser's pro-Soviet foreign stance, and his apparent undermining of British Middle Eastern interests, led the Western powers to withdraw support. In retaliation Nasser nationalized the Suez Canal, leading to the 1956 "Suez Crisis." The dam was finally completed in 1970 with Soviet aid, creating a huge reservoir named after Nasser, who died that year. The dam provides about half of Egypt's power needs, and regulates the Nile floods, which frequently had caused damage along the flood plain. Navigation on the river has been aided by a more consistent water flow. But there are also problems associated with Aswan, including the dislocation of thousands during its construction In addition, it has caused poor drainage affecting farmland, erosion of the Nile Delta, a rise in fertilizer use to replace natural sediments, and an alleged increase in disease linked to stagnant water.

David J. Clarke

Egyptian entrepreneurs also built sugar factories to process locally grown cane, selling it throughout the Middle East.

Egypt's economic independence and its vital place in the world economy began to be threatened in the late 1700s. Although the French invasion of the country lasted only from 1798 to 1801, it foreshadowed a growing European interest in this part of the world. Egypt's modernizing ruler, Muhammad Ali (r. 1805–1848), brought great economic and political advances to the country, but his irrigation reforms and efforts to stimulate exports of long-staple cotton to European textile manufacturers intensified European involvement in Egypt. When his successor Isma'il Pasha, khedive of Egypt from 1863 to 1879, allowed the state to fall heavily into debt to European bankers, this led inexorably to the loss of Egypt's political

autonomy. The opening of the Suez Canal in 1869 drew the European powers further into Egyptian affairs, especially the British, whose shippers came to dominate canal traffic. Fearing French intervention, the British sent an army of occupation into Egypt in 1882. Although a speedy evacuation was promised, the British army was not withdrawn until 1956.

British control benefited large Egyptian landowners, who expanded cotton cultivation and increased exports to Europe. By 1900, cotton exports accounted for more than 80 percent of the value of Egypt's exports. Meanwhile, European merchant and investment groups took over most of the large-scale businesses in Egypt. By the beginning of the twentieth century almost 90 percent of the funds invested in Egypt's large-scale business firms came from overseas, and foreign economic interests dominated the banking, insurance, and trading firms that were vital for Egypt's export-oriented economy.

This lopsided development troubled Egyptian nationalists, the most outspoken of whom, Tal'at Harb (1876–1941), led a drive to promote Egyptian businesses and to diversify the economy through industrialization. In 1920 he founded Bank Misr, which was an entirely Egyptian-financed and -run banking establishment, which sponsored the foundation of numerous Misr industrial and commercial companies. These companies established a local textile industry, which began to consume raw Egyptian cotton. Although Egypt continued to be the world's most important exporter of long-staple cotton, the share of cotton in Egypt's total exports declined. During the 1930s and 1940s Egypt followed import-substituting industrialization, founding local textile, food processing, glassware, and other industries for which there was already a substantial consumer market.

TRADE SINCE INDEPENDENCE

The 1952 military coup d'état brought to power young, energetic army officers who wanted to rapidly advance the political independence and the economic development of the country. In 1954 they signed an agreement for the withdrawal of British forces based in the Suez Canal area, thus achieving one of Egypt's most vital nationalist goals. The Free Officers government also promised rapid economic growth, which they initially hoped could be accomplished through the private sector and with the aid of foreign and local capital. When, however, economic progress languished and Western powers refused to finance the Aswan High Dam, the government of Gamal Abdel Nasser (1918–1970) nationalized the mainly French-run Suez Canal Company. The ensuing British, French, and Israeli invasion of the country in November 1956 prompted the government to turn against the private sector. A series of nationalization decrees en-

A photo from 1885 showing equipment used to enlarge the Suez Canal in Egypt. *The canal is a 118-mile waterway that connects the Mediterranean Sea and Red Sea; it opened an important trade route between Europe and Asia that eliminated the need to sail around Africa.* © BETTMANN/CORBIS. REPRODUCED BY PERMISSION.

acted between 1957 and 1962 placed almost all large-scale private firms in state hands. Egypt also turned to the Soviet Union for aid and redirected its trade toward the Soviet bloc. The Soviets financed the Aswan High Dam and helped Egypt establish many state-run industries. An economy that once had been open to foreign trade and exchanged a single cash crop—cotton—for a wide range of European manufactures now closed itself off, striving instead for economic self-sufficiency.

The experiment failed. Local industries lost money. Products that the middle class had once taken for granted became scarce. Above all, the alignment with the Soviet Union did not enable the Egyptians to deal militarily with their chief antagonist in the Middle East—Israel. In fact, the 1967 war with Israel, which the Egyptian military high command was sure it could win, proved to be a catastrophe. Egyptians forces were destroyed, the army was humiliated, and the entire Sinai Peninsula came under Israeli rule.

The death in 1970 of Egypt's charismatic leader, Nasser, and the rise of Nasser's vice president, Anwar al-Sadat (1918–1981), prepared the way for a sea change in Egypt's political, military, and economic arrangements. In 1973 President Sadat attacked the Israelis, getting Egyptian troops across the Suez Canal, where they inflicted heavy losses on the Israelis. Although the Israelis repulsed the invasion, the Egyptian effort was sufficiently successful that Sadat could announce the ending of ties with the Soviet Union and a new alliance with the United States. Sadat expelled Soviet technicians and economic advisers and invited American advisers to help in dismantling the public sector, privatizing public-sector companies, and opening the country to foreign investment and trade. Under Sadat, who was assassinated by a disaffected Muslim group in 1981, and his successor, Husni Mubarak (b. 1929), Egypt looked to the West, particularly to the United States, the World Bank, and the International Monetary Fund, to provide technical advice and much-needed investment to spur the economy.

Like most economic programs in Egypt's recent past, the turn to the West did not realize all of the goals that its advocates had hoped for. In 2004 Egypt had over 70 million people crammed into a relatively small usable area with limited natural resources. Nonetheless, the economy has grown significantly during the last twenty-five years, with tourism, foreign remittances, and Suez Canal receipts providing most of the country's hard currency. Egypt has also become a significant exporter of textiles, vegetables, fruits, and flowers throughout the Middle East and into Europe.

SEE ALSO ALI, MUHAMMAD; BONAPARTE, NAPOLEON; CARAVAN TRADE; COTTON; EMPIRE, BRITISH; EMPIRE, FRENCH; EMPIRE, OTTOMAN; IMPORT SUBSTITUTION; INTERNATIONAL MONETARY FUND (IMF); LEVANT COMPANY; MEDITERRANEAN; NATIONALIZATION; PASHA, ISMA'IL; SUEZ CANAL; TEXTILES; UNITED STATES; VENICE; WHEAT AND OTHER CEREAL GRAINS.

BIBLIOGRAPHY

Daly, M. W., ed. *The Cambridge History of Egypt*, vol. 2: *Modern Egypt from 1517 to the End of the Twentieth Century.* Cambridge, U.K.: Cambridge University Press, 1998.

Hanna, Nelly. *Making Big Money: The Life and Times of Isma'il Abu Taqiyya, Egyptian Merchant.* Syracuse, NY: Syracuse University Press, 1998.

Issawi, Charles. *An Economic History of the Middle East and North Africa.* New York: Columbia University Press, 1982.

Owen, Roger. *Cotton and the Egyptian Economy: A Study in Trade and Development, 1820–1914.* Oxford, U.K.: Oxford University Press, 1969.

Owen, Roger. *The Middle East in the World Economy, 1800–1914.* London: Methuen, 1981.

Robert L. Tignor

ELIZABETH I
1533–1603

Elizabeth Tudor, daughter of Henry VIII (1491–1547) and Anne Boleyn (1507–1536), was born on September 7, 1533, became queen on November 17, 1558, and died on March 24, 1603. Her diplomatic skills brought stability to a nation riven by political and religious discord, and contributed to the strong growth of England's international trading interests. Whereas in the 1530s the export of raw wool from London to Antwerp accounted for over 90 percent of English trade, a range of overseas commercial links had been established by 1603. The Baltic and Iberian trades expanded, and joint stock companies promoted commerce with Muscovy and the Levant. Fishermen annually returned an abundance of cod from New-foundland to southern Europe, while the Roanoke settlers imposed an English footprint on North America, and venturers such as John Hawkins (1532–1595) and Francis Drake (1540–1596)—sometimes with Elizabeth's covert approval—traded with, or raided, Spanish America. War with Spain (1585–1603) further stimulated maritime activity. As well as fighting in the Armada campaign, privateers added a potentially profitable dimension to overseas trade and therefore proliferated. Shipbuilding flourished, and the number of seafarers increased from 15,000 to 50,000 during the war. Crowning the substantial commercial development of Elizabethan England, the East India Company was founded on December 31, 1600.

SEE ALSO EMPIRE, BRITISH; EMPIRE, SPANISH; GILBERT, HUMPHREY; HAKLUYT, RICHARD, THE YOUNGER; HAWKINS, JOHN; PHILIP II; PRIVATEERING; SLAVERY AND THE AFRICAN SLAVE TRADE; SPAIN.

BIBLIOGRAPHY

Andrews, Kenneth R. *Trade, Plunder, and Settlement: Maritime Enterprise and the Genesis of the British Empire, 1480–1630.* Cambridge, U.K.: Cambridge University Press, 1984.

Fury, Cheryl A. *Tides in the Affairs of Men: The Social History of Elizabethan Seamen, 1580–1603.* Westport, CT: Greenwood Press, 2002.

David J. Starkey

EMPIRE, BELGIAN

In 1884 to 1885 Leopold II, king of the Belgians, finally realized one of his many expansionist dreams: the great powers had recognized the existence of the Congo Free State, an enormous domain in Central Africa created by his obsessive quest for a lucrative colony. Belgium itself had no official links with this atypical colony, over which Leopold II ruled as an absolute monarch for the next twenty-three years. But in 1908, after severe international criticism of the inhumane treatment of the native population, the Belgian State took over Leopold's free state, and the Congo remained a Belgian colony until 1960.

FREE-STATE STATUS

The recognition of the Congo Free State by the foreign powers coincided with the Berlin Conference (1884–1885), which determined the international attitude towards the breaking up of Africa. The Berlin Act introduced, among other dispositions, an international regulation for the so-called "Conventional Congo Basin." This vast region, which included not only the recently founded Congo Free State but also large parts of the neighboring colonies, was declared a free-trade zone. In-

Leopold II, King of Belgium, c. 1900. Leopold's drive to create overseas markets for Belgium led to the founding of the Congo Free State in 1885. © BETTMANN/CORBIS. REPRODUCED BY PERMISSION.

ternal navigation was entirely free, any form of differential treatment of trading nations was prohibited, and no import or transit duties could be levied. At the request of the Congo Free State, which struggled with huge budgetary deficits, the last provision was altered some years later. Indeed, during the 1890 international conference held in Brussels, it was agreed that an import tax of no more than 10 percent could be levied, provided no country was discriminated against. After World War I the Convention of Saint-Germain-en-Laye (1919) replaced the Berlin Act. This new regulation maintained the essential provisions regarding free trade in the Congo Basin, but abolished the 10 percent limit on import taxes. Discriminatory treatment of any country was still explicitly prohibited. As with the Berlin and Brussels Acts, the 1919 Convention did not regulate export duties. Thus, during the seventy-five years of colonial rule (1885–1960) Congolese trade was characterized, at least in theory, by a genuine open-door policy. Belgium was not allowed to favor its own commercial or industrial interests.

TRADE POLICY

Nevertheless, during the free-state period the provisions of the Berlin Act were not scrupulously applied. In practice, free trade was curtailed by the king's economic policy, which was designed to secure maximum revenue for the state's treasury and for the king's own private Congolese possessions. The monopolization of vast stretches of land—indeed, of the richest areas—by the Congo Free State, by some private concessionary companies, or by Leopold himself, *de facto* impeded the development of free enterprise and free trade. As an astute observer humorously remarked, Congolese trade policy under Leopold was governed by the following rules: "Article 1. Trade is entirely free. Article 2. There is nothing to buy or to sell" (cited in Stengers 1989, p. 96). After the takeover by Belgium in 1908 these practices were abolished; henceforth, Belgian and foreign businessmen could invest and trade freely in the Congo. During the crisis of the 1930s, when trade volumes and values plummeted, some voices in Belgium advocated the abolishment (or at least the bypassing) of the Berlin/Saint-Germain-en-Laye rules in order to defend Belgian industrial and commercial interests in the Congo. The colonial authorities rejected these demands. On the contrary, during the interwar years, they even pleaded for the extension of the Congo Basin regime to the whole of Africa.

Over time, trade regulations rates varied quite often. Most tariff changes were inspired by purely fiscal considerations. Indeed, import and export duties represented an important part of Congolese public revenues. During free-state status, their share fluctuated around 20 percent between 1900 and 1907, but had reached far higher levels in earlier years (e.g., almost 40% in 1895). After the Belgian takeover customs levies generally represented between 30 and 42 percent of public revenue (with a minimum of about 16% during the crisis of the early 1930s). In 1950 export duties alone represented as much as 25 percent of all Congolese budgetary incomes. Nevertheless, in some instances tariff-policy measures resulted from other than purely fiscal motives. During the 1920s capital goods could be imported duty free or at very low rates—a policy designed to stimulate the colony's equipment. During the 1950s import duties of some consumer goods were introduced or raised in order to protect the burgeoning local industrial production against import from abroad, be it from Belgium or from other countries.

GLOBAL TRENDS OF CONGOLESE TRADE

Congolese trade statistics were almost nonexistent during the free-state period; they remained extremely rudimentary, incomplete, and unreliable before the beginning of the 1920s. Only the last four decades of colonial Congo's trade evolution can therefore be analyzed in some detail, but even then, important methodological shortcomings hamper correct observation.

After a steep takeoff, due especially to the rubber boom (1.9 million Belgian francs, or BEF, in 1887; 50.4 million BEF in 1901), Congolese export stagnated during the first years of the twentieth century (55.1 million BEF in 1913). The integration of the Congo into world trade really began in the 1920s. The export volume index (100 in 1948–1950) represented 10 in 1920 and 44 in 1930. The world economic crisis interrupted this growth for some years (28 in 1932, 41 in 1934), but the recovery during the second half of the 1930s and, more importantly, the enormous demands for strategic primary products during World War II, generated an important growth (60 in 1939 and 80 in 1945). Nevertheless, the most spectacular export breakthrough took place in the postwar period, and especially the first half of the 1950s (105 in 1950, 145 in 1956, and 162 in 1959). The Congo's share in world trade more than doubled between 1938 (2.4%) and 1953 (5.33%). Except for the initial period of the Congo Free State (1885–1898) and for several years during the 1920s (when Congolese infrastructure dramatically expanded), export values always exceeded import values. Particularly during and after World War II, Congo produced important surpluses on its trade balance. The terms of trade deteriorated from the beginning of the 1920s to 1946, but afterward, they rapidly and significantly improved, thanks to the price increase of Congo's most important export products (86 in 1921, 66 in 1931, 50 in 1945, 132 in 1955).

GEOGRAPHICAL FLOWS AND COMMODITY COMPOSITION

The Congo's particular international status had an important impact on geographical trade flows. Compared to other colonies, where the "mother country" played a far more important role in the trade of its dependencies (e.g. France, and its colonial empire), the Belgian Congo did not develop an exclusive trade link with Belgium. According to trade statistics, in 1921 Belgium absorbed 48 percent of Congo's export value (Great Britain came second with 44%). During the 1930s this proportion peaked at 76 percent, but after the war the Belgian share receded and fluctuated at around half of Congo's total exports (e.g., 51% in 1955). Nevertheless, these official figures blurred the real picture because they did not take into consideration that many goods only passed through Belgium on the way to other countries. Corrected statistics showed that actually Belgium absorbed a far more modest proportion of Congolese exports (25% in 1955). During and after World War II the United States became Congo's second export partner, with a "real" share comparable to that of Belgium (e.g., 22% in 1955). During

the interwar period Belgium's part in total Congolese import value fluctuated between 38 and 55 percent, but here again trade statistics overestimated Belgium's real share, because many goods counted as "Belgian" (because they were embarked at the port of Antwerp) were in fact coming from other countries. Especially during the decade of crisis, Belgian politicians and business leaders tried to stimulate the so-called "interpenetration" of the Belgian and Congolese economies, but these efforts did not meet with real and lasting success. During World War II the links between occupied Belgium and its colony were severed, and the Congo was obliged to buy most of its goods in the United States. After the war Belgium could recapture an important part of trade flows to the Congo, but its share oscillated around 36 to 40 percent, less than before the war.

Some important changes occurred in the commodity composition of Congolese export trade. During the freestate period Leopold's colony was saved from bankruptcy thanks to the export boom of wild rubber (and, to a lesser extent, of ivory) because heavy export duties were levied on these goods. Ivory made up 55 percent of Congo's total export volume in 1895, 10 percent in 1919, and 0.4 percent in 1935. Rubber represented 19 percent in 1895, 76 percent in 1901, 14 percent in 1916, and 0 percent in 1930. After these ephemeral export booms the Congolese trade pattern definitively took shape from the 1920s onward, with the expansion of the mining sector. During the four last decades of Belgian colonization copper constituted Congo's main export (about one-third of total export volume). Tin (between 5 and 8%) and cobalt (between 8 and 15%) were two other important mineral export products. Though far from nonexistent, export of agricultural products was less important. The main commodities were palm oil and nuts (14% of total trade volume in 1948), cotton (14%), and coffee (8.5%). Congo's role in world primary commodity markets was far more important for mineral than for agricultural products. In 1929 Congo was the world's third-largest copper producer, and first in cobalt and industrial diamonds. The Belgian Congo was a major player in the international copper and tin cartels. The uranium used for the first U.S. atomic bombs was of Congolese origin. Thanks to its prominent position in the world trade of some essential primary products, independent Congo played an important international role from the 1960s to the 1980s. The subsequent collapse of state power and civil wars caused the dramatic breakdown of export—and the virtual disappearance of the Congo from world trade networks. Today, only the illegal trade of some products such as diamonds and columbo-tantalite reminds us of the Congo's past commercial glory.

BIBLIOGRAPHY

Congo Belge, Secrétariat général. *Statistiques du commerce extérieur de l'Union douanière du Congo Belge et du Ruanda-Urundi* (*Foreign Trade Statistics of the Belgian Congo and Ruanda-Urundi Customs Union*). Brussels: Ministry of Colonies, 1941–1959.

Royaume de Belgique, Ministère des Colonies. *La situation économique du Congo Belge et du Ruanda-Urundi en 1950–1959* (*The Economic Situation of Belgian Congo and Ruanda-Urundi in 1950–1959*). Brussels: Author, 1951–1960.

Stengers, Jean. *Congo. Mythes et réalités: 100 ans d'histoire* (*Congo. Myths and Realities. 100 Years of History*). Paris-Louvain-la-Neuve: Duculot, 1989.

Van de Velde, Marcel. *Economie belge et Congo belge* (*Belgian Economy and Belgian Congo*). Antwerp, Belgium: Lloyd Anversois, 1936.

Vandewalle, Gaston. *De conjuncturele evolutie in Kongo en Ruanda-Urundi van 1920 tot 1939 en van 1949 tot 1958* (*The Conjectural Evolution of Congo and Ruanda-Urundi from 1920 to 1939 and from 1949–1958*). Ghent, Belgium: Rijksuniversiteit, 1966.

Guy Vanthemsche

EMPIRE, BRITISH

This entry consists of the following articles:
EMPIRE, BRITISH: 1450–1783
EMPIRE, BRITISH: 1783–PRESENT

EMPIRE, BRITISH: 1450–1783

Britain was a latecomer in the European race for empires, left behind by its rivals Spain and Portugal. Even in the 1650s English overseas possessions amounted to no more than a few Caribbean islands, a number of North American "plantations," and some Indian ports. The English envied Portugal, whose eastern possessions brought in valuable spices, sugar, and slaves. Even more enticing was Spain's Central and South American empire, which yielded vast amounts of gold and silver.

In 1497 King Henry VII (1457–1509) sponsored an expedition under the Venetian John Cabot (c. 1450–1499) to find a route to Asian commodities. Instead, Cabot "discovered" the island of Newfoundland, with its rich cod fishing grounds. From the sixteenth century, Englishmen such as Martin Frobisher (1535?–1594)

VENTURES TO NORTH AMERICA

After Christopher Columbus's journey in 1492, Europeans made many attempts to found colonies in North America. A good many of these enterprises were private ventures, and not all of them succeeded. England's first American colonial venture was made by Sir Walter Raleigh at Roanoke Island in 1585. Raleigh's expedition left about 100 men on the island. Relations with the local population were friendly at first, but soon deteriorated. In 1586, low on food and discouraged that a promised relief expedition had not appeared, the colonists took passage home with Sir Francis Drake. In 1587 another attempt was made to settle Roanoke, but when their relief expedition arrived in 1590 all the colonists had vanished mysteriously, perhaps having integrated with the local Indians. These underfunded ventures were not the last colonial schemes to fail. In 1775 the Transylvania Company sent Daniel Boone to colonize the area that is now Kentucky and Tennessee, although the enterprise did not have British sanction. The Continental Congress later refused to recognize Transylvania as the fourteenth state. The company's land grants were voided by Virginia and North Carolina, but promoter Richard Henderson and his associates received new grants for their troubles.

David J. Clarke

searched for precious metals and routes to China in the north. Such projects came to nothing. A pair of underfunded colonies established at Roanoke Island and Newfoundland in the 1580s also failed. For a time the English simply allowed mariners such as Sir Francis Drake (1540?–1596) to harass and capture Spanish traders.

A more ambitious colonization plan centered on Virginia's Chesapeake Bay was licensed by King James I (1566–1625) in 1607. The London (or Virginia) Company hoped to supply England with products as diverse as wine and ship timber. Eventually trade in a new commodity, tobacco, made Virginia, though not the Virginia *Company*, a success. King James, who detested smoking, established a royal monopoly over the profitable trade in 1624. By the 1690s tobacco use was widespread in England. Virginia and another tobacco colony, Maryland, were soon home to tens of thousands of settlers. In other southern colonies such as South Carolina products such as rice and indigo became important export goods. To the north the Massachusetts Bay Colony enjoyed commercial success through a cod fishery broadly similar to Newfoundland's.

Newfoundland itself was sparsely settled, but an English fishing fleet operating off its coasts supplied Iberian markets from the 1520s on. The trade in cod was later important to another English colony, Nova Scotia. Other portions of modern Canada were also claimed by England. In 1670 a private enterprise, the Hudson's Bay Company, was founded with rights to all territory draining into Hudson's Bay. It pursued a fur trade with native peoples that supposedly was a monopoly, but until the Seven Years' War (1756–1763) it was often in conflict with French rivals. Victory over France gave Britain control of eastern North America from Canada to the Carolinas.

Before 1783 the British Empire was Atlantic-oriented, and the American colonies were not its only valuable possessions. In the 1600s English settlers occupied a number of Caribbean islands including Barbados, the Leeward Islands, and Jamaica. From the 1750s to 1825 their chief export, sugar, was Britain's most valuable import. Sugar cultivation occurred on large plantations whose owners could make sizeable fortunes. The crop, though lucrative, was labor-intensive. By the mid-seventeenth century the need for low-cost workers led to an extensive slave trade from Africa's Atlantic coast. Originating in the Caribbean sugar islands, a slave economy also developed in Britain's southern American colonies after 1680. More than 3 million Africans were forcibly transported in British empire vessels from the 1660s until 1807, and many died en route. Britain's Atlantic empire became based on a "triangular" trade in which the northern fisheries also played a role. West Africa supplied the labor, low-grade cod kept the slaves fed, and sugar and tobacco returned to Britain for home use and re-export. As more and more Britons immigrated to the colonies, the colonies in turn became important destinations for British manufactured goods.

The American colonies were an important link in this chain, but by the later 1700s a number of grievances arose against the British Crown. Many were based on trade concerns. The Acts of Trade and Navigation, originating in the mid-1600s, recognized English possessions as a single trading sphere, basically creating a jurisdiction of the Empire. The acts also gave British vessels a monopoly over colonial trade. Thus they were a source of friction with the colonists, who wanted more freedom to trade outside the Empire on their own account. A series of taxes on trade goods such as sugar and Madeira were also enacted, but by 1773 most were repealed. Still, the principle that the English Parliament could tax its colonies without their consent remained. Though the issues were more complex, this was certainly a factor in starting the American Revolution (1775–1783). Though America gained its independence, the nation remained bound to Britain by commercial, if not political, ties.

With the loss of its American colonies British attention turned eastward. From the 1600s the English, through the monopolistic East India Company, tried to copy Dutch success in the Indian spice trade, but found their niche instead in coffee and textile trading. The English acquired bases at Madras and, through the dowry of King Charles II's Queen, Catherine of Braganza (1638–1705), the port of Bombay. A trade in China tea also began, adding another must-have product to the list of English overseas imports. At first company traders were no more than small players on the fringes of an advanced civilization, but by the early 1700s things were changing. India's rulers, the Muslim Mughal emperors, were in decline, and France was Britain's main Indian commercial rival. It was largely fear of French competition that sent company armies on the march; the East India Company's aim, after all, was to further its trade, not fight battles. The Seven Years' War changed everything, though this was not the company directors' intention. Under employee Robert Clive (1725–1774), their army won a series of victories cementing their supremacy in India. In 1764 the company took formal charge of Bengal. Rival French traders folded in 1769, and the British soon won Ceylon from the Dutch. By the 1780s British governments took a direct interest in India, setting up a system of "dual control" with the company that ended only in 1858. Whether planned or not, British territorial acquisitions in India continued. The East India Company's wish to trade eventually led to British rule over millions of Indian subjects, laying the foundations for the Indian Empire, or *raj,* that lasted until 1947.

SEE ALSO Board of Trade, British; Boston; Bristol; Canada; Charleston; East India Company, British; Empire, Spanish; Free Trade, Theory and Practice; Gilbert, Humphrey; Hakluyt, Richard, the Younger; Hawkins, John; India; Jamaica; Liverpool; London; Mercantilism; Navigation Acts; Newport; New York; Philadelphia; Philip II; Population—Emigration and Immigration; Privateering; Slavery and the African Slave Trade; Spain; Sugar, Molasses, and Rum; Treaties; United Kingdom; United States; Wars.

BIBLIOGRAPHY

Canny, Nicholas, ed. *The Oxford History of the British Empire*, vol. 1: *The Origins of Empire*. Oxford, U.K.: Oxford University Press, 1998.

Ferguson, Niall. *Empire: The Rise and Demise of the British World Order and the Lessons for Global Power*. New York: Basic Books, 2004.

Harper, Lawrence A. *The English Navigation Laws: A Seventeenth-Century Experiment in Social Engineering*. New York: Columbia University Press, 1939. Reprint 1964.

James, Lawrence. *The Rise and Fall of the British Empire*. New York: St. Martin's Press, 1996.

Kurlansky, Mark. *Cod*. Canada: Vintage Canada, 1998.

Marshall, P. J., ed. *The Oxford History of the British Empire: The Eighteenth Century*. Oxford, U.K.: Oxford University Press, 2001.

Roberts, J. M., ed. *The Penguin History of the World*. Toronto: Penguin Books Canada, 1995.

David J. Clarke

EMPIRE, BRITISH: 1783–PRESENT

By 1783 France had been an aggressive enemy of Britain for nearly a century, planning invasions, supporting Jacobite rebels, challenging Britain in India and the Caribbean, smarting from defeats in 1757 to 1763, seizing every chance to strike at the great organizers of anti-French coalitions. For the British Empire the American Revolution was a stab in the back by rebels who made an alliance with the French enemy, as Irish rebels did occasionally, and attacked Canada. In 1775, while 40,000 Americans were moving to Canada as empire loyalists, armies led by Benedict Arnold and the Irish-born brigadier general Richard Montgomery seized Montreal and besieged Quebec City. Republican France attacked Britain in 1793 and in 1812 American rebels stabbed again while the empire was grappling with Napoleon's "Continental System." But losing the thirteen colonies did not stop Anglo-American trade from growing: English hardware, housewares, and textiles flowed westward in exchange for cotton, foodstuffs, tobacco, and timber.

The empire's enormous wealth and dominion during the next century stemmed from the first modern industrial revolution, a liberal constitution encouraging personal freedom, and a strong maritime tradition. Lord North's reforming efforts, which provoked the American colonies to rebel, were part of a movement to make government more efficient and accountable, less corrupt and oppressive. British merchants, bankers, investors, and shipping interests grew stronger and warded off the demoralizing effects of French revolutions, with their bureaucratic dirigisme. Abundant cheap capital encouraged British businessmen to venture overseas while monopolies of chartered companies were removed one by one. Provoked by a bloody mutiny in 1857 to 1858, the British

government even took India away from the East India Company. Between 1835 and 1845 an unrivaled network of "mail lines" spread across the seven seas, such as the Peninsular and Oriental Line linking England with Egypt, India, and the Far East. In the 1870s and 1880s British shipping left competitors far behind as strong firms absorbed weaker ones and wooden sailing ships gave way to iron steamers. In 1914 Britain owned around 40 percent of the world's steam tonnage. Britain dominated world cable communications even in 1914, and the trans-Pacific cable as late as the 1930s.

The Indian mutiny of 1857 to 1858 again showed the colonies to be troublesome. Britain put up with the refusal of Australia, Canada, New Zealand, and South Africa to contribute to imperial defense except when wartime dangers revived popular imperial patriotism. The Royal Navy turned to protecting commercial shipping more and more as free-trade principles formed foreign policy from the 1830s. By mid-century colonial "annexations were to be avoided if possible" (Robinson and Gallagher, p. 5). An informal British Empire of commercial ventures and investments in China, Egypt, the Middle East, and South America was added to colonial possessions marked red on the map. British forces were continually fighting small wars, usually of pacification, in the wilder parts of the empire.

The empire's history is clogged with outdated prejudices of liberal, socialist, and foreign enemies, and friendly voices among historians are rare indeed. J. A. Hobson's *Imperialism, A Study* (1902) and V. I. Lenin's *Imperialism, the Highest Stage of Capitalism* (1916) taught imperial history as a capitalist conspiracy. Among their disciples was Eric Williams (1911–1981), whose *Capitalism and Slavery* (1944) persuaded many that Parliament suppressed the slave trade from 1807 and plantation slavery from 1833 only because they ceased to be profitable, a claim discredited by later research.

The public conscience behind antislavery gradually affected other parts of imperial life, transforming colonies into tutorial regimes for overseas development. Railways, canals, irrigation systems, famine relief, vast surveys, experimental farms, public health, and forest management schemes, improved very little by post independence governments, gradually turned the empire into an agency for Third World assistance. "Gentlemanly capitalists," identified in studies by Cain and Hopkins, encouraged these developments. British conscientious scruples ultimately killed the empire.

Meanwhile, personal freedom in a monarchy nourished aristocratic hierarchy. Popular pageants celebrating imperial trade and industry were organized around the empire for twenty-five years by Frank Lascelles (1875–1934), but success in business led to knighthoods, the

SIR WINSTON CHURCHILL

By the end of the nineteenth century the proud boast of Great Britain was that the sun never set on the British Empire! A century later, it had disappeared. Sir Winston Churchill (1874–1965) was a lifelong believer in Britain's "imperial mission." As a youth he served in Queen Victoria's armies, later defending the empire in World War I as both parliamentarian and soldier. From 1929 to 1935, a low point for Churchill and the nation, he railed against the perceived erosion of British imperial authority. As a wartime leader he made one of his most definitive statements on the empire: when in 1942 Franklin Roosevelt asserted that the United States had entered World War II to defeat fascism, not to maintain British dominion over colonial peoples, Churchill retorted that he had not become the king's prime minister "for the purpose of presiding over the dissolution of the British Empire." Even so, during his second term (1951–1955) Churchill could not escape the reality of Britain's gradual retreat from empire. He agreed to drop the name "British" from the Commonwealth of Nations, and in 1954 his government negotiated the withdrawal of British troops from the Suez Canal zone. The subsequent Suez Crisis (1956) proved that Britain could no longer act decisively on the world stage, and by the time Churchill died in 1965, almost all the former colonies were independent nations.

David J. Clarke

peerage, and life in privileged families, independent "public" schools, regiments, and clubs. The ruling class enjoyed education and travel, languages, and literacy, which qualified them beyond what is normally achieved in a democracy. Many adventurous Arabists from Oxford and Cambridge Universities familiar with Middle Eastern countries and friendly with sheiks and other powerful families helped to win control of Persian oil, Iraq, Kuwait, and Transjordan, and to forestall aggressive German and Turkish plans. Most knew—or knew of—one another, and could cut through bureaucratic obstacles and delays, as did Gertrude Bell (1868–1926), a leading Arabist whose advice and influence were decisive in creating Iraq out of what had been called Mesopotamia while keeping in touch with sheiks, soldiers, and archae-

ologists in the desert, as well as high-ranking relatives and friends in London.

The English ruling aristocracy recognized the virtues of "natural gentlemen" such as Donald Alexander Smith (1830–1914), a Scot who began life as a Hudson's Bay Company clerk in Canada but died in London as Lord Strathcona, rich railway baron, founder of a famous cavalry regiment, chairman of the Anglo-Persian Oil Company (later British Petroleum), and a neighbor in London's Grosvenor Square of that company's principal founder, William Knox D'Arcy (1849–1917). With profits from the Mount Morgan gold mine in Australia, D'Arcy funded Burmah Oil's 1909 discoveries in Persia near Basra, Mesopotamia, and so launched the Middle East oil business, which supplied the navy as it converted to oil after 1904. England's ruling elite likewise befriended the Wild West Indian fighter Frederick Russell Burnham (1861–1947), a major in the British army during the South African War (1899–1902). "The kind-hearted Queen [Victoria] invited me to visit her at Osborne," he recalled, "and . . . we were treated as real friends" (Burnham 1926, 350–352). Imperial decorations, such as the Distinguished Service Order awarded to Burnham in 1901, created a hierarchy of merit, as well as privilege, and made room for money without glorifying it.

From the 1870s Britain fell behind Germany and the United States in the production of industrial steel, chemicals, and electrical goods. What sustained the empire during its last half-century was its worldwide shipping, banking and other financial services, international insurance companies, and an immense accumulation of overseas investments, particularly in North and South America. As the world's banker and the first industrial country, Britain was challenging other Western powers to industrialize and helping them to do so with huge investments abroad, spent at last in the world wars of 1914 to 1918 and 1939 to 1945 defending the empire with its allies in a centuries-old British practice. Postwar governments launched a decolonization process leading to Indian independence in 1947, the simultaneous formation of Pakistan by Indian's Muslims after a murderous civil war against the Hindu majority, Egypt's liberation by stages in the 1950s, and the independence of most African colonies during the 1960s. But fixing chronologies of colonial independence distorts British imperial history. London has always granted some self-governance to overseas territories. It did not hold New England or New York in as firm a grip as Paris held New France or, later, Algeria. Canada, New Zealand, Australia, New Zealand, and South Africa were self-governing for generations before the Statute of Westminster (1931) recognized their formal independence in a commonwealth. The monarchical polity allowed for an exceptionally loose imperial structure. Prime Minister W. E. Gladstone was planning for Irish home rule as early as 1886. By then the anti-imperial "Little Englanders" in Britain were already formidable and arguing that colonies were held in trust. Defending the poor against oppressive and corrupt indigenous rulers was already one of London's guiding principles. As a result, the British Empire had many collaborators among its colonial subjects.

SEE ALSO BOARD OF TRADE, BRITISH; BOSTON; BRISTOL; CANADA; CHARLESTON; EAST INDIA COMPANY, ENGLISH; EMPIRE, SPANISH; FREE TRADE, THEORY AND PRACTICE; GILBERT, HUMPHREY; HAKLUYT, RICHARD, THE YOUNGER; HAWKINS, JOHN; INDIA; JAMAICA; LIVERPOOL; LONDON; MERCANTILISM; NAVIGATION ACTS; NEWPORT; NEW YORK; PHILADELPHIA; PHILIP II; POPULATION— EMIGRATION AND IMMIGRATION; PRIVATEERING; SLAVERY AND THE AFRICAN SLAVE TRADE; SPAIN; SUGAR, MOLASSES, AND RUM; TREATIES; UNITED KINGDOM; UNITED STATES; WARS.

BIBLIOGRAPHY

Boyce, Gordon. *Information, Mediation, and Institutional Development: The Rise of Large-Scale Enterprise in British Shipping, 1870–1919.* Manchester, U.K.: Manchester University Press, 1995.

Bridge, Carl, and Fedorowich, Kent, eds. *The British World: Diaspora, Culture, and Identity.* London: Frank Cass, 2003.

Burnham, Major (sic) Frederick Russell, D.S.O. *Scouting on Two Continents,* ed. Mary Nixon Everett, The Haynes Corporation, 1926; Prescott, Arizona: Wolfe Publishing Co., 1994.

Cain, P. J., and Hopkins, A. G. *British Imperialism, 1688– 2000.* 2nd ed. Harlow, U.K.: Longman, 2002.

Carrington, C. E. *The British Overseas: Exploits of a Nation of Shopkeepers.* Cambridge, U.K.: Cambridge University Press, 1950.

Davis, Lance E., and Huttonback, Robert A. *Mammon and the Pursuit of Empire: The Economics of British Imperialism,* abridged edition. Cambridge, U.K.: Cambridge University Press, 1988.

Drescher, Seymour. *Capitalism and Slavery: British Mobilization in Comparative Perspective.* New York: Oxford University Press, 1987.

Ferguson, Niall. *Empire: The Rise and Demise of the British World Order and the Lessons for Global Power.* London: Allen Lane, 2002.

Fischer-Tine, Harald, and Mann, Michael. *Colonialism as Civilizing Mission: Cultural Ideology in British India.* London: Anthem Press, 2004.

Gann, L. H., and Duignan, Peter. *The Rulers of British Africa, 1870–1914.* London: Croom Helm, 1978.

Hopkirk, Peter. *The Great Game: On Secret Service in High Asia.* London: John Murray, 1990.

Mathias, Peter, and Davis, John A., eds. *The Nature of Industrialization,* vol. 5: *International Trade and British Economic Growth from the Eighteenth Century to the Present Day.* Oxford, U.K.: Blackwell, 1996.

Robinson, Ronald, and Gallagher, John. *Africa and the Victorians: The Climax of Imperialism.* New York: Doubleday Anchor, 1968.

Tripp, Charles. *A History of Iraq.* Cambridge, UK: Cambridge University Press, 2000.

Woodruff, Philip. *The Men Who Ruled India.* 2 vols. London: Jonathan Cape, 1953–1954.

J. F. Bosher

EMPIRE, DUTCH

In the 1590s merchants from the young Dutch Republic started the first significant commercial ventures outside Europe. After one fleet had successfully rounded the Cape of Good Hope and returned from the East Indies with spices in 1597, companies trading with Asia shot up like mushrooms. Competition was so intense that the profit margin fell to a minimum, as the cost price of spices in Asia rose while the sales price in Europe dropped. At this point, the Estates General (Dutch Parliament) intervened, founding the Vereenigde Oost-Indische Compagnie (United East India Company, or VOC). It was allowed to enter into treaties, declare wars, and build fortresses in Asia.

From the outset, military actions paved the way for commercial success. The VOC used force against natives of the Moluccas, Indian merchants, and Portuguese and English rivals to secure footholds and obtain spice monopolies. Dutch conquests in Asia included the Spice Islands of Amboina, Tidore, and Ternate (1605), Taiwan (1623), part of coastal Ceylon (1641), strategically located Malacca (1641), and parts of southwest India (1663). In addition, a way station was founded at the Cape of Good Hope (1652).

Such expansion enabled the formation of a network of factories from Japan and Siam to Ceylon, linked by a regular exchange of information and commodities. Batavia, on the island of Java, was set up in 1619 as the nerve center of the Dutch empire in Asia, to which all Dutch factories were subordinated, and as the general warehouse for goods to be exported to Europe. From the late 1650s, the Dutch monopolized the global cinnamon trade, and by the late 1660s, they had near-total control of the production and marketing of nutmeg, mace, and cloves. By contrast, pepper remained elusive, since it was cultivated over a vast area. All pepper was destined for the European market, while cloves, nuts, and mace were only shipped back after Asian demand had been satisfied. The spice monopsony that enabled the VOC to fix prices left the Company with huge profits, needed to offset the large overhead costs. The Company's policy in Europe was to slightly oversupply the market, driving down prices and thus usually discouraging competitors.

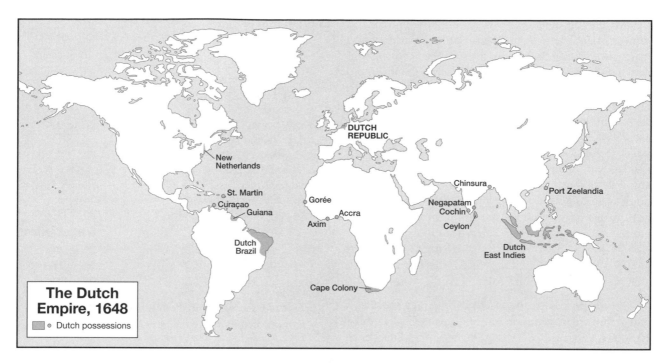

The Dutch Empire, 1648
□ ● Dutch possessions

XNR PRODUCTIONS. REPRODUCED BY PERMISSION OF THOMSON GALE.

After 1680 the share of pepper and spices in the VOC's revenues began to decline, while trade in cotton and silk fabric from India, coffee (cultivated on Java after 1711), and Chinese tea rose. After 1690 Asian profits turned into losses, as expenses kept rising and income did not increase commensurately. The VOC remained the world's largest company throughout the eighteenth century, offering a wide array of Asian goods for sale in Europe, but it was gradually cut down to size. Nevertheless, its role as supplier of colonial goods helped Dutch merchants maintain themselves in the European markets.

After huge losses had led to the demise of the VOC in 1795, the Napoleonic Wars saw the British occupation of all Dutch colonies East and West, around 1800. By the time the Dutch retook control of their possessions in 1816, their empire had shrunk, since Britain did not restore Ceylon and the Cape Colony. More importantly, Dutch commercial hegemony in eastern Asia was now a thing of the past. After the Acultivation system, which obliged the local population to grow several cash crops, was introduced on Java in the first half of the 1830s, the Dutch recovered some lost ground. Until 1870 large amounts of coffee, sugar, indigo, tobacco, and tea were sent from Java to the Netherlands. Total proceeds from the sale of the East Indian products amounted to 451 million guilders from 1830 to 1850, almost half of which directly enriched the national treasury. East Indian revenues were partly used to finance the abolition of slavery in Dutch America.

After 1873 the Dutch expanded the territory under control in the East Indies in an often ruthless way, especially in Aceh, where a bloody war was fought with natives. By the early years of the twentieth century, a *pax neerlandica* prevailed from the northern tip of Sumatra to Australian New Guinea. Although benefiting from the extraction of petroleum in Sumatra and on Borneo's east coast, overall Dutch trade with the East Indies declined. After the Dutch authorities failed to extend any form of autonomy in the 1930s to an increasingly assertive colonial population, the Japanese invasion of 1942 changed conditions drastically. Nationalists declared independence in 1945, and in 1949, after four years of warfare, the Dutch abandoned what was henceforth called Indonesia. New Guinea, the last Asian territory under Dutch rule, was given up in 1962.

THE ATLANTIC COLONIES

Dutch expansion in the Atlantic world was also as much a military as a commercial affair. The Dutch conquered the Spanish colonies of St. Martin (1631) and Curaçao (1634) and the major Portuguese strongholds in Africa: São Jorge da Mina or Elmina (1637–1872) and Luanda (1641–1648). In addition the Dutch conquered the Brazilian capital of Bahia (1624–1625) and an expanding and then contracting area in northern Brazil (1630–1654). Another large territory under Dutch control was New Netherland (1624–1664), a fur-trading colony made up of settlements on the Hudson, Delaware, and Connecticut Rivers and on Long Island.

More enduring colonies were established on the Caribbean islands and in northern South America. Apart from Curaçao and St. Martin, the Caribbean colonies included the Windward Islands Aruba and Bonaire (1636) and the Leeward Islands St. Eustatius (1636) and Saba (1640). In Guiana, the unsettled region between the Amazon and Orinoco rivers, permanent Dutch settlements arose along the Berbice, Essequibo, Demerara, and Suriname (1667) rivers, partly in an attempt to recreate the Golden Age of Brazil. Brazil had produced prodigious amounts of sugar, tobacco, and brazilwood, filling the holds of ships bound for the United Provinces year after year. Investments in Brazil did not pay off, however, as a nine-year war ousted the Dutch from Brazil. The commercial losses sustained in Brazil eventually led to the bankruptcy in 1674 of the West India Company, the VOC's counterpart in the Atlantic world since 1621.

Suriname boasted hundreds of sugar, coffee, cacao, and cotton plantations in the mid-eighteenth century. However, unlike other empires, the produce of the Dutch plantation colonies did not receive preferential treatment in the home market. After 1780 the smaller Dutch Guiana colonies of Berbice, Essequibo, and Demerara prospered, perhaps eclipsing the cash crop output of Suriname. Although no crops were grown commercially on Curaçao and only minor amounts on St. Eustatius, a steady traffic in colonial goods took place from these islands to the mother country. In exchange for African slaves and European commodities, Curaçao obtained cocoa, tobacco, indigo, sugar, coffee, and hides from the Spanish Main and the Spanish and French islands in the Caribbean. The second quarter of the eighteenth century saw the rise of St. Eustatius, from where French Caribbean sugar and coffee and British North American tobacco were sent to the United Provinces. In 1791 the second West India Company, which had been founded after the demise of the first, went bankrupt. The subsequent onset of the Napoleonic Wars was the kiss of death for the two islands, which lost their niche in the region's contraband trade. Great Britain did not restore Berbice, Essequibo, and Demerara, which came to make up British Guiana. And although Suriname was returned to Dutch rule, its economic weight for the metropolis had declined by the nineteenth century. While all Dutch colonies in America received autonomy in 1954, only Suriname was given its independence, in 1975.

SEE ALSO AMSTERDAM; CANADA; EAST INDIA COMPANY, DUTCH; HOPE FAMILY; INDIA; INDONESIA; MARKETS, STOCK; POPULATION—EMIGRATION AND IMMIGRATION; ROTTERDAM; SHIPPING, INLAND WATERWAYS, EUROPEAN; SHIPPING, TECHNOLOGICAL CHANGE; SHIPS AND SHIPPING; WEST INDIA COMPANY, DUTCH.

BIBLIOGRAPHY

Boogaart, Ernst van den; Emmer, Pieter; Klein, Peter; and Zandvliet, Kees. *La expansión holandesa en el Atlántico.* Madrid: Mapfre, 1992.

De Vries, Jan, and Woude, Ad van der. *Nederland 1500–1815: De eerste ronde van moderne economische groei.* Amsterdam: Balans, 1995.

Gaastra, Femme. *De geschiedenis van de VOC.* Zutphen, Netherlands: Walburg Pers, 1991.

Israel, Jonathan I. *Dutch Primacy in World Trade, 1585–1740.* Oxford: Clarendon Press, 1989.

Postma, Johannes, and Enthoven, Victor, eds. *Riches from Atlantic Commerce: Dutch Transatlantic Trade and Shipping, 1585–1817.* Leiden, Netherlands: Brill, 2003.

Wim Klooster

EMPIRE, FRENCH

This entry consists of the following articles:
EMPIRE, FRENCH: 1450–1815
EMPIRE, FRENCH: 1815–PRESENT

EMPIRE, FRENCH: 1450–1815

France acquired its first colonial empire during the seventeenth century and lost it piecemeal between 1713 and 1815. This empire consisted of several different imperfectly connected parts. The colonies consisted of population centers in North America, plantations in the West Indies, slave trading posts on the coast of Africa (Senegal, Gorée), and trading posts in India.

To counteract Spanish and Portuguese power, in the sixteenth century French kings supported voyages of exploration and colonization by Jacques Cartier (1491–1557) in Canada, Nicolas Durand de Villegagnon (1510–1571) in Brazil, and Jean Ribault (1520–1565) and René Goulaine de Laudonnière (d. 1582?) in Florida. These endeavors, like those by the English at the same time, failed. However, cod fishing, whaling, and the fur trade in Newfoundland had retained French interest in North America: acquisition of fur trade monopoly became the object of lobbying. With the end of France's Wars of Religion (1598) and against Spain (1603), colonial undertakings could be resumed. In 1608 Samuel de Champlain (c. 1567–1635) founded Quebec, which became a hub for trade relations between Canada and France and a base for expeditions further into the continent in the seventeenth century, culminating in the colonization of Louisiana in 1682 and 1698–1702.

The French empire on the American continent was gradually lost as a result of clashes between Britain and France during the eighteenth century: Newfoundland and the Maritime Provinces in 1713, Canada and Louisiana in 1763. France retained only Guyana, which was poorly developed. Despite these losses, France preserved fishing rights in Newfoundland, mounting around 350 fishing expeditions per year in the eighteenth century, compared to 500 per year a century earlier. The loss of New France did not do drastic damage to French colonial trade, even if it did affect La Rochelle, the main port for trade with Canada.

The mainstay of the French colonial empire, from a trading perspective, was the West Indies, occupied by the French between 1620 and 1650 (Saint-Christophe beginning in 1624, Guadeloupe in 1635, Martinique in 1638). These acquisitions served to enhance the power of the French Crown as well as national trade. France acquired the western part of Hispaniola with the Treaty of Ryswick (1697). Tobacco and later sugar cultivation were introduced.

France had established trading posts on the African coast to develop the slave trade (Gorée, Senegal), but this trade was not restricted to these places. From the final quarter of the eighteenth century, French slavers rounded the Cape of Good Hope and set up posts on the Ile Bourbon (occupied in 1649) and the Ile de France (Mauritius, Dutch until 1715). Out of a total of around 4,200 French slaving expeditions in the seventeenth and eighteenth centuries, Nantes was responsible for around 40 percent, and Bordeaux, Le Havre, and La Rochelle for around 10 to 12 percent each.

The French presence in Asia was rather disjointed and mainly restricted to the Indian subcontinent. After extending its influence over a large part of it, in 1763 the French imperial presence in Asia was restricted to just five trading posts, including Pondicherry. French trade in Asia was organized under the auspices of the Compagnie des Indes Orientales (CIO; 1664–1769, 1785–1790). The trade was all centered on Lorient, a purpose-built port established in 1666. Trade in Asia was never as important to France as it was to Britain, hence while the trade of the East India Company increased enormously during the second half of the eighteenth century, the French CIO declined.

Despite these fundamental weaknesses, the eighteenth century was the high point of colonial trade, the driving force behind the growth of French trade. While this quadrupled between the 1720s and the outbreak of the French Revolution in 1789 colonial trading increased tenfold over the same period. During the 1780s colonial produce amounted to 40 percent of total French imports.

This trade benefited the main French ports: Bordeaux, Nantes, Le Havre, and Marseille. In 1788 France imported 98,000 tons of sugar and 40,000 tons of coffee. Indigo, dyewood, and cocoa completed the cargoes.

Trade with the colonies was restricted solely to French merchants and ships as a result of legislation known as the *Exclusif.* Under it, French colonists were obliged to buy their foodstuffs, manufactured goods, and slaves from French merchants. This monopoly, which was established since the beginning of colonization (1626), constantly reaffirmed thereafter (1664, 1698) and fully developed in 1717 and 1727, did not prevent smuggling with the West Indies and North America. The *Exclusif* was relaxed in 1767, and even more in 1784, partly because the loss of New France ended the supply of Canadian fish, cereals, animals, and wood to the West Indies, and also because colonies were opened up to foreigners during the wars (1756–1763, 1778–1783) and it became more difficult to reintroduce a set of rules that ran contrary to colonial interests. Despite this partial opening of the French West Indies, trade in sugar, coffee, and indigo, and the import of flour, wine, and manufactured good to the West Indies was still, at least in theory, the sole preserve of French commerce.

From the 1740s most of the goods imported to France from the West Indies were re-exported to Northern Europe (Holland, Hamburg, and the Baltic). This trade was managed by foreign merchants, who had large numbers of agents in French ports. They brought with them some goods, which were re-exported to the colonies (Irish butter, Swedish iron, German cloth), and they took away sugar and coffee.

The rapid expansion of colonial trade in the eighteenth century was based upon a structure of slave labor in the West Indies. The number of slaves in Saint-Domingue on the eve of the French Revolution was around half a million; Guadeloupe and Martinique had 80,000 each. The ratio of colonists to slaves, which had been one to two at the beginning of the eighteenth century, was one colonist for twenty slaves on the outbreak of the French Revolution. The revolts by the colored people in 1791 and 1793, followed by the independence of Haiti in 1804, dealt a fatal blow to French colonial trade. In 1815 France regained Martinique, Guadeloupe, and Reunion, but these islands produced much less than Saint-Domingue/Haiti. In 1815, at the end of the so-called "Second Hundred Years' War" between France and England, the first French colonial empire had virtually vanished. The Île de France, which became Mauritius, passed to Great Britain. With the Paris treaty France reverted to the borders of 1792, losing all the lands in Europe that Napoleon had annexed during his European expansion—the "French Empire" was created in 1804—as well as the left bank of the Rhine.

SEE ALSO BORDEAUX; COLBERT, JEAN-BAPTISTE; EAST INDIA COMPANY, OTHER; FRANCE; LA ROCHELLE; MARSEILLES; NANTES; PARIS; POPULATION— EMIGRATION AND IMMIGRATION; SLAVERY AND THE

African Slave Trade; Sugar, Molasses, and
Rum; Treaties; United States; Wars.

BIBLIOGRAPHY

Haudrère, Philippe. *La Compagnie française des Indes au XVIIIe siècle.* 4 vols. Paris: Librairie de l'Inde, 1989.

Meyer, Jean, Tarrade, Jean and Rey-Goldzeiguer, Annie. *Histoire de la France coloniale.* Vol. 1: *La conquête, des origines à 1870.* Paris: Pocket, 1996.

Pluchon, Pierre. *Histoire de la colonisation française.* Paris: Fayard, 1990.

Tarrade, Jean. *Le commerce colonial de la France à la fin de l'Ancien Régime: L'évolution du régime de l'exclusif de 1763 à 1789.* 2 vols. Paris: Presses universitaires de France, 1973.

Silvia Marzagalli

EMPIRE, FRENCH: 1815–PRESENT

The establishment of a second colonial empire was undertaken without an overall plan, but France sought to acquire the territorial possessions as a world power in order to compensate for its loss of significant parts of its first empire during the period 1713 to 1815 and later (1870–1871). Military forces accompanied the bridgeheads established by overseas traders in Algeria (starting from the 1820s), in Senegal and Sudan (in the 1850s and 1860s), or in Indochina (from the 1850s to 1880s), nominally to keep the peace along trade routes and ports. Finally, the rivalry between European powers compelled the French Third Republic to take part in the "scramble for Africa" at the end of the nineteenth century. Beyond notions of "civilizing" these places, the establishment of overseas economic power became a means of reinforcing colonial rule. The theory (*mise en valeur*, or development in profit of both local populations and French economy) behind setting up colonies developed during the years 1890 to 1920: The empire would make it easier to provide France with agricultural, forestry, and mineral staples, and it would provide outlets for industry, which was suffering as a result of the slight growth of the French population. Pressure groups formed among Parisian and regional businesses (chambers of commerce and industry, professional federations) or in parliament (the "colonial party"), who found vehicles for their opinion in the media, in the propaganda of the *Union coloniale* (where businessmen were influential), and in the exhibitions and fairs which stressed the resources and wealth of empire.

An overseas trading economy was established. In Black Africa, trading companies were established during periods of expansion by a number of small businessmen, and then, in the interwar (1919–1939), by Syrian and Lebanese from the French Levant. These companies became the foundation for the collection and purchase of "goods" (under the name of *Traite,* that is the seasonal trade of commodities), as gradually commercial agriculture developed, practiced by traditional villagers, by smallholders, or by plantation companies established by the mother country. Merchants established networks of trading posts which were gradually assisted by the authorities (such as Abidjan in the Ivory Coast), and inland trading stations for wholesale and retail distribution of imported manufactured goods including, for example, articles of clothing, ironware, agricultural equipment, and vehicles. The three main firms behind this were the CFAO (Compagnie française de l'Afrique occidentale), the SCOA (Société commerciale de l'Ouest africain), and Optorg. These controlled Black Africa, where there were also some twenty family businesses from Bordeaux (e.g., Maurel et Prom, Devès et Chaumet, and Buhan et Teisseire). They held commercial sway over French Black Africa, but in the Niger River basin an agreement with the United Kingdom maintained an "open port" arrangement between 1898 and 1936, which explains that British firms were also active there, joined by Anglo-Dutch Unilever, equipped with subsidiaries in French Black Africa.

In other countries, there were two kinds of trade: robust, home-grown organizations were mostly responsible for wholesale and retail trade; commercial companies restricted themselves to wholesale transactions via a framework of warehouses. They frequently supported various light industry, particularly for consumables (brewing, cement works, etc.). Family businesses (e.g., Denis frères, from Bordeaux, in Indochina; Brossette, Descours, et Cabaud, from Lyon, in North Africa) or large companies (e.g., Compagnie du Maroc) operated side by side with hundreds of small businessmen. Throughout the territories expansion of trade was assisted by an infrastructure of transport (railways, roads, ports) and finance with specialized overseas banks including Banque de l'Afrique occidentale, Banque de l'Indochine, Crédit foncier d'Algérie et de Tunisie, and Compagnie algérienne. This was complemented in France by banks, agents, staging posts, and transport networks, which promoted the development of overseas trade.

The occurrence of "economic war," which grew during the depression of the 1880s and 1890s, and then again in the period of the interwar, explains why the overseas territories came to be part of a protectionist or even prohibitionist rationale, a revival of the so-called *pacte colonial.* Legislation in 1892 had created a zone of semi-free trade between colonies that were "*assimilées*" (Antilles, La Réunion, New Caledonia, Indochina, then Madagascar) and the home country, and this principle was extended throughout the empire by the customs law of 1928. This attitude of *chasse gardée* (protected competition) generally supported a large number of industries producing consumables, particularly clothing and everyday goods. However, French civil and electrical engineering companies obtained many overseas contracts, which led to the export of equipment, expanding as a result of state-supported finance of basic equipment (during the 1930s, then between 1945 and 1960). At the same time, the expansion of commercial agriculture and the extraction of mineral deposits led to the extensive import of natural produce (rubber, wood, cocoa, coffee, bananas, rum, nuts, cotton, etc.) and minerals (iron, manganese, copper, coal).

The protectionist theory of "security through empire" can be seen in the increasing role of French trade with overseas territories. From 1908 to 1912 the empire accounted for 13 percent of exports and provided 11.3 percent of total French imports. The high point was during the years 1948 to 1952, when French exports to the countries in the Zone Franc—that is countries using the franc as currency and the support from French central banking institutions—amounted to 44.3 percent of French exports in 1948; they still constituted 37.4 percent in 1958. A debate arose during the 1930s, then again more strenuously between 1952 and 1962 on the negative effect of colonial trade on the competitiveness of French businesses, which benefited from *chasses gardées*, except in areas, which were open to more competition (the Niger River basin, Morocco under the Algesiras Agreement of 1906, Cameroon and Togo under French mandate after 1918). Buying within the empire took place at prices that were often higher than the average world price. Sales within the empire generally relied upon subsidies provided by the Exchequer to make up the deficit of the particular territory; hence this was a somewhat artificial economy. In the end, the empire produced little revenue, because it sold very little externally (besides, for example, Indochinese rice in China, North African minerals and phosphates to the United States) and imported more and more material bought outside France. The independence movement plunged French capitalism back into a trade war which lay outside the protection afforded by colonial trade, producing the rapid shift of the geography of French trade during the years 1960 to 1980.

SEE ALSO Colbert, Jean-Baptiste; East India Company, Other; France; La Rochelle; Marseilles; Morocco; Nantes; Paris; Population—Emigration and Immigration; Shipping, Inland Waterways, European; Slavery and the African Slave Trade; Sugar, Molasses, and Rum; Treaties; United States; Vietnam; Wars.

BIBLIOGRAPHY

Bonin, Hubert. *CFAO (Compagnie française de l'Afrique occidentale): Cent ans de compétition (1887–1987).* Paris: Économica, 1987.

Bonin, Hubert, and Cahen, Michel, eds. *Négoce blanc en Afrique noire: L'évolution du commerce à longue distance en Afrique noire du 18e au 20e siècles.* Paris: Publications de la Société française d'histoire d'outre-mer, 2001.

Daumalin, Xavier. *Marseille et l'Ouest africain: L'outre-mer des industriels (1841–1956).* Marseille, France: Publications de la Chambre de commerce and d'industrie, 1992.

Dike, K.O. *Trade and Politics in the Niger Delta, 1830–1885,* Oxford: Clarnedon Press, 1956.

Fieldhouse, D.K. *Unilever Overseas.* London: Croom Helm, 1978.

Law, R., ed. *From Slave Trade to "Legitimate" Commerce: The Commercial Transition in Nineteenth-Century West Africa.* New York: Cambridge University Press, 1995.

Marseille, Jacques. *Empire colonial et capitalisme français: Histoire d'un divorce,* Paris, Albin Michel, 1984.

Topor, Hélène d'Almeida, and Monique Lakroum. *L'Europe et l'Afrique: Un siècle d'échanges économiques.* Paris: Armand Colin, 1994.

Hubert Bonin

EMPIRE, JAPANESE

The Japanese "Empire" from 1895 to 1937 comprised two types of territory. The first were the territories where Japan had direct colonial jurisdiction recognized in international law, including Taiwan, Korea, the Kwantung Leased Territory (KLT), Karafuto, and the Nanyō territories. Second were the territories controlled by indirect, "informal" means, including Manchukuo (Manchuria), which was controlled by a puppet government and the Japanese military; the Chinese Treaty Ports, where Japan held various rights; parts of the Yangtze Valley, where the Japanese had substantial *de facto* control through a combination of economic and gunboat influence. Of all these territories, Manchuria/KLT, Korea, and Taiwan were by far the most important from the viewpoint of trade.

Japan invaded China in 1937 and then extended its control into Southeast Asia during the Pacific War (World War II), which ended in 1945. During the Pacific War the empire briefly expanded to include major territories, including Malaya, Singapore, Indonesia, and the greater part of China.

Within the pre-1937 empire the KLT was a rather special case, being a finger-like extremity of what was formerly part of Liaoning province (Manchuria). Although only 3,462 square kilometers, it was important for two reasons: it included the ports of Port Arthur and Darien, and it was the southern terminal of the South Manchurian Railroad. The railroad opened up the whole of the

Shares of total foreign trade of the Japanese Empire, 1935 (percentages)	
Japan Homeland	41
Karafut	2
Taiwan	9
Korea	23
Nanyō	1
KLT	14
Manchukuo	10
Total	100

SOURCE: Adapted from Nakamura et. al, 1989.

THE GALE GROUP.

Shares of net domestic product in the Japanese Empire, 1937 (percentages)	
Japan Homeland	72
Karafut	1
Taiwan	3
Korea	9
Nanyō	–
KLT	1
Manchukuo	14
Total	100

SOURCE: Adapted from Nakamura et. al, 1989.

THE GALE GROUP.

northeast and formed part of a rail network extending from Europe to Japan. It was built on a 62-meter-wide zone controlled by Japan and economically developed after the Russo-Japanese War (1905–1906).

INTERNATIONAL CONTEXT FOR COLONIAL TRADE POLICIES

To understand Japan's trade policies within its empire, we need to recall the world and East Asian context within which they evolved. Traditional intra-Asian trade was conducted clandestinely between mutually hostile major partners—especially China and Japan—through networks of Chinese and Japanese traders located in entrepôts such as Taiwan, the Ryukyu Islands, and other points in Southeast Asia. Much trade also flowed in the guise of "tributary" trade to the Japanese and Chinese courts.

In the nineteenth century Westerners forcibly arrived, first in China (from the 1830s) and then in Japan (from the 1850s). Based in the treaty ports with extraterritorial powers, the Westerners developed new trade in Asia without needing full territorial control. This Western trade gave added stimulus to Asian production and trade as new sources of demand grew for consumer, intermediate, and primary products.

After the golden age of the pre–World War I decades, when international trade expanded under relatively stable and liberal conditions, the world system entered a crisis in the 1920s and 1930s. Out of their semiformed colonial systems the Western powers moved to form protectionist blocs that would give them more predictable environments and market assurance.

Underlying these nineteenth- and twentieth-century trends was the relative technological superiority held by the West. This not only provided the basis for industrial and military advantage, but also encouraged organizational innovation in the form of modern corporate organization and worldwide banking networks based on telegraphic communications.

Japanese colonial policies, therefore, have to be seen as part of a wider strategy of economic and political survival. From the 1860s to the 1890s Japan's priorities were to resist further Western control of the Japanese economy; to recover lost legal status and effective control over commerce and tariff policy; and to achieve rapid import substitution in consumer and producer goods industries.

From the 1900s the Japanese economy was increasingly participating in the division of international labor—with Japan's comparative advantage moving rapidly from agricultural and primary commodities towards manufactures. This change required new markets for exports and assured supplies of food and raw materials. These requirements were even more pressing by the 1920s, by which time Japan required substantial imports of sugar, rice, and raw cotton, and of coal, coke, and iron ore for the metallurgical industries. In terms of export markets, even as late as 1936, 56 percent of all Japanese export markets were controlled either by the United States or by Great Britain.

Japan acquired its empire in the course of a series of conflicts: Taiwan and commercial rights in China after the Sino-Japanese War (1895); the KLT, railway, and other rights in Manchuria after the Russo-Japanese War (1905); Korea after 1895 and a final annexation in 1910; and further territories after World War I, including Manchuria after 1931. All of the postwar settlements included commercial and economic treaties that were constantly renegotiated according to Japanese priorities to expand export markets, invest in industry and in rail, harbor, and transportation infrastructures, and to secure controlled supplies of necessary imports.

The development of the colonial trade and economic systems were supported not only by war and diplomacy but also by distinctive institutions that blended public and private sectors in ways unprecedented for economies based on private ownership and market transactions. These included state-sponsored shipping (the Nippon Yusen Kaisha and other lines); the South Manchurian Railroad Company; state-nurtured trading companies (especially Okura and Mitsui); tightly knit industrial associations; and banking institutions, notably the Bank of Chosen (Korea), the Bank of Taiwan, the Central Bank of Manchukuo, and the Yokohama Specie Bank.

In spite of the clear economic dimensions of the Japanese Empire, the consensus view is that economic motivation was fundamentally subordinate to wider strategic concerns. However, after 1937, the building of a strategically self-sufficient trade and economic base became an integral part of the wider drive for a new Japanese political order in Asia. The distinction between politics and economics then disappeared.

MAIN TRENDS IN COLONIAL TRADE

Taiwan was the first case in which a colonial economy was systematically developed to support a pattern of foreign trade favorable to the home economy of Japan. The two commodities central to these efforts were sugar and rice. Japan had experienced a long-term sugar "deficit," and Taiwan, as a semitropical economy, had the potential to solve this problem with cane-sugar output. Large investments were made in land consolidation and improvement, in mechanization, and in processing and transportation. These developments were supported by the Mitsui Bank and the Bank of Taiwan, and undertaken initially by the state-sponsored Taiwan Sugar Company. Taiwan eventually was responsible for 87 percent of all the sugar produced in Japan and its colonies.

Investment in rice got under way somewhat more slowly, but by the 1920s it was considerable. Not only did the government invest in huge irrigation works, but it also transferred to Taiwan seed development and other agronomic technology in which, by this time, Japan had become a world leader. As a result of these colonial policies foodstuffs rose from 75 percent of Taiwan's total exports in 1911 to 1913 to 90 percent by 1936 to 1938. Of total exports, by 1935, 87 percent were being sent to Japan. On the import side, Taiwan's major items were fertilizer, textiles, steel, machinery, and transport equipment, again virtually all from Japan.

Only in the late 1930s did this pattern begin to change. This partly reflected Taiwan's industrial development and its potential as a central "pole" in the emerging plans for a new Asia-based war economy. But also important was the rise in protection for Japanese rice farmers and the growing competitiveness of sugar producers in Java and other zones more favorable to sugar production than Taiwan.

The high degree of specialization and Japan-oriented export concentration was even more striking in Korea. There, by 1936, 96 percent of exports were to Japan and 92 percent of imports were from Japan. Rice was by far the biggest export commodity, accounting for 80 percent of the total by 1936. Korea's strategic role as a buffer against Russia was reflected in the scale of heavy-industry– and transportation-related imports. Steel, machinery, and fertilizer, followed by textiles, were the top three imports in 1936.

Although Manchuria was part of the "informal" empire, its controls and policies were substantially exercised by Tokyo, except that the expatriate Japanese administrators were more inclined to Soviet-type planning and were anxious to replace the "old" Japanese *zaibatsu* with state corporations and "new" *zaibatsu* such as Nissan.

The early key to Manchurian development was the soybean; its trade had developed strongly beginning in the mid-nineteenth century, pioneered mainly by the Mitsui Trading Company. Subsequently, as Japan's needs became clearer, coal, ores, and coke became important products. Finally, in the late 1930s, Manchuria graduated to the production of advanced engineering and high-technology products. But by 1935 exports of soya beans and soy-derived products reached a peak of 45 percent of total exports, at which stage Manchuria was the world leader in this product. Other exports were also mainly agricultural. The import side of Manchuria's trade was also quite striking. Between 1925 and 1939 Japan's total exports were growing in the range of 5 to 6 percent per annum, but heavy-industry exports in the same period were growing at 14 percent per annum. At this stage Japanese heavy-industry exports were not in fact strongly competitive in world markets, but the "protected" markets of Korea, Taiwan, and Manchuria were the outlets that made this expansion possible. By the late 1930s these economies were accounting for two-thirds of all Japanese heavy-industry exports.

Japan's colonial trade had mixed results. It did improve Japanese food security, but it did not provide the comprehensive economic security required for a self-sufficient, aggressive political empire. This was partly because the variety of raw materials needed by modern industrial economies is so large that global market access is needed to satisfy them, and partly because Japan's technological level, remarkable though it was, still needed access to the higher levels of capability only available in the United States and Europe.

The impact of colonial trade on the colonies varied. In Taiwan incomes rose, and health, education, and other welfare indicators improved. (Life expectancy was actually higher in Taiwan towards the end of the colonial period than in Japan proper). It is true that professional opportunities for Taiwanese were tightly restricted, but there was learning and skill accumulation, and a strong small-scale commercial culture developed. In Korea, by contrast, income and welfare indicators for the Korean population told a much more negative story, and the displacement of Korean cultivators by Japanese immigrants was a desperate social problem. Manchukuo's high growth rate, on the other hand, achieved a level of per capita income some 40 percent above the average for the rest of China proper, and, in spite of Russian thefts at the end of the war, the industrial foundations laid by Japan left the three Manchurian provinces as leaders of China's heavy industry until the 1980s, when reform and market forces led to the rise of the eastern and southern seaboard regions.

THE PACIFIC WAR TRADE

Japan's entry into China and Southeast Asia was only partly motivated by economic factors. Of these, the most pressing was the wartime need for oil, for Malaysian tin, and for other raw materials needed to supply the war effort. Oil was particularly crucial because of the embargoes on regular trade at the outset of the war. The war also accelerated the process of specialization within the Greater East Asia Co-Prosperity Sphere as a whole. The principle indicator of this was the transformation of Taiwan's economy from mainly producing food and raw materials to focusing increasingly on industrial activity and serving as a logistics hub.

Although in a crude sense the war "completed" Japan's policy of seeking a self-sufficient East Asian trading block under its control, the result was not a success by any measure. After the war the Japanese discovered that diplomacy, direct investment, and trade in conditions of peace were more effective as agents of Japanese economic development.

SEE ALSO Blockades in War; Boycott; Burma; China; Cotton; Developmental State, Concept of the; Drugs, Illicit; Empire, British; Empire, Dutch; Empire, French; Empire, Qing; Great Depression of the 1930s; Hong Kong; Imperialism; Imperial Preference; Indonesia; Japan; Korea; Laborers, Coerced; Manchuria; Mitsui; Petroleum; Philippines; Rice; Rubber; Shanghai; Singapore; South China Sea; Sugar, Molasses, and Rum; Sumitomo; Taiwan; Textiles; Tobacco; United States; Vietnam; War, Government Contracting.

BIBLIOGRAPHY

Beasley, W. G. *Japanese Imperialism.* Oxford, U.K.: Oxford University Press, 1987.

Duus, Peter; Myers, Ramon H.; and Peattie, Mark. *The Japanese Informal Empire in China, 1895–1937.* Princeton, NJ: Princeton University Press, 1989.

Howe, Christopher. *The Origins of Japanese Trade Supremacy: Development and Technology in Asia from 1540 to the Pacific War.* Chicago: Chicago University Press, 1999.

Ka, Chih-Ming. *Japanese Colonialism in Taiwan: Land Tenure, Development, and Dependency, 1895–1945.* Taipei, Taiwan: SMC Publishing, 1995.

Mitsubishi Keizai Kenkyujō. *Taiheiyō ni okeru Kokusai Keizai Kankei* (International Economic Relations in the Pacific). Tokyo: Nihon Hyōronsha, 1937.

Myers, Ramon H., and Peattie, Mark R. *The Japanese Colonial Empire, 1895–1945.* Princeton, NJ: Princeton University Press, 1984.

Takahashi Kamekichi. *Gendai Taiwan Keizairon* (The Economy of Modern Taiwan). Tokyo: Ōkura Shōbō, 1937.

Townsend, Susan C. *Yanaihara Tadao and Japanese Colonial Policy: Redeeming Empire.* London: Curzon, 2000.

Young, Louise. *Japan's Total Empire: Manchuria and the Culture of Wartime Imperialism.* Berkeley: University of California Press, 1998.

Christopher Howe

EMPIRE, MING

The Ming dynasty (1368–1644) emerged out of fifteen years of destructive civil war as Chinese rebels fought among themselves and the victor expelled the Mongols from China, ending their Yuan dynasty (1279–1368). The destruction and disruption were especially severe in Jiangnan, the lower Yangzi region that was the most commercialized and urbanized region in China and probably in the world in the 1200s and 1300s. The effects of war on commerce were compounded by the disruption of inner Asian trade routes by the collapse of the Mongol Empire and by mismanagement of the paper currency system inherited from the Yuan, which rendered that currency worthless and left China with no adequate medium for large-scale interregional trade.

The rulers and bureaucratic elite of the new dynasty had some degree of anticommercial prejudice, but probably were justified in making their first priority the rebuilding of the ravaged agrarian economy and rebuilding and systematization of an educational system designed to produce scholar-officials with a large fund of shared ideas and texts. Early hopes for an enduring systematic harmony of rulers and scholar-officials soon gave way to alternating periods when imperial politics were dominated either by military men and court eunuchs, or by scholar-officials. But these quarrels did not affect local economic recovery, and taxes remained low. The very substantial economic revival in the 1400s affected most areas of the

Chinese enameled porcelains from the Ming and Qing Dynasties. *The skilled craftsmanship behind these objects made them valuable items and also created a trade based on imitation goods that were made to replicate the originals.* © ROYAL ONTARIO MUSEUM/CORBIS. REPRODUCED BY PERMISSION.

empire, in contrast to the growth of the 1100s and 1200s, which had been heavily concentrated in Jiangnan and some south coast areas. Specialization of agricultural production fed into growing interregional trade.

Although most trade was lightly taxed and regulated, certain branches were profoundly shaped by government policies. Salt could be legally sold only with a government license, simply purchased, or granted in compensation for service to the state such as transportation of grain to a frontier garrison. After the capital was moved from Nanjing to Beijing in the1420s, transportation of grain from Jiangnan was managed by nonmarket means, collected as heavy surcharges on the richest prefectures and transported up the Grand Canal, with maintenance and haulage by corvée labor. The legal segment of foreign trade was managed in conjunction with tribute embassies, which the Ming understood as acknowledging the ceremonial supremacy of their emperor and which involved a great deal of exchange of gifts and regulated trade from foreign rulers; court agents took a fixed share of imported luxuries, and closely supervised trade by the embassy party in its port of entry and at the capital. A government agency monopolized the trade in tea in several northwestern provinces in order to have an adequate supply to trade with frontier peoples for strategically vital supplies of horses.

Government interventions might unintentionally support private trade. Great merchant fortunes were made in the salt monopoly. The Grand Canal was open to private shipping, and government grain barges heading south routinely carried private goods. Taxation of this trade recovered only a small part of the maintenance costs. Manufactures of luxury silk goods, especially at Suzhou, and the famous porcelain manufactories at Jingdezhen were managed by imperial agencies to provide a steady flow of these goods to the imperial court, but they also produced large quantities for export and for private purchase within the empire. Even trade in conjunction with tribute embassies facilitated duty-free imports and provided a safe and scrupulously fair environment for trade in luxury goods.

Until about 1350, the south coast of China, with its great port at Quanzhou, Fujian, had been one of the most vigorous centers of maritime commerce in the world. Chinese shipping had reached all over Southeast Asia and to India, the Arabian Peninsula, and East Africa. The famous early Ming voyages (1402–1435) under the eunuch admiral Zheng He are best seen as a continuation and culmination of this earlier phase, combined with a hostility to private maritime trade and an effort to force it into an officially controlled channel. By 1400 private maritime trade had been forbidden on the grounds that it gave aid and comfort to Japanese pirates and their Chinese allies. Thereafter the only legal trade conducted in Chinese ports was in connection with tribute embassies sent by some Southeast Asian sovereign. Chinese who had settled in Southeast Asia, especially at Melaka and at Ayutthaya, the capital of Siam, often managed the embassies and their trade. Clandestine trade in Chinese shipping from south Chinese harbors never entirely ceased, and it was flourishing by 1500. Official sources suggest a good deal of trade on inner Asian routes in connection with more or less genuine embassies; the lack of such records in the late Ming period may reflect the escape of this trade from the tribute matrix, not its decline.

By 1500 the broad revival of the agrarian economy was producing large quantities of consumer goods—silks, porcelain, lacquerware, fine furniture, and much more—and a prosperous local elite all across the empire eager to purchase them. Culture and trade were especially closely entwined in the rise of a very substantial publishing industry that produced everything from fine editions of the Chinese classics to cheap handbooks for travel and daily life and novels full of sex and fighting. Much of this general prosperity and increase in the production of consumer goods can be seen as revivals and extensions of trends and types already visible before the civil wars around the founding of the Ming, mentioned at the beginning of this entry, the Yuan-Ming disorders. A newer

contribution to trade within the empire was the spread of the cultivation of cotton on the north China plain. In the 1500s large amounts of raw cotton were being shipped south to weaving centers in Jiangnan, and some Jiangnan areas ill-suited for rice were shifting to growing cotton.

The collapse of the paper money system around 1400 had left Ming China without an adequate means of exchange for large-scale and long-distance trade. The need became more acute as trade expanded. Some silver was available from Chinese mines, and the rulers became interested in commuting their cumbersome system of taxation in goods and labor services into consolidated taxes payable in silver. The result was a demand for silver that produced a premium in exchange with other metals and goods for anyone who could import silver to China. As world production of silver increased after 1550 with the opening of mines in the Americas and in Japan, much of the increased stock eventually made its way to China. In the Chinese commercial economy and in the payment of commuted taxes, silver was not coined but circulated in ingot, subject to repeated weighings and assays but not to official manipulations and debasements. The transition to a silver economy was much more rapid and far-reaching along the south coast and in the great cities of the lower Yangzi valley. Consequences included price inflation that put increasing pressure on the living standards of officials on fixed salaries, the resulting corruption, and the ability of wealthy land-holding families to suborn the land registration process and keep much of their land off the tax rolls. Military emergencies in the 1590s were a further stimulus to court efforts, frequently managed by eunuchs and vehemently resisted by scholar-officials, to find new sources of revenue.

In the late Ming period the cities of Jiangnan were centers of an intense and sophisticated elite consumerism. Manuals were printed to help the newly rich buy the right things; the contemporary famous novel *Jin Ping Mei* (Plum in the Golden Vase) may contain as many descriptions of fine clothes as it does of sexual acts. In the great mansions and gardens of Suzhou rich men invited their friends to see their new treasures and wrote poems about the joys of modest retirement from the striving world, almost within earshot of big silk warehouses and workshops, labor unrest, and demonstrations against government efforts to impose new taxes. Amid private affluence, tax revenues were not keeping pace with government expenditures. Confucian moralists railed both at corruption and at lavish consumerism. After about 1620 trade sometimes was disrupted by coastal warfare, by mounted rebels coming out of the northwest, and by the incursions of the rising Manchu people on the northeast. Imports of silver did not fall radically, but became less consistent.

At least as important in its effects on the stock of silver in circulation, and even less measurable, was the increase in hoarding of private stocks as law and order declined. The fall of Beijing, first to rebels and then to the Manchu Qing dynasty in 1644, was followed by years of civil war, disruption of trade, and state policies that were anticommercial in effect but not in intention, and then by a remarkably solid and long-lasting recovery after about 1700 that built on Ming foundations.

SEE ALSO BULLION (SPECIE); CHINA; COEN, JAN PIETERSZOON; COMMODITY MONEY; EAST INDIA COMPANY, DUTCH; EMPIRE, SPANISH; EMPIRE, PORTUGUESE; ENTREPÔT SYSTEM; ETHNIC GROUPS, CANTONESE; ETHNIC GROUPS, FUJIANESE; GOLD AND SILVER; GUANGZHOU; JAPAN; KOREA; MELAKA; PHILIPPINES; PIRACY; POTOSÍ; SILK; SMUGGLING; SOUTH CHINA SEA; SPICES AND THE SPICE TRADE; TAIWAN; TEA; TEXTILES; THAILAND; TOBACCO; TRIBUTE SYSTEM; ZHANG HAN; ZHENG FAMILY.

BIBLIOGRAPHY

Brook, Timothy. *The Confusions of Pleasure: Commerce and Culture in Ming China.* Berkeley, Los Angeles, and London: University of California Press, 1998.

Chia, Lucille. *Printing for Profit: The Commercial Publishers of Jianyang, Fujian (11th–17th Centuries).* Cambridge, MA, and London: Harvard University Asia Center, 2002.

Clunas, Craig. *Superfluous Things: Material Culture and Social Status in Early Modern China.* Urbana and Chicago: University of Illinois Press, 1991.

Flynn, Dennis O., and Giráldez, Arturo, eds. *Metals and Monies in an Emerging Global Economy.* Aldershot, U.K., and Brookfield, VT: Ashgate Variorium, 1997.

Twitchett, Denis, and Fairbank, John K., eds. *The Cambridge History of China*, vols. 7 and 8: *The Ming Dynasty, 1368–1644, Parts I, II.* Cambridge, U.K., and New York: Cambridge University Press, 1988, 1998.

Von Glahn, Richard. *Fountain of Fortune: Money and Monetary Policy in China, 1000–1700.* Berkeley, Los Angeles, and London: University of California Press, 1996.

John E. Wills Jr.

EMPIRE, MUGHAL

The Mughal Empire was one of the three major Asian states of the early modern period—the other two being Safavid Persia and Ming/Qing China. It was one of the largest centralized states known in the early modern world, with political authority over a population numbering between 100 and 150 million in the late 1600s and lands covering most of the Indian subcontinent. The wealth of Hind was proverbial in the relatively less fertile and sparsely settled lands of the medieval Islamic world

to the west. Overland, coastal and high-seas trade routes linked regional Mughal Indian economies with the wider world. The Indian population was long accustomed to a money economy using gold, silver, and copper coinage. Insufficient domestic production of gold and silver was augmented by large imports of these metals, paid for by India's substantial commodity trade surplus. Indeed, the port of Mocha in the Red Sea was often described as the "treasure chest" of the Mughal empire.

There was also a considerable amount of trade among the constituent parts of the empire, both overland and along the coast. The major regions with important trading links among themselves were Bengal and the Coromandel coast on the east coast and Gujarat on the west coast. Bengal rice was sent up the Ganges to Agra via Patna, to Coromandel, and round the Cape to Kerala and various port towns on the west coast. The Gujarat silk industry was almost entirely dependent on the import of raw silk from Bengal. Gujarat, in turn, provided large quantities of cotton for the Bengal textile industry. Surat was the premier commercial and financial center of the Mughal Empire. A document dating from 1661 records that the cotton piece goods annually exported by the Armenian and Mughal merchants to Persia through Surat came from as far as Benares and Patna, and their value was no less than 1 million rupees. The Gujarati trader was just as active in the coastal trade of India and in trade to Southeast Asia and East Africa as he was in the commerce with the Middle East. Both Tomé Pires and Duarte Barbosa (Portuguese authors of major accounts of early sixteenth-century Indian Ocean trade) mention the presence of Gujarati merchants in Bengal, Pegu, Malacca, Sumatra, and even China.

MUGHAL INDIA IN ASIAN TRADE

Mughal India had traditionally played a central role in the structure of Asian trade. In part, this was a function of the midway location of the subcontinent between western Asia on the one hand and Southeast and East Asia on the other. But perhaps even more important was the subcontinent's capacity to put on the market a wide range of tradable goods at highly competitive prices. These included food items such as rice, sugar, and oil as well as raw materials such as cotton and indigo. Although most of this trade was coastal, the high-seas trade component was by no means insignificant. The real strength of the subcontinent, however, lay in the provision of large quantities of manufactured goods, the most important of which were textiles of various kinds. These included high-value varieties such as the legendary Dhaka muslins and the Gujarat silk embroideries, but the most important component for the Asian market was the coarse cotton varieties manufactured primarily on the Coromandel coast and in Gujarat. There was great demand for these varieties both in the eastern markets of Indonesia, Malaya, Thailand, and Burma and in the markets of the Red Sea, the Persian Gulf, and East Africa. Although it is impossible to determine precisely what proportion of total demand for mass-consumption textiles in these societies was met by imports from India, the available evidence suggests that it was not insignificant. India's capacity to manufacture these textiles in large quantities and to put them on the market at highly competitive terms made it in some sense the "industrial" hub of the region surrounded by western Asia on one side and Southeast Asia on the other.

This circumstance also largely determined the nature of India's demand for imports from the rest of Asia. This demand consisted essentially either of consumption goods which were not produced domestically for soil, climatic, or other reasons, or of minerals and metals of various kinds whose domestic supply was either nil or substantially below the total demand. In the first category were items including fine spices such as cloves, nutmeg, and mace from Indonesia, and horses and rosewater from western Asia. The second category included rubies and other precious stones from Burma, as well as metals, both precious and nonprecious. By far the most important nonprecious metal imported was tin from Malaya. Precious metals, mainly silver, were imported overwhelmingly from western Asia. Trade satisfied different kinds of consumption needs for India as compared with her numerous trading partners in the Indian Ocean region. This by itself provided an excellent basis for a significant and growing level of trade.

From the vantage point of Mughal India, the two principal segments of maritime Asian trade were the Bay of Bengal and the western Indian Ocean. The Bay of Bengal littoral extended through the Straits of Malacca to the South China Sea all the way to Japan. Westward, however, the link with the Mediterranean through the Persian Gulf and the Red Sea channels involved the use of a certain amount of river-cum-land transportation, more so in the Persian Gulf route than in the Red Sea route. Asian goods brought to the Persian Gulf and the Red Sea ports, mainly by Indian merchants, were taken over at these ports by the merchants of the Middle East, who transported some of them to the southern coast of the Mediterranean, to which Italian and other European merchants had traveled to buy them and carry them back to Europe.

EURO-ASIAN TRADE

This pattern of trade between Mughal India and Europe, which had been in operation for centuries, underwent a structural modification following the discovery by the Portuguese at the end of the fifteenth century of the route to the East Indies via the Cape of Good Hope. The procurement of the Asian goods came to be organized by the Europeans themselves, who had arrived in the East in any number for the first time. Most of the goods had to be paid for in precious metals because Europe was unable to supply goods, which could be sold in Asia in reasonably large quantities at competitive terms. Spanish-American silver mines had tremendously expanded the European silver stock, a part of which was available for diversion to Asia for investment in Asian goods, so expansion in the volume and the value of the Euro-Asian trade continued.

Throughout the sixteenth and the first half of the seventeenth century the Euro-Asian trade carried on by the Portuguese was centered on southwestern India. The Portuguese were followed by the British and the Dutch East India Companies, which were established in 1600 and 1602, respectively. But because both the Dutch and the English procured their pepper and other spices mainly in Indonesia, the Asian loci of the Euro-Asian seaborne trade shifted at the beginning of the seventeenth century from southwestern India to the Indonesian archipelago. It was nearly three-quarters of a century before the Asian loci shifted decisively to Mughal India. This was a consequence of the change in European fashions that assigned an increasingly important role to Mughal Indian textiles and raw silk in the Asian imports into Europe. Mughal India also played a key role in the extensive Dutch intra-Asian trade. Indeed, it was the long-established pattern of the Indonesian spice growers asking for Coromandel textiles in exchange for their wares, which had set the Dutch East India Company on the path of participation in intra-Asian trade in the first place. Later in the seventeenth century Bengal raw silk and opium played an extremely important role in the successful functioning of the Dutch network of intra-Asian trade. The largest group of the private European traders engaged in this trade, the English private traders, also operated overwhelmingly from Mughal India.

PROCUREMENT AND TRADE The organizational structure of procurement and trade that the European trading companies and private traders encountered in Mughal India was both efficient and sophisticated. The production for the market was organized mainly on the basis of contracts between merchants and producers that specified the quantity to be supplied, the price, and the date of delivery. A highly developed credit organization contributed to the efficient working of the system. Merchants could raise short-term loans at remarkably low rates of interest. The institution of the respondentia loans (a loan on a ship's cargo payable only upon safe arrival) was also quite widespread. Funds could be transferred from one place to another relatively cheaply by using the *hundi* (bill of exchange). The *sarrafs* (dealers in money) who ran the credit and the banking structure were also indispensable to the working of the currency and the monetary system. The Mughal coinage system, with its uniform imperial standards of weights and measures, was imposed throughout the empire over dozens of local monetary systems. Centrally appointed functionaries of the imperial mints accepted bullion or coin from local *sarrafs* or other private individuals. The system of free minting ensured that the Mughal coins retained their high degree of fineness without any known debasement for nearly two centuries. Overall, a sophisticated infrastructure of institutions and services, which rendered the system of production and exchange highly efficient, dynamic, and fully market responsive, was available in Mughal India. The principal constituent elements of this infrastructure were a high degree of labor mobility and the existence of a labor market, merchant groups capable of collective defense and good organization, the development of accountancy skills, and highly developed and price-responsive marketing systems.

PROFILE OF THE EUROPEAN COMPANIES' TRADE From a modest figure of less than f.3 million (1 florin = 0.66 rupees) over the three-year period 1619 to 1621, the total Dutch imports from Asia had crossed the f.10 million mark by 1668 to 1670 and stood at f.15 million from 1698 to 1700. The figure in 1738 to 1740 was in excess of f.19 million, and nearly f.21 million in 1778 to 1780. Pepper and spices together came down from an imposing 74 percent of the total imports in 1619 to 1621 to a mere 12 percent during 1778 to 1780. On the other hand, textiles and raw silk went up from 16 percent in 1619 to 1621 to an incredible 55 percent at the end of the seventeenth century. There was a decline thereafter, but in 1778 to 1780 textiles and raw silk again accounted for half of the total imports. Because Bengal alone accounted for more than 50 percent of the total of textiles and around 80 percent of the total of raw silk imported from Asia, the share of this region in the total Asian imports at the end of the seventeenth century was approximately 40 percent. This proportion was much higher for Mughal India as a whole.

The story of the British East India Company was broadly similar. Starting out very much behind its Dutch rival, the British Company had almost caught up with it by the end of the seventeenth century and actually forged ahead of it by 1738 to 1740. By the end of the 1770s the three-year total British figure stood at f.69 million, against the Dutch figure of f.21 million. Between the periods 1668 to 1670 and 1738 to 1740, the share of textiles in total British imports had become as much as 70 percent. India was central to the British Company trade

throughout, accounting for 95 percent and 84 percent of total Asian imports during the periods 1698 to 1700 and 1738 to 1740, respectively, when the textile trade was at its peak.

TRADE AS AN INSTRUMENT OF GROWTH The substantial amount of trade carried on from Indian ports by the Europeans, both with Europe as well as with other parts of Asia, served to strengthen Mughal India's status considerably as a premier trading and manufacturing nation in Asia. At the turn of the eighteenth century India was probably the largest and the most cost-competitive textile-manufacturing country in the world. The "bullion for goods" character of the European trade considerably enhanced its positive implications and indeed turned it into an important instrument of growth in the Mughal Indian economy. The gold and silver the Europeans imported from Europe and Asian countries such as Japan led to a substantial increase in the supply of money in the country. The growing level of monetization in the economy in turn facilitated reform measures such as the growing conversion of the land-revenue demand from kind into cash, which led to a further increase in market exchange and trade.

Because the "bullion for goods" European trade did not produce a decline in the domestic output of import-competing goods, the positive implications of the growth in trade for the level of income, output, and employment in the economy were considerably greater than they would have been if the trade had been of the ordinary "goods for goods" variety. The increase in output and employment in the manufacturing sector was clearly significant. In addition, the fact that, on average, the rate of growth of the European demand for Mughal Indian goods such as textiles and raw silk was greater than the rate of growth of their supply increasingly turned the market into a sellers' market.

This scenario, however, underwent a drastic change in the second half of the eighteenth century when the British East India Company managed to acquire *diwani* revenue collection rights in Bengal. Insofar as the relationship between the British East India Company and the Indian intermediary merchants and producers was no longer governed by the market but by the company, the company appropriated a good part of the legitimate share of the producers and the merchants in the total output. Also, by siphoning off a part of the province's revenues for the procurement of the export goods, the British Company was increasingly able to manage without importing much bullion from home.

SEE ALSO ARMS, ARMAMENTS; BENGAL; BULLION (SPECIE); CALCUTTA; CARAVAN TRADE; CHINA; COMMODITY MONEY; COTTON; COWRIES; EAST INDIA

COMPANY, BRITISH; EAST INDIA COMPANY, DUTCH; EAST INDIA COMPANY, OTHER; EMPIRE, BRITISH; EMPIRE, DUTCH; EMPIRE, FRENCH; EMPIRE, PORTUGUESE; ENTREPÔT SYSTEM; ETHNIC GROUPS, GUJARATI; FACTORIES; FAIRS; GAMA, VASCO DA; GOLD AND SILVER; GUILDS; GUJARAT; INDIA; INDUSTRIAL REVOLUTION; MADRAS; MERCANTILISM; MUMBAI; PAKISTAN; SILK; SPICES AND THE SPICE TRADE; SRI LANKA; TEXTILES; TOBACCO; WAR, GOVERNMENT CONTRACTING.

BIBLIOGRAPHY

Chaudhuri, K. N. *The Trading World of Asia and the English East India Company, 1660–1760.* Cambridge, U.K.: Cambridge University Press, 1978.

Prakash, Om. *The Dutch East India Company and the Economy of Bengal, 1630–1720.* Princeton, NJ: Princeton University Press, 1985.

Prakash, Om. *European Commercial Enterprise in Pre-Colonial India.* Cambridge, U.K.: Cambridge University Press, 1998.

Prakash, Om. *Bullion for Goods: European and Indian Merchants in the Indian Ocean Trade, 1500–1800.* Delhi, India: Manohar Publishers, 2004.

Richards, John F. *The Mughal Empire.* Cambridge, U.K.: Cambridge University Press, 1993.

Om Prakash

EMPIRE, OTTOMAN

The Ottoman Empire (1300–1918) was an important conduit of trade throughout its history because it straddled Europe and Asia, but its largest volume of trade was not international but domestic. The Ottoman Empire endured as long as it did because of its stable agrarian economy. Its government was organized around a land-tenure system that funded a military bureaucracy designed to preserve order and prosperity.

Trade in the Ottoman Empire was often seen as less important than agriculture. As described in the Ottoman "circle of justice," the ruler defended the peasants so they could work the land. The land produced crops, which supported the ruler, who in turn protected the peasants. Even in this agrarian system, though, the steadily growing importance of international commerce to the Ottoman economy can be traced through five distinct periods in the early modern era.

CREATING THE OTTOMAN SYSTEM, 1453 TO 1606

The Ottoman Empire arose in Western Anatolia in the mid-fourteenth century as one of several Turkish frontier principalities. Its establishment of power in both Europe and Asia gave it control of strategic entrepôts of trade, particularly after it took Constantinople (later, Istanbul) in 1453. Early Ottoman rulers built a land-tenure system for collecting revenue, the proceeds from which they supplemented with taxes on trade. Genoa and Venice were among their first foreign trading partners, each with merchant communities long resident in Ottoman lands.

By the middle of the sixteenth century the Ottomans had secured the main territories of the Middle East (excluding Iran) and were trying to control the export and import of precious metals, wheat, and cotton to secure social stability. Their goals stood in sharp contrast to the mercantilism of rising European trading nations, which were striving through economic competition to gain power and wealth.

In late medieval times a north-south trade in furs, slaves, and sugar had dominated international commerce between the Arab lands and Central Asia, and this continued strong through the early Ottoman era. This trade eventually began to be eclipsed in the fourteenth and fifteen centuries by the continual flow of silk, precious metals, spices, and textiles on east-west caravans. Among the most important centers for this new trade were the coastal cities of western Anatolia and Syria: Izmir, Bursa, Aleppo, and Damascus.

In all the major Ottoman cities, strong artisan guilds that played significant roles in trade were promoted. Such groups retained their importance through the early modern era, given that the state supported their systems of self-regulation and governance. As in many other areas, Ottoman official policy toward the guilds was essentially conservative, attempting to preserve continuity with past practice and to innovate only with great caution. Regional trade fairs that resembled fairs in other premodern economies thrived for many centuries, particularly in the Balkans.

In the sixteenth century merchant networks, particularly of non-Muslim groups, such as Greeks, Armenians, and Jews, also began to expand and flourish as the Ottomans consolidated control over areas they had conquered. The relative political and social autonomy of these minority groups was reinforced by their status within the Ottoman *millet* system, which recognized the legal status of Jews and Christians within the empire and allowed these groups to practice their religions privately while requiring a special annual tax from them. In addition, all of these minority groups had family connections beyond the Middle East, further increasing their importance as networks for international trade.

With the rise of maritime empires such as those of the Portuguese and Spanish, the Ottomans began to confront new rivals in international trade who threatened to rearrange long-standing patterns of commerce. In the

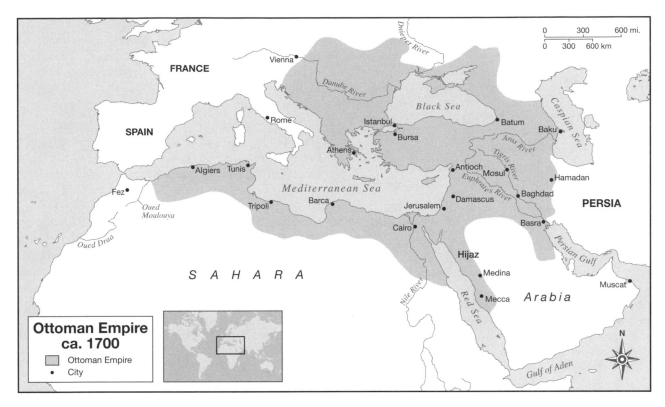

Ottoman Empire ca. 1700
☐ Ottoman Empire
• City

XNR PRODUCTIONS, INC. REPRODUCED BY PERMISSION OF THOMSON GALE.

sixteenth century, for example, the Portuguese tried but failed to divert the long-standing trade in spices between India and the Ottoman Empire that had flowed through the Persian Gulf and the Red Sea. The Portuguese also could not displace enduring trade relationships that the Ottomans had built with their Mediterranean trade partners.

Various Mediterranean trade cities such as Ragusa (modern Dubrovnik) flourished even in times of hostility. Ragusa was an Ottoman vassal city-state that was given political autonomy in exchange for an annual tribute payment in gold. It was permitted to function independently for centuries, enabling Ragusan merchants to establish a network of cloth distribution through the Ottoman Balkans, with branches in cities such as Sofia, Belgrade, Sarajevo, and Edirne.

During this era the Ottomans also began to use capitulations treaties to pursue their foreign-policy goals. Although their trade agreements with Italian city-states dated back several centuries, the Ottomans signed the first full-capitulations treaty with a major Western European power, France, in 1569. The capitulations system allowed certain European nations to receive varying rates of tax exemption on their imports and exports to and from the Ottoman Empire. The Ottoman goal in granting capitulations was to permit a cheap supply of Europe-

an finished goods to promote their subjects' welfare, whereas the European goal was to maximize exports and reduce imports to decrease the flow of precious metals away from Europe. Both sides saw benefits from this system.

OTTOMAN CONSOLIDATION, 1606 TO 1699

By the beginning of the seventeenth century, Ottoman territorial expansion had ended as the empire entered a period of consolidation. Soon after the French had established a competitive advantage through their capitulations agreement with Istanbul, the English and Dutch negotiated similar treaties. European competition took the form of merchant companies such as the English Levant Company, whose members were drawn from the same class of people who would later build similar enterprises in the New World. One such merchant/adventurer was Captain John Smith (c. 1580–1631), founder of the Virginia Company, who had spent considerable time as a merchant in Ottoman ports before his move across the Atlantic.

These merchant companies initially focused on importing cloth, cotton, spices, and silk from Ottoman ports, but their trading activities were overshadowed during the seventeenth century by the rise of New World sources of such raw materials. The burgeoning supply of silver from new mines in Latin America and Central Europe led to the virtual collapse of the Ottoman monetary system in the 1580s. This period also saw the establishment of colonial plantations producing goods traditionally imported from the Ottomans, particularly sugar, tobacco, coffee, and cotton. More and more, the Ottoman Empire came to be perceived as a market for European finished goods, as well as a strategic transit point for more attractive commodities coming from farther east. Egypt in particular became important as a conduit for goods from India and South Asia to Europe.

The late seventeenth century also saw rivalry between two major British overseas trading companies, the East India Company and the Levant Company, in which trade through Ottoman territory played an important part. The East India Company was criticized for exporting too much silver to India, and the British government demanded that it ship more English cloth there. With low demand in India for English woolens, the East India Company tried to comply by marketing its goods more aggressively in Iran. This tactic brought it into conflict with the Levant Company, which had already established its own textile trade through Aleppo to Iran via networks of Armenian merchants. In the eighteenth century, when the Levant Company reduced its activities in Aleppo due to political unrest, the East India Company still had not displaced the Armenian trading networks that linked Iran with Aleppo, because the Armenians simply began working with French textile merchants from Marseilles instead of with the English who had been there before.

FURTHER ADJUSTMENTS IN THE EIGHTEENTH CENTURY, 1699 TO 1798

The Ottomans perceived a decline in their international standing as early as the mid-seventeenth century, when various commentators began to explore the causes of the military and financial problems that had started to affect them. The steady Austrian advance into the Balkans, culminating in the Long War (1683–1699), further exacerbated Ottoman concerns. The Treaty of Karlowitz, signed after that war, marked the first permanent and substantial Ottoman loss of territory to a European power. This encroachment was soon followed by further capitulations agreements with Austria's European rivals. Another factor that weakened the Ottoman central authority at that time was the rise of independent local hereditary landlords, particularly in such places as Lebanon that were no longer under the full control of the central government.

At the same time, there was a new drive to modernize Ottoman society in various ways. The "Tulip Period" of the 1720s was a time when the Ottoman elite became enamored with Western tastes and fashions. The cultivation of rare tulip gardens became a way for the Ottoman

elite to display wealth and sophistication. Over the next few decades more substantial changes were introduced, such as the first attempts to modernize the Ottoman military. This began in the 1730s and eventually culminated in the remaking of the Ottoman army into a modern European army by the middle of the nineteenth century.

The impact of Western global expansion was also felt gradually in Ottoman domains during the eighteenth century through an increasing European presence in the Black Sea, the Mediterranean, and the Indian Ocean. One traditional economic system that began to be challenged by European powers was maritime piracy, which for centuries had functioned in the Mediterranean, particularly off the coast of North Africa, as an unorganized method of collecting revenue from maritime commerce. Beginning in the late eighteenth century European navies took steps to suppress it as they tried to establish more regular systems of international maritime law.

CONFRONTING THE MODERN GLOBALIZING ECONOMY, 1798 TO 1858

Global geopolitical and economic rivalries had their most direct impact on the Ottomans with Napoleon's invasion and occupation of Egypt in 1798. This unprecedented event caused the Ottomans to review how their militaries were organized, given the weaknesses that it had exposed. The long-term impact of French involvement in politics and trade in the region was felt most keenly in North Africa, where the local governors of Tunisia and Algeria were brought gradually under French colonial control and disassociated from their original Ottoman rulers.

In the central Ottoman lands, the governor of Egypt, Muhammad Ali Pasha (who ruled 1805–1849), took the French invasion as the starting point to begin a thorough fiscal and military modernization of his domains. Over the next twenty years he asserted his independence, consolidated his own power, and nearly defeated the Ottomans in an attempt to make himself the main ruler of the region. Taking lessons from the French Revolution, he organized a mass army and inaugurated a program of military construction and industrial production that went against European plans for Egypt, which, in a mercantilist system dominated by Europe, could only be a source of raw materials and a consumer of finished goods.

Ultimately, Muhammad Ali's rising economic autonomy so alarmed the European powers that they united to curb his ambitions. They forced first the Ottomans and later, Muhammad Ali and his successors, to sign far more extensive capitulations agreements than before, such as the 1838 Balta Limanı Treaty. During the early nineteenth century two-thirds of British exports to the Ottoman Empire were textiles. This period also witnessed the most serious debasement of the Ottoman currency in the history of the empire, with the exchange rate on the British pound reduced from 8 to 104 kuruş (the standard Ottoman silver coin of this era) between 1808 and 1839. European trade and monetary policies that promoted exports at all costs exacerbated the general weakening of the Ottoman financial situation.

ON THE MARGINS OF THE WORLD SYSTEM, 1858 TO 1918

During the first half of the nineteenth century roughly 75 percent of Ottoman trade was still domestic, so the Ottoman economy was shielded considerably from the market forces of the outside world. The Ottomans began to enter into the European financial system and borrow significant amounts of money from European lenders starting in the 1850s, a process initially facilitated by European powers who wished to acquire more leverage over the Ottomans to guard against the southward expansion of Russia, as well as to promote sales of their exports. This helped create the conditions for the outbreak of the Crimean War, and involved European financial interests in the Ottoman economy to secure loan repayment. By the 1870s European bankers had formed public debt commissions in Egypt and in Istanbul to control local economic policy to ensure the repayment of debts owed them.

Also at this time, foreign powers began to sell *berats* to local non-Muslim *millet* community members. *Berats* were diplomas granting the status of foreign citizenship, which conferred various tax privileges on Ottoman non-Muslims based on the capitulations system. This change in status helped create resentment of *millet* community members among Muslim merchants who suddenly had to compete with them on less favorable terms.

The Egyptians thought at first that the Suez Canal, completed in 1867 under Muhammad Ali's successor, Isma'il Pasha, would help Egypt bolster its own trade status, which had been lifted by the increased importance of Egyptian cotton because of the blockade of U.S. cotton during the Civil War. Ultimately, though, British and French financial interests controlled the Suez Canal project. The increasing European commercial presence in Egypt precipitated an antiforeign revolt in 1882, after which the British established a shadow government there to maintain stable access to the canal. This was necessary to defend Britain's vital link to India, a global connection that more and more defined Britain's place in the world.

After the tumultuous military and governmental modernizations of the first half of the nineteenth century, the Ottomans introduced another set of sweeping economic and social reforms during the period known as the *Tanzimat* (1839–1876). In economic terms, some of the most important changes occurred as a result of the Ottoman Land Law of 1858, a statute that dramatically expanded the potential for the private ownership of land. Large tracts of land could now be bought, sold, and held by absentee landlords, and, in some cases, transferred to foreigners. This caused some upheaval because not all segments of the population were brought into a monetary economy at the same rate and with the same resources. After the experiments in political and economic modernization of the Tanzimat period, Sultan Abdül-hamit II ruled for three decades (1876–1909) with an authoritarian style that limited further changes and modernizations.

As a result of the constraints imposed by this late Ottoman political and economic contraction, the Ottoman Empire became marginalized in the larger global struggle being waged by European powers for colonial expansion, particularly as they carved up Africa for its raw materials. The Ottomans retained their roles as a secondary market for finished goods and as a source for certain raw materials. Their main role in the global economy by the late nineteenth century was to reclaim their perennial status as a transit point for east-west commerce. The Middle East, in general, occupied this position until the discovery of oil in Iran in 1908 and in Iraq after World War I. The economic implications of this critical development, however, would not be felt until the 1940s and 1950s, decades after the collapse of the Ottoman Empire in 1918.

SEE ALSO ALI, MUHAMMAD; ARMS, ARMAMENTS; BLOCKADES IN WAR; BULLION (SPECIE); CALCUTTA; CARAVAN TRADE; COMMODITY MONEY; COTTON; COWRIES; EGYPT; EMPIRE, BRITISH; EMPIRE, FRENCH; EMPIRE, PORTUGUESE; EMPIRE, SPANISH; ENTREPÔT SYSTEM; ETHNIC GROUPS, AFRICANS; ETHNIC GROUPS, ARMENIANS; ETHNIC GROUPS, JEWS; FAIRS; GENOA; GOLD AND SILVER; GREECE; GUILDS; LEVANT COMPANY; MERCANTILISM; MILLETS AND CAPITULATIONS; PASHA, ISMA'IL; PERSIAN GULF; PIRACY; SILK; SLAVERY AND THE AFRICAN SLAVE TRADE; SPICES AND THE SPICE TRADE; SUEZ CANAL; TEXTILES; TOBACCO; WAR, GOVERNMENT CONTRACTING; WARS; WHEAT AND OTHER CEREAL GRAINS.

BIBLIOGRAPHY

Goffman, Daniel. *The Ottoman Empire and Early Modern Europe.* Cambridge, U.K., and New York: Cambridge University Press, 2002.

Inalcik, Halil. *The Ottoman Empire: The Classical Age, 1300–1600,* tr. Norman Itzkowitz and Colin Imber. New York: Praeger Publishers, 1973.

Inalcik, Halil; Faroqhi, Suraiya; McGowan, Bruce; Quataert, Donald; and Pamuk, Şevket. *An Economic and Social History of the Ottoman Empire, 1300–1914.* Cambridge, U.K., and New York: Cambridge University Press, 1997.

Pamuk, Şevket. *The Ottoman Empire and European Capitalism, 1820–1913: Trade, Investment, and Production.* Cambridge, U.K., and New York: Cambridge University Press, 1987.

Pamuk, Şevket. *A Monetary History of the Ottoman Empire.* Cambridge, U.K., and New York: Cambridge University Press, 2000.

Ernest Tucker

EMPIRE, PORTUGUESE

The Portuguese Empire, the first of the European colonial empires, was also the last to come to an end. From the 1415 conquest of Ceuta, a Moroccan port in the Strait of Gibraltar, to the independence of the African colonies in 1974 and 1975, it underwent many fundamental changes in geographical boundaries and institutional framework. It was never a purely merchant empire, for Church and Crown always played important roles, but in the long run trade was probably the most important single factor for the empire's breadth and subsistence.

Before Columbus reached America the Portuguese already held a few fort-towns in Morocco; they had discovered and peopled the Atlantic islands of Madeira and Azores (and later Cape Verdes and São Tomé) and explored the west coast of Africa all the way down to the Cape of Good Hope. This was a vast base for long-distance trade. In Morocco they dealt in local textiles, corn, and horses; they grew wheat in the Azores and sugarcane in Madeira; and they traded in slaves and malagueta pepper in West Africa. At the fort of Elmina, on the coast of present day Ghana, the acquisition of gold formed a Crown monopoly.

These early forays set a precedent for European overseas trade and ultimately prepared the way for Vasco da Gama's voyage to India (1498). Trade on the Cape route to the East Indies immediately became the leading merchant enterprise. Luxuries, which were mostly paid for in silver, were brought to Lisbon—which grew to be one of the largest cities in Europe—and then circulated through a trading post in Antwerp. This business was largely run for the benefit of the Crown, but it also interested the largest international merchant houses. The Cape route was not, however, the only concern of the Portuguese in the East. They established a network of forts and trading posts centered in Goa and extending from Mozambique to Macao and East Timor—the *Estado da Índia*—and tried to tax and control all navigation in the Indian Ocean. They also engaged in Asian carrying trade by outfitting expeditions to China (Macao) and Japan (Nagasaki). In time, this became even more important than the sea route to Lisbon.

Portuguese endeavors facilitated the displacement of long-distance trade from the Mediterranean to the Atlantic. However, the Levant spice route was never completely shut down, and it even recovered after 1570. At the same time, the Portuguese monopoly over the Cape route was challenged by Dutch and English interlopers, and later by the East India Companies they established. Eventually, the Portuguese spice trade decreased to less than one-third what it had been. Eastern trade never regained its former prominence.

In the meantime, Portugal had set up a colony in America. For the first thirty years after its discovery in 1500, Brazil provided little more than dyewood. After the introduction of sugarcane, colonization progressed but was still hindered by the shortage of labor, as disease, native resistance, and missionary interference hampered the enslavement of the Indians. Merchants and planters resorted to importing slaves from Africa. By 1570 there were 2,000 to 3,000 Africans in Brazil. After that, the slave trade and sugar mills (later supplemented by tobacco growing and cattle raising) lay the foundation for the Atlantic Empire, which joined Brazil and West Africa.

In 1580 Portugal entered a dynastic union with Spain and soon the empire came under attack from the United Provinces, known today as the Netherlands. In the East most of the dominions were permanently lost, and so was Elmina. Angola and São Tomé were also temporarily captured. In Brazil, Bahia was taken and promptly recovered, but Pernambuco remained under Dutch control for more than twenty years. For a time, the very subsistence of the empire seemed at stake, but after successful secession from Spain in 1640, diplomatic and military efforts restored the best part of the Atlantic domains to Portuguese control. The Dutch were expelled from Angola by an expedition from Rio de Janeiro (1648), and from Pernambuco (1654) by the settlers themselves, with the assistance of the short-lived General Company for the Trade of Brazil, founded in 1649 to protect the Atlantic fleets.

The empire was now anchored in Brazil and the Atlantic. By 1680 even ships on the Cape route stopped at Bahia, and the sale of tobacco in Asia helped sustain the *Estado da Índia*. Brazilian exports of sugar and tobacco were growing, but the instability of European demand could cause long recessions, as in 1668 to 1690. The commercial upturn was facilitated by the discovery of gold and later of diamonds. Brazil continued to be a plantation economy, but during the first half of the eighteenth century gold was a fundamental resource for the empire and a prime source for the European supply of bullion. British merchants, who enjoyed a privileged status, exported most of the gold, and indirectly came to control a large part of the Brazilian trade.

Reforms adopted under the government of the marquis of Pombal (1750–1777) intended to reclaim that

MACAU

Europe's oldest Far Eastern settlement was established by Portuguese traders on the southeastern Chinese coast, at a place they referred to as Macau. The Portuguese arrived in China in the early sixteenth century, establishing a permanent settlement at Macau in 1557. The settlement became an important base in Portugal's Asian trade network. Though officially Chinese, Macau was administered by Portugal, which paid an annual rent until 1849. In 1685 China officially recognized the city a foreign-trade port. For many years Macau was a vital entrepôt for Sino-Japanese trade, and for regional trade to Europe. By the nineteenth century, however, the decline of Portugal as a commercial power, and the establishment of Hong Kong, eroded Macau's economic importance. Macau was declared a Portuguese colony in 1862, but China never really accepted this status. Macau briefly regained its commercial importance early in World War II as a neutral port, but it came under Japanese domination from 1943 to 1945. China's postwar Communist government let Macau's status as a Portuguese possession remain unchanged until the future of Hong Kong was resolved. In 1999, following the British handover of Hong Kong, Macau was returned to China as a special administrative region.

David J. Clarke

trade from foreign control (by setting up chartered companies and new trade regulations) and to offset diminishing gold receipts. After a period of uncertainty, trade with Brazil again prospered, favored by the widening European market for sugar and cotton. Portuguese neutrality in the wars that followed the French Revolution proved particularly rewarding until 1807, when the Napoleonic armies invaded Portugal to enforce the Continental System. The royal family retired to Brazil and as a result, the colonial system was suspended. Portugal could no longer serve as the entrepôt for the produce of Brazil. Widespread discontent triggered a revolution in 1820 that forced the king to return to Portugal and eventually led to the independence of Brazil (1822).

The sudden collapse of the colonial system caused a severe crisis. No other empire had been as important to the metropole as the Portuguese, in financial and economic terms. But now Eastern trade, after a brief revival, was almost irrelevant, and so was intercourse with the African possessions, which continued to work as slave-trade stations for Brazil. Only when that traffic was effectively stopped (after 1851) did trade begin to flow. Nevertheless, until the 1880s it did not did not exceed 6 percent of foreign trade. Portugal was then involved in the scramble for Africa and obtained international approval for territorial expansion, even though the grand project of the rose-colored map joining Angola and Mozambique was ultimately thwarted. The resulting national commotion, combined with a serious financial crisis, generated a protectionist atmosphere that favored colonial business. Nevertheless, with the exception of São Tomé, where coffee and cocoa plantations prospered, this was a largely predatory growth based on the extraction and re-export of wild rubber and coffee from Angola and on labor exports from Mozambique to the South African mines. African possessions nonetheless became an important source for international currency.

Subsequent development depended heavily on foreign investment in chartered companies, particularly in Mozambique, and on public expenditure, which resulted in large budgetary deficits, mostly in Angola. This was unacceptable for the autocratic regime established in 1926, which valued strict financial discipline, even at the cost of slowing down economic growth in the colonies. After World War II, growth and emigration resumed and, oddly enough, even accelerated after the outbreak of nationalist guerilla wars (1961). During the 1960s the colonies took up 24 percent of Portuguese exports and supplied raw materials at privileged prices. Yet, this exchange grew less important as foreign trade expanded and diversified in both Portugal and the colonies. By then, however, the reigning political regime had tied its destiny to the defense of the overseas possessions, and so emphatically rejected any possibility of decolonization. This would only come about in the aftermath of the Revolution of 1974, which intended from the outset to put an end to the colonial wars.

SEE ALSO ANGOLA; BAHIA; BRAZIL; EAST INDIA COMPANY, OTHER; EMPIRE, DUTCH; EMPIRE, SPANISH; GAMA, VASCO DA; INDIA; POMBAL, MARQUÊS DE; RIO DE JANEIRO; SLAVERY AND THE AFRICAN SLAVE TRADE.

BIBLIOGRAPHY

Bethell, Leslie, ed. *Colonial Brazil.* Cambridge, U.K.: Cambridge University Press, 1987.

Clarence-Smith, Gervase. *The Third Portuguese Empire, 1825 1975: A Study in Economic Imperialism.* Manchester, U.K.: Manchester University Press, 1985.

Godinho, Vitorino Magalhães. *L'Économie de l'empire portugais, XVe–XVIe siècles (The Economy of the Portuguese Empire, 15th–16th centuries)*. Paris: SEVPEN, 1968. Enlarged Portuguese edition: *Os Descobrimentos e a Economia Mundial (The Great Discoveries and the World Economy)*. 4 vols. Lisbon: Presença, 1981–1983.

Miller, Joseph C. *Way of Death: Merchant Capitalism and the Angolan Slave Trade, 1730–1830*. Madison: University of Wisconsin Press, 1988.

Newitt, Malyn. *Portugal in Africa: The Last Hundred Years*. London: C. Hurst, 1981.

O'Brien, P. K., and Prados de La Escosura, Leandro, eds. "The Costs and Benefits of European Imperialism from the Conquest of Ceuta, 1415, to the Treaty of Lusaka, 1974." *Revista de Historia Económica* 16, no. 1 (Winter 1998).

Pearson, Michael N. "The Portuguese in India." *The New Cambridge History of India*, vol. 1. Cambridge, U.K.: Cambridge University Press, 1987.

Jorge M. Pedreira

EMPIRE, QING

The Qing (Ch'ing) dynasty ruled China from 1644 to 1911. The present boundaries of the People's Republic of China are the results of its military prowess and masterful frontier administration. At the apex of an ethnically complex power elite were the Manchu people, originally from what is now northeast China, who provided the imperial ruling house, a highly disciplined military elite, and many high officials. Mongols also had an important share in the military structure and the life of the imperial court. The Han Chinese scholar-official elite provided most of the bureaucracy, including some at the highest levels. The vast majority of the subjects of the empire were "Han," ethnically Chinese. The most conspicuous symbol of the foreignness of Qing rule was the requirement that all male subjects adopt the Manchu queue, shaving the fronts of their heads and wearing a long braid down the back. Its imposition was bitterly resisted in a few places during the wars of the conquest, but fairly soon most of the elite saw that they could pursue their scholar-official vocations under Manchu rule at least as effectively as they had under the Ming (1368–1644), and commoners pursued the opportunities for settlement and enterprise opened up by the expanding Qing peace.

The Qing were thoroughly in control of the capitals and great commercial cities of the coastal provinces by 1650, but until 1683 the threat of Zheng Chenggong (1624–1662) and his successors in coastal strongholds and on Taiwan stimulated severe restrictions on coastal and maritime trade. The revolt of three great generals against the Qing from 1673 to 1681 made the roads unsafe and generally discouraged commerce. Some merchants prospered through clientage connections to court grandees or high provincial officials.

In the long peace of the 1700s the population of the Qing Empire grew from about 200 million to 400 million. Areas that had been peripheral to Ming China, such as Yunnan, or devastated during the Ming-Qing wars, such as Sichuan, filled up very rapidly. In the 1720s and 1730s the Qing authorities encouraged the immigration of Han settlers into the highlands of Yunnan, which previously had been populated mostly by non-Han peoples related to those of modern Burma, Laos, and Thailand. Copper mining developed rapidly, providing an increasingly adequate supply of small currency for the bimetallic copper/silver system. In addition to this growth of trade and settlement to the west and southwest, the rich rice lands of the central Yangtze Valley, especially Hunan, developed rapidly. The effects of this growth were dramatically apparent at Hankou, today a part of the great multiplex city of Wuhan, on the middle Yangtze. Vigorous urban growth on the lower Yangtze, and the beginnings of a shift from rice to cotton in the agriculture of that region, opened up great markets for rice from upriver. In addition, Hankou was the great center for shipment of tea, which was formed into bricks for easier transportation, and destined for consumption by the Mongols and, increasingly, by Siberians and even European Russians. A great Mongol trading house had a branch in Hankou. Unlike most Chinese cities, Hankou was primarily a creation of trade not a center of bureaucratic power. It had a minimal official presence and very powerful guilds. It reached one of its peaks of prosperity and commercial volume before 1750, and survived many ups and downs into the late 1800s, when foreigners settling there under provisions of the treaties found that the only way to do business was to plug into the highly developed trade networks already developed by the Chinese merchants.

Another example of Qing commercial growth is Xiamen, known in the 1800s as the treaty port of Amoy. On an island in a Fujian estuary, it had been the base of the power of the Zheng family in the 1600s. Some foreigners came there to trade, but it was primarily a center from which Chinese ships went out to Southeast Asian ports. The silver of the Manila galleons found its way into China primarily by way of Xiamen. Xiamen ships carried large quantities of tea to Batavia. Among their important imports were pepper, incense woods, and tin, made into foil for the "spirit money" burned in Chinese ceremonies and packaging for tea. It is estimated that the volume of this trade equaled that of the foreigners trading at Canton until at least 1750. Some recent scholarship suggests that it was far more important in the early 1800s than previously assumed. And Xiamen, like Hankou, had a minimal official presence and very powerful guilds.

The trade of the foreigners at Canton was the source of the supplies of silver that facilitated continued com-

Engraving after Amoy, from the Outer Anchorage, by Thomas Allom, c. 1843. The port Amoy (Xiamen) was the base of power of the Zheng family in the 1600s. © BETTMANN/CORBIS. REPRODUCED BY PERMISSION.

mercial expansion. The Chinese managed deliveries of tea to buyers at Canton through a series of market transactions, from cultivator to upcountry processor to wholesale merchant to licensed exporter in Canton. Until 1760 or later, 90 percent of the payment for tea and other exports was in silver. After that silver exports seem to have reached a plateau, and continued growth of exports was covered by growing imports of Indian cotton, English woolens (which found some markets in the northern and western reaches of the Qing Empire), and opium. We can estimate that China exported 30,000 piculs (the Asian trade "hundred-weight" of about 60 kilograms) of tea in 1720, 60,000 in 1740, 120,000 in 1765, and 240,000 in 1795.

Tea, porcelain, silks, and many other fine consumer goods exported to Europe had been produced and traded inside China for centuries. Relatively new in China was the spread of cotton growing and the gradual adoption of cotton, including padded clothing for cold weather, as the general wear of ordinary Chinese. Parts of the lower Yangtze region with sandy soil unsuitable for rice cultivation and a damp climate that was said to facilitate spinning and weaving with yarns of higher and more uniform

strength came to specialize in cotton growing and textile production, but there were many other textile-producing areas. As late as 1895, for example, hundreds of thousands of bales of raw cotton and handwoven piece goods were moved every year from Hupei into Sichuan. Around 1800 even England imported substantial quantities of *nankeens,* Chinese hand-loomed cotton fabrics.

In the late 1700s China began to import increasing quantities of opium, which was produced primarily in Bengal and brought by British traders in channels separate from the legal trade at Canton. The growing demand for opium began as a result of the practice of mixing it with tobacco, which later led to the inhaling of a vaporized pure extract, which was much more addictive than ingestion; this may have been spread to China by Chinese settlers in Java. The silver paid for opium imports helped to finance the tea trade, and at some point in the early 1800s it reversed China's long-positive balance of trade and led to a net outflow of silver. Qing officials noted this, along with the effects of addiction and corruption, as they decided to try to stop the trade. The resulting Opium War (1839–1842) ended in an imposed treaty that opened four more ports (in addition to Canton) to foreign trade and fixed a low tariff. The Western powers, with the English in the lead, had taken the first big step in "opening China" to foreign trade.

In fact, the Opium War did not lead to any major change in China's commerce. Opium imports, now implicitly legalized, grew. The great Taiping Rebellion, which started west of Canton in 1850 and swept into the Yangtze Valley, did far more to alter patterns of trade: Canton lost commercial dominance, and Shanghai, one of the newly opened ports and the gateway to the Yangtze Valley, began to grow. After the Second Opium War (1856–1860) more ports were opened, and the Yangtze was opened to foreign navigation. Foreign business firms, modern banks, and Chinese working closely with them were agents of change. An Imperial Maritime Customs staffed by foreigners advised the Qing rulers on this order and provided to the state a very important and reliable stream of revenue, which made the rulers much more interested in commercial matters than they had been. Opium imports stagnated as the Chinese grew more of their own. Tea exports lost out to the new plantation industries of India and Ceylon. By Albert Feuerwerker's estimate the foreign trade of China increased by 300 percent between 1870 and 1911, but it still was a very small amount per capita, and traditional patterns of trade within China continued with only a few major changes. Traditional handcraft methods of cotton-cloth production were efficient and market sensitive; foreign goods made little headway. But from the 1880s on machine spinning of cotton thread, especially in Japan, produced a cheap and superior product that began to displace Chinese hand-spun yarn; this was the largest component of the post-1870 increase.

The Treaty of Shimonoseki at the end of the Sino-Japanese War in 1895 permitted the establishment of foreign-owned industries in China. The first major railroad projects opened new lines of trade. Chambers of commerce in major cities were among the more important forms of modern political organization. Commercial growth, imperialist encroachment, and new forms of political and social organization marked the last years of the Qing dynasty. Still, observers everywhere in China commented on the continued scale and vigor of the nation's traditional commerce, and foreigners wanting to sell kerosene, tobacco, and many other products found that their best strategy was to tie into existing commercial networks.

SEE ALSO ALCOCK, RUTHERFORD; BOYCOTT; BULLION (SPECIE); CANTON SYSTEM; CHINA; COMMODITY MONEY; DRUGS, ILLICIT; EAST INDIA COMPANY, BRITISH; EAST INDIA COMPANY, DUTCH; EMPIRE, BRITISH; EMPIRE, DUTCH; EMPIRE, FRENCH; EMPIRE, JAPANESE; EMPIRE, MING; EMPIRE, PORTUGUESE; ENTREPÔT SYSTEM; ETHNIC GROUPS, CANTONESE; ETHNIC GROUPS, FUJIANESE; FACTORIES; FURS; GOLD AND SILVER; GUANGZHOU; GUILDS; HART, ROBERT; HONG KONG AND SHANGHAI BANK; IMPERIAL MARITIME CUSTOMS, CHINA; IMPERIALISM; JAPAN; JARDINE MATHESON; KOREA; LABORERS, CONTRACT; LIN ZEXU; MANCHURIA; MOST-FAVORED-NATION PROVISIONS; PHILIPPINES; PIRACY; RICE; THAILAND; SHANGHAI; SILK; SINGAPORE; SMUGGLING; SOUTH CHINA SEA; SPICES AND THE SPICE TRADE; TAIWAN; TEA; TEXTILES; TOBACCO; TRIBUTE SYSTEM; ZHENG FAMILY.

BIBLIOGRAPHY
Feuerwerker, Albert. "Economic Trends in the Late Ch'ing Empire, 1870–1911." In *The Cambridge History of China, Vol. 11: Late Ch'ing, 1800–1911, Part 2,* ed. John K. Fairbank and Kwang-ching Liu. Cambridge, U.K., and New York: Cambridge University Press, 1980.
Rowe, William T. *Hankow: Commerce and Society in a Chinese City.* Stanford, CA: Stanford University Press, 1984.

John E. Wills Jr.

EMPIRE, SPANISH

Spain was commercially active in the Mediterranean Sea and down the Atlantic coast of Africa for many decades before 1492. Most notably, it had begun its takeover of the Canary Islands nearly a century before Christopher Columbus's voyage. The only valuable resource on the Canaries was *orchilla*, a dyestuff, but soon after taking over, the Spanish established sugar plantations, complete with black slaves imported from Africa, that produced for the European market.

In the Americas, Spain first colonized the major islands of the Caribbean, but by 1550, after turning out only modest amounts of gold, these islands became an economic backwater in the still expanding empire. In 1494, by signing the Treaty of Tordesillas, Portugal and Spain ended their emerging rivalry over the South Atlantic. Portugal protected its exclusive sea route to India, and Spain assured its dominance in the Americas. Spanish expeditions conquered Mexico in 1521 and Peru in 1532. These lands, rich with silver and large native populations, became Spain's primary centers for trade until the 1700s, when the emergence of the economies of other Spanish American colonies, including Cuba, Venezuela, and Buenos Aires, required a shift of Spain's patterns of trade with its American colonies. By the 1570s all of the less prosperous colonies, such as Central America, Colombia, Paraguay, and Chile, had been established, but their primary products, including indigo, yerba mate (a kind of tea), and wheat, were marketed primarily to other American colonies, rather than overseas.

Spain soon established a monopoly over trade with its American colonies. In 1503 a Board of Trade (*Casa de la Contratación*) was established in Seville to govern commercial relations with the colonies. In 1543 the Crown legally incorporated the powerful merchant houses of Seville into a merchants' guild (*consulado*) in which a monopoly over trade was formally invested. It was also granted juridical authority over civil disputes concerning trade, a tremendous legal advantage. In the 1560s, to protect its trade with its colonies against marauding ships from other European powers, Spain established the Fleet System, wherein two substantial fleets escorted by warships departed Spain each year, one bound to Mexico's primary port of Veracruz, and the other to the Isthmus of Panama, where its goods were offloaded to be shipped down the Pacific coast to Peru. The two fleets remained at their American ports until loaded with silver from Mexico and Peru, whereupon they departed for Spain. Though very expensive and limiting in the amount of merchandise that the colonies could legally receive, the Fleet System worked quite well for Spain's purposes. European rivals seized the fleets only twice, in 1628 and in 1656.

In 1561 an expedition organized in Mexico sailed across the Pacific Ocean and occupied the Philippine Islands. This gave Mexico access to prized Chinese goods, which had been shipped to Manila for centuries by Chinese merchant houses. Each year Mexican trading firms dispatched from Acapulco one galleon loaded with silver to Manila, where the contents were exchanged for Chinese fineries for the shipment back. The trade of the Manila galleon persisted until the end of the colonial period. It was so lucrative that often more than one-third of Mexico's annual silver production was routed to Manila rather than to Spain.

Contraband trade sprung up in Spanish America against this very restrictive trading and spread rapidly. Spain could control neither the vast American coastline nor its profit-seeking colonial officials. Contraband clearly worsened in the second half of the seventeenth century and throughout the eighteenth. By the early seventeenth century, Spain's economy had declined compared to those of the Netherlands, England, and France, and after mid-century these latter countries seized lightly occupied Spanish Caribbean islands to establish their own complexes of sugar plantations.

Around three million black slaves were imported into Spanish American over the course of the colonial period, largely to work on plantations, but Spain itself shipped very few of them from the African mainland. Instead, it entered into agreements (*asientos*) with other European nations whose traders were more firmly based in Africa. Portugal was the first country to gain such an

asiento. The fact that Spain and Portugal were ruled by the same monarch between1580 and 1640 facilitated that agreement. After Portugal successfully rebelled against Spain to obtain a Portugal-based ruling family, Spain turned eventually to France and then England as replacement suppliers.

By the early eighteenth century Spain's economy had declined badly when compared to its European rivals because it did not participate in the incipient Industrial Revolution and it suffered from a weak governmental financial system and a declining navy. Spain could not prevent a rapid expansion of contraband trade with its colonies. The Fleet System was now badly outdated and was gradually abandoned until its final dissolution in the 1760s.

After repeatedly losing both military conflicts and trading concessions to its more innovative and productive rivals, Spain finally undertook various trading reforms with its colonies. Far and away the most important was permitting free trade within the empire. In 1778 all colonies except for Mexico and Venezuela were allowed to trade with each other, plus any port in Spain could now send any number of ships at any time of the year to any colonial ports. The free-trade system was finally extended to Mexico and Venezuela as well in 1789. Nonetheless, because of Spain's enduring industrial weakness, the amount of foreign-made goods shipped to the Americas continued to increase. In addition, Spain never entertained allowing its colonies to trade legally outside of the empire.

In the eighteenth century, colonies that had been of peripheral economic importance to Spain over the previous two centuries saw their economies expand quite rapidly because of Western Europe's commercial revolution and heightened demand for primary products, including sugar from Cuba, cacao from Venezuela and Ecuador, and cattle hides from the Buenos Aires region.

Following the Napoleonic invasion of Spain in 1808, most of the American colonies moved quickly to independence, with Mexico and Venezuela gaining their freedom in 1821, Ecuador in 1822, Peru in 1824, and Bolivia in 1825. Cuba, Puerto Rico, and the Philippines remained as colonies until 1898. As Spain lost its political control over its former colonies, it also lost most of its trade with them to its major commercial rivals England, France, and the United States. These countries enjoy the advantage of having entered the industrial revolution. Spain lagged badly.

SEE ALSO BOARD OF TRADE, SPANISH; CÁDIZ; CARTAGENA; COLUMBUS, CHRISTOPHER; CONQUISTADORS; EMPIRE, BRITISH; EMPIRE, PORTUGUESE; ENCOMIENDA AND REPARTIMIENTO;

ETHNIC GROUPS, JEWS; GOLD AND SILVER; HAVANA; LABORERS, AZTEC AND INCA; LABORERS, COERCED; MEXICO; MINING; NEW SPAIN; PHILIP II; PERU; POPULATION—EMIGRATION AND IMMIGRATION; PORTUGAL; SEVILLE; SLAVERY AND THE AFRICAN SLAVE TRADE; SUGAR, MOLASSES, AND RUM.

BIBLIOGRAPHY

Brading, D. A. *Miners and Merchants in Bourbon Mexico, 1763–1810.* Cambridge, U.K.: Cambridge University Press, 1971.

Fisher, John R. *The Economic Aspects of Spanish Imperialism in America, 1492–1810.* Liverpool, U.K.: University of Liverpool Press, 1997.

Hoberman, Louisa Schell. *Mexico's Merchant Elite, 1590–1660: Silver, State, and Society.* Durham, NC: Duke University Press, 1991.

Kamen, Henry Arthur Francis. *Spain's Road to Empire: The Making of a World Power, 1492–1763.* London: Allen Lane, 2002.

Kicza, John E. *Colonial Entrepreneurs, Familis and Business in Bourbon Mexico City.* Albuquerque: University of New Mexico Press, 1983.

Parry, J. H. *The Spanish Seaborne Empire.* New York: Alfred A. Knopf, 1970.

Socolow, Susan Migden. *The Merchants of Buenos Aires, 1778–1810: Family and Commerce.* Cambridge, U.K.: Cambridge University Press, 1978.

John E. Kicza

ENCOMIENDA AND REPARTIMIENTO

Encomiendas were royal grants made to individual Spanish colonists in the Americas. Recipients of such grants (called *encomenderos*) thereby personally owned the labor and tribute (tax) payments—but not the land—of Indians who lived in a particular village or region. The *encomienda* influenced several kinds of colonial economic relations, although it varied geographically in Spanish America, and chronologically between 1493 and the early nineteenth century.

Geographical variation in *encomienda* practice depended on what kind of indigenous society the Spanish encountered in the course of establishing colonial rule. In the most densely populated regions of the Americas, the institution did not last much beyond 1700. In New Spain and Peru, for instance, the Crown eliminated *encomienda* rights to labor by the second half of the sixteenth century. Moreover, by the end of the seventeenth century, the Crown had ended the institution altogether. By contrast, in regions with less complex Indian societies, the institution survived for much longer, and in those places it included labor obligations until well into the eighteenth century. The difference stemmed from the na-

ture of the Indian economy. In the fringe regions, existing indigenous societies did not produce sufficient surplus to support *encomiendas,* leaving *encomenderos* unable to extract more than just forced labor from their grants, while also attracting fewer Spanish colonists to compete for the use of that labor.

In regions with more complex pre-Conquest economies, colonial labor relations changed as *encomenderos* lost their exclusive claim to Indian labor. First, a new institution called *repartimiento* emerged, which required that a certain number of Indians from each community hire themselves out weekly to Spanish employers. As a result, more colonists enjoyed access to Indian labor, while the Crown could regulate labor relations more directly. Particularly because the Indian population continued to decline due to disease, though, the labor version of *repartimiento* followed the *encomienda* into extinction. Despite the continued availability of *repartimiento* laborers, by about 1630 Spanish employers instead competed for Indian laborers by offering individual Indians wages or land.

Subsequently, in the core regions of Spanish America, little survived of these two institutions. One legacy was Indian tribute payment to the Crown—since even after the end of the *encomienda,* the Spanish Crown did not release Indians from their obligation to pay tribute. Instead, the Crown posted royal magistrates in former *encomiendas* to collect tribute. Another surviving practice was the *mita* (rotating draft labor obligations in the Andes specifically to support silver and mercury mining). Finally, the decline of the *encomienda* also contributed to the rise of an unofficial colonial institution that was also called *repartimiento* (the *repartimiento de mercancías,* or in the Andes often just *reparto*). This involved Spanish officials illegally distributing to Indians under their jurisdiction either money to acquire future production of goods, or else commodities to acquire future payment in cash. Thus, even in core regions, the *encomienda*'s impact continued until the early nineteenth century, when the colonial bureaucracy was dismantled by newly independent Latin American nations.

Between them, these institutions altered commerce in the Americas in several related ways, all focused on encouraging Indians to produce goods that the Spanish perceived to be valuable. For instance, export-oriented production of a variety of cash crops (such as sugar, cacao, cotton, tobacco, and indigo) depended on Indian laborers recruited via *encomienda* and *repartimiento*. This was less true for silver mining, although many Indian laborers on colonial Spanish-American landed estates produced goods (such as maize and wheat) that served to support silver mining indirectly.

In addition, Indians changed their productive habits in response to tribute collection. At first, for example, tribute was collected in commodities, but because Spaniards had no use for many of the items paid to previous rulers (for instance, quetzal feathers demanded by Aztec emperors), the specific goods produced had to conform to what the colonists desired instead. Later, the Crown demanded tribute payments in cash, potentially drawing Indians more thoroughly into labor and commodity markets.

Like changing commodity production, the legacy of *encomienda* and *repartimiento* also influenced Indians to alter their market exchange habits, especially by facilitating the introduction of new goods to indigenous markets. This occurred primarily via the *repartimiento de mercancías*. Because this operated on credit (future payment in commodities or money), Indians accepted new goods more readily, even if they later resisted repaying their debts. As it turns out, this form of *repartimiento* also affected global trade, as it was virtually the only way for Europeans to stimulate Indian production of cochineal dye (primarily in southern New Spain, centered in Oaxaca) to meet the demand for that high-quality red dyestuff in Europe.

Finally, trade routes also changed in response to *encomienda* and *repartimiento* practice. These institutions provided workers to produce American agricultural and mineral exports. These exports, in turn, promoted the development of new routes of long-distance trade within the Americas to link supply (of cotton textiles or livestock products, for instance) to new centers of demand (silver mines). Meanwhile, those exports linked the Americas to Europe (via Seville), as well as to Asia (via Manila). Thus, these local colonial institutions reflected and helped to constitute more complex global trade between 1493 and the early nineteenth century.

SEE ALSO Africa, Labor Taxes (Head Taxes); Argentina; Chile; Colombia; Conquistadors; Empire, Spanish; Gold and Silver; Haiti; Laborers, Aztec and Inca; Laborers, Coerced; Laborers, Contract; Mercantilism; Mexico; New Spain; Peru; Philippines; Potosí; Smuggling; Textiles; Tobacco.

BIBLIOGRAPHY

Baskes, Jeremy. *Indians, Merchants, and Markets: A Reinterpretation of the Repartimiento and Spanish-Indian Economic Relations in Colonial Oaxaca, 1750–1821.* Stanford, CA: Stanford University Press, 2000.

Gibson, Charles. *The Aztecs under Spanish Rule: A History of the Indians of the Valley of Mexico, 1519–1810.* Stanford, CA: Stanford University Press, 1964.

Patch, Robert W. "Imperial Politics and Local Economy in Colonial Central America, 1670–1770." *Past and Present* 143 (1994): 77–107.

Spalding, Karen. *Huarochirí: An Andean Society under Inca and Spanish Rule.* Stanford, CA: Stanford University Press, 1984.

Stern, Steve J. *Peru's Indian Peoples and the Challenge of Spanish Conquest: Huamanga to 1640.* Madison: University of Wisconsin Press, 1982.

Jason L. Ward

FRIEDRICH ENGELS
1820–1895

When Friedrich Engels (1820–1895) and Karl Marx (1818–1883) formed their revolutionary partnership in 1844, they agreed that the world was their unit of analysis and theater of action. Five years later they concluded, with remarkable foresight, that the

> most important thing to have occurred (in America) . . . is the discovery of the California goldmines. . . . (As a result, the) center of gravity of world commerce . . . is now the southern half of the North American peninsula. . . . (T)he Pacific Ocean will have the same role as the Atlantic has now and the Mediterranean had in antiquity . . . that of the great water highway of world commerce. (Marx and Engels, vol. 10, pp. 265–266, originally published January 31, 1850).

The cotton trade figured significantly in the analysis the two made of the U.S. Civil War (1861–1865) and the political response in Britain. Engels, who worked as a bookkeeper in his family's textile mill in Manchester, England, had access to data that were invaluable for Marx's insightful writings on the war as well as for Marx's magnum opus, *Capital*.

Following Marx's death, Engels publicized and defended their views on the free-trade-versus-protectionism issue, as it continued to be debated in Europe and the United States. Though the debate was entirely within the framework of capitalism, he argued that the working class had an inherent interest in free trade. The latter accelerated capitalist development and, hence, all of its contradictions, which could only be resolved by workers seizing political power and embarking on the road to socialist transformation.

SEE ALSO Cuba; China; Cotton; Free Trade, Theory and Practice; Germany; Gold and Silver; Korea; Marx, Karl; Protectionism and Tariff Wars; Russia; Socialism and Communism; Vietnam.

BIBLIOGRAPHY

Marx, Karl, and Engels, Frederick. *Collected Works.* New York: International Publishers, 1975–2004.

Nimtz, August. "Marx and Engels": The Prototypical Transnational Actors." In *Restructuring World Politics:*

Transnational Social Movements, Networks, and Norms, ed. Sanjeev Khagram, James V. Riker, and Kathryn Sikkink. Minneapolis: University of Minnesota Press, 2002.

August H. Nimtz Jr.

ENTREPÔT SYSTEM

An entrepôt is a location, often a port, in which an unusually large range of goods and services are available and an unusually large variety of traders from other places gather, so that as a result the place gains in attractiveness, efficiency, and staying power as a commercial center. A clear example is Amsterdam in the seventeenth century, where Asian spices and textiles, sugar from the Americas, Baltic grain and timber, and North Sea herring were among the goods traded by merchants from every part of Europe, including a large group of Sephardic Jews. Amsterdam's eminence as an entrepôt owed something to its location on the North Sea near the mouth of the Rhine, but more to the stable and commerce-friendly rule of the city's elite, including its tolerance of Jews and, less openly, of Roman Catholics.

Our understanding of entrepôts in Asian seas is more likely to begin with geographical imperatives. There were certain locations where the alternations of the monsoon winds and the constraints of sea passage between land masses almost always led to the presence of an entrepôt, especially the straits that lie at the mouth of the Red Sea and the Persian Gulf, and those between Sumatra and Java and between Sumatra and the Malay Peninsula. Rich zones of agricultural and craft production near sea lanes, as in Gujarat, Bengal, Siam, and Guangdong, also were very hospitable to the growth of entrepôts. An entrepôt might flourish in a less "natural" location, such as the coast of Taiwan, when alternatives are inhibited by warfare or anticommercial policy.

At the choke points for maritime trade on the two southern corners of the Arabian Peninsula, at the Straits of Hormuz and of Bab-el-Mandeb, this positional logic was undercut by the rigors of an immediate environment where heat and disease made the coast nearly uninhabitable for part of the year, and food and even water were in very short supply. Thus, although there always was a port at each—Aden and later Mocha at Bab-el-Mandeb; Hormuz, then Bandar Abbas, then Muscat on the Straits of Hormuz—they often resembled vast camps of tents and compounds during a trading season and were almost deserted in the hottest months.

On the west coast of India, Gujarat was the usual departure point for voyages to the Arabian ports to the west, and had in its hinterland abundant food stocks and a flourishing textile industry. The best known and most enduring early modern entrepôt in this region was Surat, where great Hindu and Muslim merchant houses and the Dutch and English companies all prospered under Mughal governors. Bombay rose to prominence as a center of English power and trade, and eclipsed Surat as the breakdown of law and order inhibited land trade in South Asia and in the Middle East after 1750. Far to the south on the west coast of India, ports such as Cochin and Calicut, which had a great heritage of local pepper production and entrepôt activity and a striking variety of ethnic stocks and religions, prospered only unevenly amid wars between Portuguese and Dutch, Mughals and local Hindus. On the east side of southern India, entrepôt connections to the east and local cloth industries offered great opportunities; the English Company at Madras was especially successful in encouraging private trade by the English and joint ventures among the English, local Portuguese, Hindus, and Muslims of many origins. In the lowlands of Bengal, exports of cotton and silk textiles from the densely settled countryside were the key to the prosperity of Hugli and Dacca and to the rise of Calcutta as a great British center. In the late 1700s the export of opium to Southeast Asia and China was a growing source of the prosperity of this great port.

The most dramatic example of entrepôts that responded to geographical imperatives are those that commanded the passages between the Indian Ocean and the South China Sea to the north and south of the island of Sumatra. Until about 1400 both straits were dominated by Srivijaya, in the neighborhood of Palembang on the southeast coast of Sumatra. In the early 1400s Melaka took over entrepôt functions as an independent sultanate on the eponymous strait. This is the best-studied case of classic Southeast Asian ways of nourishing entrepôt activity. Each community of traders—Javanese, south Indians, Chinese, Malays—lived in a separate quarter under its own *hahbandar*s ("lord of the market") and administered its own laws, especially in matters of family and property. The sultans sent tribute embassies to Ming China, sometimes managed by locally based Chinese. Because maritime trade in Chinese shipping from Chinese ports was illegal under the early Ming, this was a case of enhancing entrepôt function in one place while strangling it by policy in another. The powerful Chinese community seems to have been at odds with the sultan and the Malays in the early 1500s, and reportedly assisted the Portuguese in their conquest of Melaka in 1509. Much of the old entrepôt structure was preserved under the new regime, but Portuguese Melaka faced repeated attacks from its Muslim neighbors, especially by the descendants of the former sultans of Melaka who were based in Johor near modern Singapore, and by Aceh on the north end of Sumatra, which emerged as a potent west-facing and Islam-oriented entrepôt. After the Dutch conquered Melaka in 1641 they showed little interest in encouraging its entrepôt functions, preferring their own great center at Batavia near the Sunda Straits between Sumatra and Java. Melaka and its rivals shifted to more local trades until the rise of British power and the opium trade led to new entrepôts—Penang in 1786 and Singapore in 1819.

Banten, very near the Sunda Strait on the northwest coast of Java, was as classic a Southeast Asian entrepôt as Melaka. Here too there were thriving Chinese, south Indian, and Malay trading communities under a local Muslim ruler. Here the Portuguese, and later the English, the Dutch, and the Danes, had to fit into this multiethnic framework. The Dutch Company built its headquarters at Batavia (modern Jakarta), about 50 miles east of Banten. Even here the Dutch allowed a great deal of Chinese trade and a highly organized Chinese community, but it sought a stronger form of control of the Sunda Strait than that of the traditional Southeast Asian entrepôt. In 1682 it intervened in a quarrel in Banten's ruling family, took the town, and closed its port to its competitors.

As the Siamese kingdom developed its wealth and power in the 1400s, its capital, Ayutthaya, adopted much of the Southeast Asian entrepôt pattern. The Chinese were the most vital participants, managing Siamese tribute embassies to Beijing and the maritime trade of the royal house. At its multicultural height in the seventeenth century, Ayutthaya also had communities of Persians, Malays, Portuguese, and Dutch and English trading posts.

China was the world's greatest center of commercial activity and fine craft production between about 700 and 1700, and when its political situation permitted it had some of the world's great entrepôts. In the 700s and 800s large numbers of Arabian and Persian merchants traded at Guangzhou. From about 1000 to 1350, Quanzhou in Fujian had communities of Hindu, Muslim, Nestorian Christian, and even Roman Catholic traders. But after about 1400 the Ming authorities imposed such drastic restrictions on foreign trade, whether by Chinese ships or by foreigners coming to China, that much interchange and commercial coordination had to take place offshore. Siam, Melaka, the Ryukyu Islands, and Champa in the south of modern Vietnam all played this role to some degree. In the great surge of maritime trade around 1600, new entrepôts emerged at Hoi An in the Hue-Danang region of modern Vietnam, where the Nguyen lords built up their own power in opposition to rivals in the north and depended greatly on the revenue from thriving colonies of Chinese and Japanese traders; at Macao; at the great Dutch trading center Casteel Zeelandia, in the vicinity of modern Tainan, Taiwan; and most improbably at Manila, with its new connection across the Pacific. In

all of these places highly organized communities of emigré Chinese were crucial. Casteel Zeelandia fell to Zheng Chenggong in 1662; Macao never recovered from the loss of its Japan trade in 1640; Manila and Hoi An had phases of unstable prosperity well into the eighteenth century. But the great east Asian entrepôt of that century was again in Chinese territory, at Guangzhou, where European demand for tea stimulated an immense trade. The large numbers of English, Dutch, French, Swedish, Danish, Armenian, and Indian merchants who participated were much more closely controlled than in earlier entrepôts in China or elsewhere, and they were supposed to leave at the end of the trading season; many of them went no further than Macao. But in its good order, the sophistication of its commercial organization, and the wide range of commodities available, Guangzhou in the great days of the "Canton trade" did fulfill many classic entrepôt functions.

SEE ALSO Albuquerque, Afonso de; Balance of Payments; Bengal; Bullion (Specie); Burma; Calcutta; Canton System; Caravan Trade; China; Coen, Jan Pieterszoon; Cowries; East India Company, British; East India Company, Dutch; East India Company, Other; Empire, British; Empire, Dutch; Empire, French; Empire, Ming; Empire, Mughal; Empire, Ottoman; Empire, Qing; Empire, Spanish; Ethnic Groups, Armenians; Ethnic Groups, Cantonese; Ethnic Groups, Fujianese; Ethnic Groups, Gujarati; Ethnic Groups, Jews; Free Ports; Gold and Silver; Guangzhou; Guilds; Gujarat; Imperialism; India; Indian Ocean; Indonesia; Iran; Institutional Aspects of World Trade; Japan; Kenya; Madras; Melaka; Millets and Capitulations; Mumbai; Nagasaki; Persian Gulf; Philippines; Piracy; Raffles, Sir Thomas Stamford; Shipping, Coastal; Silk; Singapore; South China Sea; Spices and the Spice Trade; Sri Lanka; Tea; Textiles; Tribute System; Women Traders of Southeast Asia; Zheng Family.

BIBLIOGRAPHY

Barendse, R. J. *The Arabian Seas: The Indian Ocean World of the Seventeenth Century.* Armonk, NY, and London: M. E. Sharpe, 2002.

Chaudhuri, K. N. *Trade and Civilisation in the Indian Ocean: An Economic History from the Rise of Islam to 1750.* Cambridge, U.K., and New York: Cambridge University Press, 1985.

Israel, Jonathan I. *Dutch Primacy in World Trade, 1585–1740.* Oxford, U.K.: Clarendon Press, 1989.

Meilink-Roelofsz, M. A. P. *Asian Trade and European Influence in the Indonesian Archipelago between 1500 and about 1630.* The Hague, Netherlands: Nijhoff, 1962.

Reid, Anthony. *Southeast Asia in the Age of Commerce, 1450–1680,* 2 vols. New Haven, CT, and London: Yale University Press, 1988, 1993.

Wills, John E., Jr., ed. *Eclipsed Entrepots of the Western Pacific: Taiwan and Central Vietnam, 1500–1800.* Aldershot, U.K., and Burlington, VT: Ashgate Variorum, 2002.

John E. Wills Jr.

ETHNIC GROUPS, AFRICANS

Although the African environment is very diverse, it primarily consists of the desert, sahel (a dry grass steppe region or desert edge), savanna, and forest zones. With differing climatic and other ecological conditions, each of these areas necessarily specializes in the production of different commodities as well as in different economic activities. In the face of specialization, foreign merchants, at least since the medieval era, have settled largely along the coasts of the Sahara, East Africa, and western Africa, thereby introducing several foreign products such as cowries, alcohol, tobacco, and firearms. Over time, economic specialization and the concentration of foreign merchants in these particular regions provided the basis for internal trade in Africa. Since 1450 this internal African trade has been monopolized by a relatively few ethnic groups who operated largely outside their homelands.

Up to recent times, the main African ethnic group that facilitated the movement of goods from the Sahara, through three major trade routes from the sahel to the savanna and vice versa, has been the Tuareg. Jellaba and Jabarti traders controlled other trade routes within the northeastern horn of Africa, especially around the Nile Valley and Ethiopia. Once the Tuareg merchants moved goods from the Sahara to the savanna, native merchants in the Central Sudan were primarily responsible for the distribution of these and other commodities within the region. From the mid-fifteenth century these local merchants included the Juula of the Western Sudan and the Wangarawa, Hausa, and Kanuri merchants of the central savanna. In the central and eastern African region, native merchants played significant roles in commerce, too. The major ethnic groups involved in this region by the nineteenth century were the Kamba, Nyamwezi, Yao, Bisa, Cokwe, and Thonga. African merchant groups traded in commodities such as gold, ivory, wax, rubber, copper, salt, goats, sheep, camels, and cattle, and different groups tended to specialize in certain goods. For example, it was the Hausa merchants who were most closely associated with the kola trade.

Most, if not all, ethnic groups that dominate trade in Africa have not been homogenous social units. For instance, the Kel Air, Kel Tadmekka, and Kel Gress were among the numerous subethnic groups that constitute the Tuareg. In addition, at least up to the early twentieth century, the Tuareg merchant also had several gradations of status: below the aristocrats were various categories of dependents including tenant farmers, herders who worked on contract, vassals, and slaves, who did most of the hard work including tending animals, drawing water from wells, cooking, and transporting goods by head.

The heterogeneity of the groups and the unequal positions of members of the Tuareg and other ethnic groups that dominated trade in Africa produced tension that sometimes resulted in emancipation from servile obligations and or assumption of new identities. The *irewelen* (people of servile ancestry) of the Tuareg, for instance, emigrated to the region that is now northern Nigeria and ultimately, in the nineteenth century, by assimilating Hausa culture. At the same time, they adopted another separate identity, through the adaptation of the Asali (common, usually distant, place of origin) institution, the use of facial markings and a corporate name, Agalawa, so as to maintain a corporate exclusiveness necessary for the establishment of effective marketing networks as well as the enhancement of their enterprise in general. Ethnicity was a tool used, at least up to the twentieth century, by the African merchant groups to protect their economic rights, occupational privileges, and political position. Groups emphasized their ethnicity as distinct from the surrounding populations while also attempting to bring people across ethnic boundaries, mostly to serve as laborers, especially in salt mines, plantations, and in other activities closely tied to commerce that in turn enhanced the interests of the ruling elements in each merchant group.

Although merchant groups recruited labor through several means, since 1450 many laborers have been, up to the twentieth century, slaves obtained through warfare, breeding, purchase, and other means. In general, loyal and hardworking slaves were assimilated into the dominant merchant culture, and recalcitrant ones could face several forms of punishment, including sale. As well as selling slaves as punishment, African merchant groups also exported slaves across the Atlantic and Indian Oceans, the Red Sea, and the Mediterranean for profit.

Besides rewarding or disciplining laborers and manipulating ethnicity, African merchant groups relied on other mechanisms for protection to maintain control and solidarity and to foster their operations in general. One of the key instruments was religion. Most African merchants were Muslims, hence it is varying versions of Islam that they have used to encourage necessary honesty, frugality, commercial literacy, and credit arrangements among themselves. Another instrument is the institution known widely as trade settlement. Some

Baling hay for salt trading in Niger, 1999. *The Tuaregs are the main African ethnic group to facilitate the movement of goods, including salt, across the Sahara Desert.* © MICHAEL S. LEWIS/CORBIS. REPRODUCED BY PERMISSION.

merchants settled permanently as aliens in significant towns outside their homelands, where they learned the languages and cultures of their host societies. Eventually they became cross-cultural brokers, helping and encouraging trade between the host societies and traders from their own countries of origin who traveled between the regions. At the trade settlements, leading merchant families assumed an ethnic minority status, which, among other benefits, enabled them to maintain their international connections, especially to related itinerant merchants, and it was this that permitted them to fulfill the two main needs of trade—brokerage and agency.

In their daily operations Muslim merchants normally competed with each other. Also, especially between 1450 and the early twentieth century, they had to contend not only with centralized states such as Oyo, Dahomey, and Asante, which were relatively more closely linked with trade, but also with merchants from federations of diverse ethnic groups such as the Aro and Nzabi, in southeast Nigeria and coastal regions of Gabon and the Congolese Republic respectively, who used fictitious kinship and secret societies to overcome problems that impeded trade, especially that of ethnic diversity, and consequently to dominate specific trade networks. Today, competition between trading groups in Africa has

changed in response to changes in technology and to the interplay of political and military events. Also, laws and bilateral and multilateral treaties now more seriously govern the status of traders in the Diaspora.

SEE ALSO ANGOLA; BRAZIL; CARAVAN TRADE; COFFEE; COTTON; CUBA; DAHOMEY; EMPIRE, BRITISH; EMPIRE, DUTCH; EMPIRE, FRENCH; EMPIRE, PORTUGUESE; EMPIRE, SPANISH; GHANA; GOLD COAST; HAITI; JAMAICA; KENYA; KONGO; LABORERS, COERCED; LABORERS, CONTRACT; NIGERIA; POPULATION—IMMIGRATION AND EMIGRATION; RELIGION; SENEGAMBIA; SLAVERY AND THE AFRICAN SLAVE TRADE; SOUTH AFRICA; SUGAR, MOLASSES, AND RUM; TOBACCO; TRAVELERS AND TRAVEL; UNITED STATES.

BIBLIOGRAPHY

Curtin, Philip D. *Cross-cultural Trade in World History.* Cambridge, U.K.: Cambridge University Press, 1984.

Gemery, Henry A., and Hogendorn, Jan S., eds. *The Uncommon Market: Essays in the Economic History of the Atlantic Slave Trade.* New York: Academic Press, 1979.

Gray, Richard, and Birmingham, David, eds. *Pre-Colonial African Trade: Essays on Trade in Central and Eastern Africa before 1900.* London and New York: Oxford University Press, 1970.

Lovejoy, Paul E. *Transformations in Slavery: A History of Slavery in Africa.* Cambridge, U.K., and New York: Cambridge University Press, 2000.

Lovejoy, Paul E. *Salt of the Desert Sun: A History of Salt Production and Trade in the Central Sudan.* Cambridge, U.K.: Cambridge University Press, 2002.

Pankhurst, Richard. *An Introduction to the Economic History of Ethiopia from Early Times to 1800.* London: Lalibela House, 1961.

Mohammed Bashir Salau

ETHNIC GROUPS, ARMENIANS

The Armenians are an ethnic group of ancient culture whose historic homeland is situated at the trading crossroads of Transcaucasia, eastern Turkey, and northern Iran; the region has been the object of competing powers since the fifth century B.C.E. The Armenians share a common culture and faith and, except for brief periods as an independent state, have generally lived as a Christian minority within primarily Muslim nations or empires. Their commercial successes, religious devotion, church-sponsored schools, and perceived patronage by political leadership have, however, stirred resentment at times in majority populations among which they have lived. Today there are two Armenias: one, an internationally recognized sovereign nation; the other, an informal community of Armenians who, over two millennia, have left their homeland under various circumstances and constitute a worldwide diaspora.

For most of its history, Armenia has been a geographical expression rather than a country with fixed and formal borders. For this reason, Armenians often have prospered more readily outside their homeland than within it. As early as the sixth century there is evidence of Armenian migration from the Byzantine Empire. After the destruction of the only recorded Armenian kingdom, the medieval Bagradid dynasty (885–1045), thousands of Armenians fled to southwestern Europe, and from the eleventh century Armenian traders and craftsmen were welcomed in western European cities including Venice, Marseilles, Paris, Bruges, and London. By the fifteenth century Armenian communities existed in Poland, Romania, Ukraine, and the Crimea, and the expansion of the maritime trade in the sixteenth century established Armenians in Amsterdam and eventually the Far East.

By the seventeenth century an informal Armenian trading network existed based on long-standing diaspora settlements. It is unclear how much, if any, functional cooperation existed between distant Armenian communities, or how kinship ties dictated trade flows. There is evidence, however, of Armenian trade activity from Transcaucasia eastward to China through India and Ceylon (Sri Lanka), Tibet and Central Asia as far as the Philippines; northward into Russia and the Baltic states, and westward into Europe. Voluntary Armenian emigration from the homeland was as much a response to uncertainty and danger at home as it was a search for opportunity abroad. In this sense, the Armenians followed a pattern similar to the Chinese, Jewish, Irish, or Vietnamese diasporas, whose migrants have chosen to leave their places of origin yet maintain ties to a homeland.

Armenia has had to balance its position with great powers that have overrun the Armenian homeland for two millennia—including the Assyrians, Persians, Parthians, Byzantines, Arabs, Mongols, Turks, and Russians. The Armenians have sustained themselves through this turbulence at great cost through the bulwark institutions of the church and church-sponsored schools, as well as through success in commercial endeavors. They became associated with the affairs of business and trade within the various ruling empires because, as Christians, they could handle money at interest in ways religiously forbidden to the Muslim majority. Armenian commercial abilities were honored by privileges bestowed by different groups, including the Safavid shahs of sixteenth-century Persia (now Iran), who granted Armenian merchants a monopoly on the imperial silk trade. In neighboring Russia, where Armenians had long served as doctors and merchants, the empire's expansion in the 1560s opened new opportunities for Armenian enterprise as well. With the Persian silk monopoly secured, Armenian traders established links with Moscow in the seventeenth century, and the tsar granted them exclusive rights to sell Persian goods throughout Russian lands. By the early eighteenth century Armenians—by then part of the Ottoman Empire—had cornered the Russian textile market.

Throughout the nineteenth century Armenian fortunes ebbed and flowed to a large degree with the character of Ottoman leadership, and despite discrimination and oppression against the Armenian population through exploitative taxes, forced resettlements, and restrictions under Islamic law, the Armenian people made notable contributions to the public life of the Ottoman Empire. The rulers under whom they lived esteemed Armenians as entrepreneurs, traders, and craftsmen. Ironically, this esteem led to occasional forced population transfers of Armenians to unproductive areas of the empire, where rulers expected them to stimulate the economies by their abilities and industry. Self-governing communities called *millets*—ostensibly free from Turkish or Muslim interference—dictated much Armenian life in the empire outside Istanbul. In these relatively safe but increasingly restricted *millet* communities, Armenians crafted splendid examples of carpets, gold- and silverware, ceramics, and jewelry sought internationally from the sixteenth century onward.

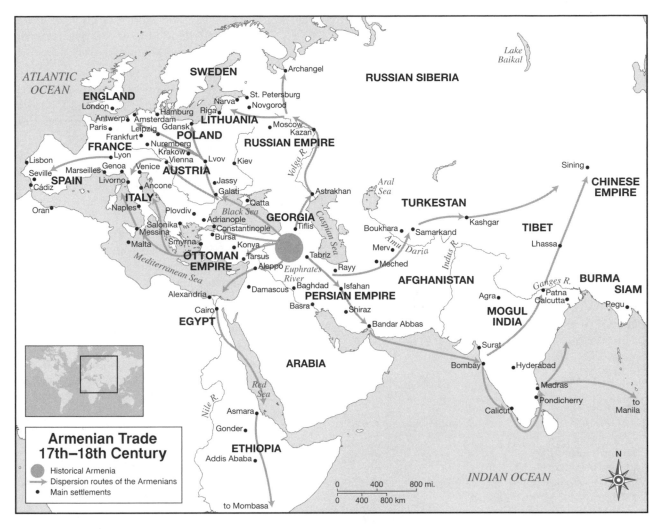

Armenian Trade 17th–18th Century

- Historical Armenia
- Dispersion routes of the Armenians
- Main settlements

MAP BY XNR PRODUCTIONS. THE GALE GROUP.

Quite apart from those in the so-called Turkish-Armenian interior, many Armenians in the capital, Istanbul, held high posts of political, economic, and cultural significance. Armenian capital undergirded many imperial factories before the 1850s, and Armenians ran iron, silk, paper, and gunpowder industries as well as several shipyards. The designated "architects of the empire" came from an Armenian family, Balian, who dominated Ottoman architecture, adorning the imperial capital with official commissions—none so grand as the still-extant palace of Dolmabahche. Armenians established the first printing press in Istanbul, and for over a century, the Duzian (Duzoglu) family directed the Ottoman mint, whose records were kept in Armenian from the 1750s to the 1880s.

In Istanbul and the wider territories of the Ottoman and Persian empires Armenians filled posts of distinction in, for example, Azerbaijan, Afghanistan, and Egypt. By the 1870s Armenians were the dominant commercial

class in Transcaucasian cities such as Tiflis (Tblisi), and by the 1890s Armenians controlled half the oil wells in the petroleum city of Baku (in present-day Azerbaijan). For two centuries Armenian merchants and financiers were the dominant commercial force in the Ottoman Empire, until they were displaced by British companies in trade, and British and French capital in Ottoman finance in the nineteenth century.

From the 1870s Ottoman Turkey sustained a series of military defeats that contributed to a radicalization of Ottoman leadership and increased hardships for Armenians as Turkish regimes looked for legitimacy by sanctioning oppression of minorities throughout the empire. Attacks against Armenians in the 1880s and 1890s culminated in the 1915 to 1916 genocide during World War I that eliminated half the population of Turkish Armenia. Those who survived and escaped enlarged the Armenian diaspora populations of Paris, Fresno, Boston, Beirut, Buenos Aires, and southeastern Australia.

From 1921 to 1991 Armenia was part of the Soviet Union and had the highest per capita income of any Soviet republic. Today, Armenians have a nation of their own for the first time in 900 years. In 2004 Armenia had a population of just over 3 million and, as a landlocked state, was struggling to prosper. There remains great interest in Armenia from the approximately 2 million members of the diaspora. Since independence, however, Armenia has experienced a net outflow of population to other parts of the world. Armenians remain spread out across the globe, as they have been for 2,000 years.

SEE ALSO AMSTERDAM; CARAVAN TRADE; EAST INDIA COMPANY, BRITISH; EAST INDIA COMPANY, DUTCH; EMPIRE, BRITISH; EMPIRE, DUTCH; EMPIRE, MUGHAL; EMPIRE, OTTOMAN; ETHNIC GROUPS, GUJARATI; GREECE; GUILDS; GULBENKIAN, CALOUSTE; INDIA; INDIAN OCEAN; IRAN; LEVANT COMPANY; MEDITERRANEAN; MILLETS AND CAPITULATIONS; PERSIAN GULF; POPULATION—EMIGRATION AND IMMIGRATION; RUSSIA; SHIPPING, MERCHANT; SILK; SPICES AND THE SPICE TRADE; UNITED STATES; VENICE.

BIBLIOGRAPHY

Bauer, Elisabeth. *Armenia, Past and Present.* New York: The Armenian Prelacy, 1981.

Chaliand, G., and Rageau, J. *The Penguin Atlas of Diasporas.* New York: Viking, 1995.

Walker, Christopher J. *Armenia: The Survival of a Nation.* New York: St. Martin's Press, 1990.

Peter E. Austin

ETHNIC GROUPS, CANTONESE

Centuries of overseas Chinese emigration have created one of the largest and most extensive diasporas in world history. That emigration was generated by historical processes that connected local economies in both the emigrant and host regions to global markets. As active participants in such processes, emigrants and their descendants helped to transform the economies of their adopted homeland. Having played an extremely critical role in China's economy, their financial resources and expertise represent a driving force in China's phenomenal growth in recent years since the 1980s.

Until recent decades, an overwhelming majority of emigrants originated from Guangdong and Fujian. Of these two provinces, Guangdong has played an arguably greater role in creating the global Chinese diaspora. Of today's estimated 30 million ethnic Chinese in the diaspora, more than half are believed to be of Cantonese descent. Moreover, although the destination of most early

Fujianese emigrants was Southeast Asia, Cantonese emigrants not only migrated to Southeast Asia but also established settlements elsewhere the modern world, such as North America and Australia.

Commerce is an important impetus for emigration, and the major emigrant communities are all located in regions that were affected by long-standing maritime trade. Located at the southeast end of mainland China on the west side of the South China Sea, Guangdong has occupied an important place in China's interactions with the outside world. Its capital, Guangzhou (also known as Canton), in particular, has been one of the most significant ports of international trade in Chinese history. By 1450, the first year of the reign of the seventh emperor of Ming dynasty (1368–1644), Cantonese merchants, along with their compatriots from Fujian, had developed well-established trade relations with Southeast Asia—relations that may date as early as the third century BCE. Traveling back and forth with commodities such as spices, silk, and chinaware, these merchants helped to turn the South China Sea region into one of the world's busiest zones of international trade. By the mid-fifteenth century, stranded merchants, along with exiles and adventurers, had long established Chinese settlements in different parts of Southeast Asia.

The expansion of Western colonialism and capitalism to the South China Sea created new markets for commodities and labor, generating new waves of Chinese emigration. In Southeast Asia, Europeans established colonial rule and economies during the sixteenth and seventeenth centuries. Many Chinese, including a growing number of people from Guangdong, went there as agricultural workers and miners. At the fall of the Ming dynasty they were joined by Ming Loyalists who refused to accept the new Qing dynasty (1644–1911).

During the Qing dynasty the significance of Guangdong in China's international affairs increased. The Qing Court designated Guangzhou as China's sole port for international trade between 1757 and the end of the Opium War (1840–1842). Europeans and, later, Americans who came to China during that period congregated in Guangzhou, making the city a hub for international commerce and cultural encounters. Emigration from the Pearl River Delta region, which centered around Guangzhou, for destinations outside Southeast Asia accelerated after the Opium War. By the early twentieth century, emigrants from the delta had established communities in places such as the United States, Canada, Mexico, Peru, Cuba, Australia, and Hawaii.

Individual emigrants followed what scholars of immigration call "migrant networks," sustained largely by geographical, linguistic (dialectic), and kinship ties. Emigrants with such ties tended to have a concentrated pres-

New Year's lion dance parade on Mott Street in New York's Chinatown, 2002. *The Cantonese have helped to develop the economies in both their adopted homelands and in China; today they provide 80 percent of overseas investment in their province of origin, Guangdong.* PHOTOGRAPH BY GRAHAM MORRISON. AP/WIDE WORLD PHOTOS. REPRODUCED BY PERMISSION.

ence in certain locations and even occupations. Although emigrants from the Pearl River Delta founded numerous predominantly Cantonese communities beyond the South China Sea, for instance, the most populous Cantonese group in Southeast Asia originated from Chaozhou and the surrounding areas, another important emigrant region in Guangdong, located south of Fujian. Early in the 1930s Chaozhou people represented a majority of the ethnic Chinese population in Thailand. They also had a significant presence elsewhere, such as in Indonesia, where a large number of them were employed in agriculture and mining. Moreover, geographical, linguistic, and kinship ties influenced the organization and operation of small and large Cantonese business enterprises. Small businesses in the early twentieth century, ranging from laundry shops in Chicago to retail stores in Batavia (now Jakarta), often functioned as family operations and relied on labor recruited among relatives or friends. Meanwhile, many large firms and corporations that began to emerge then, such as banking institutions in British Malaya, were also built along ethnic lines.

Ethnic Cantonese have made important contributions to the economic development of their countries of residence. It is common knowledge that in Southeast Asia, Cantonese, along with Fujianese, have been prominent in numerous sectors such as trade, retail, banking, and transportation. It must also be noted that many Cantonese were laborers, a significant number of whom had been kidnapped from China. Ethnic Cantonese in regions outside Southeast Asia did not have the same economic prominence in part because their Chinese settlements were much smaller. In the United States, for example, the Chinese population has never exceeded 1 percent of the national population.

For centuries, Cantonese emigrants have been sending remittances to their families, first relying primarily on individual couriers, then by private postal agencies and financial institutions that multiplied during the nineteenth century, and finally by modern banking institutions during the early twentieth century. Their transmissions form an extensive web for transporting diasporic capital, often by way of Hong Kong, to China. Around the mid-nineteenth century, ethnic Cantonese began to invest directly in Guangdong's economy.

Such diasporic capital provided much-needed foreign currency for the national economy. From 1937 through 1939, for instance, remittances were more than four times the size of the country's international trade deficit, and more than half of the remittances in the 1930s came from Cantonese communities in the United States. Since World War II, the Chinese diaspora has become even more complex and expansive. Cantonese communities, now found in more than 100 countries, have an increasingly visible presence in the global economy, and continue to inject capital into Guangdong. Since China began its economic reform late in the 1970s, ethnic Chinese have provided 80 percent of all overseas investments in Guangdong, and have contributed management skills and access to global markets, making the province a locomotive of China's fast-growing and fast-changing economy.

SEE ALSO AGRICULTURE; BURMA; CANADA; CANTON SYSTEM; CHINA; CUBA; DRUGS, ILLICIT; EAST INDIA COMPANY, DUTCH; EMPIRE, BRITISH; EMPIRE, DUTCH; EMPIRE, FRENCH; EMPIRE, JAPANESE; EMPIRE, MING; EMPIRE, PORTUGUESE; EMPIRE, QING; EMPIRE, SPANISH; ETHNIC GROUPS, FUJIANESE; FAMINE; GOLD RUSHES; GUANGZHOU; GUILDS; HONG KONG; HONG KONG AND SHANGHAI BANK; IMPERIALISM; INDONESIA; INDUSTRIALIZATION; JAPAN; JARDINE MATHESON; LABORERS, CONTRACT;

MELAKA; MINING; NAGASAKI; NANYANG BROTHERS
TOBACCO; NATIONALISM; NATIONALIZATION;
PEDDLERS; PERU; POPULATION—EMIGRATION AND
IMMIGRATION; RUBBER; SEX AND GENDER; SHIPS AND
SHIPPING; SINGAPORE; SOUTH AFRICA; SOUTH CHINA
SEA; TEA; THAILAND; TRAVELERS AND TRAVEL;
TRIBUTE SYSTEM; UNITED STATES; VIETNAM;
YOKOHAMA.

BIBLIOGRAPHY

Barnett, Milton. "Kinship as a Factor Affecting Cantonese Economic Adaptation in the United States." *Human Organization* 19 (1960): 40–46.

Chen, Yong. "The Internal Origins of Chinese Emigration to California Reconsidered." *The Western Historical Quarterly* 28 (1997): 520–546.

Gomez, Edmund Terence, and Hsiao, Hsin-Huang Michael. "Introduction: Chinese Business Research in Southeast Asia." In *Chinese Business in Southeast Asia,* ed. Edmund Terence Gomez and Hsin-Huang Michael Hsiao. Richmond, U.K.: Curzon, 2001.

Hamilton, Gary, and Waters, Tony. "Ethnicity and Capitalist Development: The Changing Role of the Chinese in Thailand." In *Essential Outsiders: Chinese and Jews in the Modern Transformation of Southeast Asian and Central Europe,* ed. Daniel Chirot and Anthony Reid. Seattle: University of Washington Press, 1997.

Li, Ji; Khatri, Naresh; and Lam, Kevin. "Changing Strategic Postures of Overseas Chinese Firms in Emerging Asian Markets." *Management Decision* 37 (1999): 445–456.

Mei, June. "Socioeconomic Origins of Emigration: Guangdong to California, 1850 to 1882." In *Labor Immigration under Capitalism,* ed. Lucie Cheng and Edna Bonacich. Berkeley: University of California Press, 1983.

Wang Gung-Wu. "Confronting Myths." In *China and Southeast Asia: Myths, Threats and Culture.* Singapore: World Scientific and Singapore University Press, 1999.

Yen Ching-hwang. "Modern Overseas Chinese Business Enterprise: A Preliminary Study." In *The Chinese Diaspora,* ed. Wang Ling-chi and Wang Gungwu. Singapore: Times Academic Press, 1998.

Wu, David Y. H. "To Kill Three Birds with One Stone: The Rotation Credit Association of the Papua New Guinea Chinese." *American Ethnologist* 1 (1974): 565–584.

Yong Chen

ETHNIC GROUPS, FUJIANESE

Fujianese as an ethnic designation does not denote all people from Fujian province, but only those of the Quanzhou-Zhangzhou region in South Fujian. In Southeast Asia they are also known as *Hokkien* (literally, "Fujianese"). In Taiwan they are also called *Minnanren* ("South Fujianese"). They speak a common dialect, but with varying accents.

South Fujian, long known for its seafaring activities, was connected to the wider maritime world when its major seaport, Quanzhou, became an important port of call for Middle Eastern traders during the ninth century. The city had many Arab merchants, and the early-fourteenth-century Morrocan traveler Ibn Battuta described it as the world's largest seaport. Junks from Quanzhou were visiting maritime Southeast Asia by the thirteenth century, and India by the early fourteenth century. Small South Fujianese communities soon appeared overseas.

The fifteenth century brought a new era in Chinese maritime history after early Ming attempts failed to impose rigid state control over overseas trade. Seven spectacular imperially sponsored expeditions left China under the command of Admiral Zheng He (1371–1435) from 1405 to 1433; he traveled as far as the east coast of Africa. However, high costs ended this state initiative, and private commerce soon dominated China's overseas trade. By the late fifteenth century, the city of Yuegang in Zhangzhou became a bustling center of private trade and of smuggling, and it remained the province's preeminent port for about two centuries before it was overtaken by its neighbor Xiamen (Amoy).

During the sixteenth to eighteenth centuries the Fujianese were the undisputed maritime traders in China, Japan, and maritime Southeast Asia, and they formed complex, multilayered networks that extended across Southeast and Northeast Asia. The arrival of European traders in East Asian waters in the sixteenth and early seventeenth centuries helped extend Fujianese links to markets outside the region. The Fujianese became indispensable facilitators for multinational trade enterprises in this huge region. Their communities blossomed in Western colonial towns such as Batavia and Manila, and in Japanese port cities such as Hirota and Nagasaki. The Fujianese maritime trade had its golden age during China's prosperous eighteenth century, when hundreds of Quan-Zhang junks plied the China and Taiwan coasts and the South China Seas. The Quan-Zhang people had become an overwhelming majority in Taiwan, and they migrated overseas in growing numbers.

The Fujianese engaged in all kinds of trade, and their low overheads gave them a competitive edge. They imported spices and medicinal herbs from Southeast Asia and silver from Japan and from Spanish America through Manila. American silver was mainly for the purchase of silk from South Fujian; Spanish galleons subsequently carried it to Acapulco and on to European markets. The overseas trade of the Fujianese helped accelerate late Ming commercialization.

Besides silks, Fujianese junks also exported porcelain, low-grade earthenware, and various small handicraft items.

Junks in Xiamen's harbor, 1985. *Overseas Fujianese played an important role in the economic development of Xiamen in the 1980s and 1990s.* © DEAN CONGER/CORBIS. REPRODUCED BY PERMISSION.

In the eighteenth century bulky items entered the flow of coastal trade, such as rice and sugar shipped from Taiwan. Ships embarking from Xiamen for other Chinese ports carried earthenware, preserved fruits, candies, tea, tobacco, pine boards, paper, indigo, pepper, marine delicacies, shark's fins, medicinal herbs, myrrh, sapanwood, frankincense, and tin. Fujianese junks trading with Southeast Asia exported tea, silk, porcelain, and hundreds of manufactured items for popular consumption, and brought back "straits produce"—which included a wide range of agricultural and mineral products from the Malayan Archipelago—and rice from Siam.

After the Opium War (1839–1842) the Chinese junk trade faced a strong challenge from Western shipping, and the arrival of steamers in the following decades effectively sidelined junk traders. However, the Fujianese in Southeast Asia benefited from expanding trade. Late-nineteenth- and early-twentieth-century examples included the rice merchant Tan Kim Ching (1829–1892) in Singapore; southern Siam's Khaw Sim Bee (1857–1913), whose business covered tin mining, shipping, insurance, and opium farms; the "sugar king," Oei Tiong Ham (1866–1924), in the Dutch Indies; the "rubber king," Tan

Kah Kee (1874–1961), in Singapore; and the "timber king," Dee C. Chuan (1889–1940), in the Philippines. They were among the richest men in Asia.

So-called "Straits Chinese," descendants of Hokkien settlers in the British Straits Settlements of Penang, Melacca, and Singapore, also operated in the treaty port of Xiamen itself. Their status as British-protected subjects helped them avoid interference from local Chinese officials. And in the late nineteenth century many Fujianese also emerged in response to rising labor demand in Southeast Asia.

In the early twentieth century overseas Fujianese became investors in modern industries in Fujian such as railroad construction and mining, but most of these ventures failed. In light industry such as canned food there were a few successes. Prior to 1949 virtually all outside investment in Fujian originated from Southeast Asia, especially the Philippines, Indonesia, and Malaya. Funds went to industry, agriculture, mining, communications, commerce, finance, services, property, and other sectors. Xiamen absorbed most of the capital invested.

After three decades of low overseas investments in China, Southeast Asian Fujianese again invested substantial sums in Xiamen beginning in the 1980s, when it was designated a Special Economic Zone to attract investment. By the late 1990s Xiamen was classified as "upper-middle-income" by the World Bank standards, an achievement made possible by the investment of overseas Chinese capital.

The unassailable position of the Fujianese among their collaborators/competitors, including European traders, over the past few centuries is largely due to their widespread and intricately interconnected networks. Family lineages in rural Fujian offered manpower and resource pooling for seafaring endeavors in late imperial times. Away from their native villages, the Fujianese formed native-place associations known as *huiguan,* flexibly extending organizational boundaries to achieve group solidarity. These associations are still highly influential in the Chinese communities of the Philippines, Indonesia, Malaysia, and Singapore. From the 1980s, Chinese native-place or same-surname associations have organized various world congresses, and Fujianese associations have been active participants. These efforts have strengthened ties with other associations worldwide, and also with the *qiaoxiang* (ancestral hometowns). Although the reasons for this involvement are partly sentimental, the process also builds new connections and constitutes yet another adjustment on the part of the Fujianese to a rapidly changing business environment.

SEE ALSO AGRICULTURE; BURMA; CANADA; CANTON SYSTEM; CHINA; CUBA; DRUGS, ILLICIT; EAST INDIA COMPANY, DUTCH; EMPIRE, BRITISH; EMPIRE, DUTCH; EMPIRE, FRENCH; EMPIRE, JAPANESE; EMPIRE, MING; EMPIRE, PORTUGUESE; EMPIRE, QING; EMPIRE, SPANISH; ETHNIC GROUPS, CANTONESE; FAMINE; GOLD RUSHES; GUILDS; HONG KONG; HONG KONG AND SHANGHAI BANK; IMPERIALISM; INDONESIA; INDUSTRIALIZATION; JAPAN; JARDINE MATHESON; LABORERS, CONTRACT; MELAKA; MINING; NAGASAKI; NANYANG BROTHERS TOBACCO; NATIONALISM; NATIONALIZATION; PEDDLERS; PERU; RUBBER; SHIPS AND SHIPPING; SINGAPORE; SOUTH AFRICA; SOUTH CHINA SEA; TEA; THAILAND; TRAVELERS AND TRAVEL; TRIBUTE SYSTEM; UNITED STATES; VIETNAM; YOKOHAMA.

BIBLIOGRAPHY

Australia Department of Foreign Affairs and Trade. *Overseas Chinese Networks in Asia.* Parkes Australian Capital Territory–Australia: 1995.

Blusse, Leonard. *Strange Company: Chinese Settlers, Mestizo Women, and the Dutch in VOC Batavia.* Dordrecht, Netherlands: Foris Publications, 1986.

Cartier, Carolyn. *Globalizing South China.* Oxford, U.K.: Blackwell, 2001.

Chin Kong, James. "Merchants and Other Sojourners: The Hokkiens Overseas, 1570–1760." Ph.D. diss., University of Hong Kong, 1998.

Cushman, Jennifer W. *Family and State: The Formation of a Sino-Thai Tin-mining Dynasty, 1797–1932.* Singapore: Oxford University Press, 1991.

Leo Douw, Cen Huang, and Godley, Michael R. *Qiaoxiang Ties: Interdisciplinary Approaches to "Cultural Capitalism" in South China.* London and New York: Kegan Paul International, 1999.

Menkhoff, Thomas, and Gerke, Solvay, eds. *Chinese Entrepreneurship and Asian Business Networks.* London and New York: Routledge, 2002.

Ng Chin-keong. *Trade and Society: The Amoy Network on the China Coast, 1683–1753.* Singapore: Singapore University Press, 1983.

Pan, Lynn, ed. *The Encyclopedia of the Chinese Overseas.* Singapore: Archipelago Press and Landmark Books, 1998.

Vermeer, E. R., ed. *Development and Decline of Fukien Province in the Seventeenth and Eighteenth Centuries.* Leiden, Netherlands: E. J. Brill, 1990.

Chin-keong Ng

ETHNIC GROUPS, GUJARATI

Traders from Gujarat, on the west coast of India north of Mumbai, have long played a major role in trade in the Indian Ocean area and further afield. Some are Muslims, and they themselves are internally divided: some are known as *khojas* (or Nizari Isma'ilis, whose head is the Aga Khan), and *bohras,* who are minorities within the Shi'a sect of Muslims; others are Parsis, descendents of people who migrated from Iran, who follow the pre-Islamic religion of Persia, Zoroastrianism. However, the most important merchants are followers of two other religions, who collectively are called *vanias.* Some *vanias* are Jains, who follow a particularly ascetic religion dating back over 2,500 years, but most are Hindus. In total, these groups make up less than 10 percent of the population of Gujarat state today. Over the last six centuries these people have emigrated to conduct trade in foreign nations, but they nearly always retain ties with their family groups back in Gujarat. If possible, they visit "home" from time to time, marry women from their own group in Gujarat, and sometimes (though less frequently in the last fifty years) send their children back home for schooling. This is not so much a matter of migration to escape poverty at home, but rather to seek better opportunities abroad and to establish a foreign base for their kin members back home.

Gujarat has long been an important producing area in India. From the fifteenth to the early nineteenth centuries it produced indigo dye, saltpeter, and handicrafts, but the main export was cotton cloths, ranging from coarse stuff for everyday wear for poor people to very fine and intricately dyed cloths for the elite. These cloths were important trade items from Southeast Asia to the east coast of Africa; indeed, in some areas Gujarati cloths were used as currency. Gujarati merchants—at this time mostly Muslims, but also some Hindu and Jain *vanias*—exchanged their cotton cloths for spices from Indonesia and ivory and gold from East Africa. When the Portuguese arrived at the end of the fifteenth century they found that the only trade item with a market in East Africa was cloths from Gujarat.

The arrival of Europeans—first the Portuguese in 1498, and then the Dutch and English late in the sixteenth century—affected Gujarat's trading communities in several ways. Traders in the area's great ports—Surat, Cambay, Broach, Diu, and Gogha—had to pay a levy to the Portuguese. Monopolistic Portuguese policies in Southeast Asia prompted Gujarati traders to move their trade to the Red Sea area. Despite Portuguese opposition, they were able to transport spices and cotton cloths to Middle Eastern markets. When the Dutch and English arrived they soon realized the necessity of acquiring cloths from Gujarat to trade all around the Indian Ocean littoral. Gujarati traders often used European ships to transport their goods because they were stronger and safer from pirates. Great Jain magnates in Gujarat disposed of considerably greater capital than did the European trading companies.

As English control in India advanced late in the seventeenth century, many Gujarati traders moved to the new English port city of Bombay (now Mumbai). It is from this time that Parsis, *khojas,* and *bohras* began to flourish. The Parsis acted as middlemen between the English and Indians, but in the nineteenth century they became independently wealthy from trade and shipbuilding, and later from professions such as medicine. However, for most other trading communities in the nineteenth century it was very difficult to compete with the economic power of industrialized Britain. Nevertheless, *vanias* and members of the Hindu *bhatia* group from Kutch were able to trade successfully in East Africa, dominating the supply of credit and many trade items. Gujarati traders produced tightly knit and exclusive family firms that did very well within the imperial structure of the British; their members operated far inland in East Africa, buying trade goods and running small businesses.

From late in the nineteenth century Indian industry slowly began to compete with machine-made goods from England. The first modern textile mills were established by trading groups in Gujarat, and they were the original bases for many of the great industrial families in India that continue to this day. One example is the Tata family, who owns a vast conglomerate of businesses in India run by Parsis, and has expanded some of their activities worldwide.

India became independent in 1947, but Gujaratis continued to trade successfully around the shores of the Indian Ocean, and especially in Kenya, South Africa, and Tanzania. However, as African countries became independent they often resented the economic dominance of the Indians and took measures against them. The most extreme example of this was the expulsion by Idi Amin (1925–2003), the dictator of Uganda, of the entire Asian population of the country in the early 1970s. Most of the expelled moved to England, where they play an important role in retail trade.

In more recent times different Gujarati groups have expanded successfully into Western markets while remaining important within India. The *khojas* are a closely-knit and very successful business community who often use their wealth for charitable and educational purposes. They are very widely dispersed throughout the world, as far away as New Zealand and Sweden. Jains, who number only perhaps 5 million worldwide, play a role of importance out of all proportion to their numbers—they dominate the world diamond trade. Hindu *vanias* have expanded their activities similarly. About one-fifth of all Indians resident in the United States today are Gujaratis, including many *patels*—that is, people not from the traditional trading castes—who own a large number of motels and hotels in the United States, as well as many news agencies and small retail stores. In England, Gujaratis own many convenience stores and other shops. Many Parsis, whose numbers and wealth are declining in India, have migrated to the West, where they are professionals rather than businessmen.

SEE ALSO AGRICULTURE; BANKING; BOMBAY; BENGAL; BURMA; CALCUTTA; CARAVAN TRADE; EAST INDIA COMPANY, BRITISH; EAST INDIA COMPANY, DUTCH; EMPIRE, BRITISH; EMPIRE, DUTCH; EMPIRE, MUGHAL; EMPIRE, OTTOMAN; EMPIRE, PORTUGUESE; FAMINE; GOLD RUSHES; IMPERIALISM; INDIA; INDIAN OCEAN; INDONESIA; IRAN; KENYA; LABORERS, COERCED; LABORERS, CONTRACT; LONDON; MADRAS; NATIONALISM; NATIONALIZATION; PAKISTAN; PERSIAN GULF; SINGAPORE; SOUTH AFRICA; TATA FAMILY ENTERPRISES; TRAVELERS AND TRAVEL; UNITED KINGDOM; UNITED STATES.

BIBLIOGRAPHY

Brown, Judith, and Foot, Rosemary, eds. *Migration: The Asian Experience.* Houndmill, U.K.: St. Martin's Press, 1994.

Luhrmann, T. M. *The Good Parsi: The Fate of a Colonial Elite in a Postcolonial Society,* Cambridge, MA: Harvard University Press, 1996.

Sorrell, Thomas. *Migrations and Cultures: A World View.* New York: Basic Books, 1996.

Michael N. Pearson

ETHNIC GROUPS, HUGUENOTS

The Huguenots were the French followers of a Protestant reformer, John Calvin (1509–1564), who fled from Paris to Geneva, where he took command in 1555 and launched a second Reformation. Calvin's influential *Institutes of the Christian Religion* (1536), a coherent manual of Bible teachings, alarmed Catholic governments, as did the Calvinist republican organization of ministers and elders in parish consistories, regional colloquies, and the twenty-nine national synods held from 1559 to 1659—all independent of princes and bishops. Huguenots set up the *Église réformée* in France, while fellow Calvinists organized as the Dutch Reformed Church in the Netherlands, the Presbyterian Church in Scotland, the Puritans in England, and the *Reformierten Kirche* in parts of Germany. For two centuries, all followed Calvin's example by escaping abroad when persecuted by Catholic authorities; the term "refugees" (*réfugiés*) was invented to describe them. In London the first of many Huguenot and Walloon (French-speaking Dutch) churches appeared in 1550. Soon after the infamous Catholic massacres of Huguenots on St. Bartholomew's Day in 1572, there were ten thousand foreign Protestants in England; other churches were forming in Dutch, German, and Swiss towns.

Emigration rose and fell in response to variable persecution at home. Between 1562 and 1598 fighting noblemen led the Huguenots in "Wars of Religion" against Catholic oppressors, but many gave up the reformed faith when their leader, Henry of Navarre, turned Catholic in 1593 and was murdered in 1610. As King Henry IV, he signed a famous Edict of Nantes (1598), granting Huguenots temporary protection, mainly in certain fortified towns, but beginning in 1620 his Catholic successor, Louis XIII, conquered and catholicized them all in four military campaigns. The last stronghold, La Rochelle, fell in 1628, and thereafter Huguenots led a precarious, harried existence until October 1685, when Louis XIV outlawed them by repealing the Edict. Many escaped abroad, of whom 50,000–60,000 found shelter in the Dutch Republic; 40,000–50,000 in England; 25,000–30,000 in Germany; 22,000 in Switzerland; 10,000 in Ireland; 10,000 in America; 2,000 in Denmark and northeastern Europe; and 400 in the Cape of Good Hope.

A DIASPORA

These refugee communities had not only merchants, but also craftsmen, laborers, mariners, soldiers, professional

THE ACADIANS

In 1603 Henri IV appointed Huguenot Pierre Du Gua, Sieur de Monts, as viceroy of the North American colony "La Cadie" (Acadia). By 1605 de Monts, aided by explorer Samuel de Champlain, founded Port Royal on the Bay of Fundy. Their successors continued to promote the colony. By the late seventeenth century small communities had taken root throughout Acadia, which possessed some of North America's most fertile soil. The French-speaking, Catholic Acadians became prosperous farmers who also fished and traded furs. The British acquired Acadia (renamed Nova Scotia) in 1713 under the Treaty of Utrecht. Most Acadians remained on their productive farms, taking an oath of allegiance that allowed them to remain neutral in the conflict against the French and Indians. With another Anglo-French war looming in 1755, British authorities feared that the "French neutrals" would form a dangerous fifth column in their midst. After the Acadians refused a new oath without reservations, Nova Scotia's Governor Charles Lawrence decided that they had to be removed. Deportations began in October, with 10,000 Acadians eventually forced off their lands. Of their number, about one-third died of disease. The rest were eventually scattered among the American colonies, Louisiana, France, and the Caribbean.

David J. Clarke

men, intellectuals, artists, and clergy, but there were no peasants, vagrants, or urban proletariat. This was because Calvinists were committed to an austere ethic of self-help, which later inspired Samuel Smiles (1812–1904) to write his famous *Self-Help* (1858) and a popular history of the Huguenots. He had in mind the evident success which Huguenot merchants owed partly to their overseas networks of trading relatives, built up abroad as a result of persecution in France; partly to their intermarriage with Dutch and English Protestants who more and more dominated maritime commerce in the seventeenth century; and partly to being forbidden to buy their way into the lower ranks of French nobility.

Only Catholics could buy the royal offices of *secrétaire du Roi, trésorier du Roi, receveur général,* and others, with the anomalous result that successful Catholic merchants tended to rise beyond the ranks of shopkeepers *(marchands),* and even of respectable wholesale shipping merchants *(négociants),* to become minor noblemen pretending to despise trade—*bourgeois gentilhommes,* in Molière's satirical play (1670). Their Huguenot competitors perforce carried on trading between ports on the North Sea, the Baltic, the Atlantic Ocean, and the Mediterranean, as well as Geneva, and certain inland towns in Germany, the Dutch Republic, and the British Isles. Hoping for better times later, their families posted members at Bordeaux, La Rochelle, Bayonne, Rouen, and other towns as trading partners and to hold on to family property by conforming as "new converts," sometimes discreetly tolerated by French authorities anxious to promote French trade.

A cosmopolitan freemasonry or "Protestant international" prospered during the seventeenth and eighteenth centuries. Great colonies of Huguenot merchants flourished in Amsterdam, Rotterdam, London, and Geneva, and smaller ones flourished in Norwich, Southampton, Dublin, New York, Boston (New England), Charleston (South Carolina), Lisbon (under British protection), and elsewhere. Wealthy Huguenot bankers lived in Geneva freely but also in Paris disguised as "new converts."

Three years after the Revocation of the Edict of Nantes in 1685, Prince William of Orange, the Dutch Statholder, embarked thousands of mixed Protestant refugees—Huguenot, Dutch, Walloon, Swiss, Swedish, and English (victims of James II's oppressive Catholic reign)—in an armada to invade England, where Parliament offered the throne to him and his Anglican wife, Mary, James II's daughter.

England and the Dutch Republic, thus linked until William died in 1702, witnessed a huge commercial, financial, and military expansion, with Huguenots playing big parts, along with Jews, Quakers, and other minorities. Seven of the twenty-four founding investors in the Bank of England established in 1694 were Huguenots, as were many investors in the New East India Company, the South Sea Company, the Royal Exchange, and other new insurance companies. Beginning in April 1697, Jean Castaing, a refugee from Bordeaux, published a twice-weekly *Course of the Exchange* in London, while business news was printed there and in Rotterdam by other Huguenots.

In the 1670s, Dutch paper mills, pioneered in Angoulême, prospered in the Zaan and Gelderland districts; in the 1680s, Huguenots brought a flourishing silk industry to towns in Holland, London's Spitalfields district, and Southampton; and after the Glorious Revolution (1688–1689) in England and the war against France, the linen trades bloomed in Overijssel, Haarlem, Waterford, and Cork; Huguenots craftsmen in textiles, leather, cotton, wool, millinery, and silver carried their trades to many towns in Protestant countries. In France, the government tended to make use of successful Huguenots while denouncing their heresies and putting less successful ones in prison or the slave galleys, imprisoning their wives and children in convents.

PROSPERITY AND SUCCESS

Leading Huguenot refugees were prominent enough in international trade to become pillars of their communities. At Amsterdam between 1590 and 1620, the Poulle brothers from Lille, Pieter, Germain, Isaac and Israel, built up a leading international trading network around the North Sea and the Baltic. Louis de Geer (c. 1586–1652), a Walloon financier born in Liège, started his business career at La Rochelle in 1608 and lived in Stockholm from 1627 until his death, busy with Swedish copper and iron exports and cannon manufacturing, which helped King Gustaf Adolf to win battles in Germany against Catholic forces in between 1630 and 1632. Two members of the Desmynières family, originally from Poitou, became Lord Mayors at Dublin, where the family settled as traders in 1638. Sir Theodore Janssen, whose father and grandfather manufactured paper in Angoulême, was educated in Holland but went with two brothers and £20,000 to London, where in 1683 he joined the Threadneedle Street Church and was soon naturalized English. He grew wealthy in trade with family and Huguenot contacts in Angoulême, Hamburg, and Amsterdam. He sent tin and lead to Genoa and the Straits; imported much paper from his father in France; was a founder and director of the Bank of England and the New East India Company of 1698; and grew rich by financing British armies on the continent.

In the eighteenth century Sir John Houblon dominated the Bank of England until he died in 1712, and in his circle were such descendants of other Huguenot refugees as Thomas Papillon, Edward Desbouverie and sons, and John Lambert (in the South Seas Company). Gabriel Bernon (1644–1736) of La Rochelle grew rich at Providence, Rhode Island, trading with relatives in Europe, New England, and New York. André Faneuil (1657–1737) and his nephew, Peter (Pierre) Faneuil (1700–1743), made their mark famously in Boston, Massachusetts, while trading with Benjamin Faneuil (1658–1719), Peter's father, who had settled in New York; with Jean Faneuil of Rotterdam and other cousins in La Rochelle; and with Thomas Bureau, a substantial London merchant, whose £500 investment in the Bank of England in 1694 made him one of its founders. To trace networks of Huguenot merchant families is to throw new light on the economic and financial life of the Western world in early modern times. Their descendants, proudly conscious of their stout collective resistance to Catholic French bullying, survive in societies all over the civilized world and publish much scholarly history, as well as genealogy.

SEE ALSO CANADA; EMPIRE, BRITISH; FRANCE; LONDON; RELIGION; UNITED KINGDOM.

BIBLIOGRAPHY

Bosher, J. F. *Business and Religion in the Age of New France.* Toronto: Canadian Scholars' Press, 1994.

Bosher, J. F. "Huguenot Merchants and the Protestant International in the Seventeenth Century." *William and Mary Quarterly,* Third Series 52 (1995): 77–102.

Butler, Jon. *The Huguenots in America: A Refugee People in New World Society.* Cambridge, MA: Harvard University Press, 1983

Caldicott, C. E. J.; Gough, H.; and Pittion, J. P., eds. *The Huguenots and Ireland: Anatomy of an Emigration.* Dun Laoghaire, Ireland: Glendale Press, 1987.

François, E. "L'accueil des refugiés huguenots en Allemagne." In *La révocation de l'édit de Nantes et les Provinces Unies, 1685,* ed. J. A. H. Bots, et al. Amsterdam: Holland University Press, 1986.

Gwynn, Robin D. *Huguenot Heritage: The History and Contribution of the Huguenots in Britain.* London: Routledge, 1985

Naphy, William G. *Calvin and the Consolidation of the Genevan Reformation.* Manchester, England: Manchester University Press, 1994.

Nash, R. C. "The Huguenot Diaspora and the Development of the Atlantic Economy: Huguenots and the Growth of the South Carolina Economy, 1680–1775." In *Merchant Organization and Maritime Trade in the North Atlantic, 1660–1815,* ed. Olaf Uwe Janzen. St. John's, Newfoundland: International Maritime Economic History Association, 1998.

Spicer, Andrew. *The French-Speaking Reformed Community and Their Church in Southampton, 1567–c. 1620.* London: The Huguenot Society of Great Britain and Ireland, 1997.

Van der Laan, P. H. J., "The Poulle Brothers of Amsterdam and the North Sea and Baltic Trade, 1590–1620," in *From Dunkirk to Danzig: Shipping and Trade in the North Sea and the Baltic, 1350–1850,* ed. W. G. Heeres, L. M. J. B. Hesp, L. Noordegraff, and R. G. W. Van de Voort. Helversum, 1988, pp. 317–330.

Van Ruymbeke, Bertrand, and Sparks, Randy J., eds. *Memory and Identity: The Huguenots in France and the Atlantic Diaspora.* Columbia, SC: University of South Carolina Press, 2003.

Veale, Elspeth. "Sir Theodore Janssen, Huguenot and Merchant of London c. 1658–1748." *Proceedings of the Huguenot Society of Great Britain and Ireland* 26, no. 2 (1995): 264–288.

J. F. Bosher

ETHNIC GROUPS, IRISH

Foreign trade at large was slight in the Middle Ages, disproportionately dominated at the higher levels by finan-

POTATO FAMINE

From 1800 to 1847 Ireland's population almost doubled, to 8.5 million. Many Irish were desperately poor, especially in the western counties. Eking out a living on tiny plots, these poor farmers were further hampered by rising rents and falling wages, often imposed by absentee landlords. Increased demand from industrial Britain had also turned Ireland into an exporter of grains. By the 1840s many Irish were fed almost entirely by potato crops, which grew well in the damp soil, but from 1845 to 1848 the potato crop failed, producing famine. Ireland had experienced famines before, but not on such a scale. In counties such as Galway and Mayo the death rate rose by 20 percent from 1846 to 1851. In keeping with contemporary economic ideas, the British government was reluctant to intervene, even in cases where oats were being exported from the famine-stricken nation. Some relief was provided, but it was not nearly enough. Between 1845 and 1850 more than 1 million Irish died from starvation or hunger-related diseases such as typhus and dysentery. A half million were evicted from their homes during the famine, and 1.5 million more emigrated to places such as the United States.

David J. Clarke

ciers (Italian and, much later, German mining magnates) who covered government deficits, and at lower levels by modest flows of timber, wool, hides, cloth, and wine. Discovery of the Americas created pressures on slender lines of supply. Peripheral areas, rich in surpluses of a few primary products or in ships and seamen (a consequence of the fishing industry), benefited from this, and in a still-backward world a highly diffuse participation, direct or indirect, quickened across the entire Atlantic expanse. In ship-rich regions such as the southwest of England, Brittany, and Cantabria whole networks of lesser ports experienced a boom despite relatively small immediate hinterlands. A few ports such as Bayonne, La Rochelle, and Saint-Malo, and in Britain, Bristol, enjoyed periods of great prominence.

The most peripheral of all these regions (and so, later to benefit) was Ireland. Its trade in the sixteenth century remained very much a medieval-style conversion of agricultural surplus, usually through supercargoes, into a

Workers roll linen at a factory in Belfast, Ireland. Belfast, a city in Northern Ireland, became a leading linen manufacturer in the nineteenth century. © SEAN SEXTON COLLECTION/CORBIS. REPRODUCED BY PERMISSION.

handful of desired imports. Hides, skins, fish (especially for the lenten markets of Europe), and some wool were shipped from minor ports all around the island. In return the main imports were salt and wine (because locally brewed beer and the nascent whiskey were poorly made products). Although ports on the Irish Sea unavoidably remained linked to trade with the nearby coasts of England, some ports profited in time from the new Atlantic world. Galway was early into the tobacco trade, and in time created the most far-flung network of Irish commercial outposts abroad. By the 1680s trade everywhere was already beginning to narrow to a smaller number of ports. In Ireland, Cork showed signs of its future prominence. Over time, Galway, like Saint-Malo, compensated for declining commodity trade with the investment of initiative and capital elsewhere. Merchants from Waterford, using Saint-Malo as springboard, settled further afield in France and Spain. Vessels from Poole added a new dimension to Waterford's trade by stopping in the port city for food and men on their outward voyage to the Newfoundland fishery.

With the emphasis in Irish external trade shifting from England to the Americas and continental Europe, the traffics retained their importance until the 1770s, a fact concealed by the dramatic development of the high-value and regionally limited trade in linen linked to Dub-

lin (for its finance) and to London (for its markets). On the Continent, repeating the domestic pattern in Ireland, Irish merchants gradually narrowed their focus to a handful of ports: Nantes, Bordeaux, and Cadiz. In Nantes a precocious presence meant that Irish business families acquired colonial property and titles of nobility, becoming part of a propertied elite who progressively withdrew from trade (as Nantes lost its impetus to other French rivals). In Bordeaux the Irish colony was the largest foreign group after the Germans, in Cádiz the largest after the French and Italians, and in the small but strategic Canary Islands, the largest foreign community of all.

The management and financing of trade likewise changed. In the past merchants, eager to acquire sought-after salt and wine, traveled with their goods; bills were endorsed on the spot, often several times over, and notarial protests were inevitably numerous. Thereafter, the medley of bills drawn on little-known figures was replaced by bills drawn on or payable to London houses. These changed hands locally in a singe transaction, immediately entering into a flow of banking operations linking Paris (or Madrid) and London. Irish houses in London were reinforced not only by the new linen trade but also by the financing of trade with Europe and America. A well-defined financial interest developed, of which the outstanding houses were the Fitzgeralds (famously important as buyers for the French tobacco monopoly), and the Nesbitts. Overall, Irish high finance, whether in London or on the Continent, was very much a case of a few large figures and a numerous but small-scale supporting cast.

Irish participation in the East India Company was slight, although Sir George Colebrooke (1729–1809), married to the heiress of an Irish fortune in the West Indies, was chairman in its fractious politics of 1769, 1770, and 1772. Laurence Sullivan (c. 1713–1786), a director from 1755, was Irish. In the 1720s, the short-lived Ostend Company was dominated by Irishmen. The French East India Company, in the 1760s, had an important Irish presence when it was led by the Irishmen Francis Rothe (whose wife was a Hay from Saint-Malo) and Thomas Sutton (comte de Clonard). They were both close associates of Choiseul, the dominant French politician of the 1760s, along with the Laborde (Bayonne) and Magon (Saint-Malo) interest. Their fortunes followed those of their political patron.

The Irish pattern in the Atlantic trades was one of a belated precocity and a relatively short-lived flourishing. It is easy to blame the Navigation Acts at large for the fading of Irish involvement. Ireland was in many ways akin to individual ports such as Bayonne and Saint-Malo, or in a longer perspective, Cádiz and Bordeaux, which in time, through economic and political change on

A horse-drawn cart brings goods to a steamer boat in the Irish port town of Cork. In the early twentieth century, Cork was the largest butter exporter among the British Isles and also became a key trading center for other commodities such as cattle, pork, copper, linen, and wool. **PHOTOGRAPH BY SEAN SEXTON. CORBIS. REPRODUCED BY PERMISSION.**

the far side of the Atlantic, were reduced to backwaters. In essence, the Irish place in Atlantic trades was determined by enhanced demand for agricultural surpluses before transatlantic surplus became abundant, and by England's standoff with France and Spain, which gave Ireland an economic and managerial role in the wine and

brandy trades. Except for the wine and brandy houses, the general trading houses all disappeared with the collapse of the Atlantic trades of Bordeaux and Cádiz. From the 1780s Irish trade began its progressive contraction to a cross-channel basis, supplying agricultural surpluses, at first in grain more permanently in cattle, bacon, and butter, to an industrializing Britain. Irish houses could still display real initiative. The cross-channel steamship trade, the first intensive use anywhere of steam power in commercial shipping, was pioneered, financed, and managed by an Irish interest, which also drew some British dissenter capital into its ventures. Dublin (or Belfast) wholesalers could still control the Irish market in exotic goods, but they bought in London, not elsewhere.

SEE ALSO DISEASE AND PESTILENCE; EMPIRE, BRITISH; FAMINE; LABORERS, COERCED; POPULATION—EMIGRATION AND IMMIGRATION; UNITED KINGDOM.

BIBLIOGRAPHY

Cullen, Louis Michael. *Anglo-Irish Trade, 1660–1800.* Manchester, U.K.: University Press, 1968.

Cullen, Louis Michael. "Economic Trends 1660–1691." *A New History of Ireland Volume III: Early Modern Ireland 1534–1691,* ed. Theodore William Moody, Francis-Xavier Martin, and Francis John Byrne. Oxford, U.K.: Clarendon Press, 1976.

Cullen, Louis Michael. "Economic Development, 1691–1800." *A New History of Ireland Volume IV: Eighteenth-Century Ireland, 1691–1800.* ed. Theodore William Moody and William Edward Vaughn. Oxford, U.K.: Clarendon Press, 1986.

Cullen, Louis Michael. "Colonial and Exotic Products: Their Place and Role in Irish Economy and Society." *Prodottie e techniche d'oltremare nelle economie europee secc. XIII–XVIII* (Overseas Products and Techniques in the European Economies in the XIII–XVIII Centuries), ed. Simonetta Cavaciocchi. Prato, Italy: Le Monnier, 1998.

Cullen, Louis Michael. "Irish Businessmen and French Courtier: The Career of Thomas Sutton, comte de Clonard, c. 1722–1782." *The Early Modern Atlantic Economy,* ed. John J. McCusker and Kenneth Morgan. New York; Cambridge, U.K.: Cambridge University Press, 2000.

Dickson, David. *Old World Colony: Cork and South Munster 1630–1830.* Cork, Ireland: Cork University Press, 2005.

Solar, Peter. "Irish Trade in the Nineteenth Century." *Refiguring Ireland,* ed. David Dickson and Cormac O'Grada. Dublin: Lilliput, 2003.

L. M. Cullen

ETHNIC GROUPS, JEWS

The Jews were one of the most numerous and important ethnic groups involved in trade (local, long-distance, and international) from 1450 onward. Although they shared some of the characteristics of other ethnic groups engaged in commerce—for example, the Parsi diaspora from Iran, the Armenians, the Greeks of the Ottoman Empire, the Chinese in many areas of Southeast Asia from the fifteenth to the twentieth century, the Indian middleman minorities of East Africa and Malaya, the Pakistanis in Britain, and the Lebanese Christians in eighteenth-century Egypt and contemporary West Africa—Jewish merchants and traders also had some distinctive features.

Jews were engaged in trade even in ancient times, but their extensive involvement in commercial and trade activities occurred with the establishment of the Muslim Empire in the eighth and ninth centuries. Since then, they have been associated with trade, commerce, moneylending, and other urban skilled occupations.

HISTORY OF JEWISH TRADE

The largest share of the Jewish population in the fifteenth century lived in western Europe. The two main cultural groups were the Sephardim, who descended from the Spanish-Portuguese Jews, and the Ashkenazim, who were the descendents of the Eastern European and German Jews. In the sixteenth and seventeenth centuries most Sephardi Jews lived and engaged in crafts and trade in the cities and commercial centers in Europe, whereas the Ashkenazi Jews engaged in a variety of occupations in towns and villages in central and eastern Europe.

From the twelfth century to 1492, Spain was one of the main centers of Jewish settlement and business activities. In the main cities such as Seville, Cordoba, Saragossa, Valencia, Toledo, and Barcelona, as well as in smaller towns, there were Jews involved in all sectors of the urban economies, as swordsmiths, goldsmiths, tailors, shopkeepers, cloth producers, owners of tanneries, moneylenders, medical doctors, and tax farmers. Many Jews in Spain also were engaged in commercial and trading activities connecting central and eastern Europe to North Africa, the Levant, and the Near East. Spices, bullion, silk, and carpets were only some of the many items the Jews moved from one part of the world to the other. Involvement with the slave trade was also substantial.

Most of the Jewish craftsmen and merchants who left Spain after the edict of expulsion in 1492 went first to Portugal, until their expulsion from there in 1496. Those who remained in the Iberian Peninsula and converted to Christianity but secretly kept their Jewish religious traditions became a distinct group called *Marranos.* Many of them and their descendants became leading traders and merchants all over the world from the sixteenth century to the eighteenth century. Marrano traders from the East Indies and the Americas to western Europe traded spices, luxury goods, textiles, and precious stones. Other Marrano merchants were heavily involved in trading and commercial activities in Africa (slave trade), and Brazil and the West Indies (sugar production and trade).

A woodcut from 1531 shows a farmer visiting a Jewish moneylender, who uses an abacus for his transactions. Many Jews across Europe played a crucial role in developing commerce and lending systems that helped expand trading among nations during the sixteenth century. © CHRISTEL GERSTENBERG/CORBIS. REPRODUCED BY PERMISSION.

In addition to Portugal and Spain, where the spice trade represented a very important share of the Marrano business, the main centers in which Marrano traders established their business in the sixteenth and early seventeenth century were Leghorn and Venice in Italy, Antwerp in the Low Countries (especially for the jewel trade), Amsterdam in the Netherlands, and Hamburg in Germany. Textiles, sugar, and grain were the other main items imported and exported by Marrano merchants.

In the second half of the seventeenth century and during the eighteenth century Amsterdam, London, Poland, and Lithuania became the main centers from which Jewish traders brought their business all over the world. The community of Portuguese Jews in Amsterdam was involved in the colonial trade, as well as in speculative trade in commodities and company shares. At the same time, the Sephardi Jews in London were actively involved in long-distance trade with West Africa and the West Indies. The Jews in Poland and Lithuania connected trade in eastern Europe to western Europe and the rest of the world.

Among the various goods dealt with by Jewish merchants and traders, diamonds occupy a special place because the Jews became almost the dominant workers and traders of diamonds from the early modern period up until recent times. First Amsterdam, then Hamburg, and later London became the headquarters for Sephardi Jewish traders of Portuguese descent, and later for Ashkenazi Jews, who imported diamonds from India. The records and account books of the British East India Company indicate that most merchants involved in the diamond trade from India in the eighteenth century were Jews. The dominance of Jewish traders in the diamond industry and trade continued when Brazil in the mid-eighteenth century and South Africa in the late nineteenth-century became the main suppliers of uncut diamonds.

As for Ashkenazi Jews in Eastern Europe, they gained prominence in forming and running mints, especially in Hamburg and Prague. In the late seventeenth and in the eighteenth century Jews in Germany, Poland, Russia, Bohemia, Moravia, Hungary, and Galicia were actively involved in crafts and local trade providing various goods and services to the local population. Jewish entrepreneurs and traders were particularly active in German and Russian towns in the mining and metal industries, especially in the copper, zinc, tin, nickel, aluminum, silver and gold trades. The Jews were also the first to develop coal mines in Eastern and Central Europe and export coal to England in the eighteenth and nineteenth centuries.

In the Ottoman Empire Jews kept a very important role in the silk, spice, and jewel trades connecting Europe to East and South Asia. Moreover, many Jews who left Portugal after their expulsion in 1496 were expert producers of arms, guns, and cannons, and they brought their skills to Constantinople. Jews continued as metalworkers in many lands under Muslim rule for centuries.

In the United States, since their early arrival in the mid-seventeenth century the Jews were involved in trade as shopkeepers and merchants bringing European goods (e.g., textiles, wine, tea, and hardware) to the cities on the East Coast of the North American continent, and bringing back to Europe grain, furs, fish, and lumber. The movement westward and the expansion of the frontier brought many more opportunities for the Jews to enter other branches of industry and trade such as insurance, banking, mining, shipping, railroad investment and construction, and land development. In the middle of the nineteenth century Jewish merchants and traders could be found in all large cities and also in many villages, forming a commercial network all over the United States. In the late nineteenth century Jewish entrepreneurs were the founders of the most successful and famous department stores in the United States, such as Sears Roebuck.

The involvement of the Jews in trade and commercial activities continued in the twentieth century. They actively participated in the industrialization of countries in Western and Eastern Europe, and in even greater numbers they entered the banking, stock exchange, and brokerage businesses. According to data provided by the economist Simon Kuznets (1960), almost all the Jews in all the countries of Eastern Europe and in the United States and Canada in the early twentieth century were engaged in nonagricultural occupations. Moreover, of these nonagricultural occupations, trade and finance were the ones chosen by most Jews in all countries before World War II.

THEORIES OF JEWISH PARTICIPATION IN TRADE

There are two main explanations for the unusually extensive involvement of the Jewish people in trading and commercial activities. A common view among scholars maintains that from the Middle Ages until modern times, Jews specialized in crafts, trade, and banking because they were prohibited from owning land, and therefore they could hardly engage in agriculture. From a similar but slightly different point of view, other scholars asserted that as a persecuted minority in many areas where they settled, the Jews did not opt for investing their wealth in land, but preferred to invest in trade and crafts where the capital invested (human capital and goods to sell) was highly portable and less subject to confiscation or expropriation.

To the contrary, Max Weber (1917) argued that the Jews voluntarily chose to segregate themselves in urban occupations such as trade, moneylending, and crafts in order to maintain their ritualistic correctness, dietary prescriptions, and Sabbath rules, which would have been impossible to follow in rural areas. Similarly, the explanation presented by Kuznets for the Jewish occupational selection into crafts and trade relies on what he called "the economics of small minorities." The noneconomic goal of maintaining cohesion and group identity leads members of a minority, such as the Jews, to prefer to be concentrated in selected industries and selected occupations.

SEE ALSO CARGOES, PASSENGER; CORRESPONDENTS, FACTORS, AND BROKERS; EMPIRE, OTTOMAN; MEDITERRANEAN; MILLETS AND CAPITULATIONS; WALLENBERG FAMILY.

BIBLIOGRAPHY

Baron, Salo Wittmayer. *A Social and Religious History of the Jews,* 2nd edition. Philadelphia: Jewish Publication Society of America, 1952.

Israel, Jonathan Irvine. *Diasporas Within a Diaspora: Jews, Crpyto Jews, and the World of Maritime Empires (1540–1740)*. Boston, MA: Brill, 2002.

Kahan, Arkadius. "Economic History." In *Encyclopedia Judaica*, ed. Cecil Roth. New York: Macmillan, 1972.

Katz, Israel J., and Serels, M. Mitchell, eds. *Studies on the History of Portuguese Jews from Their Expulsion in 1497 Through Their Dispersion*. New York: Sepher-Hermon Press, 2000.

Kellenbenz, Hermann. "Trade and Commerce." In *Encyclopedia Judaica*, ed. Cecil Roth. New York: Macmillan, 1972.

Kuznets, Simon. "Economic Structure and Life of the Jews." In *The Jews: Their History, Culture, and Religion*, ed. Louis Finkelstein. New York: Harper, 1960.

Roth, Cecil. *A History of the Marranos*. Philadelphia: Jewish Publication Society of America, 1941.

Weber, Max. *Ancient Judaism*, tr. and ed. Hans H. Gerth and Don Martindale. (First German edition 1917). Glencoe, IL: Free Press, 1952.

Maristella Botticini

ETHNIC GROUPS, NATIVE AMERICANS

Following the arrival of Europeans in North America at the end of the fifteenth century there was much dislocation among native peoples. New infectious diseases unwittingly introduced by Europeans led to declines in the native population of as much as 90 percent in some areas. The estimated native population east of the Mississippi in 1500 was 561,000; this had declined to about 177,000 by 1800 (Ubelaker 173). Some native groups stayed in roughly the same areas for centuries, whereas others migrated or were driven out of their territories by Europeans or other native peoples with new technologies such as guns or horses. Some tribes disappeared, and new tribes were formed by refugees from displaced populations.

Many of the early European expeditions came to North America expecting to explore, claim territory, seize goods, and sometimes take captives as slaves. Indians in turn would raid for goods or horses. Sometimes these armed expeditions traded for goods when force was not an option, and at other times gifts were exchanged between Europeans and native leaders to secure alliances. Thus, even aggressive expeditions could lead to a two-way exchange. There were also other peaceful exchanges of goods and gifts. European fishermen in the North Atlantic traded with Indians for fresh food, for example.

Trade between Indians and the English was centered on the East Coast. Indians traded with the Spanish in the South and Southwest; the French in the Great Lakes and along the Mississippi River; and with Russian fur traders in the Pacific Northwest. The English also traded for furs in Canada around Hudson Bay.

TRADE TO 1763

Based on evidence from archaeological finds, long-distance trade in small, high-valued items existed prior to 1492. Trade seems to have occurred largely between native people who lived close to each other, but by repeated exchanges goods could travel great distances. Stone tools have been discovered 1,000 miles from the point where the materials were quarried. Some of the items exchanged, had spiritual value; for example, copper was valued for its color and for the fact that it reflected light, which suggested spiritual properties. Many of the goods acquired from Europeans also were seen as having spiritual value.

Over time, trade became more regularized. Indians traded beaver and deerskins for European-manufactured goods such iron tools, guns, cloth, blankets, beads, mirrors, and alcohol. In Europe, beaver pelts were highly valued in making hats, and deerskin was used to make gloves and other soft-leather items. By the mid-seventeenth century, European steel tools and other useful items had become essential to many Indian societies. Alcohol was also highly sought after and was a source of conflict along the frontier, where drunkenness often led to bloodshed.

The trade in beaver pelts was the most valuable trade, and was concentrated in the North and Canada, but the trade in deerskins was also very important to native peoples and the colonists in the South. Indians hunted or, later, trapped the game, then prepared the pelts or skins. In the Northeast, Indians sometimes came to trading posts to sell the beaver pelts, but often traders traveled to the Indians with goods to trade. In the South, traders usually traveled to Indian towns to acquire deerskins, which required extensive processing by Indian women. Traders had more horses and could more easily transport the goods than could Indians.

Major trading companies organized trade with the Indians. Prices were set by negotiations between Indian leaders and leading traders or government officials. The fact that prices were fixed meant that Indian hunters knew in advance the price they would receive and did not have to haggle with traders. Traders also offered credit to individual Indians, who sometimes accumulated large debts to traders.

The fur trade was an important source of export earnings for English settlers in Massachusetts during the seventeenth century. This trade was later dominated by the Dutch in New Amsterdam (New York) until that colony was taken over by the British. Furs and skins, especially the beaver skins used to make hats, were so important to the English that the Navigation Acts included these on the list of enumerated goods that could only be sent to England.

Native traders at Eskimo Point along Hudson Bay hang fox pelts to dry. *Natives hunted, then prepared the pelts for trade. Due to the lack of horses among the natives, traders generally came to collect pelts at the natives' camps.* © HULTON-DEUTSCH COLLECTION/CORBIS. REPRODUCED BY PERMISSION.

Over time beavers were hunted to extinction in New England, and the source of pelts shifted to western tribes. The Iroquois Confederacy became a power on the frontier in the Northeast and dominated the fur trade by positioning themselves as middlemen between the English and western tribes that gathered the furs. They also allied themselves with the English in rivalry with the French. Other tribes were allied with the French or Spanish. French traders were active throughout the Mississippi and Great Lakes region, and Spanish traders and missions were in Florida. Tribes received goods and support from their European allies and sometimes strategically shifted alliances.

In the South, deer were also overhunted, and depletion of game was a continuing problem for tribes that increasingly relied upon European manufactured goods.

Tribes in the East closest to the English were forced to look further west for game.

1763 TO 1890

With the defeat of the French and their Spanish allies in 1763, England took control of Canada and Florida, and Louisiana was transferred to Spain. This meant that Indians east of the Mississippi River could only trade with English or colonial traders. Beginning with the Proclamation of 1763, Britain tried to restrict settlement in the West to limit conflict between settlers and Indians and to protect the fur trade, but these efforts largely failed. During the American Revolution many tribes sided with the British, and this led to war on the frontier. Following the Revolution, the new U.S. federal government tried to regulate trade and preserve peace with Native Americans with a system of licensed traders and federally funded trading posts. Private traders, however, continued to dominate the fur trade.

The largest fur trading company was the American Fur Company of John Jacob Astor, who became the richest man in the United States in the early nineteenth century. Astor also tried to develop a fur trade from Oregon to China, but this failed as a result of the War of 1812. In addition to the fur trade, some members of Southeastern tribes adopted to commercial agriculture along American lines and sold cotton and other agricultural products on the world market. Trade (and raids by Southern Plains tribes) also occurred in the Southwest along the Santa Fe Trail, which was a major trade route from Missouri to what was then northern Mexico.

Until fashions changed and the demand for beaver pelts fell drastically, beaver pelts were the highest-valued item traded with western Indians. As the frontier moved west and game was depleted, the source of the pelts shifted first to the upper Missouri River basin and then to Oregon. Fur traders and trappers often were the first Europeans to explore the western United States. St. Louis on the Mississippi River developed as a port for the export of furs and import of trade goods. There was also a trade in bison (buffalo) hides. Indians continued to receive guns, tools, blankets, and alcohol in exchange. The beaver trade declined after 1840 and the trade in bison hides ended with the near-extinction of bison by the mid-1870s.

U.S. policy was to encourage or coerce tribes to cede their land in the East and move to lands west of the Mississippi River, although isolated bands of Indians continued to survive in the East. This evolved into a reservation system by the mid-1850s, with tribes having defined territories reserved for their use. Typically, the federal government agreed to provide food, tools, and educational opportunities because the specified territories were too small to allow the Indians to support themselves through hunting.

1890 TO 2000

The last Indian "battle" occurred in 1890, which is also the date that the U.S. Census stopped defining a *frontier* as the area between the settled and unsettled regions of the country. By 1900 the Indian population in the continental United States was about 270,000 out of a total population of 76 million. The goal of U.S. Indian policy from 1887 to 1934 was to divide land among members of the tribe and invite non-Indians to settle among Indians as a way of assimilating Indians into the larger culture. This was carried out most completely in Oklahoma, where many Indians lived. Indian reservations remained most intact in Arizona and New Mexico, in the Northern

Plains, and in the Pacific Northwest. Federal policy took a different course in the years from 1934 to 1945, when the federal government drafted legal constitutions for tribes and recognized that tribal governments had a degree of autonomy. In 1946 federal policy shifted again to move to eliminate separate tribal governments and have state governments provide services for Indians.

The federal government renounced the policy of trying to eliminate tribal governments in 1970, and since then the federal government has officially recognized more tribes. Artworks and handicrafts are a visible export from some reservations, and Indian farmers and ranchers sell in national markets. Some tribes also sell oil, coal, and other minerals produced on reservation lands.

Indian tribes are exempt from state laws and taxes, and this has proved profitable as, for example, tribal stores on some reservations sell cigarettes to non-Indians without having to pay state taxes. In the 1970s and earlier some tribes opened bingo halls or offered other forms of gambling on their reservations. State governments at times tried to stop these activities, but their efforts were challenged in court and the right of tribes to have gambling facilities was affirmed. The federal Indian Gaming Act of 1988, by which Congress hoped to promote "tribal economic development, self-sufficiency, and strong tribal governments," recognized that some tribes were quite poor, and made it easier for tribes to open casinos on tribal land in many states. More than 200 of the 556 federally recognized tribes have gaming facilities, often run by outside contractors. Indian gaming accounted for about $10 billion, or one-sixth of legal gambling in the United States in 2000 (Evans and Topoleski 2002, 3). The proceeds from a gaming enterprise go to the individual host tribe for the benefit of its members, which means that tribes with prime locations gain the most, and that other tribes, particularly those in isolated rural areas, receive nothing from gaming.

Individual tribes have developed other industries. In Mississippi, the Choctaw tribe has become the largest single employer in the state, with manufacturing jobs as well as casinos. But most of the 2.45 million people who identified themselves as Indians or Alaska Natives in 2000 do not live on reservations, and their economic activities are blended with the general population.

SEE ALSO Astor Family; Laborers, Native American, Eastern Woodland and Far Western.

BIBLIOGRAPHY

Barrington, Linda, ed. *The Other Side of the Frontier: Economic Explorations into Native American History.* Boulder, CO: Westview Press, 1999.

Evans, William, and Topoleski, Julie. "The Social and Economic Impact of Native American Casinos." National

Bureau of Economics, Cambridge, MA: working paper 9198. September 2002.

Prucha, Francis Paul. *The Great Father: The United States Government and the American Indian.* Lincoln: University of Nebraska Press, 1986.

White, Richard. *The Roots of Dependency: Subsistence, Environment, and Social Change among the Choctaws, Pawnees, and Navajos.* Lincoln: University of Nebraska Press, 1983.

Wishart, David. *The Fur Trade of the American West, 1807–1840.* Lincoln: University of Nebraska Press, 1979.

Leonard A. Carlson

ETHNIC GROUPS, SCOTS

This entry consists of the following articles:
ETHNIC GROUPS, SCOTS BEFORE 1800
ETHNIC GROUPS, SCOTS SINCE 1800

ETHNIC GROUPS, SCOTS BEFORE 1800

Scots contributed to and profited from an expanding world trade system over the course of the eighteenth century. In 1707 Scotland's and England's parliaments merged, creating a single British state. One of this Union of Parliaments' most significant impacts was to provide the Scots access to England and, as importantly, to its American colonies, including those in the Caribbean. (Before 1707, such access had been forbidden to all foreigners, including the Scots.) By opening up the colonies, the Union of Parliaments provided social and economic opportunities for Scots. Because Scotland had one of Europe's best educational systems but only limited ways for educated people to improve the conditions of their lives, access to the Atlantic economy ensured the Scots a prominent role in its eighteenth-century operation and expansion. They would continue to play a prominent role as Britain's Atlantic economy globalized by moving into Asia—especially India—and, in the late nineteenth century, Africa.

The Scots played several major roles in the Atlantic American colonies. The first transformed the way in which the tobacco economy in the Chesapeake operated. Before the Scots began to dominate the tobacco trade, English merchants purchased tobacco from colonial farmers on consignment. This meant that the farmers bore all of the costs of transportation and insurance until the tobacco could be sold in European markets. The costs of getting the tobacco to market were then deducted from the purchase price, along with a sales commission; only then did planters learn how much profit their crops had yielded. The Scottish innovation was in buying the tobacco outright from the planter, who could then purchase British goods directly from the same agents. Many purchased more British products than their tobacco was worth and, as a result, Scottish merchants held a large share of these colonists' debts.

"NEW EDINBURGH"

The 1707 Anglo-Scottish Union was effected partly through the failure of a Scottish trade venture. The Company of Scotland Trading to Africa and the Indies, founded in 1695, proposed a South American colony on the Isthmus of Panama's Darien coast that would become a nexus of East-West trade, eliminating the journey around Cape Horn. The first settlers departed in 1698, but both backers and colonists were disillusioned. Storms and disease beset the venture during the Atlantic crossing, and upon arrival settlers found that their "New Edinburgh" was little more than a malarial swamp, where dozens perished. Spanish raiders, encouraged by resentful English traders, finished the job. The fiasco was a serious blow to both Scottish pride and national finances.

Although English mercantile interests were reviled by the Scots, the affair ultimately pushed the two nations closer. Many Scottish leaders realized that some accommodation with England was needed, so they acquiesced to English pressure—and the offer of almost £400,000 to make good the Darien losses—and agreed to the Act of Union in 1707.

David J. Clarke

If Scottish merchants and factors came to dominate the tobacco trade before 1776, many young and educated Scots also went to Britain's new, and expanding, Caribbean colonies. In these islands, which had large slave populations, skilled white people were in great demand to keep the local economies, dominated by sugar, in operation. Scots served as doctors, attorneys, managers, merchants, and bureaucrats in islands with large frontiers, such as Jamaica, or in formerly French islands, such as Grenada and Tobago, which were ceded to the British in 1763. Bringing with them a high level of education as well as trading connections, Scottish men worked hard on integrating their new island residences into Britain's expanding imperial economy. Many filled important managerial and entrepreneurial roles, and others held important governmental positions.

The Scots understood that the imperial economy in which they operated guaranteed their upward economic mobility. During the American War for Independence, in 1776, many mainland colonists began to vilify the Scots as traitors to the cause of independence, and refused to pay the debts they owed to their Scottish traders. As a result, many Scottish companies recalled their employees on the American mainland to sit the war out at home. Most of them expected an easy British victory. When the war ended in British defeat, opportunities for migration to the mainland colonies were far fewer. A few Scots merchants sent employees back to collect the delinquent debts, but most of those met with very limited success. Because the island colonies did not rebel, many Scots continued to migrate to the Caribbean. Opportunities there were also more limited as the eighteenth century drew to a close.

Because Scots tended to migrate in groups, employing networks of family and friends as they decided where to go, new opportunities for economic improvement elsewhere presented themselves as those in the Americas dwindled. Scots built networks, and this led to further opportunites, since migrants created jobs for each other. So where one went, others inevitably followed. Educated Scots, as well as younger sons from wealthier families, began to purchase commissions in the British East India Company, which began an extended push for control of the Indian subcontinent in the 1760s and 1770s. This effort lasted through much of the nineteenth century. Scots in India participated in the growing and highly lucrative tea trade, both as officers of the East India Company and as private traders engaging in commerce. Scotland's residents, as a result, continued to reap the rewards of participating in the British imperial economy. Though Scotland itself remained relatively poor, the profits amassed by Scots professionals in the East and West Indies allowed Scotland's wealth, as a whole, to increase.

Perceived as clannish by many of their colonial neighbors, the Scots successfully used personal networks based in ethnicity and regionalism to help their countrymen thrive in an empire that was still dominated by the English. Indeed, Scots professionals were at the vanguard of imperial and commercial expansion in that they were among the first British subjects to arrive in a newly conquered area. They thus innovated on the margins of empire; as a result, they played a significant part in developing the way that the British imperial economy increasingly linked the world before 1800.

SEE ALSO CORRESPONDENTS, FACTORS, AND BROKERS; EMPIRE, BRITISH; GLASGOW; POPULATION– EMIGRATION AND IMMIGRATION; TOBACCO; UNITED KINGDOM.

BIBLIOGRAPHY

Devine, T. M. *The Tobacco Lords.* Edinburgh, U.K.: Edinburgh University Press, 1975.

Hancock, David. *Citizens of the World: London Merchants and the Integration of the British Atlantic Community,* New York: Cambridge University Press, 1995.

Karras, Alan L. *Sojourners in the Sun: Scots Migrants in Jamaica and the Chesapeake.* Ithaca, NY: Cornell University Press, 1992.

Price, Jacob. *Capital and Credit in the Tobacco Trade: The View from the Chesapeake.* Cambridge, MA: Harvard University Press, 1980.

Alan L. Karras

ETHNIC GROUPS, SCOTS SINCE 1800

The Scots were able to build on their formidable reputation as traders as a result of the extensive links they had been built up during the eighteenth century. By 1800 they were firmly established in British North America, India, and other parts of the British Empire. The Scots used family and local connections to build up individual trading empires; this method was an effective way of ensuring coherence and loyalty in trading organizations. People from the island of Orkney, for example, largely staffed the North British Trading Company. The Scots' clannishness drew frequent accusations of unfair, preferential treatment, and it also gave rise to the popular caricature of the Scot as mean and penny-pinching.

From 1800 to about 1870 Scotland's principal exports were the low-grade industrial products that were characteristic of the early Industrial Revolution: coal, iron, and cotton.

After 1870 Scottish trade increasingly specialized in high-quality and specifically designed heavy industrial products such as shipbuilding, heavy engineering, and marine technology. World trade was the key stimulus to Scottish economic growth in the late nineteenth century as the Scots built the ships and trains that would transport goods, and often the heavy industrial machinery that would manufacture those goods. A critical element in Scottish success was the economy's ability to utilize skilled, cheap labor. As the world moved increasingly toward a mass-production economy, the Scots sought protection in the production of goods that could not be mass produced. Low labor costs were crucial to maintaining profitability. This had a number of consequences for the Scots. Firstly, it meant that the Scottish economy was locked into the fortunes of the global economy to a greater extent than other advanced economies. Secondly, the importance of low wages meant that the domestic economy failed to develop, leaving society overreliant on the export economy, which in turn impeded the development of the domestic sector. It was a self-reinforcing cycle.

One consequence of the low-wage economy was extensive emigration. It is estimated that about 2.5 million

Scots migrated in the period 1800 to 1950, and along with Norway and Ireland, Scotland had one of the highest per-capita emigration rates of the modern era. A distinguishing feature of Scotland was that it was an advanced industrial society, in contrast to most other high-emigration European nations, which were agrarian and rural. The average Scottish emigrant was skilled, urban, and working class, although the Scots also exported a disproportionate number of professional and middle-class emigrants.

Such reliance on the international economy had a devastating effect on Scottish society following the dislocation of world trade after World War I. The staples of Scottish trade—shipbuilding, heavy engineering, locomotives, textiles, and coal—all suffered from either a downturn in world trade or from markets lost during the war. An example of the latter is the jute industry, which lost markets in the Far East because Scottish production was converted to supply war needs. Shipbuilding suffered due to advances in prefabrication techniques, the glut of ships left at the end of the war, and a lack of confidence in the global economy that hit capital investment goods. The traditional Scottish industries languished for most of the interwar period, and the Scots failed to diversify their economy to any great extent, but those same industries recovered with rearmament and the onset of World War II.

Scotland still relied on the traditional industries in the period after 1945, and state intervention and support was the critical factor in shoring them up. Poor productivity, lack of modernization, and poor marketing techniques were responsible for a gradual decline in shipbuilding and heavy engineering. In an endeavor to offset this decline, state intervention promoted the growth of inward investment in the form of branch-plant manufacturing. By the 1970s almost three-quarters of all manufacturing in Scotland was foreign-owned. Global uncertainty in the 1970s and early 1980s witnessed the diminution of the Scottish manufacturing base as a result of branch-plant closures and the decision of the Thatcher government (1979–1992) to withdraw state aid for the traditional industries.

The period after the mid-1980s witnessed a transformation in the Scottish economy as it moved more towards the financial-services industry. Yet, trade was an essential part of the Scottish economy. Electronic assembly work in what is known as "Silicon Glen," the Scottish version of Silicon Valley in California, meant that the Scots had a higher export per capita than Japan, and it was responsible for much of Western Europe's production of personal computers, televisions, automatic money-transfer machines, and so on.

SEE ALSO CORRESPONDENTS, FACTORS, AND BROKERS; EMPIRE, BRITISH; GLASGOW; POPULATION—EMIGRATION AND IMMIGRATION; TOBACCO; UNITED KINGDOM.

BIBLIOGRAPHY

Campbell, R. H. *Scotland since 1707: The Rise of an Industrial Society.* Edinburgh: John Donald, 1985.

Devine, Thomas Martin. *Scottish Nation, 1700–2000.* London: Allen Lane, 1999.

Devine, Thomas Martin. *Scotland's Empire, 1600–1800.* London: Allen Lane, 2003.

Finlay, Richard J. *Modern Scotland, 1914–2000.* London: Profile Publishers, 2003.

Fry, Michael. *Scottish Empire.* Edinburgh: John Donald, 2000.

Lenman, Bruce P. *An Economic History of Modern Scotland.* London: Batisford, 1979.

Richard J. Finlay

FACTORIES

The *feitoria,* or trade factory, has roots dating back to the thirteenth century Mediterranean trade diasporas of the Genovese and Venetians, who opened up trading posts on foreign soil after having gained permission from the local rulers. In medieval times the Hanseatic traders also established permanent trading posts along the coasts of the Baltic—or as far away as Novgorod—in order to become more familiar with local conditions so that they could buy up the local harvest at the right time of the year, cut the timber they needed for house- and ship-building, and collect the furs from the trappers. At "counters" (trading posts) a strict discipline was enforced to preempt any disturbance with the local people. Out of these early experiences in the periphery of Europe grew the network of trading posts that the Portuguese and subsequently the East India Companies established along the coastal rims of Asia.

After their arrival in Asian waters in 1498 the Portuguese pioneers established their *feitoria* by means both peaceful and forceful. A seventeenth-century book lists more than 100 of these settlements strategically situated around the rim of the Indian Ocean. Muslim competitors in the pepper trade stormed the first trade factory, in Calicut, which had been established with the ruler's consent, in 1501, and its complete staff was murdered. The Portuguese fleet bombarded the city in retaliation. A friendlier welcome was received at the hands of the ruler of Cochin, who saw the Portuguese as potential allies and protractors against his Calicut neighbor. As a result, one can make a distinction between factories, which were basically fortresses, and enclaves that were under the protection of local rulers.

The trading factories, which were founded by the East India Companies, also came in all types and sizes. These factories often were built at places designated by the local rulers, such as the *pangeran* of Banten (western Java), who ordered the Dutch and English to build their warehouses outside the town walls. Because of the relative insecurity of these locations, the factories were often walled compounds that could be defended easily against robbers. In the well-regulated societies of China and Japan the traders were suffered in small isolated enclaves outside the city of Canton and on the tiny man-made island of Deshima in the bay of Nagasaki, where they were closely guarded and spied upon by local officials.

A very different factory system was introduced in the 1790s in the United States, where Congress voted to establish factories in the frontier areas to enable the American Indians to barter their furs and skins for Western goods. In the United States the trade factory was introduced basically to assimilate the Indians into the culture of the white settlers. In Asia, where small minorities of Western merchants were operating within a millennia-old trading world, such considerations were out of the question.

There was a great variety in the layout of the various trading factories. A very detailed 1665 painting of the Dutch East India Company's factory in Houghly on the River Ganges clearly shows day-to-day activities. Dutch ships are at anchor in the background, and within the walled compound Europeans and Indians enter and exit offices and warehouses. A medicinal herbal garden shows

FORT YUKON; HUDSON'S BAY COMPANY'S POST.

Alaskan indigenous people outside the Hudson's Bay Company trading post at Fort Yukon. *The fort was an example of a trading factory, a location established to integrate trading practices between Native Americans and European settlers.* © CORBIS. REPRODUCED BY PERMISSION.

the care given to the health of Europeans living in this murderous tropical climate. Outside the walls horses are bathed, and elephants and camels parade. Close to the river there are piles of timber ready to be used by the local shipyard. In the background a Hindu widow joins her deceased husband by throwing herself on the funeral pyre. No less intriguing is the encampment of a Mughal local official, who is ceremoniously greeted by Dutch company officials. By their presentation of gifts they ensure that they can continue to trade.

How different was the situation on Deshima. Japanese authorities originally constructed this artificial island with a surface area of about two football fields to house Portuguese merchants, but when the latter were expelled in 1639, the Dutch were ordered to dismantle their offices at the nearby port of Hirado and move to Deshima, where they were put under close surveillance. The houses, offices, and warehouses were leased to the Dutch East India Company by Japanese landlords and were wholly Japanese in appearance. During the summer

when the Dutch ships were in port, the island bristled with activity as import goods from overseas were discharged and export goods such as precious metals, camphor, porcelain, and lacquerware were loaded onto the ships that had to leave on a strict schedule. About a dozen company employees, served by house slaves from Southeast Asia, stayed on the island during the winter, playing billiards, reading books, talking to occasional Japanese visitors, cultivating an herb garden, and looking after imported exotic animals, which were kept to give as presents to Japanese officials. Early in the year the chief merchant of the factory went to the court in Edo (present-day Tokyo) with a surgeon and a secretary to pay homage to the shogun. There was probably no safer place on earth than this heavily guarded trade factory, which the Dutch likened to a chicken coop.

In the port principality of Banten on the western tip of the island of Java, the English and Dutch faced a totally different situation when they arrived there at the end of the sixteenth century. After first being housed in the Chinese settlement outside the city walls, they were allowed to build their own quarter. There they built fireproof brick warehouses to protect themselves from occasional raids from the predatory local nobility and their followers. In 1618 the Dutch were so annoyed by their insecure living conditions and the monopolistic behavior of the local ruler that they moved out to the nearby port principality of Jacatra. When this trade factory was attacked by the Bantanese in 1619 and by the English and the local people in 1620, the garrison held out until a Dutch fleet from the Moluccas arrived. The *kraton* of Jacatra was razed, and on its ruins Governor-General Jan Pieterszoon Coen built a veritable castle and a walled colonial town, Batavia. This became the headquarters of the emerging Dutch trading empire in Asia.

In Canton and Deshima, where Western women were explicitly forbidden entry by the local governments, the company servants sought solutions to their solitude. On Deshima courtesans regularly visited them from Nagasaki. The merchants who spent the winter in Canton carrying out their trade moved out in summer to the tiny Portuguese colony of Macao to spend the slack period with their mostly Chinese wives. Following the Portuguese example, many company servants living elsewhere in Asia cohabited with local women, and if there were no religious impediments, married them. In Siam the Dutch were explicitly denied the right to take their children out of the country and raise them as Christians.

Because the prevailing monsoon winds dictated the flow of correspondence between the overseas trading factories and headquarters, the chief merchants were required to keep diaries in which they noted down all daily activities. These diaries, insofar as they have been preserved, together with the business correspondence written by the factory heads, provide an intimate view of the social and political scene of early modern Asia.

SEE ALSO Angola; Burma; Calcutta; Canton System; Dahomey; East India Company, British; East India Company, Dutch; East India Company, Other; Empire, British; Empire, Dutch; Empire, French; Empire, Ming; Empire, Mughal; Empire, Ottoman; Empire, Portuguese; Empire, Qing; Gold Coast; Guangzhou; Indonesia; Japan; Kenya; Kongo; Madras; Melaka; Millets and Capitulations; Mumbai; Nagasaki; Senegambia; Thailand.

BIBLIOGRAPHY

Blussé, Leonard; Remmelink, Willem; and Smits, Ivo; eds. *Bridging the Divide: 400 Years, The Netherlands–Japan.* Amsterdam: Hotei Publishing, 2000.

Blussé, Leonard; Remmelink, Willem; and Viallé, Cynthia. *The Deshima Diaries, 1700–1800,* 2 vols. Tokyo: Japan-Netherlands Institute, 1992–2004.

Coolhaas, Willem Philippus. *A Critical Survey of Studies on Dutch Colonial History.* Netherlands: The Hague, 1980.

Curtin, Philip. *Cross-Cultural Trade in World History.* Cambridge, U.K.: Cambridge University Press, 1984.

Simkin, Colin George Frederick. *Traditional Trade of Asia* Oxford, U.K.: Oxford University Press, 1968.

Van Oers, R. *Dutch Colonial Town Planning Overseas during VOC and WIC Rule.* Zwolle, Netherlands: Waanders Publishers, 2000.

Winius, George. *Portugal, The Pathfinder.* Madison: University of Wisconsin Press, 1995.

Zandvliet, Kees. *The Dutch Encounter with Asia, 1600–1950.* Zwolle, Netherlands: Waanders Publishers, 2002.

Leonard Blussé

FAIRS

Fairs are periodical markets held in a central location often close to major trading routes, bringing together producers or merchants and customers from a pool that is larger than just local. Fairs are only one form of organizing commercial exchange; others include local markets, which range from forms of continuous international commercial exchange within a designated space, such as a commodity exchange or a permanent store.

Fairs have some of the same attributes as other marketplaces. Seller and buyer, who may be complete strangers, meet in a market both know to take place at a particular time in a particular location. In common with most other forms of markets, fairs also tended to rely on some form of political protection, whether from a town, religious authority, regional overlord, or the state. Historically, political authorities favored fairs with special privileges concerning taxation of trade and other commercial issues.

Other characteristics set fairs apart from more local or more permanent places of exchange. Fairs are distinct from regularly held village or town markets in that they take place only once or twice a year (in some cases even less often) and attract sellers and buyers from a larger geographical area. Whereas female traders often dominated local markets, international and interregional trade—including that conducted at fairs—was more likely to be conducted by men. Fairs also typically attract a larger variety of both agricultural and nonagricultural goods. Compared to more permanent places of commercial exchange, fairs offer a central marketplace to meet large numbers of potential buyers at a relatively low cost for the seller, who does not have to establish a permanent shop or other representation.

FUNCTIONS AND ORIGINS

The main function of fairs is to reduce transaction costs. These costs of doing business increased over time as mar-

La Feria de Marena (The fair at Mayrena), engraving by Adolphe Jean-Baptiste Bayot, 1842. Starting in the medieval period, regional fairs served as important points of commercial exchange. © ARCHIVO ICONOGRAFICO, S.A./CORBIS. REPRODUCED BY PERMISSION.

kets became integrated over larger distances. The costs of acquiring information about prices, availability and quality of goods, the reliability of trading partners, and different monetary, credit, and measurement systems, as well as transport costs, enforcement of contracts costs, and insurance increased significantly as merchants moved beyond strictly confined local and regional markets. Experienced merchants were on hand to witness transfers of property rights and even where law and custom did not require such witnesses, they added security to a transaction.

Fairs offered distinct advantages in this context. By concentrating business into a short period of time—maybe two or three weeks—traders traveling to the fairs from various directions could organize joint transport and protection, thus reducing costs for the individual. The presence of a multitude of merchants guaranteed a large variety of products, improving information about quality and prices. The political and religious authorities endowed fairs with exemptions from general rules of trading. Religious or ethnic minorities and foreign merchants, who were usually barred from trading by the privileges enjoyed by local merchants, were often allowed to trade during fair periods.

In many cases rulers gave fairs special privileges regarding commercial jurisdiction. This allowed the mercantile community to create its own commercial arbitration independent of the local courts. In England, for instance, so-called courts of pie powder (a corruption of a French term for "dusty feet" in referring to itinerant merchants) were established at regional fairs to settle commercial disputes swiftly. Mercantile arbitration gave merchants incentives to deal honestly, because having been found to be dishonest by a commercial court ruined a merchant's reputation within the fair-visiting community of traders and hurt his trade. Rulers could provide military protection and policing during short fairs at a relatively low cost.

By attracting long-distance merchants, goods fairs also became places of money exchange and credit transactions. The increasing sophistication of trading and credit instruments such as bills of exchange became intimately linked to interregional and international fairs. Regular fairs enabled merchants to settle payments with bills to be paid at a future fair in the same town or at another one within the networks of fairs. When such bills became tradable themselves, they functioned as commercial credit and enabled merchants to reduce risks considerably by creating cash-free long-distance trading. Sixteenth-century traders in Peru could have debts paid to their agents at the Castilian fair of Medina de Campos, where the money could then be used to buy merchandise to be shipped to Peru, or to any other place.

REGIONAL FAIRS, INTERCONTINENTAL EXCHANGE MARTS, AND WORLD FAIRS

Some historians have seen fairs essentially as a stage within the development of more integrated interregional and global markets. Fairs have been portrayed as a way to reduce transaction costs in relatively thin markets, for example in areas of low population density, in weak states, or where demand for more valuable products supplied over long distances is limited (see e.g., Abu-Lughod 1989). The persistence of fairs in many parts of the world is therefore seen as a sign of less developed markets and states.

The decline of the most famous medieval precedents of European fairs, the Champagne fairs, which were the heart of Europe's overland trade. including that with northern Africa and the Middle East in the twelfth and thirteenth centuries, has been interpreted as part of a shift to more modern forms of markets. More sophisticated, permanent urban trading networks are said to have replaced the temporary fairs (Pirenne 1947, Weber 1923). More efficient maritime trade, which replaced overland routes all over the world, made joint travel unnecessary and therefore favored the establishment of permanent markets. Emerging nation-states, which provided more centralized and more efficient protection of commercial activity, also meant that fairs were eventually superseded by year-round selling and buying in large commercial centers (Milgrom, North, and Weingast 1990).

Other historians have suggested that it is too simplistic to see fairs as little more than a second-best solution to reduce transaction costs in the absence of dense enough markets and strong enough states. After all, "international" fairs such as those of Lyon, Besançon, Piacenza, Medina de Campo, Geneva, Antwerp, Frankfurt, and Leipzig continued to rise and decline in various parts of Europe. And they were only part of an ever-changing network of fairs reaching to the Russian fairs at Nizhni Novgorod and into the Balkans and Ottoman Empire. At the same time, large numbers of regional fairs emerged as well.

Fairs were not necessarily competing with other forms of markets, but instead were complementary (Epstein 1994, Munro 2001). They were flexible and more easily adapted to changing circumstances. Fairs continued to be particularly important in organizing the seasonal exchange between different ecological zones. Fairs linked the highlands of modern southern Bolivia and the lowlands of modern northern Argentina in an exchange of mining products, agricultural products, and livestock throughout the colonial period and far into the nineteenth century (Langer and Conti 1991). Fairs also played a crucial role in providing financial services such as credit and insurance, and some, such as Lyon and Medina de Campo, became very important in providing state finance.

In return, states continued to protect fairs; in some cases, state-sponsored monopoly trade was the very reason why fairs emerged. The Nombre de Dios/Portobelo fairs of the sixteenth and seventeenth centuries existed only because within the strongly regulated Spanish colonial trade goods had to be transhipped from the Atlantic to the Pacific via the Isthmus of Panama. Hence, for twenty or thirty days a year the inhospitable and largely uninhabited Portobelo buzzed with thousands of merchants, sailors, and officials trading in the merchandise brought in on the Spanish *flotas* and transhipping bullion to Spain (Vila Vilar 1982). Regulated long-distance trade created similar markets around the world. Unless rulers kept long-distance merchants separated from locals, as for example in Canton, fairs tended to combine the roles of local, regional, and interregional markets.

During the nineteenth century fairs became less important as points of commercial exchange. Instead, since the pathbreaking Crystal Palace (London) world exhibition of 1851, such events became tools of political and ideological representations in which the industrializing countries demonstrated their technological competitiveness and imperial ambitions, while some Asian countries for the first time represented themselves outside their own territories. Today, world expositions are a mass cultural event, and trade fairs have become places of exchange of technological and cultural novelties, and exist for almost every sector of modern economies.

SEE ALSO AGRICULTURE; CANTON SYSTEM; CARAVAN TRADE; EMPIRE, MUGHAL; EMPIRE, OTTOMAN; INDIA.

BIBLIOGRAPHY

Abu-Lughod, Janet L. *Before the European Hegemony: The World System, AD 1250–1350.* Oxford, U.K.: Oxford University Press, 1989.

Braudel, Fernand. *Civilisation and Capitalism,* Vol. 2: *The Wheels of Commerce.* London: Collins 1982.

Epstein, Stephan R. "Regional Fairs, Institutional Innovation, and Economic Growth in Late Medieval Europe." *Economic History Review* 2nd series, no. 47 (August 1994): 459–482.

Langer, Erick D., and Conti, Viviana E. "Circuitos comerciales y cambio económico en los Andes centromeridionales 1830–1890 (Commercial Circuits and Economic Change in the South Central Indies 1830–1930)" (trans.). *Desarrollo Económico* 31, no. 121 (April–June 1991): 91–111.

Milgrom, Paul D.; North, Douglas C.; and Weingast, Barry R. "The Role of Institutions in the Revival of Trade: The Law Merchant, Private Judges, and the Champagne Fairs." *Economics and Politics* 2 (March 1990): 1–23.

Munro, John H. "The 'New Institutional Economics' and the Changing Fortunes of Fairs in Medieval and Early Modern Europe: The Textile Trades, Warfare, and Transaction Costs." *Vierteljahrschrift fuer Sozial- und Wirtschaftsgeschichte* 88, no. 1 (2001): 1–47.

Pirenne, Henri. *Economic and Social History of Medieval Europe.* London: Paul, Trench, Trubner, 1947.

Tracy, James D., ed. *The Rise of the Merchant Empires: Long-Distance Trade in the Early Modern World, 1350–1750.* Cambridge, U.K.: Cambridge University Press, 1990.

Vila Vilar, Enriqueta. "Las ferias de Portobelo: Apariencia y realidad del comercio con Indias" (trans.). *Anuario de Estudios Americanos* 39 (1982): 275–340.

Weber, Max. *General Economic History.* London: Allen and Unwin, 1923.

Regina Grafe

FAMINE

A famine (from the Latin *fames,* hunger) may be defined as an extreme scarcity of food causing a populace to suffer from constant hunger, large-scale loss of weight, a

A Congolese mother with her malnourished child in Kabinda, 2001. Famine often follows on the heels of war, such as has been the case in the Congo since the 1990s. PHOTOGRAPH BY CHRISTINE NESBITT. AP/WIDE WORLD PHOTOS. REPRODUCED BY PERMISSION.

general deterioration in health, and a significant increase in mortality rates. Famine, a relatively rare catastrophe, must not be confused with the numerous food shortages that humanity had to face in history.

Discussion of famines has one main difficulty: it is impossible, in most instances, to separate the human and natural causes of nutrition disasters. Indeed, the effects of "natural" phenomena such as drought are largely dependent upon the socioeconomic level of the population, its "famine culture," and the development (or failure) of support networks. In other words, "famine lands" do not exist, even if between 1870 and 1914—one of the golden ages of liberal capitalism—Southeast Asia suffered from an international economic drive centered on London which, by putting pressure on its food production processes, created the conditions for Asia's underdevelopment.

For the sake of clarity, however, we should distinguish three kinds of famine: those principally caused by humankind, those in which natural factors play a relatively important part alongside human factors, and those

where a natural disaster is the main cause, even if human factors do always play their part.

THREE KINDS OF FAMINE

The great famine that struck Bangladesh in 1943 is typical of the first sort, but world trade was not the cause. In 1942 successive hurricanes caused severe damage to the rice harvest in Bangladesh, but the supply of food remained 9 percent greater than in 1941. The Japanese were occupying Burma, depriving India, and thus Bengal, of additional emergency food supplies. Rice supplies were transported out of Bengal so that they would not fall into enemy hands in the event of occupation. But the floods alarmed the population, unleashing the frenzy of speculators. The price of rice rose sixfold locally, and tragedy struck. Between 2 and 6 million people lost their lives. Bengali economist Amartya Sen (b. 1933), the 1998 Nobel Prize winner for economics for his work on famine, wrote about the 1943 Bengal tragedy, "I had been struck by its thoroughly class-dependent character . . . . it was not a famine that afflicted even the lower middle classes—only people much further down the economic ladder, such as landless rural labourers" (Sen 1976). Some famines have had purely political causes. Thus, several years after the famine in the U.S.S.R., which had been caused by civil war and foreign intervention, a severe famine occurred in Ukraine (December 1932 to August 1933) following a senseless agricultural reform: in 1930, just a few months after the start of collectivization on a grand scale, 65 percent of holdings were collectivized on the orders of Joseph Stalin (1879–1953) and against the wishes of the people. Output plummeted. Half the livestock was lost. In 1932 to 1933 this famine caused 5 million deaths.

Apart from the disaster (20 million deaths) caused by the calamitous policies of Mao Zedong between 1959 and 1961, which is similar to the Ukrainian famine in terms of political cause, most of the famines that struck China in the twentieth century fall into the second category of famine—those caused by some combination of human action and climatic intervention. The international demand for cotton, tobacco, and opium encouraged Chinese farmers to abandon food crops that were less profitable than rice. In addition, China has always been debilitated by difficult climatic conditions: the vast northern China plain is constantly threatened by drought. The monsoon rains, which occur two years out of three, do not completely cross the mountains to the south of the region. Furthermore, the Yellow River, which has its source in Tibet, floods when the snows thaw at the height of summer. Famine is thus a part of Chinese civilization, which as a defense mechanism developed alternative foodstuffs such as barks, root vegetables, and *guanyintu*, a clay that may be eaten to stave off hunger. In the eighteenth century the struggle against famine was relatively well organized: granaries were situated along navigable routes to allow the swift distribution of relief supplies of grain. By the twentieth century this system could no longer resist warlords and bandits; in 1921 relief grain supplies were transported by rail, which reduced the number of victims, but the famine of 1928 broke out at the height of a civil war.

The famine that arose in the Sahel (the vast savannah region which borders the Sahara Desert to the south) in 1983 to 1984 fell into the third category: its causes were essentially climatic. World trade does not seem to have played an important part in the catastrophe. In the Sahel droughts are frequent and long because of severe water stresses that have existed in the region since the end of the 1960s. Indeed, Sahel agriculture enjoys "sufficient humidity" for only two to three months per year. In this part of the world, the soil is not very fertile: it lacks minerals, it is not fertilized, and it is very dry and vulnerable to the winds and surface flow, like the soil at the time of the Dust Bowl storms in the United States (1934–1942).

Beginning in 1961 the Sahel's increase in production was less than the growth in population—around 50 million people. This scenario makes clear why the secure food supply for the Sahel was a difficult objective to achieve. The previous two famines had a deadly effect. Thus, between 1978 and 1973 cereal production fell by 600,000 metric tons and 80 percent of livestock disappeared, causing more than 100,000 deaths.

REGIONALISM OF FAMINES

The above examples illustrate the profile of a country vulnerable to famine: a poor country, generally tropical, which possesses inadequate reserves of food. It is a country that does not use advanced agricultural techniques, is relatively isolated from the rest of the world in terms of trade, and is unable to deal with the shockwaves of trade on a global scale, although often it is affected by water stress that is not strictly necessary if other factors are present to a great extent. For example, the 1693 to 1694 famine in France was not caused by drought but by long periods of winter frost and by summer rains that ruined the poor cereal crops.

Famines strike regionally, not globally. The relative commercial isolation of the countries involved explains the lack of influence of world trade. It is true, however, that a developing country with an intensive monoculture such as rice, sugar, or cocoa may find itself in difficulty when prices collapse, whether because of speculation or otherwise. And in this case, world trade, in the guise of the "free market" of cereals, plays a significant role in weakening entire agricultural regions. As far as controlling the effects of famine, international trade plays a much less important role than one might think. Food aid is generally "humanitarian" and is most often provided by nongovernmental organizations (NGOs). However, agencies of the United Nations or states can take some control of matters: for example, if the means of transport are not specifically hired for this kind of operation, food aid is delivered using the means and routes normally used for international trade.

The staggering famines that struck the Indies during the nineteenth century because of inadequate or delayed monsoons (25 million dead in the eighteen major crises which occurred between 1874 and 1900), as well as the Chinese famines, have led us to believe that famines are principally an Asian phenomenon. This is not correct, as can be seen from the Great Famine in Ireland, which resulted from potato blight and caused more than 1 million deaths between 1846 and 1850, as well as the famines that plagued Africa during the second half of the twentieth century (2 million dead in Biafra between 1967 and 1970, and 800,000 dead in Ethiopia in 1984 to 1985).

SEE ALSO Bangladesh; China; Disease and Pestilence; India; Population—Emigration and Immigration; United Kingdom; United States; Wars.

BIBLIOGRAPHY

Acot, Pascal. *Histoire du Climat (History of Climate)* (trans.). Paris: Editions Perrin, 2003.

Brunel, S., and Bodin, J. L. *Géopolitique de la faim (Geopolitics of Famine)* (trans.). Paris: Presses Universitaires de France (PUF), 1998.

Burroughs, W. J. *Does the Weather Really Matter? The Social Implications of Climate Change.* Cambridge, U.K.: Cambridge University Press, 1997.

Daly, M. E. *The Famine in Ireland.* Dundalk, Ireland: Dundalgan, 1986.

Davis, Mike. *Génocides tropicaux: Catastrophes naturelles et famines coloniales (1870–1900).* Paris: La Découverte, 2003. Published in English translation as *Late Victorian Holocausts, El Niño Famines and the Making of the Third World.* London; New York: Verso, 2001.

United Nations Development Programme. *Global Report on Human Development 1998.* New York: Author, 1998.

Robson, J. R. K., ed. *Famine: Its Causes, Effects, and Management.* New York: Gordon and Breach, 1981.

Sen, Amartya. *Famines, Food Availability, and Exchange Entitlements: The Case of the Bengal Famine.* London: London School of Economics, 1976.

Pascal Acot

FINANCE, CREDIT AND MONEY LENDING

Trade growth was greatly supported by credit, because the invention of credit facilities increased the turnover of goods. The exchange of money and credit increased the confidence between purchasers and sellers which was the basis of business transactions in modern times.

UP TO THE EIGHTEENTH CENTURY

The growth of commercial exchanges in Europe at the end of the Middle Ages went with the creation of adequate monetary instruments that could speed up the transmission of payment. The Italians, who were the driving force behind the first major international trade networks, introduced the bill of exchange in the thirteenth century. Like public-debt bonds, these documents could be transferred by one merchant to another, thus creating a paper currency; in the seventeenth and eighteenth centuries the volume of paper currency exceeded the amount of metal currency in circulation by ten to twenty times. This resort to bills of exchange offered several advantages and fulfilled several needs. It was a means of compensation and payment that avoided transfer of payment in cash, which was always risky stimulating trade whenever the dispatch of return goods was not immediately possible. In addition, it allowed the settlement of business between places that did not have the same currency—indeed, this was theoretically its sole purpose. Very quickly, this means of payment and exchange also allowed the granting of credit, short-circuiting the ban on lending at interest imposed by the church. Discount on bills of exchange—that is, their transfer for cash before their due date—gave rise to the levy of interest by the person making the advance. Via the issue, discount, and transfer of bills of exchange, every *ancien régime* merchant took on the role of credit lender and banker, in the absence of formal institutions offering credit. The Banks of Amsterdam (1609), Hamburg (1619), and London (1694) did not permit any kind of loans to private individuals.

Bills of exchange were available to the majority of merchants, but speculation on the exchanges and possible gains was only within the grasp of a few important merchant banker families, having an extended network of informants in the main world trading places, such as the Arnolfinis (Antwerp and Lyon) and the Fuggers (Augsburg) in the sixteenth century, and the Hopes, the Parishs, and the Rothschilds in the eighteenth century. The existence of paper currency of this kind underpinned merchant credit. North American and Caribbean trade relied upon long-term credit being available to the colonists. The purchase of slaves at Saint-Domingue at the end of the eighteenth century, for example, was settled over three years. The indebtedness of the colonies was widespread and led to the allowance of longer credit, although this sometimes posed problems with liquidity, even for important trading houses, which could offer credit thanks to their commercial and financial profits and the credits that they themselves could obtain from their backers. Credit was also the basis of the tobacco trade in Chesapeake Bay: British merchants exported goods produced in the American colonies, leaving their correspondents to make payment by bills of exchange that could be cashed several months later. This delay allowed the colonial producer to realize the income from his sales before having to pay for his purchases. Alternatively, to ensure the deal, the British merchant could also pay for the goods with bills of exchange upon receipt, even before having completed their resale. The interest rate was normally around 5 percent, but it could rise suddenly in the event of war or a crisis. The collapse of certain important trading houses (Amsterdam in 1773, Hamburg in 1799) had repercussions for all the main markets, with merchants reluctant to rely upon bills of exchange for fear that they would not be paid.

The circulation, transfer, and conversion of this paper currency into cash and vice versa was facilitated by

The interior of Lloyd's of London in the Royal Exchange in the Cornhill section of the city. *The exchange was a center for a variety of business dealings that involved insurance premiums, investment instruments (stocks and bonds), and capital funding.*
© BETTMANN/CORBIS. REPRODUCED BY PERMISSION.

the wide availability of stock exchanges, which allowed merchants to meet informally in one place at a fixed time. Such regular meetings became widespread throughout European trading places from the fifteenth century (Bruges in 1409, Antwerp in 1460, Toulouse in 1469, Amsterdam in 1530, London in 1554, and Hamburg in 1558). Before buildings were erected for the purpose, merchants often met in the open. In London, Thomas Gresham (1519–1579) established the Royal Exchange, which was officially opened in 1571. Besides the writing of shipping insurance, the buying and selling of goods, and the exchange of information, all kinds of other business transactions took place at the stock exchange. The stock exchange was thus both a market for stocks and shares and a financial market. Amsterdam and London were preeminent in this sphere in the seventeenth and eighteenth centuries. By the end of the seventeenth century, London speculators in stocks, shares in the India companies and in several dozen other companies, and in

Bank of England bonds moved first to Exchange Alley (1698–1700), then into the Stock Exchange (1773). The spatial separation between commercial business (goods and credit) and finance points to the opening of a new era.

FROM THE NINETEENTH CENTURY

As soon as a peacetime economy was restored in Europe, and between the United States and the United Kingdom, at the start of the 1820s, the flow of credit underpinning international trade benefited from an increasing number of exchanges and a reduction in the price of silver. London (backed up by Glasgow) and Paris were the main places for the bills-of-exchange business because they were the focal points of their respective countries, and above all because they acted as conduits for international clearing of bills. Paris became less important when, in order to pay the indemnity of war to Germany, the French state ordered the banks to settle almost 5 billion francs of accounts and transfer them to Berlin in 1873 and 1874. Thus London was confirmed until World War I as the worldwide location for clearing bills of exchange. An international round of remittances was put together and ended up in London, after various endorsements, on the heels of an enormous influx of shipping and trade—from Latin America and North America, often relayed via New York; from the Far East via India and Egypt; and from the ports and markets of continental Europe. Two-thirds of the bills issued in London were destined for overseas during the years 1911 to 1913.

In addition to the strengths of British industry and shipping, the leading role of London may be explained by the fact that merchant banks added to discounting the practice of acceptance, by which they pledged their signatures as guarantees of the transfer of bills of exchange, while becoming key players in the primary financial market (underwriting and issuing) and the secondary trading of shares. Kleinwort (covering northwest Europe), Baring (covering Latin America), Morgan Grenfell (very active in North America, on account of its links with J. P. Morgan), Schroder, Hambro, Brown-Shipley, Rothschild, and altogether about thirty large banking houses formed the cornerstone of the system of credit connected with world trade until the 1930s. The bill brokers and commercial banks supplemented this system with their discounting. The Great Depression in the 1930s, followed by the war years, weakened these merchant banks because many of their accounts were frozen. All over Europe, the deposit and clearing banks were endowed with strong departments for wholesale finance within their own countries, where they centralized interbank rediscounts related to trade. They became key players in credit on warrant beginning from the middle of the nineteenth century, thanks to customs-bonded warehouses. Places of credit were established where industrial materials could be traded, like Marseilles and Hamburg for colonial commodities. In the meanwhile, in order to prop up trade abroad, modern banks were equipped with a network of overseas "correspondents," or partner banks, which may be used to build up a worldwide system of "documented credit," whereby loans to importers or exporters were dependent upon the interbank production of "documentation" on the transport of goods. Some banks were supplied with advice from overseas subsidiaries, such as Deutsche Bank, BOLSA (Bank of Latin and South America), and Barclays DCO (Dominion, Commonwealth, Overseas). Beginning in the 1920s Lloyds sponsored BOLSA and the British Bank of West Africa, and was stationed in India and Egypt. Specialized international banks (e.g., the Hong Kong and Shanghai Bank Corporation or Standard Chartered) lent support to British influence. France found outlets via its Banque de l'Indochine (for Southeast Asia) and banks dealing with

Africa. A scramble for Asia rallied European and Japanese banks to finance trade between Russia and China and between China and its Asian neighbors, and to take part in flows with other continents, hence the pivotal role of credit in Hong Kong and Shanghai. The development of Asian territories led to financing the flow of materials and goods with India, Malaysia, and Indonesia. Networks of banking relationships were set up between London, Hong Kong, Yokohama and San Francisco.

Central banks promoted such trade by their rediscounting, but the city benefited also from its genuine interbank monetary market ("open market"). These interbank markets also relied upon treasury bills to sustain a state's liquid assets, which broadened the size of the monetary markets. Defending the position of the main market thus was essential in the event of a crisis of confidence or payments: the central bank was obliged to save the banks involved in order to preserve the financial trading system. The Banque de France intervened on several occasions during the years 1820 to 1860 to support the Parisian market, which had been weakened by recessions, then ensured the continued survival of the market during the crashes in 1882 and 1889. The Bank of England was involved in alleviating the 1878 crisis and organized the rescue of merchant bank Baring in 1890. Finally, central banks oversee the "settlement" of intercountry balances and the transfer of gold (or gold and silver, before the single currency succeeded bimetallism at the end of the nineteenth century). The gold market in London is the symbol of this ultimate guarantee of the balance of payments.

In the twentieth century the New York market established itself as U.S. banks financed North American trade and expanded their role in financing trade with Latin America. Certain private groups supported intergovernmental loans between the allies during World War I to finance purchases in the U.S. The onslaught of U.S. bankers in Europe and China during the 1920s demonstrated their new power. The European markets had also been reconstructed. From the start of the century the markets of Antwerp and Brussels flourished as they financed Belgian commercial expansion in Africa (Kongo), Asia, and Central Europe, and Antwerp took advantage of its role as gateway to the Rhine economy and the Belgian hub with Latin America (with the Belgo-Argentine trading company Bunge and Born). Further east, although Vienna lost influence with the fall of the Austro-Hungarian Empire, and its territory on the Danube was now shared with Romanian and Czech bankers, markets such as Trieste, Genoa, and Thessaloníki continued to expand, and Piraeus advanced and became the staging post of trade in the northeast Mediterranean.

The realignment of commercial forces after World War II explains the vigor of U.S. banks in financing inter-American and transatlantic trade, the breakthrough of Japanese banks connected to trading companies (*sogo-soshas*) which were members of the same business groups (or *keiretsus*), and the relative decline of European banks in the face of these inroads. Confronted by the U.S. bank EximBank, the major European countries looked to a public or semipublic institution (such as the BFCE, or Banque française du commerce extérieur). Banking practices varied, with medium-term credit formulas, via "credit sellers" (assigned by the banks to exporters), and, from the 1960s, "credit buyers" (assigned to foreign importers by the business clients of these banks). Public authorities supported these efforts because central banks refinanced these credits in the medium term. In order to increase East-West trade, various interstate "protocols" were concluded, and banks relied upon interest-rate reductions from their national exchequers and on generous refinancing by their central banks. This system culminated in the financing of energy equipment and key factories in the U.S.S.R. between 1970 and 1980.

London remained the world center for credit to business. With its organization, its telecommunications network, its accumulated expertise, and its flexible legislation, London had hosted U.S. and Japanese banks since the 1960s. After its foreign exchange market (*forex*) reopened in 1951 it once more became the pivotal point for exchange payment, with its modernized dealing floor. London was involved in large-scale project financing (of overseas equipment, export of materials, then aircraft) via credit syndicates linking up to several hundred banks behind lead-managing banks, hence stiff competition between banks to get the mandates for managing such financing of international trade. Even when its merchant banks were bought out by some German and U.S. commercial banks, the key role of London was confirmed when front offices were created during the years 1980 to 1990. The confusion of the silver and commodities markets by the slant of the markets in terms of goods, materials and raw materials, energy, derivatives, and futures gave rise to the commodization of finance, producing enormous fluidity in the finance of commodities, with currency swaps and a secondary credit market for transnational companies (by securitization), which encouraged the spread of globalization. London remains at the heart of the changes, with one-third of the global currency trading business in 2003, before Tokyo and New York. From the 1980s these markets supported trading in derivatives/futures, and their vast extent provide growing independence with regard to the financing of the trading exchanges themselves. In addition to speculating in trade commodity futures, they started speculating in nonmaterial goods, thus taking greater risks.

SEE ALSO Balance of Payments; Banking; Developmental State, Concept of; Finance, Insurance; Great Depression of the 1930s; Gresham, Sir Thomas; Hamilton, Alexander; Home Charges (India); Germany; Hong Kong and Shanghai Bank; Hope Family; Japan; Money and Monetary Policy; Morgan, J. P.; Quantity Theory of Money; Treaties; United Kingdom; United States.

BIBLIOGRAPHY

Baker, James. *Financing International Trade*. Westport, CT: Greenwood Press, 2003.

Bonin, Hubert. *La Banque de l'union parisienne: Histoire de la deuxième banque d'affaires française (1874/1904–1974).* (*The History of the Second French Investment Bank*). Paris: P.L.A.G.E, 2001.

Braudel, Fernand. *Civilization and Capitalism, 15th–18th Century*, Vol. 2: *The Wheels of Commerce*. Berkeley: University of California Press, 1992.

Burk, Kathleen. *Morgan Grenfell, 1838–1988: The Biography of a Merchant Bank*. Oxford, U.K.: Oxford University Press, 1989.

Bussière, Eric. *Paribas, l'Europe et le monde, 1872–1992.* (*Paribas, Europe and the World*). Anvers: Fonds Mercator, 1992.

Carosso, Vincent. *The Morgans: Private International Bankers*. Cambridge, MA: Harvard University Press, 1987.

Collins, Michael. *Money and Banking in the United Kingdom: A History*. London: Croom Helm, 1988.

Holtferich, Carl L. *Frankfurt as a Financial Centre: From Medieval Trade Fair to European Banking Centre*. Munich: Beck, 1999.

Jeannin, Pierre. *Change, crédit et circulation monétaire à Augsbourg au milieu du 16e siècle.* (*Exchange, Credit and Monetary Circulation in Augsburg in the midst of the 16th Century*). Paris: Armand Colin, 2001.

Jones, Geoffrey. *Banks as Multinationals*. London: Routledge, 1990.

Jones, Geoffrey. *British Multinational Banking, 1830–1990*. Oxford, U.K.: Oxford University Press, 1993.

King, Frank. *The History of the Hong Kong and Shanghai Banking Corporation*. 4 vols. Shanghai; New York: Cambridge University Press, 1987–1991.

Klebaner, Benjamin. *American Commercial Banking: A History*. Boston: Beard Books, 1990.

Kynaston, Niall. *The World's Banker: The History of the House of Rothschild*. London: Weidenfeld and Nicolson, 1998.

Lévy-Leboyer, Maurice. *Les banques européennes et l'industrialisation internationale dans la première moitié du XIXe siècle.* (*European banks and international industrialization in the first half of the 19th century*). Paris: Presses universitaires de France, 1966.

McCusker, John J. *Money and Exchange in Europe and America, 1600–1775: A Handbook*. 2nd edition, rev. Chapel Hill: University of North Carolina Press, 1992.

Michie, Ranald C. *The City of London: Continuity and Change since 1850*. London: Palgrave, 1991.

Price, Jacob M. *Capital and Credit in British Overseas Trade: The View from the Chesapeake, 1700–1776.* Cambridge, MA: Harvard University Press, 1980.

Roberts, Richard. *Schroders: Merchants and Bankers.* Basingstoke, U.K.: Macmillan, 1992.

Tamaki, Norio; Checkland, Olive; and Nishimura, Shizuya, eds. *East Meets West: Banking History in the Pacific Area (1859–1959).* London: Macmillan, 1994.

Silvia Marzagalli
Hubert Bonin

FINANCE, INSURANCE

The emergence of modern premium insurance is commonly dated to fourteenth-century Italy: the earliest recorded insurance policy covered a ship traveling from Genoa to Majorca in 1347. In the late fourteenth century the Prato merchant Francesco Datini regularly insured textiles between Spain, Italy, and Tunis, and wine carried to Flanders and England. Private merchants acted as underwriters, but public notaries were employed to draw up the contracts. By 1450 there were several hundred notaries working in Genoa, Pisa, Florence, Marseilles, and Milan. During the following two centuries specialized communities of insurance brokers also emerged in London, Antwerp, Amsterdam, Bruges, and Hamburg.

The growth of marine underwriting, and its concentration in the hands of specialized notaries and brokers, was accompanied by an international convergence of practices. By the sixteenth century the marine insurance policy had acquired a standard form. The policy commonly offered compensation for loss or damage to hull and/or cargo due to the "perils of the seas" such as wreck, stranding, burning, sinking, and deliberate damage by masters or crew, as well as losses by "men-of-war. . .enemies, pirates, rovers, thieves, jettisons, letters of mart. . .takings at sea, arrests, restraints and detainments of all kings, princes and people" (Cockerell and Green 1994, p. 4). Policies could cover either single voyages or provide cover for a specified period of time.

Marine underwriting was also regulated at an early date. Ordinances issued at Barcelona between 1435 and 1484 placed maritime insurance under the *Consolat de Mar* which formed the basis for international commercial law in the Mediterranean. Further ordinances were passed in Italy, Spain, Flanders, and England during the sixteenth and early seventeenth centuries, and chambers of insurance were set up in several ports. The chief purposes of these institutions were to prevent fraud, to reduce the costs of disputes, and to secure an important source of tax revenue.

The insurance of ships and cargoes at sea reached a new level of efficiency with the rise of Lloyd's of London beginning in the 1690s. Lloyd's advantage lay not only in its concentration of underwriters and brokers in close proximity, but also in the reliable flows of shipping intelligence gathered in *Lloyd's List,* first published in 1692. Although it continued to be difficult to measure accurately all the perils faced on long-distance voyages, currents, tides, and climate, the incidence and geography of piracy and privateering, and the reputations of ships' captains and merchants' agents became generally well known. This kind of risk information probably helped premium insurance to keep pace with the rapid expansion of trade. English foreign trade alone grew by a factor of about five during the course of the eighteenth century.

Wars increased the losses to merchant shipping and raised premium rates, but they also increased the demand for insurance cover. Insurance profits and their volatility rose. The prospect of profits, as well as the long distances involved in placing overseas risks in London, encouraged the establishment of marine insurance companies in Hamburg and other northern European ports, as well in India and North America. From the 1850s the dominance of Lloyd's in English marine underwriting was also challenged by the rise of large marine or composite insurance companies such as the Commercial Union and the Union Marine. Overseas insurance markets became increasingly crowded. On the U.S. Pacific coast, for instance, by the 1880s British and U.S. marine insurers jostled not only with their European rivals, but also with insurance companies from China, Japan, and New Zealand. Not all ships and voyages, however, were insured by the market. Some shipping and trading companies, for example the British East India Company, the Peninsular and Oriental Steam Navigation Company, and the Mitsubishi Shipping Company in Japan, operated their own insurance funds, and in some countries smaller shipowners clubbed together to form mutual marine insurance associations.

The age of steamships brought with it new risks, including greater tonnage and more valuable cargoes at sea, more crowded shipping lanes, and the risk of boiler explosions. Marine underwriting thus remained highly volatile. Growing competition ensured long periods of falling premiums and profits in the third quarter of the nineteenth century. Losses through naval and military action increased, for example during the Russo-Japanese War of 1905, and underwriters became increasingly reluctant to continue to include war-related risks in their policies. At the outbreak of World War I in 1914 the insurance of all British ships was transferred to a new government war-risks scheme, though private insurers continued to cover foreign shipping. This heralded the expansion of the state's role in insurance markets.

Between the world wars the stagnation of international shipping left marine underwriters subject to wildly gyrating markets. Economic nationalism, increasing restrictions on foreign companies, political instability, social conflict, currency fluctuations, and the Great Depression also made life difficult for insurers in new lines such as trade-credit insurance. Their services were increasingly supplemented by the state. The U.K. Board of Trade established the first government export-credit insurance program in 1919. This was designed to complement rather than replace private trade-indemnity insurance. Other countries also turned to export-credit and guarantee programs. In 1934 a group of public agencies came together in Berne, Switzerland, to form the International Union of Credit and Investment Insurers to regulate their business, but this had little impact in the turbulent 1930s. After World War II the process of decolonization opened up new investment and trading possibilities, but also brought with it new political uncertainties. A range of new public-insurance and investment-guarantee plans was established in both industrialized and developing countries to stimulate capital and trade flows. Although their collective regulatory impact remained weak, the volume of trade and political-risk insurance they acquired came to dwarf that of the private insurers—by 1984, U.S.$200 billion (Berne union members alone) compared to U.S.$150 million.

Burgeoning defaults on debt in the Third World pushed many of the public export-credit and insurance agencies into financial difficulties in the mid-1980s, and by the end of the decade the private insurers had recaptured a portion of the market. Export credits, however, had by this stage become a tool of foreign policy by some governments, notably the United States, and plans were often reformed rather than abandoned. Public and private provision of trade insurance continues to be complementary. The latter is flexible but restricted—private insurance of war, terrorism, and inconvertibility risks is rare. The former offers such types of insurance but restricts coverage on a political basis, and the contracts require more bureaucracy to complete. The debt crisis and recent wars in the Middle East, however, demonstrate that both public and private insurance can encourage the continuance of trading in high-risk environments.

SEE ALSO BALANCE OF PAYMENTS; BANKING; BUNGE AND BORN; FINANCE, CREDIT AND MONEY LENDING; GREAT DEPRESSION OF THE 1930S; JARDINE MATHESON; LLOYD'S OF LONDON; MITSUBISHI; MITSUI; TREATIES.

BIBLIOGRAPHY

Cockerell, H. A. L. and Green, Edwin. *The British Insurance Business,* 2nd edition. Sheffield, U.K.: Sheffield Academic Press, 1994.

Haufler, Virginia. *Dangerous Commerce: Insurance and the Management of International Risk.* Ithaca, NY and London: Cornell University Press, 1997.

McCusker, John J. "The Early History of 'Lloyd's List'." *Historical Research: The Bulletin of the Institute of Historical Research* 64 (October 1991): 427–431.

Pearson, Robin. "Insurance: An Historical Overview." In *The Oxford Encyclopaedia of Economic History,* vol. 3, ed. Joel Mokyr. New York: Oxford University Press, 2003.

Raynes, Harold E. *A History of British Insurance.* London: Pitman, 1948.

Supple, Barry. *The Royal Exchange Assurance: A History of British Insurance, 1720–1970.* Cambridge, U.K.: Cambridge University Press, 1970.

Trebilcock, Clive. *Phoenix Assurance and the Development of British Insurance, Vol. 2: The Era of the Insurance Giants, 1870–1984.* Cambridge, U.K.: Cambridge University Press, 1998.

Robin Pearson

FINLAND

A remote and sparsely populated corner of Europe, Finland was for centuries a supplier of northern forest and other primary products, such as furs, fish, tar, and timber. As the Baltic Sea and its gulfs joined it with Central and Western Europe, it was, however, relatively easy to carry even bulkier products to the international markets.

The first Finnish exports seem to have been furs. Possibly such trade already existed in prehistoric times—at least it was important during the Middle Ages, when the provinces of present Finland were gradually incorporated into Sweden. Yet it seems that, in the beginning, Low-German mercantile influence was more dominant than the Swedish: Evidence of a German fur-trading system has been found in the Finnish interior, and the major burghers in the few medieval towns were of German origin. Gradually, the Swedish capital Stockholm gained control over Western Finland—the Bothnian coast, in particular—but the southern coast remained in the sphere of the Hanse and, specifically, Tallinn, until the late sixteenth century. In comparison, Finnish trade with Russia was very modest.

Another important medieval export commodity was fish, which mainly found markets in Estonia and around Stockholm, typically in exchange for grain; this trade also induced the import of salt, which was to remain the number one import article until the nineteenth century. Salt also was the first bulk commodity in the Finnish foreign trade, which meant that, until the late sixteenth century, imports required much more cargo space than exports. In this respect, however, a major change was brewing in the sixteenth century, with the growth of West European demand for "naval stores." While the Southern

MAP BY XNR PRODUCTIONS. THE GALE GROUP.

By the late seventeenth century, the increasing West European demand for timber had boosted the price of sawed wood so much that it became possible to transport it from the Gulf of Finland area. Dutch entrepreneurs built the first big water-powered sawmills at the mouth of the Narva River (in Estonia) in the 1680s, and after the Great Northern War this new industry also became established in the province of Wiborg, which had been incorporated with Russia in 1722. During the eighteenth century, Russia, Finland, and Ingria developed into a major center for the sawmill industry, with outlets in the ports of Wiborg, St. Petersburg, and Narva. Even in Swedish Finland the export of sawed wood increased, but faster growth was experienced only in the nineteenth century—after all of Finland had been incorporated with Russia as an autonomous Grand Duchy. Around 1830, the value of exported wood products already exceeded that of tar, but even the export of tar grew slowly until the 1860s.

As before, these exports went mainly to Western Europe, but with Britain favoring its North American colonies, the Spanish and Mediterranean markets increased their importance from the late eighteenth century onward. This development was also connected with the fact that salt (from southern Europe) remained the number one import article until the early nineteenth century, when grain—mainly from Russia—surpassed it in value. Iron from Sweden also was an important import item in the seventeenth and eighteenth centuries, but after the political separation its role diminished, as did all trade with Sweden.

FROM PRIMARY TO INDUSTRIAL EXPORTS

The real breakthrough of forestry industries took place after the 1860s. Growing West European demand, the decrease of British timber dues, and the abandonment of former restrictions of forestry exploitation made Finnish sawed wood production and exports grow faster than ever before: Between 1860 and 1913, the export volume grew about twelvefold and the value twentyfold. The birth of the modern pulp and paper industry further increased the importance of the forest sector: From almost nil, the export value of pulp and paper boosted to about 45 percent of that of sawed wood. Even the export of raw timber, pit-props, paper-wood—in addition to the traditional export of firewood to Stockholm and St. Petersburg—expanded with the cheapening sea transport. Overall, while the volume of exports grew almost ninefold, the proportion of all forest produce (by value) increased from about 35 to 70 percent between 1860 and 1913. Sawed and raw wood mainly went to Central and West Europe, while the paper industry found its markets in Russia.

shores of the Baltic and Norway exported sawed wood and timber, Finland gradually became the prime producer of tar, which, being more valuable in relation to bulk, was cheaper to transport from far afield. Finnish tar production grew quickly during the first four decades of the seventeenth century. Finland became the number one producer of tar in Europe, albeit most Finnish tar was sold abroad from Stockholm. Tar exports grew so large that they changed the transport balance of Finnish foreign trade: Exports now required more cargo space than imports. Tar production also connected the Finnish economy with the West European "world system."

Expanding exports also enabled expanding imports and widened the scope of the latter. Thus, the proportions of raw materials and machines increased, while those of grain and other foods decreased slightly. On the other hand, the import of salt, which already had been surpassed by sugar before 1860, increased, but that was because it was increasingly used as an industrial raw material.

After Finland in 1917 became independent from Russia, its trade with its former mother country (now Soviet Russia) dwindled to a fraction of previous levels; in exports, the proportion of trade with Britain increased, and, in imports, that of Germany increased. The structure of exports remained similar, although the proportion of forest produce further increased, approaching 80 percent. In imports, raw materials and investment goods also increased their share to about 70 percent of the total.

After World War II, a number of important developments took place. First, the Soviet Union's share of Finland's total foreign trade grew, reaching to over 20 percent just before the collapse of the Soviet system. Nevertheless, Central and Western Europe's share remained high, seldom sinking below 50 percent and sometimes exceeding 60 percent. Trade with non-European countries remained relatively small until the 1990s.

Overall, this was a period of improving value-added of exports, resulting from a sustained move from timber to paper products in forest industries. The exports by metal industries also increased, partly because of the growth of Soviet trade, and the electronic and information technology industries experienced further development. The move from bulky to high value-added products was also reflected by the fact that exports required less cargo space in proportion to imports—a trend that was strengthened by increasing oil (and later coal) imports. Already in the 1960s, the volume of imports (in tons) exceeded that of exports.

In the span of about five centuries, the role of foreign trade in the Finnish economy has grown hugely. Around 1630, with tar trade already affecting large rural areas, the annual value of exported tar corresponded to the annual grain consumption of some 20,000 people, or 5 percent of the population, suggesting a trade ratio (exports/GDP) of only 2 percent. Around 1860, exports amounted to almost 10 percent of GDP, and they exceeded 20 percent by 1880. After that, however, the ratio remained stable: From around 25 percent in the 1920s and 1930s, it sunk below 20 percent after World War II and increased only slowly since then. After about 1975, however, the trade ratio exceeded the earlier proportions; it reached over 30 percent at the turn of the millennium.

SEE ALSO Agriculture; Balance of Payments; Baltic States; Cargoes, Freight; Cargoes, Passenger; Common Market and the European Union; Denmark; Free Trade, Theory and Practice; GATT, WTO; Great Depression of the 1930s; Industrialization; International Trade Agreements; Norway; Regional Trading Agreements; Russia; Sweden.

BIBLIOGRAPHY

Åström, Sven Erik. *From Tar to Timber: Studies in Northeast European Forest Exploitation and Foreign Trade.* Helsinki: Societas Scintiarum Fennica, 1988.

Hjerppe, Riitta. *The Finnish Economy, 1860–1985: Growth and Structural Change.* Helsinki: Bank of Finland, 1989.

Kaukiainen, Yrjö. "Finland and the World Economy, c. 1600–1950: Some Perspectives." In *Nordwesteuropa in der Weltwirtschaft: 1750–1950,* ed. Michael North. Stuttgart: In Kommission bei F. Steiner, 1993.

Oksanen, Heikki, and Pihkala, Erkki. *Suomen ulkomaankauppa / Finland's Foreign Trade: 1917–1949.* Helsinki: Bank of Finland, 1973.

Pihkala, Erkki. *Suomen ulkomaankauppa, 1860–1917 / Finland's Foreign Trade, 1860–1917.* Helsinki: Bank of Finland, 1969.

Yrjö Kaukiainen

FLOWS OF FACTORS OF PRODUCTION

Factor flows refer to the movements of capital and labor, two of the conventional factors of production, within the world economy. These can take various forms. There are short- and long-term capital flows; long-term capital may be direct or portfolio; capital may come from private sources, the public sector or institutional agencies. Similarly, labor flows, measured by emigrant and immigrant data, can be both short- or long-term. Although the common view is that emigrants remain in the reception country, where they raise the next generation, the evidence is that many return to their country of origin after a number of years of work or upon reaching retirement age. In the case of labor movements between southern Europe and South America, so-called *golondrinas* (swallows) left Italy and Spain at the end of their harvest cycle in autumn for six months' agricultural work in the Southern Hemisphere, only to return home in time for spring sowing in Europe. Similarly, many merchants in Puerto Rico's sugar and coffee trades were Mallorcan immigrants who returned to Europe with their financial gains.

PUSH AND PULL

One traditional approach in explaining factor flows is via "push and pull" analysis. "Push" refer to forces originat-

A 1915 photo shows immigrants arriving at Ellis Island after a voyage across the Atlantic Ocean. The island was the major immigration checkpoint for the United States from 1892 to 1943. Documents of around 20 million immigrants were processed here and provided a pool of labor that helped fuel the rapid growth of the country during that era. © BETTMANN/CORBIS. REPRODUCED BY PERMISSION

ing in the country of origin, which effectively encourage outward movement. "Pull" factors are those that attract labor and capital into the reception countries. In the case of capital, the push and pull influences are likely to involve expectations about the relative level of financial returns, taking into account issues of capital appreciation and the perceived degree of risk. Low returns at home and the expectation of higher profits abroad encourage outward movement of capital. Labor movement is somewhat more complicated insofar as economic explanations—the prospects of better jobs, higher incomes, or cheap land—may not be the whole story. Social, cultural, and political factors come into play as emigration is also the result of persecution, religious intolerance, and cultural deprivation at home. Pogroms, most notably in tsarist Russia, forced Eastern European Jews to flee their homes; Welsh settlers, fearing their culture was under threat in the United Kingdom, preserved their way of life in the Chubut in Argentina, free from English domination.

HISTORY OF FACTOR FLOWS

Before 1800 factor flows were marginal to the world's total capital and labor supplies, with a number of exceptions. One was the slave trade. Plantations in the West Indies at first exploited indentured labor from the mother country (particularly in the case of the United Kingdom), but white European settlers could not be attracted to tropical and subtropical regions. Consequently, the Caribbean Islands and European colonies in the Americas imported African slave labor. Such were the riches of the transatlantic slave trade, despite the appalling human losses of the middle passage, that some scholars hold that profits thus accumulated supplied the essential funding for Britain's early industrialization. What became the United States was another exception, as the British colonies there attracted both settlers and capital. Elsewhere, large-scale demographic and capital movements remained modest, the former usually associated with the transportation of criminals, for example from the United Kingdom to Australia.

The second half of the nineteenth century, when the slave trade had been brought to an end, marked a new departure in factor movement. Capital flows responded rapidly to the changing economic conditions in the world economy, and migration quickly followed. Cheap transport by railway and steamship, improved information flows about opportunities abroad, and the demonstration effect of the success of earlier settlers soon encouraged large numbers of European emigrants. Data on such demographic movement comes from immigration records in the reception countries and from steamship companies' passenger manifests. Of the 45 to 50 million who left Europe in the century before the outbreak of World War I, the United Kingdom supplied about one-third, mainly from the "Celtic fringe" of Ireland and Scotland but also from the agricultural areas of England. Italy was the next most important departure country. The reception countries were overwhelmingly in the temperate, sparsely populated areas of the globe where overseas European communities could be established. The United States received about two-thirds of the migrants from practically every departure country. Destination countries such as Canada, Australia, Argentina, and Brazil were more exclusive. Not surprisingly, Canada and Australia overwhelmingly attracted British-based emigrants, whereas Argentina and Brazil received mainly Southern Europeans from Italy, Spain, and Portugal.

Labor flows in the nineteenth century were not confined to Europeans. Workers left Asia and the Far East to work in tropical locations, where European survival rates were poor. Although the numbers of Asian emigrants were probably lower than those of Europeans, there is much uncertainty about the extent of Asian migration, as records are poor. Movement was not always entirely voluntary, as overpopulated Indian and Chinese villages forced communities to leave. Migrants were often indentured laborers who agreed to work abroad for a fixed period in return for pay and lodging and a guaranteed passage home. Labor and living conditions were usually harsh. Chinese villagers worked in Peru, Indian communities sprang up in Africa and the Far East, and Japanese migrants went to South America.

Factor flows slowed after World War I as economic nationalism spread to emigration controls and the world depression deterred capital movement, especially in the 1930s. Both capital and labor continued to move across borders, but at a reduced rate. After World War II, which itself contributed to the migration eastward of millions of Europeans, factor flows assumed a new intensity. Multinational investment and public funding pumped capital around the world. Similarly, migration flows became stronger, although both departure and destination countries changed. There was movement within Europe as

southern Italians sought work elsewhere, many Turks obtained jobs in Germany, and Eastern Europeans moved westward. Whereas in the nineteenth century Europeans emigrated to their imperial possessions, now workers from the Caribbean and the Indian subcontinent came to the United Kingdom; North Africans from Morocco, Tunisia, and Algeria entered France; and people from former colonies in sub-Saharan Africa also moved to their respective mother countries in Europe.

EFFECTS OF FLOWS

It is tempting to link the movements of the two factors, but the correlations are imperfect. A country receiving large numbers of emigrants will inevitably import capital for the social infrastructure its new residents will demand in the form of housing, schools, transport, and jobs. Many emigrants bring capital with them to start their new lives as farmers or entrepreneurs. At the same time, a country importing capital is likely to create new economic opportunities and enhanced job prospects that will inevitably attract immigrants. In the nineteenth century, for example, both capital and labor flowed to resource-rich temperate areas of the globe. But the reality of factor flows is more complicated. France supplied funds to the rest of the world second only to the United Kingdom's capital exports but provided few emigrants; Italy supplied emigrants but little capital; India imported huge quantities of mainly British capital but received few immigrants. In the late twentieth century, too, the factors flows are not well correlated. From the 1990s, for example, Britain has continued her policy of exporting capital but has now become a net importer of people.

Factor flows exercise considerable influence over the direction and timing of international trade. Emigrants naturally attract imports into their reception country from the country of departure. Overseas lending tends to return to the supplier country through return orders for equipment and capital goods, sometimes by arrangement in the shape of "tied" loans. Furthermore, countries of recent settlement exploited inward factor flows to supply the rest of the world with a wider range and greater quantity of foodstuffs and raw materials. Canada, largely peopled by British emigrants and supplied by British and U.S. investment, revolutionized the world wheat trade around 1900 and helped keep down the cost of imported food in Britain.

The freedom of factor flows is one sign of an integrated and open international economy. Both capital and labor moved freely across borders in the nineteenth century, and factor flows are an important feature of a global economy. It is true, however, that at the start of the twenty-first century capital probably moves more freely than labor. While countries have largely removed exchange controls and permit currency convertibility, they are busy devising the means to restrict labor flows and limit the social consequences of large-scale immigration.

SEE ALSO CAPITAL FLOWS; LABOR, TYPES OF; LABORERS, CONTRACT; POPULATION—EMIGRATION AND IMMIGRATION.

BIBLIOGRAPHY

Foreman-Peck, James. *A History of the World Economy: International Economic Relations since 1850,* 2nd edition. London: Harvester-Wheatsheaf, 1995

Kenwood, George, and Lougheed, Alan L. *The Growth of the International Economy, 1820–1913: An Introductory Text,* 4th edition. London: Routledge, 1999.

Richardson, H. W. "British Emigration and Overseas Investment, 1870–1914." *Economic History Review* 25, no. 1 (February, 1972): 99–113.

Vecoli, Rudolph J., and Sinke, Suzanne M., eds. *A Century of European Migrations, 1830–1930.* London: University of Illinois Press, 1991.

Woodruff, William. *The Impact of Western Man.* London: Macmillan, 1982.

Robert G. Greenhill

HENRY FORD
1863–1947

Henry Ford was a pioneer in the international production and marketing of automobiles. The Ford Motor Company began production in the United States in 1903. Ford constructed his first foreign factory in Canada in 1904 and began production in Britain in 1911. By 1939 Ford was assembling vehicles in twenty-two other countries and had major manufacturing sites in Canada, Britain, France, and Germany. Ford was part of a broader U.S.-led initiative to lower the price of cars by using interchangeable components and producing vehicles in large numbers. He revolutionized the industry in 1908 with the introduction of the Model T, the first internationally marketed low-cost automobile. Demand for the Model T was so great that it required a revolution in production methods. Between 1908 and 1913 Ford reduced his reliance on skilled labor and divided the process of producing cars into increasingly narrow tasks, culminating with the introduction of the moving assembly line in 1913. This led to a social crisis as Ford workers rebelled at the new conditions of work. Suffering excessive rates of labor turnover, Ford moved to reduce the hours of work from nine to eight hours per day and doubled wages to $5.00 per day in 1914. Despite Ford's interest in improving the standard of living of his workers he resisted unions, becoming the last of the major automobile makers to accept collective bargaining. Although ex-

tremely successful as a product and process innovator, Ford was much less successful as an organizational innovator. His failure to keep pace with the organizational changes adopted by General Motors and Chrysler resulted in Ford being surpassed by General Motors in the 1930s.

SEE ALSO AUTOMOBILE.

BIBLIOGRAPHY

Nevins, Allan. *Ford: The Times, the Man, the Company.* New York: Scribner, 1954.

Wilkins, M., and Hill, F. F. *American Business Abroad: Ford on Six Continents.* Detroit: Wayne State University Press, 1964.

Wayne Lewchuk

FRANCE

Among European countries, except Russia, France is the largest geographically and, until the nineteenth century, had the largest population. Despite the temptation of autarky, external trade played an important role in its history, reflecting both the specificities of its economic development and global trends.

1450s TO THE 1780s

France underwent a period of economic recovery and territorial consolidation in the second half of the fifteenth century. Its external trade grew till the 1560s. The establishment of the Lyon fairs revived the French isthmus linking the Mediterranean Sea with Northern Europe through the Rhône Valley. Most major French ports were definitively added to the territory only at that time (Rouen in 1449, Bordeaux in 1453, Marseille in 1481, and Nantes and Britanny in 1491).

France was traditionally exporting salt and wine. Other exports were mainly wheat, light cloths, and dyestuff. A large part of French trade, especially on the Mediterranean, was by and large under the control of Italian merchants. Competition from the Netherlands and England, along with civil and foreign wars, impeded external trade between the 1570s and the 1650s. The decline in the role of Italian merchants contrasted with the rise of the role of Dutch merchants in the Atlantic trade.

Headed by Jean-Baptiste Colbert (1619–1683) and others, the French state conducted a mercantilist policy from the 1660s to the 1780s. This consisted in encouraging domestic industries, creating and promoting colonies, and challenging Dutch supremacy. Many of Paris-based initiatives, especially monopolist companies, failed. Yet, in the second half of the seventeenth century the available evidence shows a robust growth of French trade

Geography and composition of French external trade (1550s and 1787)

All numbers are approximations

1550s imports
Total 35 million livres
Total GDP: between 200 and 400
million livres (openness rate: between 8 and 15%)

Italy and Near East	40%	Silk products	40%
German and northern states	19%	Gold and silver	26%
Spain	16%	Metals, weapons and hardware	15%
Low Countries	10%	Spices, alum and sugar	6%
England	8%	Leather products	4%
Portugal	6%	Other	8%

1787
Total imports: 645 million livres;
total exports: 530 million livres.
Total GDP: between 5 and 6 billion
livres (openness rate: between 10 and 12%)

	Imports	Exports		Imports	Exports
West Indies	29%	15%	Industrial goods	20%	34%
Great-Britain and United States	23%	12%	Agricultural goods	20%	30%
Italy, Spain and Portugal (incl. their empires)	20%	24%	Raw materials	28%	6%
Other European countries	20%	42%	Colonial goods	32%	30%
Asia and Africa	18%	9%			

SOURCE: Compiled from Braudel and Labrousse (1970–1982), Daudin (2004), and Spooner (1972).

THE GALE GROUP.

despite the wars of Louis XIV (1638–1715); for example, the number of French merchant ships of more than 100 tons doubled from 350 to 700 between 1664 and 1704.

The relatively peaceful first half of the eighteenth century was even more favorable to the growth of French external trade, which was not stopped by the wars of the second half of the century. French traders, protected by the system of the *Exclusif*, which banned foreigners from trade with the French colonies, were able to exploit the slavery-based prosperity of the West Indies (especially in what later became Haiti) to supply Europe with sugar and other colonial goods. France's traditional industries were widely exported to continental Europe. At the eve of the French Revolution, France had just overtaken Great Britain as the leading Western trading country. However, the consequences of the trade treaty (Eden-Rayneval) signed with Great Britain in 1786 revealed the weakness of France in the new sectors of the Industrial Revolution.

1790s TO THE 1910s

Civil disorder and external war had a catastrophic effect on French trade during the Revolution and the Empire, when the basis of the prosperity of the eighteenth-century colonial empire was destroyed. Trade policy became protectionist. France's 1787 openness was not recovered before the 1840s, when from that date, a number of custom duties were repealed. In 1860 France and Great Britain signed the Cobden-Chevalier treaty, which set off a movement toward free trade in Europe. In 1880 total custom duties were equal to only 8 percent of French imports. However, France came back to moderate protectionism during the Great Depression.

Imports were mainly raw materials or the new products of the Industrial Revolution. Export specialization was either in traditional agricultural exports (especially wine), luxury and semi-luxury goods, or, in the early twentieth century, new products such as cars. The new colonial empire created in Africa and Indochina provided raw materials and served as a shelter for the less-competitive French sectors. The rise of new industrial countries and France's lack of demographic and economic dynamism resulted in a relative regression of French trade, which was overtaken by the United States and Germany.

1920s TO THE PRESENT

The strength of the modern French sectors was confirmed in the trade upturn of the 1920s, but the worldwide reduction in trade in the 1930s did not spare France. After World War II the modernization of the French economy lessened the need for the protected markets supplied by the colonial empire and protectionist policy. France was able to liberalize successfully, especially with its partners in the European Economic Community (created by the Treaty of Rome in 1957). Only its agricultural sector is still protected (by the Common Agricultural Policy) against non-European producers.

The increase of the share of industrial products in imports—and the concomitant decline of the share of raw materials—is a sign of French integration in intra-industry trade patterns, in contrast with the cross-industry trade pattern of the nineteenth century. This is linked to the rising importance of Europe as a trade partner. France is in 2003 the world's fifth-largest merchandise exporter and importer.

SEE ALSO Agriculture; Balance of Payments; Blockades in War; Bonaparte, Napoleon; Bordeaux; Canals; Cargoes, Freight; Cargoes, Passenger; Colbert, Jean-Baptiste; Common Market and the European Union; Condorcet, Marie-Jean-Antoine-Nicolas de Caritat,

Marquis de; De Rhodes, Alexandre; Empire, French; Ethnic Groups, Hugenots; Free Trade, Theory and Practice; GATT, WTO; Great Depression of the 1930s; Haiti; Imperialism; Industrialization; International Trade Agreements; Iron and Steel; La Rochelle; Law, Common and Civil; Marseilles; Mediterranean; Mercantilism; Monnet, Jean; Morocco; Nantes; Nationalization; New Orleans; Paris; Pasha, Isma'il; Physiocrats; Privateering; Regional Trade Agreements; Rothschild Family; Schlumberger Family; Senegambia; Shipbuilding; Suez Canal; Vietnam; Wars; Wine.

BIBLIOGRAPHY

Braudel, Fernand, and Labrousse, Ernest. *Histoire économique et sociale de la France (French Economic and Social History)*. 4 vols. Paris: Presses Universitaires de France, 1970–1982.

Crouzet, François, ed. *The Economic Development of France since 1870*. Aldershot, U.K.: Edward Elgar, 1993.

Daudin, Guillaume. *Commerce et prospérité: La France au XVIIIe siècle (Commerce and Prosperity: 18th Century France)*. Paris: Presses Universitaires de Paris–Sorbonne, 2005.

Dormois, Jean-Pierre. *The French Economy in the Twentieth Century*. Cambridge, U.K.: Cambridge University Press, 2004.

Heywood, Colin. *The Development of the French Economy, 1750–1914*. Basingstoke, U.K.: Macmillan, 1992.

Lévy-Leboyer, Maurice, and Bourguignon, François. *The French Economy in the Nineteenth Century: An Essay in Econometric Analysis*. Cambridge, U.K.: Cambridge University Press, 1990.

Spooner, Frank. *The International Economy and Monetary Movements in France, 1493–1725*. Cambridge, MA: Harvard University Press, 1972.

Guillaume Daudin

The front of a McDonald's restaurant in Beijing, China. *McDonald's, the world's largest food-service retailer, opened its first international franchise in British Columbia, Canada, in 1967. The company's business model charges a franchise fee to individual locations, allowing them to profit from the existing brand and systems, while adhering to specific guidelines. This franchising model was used to expand overseas after the U.S. market became saturated. McDonald's first came to China in 1990.* © EYE UBIQUITOUS/CORBIS. REPRODUCED BY PERMISSION.

FRANCHISING, INTERNATIONAL

The word *franchising* comes from Old French, meaning "privilege" or "freedom." In the Middle Ages a franchise was a privilege or a right. Over the centuries the franchising concept has evolved, and this business innovation has become a remarkable success.

There are two main types of franchises: product distribution, and business format. Franchising is characterized by a network of firms in which a manufacturer or marketer of a product or service (a franchiser) grants exclusive rights to local entrepreneurs (franchisees) to conduct business in a defined area using prescribed methods over a specified time period. Franchising agreements generally create a license to use a predefined business format for the distribution of goods and services. An important part of this is a license to use intellectual-property rights related to trademarks, signs, and know-how. The franchiser who grants the license is paid a royalty by the franchisee for the use of the intellectual-property rights, the specific business format, and often a model business plan. Such agreements provide the franchiser with a low-cost, effective method of setting up a uniform network of outlets for distributing its goods or services, and access to a comparatively low-risk and well-tested method of initiating a new business. Franchise agreements are often combined with vertical restraints that may include non-compete clauses and combinations of elements of selective distribution and exclusive distribution. Many people think of fast-food restaurants such as McDonald's when they think of franchising, but there are many other types of franchising businesses: homes are bought and sold through franchised real-estate companies, and we can have our hair cut, clothes cleaned, pets cared for, or travel across the world using franchised businesses.

Product-distribution franchises sell the franchiser's products; they are supplier-dealer relationships. In product distribution the franchiser licenses its trademark and logo to the franchisees, but usually does not supply them with an integrated system to run their businesses. This is the model for soft-drinks distributors, automobile dealers, and gas stations.

The first wave of business franchises, known as tied-house systems, sprang up in the eighteenth century among German brewers, who contracted with taverns to sell their brand of beer exclusively. The second wave appeared in the nineteenth century when the U.S.-founded Singer Sewing Machine Company sold their products to its sales force, who in turn had to find markets for them. This type of arrangement, known as product–trade name franchising, involves using franchisees to distribute a product under a franchiser's trademark. Around the turn of the nineteenth century oil-refinery firms and automobile manufacturers began to grant the rights to sell their products, and gas stations and automobile dealerships grew rapidly as franchises after World War I.

It is no coincidence that this second wave of franchising—product–trade name franchising—occurred at the time when branded products were coming into vogue. Improvements in transportation and communications made it possible to cost-effectively stimulate the broad demand for branded products for the first time in history. Franchisers of this era discovered that franchising could solve distribution problems with someone else's capital while simultaneously expanding the reach and value of their brands.

A&W Restaurants developed the third wave of franchising, known as the business format, or "package," in the twentieth century. This type of franchising has franchisees replicate in their local communities an entire business concept, including product, trade name, and methods of operation. For example, McDonald's provides its franchisees with a tested menu, a global brand-name, store location and design, operating procedures, specialized equipment, advertising, and continuous training through its Hamburger University. This entire "package" is the format. This form has accounted for most of the unit growth of franchising since 1950, and became the most common type of franchise by the 1980s.

The postwar U.S. baby boom and consumer boom contributed to the expansion of the hotel/motel and fast-food industries. The fast-growing franchise industry in the 1960s and the 1970s created opportunities as well as

Local citizens in Kuwait stand outside a Starbucks coffee shop. Starbucks, founded in Seattle in 1971, expanded its concept of retail coffee shops across the country without franchising its locations. However, the company has franchised with local partners in various countries, such as in Kuwait, which was the first outlet to open in the Middle East. © ED KASHI/CORBIS. REPRODUCED BY PERMISSION

abuses (e.g., fraudulent companies that took peoples' money and did not deliver). The International Franchise Association was founded in 1960 with the goal of strengthening the entire industry.

The fourth wave of franchising offers "innovative" solutions, including the use of strategic alliances based on franchising principles to cut costs while generating new sources of revenues. Introducing movie-based action figures through fast-food outlets is one example. Franchising has emerged in recent years as a highly significant strategy for business growth, job creation, and economic development. As a result, franchising is becoming one of the most popular entry strategies for international retail companies moving into international markets. It can provide increased control over distribution and marketing without the obligations of ownership. It provides an evolved way of managing intangible assets, such as quality and brand, often more successfully than traditional in-house processes and systems.

In addition, economic developments play a major role in the formation and success of franchising. Over the last several decades the West has witnessed a major shift from what was primarily a manufacturing economy to one dominated by service businesses. During this same period, the franchising concept has matured with the development and rapid success of business-format and strategic alliances. The parallel growth in the service sector and in franchising has demonstrated how franchising's primary attributes (capital formation, motivated entrepreneurs, standard systems and procedures of control operations) can solve the inherent problems faced by most service firms (small size, intangibility of services, and quality control).

As franchising has matured in the United States, and as markets for certain franchised products and services have become saturated (such as fast-food franchisers), international opportunities have developed at an unprecedented rate. Many other countries are experiencing trends similar to those that made franchising so successful in the United States. Improvements in transportation and communication systems have made controlling foreign franchisees easier, and many Western innovations have met with rapid consumer acceptance, facilitating high levels of global standardization.

The format franchise has grown enormously in recent years. The 1980s and 1990s were periods of rapid international expansion for business-format franchises. The success of U.S. franchisers abroad often spawned imitators who set up franchising systems of their own. The development of international franchising by non-U.S. franchisers has been swift (e.g., Benetton, the Italian-based clothing franchiser with licensed outlets worldwide).

The most common foreign-entry modes used by franchisers have been by direct investment (subsidiary), joint ventures, and granting rights to a master franchisee that in turn subcontracts to local franchisees. Of these, selling a master franchise is currently the most popular and fastest way of entering foreign markets. Although there may be a danger of loss of control and relaxed standards, this entry mode can be used when foreign regulations are relatively restrictive, political and economic risk is high, and the franchiser lacks resources in a particular country.

Format franchisers have expand internationally by "rolling out" the standardized "packages" that have been successful in their home markets. Therefore, initial foreign markets have been selected because they are proximate and similar to the home market. However, as fran-chisers have expanded across foreign borders to more distant markets and diverse cultures, such as Southeast Asia or Eastern Europe, some franchising systems have been adapted from their original uses in the home markets in terms of product, place, price, and marketing strategy.

SEE ALSO Globalization, Pro and Con; Jardine Matheson.

BIBLIOGRAPHY

Alon, I. "Global Franchising and Development in Emerging and Transitioning Markets." *Journal of Macromarketing* 24, no. 2 (December 2004): 156–167.

Preble, John F., and Hoffman, C. R. "Franchising Systems Around the Globe: A Status Report." *Journal of Small Business Management* 33, no. 2 (April 1995): 80–88.

Stanworth, J., and Curran, J. "Colas, Burgers, Shakes, and Shirkers: Towards a Sociological Model of Franchising in the Economy." *Journal of Business Venturing* 14 (July 1999): 323–344.

Welch, Lawrence S. "Diffusion of Franchise Systems Use in International Operations." *International Marketing Review* 6, no. 5 (1989): 7–19.

Alfredo Manuel Coelho

FREE PORTS

Free ports—in which merchants of all nationalities could establish themselves without fear of discrimination and where the entrance of goods, especially those intended for reexportation, was free of taxes—constitute an extremely important phenomenon in the history of world trade. They date from the early modern period. Although previously there had been franchises and privileges in several ports, their limited character, in the double sense that they only affected merchants of a given nationality and that they did not involve the suppression of customs duties, means that there were no free ports before the sixteenth century.

Livorno (sometimes called Leghorn in English), Italy, constitutes one of the earliest and best examples of an early modern free port. An outer port of Pisa, and of Tuscany in general, Livorno owes its importance to the decision by Cosimo I (1519–1574) and Fernando I de Medici (1541–1587) to facilitate the establishment of foreign merchants in the city, regardless of their nationality or religion. The first regulations to achieve this were enacted in 1566, 1592, and 1593, although the franchising of goods coming into the city did not become general practice until 1676.

Livorno's fortune could not go unnoticed by its neighbors, especially since at that time markets were considered to be static, so that the growth of any one port

Gibraltar, a British territory located on the southern coast of Spain. *Gibraltar is a major port linking the Mediterranean Sea and the North Atlantic Ocean. Because of its free-port status, many of the world's shipping lines use it as a key destination along their trade routes.* © STEPHANIE COLASANTI/ CORBIS. REPRODUCED BY PERMISSION.

had to come at the expense of its neighbors; thus Genoa and Marseilles competed with Livorno for commercial supremacy in the western Mediterranean. The method used was the Declaration of Free Ports, a measure taken in 1609 for Genoa and in 1669 for Marseilles. However, neither of them was ever quite as open as Livorno, especially in relation to foreign merchants; this helped Livorno remain the region's main port for merchants from Northern Europe and the western Mediterranean. The franchises awarded to Marseilles did nevertheless stimulate industrial as well as commercial activity there.

From the seventeenth century onward the number of free ports continued to increase. The authorities intended the franchises granted to certain ports—always in limited numbers, so as not to reduce the income from customs duties—to be used to modify the direction of international traffic to the benefit of the country. During the late eighteenth century the main free ports of the Mediterranean region from west to east were: Gibraltar (1706), Marseilles (1669), Nice-Villefranche (1613 and 1666), Genoa (1609), Livorno (1676), Civitavecchia (1630 and 1696), Messina (1732), Ancona (1732), Trieste (1719), Fiume (1719), and Malta (1800). On the Atlantic coast, from south to north, they were Bayonne (1784), Lorient (1785), Dunkirk (1662, 1681), Ostend (1719), the Hanseatic cities Altona, Denmark (1664), and Marstrand, Sweden (1772).

The two greatest commercial powers of early modern Europe—the United Provinces and Great Britain— did not consider the existence of free ports to be necessary. The duties demanded in Dutch ports and, to a lesser extent, in British ports, were so low that there was no need for free ports to maintain competitiveness. The proof that the Dutch and British were not hostile towards the establishment of free ports *per se* can be found in America. All the commercial powers in the Caribbean and West Indies—with the exception of Spain— established free ports in order to vie with their rivals for the continent's markets and to channel the outward silver and colonial products. The main ports enjoying this status were: Curaçao (1675) and St. Eustatius (1737), belonging to the United Provinces; St. Thomas and St. John (1764), which belonged to Denmark; Martinique and Guadeloupe, which belonged to France; Jamaica and Dominica (1766), belonging to Great Britain; and St. Bartholomew (1784), which belonged to Sweden.

FROM FREE PORTS TO FREE ZONES

The end of the *ancien régime* (old regime) and the reorganization of the European and American political maps ended free ports as they had been known before. In the name of equality among all French citizens, but also as a means to combat contraband and to reduce competition from foreign products, the Government of the Convention abolished free ports in 1794. The unification of Italy, likewise, brought with it the disappearance of free ports from 1866 to 1872 onward, as the national government claimed Italy's political and economic unity was incompatible with the maintenance of special customs regimes. Meanwhile, free ports in the Caribbean and West Indies declined as the new Latin American states opened direct trade with the United States and maritime powers of Europe.

The place that was once occupied by free ports was taken over, from the end of the nineteenth century, by other forms of organization of international trade, including free zones. Unlike free ports, whose franchises extended to entire cities, free zones are clearly demarcated spaces within a port or city, where goods can be introduced without paying customs duties and without being subject to any type of fiscal inspection. These goods can be stored, classified, manufactured, and finally exported without paying customs duties, unless they are going inland, in which case the relevant taxes must be paid.

Before World War I, European free zones were in the old Hanseatic cities of Hamburg and Bremen, which only entered the German customs union in 1888 in exchange for free-zone status and large investments in their port facilities. Copenhagen (1892), Genoa (1877), Trieste

(1891), and Fiume (1891) had similar arrangements. France and Spain had extensive debates about the establishment of free zones in some of their ports beginning in the late nineteenth century. The opponents of free zones claimed the franchises awarded to certain ports in the country would have a negative effect on the others: they would facilitate contraband and they would intensify the competition from foreign products. Besides, to what extent could the success of ports such as Hamburg be attributed to the existence of a free zone? Had the ports of Antwerp and Rotterdam not experienced growths similar to—if not greater than—that of the port of Hamburg, without the existence of a free zone? Could profits similar to those expected from the free zones not be obtained through a different set of measures, such as the establishment of a temporary admissions regime for goods, that is, the free import of goods as long as they are exported in the same conditions or remanufactured within a short period of time?

The increase in the number of free zones in countries where they already existed, and the spread of the system to many others that previously lacked them, leaves little doubt that those in favor of free zones managed to convince public opinion and governments of the advantages. In the United States the 1934 Foreign Trade Zones Act authorized the establishment of "free ports" in the country, but with a prohibition on manufacturing. The first to open was New York, in 1937. Since then the number of foreign trade zones has continued to increase, and currently there are more than 600 worldwide. Many of them are no longer found on coasts, but inland, near international airports or near borders. The franchises that Singapore and Hong Kong have offered since 1823 and 1841, respectively, extend to the totality of their territories, making them authentic free ports. Singapore and Hong Kong head the ranking of the most active ports in the world. Along with their excellent geographical locations and their free-port status, their success can also be explained by the perfection of their infrastructures and the efficiency of the banking and insurance services they provide to economic agents operating there, as well as by their intense industrial activity.

SEE ALSO CALCUTTA; CARTAGENA; CHARLESTON; GDANSK; HARBORS; HAVANA; HONG KONG; LA ROCHELLE; LISBON; LIVERPOOL; LONDON; LOS ANGELES–LONG BEACH; MADRAS; MELAKA; MUMBAI; NAGASAKI; NANTES; NAVIGATION ACTS; NEW ORLEANS; NEWPORT; NEW YORK; ROTTERDAM; SHANGHAI; SHIPPING LANES; SHIPS AND SHIPPING; SINGAPORE; SMUGGLING; SYDNEY; VERACRUZ; YOKOHAMA.

BIBLIOGRAPHY

Armytage, Frances. *The Free Port System in the British West Indies: A Study in Commercial Policy, 1766–1822.* London: Longman, Green and Company, 1953.

Kirk, Thomas. "Genoa and Livorno: Sixteenth- and Seventeenth-Century Commercial Rivalry as a Stimulus to Policy Development." *History*, vol. 86, issue 281 (January 2001): 3–17.

Masson, Paul. *Ports francs d'autrefois et d'aujourd'hui (Yesterday and Today Free Ports)* (trans.). París: Hachette, 1904.

Trampus, Francesca. *Free Ports of the World.* Trieste, Italy: Edizioni Universitá di Trieste, 1999.

José-Ignacio Martínez Ruiz

FREE TRADE, THEORY AND PRACTICE

The term *free trade* usually refers to the free exchange and movement of goods without any restraints from the state. In its purest form, free trade in international commerce would imply a complete lack of tariffs, quotas, or other barriers to the import and export of goods.

THEORY AND PRACTICE THROUGH THE NINETEENTH CENTURY

Although it is almost never observed in practice, free trade and the general problem of optimal commercial policy have been of interest wherever cities, kingdoms, regions, and nation-states have had jurisdiction over the economy. Coherent arguments over the desirability of free trade or trade restrictions were mostly coincident with the birth of modern economic thought in seventeenth- and eighteenth-century Europe.

The modern nation-state, with its expanded administrative capacity and its overarching need for revenue to maintain large armies and to conduct increasingly expensive wars, found that commercial policy often overlapped with questions of foreign policy. Considerations of trade and tariff were often interspersed with concerns about which countries the people should be allowed to trade with. Early arguments about free trade were mostly advanced in a negative form. Many writers in the seventeenth century felt that trade should be an extension of foreign policy, and that restricting trade to ensure a surplus of exports over imports contributed to a nation's prosperity.

The clearest statement of this view comes from Thomas Mun (1571–1641), who wrote that "the ordinary means therefore to increase our wealth and treasure is by foreign trade, wherein we must ever observe this rule; to sell more to strangers yearly than we consume of theirs in value" (1664, p. 11). This view—often labeled *mercantilism*—associated wealth with the hoarding of precious metals and coin or specie. For the mercantilists, trade was war, and they assumed that for every trade winner there was a trade loser.

Other writers criticized this view, but the mature expression of this view came about with the work of Adam Smith (1723–1790) in his book *An Inquiry into the Nature and Causes of the Wealth of Nations* (1776). Smith noted that wealth did not rely on specie or bills of exchange, but instead came about through the enrichment of a nation's inhabitants through trade. Voluntary trade was mutually beneficial, and extensive trade served to promote specialization, which led to greater gains from trade. Furthermore, it made no sense to think about promoting permanent surpluses because countervailing forces existed that moved in the opposite direction. It was the circulation of goods and services that was the true lifeblood of the nation. Modern economists would say that the mercantilists ignored the equilibrium considerations of world trade, in which surpluses would be self-correcting. Mercantilists were also mistaken in that trade was really a positive-sum game that enhanced the welfare of both parties to the exchange.

David Ricardo (1772–1823) further advanced these ideas and developed the theoretical models that were to establish the modern literature on international trade. All nations would benefit if they produced goods in which they had a comparative advantage while trading with each other. This idea is especially deep and profound, and it is often mistakenly confused with absolute advantage, in which one nation can produce all goods more cheaply than any other. But comparative advantage merely requires that one produce goods which have the lowest relative opportunity cost. Hence, all nations have a comparative advantage in something.

Despite the theoretical interest in free trade, and the immense importance accorded by intellectuals and politicians to the influences of Smith, David Hume (1711–1776), and other thinkers of the Scottish Enlightenment, few nations cared to adhere to such a policy. Often this did not stem so much from any ideological considerations as from practical ones. The state needed revenue, and taxing trade—both international and domestic—was often the most convenient means of acquiring income. Furthermore, then as now, special interests often benefited from restricting or controlling commerce, and were able to influence national policy to suit their demands.

Prior to the eighteenth century, only the Netherlands worked to promote anything vaguely resembling a free-trade policy with relatively modest mercantilist restrictions. Scholars have usually attributed its economic success to Holland's development of both domestic and international trade, and especially to the gains derived from the nation's leadership in expanding European trade.

Nonetheless, Holland was no doctrinaire free trader, and used tariffs and regulations to suit the needs of the state.

There are exceptions to the general arguments about free trade, notably the cases in which a nation has a high degree of monopoly power in the world market, or in which tariffs are used to protect infant industries for a limited time period. The former case requires that the market leader establish an optimal tariff but go no higher, and it presumes that other states do not retaliate by imposing tariffs in return. Ironically, it is often the states that have no market power to influence world prices, and hence gain nothing from protection, that are among the likeliest to impose tariff barriers. Similarly, the rare case of infant-industry protection requires temporary tariff protections for some fledgling industries. Again, the political economy of government regulation usually leads to established industries in decline getting the bulk of protection. Even when infant industries are properly shielded, the temporary restrictions turn into permanent barriers that are difficult to remove once they have exceeded their usefulness.

Customs duties, and to a lesser degree, prohibitions and quotas, were the central tools of the state. The income derived therefrom accounted for a significant share of the budgets of the leading Western nations. Britain became especially dependent on customs and excise duties of various sorts, particularly on goods such as wines, linens, and silks, which featured prominently in the trade of her great, rival France. This policy of restricting wine imports, especially French, was the outcome of the almost continual struggles between Britain and France from the late 1600s to the end of the Napoleonic Wars in 1815. These wars led to nearly prohibitive duties on French products, notably wine and spirits that were meant to discriminate against the French and in favor of British beer and spirits, colonial products, and alcohol from friendly nations, especially Portugal.

When changes in the political and ideological climate moved Britain toward the promotion of free trade in the nineteenth century, the nation was hindered in these efforts by the importance of special interests arising from long-standing restrictions on trade. Efforts to lower tariffs dramatically began to take effect after the 1840s when a variety of agricultural restrictions known as the Corn Laws were removed. The period from 1842 to 1860 saw the removal of virtually all the major tariffs except those on coffee, tea, sugar, tobacco, wine, and spirits, which remained important obstacles to full free trade.

Eventually, the rise of a promarket ruler in France—Napoleon III (1808–1873)—coupled with a much weakened agricultural and brewing lobby in Britain led to the signing in 1860 of the Anglo-French Treaty of Commerce, a bilateral trade agreement of truly historic significance. This treaty between the leading powers of Europe caused almost all the other European nations to sign bilateral, most-favored-nation agreements with Britain and France throughout the 1860s, thus linking Europe into an extremely free and open market—in some ways, more open than the European Union today. The late nineteenth century was also a period of unprecedented economic growth in Western Europe, with rising standards of living at all levels of society, interrupted only by the coming of World War I.

THEORY AND PRACTICE IN THE TWENTIETH CENTURY

Today, arguments for and against trade have shifted away from issues of economic growth towards social concerns. The most notable of these objections comes in the form of the anti-globalization movement. This is a difficult group to pin down because globalization is a rather vague concept, and the objections to it are varied and often incoherent. Oftentimes, the objections amount to criticisms of markets *per se,* whether or not international commerce is involved.

The most focused of the arguments against globalization and increased international trade either rehash old protectionist arguments or point to the plight of those working in inefficient industries that are displaced by trade. The latter is a serious issue that should be addressed properly by aiding the workers retraining, moving, and transferring to different industries. Most of the time, however, attempts to shield people in such industries merely postpone the inevitable, and create widespread harm throughout the economy that is less concentrated and visible but that is more damaging in the long run. Moreover, most of the changes in industry that lead to moving factories or work abroad have less to do with international trade than with technological change. Even in a world of limited international trade, high rates of technological innovation would mean that certain industries would decline. New innovations often work by destroying old markets and old ways of doing business. This, more than trade, is responsible for the unrest associated with globalization.

A more serious set of potential problems arises with the environment. If there are externalities rising from missing markets, as is the case with airborne pollutants, then trade will tend to exacerbate these problems. But here again, the culprit is not trade *per se,* but rather externalities. Air pollution due to missing markets is a problem whether or not international trade is brought in. Moreover, complaints about the environmental effects of trade often mask the conflict between rich and poor nations. Richer nations are liable to be more willing to trade economic growth for lower pollution. Poor countries

might reasonably worry less about clean air when the problem of simply feeding their populations is most acute. Here too, the market solution would encourage tradable pollution rights, which would benefit all participants, and it would encourage rich nations with a stronger interest in a cleaner environment to make side payments to the poorer ones.

Most of all, cutting off trade has dynamic effects. Most of the time, the poorest nations are those with the most dysfunctional governments, full of corruption, inefficiency, and nonliberal institutions. Trade tends to put some pressure on nations and firms to become more efficient. The more open the trade, the harder it is to keep weak industries going purely for the benefit of a small group. Vested interests work to limit change. Historians Stephen Parente and Edward Prescott (2001) noted that laws were often used to stifle innovation, such as the limits on increasing the number of looms per worker in India in the early twentieth century. This, coupled with high textile tariffs, contributed to the relative decline of Indian textiles in competition with Japan. It is not a surprise that all of the most closed economies today—such as North Korea—are also among the poorest and most backward.

Despite all the arguments for and against free trade, it is not the science that seems to matter. Unsurprisingly, the tariffs most often observed in the real world do not conform to any theoretically efficient regime, and are better explained in terms of interest-group politics rather than putative efficiency. Furthermore, the professional consensus notwithstanding, free trade has always had very mixed public support, as the benefits are usually diffuse and slow in spreading, whereas those adversely affected are visible and concentrated.

SEE ALSO GLOBALIZATION; MOST-FAVORED-NATION PROVISIONS; THEORIES OF INTERNATIONAL TRADE.

BIBLIOGRAPHY

Irwin, Douglas A. *Against the Tide: An Intellectual History of Free Trade.* Princeton, NJ: Princeton University Press, 1996.

Mun, Thomas. *England's Treasure by Forraign Trade.* [1664], Fairfield, NJ: A. M. Kelley, 1986.

Nye, John V. C. "The Myth of Free Trade Britain and Fortress France: Tariffs and Trade in the Nineteenth Century." *Journal of Economic History* 51, no. 1 (March 1991): 23–46.

Parente, Stephen L., and Prescott, Edward C. *Barriers to Riches (Walras-Pareto Lectures).* Cambridge, MA: Massachusetts Institute of Technology, 2001.

Schonhardt-Bailey, Cheryl, ed. *The Rise of Free Trade,* Vol. 1: *Protectionism and Its Critics, 1815–1837.* London: Edward Elgar, 1997.

Smith, Adam. *An Inquiry into the Nature and Causes of the Wealth of Nations.* [1776]. 1981, 1976 Liberty Classics reprint of the Oxford Press edition of 1976, Indianapolis, Indiana. 2 vols.

John V. C. Nye

FUGGER FAMILY

The Fugger family dates back to fourteenth-century Augsburg, Swabia, where they worked in the textile business (fustions). In the following century they founded a merchant house (*Handlung*) and entered into investments in silver and copper mining. They became famous in 1488 when they received the use of the silver mine at Schwaz in exchange for a loan of 150,000 florins to Archduke Sigismund the *Münzreiche* of Tyrol, who became famous for his monetary reform, such as a the creation of heavy silver coins. They acquired a silver and later a copper monopoly in Tirol and Hungary (Slovakia) because neither Sigismund nor his successor Maximilian paid back the growing debt. This encouraged the Fuggers into further lending, led by Jacob Fugger the rich (1459–1525) in favor of Habsburg rulers. In 1519 Jacob Fugger raised 543,585 florins of the bribes necessary for the royal election of the young King Charles (the later Emperor Charles V). By this means the Fuggers hoped to gain royal imperial support against the anti-monopoly and anti-usury campaign directed by the German *Reichstag* against the South German merchant houses.

The imperial military expeditions against the Turks, France, and later of Spain during the Dutch revolt required continuous credits. The Fuggers lent the Emperor money at Antwerp or supplied him with money via an exchange market elsewhere. The money was to be redeemed on the Castilian Fairs (Medina del Campo) or in Seville by assignments to Spanish fiscal income or the expected silver fleets. However, with the first Spanish state bankruptcy decree (1557), all payments of assignments to fiscal income were suspended, the precious metals of the incoming fleets confiscated. Since the Fuggers remained with the Spanish crown, trying to realize at least some of the claims, they witnessed more losses in the following Spanish state bankruptcies of 1575 and 1607. However, they avoided the fate of the Welsers, who went bankrupt in 1614, due to the suspension of payments by France and Spain. The Fuggers later retired to their landed estates. They were replaced by other Augsburg merchant bankers such as the Paler, who tried to combine foreign trade with (deposit) banking and industrial development, avoiding the risks of credits to a sole powerful debtor. There was neither specialization nor innovation in the business of the Fuggers, which represented, above all, the most developed form of the late-medieval family companies, differing from their predecessors only with respect to their worldwide activities and the concentra-tion on Habsburg rulers. With regard to their exchange business they resembled the Italian merchant bankers of the Middle Ages. They maintained a wide network of branches and factors in the major markets and exchange places of Europe, aiming primarily to advance funds by bills of exchange, making big profits by exploiting the fluctuations of the money markets.

SEE ALSO BANKING; FINANCE, CREDIT AND MONEY LENDING; GERMANY.

BIBLIOGRAPHY

Ehrenberg, Richard. *Das Zeitalter der Fugger: Geldkapital und Kredite im 16. Jahrhundert*, vol. 1: Die Geldmächte des 16. Jahrhunderts, Hildesheim 1990, p. 185f.

Kellenbenz, Hermann. *Die Fugger in Spanien und Portugal bis 1560 – ein Großunternehmen des 16. Jahrhunderts*, vol. 1, München 1990, pp. 98ff., pp. 245ff.

North, Michael. "The Great German Banking Houses and European Merchants, 16th–19th Centuries." In *Banking, Trade, and Industry, Europe, America, and Asia from the Thirteenth to the Twentieth Century,* ed. Alice Teichova, Ginette Kurgan van Hentenryk, and Dieter Ziegler. Cambridge, U.K.: Cambridge University Press, 1997.

Van der Wee, Herman. "Monetary, Credit, and Banking Systems." In *The Cambridge Economic History of Europe,* vol. 5: *The Economic Organization of Early Modern Europe,* ed. E. E. Rich and C. Wilson. Cambridge, U.K.: Cambridge University Press, 1977.

Michael North

FURS

Furs can be classified as either fancy or staple. Fancy furs are those demanded for the luster and beauty of their pelts—fox, mink, or ermine—and are fashioned by furriers into garments. Staple furs are sought for the quality of their wool, which is the short, softer hair that grows next to the animal skin protected by long, stiff hair called guard hairs. Although a commercial trade in both of these types of furs has existed for centuries, from the early sixteenth century the commercial trade shifted to North America. Starting from a haphazard exchange between fishermen and Native Americans, by the end of the seventeenth century there was an organized trade through Montreal, Albany, and Hudson Bay. Trade from Montreal went north and southwest. Only with Jay's Treaty was this separated into two distinct trades. Jay's Treaty in 1794 defined the boundary between the United States and Canada. The trade from Montreal, which had gone southwest, became the American Fur Company, and the trade to the northwest became the Northwest Company.

The shift from Europe to North America was due to depletion and over-exploitation of the European stocks.

What made North America an excellent source of supply was both the relatively unexploited nature of the area and the severity of the winters in the subarctic regions of the continent. In addition, prior to the introduction of a commercial trade, animal pelts were used for clothing and internal trade; with a commercial trade, pelts could be used to purchase European trade goods. Indians were the primary agents in the North American commercial fur trade; they hunted and traded the pelts to European intermediaries in a voluntary exchange.

Native American traders were astute, purchasing only those commodities that met their specifications. In addition to necessities such as iron pots, awls, blankets, and guns, Indians consumed a remarkable variety of luxury goods—beads, combs, mirrors, rings, shirts, and hats. The share of their expenditure on luxury goods increased dramatically.

The ability of native traders to purchase such a wide range of European commodities was the result of a strong and growing demand in Europe for beaver and felt hats and thus for the staple pelts used in their manufacture. Although styles changed, the material used to make men's hats remained a constant—wool felt. By the sixteenth century, beaver wool came to dominate. The beaver hat remained the height of fashion until the introduction of the silk hat in the nineteenth century.

The transformation of beaver skins into felt and then hats is a highly skilled process. First the short hairs must be separated from the pelt. In Russia, where there was a long tradition of working with beaver, felters had perfected a technology of combing the beaver pelts to remove the wool hairs. Despite attempts to keep the technology secret, combing became known in Western Europe by 1700 and brought an end to the export of English and French pelts to Archangel, Russia, and reimportation of combed wool.

Separating the beaver wool was only the first step. Normally these hairs are covered in keratin, but to make felt some of the barbs on the hairs must be open. Felters experimented, often unsuccessfully, with ways to do this. Furs imported from North America generated a subset of furs whose guard hairs had been removed and the keratin broken down. These were pelts worn by the Indians and called *coat beaver*, or *castor gras*. Parchment beaver, or *castor sec*, were those furs which were simply dried before being traded. The constraint of fixed proportions of coat and parchment beaver was relaxed with the introduction of a chemical process called *carrotting*, which turned parchment into pseudo-coat beaver. The process consisted of diluting salts of mercury in nitric acid, which was brushed on the pelt. Unfortunately, felters and hat-ters were forced to breathe the mercury vapor, with serious consequences for their nervous systems—thus the phrase *mad as a hatter.*

A commercial trade continued in Canada through the twentieth century. The influence of animal-rights organizations led the Hudson's Bay Company to close its fur division in the 1990s, with serious losses for Canada's First Nations, a generic Canadian term meaning the aboriginal peoples collectively.

SEE ALSO ASTOR FAMILY; CANADA; LABORERS, NATIVE AMERICAN, EASTERN WOODLAND AND FAR WESTERN; TEXTILES; UNITED STATES.

BIBLIOGRAPHY

Carlos, Ann M., and Lewis, Frank D. "Indians, the Beaver, and the Bay: The Economics of Depletion in the Lands of the Hudson's Bay Company 1700–1763." *Journal of Economic History* 53, no. 3 (1993): 465–494.

Carlos, Ann M., and Lewis, Frank D. "Trade, Consumption, and the Native Economy: Lessons from York Factory, Hudson Bay." *Journal of Economic History* 61, no. 4 (2001): 465–494.

Carlos, Ann M., and Lewis, Frank D. "Marketing in the Land of Hudson Bay: Indian Consumers and the Hudson's Bay Company, 1670–1770." *Enterprise and Society* 2 (2002): 285–317.

Crean, J. F. "Hats and the Fur Trade." *Canadian Journal of Economics and Political Science* 28, no. 3 (1962): 373–386.

Corner, David. "The Tyranny of Fashion: The Case of the Felt-Hatting Trade in the Late Seventeenth and Eighteenth Centuries." *Textile History* 22, no.2 (1991): 153–178.

De Vries, Jan. "Between Purchasing Power and the World of Goods: Understanding the Household Economy in Early Modern Europe." In *Consumption and the World of Goods,* ed. John Brewer and Roy Porter. London: Routledge, 1993.

Ginsburg, Madeleine. *The Hat: Trends and Traditions.* London: Studio Editions, 1990.

Harte, N. B. "The Economics of Clothing in the Late Seventeenth Century." *Textile History* 22, no. 2 (1991): 277–296.

Heidenreich, Conrad E., and Ray, Arthur J. *The Early Fur Trade: A Study in Cultural Interaction.* Toronto: McClelland and Stewart, 1976.

Innis, Harold. *The Fur Trade in Canada,* revised edition. Toronto: University of Toronto Press, 1956.

Lawson, Murray G. *Fur: A Study in English Mercantilism.* Toronto: University of Toronto Press, 1943.

Ray, Arthur J., and Freeman, Donald Freeman. *"Give Us Good Measure": An Economic Analysis of Relations Between the Indians and the Hudson's Bay Company before 1763.* Toronto: University of Toronto Press, 1978.

Ann M. Carlos

VASCO DA GAMA
1469?–1524

Vasco da Gama was born in Portugal, probably in 1469, and died in India, at Cochin on the southwest coast, on Christmas Eve, 1524. From 1497 to 1499 he commanded a fleet that made the first direct sea voyage from Europe to Asia via the Cape of Good Hope. Gama's voyage from Lisbon to Calicut in India was the culmination of a century of Portuguese expeditions, which slowly advanced down the west coast of Africa until the Cape of Good Hope was rounded in 1488. Ten years later Gama also rounded the Cape, and then sailed up the East African coast and over the Arabian Sea to India. He returned to India twice as head of the Portuguese in Asia.

For many centuries before Gama there had been extensive trade between the Indian Ocean and the Mediterranean. Goods were transported from the Indian Ocean through either the Persian Gulf or the Red Sea, and then overland to the Mediterranean. The route via the Cape made it much easier to transport goods from the Indian Ocean to Europe, for this was a nonstop route that did not require goods to be transferred from ship to land transport and back to ship.

SEE ALSO EMPIRE, PORTUGUESE; INDIA; LISBON; SHIPS AND SHIPPING.

BIBLIOGRAPHY
Disney, Anthony, and Booth, Emily, eds. *Vasco da Gama and the Linking of Europe and Asia.* New Delhi: Oxford University Press, 2000
Subrahmanyam, Sanjay. *The Career and Legend of Vasco da Gama.* New York: Cambridge University Press, 1997.

Michael N. Pearson

BILL GATES
1955–

Bill Gates is one of the wealthiest and most successful entrepreneurs in world history. His biography is inseparable from Microsoft, a globally dominant corporation that he cofounded and for which he serves as the "chairman and chief software architect." Gates's interest in computer programs first developed when he was a teenager at the Lakeside School in Seattle, Washington. Gates entered Harvard University but left in his junior year. He and Paul Allen launched the Microsoft company in 1975. Microsoft bought the rights to BASIC programming software and adapted it to the Altair personal computer. This first venture showed foresight, innovation, and impeccable judgment, and Gates subsequently applied the same business model to garner a commanding lead over competitors in the software industry. In 1980 Microsoft entered into a critical contract with IBM to license the DOS operating system for use on IBM personal computers. Microsoft went public in 1986 at an initial public offering of $21 per share (valued around $8,000 in 2004). In the 1990s the company introduced its flagship Windows program and successfully promoted the Internet Explorer web browser. Federal, state, and international antitrust agencies since 1990 have engaged in persistent scrutiny into the legality of Microsoft's business practices. The Bill and Melinda Gates Foundation has made unparalleled philanthropic contributions to global health, education, and welfare, employing innovative policies that remedy existing market failures in areas such as the development and delivery of vaccines against tropical diseases.

SEE ALSO CAPITALISM.

BIBLIOGRAPHY

Gates, Bill, with Nathan Myhrvold, and Peter Rinearson. *The Road Ahead.* New York: Viking Press, 1995.

B. Zorina Khan

GATT, WTO

Between the collapse of the New York Stock Exchange in 1929, sparking the Great Depression, and the end of World War II in 1945, international trade came to a virtual standstill. A war immediately stops trading activities between the nations at war with one another, and it reduces international trade by sea between allied nations because there is a greater risk of vessels being attacked. Also, during an economic downturn, many companies fail, and those that remain functioning tend to focus on less risky transactions with known customers who are usually domestic rather than international.

A priority for trading nations at the end of World War II was to promote the recovery of international trade as soon as possible. Another priority was to put in place measures that would prevent another catastrophe like the Great Depression. In an effort led by the United States, which had taken over from Britain as the leader in world trade, three international organizations were planned to regulate global economic and trade activities.

POST–WORLD WAR II ORGANIZATIONS

The International Trade Organization (ITO) was designed to regulate international trade and to dissolve barriers to trade. The International Monetary Fund (IMF) was to address the balance-of-payments problems (of countries that spent more than they earned). The World Bank was to regulate international investment (regarding companies that invest their money in commercial operations in another country). Although the IMF and the World Bank came into existence, the ITO did not.

The charter proposed for the ITO, known as the Havana Charter, was completed in 1948. It provided for the establishment of a permanent trade organization that would create legal obligations for the United States, and for this reason the U.S. Congress would not approve it. Even though the United States was to be just one member of the ITO, it was the dominant trading nation, and a trade organization without it as a member would not hold much influence. Therefore, the ITO was not established.

THE GATT

While the Havana Charter was being drafted, governments negotiated with one another to reduce their trade barriers. An example of a trade barrier is a quota restriction, where a country places a limit on the quantity of a particular type of good that can be imported. Another example of a trade barrier is a customs tariff, which is a charge a country taxes on goods that are imported. That charge is paid by the importer of the goods, who then has to charge more for the goods in order to recover the cost. This has the effect of making the foreign imported goods sell at a higher price, which means they are less competitive compared to domestically made goods, which have no such additional charge attached to them. Therefore, the customs tariff was a barrier to trade because foreign companies were more likely to consider it unprofitable to export their goods, and as such, the domestic industry was protected.

The negotiations between governments led to the signing in 1947 of a provisional international agreement for the lowering of trade barriers, known as the General Agreement on Tariffs and Trade (GATT). The main aims of the GATT were to reduce the ways nations favored their domestic industries to just one type of trade barrier, the tariff, and secondly, to progressively negotiate the reduction of tariffs.

When the ITO failed to come about, the GATT became the main way international trade was regulated. The nations that were part of it were called *contracting parties* rather than *member states* because there was no organization of which to be members; rather, each GATT was a contract between them. Decisions on the GATT were made collectively, and the GATT was updated over a forty-eight-year period in a series of negotiations known as *rounds*.

There were eight rounds of the GATT, in 1947, 1949, 1951, 1956, 1960 to 1962, 1962 to 1967, 1973 to 1979, and 1986 to 1994. The rounds took gradually more time, with the eighth round taking eight years, because they became more complex. Over time, the focus expanded from trade in goods to trade in services, then to new issues such as intellectual property (protection of things such as trading names and symbols, known as trademarks, and inventions that were patented to allow the inventor time to trade without competition). Also, other groups were created that fed into the negotiations, such as the United Nations Conference on Trade and Development (UNCTAD), which focused on the special needs of the poorer, developing countries.

THE WTO

The eighth round (1986–1994), known as the Uruguay Round, resulted in agreement to create the World Trade Organization (WTO), which in some ways was the realization of the plans for the ITO nearly fifty years earlier. The WTO was established in 1995 by the Final Act Embodying the Results of the Uruguay Round of Multi-

The main meeting room inside the World Trade Organization building in Geneva, Switzerland features nameplates of member countries. *The World Trade Organization was established in 1995 as an international body to create and enforce rules of trade between nations.* © JOUANNEAU THOMAS/CORBIS SYGMA. REPRODUCED BY PERMISSION.

lateral Trade Negotiations, otherwise known as the Marrakech Agreement, or the WTO Agreement. This agreement provided for an institutional arrangement that would encompass the GATT.

In addition to the WTO Agreement establishing the WTO, there were several other agreements, including:

The Agreement on Agriculture. This agreement aims to restrict trade barriers such as export subsidies and domestic support to just the tariff, and then to successively reduce the tariff levels.

The Agreement on Sanitary and Phytosanitary Measures (SPS measures). These measures, which protect animal and plant health and are required for food safety (for example, requirements for the packaging and storage of food to be traded for sale) are considered to be a legitimate barrier to free trade, provided the requirements are indeed necessary.

The Agreement on Textiles and Clothing. Its aim is to reduce the quota restrictions applied by countries in the trade of fabrics and clothing.

The Agreement on Technical Barriers to Trade. Requirements that goods be tested and certified before they can be imported into a country can also serve as a barrier to trade. These are considered legitimate provided they are necessary.

The Agreement on Trade Related Aspects of Investment Measures (TRIMS). This aims to reduce investment measures that restrict international trade. For example, some countries require companies to buy local products to use in manufacture, or put quota restrictions on imports, and these restrict free trade.

The Agreement on Subsidies and Countervailing Measures. Its aim is to reduce the amount of subsidies governments give to their domestic producers. It is considered acceptable to fund research, but not to pay subsidies based on the amount of goods exported by the local company.

The General Agreement on Trade in Services (GATS). GATS aims to free up trade restrictions in services such as tourism, education, banking, air transport, and telecommunications. It also covers the movement of service providers to offer their services in other countries.

The Agreement on Trade Related Aspects of Intellectual Property Rights, Including Trade in Counterfeit Goods (TRIPS). This agreement covers intellectual property and related rights, such as trademarks, copyright, designs, and patents. The inventor has sole rights to trade in their invention for a period of time, to enable them to recoup the costs and reap the benefits from the work they have done.

The Understanding on Rules and Procedures Governing the Settlement of Disputes (DSU). The DSU provides a forum where disputes between states, or actions brought by states on behalf of their members, can be resolved. The states negotiate with one another, often with the assistance of a third party. If negotiations fail, a panel may be established to hear the dispute and determine the outcome.

The WTO is different from the GATT in several ways. Whereas the GATT is just an agreement, the WTO is an organization. Whereas the GATT was international, the WTO is global. Whereas the GATT was welcoming of nations to join the negotiations, the WTO expects them to bring their trade policy into line with WTO standards and state other commitments in a WTO Access Agreement before they can join. And finally, the GATT mainly focused on trade in goods, and to a lesser extent, services and intellectual property. In contrast, the WTO covers a plethora of things, including goods, services, and intellectual property, but also investment measures, agricultural trade, textiles and clothing, technical standards and certification procedures, and it has a specific body to handle the settlement of disputes between WTO member nations.

The WTO has been the subject of much controversy. While those in favor of it consider free trade to be the best way to help poorer countries raise their standard of living, others believe that the WTO is focused only on profit from trade, and does not take into account important social, cultural, and environmental factors. For example, a refusal to accept fish imported from countries that used nets that caught not only fish but also turtles and dolphins was considered by the WTO Dispute Settlement Body to be an unreasonable restriction to trade.

In 2002 a further round of trade negotiations, referred to as the Millennium Round, was launched to further the aim of free trade. Its goal has yet to be realized.

SEE ALSO INTERNATIONAL MONETARY FUND (IMF); WORLD BANK.

BIBLIOGRAPHY

Jackson, John Howard. *The Jurisprudence of GATT and the WTO.* Cambridge, U.K.: Cambridge University Press, 2000.

Kirshner, Orin; Bernstein, Edward M; and Institute for Agriculture and Trade Policy. *The Bretton Woods-Gatt System: Retrospect and Prospect after Fifty Years.* Armonk, NY: M. E. Sharpe, 1995.

Wallach, Lori; Woodall, Patrick; and Nader, Ralph. *Whose Trade Organization?: A Comprehensive Guide to the World Trade Organization,* 2nd edition. New York: New Press, 2004.

INTERNET RESOURCES

World Trade Organization web site. Available from www.wto.org.

Michelle Sanson

GDANSK

Gdansk (German, Danzig), a major Polish city on the Bay of Gdansk at the mouth the Vistula River on the Baltic Sea, has been a trade center for northeastern Europe since the fourteenth century. As early as the thirteenth century Gdansk was an important link in the chain of northern Germanic trading towns that comprised the mercantile organization known as the Hanseatic League, which virtually monopolized the trade of the Baltic and North Seas until the seventeenth century. Throughout this time, Gdansk was the main port of Poland and experienced rapid growth as an exchange hub, eventually surpassing in size other trading cities on the Baltic seaboard such as Lubeck and Hamburg. In 1500 the number of ships entering Gdansk reached nearly 800, importing and exporting such staples as furs, wax, honey, salt herring, silks, spices, and cloth. The city maintained a large trade with the Netherlands and Russia, particularly in grain, and handled most of Poland's seaborne commerce transported northward from the Polish interior via the Vistula River. The city's fortunes were damaged severely, however, by the Thirty Years' War (1618–1648), by the Northern Wars (1655–1660), and by bubonic plague in 1709.

The eighteenth century was turbulent for Gdansk and the rest of Poland. Between 1772 and 1774 Prussia and Russia acquired large portions of Poland in the so-called First Partition of Poland, and they made Gdansk temporarily a free city. In 1792 Russia and Prussia carved out further territory from Poland, and the crushing of a Polish revolt against foreign occupation caused the third, and final, partition by Prussia, Austria, and Russia, which obliterated the Polish state from the map of Europe.

At the end of the Napoleonic Wars (1799–1815), the Congress of Vienna upheld the Polish partitions. Gdansk became part of the German Empire as Danzig, the fortified provincial capital of West Prussia. Cut off from its natural hinterland until 1919, Danzig ceased to be a center of the Baltic trade and entered a period of economic decline, though shipbuilding provided some compensation. After World War I, Danzig once again became a free city with its own legislature under the protection of the League of Nations, with a territory of 730 square miles and a registered population of 407,000 (1929 census). Though Danzig at that time was only 4 percent Polish, the city was included in the Polish customs frontiers, and Poland was granted free use of all waterways and of all railways to Danzig and authority to conduct the city's foreign affairs.

Though overshadowed by large oceanic ports such as Amsterdam and London, Danzig flourished during the interwar years as a regional port serving the Baltic Sea area. Shipping tonnage entering Danzig quadrupled between 1913 and 1938 to nearly 5 million metric tons, and annual combined imports and exports rose more than threefold to 7 million metric tons. In 1939, however, Germany annexed Poland and Danzig, which saw heavy fighting during World War II.

In 1945 Danzig was unconditionally returned to a reconstituted Poland, and once again became Gdansk. The city had suffered terribly during the war and, though independent, was in the sphere of the communist Soviet Union. In 1980 highly publicized workers' strikes centered at Gdansk caused major political changes that eventually resulted in free elections in 1990 and 1991.

With political liberalization, Gdansk benefits from a surge of investment into greater Poland, and is in the process of privatizing and modernizing its shipyards, rail facilities, and road system. The city remains a major regional shipbuilding center as well as a container port and petrochemical processing hub, and its economy is diversifying into electronics and telecommunications. In May 2004 Poland joined the European Union. Gdansk is well-situated to recapture an increasing part of the quickly growing maritime trade through the Baltic Sea area.

SEE ALSO Agriculture; Cargoes, Freight; Cargoes, Passenger; Chambers of Commerce; Containerization; Free Ports; Hanseatic League (Hansa or Hanse); Harbors; Port Cities; Shipbuilding; Russia.

BIBLIOGRAPHY

Davis, Norman. *Heart of Europe: A Short History of Poland.* Oxford, U.K.: Oxford University Press, 1985.

Kirby, David. *The Baltic World, 1772–1993.* London: Pearson Educational, 1995.

Peter E. Austin

GENOA

Genoa's commercial development has always been linked to its harbor and its proximity to the traffic routes toward northern Italy and Central Europe. By the mid-1400s Genoa was the heart of a vast and integrated trade network extending from the Black to the North Seas. Genoese merchants bought spices, sugar, dyeing products, alum, silk, and cotton in the Black Sea's emporiums; grain, wine, and fabrics in Sicily and southern Italy; coral and cork in Sardinia. Once collected in Genoa, the lighter and most valuable of these goods were sent overland to Lombardy, Germany, and Flanders. Heavier and less valuable cargoes followed instead the longer but cheaper coastwise route along the Iberian Peninsula, where olive oil, soap, and wine were purchased, to England and the North Sea. Fabrics were brought back on the return voyage. From the second half of the 1400s, the Ottoman conquest of the eastern Mediterranean forced Genoa to concentrate its commercial activities on the central-western part of it, and on the Atlantic and the North Sea. Business relations with the several Italian states, Provence, the Iberian Peninsula, and the archipelagos of the Atlantic were therefore strengthened.

From the mid-1500s Genoa's economic interests shifted decidedly from trade to finance. Profits accumulated thanks to international trade, allowing a powerful aristocracy of merchant-banking families such as the Dorias, the Spinolas, the Giustianianis, the Grimaldis, the Lomellinis, and the Balbis to dominate the Spanish Crown's finance and to become, between 1550 and 1630, the protagonists of the European capital markets. The bankruptcy in 1627 of Philip IV of Spain (1605–1665) caused very heavy losses and renewed interest in trade, which also was fostered by the institution of duty-free facilities in 1609, and by the availability of export products manufactured in the city, such as valuable fabrics and paper. However, financial activities remained predominant: At the end of the 1700s the Genoese financiers extended their loans to nearly all European countries.

During the first decades of the 1800s Genoa's import trade consisted mainly in foodstuffs, groceries, and raw material for urban consumption. Its exports were local finished goods (paper, pasta, and fabrics) and agricultural products (olive oil and citrus fruit).

Following Italian unification (1861), Genoa became one of Italy's most industrialized cities and the maritime terminal for northern Italy, the country's most economically advanced area. Since the early 1900s its trade has involved above all the importation of industrial raw materials and fuels needed to supply both the city's and Italy's production system, such as coal and oil, cast and scrap iron, and textile fibers. Grain also was imported from North and South America.

At the beginning of the twenty-first century Genoa still is the premier port serving Italy's major industrial centers and one of the leading ports along the routes that, through the Suez Canal and the Strait of Gibraltar, link the Mediterranean to Asia, Africa, and the American continents. It is also the major European terminal for petroleum products. Its network of oil pipelines supplies the refineries of northern Italy, Switzerland, and Germany.

SEE ALSO AGRICULTURE; BLACK SEA; CARGOES, FREIGHT; CARGOES, PASSENGER; CHAMBERS OF COMMERCE; CONTAINERIZATION; FREE PORTS; HARBORS; ITALY; MEDITERRANEAN; MILLETS AND CAPITULATIONS; PORT CITIES; SPICES AND THE SPICE TRADE.

BIBLIOGRAPHY

Braudel, Fernand. *The Mediterranean and the Mediterranean World in the Age of Philip II.* Berkeley: California University Press, 1996.

Epstein, Steven A. *Genoa and the Genoese, 958–1528.* Chapel Hill: North Carolina University Press, 2001.

Tonizzi, Maria Elisabetta. "Economy, Traffic and Infrastructure in the Port of Genoa, 1861–1970." In *Resources and Infrastructures in the Maritime Economy, 1500–2000,* ed. G. Boyce and R. Gorsky. St. John's, Newfoundland: International Maritime Economic History Association, 2002.

Maria Elisabetta Tonizzi

GERMANY

During the late Middle Ages, urban landscapes emerged in Germany that developed a regional specialization in interregional and international trade. Most important in this respect were the Rhineland, Upper Germany, the Hanseatic coastal area, and Central Germany. In the Rhineland, Cologne had become the major center of production and distribution, while Frankfurt emerged as the leading fair for the continental land trade between Flanders and Brabant and the German South and Upper Italy. With the rise of Antwerp in the fifteenth century, the ties between Frankfurt and Antwerp strengthened, while Cologne profited from Amsterdam's rise into the world's entrepôt. Although Cologne's merchants were pushed out of several direct trades (for example with England) in the seventeenth century, Cologne became most important for Dutch purchases and sales upstream on the Rhine. From the hinterlands came wine, grain, and timber, while English cloth and herring were shipped in the opposite direction. Frankfurt owed its rise to immigrants from the Netherlands during the Dutch Revolt, who turned Frankfurt into the leading fair and money market of the Holy Roman Empire. Although Frankfurt faced se-

vere losses during the Thirty Years' War and was superseded by the Leipzig fair during the second half of the seventeenth century, it remained a leading banking place and a luxury market for the German courts.

Upper Germany was characterized by the textile production of linen and fustians. From larger towns, such as Nördlingen, it spread to the countryside, were entrepreneurs, circumventing urban guild restrictions, found cheaper sources of labor. Thus it is no wonder that the Fuggers started their enterprise in the Augsburg fustian business and then founded their merchant house and made investments in silver and copper mining in the late fifteenth century. The major technical innovation in the latter field was the invention of liquation (*Saigerverfahren*), whereby silver was extracted from argentiferous raw copper through the admixture of lead. This innovation led, together with the discovery of argentiferous copper deposits in Thuringia (Mansfeld, Hettstedt), Tyrol (Schwaz), and Upper Hungary (Neusohl), to the Central European silver mining boom.

The Fuggers owned smelteries and maintained factories in these areas, as they had acquired a silver and copper monopoly in exchange for credits to Habsburg rulers. The Fuggers channeled the metals on the European markets for precious metals: the Frankfurt and the Antwerp fairs and the workshops of Nürnberg metalworkers. Nürnberg was the most advanced industrial area, where such processes as liquation, tinplating, and wiredrawing had been invented. The city and its entrepreneurs organized the hinterland into a zone of mass production. Craftsmen of the hinterland supplied in a putting-out system semifinished ironware for finished Nürnberg products (hooks, blades, knifes, needles, armors, wires, etc.) destined for the European markets. So it was the combination of different factors, such as trade, mining, and industrial production, together with technical innovations and the introduction of Italian bookkeeping and banking practice, that gave Upper Germany superiority in the German economy of the fifteenth and sixteenth centuries. However, with the increasing importance of Amsterdam and the maritime trade and the setbacks caused by the Thirty Years' War, Augsburg and Nürnberg declined in economic power.

In the late Middle Ages, only the Hanseatic trading system in the North was comparable to Upper Germany. The Hanseatic League, a powerful association of towns and cities, led by Lübeck, dominated trade, shipping, and politics around the North Sea and the Baltic from the thirteenth to the sixteenth century. Its trade ran on an East-West line (Novgorod-Reval-Riga-Visby-Danzig-Stralsund-Lübeck-Hamburg-Bruges-London) and had as its basis the exchange of food and raw materials from Northern and Eastern Europe with manufactured goods

Germany

— International border
⊛ National capital
• Other city

DENMARK

Baltic Sea

North Frisian Islands

Fehmarn Island

Mecklenburg Bay

Rügen Island

Kiel

North Sea

East Frisian Islands

Hamburg

Elbe River

Bremen

POLAND

Oder River

⊛ Berlin

Hanover

Braunschweig

NETHERLANDS

Weser R.

Münster

Bielefeld

Gelsenkirchen
Duisburg
Krefeld
Mönchengladbach

Dortmund
Essen Bochum
Wuppertal
Düsseldorf

Halle

Leipzig

Cologne

Rhine R.

Aachen
Bonn

Chemnitz

Dresden

Elbe River

BELGIUM

Moselle River

Frankfurt am Main

Wiesbaden

Main R.

CZECH REPUBLIC

LUX.

Mannheim

Nürnberg

Rhine R.

Karlsruhe

Stuttgart

Danube River

Lech River

Augsburg

FRANCE

Munich

AUSTRIA

0   40   80 mi.
0   40   80 km

Bodensee

LIECH.

SWITZERLAND

MAP BY XNR PRODUCTIONS. THE GALE GROUP.

from Northwest Europe, thus creating a prospering trading area. However, in the fifteenth and sixteenth centuries this system, based on trade privileges and not on competition, was challenged by such competitors as the Dutch, the Upper Germans, and the emerging power states (England, Denmark, Sweden, and Russia), canceling the privileges of the Hanseatic merchants. Thus only cities such as Hamburg or Gdansk that could fulfill indispensable services (such as grain supply) for the rising Atlantic economy and at the same time successfully adapt

Western know-how were able to maintain and promote their position in international trade in the early modern period. Hamburg especially, which hosted Flemish and Sephardic emigrants after the Dutch revolt, integrated itself into the exchange between West and East. Hamburg was linked by a 500-mile waterway (and by the Oder) with Central Germany and Central Europe and thus maintained close connections with the Leipzig fairs, whose importance was based on the exchange of Western cloth for linen, copper, and silver. The links with the linen-producing areas of Silesia, Bohemia, Saxony, and Lusatia proved to be particularly useful. Thus hinterland resources in Central Germany and Central Europe could be brought into line with Hamburg's export demands. Moreover, the Elbe-Oder waterways provided Hamburg, dealing in western European and colonial goods, a profitable channel into the emerging capitals of Prussia (Berlin) and Saxony (Dresden). Due to the city's consistent neutrality and to its fortifications, Hamburg prospered during the Thirty Years' War. Besides the Netherlands, England and the Iberian Peninsula were Hamburg's most important trading partners. Hamburg also was engaged in the Russian trade and in France's re-export trade (sugar, coffee), which boomed in the second half of the eighteenth century. In 1783, Hamburg merchants profited from American independence, and in the 1820s trade connections were established with the independent Central and South American states. Around 1850, Hamburg had become the second most important European port (in terms of volume), behind London, and by the end of the nineteenth century it had expanded its trade to Southeast Asia and Australia as well as Africa. Under the German Empire, Hamburg built a large toll-free port and supported the settlements of industries closely connected with the import trade (food industries, coffee roasters, refineries for copper and mineral oil, rubber processing). Around 1900, 4.5 percent of the world's trade volume was loaded and unloaded in Hamburg. The world's largest shipping company, the HAPAG, had its seat there.

At the same time (around 1900), Germany as a whole contributed to 11 percent of world trade. However, during the nineteenth century the composition of Germany's export had changed significantly. By the end of the eighteenth century (according to the Prussian statistics), the German export trade had consisted mainly of foodstuffs and textiles (linens). By the end of the nineteenth century, manufactured goods, metal products, and especially machinery products played the most important role. Germany dominated this trade along with the United Kingdom. Chemicals, especially synthetic dye stuffs, were also important. As a result of the world wars, German trade fell into a deep crisis; it recovered its 1913 volumes only in the mid-1950s. Since then, trade levels have continued to rise. In 1913, Germany had an export/

GDP ratio of 15.6, ranking behind the Netherlands (17.8) and the United Kingdom (17.7). In 1992 it had a ratio of 32.6, ranking third behind the much smaller Netherlands (55.3) and Taiwan (34.4).

SEE ALSO AGRICULTURE; BALANCE OF PAYMENTS; BALTIC STATES; BANKING; BOOKS; BOYCOTT; CANALS; CARGOES, FREIGHT; CARGOES, PASSENGER; COMMON MARKET AND THE EUROPEAN UNION; DEPRESSIONS AND RECOVERIES; ETHNIC GROUPS, JEWS; FREE TRADE, THEORY AND PRACTICE; FUGGER FAMILY; GATT, WTO; GDANSK; GREAT DEPRESSION OF THE 1930S; HAMBURG; HANSEATIC LEAGUE (HANSA OR HANSE); IMPERIALISM; INDUSTRIALIZATION; INTERNATIONAL TRADE AGREEMENTS; IRON AND STEEL; KRUPP; MARKETS, STOCK; MEXICO; MINING; NATIONALIZATION; PHARMACEUTICALS; REGIONAL TRADING AGREEMENTS; ROTHSCHILD FAMILY; RUBBER; RUSSIA; SHIPBUILDING; SIEMENS; TOYS; WARS; WINE.

BIBLIOGRAPHY

Foreman-Peck, James. "Long-Distance Trade since 1914." In *The Oxford Encyclopedia of Economic History*, Vol. 3, ed. Joel Mokyr. Oxford, U.K.: Oxford University Press, 2003.

Kriedte, Peter. "Trade." In *Germany: A New Social and Economic History*, Vol. 2: *1630–1800*, ed. Sheilagh Ogilvie. London: Arnold, 1996.

North, Michael. "Hamburg: The Continent's Most English City." In *From the North Sea to the Baltic: Essays in Commercial, Monetary and Agrarian History, 1500–1800*, ed. Michael North. Brookfield, VT: Variorum, 1996.

North, Michael. *Kommunikation, Handel, Geld und Banken in der Frühen Neuzeit*. München: R. Oldenbourg, 2000.

North, Michael, ed. *Deutsche Wirtschaftsgeschichte: Ein Jahrtausend im Überblick*. München: C. H. Beck, 2000.

Pohl, Hans. *Aufbruch der Weltwirtschaft: Geschichte der Weltwirtschaft von der Mitte des 19. Jahrhunderts bis zum Ersten Weltkrieg*. Stuttgart: Franz Steiner Verlag, 1989.

Michael North

JEAN PAUL GETTY
1892–1976

Jean Paul Getty inherited his father's oil business, George Getty Inc., and became its president and general manager in 1930. His fortune came from profitable acquisitions on the stock market, beginning during the Great Depression. In 1937 he took control of the Tidewater Association Oil Company; subsequently, he acquired Skelly Oil Company and Missouri Oil Company. The three companies were merged in 1956 to form Getty Oil, whose assets were worth more than U.S.$3 billion in 1967. In 1949 Getty paid U.S.$9.5 million for a sixty-year concession on half of a neutral barren tract between Saudi Arabia and Kuwait. After an initial investment of U.S.$30 million, Getty's speculation paid off. He found enormous quantities of oil in the tract, which came to produce over 16 million barrels of oil per year. By the early 1960s Getty's financial empire included holdings in oil and natural gas, as well as gold and uranium mines, a copper deposit, vineyards, orchards, grazing lands, timberlands, refineries, and chemical plants. He was declared the richest man on earth by *Fortune* magazine in 1957. Always an avid art collector, Getty left a large portion of his wealth to the J. Paul Getty Museum Trust. Designed as a replica of a Roman villa, the Malibu museum houses paintings, sculpture, and eighteenth-century French furniture.

SEE ALSO PETROLEUM.

BIBLIOGRAPHY

Getty, J. Paul. *My Life and Fortunes.* London: Allen and Unwin, 1953.

Yergin, Daniel. *Prize: The Epic Quest for Oil, Money & Power.* New York: Free Press, reissued 1993.

Federico Boffa

GHANA

The Gold Coast was one of the three key areas for international trade on the west coast of Africa at the end of the Middle Ages. Trading posts and forts were established there by the Portuguese (Cape Coast Castle, El Mina in 1482, Accra in 1515) and the Dutch (1598), and then also by the Danes (beginning from 1650), who in 1661 founded Christiansborg in the heart of modern Accra, while the British also gained a foothold there (Accra in 1644). Merchants traded extensively in slaves. The mainstay of trade in what would become modern Ghana was focused on the interior: gold and slaves were traded in the north via the Saharan trails because the southern region was covered in thick tropical forests. It was here that the Ashanti state became established at the end of the seventeenth century, developing rapidly until the early nineteenth century. It controlled the Fanti coastal principalities, and in the north it kept a check on the inroads of Hawsa merchants in the trading towns on its borders. Accurately termed a "slave state," the kingdom controlled the slave trade with the Sudan and the Islamic nations, the caravans that headed toward the ports, and trade in gold dust and the kola nut (for export) and in salt, skins, and grass skirts (for import). The Ashanti handled vast quantities of cowrie shells, symbols of their wealth.

THE COLONIAL PERIOD

The European slave trade ended between 1803 and 1807; gold, wood, and palm oil became the main trading commodities. Beginning in the 1830s the Gold Coast came under the influence of the British, starting with their base at Accra and advancing northward until they met with Ashanti resistance until 1901. The British established a colony in the south in 1874, occupying the Fanti regions while the Dutch and Danes surrendered their trading posts. The territory underwent two huge commercial changes: the Hawsa were able to trade freely there, and supplied the south with livestock; and in dealings with the Sahel, port traffic became increasingly significant. The gold mines were developed from the 1870s, and British companies began exporting palm oil and, above all, cocoa. From the 1880s, Ghana rapidly became an extensive "pioneer frontier" for cocoa, thanks to the growing number of plantations and the settlement of a large population of planters and middle-class traders. Cocoa sales reached 40,000 tons (16% of world production) in 1911, then 200,000 to 300,000 tons per year between 1920 and 1930 (40% of world production). This made up between 50 and 60 percent of the territory's exports, and various trade agreements governed its harvesting in the years 1903 to 1917. Finally, just as in Nigeria, following a succession of mergers between various companies, the United African Company, part of the Unilever group, occupied the leading position after 1929. But competition survived with John Holt (since 1935) or French companies CFAO (since 1909) and SCOA (since 1913) or with the UTC. The Union Trading Company (UTC) in conjunction with Swiss various groups also played a significant part there. Although the United Kingdom increased public-investment programs (e.g., ports, railways, hydraulics projects) to serve the needs of modern trade, private capital provided 60 percent of the total investment between 1870 and 1940, which shows how prosperous the Gold Coast was despite a decrease in the price of cocoa between 1928 and 1937. Its inclusion in the British Commonwealth and the postwar revival encouraged commercial growth: in 1951 exports (£91.3 million) and imports (£63.4 million) amounted to three-quarters of those in vastly more populous Nigeria (£128.4 and £84 million, respectively). As elsewhere, marketing boards controlled first the trade in cocoa (1947) then in other products (1949).

POSTINDEPENDENCE

An anti-imperialist, nationalist policy was pursued by Kwame Nkrumah (1909–1972, ruled 1951/1957–1966), who revived the name of the tenth- and eleventh-century kingdom of Ghana. Trade was gradually nationalized, and foreign companies pulled out. Ghana remained an exporter of cocoa and became a producer of bauxite, aluminium (as a result of the large Akosombo Dam), and manganese (becoming the world's eighth-largest producer in 1986). Government control of trade (particularly the monopoly of the National Office for the Cocoa Trade) and the policies of comparative self-sufficiency (with heavy import duties) followed between 1970 and 1980, resulting in a decline of the commercial infrastructure and a dearth of foreign investment, despite multilateral and British aid to re-establish Ghana's inclusion in the Lomé Convention of 1975 between the European Economic Community and African countries. Ghana's volume of British imports shrank from 2.89 percent in 1978 to 0.07 percent in 1989 to 1992, and it imported only 0.15 percent of British exports in 1984 to 1992, in contrast to 0.3 percent in 1970 to 1978. Ghanaian exports were no longer able to pay for essential imports such as consumer goods, cars, and equipment for a large population (13 million in 1985) still enjoying a relatively high standard of living for Black Africa, despite the need to import two-thirds of its corn and despite suffering from fluctuations in the price of cocoa. (Ghana remained the world's third-largest producer, with 200,000 tons in 1986, or 11%.) Ghana developed a trade deficit (U.S.$727 million imported and U.S.$610 million exported in 1985) and a foreign-debt burden (U.S.$5 billion in 1994), while factories and the transport and commercial network declined because of a lack of spare parts. Redirection of economic policy, against state control, depended upon the assistance of the International Monetary Fund and the World Bank, which negotiated several currency devaluations (in 1983–1986), a liberalization of trade, and an Investment Code (1985). However, rebuilding trade structures was a long-term process, because import licenses were difficult to obtain and commercial taxation remained very high.

SEE ALSO AFRICA, LABOR TAXES (HEAD TAXES); ARMS, ARMAMENTS; CARAVAN TRADE; COFFEE; COWRIES; DAHOMEY; DEVELOPMENTAL STATE, CONCEPT OF THE; EMPIRE, BRITISH; EMPIRE, DUTCH; EMPIRE, FRENCH; EMPIRE, PORTUGUESE; ETHNIC GROUPS, AFRICANS; GOLD AND SILVER; GOLD COAST; IMPERIALISM; IMPORT SUBSTITUTION; INTERNATIONAL MONETARY FUND (IMF); LABORERS, COERCED; LABORERS, CONTRACT; MERCANTILISM; SLAVERY AND THE AFRICAN SLAVE TRADE; TEXTILES; TIMBER; WORLD BANK.

BIBLIOGRAPHY

Bourret, F. M. *The Gold Coast: A Survey of the Gold Coast and British Togoland, 1919–1946.* London and Stanford, CA: Stanford University Press, 1949.

Carmichael, John. *African Eldorado: Gold Coast to Ghana.* London: Duckworth, 1993.

Fieldhouse, D. K. *Merchant Capital and Economic Decolonisation: The United Africa Company, 1929–1989.* Oxford, U.K.: Clarendon Press, 1994.

Guex, Sébastien. "Le négoce suisse en Afrique subsaharienne: le cas de la société Union Trading Company (1859–1918)." In *Négoce blanc en Afrique noire: L'évolution du commerce à longue distance en Afrique noire du 18e au 20e siècles (Swiss Trading in Sub-Saharan Africa: The Case of the White Trading in Black Africa. The Evolution of Long Distance in Trading in Black Africa from the Eighteenth Century to the Twentieth Century)*, ed. Hubert Bonin and Michel Cahen. Paris: Publications de la Société française d'histoire d'outre-mer, 2000.

Gunnarson, Christer. *The Gold Coast Cocoa Industry, 1900–1939: Production, Prices, and Structural Changes.* Lund, Sweden: AV–Centralen, 1978.

Lynn, Martin. *Commerce and Economic Change in West Africa: The Palm Oil Trade in the Nineteenth Century.* New York and Cambridge, U.K.: Cambridge University Press, 1997.

Southall, R. J. "Farmers, Traders, and Brokers in the Gold Coast Cocoa Economy." *Canadian Journal of African Studies* 12, no. 2 (1978): 185–211.

Hubert Bonin

HUMPHREY GILBERT
c. 1539–1583

Sir Humphrey Gilbert was a navigator, army officer, member of Parliament, and soldier. He annexed the Newfoundland territory for the British Crown and, in spite of his failure to establish a permanent British colony there, devised a brilliant, unprecedented colonization scheme focusing on European development. Early in his career, Gilbert helped to establish English settlements in Ireland in order to quell Irish rebellion. The resoluteness of his methods, often described as brutal, earned him a knighthood in 1570.

In 1566 Gilbert presented *A Discourse of a Discovery for a New Passage to Cataia* to Queen Elizabeth I of England, to gain royal patronage for voyages of exploration to China (Cataia) that sailed in a northwest direction. He believed that colonization would foster England's overseas trade, which was then dominated by the Spanish and Portuguese. In 1578, his efforts were finally rewarded by a royal charter granting him the privileges of exploration and colonization in North America. After a first unlucky expedition dispersed by the Spanish, he successfully sailed again to St. John in 1583. After two weeks in his new colony, Gilbert left because of the mutiny of the colonists. He died during his return trip to England.

SEE ALSO CANADA; ELIZABETH I; EMPIRE, BRITISH.

BIBLIOGRAPHY

Hayes, Edward. *Sir Humphrey Gilbert's Voyage to Newfoundland.* Whitefish, MT: Kessinger Publishing, 2004.

Parmenius, Stephanus. *The New Found Land of Stephen Parmenius: The Life and Writings of a Hungarian Poet,*

Drowned on a Voyage from Newfoundland, 1583. Toronto: University of Toronto Press, 1972.

Federico Boffa

GLASGOW

After being some way down the urban hierarchy in Scotland in the medieval period, Glasgow overtook Perth, the fourth-largest burgh (town), in 1649, and then Aberdeen and Dundee. By the early 1800s Glasgow was growing more rapidly than any other European city of its size, and it finally overtook Scotland's ancient capital, Edinburgh, between 1811 and 1821, when its population reached just over 147,000. By the mid-nineteenth century vessels were being loaded at Glasgow's burgeoning docks with coal mined from pits which, fortuitously, lay in and around the city, along with Glasgow-made goods, in which pig iron and iron manufactures predominated (with coal they comprised between 52 percent and 65 percent of the port's tonnage between 1905 and 1914). Glasgow still served markets in Europe; even more was shipped across the Atlantic, and ships from the Clyde regularly traveled to and from South America.

What was most striking in Glasgow's rise, particularly after the opening of the Suez Canal in 1869, was the overwhelming importance of destinations in the Middle and Far East, in India and other far-flung outposts of the British Empire—of which Glasgow had become the second city, smaller only than London. The way was led first by textiles and, in the second half of the nineteenth century, by the export of heavy metal goods: these included gas and water pipes, which were incorporated into several of the world's largest civic utilities; and boilers, steam engines, rails, and locomotives, which achieved massive sales in India and South America. Around the globe, Glasgow, the "Workshop of the Empire," and engineering were synonymous. Given the absence of any shipbuilding firms in Glasgow in 1800, the fact that Clyde yards were responsible for 66 percent of Britain's steam tonnage in the second half of the 1860s seems astonishing; the feat owed much to the proximity of coal and iron, but more to the preeminence of the city's and the region's skills and early enthusiasm for steam engines and steam navigation and, ultimately, its marine engineers. In 1913 almost one-fifth of the world's shipping tonnage was launched on the Clyde, more than the entire shipbuilding industry of either Germany or the United States. Foodstuffs and raw materials too were drawn from abroad. The first, among which grain and flour predominated, were required to feed the city's people, whose numbers continued to grow—by more than 1,000 percent between 1801 and 1911, by which time Glasgow boasted over 1 million inhabitants. It was not until the

1950s that the population level began to decline. The human price of economic growth was high, however: Scotland's industrial economy depended not only on skilled workers but also required the ruthless exploitation of low-cost manual labor, as for example the 6,000 or so casual dock laborers (42 percent of the Scottish total), employed at the Clyde Navigation Trust–run port of Glasgow in 1911. A raft of data on health, key demographic indicators such as death rates, life expectancy, and housing statistics, place Glasgow toward the top of the British league of urban distress in both the nineteenth and twentieth centuries. Raw materials including wood, cotton, and dyestuffs were devoured by industrialists and builders. Glasgow and its region dominated the Scottish cotton industry, with 168 mills at its mid-nineteenth-century peak, when one in four employees in the U.K. cotton industry worked in Scotland, mostly in and around Glasgow. On the eve of World War I the port of Glasgow handled one-third of the tonnage arriving in Scotland from overseas (with a value of some £18.5 million); in U.K. terms Glasgow ranked as the fifth-largest importer. In exports, Glasgow was third in the United Kingdom, as it was in ship-owning. From less than 2,000 tons in 1810, by 1910 Glasgow firms owned just over 2 million tons of shipping. As dramatic as the expansion in shipping and of port facilities in Glasgow—the last particularly strongly after 1875—was the remarkable transformation in the shipping fleet from one dominated by sail to one comprised increasingly of large steel hulls powered by steam-driven compound-engines. By 1895 the sail trade had virtually disappeared. This was equally true of coastal shipping, the importance of which is easily overlooked; yet this more regular commerce, carried on in smaller vessels, accounted for 85 percent of the arrivals in Glasgow in 1913, and 36 percent of the port's tonnage.

The strengthening of Glasgow's economy in the sixteenth century and its spectacular breakthrough in the seventeenth century owed more to trade within Scotland and with Ireland and England than to links overseas. Textile manufacturing featured early, as did the town's role as a market center for the western Highlands and islands and Ulster. It is clear that Glasgow's merchants had forged connections with New England's tobacco planters by 1680, England's prohibitive Navigation Acts notwithstanding. What is equally clear, however, is that union with England in 1707, which legalized Scottish trade with the colonies, provided the framework in which Glasgow merchants could exploit their favored location, the cost advantages of the store system, the practice of purchasing tobacco directly from the planters, their facility in outwitting customs officers, and London links with the French market for Virginian leaf. From the middle of the eighteenth century Glasgow vied with London to become Britain's leading tobacco port. Investment from tobacco

City chambers in Glasgow. *During the 1800s, Glasgow, Scotland, emerged as the country's largest city and established itself as the shipbuilding capital of the world. George Square, pictured here, is located in the central part of the city.* © HULTON-DEUTSCH COLLECTION/CORBIS. REPRODUCED BY PERMISSION.

and sugar merchants in banks, land, and industry boosted economic development in the city and its region, but was less important for the cotton and iron industries than is sometimes assumed. Ironically, although colonial profits encouraged diversity in manufacturing in the eighteenth century, it was the concentration of economic activity and the interconnectedness of the regional economy—in coal mining, steel production, and shipbuilding—that explains more of Glasgow's slow but far from steady decline from the pinnacle it reached around 1913; in the immediate post–World War II years around a quarter of the world's new merchant vessel tonnage was Clyde-built.

SEE ALSO EMPIRE, BRITISH; ETHNIC GROUPS, SCOTS; POPULATION—EMIGRATION AND IMMIGRATION; PORT CITIES; SUGAR, MOLASSES, AND RUM; TOBACCO.

BIBLIOGRAPHY

Cunnison, James, and Gilfillan, J. B. S., eds. *The Third Statistical Account of Scotland: Glasgow.* Collins, 1959.

Devine, Thomas M., and Jackson, Gordon, eds. *Glasgow,* Vol. 1: *Beginnings to 1830.* Manchester, U.K.: Manchester University Press, 1995.

Fraser, W. Hamish, and Maver, Irene, eds. *Glasgow,* Vol. 2: *1830 to 1912.* Manchester, U.K.: Manchester University Press, 1996.

Graham, Eric J. *A Maritime History of Scotland, 1650–1790.* East Linton, UK: Tuckwell Press, 2002.

Kenefick, William. *"Rebellious and Contrary": The Glasgow Dockers, 1852–1932.* East Linton, UK: Tuckwell Press, 2000.

Saville, Richard, ed. *The Economic Development of Modern Scotland, 1950–1980.* Edinburgh, Scotland: John Donald Publishers, 1985.

Slaven, Anthony. *The Development of the West of Scotland, 1750–1960.* London: Routledge, 1975.

Christopher A. Whatley

GLASSWARE

The technological know-how of Renaissance glass production stems from ancient techniques which, through additional contributions made by medieval glassmakers, survived with little alterations until the thirteenth century. The major Renaissance center of glassmaking was found in Venice, and it is likely that its prominence in the field was due to the fact that the technical know-how had been imported at a very early stage from the island

JOSIAH WEDGWOOD

One of the most famous names in the pottery manufacturing business is Josiah Wedgwood (1730–1795). Wedgwood came from a family of potters, and at age nine was apprenticed to his brother in the trade after their father's death. In 1759 Wedgwood opened a pottery works in his hometown of Burslem, Staffordshire. Even the loss of a leg in 1768 did not deter Wedgwood, and the following year he and partner Thomas Bentley started a new works near Stoke on Trent that included a village to comfortably accommodate workers. His career was remarkably successful, based in large part on his pursuit of more efficient modes of production. He took a hands-on approach to design and the preparation of clay mixtures, and also employed other designers, including John Flaxman. Wedgwood's classically inspired pieces were superior in design to the pottery then common, and they were noted for their durability. Among Wedgwood's important clients were George III's wife, Queen Charlotte, and Russia's Catherine II. The innovative Wedgwood became a Fellow of the Royal Society in 1783. At his death Wedgwood left a sizable fortune. Many of his designs remain in production.

David J. Clarke

of Torcello outside Venice, where recent archaeological excavations have revealed the existence of a center of production dating from the seventh century C.E.

By the thirteenth century glassmaking had become an important economic manufacture, and in 1224 Venetian glassmakers united in a well-organized guild controlled by the government of the Serenissima. A statute (*Capitulare de Fiolaris*) dated in 1271 regulated the guild and took explicit measures to preserve the secrets of the arts and to keep them under the control of the city. Accordingly, glassmakers were not allowed to leave the town and the Veneto state without a permit. The statute also regulated the production and the division of labor, the ingredients of the glass, and the combustible to be used. Since the fusion of glass requires a high and constant temperature, furnaces were active night and day for eight months a year, and the remaining four months were used to sell the products on the market. Due to the rapid expansion of the production and the increasing

danger of fire, in 1291 the glassmakers were forced to move to the island of Murano, and by the sixteenth century some twenty furnaces were active on the island. Their principal products were mirrors, glass disks for windows, glass tesserae for mosaics, and gems and pearls imitating precious stones. In the first half of the fifteenth century Angelo Barovier (1405–1460) successfully experimented with new techniques, which enabled him to create his famous "crystalline glass" (very pure potassium-calcium silicate) and other innovative products such as chalcedony and millefiori glass.

The Venetian glassmakers successfully exported sophisticated products such as large mirrors and decorated crystal items throughout continental Europe, to Germany in particular. Thanks to the migration of Venetian glassmakers to France, Bohemia, and England, Northern Europe was able to produce high-quality glass during the seventeenth and eighteenth centuries. Due to the introduction of coal as the main combustible, as well as to ingenious technical innovations in the building of furnaces, Bohemian glassmakers were soon able to produce high-quality crystal and lead glass. The improvement of the glass paste produced in these areas allowed them to develop an unprecedented skill in grinding and cutting.

In France during the second half of the seventeenth century, professional chemists were invited by Jean-Baptiste Colbert (1619–1683), the minister of finance, to superintend the glass and mirror manufacture of Saint Gobain, the first large industry that could challenge the supremacy of Venetian glass. In the same period similar policies were pursued in the Netherlands and in England, where small glass manufactures specialized in the production of single classes of items.

In 1676 George Ravenscroft (1618–1681), a glassmaker in London, introduced a new process that resulted in so-called "flint glass." This type of glass was obtained by mixing lead oxide and potash into a silica batch. Flint glass had many qualities that made it immediately successful on the European market: it was more fusible than others glass pastes, it could be easily handled and cut, and it possessed a high density and a remarkable brightness. In addition, flint glass enabled natural philosophers to manufacture more accurate optical instruments, telescopes, and, in particular, microscopes. Isaac Newton (1642–1727) was the first to understand, at the end of the seventeenth century, that flint glass successfully solved the problem of chromatic aberrations of traditional optical lenses. Following this important discovery, glassmaking become even more specialized, and instruments makers produced new and more accurate optical devices. Under the guidance of natural philosophers, artisans made systematic research in order to improve the quality of glass, and as a consequence of this scientific interest in innovation, new specialized arts of glassmaking were created. By the end of the nineteenth century these specialized crafts had developed into important industries of optical and pharmaceutical glass.

The preoccupation of scientists of finding a new and more objective way to represent reality—and to communicate this to the public—is exemplified by the invention of photography (1839). The use of telescopic images by Galileo (1564–1642) had always been regarded as the effect of a manufactured representation of reality. As early as 1839 the French physicist François Arago (1783–1853) heralded the victory of an objective representation of reality which, through the fixation of images on glass plates, unveiled the nature of objective reality.

During the nineteenth century the production of glass, following in the footsteps of other crafts and manufactures, underwent a progressive mechanization and industrialization. Whereas the most important glassmaking product during the eighteenth century had been large-size mirrors, the dominating products in the era of the Industrial Revolution were windowpanes and showcases. A spectacular demonstration of this trend was the Great Exhibition of 1851 in London. Promoted by Prince Albert (1819–1861), the Great Exhibition was held in Hyde Park in London in the specially constructed Crystal Palace, a huge iron structure covered with over a million square feet of glass. The advancement of science, technologies, and industries were thus put on display in a gigantic showcase. Since then, glass has become a central material in architecture, competing with iron and, more recently, cement.

The success of glass in industrial countries has made this material an indispensable resource, not only in architecture but also in everyday life. Even as the industrial production of glass expanded its uses enormously, the major breakthrough of the twentieth century was the 1930 invention by William Chalmers of Plexiglas, a thermoplastic synthetic resin that perfectly imitates the qualities of glass but has a chemical composition which makes it less fragile.

SEE ALSO France; Colbert, Jean-Baptiste; London; Venice.

BIBLIOGRAPHY

Macfarlane, Alan, and Martin, Gerry. *Glass: A World History.* Chicago: University of Chicago Press, 2002.

Tait, Hugh, ed. *Five Thousand Years of Glass.* London: British Museum, 1991.

Marco Beretta

GLOBALIZATION, PRO AND CON

Advances in communications, information processing, and transportation technologies have permitted poor countries to become participants in world global markets in ways that previously were not possible. They now can be large-scale exporters of manufactured goods. Because this is so, both foreign direct investment (FDI) and financial capital are attracted to these previously neglected countries, particularly to those that are large and effectively governed (Mandle 2003).

A PATH TO MODERN ECONOMIC GROWTH

After a long period of skepticism, the leaders of many developing countries have come to believe that global market integration is an effective means to promote economic growth. Today representatives of such nations typically do not stand in opposition to globalization, but rather complain that the developed world often fails to adopt sufficiently liberal trade policies. In particular the European Union, the United States, and Japan are taken to task for using subsidies as no-tariff barriers impeding agricultural imports.

The empirical record generally suggests that the poor nations have benefited from their embrace of globalization. Although high levels of exports and substantial capital inflows do not ensure economic growth, the fact remains that for numerous developing countries the ability to attract FDI and to export intermediate and final manufactured goods has been effective in accelerating economic development. Typically, their growth has been associated with success in reducing poverty. Even the textile and apparel industries, much maligned for the relatively poor wages and working conditions they provide, almost always offer higher levels of income than the alternative opportunities available to their workers.

Even so, there are those who deny that globalization provides a path to development for poor nations. Such critics point to numerous cases in which the policy recommendations advanced by the World Bank and the International Monetary Fund concerning developing countries have been ill advised. These multinational institutions have frequently insisted upon the privatization of public assets before functioning markets are in place; the liberalization of capital markets before needed regulatory mechanisms are present; and in the name of fiscal austerity, the curtailing of health and education programs, though such expenditures are essential for success in globalization.

Policies such as these—often referred to as "the Washington Consensus"—are subject to legitimate criticism, but they themselves are not integral to globalization. Indeed, many of the most successful globalizers,

Activists protest U.S. control over the World Trade Organization (WTO) at a rally near the U.S. embassy in Manila, Philippines, 2003. The view that the WTO is steered by (mostly U.S.) corporations undermines the legitimacy of the organization.
PHOTOGRAPH BY BULLIT MARQUEZ. AP/WIDE WORLD PHOTOS. REPRODUCED BY PERMISSION.

particularly in Asia, have rejected the Washington Consensus, yet have successfully penetrated export markets and attracted foreign capital (Stiglitz 2002).

CRITICS IN DEVELOPED NATIONS

It is in the developed world that doubts about global market integration are most strongly expressed. There are three distinct sources of this opposition. First, globalization's critics believe that trade and investment agreements between poor and rich nations harm the interests of the working class and the poor in the wealthier nations. They argue that the people of the developed nations suffer because open product markets and capital mobility drive down wages, undermine labor rights, and put environmental regulations at risk. They insist that such agreements should be entered into only if they contain provisions to offset this presumed "race to the bottom" (Greider 1997).

There is no convincing evidence to suggest that globalization has had a negative impact on environmental standards (Bhagwati 2004). But trade relations between a developed and an underdeveloped nation can result in reduced wages for unskilled workers in the rich nations. As manufacturing spreads to poor countries, increased competition means that some industries in the rich nations are forced to close or cut back on production. Job losses occur, and this generates downward pressures on wages. Though most empirical research into the causes of the recent wage stagnation in the United States does not identify globalization as the major cause involved, this mechanism does have plausibility (Bhagwati 2004; Rodrik 1997).

But what this argument neglects are the gains that rich countries can secure from globalization. Most fundamentally, consumers benefit as more goods at lower prices become available. In addition, at least some producers and their labor forces also benefit. The increased income that globalization generates when poor nations expand their overseas sales means enhanced export opportunities for firms in developed countries. Markets are created where previously there were none. If seized, these opportunities mean the creation of new jobs, even as others are lost. What is crucial in this regard is that economic theory predicts that the industries that migrate to poor nations will tend to be those using labor-intensive methods of production. The jobs that are lost, therefore, will be ones that pay relatively low wages. By comparison, the wages paid in the remaining, expanding industries will very likely be relatively high. Overall, the wage structure will rise (Rodrick 1998).

A second issue animates the antiglobalization movement. The critics believe that the results are unfair. They have a strong case. The growth in compensatory and assistance programs to benefit the job losers and those put under wage pressure—the innocent victims of progress—has lagged far behind the need for such remedial efforts. In the United States, for example, job retraining is ineffective, wage insurance does not exist, and even portable health insurance is all but unavailable. Governments have provided insufficient help to those who were required to bear the costs of the dislocations associated with globalization. Thus, even as it can be maintained that, overall, globalization is wealth producing, many of those whose interests have been damaged by restructuring have not been provided with the resources necessary to allow them to become successful participants in the process (Burtless et al. 1998).

This issue of the fairness of the process is linked to a third strand of opposition—the widespread anxiety that globalization threatens national sovereignty and therefore the scope of democratic rule. At issue here are the mechanisms created to govern the increasingly integrated international economy.

Prior to the 1995 creation of the World Trade Organization (WTO), no effective dispute-settlement body existed to resolve the inevitable conflicts that occurred as trade and investment flows increased. The procedure that had existed under the General Agreement on Tariffs and Trade (GATT) was of little use because it operated under the principle of consensus. The guilty party had to agree that it was in the wrong for a conflict to be resolved. Under the WTO rules, the resolution of disagreements no longer requires unanimity, and dispute-settlement panels can have their conclusions implemented without the threat of a veto. As the WTO's proponents convincingly argue, such a mechanism is both functional and necessary in an ever-more integrated world economy (Jackson 1998).

But it is precisely the quasi-judicial pronouncements of the WTO settlement panels that draw the ire of the antiglobalization coalition in the developed world. What unites disparate groups, which on many other issues disagree with each other, is their unwillingness to cede decision-making authority to an international organization. They believe those decisions will be unjust (Eckes 1999; Wallach and Sforza 1999).

What is at issue here is the relationship between governments and multinational corporations and how that relationship is put on display in the WTO. Obviously, transnational firms are major actors in globalization. It is their technical competence, financial resources, and entrepreneurial initiatives that drive economic expansion. But what causes unease is their role in the shaping of trade rules. Negotiations under the GATT and now the WTO typically take the form of governments acting as industrial advocates. Government trade representatives lobby on behalf of firms based in their countries. In appearance, therefore, trade talks seem to be undertaken exclusively in response to and on behalf of corporate interests (O'Dell and Eichengreen 1998).

The resulting spectacle is responsible for the widely held view that multinational corporations have captured the WTO, and it is that view that places the legitimacy of the organization at risk. Its ability to be fair and responsive to more than its corporate constituency is doubted. It is one thing to argue that the technology that permits the world economy to be integrated is potentially beneficial, but it is another to claim that it is being deployed in a way that equitably distributes those benefits. And it is in this regard that the "democratic deficit" in the WTO is important (Ostrey 1999).

In sum, concerns over wages, fairness, and national sovereignty are the issues that, in reinforcing each other, have attracted the components of the antiglobalization movement: unions worry that the WTO's enforcing of global trade rules means job losses; environmentalists believe that it accelerates the process of environmental despoiling; nongovernmental organizations argue that it encourages sweatshops; defenders of traditional culture insist that it undermines indigenous ways of life; and all agree that globalization, as implemented through the WTO, represents a process whose benefits are skewed to corporate interests as opposed to all other constituencies. To be sure, latent within the coalition are conflicts. Trade unionists and environmentalists are not traditional allies. Furthermore, the movement is much stronger in opposing globalization than it is in proposing an alternative. Nevertheless, distrust of globalization has been sufficient to provide recruits to the coalition (Mandle 2003).

Despite its critics, it is very likely that globalization has reached a point of no return. But it can be made more just. Attention can be directed to the interests of its victims. The resources necessary to alleviate the price they pay are generated by the efficiencies that globalization itself creates. Further, the WTO can become a more transparent organization, and its decision-making mechanisms can become more sensitive to a broader range of constituencies. If these and other reforms are undertaken, much of what sustains the protesters will recede. But if both in appearance and substance globalization remains biased toward corporate interests, the antiglobalization movement will continue to attract adherents.

SEE ALSO FREE TRADE, THEORY AND PRACTICE; GATT, WTO; THEORIES OF INTERNATIONAL TRADE.

BIBLIOGRAPHY

Bhagwati, Jagdish. *In Defense of Globalization.* New York: Oxford University Press, 2004.

Burtless, Gary; Lawrence, Robert Z.; Litan, Robert E.; and Shapiro, Robert J. *Globaphobia: Confronting Fears about Open Trade.* Washington, DC, and New York: Brookings Institution, 1998.

Chadha, Rajesh; Hoekman, Bernard; Martin, Will; et al. "Introduction." In *Developing Countries and the WTO: A Pro-active Agenda,* ed. Bernard Hoekman and Will Martin. Oxford, U.K. and Malden, MA: Blackwell, 2001.

Dollar, David. "Globalization, Poverty, and Inequality since 1980." World Bank Policy Research Working Paper 3333. Washington, DC: World Bank, 2004.

Eckes, Alfred E., Jr. "U.S. Trade History." In *U.S. Trade Policy: History, Theory, and the WTO,* ed. William A. Lovett; Alfred E. Eckes, Jr.; and Richard L. Brinkman. Armonk, NY, and London: M.E. Sharpe, 1999.

Greider, William. *One World, Ready or Not.* New York: Simon and Schuster, 1997.

Jackson, John H. "Designing and Implementing Effective Dispute Settlement Procedures: WTO Dispute Settlement, Appraisal, and Prospects." In *The WTO as an International Organization,* ed. Anne O. Krueger. Chicago and London: University of Chicago Press, 1998.

Krueger, Anne O. *Trade Policies and Developing Nations.* Washington, DC: Brookings Institution, 1995.

Mandle, Jay R. *Globalization and the Poor.* New York. Cambridge University Press, 2003.

Odell, John, and Eichengreen, Barry. "The United States, the ITO, and the WTO: Exit Options, Agent Slack, and Presidential Leadership." In *The WTO as an International Organization,* ed. Anne O. Krueger. Chicago and London: University of Chicago Press, 1998.

Ostry, Sylvia. "The Future of the World Trade Organization." In *Brookings Trade Forum 1999,* ed. Susan M. Collins and Robert Z. Lawrence. Washington, DC: Brookings Institution, 1999.

Rodrik, Dani. *Has Globalization Gone Too Far?* Washington, DC: Institute for International Economics, 1997.

Rodrik, Dani. "Has Globalization Gone Too Far? An Interview with Dani Rodrik." *Challenge* 41, no. 2 (March–April 1998): 81–94.

Stiglitz, Joseph E. *Globalization and Its Discontents.* New York: W. W. Norton, 2002.

Wallach, Lori, and Sforza, Michell. *Whose Trade Organization? Corporate Globalization and the Erosion of Democracy.* Washington, DC: Public Citizen, 1999.

Jay R. Mandle

GOLD AND SILVER

Gold was so valuable in the fifteenth century that Portugal's Henry the Navigator sent explorations along the west coast of Africa in search for gold. Prior to the Portuguese incursions, West African gold had entered European trading circuits via the Sahara Desert. Portuguese conquests resulted in the construction in 1481 of the Sao Jorge da Mina outpost, an area since known as the Gold Coast. Gold arrivals at Lisbon's Casa da Moneda rose to 700 kilograms annually between 1500 and 1520, after which there was a downward trend for the remainder of the sixteenth century. Decline in gold arrivals to Lisbon coincided with Spanish conquests in America. Soon after their arrival in the Caribbean, conquistadors began collecting existing indigenous gold as well as organizing placer gold mining, gold collected from alluvial deposits in rivers or river beds. Greater amounts of looted gold entered Europe after the 1519 conquest of Mexico and the conquest of Peru in the 1530s. Soon mining operations were developed in Mexico, Peru, Chile, and New Granada. Gold imports into Spain peaked between 1551 and 1560.

Europe's silver came from mines located in Germany and elsewhere in the Holy Roman Empire (e.g., Bohemia, Hungary, and the eastern Alps) during the Middle Ages. Central European silver production surged, propelled by new technology. In 1451 the Duke of Saxony granted the right to implement the cupelation process, which separated silver from copper by using lead. European silver production may seem modest (100 tons of silver mined during the decade 1526–1535) compared with the fantastic subsequent output from American mines, but some argue that the Price Revolution (over a century of unprecedented price inflation) began in the second half of the fifteenth century, prior to the arrivals of the metals from America. This early price inflation is consistent with surging silver production in Central Europe.

Prior to 1530, gold was the only American precious metal to reach Spain, but by the 1540s European imports of American silver surpassed imports of American gold (in value terms). Initial Spanish silver mines were established in central Mexico, followed by discoveries in upper Peru (now Bolivia) at Porco in 1538 and at Potosí (the world's most prolific source of silver) in 1545. The main mining districts were in the central Andes and in northwest Mexico (containing mines at Pachuca, Santa Barbara, Guanajuato, Zacatecas, and Sombrerete). Mining operations in the Andes initially used indigenous technology such as the smelting furnace (*wayra*). Central European technology inspired the *patio* method, based on the amalgamation of silver ores with mercury. The mercury amalgam process was introduced in Mexico during the 1550s and in Peru during the 1570s. An im-

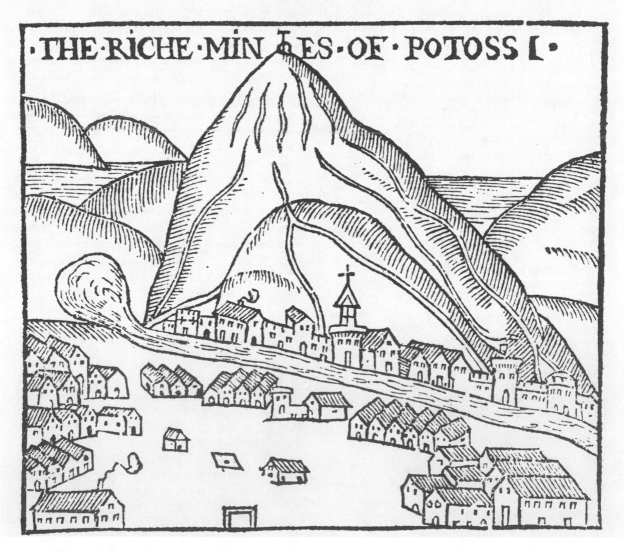

THE
DISCOVERIE AND CONQVEST
of the Prouinces of *PERV*, and
the *Nauigation in the South*
Sea, along that Coaſt.
And alſo of the ritche Mines
of *POTOSI*.

·THE·RICHE·MINES·OF·POTOSSI·

The town of Potosí. *A 1581 illustration showing a small South American town located beneath mountains containing a wealth of precious metal resources. Mining operations were established throughout the central Andes and in areas like Potosí, where a wealth of silver was discovered.* © BETTMANN/CORBIS. REPRODUCED BY PERMISSION.

mense silver mining boom ensued, because amalgamation permitted processing of lower-quality ores. Longer and deeper mines were excavated, requiring innovations in drainage and ventilation. Mills were powered by animals or water, which implied large capital investments.

The world's second most important producer of precious metals was Japan, the source of perhaps half as much silver as all of Spanish America during the sixteenth and seventeenth centuries. The Japanese mines soon came under the control of Tokugawa *shogunate,* and their profits financed unification of Japan. The main exports of Japan in the seventeenth century were silver and, later, gold and copper. The principal mines were Yamagano, Besshi, Ikuno, Hodatsu, Hodatsu, Aikawa and Tsurushi (Sado), Umegajima, Nobezawa, Innai, Ani, and most notably Omori in Iwami. A new technology for smelting silver using lead, *haifuki,* was introduced from China via Korea. Gold was extracted using the same procedure. The technology for smelting copper ores, *mabuki,* also arrived from Korea. A chlorination process was imported from China before 1643 that allowed separation of silver from gold. The Japanese knew about the mercury amalgamation process that was so important in Spanish America; indeed, they used the *patio* process in the Sado mines by 1610. Due to availability of lead and the alternative uses of mercury, however, the cupellation process was preferred. Japanese miners used new excavation techniques, including mine drainage, ventilation, and surveying. New methods in refining precious metals and mining engineering resulted from trade with Korea and China as well as from the Portuguese and Spaniards. Between 1550 and 1650 Japan's production of silver and gold reached levels unsurpassed until the Meiji Era of the nineteenth century.

According to Ward Barrett, from 1493 to 1700 America produced 79.5 percent of the world's silver and 52 percent of the world's gold. American silver production had tremendous repercussions in the world economy, for it was the crucial commodity that connected America, Europe, Asia, and Africa (indirectly). The reason is simply that the price of silver was much higher in China than in the rest of the world. A century of vigorous transshipment of silver through trade circuits worldwide finally depressed the price of silver in China down to the world price by 1640. The first global trade cycle (1540s–1640) ended when silver's value could fall no further because extraordinary profits had been squeezed out. The "price revolution" also ended by 1640 because silver's value could fall no further (and a fall in money's value is price inflation by definition).

A great deal more silver was produced in the eighteenth century—most of which came from Mexico—than in the previous two centuries combined. The dominant end-market for silver during the eighteenth century was once again giant China, which had doubled in population and landmass, thanks in large part to introduction of American foodstuffs. Silver again flowed overwhelmingly to China because the price of silver in China rose to a level 50 percent higher than in the rest of the world by 1700. Massive Chinese imports of silver depressed its price there to the world level again by 1750. Aside from depressed silver prices, the Independence Wars in America rendered more difficult the exploitation of silver mines in Mexico and Peru and the gold mines of Brazil.

Gold production, perhaps 85 percent of which came from the Americas, also peaked during the eighteenth century. Gold mines were discovered in 1744 in the Urals region of Siberia, where mining activity continued into the nineteenth century, thanks in part to German technological expertise. From 1831 to 1840 Siberian mines accounted for one-third of world output. In other words, Russia became the world's greatest producer of precious metals, following the preeminence of Spanish America earlier on and prior to California's mid-nineteenth-century gold rush.

From 1848 to 1856 California produced 752,400 kilograms of gold. Mining activities began soon thereafter in British Columbia, Colorado, Nevada, Idaho, and Montana. There were also significant gold rushes in Australia and New Zealand. During the second half of the nineteenth century 11,000 tons of gold were produced, perhaps double the amount of the yellow metal produced since the discovery of America in the fifteenth century. The gold standard was adopted in many important countries around the world during the second half of the nineteenth century, and gold finally replaced silver as the world's dominant monetary substance. By the 1870s gold had become relatively scarce, but the South African Witwatersrand was discovered in 1886. Industrial technology allowed deep excavation in South African mines, and discovery of the Mac Arthur-Forrest cyanide process in 1890 permitted extraction of gold from ores with low gold content. This South African source produced 120 tons of gold in 1898, 25 percent of world production. South Africa mined one-third of world gold production in the twentieth century.

As was true earlier, when silver was the world's dominant monetary substance, nineteenth- and twentieth-century gold rushes occurred when gold's price rose significantly above its cost of production. Between 1810 and 1848 gold was expensive relative to merchandise, but the 1848 to 1851 "gold rushes" unleashed large quantities of new gold that pushed down its market value; that is to say, there was a general increase in prices because the value of gold monies declined. The period 1896 to 1920, which saw gold discoveries in South Africa, Alaska, and the Klondike, likewise witnessed an inflationary period.

Mexico was the largest silver producer during the nineteenth century, but discoveries in the Comstock and Eureka districts of Nevada, Utah, and Arizona subsequently elevated the United States to world preeminence. This great U.S. silver output resulted from new technologies (developed between 1842 and 1869) for separating silver from lead ore. Again, a predictable consequence of the resultant flood of silver reaching the global marketplace was a depreciation in the value of silver. Asian countries with traditional silver-based monetary systems, such as India and China, finally abandoned the white metal. India pegged the rupee to gold in 1898, and China began printing paper money after the Sino-Japanese war of 1894 to 1895. On August 15, 1971, the United States abolished the international convertibility of the dollar for gold. After many centuries of global dominance, silver and gold no longer served as foundations for world monetary systems.

SEE ALSO BULLION (SPECIE); EMPIRE, SPANISH; MINING; MONEY AND MONETARY POLICY; POTOSÍ; PRICES AND INFLATION; SOUTH AFRICA; UNITED STATES.

BIBLIOGRAPHY

Bakewell, Peter, ed. *Mines of Silver and Gold in the Americas.* Aldershot, U.K.: Variorum, 1997.

Barrett, Ward. "World Bullion Flows, 1450–1800." In *The Rise of Merchant Empires: Long Distance Trade in the Early Modern World, 1350–1750,* ed. James D. Tracy. New York: Cambridge University Press, 1990.

McGuire, John; Bertola, Patrick; and Reeves, Peter, eds. *Evolution of the World Economy, Precious Metals and India.* New Delhi: Oxford University Press, 2001.

Richards, John. F., ed. *Precious Metals in the Later Medieval and Early Modern Worlds.* Durham, NC: Carolina Academic Press, 1983.

Richards, John F., ed. *The Imperial Monetary System of Mughal India.* Delhi: Oxford University Press, 1987.

Von Glahn, Richard. *Fountain of Fortune: Money and Monetary Policy in China, 1000–1700.* Berkeley: University of California Press, 1996.

Dennis O. Flynn
Árturo Giraldez

GOLD COAST

The Gold Coast of West Africa included the land between the Tano River and the Volta River, approximately 250 miles of coastline between longitude 3.5 degrees west and longitude 1.5 degrees east. The Gold Coast lay between the modern countries of the Ivory Coast and Togo. Two main trends may be perceived in the history of the Gold Coast. First, people living on the Atlantic Ocean participated in an international trading system that included the exchange of products from parts of Africa, Asia, the New World, and Europe. Second, one consequence of participation in this international economic system was a prolonged, intense interaction between Africans and Europeans residing in forts and trading posts, most notably at Elmina, Cape Coast, and Accra.

Recent research confirms connections between the Niger River in the West African interior (today's Mali) and the Gold Coast before the European arrival. These trade connections brought Manding-speaking traders from interior West Africa to the Gold Coast after about 1350, primarily to acquire gold. Also, circumstantial evidence suggests a sea trade between the Gold Coast and the Benin kingdom (Nigeria) exchanging gold for Benin beads, cloth, and slaves.

The Portuguese were the first Europeans to trade with Gold Coast residents (1471). In 1482 they constructed a fort at Elmina and, later, smaller structures along the coast. Other Europeans followed the Portuguese example in the seventeenth century, most notably companies from the Netherlands, England, and Denmark. The Europeans constructed these forts to store their trade goods, provide housing for their employees, and, most important, protect themselves from other Europeans, not from the Africans. Trade could prosper only if peace was maintained between the Europeans and their African hosts and neighbors, and the Africans could easily blockade a fort if a dispute arose. The Europeans lived on the Gold Coast for business reasons only. Usually, a sizable town grew up around a major fort, like Elmina, where a multiethnic population in the eighteenth century ranged from 12,000 to 16,000.

Gold Coast Africans brought the major exports—gold, ivory, and slaves (especially during the eighteenth century)—from the interior to the coastal towns, where the Africans and Europeans negotiated prices and the exchange of goods. The Europeans did not enter the interior to buy directly from the producers. The Gold Coast was not a major center for slave exports, accounting for only about 9 to 10 percent of the total of all exports. Imports included large quantities of Indian- and European-manufactured cloth; metals and metalware such as iron bars, pots, and pans; firearms, gunpowder, and flints; alcohol; and small amounts of trinkets, such as mirrors and beads. Eventually, the Portuguese also brought tobacco from the New World. The main currency was pure gold dust or gold dust adulterated with copper filings. The economies of the coastal towns benefited from their middleman positions because the Europeans and the interior traders demanded goods and services. Coastal farmers

Gold Coast village, c. 1920s. *By the end of the nineteenth century the Gold Coast had turned from exporting mostly slaves to exporting palm oil, rubber, and cocoa.* © BETTMANN/CORBIS. REPRODUCED BY PERMISSION.

produced surplus food for the Europeans in the forts and the people on the ships (including the slaves), and others collected fresh water and firewood for the ships. Fishermen, who knew about the surf, supplemented their income by providing ship to shore transportation and communication along the coast between the forts. The interior businessmen required housing, food, and protection. Both sides hired local interpreters and middlemen to aid in the negotiations. In most places, the Europeans paid rent for the land on which the forts or trading posts were constructed. One important result of this economic situation was the development of what Kwame Daaku called a new class of Gold Coast entrepreneurs, wealthy men who also had political influence in their communities (Daaku 1970). Another result was miscegenation, leading to the growth of an Afro-European population.

During the nineteenth century the slave trade declined and new economic opportunities emerged for individual Africans. There was a transition from selling

human beings to selling primary products, such as palm oil and natural rubber, and a renewed gold trade. The Gold Coast was not a major exporter of palm oil, but it became one of the major African producers of rubber at the end of the nineteenth century, exporting two to three million pounds (in volume) in the early 1890s. In addition, toward the end of the nineteenth century the cultivation of cocoa, a New World crop, was introduced into the Gold Coast; it became the dominant agricultural export from the Gold Coast in the twentieth century.

Many of the African exporters, such as John Sarbah (c. 1834–1892), also developed retail businesses and became successful entrepreneurs. The shift to the export of primary products and the continued import of cloth, hardware, alcohol, tobacco, and other European goods contributed to the growth of a prosperous business class within Gold Coast society. Entrepreneurs were aided by the development of the steamship, which allowed them to import small quantities at cheaper rates, and the availability of credit from European suppliers. The shift to primary products grown mainly in the forest interior of the Gold Coast spread the effects of the production of these products beyond the coastal towns. Individuals and societies entered the business of collecting, processing, and transporting palm oil, palm kernels, or rubber, all of which were labor-intensive efforts. The owner of the trees had to be convinced to enter the market economy, and potential laborers had to be encouraged to work for pay in addition to their usual farming responsibilities. Women in certain areas became involved in processing palm oil. Toward the end of the nineteenth century entrepreneurs such as Africanus Horton, M.D. (1835–1883), created companies to introduce deep mining into the Gold Coast. Horton also hoped to construct a railroad into the interior. However, these companies failed to attract the necessary capital to translate their ideas into action.

By the late nineteenth century, before colonial rule, the Gold Coast had a vibrant economy linked to international trade. A small, successful business class had emerged, and Gold Coast farmers had laid the foundation for the export of an important cash crop, cocoa. The children of many businessmen trained as professionals in British universities, and educated Gold Coast citizens began cooperating with traditional leaders in modern constitutional experiments.

SEE ALSO Africa, Labor Taxes (Head Taxes); Arms, Armaments; Caravan Trade; Coffee; Cowries; Dahomey; Empire, British; Empire, Dutch; Empire, French; Empire, Portuguese; Ethnic Groups, Africans; Ghana; Gold and Silver; Imperialism; Laborers, Coerced; Laborers, Contract; Mercantilism; Sarbah, John; Slavery and the African Slave Trade; Textiles; Triangular Trade.

BIBLIOGRAPHY

Daaku, Kwame Y. *Trade and Politics on the Gold Coast, 1600–1720.* Oxford, U.K.: Clarendon Press, 1970.

Davies, K. G. *The Royal African Company.* London: Longman, 1957.

Feinberg, Harvey M. *Africans and Europeans in West Africa: Elminans and Dutchmen on the Gold Coast during the Eighteenth Century.* Philadelphia: American Philosophical Society, 1989.

Kea, Ray E. *Settlements, Trade, and Politics in the Seventeenth-Century Gold Coast.* Baltimore, MD: Johns Hopkins University Press, 1982.

Kimble, David. *A Political History of Ghana.* Oxford, U.K.: Clarendon Press, 1963.

Nørregård, Georg. *Danish Settlements in West Africa.* Boston: Boston University Press, 1966.

Priestley, Margaret. *West African Trade and Coast Society: A Family Study.* London: Oxford University Press, 1969.

Harvey M. Feinberg

GOLD RUSHES

Gold was prized for thousands of years. What caused the phenomenon of the large-scale gold rush from the mid-nineteenth century to the end of the nineteenth century? Four factors played a role. The first was denser settlement of previously lightly settled areas in North America, Australia, Asia, and South Africa, leading to new mineral discoveries. The second was the widespread availability of newspapers and a literate population to read them. These newspapers transmitted large amounts of information about gold rushes to readers. Some, excited by the prospect of riches and adventure, decided to go. Thirdly, the period also featured greatly enhanced possibilities of large-scale movement. Historically, many people had been bound to the land, and not allowed to move, but by the mid-nineteenth century most people of European ancestry were free to move, as were Chinese. People also had to be able to reach the site of the rush. International and long-distance migrants had to travel mostly by water. Fortunately, ongoing improvements in sailing and, later, steam ships made the trips feasible. Finally, these gold rushes occurred in settings where the government chose not to unduly tax or regulate gold mining, thus allowing miners to capture most of the proceeds from their efforts. These four factors kicked off an era of large and small gold rushes.

The first major gold rush began in California in January 1848 at the famed Sutter's Mill. A second followed rapidly at Ballarat and Bendingo in Victoria, Australia, in 1851. A spate of smaller rushes followed: Otago in New Zealand (1857), Queensland in Australia (1858), Fraser River in British Columbia (1858), the Comstock in Nevada (1859–1860), Pikes Peak in Colorado (1858), Boise in Idaho (1860), Montana (1862), the Black Hills of South Dakota (1876–1878), the Amur River (1883) on the Russian-Chinese border, and Western Australia (1886). The third major gold rush began in South Africa in 1886 in the Witwatersrand ("Rand") district of the Transvaal. The last major gold rush, in the Klondike, began in 1896 and encompassed finds on both the U.S. and Canadian sides of the border.

MIGRATIONS

The scales of the migrations associated with the four major gold rushes are not particularly well documented. Many more people set out than actually reached their destinations or became miners. Some died along the way; some turned around en route. Others reached a major jumping-off site to the more remote regions and decided to stay. Even among those who reached the mines, many died, turned around, or took up other occupations.

The California gold rush began in earnest in May 1848 when Sam Brannan (1819–1889) appeared in San

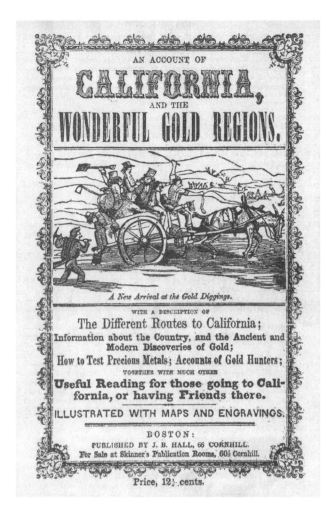

The title page of An Account of California and the Wonderful Gold Regions, **published by J. B. Hill in 1849.** *The book served as a guide to would-be prospectors who traveled to California after the discovery of gold at Sutter's Mill in 1848. Over 40,000 people immigrated to the West Coast with hopes of striking it rich, but few profited from their ventures.* © BETTMANN/CORBIS. REPRODUCED BY PERMISSION.

Francisco waving a bottle of gold dust. Crewmen in San Francisco deserted, and whole towns emptied. The rush was given further momentum when President James K. Polk (1795–1849) confirmed the discovery of gold in his message to Congress. In 1849 81,000 gold rushers reached California, and in 1850 another 91,000 arrived. By 1852 the population of the state had gone from roughly 40,000 (including Native Americans) to 260,000. This increase equaled roughly 1 percent of the population of the United States during this period. A much greater share of young white males picked up and permanently moved West within the period of a few years. Estimates suggest that one-quarter of the participants in the gold rush were foreign-born.

With the gold rush, the population in Australia and in Victoria exploded; the total population of Australia nearly tripled from 430,000 in 1851 to 11.2 million in 1861. In 1852, 370,000 immigrants arrived in Australia, largely from the British Isles. Victoria's population jumped from 77,000 to 540,000 in two years. Chinese men began to arrive at the mines in 1853, and by 1858 they represented 20 percent of the mining population.

South Africa also boomed with the discovery of gold. Between 1870 and 1904 the white population quadrupled from fewer than 250,000 to 1 million. Most of the immigrants were British and Dutch. Johannesburg increased from essentially nothing in 1886 to 102,000 in 1896, and the number of black laborers in the mines increased from 14,000 to 97,000 between 1890 and 1899.

Although an estimated 100,000 left for the Klondike, only 35,000 to 40,000 people actually reached the gold fields because of the difficulty of getting there. Compared to the previous three rushes, a far smaller number of people participated.

LIFE IN THE GOLD FIELDS

In the initial stages of the gold rushes in each of these regions, huge numbers of people from the surrounding areas dropped what they were doing and headed to mine. Almost immediately, wages increased, often doubling or even tripling, but frequently this was not enough to keep people on the job. Over time, the hardship of mining in remote locations and the high levels of wages and prices led to a reallocation of labor toward activities such as agriculture in California, Australia, and South Africa. In Alaska and the Yukon the majority of miners chose not to stay for the winter, heading south to places such as Seattle. Many did not to return the next year. Rushes proved to be a significant spur in the development of cities such as San Francisco, Melbourne, Seattle (the gateway for the Klondike), and Johannesburg. In the mountainous mining regions there was little lasting settlement and often significant environmental damage.

Prices in the mines went up dramatically with the initial rush of people to the area and then fell over time. This pattern reflects the fact that all of the miners had to be outfitted from the available stocks of food, clothing, and equipment, and supply took a while to respond. Another factor in the high prices in the mines, and one that did not disappear over time, was the cost of supplying remote areas. All products had to be brought in over rugged terrain, sometimes by water, but more often by horses, dogs, or humans.

Property rights were generally similar across gold rushes in that mineral claims consisted of a plot of land of a specific size, claims could be bought and sold, and continued control of a claim depended on the claim being actively mined. California, Australia, and the Klondike all had significant amounts of gold near the surface, which could be mined by small numbers of individuals with relatively little capital investment. In California and Alaska, claim sizes were decided by miners in the mining district and were typically larger than the claims in Australia and Canada, where the government specified claim sizes. In the United States miners were not taxed or otherwise required to pay to mine, whereas in Australia and Canada the miners had to pay substantial taxes. In South Africa relatively little of the gold was near the surface. Thus, most of the mining was undertaken by corporations, which invested heavily in the mining equipment necessary to bring the rock to the surface and crush the rock to extract the gold. Many of these corporations were also heavily involved in diamond mining.

Ethnic conflict was a common feature of most rushes, with sentiment against non-English-speakers and the Chinese in particular running high. In California this antiforeigner sentiment was manifest in the Foreign Miners Tax. Originally $20 per month in 1850 for foreign miners, the tax was repealed in 1851 and then reinstated in 1852 at a monthly rate of $3. Foreign miners also were more likely to be pushed off by threat of violence by Americans. Generally, the foreign miners in Canada and Australia were more likely to be of British origin than were those in California, although immigration restrictions were put in place in Australia to limit Chinese inflow. In South Africa political conflict between the Dutch Boers and the British over the rights of the British in the Boer-controlled gold-rush area in the Transvaal led to the Boer War (1899–1902), and ultimately to British control. Because the vast majority of the workers in the South African mines were black, ethnic conflict tended to be between various tribal groups, and it was exacerbated by recruitment of laborers in neighboring countries who were often willing to work for lower wages.

MACROECONOMIC EFFECTS

As a result of these major and minor gold rushes, the annual world production of gold tripled over the fifty-year period 1848 to 1898. Before then, the ratio of the world silver stock to the world gold stock had been roughly constant since 1600. In 1850 most countries were on a gold standard, a silver standard, or a bimetallic standard, in which silver and gold were accepted in a fixed ratio. The discovery of large amounts of gold and the failure to discover even larger deposits of silver caused the ratio of the world stock of silver to gold to fall rapidly. By the mid-1870s the increase in the gold supply had largely driven out the bimetallic standard, and bimetallic-standard countries and some silver-standard countries moved to the gold standard.

SEE ALSO Africa, Labor Taxes (Head Taxes); Anglo American Corporation; Australia; Bullion (Specie); Canada; Empire, British; Empire, Japanese; Gold and Silver; Gold Standard; Guggenheim Family; Labor, Types of; Laborers, Coerced; Laborers, Contract; Manchuria; Mexico; Mining; Population— Emigration and Immigration; Rates of Exchange; San Francisco–Oakland; Smuggling; South Africa; United States.

BIBLIOGRAPHY

Eichengreen, Barry, and McLean, Ian W. "The Supply of Gold Under the Pre-1914 Gold Standard." *The Economic History Review* new series, 47, no. 2. (May 1994): 288–309.

Fetherling, Douglas. *The Gold Crusades: A Social History of Gold Rushes, 1849–1929.* Toronto: University of Toronto Press, 1997.

Morrell, William P. *The Gold Rushes.* Chester Springs, PA: Dufour, 1968.

Schmitz, Christopher J. *World Non-Ferrous Metal Production and Prices, 1700–1970.* London: Frank Cass, 1979.

Velde, Francois R., and Weber, Warren E. "A Model of Bimetallism." *The Journal of Political Economy* 108, no. 6 (December 2000): 1210–1234.

Karen Clay

GOLD STANDARD

A gold standard is a system in which money is meaningfully denominated in units of gold. *Denominated* means that a piece of money may be a full-bodied gold coin, or it may be a claim redeemable for gold coins or bullion.

Ancient economies adopted various commodities (including oxen, salt, and shells) as media of exchange. As trade networks grew, metals (silver, gold, and copper) displaced other commodity monies because of their greater convenience for hand-to-hand exchange: they were more portable (precious), durable, and divisible. An inconvenience of trading silver or gold in raw form was the difficulty of assessing the quality of any particular nugget. The development of coinage, which certified the weight and fineness of the metal being offered, overcame that problem. The use of silver and gold coins spread across the trading world after about 600 B.C.E.

Where modern banking developed, the public came to hold most of its money in the form of redeemable claims (token coins, banknotes, and transferable deposits), with the precious metals residing mostly in bank vaults. Bank-issued money avoided the major problems associated with full-bodied coins: bulkiness (for large payments), wear and tear, and lack of uniformity due to clipping (lightening by the public) and debasement (lightening by royal mints). Because the mints faced more competition in producing the large-value gold coins that circulated internationally, they debased silver coins more extensively.

Although some authors define the gold standard by reference to central bank or treasury policies, no government role in money is required for a gold standard in the general sense. If a central bank or treasury *does* issue money under a gold standard, it denominates and redeems (or mints) that money in gold. The business of minting silver and gold coins was commonly nationalized to reap the profit available from minting monopoly, but in a few places (e.g., California during the 1850s gold rush) it was left to private competition. The business of issuing redeemable banknotes was normally left to private commercial banks before central banks nationalized it in the nineteenth and twentieth centuries. Deposit banking remained largely private throughout the period.

Silver standards predominated from ancient times until the nineteenth century, with gold coins limited to large-value payments. As gold payments grew in importance through the Renaissance and the Industrial Revolution, some national governments tried to fix unit-of-account values for *both* precious metals. *Bimetallism* gave the dollar both a defined silver content and (alternatively) a defined gold content. Bimetallism was unsustainable when the world market exchange ratio moved too far from the official silver/gold ratio implied by the dual definition of the dollar. People would pay dollar debts in whichever metal was cheaper to get in the market. They would hoard or export the legally undervalued metal, leaving only the legally overvalued metal in circulation (the famous "Gresham's Law"). In 1717 Isaac Newton (1642–1727), as master of the Royal Mint, inadvertently moved the United Kingdom from silver to gold by overvaluing gold. The United States government overvalued gold in 1834, with similar results. Several European nations led by Germany—either seeking to emulate the United Kingdom and the United States or fearful of a decline in the relative value of silver—deliberately switched from silver to gold standards in the 1870s.

The heyday of the international gold standard ended with World War I. Central banks and treasuries abandoned their commitments to gold redemption so as to finance war expenditures with issues of unbacked money. They established and then broke more tenuous links to gold in the interwar period. Under the Bretton Woods system after World War II, the U.S. government allowed foreign central banks (but not U.S. citizens) to redeem dollars for gold, until President Richard Nixon (1913–1994) finally "closed the gold window" in 1971. Gold today serves as a parallel currency for few transactions.

THE QUANTITY AND PURCHASING POWER OF MONEY

In most countries on gold, the unit of account had a distinct name. For example, the U.S. economy before 1933 used the *dollar,* defined as .04838 troy ounce (or equivalently 23.22 grains) of gold 90 percent fine. With prices quoted in dollars, and the dollar defined as an amount of gold, the consumer price level (dollars per goods-basket) was the product of two factors: (1) the defined ratio between dollars and gold (dollars per ounce Au), and (2) the relative price of the goods-basket in terms of gold (ounce Au per goods-basket).

Law or convention fixed the first ratio. The second was governed by supply and demand conditions in the world market for gold. An increase in demand for monetary gold (e.g., a large country switching to the gold standard and amassing gold reserves) would increase the purchasing power of gold (lower the relative price of goods in gold), and thereby lower the dollar price level proportionally. In a decade or two the higher purchasing power of gold would stimulate enough extra mining for the stock of gold to catch up with demand, reversing the initial price level movement. A fall in monetary gold demand would conversely cause a drop and then recovery of the purchasing power of gold (ppg) by discouraging mining. In the long run the ppg was governed by the output of gold from the world's mines and the consumption of gold by industrial uses. A major boost to output at the existing ppg (the California gold discovery) could lower the equilibrium ppg and raise the path of the price level.

But events such as the California discovery were rare. Actual growth of the world monetary gold stock was gradual. Hugh Rockoff reports that the gold stock grew at an average annual rate of 6.39 percent from 1849 to 1859, the decade of the California and Australian gold rushes (1984, p. 621). In no other decade between 1839 and 1929 was the growth rate above 3.79 percent. The smaller gold strikes in South Africa (1874–1886), Colorado (1890s), and Alaska (1890s), following years of intense prospecting prompted by a high ppg, helped grow the gold stock to meet growing world demand for gold. The cyanide process for extracting pure gold from ore, a breakthrough allowing profitable exploitation of the South African gold deposits, did likewise. The U.S. fiat monetary base, by contrast, has grown more than 7.4 percent in each decade since 1969. The standard deviations of annual percentage rates of change (around decade-average rates of change) have also been consistently larger for the fiat monetary base since 1949 than for the world's stock of monetary gold from 1839 to 1929.

THE BENEFITS AND COSTS OF A GOLD STANDARD

Defenders of a gold standard emphasize that the natural stability of gold supply limits inflation. The expected inflation rate has close to a zero mean over long-time horizons where the gold standard prevails and is expected to be left alone. Arthur J. Rolnick and Warren E. Weber (1997), studying the histories of fifteen countries, report that their average annual inflation rate under silver or gold standards was 1.75 percent. In the same countries inflation has averaged 9.17 percent under fiat standards.

Bond-market participants had greater confidence in their ability to predict the price level at long horizons under the historical gold standard, judging by the much thicker market for long-maturity bonds. Nineteenth-century railroads found ready buyers for fifty-year bonds. Such bonds are unknown today. Overall, the maturity of new corporate debt issued shrank substantially with the move to fiat standards in the postwar United States.

Gold redemption at a fixed parity prevents governments from printing money without limit to finance its spending. Classical liberals viewed strict commitment to the gold standard as an important constitutional constraint against those activities of governments, particularly war-making, that might be financed by the burst of revenue available from issuing unbacked money.

The leading objection economists have made to a gold standard is the resource cost involved: alternative uses are foregone for the gold tied up in coins and bullion, and resources are devoted to ongoing gold mining. Unbacked (fiat) paper money is much cheaper to produce. Fiat monetary expansion can in principle be constrained to keep inflation to whatever level is desired.

The world's actual switch to fiat regimes has not realized the potential resource cost savings, for two reasons. First, central banks have sold off only a small fraction of their gold stocks. (They *have* at least stopped accumulating gold.) Second, the uncertain reliability of fiat money has prompted the public to accumulate gold coins and bullion as an inflation hedge. The purchasing power or real price of gold is actually higher today than it was in the gold standard era. ($400 per ounce in 2004 is equivalent to about $73 at 1967 U.S. consumer prices, whereas gold was $35 per ounce in 1967. It is equivalent to about $37 at 1929 prices, whereas gold was $20.67 per ounce in 1929.) At a higher real gold price, *more* resources are devoted to gold mining. The switch to fiat standards may ironically have *increased* the resource costs of the monetary system.

An oft-cited estimate of the resource cost of a gold standard is Milton Friedman's (1953) back-of-the-envelope calculation that acquiring new gold to satisfy growing real money demand would annually consume 2.5 percent of national income. Friedman's calculation, however, assumed a "pure" gold standard in which banks hold 100 percent gold reserves even against time deposits. In sophisticated real-world gold-based banking systems, such as Scotland's in the nineteenth century, bank reserves equaled about 2 percent of demand liabilities. The estimated resource cost of a gold standard for such a system is about *one-fiftieth* of Friedman's figure (0.05%) of annual national income. Using standard estimates of the deadweight cost of inflation, the welfare cost of inflation begins to exceed the estimated resource cost of a gold standard (0.05% of national income) at an inflation rate of about 4 percent. If these are the only costs and benefits considered, a gold standard's cost is worth bearing if the alternative is a fiat standard with 4 percent or greater inflation.

SEE ALSO Bullion (Specie); Money and Monetary Policy.

BIBLIOGRAPHY

Friedman, Milton. "Commodity Reserve Currency." In *Essays in Positive Economics,* ed. Milton Friedman. Chicago: University of Chicago Press, 1953.

Rockoff, Hugh. "Some Evidence on the Real Price of Gold, Its Costs of Production, and Commodity Prices." In *A Retrospective on the Classical Gold Standard, 1821–1931,* ed. Michael D. Bordo and Anna J. Schwartz. Chicago: University of Chicago Press, 1984.

Rolnick, Arthur J., and Weber, Warren E. "Money, Inflation, and Output under Fiat and Commodity Standards." *Journal of Political Economy* 105 (December 1997): 1308–1321.

Lawrence H. White

GREAT DEPRESSION OF THE 1930S

The Great Depression, which began in 1929, engulfed the most powerful manufacturing countries and producers of food and raw materials, in a vicious downward spiral that lasted until a sustained recovery began in late 1932 or early 1933. During this period the volume of world trade declined by one-fourth. The severity of the crisis was such that both the structure and the means of conducting international business were dramatically changed. The 1930s was a time of trade restrictions, quotas and tariffs, currency depreciation, and the pursuit of self-sufficiency. Moreover, international lending, which had played a crucial role in sustaining the prosperous international economy in the half century before 1914, was no longer significant. Foreign trade, which had been regarded as the engine of growth in the recent past, had lost its vigor.

This account will outline the important trade and financial links that determined international economic

FRANKLIN D. ROOSEVELT

Franklin D. Roosevelt won the 1932 U.S. presidential election during the Great Depression. Roosevelt's first term was marked by radio addresses, known as the "Fireside Chats," in which he made a point of explaining economic matters in terms all his listeners could understand, reassuring them about the nation's future with a combination of confidence and humor. Roosevelt's 1933 inaugural address was more low-key, yet still optimistic. The economic breakdown was not due to a lack of plenty, he said, but to a larger failure in world trade flows and the inability of leaders and bankers to find rational solutions. Roosevelt intended to approach the crisis as though his nation were at war, waging a vigorous campaign to put ordinary Americans back to work, making more productive use of national resources, and coordinating relief efforts; these strategies were implemented as part of his "New Deal" program. In this inaugural address Roosevelt famously reassured Americans that "this great Nation will endure as it has endured, will revive and will prosper. So, first of all, let me assert my firm belief that the only thing we have to fear is fear itself...."

David J. Clarke

forces. These relationships help explain why hard times spread so rapidly throughout the world.

THE INTERNATIONAL SLUMP: 1929–1933

One of the most destabilizing features of the Depression was the dramatic fall in prices, which both consumers and businesses came to regard as a curse. Over these few years, wholesale prices in the majority of the world's most advanced industrial countries declined by 30 to 40 percent. The situation in economies that depended heavily on the production and export of primary products—unprocessed foodstuffs and raw materials—was worse, as prices fell by 60 to 70 percent. Many primary producers were seriously disadvantaged after 1929: by 1932 they had to sell more of their exports to purchase the same quantity of manufactured imports as they had before the Depression.

Once the Depression gathered force, factories and construction companies reacted to the falling demand for their products by reducing purchases of raw materials, by cutting production, and by firing workers. But rising unemployment led to even lower sales, declining profits, and a further reduction in the demand for raw materials. For example, as U.S. auto manufacturers dramatically cut the numbers of vehicles that they produced, the need for rubber, imported from Southeast Asia to manufacture tires, declined. Unfortunately the rubber-producing countries relied heavily for the bulk of their export earnings on the international sales of that single commodity. Even very low prices failed to stimulate demand. Many primary producing countries were in that situation, facing a growing balance-of-payments deficit.

While manufacturing, mining, and construction companies reacted to falling demand by reducing output, the majority of food and raw material producers found it impossible to follow this path. Throughout the world, the most common unit of production in agriculture was the family, and farmers could not cut costs by dismissing family members. Nor did individual farmers react to falling sales and lower prices by cutting back on production. On the contrary, many strove to increase output, hoping that additional sales would compensate for lower prices. Unfortunately, the outcome was that by 1932, large stocks of a wide range of commodities—cotton, wheat, wool, sugar, and rubber, for example—served to further depress primary-product prices. The growth of stocks is one reason why the price falls for primary products were more severe than the decline in manufacturing prices.

A further problem facing primary producers was that most were in debt. Countries had borrowed heavily during times of war-induced prosperity, especially from investors in the United States. Then in the twenties they borrowed from private citizens in the United States, the world's leading lender, or from the United Kingdom. Borrowing made it possible to fund the purchase of imports that the earnings from exports could not cover. However, the disproportionate primary-product price falls after 1929 had a devastating effect on debtors, many of whom struggled to meet their financial obligations. It is important to remember in this context that while inflation lessens the burden of debt, deflation actually increases it.

In 1929, the United States was the leading exporting nation, accounting for almost 16 percent of the world's total exports and with just over 12 percent of the world's total imports, second only to the United Kingdom. During the 1920s, the United States had also become the world's leading provider of international capital. By purchasing imports and by lending freely, it was able to provide the rest of the world with a regular flow of dollars, on which many countries became dependent.

Massive crowds march in Trafalgar Square, London, as part of a hunger protest in 1932 during the Great Depression. In addition to the economic downturn in the United States, a financial decline spread across Europe as countries were still in recovery from World War I. In 1931, Britain reacted by devaluing its currency and departing from using the gold standard with its trading partners. AP/WIDE WORLD PHOTOS. REPRODUCED BY PERMISSION.

These dollars could be used either to purchase imports directly from the United States, to meet debt repayments, or, since the dollar was widely accepted as an international currency, to purchase goods and services from anywhere in the world. However, once the U.S. economy slid into deep depression, its importing and international lending went into a steep decline, with serious consequences for the international economy. The situation was exacerbated as other rich industrial nations also cut their imports, especially of raw materials, as well as their lending.

THE GOLD STANDARD: A SOURCE OF INSTABILITY

In the decades before 1914, both international trade and lending grew rapidly, but within a fairly stable frame-work. Contemporaries came to the conclusion that this stability had been made possible by the gold standard, which many of the world's major trading nations had adopted. The central banks of countries on the gold standard were required to convert domestic currency into gold at the specified fixed exchange rate. Furthermore, gold could be imported or exported without restriction. Under the rules of the gold standard, when a country ran a balance-of-payments deficit, gold would be exported to fund the deficit. The loss of gold would lead to a contraction of the money supply, which would bring about a gradual deflation, which in turn would lower the costs of production. As a result, exports would become more competitive, and the balance of payments deficit would be rectified. Countries running balance-of-payments surpluses would attract gold, and the consequent increase in the money supply would raise production costs. Exports would become more expensive, and soon the surplus would be reduced.

The appeal of this very simplistic view of the operation of the international gold standard was that it worked automatically. There were clear rules, there was no need for government intervention, and if economies moved toward either surplus or deficit on their balance of payments, the operation of the gold standard ensured that neither movement was extreme.

Most countries abandoned the gold standard during or shortly after World War I, but all major trading nations showed a great determination to readopt it during the 1920s. Unfortunately, by the late twenties most of the world's stock of gold was held by the United States and France. Neither country allowed their gold stock to inflate their domestic economies, so part of the self-correcting mechanism did not operate. Just as significant, the strict adherence to fixed exchange rates played a crucial role in worsening the Depression.

Consider the position of a primary producing country with an international debt that had to be serviced but also with a growing balance-of-payments deficit. How could exports be made more competitive? Could the import bill be reduced? Would it be possible to borrow more from overseas investors during this difficult period? The room to maneuver was limited.

Many countries attempted to force down wages and prices in a desperate attempt to increase export sales. Such measures could result in political instability, and in any case, reduced export prices could not guarantee additional earnings. Imports could be reduced easily by the imposition of quotas or tariffs, but the advantage was often quickly eroded as such action invited and received retaliation. In 1930 the United States introduced the Hawley-Smoot Tariff, which led to a wave of retaliation across the world. Little wonder that one by-product of the Depression was the increase in barriers to trade. As one country's imports are another's exports, swift reaction to any exclusion was inevitable.

As the Depression deepened, international investors became concerned about the ability of debtor countries to continue servicing their debts, and this growing uncertainty led to a repatriation of capital. Debtor counties sought to retain the confidence of foreign investors by pursuing deflationary policies and raising interest rates in the hope that this would make investment more attractive. Unfortunately, the strategies employed to appease overseas investors had the effect of worsening the Depression domestically, and this tended to accelerate the outflow of foreign capital. Eventually, economies with little gold or foreign currency reserves could not sustain the defense of their exchange rates, and devalua-

tion became unavoidable. One result of devaluation was retaliation, and therefore the advantage of this policy was often short-lived. Devaluation also resulted in a loss to foreign lenders, who reacted by withdrawing their capital from all countries that seemed to be in grave difficulties, a course of action that made devaluation even more likely.

In 1931 a major financial crisis affected several powerful economies. The crisis started in Austria, then spread to Germany before moving to Great Britain. Germany did not devalue the mark but instead imposed strict import and foreign-exchange controls. In a move that stunned contemporaries, Britain was forced to devalue sterling in the fall of 1931 and to abandon the gold standard. Many countries that had strong trading links with Britain also left the gold standard and allowed their currencies to depreciate. In the spring of 1933 the United States devalued the dollar and abandoned the gold standard. A few countries stubbornly remained on gold, but by 1936 they too were forced to quit.

The exchange rate rigidity that the gold standard had imposed helped to exacerbate the effects of the Depression through deflation. Once Britain devalued sterling, economic recovery was relatively vigorous. Those nations, such as France, that clung to gold endured a long-lasting economic decline.

Post-1945 policy makers realized that international cooperation was essential if actions determined by short-term national self-interest were to be avoided and the barriers to trade reduced. The Bretton Woods Agreement (1944) set up the International Monetary Fund (IMF), which was designed to encourage international cooperation and offer support to countries facing exchange-rate difficulties.

SEE ALSO DEPRESSIONS AND RECOVERIES; HOOVER, HERBERT; KEYNES, JOHN MAYNARD; ROOSEVELT, FRANKLIN DELANO.

BIBLIOGRAPHY

Clarke, Stephen V. O. *Central Bank Cooperation: 1924-31.* New York: Federal Reserve Bank of New York, 1967.

Costigliola, Frank. *Awkward Dominion: American Political, Economic, and Cultural Relations with Europe, 1919–1933.* Ithaca, NY: Cornell University Press, 1984.

Eichengreen, Barry. *Golden Fetters: The Gold Standard and the Great Depression, 1919–1939.* New York: Oxford University Press, 1992.

Fearon, Peter. *War, Prosperity and Depression: The U.S. Economy 1917–45.* Lawrence: University Press of Kansas, 1987.

Foreman-Peck, James. *A History of the World Economy: International Economic Relations since 1850.* Brighton: Harvester Press, 1983.

James, Harold. *The End of Globalization: Lessons from the Great Depression.* Cambridge, MA: Harvard University Press, 2001.

Kindleberger, Charles P. *The World in Depression, 1929–39.* Harmondsworth: Pelican Books, 1987.

Rothermund, Dietmar. *The Global Impact of the Great Depression, 1929–1939.* London: Routledge, 1996.

Saint-Étienne, Christian. *The Great Depression, 1929–1938: Lessons for the 1980s.* Stanford, CA: Hoover Institution Press, 1984.

Temin, Peter. *Lessons from the Great Depression.* Cambridge, MA: Harvard University Press, 1989.

Peter Fearon

GREECE

Greece has historically been an active trading nation. In 2002 trade accounted for 12.6 percent of the nation's gross national product (€514 million=U.S.$621 million). Half of that was retail trade, but imports represented the largest part, so there was a large trade deficit. The country's trade deficit had increased drastically after it joined the European Economic Community in 1981. Nonetheless, Greek traders have always been adaptable; a contemporary example of this was the quick Greek commercial penetration, backed by governmental encouragement, into the countries of the Balkans and the Black Sea to capitalize on new markets in former Communists countries.

Greece is a traditionally maritime country with thousands of islands. Merchant shipping is a dynamic factor in the national economy, and the industry represents Greece to the world mainly through the exciting images of Greek tycoons such as Aristotle Onassis (1900–1975) and Stavros Niarhos (1909–1996). Greek-owned ships sailing under foreign flags comprised 17.4 percent of the world merchant marine in 2000. Most Greek ships are tramp ships carrying mainly dry products such as iron ore, coal, grains, bauxite, alumina and phosphate fertilizers, as well as ocean liners. Merchant shipping steadily supported the Greek economy in the twentieth century, offering a net exchange at no cost to the national economy. In 1995 shipping operations contributed a significant U.S. $2.191 billion to the national balance of payments of Greece.

GREEK TRADE IN THE OTTOMAN PERIOD (1453–1828)

From the mid-eighteenth century up to the first decades of the nineteenth century, Greek merchants controlled the external trade of the Ottoman Empire with Western Europe and conducted a large part of the intra-Ottoman trade. Greek business enclaves developed along sea routes in the Ottoman Smyrna in Asia Minor and in the ports of southern Russia in the Black Sea. Communities were made up of emigrants from Greek regions in the Ottoman Empire who participated in the maritime trade with Western European ports such as Leghorn, Trieste, Marseilles, and Amsterdam. The trade products were foodstuffs, textiles, natural dyestuffs, and minerals.

The growth in the nineteenth century of the European economy—preponderantly in France and Britain—and with it the Ottoman markets compelled the Ottoman Porte to make civil and commercial reforms and treaties that created a favorable socioeconomic milieu for Greeks and other non-Muslim minorities. Trade in agricultural products and raw materials had increased in the markets of the Ottoman Empire, which were in frequent contact with ports on the Italian peninsula, in France, in Great Britain, in the Netherlands, and in Russia. The need for access to centers of distribution for the treatment and consumption of agricultural and semi-processed products led to the organization of family-based entrepreneurial networks whose members were dispersed in different cities. Thus merchant enterprises constituted the heart of the economy in port cities handling together a wide range of activities: buying and selling; commissioning; transaction financing; insurance of goods.

At the same time, Greek commercial migration of the same organizational type spread overland in the Ottoman Empire, mainly departing from towns in Thessaly, Epirus, and Macedonia and heading to transit stations and economic centers in the Balkans and Central Europe. The main carrying goods were foodstuffs, furs, leathers, and textiles. Thus small mountain towns with domestic wool industries, commercial connections, and experience in organizing overland transport produced a number of famous expatriate merchants, including the three generations of the Sinas family of Budapest and Vienna.

NATIONAL GREEK TRADE IN THE NINETEENTH AND TWENTIETH CENTURIES

The formation of an independent Greek state in 1828 provided psychological and economic incentives for many expatriate merchants to settle in Greece. From its early days, the new state offered opportunities for free entrepreneurial expansion backed by a policy of protectionist measures based on national and economic considerations. The capital invested by these businessmen in the fledgling state was directed mostly to commercial ventures and secondly to banking and industrial activities.

The establishment of the Greek state and its interest in national trade did not change trade practices and organization patterns, but it did create new markets. By 1830 the port of Hermoupolis, on a small Cycladic island, was the center for transit trade in the Eastern Mediterranean,

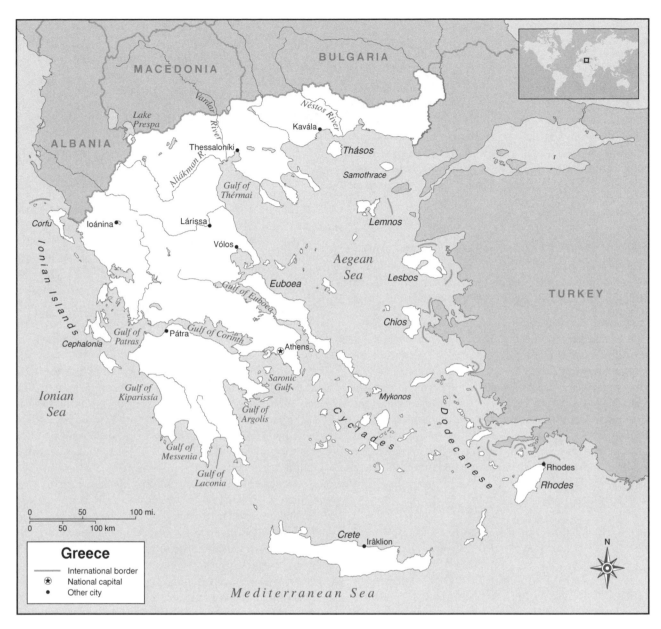

MAP BY XNR PRODUCTIONS. THE GALE GROUP.

dealing in foodstuffs, silk, leather, cotton, and hardware. Consequently, a local banking and credit system and shipping, manufacturing, and building industries developed in the new city-port. At the end of the nineteenth century the port of Piraeus, next to the Greek capital, Athens, became Greece's main trade port. The port of Patras, in north Peloponnesus, developed spectacularly in the nineteenth century due to its trade in currants.

In the first decades the Greek state was oriented to a tariff-collecting policy, and between 1851 and 1871 state revenue from the country's custom houses quadrupled. The most valuable export products were currants, figs, olive oil and olives, silk, and valonia (used in tanning leathers). The main import products were grains, stockfish, sugar, coffee, and textiles. Trade fairs of all sizes were the main venues of import and distribution, meeting the needs of the population. In 1862 twenty-two trade fairs were registered in central Greece and Peloponnesus.

In the beginning of the twentieth century retail trade began to flourish in Greece's main urban centers. In 1914, soon after the Balkan Wars (1912–1913) and before World War I, Greece's external trade was valued in 196.777,046 francs, equivalent to the same amount in golden drachmas, and her main trade partners were Austria-Hungary, Italy, and Britain. The external trade was comprised of agricultural products, textiles, and oils.

The interwar period in Greece saw the arrival of 1.5 million refugees of the Asia Minor catastrophe in 1922. The massive settling of refugees in the Greek state enlarged the national market, especially as far as the alimentary goods and garment products were concerned. Between 1920 and 1929, the export growth of the country was marked by the tobacco boom. The National Bank of Greece begun to operate in 1928, marking a major turning point in Greek banking system, bringing the country to the gold standard. The world economic crisis of 1929 was crucial for the country's trade balance. Autarchy became the main scope of all interwar Greek governments and the already difficult relationship between free trade and national industry was aggravated (by new state policy partial to Greek industry.) Import tariffs were increased, enabling national industry to cover 75 percent of the Greek market. Thus, Greek nationalism promoted the triptych of modernization, interventionism, and protectionism.

World War II completely changed the political and economic scene in Greece, but the existing economic conflict not only didn't cease, but also gained a new political apparatus. In the postwar period, under the Marshall Plan from the United States poured millions of dollars into Greece's economic reconstruction. Nonetheless, the economic sector that showed the most spectacular growth was the merchant marine. In becoming the largest fleet in the world, the Greek-owned merchant marine employed many Greeks and provided promising private and state revenues.

SEE ALSO AGRICULTURE; BALANCE OF PAYMENTS; BLACK SEA; CARGOES, FREIGHT; CARGOES, PASSENGER; COMMON MARKET AND EUROPEAN UNION; CONTAINERIZATION; EMPIRE, OTTOMAN; ETHNIC GROUPS, ARMENIAN; FREE TRADE, THEORY AND PRACTICE; GATT, WTO; GREAT DEPRESSION OF THE 1930S; INDUSTRIALIZATION; INTERNATIONAL TRADE AGREEMENTS; MEDITERRANEAN; ONASSIS, ARISTOTLE; REGIONAL TRADING AGREEMENTS; SHIPPING, MERCHANT.

BIBLIOGRAPHY

Chatziioannou, Maria Christina. "Commerce in the Greek State (1833–1871)." In *History of Neohellenism, 1770–2000*, vol. 4: *The Greek State, 1833–1871*, ed. Vassilis Panayotopoulos. Athens: Ellika Grammata, 2003.

Clogg, Richard. *A Concise History of Greece.* Cambridge, U.K.: Cambridge University Press, 1992.

Harlaftis, Gelina. *Greek Shipowners and Greece, 1945–1975: From Separate Development to Mutual Interdependence.* London: Athlon Press, 1993.

Mazower, Mark. *Greece and the Interwar Economic Crisis.* London: Oxford University Press, 1991.

Strong, Frederic. *Greece as a Kingdom.* London: Brown, Green & Longmans, 1842.

Maria Christina Chatziioannou

SIR THOMAS GRESHAM
c. 1518–1579

Sir Thomas Gresham, one of the leading merchants and financiers of the sixteenth century, owes his reputation to the manipulation of the foreign exchanges in managing the credit of the Tudor monarchy. The son of a former lord mayor of London, he made his fortune exporting cloth in the favorable market conditions of the 1540s, but he came to prominence in 1551 when he became the king's agent, responsible for obtaining loans for the Crown from continental bankers based at the Antwerp entrepôt. His skill lay in forcing the association of English cloth exporters, the Merchant Adventurers, to pay over their receipts in Antwerp to himself for repayment in London in sterling at an artificially high fixed rate. Although he lost favor at the accession of the Catholic Queen Mary in 1553, his indispensability ensured that he was soon back in post. The zenith of his influence was in the early years of Queen Elizabeth I, when he advised her chief minister, Sir William Cecil, on economic matters such as the recoinage of 1560–1561, and also became an important conduit of diplomatic information. In 1568 he opened the Bourse, a building dedicated to the exchange of foreign credit, which was built at his expense on land provided by the City of London and rechristened the Royal Exchange after a visit from the queen in 1571. He is known mistakenly as the author of "Gresham's Law," the notion that when coins are in circulation whose relative face value differs from their relative bullion content, the "bad money will drive out the good" because it is less expensive to pay for foreign purchases in poor quality money. Although Gresham made the point, he was not the only person to do so, and by no means the first.

SEE ALSO ELIZABETH I; EMPIRE, BRITISH; FINANCE, CREDIT AND MONEY LENDING; MARKETS, STOCK; MONEY AND MONETARY POLICY.

BIBLIOGRAPHY

De Roover, Raymond, ed. *Gresham on Foreign Exchange.* Cambridge, MA: Harvard University Press, 1949.

Ramsay, George. *The City of London in International Politics at the Accession of Elizabeth Tudor.* Manchester, U.K.: Manchester University Press, 1975.

Saunders, Anne, ed. *The Royal Exchange.* London: London Topographical Society, 1997.

Ian W. Archer

GUANGZHOU

By 1450 Guangzhou (Canton) had long established its position as one of China's most important ports of international trade. During the Qing dynasty (1644–1911) China's growing maritime trade activities further enhanced the importance of Guangzhou, which existed as the country's sole port for foreign commerce between 1757 and 1842 and which was the site of a customs office established by the government. During much of the Qing period a few firms known collectively as the *Hong* were in charge of international trade with their Western counterparts, who leased facility spaces in the city. During the first half of the twentieth century foreign trade in Guangzhou was often controlled by Westerners and Japanese, who occupied Guangzhou from 1938 to 1945. Shortly after the founding of the People's Republic of China in 1949 the government took over the running of all foreign trade activities, which were managed by state-owned industry-based trade firms.

Of the different products exported from Guangzhou during the Ming dynasty (1368–1644), silk and china were the two most important, and the famous Ming chinaware developed a strong international reputation. During the Qing dynasty, silk remained a top export commodity, and tea became more important, becoming the number one export commodity before the Opium War (1840–1842). The growth of tea exports reflected China's increasing interaction with Britain, where tea drinking had become a national pastime.

Over time, export activities increased, but most of the goods were handicrafts and other nonmanufactured products such as raw materials, medicine, and food. This changed in the late twentieth century, when China's post-1978 reform policies revitalized the Chinese economy and multiplied exports in both volume and variety, including exports in manufactured goods such as machinery and electronic products.

Many pre-twentieth-century imports were luxury consumer goods such as pearls, precious stones, spices, and sea otter skins. Without enough salable goods to balance its trade with China, the British turned to opium. Its import dramatically increased after the Opium War, which the British launched in order to legalize its opium trade. Much of the British opium went to China through Guangzhou. After the Opium War, Guangzhou also witnessed a significant increase in the importation of consumer goods, especially textiles. During the first half of the twentieth century a variety of goods ranging from textiles to food, machinery, and transportation vehicles were imported, reflecting a weak national economy. Imports, under tight control because of the lack of foreign currency in the early decades of the People's Republic of China, proliferated after the country's economic reform began in the late 1970s, primarily meeting the needs of a fast-growing, export-oriented economy.

Southeast Asia, a long-time trade partner with Guangzhou, was outstripped by Western nations, especially Britain, during the Qing dynasty, and by Japan in World War II. After the war the United States became the primary source of imports. From the 1950s through the 1970s, Guangzhou conducted almost all its international trade through Hong Kong. In 1990 it traded directly with more than 100 countries.

Because of its position in international trade, Guangzhou has had a profound impact on the region as well as the nation. By the nineteenth century the surrounding Pearl River Delta had developed a dynamic market-oriented economy, and had become a hub for international commerce migration and for information about the outside world.

SEE ALSO AGRICULTURE; CANTON SYSTEM; CHINA; CARGOES, FREIGHT; CARGOES, PASSENGER; CHAMBERS OF COMMERCE; COMPRADORS; CONTAINERIZATION; COTTON; DENG XIAOPING; DRUGS, ILLICIT; EAST INDIA COMPANY, BRITISH; EAST INDIA COMPANY, OTHER; EMPIRE, JAPANESE; EMPIRE, MING; EMPIRE, QING; ENTREPÔT SYSTEM; ETHNIC GROUPS, CANTONESE; FACTORIES; FREE PORTS; HARBORS; HART, ROBERT; HONG KONG; IMPERIAL MARITIME CUSTOMS, CHINA; JAPAN; JARDINE MATHESON; LIN ZEXU; PHILIPPINES; PORT CITIES; RICE; SINGAPORE; SOUTH CHINA SEA; RUSSIA; SPICES AND THE SPICE TRADE; TEA; THAILAND; ZHENG FAMILY.

BIBLIOGRAPHY

Cheong, W. E. *The Hong Merchants of Canton: Chinese Merchants in Sino-Western Trade.* Richmond, Surrey, U.K.: Curzon, 1997.

Downs, Jacques M. *The Golden Ghetto: The American Commercial Community at Canton and the Shaping of American China Policy, 1784–1844.* Bethlehem, PA: Lehigh University Press, 1997.

Johnson, Graham. "Open for Business, Open to the World: Consequences of Global Incorporation in Guangdong and the Pearl River Delta." In *The Economic Transformation of South China: Reform and Development in the Post-Mao Era,* ed. Thomas P. Lyons and Victor Nee. Ithaca, NY: Cornell University Press, 1994.

Sit, Victor F. S., and Yang, Chun. "Foreign-Investment-Induced Exo-Urbanization in the Pearl River Delta, China." *Urban Studies* 34, no. 4 (1997): 647–677.

Wakeman, Frederic Jr. "The Canton Trade and the Opium War." In *The Cambridge History of China,* vol. 10, part 1, ed. Denis Twitchett and John King Fairbank. Cambridge, U.K.: Cambridge University Press, 1978.

Yearbook of China's Foreign Economic Relations and Trade. Beijing: China Foreign Economic Relations and Trade Publishing House, 2002.

Yong Chen

GUGGENHEIM FAMILY

Meyer Guggenheim (1828–1905) was the patriarch of the Guggenheim family. A native of Switzerland, he migrated to the United States in 1847. He began his entrepreneurial carrier by selling shoelaces and manufacturing stove polish in Philadelphia. In 1872 he established Guggenheim & Pulaski, a firm importing embroideries from Switzerland. The business prospered, allowing him to turn his interests to other fields. In 1888 he and his second son, Daniel Guggenheim (1856–1930), acquired copper mines in Colorado and established the Philadelphia Smelting and Refining Company, which became a worldwide copper market leader.

In 1891 they consolidated some of their refining operations in a trust named Colorado Smelting and Refining Company. A decade later they assumed industry leadership by taking control of a competitor trust, the American Smelting and Refining Company. Daniel directed the trust until 1919. By placing mining operations and metal processing under one entity, they gained better control of supply. New exploration companies were created and, as a result, family interests were expanded to include Bolivian tin mines, African diamond mines, Chilean nitrate fields, and Congolese rubber plantations.

Simon Guggenheim (1867–1941), Meyer's youngest son, was an eminent figure in U.S. politics. Elected a senator from Colorado in 1906, he assumed control of the family firm in 1919. As an active philanthropist, he established the John Simon Guggenheim Memorial Foundation in 1925 in his son's memory.

SEE ALSO CHILE; COPPER; CORPORATION, OR LIMITED LIABILITY COMPANY; GOLD RUSHES; MEXICO; MINING; NITRATES; UNITED STATES.

BIBLIOGRAPHY

Davis, John H. *The Guggenheims: An American Epic.* New York: William Morrow, 1978.

Lomask, Milton. *Seed Money: The Guggenheim Story.* New York: Farrar, Straus, 1964.

O'Connor, Harvey. *The Guggenheims: The Making of an American Dynasty.* New York: Covici-Friede, 1937.

Fabio Braggion

GUILDS

From the eleventh century, associations of tradesmen in Europe acquired the privilege of governing themselves at the local level. City administrations soon evolved to where each trade was under the control of a recognized association, which was called a *guild.* While guilds performed many roles, such as acting as benevolent societies and ensuring product quality, their defining characteristic was that they restricted the entry of human and physical capital inputs.

ORIGIN AND RISE OF GUILDS

From late in the eleventh century, merchant guilds rapidly spread from northern Italian cities across Western and West-Central Europe. Significantly, their rapid rise corresponded with unusually high rates of immediate and continuing economic growth. About a hundred years later, this pattern was repeated when craft guilds experienced a similar growth. Typically, each city adopting the guild system received from the king or local prince a charter, which was called a *firmi burgi,* that granted local autonomy in return for regular lump-sum tax contributions, and periodic extraordinary tax contributions in times of military threat.

The origin of guilds can be traced to the Roman merchant and craft associations called *collegia.* The *collegia,* which were preceded by associations acting as benevolent societies, were an instrument of the emperor to exact taxes, and as such, were placed under a government-appointed prefect. This practice continued in the Eastern Roman Empire, including in the Italian protectorates, the most important of which were Amalfi, Naples, and Venice. However, unlike in classical Rome, in Constantinople *collegia* were primarily located in the foreign-trade sector, which may explain why they were encouraged to develop entry-restricting practices to better exploit the city's trading monopoly. Through its system of regular lump-sum taxes combined with periodic extraordinarily taxes, the regime would have ensured that most of the gains accrued to it.

Up to the mid-eleventh century, Constantinople prospered through trade. Consequently, the city's policies regarding the *collegia* were also adopted in its Italian protectorates, where Byzantium even encouraged merchant-oligarchic governments, which subsequently also flourished. The success of the Byzantine-protected cities contrasted favorably with other Italian centers under Frankish control, so merchant-oligarchic governments, which enjoyed a large degree of autonomy, were also adopted during the early ninth century in Frankish cites such as Genoa, Florence, and Pisa. In all such centers, the Frankish emperor encouraged the establishment of independent merchant and craft associations in return for annual fixed tax payments. Subsequently, the Frankish cities also prospered. Such a charter may have been necessary to protect town merchants and craftsmen from

The Houses of Business, or Guildhalls, in old Brussels, Belgium, c. 1885. *Tradesmen formed organizations called guilds that flourished between the eleventh and sixteenth centuries. By the end of the nineteenth century, most guilds had lost their power as nations introduced central banks and convertible currencies.* © MICHAEL MASLIN HISTORIC PHOTOGRAPHS/CORBIS. REPRODUCED BY PERMISSION.

any predatory actions on the part of local lords or church bureaucrats.

The Frankish emperor's policy of granting guild-dominated cities local autonomy in return for regular lump-sum taxes and occasional extraordinary taxes was copied elsewhere. Charters in other European cities likewise extended legal protection to tradesmen by ceding jurisdiction relating to any trade dispute to the particular guild court. City governments, moreover, were typically dominated by the wealthiest guilds.

Where central power proved weak, some cities during the Middle Ages gained *de facto* independence. Examples of such cases include the Italian cities of Florence, Venice, and Genoa, and the Flemish city of Bruges. Some cities even formed alliances to gain independence. The most notable examples are the cities of the Swiss Federation such as Lucerne, Zurich, and Berne, and the cities of the Hanseatic League such as Lubeck, Hamburg, and

Rostock, which combined to form strong trading and military alliances in the same period. Both federations gained independence from a weakened Holy Roman Empire at the beginning of the late thirteenth century.

MATURE MEDIEVAL GUILDS

Controversially, guilds imposed a comprehensive set of restrictions on their members. For example, rather than allowing their members to compete on the basis of product price, guilds invariably fixed a maximum price. In addition, guilds comprehensively regulated output quality, examples of which included the clothiers' rule against patched-up work being passed off as new, rules that required members to purchase only in quality input markets rather than from street hawkers, and the rules of the London poulters that required members to purchase inputs only at times of the week when quality was highest.

Failure to comply with any guild regulation often resulted in a heavy fine for the transgressor.

In light of these guild practices, scholars such as Charles Gross, Henri Pirenne, and Michael Poston have argued that guilds were inefficient monopolistic cartels. Yet, effective cartels, in order to preventing cheating, enforce only minimum prices and maximum quality levels. But as guilds set only maximum price restrictions and minimum quality restrictions, their rules seem to conform more to antimonopoly practices.

A more consistent monopoly view is to argue, as the eighteenth-century French Physiocrats and the Scottish economist Adam Smith did, that guilds worked mainly through restricting inputs of both human and physical capital. In regard to human-capital restrictions, guilds generally required long apprenticeships beginning at a minimum age of seven years, and a minimum age of twenty-five in order to qualify as a regular guild journeyman. Guilds also set high initiation fees for journeymen to progress to master status. Such fees were continually increased and eventually became prohibitively high for all but a few journeymen. Also, guilds typically set discriminatory entry fees for any master desiring to relocate from another city.

In regard to physical-capital restrictions, there were rules restricting the operation of shops to only guild masters, and each master could own only one shop. In addition, many craft guilds imposed restrictions on the number of machines any one master could employ. Finally, there were also rules that worked to restrict more intensive use of physical capital. For example, there were restrictions on the maximum number of apprentices and journeymen any one master could employ, and there were rules against night work and working on declared holidays.

Although such restrictions are consistent with a monopoly view of guilds, there is an alternative explanation. Generally, medieval societies had no regular income-tax system (except for those existing in the export-oriented independent cities mentioned above). Consequently, the annual fixed lump-sum tax contributions of guild members in the nonindependent cities were an important source of cash revenue for the king. Guild members were also required to provide substantial emergency tax contributions in times of war, and those contributions take on particular importance when we remember that most wealth in the period was in the form of land. Thus, cash contributions from the towns would have been an important source of available cash to the king, particularly during military emergencies.

There is an additional, subtle explanation for the existence for guild entry restrictions. From a societal perspective, in a modern economy an individual is prevented from over-investing by being required to pay a proportional wealth or income tax. Without such a tax, an investor would ignore any extra cost to the society generated by their increased wealth. As such a tax was absent in most medieval societies, guild rules restricting shop size as well as the maximum number of machines per master may have served as an effective substitute.

Weighing against the monopoly view is the fact that a full set of guild entry restrictions were employed even in cities that were particularly controlled by the king, such as London and Paris. Moreover, entry-restricting regulations were also a characteristic feature of guilds located in cities whose customers were politically powerful members of the aristocracy. In addition, the monopoly view is not compatible with other antimonopoly provisions typically employed by guild cities, such as laws against forestalling, regrating, and engrossing. The first two of these were safeguards against speculation by middlemen, particularly in victuals, whereas the last was a safeguard against hoarding in order to corner the market, which was a particular problem during the medieval era given uncertain harvests and other supplies. Finally, the monopoly view is inconsistent with the timing of the demise of guilds.

THE DECLINE OF GUILDS

Guilds lost their local autonomy with the coming of the nation-state. Holland dramatically weakened its guilds in the sixteenth century. Later, during the Elizabethan era, England passed the Statute of Artificers, which allowed guilds to maintain their entry restrictions but placed tradesmen under local magistrates. National guild regulation occurred in France during the mid-seventeenth century under the reforms of Jean-Baptiste Colbert (1619–1683). These also placed guilds under the control of central-government representatives. Other countries forming strong central governments soon followed their lead.

Significantly, there is a strong correlation between the elimination of guild entry restrictions and the adoption of a modern income-tax system. For example, the Netherlands introduced an income-tax system late in the seventeenth century, and soon after eliminated guild entry restrictions. England followed suit when it eliminated guild input regulations after adopting an income tax in the eighteenth century. French guild entry restrictions persisted until guilds were eliminated at the end of the eighteenth century during the Revolution, at which time France also introduced an income-tax system. The French pattern was repeated first in those counties adopting the Napoleonic Code as a consequence of French domination, and eventually elsewhere.

Though effectively guilds lost most of their power during the Napoleonic period, in some countries they continued to exist for a few decades more, particularly in parts of Germany, Austria-Hungary, Scandinavia, and Southern Europe. But as part of their centralization during the third quarter of the nineteenth century, these areas, too, introduced central banks and convertible currencies, so any potential need to use guilds as a source of emergency revenue became unnecessary, and they eliminated guilds. Indeed, guilds lasted longest in Russia, where they were not eliminated until the turn of the twentieth century when, significantly, it too introduced a central bank.

SEE ALSO EDUCATION, OVERVIEW; LABOR, TYPES OF; POPULATION—EMIGRATION AND IMMIGRATION.

BIBLIOGRAPHY

Gross, Charles. *The Guild Merchant.* Oxford, U.K.: Clarendon Press, 1890.

Hickson, Charles, and Thompson, Earl. "A New Theory of Guilds and European Development." *Explorations in Economic History* 28, no. 2 (April 1991):127–168.

Pirenne, Henri. *Economic and Social History of Medieval Europe.* New York: Harcourt, 1933.

Postan, Michael M. *The Medieval Economy and Society.* Berkeley: University of California Press, 1972.

Renard, Gerard. *Guilds in the Middle Ages.* London: Kelley, 1969.

Thompson, Earl, and Hickson, Charles R. *The Ideology and the Evolution of Vital Institutions: Guilds, the Gold Standard, and Modern International Cooperation.* Boston: Kluwer Academic, 2001.

Thrupp, Sylvia. *The Merchant Class of Medieval London.* Chicago: University of Chicago Press, 1948.

Charles R. Hickson
John D. Turner

GUJARAT

Strategically situated between the western and eastern extremities of the Afro-Eurasian continents, Gujarat played a central role in world-trade networks dating back at least to the third millennium BCE. Located at the eastern end of the Arabian Sea, sailors plying along its extensive coastline found safe routes through the shifting sea bed on the predictable winds of the southwest and northeast monsoons to land at the dozens of ports established over the centuries, most importantly in modern times at Broach, Cambay, and Surat.

In the mid-fifteenth century Gujarat was a major entrepôt for the direct exchange of goods and people by sea between the Near East, western Asia, and eastern coastal Africa in one direction, and eastern and southeastern Asia in the other. Some of the trade goods arriving in Gujarat were locally consumed or used in manufacturing; others traveled along the great land routes to Agra and thence across all of northern India and into Afghanistan; but the bulk was re-exported across the seas.

Trade between Gujarat and East Africa extended from Mogodishu in the north to Sofala and Madagascar in the south. This trade was often direct and bilateral, with Gujarati-manufactured carnelian beads and cotton cloth exchanged for African ivory, gold, and slaves. Trade along the Red Sea and Persian Gulf involved the export of Gujarati carnelians, a wide range of coarse and fine, and dyed and embroidered cotton and silk cloths, carpets and furnishings, tanned hides and shoes, indigo, ginger and pepper, wheat and rice, and the re-export of spices, aromatic woods, and pearls from Malabar, Ceylon, and Southeast Asia, and silk and porcelain from China. In exchange, Gujarat took primarily gold and silver, and some horses. To the east, Gujarat exported her manufactures and raw materials in exchange for spices and silk.

Gujarati long-distance trade provided extensive employment opportunities for a wide range of castes. Tribals collected and processed agates, tannins, aromatics, wild animals, and materials for mats and construction. Agriculturalists grew and processed indigo, cotton, and foods. Artisans turned agates into carnelians and beads, wood into boats, cotton into sails and cloth, and leather into shoes, and they built the substantial public and private structures found in all the major port towns. Merchants owned ships, contracted with producers, made loans, exchanged monies, and provided insurance. Gujarat was prosperous, thriving, and impressive to Western travelers.

Over the next five and a half centuries Gujarat's external trade changed dramatically in response to new political conditions and technological innovations. When the Portuguese entered the Indian Ocean trading system in 1498 the Chinese had recently withdrawn, the Arabs were preeminent, and Gujarati merchants were in virtually every port. Portuguese control of Indian Ocean trade, which peaked in the sixteenth century, was contested everywhere by Ottoman Turks, Safavid Persians, Indian Mughals, and Omani Arabs. In Gujarat the Portuguese bypassed the leading port at Cambay, fortified themselves in Diu and Daman, and controlled a significant portion of Gujarat's long-distance trade. There was little change in the kinds of goods produced for trade, although the volume increased and trade flowed more east-west than north-south, and Gujarati merchants, farmers, and artisans continued to prosper.

During the seventeenth century the Portuguese faced new competitors as the English, Dutch, and French East India Companies aggressively forced their way past Portuguese blockades and were granted trade privileges by the Mughals, most notably at Surat. These Europeans entered the internal Indian markets, joining their indigenous merchant competitors in contracting for trade goods, notably cotton, tobacco, opium, and cotton cloth. By the mid-eighteenth century both the French and Dutch had withdrawn from Gujarat, the Portuguese were left in their port enclaves, the Mughal empire was disintegrating, and various Maratha leaders were contesting for control of Gujarat's revenues. By the first decades of the nineteenth century all of Gujarat was under the direct or de facto control of the English, and it remained so until India gained its independence in 1947.

From the seventeenth century onward, technological advances in shipping reduced the necessity for frequent landfalls and the transshipment or re-export of goods across the Indian Ocean. Gradually, once great ports fell into disuse and new ones with significantly improved port facilities monopolized intra-ocean trade. Most of Gujarat's ports continued to play a major role in regional shipping and transshipment of goods to and from Bombay well into the mid- and late nineteenth century, but large-scale commercial activity shifted south, and Gujarat's merchant communities mostly followed. The extension of the railroad from Bombay to Delhi from the 1860s also redirected Gujarat's internal and foreign trade away from the sea.

Technological changes in European production dramatically altered the terms of trade between Gujarat and the rest of the world. By the nineteenth century indigo was replaced by new, more permanent dyes, and Indian cotton goods were no longer relatively cheap. Their export declined continuously even after modern mills flourished in Ahmedabad from the early twentieth century. Perhaps even more important were changes in consumption patterns as the demand for luxury items by the very wealthy was replaced by rapidly growing demand for new products and services by large middle-classes and industrial firms around the world. Many tribals, artisans, and farmers had to adjust to these changing circumstances. By 2000 Gujarat's most active ports were in Saurashtra, where freighters and tankers are salvaged, and industrial diamond cutting and polishing in Surat has replaced carnelian beads, the staple of trade since antiquity.

SEE ALSO AGRICULTURE; BENGAL; CARAVAN TRADE; COTTON; EAST INDIA COMPANY, BRITISH; EAST INDIA COMPANY, DUTCH; EAST INDIA COMPANY, OTHER; EMPIRE, BRITISH; EMPIRE, DUTCH; EMPIRE, MUGHAL; EMPIRE, PORTUGUESE; ETHNIC GROUPS, GUJARATI; FACTORIES; GOLD, SILVER AND OTHER PRECIOUS METALS; IMPERIALISM; INDIA; INDIAN OCEAN; MUMBAI; NATIONALISM; PAKISTAN; PERSIAN GULF; SHIPBUILDING; SOUTH AFRICA; TEXTILES; TOBACCO; WHEAT AND OTHER CEREAL GRAINS.

BIBLIOGRAPHY

Chandra, Satish, ed. *The Indian Ocean: Explorations in History, Commerce, and Politics.* New Delhi: Sage Publications, 1987.

Das Gupta, Ashin, and Pearson, M. N., eds. *India and the Indian Ocean, 1500–1800.* Calcutta: Oxford University Press, 1987.

Gopal, Surendra. *Commerce and Crafts in Gujarat, 16th and 18th Centuries: A Study in the Impact of European Expansion on Precapitalist Economy.* New Delhi: People's Publishing House, 1975.

Pearson, Michael. *The Indian Ocean.* London: Routledge, 2003.

Marcia J. Frost

CALOUSTE GULBENKIAN
1869–1955

Calouste Gulbenkian, a Turkish-born British businessman of Armenian descent, helped to found in 1911 the Turkish Petroleum Company (later the Iraq Petroleum Company), which was the first to produce oil in Iraq and eventually produced oil and laid pipeline in Saudi Arabia and many Persian Gulf emirates. In 1891 Gulbenkian published *Transcaucasia et la Peninsule d'Apcheron—Souvenirs de voyage* (Transcaucasia and the Peninsula of Apcheron—Memories of Travel), an account of his voyages to the oil fields of Baku; the book brought Gulbenkian to the attention of the Ottoman government, and a subsequent report led the Ottoman Empire to begin drilling for oil in Iraq. Gulbenkian was known in the press as "Mr. Five Percent" because he frequently retained a 5 percent share in the oil companies he developed. Gulbenkian set up a consortium between the Anglo-Persian Oil Company, Royal Dutch Shell, and Deutsche Bank, and Gulbenkian's partners went on to become the world's largest energy companies: British Petroleum, Shell, Total, and ExxonMobil. Gulbenkian was the economic advisor to the Turkish embassies in Paris and London and, in this capacity, found entrepreneurs willing to set up oil pipelines in the Ottoman Empire. During World War I, Gulbenkian advised a committee in the French government and, by 1920, France had oil sources in the Middle East for the first time.

SEE ALSO EMPIRE, BRITISH; EMPIRE, OTTOMAN; ETHNIC GROUPS, ARMENIAN; IRAN; PETROLEUM.

BIBLIOGRAPHY

Hewins, Ralph. *Mr. Five Percent: The Story of Calouste Gulbenkian.* New York: Rinehart, 1958.

Jeffrey Wood

Haiti

The first export product from Haiti was gold, but the gold mines were exhausted during the early decades of the sixteenth century. Sugar was introduced around the same time, without much success. The Indians were dying out, and enough African slaves could not be imported. Toward the end of the century ginger became the most important export product from Hispaniola (the island today divided into Haiti in the west and the Dominican Republic in the east), but mainly from the east. The western third of the island remained more or less uncolonized for the first century after the European conquest. Spain had a trade monopoly with its colonies, but during the seventeenth century contraband exports of livestock products took over, to Portuguese, Dutch, French, and English traders, notably on the western and northern coasts. The Portuguese supplied slaves.

As a result, in 1605 to 1606 the Spanish depopulated western Hispaniola. Beginning in 1630, the French gradually filled this vacuum. In 1664 La Compagnie des Indes Occidentales (West Indian Company) was founded in France and was given a monopoly of West Indian trade. The French colony—called Saint-Domingue—was consolidated over the next twenty years, and contraband trade with the Spanish colony in the east expanded. (The Spanish called their colony Santo Domingo.) Saint-Domingue received horses, meat, and hides, and supplied the Spanish with French manufactures. After the Treaty of Ryswick in 1697 Spain did not present any further claims to the western part of the island.

The golden age of Saint-Domingue had begun. After 1680 sugar, a staple, became the main export product; indigo and cocoa were added toward the end of the seventeenth century. Cotton was exported for a while but suffered heavy competition from sugar, and did not come back until the 1750s. The overall value of exports expanded rapidly. In 1743 Saint-Domingue produced more sugar than all of the British Antilles together. Saint-Domingue developed into France's most valuable colony: in 1789 it accounted for more than 40 percent of the foreign trade of France, and some 5 out of 27 million French were estimated to depend directly on this trade, which rested on the labor of some 450,000 slaves. In the same year coffee exports, which had begun in the late 1730s, had expanded to the point where their value equaled two-thirds of the exports of raw sugar.

During the wars of liberation (1791–1803) Haiti's foreign trade was virtually wiped out. Plantations, sugar factories, and irrigation works lay in ruins, and the population was declining. In 1804 a recovery had set in, except for the indigo trade, which remained close to extinction, but none of the crops was even close to half of the 1789 volume. Both capital and manpower were lacking, and the war cut off the export markets. The old export economy could not be maintained. The system was crushed from both the demand and the supply sides, and, after the 1809 land reform, Haiti became a peasant economy with low-quality coffee as the dominant export product. The country was ostracized internationally. Export volumes fell, and then climbed back almost to the colonial level in the 1860s and 1870s, and remained more or less there until the advent of World War I. Coffee failed to become a staple. At the end of the nineteenth century Haitian government revenues consisted almost exclusively of taxes on foreign trade.

A worker at the U.S.-based Rawlings baseball plant in Port-au-Prince, Haiti, 1986. Haiti's export of baseballs and other light-assembly products was crippled by international sanctions in the 1990s, but has struggled back. PHOTOGRAPH BY MICHAEL RODDY. AP/WIDE WORLD PHOTOS. REPRODUCED BY PERMISSION.

Cotton exports increased during the U.S. Civil War, but fell back rapidly after the war, when prices came down. Cocoa also continued to be an export product. Exports of precious woods, notably logwood, saw a boom in the 1890s and the first two decades of the twentieth century. Thereafter, reserves were depleted.

During the U.S. occupation of Haiti (1915–1934) sugar and sisal plantations were established, but few remained after the end of the occupation. Coffee continued to be the dominant export crop. Exports would also be influenced by political factors, by more or less predatory regimes. In the 1930s and the first half of the 1940s bananas began to be exported, but the removal of the private export monopoly thereafter killed the new product. A politically driven attempt to export rubber from a domestic plant in 1941 failed as well.

The latter half of the 1940s were successful export years. Coffee and sisal prices were good. In 1949 Haiti

was the third-largest sisal producer in the world, but after the Korea boom the sisal price fell 50 percent within a few months in 1951 to 1952. In 1953 bauxite exports were begun. In 1955 coffee accounted for 65 percent of total exports, followed by sisal (16%), sugar, cocoa, and essential oils. Subsequently, however, these exports shrunk, one by one. Bauxite reserves were depleted. Sisal was finished by the mid-1970s, outcompeted by synthetic fibers. The sugar trade lasted for another decade before low yields and political mismanagement strangled it. Cocoa exports declined as a result of unfavorable prices in relation to domestic food crops. Essential oils, which had shown an upward trend from the late 1950s to 1974, when they accounted for almost 10 percent of the total export value, were priced out of the market by a government export monopoly. Coffee production, finally, declined as the population grew and food crops gradually took over the land.

In the early 2000s, Haitian exports are dominated by manufactures. The industry in light assembly of products made from imported raw materials (electronics, textiles, baseballs, toys) increased sales abroad from the mid-1960s to the beginning of the 1990s, but the sector was almost killed by international sanctions from 1991 to 1994 and struggled to come back; in 2004 it consisted virtually exclusively of textiles. In 1999 the sector accounted for almost 85 percent of total Haitian exports, compared with 11 percent for agricultural goods (coffee, essential oils, and mangoes). Due to the severe land erosion caused by population growth, Haiti has lost its comparative advantage in agriculture, and exports (manufactures) are now based on low labor costs.

SEE ALSO Bonaparte, Napoleon; Bordeaux; Coffee; Conquistadors; Drugs, Illicit; Empire, French; Empire, Spanish; Encomienda and Repartimiento; Ethnic Groups, Africans; Imperialism; International Monetary Fund (IMF); Laborers, Coerced; Mercantilism; New Orleans; Slavery and the African Slave Trade; Sugar, Molasses, and Rum; United States.

BIBLIOGRAPHY

Benoît, Pierre. *1804–1954. Cent cinquante ans de commerce extérieur d'Haïti (One hundred years of commerce in Haiti).* Port-au-Prince, Haiti: Institut Haïtien de Statistique, 1954.

Lundahl, Mats. *Peasants and Poverty: A Study of Haiti.* London: Croom Helm, 1979.

Lundahl, Mats. *Politics or Markets? Essays on Haitian Underdevelopment.* London and New York: Routledge, 1992.

Lundahl, Mats. "Poorest in the Caribbean: Haiti in the Twentieth Century." *Integration and Trade* 5 (2001): 177–200.

Lundahl, Mats. "The Economic Consequences of 1809, or 'Was Haiti Doomed to Fail?' A Story of Factor Proportions, Labor Market Institutions, and Politics." In *Currents of Change: Globalization, Democratization, and Institutional Reform in Latin America,* ed. J. Behar, U. Jonsson, and Mats Lundahl. Stockholm: Institute of Latin American Studies, Stockholm University, 2002.

Mats Lundahl

RICHARD HAKLUYT THE YOUNGER
c. 1553–1616

The English geographer Richard Hakluyt the Younger compiled maps of British voyages to North America to aid traders and colonists. Principal works include "Divers Voyages Touching the Discoverie of America," published in 1582; "The Discourse on the Western Planting," published in 1584, which outlines Hakluyt's ideas on "planting" English colonists in North America; and "Principal Navigations," which describes the early English voyages to North America and is considered to be Hakluyt's greatest work. It was published in 1589 as a folio in one volume and republished as three volumes in 1598 to 1600. Hakluyt was a clergyman and the first professor of modern geography at Oxford University, where he taught seamen the science of their profession. Devoted to preserving old maps and accounts of historic voyages, Hakluyt spoke seven languages, including English, to aid him in his research. In 1583 Hakluyt was sent to Paris and there gathered information on historic voyages and the Canadian fur trade. Hakluyt personally gave a copy of "The Discourse" to Queen Elizabeth I, and after 1600 advised her on colonial affairs. Hakluyt was a member of the Skinners' Company, an organization of fur traders, as well as a patentee of the Virginia Company and a charter member of the Northwest Passage Company.

SEE ALSO ELIZABETH I; EMPIRE, BRITISH; FURS; INFORMATION AND COMMUNICATIONS; TRAVELERS AND TRAVEL.

BIBLIOGRAPHY

Markham, Clements R. *The Hakluyt Society: Address by Sir Clements R. Markham, on the Fiftieth Anniversary of the Foundation of the Society, December 15th, 1896.* London: Bedford Press, 1911.

Jeffrey Wood

HAMBURG

The port of Hamburg, currently Germany's largest port, lies about 100 kilometers from the ocean on the Elbe River. It has the added advantage that the Elbe in winter typically is free of ice. Via the Elbe River, Hamburg is connected to various parts of Central Europe. For centuries, Hamburg has served as a significant entrepôt.

Founded around 800 C.E. as a fortress, Hamburg's early prominence stems from its position as an important trading nexus in the Hanseatic League, a trading network and association of almost 200 cities and towns in Northern Europe. In 1189 Emperor Frederick I (c. 1123–1190) extended to the city and its port special privileges that allowed for duty-free shipping between Hamburg and the North Sea.

Besides its geographical and political advantages, Hamburg also benefited from close proximity to Lübeck, the principal city of the Hanseatic League and one of the largest cities in northern Germany during the Middle Ages. During the centuries that followed, trade flowing through Hamburg expanded. Its largest export was beer brewed in Hamburg.

Prior to the demise of the Hanseatic League in 1669, many of the Hansa towns had experienced economic decline. In contrast, the ports of Hamburg and Bremen continued to grow in terms of total trade handled. By 1650 Hamburg had the third-largest population in German-speaking Europe; only Vienna and Danzig had greater populations. Hamburg grew between 1618 and 1648, during the Thirty Years' War, because it welcomed many refugees and experienced few war-related losses. Over time, Hamburg's openness to foreigners ensured an ample supply of merchants with different talents and connections, as well as an ability to adjust. The rights of citizenship and property ownership, though, were off limits to noblemen.

Trade continued to expand over the 1600s and 1700s. Domestically, Hamburg benefited from its easy access south to the growing city of Leipzig and its trade fairs. Internationally, Britain was Hamburg's most important trading partner. Other important partners included France, Spain, Portugal, Holland, Russia, and each of those nation's respective colonies. Hamburg imported sugar, coffee, and wine from France; textiles, sugar, tobacco, and Indian calicoes from Britain; Brazilian sugar from Portugal; and wine, oil, fruits, and wool from the Mediterranean regions. Russian and Baltic exports to Hamburg consisted of grain, flax, and timber. Linen remained one of Hamburg's chief exports.

By 1800 Hamburg was one of the largest German cities and its richest by far. With the growth in international trade over the nineteenth century, Hamburg established business ties to ports in Asia, Australia, South America, and Africa. Whereas trade with Britain had been of utmost importance before the American Revolution, Hamburg's trade relations with the United States blossomed after 1815. At first, Hamburg imported mostly cotton and tobacco, and exported immigrants. Later it imported grain from the United States and other nations. By the 1850s German and Central European emigrants used either Hamburg or Bremen as their port of embarkation for overseas destinations. Between 1815 and 1930, it is estimated that at least 10 million people left Germany and Austria-Hungary alone, most through one of these two ports.

After 1860 Germany experienced tremendous industrial growth in chemicals, electrical and optical equipment, and precision instruments. In the early 1900s the German economy grew into one of the largest in the world, and Hamburg played a large role. Exports leaving Hamburg included many types of manufactured goods. Hamburg and its business people adapted quickly by expanding the port facilities, establishing a shipbuilding business, making the transition from sailing ships to steam ships, and promoting tourist and cruise traveling. With such flexibility and forward thinking, Hamburg today remains Germany's largest and most important port.

SEE ALSO AGRICULTURE; CARGOES, FREIGHT; CARGOES, PASSENGER; CHAMBERS OF COMMERCE; CONTAINERIZATION; FREE PORTS; GERMANY; HANSEATIC LEAGUE (HANSA OR HANSE); HARBORS; PORT CITIES.

BIBLIOGRAPHY

Assion, Peter. *Über Hamburg nach Amerika (To America by way of Hamburg* (trans.). Marburg, Germany: Institut für Europäische Ethnologie und Kulturforschung der Universität Marburg, 1991.

Dollinger, Philippe. *The German Hansa,* tr. and ed. D. S. Ault and S. H. Steinberg. Stanford, CA: Stanford University Press, 1970.

Holborn, Hajo. *A History of Modern Germany, 1648–1840.* Princeton, NJ: Princeton University Press, 1964.

Holborn, Hajo. *A History of Modern Germany, 1840–1945.* Princeton, NJ: Princeton University Press, 1969.

North, Michael. "Hamburg: The Continent's Most English City." In *From the North Sea to the Baltic: Essays in Commercial, Monetary and Agrarian History, 1500–1800,* ed. Michael North. Brookfield, VT: Variorum, 1996.

Simon, Edelgard. *Hamburg, a Gateway for the World, 1189–1989.* Colchester, Essex, U.K.: Lloyd's of London Press, 1989.

Simone A. Wegge

ALEXANDER HAMILTON
1755–1804

Alexander Hamilton, first secretary of the United States Treasury, recommended the state encouragement of manufactures as part of a broader plan both to stabilize a debt-ridden and stagnant American economy and to lay the foundations for future growth. While generally favoring free trade, Hamilton took issue with parts of Adam Smith's free-trade doctrine. Hamilton's most immediate practical contribution was to revive the new nation's public finances, but he also wrote the landmark "Report on Manufactures" (December 5, 1791). The Report made the case for manufacturing on both economic and moral grounds. It argued that an American economy solely dependent on agricultural exports would be both more unstable and less dynamic than an economy in which a manufacturing sector provided a domestic market for agricultural surpluses. Hamilton also argued that manufacturing would have a positive impact on the citizenry by diversifying the outlets for entrepreneurs and sparking technological progress. To encourage manufactures, Hamilton recommended a series of measures, chiefly temporary and modest tariffs and subsidies, to encourage infant industries. Hamilton's proposals were not implemented by Congress, but his Report exercised a lasting influence on U.S. economic policy through the likes of Henry Clay, Abraham Lincoln and, especially, the post-Civil War Republican Party.

SEE ALSO FINANCE, CREDIT AND MONEY LENDING; INDUSTRIALIZATION; MONEY AND MONETARY POLICY; SMITH, ADAM; PROTECTIONISM AND TARIFF WARS; UNITED STATES.

BIBLIOGRAPHY

McDonald, Forrest. *Alexander Hamilton: A Biography.* New York: W. W. Norton, 1979.

McNamara, Peter. *Political Economy and Statesmanship: Smith, Hamilton, and the Foundation of the Commercial Republic.* DeKalb: Northern Illinois University Press, 1998.

Peter McNamara

HANSEATIC LEAGUE (HANSA OR HANSE)

The Hanseatic League, or German Hansa, began in the twelfth century as a community of merchants trading on the Baltic and North Seas. From the thirteenth through the fifteenth centuries it developed a powerful commercial axis stretching from Novgorod in Russia to London and other English ports in the West. About 1157 Cologne merchants gained commercial privileges in London giving them a preferred position there. Bremen merchants also gained privileges in England. Other German merchants competed effectively in Scandinavia and organized a community at Visby, on the island of Gotland,

An interior view of a Hanseatic League Supreme Court and Town Hall in Lubeck, Germany. *The Hanseatic League was formed during the Middle Ages as an alliance of German cities in order to establish a trade monopoly in Northern Europe and the Baltic region. During the sixteenth century, a number of elements, such as internal conflict and shipping developments by the Dutch and English, started the decline of the league's influence and existence.* © DAVE BARTRUFF/CORBIS. REPRODUCED BY PERMISSION.

that traded actively throughout the Baltic. Following earlier examples of the French Rolls of Olèron (1152) and the thirteenth-century Book of the Consolat de Mar of Barcelona, the Laws of Visby became widely accepted as a maritime code throughout the northern commerce. The Laws of Visby were included in the Hansa's ordinances published in 1591, and later were expanded and revised in 1614 in Lübeck as the *Jus Hanseaticum maritimum.* Access to Novgorod allowed these merchants to become a major conduit for goods from the East into Western Europe. By 1205 they had established a merchant community, or *kontor,* known as the Peterhof, at Novgorod. Lübeck eventually replaced Visby as the most important commercial city on the Baltic, especially after it became an imperial city in 1226 and formed its first alliance with Hamburg in 1230.

RISE OF THE HANSA

This loose league was highly decentralized, so although seventy-two was often cited as the number of active member ports and inland towns, that number was never absolute. There were about 200 towns affiliated with the Hansa at one time or another, stretching from the Zuider Zee to the Gulf of Finland and south to Thuringia. The league emphasized freedom and security of commerce and the equality, rights, and privileges of all of its merchants. Lübeck's importance rose as, together with Hamburg, it maintained the route across the Danish peninsula, avoiding the voyage around Denmark and the frequent pirates in the straits between Sweden and Denmark. Salt, textiles, and fish from the West were traded for Russian furs and forest products. In 1252 Lübeck, Brunswick, Danzig, Cologne, and other free North German cities formed the Teutonic Hansa confederation, or what later became known as the Hanseatic League.

Hanseatic merchants gained privileges in the wool trade in Flanders in 1252 to 1253 and the Hanseatic *kontor* at Bruges became a powerful center of Hanseatic influence there. In 1281 Hanseatic merchants organized a *kontor* at the *Stalhof* (corrupted to "Steelyard" in English) in London. In 1293 control of the Novgorod *kontor* passed from Visby to Lübeck. Hanseatic colonization of the eastern Baltic established new ports and inland towns, widening the trade and increasing agricultural production and exports. By the end of the thirteenth century the Hansa traders dominated the trade from England and the Low Countries through Scandinavia to Russia. The largely autonomous Hansa towns found protection in their mutual alliances. Their municipal governments defended merchant interests, yet the league remained loose and decentralized, always more economic than political. It never claimed sovereignty, remaining within the framework of the Holy Roman Empire, although it was effectively independent of it.

In the fourteenth century the Hanseatic League reached its greatest strength and influence, as trade grew rapidly in both volume and variety of merchandise. The Black Death (1349–1351) was a setback, causing population decline and dislocation, but cooperation among the Hansa towns helped the region rebound quickly. Tighter regulations resisted foreign competition. The league sometimes resorted to war to maintain privileges and advantages in foreign markets, but more often used embargoes or other economic weapons against its rivals. In 1356 delegations from the Hansa towns met together for the first time in a diet (*Hansetag*) to deal with difficulties in Flanders. This and subsequent diets also reflected the transition of the Hansa from an association of merchants to a league of towns. The Hanseatic diets subordinated the *kontore* in foreign cities—the most important were at Novgorod, Bruges, Bergen, and London—to their will. Diplomacy and war brought trade agreements with Flanders and Denmark and resulted in stronger alliances among the Hanseatic towns, Dutch towns, and the Order of Teutonic Knights in Prussia, leading to formation of the Hanseatic Confederation at the 1367 diet at Cologne. Defeat of Denmark and the Peace of Stralsund in 1370 allowed the Hanseatic League to extend its power further through blockades and war.

DECLINE FROM THE FIFTEENTH CENTURY

Subsequent rivalry with English, Dutch, Russian, and Flemish merchants began to challenge Hanseatic control of the Baltic by the beginning of the fifteenth century. In 1410 Poland and Lithuania defeated the Teutonic Knights at Tannenberg, weakening its support of the Hansa. Repeated wars with Denmark took a toll on the Hansa, as did a long war with Castile (1419–1441) and with the Dutch (1438–1441). The Hansa were at war with England in 1470 to 1474, during which the Hansa excluded Cologne from its membership because of its close ties to England. These conflicts weakened the league, making it harder to maintain the privileges and agreements that had tied the community together earlier. The Dutch and the Flemish first succeeded in reducing the Hansa's privi-

leges, but eventually the English, Russians, and Scandinavians did also. Moscow conquered Novgorod in 1478 and encouraged Russian merchants to replace the Germans. In 1494 the tsar closed the Peterhof at Novgorod. Although it reopened twenty years later, by that time the Hansa merchants had lost their advantages there.

In the sixteenth century the turmoil of the Protestant Reformation further undermined the Hansa in the face of rising national states and principalities. Continuing difficulties with Flanders caused the Hansa to move the *kontor* of Bruges permanently to Antwerp in 1520 in collaboration with local merchants there. In the process, Hansa influence declined. The Bergen *kontor* also faded, as Norwegian merchants demanded a larger share of the trade, along with Danish participation. The Steelyard in London remained important, but it, too, eventually weakened before English merchant competition. Southern German commercial houses, notably the Fuggers, also eroded Hanseatic strength by opening East-West routes through Central Europe. The Dutch and the English, improving on Hanseatic ship designs, expanded their trade in the Baltic at the expense of the Hansa. Their successful trade with the Americas also added to their capital resources. The Hansa responded with more stringent regulations on foreign traders, but could not stem the tide of new traders moving into its region. Moreover, many Hanseatic towns began to form political alliances apart from the common commercial interests of the Hansa. Even so, Hansa trade grew, reaching into the Atlantic to trade with France, Portugal, Spain, and the Mediterranean. But the Hansa failed to modernize its technology and structure to compete effectively with the larger nation-states emerging all around.

In an effort to restore its former grandeur, the 1557 diet at Lübeck established membership fees, more stringent rules for membership, and detailed regulations on trade. It named a *syndic,* a full-time legal officer who worked to protect and extend the diplomatic and commercial agreements among the members and in foreign ports. There was some revitalization of Hanseatic trade during the latter half of the sixteenth century, but this growth was probably due more to the general growth of European trade, stimulated by American gold and silver, than to the league's reorganization. The long Dutch war against Spain (1568–1648) allowed the Hansa to regain some of the trade that it had lost to the Dutch, but the East-West trade increasingly bypassed the Hanseatic towns. The English moved heavily into the Baltic, and each Hansa town began to make its own arrangements with the English or Dutch traders. Lübeck lost a major naval battle against a Scandinavian force off Gotland in 1566, and in 1567 Hamburg granted privileges to English merchants, as did Elbing in 1579. Elizabeth I closed the London Steelyard in 1598. More defeats for the Hansa came in the early seventeenth century, and the Thirty Years' War (1618–1648) finally destroyed it. An alliance between Lübeck, Hamburg, and Bremen in 1630 was all that was left of the Hansa, although the last Hanseatic diet convened at Lübeck in 1669 in an unsuccessful effort at restoration.

In the eighteenth century the Hansa was all but forgotten, but in the nineteenth century Lübeck, Hamburg, and Bremen reunited to promote their trade and diplomatic presence abroad. The Hanseatic League was essentially a medieval institution that had failed to compete with the larger political units and private corporations of early modern Europe.

SEE ALSO GERMANY; GUILDS.

BIBLIOGRAPHY

Braudel, Fernand. *Civilization and Capitalism, 15th–18th Century,* 3 vols., tr. Siân Reynolds. New York: Harper and Row, 1982–1984.

Dollinger, Philippe. *The German Hansa,* tr. D. S. Ault and S. H. Steinberg. London: Macmillan, 1970.

DuBoulay, F. R. H. *Germany in the Later Middle Ages.* New York: St. Martin's Press, 1983.

Fudge, John D. *Cargoes, Embargoes, and Emissaries: The Commercial and Political Interaction of England and the German Hanse, 1450–1510.* Toronto: University of Toronto Press, 1995.

Haenens, Albert d'. *Europe of the North Sea and the Baltic: The World of the Hanse,* tr. E. J. L. Bacon. Antwerp, Belgium: Fonds Mercator, 1984.

Lloyd, Terrence H. *England and the German Hanse, 1157–1611: A Study of their Trade and Commercial Diplomacy.* Cambridge, U.K.: Cambridge University Press, 1991.

Sartorius, Georg. *Geschichte des Hanseatischen Bundes (History of the Hanseatic League)* (trans.), 3 vols. Göttingen, Germany: H. Dieterich, 1802–1808.

Shildhauer, Johannes. *The Hansa: History and Culture,* tr. Katherine Vanovitch. Leipzig, Germany: Edition Leipzig, 1985.

Thompson, James W. *Economic and Social History of Europe in the Later Middle Ages.* New York: Ungar, 1960.

Ralph Lee Woodward Jr.

HARBORS

Ports were, literally, the gateways of trade. From early times, regional or national development depended on exchanging favorable factor products: raw materials, manufactures, and foodstuffs. Against inadequate overland transport, river and sea ports offered an easier system linking hinterland, coastwise, and overseas trading. Although from ancient times ports worldwide offered regional trade, bases for imperial adventures, and centers for human migration, most important for long-term oceanic and international trade were those in Europe. After the Dark Ages intra-European trade grew, and by 1450 there was an established exchange of wine, fruit, and salt from the warm south and woolens, raw materials, and fish from the cooler north, organized principally by Amsterdam. The strength of such entrepôts lay partly in geographical advantages, but equally in knowledge, connections, finance, and general mercantile expertise. "Port People," merchants, shipowners, and explorers, created trades, and their factors in foreign ports searched for goods and markets to support home industries, which were actively encouraged. By the 1490s their cosmopolitan societies were spreading ideas about "round earth" geography, encouraging exploration to secure goods from different climatic zones. They were further encouraged by scientific and technical advances, including efficient cargo vessels (following the Dutch *fluijt*), compasses, and sea cannons. Adventurers and mapmakers following Christopher Columbus opened the rich potential of the tropical East and West Indies and the temperate grasslands of the Americas. Mercantile capital (rather than kings and aristocrats) created "plantations" (colonies) on new land, employing African slaves and European emigrants. By 1700 Dutch, British, French, Spanish, and Portuguese ports were establishing oceanic trade routes and stimulating a nascent international economy, interacting in the eighteenth century with the technical and economic dynamism of the British Industrial Revolution, which was largely dependent on ports for raw materials and export (and re-export) markets.

Oceanic trade required partner/client ports established by European agents with access to market knowledge, shipping, and credit, stretching from Lima, Rio de Janeiro, and New York in the West to Jakarta and Sydney in the East. Although Japan refused entry until 1854, China, which confined European "factories" (trading stations) to Canton, was gradually forced after 1842 to allow Britain, Germany, France, Italy, and Russia to build their own ports, of which the prize was Shanghai on the Yangtze which, like the Irrawaddy, was "opened" by British shipping. Elsewhere mercantile, settler, or military penetration from partner-ports developed Europe-oriented economies, while demand for "settler goods" encouraged Europe's industrialization. Continents were now linked to Spanish, Dutch, and British ports, especially Glasgow, Liverpool, London, Amsterdam, and Rotterdam. Those ports in turn accumulated huge wealth, increasing their countries' economic leadership and indirectly funding imperial and naval adventures. Quite remarkably, the Americas were shared between Portugal, Spain, and Britain, and the British and Dutch East India Companies eventually controlled large areas of India and Indonesia.

The port city of Genoa, Italy. *Located in the northwest part of the country, Genoa is Italy's chief seaport and a prominent center for shipbuilding. Facilities along the coast were badly damaged during World War II, but then rebuilt and modernized to accommodate a strong merchant trading community.* © THE MARINERS MUSEUM/CORBIS. REPRODUCED BY PERMISSION.

Many imperial staging posts became international entrepôts: Singapore and Hong Kong are still the leaders.

Whereas major ports dominated international trade, smaller ports contributed to general trade by supplying seamen, ships, and apprentices, and by handling coastal and short-haul trade in groceries, wood, and minerals. Many unimportant ports employed shipping primarily in cross-trading. Holland relied on foreign seamen, and twentieth-century Norwegian ports manned the bulk of world whalers.

Ports changed over time with the interrelated development of hinterlands, trade schedules, and transport technology. Tidal havens and minimal facilities no longer served. When, by about 1770, vessels reached around 350 tons, and East Indiamen engaged in Far Eastern trades around 700 tons, concurrent advances in hydraulic engineering facilitated substantial piers and wet docks, and large sea-locks were perfected around 1800. Massive quayside warehousing also became possible. However, the most influential novelty on sea and land was steam power. From the 1830s ports were equipped with larger

steamship piers or docks, and from the 1840s, with open space and transit sheds for railway working. Hydraulic power from around 1856 facilitated ever-larger lock gates and cranes, and inaugurated trade in heavy unit goods such as railway engines to open up "new" economies. Railway expansion also ended ports' private hinterlands, forcing competition in facilities that led to over-provision and massive port-authority debts. Some railway companies created their own, better-organized ports, though shipowners' attachments to established routes often thwarted success, except with minerals, which generally went to the nearest dedicated port facilities, to which ships had to go for both bunkers and cargo. A final burst of port building occurred beginning in the 1880s as both international economy and ports expanded enormously in business and area. Steel ships with triple-expansion engines grew rapidly in size, forcing ports to extend into deeper water and producing miles of expensive waterfront. Vast amounts of money were spent around the world creating harbors, docks, and piers for huge passenger liners, especially on the Atlantic, and for booming coal traffic, though many—especially shallow—ports in Africa and Asia required cargo liners to carry their own derricks for loading to or from barges. Many ports were over-resourced and financially overstretched when wars and depression between 1914 and 1945 upset trade expectations.

Dramatic changes began again after 1945 when the application of wartime cargo handling methods, principally roll-on/roll-off (Ro/Ro) vehicle transporters, demanded unprecedented changes in port facilities. Giant vessels required very deep water, novel handling equipment, vast areas of leveled ground, and new, integrated hinterland transports systems. Many ports abandoned or expanded beyond historic centers, especially for oil jetties and related refineries. Unfortunately, for topographical or financial reasons many great ports, including London, could not respond adequately, and most ports abandoned outdated facilities or used them for short-haul vessels. More seriously, globalization of shipping removed control over trade from local port people to international shipowning combines with their own back-carriage systems and little port loyalty. Computerized container vessels required a minimal number of hub ports connected by smaller vessels to feeder ports. Because many major ports lacked adequate water depth and back-carriage, success or failure in interport rivalry was often determined by the speed with which governments recognized and reacted to the reality that their trade might depend upon foreign hubs unless port or transport subsidies were offered. Successful ports were also likely to be those with the most productive or demanding hinterlands, so the busiest ports are now in the Far East—Hong Kong, Singapore, Kaohsiung (Taiwan), Pusan, Kobe, and Yokohama. Many ports, such as Dubai, have expanded with the exploitation of oil fields. By comparison, Rotterdam is the only top-rank port in Europe, once the prime mover in international trade. Many declining ports are now feeders for foreign hubs, though currently private and public enterprise is trying to provide adequate facilities to re-enter the big league: Clydeport (Glasgow), Hamburg, and Antwerp, for instance, hope to rival Rotterdam. Ironically, many small ports have actually revived by acting as low-level importers because their land and labor is relatively cheap, and small-scale Ro/Ro facilities are more easily provided.

Port people were obviously in control of their own destinies—and that of many people in developing areas—until around 1850, when railway companies began to control or shift hinterland trade flows, or build their rival ports. But the failure of traditional port-city authorities to build appropriate facilities in line with changes in transport technology and trade schedules started in the eighteenth century, and for generations

new facilities were quickly overtaken by trade volumes and ship sizes. Lack of foresight and reluctance to spend money raised from dues are often blamed, but providing appropriate facilities in an ever-changing world was never easy. Interestingly, port towns have exerted themselves more efficiently to reclaim the "land-sea interface" for recreation or building than ever they did to maintain working ports.

In considering ports as a collection of docks, it is easy to overlook their special characteristics as cities. They were among the largest in their countries, and many created very large industrial capacities, building ships, processing imports, and manufacturing exports. Glasgow ("Second City of the Empire") was perhaps the greatest port/industrial city, but Genoa was very similar, as are many of the great Asian ports today. They also engaged in capitalized fishing on a larger scale than in isolated fishing ports. In social terms their very large labor forces were irregularly employed, poorly paid, overcrowded, and suffering from higher levels of malnutrition, disease, and mortality than inland cities. "Sailor towns" were commonly isolated units within them, and ghettoes existed for inland and foreign immigrants escaping from even worse conditions. In many countries dockers' dissatisfaction bred strong unions whose only weapon was total strikes that affected port competition. Recurrent opposition to modernization alienated ports such as London from shipowners or governments. The consequences of mechanization on workforces were devastating everywhere. Port communities experienced massive unemployment, and even ports with major (low-labor) facilities experienced the break-up of traditional communities and suffered economic and social privation for a decade or more before adjusting to the new world of feeder port operations.

SEE ALSO Amsterdam; Antwerp; Bahia; Baltimore; Barcelona; Bordeaux; Boston; Bristol; Cádiz; Calcutta; Cargoes, Freight; Cargoes, Passenger; Cartagena; Charleston; Containerization; Free Ports; Gdansk; Genoa; Glasgow; Guangzhou; Hamburg; Havana; Hong Kong; Indian Ocean; La Rochelle; Los Angeles–Long Beach; Marseilles; Mediterranean; Mumbai; Nagasaki; Nantes; New Orleans; New York; Petroleum; Philadelphia; Port Cities; Porto; Rio de Janeiro; Rotterdam; Salem; San Francisco–Oakland; Shipping, Aids to; Shipping, Coastal; Shipping, Inland Waterways, Europe; Shipping, Inland Waterways, North America; Shipping Lanes; Shipping, Merchant; Shipping, Technological Change; Ships and Shipping; Ship Types; Singapore; Veracruz; Yokohama.

BIBLIOGRAPHY

Bird, James Harold. *The Major Seaports of the United Kingdom.* London: Hutchinson, 1969. Offers a geographer's model of the physical evolution of major ports.

Broeze, Frank, ed. *Gateways of Asia: Port Cities of Asia in the 13th–20th Centuries.* London and New York: Kegan Paul, 1997.

Devine, Thomas. M., and Jackson, Gordon, eds. *Glasgow,* vol. 1. Manchester, U.K., and New York: Manchester University Press, 1995. Examines the role of a major industrial and port system in the context of "Second City of the Empire."

Fischer, Lewis R., and Jarvis, Adrian, eds. *Harbours and Havens: Essays in Port History in Honour of Gordon Jackson.* Research in Maritime History no. 16. St. John's, Newfoundland: International Maritime Economic History Association, 1999.

Jackson, Gordon, and Williams, David M., eds. *Shipping, Technology, and Imperialism.* Brookfield, VT: Scholars Press, Aldershot, and Ashgate Publishing, 1996.

Jackson, Gordon. "Some Problems of Decision-Making in a Changing World." *International Journal of Maritime History* 6, no. 2 (1994) 260–277.

Jackson, Gordon. "The Significance of Unimportant Ports." *International Journal of Maritime History* 13, no. 2 (2001): 1–17.

Jackson, Gordon. *The History and Archaeology of Ports.* Tadworth, U.K.: World's Work, 1983. A general survey of the typography and evolution of ports in Britain.

Starkey, David J., and Harlaftis, Gelina, eds. *Global Markets: The Internationalization of the Sea Transport Industries since 1859.* Research in Maritime History no. 14. St. John's, Newfoundland: International Maritime Economic History Association, 1998. Contains many relevant articles.

Gordon Jackson

HARDWARE

The making of hardware—that is, ferrous tools, fasteners, and mechanisms—was common across most regions of Eurasia and Africa in the early modern era. The indigenous peoples of America and Australasia, on the other hand, had no knowledge of ferrous metallurgy prior to their contact with Europeans, and were restricted to implements of stone, animal bone, or vegetable matter, or to items fashioned from softer, nonferrous metals.

Expertise in smelting and smithing was widely spread. Indeed, the ubiquity of these skills may have inhibited the exchange of basic ironwares. Ironworking was to be found in many parts of sub-Saharan Africa, for example, exploiting the ore-rich lateritic crust that covers much of the continent. An exceptional concentration of resources did lead to the emergence of specialized production zones, such as that of the Upemba Depression in the south of the Congo Basin, but the axes and hoes crafted by African smiths were traded within Africa, not beyond it. Central Europe, too, was home to specialized industrial districts, such as those in Bohemia and Westphalia, which produced a range of agricultural tools and implements for markets across the north and east of the continent. Other centers were dedicated to the making of new or prestige products. The Liège district, for example, became a major center for the manufacture of gun locks, while Innsbruck and Brescia were renowned for their armor workshops.

The opening up of the Atlantic economy in the sixteenth and seventeenth centuries led to a reordering of production within Europe, with a swing away from central and alpine Europe and toward manufacturing districts in the north and west. The Americas provided an entirely new market for European manufacturers, and one that expanded greatly in the seventeenth and eighteenth centuries. An intercontinental maritime trade in hardware got under way, given impetus by the growth of plantation agriculture in the tropics and semitropics and by the extension of European settlement in the more temperate zones of the New World. The ecological transformation of America, whether carried out by enslaved Africans or European migrants, depended upon steel-edged tools of English or Walloon provenance—axes, saws, scythes, hoes, and woodworking tools. Only in the later eighteenth century was there significant import substitution, as North Americans began to produce nails and axes of their own.

A maritime trade in metalwares was already a feature of the Indian Ocean in the fifteenth century, although in Asia, as elsewhere, most smiths catered for local markets. Metalworking traditions of great antiquity were to be found in China, India, and the Islamic world. Casting techniques, both in iron and bronze, were highly advanced in China. High-grade steel was a speciality of southern India and Ceylon, supporting the manufacture of swords that circulated throughout the Middle East. During the early modern era, however, European merchants insinuated their way into the trading networks of the Indian Ocean. By the 1660s, for example, the Dutch were organizing the export of nails and other wrought iron articles from the Coromandel Coast to Indonesia.

It is not clear whether the trade in nails to Batavia was a creation of the Dutch or whether they were building upon an established commerce. Where the Dutch were unquestionably innovative was in the organization of Indian labor. They put into operation European-style factories with Dutch or Swedish overseers in charge of dozens of local smiths at a time. Elsewhere, production systems were relatively stable. Smiths in Africa tended to be a caste apart—independent workers who were often credited with powers of divination. In Europe guild organizations remained powerful throughout the period, although putting-out networks, which mobilized the labor of women as well as men, grew in significance, especially for employers oriented upon the more dynamic transatlantic markets.

SEE ALSO COPPER; INDUSTRIALIZATION; IRON AND STEEL.

BIBLIOGRAPHY

Braudel, F. *The Structures of Everyday Life: The Limits of the Possible.* London: Collins, 1981.

Chaudhuri, K. N. *Asia before Europe: Economy and Civilisation of the Indian Ocean from the Rise of Islam to 1750.* Cambridge, U.K.: Cambridge University Press, 1990.

Schmidt, Peter R., ed. *The Culture and Technology of African Iron Production.* Gainesville: University of Florida Press, 1996.

Chris Evans

ROBERT HART

1835–1911

Robert Hart was born in 1835 in Northern Ireland. He graduated college with honors at age 19 and accepted an internship with the British governor in Hong Kong. The same year (1854), a rebellion paralyzed customs operations at Shanghai, and British diplomats convinced China's Qing dynasty to establish an Imperial Maritime Customs Service (IMC) staffed by foreigners but subordinate to the Qing. Hart became Canton deputy commissioner in 1857, and inspector general for the entire system in 1861.

Hart developed close ties with reformers in China's foreign ministry. Whereas his predecessor consistently pushed British interests, Hart strove to make the service impartial and professional, and insulate it from political crises. But the importance of customs revenue (which rose 700% in local currency during Hart's tenure) made Hart politically important; his policy that all revenues went to Beijing, none to regional authorities, remained until 1942, greatly influencing various power struggles. Fourteen ports were open in 1861; forty-nine when he retired in 1908. He helped to modernize port procedures and facilities, and advised the Qing on foreign relations. Nonetheless, the system which the IMC helped to operate—in which China lacked tariff autonomy, could not ban opium imports, and so on—made it an imperialist institution to many. Hart died in 1911; the Qing fell four months later.

SEE ALSO CHINA; EMPIRE, BRITISH; EMPIRE, QING; FREE TRADE, THEORY AND PRACTICE; GUANGZHOU; HONG KONG; IMPERIAL MARITIME CUSTOMS, CHINA; JARDINE MATHESON; MOST-FAVORED-NATION PROVISIONS; SHANGHAI.

BIBLIOGRAPHY

Fairbank, John K., et. al. *The IG in Peking: Letters of Robert Hart, Chinese Maritime Customs, 1868–1907.* Cambridge, MA: Harvard Belknap, 1975.

Wright, Stanley F. *Hart and the Chinese Customs.* Belfast: William Mullan and Son, 1950.

Kenneth Pomeranz

HAVANA

In 1517 Spanish conquerors founded the town of Havana on the northern coast of Cuba facing one of the best harbors in the world. The port commanded the Caribbean sea lanes between Spain and its American colonies, making Havana a key administrative and commercial hub of the Spanish Empire. From the 1560s into the 1700s Spain's Atlantic trade circulated in annual convoys of ships that gathered in Havana before carrying the fruits of Spain's global empire back to the peninsula—precious metals, tobacco, sugar, cochineal, and cacao from the Americas, and textiles, spices, and porcelains from Asia. The return voyages from Spain brought wheat and other foodstuffs, wines and brandies, and European manufactured goods. Spanish merchants monopolized this imperial trade into the 1800s, with the exception of the Crown's concessions to foreign traders to supply the empire with African slaves. Cuba received some 130,000 slaves between 1511 and 1789. Until the late 1700s imperial trade and defense drove economic activity in Havana and its hinterland.

Two events in the second half of the eighteenth century brought profound change to the Spanish Empire and to the city of Havana—the British occupation of the city in 1762 and 1763 and the Haitian Revolution, which began in 1791. The occupation forced Spain to increase spending for imperial defense and to find new sources of revenue. In Cuba the Crown encouraged the expansion of sugar production for export and allowed the increased importation of enslaved Africans (over 250,000 between 1790 and 1820). Revolution in Haiti ended the plantation economy there, opening a significant share of the world's market to Cuban sugar. The Crown also liberalized imperial trade, eventually granting Cuba the right of free trade in the world market by 1818. Cuba was transformed into a sugar plantation colony, producing 25 percent of the world's sugar by 1856. Yet, as sugar production expanded south and east of Havana, the city's dominance in the island's trade decreased.

From the early 1800s until the 1990s sugar dominated Cuba's economy, and Cuban trade continued to depend upon a principal trading partner—first Spain, then the United States, and finally, the Soviet Union. By 1898, when Cuba became independent from Spain, the island was already dependent on U.S. markets and investment capital. By the 1920s U.S. firms controlled 75 percent of the sugar industry, along with mines, railroads, and public utilities. By the 1950s, 69.1 percent of Cuban trade was with the United States, and almost 55 percent of Cuban sugar was exported to the United States. This economic dependence on the United States ended with the U.S. embargo against the 1963 Socialist revolution of Fidel Castro (b. 1926), but it was replaced by a similar dependence on trade, credit, and capital from the Soviet Union. The collapse of the Soviet Union and its Eastern European satellites by 1991 closed their protected markets for Cuban sugar, forcing the Cuban government to reorient the economy toward tourism. By 1994 tourism was earning more hard currency than sugar and was a greater proportion of gross domestic product. Tourism will likely expand further whenever the U.S. embargo is lifted. Havana is still an active port, but it also has become a tourist attraction since UNESCO designated the old colonial part of the city a World Historical Site in 1982.

SEE ALSO AGRICULTURE; CARGOES, FREIGHT; CARGOES, PASSENGER; CHAMBERS OF COMMERCE; CONQUISTADORS; CONTAINERIZATION; CUBA; EMPIRE, SPANISH; ETHNIC GROUPS, AFRICANS; FREE PORTS; HARBORS; PORT CITIES; RUSSIA; SPAIN; UNITED STATES.

BIBLIOGRAPHY

Kuethe, Allan. "Havana in the Eighteenth Century." In *Atlantic Port Cities, Economy, Culture, and Society in the Atlantic World, 1650–1850*, ed. Franklin W. Knight and Peggy K. Liss. Knoxville: University of Tennessee Press, 1992.

Leogrande, William M., and Thomas, Julie M. "Cuba's Quest for Economic Independence." *Journal of Latin American Studies* 34 (2002): 325–363.

McNeill, John Robert. *Atlantic Empires of France and Spain, Louisbourg and Havana, 1700–1763*. Chapel Hill and London: University of North Carolina Press, 1985.

Segre, Roberto; Coyula, Mario; and Scarpaci, Joseph L. *Havana. Two Faces of the Antillean Metropolis*, rev. edition. Chapel Hill: University of North Carolina Press, 2002.

Evelyn Powell Jennings

JOHN HAWKINS
1532?–1595

John Hawkins was born in Plymouth, England, in 1532 or 1533, the son of William and Joan (neé Trelawney)

Hawkins. His father was a merchant and shipowner who sailed to the Spanish Indies on several occasions. When William died in 1554, John and his older brother William inherited the family business. John made several trips of his own to the West Indies, carrying African slaves and English woolens to trade for gold, pearls, hides, and anything else of value that might be available. Foreigners were forbidden to trade in the Spanish Indies. Hawkins's attempt to trade ended in disaster in 1568 at San Juan de Ulloa. There Spanish forces attacked and burned most of his ships, killing or capturing more than a hundred of his men. His son Richard was born in 1560, while Hawkins was still unmarried. In 1564 John married Catherine Gonson, who died in 1591, whereupon he married Margaret Vaughn. In 1570 Hawkins attempted to strike a deal with Philip II of Spain: Hawkins offered to give Philip English royal navy ships and sailors, with himself as commander in exchange for the release of his previously captured men. The attempt was aborted when English officials discovered what Hawkins planned to do. Whether this was a clever ruse or base betrayal by Hawkins is still in dispute. Even so Hawkins was such a talented seaman that he was soon allowed to take charge of English naval construction. Within a few years he managed to rebuild the navy, making it possible for England to withstand the Spanish invasion threat in 1588. Knighted for bravery against the Spanish Armada, Hawkins kept his earlier coat of arms, a slave bound with a rope. He died on November 11, 1595, during a raid on the Spanish Indies in partnership with his cousin Sir Francis Drake (1540?–1596), who also died on the voyage.

SEE ALSO ELIZABETH I; EMPIRE, BRITISH; PRIVATEERING; SLAVERY AND THE AFRICAN SLAVE TRADE.

BIBLIOGRAPHY

Kelsey, Harry. *Sir John Hawkins, Queen Elizabeth's Slave Trader*. New Haven, CT, and London: Yale University Press, 2003.

Harry Kelsey

WILLIAM RANDOLPH HEARST
1863–1951

William Randolph Hearst was a news baron and media entrepreneur who exerted a critical influence on the world during the first half of the twentieth century through his manipulation of media. Although he never completed his degree at Harvard University, his first journalism experience was in 1883 at the *Harvard Review*. In 1887 his father gave him control of the *San Francisco Examiner*, which he saved from the brink of collapse and made profitable. Hearst eventually became the owner of an empire of forty publications with 20 million readers. Hearst claimed to have started single-handedly the Spanish-American War with sensational—"yellow" journalistic—headlines. Soon this influence spread to political circles, and Hearst served as a New York congressman from 1903 to 1907. Always seeking to vertically integrate while increasing circulation, Hearst founded several news services (alternative to the Associated Press; the foremost was the International News Service, now United Press International) to serve as sources of information for his papers. Hearst also popularized color comics. As he was generally antagonistic toward immigrants and minorities, Hearst sympathized with Adolf Hitler during the early 1930s. This, in addition to Hearst's unpopular criticism of Franklin D. Roosevelt's New Deal, and an unflattering, thinly disguised portrayal of him in the film "Citizen Kane," put an end to the extraordinary influence he had on Americans in the early 1900s.

SEE ALSO INFORMATION AND COMMUNICATIONS.

BIBLIOGRAPHY

Davies, Marion. *The Times We Had: Life with William Randolph Hearst.* Indianapolis: Bobbs-Merrill, 1975.

Nasaw, David. *The Chief: The Life of William Randolph Hearst.* Boston: Houghton Mifflin, 2000.

Benjamin Passty

HECKSCHER-OHLIN

In the first decades of the twentieth century, two Swedish economists, Eli F. Heckscher (1879–1952) and Bertil Ohlin (1899–1979), developed the factor proportions model of international trade, which has dominated trade theory ever since. Heckscher's contribution was an article published in 1919, while Ohlin's came in his doctoral dissertation, published in 1924. Both pieces were concerned with the underlying causes underlying causes of international trade, and their insight was that this trade could be due to differences across countries in the endowments of factors of production—that is to say, to cross-country differences in the relative amounts of land, labor, skills, capital, natural resources, and other inputs available for production.

Formally, the Heckscher-Ohlin theorem states that a country will export those commodities that use relatively intensively the factors of production with which it is relatively abundantly endowed, and that it will import those commodities that use relatively intensively those factors of production that are relatively scarce in the country. It is easiest to give a flavor of the theorem by means of an example, provided in Ohlin's dissertation.

Suppose that there are two regions in the world, Australia and Europe; and that Australia is abundantly endowed with land, but has only a small population. In Europe, on the other hand, suppose that the land endowment is no bigger than in Australia, while its population is much bigger than Australia's. Under these assumptions, the ratio of land to labor will be higher in Australia than in Europe; in the language of the theorem, Australia is relatively land-abundant, while Europe is relatively labor-abundant.

Suppose also that there are two industries in each country, agriculture and manufacturing; and that production in agriculture involves high inputs of land relative to labor, whereas production in industry involves high inputs of labor relative to land: Agriculture is then said to be relatively land-intensive, whereas industry is said to be relative labor-intensive. The theorem states that relatively land-abundant Australia will export the relatively land-intensive good, agricultural output, to Europe; while relatively labor-abundant Europe will in exchange export the relatively labor-intensive good, manufacturing output, to Australia.

Formally proving this theorem requires a significant amount of work, and an array of technical assumptions (for an introduction, see Krugman and Obstfeld 2003); however, it makes intuitive sense. Land in Australia should be much cheaper than in Europe, since it is relatively more abundant there; and so it should be relatively cheap to produce commodities such as wool and wheat, which require large inputs of land. On the other hand, labor will be cheaper in Europe than in Australia, and it will be cheaper to produce labor-intensive commodities in Europe.

This discussion may seem abstract, and indeed it is, but common sense tell us that factor proportions do in fact matter for trade patterns in the real world. For example, low-wage economies such as China have an advantage over rich countries such as the United States when it comes to producing simple industrial commodities such as clothing and textiles, since wage costs are a large proportion of total costs in these industries; on the other hand, aircraft production requires skilled labor as well as large capital investments, and so it tends to be located in rich countries, where skills and capital are relatively abundant.

If this theory does indeed explain international trade patterns, then an important corollary follows: international trade will help to equalize factor prices (such as unskilled or skilled wages, land rents, or the returns to capital) across countries. Take again the stylized example of land-abundant Australia trading with labor-abundant Europe. As mentioned before, land rents will be higher in Europe than in Australia, and wages will be higher in

Australia than in Europe; but now consider what happens when trade between these two countries takes place.

As Australian agriculture finds new markets overseas, its output will expand, and this will raise the demand for Australian land, and hence its price. On the other hand, as Europe starts to import food its agriculture will contract, and this will lead to the demand for land, and hence land rents, falling there. The gap between high European land rents and low Australian land rents will thus decline. Similarly, expanding European industry will hire workers and raise European wages, while imports of manufactured goods will lead to Australian industry contracting and to the demand for Australian labor, and Australian wages, falling. The gap between high Australian wages and low European wages will also decline: trade between the two regions thus leads to factor price convergence. It may even, under certain rather strict theoretical assumptions, lead to factor prices being equalized across countries; but this is clearly not something that can be observed in the highly unequal world of the early twenty-first century.

Despite the intuitive appeal of Heckscher-Ohlin theory, there are several facts about international trade in the late twentieth century that have made some economists doubt its validity in practice. For example, according to the theory, trade should be greatest among countries with very different factor endowments, whereas in fact the bulk of international trade takes place among rich countries. The theory also has trouble explaining what is known as intra-industry trade, which occurs, for example, when two countries exchange different makes of automobiles with each other (since presumably factor proportions in the two industries will be very similar). Indeed, the 1980s saw the development of so-called *new trade theory,* which allowed economies of scale to play an independent role in determining trade patterns (see for example Helpman and Krugman 1985). The 1980s also saw the development of a highly technical econometric literature trying to test Heckscher-Ohlin theory; while early contributions (for example Bowen, Leamer, and Sveikauskas 1987) questioned the usefulness of the theory in explaining the real world, more recent work (for example, Davis and Weinstein 2001) suggests that Heckscher-Ohlin theory does indeed help to explain trade patterns, so long as the researcher bears in mind the facts that countries are not distinguished by differences in factor endowments alone (for example, technology differs across countries), that some goods are not traded between countries at all, and that international trade is not costless.

Heckscher and Ohlin were in large part trying to understand the highly globalized world of the late nineteenth century (roughly 1870–1913) when developing their theory, and economic historians have shown that factor proportions theory is particularly useful in understanding this period (O'Rourke and Williamson 1999). Labor-abundant Europe did indeed exchange manufactures in exchange for food and raw materials with the land-abundant New World, just as the theory predicts. Moreover, this led to factor price convergence, in accordance with Heckscher-Ohlin logic. Land prices rose in real terms by more than 400 percent in Australia between 1870 and 1910 and by more than 250 percent in the United States during the same period, while they fell in European countries such as Britain, France, and Sweden. European wages on average caught up with high New World wages during the late nineteenth century. More generally, in land-scarce economies such as Japan, Korea, and Taiwan, as well as in many European countries, wages rose substantially, relative to land rents, between 1870 and 1913, while the ratio of wages to land rents fell sharply in land-abundant food-exporting nations such as Argentina, Australia, the United States, Uruguay, Burma, Siam, Egypt, and the Punjab. In the former regions, rising wage-rental ratios implied more equal societies (since landowners were typically closer to the top of income distributions than landless workers); in the British case, the rise in the wage-rental ratio from the 1850s onwards marked a historic turning point, since wage-rental ratios had been declining from 1500 to 1850 as a result of a rising population pressing against a fixed land endowment (O'Rourke and Williamson 2002).

Elsewhere, these forces led to a backlash against globalization, as losers obtained tariff protection in an attempt to insulate themselves against world market forces. The classic example can be found in European decisions to impose tariffs on food imports from the 1870s or 1880s onward. The distributional effects of international trade identified by Heckscher and Ohlin remained a source of political tension in the early twenty-first century, as unskilled workers in rich countries protested against imports from labor-abundant low-wage economies, and rich countries continued to block agricultural exports from land-abundant developing countries.

SEE ALSO Stolper-Samuelson Theorem; Theories of International Trade.

BIBLIOGRAPHY

Bowen, Harry P.; Leamer, Edward E.; and Sveikauskas, Leo. "Multicountry, Multifactor Tests of the Factor Abundance Theory." *American Economic Review* 77 (1987): 791–809.

Davis, Donald R., and Weinstein, David E. "An Account of Global Factor Trade." *American Economic Review* 91 (2001): 1423–1453.

Flam, Harry, and Flanders, M. June. *Heckscher-Ohlin Trade Theory.* Cambridge, MA: MIT Press, 1991.

Helpman, Elhanan, and Krugman, Paul R. *Market Structure and Foreign Trade.* Cambridge, MA: MIT Press, 1985.

Krugman, Paul R., and Obstfeld, Maurice. *International Economics: Theory and Policy,* 6th edition. Addison-Wesley-Longman, 2003.

O'Rourke, Kevin H., and Williamson, Jeffrey G. *Globalization and History: The Evolution of a Nineteenth Century Atlantic Economy.* Cambridge, MA: MIT Press, 1999.

O'Rourke, Kevin H., and Williamson, Jeffrey G. "From Malthus to Ohlin: Trade, Growth and Distribution Since 1500." NBER Working Paper No. 8955. Cambridge, MA: National Bureau of Economic Research, 2002.

Kevin H. O'Rourke

HOME CHARGES (INDIA)

From November 1, 1858, to August 14, 1947, the British Parliament in London directly ruled India. For much of that period "British India" included today's Republic of India, Pakistan, and Bangladesh, and also Myanmar (previously known as Burma). The budget of the government of India for most of that period included what were called "Home Charges," consisting of items for which money had to be spent in London by the British Indian government. They included (a) debt payment; (b) charges for the military and naval establishment, including pensions for retired officers, soldiers, and sailors; (c) charges for the civil establishment maintained by the British Indian government in London; (d) the cost of purchases of materials and equipment bought in the United Kingdom by the same government; and (e) the cost of mail, telegraph services, and so on charged to the Indian budget. Up to the early 1870s they also included dividends on the shares of the East India Company, from which Parliament had taken over the right to rule India in 1858.

The external debts of the British Indian government had some peculiarities, including the charge for the shares of the East India Company, which had stopped being a trading firm after 1833 but whose shareholders had still to be paid out of the taxes imposed on their Indian subjects by the British. They also included the loans raised by the British government for suppressing a large-scale peasant revolt in 1857 to 1858 led by recruits of the British Indian army. When the expenditure for a war could not be met out of the current revenues of the government, loans were raised for financing it. Most of these wars had little to do with the defense of India, but were waged to expand the British Empire in Asia or even in Africa. For example, the cost of the British conquest of Burma between the 1850s and 1880s was entirely borne by the Indian government. Most of the cost of patrolling the Indian Ocean, as a part of defense of the British Empire, was put on the Indian budget. Lord Salisbury (1830–1903), a prime minister of Britain and at one time secretary of state for India, put his finger on the real situation when he said: "India is an English barrack in the

AN ARMY OF SEPOYS

In the 1740s Britain's East India Company began recruiting a security force among the native warrior castes of India to protect the company's trading interests. The force soon grew into a private army. In the 1750s company troops and regulars under Robert Clive won a number of victories that cemented the British presence in India. In the Napoleonic Wars the company's native troops (sepoys) again fought gallantly alongside British regulars. By the 1850s the army consisted of well over 300,000 men, with a ratio of almost eight sepoys to every one British soldier (top-ranking officers were always British). In 1857 a section of the army mutinied, partly due to British contempt for native religious practices. With the mutiny suppressed, the Indian army became part of the regular establishment, and the ratio of British to native troops was increased. From the late 1800s to 1914 this force fought in more than a dozen campaigns worldwide, usually with great success. Its importance to the empire continued almost to the end of "British India." Thereafter, the Indian army fought bravely in Mesopotamia during World War I, and in 1944 soundly defeated the Japanese at Imphal during World War II.

David J. Clarke

Oriental seas from which we may draw any number of troops without paying for them" (Howard 1972, p. 18, in Tomlinson 1975, p. 341) Only a small part of the Indian debt was incurred for building the railways and irrigation works that raised the productivity of the country.

In 1894 to 1895, a typical year, home charges accounted for £15.7 million out of a total revenue expenditure by the Indian government amounting to £67.5 million. The total amount of home charges between 1858 to 1859 and 1897 to 1898 came to £573.1 million; of this, only £27.5 million was spent for financing the building of railways and irrigation works in India (Banerji 1982; Reserve Bank of India 1954). The expenditures in India also were mainly incurred for administration and defense, and thus, from the perspective of Indian development, largely wasted.

Some scholars have argued that the home charges were too small relative to India's overall economy to matter much, but that does not capture their full significance. Home charges had to be paid every year, come hail, flood, drought, or famine. That meant that India had to have a substantial surplus in its balance of trade every year, and a major part of that surplus yielded no benefits in the future. The only exceptions to the surplus requirement occurred when imperial interests involving war or preparations for war demanded the raising of a loan, generally in London. This lent a deflationary bias to its monetary and fiscal policy and further held back India's development. Home charges were also a part of the surplus that was systematically transferred from India and other dependent colonies to the imperial countries. This surplus in turn helped to sustain the massive flows of investment from Britain to the United States, Canada, Australia, and other countries to which Europeans migrated and settled in large numbers, especially between 1870 and 1924 (Bagchi 2002).

SEE ALSO Bengal; Bullion (Specie); Drugs, Illicit; East India Company, British; Empire, British; Empire, Mughal; Finance, Credit and Money Lending; Gujarat; Imperialism; India; Industrialization; Mercantilism; Nationalism; Rates of Exchange; Textiles.

BIBLIOGRAPHY

Bagchi, Amiya K. *The Political Economy of Underdevelopment.* Cambridge, U.K.: Cambridge University Press, 1982.

Bagchi, Amiya K. "The Other Side of Foreign Investment by Imperial Powers: Transfer of Surplus from Colonies." *Economic and Political Weekly* (Mumbai) 37, no. 23 (June 8, 2002): 2229–2238.

Banerji, Arun K. *Aspects of Indo-British Economic Relations, 1858–1898.* Oxford, U.K.: Oxford University Press, 1982.

Reserve Bank of India. *Banking and Monetary Statistics of India.* Bombay: Author, 1954.

Sen, Sunanda. *Colonies and the Empire: India, 1890–1914.* New Delhi: Orient Longman, 1992.

Amiya Kumar Bagchi

HONG KONG

Hong Kong is a global financial center that has evolved from a small trading port in the past 160 years. There are many factors that explain its economic success: a British-style bureaucracy and regulatory system, stable political and legal institutions with effective protection of private property rights, a relatively uncorrupt government, a reputation as the freest economy in the world, free flow of information, no restrictions on capital flows, a level playing field for foreign and local investors, excellent infrastructure, established international network and professional expertise, a fast-growing China market nearby, low tax rates, no quotas, no antidumping policy, low frequency of labor disputes, and a prime location with a time-zone advantage. Hence, Hong Kong has become a hub for major financial, legal, accounting, and engineering transnational corporations that locate specialists and send staff to projects in the region. Hong Kong's citizens (6.8 million) are proud of the city's large economic performance (GDP growth rate about 5.3%; per capita GDP about U.S.$24,200 in 2004) on such a small piece of land (1,103 square kilometers).

There is plenty of evidence that Hong Kong is a paradise for capitalists. In 2004 there were 279 foreign-owned licensed banks, restricted-license banks, deposit-taking companies, and bank representative offices from thirty-seven countries conducting business in Hong Kong. Seventy-five percent of the world's top 100 banks have operations in the city. It is the world's seventh-largest center for foreign-exchange transactions. Its stock market is ranked among the world's top ten in terms of market capitalization. In 2004 a total of 863 companies with a market capitalization of U.S.$679 billion were listed on the Main Board of the stock market in Hong Kong. Among these companies, 274 enterprises are from mainland China (accounting for about 29% of the total market capitalization in the city). From 1993 to 2004 mainland Chinese enterprises have raised over U.S.$102 billion in Hong Kong. In addition, many foreign companies have set up their regional headquarters in Hong Kong; among the 966 regional headquarters in 2003 in Hong Kong, some 830 were responsible for business in mainland China.

RELATIONSHIP WITH MAINLAND CHINA

Although Hong Kong tries to keep its distance from mainland China politically, it could not survive if it were disconnected from China economically. Economic cooperation and linkage with the mainland has transformed Hong Kong from an export-oriented manufacturing location to a service-based economy. In the late 1970s, with Deng Xiaoping's Open Door Policy, the thriving manufacturing industries moved from Hong Kong, where rents were high and labor expensive, to the land-rich Pearl River Delta (PRD), where labor costs were low. In 2004 about 53,000 Hong Kong–linked companies employed nearly 10 million workers in and around the PRD. Meanwhile, the services sector accounted for 88 percent of the city's GDP. For many investors, the ideal way to enter the China market is to establish a manufacturing base in the PRD while maintaining management and finance functions in Hong Kong. This combines the competitiveness of the PRD's workforce with Hong Kong's

Hong Kong's skyline from Victoria Peak, 2002. Once a small trading port under British control, Hong Kong is today a global financial center, returned to Chinese sovereignty in 1997. PHOTOGRAPH BY ANAT GIVON. AP/WIDE WORLD PHOTOS. REPRODUCED BY PERMISSION.

highly trained managers and Western-style regulatory framework. Hong Kong is the PRD's largest trading partner, handling about 80 percent of the PRD's exports. Total trade with Guangdong province was valued at U.S.$48 billion in 2002.

TRADE IN GOODS

One of the cornerstones of Hong Kong's commercial policy is the rule-based multilateral trading system of the World Trade Organization (WTO), of which it is a member (as "Hong Kong, China"). The total value of all trade in goods in 2003 was U.S.$455 billion (imports U.S.$231.5 billion, domestic exports U.S.$15.6 billion, reexports U.S.$207.8 billion.), an increase of 11.6percent over 2002. Hong Kong's principle trading partners in 2003 were mainland China (43.1%), the United States (11.9%), and Japan (8.7%).

Hong Kong's main imports are electrical machinery, apparatus, appliances, and electrical parts thereof (comprising 19.4% of total imports in 2003); telecommunications; and sound recording and reproducing apparatus

and equipment (11.6%). Most imports came from mainland China (43.5), Japan (11.9%), and Chinese Taipei (6.9%). Major domestic exports are articles of apparel and clothing accessories (52.5% of total domestic exports in 2003); and electrical machinery, apparatus, appliances, and electrical parts thereof (8.4%). Domestic exports went mostly to the United States (32.2%), mainland China (30.2%), and the United Kingdom (6.4%). For re-exports, major items included electrical machinery, apparatus, appliances, and electrical parts thereof (18.7% of total re-exports in 2003); telecommunications; and sound recording and reproducing apparatus and equipment (13.5%). Most reexports went to mainland China (43.5%), the United States (17.6%), and Japan (5.6%).

The total value of trade in services in 2003 was U.S.$70.3 billion, an increase of 2.4 percent over 2002. Key services subsectors in Hong Kong include the wholesale, retail, and import/export trades; restaurants and hotels (26.9% of GDP, 2002); community, social, and personal services (22.2%); and financing, insurance, real estate, and business services (22.2%).

HONG KONG'S HISTORY

Hong Kong was colonized by Britain in 1842 to consolidate the power of British merchants (*hongs*) in the China trade. For much of its history, the utility of the colony lay not in its own economy but in the functions it performed for the wider British interest in China. The fast-growing British economic presence in China began in the seventeenth century with the British East India Company, which established its first foothold in Canton in 1684. Tea and opium were the major trading items during that period. Hong Kong was established as the headquarters of the China trade, providing secure access to the Canton import and export market. It also became an important naval station and the first port of call for Europeans in East Asia after Singapore. The diplomatic, military, and commercial uses of the island were essential to British, and the governor of Hong Kong supervised the British consuls in the five treaty ports in China in the nineteenth century.

Before the two world wars Hong Kong became an East Asian entrepôt, a transshipment point for the British merchant houses' exports and imports to and from China and other parts of the region. Gradually it also became a regional center for finance, banking, and service transactions between Europeans and Chinese. Despite the massive disruption of entrepôt trade by the Japanese occupation of the territory (1941–1945) and the violent civil war on the Chinese mainland, two-thirds of Hong Kong's exports (mostly reexports) were sent to China in the first half of the century.

Hong Kong's trading activities recovered more quickly than expected after World War II due to the promotion by the large British *hongs* (such as Jardine, Matheson, the Swire, and the Hong Kong and Shanghai Bank). The British Empire's share of trade passing through Hong Kong also increased after the war. In 1938 only 16 percent of the colony's imports and 17 percent of its exports were with countries in the empire (including Malaya, Australia, India, etc.), but in 1947 these figures increased to 28.6 percent for imports and 29.5 percent for exports.

The postwar economic recovery of Hong Kong lasted for only five years (1946–1950). Due to the Korean War and the United Nations embargo against China, 193 registered factories ceased operations in 1951, increasing unemployment by about 30,000 workers. Much foreign capital was withdrawn from Hong Kong due to the unstable political environment in China in that period.

When the Chinese Communist Party (CCP) took power in 1949 it was faced with a dilemma—on the one hand, it required economic resources for state-building, with colonial Hong Kong as a convenient link with the outside world; on the other hand, it needed to manage its strong domestic anticolonial mood. Its solution from the 1950s to the 1970s was to allow Britain to maintain a *de facto* administration and the status quo. The CCP recognized that Hong Kong could serve as a channel linking Communist China with the capitalist world, so it left the colony in British hands in 1949, when it could easily have taken it back by force. During the Korean War China imported most of its strategic and military supplies via Hong Kong. Although the United Nations embargo prevented China's trading ties with capitalist nations, China continued to trade with them via Hong Kong.

China sought to earn hard currency (because its *renminbi* was not recognized by most Western nations) by exporting to Hong Kong (because the Hong Kong dollar was linked with the sterling pound during the 1950s and 1960s). Hong Kong's imports from China grew in the late 1950s, accounting for 11 percent of China's total exports. And in 1966, just before the Chinese Cultural Revolution, it increased to 21 percent.

The CCP victory on mainland China resulted in a huge flow of Chinese capital and entrepreneurs escaping from Shanghai to Hong Kong; this revitalized the colony. The Shanghainese brought industrial know-how on textiles and advanced machines, as well as a large pool of skilled and unskilled labor as refugees flooded into Hong Kong. This Shanghainese capital, entrepreneurship, and technology, and the hard-working, fast-learning, and cheap labor, proved to be the key factors in Hong Kong's "industrial taking-off" in the 1950s to 1970s.

The colonial government faced a crisis of political legitimacy in the mid-1960s because of the discontent of the frustrated working class. Riots and political instability led to a new round of policy reforms in Hong Kong, including a public-housing program, better chances of education at primary and secondary level, the establishment of an anticorruption agency, and great improvement in social welfare, public health, infrastructure. These reforms, termed "the developmental state strategy," brought rapid economic development for the sake of enhancement of political legitimacy of the colonial state.

Although Hong Kong was handed over to China in 1997, the new "Special Administrative Region" (SAR) maintains the legacy of British-style administration, the rule of law, and a pluralistic/democratic civil society. The highly institutionalized respect of private-property rights, the common-law system, the separation of powers, and consistent regulations distinguish the Hong Kong SAR from its sister cities such as Shanghai and Guangzhou in the eyes of foreign investors. The economic competitiveness of Hong Kong will be maintained as long as it can preserve its Western capitalist political legacy.

SEE ALSO ALCOCK, RUTHERFORD; BANKING; BULLION (SPECIE); CANTON SYSTEM; CHINA; CONTAINERIZATION; DENG XIAOPING; DRUGS, ILLICIT; EAST INDIA COMPANY, BRITISH; EMPIRE, BRITISH; EMPIRE, JAPANESE; EMPIRE, QING; EMPIRE, PORTUGUESE; ENTREPÔT SYSTEM; ETHNIC GROUPS, CANTONESE; ETHNIC GROUPS, FUJIANESE; FREE PORTS; GUANGZHOU; HART, ROBERT; HONG KONG AND SHANGHAI BANK; IMPERIAL MARITIME CUSTOMS, CHINA; IMPERIALISM; JAPAN; JARDINE MATHESON; LIN ZEXU; MARKETS, STOCK; RICE; SHANGHAI; SHIPBUILDING; SILK; SINGAPORE; SOUTH CHINA SEA; TAIWAN; TEA; TEXTILES; TUNG CHEE-HWA; UNITED STATES.

BIBLIOGRAPHY

Chan, Cheuk-wah. "The Politics of Banking in Hong Kong." Ph.D. diss., Chinese University of Hong Kong, 2002.

Chan, Cheuk-wah. "Hong Kong's Economic Path and Its Strategic Value for China and Britain 1946–56: A Rational-Strategic Approach." *Issues and Studies* 33, no. 6 (June 1997): 88–112.

Endacott, G. B. *A History of Hong Kong.* New York: Oxford University Press, 1964.

Sung, Y. W. *China–Hong Kong Connection.* Cambridge, U.K.: Cambridge University Press, 1991.

Scott, Ian. *Political Change and the Crisis of Legitimacy in Hong Kong.* Hong Kong: Oxford University Press, 1989.

Cheuk-Wah Sunny Chan

HONG KONG AND SHANGHAI BANK

The Hong Kong and Shanghai Banking Corporation Limited (HSBC) is the foremost financial institution in the Asia-Pacific region and one of the world's largest banks. Before the establishment of the bank, native banks and the European trading houses, or *hongs* handled most financial transactions in East Asia. The bank was founded in March 1865 in Hong Kong, and a second branch office was opened in Shanghai in April by a Scotsman, Thomas Sutherland (1834–1922), to service foreign firms on the China coast and to deal with increased demand for money and banking facilities in the region due to the growing international trade. It was incorporated in Hong Kong under a special decree. HSBC enjoyed a period of sustained growth and expansion for many years. The history of the bank and its survival in an increasingly nationalistic East, and in the context of intense international banking competition, illuminates the history of intra-Asian trade, growth of the Chinese diaspora, and the spread of modern banking practices.

HSBC's early role was in providing local merchant-banking facilities in Hong Kong and the China coast, of-

The headquarters of the Hong Kong and Shanghai Bank tower over Hong Kong Harbor. *Established in 1865 to assist in the growing trade between Europe, India, and China, the financial institution played a key role in working with Asian governments to develop banking and currency systems. In 2002 it adopted the tagline, "the world's local bank," after expanding internationally while maintaining a focus on local markets and cultures.* © MARTIN JONES; ECOSCENE/CORBIS. REPRODUCED BY PERMISSION.

fering short-term merchant finance, and handling remittances from overseas Chinese between China and Southeast Asia. It extended its network from coastal Chinese cities to Yokohama (1866), Calcutta (1867), Kobe and Bombay (1869), Saigon (1870), Manila (1875), Singapore (1877), Penang and Batavia (1884), Bangkok (1888), Nagasaki and Rangoon (1891), Colombo (1892), and Sourabaya (1896). Trade finance was originally the main area of business for HSBC with bullion, exchange, and note issuing. The bank also handled China's first public loans, the 8 percent Fuzhou loan of 1874. HSBC was very successful and became a very reputable organization.

In the early twentieth century the bank increased its involvement in the issuing of public loans in China and other countries for infrastructure and other nation-building projects. After World War I the bank entered a difficult period that continued until the end of World War II. In the 1920s instability in China forced it to close down its merchant-banking division there. There was a movement within the bank to distance itself from politics and international ties. There was also friction between the bank's new head office in Hong Kong and its London office. The London manager was the very prominent Charles S. Addis, and many in the bank resented his insistence in trying to compete constantly with the head office. Addis was effectively sidelined in 1930. The London office stopped trying to initiate policy, and the company became essentially an Eastern bank.

The bank was a profit-making, dividend-paying corporation whose long-term interests happened to coincide with China's development. It became the premier foreign bank in China in the 1930s. In the period 1935 to 1941 the bank's big concern was that China's currency system would collapse, taking with it much of the capital the bank had permanently invested in China. These fears were based on China's high military expenditures, the large budget deficit, the country's large silver exports, and Japan's military aggression. It was during this period that the bank's Shanghai branch became instrumental in stabilizing China's currency and financial markets. But economic depression, political instability, and growing Japanese aggression forced the bank to begin curtailing its business in the region. By World War II, with much of the bank's operations and staff in Japanese hands, the head office was moved to London and the company was forced to wait for the end of the war before it could rebuild. At the end of the war the bank reestablished its head office in Hong Kong.

The bank played a key role in Hong Kong's postwar development, and today has more than 200 offices in Hong Kong. Most of the offices in China were closed between 1949 and 1955, but the bank reopened an office in Beijing in 1980. It has a strong presence in overseas Chinese communities, especially in Toronto, Vancouver, New York, and Sydney.

In 1959 HSBC began expanding beyond East Asia, acquiring the British Bank of the Middle East and the India-based Mercantile Bank. It established the Hong Kong and Shanghai Banking Corporation of California in 1955 and took over Hong Kong Hang Seng Bank Limited in 1965. In 1987 HSBC purchased Marine Midland Bank in the United States, and acquired full ownership of Midland Bank of Birmingham in the United Kingdom in 1992. In the 1980s HSBC moved successfully into the Swiss, Pakistani, Thai, Spanish, Italian, Swedish, Australian, and Canadian markets, and extended its business to New Zealand in 1994. It also became the largest foreign

bank in Malaysia and established four new offices in Macau. In 1984 the bank was the fourteenth-largest banking group in terms of shareholders' funds.

There were setbacks as well. Hong Kong boomed in the 1980s, but the uncertainty of its future was a challenge. However, the bank coped with the transition from British rule to Special Administrative Region of the People's Republic of China (SAR) status under China. In 1991 HSBC Holdings was created, with shares trading on the London and Hong Kong stock markets. Over the next ten years HSBC acquired a large number of companies throughout the world, including the Republic Bank of New York (1999) and Crédit Commercial de France (2000). These acquisitions enabled HSBC to be traded on the New York and Paris stock exchanges. From 1991 to 2004 HSBC acquired companies in Turkey, Mexico, the United States, Bermuda, Argentina, and the United Kingdom. Today HSBC provides financial services ranging from personal financial services and private banking to investment banking and corporate and commercial banking. HSBC has 9,500 offices in more than 79 countries and territories around the world, with 70 percent of its income coming from outside the United Kingdom (where HSBC headquarters is located). In June 2003 the HSBC Holdings had total assets amounting to U.S.$983 billion, 218,000 employees, and nearly 200,000 shareholders around the world. Today HSBC is the world's second-largest bank group, behind Citigroup.

SEE ALSO Banking; Bullion (Specie); Capital Flows; China; Drugs, Illicit; Empire, British; Empire, Qing; Ethnic Groups, Cantonese; Ethnic Groups, Fujianese; Ethnic Groups, Scots; Finance, Credit and Money Lending; Gold and Silver; Hart, Robert; Hong Kong; Imperial Maritime Customs, China; Imperialism; India; Indonesia; Japan; Jardine Matheson; Laborers, Contract; Nationalization; Rates of Exchange; Shanghai; Singapore; United Kingdom; United States.

BIBLIOGRAPHY

Jones, Geoffrey. *The History of the British Bank of the Middle East.* 2 vols. Cambridge, U.K.: Cambridge University Press, 1986–1987.

King, Frank H. *The History of the Hong Kong and Shanghai Banking Corporation.* 4 vols. Cambridge, U.K.: Cambridge University Press, 1987–1991.

HSBC Holdings plc. *The HSBC Group: A Brief History.* London: Author, 2003.

INTERNET RESOURCES

HSBC web site. Available from http://www.hsbc.com.

Chi-Kong Lai

HERBERT HOOVER
1874–1964

Herbert Clark Hoover, the thirty-first president of the United States, was born August 10, 1874 and died on October 20, 1964. He was a very successful engineer before entering public service. Although Hoover was a great humanitarian, his name will forever be associated with the Great Depression that occurred during his one term as president, and with the notorious Smoot-Hawley Tariff of 1930, which is frequently cited as a factor in making the Depression longer and more severe than it might have been. Surprisingly, there was no general call for tariff increases before Hoover proposed increased protection for farmers in the 1928 presidential campaign. Hoover mistakenly thought that tariff changes could be limited to agricultural commodities. Following the stock market crash in 1929 Hoover initiated a number of misguided measures in confronting the collapsing economy, calling for wage freezes and reduced hours of work rather than layoffs, arguing that the shock of the contraction should be absorbed by reduced corporate profits. But he also believed that voluntary cooperative efforts were the best means of combating the Depression. In 1932 he engineered a massive increase in federal income tax rates to balance the budget. During the spring of 1932 a "Bonus Army" of unemployed World War I veterans marched on Washington, D.C., demanding early payment of bonuses promised to them. His handling of the Bonus Army's expulsion from Washington, D.C., doomed his reelection chances.

SEE ALSO GREAT DEPRESSION OF THE 1930S; ROOSEVELT, FRANKLIN DELANO.

BIBLIOGRAPHY

Eichengreen, Barry. "The Political Economy of the Smoot-Hawley Tariff." *Research in Economic History* 11 (1989): 1–44.

Hoover, Herbert. *The Memoirs of Herbert Hoover: The Cabinet and the Presidency, 1920–1933*. New York: Macmillan, 1951–1952.

Mitchell, Broadus. *Depression Decade: From New Era through New Deal, 1929–1941*. New York: Rinehart, 1947.

Smiley, Gene. *Rethinking the Great Depression*. Chicago, IL: Ivan R. Dee, Inc., 2002.

Temin, Peter. *Lessons from the Great Depression*. Cambridge, MA: Massachusetts Institute of Technology Press, 1989.

Gene Smiley

HOPE FAMILY

Members of the Hope family, including Archibald (1664–1743), Thomas (1704–1779), Adrian (1709–1781), Henry (1735–1811), and John (1737–1784), played a pivotal role in the emerging Amsterdam capital market of the eighteenth century. In this process a division developed between traditional cross-border commerce and the financing thereof. This led to the establishment of merchant-banking houses, which specialized in various financial services. Their capital included family wealth as well as investment loans from other private individuals.

The merchant house Hope started in the classic Baltic grain and timber trade, but by the 1760s these activities had stopped. In 1762 the family business expanded and was renamed Hope and Company. During the Seven Years' War (1756–1763) the firm acted as broker for the British government in paying their overseas allies and army commanders. They also financed the British war effort. From then on, most of the profit came from commissions, including financial services such as bills of exchange and loan issues; for instance, they issued loans on behalf of the Swedish Crown and Russia. By 1800 Hope and Company had capital of 15 million guilders with a balance sheet of 25 million guilders. By then, they had become the undisputed leader of the Amsterdam merchant houses.

SEE ALSO AMSTERDAM; BANKING; EMPIRE, DUTCH; FINANCE, CREDIT AND MONEY LENDING.

BIBLIOGRAPHY

Buist, Marten G. *At Spes Non Fracta: Hope & Co., 1770–1815. Merchant Bankers and Diplomats at Work*. The Hague, Netherlands: Martinus Nijhoff, 1974.

Victor Enthoven

DAVID HUME
1711–1776

David Hume, the great philosopher and historian, was born in Scotland in 1711, and died in 1776. He is widely credited with providing the basis for international trade theory for almost the next two centuries in a series of essays published in 1752. Hume challenged the mercantilist concern with preserving the domestic stock of money by restricting trade. Others in Scotland had advocated free trade before Hume, but it was he who set out the mechanism whereby an outflow of specie (gold or silver) due to a trade deficit would bring about a correction in the form of a fall in the general price level. This would continue until trade returned to balance and the value of the stock of specie was restored: the price-specie-flow mechanism. This mechanism provided the basis for the theory of global monetarism that emerged in the 1970s. But for Hume the ultimate determining factors behind trade (and the money stock) were the conditions for economic growth in the historical degree of "industry and innovation." The capacity to produce cheaper exports induced inflows of specie, which added a further spur to industry, and further exports. Finally, although a free-trader, Hume allowed for the possibility of tariffs.

SEE ALSO RATES OF EXCHANGE; THEORIES OF INTERNATIONAL TRADE.

BIBLIOGRAPHY

Hume, David. *Political Discourses.* London: Andrew Millar, 1752. Reprinted in *Essays Moral, Political, and Literary.* Edinburgh, U.K.: Cadell, Donaldson, and Creech, 1977; and in E. F. Miller, ed., *David Hume: Essays Moral, Political, and Literary.* Indianapolis, IN: Liberty Fund, 1985.

Sheila C. Dow

WILLIAM HUSKISSON
1770–1830

William Huskisson was an English financier and politician whose ideas inspired the trade and tariff reforms initiated by British prime minister Sir Robert Peel in the 1840s.

Elected to Parliament in 1796, Huskisson first entered government based on his writings on finance, currency issues, and trade; he held office during the Napoleonic Wars and during several postwar decades of great economic, political, and social change in British life. After serving as secretary of the treasury (1804–1809), Huskisson spent an interval as a private citizen. He joined Lord Liverpool's administration in 1814, holding minor office until appointed president of the Board of Trade and treasurer of the navy in 1823. Though a Tory, Huskisson was an advocate for free trade, and did much to liberalize Great Britain's trading regulations. He reformed the Navigation Acts (which had originated in Tudor times), reduced customs duties, and attempted to introduce a sliding scale to relax the set of regulations known as the Corn Laws that had long protected British agriculture from foreign trade competition.

Huskisson's positions on "freer" trade were generally ahead of their time. In the years after his death, however, the momentum created by his ideas led to reforms such as the abolition of the East India Company trade monopoly in 1833, and other measures that spurred an unprecedented expansion of world commerce in the nineteenth century and later.

SEE ALSO CANADA; CARGOES, FREIGHT; CORN LAWS; EDUCATION, OVERVIEW; FREE TRADE, THEORY AND PRACTICE; PEEL, SIR ROBERT; PROTECTIONISM AND TARIFF WARS; UNITED KINGDOM.

BIBLIOGRAPHY

Briggs, Asa. *The Age of Improvement.* London: Longman, 1979.

Thomson, David. *England in the Nineteenth Century.* London: Penguin, 1986.

Peter E. Austin

HYUNDAI

Hyundai Group, now formally divided into a number of independent firms including Hyundai Motor Company, Hyundai Heavy Industries, and Hyundai Engineering and Construction Company, is one of the leading players in global business world. In 2003 it was the second-largest car exporter in the world after Japan's Toyota; the world's largest shipbuilder; and its fourteenth-largest construction firm, with worldwide activities. These achievements are all the more impressive when they are viewed against the group's short history: it took just half a century for Hyundai to grow from virtual nonexistence to its present standing. Indeed, Hyundai's development came hand in hand with South Korea's emergence as one of the "Asian dragons."

When the Korean War ended in 1953, South Korea was one of the poorest nations in the world. Throughout the 1950s South Korea exported only primary products such as tungsten, raw silk, and fish. In 1962 General Park Chung Hee (1917–1979), who had come into power through a military coup in 1961, launched the export-oriented economic development plan, and light-industrial products such as textiles and shoes became the major export items. From the early 1970s Park promoted heavy industries by allocating great resources to a small number of firms (known as *chaebol*) that he thought could produce competitive exports. The oil shocks of the 1970s led to a painful setback, but also provided a good opportunity. The Middle Eastern construction boom earned South Korea invaluable dollars that were invested in heavy industries and in new technology-intensive industries. In the 1980s products of heavy industries accounted for over half of South Korea's exports. Despite an economic hiccup as a part of the East Asian economic crisis of 1997, production and foreign trade of South Korea continued to grow. The top five export items today are semiconductors, automobiles, mobile phones, ships, and computers.

In this so-called "miracle of the Han River," Hyundai played a pivotal role, together with other conglomerates such as Samsung, LG, and Daewoo. Hyundai was especially crucial in automobiles and ships.

Hyundai's founder, Chung Ju Yung (1915–2001), was an ingenious entrepreneur and aggressive leader.

Hyundai cars are ready to be shipped to international destinations from Ulsan, Korea, a port 256 miles south of Seoul.
Hyundai was founded in 1947 as a construction company and entered the U.S. auto market in 1986. It set a record for selling the most cars during its first year in the American market. © REUTERS/CORBIS. REPRODUCED BY PERMISSION.

Chung pushed ahead with business projects in which he had little previous experience, and he succeeded in many of them. In 1967 Chung entered into the Hyundai Group's principal business—car manufacturing—based on technical assistance from Ford. But the relationship did not last long, as Chung's ambitious proposition to have Hyundai-made Fords sold through Ford's global distribution network clashed with Ford's intention to confine Hyundai's role to manufacturing parts and assembling sets. As the South Korean government announced plans to promote heavy industries, Hyundai searched all over the world for new sources of technology transfer. Having learned valuable technological know-how from England, Japan, and Italy, it finally found what it needed in Mitsubishi in 1973. Facing tough competition from Toyota and Nissan, Mitsubishi desperately wanted to expand its operation, and it offered an agreement whereby Hyundai would retain all managerial control and Mitsubishi would give only technical assistance. Soon, under another government initiative and with favorable financial support, Chung ventured to build a citizens' car made almost entirely with Korean parts. This

led to the production of the "Pony" in 1976 and its subsequent export, an important milestone in the rise of both Hyundai and the South Korean economy. The following success of the "Excel" in 1986 consolidated Hyundai's position in the global car market. But the company's bold attempt at incorporating as many Korean-made parts as possible into its cars faltered in the late 1980s. Quality deteriorated and sales dropped, together with the corporate reputation. Another setback came from Chung's unsuccessful bid to become president of South Korea in 1992. Facing less favorable political conditions, the Hyundai Group had to find its own way for survival and further growth. In the new millennium Hyundai's ordeal continued with Chung's death, financial problems that led to selling off some companies, and the death of Chung's son, who had been in charge of investment and development projects in North Korea, one of the long-time ambitions of Hyundai. Despite these difficulties, Hyundai has so far proved itself capable of competing with foreign rivals, and is trying hard to maintain and enlarge its competitive edge in the ever-tougher global business environment.

SEE ALSO AUTOMOBILE; DEVELOPMENTAL STATE, CONCEPT OF THE; INDUSTRIALIZATION; KOREA.

BIBLIOGRAPHY

Amsden, Alice H. *Asia's Next Giant: South Korea and Late Industrialization.* Oxford, U.K.: Oxford University Press, 1989.

Chang, Sea-Jin. *Financial Crisis and Transformation of Korean Business Groups: The Rise and Fall of Chaebols.* Cambridge, U.K.: Cambridge University Press, 2003.

Jeong, Seung-il. *Crisis and Restructuring in East Asia: The Case of the Korean Chaebol and the Automotive Industry.* London: Palgrave, 2004.

Kirk, Donald. *Korean Dynasty: Hyundai and Chung Ju Yung.* Armonk, NY: M. E. Sharpe, 1994.

Steers, Richard M. *Made in Korea: Chung Ju Yung and the Rise of Hyundai.* New York: Routledge, 1999.

Byung Khun Song

IMPERIALISM

Empire (Latin "imperium") is an old and complex word; *imperialism* a quite recent and more treacherous one. At its simplest, an empire is a territory within which there is one supreme military and legal authority. By the end of the fifteenth century, empire in this strict sense was not fully achieved in Europe until the unifications of Italy (1860) and Germany (1870) swept away the petty states and overlapping jurisdictions of Central Europe and completed the division of most of the continent into large competing territorial states, marking the onset of modern "imperialism" as distinct from mere "empire." For the defining feature of imperialism is not the mere presence of empires in a state system, but the domination of that system by struggles between empires. But by the end of the fifteenth century, this very limited sense of empire was about to be vastly extended as petty European kings began to develop extensive overseas realms to rival, or even supplant, the longer established, extensive, and wealthy empires of Asia and the Americas.

Throughout the next three centuries, these European "empires" grew steadily. Struggles arising from an uneasy balance of power between the leading European states were worked out on battlefields in India and Canada; commercial disputes far from Europe renewed conflict in the heart of Europe. To thinkers of the late seventeenth and early eighteenth centuries the close interaction of state power and commercial interest became known as *mercantilism*. Under this system European powers tried to maintain their empires as exclusive trading zones. In the later eighteenth century mercantilism came under attack. Liberals argued that the public interest would be better served by a much more restricted use of state power, at home and abroad, allowing unrestricted access to and operation of markets, including free trade between nations. War and conquest were disparaged as exploitative activities associated with hereditary aristocracies and monarchies; the future lay with the more peaceable middle classes.

IMPERIALISM AND NEW IMPERIALISM

It is important to draw a distinction between the history of thought and the pattern of mundane events. *Imperialism* is a term closely associated with the revival of enthusiasm for empire in the late nineteenth century; it describes a popular sentiment. Yet it is also a descriptive term, implicated in interpretations of history that accept and proceed to account for an accelerated pace of European expansion around this time. British historians of the second half of the twentieth century therefore readily assumed that the classic theorists of imperialism, who had written between 1900 and 1920, must have been trying to explain a spurt in the growth of colonial empires. This assumption was made without first clarifying whether accelerated growth had in fact been the leading feature of what contemporaries named the *New Imperialism* of the 1880s, let alone whether this had been what the classic theorists had been primarily concerned with explaining.

Regarding the first of these issues, there may well have been aversion to the idea of empire in the salons of Europe following the defeat of the French in India and Canada and the successful American wars of independence waged by colonists against Britain and Spain. Yet, there is little sign of it on the ground. After the French

369

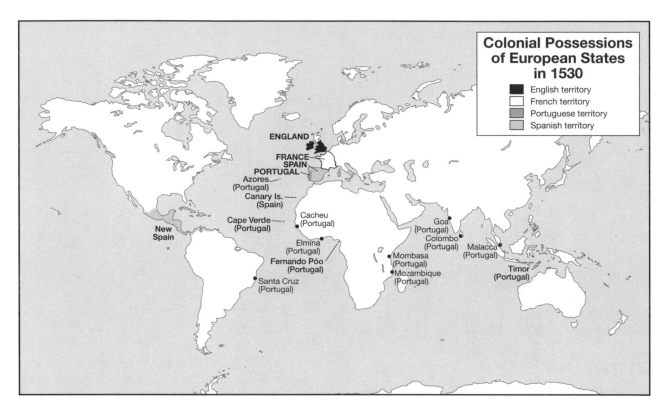

**Colonial Possessions
of European States
in 1530**

- ◼ English territory
- ◻ French territory
- ▨ Portuguese territory
- ▩ Spanish territory

ENGLAND

FRANCE
SPAIN
PORTUGAL
Azores
(Portugal)

Canary Is.
(Spain)

Cacheu
(Portugal)

Cape Verde
(Portugal)

New
Spain

Elmina
(Portugal)

Fernando Póo
(Portugal)

Santa Cruz
(Portugal)

Goa
(Portugal)
Colombo
(Portugal)

Malacca
(Portugal)

Mombasa
(Portugal)

Mozambique
(Portugal)

Timor
(Portugal)

MAP BY XNR PRODUCTIONS. THE GALE GROUP.

Revolution the French compensated by attempting to recreate a vast empire in and beyond Europe, which was not entirely extinguished by the defeat of Napoleon. The conquest of what was to be an immense African empire began with the invasion of Algeria in 1830. Meanwhile, massive conquests were being made by other European powers and their successor states throughout the nineteenth century. So it can certainly be argued that there was continuous imperial expansion by Europeans throughout what has often been referred to as a liberal interlude. It is also the case that for the established powers, the territories acquired before 1870 were of greater economic salience than those acquired afterward, and that, for Britain, trade and investment outside the British Empire, chiefly in the United States and Latin America, were far more important than post-1870 conquests in Africa and Asia.

Far from disposing of the New Imperialism, this interpretation helps to isolate its essential feature more clearly. Expansion in the earlier period had led to relatively little conflict between the major powers, which indeed enjoyed a period of relative peace between 1815 and 1870. All this changed after 1870. It was the conflicts between the imperial powers rather than expansionism itself that defined the New Imperialism and provided the focus of the classic theories. So although colonial historians can be forgiven for pointing to the European partition of Africa—which was almost entirely gobbled up by seven European states in a mere twenty years—as the most spectacular symptom of imperialism, its most fundamental characteristic in this period was not expansion *per se,* but the rivalries that developed between the major powers.

New states had after 1870 entered the rivalry; Belgium, Italy, and Germany jostled with newly assertive powers, such as the United States of America and reformed and modernizing Japan, to test British hegemony. British manufacturing and commercial supremacy was on the wane, challenged most effectively by Germany and the United States. A second industrial revolution was under way, based on steel, petroleum, electricity, and synthetic chemicals, and this created fresh anxieties about the security of supplies of raw materials. With industrialization in Europe came urbanization, bringing a growing need for imported foodstuffs and concerns about the effects of internal migration on social and political order. Even in Britain, which had pursued a policy of free trade since 1846, pressure was building by the 1890s for tariff reform, by which was meant a system of preferential trading within the British Empire. Other powers were less squeamish, and ran their empires as unashamedly economic units.

At the same time, the effect of new transport and communications technologies—submarine telegraphy,

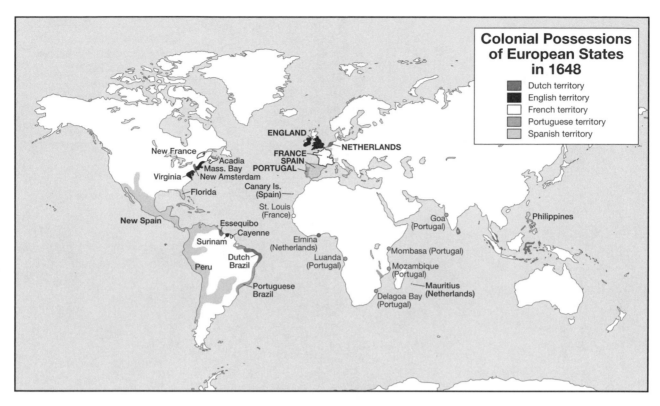

MAP BY XNR PRODUCTIONS. THE GALE GROUP.

railroads, and regular steamship lines—had been to bind together the empires that adopted them and, almost unavoidably, to degrade links between their respective dependencies. Moreover, all these developments first required, yet subsequently also generated, enormous accumulations of capital as well as new financial intermediaries, institutions, and forms of asset. Investment of this capital overseas in infrastructure and, later, in the extractive and manufacturing sectors—above all by the British, but also by the French and other Europeans—was the means by which the global trading system was modernized, expanded, and, up to a point, integrated. Without it, world trade could not have risen at the astonishing rate and to the unprecedented level, relative to output, that it attained shortly before World War I. So it is no wonder that some theorists and historians have pondered the connections between trade, investment, and empire. Did trade follow the flag, or vice versa?

CLASSICAL THEORIES

It is important to recognize that the reflections upon this state of affairs by J. A. Hobson (1858–1940), Joseph Schumpeter (1883–1950), and V. I. Lenin (1870–1924)—each of whom tried to provide a general theory of imperialism in the early twentieth century—were not motivated by concern for the downtrodden masses of the world's poorest countries. Their political constituencies were the

middle and working classes of Europe; their central task was to explain deteriorating relations and, finally, war, between the Great Powers (Britain, Germany, France, Austria-Hungary, and Russia). For the liberal thinkers Hobson and Schumpeter this posed a problem, because liberals had long regarded capitalism as a pacific influence. They overcame this difficulty by arguing that it was not capitalism as such but rather its incompleteness or corruption that had brought about catastrophe. Reform was possible. Lenin, by contrast, thought that conflict among capitalist states was inevitable. Lenin, arguing against fellow Marxist Karl Kautsky, was concerned with explaining why the European working class in 1914 had supported a war so plainly against their collective interest. He found his answer in the resources available to metropolitan states from their colonial empires with which, in effect, they bribed the workers. But unlike his liberal contemporaries, Lenin neither saw nor wanted to see any possibility of reform, anticipating instead that imperialism (which he described as the "Highest Stage of Capitalism") must lead to the destruction of the capitalist state system and herald the revolution.

Hobson, writing in England in the shadow of the South African (Boer) War (1899–1902), based his argument on what he regarded as a generic problem of industrialized economies. Unrestricted capitalism, he believed, had led to impoverishment of the working class and con-

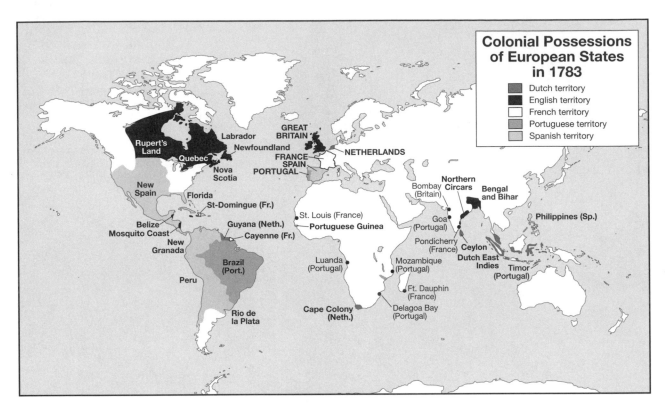

**Colonial Possessions
of European States
in 1783**

- Dutch territory
- English territory
- French territory
- Portuguese territory
- Spanish territory

Rupert's Land · Labrador · Newfoundland · GREAT BRITAIN · Quebec · Nova Scotia · NETHERLANDS · FRANCE · SPAIN · PORTUGAL · New Spain · Florida · St-Domingue (Fr.) · Belize · Mosquito Coast · New Granada · Guyana (Neth.) · Cayenne (Fr.) · Peru · Brazil (Port.) · Rio de la Plata · St. Louis (France) · Portuguese Guinea · Luanda (Portugal) · Cape Colony (Neth.) · Delagoa Bay (Portugal) · Ft. Dauphin (France) · Mozambique (Portugal) · Bombay (Britain) · Northern Circars · Goa (Portugal) · Pondicherry (France) · Bengal and Bihar · Ceylon · Dutch East Indies · Timor (Portugal) · Philippines (Sp.)

MAP BY XNR PRODUCTIONS. THE GALE GROUP.

sequent underconsumption. Markets did not clear, as predicted by the classical economists. Instead, goods and capital accumulated in the hands of uncompetitive manufacturers and investment bankers, who lobbied government for exclusive access to overseas markets in which these surpluses could be dumped or deployed. Hobson argued that only macroeconomic management and redistributive fiscal policies—what might be called *compensatory* or *welfare liberalism*—could reduce this lobbying pressure and allow foreign policy to be formulated in response to national rather than sectional interest. The chief problem with Hobson's theory was the empirical implausibility of the alleged lobbying system. Extensive recent scholarship suggests that manipulation of the state by sectional interests was not that simple, and that concentration of overseas investment and trade in dependent territories, and the desire to achieve this, were least marked in the longer established industrial economies, such as Britain, France, and Belgium.

The Austrian Schumpeter had been thinking along similar lines. Defining imperialism as an objectless disposition on the part of the state toward violence (no reference here to colonies!), he laid the blame squarely on the aristocracy, whose militarism he regarded as a social atavism. For several generations writers as disparate as Thomas Paine (1737–1809) and Immanuel Kant (1724–1804) had agreed that the dependence of a warmongering

aristocracy on industrial and commercial wealth and technology would inevitably lead to a transfer of power to the more representative and pacific middle classes, and therefore to less violent relations between states. Schumpeter accepted this theory and argued that where there was no aristocracy, as in the United States, there could be no imperialism. (It should be noted that Schumpeter excluded from the category of imperialism any war, however aggressive, undertaken for rational ends.) But he believed that in the Hapsburg Empire and other European states the capitalist revolution had been distorted as monarchs allied with the new industrial classes to curb the power of traditional aristocracies, with the undesirable consequence that certain sections of industry became heavily reliant on state procurement and greedy for tariff protection. On this foundation Schumpeter mounted an argument in which conflict between states arose from protectionism and the competitive dumping of surplus goods in third-country export markets. This was not dissimilar to Hobson's argument, and rather more plausible, given the typically more mercantilist style of late-industrializing states such as the Hapsburg Empire.

Though Lenin drew on Hobson, his core argument was very different. Lenin argued that capitalism, and the system of states in which it was embedded, was a necessarily dynamic system. It would never find equilibrium, only a limit. Lenin believed that the final stage of European territorial expansion between 1870 and 1900 had coincided with a final division of world markets. Imperialism for him did not mean colonization; it described the whole integrated and multifaceted process of expansion of the European capitalist system, of which colonialism was merely one facet, and which he believed had effectively reached its end by 1900. With no remaining unexploited markets or unclaimed territories, he maintained, the major firms and states of Europe now had no option but to turn on one another, the former seeking the support of the latter. Hence, the progressive deterioration in international relations that led to World War I (1914–1918). It is not hard to see that this argument was, if not entirely specious, then certainly premature, because it neglected the many ways in which technological innovation and the creation of new desires can spin out the process of economic growth almost indefinitely.

All three of the classic theorists, as well as their contemporaries Rudolf Hilferding, Rosa Luxemburg (1870–1919), and Nikolai Bukharin (1888–1938), had been concerned with the consequences of territorial expansion for relations with the European powers rather than with its causes. Yet, although imperialism did not end with World War I, nor even with the near completion of European decolonization by the mid-1960s, debate about it divided into two strands: one concerned with relations between imperial powers and their dependencies, and the other with the mutual relations of the Great Powers. Only in the first strand did the term *imperialism* retain currency.

POSTWAR IMPERIALISM

Imperialism before 1914 had been in many ways simply a variant of nationalism. The means used to bind a nation together were not so very different from those used to bind together a multinational empire. For liberals of the mid-nineteenth century, nationalism had been quintessentially about bringing together politically fragmented nations into larger united states, with Italy and Germany as examples. Increasingly, throughout the twentieth century, nationalism came to be pitted against imperialism, as component elements of empires—whether Quebec, Catalonia, or Scotland—sought self-determination or autonomy. Increasingly, therefore, *imperialist* came to be used, almost exclusively by the political Left, to designate those who sought to gain or retain control over dependent states by any form of interference, be it armed intervention, economic manipulation, or mere inertia.

SEE ALSO CAPITALISM; EMPIRE, BELGIAN; EMPIRE, BRITISH; EMPIRE, DUTCH; EMPIRE, FRENCH; EMPIRE, JAPANESE; EMPIRE, MING; EMPIRE, MUGHAL; EMPIRE, OTTOMAN; EMPIRE, PORTUGUESE; EMPIRE, QING; EMPIRE, SPANISH.

BIBLIOGRAPHY

Cain, P. J., and Hopkins, A. G. *British Imperialism, 1688–2000,* 2nd edition. Harlow, U.K.: Longman, 2002.

Hobson, J. A. *Imperialism: A Study.* London: George Allen and Unwin, 1902.

Schumpeter, Joseph A. *Imperialism and Social Classes.* [1917]. Tr. Heinz Norden, ed. and intro. Paul M. Sweezy. Oxford, U.K.: Oxford University Press, 1951.

Lenin, V. I. *Imperialism, the Highest Stage of Capitalism.* [1917]. New York: International Publishers, 1939.

Luxemburg, Rosa, and Bukharin, Nikolai. *Imperialism and the Accumulation of Capital.* [1915, 1924]. Ed. and intro. Kenneth J. Tarbuck, tr. Rudolf Wichmann. London: Allen Lane, Penguin, 1972.

Hilferding, Rudolf. *Finance Capitalism: A Study of the Latest Phase of Capitalist Development.* [1910]. Ed. and intro. Tom Bottomore, tr. Morris Watnick and Sam Gordon. London: Routledge and Kegan Paul, 1981.

Charles Jones

IMPERIAL MARITIME CUSTOMS, CHINA

The Chinese Imperial Maritime Customs was unique. Although a government organ, its inspector general was invariably British, except for the last one, who was American. Its senior management was also predominantly British, although the Americans, French, Germans, Russians, Japanese and other foreigners were included. The Chinese occupied only the most junior positions.

The Maritime Customs began in 1854, after insurgents destroyed the Shanghai customhouse. Foreign ships came and went without paying taxes, in defiance of treaty stipulations. Anxious that the treaties be kept, the British, U.S., and French consuls persuaded the Chinese authorities to reopen the customhouse in the British-controlled part of Shanghai. Each consul offered to provide one man to assist in the collection of duties. An agreement was duly signed, and the customhouse reopened on July 12, 1854, with a strong foreign contingent that was "English-speaking, unafraid of British, American, or Chinese bullies or scallywags, impervious to threats, and uninterested in bribes," (Fairbank 1975, vol. 1, p. 6) enforcing treaty tariffs on all comers. Revenue increased dramatically. The Chinese authorities were pleased. Whatever reservations they might have for Britain's desire to extend the system to all treaty ports nationwide were made irrelevant by China's defeat in the Arrow War (1856–1860). The Maritime Customs as we know it was formally established on June 21, 1861, with the appointment of H. N. Lay (b. 1832) as its first inspector general. Robert Hart (1835–1911) succeeded him for the crucial years of 1868 to 1907.

This foreign-controlled Chinese customs ensured low tariffs and equal foreign access to Chinese markets, forestalling any Chinese protectionist strategy to give local industries a fair chance to grow. But, for the time being, its revenue gave the Qing dynasty a new lease on life, paying off the war indemnities and contributing to the Self-Strengthening Movement (1861–1894), which included the creation of a Chinese postal service, the setting up of an interpreters' college in Peking, the establishment of legations abroad, and the provision of such services as coastwise lights, charts for navigation, buoys and markers in harbors, pilotage and berthing of ships, appraisal of goods, and the publication of trade statistics.

China was defeated again in 1894 to 1895, this time by the Japanese. The revenue of the Maritime Customs was used as security for large foreign loans to pay off the hefty war indemnities. The Boxer catastrophe of 1900 incurred even more hefty indemnities, and the same revenue was similarly used as security for foreign loans to pay for them. This practice inspired the pledge of other revenues, such as the salt monopoly as collateral for further foreign loans, until the Qing was toppled by the 1911 revolution.

The revolution prompted the powers to put the remainder of the customs revenue, after all obligations had been met, into trust accounts of foreign banks in Shanghai until they decided to which party the surplus should be paid. The leader of the revolution, Sun Yat-sen (1866–1925), who was elected provisional president at Nanking on January 1, 1912, promptly offered to resign and have Yuan Shih-k'ai (1859–1916) elected president by the provisional parliament should the latter agree to preserve the republic. Yuan agreed, so all the surplus went to his government. In 1915 Yuan dishonored his pledge, and the southwestern provinces rebelled. His death in 1916 threw China into the "warlord period." The powers continued to pay the remainder of the customs revenue to the government in Peking, which effectively meant whichever warlord strong enough to control the capital and whose government received their recognition.

Thrice—in 1917 to 1918, 1920 to 1922, and 1923 to 1925—Sun Yat-sen set up in Canton an independent "constitutional" government—"constitutional" on the grounds that his government was elected by members of the parliament dissolved by the northern warlords in Peking. On January 21, 1921, he asked the Corps Diplomatique in Peking for the share due to Guangdong of the remainder of the customs revenue, but he was refused. He threatened to take over the Canton customhouse. Instantly, the Hong Kong government sent two gunboats to Canton for its protection. In September 1923 Sun Yat-sen tried again, this time asking the inspector general, Sir Francis Aglen (1869–1932). Aglen ignored him, eventually driving him to make the same threats. By January 1924 a total of sixteen foreign gunboats congregated at Can-

ton: six U.S., five British, two French, two Japanese, and one Portuguese. An aggrieved Sun Yat-sen continued to complain bitterly that the inspector general financed the wars launched by wicked northern warlords against his "constitutional" government.

On August 10, 1924, the Norwegian freighter S.S. *Hav* entered Whampoa Harbor of Canton. On board was a huge consignment of arms and ammunition disguised as machinery. The acting commissioner of customs at Canton, an Englishman named W. O. Law, insisted that the goods be accurately manifested, although he had been secretly approached to keep quiet. His insistence exposed a plot by the Canton Merchant Volunteers Corps to overthrow Sun Yat-sen. Apparently, those aware of this gunrunning included the senior management of the Hong Kong and Shanghai Bank, the British consul-general at Canton, the governor of Hong Kong, and Inspector General Aglen himself, who promptly dismissed his acting commissioner at Canton. This incident and the British consul's August 28, 1924, ultimatum to Sun Yat-sen not to use force against the Merchant Volunteers Corps formed the basis of Sun's protest to the British prime minister and the League of Nations.

The *Hav* affair marked the height of the Maritime Customs' political influence. From that point onward it could only decline, as Chinese indignation continued to fuel Chinese nationalism. Once Sun Yat-sen's successor, Chiang Kai-shek (1887–1975), reestablished a republican government at Nanking, negotiations were afoot to regain for China its sovereignty over the Maritime Customs. The subsequent Japanese invasion eliminated British influence in China. The Pacific War and the increase of U.S. influence saw the appointment of the first American, L. K. Little, as the inspector general, now based in Chungking. After the war, the office of the inspector general was moved to Shanghai and, together with the retreat of the nationalists, next to Canton, and finally to Taipei, where Little resigned in 1950. He was the last foreign inspector general of this Chinese service.

SEE ALSO Alcock, Rutherford; Canton System; China; Drugs, Illicit; Empire, British; Empire, French; Empire, Japanese; Empire, Qing; Free Ports; Guangzhou; Hart, Robert; Hong Kong; Hong Kong and Shanghai Bank; Imperialism; Japan; Jardine Matheson; Korea; Manchuria; Most-Favored-Nation Provisions; Port Cities; Shanghai; Treaties; United States.

BIBLIOGRAPHY

British Foreign Office. Records FO17 for the years 1854, 1858, 1860, and 1861.

British Foreign Office. Records FO371 for the years 1921, 1923, and 1924.

Canton Customs Archives. On deposit at the Guangdong Provincial Archives, Canton.

Chen Xiafei, ed. *Zhongguo haiguan midang: Hede, Jindenggan handian huibian, 1874–1907* (The secret files of the Chinese Maritime Customs: Letters and telegrams between Robert Hart and James Duncan Campbell, 1874–1907). 2 volumes. Beijing: Zhonghua shuju, 1999.

Fairbank, J. K., et al., eds. *The I.G. in Peking: Letters of Robert Hart, Chinese Maritime Customs, 1868–1907.* 2 volumes. Cambridge, MA: Harvard University Press, 1975.

Wong, John Y. *Deadly Dreams: Opium, Imperialism, and the Arrow War (1856–60) in China.* Cambridge, U.K.: Cambridge University Press, 1998.

Wong, John Y. *Zhongshan xiansheng yu Yinguo, 1883–1925* (Sun Yat-sen and the British, 1883–1925). Tapei: Xuesheng Shudian, 2005.

John Y. Wong

IMPERIAL PREFERENCE

Imperial preference is a system of rules for managing trade within the British Empire introduced in Ottawa in 1932, mainly in response to the sustained unemployment and virulent economic nationalism that plagued the industrial world during the period between the world wars. Member states of the empire, already having embraced protectionist measures to bolster their domestic economies and thereby their employment, agreed to *preferentially* reduce their tariffs, lowering the rates imposed on imports from other countries of the empire while retaining higher rates on imports from countries outside the empire.

ESTABLISHMENT OF IMPERIAL PREFERENCE, 1932

The Ottawa Conference hammered out a compromise between the vision of an empire-wide free-trade area desired by England, which had hewed to free trade between 1846 and 1932, and a partial customs union desired by protectionist dominions such as Australia, which wanted a system of differential tariffs (lower tariffs for members of the unions, higher tariffs for all other countries). The result was the establishment of one of the most important interwar trading/monetary blocs. Its heyday was during the mid-1930s; by 1938 it was coming apart at the seams.

Political debate concerning the creation of imperial preference raged in England and throughout the empire from the 1890s. The Tariff Reform League was active in pushing the idea within England, and the Unionist Party adopted the concept in its platform during the early twentieth century. Nonetheless, resistance to imperial preference was well entrenched, only giving way to acceptance under the extraordinary conditions of the Great Depression in the 1930s.

To understand the difficulties of forging, and holding together, the imperial preference system, the comparative advantages of the various members of the customs union must be appreciated. The United Kingdom was the first major industrial nation, exporting manufactures such as cotton textiles, steamships, and machinery, and the employment of its labor force was closely tied to the performance of its manufacturing sector. Complementing its export profile was its voracious appetite for raw materials and foodstuffs, an appetite partially satisfied by importing from countries within its empire. The other major members of the imperial preference union—Australia, Canada, India, the Irish Free State, New Zealand, and South Africa—mainly produced foodstuffs and raw materials, but sought to develop their nascent industrial sectors through infant-industry protection.

As the first industrial nation and the workshop of the world in the mid-nineteenth century, free trade was in the interests of the United Kingdom. By bringing in raw materials and foodstuffs without duty, domestic prices for imported raw cotton, wheat, coffee, and tobacco were kept relatively low. By eliminating duties on its modest imports of foreign-manufactured items, the United Kingdom encouraged its trading partners to do likewise, promoting the spread of a global system of unfettered commercial intercourse. To enter into an imperial preference system aimed at binding together the empire economically meant slapping tariffs upon foodstuffs and raw materials produced in countries outside the empire such as Argentina and the United States. There was great political resistance within England to doing this, especially among the ranks of the Liberal Party.

In the self-governing dominions (Australia, Canada, New Zealand, and South Africa) the political problem was the mirror opposite. Protectionism achieved through tariffs, quotas, or exchange-rate manipulations helped the small, struggling manufacturing industries to stay viable in their competition with British products. Advocates of industrialization within the empire resisted giving special preference to British goods. But the wheat farmer, the sheep or cattle raiser, and the dairy owner selling butter were of a different mind: linking the fate of their markets to integration within the empire had great appeal.

In short, political resistance to creating an imperial preference system was strong in both the United Kingdom and the empire. But a strong trend in international trade between the 1870s and the 1930s undercut resistance, at least in England. The share of the United Kingdom was steadily slipping as the United States, Germany, and, later, Japan emerged as important industrial giants challenging the dominance of British goods on global markets. In 1870 the U.K. share of world export trade was

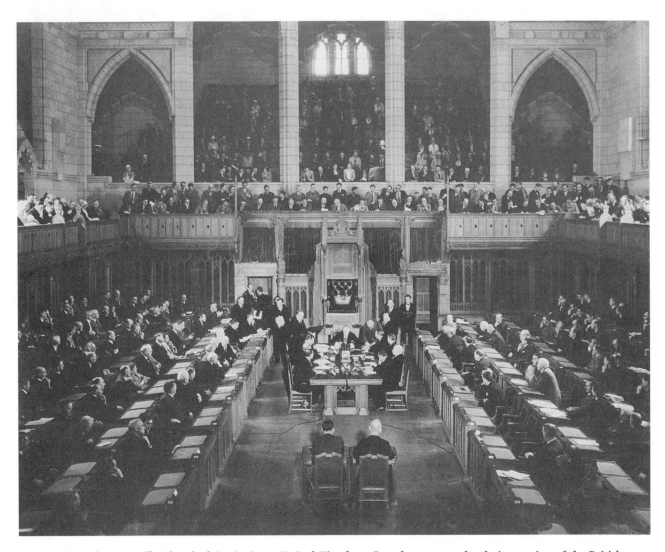

A 1932 photo shows Neville Chamberlain signing a United Kingdom–Canada treaty at the closing session of the British Imperial Conference. *The agreement established a preferred trading arrangement reducing tariffs on exports between Britain and its former colonies. Those involved hoped the treaty would stimulate economies throughout the British Empire and increase worldwide demand for their goods.* © BETTMANN/CORBIS. REPRODUCED BY PERMISSION

22 percent, the German share 12 percent, and the U.S. share 4 percent; by 1913 the U.K. share had fallen to 17 percent, or about equal to the German share, and the U.S. share had reached 8 percent. By 1929 all three shares were about 10 percent. Moreover, unlike the United Kingdom, which was committed to free trade, the United States and Germany had fairly high tariffs, especially after 1900.

In addition to the general secular increase in international competition, three other phenomena peculiar to the early 1930s pushed the dominions and the United Kingdom into cementing a deal in Ottawa in 1932: a sharp fall in the relative price of foodstuffs and raw materials; an acceleration in the drift toward autarky (economic nationalism) as the gold standard floundered and country after country introduced "beggar-thy-neighbor"

protectionism; and rising unemployment in the industrial world during the late 1920s, especially during the early 1930s, and especially in the United States. The United States implemented the highly protectionist Smoot-Hawley Tariff in 1930 as it slid into the Great Depression. Countries on the European continent variously experimented with embargoes, barter, devaluation, quotas, and clearing and payment agreements in an effort to protect their domestic employment levels.

Stung by the declining terms of trade for their exports (raw materials and foodstuffs), concerned about an apparently inexorable drift into autarky or trade blocs, and wanting to promote employment expansion through a mixed strategy of protectionism tempered by trade promotion, the dominions began to see advantages in linking their individual national fates with the rest of the British Empire.

In theory, the signatories to the Ottawa Conference agreements—while acknowledging that the immediate impact of preference was to divert the trade of members of the empire toward one another—were committed to expanding global production, thereby reducing global unemployment. On the final day of the conference in August 1932 a declaration was issued asserting that reducing tariffs within the empire would stimulate the economies of the empire (reducing their unemployment), thus expanding the demand of the empire countries as a group for the products of countries outside the empire.

DECLINE OF IMPERIAL PREFERENCE, 1938

Contrary to British expectations, the dependence of the rest of the empire upon United Kingdom exports fell between 1927 and 1938, while United Kingdom dependence on its empire for export markets increased. Moreover, as the United Kingdom diverted its trade from nonempire to empire countries, the flow of British sterling to countries outside the empire plummeted, while sizeable amounts of the increased volume of sterling flowing to the empire were used to repurchase British-held investments in the empire, thereby reducing demand for British exports.

Was this seemingly perverse turn of events responsible for the gradual unraveling of imperial preference in 1938? Probably not; three other factors seem to have played more decisive roles. First, revulsion against the breakdown in world trade was creating movement, however tentative, toward a more open international economic order. In 1936 the tripartite agreement between the United States, the United Kingdom, and France stabilized exchange rates between the dollar, the pound, and the franc. The tripartite agreement did not challenge imperial preference per se, but it did pave the way for the 1938 negotiations between the United States, the United Kingdom, and Canada aimed at reducing the tariffs imposed on U.S. products by imperial preference through the give-and-take of reciprocity. Second, the breaking down of barriers to intraempire migration, which was meant to parallel what was being achieved within the arena of intraempire trade, never occurred. Citizens of low-wage countries such as India who sought richer opportunities through emigration were barred from moving to the self-governing dominions. Third, the United Kingdom was losing interest in using imperial preference to promote its own internal growth in order to drive down its unemployment. Indeed, the average annual growth rate for the British economy between 1932 and 1937 was 3.9 percent; in the same period unemployment fell from around 15 percent to a comparatively low 8 per-

cent. Imperial preference was outliving its utility even before its tenth anniversary.

Still, imperial preference did not die in 1938. With the breakup of the empire after 1945 and the creation of the Commonwealth, imperial preference became the basis for a system of commonwealth preference, which in turn came under fire with the creation of the General Agreement on Tariffs and Trade (GATT), whose bedrock was the most-favored-nation principle of nondiscrimination promoted by the United States, and by Britain's negotiation for entry into the European Economic Community.

SEE ALSO EMPIRE, BRITISH.

BIBLIOGRAPHY
Arnold, Guy. *Economic Co-operation in the Commonwealth.* New York: Pergamon Press, 1967.
Benham, Frederic. "The Muddle of the Thirties." *Economica* 12, no. 45 (1945): 1–9.
Campbell, R. M. "Empire Free Trade." *Economic Journal* 39, no. 155 (1929): 371–378.
Drummond, Ian. *Imperial Economic Policy, 1917–1939: Studies in Expansion and Contraction.* London: Allen and Unwin, 1974.
Glickman, David L. "The British Imperial Preference System." *Quarterly Journal of Economics* 61, no. 3 (1947): 439–470.
Miller, Frederic M. "The Unemployment Policy of the National Government, 1931–1936." *Historical Journal* 19, no. 2 (1976): 453–476.
Thompson, Andrew S. "Tariff Reform: An Imperial Strategy." *Historical Journal* 40, no. 4 (1997): 1033–1054.
Trentmann, Frank "The Transformation of Fiscal Reform: Reciprocity, Modernization, and the Fiscal Debate within the Business Community in Early Twentieth-Century Britain." *Historical Journal* 39, no. 4 (1996): 1005–1048.

Carl Mosk

IMPORT SUBSTITUTION

Import substitution refers to a strategy of restricting import in order to encourage domestic production. It has been used to protect high-cost domestic producers, to improve the balance of payments, and as a paradigm of development and industrialization. The classic instrument of import substitution is the import tariff. However, import-substituting industrialization strategies (ISI) have also used export subsidy, exchange control, credit subsidy, preferential access to scarce inputs, preferential access to scientific and technical knowledge, and industrial parks.

PROTECTION AND PROMOTION

Import substitution was endorsed in the seventeenth and eighteenth centuries by "mercantilists" and "bullionists," who treated net inflow of bullion or export surplus as a sign of prosperity. Perhaps the most famous example of contemporary import substitution was the English Corn Law (1804), the repeal of which formally inaugurated a free-trade regime in Britain along the lines advocated by Adam Smith (1723–1790) and David Ricardo (1772–1823). As Britain's industrial exports grew, fears of de-industrialization led to protection for domestic industry in parts of Europe and the Americas. More recently, postwar industrial societies have protected their agriculture from cheap imports.

These variations arose in part because free trade tended to hurt the relatively scarce factors pf production in a country, which then lobbied for protection from foreign imports. Thus, land-scarce Europe might want protection against agricultural import from the land-rich United States. The strength of such demands and the level of sympathy for them have varied over time. The world in general was moderately protectionist in the nineteenth century, and aggressively protectionist in the interwar period. In the postwar world, the term *import substitution* has more often referred to the context of economic development. In both usages—protectionist or developmental—import substitution hurts consumers and helps producers of import-competing goods, redistributes incomes, and creates inefficiency. These costs may still be worthwhile if it works as a development paradigm.

ROOTS OF ISI

There were several intellectual roots of import substitution as a development paradigm. One was a critique of liberal theories of trade. Trade theory suggests that countries should specialize in those products, which they can produce relatively cheaply, and that comparative advantage is related to a country's relative factor endowment. Poorer countries, with relatively little capital or skilled labor, should specialize in exports intensive in natural resources such as land. In the 1950s, "export pessimists" argued that land-intensive trade was not a sustainable road to prosperity because terms of trade between agriculture and manufacturing were likely to fall. Industrialization, by protectionist means, was necessary. An older root of ISI was the infant-industry argument, first proposed in the nineteenth century by Friedrich List (1789–1846), which claimed that protection would help small new firms acquire efficiency and reduce cost. The historical experience of the United States, Germany, and Japan, all of which used tariffs during their industrialization, seemed to illustrate the point. Lastly, the shared experience of colonialism had created in the 1950s a consensus among Third-World economists and politicians on the need to restrain trade and build a strong government.

Free trade and a noninterventionist state, tenets of liberalism which were associated with colonial governments, were held to have impoverished and "drained" domestic resources of the colonies.

MODELS

In practice, there seem to be two distinct models of ISI in the postwar world. The milder variant was practiced in the "miracle" economies of East Asia, such as South Korea and Taiwan. The stronger variant was practiced in South Asia and the larger Latin American countries, particularly Brazil and Mexico. Both variants used ISI as a means to promote capital-intensive industry. Both introduced state control and direction in the use of scarce resources such as capital and imported equipment. However, the East Asian variant was not export pessimist like the South Asian one, and it enabled a macroeconomic environment in which the export of labor-intensive manufactures could grow. The two variants also differed in the degree of protection and control erected. In the second variant, ISI involved extremely high levels of tariff, large-scale government investment, extensive regulation of finance and trade, and "crowding out" of private investment.

ASSESSMENT

ISI generated quick returns for about fifteen years, followed by economic slowdown. The point of transition came when prospects of manufacturing growth by selling at the limited home market was exhausted. The high cost and poor quality of domestic goods discouraged demand growth. Extreme forms of ISI led to macroeconomic crises and failed to reduce poverty. There were several reasons for this. First, extreme import protection hurt export. Whereas freer trade gave domestic industry access to new technologies and helped them learn, restricted trade made learning difficult and reduced competitiveness. Second, limited exports and high budget deficits worsened inflation and trade deficits. Third, inefficiency "spilled over." For example, the high cost of locally produced machines raised the cost of goods made by using those machines. Fourth, comparative advantages were ignored. As resources were channeled into noncompetitive capital goods, potentially exportable labor-intensive manufactures were denied capital. Resources, thus, moved to sectors with lower return to capital and lower employment potential. Fifth, controls were often seen by the people as unjust, as a means of distributing favors by politicians.

The infant-industry argument accepts that protection should gradually ease as domestic industry matures. In practice, protection created political lobbies, tended to become self-sustaining, and freed domestic industry from pressure to learn faster.

END OF IMPORT SUBSTITUTION

Pushed by episodes of macroeconomic collapse, country after country gave up or reformed import-substitution programs. Early reformers (1975–1980) included countries in Southeast Asia, some in Latin America, and Sri Lanka. Among the last to reform were Brazil, Mexico, and South Asia (1985–1990 onward). The reform package has had a fairly uniform composition: liberalization of exchange rates, reduction in tariffs, easing industrial regulation, and rollback of state investment. The design of a new framework for world trade negotiated by World Trade Organization through the 1990s and beyond encouraged the transition. The end of ISI saw rises in income, employment, and export growth rates, provided there were no serious macroeconomic and political crises. But the rollback of government spending sometimes worsened inequality.

The golden age of import substitution is largely over, though economists continue to debate its historical role in promoting or delaying industrialization.

SEE ALSO Ali, Muhammad; American System; Argentina; Balance of Payments; Brazil; Bullion (Specie); Burma; Chile; China; Developmental State, Concept of the; Egypt; Empire, Japanese; Empire, Ottoman; GATT, WTO; Globalization, Pro and Con; India; Iran; Japan; Korea; Mexico; NAFTA; Nanyang Brothers Tobacco; Nationalism; Pasha, Isma'il; Russia; South Africa; Subsidies; United States; Venezuela.

BIBLIOGRAPHY

Bruton, H. J. "A Reconsideration of Import Substitution." *Journal of Economic Literature* 36 (June 1998): 903–936.

O'Rourke, Kevin, and Williamson, Jeffrey G. *Globalization and History: The Evolution of a Nineteenth-Century Atlantic Economy.* Cambridge, MA, and London: Massachusetts Institute of Technology Press, 1999.

Tirthankar Roy

INDIA

In the past, the Indian subcontinent was a major link in the maritime trade between Asia and Europe. A coastline 4,600 miles long, easy access from both west and east Asia, local availability of textiles and other goods in demand worldwide, a well-developed shipbuilding industry, and strong mercantile tradition contributed to India's strategic position in the Indian Ocean trade. For four centuries after the Portuguese mariner Vasco da Gama (1469?–1524) discovered the sea route between Europe and India around the Cape of Good Hope (1497),

European traders played a pivotal role in Indian Ocean trade. Some historians believed that the Indian Ocean became a really important location in world trade only after the Europeans entered the stage. The current consensus is that Asia was already a prominent trading zone before European entry, and the Europeans for a long time utilized commodities, routes, and systems established in that trade in partnership with local merchants. However, by 1870, maritime trade of the region was strongly Europe-centered, in respect to participants, composition, and direction of trade.

What were the characteristics of Indian Ocean trade before European entry and after? What was the relationship between Indian and European merchants in the three centuries of coexistence? Did trade in the nineteenth century represent a decline of Indian enterprise, or a transformation? What was the relationship between trade and economic development in the region? The rest of this essay, which is organized chronologically, will return to these themes from time to time.

INDIA AND THE INDIAN OCEAN, 1450–1800

Before the arrival of the Portuguese, India's mercantile marine was largely in the hands of Gujarati Muslim merchants. Indian ships called on the ports of Red Sea and the Persian Gulf. The market of the *hajj* (Islamic pilgrimage), wherein converged caravan trade from a large area, was "the conveyor belt" through which Indian goods, chiefly textiles, found their way to European markets. In the East, Javanese shipping carried Indian textiles to the Spice Islands in eastern Indonesia in exchange for spices. The linking of sea routes and land routes, or the port cities with the interior, was as yet weak. In turn, the territorial powers did little to create and sustain port towns. These were rather the creation of the Indian Ocean.

Two new variables were added in the sixteenth century: Portuguese control of the sea routes, and the rise of continental monarchies in the western part of the ocean—the Mughal, the Safavid, and the Ottoman Empires. The second factor strengthened the *hajj* network and built stronger links between the sea and the land-based trades. Although the Ottoman and the Portuguese tried to redirect and monopolize trade routes, these attempts waned in the sixteenth century, bringing in a relatively undisturbed era of expansion.

The formation of the English East India Company in 1600 and the merger of several firms trading in the East Indies into the Dutch East India Company (Vereenigde Oost-Indische Compagnie) in 1602 announced an era that saw India drawn more firmly into the Indian Ocean trade. These enterprises had an interest in buying spices from the Indonesian archipelago, and found Indian cotton textiles a convenient means of payment. Initial-

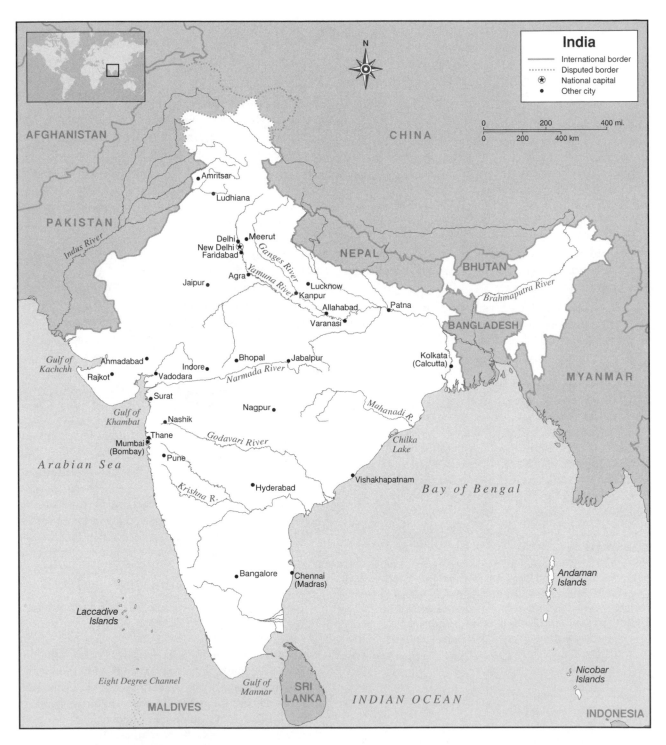

MAP BY XNR PRODUCTIONS. THE GALE GROUP.

ly, therefore, north Europeans remained part of the traditional structure. That is, they carried Asian freight for Asian markets and built ties of dependence and cooperation with Asian merchants. However, by the third quarter of the century, Europe was a more important market for Indian cotton textiles, the so-called "calicos" and "muslins," than Asia. By then, the Dutch and the English, unlike the Portuguese, had penetrated from the sea into the inland, which was the source of supply of Indian textiles.

A customer support call center in Bangalore, India, provides growing job opportunities in the technology sector for local residents in 2004. Companies from the United States and Britain discovered they could cut costs by using cheaper, skilled labor from overseas countries like India for portions of their business. India is the leader in an industry based on outsourcing high-tech jobs to other countries. © SHERWIN CRASTO/REUTERS/CORBIS. REPRODUCED BY PERMISSION.

The four great cloth-exporting regions in India in the eighteenth century were Punjab, Gujarat, Coromandel, and Bengal. Some of these regions possessed resources needed for high-quality textiles such as long-staple cotton, or water believed to be good for dyeing. That apart, these regions already had well-developed textile production systems catering to older trade networks. Punjab traded overland with Central Asia and the Middle East, Gujarat had ties with Red Sea ports, Coromandel with Southeast Asia, and Bengal used its waterways to trade with northern India. The Europeans built trading stations in these regions. The English called theirs "factories." Together with stations in ports such as Surat on the western coast and Masulipatnam on the eastern, these factories formed networks of circulation of money, merchants, and material. Within these regions, weaver settlements changed continually according to famines or political instability. European factories sometimes had a powerful attraction for artisans as sites that could offer them greater security of life and livelihood.

By 1750 the English had outpaced the Dutch in terms of presence in the hinterland. These moves into the land carried promises as well as hazards. There were incidents of dispute, even armed conflict, between the territorial powers and the English East India Company. When threatened inland, the company blockaded sea routes for the Indian merchants, which usually produced the desired effect. The extraordinary success of the European companies, thus, partly derived from what Ashin Das Gupta called a "balance of blackmail between land and sea" (Das Gupta 2001, p. 230).

Through these two centuries there were a few significant differences between the worlds of the European traders and their Indian counterparts. The latter was not a small-scale enterprise. At its peak, the Gujarati merchant marine based in Surat consisted of about 100 vessels of 200 to 400 tons each. Still, relative to European enterprise, Indian shipping declined. Although Indian ships charged lower freight rates, European ships were sturdier and better defended. Naval superiority, based on a partnership between the parent state and the merchant firms, was an important factor in European success. At key points of trade, the Europeans erected fortified settlements backed by strong fleets. These fleets not only kept the sea routes open and safe, but also restrained land power. Furthermore, European trade was organized around a large joint-stock company, whereas Indian trading firms developed around families or individuals. The stability of such a firm was too dependent on the resources and talents in the family. The English East India Company not only brought a large number of persons and stakeholders to work together, but also it had an identity independent of persons, which gave it more stability and power. Although the company had an official monopoly of commerce, in practice private European traders, including covenanted servants of the company, captured a much bigger share of the trade. The company, however, survived because of its organizational strengths.

As the eighteenth century drew to a close, the high roads of the Indian Ocean had become Europe-directed, in which European shipping and traders increased their control. The weakening of Mughal power inland saw the English East India Company drawn into territorial disputes. Eventually, as the English East India Company assumed power in Bengal (1757–1765), the land-sea political cleavage began to weaken. Native shipping and trade, prominent among them being the Gujaratis, went in a decline, even as they reasserted themselves in the hinterland. The age of partnership ended.

Interestingly, the India trade at its peak involved an exchange of goods, not for goods, but for bullion. The sustainability of the trade depended on circulation of gold and silver that came from Spanish America. More directly, the economies of regions such as Bengal and Coromandel were influenced by maritime trade for over three centuries. But there is considerable doubt about how important the Indian Ocean was for the economy of South Asia as a whole. The most generous estimates suggest that the proportion of export in national income was between 1 and 2 percent at the end of the eighteenth century, which was small indeed relative to the massive scholarship that this episode in South Asian history has produced.

TOWARD COLONIAL INDIA, 1800–1947

At the close of the Napoleonic wars, the market for Indian textiles had shrunk owing to tariffs on Indian goods in England, which were steeply raised between 1797 and 1814. Almost simultaneously, technological changes in weaving, principally Horrock's power-loom, reduced the difference in cost of production. The company's commercial monopoly ended in 1813. Already the company had become a territorial power living on land revenue. Many former employees and other individuals had established partnerships with Indians to carry on export of cotton, indigo, opium, and sugar. Profit from these trades sustained new commercial-cum-port towns such as Calcutta, Bombay, and Madras, helped some Indian groups to accumulate capital that later found its way into industrial ventures, and built close trading links between India and China, which was a market for Indian opium sold in exchange of tea. These trades had dwindled by 1900 to 1914. Natural indigo was steadily displaced by synthetic indigo. Although Lancashire rediscovered Indian cotton during the U.S. Civil War (1861–1865), subsequently more cotton was used by the newly established Indian mills themselves. The Sino-Indian opium trade declined from 1906 in the wake of a worldwide antiaddiction movement. And India emerged for Britain a more important source for tea than China.

Assumption of political power in India by the British Crown (1858) and the opening of the Suez Canal (1869) integrated India more closely with the now solidly Eurocentric world economy. Ocean freight rates on bulk goods from India fell by 60 percent or more between 1873 and 1893; by the latter date, more than two-thirds of export from India passed Suez. Between 1880 and 1925 the real volume of trade to and from India doubled. About 1890, more that half of Indian exports consisted of agricultural goods such as grains, seeds, raw cotton, and raw jute. The age of the artisan had ended, and the age of the peasant arrived. Close to half of Indian imports consisted of manufactured consumer goods, chiefly cotton textiles. The ratio of trade to national income increased from less than 10 percent in the 1860s to about 20 percent in 1914.

The pattern of trade did not remain static through this impressive expansion. As industrial capability improved in a number of directions, so did manufactured exports. Cotton yarn, for example, was a successful export to China, until the cotton mills of Japan ousted Indian goods from that market (1890s). Jute textiles, semiprocessed hides and skins, and tea increased their share in export between 1870 and 1914. In the interwar period, Indian fiscal policy and industrialization reshaped the composition of imports. Protective tariffs encouraged an import-substituting industrialization. The share of cotton textiles declined, and the share of machinery, metals, and chemicals increased as a result.

In direction of trade, a great deal of Indian exports went to Britain or were re-exported from Britain. India was almost exclusively dependent on Britain as a source of imports until World War I. In the interwar period there was a drop in Britain's share and increase in those of Japan, the United States, Germany, and Italy. The latter change reflected tendencies in Asian trade and industrialization. In the early twentieth century intra-Asian trade expanded, based on the emergence of a modern cotton textile industry in Japan. A three-way cotton-oriented trade and division of labor between India, China, and Japan emerged as a result. Japanese textiles began to penetrate Indian markets as part of this larger process, aided by an overvalued rupee. Tariffs on cotton and silk textiles were partly directed at imports from Japan. Britain's share of India trade increased somewhat late in the interwar period due to attempts to set up a preferential trade zone within the empire (Imperial Preference).

IMPORT SUBSTITUTION, 1947–1985

The present territory of the Indian Union attained independence from British colonial rule in 1947. For about forty years after that date, government policy of economic development played a large role on the pattern of foreign trade. From the nineteenth century, mainstream Western political economy advocated "free trade," and equally, the advocacy of free trade provoked sharp reaction in the Third World. India, indeed, was a stage where such battles were fought. In the 1930s an Indian concept of development emerged. There were many schools within this broad current of economic nationalism, but these traditions had a common core: a rejection of Western economics' faith in trade as an engine of growth. Consequently, these schools tended to put stress on the ideal of self-sufficiency.

Inspired by this ideology, the policy regime in force for the next 35 years protected Indian goods against imports by means of (a) rates of tariff that were among the highest in the world, (b) a licensing system wherein it was practically impossible to import anything without a government license, which was hard to get, and (c) government monopoly on the import of necessities such as oil and food. While the private sector was effectively prevented from importing, exchange rates were controlled and overvalued, which subsidized government import but reduced the competitiveness of exports. No significant shifts took place in this period in the composition of trade. In terms of direction, there was increasing presence of the Soviet bloc, which was not only politically closer to the neo-Socialist regime of India, but also willing to carry on bilateral trade.

For India's leaders at independence, looking back at the collapsing international trade of the 1930s, the cost of isolation seemed of little consequence. However, the world market revived soon after World War II, and proved a more powerful engine than ever in leading parts of Asia and Latin America into a rapid growth trajectory. India's isolation hurt her in two ways. It denied traditionally successful exports such as textiles, leather, or foodgrain access to the world market. And it made the protected sectors, including machinery, inefficient due to lack of access to technology and capital, absence of competition, bureaucratic "rent-seeking," and the existence of a black market in exchange. Between the early 1950s and the late 1970s India's share in world export fell from 2.5 to 0.4 percent, and the scale of foreign trade in relation to national income fell from 15 to 10 percent.

ECONOMIC REFORMS, 1985–2000

Discontent over isolationist policy was growing, and in the 1980s one key aspect of policy was relaxed: exchange rates were steadily depreciated to levels close to the market rates. The impact on private sector export was spectacular. From the early 1990s, licenses began to be removed and tariffs reduced. The new regime destroyed several old, overprotected firms, but it encouraged new entry and made it easier for incumbents to export, access foreign investment, and access new technologies. Between the late 1970s and 2000 India's share in world trade increased from 0.4 to 1 percent, and the ratio of trade to national income from 10 to 20 percent. The coincidence of the reforms with the end of socialism saw India leaving the Soviet bloc and returning to the market economies, including East and Southeast Asia. Composition of trade changed, too. The main exports were textiles and clothing, leather, polished gems, and processed foods—in short, goods intensive in low-wage labor or natural resources. Between 1985 and 1997, an estimated one million jobs were created in textiles and clothing, largely driven by export.

Regarding the composition of export, the postreform trade scenario was a late reversion to the colonial pattern, with one notable difference: India's principal exports in the later years of the reform were intensive not only in manual labor but also in knowledge such as software development skills. India's share in world services export was double its share in world merchandise export in 2003. The importance of knowledge-based goods in the export basket illustrated the success of one part of the old isolationist development strategy—its accent on building domestic capability in technical and scientific manpower. But it also raised entirely new challenges related to trade in services, where property rights were often vaguely defined. The position of India in world trade in future depends largely on how these problems are resolved.

SEE ALSO BANGLADESH; BENGAL; BOYCOTT; BULLION (SPECIE); CALCUTTA; COAL; COTTON; COWRIES; EAST INDIA COMPANY, BRITISH; EAST INDIA COMPANY, DUTCH; EAST INDIA COMPANY, OTHER; EMPIRE, BRITISH; EMPIRE, DUTCH; EMPIRE, MUGHAL; EMPIRE, PORTUGUESE; ENTREPÔT SYSTEM; ETHNIC GROUPS, GUJARATI; FACTORIES; FAIRS; FAMINE; GLOBALIZATION, PRO AND CON; GOLD AND SILVER; GUJARAT; HOME CHARGES (INDIA); INTERNATIONAL MONETARY FUND (IMF); POPULATION—EMIGRATION AND IMMIGRATION; IMPERIAL PREFERENCE; IMPERIALISM; IMPORT SUBSTITUTION; INDIAN OCEAN; INTERNATIONAL TRADE AGREEMENTS; LABORERS, COERCED; LABORERS, CONTRACT; MADRAS; MUMBAI; NATIONALIZATION; PAKISTAN; PHARMACEUTICALS; RICE; SILK; SOCIALISM AND COMMUNISM; SPICES AND THE SPICE TRADE; SRI LANKA; TAGORE FAMILY; TATA FAMILY ENTERPRISES; TEA; TEXTILES; WHEAT AND OTHER CEREAL GRAINS.

BIBLIOGRAPHY

Banerji, Arun. *Aspects of Indo-British Economic Relations 1858–1898.* Delhi: Oxford University Press, 1982.

Chaudhuri, K. N. "Foreign Trade and Balance of Payments (1757–1947)". In *The Cambridge Economic History of India,* Vol. 2: *c. 1757–c. 1970,* ed. Dharma Kumar. Cambridge, U.K.: Cambridge University Press, 1983.

Das Gupta, Ashin. *The World of the Indian Ocean Merchant, 1500–1800.* Delhi: Oxford University Press, 2001.

Prakash, Om. *European Commercial Enterprise in Pre-Colonial India.* Cambridge, U.K.: Cambridge University Press, 2003.

Saul, S. B. *Studies in British Overseas Trade, 1870–1914.* Liverpool, U.K.: Liverpool University Press, 1960.

Srinivasan, T. N. and Tendulkar, S. D. *Reintegrating India with the World Economy.* Delhi: Oxford University Press, 2003.

Tirthankar Roy

INDIAN OCEAN

The Indian Ocean is the world's third-largest ocean, stretching from the tip of southern Africa around the East African coast, up the Red Sea and Persian Gulf, then around the coast of South Asia and down to western Indonesia and along the west coast of Australia.

Until the advent of steam-powered ships in the mid-nineteenth century navigation in the Indian Ocean was governed by regular monsoon winds. Unlike the Atlantic trade winds, these winds blow from different directions at different seasons. From June to November they blow from the southwest, and from December to April from the northeast, so, for example, one could only sail from the East African coast to India between June and November. Once the monsoon system was understood navigation was comparatively easy; if the right season for sailing were chosen, ships would have favorable winds both ways. Another consequence of this pattern was that merchants usually left agents in the ports where they traded, for the locals knew that ships had to leave at a certain time to "catch the monsoon." To avoid being charged higher prices, a local agent bought when the market was low and held the goods until the merchant returned on the next monsoon.

EARLY TRADE TO THE EIGHTEENTH CENTURY

Trade and navigation have a very long history in the Indian Ocean. Five thousand years ago Mesopotamia traded with the Indus Valley civilization in South Asia. Later, Greeks and Romans traded with people along the ocean's littoral. From around the ninth century most traders in the region were Muslim. There was always a very important trade along the coastlines carrying basic commodities such as cotton cloth, foodstuffs, and lumber. Luxury goods such as bullion and spices dominated around 1450 long-distance trade. Trade in spices was far-flung and well organized. Fine spices came only from eastern Indonesia and Sri Lanka, whereas pepper grew in several areas. These spices were in demand everywhere from China to Europe. Merchants made large profits but also paid high taxes and took great risks as their spices traveled huge distances. Merchants ranged from humble peddlers chaffering their way from port to port with a bundle of goods to very rich magnates who sent off agents to trade in all directions.

Fifteenth-century ports such as Mombasa, Aden, Hormuz, Cambay, Calicut, and Melaka were major commercial nodes. A product, such as spices bound for the Mediterranean, would change hands several times—in Melaka, then in Calicut, and again in Alexandria. This "relay" trade was generally free of political interference. Piracy was a constant problem, but no Asian land power tried to dominate the sea. Most ports treated visiting merchants fairly and let them largely govern themselves. There was keen competition to attract visiting merchants, who paid coveted customs duties. No ruler of a port could charge too much, lest merchants go elsewhere.

The first Europeans changed relatively little. The Portuguese arrived in 1498, and soon after tried to control Indian Ocean trade. They claimed a monopoly on spices for themselves, and tried to control and tax all other trade by insisting that all traders pay them for licenses. This intervention was briefly successful: for about fifty years the Portuguese controlled much of the spice trade to Europe (though this represented only about 10 percent of the total spice trade). However, by about 1550 Asian traders had learned how to circumvent the Portuguese fleets, reviving indigenous trade in spices. Nor were the Portuguese able to control and tax other trade: the ocean was too vast, Asian traders too skillful, and Portuguese manpower inadequate.

From 1600 Northern Europeans entered the Indian Ocean. The English and Dutch trading companies usually competed peacefully with local merchants but sometimes used force, particularly in the Spice Islands, where the Dutch almost monopolized trade in the fine spices. The Northern Europeans not only traded back to Western Europe, but also carried on a "country trade" within the Indian Ocean. For years Asian products, such as spices and cloths, found markets in Europe, but European products did poorly in Asia. Until the late eighteenth century the Dutch and English exported large quantities of bullion from Europe to pay for Asian goods. This bullion came from Latin America; without it Europeans might not have been able to trade at all in the Indian Ocean, for at least in the seventeenth century their country trade profits were limited. By the end of the century the Dutch and English both owned several Indian Ocean ports, but these were little different from other Asian port cities.

Asian traders continued to prosper up to the late eighteenth century. The humble coastal trade remained in their hands, and they also participated in long-distance trade (though not in trade to Europe). Often they shipped their goods in European vessels within the ocean. European ships were better armed and so safer from pirates, both European and local, and from other Europeans.

Late in the eighteenth century European events began to damage Indian Ocean trade. English industrialization profoundly affected Asian trade. Thanks to better weapons, the English trading company began to acquire land in Bengal and then elsewhere in India. Profits from this land financed more conquests and began to reverse the flow of bullion, sending money back to England.

They conquered Bihar, inland from Bengal, and established an opium-production monopoly. This was exported to China (and when the Chinese tried to stop importing this harmful product the English forced them to continue). Opium paid for tea, a new and valuable product to send back to England.

NINETEENTH AND TWENTIETH CENTURIES

In the nineteenth century Britain controlled most long-distance trade in the Indian Ocean. The British seized several vital choke points (Aden, Melaka, Cape Town, all the coast of India and Burma) from which their navy could patrol. Three technological changes related to the Industrial Revolution were even more important. First, from mid-century ships began to be built of iron and later, steel, and were powered by increasingly efficient steam engines. Thus the straitjacket of the monsoons was overcome at last. Sailing ships continued for many years but ultimately could not compete with the speed, reliability, and cost-effectiveness of steamers. Second, the Suez Canal (opened in 1869) made the passage to Europe much quicker. Third, the British (and the Dutch, to an extent) undertook massive engineering works to make harbors safer and bigger. Increasingly, Indian Ocean countries provided raw materials and tropical products—raw cotton and silk, coffee, sugar, and tea—and received manufactured goods from Europe.

But in the twentieth century, competition from other Western powers and Japan reduced British shipping dominance. Some countries, especially India, began to industrialize in the 1920s and 1930s, and intra-Asian trade grew. This accelerated after World War II, as Asian colonies began to gain independence: first India in 1947 and later, all the others. Asian countries, especially Japan, and later India and China, became increasingly competitive with Western countries. These countries, and others, also began to provide most of the merchant shipping in the ocean.

Since World War II there also have been massive changes in maritime technology. Huge container ships, freight carriers, and oil tankers now dominate in long-distance trade. The oil trade from the Persian Gulf to East Asia and Europe is particularly important. Bigger ships needed bigger ports and harbors, and container ships needed specialized dockside facilities to ensure rapid loading and unloading of the containers. All this required massive investment in port facilities. Singapore was the first in the ocean to do this, in the 1970s, and today is the most active container port in the world, taking in containers from all over the world and redistributing them to be sent on to their destinations. Colombo (in Sri Lanka) followed Singapore, and recently Mumbai and other Indian ports have become competitive. Increasingly, global integration has merged Indian Ocean trade into worldwide trends.

SEE ALSO ALBUQUERQUE, AFONSO DE; BANGLADESH; BENGAL; BURMA; CALCUTTA; COEN, JAN PIETERSZOON; CLIMATE; COWRIES; EAST INDIA COMPANY, BRITISH; EAST INDIA COMPANY, DUTCH; EAST INDIA COMPANY, OTHER; EMPIRE, BRITISH; EMPIRE, DUTCH; EMPIRE, FRENCH; EMPIRE, MUGHAL; EMPIRE, OTTOMAN; EMPIRE, PORTUGUESE; ENTREPÔT SYSTEM; ETHNIC GROUPS, AFRICANS; ETHNIC GROUPS, ARMENIANS; ETHNIC GROUPS, CANTONESE; ETHNIC GROUPS, FUJIANESE; ETHNIC GROUPS, GUJARATI; ETHNIC GROUPS, JEWS; FACTORIES; FREE PORTS; GAMA, VASCO DA; GOLD AND SILVER; GUJARAT; IMPERIALISM; INDIA; INDONESIA; IRAN; KENYA; LEVANT COMPANY; MADRAS; MAGELLAN, FERDINAND; MELAKA; MILLETS AND CAPITULATIONS; MUMBAI; PERSIAN GULF; PIRACY; PRIVATEERING; RAFFLES, SIR THOMAS STAMFORD; RICE; SHIPBUILDING; SHIPPING, COASTAL; SHIP TYPES; SINGAPORE; SOUTH AFRICA; SPICES AND THE SPICE TRADE; SUEZ CANAL; TEXTILES; THAILAND; TRAVELERS AND TRAVEL.

BIBLIOGRAPHY

Barendse, R. J. *The Arabian Seas: The Indian Ocean World of the Seventeenth Century.* Armonk, NY: M.E. Sharpe, 2002.

Broeze, Frank, ed. *Gateways of Asia: Port Cities of Asia from the 13th to the 20th Centuries.* London: Kegan Paul International, 1997.

Chandra, Satish, ed. *The Indian Ocean: Explorations in History, Commerce, and Politics.* New Delhi: Sage, 1987.

Chaudhuri, K. N. *Trade and Civilization in the Indian Ocean: An Economic History from the Rise of Islam to 1750.* Cambridge, U.K.: Cambridge University Press, 1985.

Das Gupta, Ashin, and Pearson, Michael N., eds. *India and the Indian Ocean, 1500–1800.* Calcutta: Oxford University Press. 2nd edition, 1999.

Furber, Holden. *Rival Empires of Trade in the Orient, 1600–1800.* Minneapolis: University of Minnesota Press, 1976.

Headrich, Daniel. *The Tools of Empire: Technology and European Imperialism in the Nineteenth Century.* New York: Oxford University Press, 1981.

Lombard, Denys, and Aubin, Jean, eds. *Asian Merchants and Businessmen in the Indian Ocean and the China Sea.* New Delhi: Oxford University Press, 2000.

McPherson, Kenneth. *The Indian Ocean: A History of People and the Sea.* New Delhi: Oxford University Press, 1993.

Pearson, Michael. *The Indian Ocean.* London and New York: Routledge, 2003.

Prakash, Om. *European Commercial Enterprise in Pre-Colonial India.* Cambridge, U.K.: Cambridge University Press, 1998.

Risso, Patricia. *Merchants and Faith: Muslim Commerce and Culture in the Indian Ocean.* Boulder, CO: Westview, 1995.

Tracy, James D., ed. *The Rise of Merchant Empires: Long-Distance Trade in the Early Modern World, 1350–1750.* New York: Cambridge University Press, 1990.

Tracy, James D., ed. *The Political Economy of Merchant Empires: State Power and World Trade, 1350–1750.* New York: Cambridge University Press, 1991.

Michael N. Pearson

INDONESIA

The Indonesian islands have always been important foci of international exchange because of their openness to the sea. Different emporia—on Sumatra (Srivijaja), Java (Kediri, Banten), and, most successfully, nearby Malacca—have attempted to control parts of the international trade networks that arose in the archipelago before the arrival of European traders in the sixteenth century. Rule of the famous Spice Islands (the Moluccas), the only producers of cloves and nutmeg in the world, was the main goal of the Portuguese, Spanish, English, and Dutch traders in the area. Pepper, exported on a large scale from Java and Sumatra (but also from parts of India) was the other major Indonesian export. These products found markets all over the world, particularly in China, South Asia, and Western Europe. In return, the region imported textiles from India, and the Moluccas also needed rice from the rest of the archipelago (particularly Java). Trade was already booming before the arrival of the Europeans, but increasingly, merchants came from outside the islands—from India, the Middle East, and China. The rapid Islamization of the archipelago has been attributed to their influence.

UNDER EUROPEAN CONTROL

The Portuguese did not fundamentally change the system of international exchange. The impact of the Dutch—who first arrived in 1598—was much larger, as they enforced a monopoly on the main spices produced in the Moluccas (from the 1620s onwards), established their own emporium in Batavia (in 1619), and eliminated one by one their competitors (such as Malacca in 1641, Makassar in 1669, and Banten in 1682). Batavia became the hub of a much larger trading network, which was also channeling the exports of, for example, copper from Japan to India. During the seventeenth century the main export commodities of Indonesia remained spices, but the production of nutmeg and cloves dropped markedly after the establishment of the monopoly by the Dutch East India Company (Vereenigde Oost-Indische Compagnie, or VOC). In Banda, for example, the VOC massacred the indigenous population, which was then replaced by slaves working on plantations. In general, the desire to maximize profit margins of the monopolized spices

(nutmeg and cloves) drove up prices in Europe and Asia, which severely reduced demand, eventually curtailing production in the Moluccas. In this way, the VOC monopoly significantly reduced Indonesia's share in world trade.

Outside the Moluccas the VOC had a much weaker grip on international trade. Its activities became progressively more intertwined with those of Chinese merchants, who had much better access to Chinese markets (for porcelain, for example) and were—also as intermediaries in trade within the archipelago—increasingly effective. They played a key role in the development of a new export product, sugar, which developed vigorously in the environs of Batavia from the 1640s onward; Chinese merchants worked together closely with the VOC, which was the main buyer of the product. The VOC also had an active part in the rise of another major export crop, coffee: it organized the introduction of the crop in 1699, and developed a very successful system of coerced export production by the local population (of the western part of Java, Priangan). Sugar and coffee together dominated the exports of Java—and of Indonesia—during much of the eighteenth and nineteenth centuries. Toward the end of the eighteenth century the position of the VOC became weaker, whereas the trade of other (Buginese, Chinese, and Indian) merchants and shippers, prospered. In 1775 only half of Java's trade was in VOC hands; that figure was probably much lower elsewhere in the archipelago.

After the demise of the VOC in 1800, the English interregnum of 1811 to 1816, and the return of the Dutch in 1816, major efforts were made to increase the exports of the islands. Coffee and sugar remained the staples throughout the nineteenth century, but other products, such as tea and tobacco, became increasingly important. During the 1830s a new system of forced cultivation—the Cultivation System—was introduced, leading to a huge expansion of exports of coffee and sugar (and, more briefly, of indigo). From the 1850s plantations using "free" wage labor—often concentrating on tea or tobacco—became increasingly important. The second half of the nineteenth century also witnessed the rise of the "outer islands"; first and foremost was Sumatra, which developed into one of the most dynamic parts of Indonesia thanks to exports of tobacco (from Deli), palm oil, and, from the 1900s onwards, rubber and oil. Tin from Banka and Billiton also grew in importance. Kalimantan became another major source of both oil and rubber. The first industry was dominated by a few extremely large and capital-intensive firms, which merged together to form Royal Dutch Shell in 1907. (Subsequently, U.S. competitors entered the business in Indonesia.) In the rubber industry, large plantations coexisted with small-scale cultivation by peasants.

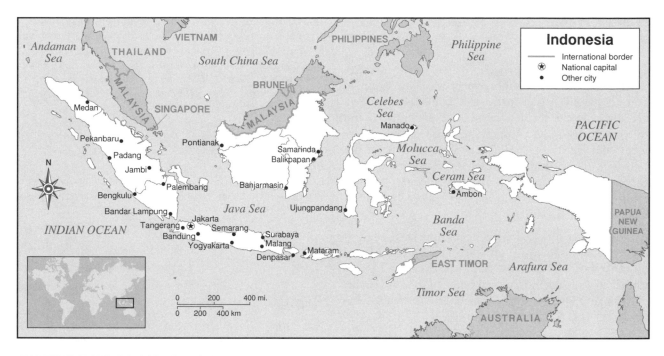

MAP BY XNR PRODUCTIONS. THE GALE GROUP.

In return for its liberal gifts to world markets, Indonesia imported manufactured goods on a large scale. The indigenous textile industry—which had been a net exporter during the eighteenth century—sharply declined during the nineteenth century due to intense international competition; only batik-making continued to prosper. Textiles manufactured in the Netherlands and Great Britain were the most important imports from the 1820s onward. Rice became another major import, whereas before the 1860s Java had traditionally been a net exporter of rice. Capital goods and consumption goods—many of them purchased by the rapidly growing foreign community—also loomed large on the import bill. Indonesia had a strikingly large surplus on the trade balance, a huge difference between exports and imports. This was, according to some, a measure of the exploitation of the economy, according to others an index of the degree to which it used foreign resources. This export-dependent economy was struck very hard by recession (after 1920) and depression (during the 1930s), but these setbacks also initiated a turn to a slightly more balanced economy through import-substitution and the related growth of industry (textiles, cigarette-production).

POSTINDEPENDENCE

After World War II and Indonesia's struggle for independence between 1945 and 1949, the economy was still highly dependent on very few export commodities—on oil, rubber, palm oil and tobacco in particular (sugar exports never recovered from the setback during the 1930s, and coffee had been declining since the late nineteenth century). Postindependence international trade was tightly controlled during the first fifteen years under President Sukarno (1901–1970) for short-run balance-of-payments reasons, as a nationalistic reaction against the colonial pattern of exports, and to promote domestic manufacturing industries. Consequently, Indonesian export volume grew by less than 1 percent per annum between 1953 and 1966, whereas world trade grew by about 7 percent per annum.

The advent of the New Order government in 1965 coincided with a dramatic acceleration in export-volume growth to over 14 percent per annum in the years 1967 to 1973. This expansion was mainly a response to the devaluation of the rupiah and other economic stabilization policies. World prices for Indonesia's major export products, which had fallen more or less continually through the latter part of the 1960s, began to recover after 1971. The dramatic growth in the world price of oil was chiefly responsible, but actually all of Indonesia's main export commodities experienced price increases in the 1970s, including rubber, timber, coffee, vegetable oils, and nonferrous metals. The real volume of export growth fell after 1973, partly because the OPEC quotas effectively placed a ceiling on petroleum production and partly because nonoil export production growth was quite modest. Nevertheless, in the 1970s Indonesian growth in export volume was faster than the growth of world trade.

Between 1981 and 1986 total commodity-export earnings contracted by 50 percent. This was entirely due to the fall in oil prices, from almost U.S.$60 in 1981 to U.S.$13 in 1986. Non-oil and non-gas exports, on the other hand, registered some growth over these years. By 1990 total export earnings had recovered slightly to above its value of 1981. This improvement was entirely due to non-oil and non-gas exports—mainly manufactures, especially plywood, textiles, garments, and footwear, and to some heavy-industry products such as fertilizer, cement, and fabricated steel. Those sectors profited from trade reforms instituted in the late 1980s and early 1990s. Indonesia thus became, like other Asian "tigers," a significant exporter of manufactures, particularly low-skilled, labor-intensive products.

The Asian financial crisis hit Indonesia in 1997, at the same time as the worst drought of the century, caused by the effect of El Niño. Sharply declining oil prices caused an acute deterioration of trade. Indonesia's export performance since the crisis has widely fluctuated. Exports totaled U.S.$48.8 billion in 1998, U.S.$48.7 in 1999, U.S.$62.1 billion in 2000, and U.S.$56.3 billion in 2001. The robust exports in 2000 stemmed from increased oil and gas as well as non-oil and non-gas exports. In 2002 total exports increased slightly, to U.S.$57 billion. Manufacturing products remained the dominant component of the total non-oil and non-gas products. The consequences of the disastrous tsunami of December 2004 are not fully clear. The World Bank estimated the costs of "replacements" (including lost income) to be in the range of U.S. $4–5 billion. The direct impact of the disaster is expected to reduce the country's 2005 economic growth rate by 0.1 to 0.4 percent. At the same time, the World Bank stressed that it is impossible to enumerate the human suffering caused by the tsunami.

SEE ALSO CHINA; COEN, JAN PIETERSZOON; COFFEE; DEVELOPMENTAL STATE, CONCEPT OF THE; EAST INDIA COMPANY, DUTCH; EMPIRE, BRITISH; EMPIRE, DUTCH; EMPIRE, JAPANESE; EMPIRE, PORTUGUESE; ETHNIC GROUPS, CANTONESE; ETHNIC GROUPS, FUJIANESE; ETHNIC GROUPS, GUJARATI; INDIA; INDIAN OCEAN; LABORERS, COERCED; LABORERS, CONTRACT; MELAKA; MERCANTILISM; OPEC; PETROLEUM; PIRACY; RAFFLES, SIR THOMAS STAMFORD; RICE; RUBBER; SINGAPORE; SRI LANKA; SUGAR, MOLASSES, AND RUM; TEXTILES; TOBACCO; WOMEN TRADERS OF SOUTHEAST ASIA; ZHENG FAMILY.

BIBLIOGRAPHY

Booth, Anne. *The Indonesian Economy in the Nineteenth and Twentieth Centuries: A History of Missed Opportunities.* London: Macmillan, 1998.

Creutzberg, Piet. *Changing Economy in Indonesia*, Vol. 1: *Indonesia's Export Crops, 1816–1940.* The Hague, Netherlands: Nijhoff, 1975.

Korthales Altes, Willem L. *Changing Economy in Indonesia*, Vol. 12a: *General Trade Statistics, 1822–1940.* Amsterdam: Royal Tropical Institute, 1991.

Dick, Howard; Houben, Vincent J. H.; Lindblad, J. Thomas; Wie, Thee Kian. *The Emergence of a National Economy: An Economic History of Indonesia, 1800–2000.* Leiden, Netherlands: KITLV Press, 2002.

Knaap, Gerrit J. *Shallow Waters, Rising Tide: Shipping and Trade in Java around 1775.* Leiden, Royal Netherlands Institute of Southeast Asian and Caribbean Studies: KITLV Press, 1996.

Reid, Anthony J. S. *South East Asia in the Age of Commerce, 1450–1680.* 2 vols. New Haven, CT: Yale University Press, 1988–1993.

Jan Luiten van Zanden
Daan Marks

INDUSTRIALIZATION

Industrialization refers to the process by which an economy's resources are transferred from the agricultural and other primary sectors into the manufacturing sector. This process involves technological change (the expansion of fixed-capital intensive mechanized production) and organizational change, meaning specialized establishments in which workers and machinery are concentrated under one roof, supervised and managed, and subject to strict discipline and quality control. The industrialization process is also typically associated with important macroeconomic changes—more rapid growth of national income and productivity, and higher rates of investment and capital formation relative to preindustrial economies. Some historians also associate with industrialization important institutional changes such as the emergence of capitalism (ownership and control of production by owners of capital), or the replacement of medieval "moral economy" wage and interest rate regulations by formal competitive markets for goods, land and resources, labor, and capital (Mokyr 1999).

INDUSTRY BEFORE THE INDUSTRIAL REVOLUTION

There were essentially three types of manufacturing enterprises in preindustrial (primarily agricultural and/or commercial) economies: the artisan workshop, the centralized mill, and the domestic or cottage industry. Each of these types played a role in future industrialization, as the more flexible of these older types of enterprise could form the foundation for modern forms of industry.

Artisan production was important because many European urban craft centers (for example, Birmingham, a center of British artisan metalworking), drawing on supplies of skilled labor and entrepreneurship, eventually became locations of modern industry. Centralized mills

Tariff rates, various nations, 1820–1950

	Great Britain		France		Germany		United States	
	Avg	Nom	Avg	Nom	Avg	Nom	Avg	Nom
1820	50%				10%		40%	46%
1830								25%
1840		34%						24%
1850		15%		12%				21%
1860		8%		5%				36%
1970		5%		4%		6%		31%
1875	0%		14%		5%		45%	
1880		5%		7%		8%		30%
1890		5%		8%		9%		24%
1900		5%		8%		8%		25%
1913	0%		20%		13%		44%	
1925	5%		21%		20%		37%	
1931			30%		21%		48%	
1950	23%		18%		26%		14%	

Note: Nom refers to the nominal tariff rate.
Avg refers to the average tariff rate.

SOURCE: Compiled from Capie (1996) and Chang (2002).

THE GALE GROUP.

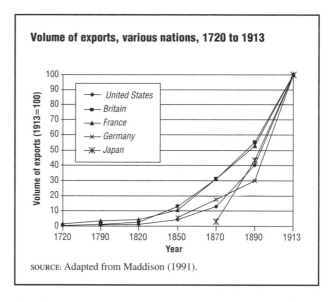

Volume of exports, various nations, 1720 to 1913

SOURCE: Adapted from Maddison (1991).

THE GALE GROUP.

carried out production processes too large or energy-intensive to be performed in the home or small shop. Fulling mills serving the European woolen industry, charcoal iron smelters and hammer forges, glassworks, breweries, early paper mills, and American grist and saw-mills were either "furnace industries" or required water power to operate, even before 1750. This kind of enterprise was especially important in Colonial America, where mills processed the output of a highly productive agricultural and natural resource economy, and mill owners were tied closely to commercial networks for marketing that output (McCusker and Menard 1991).

Perhaps most important for the course of future industrialization was rural domestic industry. Seventeenth- and eighteenth-century Europe witnessed the expansion of regionally concentrated industries connected to inter-regional or international trade in sectors including Yorkshire woolen cloth, Essex silk, Flanders linen, Lyon silk, Sambre-Meuse nails and guns, metalworks in the Siegerland, Silesian linen, and cottons, linen, and wool in the French Nord. In the United States after 1750 boot and shoe making, nail making, and some textile production, especially the high-quality specialty textile sector in the Philadelphia area, were of this nature, as were much food processing, cotton manufacturing, silk reeling, and some silk weaving in Japan. Typically, merchants distributed raw materials to domestic workers who performed manufacturing processes in the home, using traditional hand technologies. In this "putting-out" system, the merchant controlled access to raw materials and to markets. This type of industry enjoyed several cost advantages relative to the urban artisan sector, including the low opportunity cost for off-season agricultural labor, use of women and children, exploitation of an advanced division of labor, and low overhead costs.

Often associated with domestic industry were the "protofactories," which were agglomerations of workers using more-or-less traditional hand technologies that were very important in the development of the future factory sector. Calico-printing shops, wool-scribbling and -finishing mills, and handloom-weaving sheds in England, France, the Northeastern United States, and pre-industrial Japan, early centralized metalworking establishments such as Matthew Boulton's Soho works, Swiss watchmakers' workshops, early American water-powered woodworking and clock-making shops, and many others all fall into this category. In many cases these centralized workshops prepared and/or finished the work of rural outworkers. The primary rationale for these centralized workplaces was organizational. Direct process supervision allowed improved quality control, protection of valuable raw materials from embezzlement, enforcement of a more intensive work pace, improved design of work tasks to exploit the division of labor, and a greater level of secrecy for any innovations. Many of these shops also improved productivity through the introduction of small-scale machinery and water power, and by relying on cheap female and child labor. The scale of these shops could be large—several hundred workers in some (rare) cases.

There was no clear path from any one of these pre-industrial forms of industry to industrialization proper. Even "protoindustrial" rural areas might later deindustrialize for any number of reasons, especially if later industrial development elsewhere reestablished a comparative

Exports of manufactures in 1913

(percentage of country's total manufacturing exports, values at current prices)

	France	Belgium	Germany	Switz-erland	Great Britain
Chemicals	10.0%	14.3%	13.8%	6.9%	6.1%
Metals and metal goods	10.7%	31.0%	23.1%	4.4%	18.6%
Machinery	3.6%	4.6%	13.4%	10.3%	9.7%
Road vehicles and transport	6.7%	7.7%	3.8%	1.5%	6.4%
Other manufactures	27.1%	18.7%	27.1%	24.5%	10.8%
Textiles and clothing	41.9%	23.8%	18.8%	52.4%	48.4%

Note: Data for Belgium include Luxembourg.

SOURCE: Adapted from Heywood (1992).

THE GALE GROUP.

Per capita exports, 1830–1910

(current $, 3-yr. annual avg)

	1830	1860	1880	1910
Belgium	5	19	43	85
France	3	11	15	29
Germany	3	11	16	27
Switzerland	12	31	50	60
Great Britain	8	22	30	48
Europe	3		12	18

SOURCE: Adapted from Heywood (1992).

THE GALE GROUP.

advantage in agriculture for a given region. Where urban artisan or rural industrial regions were favorably located, with good transport links to markets and raw material sources, the existing supply of industrially skilled, market-oriented labor and skilled entrepreneurs with access to substantial financial resources could most likely spur full-fledged industrialization. Even then, industrialization was far from comprehensive, as many British, European, American, and Japanese industries (especially consumer-goods industries) retained their artisan or decentralized household characters well into the late nineteenth century (and even later, in the case of Japan). Industrialization and the factory system often worked in tandem with these older modes of production rather than, or prior to, fully displacing them (Pollard 1981; Hudson 2005; Crawcour 1997a, b).

INDUSTRIALIZATION AND TRADE EXPANSION

The initial burst of industrialization in continental Europe coincided with the first big wave of economic globalization that began after 1815 and ended with the onset of World War I. International capital flows, migration, and trade flows all grew rapidly during this period.

This wave of globalization was driven by three important factors—falling transport costs, declining communication costs, and changes in economic policy (reductions in trade barriers)—each of which was influenced in some way by the industrialization process. First, transport costs fell rather dramatically during this period. Both organizational and technological innovation played key roles in these cost reductions. Between 1600 and 1850 productivity growth in ocean shipping was driven by organizational changes, including improved organization and coordination of ports, which re-

duced waiting time, increased specialization in routes and cargoes, which allowed faster learning by doing, and the removal of guns from merchant ships, which allowed construction of lighter ships requiring smaller crews. After 1850 technological change moved to the fore with the development of the steamship. Between 1855 and 1910 improvements in metallurgy and mechanical-engineering technology reduced steamship coal consumption (and thus crew sizes), made masts and rigging more reliable and easier to manage (also reducing crew size), reduced breakdowns at sea, improved navigation, and permitted increased size and carrying capacity with reduced weight, all while substantially lowering the price of steamships over the period. At the same time, a new technology for overland transportation—the railroad—was helping to integrate markets within individual countries, while bringing interior areas within reach of world markets. Railroads had several advantages over inland water transportation: speed, and the capacities to deliver cargo from point of production to market without multiple loading and unloading, to be built through rugged terrain at a fraction of the cost of canals, and to operate year-round, even in cold climates. Technological change also improved inland water transportation because the diffusion of the steamboat cut upstream river transport costs during the same period (Weil 2005).

New technology also helped to expand the volume of world trade through reductions in communication costs. The advent of the steamship reduced the time required for information to flow from London to New York from three weeks in 1815 to ten days by 1860. The laying of transatlantic telegraph cables further decreased the interval to one minute by 1914. The telegraph played a fundamental role in coordinating economic activity over long distance because there were no really close alternative means for rapid long-distance communication of large amounts of information (Weil 2005).

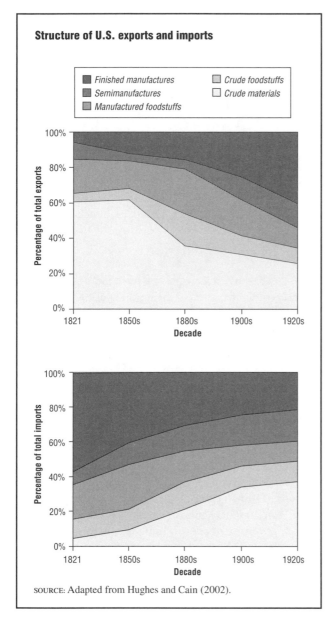

Structure of U.S. exports and imports

Finished manufactures
Semimanufactures
Manufactured foodstuffs
Crude foodstuffs
Crude materials

SOURCE: Adapted from Hughes and Cain (2002).

THE GALE GROUP.

Finally, changes in trade policy that facilitated world-trade expansion during the second half of the nineteenth century may have been partly driven by the effects of British industrialization. Reduced worldwide trade barriers would ensure ample markets for the growing output of British industry, as well as provide manufacturers access to cheap raw materials and workers with low-priced food (Gourevitch 1986).

The British tariff reductions of the 1830s and 1840s have sometimes been described as an act of "free-trade imperialism," in those British manufacturing interests were hoping to head off Continental industrialization by enforcing a worldwide free-trade regime. To an extent this was successful, as Britain and France in 1860 signed the Cobden-Chevalier trade treaty that ushered in a period of Continental trade liberalization. Between 1850 and 1870, British, French, and German exports all surged ahead of those of the United States, which until 1945 had probably the most protected manufacturing sector in the world (Chang 2002).

Other national policies that also served to reduce internal trade barriers and bring more domestic producers within reach of international markets include internal free-trade initiatives such as the establishment German Zollverein in 1834 and the U. S. Constitution's commerce clause that prohibited state-level regulation of interstate commerce, as well as public subsidies for internal transportation projects such as roads, canals, and railroads.

After 1945 a second wave of globalization began, and facets of continuing industrialization too have affected this one. Transport costs continued to fall, in part due to innovations such as containerization of ships, which led to significant increases in the speed at which ships could be loaded. The development of the airplane and airfreight sector not only reduced costs and increased speed, but also allowed new types of commodities to enter world trade. Communication costs also continued to drop with the development of new information-processing technologies. Technological change in materials and products has also resulted in large declines in the value-to-weight ratio of GDP and thus goods that are easier to transport. Finally, a series of reductions in trade barriers negotiated under the postwar General Agreement on Trade and Tariffs (GATT) and later the World Trade Organization (WTO) have seen average tariff rates fall from 40 percent in 1945 to 6 percent by 2000. As before, the cause of postwar free trade was championed by the world's industrial leader and leading economic power, this time the United States (Weil 2005).

INDUSTRIALIZATION AND TRADE PATTERNS

Because industrialization involves a change in the output mix, economies undergoing this process typically observe substantial changes in their international trading relationships as well.

BRITAIN This effect of industrialization on the direction of trade flows can be seen quite clearly in nineteenth-century Britain. As British industrialization progressed, Britain moved to a trade-surplus position based on global dominance in low-cost manufactured commodities of relatively high quality. Technological change spurred these changes in British trade patterns, as the key industries of the First Industrial Revolution—cotton textiles, pig and wrought iron, engineering, and coal—were all important export commodities. More efficient pro-

Japanese trade structure, 1890–1965

	Exports				Imports		
		Manufactured goods				Raw materials	
	Primary	Textiles	Light	Heavy	Food	(coal, oil)	Mfg
1890	32.5%	36.2%	11.5%	19.8%	24.6%	12.7%	62.7%
1913	15.3%	55.0%	16.1%	13.6%	15.2%	36.9%	47.9%
1925	12.6%	66.1%	11.2%	10.1%	19.8%	42.2%	38.0%
1935	8.6%	49.2%	17.3%	24.9%	17.2%	44.5%	38.3%
1955	15.7%	32.3%	14.3%	37.7%	28.8%	59.7%	11.5%
1965	6.0%	16.9%	13.8%	63.3%	18.7%	59.3%	22.0%

SOURCE: Adapted from Ito (1992).

THE GALE GROUP.

duction methods allowed British firms to capture export markets with cheaper goods. At the same time, the cotton-textile industry's voracious appetite for raw cotton produced a enormous demand for imports from the southern United States (Harley 2004).

Other important British export commodities in 1850 included linen goods, manufactures, silk manufactures, earthenware pottery, machinery and millwork, paper stationery, and glass manufactures, all industries that underwent significant technological or organizational changes during the first half of the nineteenth century. The most important imported goods included raw wool and cotton, sugar, corn meal and flour, tea, raw silk, coffee, and flax; later, imports of American grain and beef would grow (Temin 1997).

CONTINENTAL EUROPE Industrializing regions on the Continent typically ended up with "intermediary" trade patterns: some manufactured goods (especially "intermediate" goods such as pig iron or textile yarn) and capital equipment would be imported from advanced countries such as Britain, while their own manufactures would be exported to less-advanced regions of Eastern and Southern Europe (Pollard 1981).

UNITED STATES The industrialization of the United States in the nineteenth and early twentieth centuries—based on steel and metallurgy (including the Bessemer and open-hearth processes), rail transportation, electric power and communications (the telegraph), and the "American System" for high-volume production of complex mechanical products such as firearms, agricultural machinery, office equipment, sewing machines, bicycles, and engines—also coincided with a shift in the structure of U.S. trade away from agriculture and toward manufactured goods. There was also a shift over time in the direction of U. S. trade; in 1860 three-fourths of U.S. exports were destined for Europe, and three-fifths of U.S. imports originated there. By 1925 only about half of U.S.

exports ended up in Europe, and less than a third of U.S. imports originated there. During this period, trade with Canada, Latin America, and especially Asia grew substantially (Hughes and Cain 2002).

JAPAN The beginning of Japanese industrialization (with modern economic growth and rising levels of saving and investment) dates to two events: the opening to the West in the 1850s and, especially, the Meiji Restoration of 1868. In the 1870s significant government efforts to introduce Western production methods in textiles, iron and steel, and engineering began. Between 1880 and 1900 vertically integrated, mechanized cotton-spinning and -weaving plants were established, using modified versions of British technology. In heavy industry, the Japanese iron and steel industry was established under the aegis of government subsidy and protection, as were railway works and shipyards. Soon, indigenous Japanese efforts in textiles and engineering were beginning to bear fruit. The Toyoda firm by 1913 was operating possibly the first mass-production facility in Japanese industry, producing textile-weaving machinery with standardized, interchangeable components (Crawcour 1997a, b; Bernstein 1997).

The Japanese industrial economy truly came into its own in the aftermath of World War II, grabbing market share in industries such as steel and automobiles that had previously been dominated by the United States. In steelmaking, Japanese producers were the first to introduce continuous casting and basic oxygen furnaces, providing a large cost advantage over U.S. producers using traditional technologies. In the 1950s and 1960s Japanese automobile producers such as Toyota and Nissan pioneered a technological-organizational system known as "lean production" that allowed the production of a wider variety of very high-quality products at low prices. In the last few decades Japanese firms have gained a foothold in high-technology sectors such as advanced machine tools,

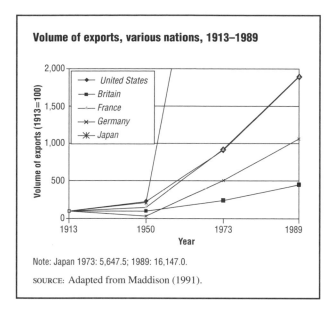

Volume of exports, various nations, 1913–1989

Volume of exports (1913=100)

- ◆ United States
- ■ Britain
- ┼ France
- ✕ Germany
- ✳ Japan

2,000

1,500

1,000

500

1913   1950   1973   1989

Year

Note: Japan 1973: 5,647.5; 1989: 16,147.0.

SOURCE: Adapted from Maddison (1991).

THE GALE GROUP.

consumer electronics, and semiconductors by making large-scale investments in research and development (R&D) and education of scientific and technical personnel, and by developing institutions to link universities, industrial R&D labs, and regional R&D centers in order to speed diffusion of best-practice technologies.

Japanese industrialization coincided, as usual, with important changes in international trading patterns. At first, primary products such as silk dominated Japanese exports, whereas imports were heavily biased in favor of industrial goods. By 1900, however, textiles and other light industrial goods had become important export commodities, and imports of these were falling. Between the world wars a similar process occurred with respect to heavy engineering—railroad equipment, shipbuilding, and so on (Von Tunzelman 1995).

ASIAN NICS In the Asian newly industrialized countries (NICs), modern economic growth in both South Korea and Taiwan preceded World War II. Both had higher GDP growth rates than did Japan during the interwar period, and the Taiwanese manufacturing sector was growing rapidly as well. Both nations were also so devastated by World War II that per-capita incomes there were no higher than in some African nations as late as 1960, but the history of relatively rapid growth (as well as both nations' histories as economic colonies of Japan) meant that Korea and Taiwan already ranked rather highly on indicators of "social capability"—especially a literate and well-educated population, a well-developed infrastructure, and openness to foreign trade relative to other developing countries at that time.

From the early 1960s to the late 1980s growth rates of Korea, Taiwan, Hong Kong, and Singapore ranged from 7 to 10 percent per year, with high growth rates of industrial output (12% per year in Taiwan during the 1950s) and manufactured exports (30 to 40% growth in Korea between 1962 and 1979). High rates of investment and capital accumulation, as well as borrowing of technologies from the more advanced economies, drove this development process. In terms of trade patterns, the East Asian industrializers reproduced the Japanese pattern described above—from exporting primary products to light industry, to heavy industry, to more technologically advanced products—but in a far shorter period of time. In the case of Korea the swift rise in manufacturing exports also coincided with significant trade liberalization in the mid-1960s (Song 1997; Vogel 1991; von Tunzelmann 1995; Wade 1990).

EXPLAINING CHANGING TRADE PATTERNS

Two concepts that may explain changing trade patterns over time will be explored here: the traditional theory of comparative advantage, and the newer "technology gap" hypothesis.

COMPARATIVE ADVANTAGE In neoclassical economic theory, international trade patterns are the result of comparative advantage, which itself is a consequence of a country's endowments of factors of production. Because one of the characteristics of industrialization is a permanent increase in the investment-to-GDP ratio, and thus in the rate of capital accumulation, it might be predicted that industrialized nations, due to a larger capital endowment, will tend to export capital-intensive goods.

At first glance the historical experiences of Britain, Europe, the United States, and Japan and Asia might seem to confirm this prediction, but at least in the case of the United States, the prediction was shown to be incorrect. The so-called "Leontief Paradox" refers to the finding that the United States was exporting relatively labor-intensive goods rather than capital-intensive ones, despite its high-wage structure. Furthermore, many observed trade patterns do not seem to coincide easily with the predictions of neoclassical trade theory. For example, what explains the fact that nineteenth-century Britain imported finished textiles from France and Switzerland, or that France and Germany both were importing textiles from each other, or that an advanced-technology country, Belgium, was exporting a primary product, coal?

TECHNOLOGY GAPS "Technology-gap" models seek to explain such trade patterns by appealing to dynamic features of technological change. In this view, learning and related feedback effects may cause nations to become "locked into" patterns of specialization. For example, regions that industrialize before others may be able to take advantage of "agglomeration economies" that prevent other locations from easily copying the new techniques. This could be the case if technologies are firm- or location-specific, in that they embody "tacit" knowledge that exists in the heads of skilled workers. The nineteenth-century British cotton-textile sector may provide one such example. It has been argued that the keys to long-term British domination of that industry include factors such as localized knowledge about technology (e.g., machine and factory design and construction), the existence of a pool of skilled labor experienced in keeping factories running and product quality high, the highly developed Liverpool cotton exchange that could ensure easy availability of a wide variety of raw cotton, and a global network of marketing specialists that other countries found difficult to copy. Thus the British started off with enormous advantages in material, production, and distribution costs (von Tunzelmann 1995; Freeman and Soete 1997).

In the "second industrial revolution" of the later nineteenth century, a similar story can be told about U.S. (Northeastern and Upper Midwestern) dominance in mass-production sectors. The success of the "American System" depended on several distinctive characteristics of the U. S. economy. One factor was access to cheap, abundant natural resources. More importantly, the U.S. economy was large and well integrated by an efficient transportation system, a single currency, a common language, and common technological standards for transportation, power systems, and so on. A third factor was the nature of "mass-production" technology—its complexity, the incremental nature of productivity-improving innovation, the need for learning by doing to master it—which militated against quick or easy imitation of these techniques. Finally, the key competitive advantage for the northern United States ultimately may have been the community of skilled engineers and mechanics that made the system work, made possible in part by public investments in compulsory education and private investments in on-the-job training. This, too, was a factor of production that was not cheap or easy to call into existence quickly (Nelson and Wright 1992).

The result may have been a "technology gap" between advanced and backward economies that plays a key role in determining trade patterns. For example, this kind of dynamic was at work in establishing the complex, ever-changing trade patterns that characterized industrializing continental Europe, in which advanced nations exported products with high modern-technology content to "backward nations" who specialized in products with low (or no) technological complexity (Pollard 1981).

OPENNESS AND RAPID ECONOMIC GROWTH

Development economists have found that countries enjoying high levels of GDP tend to be economically open to trade and foreign-capital inflows. Furthermore, poorer countries that are open to trade seem to grow faster than do rich countries, whereas poor countries that are not open to trade grow more slowly. These findings suggest that there may be linkages between economic openness, industrialization, and rapid economic growth (Weil 2005).

TRADE AND EFFICIENCY Openness to international trade permits a larger potential market that may allow domestic firms to reduce costs through specialization, comparative advantage, and scale economies. Increased competition from foreign firms also reduces market power of domestic firms and provides greater incentive for cost reductions and innovation. In Japan, for example, the effects of the 1850s opening of trade included a doubling of the production of raw silk between 1858 and 1863, as new silk-reeling technology was introduced that increased both labor productivity and quality levels (Weil 2005; Crawcour 1997a).

Despite these theoretical advantages of openness, however, most industrial countries have not followed a pure free-trade policy on the path to industrialization. Most appear to have followed some variation of a two-stage policy. At first, there is usually a temporary phase of import substitution. In early stages of British, European, American, and Asian industrialization, production for the domestic market tended to be most important at the outset, and export success came later. Britain, for example, utilized protective tariffs until the 1840s; U. S. tariffs were the highest in the world during its period of industrialization (a period which began in earnest during the Jeffersonian "embargo" of 1807 to 1809, when the United States was cut off from British manufactured goods imports). The most successful developed economies typically follow the import-substitution strategy with a more "outward-looking" growth strategy that has a number of common features across nations. Successful industrializers maintain a degree of openness with respect to the rest of the world. Often, initial protection is removed, as with Britain's move to free trade in the 1840s and Korea's trade liberalization of the 1960s. There is also a willingness to borrow production techniques from those on the technological frontier. Successful firms in these countries are allowed, or even encouraged, to compete internationally. Policies such as export subsidies and quality-control regulation for exported goods were used by Britain in the late eighteenth and early nineteenth centuries, and by Taiwan and Korea in the mid-twentieth century. Other key features of the outward-looking strategy include substantial public and private investment in physical infrastructure (transportation, communication, energy and power systems) and human capital (education, training); macroeconomic stability, with government borrowing and monetary policies constrained by international institutions such as the pre–World War I Gold Standard, or the Bretton Woods (1944–1971) system for the late industrializers; and relatively flexible labor and capital markets (Chang 2002; Perkins et al 2001).

FOREIGN INVESTMENT AND CAPITAL ACCUMULATION In theory, faster rates of investment and capital accumulation, and thus economic growth, can also be achieved by importing capital, thus breaking the constraint placed on domestic investment by domestic savings. The United States between 1850 and 1910, for example, consistently augmented its stock of national savings by borrowing one-half to one percentage point of GDP annually, and foreign investment played a key role in transportation investment and the financing of industrialization. Modern research shows, however, that there is still a high (though falling) correlation between domestic savings and investment rates, suggesting that developing countries have not taken full advantage of this potential growth accelerator (Weil 2005; Edelstein 1982).

BORROWING TECHNOLOGY Perhaps the most important linkage between openness and rapid economic growth lies in the ability of nations to increase domestic productivity by importing more efficient production and management techniques from abroad. Every successful developed economy from Britain in the eighteenth century to the Asian "Tigers" in the twentieth century have done this, although borrowed techniques almost always have to be adapted to their new economic environments, as the United States discovered when adapting British versions of coke smelting, or the steam engine, to the U.S. resource endowment (expensive labor and capital, but cheap natural resources); and as the Japanese did when they introduced British cotton-textile machinery into an environment in which labor was relatively abundant during the late nineteenth century (Weil 2005).

SEE ALSO DEVELOPMENTAL STATE, CONCEPT OF THE; INDUSTRIAL REVOLUTION; LABOR, TYPES OF.

BIBLIOGRAPHY

Bernstein, Jeffrey R. "Toyoda Automatic Looms and Toyota Automobiles." In *Creating Modern Capitalism: How Entrepreneurs, Companies, and Countries Triumphed in Three Industrial Revolutions,* ed. Thomas K. McCraw. Cambridge, MA: Harvard University Press, 1997.

Capie, Forrest. "Trade Policy and Growth: Some European Experiences (1850–1940)." In *The Nature of Industrialization,* Vol. 5: *International Trade and British Economic Growth from the Eighteenth Century to the Present Day,* ed. Peter Mathias and John A. Davis. Oxford, U.K.: Oxford University Press, 1996.

Chang, Ha-Joon. *Kicking Away the Ladder: Development Strategy in Historical Perspective.* London: Anthem Press, 2002.

Crawcour, E. Sydney. "Economic Change in the Nineteenth Century." In *The Economic Emergence of Modern Japan,* ed. Kozo Yamamura. Cambridge, U.K.: Cambridge University Press, 1997a.

Crawcour, E. Sydney. "Industrialization and Technological Change, 1885–1920." In *The Economic Emergence of Modern Japan,* ed. Kozo Yamamura. Cambridge, U.K.: Cambridge University Press, 1997b.

Edelstein, Michael. "Accumulation in the United States and its Pull on U. K. Savings." In *Overseas Investment in the Age of High Imperialism: The United Kingdom 1850 to 1914.* New York: Columbia University Press, 1982.

Freeman, Chris, and Soete, Luc. *The Economics of Industrial Innovation,* 3rd edition. Cambridge, MA: Massachusetts Institute of Technology Press, 1997.

Gourevitch, Peter. *Politics in Hard Times: Comparative Responses to International Economic Crises.* Ithaca, NY: Cornell University Press, 1986.

Harley, C. Knick. "Trade: Discovery, Mercantilism, and Technology." In *The Cambridge Economic History of Modern Britain,* Vol. 1: *Industrialization,* ed. Roderick Floud and Paul Johnson. Cambridge, U.K.: Cambridge University Press, 2004.

Heywood, Colin. *The Development of the French Economy, 1750–1914.* Cambridge, U.K.: Cambridge University Press, 1992.

Hudson, Pat. "Industrial Organization and Structure." In *The Cambridge Economic History of Modern Britain,* Vol. 1: *Industrialization,* ed. Roderick Floud and Paul Johnson. Cambridge, U.K.: Cambridge University Press, 2004.

Hughes, Jonathan, and Cain, Louis P. *American Economic History,* 6th edition. Reading, MA: Addison-Wesley, 2002.

Ito, Takatoshi. *The Japanese Economy.* Cambridge, MA: Massachusetts Institute of Technology Press, 1992.

Maddison, Angus. *Dynamic Forces in Capitalist Development: A Long-Run Comparative View.* Oxford, U.K.: Oxford University Press, 1991.

McCusker, John J., and Menard, Russell R. *The Economy of British America, 1607–1789.* Chapel Hill: University of North Carolina Press, 1991.

Mokyr, Joel. "The New Economic History and the Industrial Revolution." In *The British Industrial Revolution: an Economic Perspective,* ed. Joel Mokyr. Boulder, CO: Westview Press, 1999.

Nelson, Richard R., and Wright, Gavin. "The Rise and Fall of American Technological Leadership: The Postwar Era in Historical Perspective." *Journal of Economic Literature* 30, no. 4 (December 1992): 1931–1964.

Perkins, Dwight H., et al. *Economics of Development,* 5th edition. New York: W. W. Norton, 2001.

Pollard, Sidney. *Peaceful Conquest: The Industrialization of Europe, 1760–1970.* Oxford, U.K.: Oxford University Press, 1981.

Song, Byung-Nak. *The Rise of the Korean Economy,* 2nd edition. Hong Kong: Oxford University Press, 1997.

Temin, Peter. "Two Views of the British Industrial Revolution." *Journal of Economic History* 57, no. 1 (March 1997): 63–82.

Vogel, Ezra F. *The Four Little Dragons: The Spread of Industrialization in East Asia.* Cambridge, MA: Harvard University Press, 1991.

Von Tunzelmann, G. N. *Technology and Industrial Progress: The Foundations of Economic Growth.* Cheltenham, U.K.: Edward Elgar, 1995.

Wade, Robert. *Governing the Market: Economic Theory and the Role of Government in East Asian Industrialization.* Princeton, NJ: Princeton University Press, 1990.

Weil, David N. *Economic Growth.* Boston: Pearson Addison-Wesley, 2005.

Thomas M. Geraghty

INDUSTRIAL REVOLUTION

Britain's mid-nineteenth-century economy is often referred to as the "workshop of the world." The Industrial Revolution's modern industries dominated world markets; Paul Bairoch (1982) calculates that Britain produced two-thirds of the world's output of "new technology" products. Cotton-textile makers, who exported two-thirds of their output, were the most committed to serving word markets, but makers of other textiles and iron and iron products also sold nearly half their output abroad. These industries, greatly expanded by their successes in export markets, had transformed Britain into the world's first urban industrial society. That transformation, in turn, depended on imports of raw materials and food.

Trade has a clear association with the British Industrial Revolution. A systematic examination of the connection can usefully focus on three questions: First, to what extent did the late-eighteenth-century technological breakthroughs that established the "new technology" industries depend on Britain's position as a trading nation? Second, to what extend did trade change Britain's economic structure? Third, how greatly did Britain's expanding trade contribute to economic growth as measured by per capita income?

EIGHTEENTH-CENTURY TRADE AND THE INDUSTRIAL REVOLUTION

Late-eighteenth-century Britain was already a great manufacturing exporting nation, but cotton textile and pig and wrought iron, the great export products of the early nineteenth century, did not yet contribute. British cotton manufacture depended on the prohibition of Indian cottons, and much of the bar iron that British hardware manufacturers used was imported. Exports consisted of woolens, hardware, and other goods. These manufactured goods exports, particularly to markets in the Americas, had grown rapidly during the eighteenth century.

By the third quarter of the eighteenth century, Britain occupied the central position in a multilateral world trading system. Imports—consisting mainly of primary staple products—were paid for by exports of manufactured goods and the earnings from shipping and other international services. A disproportionate share of British manufactured exports sold in the mainland colonies in North America as part of a multilateral trading pattern. The pattern, although channeled by mercantilist regulation, reflected comparative advantage and Yankee ingenuity. New England and Newfoundland fish, the grain of the middle colonies, and the rice of the lower South fed the West Indian sugar plantations and also found eager buyers in Southern Europe. Equally important, a large portion of the tobacco from the Chesapeake Bay was re-exported through British ports to continental Europe. In turn, earnings from these exports passed to the metropolis to pay for manufactured imports, and contributed to England's access to Spanish- and Portuguese-American specie that was exchanged for textiles and tea in the trade to India and China.

Nicholas F. R. Crafts (1985) estimates that exports (already some 80% manufactured goods) amounted to nearly 15 percent of British national income in 1760—a figure comparable to the early nineteenth century (although by then the share of manufactured goods had increased to over 90%). This great expansion of trade certainly stimulated the rise of commercial and manufacturing expertise that supported the Industrial Revolution. The presence of already established export markets supported the great expansion of new sectors. It is less obvious, however, that trade made any important direct contribution to the technological breakthroughs in cotton, steam production, and iron that constitute the "Industrial Revolution." As we have already seen, these were not great exports, and foreign demand can hardly have stimulated initial breakthroughs. It would be more correct to see the breakthrough as successful achievement of an import competing strategy. Somewhat unusually, that strategy resulted in the development of great export industries.

TRADE AND ECONOMIC STRUCTURE: THE URBAN INDUSTRIAL SOCIETY

Trade has its most direct impact on an economy's structure. Fundamentally, trade allows the concentration of resources in the production of those goods in which an economy excels, and exchanges these goods to obtain imports. Britain became more industrial as a result of trade, and became an urban industrial economy by the middle of the nineteenth century as a result of the mushrooming of cities, such as Manchester, with new export industries. In 1840 the cotton-textile industry produced more than 100 times what it produced in 1760, and the metal industries (primary iron and hardware combined) produced

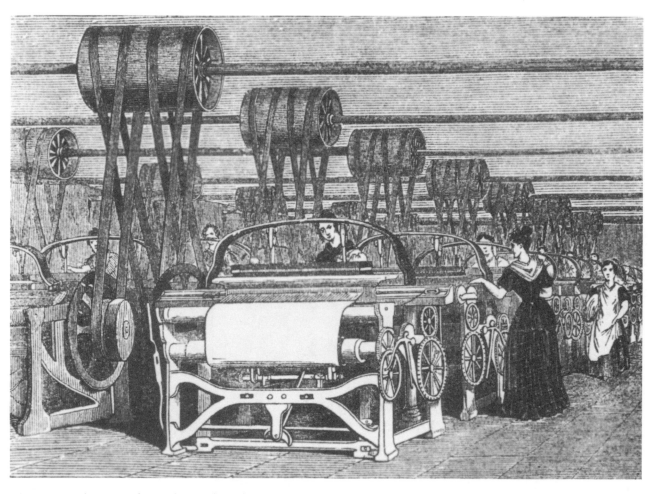

Women operating power looms during the Industrial Revolution in 1844. *As machines replaced skilled laborers, the new urban economy thrived on the toils of inexpensive workers including women and children.* HULTON ARCHIVE/GETTY IMAGES. REPRODUCED BY PERMISSION.

15 times as much as before. Without qualification, however, those figures are misleading. These industries grew because spectacular technological breakthroughs allowed British firms to produce much more efficiently (i.e., with fewer inputs) and competition drove prices down to reflect this technological improvement. Export volumes increased rapidly—British custom's unchanged official values show a nearly fivefold increase in the 1780s and the 1840s (Davis 1979); a recent calculation (Cuenca Estaben 1997) suggests a tenfold increase between 1760 and 1830. We have already seen, however, that the share of British income exported was not significantly higher in the early nineteenth century than it had been before the American Revolution. The reasons for discrepancy are twofold. First, British income nearly tripled, population roughly doubled, and per capita income increased about a quarter. Second, and more importantly, exports grew primarily as a result of technological breakthroughs that radically lowered their prices and thus their value. Urban industry was a result more of the steam engine's potential

for concentrating mechanical power than of an increase in the share of national activity going to manufacturing because of an expansion of exports.

TRADE AND GROWTH

Britain's successful industrialization went hand in hand with expansion of the volume of exports, and it is tempting, but misleading, to assert that trade caused growth. Trade allows an economy to concentrate its resources on export and obtain goods it would have otherwise produced by trade. Foreign trade should be viewed as an "industry" that produces imports in exchange for sacrifices of exports. The "productivity" of this industry (that is to say, the final goods obtained from productive resources that made exports) crucially involve the "terms of trade"—the rate at which a given amount of exports (say, yards of cloth) exchanges for imports (say, quarters of wheat). The gains from trade depends on the extent to which trade improves the terms of trade, and on the im-

An early electric motor. *As Europe shifted from an agriculturally based economy to an industrial one during the mid-eighteenth century to mid-nineteenth century, innovations in machinery supported the growth of manufacturing facilities. The electric engine became a key invention that converted electrical energy into mechanical energy that powered these factories.* © BETTMANN/CORBIS. REPRODUCED BY PERMISSION.

portance of the foreign trade "industry" relative to other, domestic, industries.

It is difficult to assess how much the terms of trade might have moved had Britain lacked trading opportunities. Terms of trade over the nineteenth century gives some guidance. They fell dramatically from an index of 170 in 1820 to 100 in 1860 because of Britain's increasing productivity. They then rose to 130 late in the nineteenth century as the full application of steam and steel lowered the cost of making and, especially, shipping food and raw materials to Britain from hitherto remote parts of the globe. This 70 percent fall and 30 percent rise in the terms of trade can, perhaps, provide a guide to the terms of trade changes implied by self-sufficiency in, for example, 1840. As an illustration, consider the effect on national income of a reduction in the price of exportables relative to importables by, say, 50 percent. The share of imports in income in 1840 was 20 percent. If all of these goods increased in real cost by 50 percent (and surely many could have been produced domestically at a much lower increase in cost), self-sufficiency in 1840, then, would have cost Britain only about 10 percent of national income.

It is also often asserted that British producers attained a monopoly in "new technology" products that conferred important gains. This too is misleading. There was no monopoly; firms were too small. As a consequence, technological improvements that lowered costs caused prices to fall as well. Lower prices passed the benefits of technology to consumers; the foreign two-thirds of cotton-textile customers shared the benefits equally with domestic customers.

CONCLUSION

Britain's Industrial Revolution intertwined with an international economy undergoing epochal change. Expanding foreign trade accompanied the increasing sophistication of the British economy in the century before the Industrial Revolution. In the eighteenth century Britain financed sugar and tobacco imports by selling a multitude of manufactured goods to the North Americans who supplied food and timber to the West Indies. When the Industrial Revolution greatly cheapened British textiles and hardware, firms in these industries found their products in demand worldwide. Although trade undoubtedly stimulated Britain's industrialization, it is difficult to develop a causal connection from trade growth to the emergence of sustained modern economic growth. Specialization and trade, of course, provided gains for the economy, but quantifying these gains show them to have been quite small compared to the growth that emerged after the Industrial Revolution.

BIBLIOGRAPHY

Bairoch, Paul. "International Industrialization Levels from 1750 to 1980." *Journal of European Economic History* 11 (Fall 1982): 269–333.

Crafts, Nicholas F. R. *British Economic Growth During the Industrial Revolution.* Oxford, U.K.: Oxford University Press, 1985.

Cuenca Esteban, Javier. "The Rising Share of British Industrial Exports in Industrial Output, 1700–1851." *Journal of Economic History* 57, no. 4 (December 1997): 879–906.

Davis, Ralph. *The Industrial Revolution and British Overseas Trade.* Leicester, U.K.: Leicester University Press, 1979.

Harley, C. Knick. "Trade: Discovery, Mercantilism, and Technology." In *Cambridge Economic History of Britain since 1700,* volume 2: *1700–1860,* ed. R. Floud and P. Johnson. Cambridge, U.K.: Cambridge University Press, 2004.

C. Knick Harley

INFORMATION AND COMMUNICATIONS

Trade depends on information. Producers, buyers, sellers, and consumers all devote time and money to finding out what goods are available, where they are, who wants them, and how much they cost. Increasing the speed and efficiency of communication systems makes the gathering of this information easier, quicker, and cheaper, thus reducing the transaction costs that are incurred at every step in a trading chain. In general, therefore, the development of new communications methods and technologies has been an important factor in increasing the volume of trade in the modern era, and also in enabling that trade to be conducted over longer distances. It is also true,

however, that there are concerns and costs associated with each new method of sending and receiving information, and that the effect of individual changes on trading systems has often seemed ambiguous, at least in the short term.

THE ERA BEFORE TELECOMMUNICATIONS

Long-distance trade expanded greatly in the early-modern centuries, as European states developed maritime connections around the Atlantic rim and in the Indian Ocean. The private information networks of merchants were fundamental to this growth, and were established and reinforced by constant letter writing. Merchants' letters did not just contain information of direct relevance to the transaction at hand, but also reported more general news about the movements of shipping, the likely implications of political developments, and the honesty of fellow merchants. Such connections remained vulnerable, however, to slow and unreliable transport systems.

These problems began to be addressed seriously beginning in the early sixteenth century, in Europe's trade with the Western Hemisphere and the Far East. Better understanding of currents and winds led to more predictable sailing schedules, and the desirability of sugar and tobacco in European markets increased traffic to the point where even the smaller West Indian colonies could expect a monthly post from Europe. In the late seventeenth century, changes in printing and publishing led to a boom in the number of newspapers, and further improvements in maritime transport steadily reduced the time needed for news to appear in those papers. Some kinds of commercial information became public knowledge. Merchants could get the latest information about crops and prices from the newspapers, but they continued to use their own letter-writing networks to spread and gather news of more direct importance to them.

One of the vital elements in the efficiency of trade was the ability to track the movements of ships, and shipowners devised strategies for keeping as close a connection with their vessels as possible. The early newspapers, and especially *Lloyd's List,* devoted considerable efforts to gathering news of shipping arrivals and departures from distant ports. Before telecommunications, captains were instructed to write at every opportunity, sending messages back to their home port by any available post. Beginning in the seventeenth century, mail-carrying "packet" ships were routinely circulating mail faster than ordinary cargo vessels could sail, so that a well-organized merchant could send letters ahead of his vessel for collection on arrival.

A communication room in the SS Wilhelmina, a combination of passenger and cargo ship from the early twentieth century. *One of the key developments the allowed the trading industry to increase volume of goods transported and travel over longer distances was the use of wireless telegraphy. This technology was based on remote wiring associated with the telegraph and later evolved into early forms of radio.* © THE MARINERS MUSEUM/CORBIS. REPRODUCED BY PERMISSION.

Cumulative improvements in the volume and speed of information distribution continued into the first half of the nineteenth century, and great gains were made as a result of the better organization of existing methods and through the use of new transport technology. Formal national postal systems were created beginning in the 1840s; steamships began to operate routinely in northern European seas beginning in the 1830s; and railway networks were built in the 1840s and 1850s. By 1860 the cumulative impact of all these changes was that international news could be transmitted in about one-third of the time it had taken in 1820, at least between major trading centers. The importance of reliable communications for both strategic and commercial purposes was recognized in an increasing number of international treaties and agreements regulating mail, culminating in the Universal Postal Union of 1878.

THE TELECOMMUNICATIONS ERA

The second half of the nineteenth century saw the spread of new telecommunications systems, with the patenting of the electric telegraph in 1837 and of the telephone in 1876. Each device was being used in a growing network within a decade of its invention. In contrast to the incremental improvements in existing technology made in earlier decades, these developments represented a fundamental shift: Telecommunications enabled messages to travel faster than they could be physically carried. This had long been recognized as a major goal in trade, and many systems of signaling using lights, beacons, and flags had been tried. The harnessing of electricity finally made telegraphy practical over long distances, however, and Samuel Morse's experimental line between Washington and Baltimore carried its first message in 1844.

The real breakthrough in international trade came with the first undersea telegraph cables. Attempts to lay a trans-Atlantic telegraph cable in 1856 and 1858 failed to provide a sustainable service, and only in 1866 had cable technology and business confidence reached a point where a successful connection could be created. Thereafter, however, undersea cables proliferated, with over 300,000 miles of cable in use worldwide by 1914.

Telegraphs and telephones still needed a physical connection between the sender and receiver, but another series of new devices and systems overcame this limitation in the twentieth century and offered another set of opportunities (and challenges) for traders. Wireless telegraphy, radio, television, and computer networks, as well as mobile telephony, enabled businesses to improve their own internal communications and also to develop new ways of interacting with customers. In the late twentieth century, advertising in the broadcast media played an important role in the creation of global brands, which had major implications for the manufacture and distribution of consumer goods. Information technology became increasingly integrated, as different elements of corporate computer networks were used to encourage demand through advertising and sales and to manage supply through improved logistics.

Many older forms of business communication took advantage of the new technology, rather than be superseded. Newspapers were important customers of the first telegraph lines, printing "flash" columns of commodity prices and shipping rates. Keeping track of transport became an even more important element in expanding international trade. Shipping companies were early adopters of successive forms of telecommunications, always with the aim of reducing the time spent in port, thereby cutting the costs of trade. Global telegraph connections enabled vessels to communicate almost instantly with their owners every time they entered port, and the great increase in shipping movements and long-distance maritime trade in the late nineteenth century was managed by these methods. With the invention of the wireless telegraph, ships could finally be contacted while they were at sea. In 1902 the Cunard liner Lucania made the first Atlantic crossing in continuous wireless contact with the shore.

With the development of global telephone and satellite systems in the late twentieth century, shipping movements could be planned, monitored, and altered with increasing precision, further driving down the time spent in port as well as the associated costs to the shipowner. The same technology was also used to track items of cargo and was an important element in the adoption of containers: International logistics systems came to depend on monitoring the whereabouts of individual containers in the course of their journeys. Such control increased the efficiency of long-distance trade and especially the ability of manufacturing industries to organize just-in-time component supply networks on an international scale.

In addition to its vital role in managing the movement of goods, telecommunications quickly became crucial to the working of stock and commodity markets. Stockbrokers were among the most enthusiastic subscribers to the first telegraph systems in the 1840s. The international cotton trade was one of the first to engage in futures trading in the 1870s, and the rapid dissemination of all kinds of prices created increasingly integrated world markets. The financial sector continued to adopt the latest technology throughout the twentieth century, most famously when the London Stock Exchange moved to computerized trading in the "Big Bangs" of 1986 and 1997.

CONCLUSION

There has been a tendency for each new form of communications technology to be hailed as bringing about a revolution in trade and business. In fact, the most important point has been the development of a multifaceted information environment, in which businesses and consumers choose from a variety of technologies and methods, depending on the task at hand.

SEE ALSO Baltic Exchange; Books; Cargoes, Freight; Climate; Condorcet, Marie-Jean-Antoine-Nicolas de Caritat, Marquis de; Eastman, George; eBay; Gates, Bill; Hearst, William Randolph; International Trade Agreements; Lloyd's of London; Marconi, Guglielmo; Packet Boats; Shipping, Merchant; Subsidies; Travelers and Travel; Watson, Thomas, Sr., and Thomas Jr.

BIBLIOGRAPHY

Crowley, David, and Heyer, Paul, eds. *Communication in History: Technology, Culture, and Society.* London: Longman, 1991.

Headrick, Daniel R. *The Tentacles of Progress: Technology Transfer in the Age of Imperialism, 1850–1940.* Oxford: Oxford University Press, 1988.

Kaukiainen, Yrjö. "Shrinking the World: Improvements in the Speed of Information Transmission, c.1820–1870." *European Review of Economic History* 5 (2001): 1–28.

McCusker, John J., and Gravesteijn, Cora. *The Beginnings of Commercial and Financial Journalism: The Commodity Price Currents, Exchange Rate Currents, and Money Currents of Early Modern Europe.* Amsterdam: NEHA, 1991.

Scholl, Lars U. "The Global Communications Industry and Its Impact on International Shipping before 1914." In

Global Markets: The Internationalisation of the Sea Transport Industries since 1850, ed. David J. Starkey and Gelina Harlaftis. St. John's, Newfoundland: International Maritime Economic History Association, 1998.

Steele, Ian K. *The English Atlantic: An Exploration of Communication and Community.* Oxford: Oxford University Press, 1986.

Winston, Brian. *Media, Technology, and Society: A History from the Telegraph to the Internet.* London: Routledge, 1998.

Graeme J. Milne

INSTITUTIONAL ASPECTS OF WORLD TRADE

Institutions are the legal, social, political, and cultural structures that condition economic activity. These institutions exist because they tend to reduce transaction costs associated with trade, either among individuals within a country or among individuals between countries. Research in what has become known as the "New Institutional Economics" has generated a great amount of literature explaining the role of institutions in economic growth and development. International trade is complementary to the growth process, and is affected by the institutional structure of trading economies. Political institutions determine the degree of democracy that a country enjoys as well as the potential for modifying existing institutions. The legal framework that defines property rights and establishes the process for enforcing contracts usually reflects the extent of individual freedom provided by the political process.

EARLY PROPERTY RIGHTS

Exchange of goods and services requires the establishment of a property-rights system, because one cannot trade something unless he or she can transfer the ownership to another person. Definition of ownership (property rights) must be established before trade can exist. A legal system that enforces property rights and contracts for the exchange of property is necessary as well. Otherwise, a person would always run the risk of having property confiscated by a more powerful market participant, possibly the government. For the same reason, businesses will be reluctant to invest in a country with a weak property-rights system.

Early international trade was frequently undertaken or controlled by the government, which determined who had the right to engage in foreign commerce as well as what goods could be traded. Most countries, for national security reasons, continue to retain the right to restrict trade, but institutional structures have evolved to increase individual freedom regarding what is traded and

Police prepare pirated CDs and video tapes for destruction in Miyun, China, 1996. The international enforcement of intellectual property rights is a key issue for the World Trade Organization. AP/WIDE WORLD PHOTOS. REPRODUCED BY PERMISSION.

with whom. Historically, some governments have established institutions to promote international trade whereas others have established institutions to diminish trade.

Mercantilism in the seventeenth and eighteenth centuries resulted in institutional structures that promoted exports but discouraged imports of finished products to generate an inflow of gold. Tax systems to confiscate excess gold inflows were necessary to prevent price adjustments under the specie-flow mechanism that would diminish the trade surplus. Governments encouraged industries that would produce export goods and protected import-competing industries from foreign competition. Colonies were founded to provide raw materials for domestic manufacturing and, in some cases, to provide markets for these domestic manufactured goods.

Establishment of colonies resulted in the spread of a particular country's institutions to new areas of the world. Colonies established by countries that used the civil-code legal system possessed different institutions than those founded by England, which used the common-law legal system. Not only were the institutions different, but the types of goods traded between the mother countries and their colonies differed as well. England tended to establish settlements that developed independent legal systems and economic structures, whereas France, Spain, Portugal, and others established outposts that were to oversee the extraction of raw materials. In the former, institutional structures evolved that promoted individual rights and enforced property rights, whereas in the latter, institutions to enforce mother-country control of economic activity were created.

England's early mercantilist objectives resulted in the Navigation Acts, the first of which were enacted in the middle of the seventeenth century. Although the United States freed itself from these acts as a result of the American Revolution, trade remained restricted between the United States and the existing British colonies. By the middle of the nineteenth century Britain had repealed the Navigation Acts and was actively promoting free trade, encouraging all countries to establish less restrictive tariff systems. Most other countries failed to see the benefits of free trade and argued that only England would gain from freer trade. As a result, these other countries maintained institutional structures that protected domestic producers.

Institutions that promoted individual risk taking and entrepreneurial activity were present in most of the countries that grew and developed in the nineteenth century. Copyright law and patent law were important institutions for promoting creative activity. Why would anyone spend time and resources to create a new invention, write a book, or compose music, if they could not claim ownership and control use of their creation, or sell it to those who were willing to pay? Eighteenth-century Britain prohibited the export of textile machinery to protect the domestic textile industry, but Samuel Slater (1768–1835) memorized the blueprints for the machinery, immigrated to the United States, and collaborated with others to produce the machinery. The lack of any international institutions to enforce property rights allowed the establishment of a textile industry in the United States, and the inventors of the textile machinery were not compensated for the use of their creations.

TRADE INSTITUTIONS AFTER WORLD WAR II

In the post–World War II period the General Agreement on Tariffs and Trade (GATT) and the International Monetary Fund (IMF) were created to promote a freer and more stable trading environment. The IMF's function was to facilitate balance-of-payments adjustment and a more stable trading environment, whereas the GATT was to be a forum in which countries could negotiate multilateral reductions in trade barriers. World Bank promotion of economic development enabled

countries to more easily participate in the world trading system. Members of GATT agreed to conduct international trade under a set of rules that prohibited predatory behavior or the enactment of laws that gave domestic firms an unfair advantage. Under the GATT, countries were prohibited from forming preferential trading agreements. However, Article 23 of the GATT provided an escape clause that allowed the formation of such institutions if certain conditions were satisfied. As a result, more than 100 preferential trade agreements have been filed with the GATT.

In 1995 the GATT was transformed into the World Trade Organization (WTO), which is a more effective institution for facilitating world trade. Under the GATT, disputes between countries over trading practices were heard and a ruling was handed down, but it was left up to the defendant country to decide whether to accept the ruling. Under the WTO, the defendant still can choose not to change its behavior after an unfavorable decision, but the plaintiff country can impose penalty tariffs on imports from the defendant in an amount set by the WTO. Under the WTO rules a country is far more likely to comply with decisions against trade practices that favor domestic producers at the expense of producers in other countries.

The international enforcement of intellectual property rights, or Trade-Related Intellectual Property Rights (TRIPs), is a major topic of discussion within the WTO. Whether a country agrees to respect the intellectual property rights of trading partners affects the inflow of foreign direct investment (FDI) as well as the volume of trade. Lack of protection of property rights by the importing country has led in the past to "reverse engineering," whereby the importing country discovers how to manufacture a product by working backwards from the final product to the manufacture of all of the parts. Reverse engineering enables the production of products without compensation to those who invested in the creation of the product and hold its patents and/or copyrights. Institutions that limit such behavior encourage trade and stimulate growth.

SEE ALSO PATENT LAWS AND INTERNATIONAL PROPERTY RIGHTS.

BIBLIOGRAPHY

Borner, Silvio; Bodmer, Frank; and Kobler, Markus. *Institutional Efficiency and its Determinants: The Role of Political Factors in Economic Growth.* Paris: Organization for Economic Cooperation and Development, 2004.

Borner, Silvio; Brunetti, Aymo; and Weder Beatrice. *Institutional Obstacles to Latin American Growth.* San Francisco: ICS Press, 1992.

North, Douglass C., and Thomas Robert Paul. *The Rise of the Western World.* Cambridge U.K.: Cambridge University Press 1973.

North, Douglass C. *Structure and Change in Economic History.* New York: W. W. Norton, 1981.

William K. Hutchinson

INTERNATIONAL LABOUR ORGANIZATION

A product of the ideological and political struggles of nineteenth-century Europe and North America, the International Labour Organization (ILO) came into formal existence on June 28, 1919, nurtured by the labor conventions of the Treaty of Versailles, signed that same date. Originally operating under the League of Nations (albeit admitting countries that did not participate in the league), the ILO had two features unique among league-affiliated organizations: its tripartite structure that brings together representatives of governments, employers' groups, and workers' groups in a common conference setting; and its ability to survive the transition from the League of Nations to the United Nations. Since 1945, the ILO has continued its operations as part of the United Nations system of international organizations, never surrendering the tripartite structure that indelibly stamped it from its inception.

ESTABLISHMENT OF THE ILO

In addition to the tripartite structure, the ILO adopted a format that combines periodic conferences, which issue both recommendations and conventions for ratification by national governments, with the ongoing operation of standing committees devoted to research and monitoring and a governing body. The reasons for this particular structure and format lie in the ILO's origins in nineteenth-century international conferences, some supported and sanctioned by governments and some not. The political pressure applied to the leaders negotiating at Versailles came from the accumulation of international efforts to create standards for employment initiated by socialists, trade unionists, and individual reformers over the course of the century from the end of the Napoleonic Wars to the end of World War I.

Individuals such as Robert Owen (1771–1858), Jerome Blanqui (1798–1854), and Daniel Le Grand (d. 1859) had appealed to governments in Europe to limit hours of work, ban child labor, and address the unsanitary conditions prevalent in textile and mining industries through international agreements. Meanwhile, Socialists and Communists, operating internationally through the First and Second Internationals. The First International (International Workingmen's Association) was founded through the efforts of activists from the English Trades Council in 1864 and gained membership until the defeat of the Paris Commune in 1871, at which point it collapsed due to infighting. Its successor, the Second (Socialist) International, was made up of representatives from political parties active in working class politics in various countries, especially Western European nations. It was formed in 1889 and dissolved in 1915 following the beginning of World War I, when nationalism trumped internationalism. Both groups were advocating the prohibition of child labor and of night work, an eight-hour workday, and weekly rest. Trade unionists, organized either within Socialist Internationals or through separate organizations, forged international trade/craft secretariats (e.g., for mining, for transport workers, for metal workers) and pushed for international labor federations capable of wielding clout across national boundaries.

Recognizing the potential for national unrest associated with these political movements, Kaiser Wilhelm II (1859–1941) of Germany invited representatives from fourteen European nations to Berlin in 1890 to discuss child labor, hours of work, accident insurance, and safety and health regulations. The idea of organizing an international response to workers' demands stemmed from fear of a "race to the bottom" that might follow if each country developed its own legislation separately. There was a genuine fear that pioneering social reform potentially creates economic penalties, driving up a nation's labor costs. Thus a country introducing reforms on its own has no guarantee that its domestic market will not be undercut by imports from unreformed countries whose labor costs remain lower. A country embracing reforms that threaten its domestic industry is inclined to introduce protective tariffs or quotas, thereby insulating its domestic market. The result could be a drift towards economic nationalism.

Against this historical background, and meeting while strikes and industrial unrest was spreading across war-devastated Europe and radical Marxists were struggling for power in Russia, the architects of the Treaty of Versailles sought to mollify the aspirations of workers with nine ringing propositions embodying many of their most salient political demands. These included:

(1) rejection of the idea of labor as a mere commodity;

(2) endorsement of the right of association;

(3) support for the notion of a minimum wage, ensuring subsistence;

(4) support for an eight-hour workday and a forty-eight-hour work week;

(5) support for a day of rest during the week, ideally Sunday;

(6) abolition of child labor;

(7) rejection of discrimination in remuneration, ensuring that females are treated equally with men;

A child making shoes in Marikina, Philippines, 1969. The founding platform of the International Labour Organization (ILO) Convention in 1919 included a proposal for the abolition of child labor. The organization estimates that in the early 2000s, there were 250 million child laborers worldwide. © BETTMANN/CORBIS. REPRODUCED BY PERMISSION.

(8) affirmation of the principle that all workers (including immigrant workers) should be on an equal footing with respect to national laws regarding workers; and

(9) commitment to setting up a system of inspection that guarantees that labor legislation is scrupulously adhered to, and that violators are punished.

This became the platform upon which the ILO began its institutional existence in 1919. Meeting for the first time in Washington, D.C., its founding conference issued draft conventions for ratification by member states, and six recommendations for considered action.

Between 1919 and 1938 the ILO developed a bureaucratic model for linking annual conferences with ongoing research and the drafting of conventions and recommendations for approval by conferences. (A majority of two-thirds was required for approval.) Key were the creation of a governing body, populated by representatives of the major industrial nations, that appoints a director; the proliferation of specialized committees with representation for workers, employers, and national governments (the standard model for the conference being one worker

representative, one employer representative, and two government representatives); and the creation of a committee of experts that reviews the actions of member governments who ratify specific conventions, thereby committing themselves to attempting legislative action within eighteen months.

Specialized industrial committees played a major role in drafting conventions. For instance, of the sixty-seven conventions passed by the ILO conferences between 1919 and 1939, more than one-fifth dealt with the plight of seafarers and workers on the seaport docks. This was no accident. In 1920 a Joint Maritime Commission consisting of fifteen representatives of workers and fifteen representatives of ship owners was established. It worked steadily to deal with the particular problems of sailors—repatriation, mandatory holiday time, sick leave compensation for accident and injury, and minimum-age restrictions—and of the workers who loaded and unloaded freight in ports. It became the model for the industrial committees that worked up conventions and recommendations for food preparation, mining, glass and glass-bottle making, textiles, nursing, and homework.

ILO BEFORE WORLD WAR II

After 1919 economic nationalism was rife; countries drifted toward autarky as the gold-standard system of fixed-exchange rates collapsed, and governments adopted "beggar-thy-neighbor" protectionism. Ideologically charged tensions persisted between communists committed in principle to the "dictatorship of the proletariat," which in fact denied workers the right to organize independent unions; fascists, who advocated corporatist solutions that banned trade unions and instead required workers to join national-front organizations in which governments, workers, and employers participated; and liberal democrats committed to some form of ILO-style reform. Countries that traditionally had accepted immigrants—including the United States, Australia, Canada, and New Zealand—all became more restrictive after World War I. The result was that international trade and migration volumes sputtered along during the 1920s, and nose-dived after the Great Depression of the 1930s brought the U.S. economy to its knees.

To gauge ILO achievement during these two difficult decades by the number of calls for national legislation that the conferences passed—sixty-seven conventions for ratification and sixty-six recommendations over a twenty-one year period—is to miss the point. Many conventions were ratified by a mere handful of countries. Ratification was no guarantee that a country would take its obligations seriously; moreover, under ILO rules, ratifying countries could selectively denounce conventions, turning their ratification into a dead letter.

Membership was another problematic issue. Two major reasons for the collapse of the international economic order after 1919 were the inability of the United Kingdom to exercise international leadership for the international monetary and trade system, and the unwillingness of the rapidly growing United States to assume a leadership role. Indeed, the United States Congress, concerned about League of Nations opposition to the draconian immigration restrictions it was planning and to its traditional policy of keeping European influence out of the Americas (the Monroe Doctrine), joined neither the league nor the ILO. Fascist Germany abandoned the ILO in 1935; Italy, Paraguay, Austria, Guatemala, Honduras, Nicaragua, El Salvador, and Japan eventually followed suit. It was not until 1934 that the New Deal administration under U.S. President Franklin Roosevelt, who was staunchly committed to social reforms such as social security and collective bargaining rights for unions, brought the United States into the ILO. In the same year the Soviet Union reluctantly joined, only to leave in 1940. As it turned out, Roosevelt's support for the ILO was crucial to its survival during World War II. During those dark days the United States cajoled its neighbor Canada into housing an ILO forced to flee Europe.

The U.S. New Deal also sheds light on the ILO's difficulties in getting its conventions ratified. U.S. unions had been active in organizing Canadian laborers from the late nineteenth century onward, because Canadian workers had great difficulty organizing with their relatively small employment base in manufacturing. After the Wagner Act was passed in 1935 in the United States guaranteeing U.S. unions collective bargaining rights, the international U.S. unions aggressively pushed labor legislation in Canada, forcing the dominion government to introduce its own version of the New Deal Canada, which had been a continuous member of the ILO from its initial founding, had ratified almost no ILO conventions prior to 1935, but ironically the dominion government, reborn as a New Deal administration, embraced the very ILO conventions it had hitherto ignored. By the early 1940s Canada had ratified a substantial number of conventions, and Montreal had become the headquarters of the beleaguered organization. The domestic economic and political circumstances of nation-states participating in the ILO strongly condition their willingness, and ability, to accede to ILO conventions and recommendations.

AFTER WORLD WAR II

Surviving World War II, the ILO was no longer a League of Nations organization, for they had given way to the United Nations. Moreover, it saw its virtual monopoly over international rules governing trade and migration slip away as new, specialized agencies that became part of the United Nations system—the World Bank, the International Monetary Fund, the General Agreement on Tariffs and Trade, the Food and Agricultural Organization, the World Health Organization, and so forth—took over many of the responsibilities that had been part and parcel of the mandate bestowed upon the ILO under the Treaty of Versailles. Indeed, in some areas—for instance, in formulating a convention on migrant workers—the ILO has seen its prerogatives seized by the United Nations itself, as newly oil-rich countries such as Mexico eschewed lobbying in the ILO (where countries with guest-worker programs such as Germany resisted the drafting of a strongly worded convention) for the United Nations, where votes could be more readily purchased.

The international economic order, invigorated by U.S. support for the United Nations system and U.S. willingness to rebuild a quasi-gold-standard system with the Bretton Woods agreement, helped usher in a golden age of economic growth in which international trade and international migration rebounded from their nadirs in the mid-1930s. In addition, many of the colonies established by the European powers or by Japan became independent nation-states in the aftermath of the war. The family of independent nations jumped from less than 70 to more than 150.

Consequently, the ILO—operating as part of the United Nations system of international organizations—saw its membership soar. Between World War II and 1970 membership in the ILO more than doubled, reaching 121 in 1969. By 2004, ILO membership exceeded 170 nation-states.

It is important to keep in mind that most of these changes occurred in the context of the Cold War, as the United States and the Soviet Union contended for leadership and allies in the developing world, in Latin America, Africa, the Middle East. and Southeast Asia. Both U.S. competition with the Communist bloc, and the influence of Communist hostility toward trade-union organizations operating independently of the state, were factors in the delicate political path the ILO followed in formulating conventions and recommendations for a membership that included both the United States and its allies and the Soviet Union and its allies (although, since the end of the Cold War in the late 1980s the international political competition has taken on new forms).

Responding to the challenge of serving a growing membership increasingly weighted toward developing (and often heavily agricultural) economies, and mindful of staying away from ideologically charged initiatives, the governing body of the ILO set up the International Centre for Advanced Technical and Vocational Training in Turin in 1965. This center has been especially active in training persons from the developing world in specific technical skills such as automobile mechanics and industrial drawing.

SUCCESS OF THE ILO

One sign of the strength of the post–World War II ILO is the successful issuing of conventions that are monitored by groups of experts in the ILO. Between 1950 and 2004 the ILO has issued eight-seven conventions, including an Equal Remuneration Convention (1951), an Abolition of Forced Labor Convention (1957), and a Worst Form of Child Labor Convention that in principle prohibits slavery, forced recruitment of children as soldiers, and exploitation of the young in prostitution and pornography. Another success has been the training of technically competent personnel from developing countries.

Against these strengths must be set weaknesses: excessive dependence on the United States for funding (one-quarter of the ILO budget in 1970 came from the United States), giving the United States excessive clout in the formulation of conventions and recommendations; political barriers to application of conventions (for ex-

ample, in federal states such as Canada, Germany, and the United States much labor-market regulation is formulated at the state or provincial level, not at the federal level); the wide dispersion in income per capita throughout the globe, with lower-income countries being far more constrained than higher-income countries in protecting the well-being of workers, due to severe limits on their taxation base; and the diversity of legal and industrial-relations systems throughout the world, which makes formulating conventions for universal usage problematic at best.

There are shortcomings to be sure. However, an international organization that generates decisions out of a tripartite political process in which labor, employers, and politician-bureaucrats participate has much to recommend itself. Although "race to the bottom" fears have not disappeared, the ILO has helped to mitigate them, thereby giving a fillip to both trade openness and social reform worldwide.

SEE ALSO Africa, Labor Taxes (Head Taxes); Disease and Pestilence; Education, Overview; GATT, WTO; Globalization, Pro and Con; Imperialism; International Trade Agreements; Labor, Types of; Laborers, Coerced; Laborers, Contract; Slavery and the African Slave Trade.

BIBLIOGRAPHY

Bohning, Roger. "The ILO and the New UN Convention on Migrant Workers: The Past and Future." *International Migration Review* 25 (Winter 1991): 698–709.

Crispo, John. *International Unionism: A Study in Canadian-American Relations.* Toronto: McGraw-Hill, 1967.

International Labour Office. *The International Labour Organisation: The First Decade.* London: Allen and Unwin, 1931.

International Labour Office. *The Impact of International Labour Conventions and Ratifications.* Geneva: Author, 1976.

Johnston, George A. *The International Labour Organisation: Its Work for Social and Economic Progress.* London: Europa Publications, 1970.

Landelius, Torsten. *Workers, Employers, and Governments: A Comparative Study of Delegations and Groups at the International Labour Conference, 1919–1964.* Stockholm: P. A. Norstedt and Söner, 1965.

Landy, E. A. *The Effectiveness of International Supervision: Thirty Years of I.L.O. Experience.* Dobbs Ferry, NY: Oceania Publications, Inc., 1966.

Lowe, Boutelle E. *The International Protection of Labour.* New York: Macmillan, 1921.

Mainwaring, John. *The International Labour Organization: A Canadian View.* Ottawa: Ministry of Labour, Government of Canada, 1986.

National Industrial Conference Board, Inc. *The Work of the International Labor Organization.* New York: Author, 1928.

Ratzlaff, C. J. "The International Labor Organization of the League of Nations: Its Significance for the United States." *The American Economic Review* 22 (September 1932): 447–461.

Stewart, Margaret. *Britain and the ILO: The Story of Fifty Years.* Kent: Headley Brothers, 1969.

Taylor, William L. *Federal States and Labor Treaties: Relations of Federal States to the International Labor Organization.* New York: Apollo Press, 1935.

INTERNET RESOURCES

International Labour Organization. "Database of International Labour Standards." Available from www.ilo.org/ilolex/english/.

Carl Mosk

INTERNATIONAL MONETARY FUND (IMF)

The International Monetary Fund (IMF, or the Fund) is an institution that oversees the international monetary system, promotes monetary cooperation and financial stability, and extends loans to its members. It is an intergovernmental organization whose members include almost all countries. Although it is a specialized agency of the United Nations (UN) and participates in the Economic and Social Council of the UN, it operates independently and has its own charter, governing structure, rules, and finances.

ORGANIZATION AND PURPOSES

As of 2004 the IMF had 184 member countries, seven fewer than the United Nations. The exceptions were Cuba, North Korea, and five tiny countries: Andorra, Liechtenstein, and Monaco in Europe, and the island countries of Nauru and Tuvalu in the Pacific Ocean. To become a member, a country must first apply and then be accepted by a majority of the existing membership as being able and willing to fulfill the obligations of membership. Cuba was an original member of the IMF but withdrew in 1964, a few years after Fidel Castro took power. None of the other six has applied.

In 2004 the IMF had around 2,800 staff from more than 140 countries, most of whom worked at the IMF's headquarters in Washington, D.C. A small number of staff work at regional or local offices around the globe. The head of the institution is the managing director, who is selected by the executive board to serve a five-year term. By tradition, the managing director has always been a European. The executive board, which sets policies and is responsible for most decisions, is chaired by the managing director and consists of twenty-four executive directors who either are appointed by their home governments or are elected for two-year terms by a constituency of countries. The five countries with the largest economies—since 1970, the United States, Japan, Germany, France, and the United Kingdom—appoint directors from their own nations, and the other 179 member countries elect directors to fill the remaining nineteen slots. Constituencies are formed by countries with similar interests and usually from the same region, such as French-speaking countries in Africa, or Islamic countries in the Middle East. They range in size from a single country to more than twenty.

Political oversight of the IMF is primarily the responsibility of the International Monetary and Financial Committee (IMFC), whose twenty-four members are mostly finance ministers or central-bank governors from the same countries and constituencies that are represented on the executive board. The IMFC meets twice a year and advises the Fund on the broad direction of policies. Most IMFC members are also members of the board of governors, on which every member country has a governor. The board of governors meets once a year, and it votes on major institutional decisions such as whether to increase the size of the Fund's financial resources or to admit new members.

One of the main functions of the IMF is to conduct surveillance over members' economic policies through annual consultations with each member country and by preparing and publishing global reports such as the semi-annual *World Economic Outlook*. For a consultation, a team of IMF staff spends up to two weeks in the country meeting with government officials and others, and then writes an assessment of the country's economic policies and prospects. The executive board then discusses the report and formulates its own assessment. Since the late 1990s, most reports and assessments have been published. The IMF also provides technical assistance and training to its members on a wide range of economic and financial issues.

The IMF lends money to countries that have difficulty financing their balance of external payments, often in response to a financial crisis. Most commonly, the Fund makes money available through a standby arrangement lasting from one to three years, during which time the country can draw up to specified amounts, subject to certain conditions on the country's economic policies and performance. The country is then required to repay the loan, usually within three to five years. The borrower pays an interest charge based on prevailing short-term interest rates in the largest industrial countries. However, some seventy-eight of the world's poorest countries are eligible to borrow for longer terms and at a lower interest rate through a subsidized lending window, the Poverty Reduction and Growth Facility (PRGF).

The Mount Washington Hotel at Bretton Woods, New Hampshire. *The International Monetary Fund was founded there by an international conference of delegates from forty-four nations in July 1944.* © BETTMANN/CORBIS. REPRODUCED BY PERMISSION.

Every member country is required to deposit at the IMF a sum of money that is determined primarily by the size of the country's economy and the amount of international trade that it does. That sum is the country's quota, which also determines the member's voting power and how much it can borrow. Close to one-fourth of the quota must be paid in liquid assets that are readily accepted in international trade and finance, such as U.S. dollars or other major currencies. The rest is paid in the country's own currency. The IMF thus gains a stock of assets that it can lend to any member. On a voluntary basis, many countries also contribute to the PRGF so that the Fund can make its loans affordable to the poorest countries. If necessary, the Fund also can borrow additional amounts from countries or other parties. In 2004 the Fund had outstanding loans to nearly fifty countries totaling around $100 billion, it held about $154 billion in usable liquid assets, and it had arrangements in place to borrow another $49 billion if needed.

HISTORY

The IMF was founded, along with the World Bank, at an international conference in Bretton Woods, New Hampshire, in July 1944. Forty-four countries sent delegations who drafted and agreed to the Articles of Agreement (the Fund's charter). Most of those countries subsequently ratified the articles and became the original members when the IMF opened for business in 1946. The major exception was the Soviet Union. Throughout the Cold War the IMF was essentially an association of non-Communist states, as its membership grew from 40 countries in 1946 to 152 in 1989. Only after the dissolution of the Soviet Union in 1991 did IMF membership become practically universal.

The IMF began lending in 1947; its first borrower was France. In its first decade, however, few countries borrowed from the IMF because the Marshall Plan and the World Bank filled most financing needs. The first big burst of lending came in 1956 to 1957, in response to the Suez crisis. From that point on, the Fund became the world's primary agency for short-term balance-of-payments financing. The IMF's main function in that period, however, was to oversee the re-establishment of multilateral trade and payments after the disruptions of the Depression era and World War II. Countries that maintained exchange restrictions on current-account transactions (which included all but a few in the 1940s and 1950s) were required to consult regularly with the Fund on their plans to eliminate them. Exchange rates for most countries were pegged to the U.S. dollar, which in turn was pegged to gold. Countries that wanted to make large changes in their rates were permitted to do so only to correct a fundamental disequilibrium in their balance of payments, and only after consulting with the IMF.

This system of fixed exchange rates came under pressure in the 1960s as the dominant position of the United States in the world economy began to wane. As other countries grew and conducted more international trade, they needed to hold ever larger stocks of U.S. dollars to ensure that they could settle their payments balances readily. To supplement these scarce dollars, the board of governors amended the articles in 1969 to enable the IMF to create a new form of international reserve asset, the Special Drawing Right, or SDR. In August 1971, however, the U.S. government terminated the convertibility of the dollar into gold, and in March 1973 the major industrial countries abandoned the dollar-based system of fixed exchange rates altogether.

The economic turmoil and stagflation of the 1970s, punctuated by two large and sudden increases in world petroleum prices, ushered in an era in which stability in international trade and payments became much more difficult to maintain. In 1978 the board of governors again amended the IMF articles to recognize that countries could choose whatever exchange regime seemed best for them. That amendment gave the Fund the authority to oversee the functioning of the international monetary system by exercising surveillance over member countries' macroeconomic and exchange-rate policies. The effectiveness of this surveillance, however, would depend on the support and cooperation of the countries involved. Unless a country needs to borrow from the Fund, it can choose to ignore any policy advice that it dislikes, though the peer pressure from the discussion of policies by the international community may foster cooperative attitudes and policies.

Since the late 1970s the influence that the IMF has over countries' economic policies has come largely from the conditions on its lending. In broad terms, those conditions are of two types. First, countries must adopt monetary and budgetary policies that are sound enough to ensure that they make adequate progress toward stabilizing the economy, financing their external payments, and sustaining a reasonable rate of economic growth. Second, in most cases they must also adopt structural reforms aimed at raising their potential growth rate by reducing bottlenecks and rigidities in the economy. Those reforms are especially important for low-income countries, which need to grow rapidly enough to reduce extreme poverty and deprivation, but they also may be of critical importance for middle-income developing countries that need to reduce their vulnerability to financial crises. If well designed, conditionality can help a government to commit itself to implementing good policies and can help overcome domestic political opposition. In some cases, though, resistance to the IMF's conditions has made it the object of protests both in the affected countries and more widely.

Helping developing countries to avoid financial crises if possible and to manage the consequences when crises do occur became a major focus of the IMF's work as a result of the international debt crisis that hit many countries in Latin America and elsewhere in the early 1980s. This focus became even more important in the second half of the 1990s, when crises hit a number of countries with emerging financial markets, including Brazil, Indonesia, South Korea, Mexico, Russia, and Thailand. In response, the IMF introduced institutional reforms aimed at strengthening its precrisis surveillance, finding innovative ways to help manage crises, and making its own procedures more open and transparent. As the IMF entered the new century and approached its sixtieth anniversary, this reform agenda was well underway but far from complete.

SEE ALSO Bretton Woods; Keynes, John Maynard; World Bank.

BIBLIOGRAPHY

Boughton, James M. *Silent Revolution: The International Monetary Fund, 1979–1989.* Washington, DC: International Monetary Fund, 2001.

James, Harold. *International Monetary Cooperation Since Bretton Woods.* Washington, DC: International Monetary Fund; New York and Oxford: Oxford University Press, 1996.

INTERNET RESOURCES

Boughton, James M. "The IMF and the Force of History: Ten Events and Ten Ideas That Have Shaped the Institution." IMF Working Paper 04/75. 2004. Available from http://www.imf.org/external/pubind.htm.

International Monetary Fund. "About the IMF." Available from http://www.imf.org/external/about.htm.

James M. Boughton

INTERNATIONAL TRADE AGREEMENTS

Agreements among trading nations have existed since ancient times and have covered many different aspects of commercial relations. As J. B. Condliffe comments in his *The Commerce of Nations,* "Commercial treaties have a long history. Early instances can be adduced from the old testament and from classical history" (Condliffe 1950, p. 216). In some cases such treaties are bilateral (between two countries) and others are multilateral (including several or many nations). Some treaties deal narrowly and explicitly with trade issues, whereas in others the impact on trade is indirect and a byproduct of agreements made to accomplish other purposes. Agreements made regarding monetary standards, international law, and labor and environmental standards can affect trade as much as those dealing solely with trade among nations.

Mutually agreed-upon regulations and reciprocal tariff reductions can be used to accomplish certain ends, serving as a sign of commitment in relation to other countries and also as a symbol of peaceful intent. But such agreements are not the only means with such ends as tariffs achieve reductions and freer trade. Much can be accomplished by an individual country's policy alone. Although trade agreements may be a political means of attracting support for tariff reduction, legislation within one country can also achieve that end. Thus the 1846 tariff reduction in the British Corn Law was a unilateral action, as was the decision to end the Navigation Acts in 1847. Much of the reduction of U.S. tariffs has reflected legislative decision, not international agreement. Although unilateral actions can be effective, agreements can help nations to achieve some desired *quid pro quo* from other countries, and thus increase the possibility of achieving such a policy.

In the beginning of the twentieth century most trade agreements were bilateral, although some, related to defining international law, were multilateral. The earliest trade agreements were intended to cover the legal rights of alien traders, providing for their safety and respecting their rights to property. Less important were agreements regarding tariff reductions, covering either all trade or only trade in specific commodities. Other treaties, either bilateral or multilateral, regarded the definition and treatment of neutrals by nations at war with each other.

As befits its role as a major trading and manufacturing nation, Britain was involved in several major trade agreements, as were its colonies that became the United States. The Methuen Treaty between Britain and Portugal in 1703 lowered the tariff on Spanish wine (port) relative to French wines, in exchange for allowing British textiles to enter Portugal. In the late eighteenth century the newly independent United States signed treaties regarding trade and shipping with several European nations. In the 1820s Britain extended its reciprocal-trade treaties with various European nations. The trade agreement that The Anglo-French Treaty of Commerce of 1860 (or the Cobden-Chevalier Treaty, after the two principal negotiators) was the nineteenth century's most famous and influential treaty, in part because of its substantial tariff reduction, in part because of its promise of peace between the nations. After 1860 France and Britain each negotiated treaties with many other European nations. Those bilateral treaties often had larger impacts on trade because most included the provision for most-favored-nation treat-

ment, meaning that the same tariff reductions were granted to every country with which there was a treaty.

In 1883 the Paris Convention for the Protection of Industrial Property established rules concerning the international protection of intellectual property, such as patents. The Berne Convention followed it for the Protection of Literary and Artistic works in 1886, and continues as the World Intellectual Property Organization.

After the nineteenth-century expansion in bilateral treaties, the Great Depression in the 1930s led to a shift away from bilateral agreements to various forms of multilateral treaties (although the United States did sign several bilateral treaties regulating tariffs with other nations, under the Reciprocal Trade Agreements Act of 1934, to encourage U.S. exports). In the postwar period the expanded use of treaties included the formation of worldwide organizations such as the General Agreement on Tariffs and Trade (GATT), and also the development of several regional organizations to influence trade within these blocs and between them and other nations. The two major financial programs for the postwar years, established at Bretton Woods, were the International Monetary Fund (IMF) and the World Bank. These institutions were intended to facilitate world trade and capital flows, and to provide for convertibility and stability between national economies.

GATT was intended to facilitate world trade by providing a forum in which to negotiate and coordinate tariffs and to adjudicate disputes on tariff terms and rates. Its object was the liberalization of world trade by lowering tariffs, reducing nontariff barriers, and monitoring national trade policies. When it was established in 1948 it included only twenty-three members, but these accounted for about 70 percent of world trade. The organization was renamed the World Trade Organization (WTO) in 1995, by which time it had at least 123 members; by 2003 membership had risen to 145. The basic goals of the WTO are still those set at its origin, but its operations have become more difficult with frequent disagreements between developed and developing nations.

As part of the ongoing tariff reforms under GATT and WTO there have been several large international meetings aimed at multilateral agreements regarding tariff reduction. These included the Kennedy Round (1964–1967) and the Tokyo Round (1973–1979), which was also concerned with the reduction of nontariff barriers. The eighth round, the Uruguay Round (1986–1993), dealt not only with tariff and nontariff barriers but also with intellectual-property rights. Two subsequent WTO meetings have collapsed because of major disputes between developed and less-developed nations. In Seattle (1999) the disagreement arose because the developed nations sought a universal application of labor standards, whereas in Cancun (2003) the dispute was over subsidized aid to agriculture in the developed nations.

The United Nations Conference on Trade and Development (UNCTAD), established in 1964, is concerned with trade and development policy to help integrate developing countries into the world economy. At present it has 192 members.

The history of regional groups resulting from trade agreements is rather complex, with changing names and memberships over time. These groups vary in their purposes, from being mainly forums for consultation among member states to attempting integration with a common currency, a single internal market, tariff uniformity, and common social and economic policies. The most ambitious of these is the European Union (EU). First organized by six nations and known as the European Coal and Steel Community in 1951, it grew to nine nations (including the United Kingdom) in 1973, fifteen in 2003, and twenty-five in 2004, and there are more still to come. Its objectives include some political concerns such as expanding rights for citizens, freedom of movement, monetary unity, and a common foreign and security policy. A counterpart to this organization, once known as the Common Market, was the European Free Trade Association, which was founded in 1960 with seven members, several of whom left to join the European Union. At present it includes only four states, with formal relations with nine members from other nations. Its aim of free trade has been achieved, and it entered into arrangements for free movement of goods, capital, and labor with the EU in 1994. The socialist nations of Eastern Europe formed COMECOM, or the Council of Mutual Economic Assistance, in 1949 to provide free trade within this bloc. It was disbanded in 1991, leaving some members free to join the EU.

In the Americas there are the Central American Common Market (1991); MERCOSUR (1991); and the North American Free Trade Agreement (NAFTA), with the original Canada–United States Treaty of 1987 expanded to include Mexico in 1993. In Asia there are the Association of South East Asian Nations (ASEAN, 1967) and the Asia-Pacific Economic Co-operation (1989). The League of Arab States was founded in 1945, and the Common Market for Eastern and Southern Africa began in 1981. All regional blocs were intended to increase trade among its members and to reduce tariffs, but the success of the groups varies with diverse economic and political factors.

In addition to treaties based on geographic location, there are also treaty-based organizations to deal with specific commodities and to influence their prices and outputs. The most important of these has been the Organization of Petroleum Exporting Countries (OPEC), founded in 1960 to control production and the revenues from oil. Less effective—because they control only a relatively small part of the world market—have been the Coffee Board Liaison Committee (established in the 1960s), the various organizations attempting to regulate international trade in textiles and in iron and steel, and the nations agreeing to deal with agricultural commodities.

SEE ALSO ACCOUNTING AND ACCOUNTING PRACTICES; BRETTON WOODS; COFFEE; COMECON; COMMON MARKET AND THE EUROPEAN UNION; DRUGS, ILLICIT; FREE TRADE, THEORY AND PRACTICE; GLOBALIZATION, PRO AND CON; GOLD AND SILVER; INTERNATIONAL LABOUR ORGANIZATION; INTERNATIONAL MONETARY FUND (IMF); LAW, COMMON AND CIVIL; MARKET INTEGRATION; MERCOSUR; MOST-FAVORED-NATION PROVISIONS; NAFTA; PATENT LAWS AND INTELLECTUAL PROPERTY RIGHTS; SLAVERY AND THE AFRICAN SLAVE TRADE; WORLD BANK.

BIBLIOGRAPHY

Condliffe, J. B. *The Commerce of Nations.* New York: W. W. Norton, 1950.

Croome, J. *Reshaping the World Trading System.* The Hague: Kluwer Law International 2nd edition, revised, 1996.

Dunham, Arthur Louis. *The Anglo-French Treaty of Commerce of 1860 and the Progress of the Industrial Revolutions in France.* Ann Arbor: University of Michigan Press, 1930.

Neal, Larry, and Barbezat, Daniel. *The Economics of the European Union and the Economies of Europe.* New York: Oxford University Press, 1998.

Stanley L. Engerman

IRAN

Iran's commercial dealings with the outside world in the early modern period essentially operated as a transit trade. This was a function of the country's strategic location between what was probably the world's most productive region, India, and what was rapidly becoming its most voracious consumer, Western Europe. India offered spices and textiles and, being largely self-sufficient, demanded bullion in return. Europe craved spices, textiles, and raw silk, and had as yet little to offer other than silver and gold, both of which were abundantly available from the New World. Little of this bullion stayed in the country, reflecting the fact that as a productive force and a consumer market, early modern Iran was of modest size. Its total population in the Safavid period (1501–1722) numbered no more than approximately 7 to 8 million people—compared to some 60 million in India and per-

Seventeenth-century Persian Isfahan-style silk panel. *Silk was Persia's largest export in the early modern period, and the main reason why the English and Dutch East India Companies entered the region's market in the early 1600s.* THE BRIDGEMAN ART LIBRARY/GETTY IMAGES. REPRODUCED BY PERMISSION.

haps 30 million in the Ottoman Empire—and this decreased to no more than 5 million in the eighteenth century, to rise to its previous level in Qajar times (1796–1925). About a quarter of Iran's inhabitants, moreover, were pastoralists, nomads who eked out lives of subsistence or near-subsistence and made only a modest contribution to economic life.

TRANSIT TRADE IN THE EARLY MODERN PERIOD

If we disregard bullion, silk was the country's largest export commodity in the Safavid period, as it had been before 1500. Mostly cultivated in the Caspian provinces of Gilan and Mazandaran, it was traditionally exported in raw form via the overland route across Anatolia or Meso-

potamia to the ports of the Levant, and, as of the seventeenth century, also via the Persian Gulf around the Cape of Good Hope, and along the Volga route to Russia and on to Europe via the White Sea or the Baltic Sea. In a good year, Iran may have exported 5,000 to 6,000 bales. Most active in the country's overland silk exports were the Armenians. Their activities received a further boost when in 1604 Shah ʿAbbas (r. 1587–1629) deported a large number from their ancestral lands in the northwest to a new suburb near Isfahan, his new capital, giving them commercial privileges and a monopoly on silk exports. Silk was the main reason why the English and Dutch East India Companies (the EIC and VOC, respectively) entered the Iranian market in the early 1600s, but their initial euphoria quickly wore off and the volume each exported rarely exceeded 500 bales annually.

India was Iran's largest trading partner in the early modern period. Despite the advent of the European maritime companies and the highly visible trade connection that developed between Iran and Europe, the volume and frequency of Iran's trade with the Indian subcontinent continued to exceed commerce with the West by far. The trade between India and Iran followed the maritime route between Surat and the ports of the Persian Gulf—principally Hormuz and in the seventeenth century, Bandar 'Abbas, or the overland route via Qandahar. Between 1507 and 1622 the Portuguese played an important role in the former link, when Hormuz was under their control and served as the main entrepôt for the Persian Gulf and western Indian Ocean.

Spices that originated in India and Southeast Asia were important Iranian imports. But pepper, cloves, mace, and nutmeg were gradually overshadowed by Indian cloth, which by the late seventeenth century became by far the dominant Indian article exported to Iran. Most eye-catching were the colorful and expensive *chits* (chintzes) from Coromandel, but the bulk of Indian exports consisted of rather coarse and cheap cotton cloth. Much of the cargo was transshipped, carried on to Basra and Mesopotamia, where the dark cloth from which the local *abayas* (women's dresses) were woven always found a good market. India also exported large amounts of indigo, sugar, and rice to Iran.

The volume and value of the goods Iran sent to India paled in comparison to what the country received from the subcontinent. Exports consisted of pearls, rosewater, some wine, pistachio nuts, almonds, carpets, velvets, and modest numbers of horses. Owing mostly to Iran's lack of viable export goods besides silk, its main export to India was bullion and specie. Thus in the 1690s Iran had become the single most important source of treasure for the VOC in its Asian operations.

Little is known about the volume of Iran's overland trade with the Ottoman Empire, about half of which may have consisted of raw silk. In a good year some 4,000 bales of silk may have been taken to the ports of the Levant, and many of the Indian textiles that entered Iran were in fact destined for the Ottoman market. A large volume of cattle, too, went west. In addition, Iran exported cotton, madder, gallnuts, goat hair, and drugs. Textiles, mostly coarse broadcloth originating in England, were among the most important of the wares that went the other way. None of this covered the value of Iran's exports, so bullion had to be brought into the country to make up the balance.

Trade with and via Russia, conducted mostly as part of diplomatic traffic, was insignificant throughout the

sixteenth century. But as of the late 1500s Armenian-Iranian and Russian merchants began to conduct a private transit trade of some significance, mostly in textiles, capitalizing on the growth of export possibilities to Western Europe. Russia, in turn, exported modest quantities of furs, wax, and metal arms. In the later 1600s the silk trade via Russia turned into a substantial export commodity, and after 1676, the year Moscow concluded a commercial treaty with Iran's Armenian merchants, silk exports took off.

The opening up of the Cape route between Iran and Europe at the turn of the sixteenth century at first had little significance for Iran. The diversion of trade from the overland to the maritime route envisioned by the European maritime companies was partial at best, and the volume of trade carried to Western Europe via the Cape, consisting of a few hundred bales of silk and a similar volume of Kirman goat's wool, remained modest.

TRADE WITH RUSSIA AND BRITAIN IN THE NINETEENTH CENTURY

The period after the fall of Isfahan to Afghan tribesmen in 1722 was marked by turmoil, with many warlords vying for power. Trade periodically came to a standstill, and most Western commercial contacts withered. Well into the nineteenth century, when the Qajar dynasty (r. 1796–1925) finally brought some stability to the country, Iran remained little affected by the growing world economy and the attendant Western influence. By 1800 most of Iran's exiguous trade was with the Ottoman Empire, Afghanistan, Central Asia, and India. But this would soon change under pressure from Russia and Britain. Russia, having twice defeated Iran in wars, forced the Qajars to open up to foreign merchants. When in 1821 the Russians imposed a treaty on Iran that gave their merchants preferential tax status, commercial links between the two countries expanded and a great volume of European goods began to be transported into Iran via the Black Sea. The Caspian Sea, too, saw increased shipping in this period, controlled by Russian companies. Following these developments, many foreign-trade representatives, mostly Greeks and Armenian and Georgian Russian subjects, took up residence in Iran's northern cities. Iran, in turn, witnessed an exodus of people going to Russia in pursuit of trade and employment.

Russia's hegemony was soon challenged, especially after the signing of the Anglo-Persian Commercial Treaty of 1841, which gave British merchants the same customs privileges as the Russians. The growing British prominence in Iran's trade that followed was facilitated by the establishment of a steamer service between India and the Persian Gulf in the 1860 as well as the opening of the Suez Canal in 1869. In the Persian Gulf Bushire became the most important port of entry, distributing its wares to Muhammara (Khurramshahr) on the Shatt al-'Arab, and later via the Karun River, which in the 1880s was opened up for navigation as far as Ahvaz.

Cheap textiles still formed the bulk of imports at this time, but by the second half of the nineteenth century consumables such as tea and sugar and accessories such as samovars, tea glasses, and kettles began to be imported in great volume. Iranian products could not compete with a flood of cheaply manufactured Western import goods on which a mere 5 percent *ad valorem* customs tariff was levied, and many local manufacturers went out of business. Until the 1860s silk made up much of exports, but its production fell drastically when the muscardine disease struck. Opium, which began to be cultivated in many parts of Iran, took up some of the slack by being exported to China as well as Europe. A large demand in Europe and the United States gave a great boost to the export of Iranian carpets in the 1870s. Cotton, too, became an export product.

By century's end, Russia managed to recapture its former position as Iran's main trading partner, so that by 1914 it provided about half of the country's imports. The process was facilitated by the completion of the Caucasian railway—which reached Baku in 1900—low Russian railway and shipping charges, and heavy subsidies for Russian export products such as tea, kerosene, and woolens.

OIL, ARMS, AND ISLAMIC REVOLUTION

World War I and the attendant turmoil in Iran halted the growth in trade; only in the 1930s did it reach the levels of the previous century. By that time oil had joined Iran's exports. Soon it would become the single most important export commodity, followed, at great distance, by carpets, cotton, and dried fruits. Until about 1950, when incomes began to grow, sugar, tea, and textiles comprised about 40 percent of Iran's imports.

Once Mohammad Reza Shah (r. 1941–1978) embarked on his project to propel Iran into First-World status, import patterns changed dramatically. Large machinery and consumer goods became an important component of imports. Increasingly considered a staunch ally of the West, Iran also became a major buyer of expensive Western, especially U.S., weaponry. U.S. arms sales to Iran between 1950 and 1979 totaled U.S.$11.2 million. The quadrupling of oil prices in 1974 and the vast financial wealth it engendered gave a further fillip to this trend, unleashing a flood of imports far exceeding the country's absorption capacity. Overnight, urban Iran took on the appearance of a consumer society, importing much of the food it used to produce itself. Oil

paid for it all, and more and more it became Iran's foreign currency earner.

The Islamic Revolution of 1978 to 1979 changed Iran's trade patterns again, though not its dependence on oil. Between 1978 and 1982 total nonoil exports fell by about half. They have since more than recovered. Iran total trade with the world in 2001 amounted to almost 47 billion. Total exports were 27.2 million (0.5% of total world trade) and imports were 19.5 million (0.4% of total world trade). Trade with the newly independent states of the former Soviet Union accounts for some of this, and the geographical distribution of Iran's nonoil exports has become more diverse and balanced, with developing countries now among the major importers of goods from Iran. Still, the European Union continues to be the largest trade partner and accounts for 30 percent of Iran's foreign trade, followed by Japan with 13.4 percent, the United Arab Emirates 7.1 percent, China 7 percent, South Korea 6.9 percent, and India, Turkey, Russia, and Philippines between 2 percent and 3 percent each. China is a new and growing trading partner for Iran, with their mutual trade topping U.S.$4 billion in 2003.

Trade relations with the United States fell precipitously following the hostage crisis of 1979 to 1981, but were never completely severed despite the disputes and the boycott that endures today. Thus, with a value of U.S.$760 million in 1992, the United States accounted for 2.67 percent of Iran's total imports and ranked eighth among the country's major trade partners. During the first half of 2004 trade exchanges between Iran and the United States stood at U.S.$120 million.

SEE ALSO Black Sea; Boycott; Caravan Trade; East India Company, British; East India Company, Dutch; East India Company, Other; Empire, British; Empire, Mughal; Empire, Ottoman; Ethnic Groups, Armenians; Ethnic Groups, Gujarati; Gold and Silver; Gulbenkian, Calouste; Imperialism; Import Substitution; Indian Ocean; International Monetary Fund (IMF); Levant Company; Nationalism; Nationalization; OPEC; Persian Gulf; Petroleum; Shipping Lanes; Russia; Sugar, Molasses, and Rum; Tea; Tobacco; United States.

BIBLIOGRAPHY

Amanat, Abbas, ed. *Cities and Trade: Consul Abbott on the Economy and Society of Iran, 1847–1866.* London: Ithaca Press, 1983.

Baghdianz-McCabe, Ina. *The Shah's Silk for Europe's Silver: The Eurasian Trade of the Julfa Armenians in Safavid Iran and India (1530–1750).* Atlanta: Scholars Press, 1999.

Barendse, R. J. *The Arabian Seas: The Indian Ocean of the Seventeenth Century.* Armonk, NY: Sharpe, 2002.

Dale, Stephen Frederic. *Indian Merchants and Eurasian Trade, 1600–1750.* Cambridge, U.K.: Cambridge University Press, 1994.

Bharier, Julian. *Economic Development in Iran, 1900–1970.* London: Oxford University Press, 1971.

Floor, Willem. *The Economy of Safavid Persia.* Wiesbaden, Germany: Reichert Verlag, 2000.

Matthee, Rudolph. *The Politics of Trade in Safavid Iran: Silk for Silver, 1600–1730.* Cambridge, U.K.: Cambridge University Press, 1999.

Matthee, RUDI. "Between Venice and Surat: The Role of Gold in Late Safavid Iran." *Modern Asian Studies* 34:1 (Feb. 2000): 231–265.

Schneider, Manfred. *Beiträge zur Wirstschaftsstruktur und Wirtschaftsentwicklung Persiens, 1850–1900 (Contribution to the Economic Structure and Development of Persia, 1850–1900).* Stuttgart, Germany: Franz Steiner Verlag, 1990.

Steensgaard, Niels. *The Asian Trade Revolution of the Seventeenth Century: The East India Companies and the Decline of the Caravan Trade.* Chicago: University of Chicago Press, 1974.

Rudi Matthee

IRON AND STEEL

At the heart of any understanding of the international diffusion of the iron and steel industry is the political economy of the product cycle. In the product-cycle model of international trade—for a particular industrial sector such as iron and steel—a country moves sequentially through four phases. Net importer (phase 1) gives way to being both importer and exporter (phase 2). In turn, entry into the second phase sets the stage for emergence as net exporter (phase 3). The conclusion of the cycle (phase 4) occurs when the country returns to being a net importer of the sector's products. At any given point in time, one or a group of countries that have made the transition to the third phase are at the technological forefront of the industry. They enjoy leadership status. However, as they slip into the fourth stage they surrender their leadership role.

How and why countries move through the product cycle in iron and steel is a story involving economics and politics deeply intertwined. From a political-economy point of view, securing and maintaining leadership in iron and steel is important because the industry exercises a strategic role in shaping economic and international power. Waging modern warfare depends on a nation's capacity to secure iron and steel products. Leadership is important because a fully developed iron and steel sector has a voracious demand for both labor and capital; because technological progress in the industry is ongoing, generating research and development investment and providing challenging opportunities for engineers; be-

Copper engraving of an eighteenth century blast furnace from Denis Diderot and Jean Le Rond d'Alembert, Encyclopédie, on Dictionnaire Raisonné des Sciences, des Arts et des Métiers. *The production design of this furnace used air combustion with high temperatures. In the resulting molten mixture, iron ore sinks to the bottom while impurities float to the top.* © CHRISTEL GERSTENBERG/CORBIS. REPRODUCED BY PERMISSION.

cause capital equipment in the sector tends to embody new technology, newer vintages trumping older; and because the industry enjoys powerful linkages, both forward (to shipbuilding, automobiles, airplanes, and construction) and backward (mining, transportation, and energy-supplying infrastructure).

U.K. LEADERSHIP

The first country in modern times to exercise leadership in iron and steel was the United Kingdom (prior to 100 BC, China was the probably the world's technological leader in the industry.) A major importer of Swedish iron during the 17th and early 18th century—the Swedish industry having made major advances in the 1600–1720 era—the United Kingdom assumed leadership during the Industrial Revolution in the late 18th and early 19th centuries. The United Kingdom was home to the Industrial Revolution, which involved simultaneous transformations in the institutions of production (manufacturing in factories supplanting the decentralized putting-out system, in which merchants served as intermediaries at virtually every stage of the production process); the harnessing of energy through mechanization, with steam power supplanting water power through mechanization; and industrial growth (especially in cotton textiles). In

A worker oversees a huge ladle of molten iron from a blast furnace as it is poured into an open-hearth furnace to be converted into steel in 1941. The facility is located in Youngstown, Ohio, a major center that fueled the development of the U.S. iron and steel industry. THE LIBRARY OF CONGRESS.

the eighteenth century the United Kingdom witnessed tremendous technical improvements in iron and steel manufacture. Particularly notable were the innovations made by Abraham Darby (1678–1717), who substituted coke for charcoal, and the inspirations of Henry Cort (1740–1800), who discovered that heating pig iron in a reverberatory furnace and stirring, or "puddling," the molten economized on the removal of impurities from the pig iron. Cort also developed a rolling mill that not only pressed out some of the carbon embodied in the iron but also generated sheets of iron that could be fashioned into boilers and plating for shipbuilding.

Drawing upon the breakthroughs of the Industrial Revolution, the United Kingdom became the workshop of the world during the first seven decades of the nineteenth century. Its entrepreneurs pioneered the creation of a nationwide railway network and converted most of

its merchant marine from wooden sailing ships to iron- and steel-plated steamships propelled by screw propellers harnessed to high-pressure steam boilers. The United Kingdom also remained the locus for most of the new technologies developed in iron and steel manufacturing. For instance, Henry Bessemer (1813–1898), took out a patent during the 1850s for a novel process of making steel in which a blast of heated air was blown through the molten mass of pig iron, burning off carbon and other impurities. And in the 1860s William Siemens (1823–1883) developed the basic concepts of the "open-hearth" method for making steel, whereby the molten was poured into shallow pans over which gases and air were passed to remove impurities. Pierre-Emile Martin (1824–1914) played a role in developing this technique. In short, until the last quarter of the nineteenth century the United Kingdom was a large exporter of iron and steel products, and enjoyed world technological leadership in the field. It exported iron and steel products extensively to the United States, Western Europe and its Empire. These exports were a considerable share of total British production. For instance, in 1900 the United Kingdom exported about a fifth of its total output of approximately 5 million tons (it exported slightly less than 1 million tons.)

U.S. LEADERSHIP

However, during the final quarter of the nineteenth and the initial decade of the twentieth century, the United States and Germany emerged as powerful trade and technological rivals in iron and steel. Sheltered by relatively high international transportation costs (in the case of the United States) and "infant-industry" and "mature-industry" protective tariffs (in the cases of both Germany and the United States), enjoying low raw-material costs, and reaping the benefits of considerable capital accumulation that embodied or was compatible with the new Bessemer and "open-hearth" technologies, the iron and steel sectors of these two new industrial giants went head to head with the British industry in both their domestic and international markets. After World War I, with German industry suffering in the aftermath of military defeat in the protracted conflict, the United States emerged as the technological and trade leader in the sector. Labor productivity advanced at such a brisk rate between 1913 and 1937 that by the later date, U.S. labor productivity was at least twice the British level. From the end of World War I until 1959, the iron and steel industry of the United States continued to cling to technological leadership and continued to export more than it imported, shipping output to Western Europe, Asia, and the rest of the Americas.

Why after 1960 did the industry of the United States move into the fourth phase of the product cycle, with its role as technological leader slipping away? Part of the reason lies within U.S. industry itself—for instance, in 1959 the United Steel Workers went on strike, initiating the longest and one of the most bitter work stoppages in U.S. history, testimony to acrimonious labor-management relations within the sector. But the major part of the story involves the massive economic rebuilding of Japan and Western Europe after World War II. Utilizing the latest technologies in iron and steel making—the basic oxygen furnace that refines molten pig iron by pumping oxygen through the molten at intensely elevated heats, and continuous casting that speeds up the time required to produce bars or sheets of steel—the iron and steel industries of Japan, Germany, Belgium, and France experienced unprecedented growth between 1950 and 1970.

ASIAN LEADERSHIP

Helping countries such as Japan emerge as the international low-cost leader were plummeting transportation costs and the development of massive bulk carriers for shipping iron ore, coal, and limestone across oceans, holding down costs in the iron and steel sector, which mainly depended on imports from Australia and Latin America for inputs. Japan's international leadership within the industry was short-lived, however. Japan confronted competition from newer producers, notably South Korea; upward pressure on production costs due to rising oil prices in the aftermath of the oil crises of the 1970s as well as escalating wages; and realignment of the yen/U.S. dollar exchange rate after the early 1970s, which pushed Japanese export prices up to heady levels. All of these contributed to Japan's drift towards the fourth phase of the product cycle in iron and steel.

How crucial were government policies during the period when leadership of the industry passed from the United States to Japan? Much has been made of Japan's industrial policy—the targeting of sunrise industries, the promotion of soft landings by sunset industries— especially the role of the Ministry of International Trade and Industry (METI) during the 1950s and 1960s. Most economists remain skeptical about the effectiveness of industrial policy, arguing that profit-driven competition was far more important than targeting in the rapid expansion of Japanese industry. More important may have been the slow growth of real wages in iron and steel manufacturing, with wage growth in unionized companies tied to general economy-wide productivity growth rather than productivity growth in a particular sector, based on the logic of Spring Offensive collective bargaining that began to dominate Japanese industrial relations during the mid-1950s. Most Japanese unions are organized along enterprise lines, one union to an enterprise. Because enterprises within any industry compete against each other, the unions in the industry are reluctant to carry out strikes unless all of the other unions in the industry strike simultaneously. In order to overcome this structural weakness, enterprise unions banded together into federations. In turn, the federations organized general coordinated offensives, all of the unions within the federation negotiating at the same time. The most famous of these coordinated wage increase offensives is the Spring Offensive, wage bargaining occurring in the first quarter of each year. In the United States the governmental response to loss of leadership and, eventually, loss of jobs as imports from Japan and Western Europe soared, was protectionism. Under the threat of U.S. quotas, Japanese iron and steel exporters agreed to impose voluntary export restraints (VERs) on their own industry. From the late 1960s onward, imports of iron and steel products to the United States from both Europe and Japan were managed under a series of negotiated agreements.

Although the importance of the Japanese government in promoting the rise to international prominence of its iron and steel sector has been much debated, the crucial role played by the South Korean government in developing Pohong Iron and Steel Limited (popularly known as POSCO) is not in doubt. Set up by the Korean government in 1968, shored by government subsidization (including the construction of harbors, roads, and electrical-supply lines), POSCO emerged as a major competitor to its Japanese rivals during the 1970s and 1980s. A product of industrial policy more aggressive and far-reaching than that pioneered by METI during the 1950s and 1960s, POSCO operated more like a private-market company concerned with maximizing profits than a government-run and -managed corporation. Perhaps it is best thought of as semipublic/semiprivate. Not only did POSCO emerge as a profit-oriented corporation that quickly increased its exporting capacity, it also served as the catalyst for the rapid expansion of shipbuilding and automobile manufacturing in South Korea. As a result, South Korean firms began to challenge Japanese corporations in a wide variety of manufacturing sectors ranging from iron and steel to the building of supertankers.

CONCLUSION

The product-cycle model best characterizes the international diffusion of iron and steel production and trade since the eighteenth century. Understanding this cycle requires appreciating the importance of government policy interventions: managing trade by protecting sunrise "infant industries" and managing trade to increase the lifespan of dying sunset industries. Ultimately, however, it is the inexorable push of technological progress in the industry, embodied in the national capital stocks of the iron and steel sector (with stocks of a more youthful vintage enjoying a technical edge over aged stocks) that drives the product cycle in country after country.

SEE ALSO AUTOMOBILE; BESSEMER, HENRY; INDUSTRIALIZATION; JAPANESE MINISTRY OF INTERNATIONAL TRADE AND INDUSTRY (METI); MINING.

BIBLIOGRAPHY

Amsden, Alice. *Asia's Next Giant: South Korea and Late Industrialization.* New York: Oxford University Press, 1989.

Bodsworth, Colin, ed. *British Iron and Steel, AD 1800–2000 and Beyond.* London: IOM Communications, 2001.

Jones, Kent. *Politics Vs. Economics in World Steel Trade.* London: Allen and Unwin, 1986.

Lindert, Peter. "U.S. Foreign Trade and Trade Policy in the Twentieth Century." In *The Cambridge Economic History of the United States: The Twentieth Century,* ed. Stanley Engerman and Robert Gallman. New York: Cambridge University Press, 2000.

Temin, Peter. *Iron and Steel in Nineteenth-Century America: An Economic Enquiry.* Cambridge, MA: Massachusetts Institute of Technology Press, 1964.

Tiffany, Paul. *The Decline of American Steel: How Management, Labor, and Government Went Wrong.* New York: Oxford University Press, 1988.

Yonekura, Seiichiro. *The Japanese Iron and Steel Industry, 1850–1990: Continuity and Discontinuity.* New York: St. Martin's Press, 1994.

Carl Mosk

ITALY

At the end of the Middle Ages the Italian peninsula was known as the most civilized region in Europe; it was the focal point of the development and economic growth of Europe between the twelfth and fifteenth centuries. During this period the Italian cities were centers for the production and circulation of goods for the whole of Europe; Italian merchants and entrepreneurs played a leading role in economic and financial activity: They laid down the rules and regulations for accountancy records; they devised working methods for the placement of their products (such as genuine joint ventures or consumer credit transactions); and they created an extensive network in the most important commercial markets.

DECLINE AND CRISIS

The preeminence of merchants from Florence, Sienna, Genoa, and Milan in European markets began to decline as the center of trading shifted from the Mediterranean to the Atlantic coast. With the ending of the Hundred Years War and in the wake of geographical discoveries, the main lines for the trade of men and merchandise shifted from the cities of the Italian peninsula to the cities of Western and Northern Europe. Portugal, Spain, and then France, England, and Holland superseded traders of Italian origin; Hanseatic merchants took the place of the Bardi, Peruzzi, Riccardi, and Medici, to name but a few.

The sixteenth century represented a period of enormous change for the Italian economy: The merchant houses that had achieved much in terms of trade in fabric, leather goods, and various foodstuffs, along with precious gold and silk cloth, slowly saw a decline in business. The magistracies concerned with commercial activity, such as the Commercial Tribunals (forerunners of the modern Chambers of Commerce) or the Savi for Venetian mercantile trade, were gradually relieved of their authority, as the volume of commerce decreased. Venice and Genoa clashed over control of the Greek islands, but until the late seventeenth century they continued to control trade with Eastern markets and around the coasts of Africa, even if the volume of goods traded on the Rialto no longer reached the level of previous centuries.

The Italian trade crisis began in the sixteenth century and continued in the seventeenth century, resulting in the peninsula's economy becoming gradually marginalized. Merchants ceased to engage in trade and withdrew to new, magnificent villas in the Italian countryside. Economically the Italian peninsula eventually became limited to internal trade, although many companies and business partnerships retained entrepôts and trading premises in many European markets.

REVIVAL

The position changed decisively with political unification in 1861. Unification was an essential prerequisite for the revival of manufacturing and trade. Barriers between the old states were abolished, currency and weights and measures were unified, and the first government after unification invested a great deal in the construction of railways, tunnels through the Alps, and an expansion of the merchant fleet.

Italy, unified, was a country with a coastline of over 5,000 miles and thus had tremendous potential to develop maritime trade. At the same time, it was a country lacking in primary resources, with no coal or iron. The switch from sail to steam and the change from ships with wooden hulls to iron ones was a long and involved process, which took the entire second half of the nineteenth century, thus slowing down the recovery of trade in an economy affected by industrialization at the turn of the twentieth century. Customs measures (in 1878 and 1887) and protectionist policies affected the movement of trade in the decades after unification. Colonial wars at the end of the century saw renewed use of Italian carriers and inaugurated a period of moderate expansion. Extensive emigration resulted in a growing requirement for passenger ships but also produced a spate of trade between the new overseas settlements and the home country.

Italy exported wine, oil, fruit, sulfur, rice, textiles, and machinery, but its balance of trade with the most developed European nations and with the United States remained negative, as a result of a lack of raw materials. The opportunity for trade between the Mediterranean and the Indian Ocean presented by the opening of the Suez Canal resulted in the development of the port of Brindisi as a transit port for Suez, but the increasing independence of shipping and the unappealing Italian infrastructure did not result in the desired takeoff.

THE TWENTIETH CENTURY

World War I saw a marked rise in the volume of trade and a growth in shipbuilding. Demand caused by the war increased the flow of trade. The postwar period was marked by a grave crisis in reorganization: Many shipyards were forced to close, and most of the few that remained were obliged to diversify their production. The shipyard crisis was made worse by the fact that Italy had acquired the territory of Trieste with the modern facilities of Monfalcone and the significant increase in the manufacturing capacity of these facilities, while the demand for new ships dropped sharply.

The years between the wars saw a terrible recession in Italy, caused by the Great Depression and made worse by the Italian decision to pursue a drastic currency reevaluation in 1926, reducing foreign demand for Italian goods. The commercial isolation resulting from the condemnation and sanctions of the League of Nations following the war undertaken in Ethiopia by Mussolini in 1935, resulted in a policy of economic self-sufficiency, while the advent of World War II shook up the existing order, revealing how weak it was.

A new chapter in the history of Italian trade was opened during the second postwar period. Italy turned its back on fascist dictatorship and adopted an Atlantic outlook. It became part of the western economy and made rapid progress in making the transition from a primarily agricultural economy to an industrial one.

The fleet was reestablished and reached a tonnage that would have been completely unthinkable in preceding decades. Italian shipyards produced beautiful but practical passenger ships. The balance of payments improved steadily, thanks to the currency resulting from tourism, and the volume of trade increased markedly.

Italy exported machinery, precision mechanical instruments, and agricultural produce, overcoming competition from countries that were much more highly industrialized. It made the most of the opportunities offered by the Marshall Plan. Italy joined GATT in 1947, opening a new avenue to the international markets, consistent with the export-led economic model. It joined the Organization for Economic Cooperation in Europe in 1948, and the European Steel and Coal Community in 1953 and signed the Treaty of Rome in 1957. The ports of Genoa, Naples, Livorno, and Venice recorded a growing volume of trade, and today Italy has become one of the strategically important countries for the exchange of people and goods, a Western gateway to those countries once under the aegis of the former Soviet Union.

To the south, Italy has continually engaged in trade with the countries of North Africa, relationships that are

MAP BY XNR PRODUCTIONS. THE GALE GROUP.

often complex and difficult because of political crises. This interchange is growing today, along with the shift of Italian business towards the new markets in the Far East, such as China and India. From 1993 to at least the beginning of the twenty-first century, Italy's balance of payments was positive, and in terms of foreign trade Italy became one of the seven leading countries in the world, a matter of some satisfaction given its past.

In short the Italian peninsula was the driving force of Europe from the twelfth to the fifteenth century in terms of trade, before undergoing a long period of decline and crisis. The revival of recent decades, presented significant opportunities for Italian goods in international markets, especially "Italian style" products, such as fashion, clothing, and furniture, as well as primary-sector produce (wine, oil, fruit, etc.) and machinery and precision instruments. In the twentieth century, scientific research and technical invention produced scientists such as Guglielmo Marconi, Enrico Fermi, and Giorgio Rubbia; there were creative masters in the field of fashion, several Italian companies have bid for and won contracts for major developments in many countries, worldwide. Italian foreign trade has a tendency to be cyclical, and it is to be hoped that it can remain in a position that is consistent with its role as one of the top seven industrialized nations.

SEE ALSO AGRICULTURE; BALANCE OF PAYMENTS; CARGOES, FREIGHT; CARGOES, PASSENGER; CLIMATE; COMMON MARKET AND THE EUROPEAN UNION; FREE TRADE, THEORY AND PRACTICE; GATT, WTO; GENOA; GREAT DEPRESSION OF THE 1930S; INDUSTRIALIZATION; INTERNATIONAL TRADE AGREEMENTS; MEDITERRANEAN; REGIONAL TRADE AGREEMENTS; SHIPBUILDING; VENICE; VOLCANIC ERUPTIONS.

BIBLIOGRAPHY

Aldcroft, Derek H. *The European Economy: 1750–1914.* London: Routledge, 1993.

Bonelli, Franco. "Il capitalismo italiano: Linee generali d'interprtetazione." In *Storia d'Italia. Annali I. Dal feudalesimo al capitalismo.* Turin, Italy: Einaudi, 1978.

Braudel, Fernand. *Espansione europea e capitalismo: 1450–1650.* Bologna, Italy: Mulino, 1999.

Castronovo, Valerio. *Storia economica d'Italia. Dall'Ottocento ai giorni nostri.* Turin, Italy: Einaudi, 1995.

Ciocca, Pierluigi. *L'economia italiana nel contesto internazionale.* Bologna, Italy: Mulino, 1976.

Fanfani, Tommaso. "The Guilds in Italian Economic Development in the Early Modern Era: Guilty or Innocent?" In *Guilds, Markets and Work Regulations in Italy: 16th–19th Centuries,* eds. Alberto Guenzi, Paola Massa, and Fausto Piola Caselli. Aldershot, U.K.: Ashgate, 1998.

Graziani, Antonio. *Lo sviluppo dell'economia italiana come sviluppo di un'economia aperta.* Turin, Italy: Einaudi, 1969.

Harlafatis, Gelina. "Storia marittima e storia dei porti." *Memoria e ricerca. Rivista di storia contemporanea* 2 (2002): 5–21.

Tonizzi, Maria Elisabetta. "Il porto di Genova: 1861–1970." *Memoria e ricerca. Rivista di storia contemporanea* 2 (2002): 23–40

Tommaso Fanfani

JAJA, KING OF OPOBO

c. 1821–1891

Enslaved as a boy, Jaja emerged as founder and ruler of Opobo (r. 1870–1887), the most important city-state in the Niger Delta in the late nineteenth century. While Jaja was undoubtedly remarkable, his career exemplifies the rise of an individual of humble origins to the top of a *house,* the basic unit of economic and political organization in the Delta. Jaja began his career in the Annie Pepple House in Bonny, then the main commercial center in the area. In 1869, when competition with a rival house leader drove Jaja to withdraw from Bonny; most of the major houses departed with him. The British consul recognized Jaja as king of Opobo and conceded that European traders could not penetrate into the interior to purchase palm oil and kernel. In 1884, when Britain signed treaties with several Delta communities, Jaja guaranteed his monopoly by insisting upon the removal of the free trade clause. Just three years later, the British kidnapped Jaja on the grounds that he was hampering British trade interests. Jaja was tried in the Gold Coast and forced into exile in the West Indies. Although British traders were unable to penetrate the interior markets until many years after Jaja's abduction and exile, his departure marked a critical point in British involvement in the area.

SEE ALSO AGRICULTURE; EMPIRE, BRITISH; ETHNIC GROUPS, AFRICANS; IMPERIALISM AND COLONIALISM; NIGERIA; ROYAL NIGER COMPANY; SLAVERY AND AFRICAN SLAVE TRADE.

BIBLIOGRAPHY

Baker, Geoffrey L. *Trade Winds on the Niger: The Saga of the Royal Niger Company, 1930–1971.* London: Radcliffe Press, 1996.

Ofonagoro, Walter. *Trade and Imperialism in Southern Nigeria, 1881–1929.* New York: Nok Publishers, 1979.

Anene Ejikeme

JAMAICA

Jamaica is the third-largest of the Caribbean Islands, with an area of 4,400 square miles. Mountains, plateaus, and plains make a diverse landscape. No point is more than 25 miles from the coast, and the sea, the ship, and overseas markets have dominated the island's trade. Columbus came to Jamaica in 1494, and the Spanish ruled the island until the British conquest of 1655. For most of Jamaica's modern history it has been a colony, gaining independence in 1962. By 2001 its population was 2.6 million.

Before the Spanish, the Taino people lived on the island's own resources, conducting limited trade with Jamaica's neighbors. The small Spanish colonial population looked further afield for its markets, selling hides and livestock to the Spanish Main, but output was insignificant. The arrival of the British and the establishment of the sugar plantation as the basic unit of enterprise by the 1670s resulted in a long-term orientation towards distant markets. Under the system of mercantilism, which was governed by the Navigation Acts, Jamaica's exports of sugar and rum went almost exclusively to Britain, whereas molasses was traded with the North Ameri-

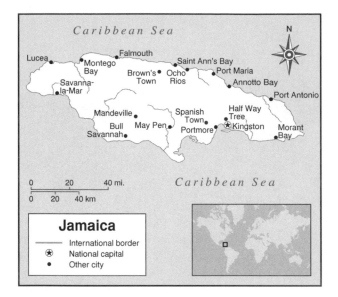

MAP BY XNR PRODUCTIONS. THE GALE GROUP.

can colonies for a range of plantation supplies including lumber, salted fish, and flour. The Atlantic slave trade brought people from Africa to work on the plantations; this system of slavery continued until 1838.

Slaveowners paid for their purchases of enslaved Africans with the proceeds received from sales of sugar in the metropolitan British market. The need to establish credit in order to make these payments resulted in the "commission system," in which planters committed future crops to particular metropolitan merchant-factors. The planters then paid for slaves with bills of exchange drawn on the metropolitan factors, who honored these bills on the condition that they received commission on the sale of the sugars shipped by the planter and on goods sent out to the plantation. The result of this system was a perpetual indebtedness that tied planters to metropolitan merchants and reduced the ability of colonial merchants to compete. Vertical integration sometimes occurred, with the merchants owning ships and eventually plantations. This metropolitan dominance of Jamaica's trade continued into the twentieth century.

In spite of Jamaica's small size, the island proved a major producer of cane sugar, exporting more than 80 percent of its total output, as well as large proportions of the byproducts rum and molasses. Sugar and rum accounted for 75 percent of the value of all Jamaican exports until 1838. Jamaica was the leading sugar exporter in the British Empire by the 1730s, and in 1805 it was the largest individual exporter in the world. Jamaica was also a major exporter of coffee, becoming famous for its high-priced Blue Mountain variety. Coffee was introduced only in the late eighteenth century, when it was given tariff protection by the British and benefited from the revo-

lution in Saint-Domingue (Haiti). The dynamics of the plantation system based on slavery were changed by the American Revolution, which disrupted the trade in plantation supplies, and by the abolition in 1808 of the British Atlantic slave trade. Coffee exports peaked in 1814, and the export of sugar declined throughout most of the nineteenth century. British import duties on sugar were equalized between 1847 and 1854, and the introduction of free trade in 1874 meant that Jamaica lost all of its former preferential advantages.

Minor export crops produced during the period of slavery included pimento (allspice), ginger, cotton, indigo and logwood (used for dye). Following emancipation, and the decline of sugar and coffee, a vigorous peasantry grew up to replace the plantation system. Some of the minor crops were developed for external trade, and new items were added. By the end of the nineteenth century logwood and bananas were among the leading exports, with oranges, ginger, and coconuts also becoming important. During the twentieth century bananas, coconuts, and citrus shifted towards large-scale plantation production, with trade encompassed by the vertical integration of production, shipping, and marketing by metropolitan corporations. Sugar revived up until the 1960s but then entered a new period of decline. Coffee expanded rapidly after 1970, tapping the Japanese market. In the last decades of the twentieth century the export of fresh fruit and vegetables became increasingly important, particularly to meet seasonal shortages in North America.

Although agriculture remained an important sector in the twentieth century, the rise of mining dramatically altered the structure of Jamaica's export trade. Jamaica has excellent reserves of bauxite, which is used to produce alumina and aluminum. Mining began in 1952 and by the 1960s Jamaica had become the world's largest exporter, accounting for 20 percent of global output. Its world ranking was quickly diminished by the entry of much larger producers such as Australia, but bauxite continued to have a major role in Jamaica's external trade. In 2000 alumina and bauxite accounted for 50 percent of Jamaica's exports, far outweighing sugar (5%) and bananas (2%). The companies that invested in the industry were North American, and it was to that region that the product was shipped. The downside of this shift to trade in bauxite was the increased dependence of Jamaica on imported fuels (a petroleum refinery was opened in 1964), machinery, and equipment. The period from 1950 also saw tourism grow as a major sector of the economy, replacing the dependence on export commodities but still requiring the import of many supplies, including some of the food consumed by visitors.

Independence was associated with efforts to increase the scale of manufacturing within Jamaica, following the strategy of import-substitution for economic growth. After the dissolution of the Federation of the West Indies (1958–1962), a move that seeking to bring the British islands into a political union, energy was put into expanding trade between the former British colonies through the establishment of the Caribbean Free Trade Area in 1968 and CARICOM (the Caribbean Community) in 1973. The result was limited. In 2000 Jamaica took only 11 percent of its imports from CARICOM countries and sent them a mere 3 percent of its exports. The United States was firmly established as Jamaica's major trader, taking 39 percent of exports and supplying 44 percent of imports. Europe, including the United Kingdom, still took 30 percent of Jamaica's exports, honoring agreements on sugar and bananas, but by 2000 supplied less than 10 percent of imports. Jamaica became a significant player in the international illegal drug trade, first as an exporter of marijuana and then as a transshipper of cocaine.

The individual indebtedness of the planters in the eighteenth and nineteenth centuries went together with a "favorable" balance of trade and a positive balance of payments. Deterioration in the balance of trade and payments became evident first in the 1870s but remained minor until the 1920s, when the gap between exports and imports began to widen. A new phase of growth in public external indebtedness began in the 1950s and was associated with heavy government borrowing, particularly in the 1970s and 1980s. This led to agreements with the International Monetary Fund and the rapid devaluation of the Jamaican dollar. By the 1990s more than 40 percent of the fiscal budget was directed to the payment of interest on external debt, and in 2000 the value of merchandise imports was double the value of exports. Tourism was central to the economy and the major legal source of foreign exchange, but new borrowing was essential.

SEE ALSO COFFEE; EMPIRE, BRITISH; EMPIRE, SPANISH; ETHNIC GROUPS, AFRICANS; INTERNATIONAL MONETARY FUND (IMF); LABORERS, COERCED; LABORERS, CONTRACT; MERCANTILISM; PIRACY; PRIVATEERING; SLAVERY AND THE AFRICAN SLAVE TRADE; SUGAR, MOLASSES, AND RUM; UNITED KINGDOM; UNITED STATES; WEST INDIA COMPANY, DUTCH.

BIBLIOGRAPHY

Eisner, Gisela. *Jamaica, 1830–1930: A Study in Economic Growth.* Manchester, U.K.: Manchester University Press, 1961.

Hall, Douglas. *Free Jamaica, 1838–1865: An Economic History.* New Haven, CT: Yale University Press, 1959.

Higman, B. W. *Slave Population and Economy in Jamaica, 1807–1834.* Cambridge, U.K.: Cambridge University Press, 1976.

Jefferson, Owen. *The Post-War Economic Development of Jamaica.* Kingston, Jamaica: Institute of Social and Economic Research, University of the West Indies, 1972.

Nettleford, Rex, ed. *Jamaica in Independence: Essays on the Early Years.* Kingston, Jamaica: Heinemann Caribbean, 1989.

Sheridan, Richard. *Sugar and Slavery: An Economic History of the British West Indies, 1623–1775.* Barbados: Caribbean Universities Press, 1974.

B. W. Higman

JAPAN

The issue of how to handle foreign trade has been crucial to the long-term economic development of Japan since 1450. Cut off by sea from mainland East Asia and often viewed as the country furthest from Europe, Japan sought to absorb technologies and institutions from more advanced civilizations while maintaining its political and economic autonomy. To achieve this, a variety of trade policies were pursued, ranging from more than two centuries of "seclusion" to aggressive export campaigns in the twentieth century. On the whole, the Japanese experience presents a good case for commitment to foreign trade. It is reflected in the nation's successful absorption of foreign technology, import substitution, and its development of competitive export industries, as well as in Japan's failure during some periods as a result of its divergence from foreign trade.

FROM TRADING NATION TO "SECLUSION"

From the fifteenth to the middle of the nineteenth centuries Japanese trade was conducted under the international environment dominated by the China-centered tributary-trade system. The Ashikaga shogunate established the practice of sending ships to China in the form of *kango* (tally) trade in 1403. This consisted both of tribute paid by the shogunate to the Ming emperor and of private trade, which was also permitted under strict conditions imposed by the Chinese. After 1465, against the background of increased piracy, the Ming government limited the tally trade to once a decade and no more than three ships per voyage. The Japanese sent gold, swords, and sulphur; the Chinese sent copper coins, silver, and silk goods in return.

After the *de facto* collapse of the Ashikaga shogunate in 1467, Japan went through a period of internal warfare. During the sixteenth century powerful regional warlords began to engage in mining operations, and with the introduction of mining and smelting technology from China by way of the Korean Peninsula, the production of silver increased rapidly. From the second half of the century, exports of silver increased so fast that Japan became one of the most active trading nations in the world. Japan imported not only raw silk and silk cloth but also advanced weaving machines from China for the development of the silk industry. On the other hand, the domestic production of cotton, which began in the late fifteenth century, expanded rapidly as the economy grew. So did rice cultivation, partly as a result of the diffusion of foreign varieties.

The Ming's strict trade ban induced the growth of alternative routes, as well as Japan's trade with Southeast and South Asia. Japanese merchants went to Southeast Asia, whereas the Portuguese brought guns and gunpowder as well as raw silk and silk cloth to Japan, all of which was paid for in silver. The introduction of guns attracted the attention of warlords, including the architects of unification, and allowed those merchants who handled arms in trade cities such as Sakai to prosper. But the primary function of the Portuguese was to intermediate intra-Asian trade.

In 1603 Tokugawa shogunate assumed power; it would rule the country until 1867. Initially, the new rulers actively promoted trade. Between 1604 and 1635 Japan sent at least 350 officially approved "read seal" ships to East and Southeast Asia, exporting silver, copper, camphor, and lacquer, and importing raw silk, silk cloth, and some Southeast Asian produce, including sugar. Meanwhile, the Dutch East India Company, a newcomer in East Asian trade, encouraged the shogunate to expel the Portuguese and to trade with the Dutch, who promised that they would not promote Christianity in Japan.

The shogunate issued a series of decrees in the 1630s to ban trade, foreign travel, and the building of ships. Only Chinese and Dutch were allowed to trade at Dejima, an island at Nagasaki, under the direct control of the shogunate. There were three other trading routes that were open: Satsuma-Ryukyu route, Tsushima-Pusan route, and Matsumae domain route in the north. The use of guns was forbidden, and a strict control of contacts with foreigners was exercised. The basic features of this "seclusion" policy lasted till the 1850s.

The implementation of this policy was motivated not only by the ban on Christianity but also by the desire to conduct intra-Asian trade to Japan's advantage within the tributary-trade system. To that extent, the aim was not so much "seclusion" as managed trade. Indeed, a substantial amount of trade, particularly exports of silver, continued throughout the seventeenth century. The profits from silver mines and export trade helped to establish Tokugawa rule. Chinese and Dutch traders were mainly engaged in intra-Asian trade, although Japanese porcelain and lacquer were popular in Europe.

After the early eighteenth century the volume of trade declined significantly as silver exports decreased.

Japan went through the process of import substitution of silk, and later of sugar. By the middle of the eighteenth century Japan probably reached a level of technology and a standard of living comparable to that of the most developed part of China. By the first half of the nineteenth century it achieved a standard of living roughly comparable to pre–Industrial Revolution Western Europe in terms of education, longevity, and basic calorific intake, although science and technology did not develop in the same way it did in the West. The sheer lack of navigation and military technology, a result of the "seclusion" policy, contributed to this difference.

FROM THE OPENING OF PORTS TO ASIA'S FIRST INDUSTRIAL NATION

The Chinese defeat in the two Opium Wars during the 1840s informed the shogunate of the imminent Western threat, and prepared it for the arrival in 1853 of Commodore Matthew Perry (1794–1858), who demanded the opening of Japan. In 1858 the shogunate signed commercial treaties with the United States, Britain, France, Holland, and Russia, and in the following year opened the ports of Kanagawa (Yokohama), near Edo (present-day Tokyo), and Hakodate in the northern-most island, in addition to Nagasaki. They became "treaty ports," where Western traders could conduct trade. The treaties were unequal in that they acknowledged extraterritorial rights of Westerners inside the ports, deprived Japan of tariff autonomy, and included the most-favored-nation clause, which tended to reinforce Japan's disadvantage arising from the lack of tariff autonomy.

On the other hand, unlike in the Chinese treaties concluded earlier, the Japanese government was able to insert an opium-prohibition clause, and it effectively banned Western traders from traveling inside Japan, which prevented them from collecting commercial information and gave Japanese traders a bargaining edge at the treaty ports. Although the lack of tariff autonomy was humiliating to the Japanese, and treaty revision became a major goal of the government, the administration of trade itself remained in Japanese hands.

After the restoration of 1868 a new government attempted a systematic introduction of Western technology and organizations. In order to earn foreign exchange, exports of raw silk and tea were promoted. Trade with other Asian countries also grew as the tributary-trade system was gradually replaced by one of forced free trade under Western domination. During the period of industrialization the bulk of exports of primary products went to the United States and Europe, and machinery and a relatively small amount of capital were imported from there. At the same time, Japan imported primary products such as raw cotton, rice, sugar, and soya-bean-

SKETCHES FROM JAPAN, BY OUR SPECIAL ARTIST : THE CUSTOM-HOUSE AT YOKOHAMA.

An 1861 sketch of men using a scale inside the customs house in Yokohama, Japan. Yokohama, one of the first ports opened to foreign trade in Japan, is the country's second largest city and a leading seaport in the Keihin Industrial Region. The country's first railroad linked the city to Tokyo in 1872. © CORBIS. REPRODUCED BY PERMISSION.

related products from India, Southeast Asia, and China, and in turn exported cotton yarn, cotton cloth, and sundries to these countries.

After an initial period of direct introduction of Western technology and organizations, which was only partially successful, the government encouraged the modernization of traditional industries and promoted exports. It collected commercial information, held exhibitions, and advised on patents and packaging through Japanese consuls overseas, trade associations, chambers of commerce, and commercial museums, and transferred the best technology and practice across the country. Combined with the growth of modern industries, especially in cotton spinning and machinery, labor-intensive industries met the growing demand for cheap manufactured goods, both at home and abroad. Chinese commercial networks helped their distribution in Asia.

Traditional merchant houses such as Mitsui amassed wealth by serving the needs of the government. Mitsui Bussan, the first general trading company (*sogo shosha*),

dealt with all major commodities and traded with all major countries. Mitsubishi, which emerged after the restoration by engaging in coastal and international shipping and shipbuilding as well as in the coal business, developed a powerful group of modern industrial enterprises. These financial and industrial business groups came to be called *zaibatsu*. The general trading company, or its functional equivalent, acted as a core organizer of the group.

During World War I European trade and shipping were disrupted, and Japan proceeded with import substitution in shipbuilding and machinery. The profit gained during the war also financed the growth of the cotton-textile industry. Although exports of raw silk to the United States stagnated during the 1920s, cotton textiles penetrated into the international markets of Asia and Africa during the 1930s, in spite of the tariffs and quotas put up to prevent it, and the effects of the Great Depression.

Japan imposed a strong assimilation policy in Taiwan and Korea and tied their economies to the mainland,

A busy city street in the Ginza section of Tokyo in 1999.
*The area is a major shopping and entertainment section of the
city characterized by its electronic signs on building fronts. It
was founded in 1612 and named after a silver coin foundry.*
© ROBERT ESSEL NYC/CORBIS. REPRODUCED BY PERMISSION.

making Japan's share in their trade overwhelming. On
the other hand, the colonies' share in Japanese trade was
not large before the 1930s. Even so, imports of cheap Korean rice helped keep down both the real wage and the
agrarian rent for the benefit of industrialists and urban
consumers. The establishment in 1931 of Manchukuo, a
puppet state in the northern-most part of China, enlarged the Japanese sphere of influence under which the
yen-denominated currencies circulated. The expansion
of the "yen bloc" was intended to ease the pressure on
the foreign exchange needed for securing raw materials
and energy.

The intra-yen-bloc trade did expand rapidly. Yet
Japanese aggression also invited Chinese resistance and
required Japan to develop heavy and chemical industries,
which meant a further increase of demand for raw materials and energy. Thus the greater the expansion, the
deeper the dependence on trade with nations outside the

yen bloc became. Japan's need to secure North China's
cotton fields was one cause of the Sino-Japanese War in
1937. The outbreak of World War II in Europe in 1939
prepared the Japanese advance into resource-rich Southeast Asia. This led to the U.S. oil embargo in 1941, and
Japan went to war with the United States in the same
year.

During World War II the Japanese-controlled areas,
which suddenly encompassed a large part of China,
Southeast Asia, and the Pacific islands, were mostly cut
off from trade relations with the West. The difficulties
caused by the loss of Western demand were eloquent re-
minders of how unrealistic it was to create an autarky in
the name of the Greater East Asia Co-prosperity Sphere.

FROM DEFEAT TO INDUSTRIAL SUPERPOWER

From 1945 to 1951 the Allied forces occupied Japan.
They initially sought demilitarization and economic democratization, but by the late 1940s, with the coming of
the Cold War, the recovery of Japanese industrial
strength was thought to be necessary. The Communist
Revolution in China in 1949 and the outbreak of the Korean War in 1950 reinforced this thinking, and the United States urged Japan to join the postwar system of free
trade. Thus, although Japan lost most of its main prewar
markets in China, Southeast Asia, and India, it was able
to import raw cotton from the United States, and revived
as the world's largest exporter of cotton textiles during
the 1950s.

The high-speed growth from 1951 to 1973 was made
possible by the national will to modernize the economy,
active industrial policy, and favorable international circumstances. The absorption of U.S. technology through
licensing, the availability of relatively low-wage labor of
good quality, and imports of cheap oil enabled Japan to
raise labor productivity in manufacturing and generate
self-sustained growth. Internationally competitive industries emerged in the relatively labor-intensive sectors of
heavy industry such as shipbuilding, automobiles, and
consumer electronics.

The Japanese firm developed various institutional
features designed to encourage both managers and workers to stay with the firm for a long time and identify
themselves with it. A tendency to value long-term relationships between firms also developed. Unlike prewar
zaibatsu, which were largely owned by a family, postwar
keiretsu groups were tied through mutual shareholding.
Keiretsu often centered around the "main bank" rather
than *sogo shosha*, reflecting the increased significance of
investment in fixed capital. There also developed subcon-
tracting relations within an industry, where recurrent
transactions were taken for granted.

To increase the efficiency in resource allocation, the Ministry of International Trade and Industry (MITI; now METI) used exchange allocation, grants, and subsidies as policy tools. Under the regime of free trade (Japan joined GATT, the General Agreement on Tariffs and Trade, in 1964) and with the reduction of transportation costs, a powerful international division of labor emerged in which the United States specialized in capital- and resource-intensive (and often military-related) industries, as well as in primary products together with other resource-rich countries, and Japan specialized in labor-intensive, resource-saving, and technologically demanding (and nonmilitary) industries.

The 1973 oil crises hit resource-poor Japan hard. Around the same time, urbanization was completed and the real wages rose. Coupled with the appreciation of the yen, Japan was rapidly transformed into a high-wage economy in dollar terms. It met this challenge by developing labor-saving and resource-saving technology. The introduction of microelectronics and "new materials" (hard plastics, versatile steel, etc.) enabled producers to reduce both labor input and energy consumption.

Even so, imports of oil remained crucial. Between 1974 and 1985 Japan imported oil from the Middle East at a very high price, and paid the bill with its huge trade surplus with the rest of the world, especially with the United States and Europe, through exports of manufactured goods (which fueled trade conflicts). This created an "oil triangle" in which the United States and Europe settled their trade deficit with Japan by absorbing the "oil dollar" into their financial markets or by selling arms to the Middle East. Japan also heavily invested abroad, mainly in U.S. bonds and securities, which acted as a counterforce of bilateral trade imbalances.

The successive growth of Newly Industrialized Economies, South Korea, Taiwan, Hong Kong, and Singapore, the Association of Southeast Asian Nations (ASEAN), and China helped Japan's economic growth, providing it with the market for manufactured goods, the venue for manufacturing investment, and, above all, the competitive pressure with lower labor costs. They also acted as partners for Asia-wide production networks by specializing in the more labor-intensive industries.

The formation of ASEAN in 1967 and the Asia-Pacific Economic Cooperation (APEC) in 1989 were intended to reinforce the commitment to free trade among the growth economies of the region. Under the framework set out by GATT (and later the World Trade Organization), the reduction of tariffs and other trade barriers was attempted. Although the United States played a leadership role in creating the postwar regime of free trade, it was the Asian countries that reinforced this principle and linked it to high-speed growth on a regional scale.

Measured in terms of emigration, immigration, and imports of capital, Japan's contacts with the outside world have been relatively limited throughout the period reviewed here. Exports of capital became important only in the most recent period. Even the size of trade has been small throughout the postwar period; the ratio of exports and imports to GDP remained below 20 percent from 1985 to 2003. Yet, trade has been both a major facilitator of the absorption of economic knowledge and the provider of vital resources unavailable. Economic development would have been unimaginable without it.

SEE ALSO AUTOMOBILES; BALANCE OF PAYMENTS; BANKING; CAPITAL FLOWS; CHINA; CONTAINERIZATION; COTTON; DEVELOPMENTAL STATE, CONCEPT OF THE; EAST INDIA COMPANY, DUTCH; EMPIRE, JAPANESE; EMPIRE, PORTUGUESE; GATT, WTO; GOLD AND SILVER; INTERNATIONAL TRADE AGREEMENTS; IRON AND STEEL; KOREA; JAPANESE MINISTRY OF INTERNATIONAL TRADE AND INDUSTRY (MITI); MANCHURIA; MITSUI; PERRY, MATTHEW; PETROLEUM; PHARMACEUTICALS; PROTECTIONISM AND TARIFF WARS; RICE; SHIPBUILDING; SILK; SONY; SUMITOMO; TAIWAN; TEXTILES; UNITED STATES; YOKOHAMA.

BIBLIOGRAPHY
Aoki, Masahiko, and Dore, Ronald, eds. *The Japanese Firm: Sources of Competitive Strength.* Oxford, U.K.: Clarendon Press, 1994.

Drysdale, Peter, and Gower, Luke, eds. *The Japanese Economy*, Part 1, Vol. III: *Trading with Japan.* London: Routledge, 1998.

Duus, Peter; Myers, Ramon H.; and Peattie, Mark R., eds. *The Japanese Informal Empire in China, 1895–1937.* Princeton, NJ: Princeton University Press, 1989.

Hall, John Whitney; Nagahara, Keiji; and Yamamura, Kozo, eds. *Japan Before Tokugawa—Political Consolidation and Economic Growth, 1500 to 1650.* Princeton, NJ: Princeton University Press, 1981.

Hayami, Akira; Saito, Osamu; and Toby, Ronald P., eds. *The Economic History of Japan, 1660–1990*, Vol. 1: *Emergence of Economic Society in Japan, 1600–1859.* Oxford: Oxford University Press, 2004.

Innes, Robert L. *The Door Ajar: Japan's Foreign Trade in the Seventeenth Century.* Ann Arbor, MI: University Microfilms International, 1980.

Myers, Ramon H., and Peattie, Mark R., eds. *The Japanese Colonial Empire, 1895–1945.* Princeton, NJ: Princeton University Press, 1984.

Mitsubishi Economic Research Bureau. *Japanese Trade and Industry: Present and Future.* London: Macmillan, 1936.

Nakamura, Takafusa. *The Postwar Japanese Economy—Its Development and Structure, 1937–1994*, 2nd edition. Tokyo: University of Tokyo Press, 1995.

Nakamura, Takafusa, and Odaka, Kônosuke, eds. *The Economic History of Japan, 1660–1990*, Vol. 3: *Economic History of Japan, 1914–1955: A Dual Structure.* Oxford, U.K.: Oxford University Press, 2003.

Okazaki, Tetsuji, and Korenaga, Takafumi. "The Foreign Exchange Allocation Policy in Postwar Japan: Its Institutional Framework and Function." In *Changes in Exchange Rates in Rapidly Developing Countries: Theory, Practice, and Policy Issues,* ed. Takatoshi Ito and Anne O. Krueger. Chicago: University of Chicago Press, 1999.

Sugihara, Kaoru. "Japan as an Engine of the Asian International Economy, c. 1880–1936." Reprinted in *The Economic Development of Modern Japan, 1868–1945: From the Meiji Restoration to the Second World War,* Vol. 1, ed. Steven Tolliday. Cheltenham, U.K.: Edward Elgar, 2001.

Sugihara, Kaoru, and Allan, J. A., eds. *Japan in the Contemporary Middle East.* London: Routledge, 1993.

Sugihara, Kaoru. *Ajia-kan Boeki no Keisei to Kozo* (Patterns and development of intra-Asian trade). Kyoto, Japan: Mineruva Shobou, 1996.

Sugihara, Kaoru. *Ajia Taiheiyo Keizaiken no Koryu* (*The rise of the Asia-Pacific economy*). Osaka, Japan: Osaka Daigaku Shuppankai, 2003.

Sugihara, Kaoru, ed. *Japan, China, and the Growth of the Asian International Economy, 1850–1949.* Oxford, U.K.: Oxford University Press, 2005.

Sugiyama, Shinya. *Japan's Industrialization in the World Economy, 1859–1899: Export Trade and Overseas Competition.* London: Athlone Press, 1988.

Toby, Ronald P. *State and Diplomacy in Early Modern Japan: Asia in the Development of the Tokugawa Bakufu.* Princeton, NJ: Princeton University Press, 1984.

Yamamura, Kozo, and Kamiki, Tetsuo. "Silver Mines and Sung Coins—A Monetary History of Medieval and Modern Japan in International Perspective." In *Precious Metals in the Later Medieval and Early Modern Worlds,* ed. J. F. Richards. Durham, NC: Carolina Academic Press, 1983.

Yamazawa, Ippei, and Yamamoto, Yuzo. *Boeki to Kokusai Shushi* (*Choki Keizai Tokei 14*) (Foreign trade and balance of payments: long-term economic statistics, vol. 14). Tokyo: Toyo Keizai Shinposha, 1979.

Kaoru Sugihara

JAPANESE MINISTRY OF INTERNATIONAL TRADE AND INDUSTRY (METI)

METI—Ministry of Economy, Trade, and Industry—is the ministry of the Japanese government most closely associated with industrial policy. Before the January 2001 reorganization of the national government it was known as MITI—Ministry of International Trade and Industry. The association of MITI with industrial policy owes much to the central role the ministry played in allocating foreign exchange under the Bretton Woods fixed-exchange-rate regime of 1946 to 1971. Antecedents of MITI played essentially the same role from 1937 through the end of the Pacific War. With the advent of floating exchange rates in 1971, and the virtual ending of Japanese government controls on foreign exchange since 1980, MITI's ability to divert resources toward favored industries and away from others was much reduced. Nevertheless, MITI—and now METI—has continued to articulate industrial policy goals. It also still implements the policies themselves, by specifically allocating industry-specific tax credits authorized by the Diet (Japan's legislature), by promoting and administering government-subsidized research and development projects, and by effecting special exemptions from antimonopoly laws so that favored industries can form export cartels or enter other such collusive arrangements.

When in the 1960s, 1970s, and 1980s Japan's economy was expanding and was an important force in the world marketplace, MITI itself occupied a prominent position in Japanese politics. Nearly all of the prime ministers since 1960 had once served as ministers of MITI. The staff of MITI/METI comprises a bureaucratic elite, the highly capable graduates of Japan's top universities.

What did MITI/METI actually accomplish? And did the industrial policies it implemented contribute any to Japan's economic success? As already mentioned, MITI's most far-reaching intervention was the allocation of foreign exchange in the 1950s and early 1960s. The foreign-exchange allocations were enforced by requiring a license issued by MITI for each foreign-currency transaction relating to imports or exports, and also by requiring MITI approval for direct investment. Given the scarcity of foreign exchange at the official exchange rate, these allocations amounted to *de facto* import restrictions in many industries. Inward direct investment was nearly choked off altogether. Export transactions, including outward direct investments, were generally allowed.

The economic effects of foreign exchange rationing in Japan are quite difficult to know precisely. Certainly the policy protected industries such as coal mining, textiles, and agriculture, in which Japan had lost its comparative advantage, and thereby diminished Japan's gains from foreign trade. Besides its direct allocative effects, foreign exchange rationing enhanced MITI influence over business policies generally. This was the origin of the notion that administrative guidance (*gyousei shidou*), private communications between bureaucrats and businesses, has projected Japanese government influence beyond the legally prescribed domains of regulation. For example, MITI used the dependence of Japan's petrochemical firms upon foreign technology, requiring its approval, to also control entry, exit, and investment in the petrochemical industry. MITI participated in the site selection, planning, and organization of the numerous petrochemical industrial complexes established in the 1950s and 1960s along the coasts of Japan.

MITI's broad authority to ration foreign exchange ended when the government made the yen convertible on current account in 1964 and relaxed restrictions on inward foreign investment in 1968. Restrictions on inward direct investment were not completely freed until 1980. In the years since then MITI/METI influence waned but was never extinguished. The Mining and Manufacturing Technology Research Association Law, enacted in 1961, authorized MITI to organize and contribute funds to joint-research ventures involving firms in the industries within its provenance. To better implement these powers, MITI's "Agency" of Industrial Science and Technology was formed in 1966 to manage the funding of large-scale projects. The most famous project under this program was the Very Large Scale Integrated-Circuits (VLSI) Technology Research Association (1976–1979), which successfully developed processes for manufacturing certain kinds of semiconductors. There have been well over 100 research consortia organized by MITI.

The ministry's role in allocating tax credits to specific firms and in garnering special exemptions from anti-monopoly laws also continues, but has probably amounted to little. Japan's antimonopoly laws are loosely enforced and have only weak penalties. And the sum total of tax credits has never been that great. In the end, the principle contribution of MITI/METI has been to give Japan's industrial policy a coherent focus. The industries targeted for promotion by the Japanese government have always been precisely the ones identified as such in MITI white papers and annual reports. In the 1950s and 1960s these were coal mining, steel, and chemical fertilizer. In the 1970s and 1980s it was semiconductors. At the beginning of the twenty-first century it is nanotechnology and aerospace.

SEE ALSO AUTOMOBILE; BALANCE OF PAYMENTS; CHINA; DEVELOPMENTAL STATE, CONCEPT OF THE; FLOWS OF FACTORS OF PRODUCTION; FREE TRADE, THEORY AND PRACTICE; GLOBALIZATION, PRO AND CON; IMPORT SUBSTITUTION; INDUSTRIALIZATION; INTERNATIONAL TRADE AGREEMENTS; IRON AND STEEL; JAPAN; KOREA; MITSUBISHI; MITSUI; PROTECTIONISM AND TARIFF WARS; RATES OF EXCHANGE; SHIPBUILDING; SONY; SUMITOMO; SUBSIDIES; TAIWAN; TEXTILES; UNITED STATES.

BIBLIOGRAPHY

Beason, Richard, and Weinstein, David E. "Growth, Economies of Scale, and Targeting in Japan (1955–1990)." *Review of Economics and Statistics* 88, no. 2 (May 1996): 286–295.

Flath, David. *The Japanese Economy.* Oxford; New York: Oxford University Press, 2000.

Johnson, Chalmers. *MITI and the Japanese Miracle, 1925–1975.* Stanford, CA: Stanford University Press, 1982.

David Flath

UNDERLYING PROFIT CONTRIBUTION IN 2004

BY BUSINESS:

Jardine Pacific: 20%

Jardine Motors Group: 8%

Jardine Lloyd Thompson: 8%

Honkkong Land: 14%

Dairy Farm: 21%

Mandarin Oriental: 2%

Jardine Cycle and Carriage: 27%

BY REGION:

Hong Kong and Mainland China: 45%

Asia Pacific: 45%

Europe: 9%

North America (including interest earned): 1%

Source: Jardine Matheson Annual Report, 2004

JARDINE MATHESON

The firm of Jardine, Matheson and Company was founded in 1832 in Canton (Guangzhou) by the Scots William Jardine (1784–1843) and James Matheson (1796–1874). At the time, Canton was the most important trading port on the South China coast, and the company's history reflects the development of foreign trade and colonial presence in nineteenth-century China. When the British East India Company lost its monopoly on trade with China in 1834, Jardine Matheson was among the first private companies that profited from the opening of the trade, shipping tea to England and importing opium from India to China. Until the 1860s the company dominated the opium trade with its fleet of clippers transporting the opium and its information network providing important market data along the China coast. Hong Kong officially became a British colony only in 1842 after the defeat of China in the first Opium War. As early as 1841, because of the island's commercial and strategic advantages, Jardine Matheson had bought land there. In 1844 it moved its headquarters to Hong Kong from Macao.

Mixing legal with nominally illegal business, Jardine Matheson's offices spread rapidly along the China coast to Shanghai (1844), Canton, Amoy (Xiamen), and Foochow (Fuzhou), establishing the company's reputation as an international trading firm importing products such as coal, machinery, and metals into China. As the company expanded, shipping became more important. In the 1850s Jardine Matheson established its presence as the first foreign trading house in Japan, with offices in Kobe and Nagasaki. The company also began to operate a steam-powered shipping line from Calcutta to various Chinese ports. Due to declining importance and diminishing profits, the firm withdrew from the opium trade in the early 1870s and focused on new opportunities in the China trade. Next to steamship lines, investment in infrastructure became the heart of the company's business portfolio in the late nineteenth century, with innovations ranging from an interoffice telegraph system in Hong Kong in 1869 to the first railroad line between Shanghai and Wusong in 1876. In order to centralize its shipping business, the company united its river, coastal, and cargo businesses under the Indochina Steam Navigation Company in 1882. At the same time, Jardine Matheson sought close business cooperation with the Chinese government by issuing loans, and thus succeeded in securing the Shanghai agency for the Kaiping coal mines and other ventures.

China's loss of the Sino-Japanese War in 1895 triggered industrialization efforts and the establishment of new economic and legal institutions to demonstrate that China could compete militarily and economically with Japan and other foreign nations. Jardine Matheson's business catered to the needs of the emerging mining operations and cotton mills and included warehouses and wharves all over the country. In Hong Kong the company opened the first sugar mill and the first spinning and weaving mill, and engaged in land reclamation and harbor services. After Britain received the ninety-nine-year lease of the New Territories in 1898, the company became involved in ferry transportation between Hong Kong island and Kowloon, which still exists today as a major landmark and tourist attraction.

The increasing involvement in transportation and industrial projects required expansion into new financial sectors for the company's portfolio. Together with the Hong Kong Shanghai Banking Corporation, Jardine Matheson formed the British and Chinese Corporation to build various lines for China's railway system. Gaining better access to capital markets, Jardine Matheson reorganized itself as a limited liability company in 1906. Despite its dominance in Hong Kong, the company chose Shanghai, the industrial, financial, and commercial hub in early twentieth-century China, as its headquarters from the 1910s. There, Jardine Matheson consolidated its cotton mills under the new name Ewo Cotton Mills, whereas the Jardine Engineering Company supplied

equipment and services for the booming industrial enterprises all over China and Hong Kong.

Like most other companies, Jardine Matheson suffered from the Japanese invasion of China and the occupation until the end of World War II. In 1941 the company had to close its offices in Hong Kong and occupied China, but it opened an office in Chongqing, in the unoccupied interior where the nationalist government had relocated. After 1945 Jardine Matheson quickly reopened for business in Hong Kong and Shanghai, and even resumed its operation in Japan only two years after the end of World War II. The establishment of the People's Republic of China at the end of the civil war in 1949 meant a drastic change in the company's business opportunities. When the new socialist government abolished private property and nationalized all business enterprises on the mainland, Jardine Matheson's headquarters moved back to Hong Kong under the protection of the British government in 1954.

Fortunately, refugees from mainland China brought new skills, capital, and labor to the colony in the 1950s, which contributed to Hong Kong's transformation from trading port to a center of industrial manufacturing in the following decades. Reorienting towards new consumer behavior and lifestyles, Jardine Matheson, which became a public company in 1961, expanded into Hong Kong's hotel business and the supermarket sector. The 1960s also saw the opening of company offices in Australia and Indonesia. Real estate, insurance interests, and merchant banking became the pillars of the company's business activities in Hong Kong and Southeast Asia. Following the opening of China after Mao Zedong's death in 1976, Jardine Matheson reaffirmed its relationship with China by opening a representative office in Beijing in 1980. After restructuring its interest, Jardine Matheson withdrew from the shipping business in 1984 and, anticipating Hong Kong's return to China in 1997, relocated to Bermuda in order to be able to remain under the British legal and tax system. In 1987 the company acquired the Pizza Hut franchise in Hong Kong and subsequently in various other places in Asia. In the 1990s expanded its supermarket operation into New Zealand and Singapore. Motor vehicle interests have become increasingly important to the group's portfolio, and the supermarket and fast-food franchising activities are still being expanded to China and Southeast Asia.

SEE ALSO Banking; Bengal; Calcutta; Canton System; China; Drugs, Illicit; East India Company, British; Empire, British; Empire, Qing; Entrepôt System; Finance, Insurance; Franchising, International; Free Ports; Guangzhou; Hong Kong; Imperial Maritime Customs, China; Industrialization; Iron and

STEEL; JAPAN; NATIONALIZATION; PORT CITIES; SHIPPING, COASTAL; SHIPPING, MERCHANT; SINGAPORE; TEA; TEXTILES; UNITED KINGDOM; VIETNAM; YOKOHAMA.

BIBLIOGRAPHY

Blake, Robert. *Jardine Matheson: Traders of the East.* London: Weidenfeld and Nicolson, 1999.

Cheong, W. E. *Mandarins and Merchants: Jardine Matheson & Co., a China Agency of the Early Nineteenth Century.* London and Malmö, Sweden: Curzon Press, 1978.

Fairbank, John K. "The Creation of the Treaty System." In *The Cambridge History of China*, vol. 10, part 1, ed. Denis Twitchett and John K. Fairbank. (Cambridge, U.K.: Cambridge University Press, 1978), 213–263.

Hao Yen-p'ing. *The Comprador in Nineteenth-Century China: Bridge Between East and West.* Cambridge, MA: Harvard University Press, 1970.

Keswick, Maggie, ed. *The Thistle and the Jade: A Celebration of 150 years of Jardine, Matheson & Co.* London: Octopus Books, 1982.

Le Fervour, Edward. *Western Enterprise in Late Ch'ing China: A Selective Survey of Jardine, Matheson and Company's Operations, 1842–1895.* Cambridge, MA: East Asian Research Center, Harvard University, 1968.

Murphey, Rhoads. *The Treaty Ports and China's Modernization: What Went Wrong?* Ann Arbor: University of Michigan, Center for Chinese Studies, 1970.

Polachek, James M. *The Inner Opium War.* Cambridge, MA: Harvard University, Council on East Asian Studies, 1992.

Elisabeth Köll

JOINT-STOCK COMPANY

A joint-stock company is a company (not usually incorporated) which has the capital of its members permanently pooled in a common fund, which is divided into shares. Transferable shares represent ownership interest, and the liability of the shareholders is limited to the par value of the shares held by them. During the early modern era there was widespread use of limited-liability stocks, including in insurance companies, but the joint-stock company matured in long-distance merchant shipping.

The origin of the joint-stock company goes back to the medieval *commenda*. This was a form of limited-liability partnership in merchant shipping to reduce risks by making specific arrangements regarding the sharing of profits (or losses) for voyages. Partners were divided into investors who stayed on land and travelers who went with the ship. The voyager did not risk any capital, only his life. Later, merchant ships were usually financed by unincorporated, risk-reducing, ship-owning partnerships. A husband, representing the shareholders, managed the finances of the venture. After every voyage the enterprise was liquidated. Shareholders shared equal responsibility for the company's profits and liabilities.

SOUTH SEA STOCK

The British (joint-stock) South Sea Company was founded in 1711, ostensibly to trade in slaves and goods in the Southern Hemisphere, but the company was really more a financial than a commercial venture. In 1719 its directors proposed taking over much of the national debt, then held by the Bank of England and bloated by war. Everyone from members of the royal court down to very humble speculators were persuaded to invest on the assumption that rapid stock appreciation would make them rich. Amidst bribery and nepotism, South Sea stock values climbed ten-fold from January to June 1720. New investors rushed in, but the venture, built on unsound commercial principles, soon imploded. By October, as prominent investors unloaded their interests, the bubble burst and stock prices plummeted. Many stockholders were ruined, and others worried about being criminally implicated. In the end Prime Minister Robert Walpole (himself a former investor) was successful in shielding most from charges. The crisis passed, and its most tangible effects were the 1720 Bubble Act and the skillful Walpole's long parliamentary ascendancy.

David J. Clarke

Exclusive trading rights to particular areas had long been enjoyed by chartered companies, which were companies organized as regulated companies (i.e., to share in the overhead costs) in which the governing body merely set broad operational parameters within which members traded on their own. Entry was relatively unimpeded. From the middle of the sixteenth century, incorporated chartered companies such as the Muscovy Company (1553) and the Levant Company (1580) emerged. Entry was by purchase of shares in the company, which exploited monopoly powers by trading as a corporate enterprise. Some shareholders were merchants actively engaged in trade, but others were passive investors who delegated management to paid officials directed by a governor elected from among their ranks. Protected by exclusive state privileges, the companies were successful as long as they could operate under the conditions of a seller's market.

DUTCH CHARTERED JOINT-STOCK COMPANIES

The wartime taxes Charles V (1500–1558), lord of the Netherlands, levied in the Low Countries led to the creation of a large and growing market of long-term securities, such as annuities. They were heritable and transferable, and therefore suitable for resale. Simultaneously, in Antwerp, safe and rapid international movement of funds was perfected in the bill of exchange. The key features of these early financial innovations were eventually successfully blended in the shares of chartered companies.

In 1568 the Dutch revolted against their lord, the king of Spain. Eventually, the Dutch became free burghers no longer subject to Habsburg regulations, restrictions, and exclusions in long-distance trade. They were free to venture outside European waters into the Atlantic and the Indian Ocean. Despite expensive and lengthy expeditions, the new trades to Asia attracted many investors. In these so-called pre-companies executive powers were delegated to a board of directors, although shareholders still influenced policy. Both directors and shareholders were partially liable. Shares were transferable, but only for the nominal value. After the ships had safely returned, the enterprise was liquidated.

In 1602, at the expense of these earlier pre-companies, the Dutch East India Company (Vereenigde Oost-Indische Compagnie, or VOC) was founded. The VOC was an incorporated joint-stock company, a chartered trading company, and a war machine. For the Dutch government the privately funded VOC had to be instrumental in their war against the king of Spain; in return, the government had to grant a charter stipulating exclusive trading rights, reducing the risks of the shareholders. In addition, in the charter all kinds of regulations about responsibilities, rights, and the relation between directors and investors were specified. The shareholders were liable only to the par value of their shares. So, the charter had a dual character: it was a statute, and it stipulated the privileges of the company.

After 1610 the combination of the large scale of the operation and the lengthy transit times to and from Asia led to the transformation of working capital, initially committed to the duration of a particular venture, into fixed capital, committed perpetually to the enterprise. This was an important institutional innovation. Investors could not recover their capital from the company, and were entitled only to whatever dividends might be declared, as well as to the right to transfer their shares to another investor. Dividends were high and stable, which made the resale market of shares attractive and enabled the company to borrow money rather easily.

Initially, the operating control of the directors was not independent of shareholders. A fierce struggle broke out over control of the company. By 1621, when the first charter was due, the directors had won, but they had to open their books before a government committee and representatives of the shareholders every four years. On these points, however, the charter was not amended. In contrast, the 1621 charter granted to the Dutch West India Company (WIC) stipulated that the executive power of the directors was independent of shareholders. The WIC shareholders, too, were granted more rights than the VOC shareholders had, but in practice, they were rather powerless.

By 1621 the combination of permanent capital and the separation of executive powers from ordinary shareholders made these shares ideal for active trading in the secondary market that arose on the Amsterdam Beurs. That they were registered in the company's ledger books made them secure, and transfers could be made very quickly and cheaply in special transfer books.

Other Dutch chartered joint-stock companies were the Muscovy Company (1608), the Guinea Company (1614), the Northern Company (1614), and the New Netherland Company (1614).

OTHER CHARTERED JOINT-STOCK COMPANIES

On October 16, 1599 Elizabeth I (1533–1603), queen of England, granted a charter to the East India Company (EIC), awarding it a monopoly on trade with the East. Until 1613 the EIC's trade was based upon the funding of separate voyages to Asia. Thereafter, three successive joint-stock ventures were established. The company partly compensated for the reduced marketability of a short-term and risky equity by making shares smaller in denomination, by not fixing the total number of shares to be sold, and by selling shares to the assembled merchants during the semiannual auctions of East India goods in London. Only in 1657 did the EIC's finances and organization become consolidated by the Cromwell regime's endorsement of the creation of a permanent joint stock.

Also in the rest of Europe, in long-distance trade, chartered joint-stock companies appeared. In 1628, for instance, the Companhia da India Oriental (East India Company) was founded in Lisbon. It enjoyed the exclusive privilege of navigation and trading between Lisbon and Asia. Its initial term was to run for twelve years, during which investment could not be returned, but interest would be paid. The board of directors would be responsible only to the Crown in Madrid. In the end, the Crown had to bear most of the expenses. After it had equipped fourteen ships, the company went bankrupt in 1635. The Companhia Geral para o Estado do Brazil (Brazil Company) was founded in 1649, but managed only five major convoys before it, too, went bankrupt. However, it almost certainly saved Brazil for Portugal by breaking the WIC blockade at a crucial time.

In the 1660s the French minister of finance Jean-Baptiste Colbert (1619–1683) established the Compagnie des Indes orientales, the Compagnie des Indes occidentales, and the Compagnie du Nord for trade with Asia, the West Indies, and the Baltic, respectively. The Crown paid a substantial amount of the initial capital, and the companies' administration was in hands of Colbert or his representatives. The state's direct involvement could be interpreted as an attempt by the king to protect his investment, but in fact it did not work. The king had to pay most of the operating expenses, and the ventures were not a success.

Also in Sweden, Denmark, and the Holy Roman Empire chartered joint-stock companies were established. Most of these ventures, however, were covered operations and financed with Dutch capital in order to circumvent the trade restrictions of the WIC.

THE BUBBLE OF 1720

From 1719 to 1721 frenzied speculation in stocks and government debts swept over Europe. It ended in France in the Mississippi Bubble, in England in the South Sea Bubble, and in the Netherlands, Germany, and Portugal in similar bubbles. For joint-stock companies the legacy was devastating. The English Bubble Act of June 1720, which prohibited any chartered joint-stock company from engaging in activities outside those authorized in its original charter, limited the use of joint-stock corporations until well into the nineteenth century. As a consequence, in many European countries only chartered joint-stock companies with clear responsibilities and rules were allowed, although in the Dutch Republic relatively small but viable unchartered joint-stock shipping companies emerged, such as the Middelburgsche Commercie Compangnie (1720) and the Sociëteit ter Navigatie op Essequebo (1771).

THE END

Economist Adam Smith (1723–1790) outlined in his *An Inquiry into the Nature and Causes of the Wealth of Nations* (1776) the unfortunate economic consequences that ensued when legal monopolies were granted to groups of merchants to set up joint-stock companies to carry out foreign trade. Smith contended that these companies were bound to fail because hired directors managing the money of others would lack sufficient motivation to succeed in such demanding businesses. Shortly afterwards, the charters of the WIC and the VOC were not renewed, and the companies were dissolved in 1791 and 1795, respectively.

During the nineteenth century new forms of limited-liability companies emerged, such as the French Société Anonieme (SA), the Dutch Naamloze Vennootschap (NV), the German Gesellschaft mit beschränkter Haftung (GmbH), the English Limited, and the U.S. Incorporated.

SEE ALSO COLBERT, JEAN-BAPTISTE; EAST INDIA COMPANY, BRITISH; EAST INDIA COMPANY, DUTCH; ELIZABETH I; LEVANT COMPANY; PARTNERSHIP; WEST INDIA COMPANY, DUTCH.

BIBLIOGRAPHY

Blussé, Leonard, and Gaastra, Femme, eds. *Companies and Trade: Essays on Overseas Trading Companies During the Ancien Régime.* Leiden, Netherlands: Leiden University Press, 1981.

Boven, Huw V. "No Longer Mere Traders: Continuities and Change in the Metropolitan Development of the East India Company, 1600–1834." In *The Worlds of the East India Company,* ed. Huw V. Bowen; Margarette Lincoln; and Nigel Rigby. Woodbridge, U.K.: Boydell Press, 2002.

Garber, P. M. *Famous First Bubbles: The Fundamentals of Early Manias.* Cambridge, MA: Massachusetts Institute of Technology Press, 2002.

Jones, Stephen R. H., and Ville, Simon P. "Efficient Transactors or Rent-Seeking Monopolists? The Rationale for Early Chartered Trading Companies." *The Journal of Economic History* 56 (December 1996): 898–915.

Neal, Larry. *The Rise of Financial Capitalism: International Capital Markets in the Age of Reason,* 2nd edition. Cambridge, U.K.: Cambridge University Press, 1993.

Rabb, Theodore K. *Enterprise and Empire: Merchant and Gentry Investment in the Expansion of England, 1575–1630.* Cambridge, MA: Harvard University Press, 1967.

Scott, William R. *The Constitution and Finance of English, Scottish, and Irish Joint-Stock Companies to 1720,* 2nd edition. Gloucester, MA: Peter Smith, 1968.

Victor Enthoven

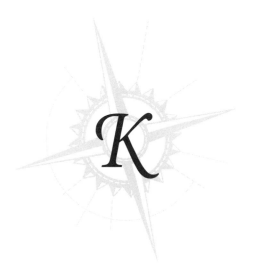

KANDY

SEE SRI LANKA

KENYA

In recent times Kenya, a former British colony on the east coast of Africa, became well known for the wildlife in its national parks and games reserves, and for its Indian Ocean beaches. Tourism is its foremost foreign-exchange earner.

In the fifteenth century the region was famous for commercial-exchange networks that linked the interior and the coast with the Arab, Persian and Indian Ocean worlds. Traditionally, Kenya's economy was based on farming, herding, hunting, and trade. But a web of regional trade routes provided the impetus for the trade goods of the interior to reach the coastal ports. Among the many groups in the region, the Kamba, who served early Arab and European explorers and traders as guides, traders, porters, and soldiers, and the seafaring Bajun of Lamu on the northern coast were particularly well positioned to facilitate the expansion of both regional and long-distance trade. Nomadic and cattle-rearing groups such as the Masai, the Turkana, the Samburu, and the Somali of the arid north, with their herds of cattle, goat, and camels, and their extended reach and mobility, carried out long-distance trade. Other groups including the Kikuyu, Luo, Kalenjin, and Luhya also participated in both age-old and modern trading arrangements.

Trade contact with the Arabs from the south of Arabia and the Persian Gulf had been established as early as the second century. By the ninth century some of these Arab and Persian traders had constructed forfeited urban settlements on the coast. In the tenth century coastal cities including Mombasa, Lamu, Malindi, and Pate had become part of the intricate Indian Ocean trading networks. They exported slaves, gum copal, mangrove poles, leopard skins, turtle shell rhinoceros horn and ivory from the interior, and gold from Kilwa (in present-day Tanzania) produced in the fields around Great Zimbabwe. Imports included silk, porcelain, salt, cloth, beads, metal goods, and a host of luxury items from Arabia, Persia, India, and China. The coastal traders did not venture far inland, but depended upon the people of the interior to bring ivory, slaves, and timber. Until the advent of this trade Africans of the interior had valued ivory as an item of ritual or ornament, rather than a commercial good. The Kamba played a crucial role in this trade. They began the sustained exploitation of elephants for ivory and gradually established a two-way caravan trade to the coast. From the late eighteenth century their trade expanded south into present-day Tanzania and west to the forests of Mount Kenya and Kikuyu territory. The depletion of the elephants and intense competition led the Kamba to turn to slave trading in the nineteenth century.

These vibrant trade networks made Mombasa the region's most prominent city by the fifteenth century, surpassing Kilwa (Tanzania) and Mogadishu (Somalia). Arab merchants who settled among the local population lived in comparative luxury and gradually evolved into the ruling class. Interaction between Arabs and the Bantu people along the coast produced a hybrid "Swahili" culture, including the language KiSwahili, now the *lingua franca* of many East African communities. Visible results of this contact include mosques and the black veil worn by Muslim women.

The arrival of the Portuguese, beginning in 1498 with Vasco da Gama (c. 1460–1524), resulted in a marked decline of trade, and many Swahili towns switched to subsistence agriculture thereafter. The Portuguese attacked and destroyed Mombasa in 1505, 1528, and 1589. With Portuguese support, the Malindi sheikh was installed as sultan of the whole region. The Portuguese constructed a fortress, Fort Jesus, in 1593, from which to police the Indian Ocean trade. Otherwise, they showed no interest in colonization. They did, however, introduce important crops from the New World: maize, cassava, and potatoes.

At the end of the seventeenth century Omani Arabs plus Dutch, English, and French traders largely supplanted the Portuguese, who were starved into submission in 1698 after a three-year siege of Fort Jesus by invading Omani Arabs, with support from Pate and Lamu. The Portuguese staged a short-lived comeback in 1728, but the Omani restored their control under the suzerainty of the Mazrui family, who after the change of dynasty in Oman in 1741 proceeded to proclaim Mombasa independent of their Omani homeland, and ruled the coast from Malindi to Pemba Island. But other Omanis and the British together whittled down Mazrui family power. The sultan of Oman, Seyyid Said, was invited to take over the Omani commercial enclave in East Africa. In 1840 he moved his capital from Oman to Zanzibar, and most of the coast of East Africa became his domain. Zanzibar became the center of flourishing trading networks and a clove industry; Kenya was largely bypassed.

The British established hegemony by 1875 and prohibited the slave trade. In 1888 the Imperial East Africa Company was chartered to administer Kenya, and many merchants abandoned Mombasa. The control of trade thereafter passed to the British; in 1895 the British government finally took over the territory. European and Asian entrepreneurs were the main beneficiaries. A railway network was completed in 1902, after which European settlers were encouraged to acquire land. Agricultural exports such as tea, sisal, and coffee became the focus of the economy. The Mombasa-Kisumu railroad undermined older trading networks, and Indian settlers built new regional networks based on the railways. Indigenous people were generally reduced to wage workers.

However, Kenyans soon created new long-distance trading networks. One significant development in this regard is the unofficial trade in cattle by livestock herders and pastoralists along the Kenya and Somali borderlands. This trade, although illegal, provides outlets for pastoral groups to sell their products, and helps feed the demand for meat in the region's growing cities. Unfortunately,

this trade sometimes goes hand in hand with commerce in illicit drugs and dangerous weapons. This vast transborder enterprise demonstrates the region's continued involvement in long-distance trade.

SEE ALSO AFRICA, LABOR TAXES (HEAD TAXES); AGRICULTURE; CARAVAN TRADE; COFFEE; EMPIRE, BRITISH; EMPIRE, PORTUGUESE; ETHNIC GROUPS, AFRICANS; ETHNIC GROUPS, GUJARATI; GOLD AND SILVER; IMPERIALISM; INDIAN OCEAN; INTERNATIONAL MONETARY FUND (IMF); LABORERS, COERCED; LABORERS, CONTRACT; NATIONALISM.

BIBLIOGRAPHY

Fage, John D. *A History of Africa*. New York: Knopf, 1978.

Flint, John E., ed. *The Cambridge History of Africa*. Vol. 5 from c. 1790–1870. Cambridge: Cambridge University Press, 1976.

Ogot, Bethwell A., ed. *Economic and Social History of East Africa*. Nairobi, Kenya: East African Literature Bureau, 1975.

Ogot, Bethwell A., ed. *Kenya Before 1800: Eight Regional Studies*. Nairobi, Kenya: East African Publishing House, 1978.

Ogot, Bethwell A., and Kieran, J. A. *Zamani: A Survey of East African History*. Nairobi, Kenya: East African Publishing House, 1978.

Salim, Ahmed I. *Swahili-Speaking Peoples of Kenya's Coast*. Nairobi, Kenya: East African Publishing House, 1973.

Olutayo Charles Adesina

JOHN MAYNARD KEYNES
1887–1950

John Maynard Keynes is considered to be the father of modern macroeconomics. He was also the co-designer of the Bretton Woods system of semi fixed exchange rates. A student of Alfred Marshall (1842–1924) and the son of economist John Neville Keynes (1852–1949), Keynes distinguished himself early for his criticism of the German reparations as a part of the settlement of World War I. Following the onset of the Great Depression, Keynes published what many economists have come to regard as the most influential economics book of the twentieth century, *The General Theory of Employment, Interest, and Money* (1936), in which he advocated that governments fight depressions by lowering interest rates and increasing government spending.

As part of a team of economists who met in Bretton Woods, New Hampshire after World War II, Keynes sought to preserve the discipline of the gold standard while overcoming its lack of flexibility. The group created a system in which exchange rates were allowed to fluctuate to a small degree so as to minimize the danger an extreme financial shock (such as the wave of bank failures that had occurred in the early 1930s) might pose to world commerce.

Keynes also had a reputation as a private financial mastermind, having assembled a personal fortune of £500,000 through judicious investing in the stock market.

SEE ALSO BRETTON WOODS; ECONOMICS, NEOCLASSICAL; GREAT DEPRESSION OF THE 1930S; INTERNATIONAL MONETARY FUND (IMF); THEORIES OF INTERNATIONAL TRADE; WORLD BANK.

BIBLIOGRAPHY

Briet, William, and Ransom, Roger L. *The Academic Scribblers.* Princeton, NJ: Princeton University Press, 1998.

Moggridge, Donald E. *Maynard Keynes: An Economist's Biography.* New York: Routledge, 1992.

Skidelsky, R. J. *John Maynard Keynes.* New York: Viking, 1986.

Benjamin Passty

KOLKATA

SEE CALCUTTA

KONGO

The Kongo Kingdom was located in what is today the west of the Democratic Republic of Congo and the north of Angola. The kingdom was founded around its capital, Mbanza Kongo (later, São Salvador), in the late fourteenth century. When Portuguese navigators under the command of Diogo Cão (flourished 1480–1486) first established ties with the Kongo in 1483, the kingdom stretched southwards from the Congo River, along coastal plains, and eastwards to a plateau of savanna woodlands in the interior. It constituted the most centralized and geographically extensive kingdom of west central Africa at that time.

Contact with the Portuguese contributed to economic, cultural, and political changes. In 1491 the king of the Kongo (or *manikongo*), Nzinga Kuwu, converted to Christianity and was baptized King João I (d. 1506). His son Affonso succeeded the throne in 1506; he was a convinced Catholic and initiated closer ties with Portugal. In exchange for the religious services of priests and a variety of luxury goods, the kingdom exported slaves, copper, and ivory. By the third decade of the sixteenth century, Portuguese and São Tomé merchants sought to circumvent control over trade exerted by the Kongo Kingdom and set up alternative trading bases. By the end of that century, the Portuguese had established the colony of Angola to the south of the kingdom as a central slave-trading entrepôt.

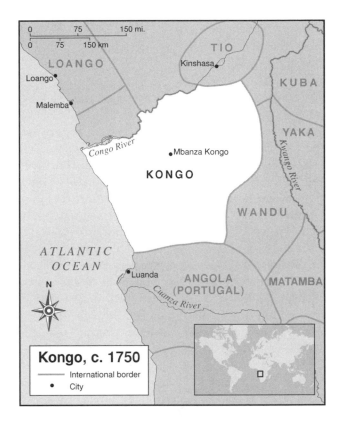

MAP BY XNR PRODUCTIONS. THE GALE GROUP.

In the Kongo Kingdom, organized trade with Portuguese merchants was facilitated by a high degree of economic and political centralization. Kongo was divided between wealthy Mbanza towns and Mabata peasant villages. Estates upon which slaves labored surrounded the Mbanza towns; the surplus from these estates fed the urban nobility and provided opportunity for local trade. Provincial governors appointed by the king extracted a portion of the surplus for themselves and for the king. In Mabata villages, corporate kin groups controlled labor and land. Some produce from villages was also traded with the towns or sent to the nobles as taxes. A monetary system based on *nzimbu* shells (found on the Kongo coastline) and cowrie shells allowed for extensive taxation and trade within the interior.

European imports such as alcohol, cloth, iron, munitions, and religious icons were luxury goods that signified status for the nobility. Although these imports were not economic necessities, their distribution helped to cement alliances and increase followings. Kongolese officials and nobles controlled trade, including the supply of slaves. Most slaves were acquired beyond the borders of the kingdom, through trade and expansionary wars in the sixteenth century. When warfare declined in the first half of the seventeenth century, the capture and export of slaves became less important. Instead, the kingdom increased exports of cloth to the interior and ivory to the Atlantic world. The small merchant class was mostly foreign and comprised of Portuguese or Africans from neighboring polities.

By the middle of the seventeenth century the kingdom was at the height of its economic and political power. Over the next fifty years, however, rivalry between the coastal town of Mbanza Nsoyo (or Sonyo) and the inland capital São Salvador, combined with Dutch and Portuguese competition over trade, led to civil war and political disintegration. Portuguese claims over exclusive trading rights on Kongo's coast and mining rights in its interior led to conflict with the kingdom and with Dutch merchants who offered superior trading goods. In 1641 the Dutch seized and occupied the Angolan port of Luanda from the Portuguese. The king of the Kongo, Garcia II (reigned 1641–1661), contacted the Dutch and sought to negotiate treaties that would end Portuguese control over trade. Garcia's rivals, based in Mbanza Nsoyo, also sent emissaries to negotiate separate treaties with the Dutch and implored them not to support Garcia. In 1648, in the midst of negotiations, the Portuguese retook Luanda and sought to punish those who had supported the Dutch. They asserted rights over the Kongo's southern province, Ndembu, and encouraged breakaways from the kingdom. Garcia's son, Antonio, who had succeeded the throne in 1661, led an army of several thousand to meet an army composed of Portuguese and their African allies at Mbwila in 1665. The Battle of Mbwila was the most significant armed conflict between Kongo and Portugal. African irregulars who supported the Portuguese, especially the fierce Imbangala warriors, proved decisive. Antonio was killed and the Kongolese army put to rout.

The collapse of Antonio's army allowed Nsoyo to gain advantage in their ongoing conflict with São Salvador. The army of Nsoyo attacked São Salvador in 1666 and 1669 in order to place their choice of king on the throne. The authority of São Salvador disintegrated and its population decreased from around 60,000 in the middle of the century to 5,000 in 1670. Warfare continued when the previous rulers of São Salvador sought Portuguese aid to attack Nsoyo. A combined Portuguese and Kongo force nearly captured Nsoyo, which was rescued by the arrival of a Dutch ship loaded with military supplies. In 1670 Nsoyo's army defeated the Portuguese and Kongo army. This battle secured the independence of Nsoyo and the remaining Kongo territories from the Portuguese for the next century, but the wars had moved the center of power in the kingdom from the interior capital of São Salvador to the coastal town of Mbanza Nsoyo.

The Kongo Kingdom would not return to the same degree of political cohesion and centralization. The slave estates surrounding the Mbanza towns, the centers of economic power in the interior, were no more, and there were few areas of dense settlement. The trade in slaves replaced the employment of slaves on vast estates. Local corporate groups usurped the nobles and officials of São Salvador as the dominant form of political authority. Although Mbanza Nsoyo provided some opportunity for the centralization of power, it could never convey its authority over the interior as effectively as São Salvador had prior to the civil wars of seventeenth century. Decentralized political units, typical of the central African interior, proliferated and prospered.

Without slave estates, the local nobility relied on international trade, especially the slave trade, to secure European goods and followings. Nobles were often supported by foreign forces that helped them to defend their lands and control lucrative trading outlets. Mbanza Nsoyo negotiated a treaty with the Portuguese in 1690, but preferred to trade with the Dutch and English, who were willing to supply munitions. There were several attempts to reunify the kingdom at the beginning of the eighteenth century. The peasant-based Antonian movement led by the self-proclaimed "Saint Anthony," Dona Beatrice Kimpa Vita 1686–1706), attempted to restore Kongo's "true" religion (an amalgam of Christian and Kongo beliefs) and enthrone a single king. It ended in 1706, when King Pedro IV (1671–1718) sentenced Dona Beatrice to burn at the stake. After the repression of the Antonian movement, Pedro IV claimed to rule a unified Kongo. His rule rested on a tenuous set of alliances with dispersed regional rulers who derived their power and wealth through trading networks that stretched to slave markets of the Atlantic world.

SEE ALSO ANGOLA; ARMS, ARMAMENTS; BRAZIL; EMPIRE, PORTUGUESE; ETHNIC GROUPS, AFRICANS; FACTORIES; IMPERIALISM; LABORERS, COERCED; LABORERS, CONTRACT; SLAVERY AND THE AFRICAN SLAVE TRADE; SUGAR, MOLASSES, AND RUM; TEXTILES.

BIBLIOGRAPHY

Hilton, Anne. *The Kingdom of the Kongo*. Oxford, U.K.: Clarendon Press, 1985.

Miller, Joseph. *Way of Death: Merchant Capital and the Angolan Slave Trade, 1730–1830*. Madison: University of Wisconsin Press, 1988.

Thornton, John K. *The Kingdom of the Kongo: Civil War and Transition, 1641–1718*. Madison: University of Wisconsin Press, 1983.

Thornton, John K. *Africa and the Africans in the Making of the Atlantic World*. Cambridge, U.K.: Cambridge University Press, 1992.

Vansina, Jan. *Kingdoms of the Savanna: A History of Central African States until European Occupation.* Madison: University of Wisconsin Press, 1968.

David M. Gordon

KOREA

By the ninth century Korean shipping dominated Northeast Asian waters. We know this by the Japanese monk Ennin's diary of his trip to China (mid-ninth century) and the excavation of a wreck (1330s) off the Korean west coast at Sin'an. The wreck contained pharmaceuticals and sandalwood from Southeast Asia; coins, ceramics, and bronzes from China; and celadons from Korea. Ceramics from six major Chinese kilns formed the bulk of the cargo. Sailing from Ningbo in China, the ship was bound for Hakata in Japan.

From the mid-fourteenth century Japanese piracy stifled trade. Civil wars and climatic crises pushed starving Japanese peasants to attack Korean tax grain shipping and even inland towns. Pirates weakened the Koryŏ (918–1392) dynasty, and a hero who gained fame against the pirates established the succeeding Chosŏn dynasty (1392–1910). As the Yuan (Mongol) dynasty (1279–1368) gave way to the Ming dynasty (1368–1644), the northern land route was also endangered.

During the early fifteenth century, Japanese piracy was quelled by incorporating pirates into a trading structure that specified ship size, crew size, and cargoes. On the northern frontier stability came after the Mongol defeat and regulation of the Jurchen trade. Trade with China was conducted in the border region and when Korean embassies visited the Ming capital. Ming demanded horses and ginseng (and even women for a brief time) and gave Korea silk. Through the fifteenth and sixteenth centuries Japanese traders brought swords, silver, gold, and copper to exchange for cotton, rice, soybeans, ginseng, books, ceramics, and copies of the *Tripitaka Koreana*, the world's most complete collection of Chinese-language Buddhist sutras. As Japan descended ever deeper into civil war, the demand for Korean cotton increased. The peace was shattered from 1592 to 1597 when the Japanese civil wars threw up a hegemon who used European arquebuses (matchlock guns) to invade Korea as the first step to conquering China.

The post-invasion settlement restricted Japanese to the single port of Pusan and greatly curtailed trade. Japanese supplied silver, copper, tin, and Southeast Asian spices and dyes to obtain Korean rice and ginseng, and Korean and Chinese silk goods. Japanese silver went to China for the Korean-Chinese trade. China was the world's leading importer of silver, from the New World

through Manila, and from Japan through Korea and Nagasaki (European and Chinese traders). In the seventeenth century Koreans passed on Japanese silver to China and Chinese silk to Japan. Japanese wanted Chinese silk because Japan lacked a silk industry until the late seventeenth century. Japanese and Chinese also wanted Korean ginseng, the finest in the world. Until the early eighteenth century private Korean-Japanese trade was dominated by Japanese silver for Korean ginseng and silk goods, while official trade exchanged Japanese copper, tin, and Southeast Asian goods for Korean rice and cotton.

In the eighteenth century Japanese policies banned silver exports, but copper and tin continued in exchange for Korean ginseng, leather, and marine products. Japanese trade drew off nearly half the rice tax income from Kyŏngsang Province, the wealthiest of Korea's eight provinces, but Japanese copper and tin were needed for Korean bronze coinage and brassware. Korean silver was exchanged for Chinese headgear, but in the nineteenth century, Korean ginseng and leather goods brought Chinese silver. These foreign connections were economically significant. Although we know trade took place, debates still rage over trade's significance to Korea's overall economy and whether it produced a deficit or a surplus.

Official ideology eschewed trade as a parasitical activity. Physiocratic preferences espoused agricultural production as the only legitimate source of wealth. The centralized and bureaucratized Chosŏn state effectively imposed an orthodoxy: self-sufficient villages practicing a moral economy produced a stable society. Urban centers never developed into huge commercial foci like China or Japan. Foreign policy suppressed the growth of trade.

A glorification of self-sufficient poverty carried into the nineteenth century, but political and economic uncertainties appeared. The 1790s to the 1880s was a "wet" century, with heavy rainfall and frequent flooding. Thereafter, the climate shifted rapidly to drought. From 1800, boy-kings controlled by in-law clans took the throne, resulting in weak leadership. Finally, the "ever-normal granaries" that stored grain for lean years and released it in fat years to stabilize prices began to empty after 1830 and became ineffectual by the 1860s. The granaries reveal the growing impotence and corruption of government. Rice prices began to rise from the 1830s and speculation increased.

The system became vulnerable and unable to respond to Japanese imperialism. Japan adopted European and U.S. mercantilist policies and in 1876 forced open the Korean economy. The Japanese sought cheap, Korean rice. Grain exports amplified the trend towards rice speculation and expanded tenancy. Exports became so great

One of three ancient entrance gates that surround Seoul, Korea, leads into the city. *Japan began occupation of Korea in 1910, marking a period of industrialization and development that was also characterized by Japanese oppression. In 1945, after the end of World War II, Japan ended its control and a new Korea emerged. It was divided into a northern state under the influence of the Soviets and a southern state influenced by the United States.* © CORBIS. REPRODUCED BY PERMISSION.

that they helped trigger an anti-foreign peasant revolt in the 1890s that led to Chinese and Japanese troops facing each other on the peninsula for the first time since the 1590s. Japanese victories in the First Sino-Japanese War of 1894 to 1895 and then in the Russo-Japanese War of 1904 to 1905 gave Japanese capital a free hand in Korea.

Korea became an agricultural colony under Japanese dictatorship. In the 1910s Japan became an industrial power on the back of spun cloth. From 1920 surplus capital from Japan was allowed into the colony. Nascent Korean industry emerged, but the rice market continued to dominate the colonial economy. After 1929 the global crash curtailed foreign demand for Japanese manufactures, and in October 1930 the Japanese rice market plunged 33 percent. The shock to the colony was extensive. Tenancy leapt over 50 percent and millions migrated to Manchuria. Until 1945 the colony continued to supply rice to the Japanese metropole and became the commissariat for the Japanese war machine in China.

Liberation in 1945 brought new problems. The first was severance from the Japanese economy. South Korea finally normalized relations with Japan in 1965, but

North Korea and Japan had not normalized relations by 2004. The worst problem was the polarization of politics, exacerbated by U.S. and U.S.S.R. troops and the birth of the Cold War. Ideological confrontation produced the Korean War (1950–1953). Millions died and nearly all cities and industry were reduced to rubble, destroying the physical plant of the first industrialization. After 1953 a military stalemate left two antagonistic states on the peninsula, and they drew aid from their sponsors.

The 1960s in North and South Korea saw changes that resulted in industrialized, successful states. The command economy in the North produced prosperity, and North Korea became a socialist success story. Politics overtook economics in the late 1970s, and the economy slid into decline from the 1980s. Russian aid was withdrawn after 1989, and severe famine appeared by the late 1990s. Chinese aid continues and is given to forestall a North Korean collapse and millions of refugees. Economic reforms made in the summer of 2002 may indicate a desire to introduce market mechanisms and make the transition from communism like China.

Traffic circles by the Namdaemun Gate in the heart of Seoul, Korea. *In the late 1980s, solid economic growth in Korea was achieved through government and business efforts that promoted the import of technology and raw materials to fuel investment in key industries. By 2005, Korea had become a global economic power, ranking thirteenth in the world in terms of nominal gross domestic product, trade, and exports.* © JOSE FUSTE RAGA/CORBIS. REPRODUCED BY PERMISSION.

In 1960 the per capita annual income in South Korea was about $60 USD. A military coup in 1961 brought strong leadership that re-created the state capitalism of the colonial period. A strong state planned the economy by apportioning soft loans to a variety of hand-picked companies that grew into export-oriented, heavy-industry combines called *chaebŏl*. Close ties between government and business directed credit to targeted sectors, kept out competing imports, suppressed labor, and instilled a competitive, export culture. Entire industries were created from scratch and paid for by strict controls over consumption and high savings rates. Successor regimes from 1980 to 1992 were corrupt and permitted high debt to equity ratios, massive foreign borrowing by business, and financial indiscipline. The Asian financial crisis from 1997 to 1999 exposed high levels of corporate debt, but the Korean post-crisis recovery was rapid.

By 1990 about a third of South Korea's gross domestic product (GDP) was involved with foreign trade. In 2002 South Korea was the world's twelfth-largest exporter and the fifteenth-largest importer. It was fifth in global research and development expenditures as a percentage of GDP, and a world leader in electronics, automobiles,

chemicals, shipbuilding, steel production, and clothing. By 2002 per capita income had reached nearly $20,000 USD, on a par with Spain and New Zealand.

SEE ALSO AUTOMOBILE; BALANCE OF PAYMENTS; CHINA; DEVELOPMENTAL STATE, CONCEPT OF THE; EMPIRE, JAPANESE; EMPIRE, MING; EMPIRE, QING; GLOBALIZATION, PRO AND CON; HYUNDAI; IMPORT SUBSTITUTION; INTERNATIONAL TRADE AGREEMENTS; IRON AND STEEL; JAPAN; MANCHURIA; PROTECTIONISM AND TARIFF WARS; RATES OF EXCHANGE; RICE; SHIPBUILDING; SOCIALISM AND COMMUNISM; TAIWAN; TEXTILES; TRIBUTE SYSTEM; UNITED STATES.

BIBLIOGRAPHY

Amsden, Alice H. *Asia's Next Giant: South Korea and Late Industrialization.* New York and Oxford, U.K.: Oxford University Press, 1989.

Chung, Sungil. "The Volume of Early Modern Korea-Japan Trade: A Comparison with the Japan-Holland Trade." *Acta Koreana* 7, no. 1 (2004): 69–85.

Eckert, Carter J., et al. *Korea Old and New: A History.* Seoul: Published for the Korea Institute, Harvard University by Ilchokak Publishers, 1990.

Gragert, Edwin H. *Landownership under Colonial Rule: Korea's Japanese Experience, 1900–1935.* Honolulu: University of Hawaii Press, 1994.

Kim, Dongchul, translated by Han Seokyung and J. B. Lewis. "The Waegwan Open Market Trade and Merchants in the Late Chosŏn Period." *Acta Koreana* 7, no. 1 (2004): 9–46.

Lee, Chul-sung. "Re-evaluation of the Chosŏn Dynasty's Trade Relationship with the Ch'ing Dynasty." *International Journal of Korean History* 3 (December 2002): 95–122.

Lewis, James B. "The Trade with Japan and the Economy of Kyŏngsang Province." *Acta Koreana* 7, no. 1 (2004): 47–68.

Oh, Doo Hwan, translated by J. B. Lewis. "The Silver Trade and Silver Currency in Chosŏn Korea." *Acta Koreana* 7, no. 1 (2004): 87–114.

INTERNET RESOURCES

"Asia: Korea, South: Economy." NationMaster.com online database, 2004. Retrieved March 19, 2004 from http://www.nationmaster.com/country/KS/Economy.

"Exhibition II." National Maritime Museum of Korea. Retrieved March 19, 2004 from http://www.seamuse.go.kr/english/index.htm.

"World in Figures: global database." World in Figures online database, 2004. Retrieved March 19, 2004 from http://www.worldinfigures.org/glo/eng/index

James B. Lewis

KRUPP

For nearly a century, from the late 1860s to 1945, the German company Friedrich Krupp A.G. epitomized both the production and the global trade of war material. In 1851, forty years after Friedrich Krupp had founded the firm in Essen (Germany), it displayed one of its first prototypes of a cast-steel gun at the inaugural world exhibition in London. It was, however, the Franco-Prussian War of 1870 to 1871 that established Krupp's name and fame as a major producer of ordnance. In the late nineteenth century governments and armies around the world clamored to acquire Krupp armaments. Although war material usually accounted for less than half of its revenues, Krupp became firmly associated with arms production during World War I, when it was Germany's main source for heavy arms. After Germany's defeat Krupp was forced to cease both production and export of war material. Under Hitler, the Nazi regime removed these restrictions, and Krupp again turned to manufacturing massive quantities of armaments for the German armed forces. During World War II, Krupp contributed heavily to Germany's war effort; after 1945 the Allies punished the firm for the part it played during the Nazi period. Krupp abandoned the production of arms, but built on its prewar experience as a major exporter to rapidly grow its foreign clientele for its wide variety of industrial products. In 1999 Krupp merged with its largest German competitor, Thyssen, to form ThyssenKrupp A.G.

SEE ALSO Arms, Armaments; Germany.

BIBLIOGRAPHY

Gall, Lothar. *Krupp: Der Aufstieg eines Industrieimperiums (Krupp: Rise of an Industrial Empire)*. Berlin: Siedler, 2000.

Gall, Lothar, ed. *Krupp im 20. Jahrhundert (Krupp in the 20th Century)*. Berlin: Siedler, 2002.

Leitz, Christian. "Arms Exports in the Third Reich, 1933–1939: The Example of Krupp." *Economic History Review,* LI 1998.

Christian Leitz